PROBLEMS AND MATERIALS

PROFESSIONAL RESPONSIBILITY

EIGHTH EDITION

by

THOMAS D. MORGAN
Oppenheim Professor of Law
The George Washington University

RONALD D. ROTUNDA
GMU Foundation Professor of Law
George Mason University

FOUNDATION PRESS

NEW YORK, NEW YORK

2003

COPYRIGHT © 1976, 1981, 1984, 1987, 1991, 1995, 2000 FOUNDATION PRESS
COPYRIGHT © 2003 By FOUNDATION PRESS

> 395 Hudson Street
> New York, NY 10014
> Phone Toll Free 1–877–888–1330
> Fax (212) 367–6799
> fdpress.com

All rights reserved
Printed in the United States of America

ISBN 1–58778–524–2

 TEXT IS PRINTED ON 10% POST CONSUMER RECYCLED PAPER

To Kathryn Morgan and Nicholas Rotunda

*

PREFACE

In less than 30 years, professional responsibility has gone from a field with few students and fewer scholars to a pervasive part of the law school curriculum. During that same time, our book has gone from the First to the Eighth Edition. Most law schools now require a course in professional responsibility, and articles by faculty and practitioners have stimulated changes in professional standards that few in the 1970s would have thought possible.

Several generations of law students have found this book a stimulating way to examine lawyer standards in the context of concrete situations. In our early editions, there were lots of questions but few authoritative answers. Now, by contrast, there are at least as many questions and even more conflicting answers.

This Eighth Edition tries to acknowledge the field's developments without losing the qualities that have made the book successful. Many of the Problems, for example, remain almost unchanged from prior editions. Jerry Harrold is still advertising for clients and Sarah Field is still trying to manage a busy practice without committing malpractice.

The Problems are still followed by Questions designed to provoke discussion. Questions are followed by case and opinion summaries designed to give examples of ways courts and rule makers have approached the issues raised. Users have suggested to us, however, that some students have had a hard time knowing what points cited cases were addressing, so in this edition, fundamental questions are presented in black letter and each of those is followed by references more clearly relevant to the issues those questions raise.

In this edition, each Problem also groups its Questions under one of four Issues, again to more clearly structure student preparation, discussion and understanding. We have not, however, reduced the rigor required to wrestle with the questions raised.

Users will also notice that material previously used as Readings is now integrated into the Questions. Users have told us that, because the Readings came at the end of each Problem, some students never took them as seriously as they should. We believe the simple change of location will help assure that the material is given the prominence it deserves.

Finally, this edition omits the lists of relevant articles that were present in earlier editions. When we began producing this book, the number of worthy articles was few and we tried to perform a service by collecting and organizing them. Now, by contrast, articles on professional responsibility number literally in the thousands, and almost all may easily be found using standard research methods. It did not seem wise to expand the page count of these materials to present information so readily available elsewhere.

Since the Seventh Edition, the ABA House of Delegates has approved major revisions to the Model Rules of Professional Conduct. Hence, in this edition, when references are to the ABA Model Rules, all citations are to the Rules as amended in 2002, unless indicated otherwise. Those new rules represent the law under which most students are likely to practice, as well as the rules that will be tested by the National Conference of Bar Examiners as early as 2004. Long-time users will also notice fewer references to the ABA Model Code of Professional Responsibility.

In addition, this edition often refers to the Restatement Third, The Law Governing Lawyers, finally published by the American Law Institute in 2000. The Restatement is likely to be an essential item on the shelves of lawyers who think about professional responsibility issues, and this edition should help make reference to it an instinctive part of addressing any important question.

We, of course, thank the authors and publishers cited, in particular the American Bar Association and American Law Institute, for permission to reprint their copyrighted material. We also thank the many professors and practitioners—in particular, Edward C. Brewer, III, Jonathan Rose and Robert Tuttle—who have offered thoughtful comments and suggestions on our materials. We try to listen to those comments and we hope you will find the Eighth Edition an up-to-date and useful successor to its predecessors.

T.D.M.
R.D.R.

Washington, DC
Arlington, VA
February 2003

SUMMARY OF CONTENTS

PREFACE -- v
TABLE OF CASES -- xi
TABLE OF STATUTES-- xxxiii
TABLE OF AUTHORITIES-- xlv

Chapter
    I.   The Legal Profession: Background and Fundamental Issues ----- 1
    II. Regulation of the Legal Profession ------------------------------ 31
   III. Fundamentals of the Lawyer–Client Relationship------------------ 83
   IV. The Requirement of Loyalty to the Client ------------------------- 158
    V. Advising Clients -- 275
   VI. Ethical Problems in Litigation----------------------------------- 368
  VII. The Delivery of Legal Services---------------------------------- 495
 VIII. Ethical Conduct of Judges-------------------------------------- 618

INDEX --- 669

*

TABLE OF CONTENTS

Preface v
Table of Cases xi
Table of Statutes xxxiii
Table of Authorities xlv

Chapter I. The Legal Profession: Background and Fundamental Issues 1
A. Introduction 1
B. Development of the American Legal Profession 2
C. The Development of Standards of Professional Conduct 11
D. Some Contributions From Moral Philosophy to the Study of Legal Ethics 14
   1. The Ethics of Duty versus the Ethics of Aspiration 14
   2. Moral People versus Moral Actions 17
   3. Role Ethics versus Common Ethical Standards 18
   4. Consequential versus Deontological Standards 20
   5. The Ethic of Care 21
   6. Personal versus Social Ethics 22
E. The Matter of Professionalism 23
F. An Introductory Problem 26
G. A Word on the Organization of this Book 28

Chapter II. Regulation of the Legal Profession 31
   Problem 1: Admission to the Bar 32
   Problem 2: Lawyer Discipline and the Disabled Lawyer 46
   Problem 3: Regulating Lawyers Outside of the Formal Disciplinary System 63

Chapter III. Fundamentals of the Lawyer–Client Relationship 83
   Problem 4: Undertaking to Represent a Client 84
   Problem 5: Billing for Legal Services 95
   Problem 6: Handling Client Property and Withdrawing From Representation 112
   Problem 7: The Duty of Confidentiality 127
   Problem 8: Confidentiality and the Organization as a Client .. 141

Chapter IV. The Requirement of Loyalty to the Client 158
   Problem 9: Representing Multiple Parties Dealing With Each Other 159
   Problem 10: The Duty of Loyalty 171
   Problem 11: Conflicts of Interest in Criminal Litigation 189
   Problem 12: Conflicts Between Client Interests and the Lawyer's Personal Interest 203

Chapter IV. The Requirement of Loyalty to the Client—Continued

Problem 13: Representing the Insured and the Insurer 215
Problem 14: The Lawyer and Her Former Client 230
Problem 15: Imputed Disqualification 244
Problem 16: Special Problems of Government Lawyers 260

Chapter V. Advising Clients 275

Problem 17: The Lawyer for an Individual Client 276
Problem 18: Advising the Business Corporation 289
Problem 19: Contact with Represented and Unrepresented Persons 302
Problem 20: The Ethics of Negotiation 318
Problem 21: The Lawyer as Evaluator 336
Problem 22: Obligations When the Client May Be Engaged in Fraud 350

Chapter VI. Ethical Problems in Litigation 368

Problem 23: The Decision to File a Civil Suit 368
Problem 24: Litigation Tactics 386
Problem 25: Disclosure of Law or Facts Favorable to the Other Side 401
Problem 26: Handling Physical Evidence 416
Problem 27: The Client Who Intends to Commit Perjury 432
Problem 28: The Verdict that May Be Tainted 453
Problem 29: The Crusading Prosecutor 464
Problem 30: The Duty to See Justice Done 486

Chapter VII. The Delivery of Legal Services 495

Problem 31: Marketing Professional Services 496
Problem 32: The Ethics of Referral to a Specialist 517
Problem 33: Roles and Responsibilities in a Modern Law Firm 530
Problem 34: Leaving One Law Firm and Forming Another 545
Problem 35: The Duty to Work for No Compensation 562
Problem 36: Problems in Class Action Representation 578
Problem 37: The Future of the Practice of Law 595

Chapter VIII. Ethical Conduct of Judges 618

Problem 38: Judges' Disqualifying Conflicts of Interest 618
Problem 39: The Judge as a Political Candidate and Public Figure 635
Problem 40: The Active Federal Judge 651

INDEX 669

TABLE OF CASES

Principal cases are in bold type. Non-principal cases are in roman type. References are to Pages.

A. v. B. v. Hill Wallack, 158 N.J. 51, 726 A.2d 924 (N.J.1999), 167, 168

Abner, State ex rel. v. Elliott, 85 Ohio St.3d 11, 706 N.E.2d 765 (Ohio 1999), 435

Abrams, In re, 689 A.2d 6 (D.C.1997), 63

Abstract & Title Corp. of Florida v. Cochran, 414 So.2d 284 (Fla.App. 4 Dist.1982), 81

Ackert, United States v., 169 F.3d 136 (2nd Cir.1999), 145

ACLU/Eastern Missouri Fund v. Miller, 803 S.W.2d 592 (Mo.1991), 529

Actel v. Quicklogic Corp., 1996 WL 297045 (N.D.Cal.1996), 242

Adams v. Aerojet–General Corp., 104 Cal. Rptr.2d 116 (Cal.App. 3 Dist.2001), 251

Adkinson, United States v., 247 F.3d 1289 (11th Cir.2001), 386

Adler, Barish, Daniels, Levin & Creskoff v. Epstein, 252 Pa.Super. 553, 382 A.2d 1226 (Pa.Super.1977), 549, 550

Adlman, United States v., 134 F.3d 1194 (2nd Cir.1998), 133

Admission of Lumumba, In re, 526 F.Supp. 163 (S.D.N.Y.1981), 604

Advisory Committee on Professional Ethics Docket No. 22–95, 144 N.J. 590, 677 A.2d 1100 (N.J.1996), 114

Aetna Life Ins. Co. v. Lavoie, 475 U.S. 813, 106 S.Ct. 1580, 89 L.Ed.2d 823 (1986), 630

A. Fred Miller P.C. v. Purvis, 921 P.2d 610 (Alaska 1996), 122

A.H. Robins Co., In re, 86 F.3d 364 (4th Cir.1996), 103

Akers v. Akers, 233 Minn. 133, 46 N.W.2d 87 (Minn.1951), 124

Alcantara, Matter of, 144 N.J. 257, 676 A.2d 1030 (N.J.1995), 305

Alexander, In re, 146 Ill.2d 83, 165 Ill.Dec. 674, 585 N.E.2d 70 (Ill.1991), 620

Allegaert v. Perot, 565 F.2d 246 (2nd Cir. 1977), 236

Allen v. Academic Games Leagues of America, Inc., 831 F.Supp. 785 (C.D.Cal.1993), 242

Allen v. Lefkoff, Duncan, Grimes & Dermer, P.C., 265 Ga. 374, 453 S.E.2d 719 (Ga. 1995), 71

Allstate Ins. Co. v. Keller, 17 Ill.App.2d 44, 149 N.E.2d 482 (Ill.App. 1 Dist.1958), 222

Allstate Ins. Co., In re, 722 S.W.2d 947 (Mo. 1987), 228, 611

Amchem Products, Inc. v. Windsor, 521 U.S. 591, 117 S.Ct. 2231, 138 L.Ed.2d 689 (1997), 581

American Airlines, Inc., In re, 972 F.2d 605 (5th Cir.1992), 170

American Can Co. v. Citrus Feed Co., 436 F.2d 1125 (5th Cir.1971), 250, 251

American Continental Corporation/Lincoln Sav. and Loan Securities Litigation, In re, 794 F.Supp. 1424 (D.Ariz.1992), 293, 355

American Home Assur. Co. v. Golomb, 239 Ill.App.3d 37, 179 Ill.Dec. 961, 606 N.E.2d 793 (Ill.App. 4 Dist.1992), 100

American Home Products, In re, 985 S.W.2d 68 (Tex.1998), 241

American Honda Motor Co., Dealerships Relations Litigation, In re, 958 F.Supp. 1045 (D.Md.1997), 80

American Ins. Ass'n v. Kentucky Bar Ass'n, 917 S.W.2d 568 (Ky.1996), 229, 611

American Tobacco Co. v. State, 697 So.2d 1249 (Fla.App. 4 Dist.1997), 153, 397

Amgen v. Hoechst Marion Roussel, Inc., 190 F.R.D. 287 (D.Mass.2000), 137

Anastaplo, In re, 366 U.S. 82, 81 S.Ct. 978, 6 L.Ed.2d 135 (1961), 36

Anders v. California, 386 U.S. 738, 87 S.Ct. 1396, 18 L.Ed.2d 493 (1967), 374, 375

Anderson v. Elliott, 555 A.2d 1042 (Me.1989), 122

Anderson, United States v., 160 F.3d 231 (5th Cir.1998), 650

Anis, Matter of, 126 N.J. 448, 599 A.2d 1265 (N.J.1992), 514

Anonymous Attorneys v. Bar Ass'n of Erie County, 393 N.Y.S.2d 961, 362 N.E.2d 592 (N.Y.1977), 63

Anonymous, Matter of, 550 N.Y.S.2d 270, 549 N.E.2d 472 (N.Y.1989), 35

Anonymous Member of South Carolina Bar, In re, 315 S.C. 141, 432 S.E.2d 467 (S.C. 1993), 218

Antar, United States v., 53 F.3d 568 (3rd Cir.1995), 634

Application of (see name of party)

Arizona v. Maricopa County Medical Soc., 457 U.S. 332, 102 S.Ct. 2466, 73 L.Ed.2d 48 (1982), 102

Armstrong v. McAlpin, 625 F.2d 433 (2nd Cir.1980), 265, 266

Arnav Industries, Inc. Retirement Trust v. Brown, Raysman, Millstein, Felder & Steiner, L.L.P., 727 N.Y.S.2d 688, 751 N.E.2d 936 (N.Y.2001), 73

Arnoff, In re, 150 Cal.Rptr. 479, 586 P.2d 960 (Cal.1978), 513

Arpadi v. First MSP Corp., 68 Ohio St.3d 453, 628 N.E.2d 1335 (Ohio 1994), 298

Artman, People v., 218 Mich.App. 236, 553 N.W.2d 673 (Mich.App.1996), 62

ASCAP, United States v., 129 F.Supp.2d 327 (S.D.N.Y.2001), 179

Atkins v. United States, 214 Ct.Cl. 186, 556 F.2d 1028 (Ct.Cl.1977), 623

Atlanta Intern. Ins. Co. v. Bell, 438 Mich. 512, 475 N.W.2d 294 (Mich.1991), 229

Attorney Grievance Com'n v. Ficker, 349 Md. 13, 706 A.2d 1045 (Md.1998), 532

Attorney Grievance Com'n v. Kent, 337 Md. 361, 653 A.2d 909 (Md.1995), 304

Attorney Grievance Com'n v. Myers, 333 Md. 440, 635 A.2d 1315 (Md.1994), 37

Attorney Grievance v. Protokowicz, 329 Md. 252, 619 A.2d 100 (Md.1993), 49

Attorney Grievance Com'n of Maryland v. Rohrback, 323 Md. 79, 591 A.2d 488 (Md. 1991), 409

Attorney Grievance Com'n of Maryland v. Vanderlinde, 364 Md. 376, 773 A.2d 463 (Md.2001), 53

Ausherman v. Bank of America, 216 F.Supp.2d 530 (D.Md.2002), 621

Austin v. United States, 513 U.S. 5, 115 S.Ct. 380, 130 L.Ed.2d 219 (1994), 374

Auvil v. Grafton Homes, Inc., 92 F.3d 226 (4th Cir.1996), 93

Avilez–Reyes, United States v., 160 F.3d 258 (5th Cir.1998), 650

Bachman v. Pertschuk, 437 F.Supp. 973 (D.D.C.1977), 581

Baird v. Koerner, 279 F.2d 623 (9th Cir. 1960), 418, 420, 484

Baird v. State Bar of Ariz., 401 U.S. 1, 91 S.Ct. 702, 27 L.Ed.2d 639 (1971), 36

Bakker v. McKinnon, 152 F.3d 1007 (8th Cir.1998), 81

Baldasarre v. Butler, 132 N.J. 278, 625 A.2d 458 (N.J.1993), 164

Balla v. Gambro, Inc., 145 Ill.2d 492, 164 Ill.Dec. 892, 584 N.E.2d 104 (Ill.1991), 534

Bane v. Ferguson, 890 F.2d 11 (7th Cir.1989), 540

BankAmerica Corp. Securities Litigation, In re, 270 F.3d 639 (8th Cir.2001), 152

Bank of America, In re, 45 S.W.3d 238 (Tex. App.-Hous. (1 Dist.) 2001), 138

Barnard v. Thorstenn, 489 U.S. 546, 109 S.Ct. 1294, 103 L.Ed.2d 559 (1989), 603

Barner v. Leeds, 102 Cal.Rptr.2d 97, 13 P.3d 704 (Cal.2000), 68

Barnett, State v., 125 N.M. 739, 965 P.2d 323 (N.M.App.1998), 234

Barnhart v. Pickrel, Schaeffer & Ebeling Co., L.P.A., 12 F.3d 1382 (6th Cir.1993), 541

Barrick, In re, 87 Ill.2d 233, 57 Ill.Dec. 725, 429 N.E.2d 842 (Ill.1981), 210

Bartlett v. Heibl, 128 F.3d 497 (7th Cir.1997), 81

Bartlett v. New York State Bd. of Law Examiners, 226 F.3d 69 (2nd Cir.2000), 45

Bates v. State Bar of Arizona, 433 U.S. 350, 97 S.Ct. 2691, 53 L.Ed.2d 810 (1977), 498, 501, 502, 503, 506, 508, 512, 523, 549

Battaglia v. United States, 349 F.2d 556 (9th Cir.1965), 458

Battle v. Thornton, 646 A.2d 315 (D.C.1994), 67

Beard v. North Carolina State Bar, 320 N.C. 126, 357 S.E.2d 694 (N.C.1987), 117

Beery v. State Bar, 239 Cal.Rptr. 121, 739 P.2d 1289 (Cal.1987), 205

Beets v. Scott, 65 F.3d 1258 (5th Cir.1995), 202

BE & K Const. Co. v. N.L.R.B., 536 U.S. 516, 122 S.Ct. 2390, 153 L.Ed.2d 499 (2002), 383

Belge, People v., 83 Misc.2d 186, 372 N.Y.S.2d 798 (N.Y.Co.Ct.1975), 427, 429, 430

Bell Atlantic Corp. v. Bolger, 2 F.3d 1304 (3rd Cir.1993), 302

Bell & Marra v. Sullivan, 300 Mont. 530, 6 P.3d 965 (Mont.2000), 126

Belli v. State Bar, 112 Cal.Rptr. 527, 519 P.2d 575 (Cal.1974), 10

Bernard v. Coyne, 31 F.3d 842 (9th Cir.1994), 625

Berner v. Delahanty, 129 F.3d 20 (1st Cir. 1997), 388

Bernhardt v. County of Los Angeles, 279 F.3d 862 (9th Cir.2002), 592

Berrios, People v., 321 N.Y.S.2d 884, 270 N.E.2d 709 (N.Y.1971), 474

Berry v. Saline Memorial Hosp., 322 Ark. 182, 907 S.W.2d 736 (Ark.1995), 232

Berrysmith, State v., 87 Wash.App. 268, 944 P.2d 397 (Wash.App. Div. 1 1997), 447

Bigelow v. Virginia, 421 U.S. 809, 95 S.Ct. 2222, 44 L.Ed.2d 600 (1975), 498

Bill Johnson's Restaurants, Inc. v. NLRB, 461 U.S. 731, 103 S.Ct. 2161, 76 L.Ed.2d 277 (1983), 91, 383

Bingham, United States v., 769 F.Supp. 1039 (N.D.Ill.1991), 468

Birbrower, Montalbano, Condon & Frank v. Superior Court, 70 Cal.Rptr.2d 304, 949 P.2d 1 (Cal.1998), 605, 606, 607

Blackwelder, In re, 615 N.E.2d 106 (Ind. 1993), 76

Blair v. Ing, 21 P.3d 452 (Hawai'i 2001), 69

Blanchard v. Bergeron, 489 U.S. 87, 109 S.Ct. 939, 103 L.Ed.2d 67 (1989), 593

Blanchard v. EdgeMark Financial Corp., 175 F.R.D. 293 (N.D.Ill.1997), 583

Bloom, In re, 241 Cal.Rptr. 726, 745 P.2d 61 (Cal.1987), 48

Bloom, People v., 259 Cal.Rptr. 669, 774 P.2d 698 (Cal.1989), 93, 94

Blum v. Stenson, 465 U.S. 886, 104 S.Ct. 1541, 79 L.Ed.2d 891 (1984), 587, 589

Boca Investerings Partnership v. United States, 31 F.Supp.2d 9 (D.D.C.1998), 145

Bohatch v. Butler & Binion, 977 S.W.2d 543 (Tex.1998), 537

Boivin v. Black, 225 F.3d 36 (1st Cir.2000), 591

Bonin, Matter of, 375 Mass. 680, 378 N.E.2d 669 (Mass.1978), 659

Bordenkircher v. Hayes, 434 U.S. 357, 98 S.Ct. 663, 54 L.Ed.2d 604 (1978), 474

Bothwell v. Republic Tobacco Co., 912 F.Supp. 1221 (D.Neb.1995), 571

Boudreau, In re, 815 So.2d 76 (La.2002), 49

Bowen v. Maynard, 799 F.2d 593 (10th Cir. 1986), 488

Boyd, United States v., 833 F.Supp. 1277 (N.D.Ill.1993), 488

Bracy v. Gramley, 520 U.S. 899, 117 S.Ct. 1793, 138 L.Ed.2d 97 (1997), 439, 624

Bradley v. State of Alaska, 16 P.3d 187 (Alaska App.2001), 627

Brady v. Maryland, 373 U.S. 83, 83 S.Ct. 1194, 10 L.Ed.2d 215 (1963), 329, 330

Brandau v. State of Kansas, 168 F.3d 1179 (10th Cir.1999), 594

Bray v. Brooks, 41 S.W.3d 7 (Mo.App. W.D. 2001), 600

Bredice v. Doctors Hospital, Inc., 50 F.R.D. 249 (D.D.C 1970), 145

Breezevale v. Dickinson, 759 A.2d 627 (D.C. 2000), 436

Brickwood Contractors, Inc. v. United States, 288 F.3d 1371 (Fed.Cir.2002), 588

Brooks, In re, 11 S.W.3d 25 (Ky.2000), 42

Brotherhood of R. R. Trainmen v. Virginia ex rel. Va. State Bar, 377 U.S. 1, 84 S.Ct. 1113, 12 L.Ed.2d 89 (1964), 557

Brown v. Artuz, 124 F.3d 73 (2nd Cir.1997), 441

Brown v. Legal Foundation of Washington, ___ U.S. ___, 123 S.Ct. 1406, ___ L.Ed.2D ___ (2003), 577, 581

Brown v. McGarr, 583 F.Supp. 734 (N.D.Ill. 1984), 46

Brown & Williamson v. Pataki, 152 F.Supp.2d 276 (S.D.N.Y.2001), 180

Buckhannon Bd. and Care Home v. West Virginia Dept. of Health, 532 U.S. 598, 121 S.Ct. 1835, 149 L.Ed.2d 855 (2001), 588, 592

Buckley v. Fitzsimmons, 509 U.S. 259, 113 S.Ct. 2606, 125 L.Ed.2d 209 (1993), 471

Buckley v. Illinois Judicial Inquiry Bd., 997 F.2d 224 (7th Cir.1993), 638

Bullard v. Chrysler Corp., 925 F.Supp. 1180 (E.D.Tex.1996), 373

Burden v. Zant, 510 U.S. 132, 114 S.Ct. 654, 126 L.Ed.2d 611 (1994), 197

Burdine v. Johnson, 262 F.3d 336 (5th Cir. 2001), 79

Burger v. Kemp, 483 U.S. 776, 107 S.Ct. 3114, 97 L.Ed.2d 638 (1987), 192

Burrow v. Arce, 997 S.W.2d 229 (Tex.1999), 75, 171

Burrows, People v., 172 Ill.2d 169, 216 Ill. Dec. 762, 665 N.E.2d 1319 (Ill.1996), 492

Busby, In re, 317 Or. 213, 855 P.2d 156 (Or.1993), 117

Bush v. United States, 375 F.2d 602 (D.C.Cir. 1967), 474

Cal Pak Delivery, Inc. v. United Parcel Service, 60 Cal.Rptr.2d 207 (Cal.App. 1 Dist. 1997), 595

Camden v. Maryland, 910 F.Supp. 1115 (D.Md.1996), 309

Campagnola v. Mulholland, Minion & Roe, 556 N.Y.S.2d 239, 555 N.E.2d 611 (N.Y. 1990), 74

Campbell v. Rice, 265 F.3d 878 (9th Cir. 2001), 195

Cantor v. Supreme Court of Pennsylvania, 353 F.Supp. 1307 (E.D.Pa.1973), 39

Caplin & Drysdale v. United States, 491 U.S. 617, 109 S.Ct. 2646, 105 L.Ed.2d 528 (1989), 483

Capoccia, Matter of, 272 A.D.2d 838, 709 N.Y.S.2d 640 (N.Y.A.D. 3 Dept.2000), 370

Cardona v. General Motors Corp., 939 F.Supp. 351 (D.N.J.1996), 235

Cardona v. General Motors Corp., 942 F.Supp. 968 (D.N.J.1996), 235

Cardwell, In re, 50 P.3d 897 (Colo.2002), 416

Carter & Johnson, In re, Exchange Act Release No. 17,597 (1981), 361

Casby, State v., 348 N.W.2d 736 (Minn.1984), 409

Case of Feld, In re, 144 N.H. 131, 737 A.2d 656 (N.H.1999), 411

Cassas, People v., 622 N.Y.S.2d 228, 646 N.E.2d 449 (N.Y.1995), 406

Castano v. American Tobacco Co., 896 F.Supp. 590 (E.D.La.1995), 397

Central Bank of Denver, N.A. v. First Interstate Bank of Denver, N.A., 511 U.S. 164, 114 S.Ct. 1439, 128 L.Ed.2d 119 (1994), 157, 349

Central Hudson Gas & Elec. Corp. v. Public Service Commission, 447 U.S. 557, 100 S.Ct. 2343, 65 L.Ed.2d 341 (1980), 509

Central States Pension Fund v. Central Cartage Co., 76 F.3d 114 (7th Cir.1996), 589

Certain Complaints Under Investigation, Matter of, 783 F.2d 1488 (11th Cir.1986), 667

Chaleff v. Superior Court, 69 Cal.App.3d 721, 138 Cal.Rptr. 735 (Cal.App. 2 Dist.1977), 568

Chambers v. Kay, 126 Cal.Rptr.2d 536, 56 P.3d 645 (Cal.2002), 527

Chambers v. NASCO, Inc., 501 U.S. 32, 111 S.Ct. 2123, 115 L.Ed.2d 27 (1991), 382

Chandler v. Judicial Council of Tenth Circuit of United States, 398 U.S. 74, 90 S.Ct. 1648, 26 L.Ed.2d 100 (1970), 665, 667

Chappell v. Cosgrove, 121 N.M. 636, 916 P.2d 836 (N.M.1996), 463

Chappell, People v., 927 P.2d 829 (Colo.1996), 281

Checkosky v. SEC, 139 F.3d 221 (D.C.Cir. 1998), 361

Cherryhomes, State v., 114 N.M. 495, 840 P.2d 1261 (N.M.App.1992), 388

Chevron Chemical Co. v. Deloitte & Touche, 176 Wis.2d 935, 501 N.W.2d 15 (Wis. 1993), 378

Chicago Council of Lawyers v. Bauer, 522 F.2d 242 (7th Cir.1975), 466, 467

Chilcutt v. United States, 4 F.3d 1313 (5th Cir.1993), 414

CHI of Alaska, Inc. v. Employers Reinsurance Corp., 844 P.2d 1113 (Alaska 1993), 222

Cho v. Superior Court, 45 Cal.Rptr.2d 863 (Cal.App. 2 Dist.1995), 232, 274

Chugach Elec. Ass'n v. United States Dist. Court, 370 F.2d 441 (9th Cir.1966), 235

Cincinnati Bar Assn. v. Kathman, 92 Ohio St.3d 92, 748 N.E.2d 1091 (Ohio 2001), 598

Cincinnati Ins. Co. v. Wills, 717 N.E.2d 151 (Ind.1999), 611

Cinema 5, Ltd. v. Cinerama, Inc., 528 F.2d 1384 (2nd Cir.1976), 173, 182

Circuit Judge Paul F. Elward, In re, Case No. 77, Illinois Courts Commission (1977), 641

City of (see name of city)

Clancy, People ex rel. v. Superior Court (Ebel), 218 Cal.Rptr. 24, 705 P.2d 347 (Cal.1985), 199

Clark v. Rowe, 428 Mass. 339, 701 N.E.2d 624 (Mass.1998), 73

Clark Capital Management Group, Inc. v. Annuity Investors Life Ins. Co., 149 F.Supp.2d 193 (E.D.Pa.2001), 86

Cleveland Bar Assn. v. Nusbaum, 93 Ohio St.3d 150, 753 N.E.2d 183 (Ohio 2001), 585

Cleveland Bar Assn. v. Rossi, 81 Ohio St.3d 195, 690 N.E.2d 501 (Ohio 1998), 306

Cleveland, City of v. Cleveland Elec. Illuminating Co., 440 F.Supp. 193 (N.D.Ohio 1976), 253

Cleveland Hair Clinic, Inc. v. Puig, 200 F.3d 1063 (7th Cir.2000), 413

Clients' Sec. Fund of State v. Grandeau, 530 N.Y.S.2d 775, 526 N.E.2d 270 (N.Y.1988), 117

Clutchette v. Rushen, 770 F.2d 1469 (9th Cir.1985), 427

Cohen, In re, 316 Or. 657, 853 P.2d 286 (Or.1993), 162

Cohen v. Lord, Day & Lord, 551 N.Y.S.2d 157, 550 N.E.2d 410 (N.Y.1989), 552, 553, 554

Cohn, In re, 10 Ill.2d 186, 139 N.E.2d 301 (Ill.1956), 528

Coles v. Marsh, 560 F.2d 186 (3rd Cir.1977), 579

Collins, In re, 252 Neb. 222, 561 N.W.2d 209 (Neb.1997), 43

Collins v. SEC, 532 F.2d 584 (8th Cir.1976), 661

Collins–Bazant, Application of, 254 Neb. 614, 578 N.W.2d 38 (Neb.1998), 43

Colorado Supreme Court, United States v., 988 F.Supp. 1368 (D.Colo.1998), 317

Colorado Supreme Court, United States v., 87 F.3d 1161 (10th Cir.1996), 317

Colorpix Systems of America v. Broan Mfg. Co., 131 F.Supp.2d 331 (D.Conn.2001), 239

Columbia/HCA Healthcare Corp. Billing Practices Litigation, In re, 293 F.3d 289 (6th Cir.2002), 135

Columbus Bar Assn. v. Brooks, 87 Ohio St.3d 344, 721 N.E.2d 23 (Ohio 1999), 97

Columbus Bar Assn. v. Zauderer, 80 Ohio St.3d 435, 687 N.E.2d 410 (Ohio 1997), 114

Comden v. Superior Court, 145 Cal.Rptr. 9, 576 P.2d 971 (Cal.1978), 462, 463

Commercial Union Ins. Co. v. Marco Intern. Corp., 75 F.Supp.2d 108 (S.D.N.Y.1999), 178

Commission for Lawyer Discipline v. Benton, 980 S.W.2d 425 (Tex.1998), 455

Committee on Legal Ethics v. Gallaher, 180 W.Va. 332, 376 S.E.2d 346 (W.Va.1988), 108

Committee on Professional Ethics v. Humphrey, 377 N.W.2d 643 (Iowa 1985), 511, 512

Committee on Professional Ethics v. Mershon, 316 N.W.2d 895 (Iowa 1982), 206

Committee on Professional Ethics v. Mollman, 488 N.W.2d 168 (Iowa 1992), 459

Commodity Futures Trading Com'n v. Weintraub, 471 U.S. 343, 105 S.Ct. 1986, 85 L.Ed.2d 372 (1985), 148

Commonwealth v.)))))) (see opposing party)

Complaint of Rook, In re, 276 Or. 695, 556 P.2d 1351 (Or.1976), 199

Complex Asbestos Litigation, In re, 232 Cal. App.3d 572, 283 Cal.Rptr. 732 (Cal.App. 1 Dist.1991), 241

Condon v. McHenry, 76 Cal.Rptr.2d 922 (Cal. App. 1 Dist.1998), 607

Conduct of Gatti, 330 Or. 517, 8 P.3d 966 (Or.2000), 331, 393, 394

Conduct of Lackey, In re, 333 Or. 215, 37 P.3d 172 (Or.2002), 367

Conduct of Loew, 292 Or. 806, 642 P.2d 1171 (Or.1982), 53

Cone v. State Bar of Florida, 819 F.2d 1002 (11th Cir.1987), 575

Conklin v. Hannoch Weisman, 145 N.J. 395, 678 A.2d 1060 (N.J.1996), 73

Conn v. Gabbert, 526 U.S. 286, 119 S.Ct. 1292, 143 L.Ed.2d 399 (1999), 480

Conn, People ex rel. v. Randolph, 35 Ill.2d 24, 219 N.E.2d 337 (Ill.1966), 568

Connell v. Clairol, Inc., 440 F.Supp. 17 (N.D.Ga.1977), 463

Conner, People v., 193 Cal.Rptr. 148, 666 P.2d 5 (Cal.1983), 198

Converse v. Nebraska State Bar Commiss, 258 Neb. 159, 602 N.W.2d 500 (Neb.1999), 36

Cook v. American S.S. Co., 134 F.3d 771 (6th Cir.1998), 398

Cook, In re, 49 F.3d 263 (7th Cir.1995), 55

Cooperman, Matter of, 611 N.Y.S.2d 465, 633 N.E.2d 1069 (N.Y.1994), 98, 99

Cooter & Gell v. Hartmarx, 496 U.S. 384, 110 S.Ct. 2447, 110 L.Ed.2d 359 (1990), 372, 375

Corboy, In re, 124 Ill.2d 29, 124 Ill.Dec. 6, 528 N.E.2d 694 (Ill.1988), 620, 621

Corona, People v., 80 Cal.App.3d 684, 145 Cal.Rptr. 894 (Cal.App. 1 Dist.1978), 201

Cottle v. State, 733 So.2d 963 (Fla.1999), 78

Cotton v. Kronenberg, 111 Wash.App. 258, 44 P.3d 878 (Wash.App. Div. 1 2002), 205

Counsel for Discipline of Nebraska Supreme Court, State ex rel. v. Wilson, 262 Neb. 653, 634 N.W.2d 467 (Neb.2001), 121

Crandon v. State, 257 Kan. 727, 897 P.2d 92 (Kan.1995), 367

Crawford & Lewis v. Boatmen's Trust Co., 338 Ark. 679, 1 S.W.3d 417 (Ark.1999), 299

Crisci v. Security Ins. Co., 66 Cal.2d 425, 58 Cal.Rptr. 13, 426 P.2d 173 (Cal.1967), 223

Croken, Commonwealth v., 432 Mass. 266, 733 N.E.2d 1005 (Mass.2000), 203

Cromley v. Lockport Board of Educ., 17 F.3d 1059 (7th Cir.1994), 258

Cross & Cross Properties v. Everett Allied Co., 886 F.2d 497 (2nd Cir.1989), 372

Crowe v. Smith, 151 F.3d 217 (5th Cir.1998), 200, 385

C.R.W., In re, 267 Ga. 534, 481 S.E.2d 511 (Ga.1997), 35

Cueto, United States v., 151 F.3d 620 (7th Cir.1998), 79

Cummings, State ex rel. Oklahoma Bar Ass'n v., 863 P.2d 1164 (Okla.1993), 124

Cunningham v. Hamilton County, Ohio, 527 U.S. 198, 119 S.Ct. 1915, 144 L.Ed.2d 184 (1999), 374

Curry, People v., 178 Ill.2d 509, 227 Ill.Dec. 395, 687 N.E.2d 877 (Ill.1997), 78

Cutler, Application of, 239 A.D.2d 269, 658 N.Y.S.2d 835 (N.Y.A.D. 1 Dept.1997), 473

Cutler, In re, 227 A.D.2d 8, 650 N.Y.S.2d 85 (N.Y.A.D. 1 Dept.1996), 473

Cutler, United States v., 58 F.3d 825 (2nd Cir.1995), 473

Cutler, United States v., 6 F.3d 67 (2nd Cir. 1993), 472

Cuyler v. Sullivan, 446 U.S. 335, 100 S.Ct. 1708, 64 L.Ed.2d 333 (1980), 191, 192, 193, 198, 202

Dalessandro, Matter of, 483 Pa. 431, 397 A.2d 743 (Pa.1979), 663

D'Alessio v. Gilberg, 205 A.D.2d 8, 617 N.Y.S.2d 484 (N.Y.A.D. 2 Dept.1994), 130

Daley, In re, 549 F.2d 469 (7th Cir.1977), 63

D'Amico v. New York State Bd. of Law Examiners, 813 F.Supp. 217 (W.D.N.Y.1993), 44

Damron v. Herzog, 67 F.3d 211 (9th Cir. 1995), 233

Davin v. Daham, 329 N.J.Super. 54, 746 A.2d 1034 (N.J.Super.A.D.2000), 328

Davis County Solid Waste Management v. Environmental Protection Agency, 169 F.3d 755 (D.C.Cir.1999), 589

Davis, State v., 504 N.W.2d 767 (Minn.1993), 388

Davis, United States v., 780 F.Supp. 21 (D.D.C.1991), 259

Dawson, Matter of, 129 N.M. 369, 8 P.3d 856 (N.M.2000), 99

DeGuerin v. United States, 214 F.Supp.2d 726 (S.D.Tex.2002), 484

DeLisio v. Alaska Superior Court, 740 P.2d 437 (Alaska 1987), 567

Denburg v. Parker Chapin Flattau & Klimpl, 604 N.Y.S.2d 900, 624 N.E.2d 995 (N.Y. 1993), 552

DePallo, People v., 729 N.Y.S.2d 649, 754 N.E.2d 751 (N.Y.2001), 450

Desilets, In re, 291 F.3d 925 (6th Cir.2002), 608

DeSisto College, Inc. v. Line, 888 F.2d 755 (11th Cir.1989), 405

Detter v. Schreiber, 259 Neb. 381, 610 N.W.2d 13 (Neb.2000), 234

DeVaux v. American Home Assur. Co., 387 Mass. 814, 444 N.E.2d 355 (Mass.1983), 90

Devlin v. Scardelletti, 536 U.S. 1, 122 S.Ct. 2005, 153 L.Ed.2d 27 (2002), 580

Dibble, Ex parte, 279 S.C. 592, 310 S.E.2d 440 (S.C.App.1983), 569

Dietz v. Doe, 131 Wash.2d 835, 935 P.2d 611 (Wash.1997), 419

Diggs, Matter of, 344 S.C. 397, 544 S.E.2d 628 (S.C.2001), 50

Disciplinary Counsel v. Campbell, 71 Ohio St.3d 1215, 644 N.E.2d 1024 (Ohio 1995), 655

Disciplinary Counsel v. Campbell, 68 Ohio St.3d 7, 623 N.E.2d 24 (Ohio 1993), 655

Disciplinary Proceeding Against Boelter, In re, 139 Wash.2d 81, 985 P.2d 328 (Wash. 1999), 121

Disciplinary Proceedings Against Bonet, 144 Wash.2d 502, 29 P.3d 1242 (Wash.2001), 476

Discotrade Ltd. v. Wyeth–Ayerst Intern., Inc., 200 F.Supp.2d 355 (S.D.N.Y.2002), 180

Doe v. Board of Education, 165 F.3d 260 (4th Cir.1998), 587

Doe v. Federal Grievance Committee, 847 F.2d 57 (2nd Cir.1988), 58

Doe v. Florida Judicial Qualifications Com'n, 748 F.Supp. 1520 (S.D.Fla.1990), 649

Doe v. Kohn Nast & Graf, P.C., 866 F.Supp. 190 (E.D.Pa.1994), 539

Doe v. Roe, 289 Ill.App.3d 116, 224 Ill.Dec. 325, 681 N.E.2d 640 (Ill.App. 1 Dist.1997), 213

Doe, In re, 117 Misc.2d 197, 456 N.Y.S.2d 312 (N.Y.Co.Ct.1982), 419

Donaldson, People v., 113 Cal.Rptr.2d 548 (Cal.App. 5 Dist.2001), 464

Dondi Properties Corp. v. Commerce Sav. & Loan Ass'n, 121 F.R.D. 284 (N.D.Tex. 1988), 398

Donnelly v. Brown, Winick, Graves, Gross, Baskerville, Schoenebaum, & Walker, P.L.C., 599 N.W.2d 677 (Iowa 1999), 554

Dove Audio, Inc. v. Rosenfeld, Meyer & Susman, 54 Cal.Rptr.2d 830 (Cal.App. 2 Dist. 1996), 383

Dowd & Dowd, Ltd. v. Gleason, 181 Ill.2d 460, 230 Ill.Dec. 229, 693 N.E.2d 358 (Ill. 1998), 546

Doyle v. Oklahoma Bar Ass'n, 998 F.2d 1559 (10th Cir.1993), 59

Doyle v. State Bar, 184 Cal.Rptr. 720, 648 P.2d 942 (Cal.1982), 117

Dresser Industries, Inc., In re, 972 F.2d 540 (5th Cir.1992), 173

Drucker's Case, 133 N.H. 326, 577 A.2d 1198 (N.H.1990), 213

Duggins v. Guardianship of Washington, 632 So.2d 420 (Miss.1993), 116

Duplantier v. United States, 606 F.2d 654 (5th Cir.1979), 624

Durie v. State, 751 So.2d 685 (Fla.App. 5 Dist.2000), 80

Dziubak v. Mott, 503 N.W.2d 771 (Minn. 1993), 68

Eastern R. R. Presidents Conference v. Noerr Motor Freight, Inc., 365 U.S. 127, 81 S.Ct. 523, 5 L.Ed.2d 464 (1961), 41

Edenfield v. Fane, 507 U.S. 761, 113 S.Ct. 1792, 123 L.Ed.2d 543 (1993), 512, 513

Edgar v. K.L., 93 F.3d 256 (7th Cir.1996), 662

Edmonson v. Leesville Concrete Co., 500 U.S. 614, 111 S.Ct. 2077, 114 L.Ed.2d 660 (1991), 388

Edwards, State ex rel. Eidson v., 793 S.W.2d 1 (Tex.Crim.App.1990), 248

Edwards, United States v., 897 F.2d 445 (9th Cir.1990), 441

Edwards, United States v., 154 F.3d 915 (9th Cir.1998), 461

EEOC v. Exxon Corp., 202 F.3d 755 (5th Cir.2000), 264

EEOC v. Sidley & Austin, 315 F.3d 696 (7th Cir.2002), 540

Eidson, State ex rel. v. Edwards, 793 S.W.2d 1 (Tex.Crim.App.1990), 248

E.I. du Pont de Nemours & Co. v. Collins, 432 U.S. 46, 97 S.Ct. 2229, 53 L.Ed.2d 100 (1977), 662

E.I. DuPont De Nemours & Co. (Benlate Litigation), In re, 99 F.3d 363 (11th Cir. 1996), 412

8182 Maryland Associates, L.P. v. Sheehan, 14 S.W.3d 576 (Mo.2000), 553

Eisen, United States v., 974 F.2d 246 (2nd Cir.1992), 382

Elane v. St. Bernard Hosp., 284 Ill.App.3d 865, 220 Ill.Dec. 3, 672 N.E.2d 820 (Ill. App. 1 Dist.1996), 526

Electro-Wire Products, Inc. v. Sirote & Permutt, P.C. (In re Prince), 40 F.3d 356 (11th Cir.1994), 171

Elliott, State ex rel. Abner v., 85 Ohio St.3d 11, 706 N.E.2d 765 (Ohio 1999), 435

Ellis, Commonwealth v., 429 Mass. 362, 708 N.E.2d 644 (Mass.1999), 201

Employers Cas. Co. v. Tilley, 496 S.W.2d 552 (Tex.1973), 222

Enron Corp. Securities, Derivative & ERISA Litigation, In re, 235 F.Supp.2d 549 (S.D.Tex.2002), 349

EPIC Holdings, In re, 28 S.W.3d 511 (Tex. 2000), 244

Essex Chemical Corp. v. Hartford Acc. and Indem. Co., 993 F.Supp. 241 (D.N.J.1998), 250

Estate of (see name of party)

Estiverne, In re, 741 So.2d 649 (La.1999), 399

Ethics Advisory Panel Opinion, In re, 627 A.2d 317 (R.I.1993), 58

Eubanks, People v., 59 Cal.Rptr.2d 200, 927 P.2d 310 (Cal.1996), 200, 201

Evans v. Jeff D., 475 U.S. 717, 106 S.Ct. 1531, 89 L.Ed.2d 747 (1986), 591, 592, 593

Evans, In re, 524 F.2d 1004 (5th Cir.1975), 604

Ex parte (see name of party)

Ezold v. Wolf, Block, Schorr and Solis-Cohen, 983 F.2d 509 (3rd Cir.1992), 539

Falanga v. State Bar of Ga., 150 F.3d 1333 (11th Cir.1998), 513

Fambo v. Smith, 433 F.Supp. 590 (W.D.N.Y. 1977), 329

FDIC v. Clark, 978 F.2d 1541 (10th Cir. 1992), 297, 346

FDIC v. Cocke, 7 F.3d 396 (4th Cir.1993), 297

FDIC v. Ferguson, 982 F.2d 404 (10th Cir. 1991), 297

FDIC v. O'Melveny & Myers, 61 F.3d 17 (9th Cir.1995), 297

FDIC v. O'Melveny & Myers, 969 F.2d 744 (9th Cir.1992), 95, 296, 346

FDIC v. Mmahat, 907 F.2d 546 (5th Cir. 1990), 95, 296

Federal Sav. and Loan Ins. Corp. v. Angell, Holmes & Lea, 838 F.2d 395 (9th Cir. 1988), 99

Federal Trade Commission v. American Nat. Cellular, 868 F.2d 315 (9th Cir.1989), 200

Federal Trade Commission v. Exxon Corp., 636 F.2d 1336 (D.C.Cir.1980), 293

Federal Trade Commission v. Superior Court Trial Lawyers Ass'n, 493 U.S. 411, 110 S.Ct. 768, 107 L.Ed.2d 851 (1990), 567

Federal Trade Commission v. TRW, Inc., 628 F.2d 207 (D.C.Cir.1980), 145

Feldman v. Minars, 230 A.D.2d 356, 658 N.Y.S.2d 614 (N.Y.A.D. 1 Dept.1997), 333, 334

Feliberty v. Damon, 531 N.Y.S.2d 778, 527 N.E.2d 261 (N.Y.1988), 224

Ferrey, In re, 774 A.2d 62 (R.I.2001), 606

Ferri v. Ackerman, 444 U.S. 193, 100 S.Ct. 402, 62 L.Ed.2d 355 (1979), 68, 569

Fiandaca v. Cunningham, 827 F.2d 825 (1st Cir.1987), 164

Ficker v. Curran, 119 F.3d 1150 (4th Cir. 1997), 516

Fickett v. Superior Court, 27 Ariz.App. 793, 558 P.2d 988 (Ariz.App. Div. 2 1976), 70

Fidelity Nat. Title Ins. Co. v. Intercounty Nat. Title Ins. Co., 310 F.3d 537 (7th Cir.2002), 119

Fields–D'Arpino v. Restaurant Associates, Inc., 39 F.Supp.2d 412 (S.D.N.Y.1999), 232

Fifteenth Judicial Dist. Unified Bar Ass'n v. Glasgow, 1999 WL 1128847 (Tenn.Ct.App. 1999), 599

Fire Ins. Exchange v. Bell, 643 N.E.2d 310 (Ind.1994), 325

Fireman's Fund Ins. Co. v. McDonald, Hecht & Solberg, 36 Cal.Rptr.2d 424 (Cal.App. 4 Dist.1994), 230

Firestone Tire & Rubber Co. v. Risjord, 449 U.S. 368, 101 S.Ct. 669, 66 L.Ed.2d 571 (1981), 169

First Miami Securities, Inc. v. Sylvia, 780 So.2d 250 (Fla.App. 3 Dist.2001), 241

First Nat. Bank of Springfield v. Malpractice Research, Inc., 179 Ill.2d 353, 228 Ill.Dec. 202, 688 N.E.2d 1179 (Ill.1997), 586

First Wisconsin Mortg. Trust v. First Wisconsin Corp., 584 F.2d 201 (7th Cir.1978), 243, 244

Flack, Matter of, 272 Kan. 465, 33 P.3d 1281 (Kan.2001), 599

Flamm v. American Ass'n of University Women, 201 F.3d 144 (2nd Cir.2000), 561

Flanagan v. United States, 465 U.S. 259, 104 S.Ct. 1051, 79 L.Ed.2d 288 (1984), 170

Flatt v. Superior Court (Daniel), 36 Cal. Rptr.2d 537, 885 P.2d 950 (Cal.1994), 177

Flores v. Flores, 598 P.2d 893 (Alaska 1979), 247

Florida Bar v. Bailey, 803 So.2d 683 (Fla. 2001), 114

Florida Bar v. Beach, 675 So.2d 106 (Fla. 1996), 598

Florida Bar v. Brown, 790 So.2d 1081 (Fla. 2001), 49

Florida Bar v. Buckle, 771 So.2d 1131 (Fla. 2000), 311

Florida Bar v. Burkich–Burrell, 659 So.2d 1082 (Fla.1995), 413

Florida Bar v. Clement, 662 So.2d 690 (Fla. 1995), 53

Florida Bar v. Cox, 794 So.2d 1278 (Fla. 2001), 438

Florida Bar v. Grosso, 760 So.2d 940 (Fla. 2000), 115

Florida Bar v. Karahalis, 780 So.2d 27 (Fla. 2001), 51

Florida Bar v. Machin, 635 So.2d 938 (Fla. 1994), 378

Florida Bar v. Martocci, 791 So.2d 1074 (Fla. 2001), 398

Florida Bar v. Weinstein, 624 So.2d 261 (Fla. 1993), 514

Florida Bar v. Went For It, Inc., 515 U.S. 618, 115 S.Ct. 2371, 132 L.Ed.2d 541 (1995), 507, 515, 516, 517

Florida Bd. of Bar Examiners v. G. W. L., 364 So.2d 454 (Fla.1978), 35

Fordham, In re, 423 Mass. 481, 668 N.E.2d 816 (Mass.1996), 100

Fornari, In re, 190 A.D.2d 379, 599 N.Y.S.2d 545 (N.Y.A.D. 1 Dept.1993), 50

Forrest, Matter of, 158 N.J. 428, 730 A.2d 340 (N.J.1999), 327

Forrester v. White, 484 U.S. 219, 108 S.Ct. 538, 98 L.Ed.2d 555 (1988), 656

Fosnight, State v., 235 Kan. 52, 679 P.2d 174 (Kan.1984), 448

Fought & Co. v. Steel Engineering and Erection, Inc., 951 P.2d 487 (Hawai'i 1998), 606

Fox Searchlight Pictures, Inc. v. Paladino, 106 Cal.Rptr.2d 906 (Cal.App. 2 Dist. 2001), 535

Franzoni v. Hart Schaffner & Marx, 312 Ill. App.3d 394, 244 Ill.Dec. 744, 726 N.E.2d 719 (Ill.App. 1 Dist.2000), 235

Frasher v. West Virginia Bd. of Law Examiners, 185 W.Va. 725, 408 S.E.2d 675 (W.Va. 1991), 35

Frazer v. United States, 18 F.3d 778 (9th Cir.1994), 78

Frazier v. Superior Court, 118 Cal.Rptr.2d 129 (Cal.App. 4 Dist.2002), 251

Fred Siegel Co., L.P.A. v. Arter & Hadden, 85 Ohio St.3d 171, 707 N.E.2d 853 (Ohio 1999), 547

Freeport–McMoRan Oil & Gas Co. v. F.E.R.C., 962 F.2d 45 (D.C.Cir.1992), 485

Freezer Services, Inc., State ex rel. v. Mullen, 235 Neb. 981, 458 N.W.2d 245 (Neb.1990), 259

Freund v. Butterworth, 165 F.3d 839 (11th Cir.1999), 197

Friedman, In re, 76 Ill.2d 392, 30 Ill.Dec. 288, 392 N.E.2d 1333 (Ill.1979), 439

Fuchs v. Schick, 2002 WL 538842 (S.D.N.Y. 2002), 240

Fuchsberg, Matter of, 426 N.Y.S.2d 639 (N.Y.Ct.Jud.1978), 622, 661

Fulton, United States v., 5 F.3d 605 (2nd Cir.1993), 195

Fund of Funds, Ltd. v. Arthur Andersen & Co., 567 F.2d 225 (2nd Cir.1977), 256

Gabbert v. Conn, 131 F.3d 793 (9th Cir. 1997), 481

Gafcon, Inc. v. Ponsor & Associates, 120 Cal. Rptr.2d 392 (Cal.App. 4 Dist.2002), 611

Gagne v. Vaccaro, 255 Conn. 390, 766 A.2d 416 (Conn.2001), 123

Gagnon v. Shoblom, 409 Mass. 63, 565 N.E.2d 775 (Mass.1991), 103

Gahan, In re, 279 N.W.2d 826 (Minn.1979), 35

Gangi, United States v., 1 F.Supp.2d 256 (S.D.N.Y.1998), 137

Gardiner v. A.H. Robins Co., Inc., 747 F.2d 1180 (8th Cir.1984), 666

Gardner v. North Carolina State Bar, 316 N.C. 285, 341 S.E.2d 517 (N.C.1986), 228, 611

Garner v. Wolfinbarger, 430 F.2d 1093 (5th Cir.1970), 149

Garr v. United States Healthcare, Inc., 22 F.3d 1274 (3rd Cir.1994), 372, 373

Gas–A–Tron of Arizona v. Union Oil Co. of California, 534 F.2d 1322 (9th Cir.1976), 253

Gaspard v. Beadle, 36 S.W.3d 229 (Tex.App.-Hous. (1 Dist.) 2001), 214

Gastineau, In re, 317 Or. 545, 857 P.2d 136 (Or.1993), 99

GATX/Airlog Co. v. Evergreen Intern. Airlines, Inc., 8 F.Supp.2d 1182 (N.D.Cal. 1998), 184

Geary v. Hunton & Williams, 257 A.D.2d 482, 684 N.Y.S.2d 207 (N.Y.A.D. 1 Dept.1999), 538

GEICO v. Forbes, 1999 WL 371625 (E.D.Pa. 1999), 229

Gellene, United States v., 182 F.3d 578 (7th Cir.1999), 171

General Cigar Holdings, Inc. v. Altadis, S.A., 144 F.Supp.2d 1334 (S.D.Fla.2001), 186

General Dynamics Corp. v. Superior Court, 32 Cal.Rptr.2d 1, 876 P.2d 487 (Cal.1994), 535

General Motors Corp. v. City of New York, 501 F.2d 639 (2nd Cir.1974), 265

Gentile v. Nevada State Bar, 501 U.S. 1030, 111 S.Ct. 2720, 115 L.Ed.2d 888 (1991), 467, 468

Georgia v. McCollum, 505 U.S. 42, 112 S.Ct. 2348, 120 L.Ed.2d 33 (1992), 388, 389, 457

Georgine v. Amchem Products, Inc., 878 F.Supp. 716 (E.D.Pa.1994), 582

Gibbs v. Breed, Abbott & Morgan, 271 A.D.2d 180, 710 N.Y.S.2d 578 (N.Y.A.D. 1 Dept. 2000), 551

Gidatex, S.r.L. v. Campaniello Imports, Ltd., 82 F.Supp.2d 119 (S.D.N.Y.1999), 394

G–I Holdings, Inc. v. Baron & Budd, 179 F.Supp.2d 233 (S.D.N.Y.2001), 435

G–I Holdings, Inc. v. Baron & Budd, 199 F.R.D. 529 (S.D.N.Y.2001), 310

Gilbert v. Master Washer & Stamping Co., Inc., 104 Cal.Rptr.2d 461 (Cal.App. 2 Dist. 2001), 587

Gilbert, United States v., 198 F.3d 1293 (11th Cir.1999), 385

Gilles v. Wiley, Malehorn & Sirota, 345 N.J.Super. 119, 783 A.2d 756 (N.J.Super.A.D.2001), 118

Gionis, People v., 40 Cal.Rptr.2d 456, 892 P.2d 1199 (Cal.1995), 130

Givens v. Mullikin, 75 S.W.3d 383 (Tenn. 2002), 376

Glenn K. Jackson Inc. v. Roe, 273 F.3d 1192 (9th Cir.2001), 110

Glover v. United States, 531 U.S. 198, 121 S.Ct. 696, 148 L.Ed.2d 604 (2001), 79

Goebel, Matter of, 703 N.E.2d 1045 (Ind. 1998), 134

Golden, Matter of, 329 S.C. 335, 496 S.E.2d 619 (S.C.1998), 400

Golden Eagle Distributing Corp. v. Burroughs Corp., 801 F.2d 1531 (9th Cir. 1986), 405

Goldfarb v. Virginia State Bar, 421 U.S. 773, 95 S.Ct. 2004, 44 L.Ed.2d 572 (1975), 10, 95, 101, 102

Goldman v. State Bar, 141 Cal.Rptr. 447, 570 P.2d 463 (Cal.1977), 513

Gonzalzles v. American Exp. Credit Corp., 315 Ill.App.3d 199, 247 Ill.Dec. 881, 733 N.E.2d 345 (Ill.App. 1 Dist.2000), 561

Goodwin, Matter of, 279 S.C. 274, 305 S.E.2d 578 (S.C.1983), 448

Goodwin, United States v., 457 U.S. 368, 102 S.Ct. 2485, 73 L.Ed.2d 74 (1982), 473

Gosselin v. Webb, 242 F.3d 412 (1st Cir. 2001), 77

Gould, Inc. v. Mitsui Min. & Smelting Co., 738 F.Supp. 1121 (N.D.Ohio 1990), 183

Government of India v. Cook Industries, Inc., 569 F.2d 737 (2nd Cir.1978), 234

Government of Virgin Islands v. Zepp, 748 F.2d 125 (3rd Cir.1984), 194

Grand Jury Proceedings, In re, 13 F.3d 1293 (9th Cir.1994), 480

Grand Jury Proceedings 88–9 Cherney, In re, 899 F.2d 1039 (11th Cir.1990), 418

Grand Jury Subpoenas dated March 9, 2001, In re, 179 F.Supp.2d 270 (S.D.N.Y.2001), 131

Grand Jury Subpoena Duces Tecum, In re, 112 F.3d 910 (8th Cir.1997), 146, 147

Grand Jury Subpeona, In re, 274 F.3d 563 (1st Cir.2001), 149

Grand Jury Subpoena, In re, 204 F.3d 516 (4th Cir.2000), 419

Grand Jury Subpoena Served Upon Doe, In re, 781 F.2d 238 (2nd Cir.1986), 479

Granewich v. Harding, 329 Or. 47, 985 P.2d 788 (Or.1999), 298

Grayson v. Wofsey, Rosen, Kweskin & Kuriansky, 231 Conn. 168, 646 A.2d 195 (Conn.1994), 66

Great Atlantic & Pac. Tea Co., Inc. v. Cottrell, 424 U.S. 366, 96 S.Ct. 923, 47 L.Ed.2d 55 (1976), 603

Greate Bay Hotel & Casino, Inc. v. Atlantic City, 264 N.J.Super. 213, 624 A.2d 102 (N.J.Super.L.1993), 180

Green, In re, 11 P.3d 1078 (Colo.2000), 100

Green, United States ex rel. v. Washington, 917 F.Supp. 1238 (N.D.Ill.1996), 490

Greene v. Grievance Committee, 444 N.Y.S.2d 883, 429 N.E.2d 390 (N.Y.1981), 513

Greenspan, United States v., 26 F.3d 1001 (10th Cir.1994), 624

Greycas, Inc. v. Proud, 826 F.2d 1560 (7th Cir.1987), 69, 347

Grievance Adm'r v. Fried, 456 Mich. 234, 570 N.W.2d 262 (Mich.1997), 50

Grievance Committee v. Rottner, 152 Conn. 59, 203 A.2d 82 (Conn.1964), 173

Grievance Proceeding, In re, 2002 WL 31106389 (D.Conn.2002), 306

Griffiths, In re, 413 U.S. 717, 93 S.Ct. 2851, 37 L.Ed.2d 910 (1973), 45

Grinnell Corp., United States v., 384 U.S. 563, 86 S.Ct. 1698, 16 L.Ed.2d 778 (1966), 632

Gross, Matter of, 435 Mass. 445, 759 N.E.2d 288 (Mass.2001), 392

GTE North, Inc. v. Apache Products Co., 914 F.Supp. 1575 (N.D.Ill.1996), 238

Guardianship of (see name of party)

Guerra v. Collins, 916 F.Supp. 620 (S.D.Tex. 1995), 488

Gulf Oil Co. v. Bernard, 452 U.S. 89, 101 S.Ct. 2193, 68 L.Ed.2d 693 (1981), 579, 580

Guralnick v. New Jersey Supreme Court, 747 F.Supp. 1109 (D.N.J.1990), 122

Gutfreund, In re, Exchange Act Release No. 31 (1992), 361

Hadix v. Johnson, 230 F.3d 840 (6th Cir. 2000), 591

Hafter v. Farkas, 498 F.2d 587 (2nd Cir. 1974), 126

Haines v. Liggett Group, Inc., 814 F.Supp. 414 (D.N.J.1993), 119

Haines v. Liggett Group, 975 F.2d 81 (3rd Cir.1992), 633

Hale, In re, 243 Ill.Dec. 174, 723 N.E.2d 206 (Ill.1999), 36

Hall v. Clifton Precision, 150 F.R.D. 525 (E.D.Pa.1993), 399

Hallinan v. Committee of Bar Examiners, 65 Cal.2d 447, 55 Cal.Rptr. 228, 421 P.2d 76 (Cal.1966), 34, 35

Halper, United States v., 490 U.S. 435, 109 S.Ct. 1892, 104 L.Ed.2d 487 (1989), 62

Hambarian v. Superior Court, 118 Cal. Rptr.2d 725, 44 P.3d 102 (Cal.2002), 200

Hammad, United States v., 846 F.2d 854 (2nd Cir.1988), 315

Hanlon v. Chrysler Corp., 150 F.3d 1011 (9th Cir.1998), 582

Hanna, Matter of, 294 S.C. 56, 362 S.E.2d 632 (S.C.1987), 100

Hansen v. Anderson, Wilmarth & Van Der Maaten, 630 N.W.2d 818 (Iowa 2001), 348

Hansen, State v., 122 Wash.2d 712, 862 P.2d 117 (Wash.1993), 296

Harper, In re, 785 A.2d 311 (D.C.2001), 609

Harper, State v., 995 P.2d 1143 (Okla.2000), 305

Harris v. New York, 401 U.S. 222, 91 S.Ct. 643, 28 L.Ed.2d 1 (1971), 436

Harris, In re, 334 Or. 353, 49 P.3d 778 (Or. 2002), 63

Haskell, Matter of, 136 Wash.2d 300, 962 P.2d 813 (Wash.1998), 532

Hastings v. Judicial Conference of United States, 829 F.2d 91 (D.C.Cir.1987), 666

Hathcock v. Navistar Intern., 53 F.3d 36 (4th Cir.1995), 634

Hawk v. State Bar, 247 Cal.Rptr. 599, 754 P.2d 1096 (Cal.1988), 127

Healy v. Gray, 184 Iowa 111, 168 N.W. 222 (Iowa 1918), 208

Hear, Matter of, 755 N.E.2d 579 (Ind.2001), 615

Hearst, United States v., 638 F.2d 1190 (9th Cir.1980), 201

Heilprin, In re, 168 Wis.2d 1, 482 N.W.2d 908 (Wis.1992), 215

Heintz v. Jenkins, 514 U.S. 291, 115 S.Ct. 1489, 131 L.Ed.2d 395 (1995), 80

Hendry v. Pelland, 73 F.3d 397 (D.C.Cir. 1996), 74, 171

Henriksen v. Great American Savings & Loan, 14 Cal.Rptr.2d 184 (Cal.App. 1 Dist. 1992), 259

Hensley v. Eckerhart, 461 U.S. 424, 103 S.Ct. 1933, 76 L.Ed.2d 40 (1983), 587, 589

Herbster v. North American Co. for Life and Health Ins., 150 Ill.App.3d 21, 103 Ill.Dec. 322, 501 N.E.2d 343 (Ill.App. 2 Dist.1986), 534

Hernandez v. Spears, 2002 WL 1205058 (S.D.Fla.2002), 203

Hernandez v. State, 750 So.2d 50 (Fla.App. 3 Dist.1999), 202

Herrera v. Collins, 506 U.S. 390, 113 S.Ct. 853, 122 L.Ed.2d 203 (1993), 491

Herron v. Jones, 276 Ark. 493, 637 S.W.2d 569 (Ark.1982), 240

H.F. Ahmanson & Co. v. Salomon Brothers, Inc., 229 Cal.App.3d 1445, 280 Cal.Rptr. 614 (Cal.App. 2 Dist.1991), 234

Hickman v. Taylor, 329 U.S. 495, 67 S.Ct. 385, 91 L.Ed. 451 (1947), 132, 133

Hilmon Co. (V.I.) Inc. v. Hyatt Intern., 899 F.2d 250 (3rd Cir.1990), 375

Himmel, In re, 125 Ill.2d 531, 127 Ill.Dec. 708, 533 N.E.2d 790 (Ill.1988), 40, 56, 58, 333

Hingle, In re, 717 So.2d 636 (La.1998), 435

Hirschfeld, In re, 192 Ariz. 40, 960 P.2d 640 (Ariz.1998), 99

Hirschfeld v. Superior Court, 184 Ariz. 208, 908 P.2d 22 (Ariz.App. Div. 1 1995), 400

Hirschkop v. Snead, 594 F.2d 356 (4th Cir. 1979), 467

Hishon v. King & Spalding, 467 U.S. 69, 104 S.Ct. 2229, 81 L.Ed.2d 59 (1984), 539

Hiss, In re, 368 Mass. 447, 333 N.E.2d 429 (Mass.1975), 35

Hizey v. Carpenter, 119 Wash.2d 251, 830 P.2d 646 (Wash.1992), 23, 71

Hoare, In re, 155 F.3d 937 (8th Cir.1998), 55

Hoff v. Mayer, Brown & Platt, 331 Ill.App.3d 732, 265 Ill.Dec. 225, 772 N.E.2d 263 (Ill. App. 1 Dist.2002), 554

Holdren v. General Motors Corp., 13 F.Supp.2d 1192 (D.Kan.1998), 307

Holloway v. Arkansas, 435 U.S. 475, 98 S.Ct. 1173, 55 L.Ed.2d 426 (1978), 190, 191, 192, 193

Holtzman, In re, 573 N.Y.S.2d 39, 577 N.E.2d 30 (N.Y.1991), 644

Hopper v. Frank, 16 F.3d 92 (5th Cir.1994), 298

Horn, United States v., 29 F.3d 754 (1st Cir.1994), 413

Horne v. Peckham, 97 Cal.App.3d 404, 158 Cal.Rptr. 714 (Cal.App. 3 Dist.1979), 65, 67

Houghton v. Department of Health, 962 P.2d 58 (Utah 1998), 267

Houston, In re, 127 N.M. 582, 985 P.2d 752 (N.M.1999), 162

Howard v. Babcock, 25 Cal.Rptr.2d 80, 863 P.2d 150 (Cal.1993), 553

Howes, Matter of, 123 N.M. 311, 940 P.2d 159 (N.M.1997), 317

Hughes v. Booker, 220 F.3d 346 (5th Cir. 2000), 375

Hughes v. Consol–Pennsylvania Coal Co., 945 F.2d 594 (3rd Cir.1991), 170

Hughes & Coleman, In re, 60 S.W.3d 540 (Ky.2001), 523

Hunoval, In re, 294 N.C. 740, 247 S.E.2d 230 (N.C.1977), 567, 568

Hunydee v. United States, 355 F.2d 183 (9th Cir.1965), 150

Idaho v. Freeman, 507 F.Supp. 706 (D.Idaho 1981), 632

Idaho State Bar v. Warrick, 137 Idaho 86, 44 P.3d 1141 (Idaho 2002), 475

Image Technical Service v. Eastman Kodak Co., 136 F.3d 1354 (9th Cir.1998), 179

Image Technical Services v. Eastman Kodak Co., 820 F.Supp. 1212 (N.D.Cal.1993), 179

Imbler v. Pachtman, 424 U.S. 409, 96 S.Ct. 984, 47 L.Ed.2d 128 (1976), 491

Inquiry of Broadbelt, In re, 146 N.J. 501, 683 A.2d 543 (N.J.1996), 658

In re (see name of party)

International Business Machines Corp., In re, 45 F.3d 641 (2nd Cir.1995), 634

IBM v. Levin, 579 F.2d 271 (3rd Cir.1978), 178, 179, 244

Iowa Supreme Court Bd. of Professional Ethics and Conduct v. Hill, 576 N.W.2d 91 (Iowa 1998), 48

Iowa Supreme Court Bd. of Professional Ethics and Conduct v. Hughes, 557 N.W.2d 890 (Iowa 1996), 281

Iowa Supreme Court Bd. of Professional Ethics and Conduct v. Lane, 642 N.W.2d 296 (Iowa 2002), 51

Iowa Supreme Court Bd. of Professional Ethics and Conduct v. Visser, 629 N.W.2d 376 (Iowa 2001), 468

Israel, State ex rel. Oklahoma Bar Ass'n v., 25 P.3d 909 (Okla.2001), 610

Iulo, Matter of, 564 Pa. 205, 766 A.2d 335 (Pa.2001), 55

Jackman, In re, 165 N.J. 580, 761 A.2d 1103 (N.J.2000), 609

Jackson, People v., 167 Cal.App.3d 829, 213 Cal.Rptr. 521 (Cal.App. 3 Dist.1985), 256

Jacobson v. Knepper & Moga, P.C., 185 Ill.2d 372, 235 Ill.Dec. 936, 706 N.E.2d 491 (Ill. 1998), 537

Jandrt ex rel. Brueggeman v. Jerome Foods, Inc., 227 Wis.2d 531, 597 N.W.2d 744 (Wis.1999), 376

January 1976 Grand Jury, In re, 534 F.2d 719 (7th Cir.1976), 424

J.E.B. v. Alabama ex rel. T.B., 511 U.S. 127, 114 S.Ct. 1419, 128 L.Ed.2d 89 (1994), 388, 457

Jeffers, In re, 3 Cal. State Bar Ct. Rptr. 211, 1994 WL 715918 (Cal.Bar Ct.1994), 408, 409

Jenkins v. Heintz, 124 F.3d 824 (7th Cir. 1997), 81

Jia v. Board of Bar Examiners, 427 Mass. 777, 696 N.E.2d 131 (Mass.1998), 43

Jimerson, People v., 166 Ill.2d 211, 209 Ill. Dec. 738, 652 N.E.2d 278 (Ill.1995), 488

John Doe Grand Jury Investigation, Matter of, 408 Mass. 480, 562 N.E.2d 69 (Mass. 1990), 139

Johnson v. Daley, 117 F.Supp.2d 889 (W.D.Wis.2000), 591

Johnson v. District of Columbia, 190 F.Supp.2d 34 (D.D.C.2002), 592

Johnson, Petition of, 322 N.W.2d 616 (Minn. 1982), 52

Jones v. Barnes, 463 U.S. 745, 103 S.Ct. 3308, 77 L.Ed.2d 987 (1983), 375

Jones v. Board of Com'rs of Alabama State Bar, 737 F.2d 996 (11th Cir.1984), 44

Jones v. Clinton, 36 F.Supp.2d 1118 (E.D.Ark.1999), 411

Jones, People v., 404 N.Y.S.2d 85, 375 N.E.2d 41 (N.Y.1978), 329

Jones Lang Wootton USA v. LeBoeuf, Lamb, Greene & MacRae, 243 A.D.2d 168, 674 N.Y.S.2d 280 (N.Y.A.D. 1 Dept.1998), 230

Jorgenson v. Volusia County, 846 F.2d 1350 (11th Cir.1988), 405

JPMorgan Chase Bankv. Liberty Mut. Ins. Co., 189 F.Supp.2d 20 (S.D.N.Y.2002), 180

Judicial Campaign Complaint Against Burick, In re, 95 Ohio Misc.2d 1, 705 N.E.2d 422 (Ohio Comm. of Judges 1999), 637

Justices of Appellate Division v. Erdmann, 347 N.Y.S.2d 441, 301 N.E.2d 426 (N.Y. 1973), 643

Kachmar v. SunGard Data Systems, Inc., 109 F.3d 173 (3rd Cir.1997), 535

Kaiser Foundation Health Plan, Inc. v. Aguiluz, 54 Cal.Rptr.2d 665 (Cal.App. 1 Dist. 1996), 115

Kala v. Aluminum Smelting & Refining Co., 81 Ohio St.3d 1, 688 N.E.2d 258 (Ohio 1998), 259

Kalina v. Fletcher, 522 U.S. 118, 118 S.Ct. 502, 139 L.Ed.2d 471 (1997), 485

Kamasinski v. Judicial Review Council, 44 F.3d 106 (2nd Cir.1994), 648

Kansas Public Employees Retirement System v. Kutak Rock, 44 P.3d 407 (Kan.2002), 297

Kaplan v. Pavalon & Gifford, 12 F.3d 87 (7th Cir.1993), 527

Kaplan v. Rand, 192 F.3d 60 (2nd Cir.1999), 595

Karahalis, Matter of, 429 Mass. 121, 706 N.E.2d 655 (Mass.1999), 51

Karan, In re Guardianship of, 110 Wash.App. 76, 38 P.3d 396 (Wash.App. Div. 3 2002), 70

Kassis v. Teacher's Ins. and Annuity Ass'n, 695 N.Y.S.2d 515, 717 N.E.2d 674 (N.Y. 1999), 260

Kastigar v. United States, 406 U.S. 441, 92 S.Ct. 1653, 32 L.Ed.2d 212 (1972), 436

Kath v. Western Media, Inc., 684 P.2d 98 (Wyo.1984), 327

Katris v. Immigration and Naturalization Service, 562 F.2d 866 (2nd Cir.1977), 402

Kay v. Ehrler, 499 U.S. 432, 111 S.Ct. 1435, 113 L.Ed.2d 486 (1991), 587

Keegan Management Co., Securities Litigation, In re, 78 F.3d 431 (9th Cir.1996), 373

Keller v. State Bar of California, 496 U.S. 1, 110 S.Ct. 2228, 110 L.Ed.2d 1 (1990), 31, 562

Kelley, In re, 276 Cal.Rptr. 375, 801 P.2d 1126 (Cal.1990), 52

Kelly v. MD Buyline, Inc., 2 F.Supp.2d 420 (S.D.N.Y.1998), 98

Kenelly, People v., 648 P.2d 1065 (Colo.1982), 378

Kennedy, In re, 442 A.2d 79 (Del.Supr.1982), 116

Kennedy v. Carlson, 544 N.W.2d 1 (Minn. 1996), 490

Kennedy v. Zimmermann, 601 N.W.2d 61 (Iowa 1999), 471

Kentucky Bar Ass'n v. Bates, 26 S.W.3d 788 (Ky.2000), 273

Kentucky Bar Ass'n v. Geisler, 938 S.W.2d 578 (Ky.1997), 327

Kentucky Bar Ass'n v. Mandello, 32 S.W.3d 763 (Ky.2000), 515

Kevlik v. Goldstein, 724 F.2d 844 (1st Cir. 1984), 238

Kirkland Const. Co. v. James, 39 Mass.App. Ct. 559, 658 N.E.2d 699 (Mass.App.Ct. 1995), 347

Kirsh, In re, 973 F.2d 1454 (9th Cir.1992), 206

Kleiner v. First Nat. Bank of Atlanta, 751 F.2d 1193 (11th Cir.1985), 580

Klubock, United States v., 639 F.Supp. 117 (D.Mass.1986), 477

Koden v. United States Dept. of Justice, 564 F.2d 228 (7th Cir.1977), 513

Koehler v. Wales, 16 Wash.App. 304, 556 P.2d 233 (Wash.App. Div. 2 1976), 547

Konigsberg v. State Bar (II), 366 U.S. 36, 81 S.Ct. 997, 6 L.Ed.2d 105 (1961), 36

Konigsberg v. State Bar (I), 353 U.S. 252, 77 S.Ct. 722, 1 L.Ed.2d 810 (1957), 36

Kooritzky v. Herman, 178 F.3d 1315 (D.C.Cir.1999), 587

Kor, People v., 129 Cal.App.2d 436, 277 P.2d 94 (Cal.App. 2 Dist.1954), 420

Kortum, State ex rel. Wal–Mart Stores v., 251 Neb. 805, 559 N.W.2d 496 (Neb.1997), 236

Koscove v. Bolte, 30 P.3d 784 (Colo.App. 2001), 606

Kramer, In re, 282 F.3d 721 (9th Cir.2002), 56

Krule, In re, 194 Ill.2d 109, 251 Ill.Dec. 665, 741 N.E.2d 259 (Ill.2000), 34

Kyles v. Whitley, 514 U.S. 419, 115 S.Ct. 1555, 131 L.Ed.2d 490 (1995), 330

Laborde v. Aronson, 112 Cal.Rptr.2d 119 (Cal.App. 4 Dist.2001), 374

Lamb, In re, 260 Cal.Rptr. 856, 776 P.2d 765 (Cal.1989), 50

Lamberis, In re, 93 Ill.2d 222, 66 Ill.Dec. 623, 443 N.E.2d 549 (Ill.1982), 50

Lansing–Delaware Water Dist. v. Oak Lane Park, Inc., 248 Kan. 563, 808 P.2d 1369 (Kan.1991), 259

Larsen, Matter of, 532 Pa. 326, 616 A.2d 529 (Pa.1992), 663

Latham v. Castillo, 972 S.W.2d 66 (Tex.1998), 81

Lathrop v. Donohue, 367 U.S. 820, 81 S.Ct. 1826, 6 L.Ed.2d 1191 (1961), 31, 562

Lawline v. American Bar Ass'n, 956 F.2d 1378 (7th Cir.1992), 598

Law Offices of Bernard D. Morley, P. C. v. MacFarlane, 647 P.2d 1215 (Colo.1982), 478

Law Students Civil Rights Research Council, Inc. v. Wadmond, 401 U.S. 154, 91 S.Ct. 720, 27 L.Ed.2d 749 (1971), 36

Lawyer Disciplinary Bd. v. Artimez, 208 W.Va. 288, 540 S.E.2d 156 (W.Va.2000), 214

Lazy Oil Co. v. Witco Corp., 166 F.3d 581 (3rd Cir.1999), 583

Lazy Seven Coal Sales, Inc. v. Stone & Hinds, P.C., 813 S.W.2d 400 (Tenn.1991), 71

Lee v. American Eagle Airlines, 93 F.Supp.2d 1322 (S.D.Fla.2000), 398

Lefcourt v. United States, 125 F.3d 79 (2nd Cir.1997), 484

Legal Services Corp. v. Velazquez, 531 U.S. 533, 121 S.Ct. 1043, 149 L.Ed.2d 63 (2001), 572, 573

Legal Services for New York City, United States v., 100 F.Supp.2d 42 (D.D.C.2000), 228

Lettley v. State, 358 Md. 26, 746 A.2d 392 (Md.2000), 193

Levine v. Bayne, Snell & Krause, Ltd., 40 S.W.3d 92 (Tex.2001), 107

Levine v. Kling, 123 F.3d 580 (7th Cir.1997), 68

Lewis, In re, 266 Ga. 61, 463 S.E.2d 862 (Ga.1995), 93

Lewis v. Superior Court, 62 Cal.Rptr.2d 331 (Cal.App. 4 Dist.1997), 199

Lichtman v. Estrin, 282 A.D.2d 326, 723 N.Y.S.2d 185 (N.Y.A.D. 1 Dept.2001), 537

Liljeberg v. Health Services Acquisition Corp., 486 U.S. 847, 108 S.Ct. 2194, 100 L.Ed.2d 855 (1988), 631

Lindsey, In re, 158 F.3d 1263 (D.C.Cir.1998), 147

Lipin v. Bender, 620 N.Y.S.2d 744, 644 N.E.2d 1300 (N.Y.1994), 397

Lisi v. Several Attorneys, 596 A.2d 313 (R.I. 1991), 621

Litchfield, United States v., 959 F.2d 1514 (10th Cir.1992), 446

Liteky v. United States, 510 U.S. 540, 114 S.Ct. 1147, 127 L.Ed.2d 474 (1994), 632, 633, 634

Litton Systems, Inc. v. AT & T, 700 F.2d 785 (2nd Cir.1983), 413

Litton Systems, Inc. v. AT & T, 91 F.R.D. 574 (S.D.N.Y.1981), 413

Litz, In re, 721 N.E.2d 258 (Ind.1999), 468

Locascio, United States v., 6 F.3d 924 (2nd Cir.1993), 197

Loggerhead Turtle v. County Council of Volusia County, 307 F.3d 1318 (11th Cir.2002), 588

Long, United States v., 857 F.2d 436 (8th Cir.1988), 448

Lopez, United States v., 4 F.3d 1455 (9th Cir.1993), 316, 317

Los Angeles Police Dept. v. United Reporting Pub. Corp., 528 U.S. 32, 120 S.Ct. 483, 145 L.Ed.2d 451 (1999), 517

Louisiana State Bar Ass'n v. Thierry, 366 So.2d 1305 (La.1978), 436

Lowery v. Cardwell, 575 F.2d 727 (9th Cir. 1978), 448

Lowery, United States v., 166 F.3d 1119 (11th Cir.1999), 476

Lowman v. Karp, 190 Mich.App. 448, 476 N.W.2d 428 (Mich.App.1991), 66

Lucas v. Hamm, 56 Cal.2d 583, 15 Cal.Rptr. 821, 364 P.2d 685 (Cal.1961), 65, 69

Lucido v. Cravath, Swaine & Moore, 425 F.Supp. 123 (S.D.N.Y.1977), 539

Luckey v. Miller, 976 F.2d 673 (11th Cir. 1992), 490

Luethke v. Suhr, 264 Neb. 505, 650 N.W.2d 220 (Neb.2002), 322

Lujan, People v., 890 P.2d 109 (Colo.1995), 53

Lupert v. California State Bar, 761 F.2d 1325 (9th Cir.1985), 41

Lustig v. Horn, 315 Ill.App.3d 319, 247 Ill. Dec. 558, 732 N.E.2d 613 (Ill.App. 1 Dist. 2000), 123

Lutz, Matter of, 101 Idaho 24, 607 P.2d 1078 (Idaho 1980), 378

Lynch, State v., 796 P.2d 1150 (Okla.1990), 568

Lysick v. Walcom, 258 Cal.App.2d 136, 65 Cal.Rptr. 406 (Cal.App. 1 Dist.1968), 225

MacDraw, Inc. v. CIT Group Equipment Financing, Inc., 138 F.3d 33 (2nd Cir.1998), 650

Mackler Productions, Inc. v. Cohen, 146 F.3d 126 (2nd Cir.1998), 385

MacMillan v. Scheffy, 147 N.H. 362, 787 A.2d 867 (N.H.2001), 69

Macumber, State v., 112 Ariz. 569, 544 P.2d 1084 (Ariz.1976), 139, 492

Madrid v. Gomez, 190 F.3d 990 (9th Cir. 1999), 591

Mahoney v. Pataki, 745 N.Y.S.2d 760, 772 N.E.2d 1118 (N.Y.2002), 589

Majorek, Application of, 244 Neb. 595, 508 N.W.2d 275 (Neb.1993), 34

Mallard v. United States Dist. Court, 490 U.S. 296, 109 S.Ct. 1814, 104 L.Ed.2d 318 (1989), 570, 571

Maloney, United States v., 71 F.3d 645 (7th Cir.1995), 439

Maness v. Meyers, 419 U.S. 449, 95 S.Ct. 584, 42 L.Ed.2d 574 (1975), 426

Manning v. Waring, Cox, James, Sklar & Allen, 849 F.2d 222 (6th Cir.1988), 258

Margow, Matter of Estate of, 77 N.J. 316, 390 A.2d 591 (N.J.1978), 601

Maritrans GP Inc. v. Pepper, Hamilton & Scheetz, 529 Pa. 241, 602 A.2d 1277 (Pa. 1992), 71, 170

Mark Marks, P.A., State v., 698 So.2d 533 (Fla.1997), 328

Marten v. Yellow Freight System, Inc., 1996 WL 568840 (D.Kan.1996), 234

Martin, United States v., 773 F.2d 579 (4th Cir.1985), 135

Mason v. Florida Bar, 208 F.3d 952 (11th Cir.2000), 510

Massachusetts School of Law at Andover, Inc. v. American Bar Ass'n, 107 F.3d 1026 (3rd Cir.1997), 41

Massengale v. Ray, 267 F.3d 1298 (11th Cir. 2001), 374

Matta–Timmins, United States v., 81 F.Supp.2d 193 (D.Mass.2000), 483

Matter of (see name of party)

Maxwell v. Superior Court, 180 Cal.Rptr. 177, 639 P.2d 248 (Cal.1982), 202

Mayol v. Summers, Watson & Kimpel, 223 Ill.App.3d 794, 166 Ill.Dec. 154, 585 N.E.2d 1176 (Ill.App. 4 Dist.1992), 71

McBryde v. Committee to Review Circuit Council Conduct, 264 F.3d 52 (D.C.Cir. 2001), 667

McCuin v. Texas Power & Light Co., 714 F.2d 1255 (5th Cir.1983), 626

McDonnell Douglas Corp., United States ex rel. O'Keefe v., 132 F.3d 1252 (8th Cir. 1998), 317

McKenzie Const. v. St. Croix Storage Corp., 961 F.Supp. 857 (D.Virgin Islands 1997), 232

McKesson HBOC, Inc. v. Adler, 254 Ga.App. 500, 562 S.E.2d 809 (Ga.App.2002), 135

McMahon v. Shea, 547 Pa. 124, 688 A.2d 1179 (Pa.1997), 66

McPhaul v. United States, 364 U.S. 372, 81 S.Ct. 138, 5 L.Ed.2d 136 (1960), 141

Meehan v. Shaughnessy, 404 Mass. 419, 535 N.E.2d 1255 (Mass.1989), 548

Mehaffy, Rider, Windholz & Wilson v. Central Bank Denver, N.A., 892 P.2d 230 (Colo.1995), 349

Melissa W., Guardianship of, 118 Cal.Rptr.2d 42 (Cal.App. 2 Dist.2002), 385

Merco Constr. Engineers, Inc. v. Municipal Court, 147 Cal.Rptr. 631, 581 P.2d 636 (Cal.1978), 602

Meredith, People v., 175 Cal.Rptr. 612, 631 P.2d 46 (Cal.1981), 425

Mergler v. Crystal Properties Associates, Ltd., 179 A.D.2d 177, 583 N.Y.S.2d 229 (N.Y.A.D. 1 Dept.1992), 72

Messing, Rudavsky & Weliky, P.C. v. President and Fellows of Harvard College, 436 Mass. 347, 764 N.E.2d 825 (Mass.2002), 309

Meyerhofer v. Empire Fire & Marine Ins. Co., 497 F.2d 1190 (2nd Cir.1974), 362

Michelman, In re, 202 A.D.2d 87, 616 N.Y.S.2d 409 (N.Y.A.D. 2 Dept.1994), 164

Mickens v. Taylor, 535 U.S. 162, 122 S.Ct. 1237, 152 L.Ed.2d 291 (2002), 192

Microsoft Corp., United States v., 253 F.3d 34 (D.C.Cir.2001), 634, 657

Microsoft Corp., United States v., 56 F.3d 1448 (D.C.Cir.1995), 634

Milbank, Tweed, Hadley & McCloy v. Boon, 13 F.3d 537 (2nd Cir.1994), 170

Miller v. Metzinger, 91 Cal.App.3d 31, 154 Cal.Rptr. 22 (Cal.App. 2 Dist.1979), 69

Miller v. Mooney, 431 Mass. 57, 725 N.E.2d 545 (Mass.2000), 69

Miller, State v., 600 N.W.2d 457 (Minn.1999), 314

Mirabito v. Liccardo, 5 Cal.Rptr.2d 571 (Cal. App. 1 Dist.1992), 71

Mireles v. Waco, 502 U.S. 9, 112 S.Ct. 286, 116 L.Ed.2d 9 (1991), 656

Mitchell v. Metropolitan Life Ins. Co., 2002 WL 441194 (S.D.N.Y.2002), 236

Mitchum v. Hudgens, 533 So.2d 194 (Ala. 1988), 224

Mittelman, United States v., 999 F.2d 440 (9th Cir.1993), 479

Mix, Matter of, 901 F.2d 1431 (7th Cir.1990), 78

Molins PLC v. Textron, Inc., 48 F.3d 1172 (Fed.Cir.1995), 177

Monsanto, United States v., 491 U.S. 600, 109 S.Ct. 2657, 105 L.Ed.2d 512 (1989), 482

Montana Department of Revenue v. Kurth Ranch, 511 U.S. 767, 114 S.Ct. 1937, 128 L.Ed.2d 767 (1994), 62

Montanez v. Irizarry–Rodriguez, 273 N.J.Super. 276, 641 A.2d 1079 (N.J.Super.A.D.1994), 219

Monument Builders of Pennsylvania, Inc. v. Catholic Cemeteries Ass'n, Inc., 190 F.R.D. 164 (E.D.Pa.1999), 627

Morales, People v., 329 Ill.App.3d 97, 263 Ill.Dec. 324, 768 N.E.2d 84 (Ill.App. 1 Dist.2002), 194

Morrell v. State, 575 P.2d 1200 (Alaska 1978), 425

Morris, United States v., 988 F.2d 1335 (4th Cir.1993), 79

Morrissey, In re, 168 F.3d 134 (4th Cir.1999), 468

Morrissey v. Commonwealth, 16 Va.App. 172, 428 S.E.2d 503 (Va.App.1993), 649

Morrissey v. Virginia State Bar, 248 Va. 334, 448 S.E.2d 615 (Va.1994), 211

Morrow v. State Bar of California, 188 F.3d 1174 (9th Cir.1999), 31, 562

Mossow v. United States, 987 F.2d 1365 (8th Cir.1993), 68

M.R., Matter of, 135 N.J. 155, 638 A.2d 1274 (N.J.1994), 284

Mrozek, Commonwealth v., 441 Pa.Super. 425, 657 A.2d 997 (Pa.Super.1995), 130

Muhammad v. Strassburger, McKenna, Messer, Shilobod and Gutnick, 526 Pa. 541, 587 A.2d 1346 (Pa.1991), 66

Mullen, State ex rel. Freezer Services, Inc. v., 235 Neb. 981, 458 N.W.2d 245 (Neb.1990), 259

Murphy, United States v., 768 F.2d 1518 (7th Cir.1985), 440

Musick, People v., 960 P.2d 89 (Colo.1998), 49

Mustafa, In re, 631 A.2d 45 (D.C.1993), 34

Mustang Enterprises, Inc. v. Plug–In Storage Systems, Inc., 874 F.Supp. 881 (N.D.Ill. 1995), 249

Nackson, Matter of, 114 N.J. 527, 555 A.2d 1101 (N.J.1989), 419

Nakasian v. Incontrade, Inc., 409 F.Supp. 1220 (S.D.N.Y.1976), 120

National Auto Brokers Corp. v. General Motors Corp., 572 F.2d 953 (2nd Cir.1978), 627

National Credit Union Admin. Bd. v. Johnson, 133 F.3d 1097 (8th Cir.1998), 99

National Medical Enterprises v. Godbey, 924 S.W.2d 123 (Tex.1996), 234

National Union Ins. Co. v. Dowd & Dowd, P.C., 2 F.Supp.2d 1013 (N.D.Ill.1998), 229

Neal v. Clinton, No. CIV 2000-5677 (Pulaski Cty. AR, Cir.Ct.2001), 411

Nemours Foundation v. Gilbane, Aetna, Federal Ins. Co., 632 F.Supp. 418 (D.Del. 1986), 258, 259

Nesse v. Pittman, 206 F.R.D. 325 (D.D.C. 2002), 148

Neuman v. Akman, 715 A.2d 127 (D.C.1998), 553, 554

Newby v. Enron Corp., 235 F.Supp.2d 549 (S.D.Tex.2002), 157

News America Pub., Inc., In re, 974 S.W.2d 97 (Tex.App.-San Antonio 1998), 305

New York County Lawyers' Ass'n v. Dacey, 28 A.D.2d 161, 283 N.Y.S.2d 984 (N.Y.A.D. 1 Dept.1967), 600

New York State Bar Ass'n v. Reno, 999 F.Supp. 710 (N.D.N.Y.1998), 282

New York Times Co. v. Sullivan, 376 U.S. 254, 84 S.Ct. 710, 11 L.Ed.2d 686 (1964), 645

Nichols v. Butler, 953 F.2d 1550 (11th Cir. 1992), 441

Nichols v. Keller, 19 Cal.Rptr.2d 601 (Cal. App. 5 Dist.1993), 91

Niesig v. Team I, 559 N.Y.S.2d 493, 558 N.E.2d 1030 (N.Y.1990), 308, 309

Nissan Motor Co., Ltd. v. Nissan Computer Corp., 180 F.Supp.2d 1089 (C.D.Cal.2002), 459

Nissenson v. Bradley, 316 Ill.App.3d 1035, 250 Ill.Dec. 370, 738 N.E.2d 586 (Ill.App. 1 Dist.2000), 410

Nitla S.A. de C.V., In re, 92 S.W.3d 419 (Tex.2002), 138

Nix v. Whiteside, 475 U.S. 157, 106 S.Ct. 988, 89 L.Ed.2d 123 (1986), 441, 446, 447, 448, 449, 453, 475

Nixon v. United States, 506 U.S. 224, 113 S.Ct. 732, 122 L.Ed.2d 1 (1993), 666

Nixon, United States v., 418 U.S. 683, 94 S.Ct. 3090, 41 L.Ed.2d 1039 (1974), 146

Nodvin v. State Bar of Georgia, 273 Ga. 559, 544 S.E.2d 142 (Ga.2001), 122

Nofziger, United States v., 878 F.2d 442 (D.C.Cir.1989), 266

Norris v. Alabama State Bar, 582 So.2d 1034 (Ala.1991), 514

North Carolina State Bar v. Graves, 50 N.C.App. 450, 274 S.E.2d 396 (N.C.App. 1981), 378, 477

Novo Terapeutisk Laboratorium A/S v. Baxter Travenol Laboratories, Inc., 607 F.2d 186 (7th Cir.1979), 252

Ockrassa, Matter of, 165 Ariz. 576, 799 P.2d 1350 (Ariz.1990), 248

Office of Disciplinary Counsel v. Ball, 67 Ohio St.3d 401, 618 N.E.2d 159 (Ohio 1993), 116

Office of Disciplinary Counsel v. Breiner, 969 P.2d 1285 (Hawai'i 1999), 399

Office of Disciplinary Counsel v. Eilberg, 497 Pa. 388, 441 A.2d 1193 (Pa.1982), 270

Office of Disciplinary Counsel v. Hazelkorn, 18 Ohio St.3d 297, 480 N.E.2d 1116 (Ohio 1985), 409

Office of Disciplinary Counsel v. Massey, 80 Ohio St.3d 605, 687 N.E.2d 734 (Ohio 1998), 484

Office of Disciplinary Counsel v. Shane, 81 Ohio St.3d 494, 692 N.E.2d 571 (Ohio 1998), 512

Ofshe, United States v., 817 F.2d 1508 (11th Cir.1987), 315

O'Hagan, United States v., 521 U.S. 642, 117 S.Ct. 2199, 138 L.Ed.2d 724 (1997), 209

Ohio State Bar Assn. v. Kanter, 86 Ohio St.3d 554, 715 N.E.2d 1140 (Ohio 1999), 525

Ohralik v. Ohio State Bar Ass'n, 436 U.S. 447, 98 S.Ct. 1912, 56 L.Ed.2d 444 (1978), 502, 503, 505, 507, 512, 513, 549, 581

Oil, Chemical and Atomic Workers Intern. Union, AFL–CIO v. Department of Energy, 288 F.3d 452 (D.C.Cir.2002), 588

O'Keefe, United States ex rel. v. McDonnell Douglas Corp., 132 F.3d 1252 (8th Cir. 1998), 317

Oklahoma Bar Ass'n, State ex rel. v. Cummings, 863 P.2d 1164 (Okla.1993), 124

Oklahoma Bar Ass'n, State ex rel. v. Israel, 25 P.3d 909 (Okla.2001), 610

Olive v. Maas, 811 So.2d 644 (Fla.2002), 567

Olwell, State v., 64 Wash.2d 828, 394 P.2d 681 (Wash.1964), 423

O'Melveny & Myers v. F.D.I.C., 512 U.S. 79, 114 S.Ct. 2048, 129 L.Ed.2d 67 (1994), 297

Omoruyi, United States v., 7 F.3d 880 (9th Cir.1993), 388

Opinion 33 of Committee on Unauthorized Practice of Law, Matter of, 160 N.J. 63, 733 A.2d 478 (N.J.1999), 607

Oracle Securities Litigation, In re, 829 F.Supp. 1176 (N.D.Cal.1993), 302

Orshoski v. Krieger, 2001 WL 1388037 (Ohio App. 6 Dist.2001), 348

Ortega v. O'Leary, 843 F.2d 258 (7th Cir. 1988), 441

Ositis, In re, 333 Or. 366, 40 P.3d 500 (Or. 2002), 394

Osprey v. Cabana Ltd. Partnership, 340 S.C. 367, 532 S.E.2d 269 (S.C.2000), 585

Outdoor Advertising Ass'n of Georgia, Inc. v. Garden Club of Georgia, Inc., 272 Ga. 146, 527 S.E.2d 856 (Ga.2000), 264

Ozer v. Borquez, 940 P.2d 371 (Colo.1997), 539

Paciulan v. George, 229 F.3d 1226 (9th Cir. 2000), 604

Panduit Corp. v. All States Plastic Mfg. Co., 744 F.2d 1564 (Fed.Cir.1984), 170

Pappas, Matter of, 159 Ariz. 516, 768 P.2d 1161 (Ariz.1988), 205

Paradigm Ins. Co. v. Langerman Law Offices, P.A., 200 Ariz. 146, 24 P.3d 593 (Ariz. 2001), 69

Paramount Communications Inc. v. QVC Network Inc., 637 A.2d 34 (Del. Supr.1994), 399

Parker v. Anderson, 667 F.2d 1204 (5th Cir. 1982), 583

Parker, United States v., 165 F.Supp.2d 431 (W.D.N.Y.2001), 394

Parrott v. Wilson, 707 F.2d 1262 (11th Cir. 1983), 459

Parsons v. Continental Nat. Am. Group, 113 Ariz. 223, 550 P.2d 94 (Ariz.1976), 219, 221, 222

Passante v. McWilliam, 62 Cal.Rptr.2d 298 (Cal.App. 4 Dist.1997), 206

Patrick v. Ronald Williams, P.A., 102 N.C.App. 355, 402 S.E.2d 452 (N.C.App. 1991), 74

Patsy's Brand, Inc. v. I.O.B. Realty, Inc., 2002 WL 59434 (S.D.N.Y.2002), 433

Patton v. Scholl, 1999 WL 431095 (E.D.Pa. 1999), 598

Pautler, In re, 47 P.3d 1175 (Colo.2002), 395

Payton v. New Jersey Turnpike Authority, 148 N.J. 524, 691 A.2d 321 (N.J.1997), 145

Peart, State v., 621 So.2d 780 (La.1993), 489

Peel v. Attorney Registration and Disciplinary Com'n, 496 U.S. 91, 110 S.Ct. 2281, 110 L.Ed.2d 83 (1990), 520, 521, 522

Pennwalt Corp. v. Plough, Inc., 85 F.R.D. 264 (D.Del.1980), 183

Pennzoil Co. v. Texaco, Inc., 481 U.S. 1, 107 S.Ct. 1519, 95 L.Ed.2d 1 (1987), 642

Penthouse Intern., Ltd. v. Playboy Enterprises, Inc., 86 F.R.D. 396 (S.D.N.Y.1980), 412

People v. _____ (see opposing party)

People ex rel. v. _____ (see opposing party and relator)

Pepsico, Inc. v. McMillen, 764 F.2d 458 (7th Cir.1985), 273

Perkins v. CTX Mortg. Co., 137 Wash.2d 93, 969 P.2d 93 (Wash.1999), 610

Perlstein, United States v., 126 F.2d 789 (3rd Cir.1942), 429

Person v. Association of Bar of City of New York, 554 F.2d 534 (2nd Cir.1977), 457, 586

Petit–Clair v. Nelson, 344 N.J.Super. 538, 782 A.2d 960 (N.J.Super.A.D.2001), 127

Petition of (see name of party)

Philip Morris, Inc., People v., 198 Ill.2d 87, 259 Ill.Dec. 845, 759 N.E.2d 906 (Ill.2001), 125

Phillips v. Washington Legal Foundation, 524 U.S. 156, 118 S.Ct. 1925, 141 L.Ed.2d 174 (1998), 576

Phoenix Founders, Inc. v. Marshall, 887 S.W.2d 831 (Tex.1994), 241

Pickens, Barnes & Abernathy v. Heasley, 328 N.W.2d 524 (Iowa 1983), 72

Picker Intern., Inc. v. Varian Associates, Inc., 670 F.Supp. 1363 (N.D.Ohio 1987), 182

Pioneer–Standard Electronics, Inc. v. Cap Gemini America, Inc., 2002 WL 553460 (N.D.Ohio 2002), 184

Pittman v. Cole, 267 F.3d 1269 (11th Cir. 2001), 638

P.J.S. v. Pennsylvania State Ethics Com'n, 555 Pa. 149, 723 A.2d 174 (Pa.1999), 267

Plaza Shoe Store, Inc. v. Hermel, Inc., 636 S.W.2d 53 (Mo.1982), 123

Plessinger v. Castleman & Haskell, 838 F.Supp. 448 (N.D.Cal.1993), 541

Pochopien v. Marshall, O'Toole, Gerstein, Murray & Borun, 315 Ill.App.3d 329, 247 Ill.Dec. 937, 733 N.E.2d 401 (Ill.App. 1 Dist.2000), 553

Polin, In re, 630 A.2d 1140 (D.C.1993), 34

Polk County v. Dodson, 454 U.S. 312, 102 S.Ct. 445, 70 L.Ed.2d 509 (1981), 68

Poly Software Intern., Inc. v. Su, 880 F.Supp. 1487 (D.Utah 1995), 232, 274

Pomerantz v. Schandler, 704 F.2d 681 (2nd Cir.1983), 125

Pounders v. Watson, 521 U.S. 982, 117 S.Ct. 2359, 138 L.Ed.2d 976 (1997), 399

Prager, Matter of, 422 Mass. 86, 661 N.E.2d 84 (Mass.1996), 35

Pressly, In re, 160 Vt. 319, 628 A.2d 927 (Vt.1993), 288

Primus, In re, 436 U.S. 412, 98 S.Ct. 1893, 56 L.Ed.2d 417 (1978), 505, 513, 549, 580, 585

Public Defender's Certification of Conflict and Motion to Withdraw Due to Excessive Caseload, In re, 709 So.2d 101 (Fla.1998), 490

Pulliam v. Allen, 466 U.S. 522, 104 S.Ct. 1970, 80 L.Ed.2d 565 (1984), 656

Pumphrey v. K.W. Thompson Tool Co., 62 F.3d 1128 (9th Cir.1995), 412

Radtke v. Board of Bar Examiners, 230 Wis.2d 254, 601 N.W.2d 642 (Wis.1999), 37

Ralls v. United States, 52 F.3d 223 (9th Cir. 1995), 484

Rand v. Monsanto Co., 926 F.2d 596 (7th Cir.1991), 584

Randolph, People ex rel. Conn v., 35 Ill.2d 24, 219 N.E.2d 337 (Ill.1966), 568

Raney v. Federal Bureau of Prisons, 222 F.3d 927 (Fed.Cir.2000), 589

Rapp v. Hawaii Supreme Court, 916 F.Supp. 1525 (D.Hawai'i 1996), 455

Ravich, Koster, Tobin, Oleckna, Reitman & Greenstein, Matter of, 155 N.J. 357, 715 A.2d 216 (N.J.1998), 514

Raymark Industries, Inc. v. Butera, Beausang, Cohen & Brennan, 1997 WL 746125 (E.D.Pa.1997), 98

Reardon v. Marlayne, 83 N.J. 460, 416 A.2d 852 (N.J.1980), 253

Reed, Matter of, 716 N.E.2d 426 (Ind.1999), 646

Regents of University of California, In re, 101 F.3d 1386 (Fed.Cir.1996), 151

Reorganization of Elec. Mut. Liability Ins. Co. (Bermuda), In re, 425 Mass. 419, 681 N.E.2d 838 (Mass.1997), 137

Republican Party of Minnesota v. White, 536 U.S. 765, 122 S.Ct. 2528, 153 L.Ed.2d 694 (2002), 639

Resnick v. American Dental Ass'n, 95 F.R.D. 372 (N.D.Ill.1982), 580

Resolution Trust Corp. v. Bright, 6 F.3d 336 (5th Cir.1993), 434

Responsible Citizens v. Superior Court (Askins), 20 Cal.Rptr.2d 756 (Cal.App. 5 Dist. 1993), 181

Reves v. Ernst & Young, 507 U.S. 170, 113 S.Ct. 1163, 122 L.Ed.2d 525 (1993), 297

Revo v. New Mexico Supreme Court, 106 F.3d 929 (10th Cir.1997), 517

Reynoso, United States v., 6 F.Supp.2d 269 (S.D.N.Y.1998), 247

Richard F. Mallen & Associates, Ltd. v. Myinjuryclaim.com Corp., 329 Ill.App.3d 953, 263 Ill.Dec. 872, 769 N.E.2d 74 (Ill.App. 1 Dist.2002), 602

Richard Roe, Inc., United States v., 68 F.3d 38 (2nd Cir.1995), 152

Richards v. SSM Health Care, 311 Ill.App.3d 560, 244 Ill.Dec. 87, 724 N.E.2d 975 (Ill. App. 1 Dist.2000), 530

Richardson, State v., 230 Kan. 23, 631 P.2d 221 (Kan.1981), 567

Richardson–Merrell, Inc. v. Koller, 472 U.S. 424, 105 S.Ct. 2757, 86 L.Ed.2d 340 (1985), 170

Rinella, In re, 175 Ill.2d 504, 222 Ill.Dec. 375, 677 N.E.2d 909 (Ill.1997), 213

Ritchie, United States v., 15 F.3d 592 (6th Cir.1994), 484

Rite Aid Corp. Securities Litigation, In re, 139 F.Supp.2d 649 (E.D.Pa.2001), 237

Riverside v. Rivera, 477 U.S. 561, 106 S.Ct. 2686, 91 L.Ed.2d 466 (1986), 594

R.M.J., In re, 455 U.S. 191, 102 S.Ct. 929, 71 L.Ed.2d 64 (1982), 523

Robbins, Matter of, 266 Ga. 681, 469 S.E.2d 191 (Ga.1996), 520

Robinson, State v., 290 N.C. 56, 224 S.E.2d 174 (N.C.1976), 448

Rock v. Arkansas, 483 U.S. 44, 107 S.Ct. 2704, 97 L.Ed.2d 37 (1987), 440

Rodgers v. Lincoln Towing Service, Inc., 771 F.2d 194 (7th Cir.1985), 404

Roe v. Flores–Ortega, 528 U.S. 470, 120 S.Ct. 1029, 145 L.Ed.2d 985 (2000), 78

Rogers v. Robson, Masters, Ryan, Brumund, & Belom, 81 Ill.2d 201, 40 Ill.Dec. 816, 407 N.E.2d 47 (Ill.1980), 224, 227

Rome, In re, 218 Kan. 198, 542 P.2d 676 (Kan.1975), 655

Romea v. Heiberger & Associates, 163 F.3d 111 (2nd Cir.1998), 81

Romley, State ex rel. v. Superior Court, 184 Ariz. 223, 908 P.2d 37 (Ariz.App. Div. 1 1995), 248

Roots, In re, 762 A.2d 1161 (R.I.2000), 37

Rose Lee Ann L., In re, 307 Ill.App.3d 907, 241 Ill.Dec. 52, 718 N.E.2d 623 (Ill.App. 1 Dist.1999), 288

Ross, Matter of, 428 A.2d 858 (Me.1981), 654

Rothman v. Emory University, 828 F.Supp. 537 (N.D.Ill.1993), 40

Rowe, Matter of, 590 N.Y.S.2d 179, 604 N.E.2d 728 (N.Y.1992), 49

Rowe, United States v., 96 F.3d 1294 (9th Cir.1996), 148

Rubenstein, In re, 637 A.2d 1131 (Del. Supr.1994), 44

Rubin v. Schottenstein, Zox & Dunn, 143 F.3d 263 (6th Cir.1998), 347

Rubin & Cohen v. Gee, 292 F.3d 396 (4th Cir.2002), 195

Ruffalo, In re, 390 U.S. 544, 88 S.Ct. 1222, 20 L.Ed.2d 117 (1968), 63

Ruiz, United States v., 536 U.S. 622, 122 S.Ct. 2450, 153 L.Ed.2d 586 (2002), 330

Runsvold v. Idaho State Bar, 129 Idaho 419, 925 P.2d 1118 (Idaho 1996), 307

Ryans, United States v., 903 F.2d 731 (10th Cir.1990), 315

Ryder, In re, 263 F.Supp. 360 (E.D.Va.1967), 421, 423, 424, 427

Saccoccia, United States v., 898 F.Supp. 53 (D.R.I.1995), 480

Sage Realty Corp. v. Proskauer Rose Goetz & Mendelsohn L.L.P., 666 N.Y.S.2d 985, 689 N.E.2d 879 (N.Y.1997), 124

Samaritan Foundation v. Goodfarb, 176 Ariz. 497, 862 P.2d 870 (Ariz.1993), 145

Sampson v. State Bar, 115 Cal.Rptr. 43, 524 P.2d 139 (Cal.1974), 114

Sandahl, Matter of, 980 F.2d 1118 (7th Cir. 1992), 170

Sanders v. Russell, 401 F.2d 241 (5th Cir. 1968), 604

Sanders, Bruin, Coll & Worley, P.A. v. McKay Oil Corp., 123 N.M. 457, 943 P.2d 104 (N.M.1997), 77

Santiago–Lugo, United States v., 162 F.R.D. 11 (D.Puerto Rico 1995), 305

Saretsky, Matter of, 179 Wis.2d 92, 506 N.W.2d 151 (Wis.1993), 604

Satcom Intern. Group PLC v. Orbcomm Intern. Partners, L.P., 49 F.Supp.2d 331 (S.D.N.Y.1999), 146

Sather, In re, 3 P.3d 403 (Colo.2000), 99

Scariano v. Justices of Indiana Supreme Court, 38 F.3d 920 (7th Cir.1994), 603

SCA Services, Inc. v. Morgan, 557 F.2d 110 (7th Cir.1977), 626

Schatz v. Rosenberg, 943 F.2d 485 (4th Cir. 1991), 350

Schiessle v. Stephens, 717 F.2d 417 (7th Cir. 1983), 257, 258

Schindler v. Finnerty, 74 F.Supp.2d 253 (E.D.N.Y.1999), 608

Schloetter v. Railoc of Ind., Inc., 546 F.2d 706 (7th Cir.1976), 253

Schmitz v. Crotty, 528 N.W.2d 112 (Iowa 1995), 71

Schreiber v. Rowe, 814 So.2d 396 (Fla.2002), 68

Schultheis, People v., 638 P.2d 8 (Colo.1981), 437

Schumacher v. Nix, 965 F.2d 1262 (3rd Cir. 1992), 604

Schware v. Board of Bar Exam., 353 U.S. 232, 77 S.Ct. 752, 1 L.Ed.2d 796 (1957), 36

Schwarz, In re, 51 Ill.2d 334, 282 N.E.2d 689 (Ill.1972), 63

Schwarz v. Kogan, 132 F.3d 1387 (11th Cir. 1998), 566

Schwarz, United States v., 283 F.3d 76 (2nd Cir.2002), 194

Scott v. Tyson Foods, Inc., 943 F.2d 17 (8th Cir.1991), 571

Scott, Matter of, 739 N.E.2d 658 (Ind.2000), 599

Scott, United States v., 909 F.2d 488 (11th Cir.1990), 446

Scruggs, In re, 164 Wis.2d 471, 475 N.W.2d 160 (Wis.1991), 50

Sealed Case, In re, 146 F.3d 881 (D.C.Cir. 1998), 132

Sealed Case, In re, 124 F.3d 230 (D.C.Cir. 1997), 140

Sealed Case, In re, 107 F.3d 46 (D.C.Cir. 1997), 153

Sealed Case (Office of Independent Counsel Contempt Proceeding), 192 F.3d 995 (D.C.Cir.1999), 470

Sears, Roebuck & Co. v. Goldstone & Sudalter, 128 F.3d 10 (1st Cir.1997), 557

SEC v. Cassano, 189 F.R.D. 83 (S.D.N.Y. 1999), 137

SEC v. Frank, 388 F.2d 486 (2nd Cir.1968), 359

SEC v. National Student Marketing Corp., 457 F.Supp. 682 (D.D.C.1978), 360

SEC v. Universal Major Industries Corp., 546 F.2d 1044 (2nd Cir.1976), 360

Security Pacific Business Credit, Inc. v. Peat Marwick Main & Co., 586 N.Y.S.2d 87, 597 N.E.2d 1080 (N.Y.1992), 70

Segal, In re, 430 Mass. 359, 719 N.E.2d 480 (Mass.1999), 62

Seidl v. Greentree Mortg. Co., 30 F.Supp.2d 1292 (D.Colo.1998), 471

Selling v. Radford, 243 U.S. 46, 37 S.Ct. 377, 61 L.Ed. 585 (1917), 56

Severson & Werson v. Bolinger, 235 Cal. App.3d 1569, 1 Cal.Rptr.2d 531 (Cal.App. 1 Dist.1991), 99

S.G., State ex rel., 348 N.J.Super. 77, 791 A.2d 285 (N.J.Super.A.D.2002), 193

Shade v. Great Lakes Dredge & Dock Co., 72 F.Supp.2d 518 (E.D.Pa.1999), 585

Shaffer Equipment Co., United States v., 158 F.R.D. 80 (S.D.W.Va.1994), 414

Shaffer Equipment Co., United States v., 11 F.3d 450 (4th Cir.1993), 438

Shapero v. Kentucky Bar Ass'n, 486 U.S. 466, 108 S.Ct. 1916, 100 L.Ed.2d 475 (1988), 506, 508, 514, 515, 516, 549, 580

Shartzer v. Israels, 59 Cal.Rptr.2d 296 (Cal. App. 2 Dist.1996), 81

Shell Oil Refinery, In re, 143 F.R.D. 105 (E.D.La.1992), 396

Shepherd v. American Broadcasting Companies, Inc., 62 F.3d 1469 (D.C.Cir.1995), 412

Sheppard v. Maxwell, 384 U.S. 333, 86 S.Ct. 1507, 16 L.Ed.2d 600 (1966), 466

Sheppard & White, P.A. v. City of Jacksonville, 827 So.2d 925 (Fla.2002), 568

Sherburne, United States v., 249 F.3d 1121 (9th Cir.2001), 386

Shuttleworth, Ruloff & Giordano, P.C. v. Nutter, 254 Va. 494, 493 S.E.2d 364 (Va. 1997), 553

Siegel, In re, 133 N.J. 162, 627 A.2d 156 (N.J.1993), 117

Silver Chrysler Plymouth, Inc. v. Chrysler Motors Corp., 518 F.2d 751 (2nd Cir. 1975), 251, 252, 253

Simac, People v., 161 Ill.2d 297, 204 Ill.Dec. 192, 641 N.E.2d 416 (Ill.1994), 392

Sindel, United States v., 53 F.3d 874 (8th Cir.1995), 484

Singleton, United States v., 165 F.3d 1297 (10th Cir.1999), 476

Skarbrevik v. Cohen, England & Whitfield, 231 Cal.App.3d 692, 282 Cal.Rptr. 627 (Cal.App. 2 Dist.1991), 298

Skolnick v. Altheimer & Gray, 191 Ill.2d 214, 246 Ill.Dec. 324, 730 N.E.2d 4 (Ill.2000), 59

Slate v. Saxon, Marquoit, Bertoni & Todd, 166 Or.App. 1, 999 P.2d 1152 (Or.App. 2000), 538

Smith v. R.J. Reynolds, 267 N.J.Super. 62, 630 A.2d 820 (N.J.Super.A.D.1993), 119

Smith v. Robbins, 528 U.S. 259, 120 S.Ct. 746, 145 L.Ed.2d 756 (2000), 375, 376

Smolen, State of Oklahoma v., 17 P.3d 456 (Okla.2000), 584

Smyth v. Rivero, 282 F.3d 268 (4th Cir.2002), 588

Snyder v. State Bar, 133 Cal.Rptr. 864, 555 P.2d 1104 (Cal.1976), 378

Snyder, In re, 472 U.S. 634, 105 S.Ct. 2874, 86 L.Ed.2d 504 (1985), 649

Sofaer, In re, 728 A.2d 625 (D.C.1999), 264

Southern Christian Leadership Conference v. Supreme Court of Louisiana, 252 F.3d 781 (5th Cir.2001), 573

Spaulding v. Zimmerman, 263 Minn. 346, 116 N.W.2d 704 (Minn.1962), 81, 492, 494

Sperry v. Florida Bar, 373 U.S. 379, 83 S.Ct. 1322, 10 L.Ed.2d 428 (1963), 607, 608

Spevack v. Klein, 385 U.S. 511, 87 S.Ct. 625, 17 L.Ed.2d 574 (1967), 51

Spraker, Matter of, 744 N.E.2d 415 (Ind. 2001), 54

Standing Committee on Discipline of United States Dist. Court v. Yagman, 55 F.3d 1430 (9th Cir.1995), 645, 650

Stanton, In re, 682 A.2d 655 (D.C.1996), 320

Starkey, Kelly, Blaney & White v. Estate Of Nicolaysen, 172 N.J. 60, 796 A.2d 238 (N.J.2002), 96

State v. _____ (see opposing party)

State Bar of Ariz. v. Arizona Land Title and Trust Co., 90 Ariz. 76, 366 P.2d 1 (Ariz. 1961), 599

State Bar of Texas v. Kilpatrick, 874 S.W.2d 656 (Tex.1994), 514

State Compensation Ins. Fund v. WPS, Inc., 82 Cal.Rptr.2d 799 (Cal.App. 2 Dist.1999), 138

State ex rel. v. _____ (see opposing party and relator)

State Farm Mut. Auto. Ins. Co. v. Traver, 980 S.W.2d 625 (Tex.1998), 229

State of (see name of state)

State Unauthorized Practice of Law Committee v. Paul Mason & Associates, 46 F.3d 469 (5th Cir.1995), 608

Stenhach, Commonwealth v., 356 Pa.Super. 5, 514 A.2d 114 (Pa.Super.1986), 426

Stern v. Supreme Judicial Court, 184 F.R.D. 10 (D.Mass.1999), 477

Stewart v. Jackson & Nash, 976 F.2d 86 (2nd Cir.1992), 538

Stolar, Application of, 401 U.S. 23, 91 S.Ct. 713, 27 L.Ed.2d 657 (1971), 36

Strasbourger Pearson Tulcin Wolff Inc. v. Wiz Technology, 82 Cal.Rptr.2d 326 (Cal. App. 4 Dist.1999), 237

Stratagem Development Corp. v. Heron Intern. N.V., 756 F.Supp. 789 (S.D.N.Y. 1991), 183

Strawser, United States v., 800 F.2d 704 (7th Cir.1986), 103

Stretton v. Disciplinary Bd., 944 F.2d 137 (3rd Cir.1991), 638

Strickland v. Washington, 466 U.S. 668, 104 S.Ct. 2052, 80 L.Ed.2d 674 (1984), 78, 79, 191, 192, 202, 489

Stropnicky v. Nathanson, 19 M.D.L.R. 39 (M.C.A.D.1997), 89

Subpoena to Testify Before Grand Jury (Alexiou v. United States), In re, 39 F.3d 973 (9th Cir.1994), 480

Sullivan County Regional Refuse Disposal Dist. v. Town of Acworth, 141 N.H. 479, 686 A.2d 755 (N.H.1996), 233

Sumitomo Corp. v. J. P. Morgan & Co., Inc., 2000 WL 145747 (S.D.N.Y.2000), 177

Superior Court (Ebel), People ex rel. Clancy v., 218 Cal.Rptr. 24, 705 P.2d 347 (Cal. 1985), 199

Superior Court (Fairbank), People v., 192 Cal.App.3d 32, 237 Cal.Rptr. 158 (Cal. App. 1 Dist.1987), 426

Superior Court (Greer), People v., 137 Cal. Rptr. 476, 561 P.2d 1164 (Cal.1977), 198

Superior Court (Laff), People v., 107 Cal. Rptr.2d 323, 23 P.3d 563 (Cal.2001), 481

Superior Court, State ex rel. Romley v., 184 Ariz. 223, 908 P.2d 37 (Ariz.App. Div. 1 1995), 248

Suppressed v. Suppressed, 206 Ill.App.3d 918, 151 Ill.Dec. 830, 565 N.E.2d 101 (Ill.App. 1 Dist.1990), 213

Supreme Court of New Hampshire v. Piper, 470 U.S. 274, 105 S.Ct. 1272, 84 L.Ed.2d 205 (1985), 45

Supreme Court of Virginia v. Friedman, 487 U.S. 59, 108 S.Ct. 2260, 101 L.Ed.2d 56 (1988), 603

Sussman v. Bank of Israel, 56 F.3d 450 (2nd Cir.1995), 373

Swedish Hosp. Corp. v. Shalala, 1 F.3d 1261 (D.C.Cir.1993), 589

Swidler & Berlin v. United States, 524 U.S. 399, 118 S.Ct. 2081, 141 L.Ed.2d 379 (1998), 140

Synthroid Marketing Litigation, Matter of, 264 F.3d 712 (7th Cir.2001), 590

Tabron v. Grace, 6 F.3d 147 (3rd Cir.1993), 571

Talao, United States v., 222 F.3d 1133 (9th Cir.2000), 312

Tallon, Matter of, 86 A.D.2d 897, 447 N.Y.S.2d 50 (N.Y.A.D. 3 Dept.1982), 76

Tarasoff v. Regents of University of California, 131 Cal.Rptr. 14, 551 P.2d 334 (Cal. 1976), 299

Taylor, Application of, 293 Or. 285, 647 P.2d 462 (Or.1982), 35, 38

Taylor v. Commonwealth, 192 Ky. 410, 233 S.W. 895 (Ky.1921), 378

Taylor v. Grogan, 900 P.2d 60 (Colo.1995), 463

T.C. Theatre Corp. v. Warner Bros. Pictures, 113 F.Supp. 265 (S.D.N.Y.1953), 231

Teague, United States v., 953 F.2d 1525 (11th Cir.1992), 446

Teichner, In re, 75 Ill.2d 88, 25 Ill.Dec. 609, 387 N.E.2d 265 (Ill.1979), 513

Tekni–Plex, Inc. v. Meyner & Landis, 651 N.Y.S.2d 954, 674 N.E.2d 663 (N.Y.1996), 233

Terzis v. Estate of Whalen, 126 N.H. 88, 489 A.2d 608 (N.H.1985), 91

Thomas v. State, 346 S.C. 140, 551 S.E.2d 254 (S.C.2001), 193

Thomas, United States v., 474 F.2d 110 (10th Cir.1973), 314

Thonert, In re, 733 N.E.2d 932 (Ind.2000), 403

Thoreen, United States v., 653 F.2d 1332 (9th Cir.1981), 391, 392

Tibbs v. United States, 628 A.2d 638 (D.C. 1993), 437

Tillman v. Miller, 133 F.3d 1402 (11th Cir. 1998), 510

TJD Dissolution Corp. v. Savoie Supply Co., 460 N.W.2d 59 (Minn.App.1990), 298

Togstad v. Vesely, Otto, Miller & Keefe, 291 N.W.2d 686 (Minn.1980), 90

Tolchin v. Supreme Court of New Jersey, 111 F.3d 1099 (3rd Cir.1997), 45

Toledo Bar Ass'n v. Fell, 51 Ohio St.2d 33, 364 N.E.2d 872 (Ohio 1977), 408

Townsend v. Townsend, 323 S.C. 309, 474 S.E.2d 424 (S.C.1996), 232

Turbin v. Arizona Superior Court, 165 Ariz. 195, 797 P.2d 734 (Ariz.App. Div. 1 1990), 248

Tutu Wells Contamination Litigation, In re, 120 F.3d 368 (3rd Cir.1997), 384

Twohig v. Blackmer, 121 N.M. 746, 918 P.2d 332 (N.M.1996), 473

Two Thirty Nine Joint Venture v. Joe, 60 S.W.3d 896 (Tex.App.-Dallas 2001), 270

Tyler v. State, 47 P.3d 1095 (Alaska App. 2001), 403

Ultramares v. Touche, 255 N.Y. 170, 174 N.E. 441 (N.Y.1931), 70

Unauthorized Practice of Law Committee v. Parsons Technology, Inc., 1999 WL 47235 (N.D.Tex.1999), 601

Unified Sewerage Agency v. Jelco Inc., 646 F.2d 1339 (9th Cir.1981), 182, 236

Unigard Ins. Group v. O'Flaherty & Belgum, 45 Cal.Rptr.2d 565 (Cal.App. 2 Dist.1995), 229

Union Carbide Corp. v. United States Cutting Service, Inc., 782 F.2d 710 (7th Cir.1986), 625

United Mine Workers of America v. Illinois State Bar Ass'n, 389 U.S. 217, 88 S.Ct. 353, 19 L.Ed.2d 426 (1967), 558

United Mine Workers of America v. Pennington, 381 U.S. 657, 85 S.Ct. 1585, 14 L.Ed.2d 626 (1965), 41

United States v. _____ (see opposing party)

United States, In re, 158 F.3d 26 (1st Cir. 1998), 621

United States Dist. Court v. Sandlin, 12 F.3d 861 (9th Cir.1993), 645

United States ex rel. v. _____ (see opposing party and relator)

United States Senate Select Committee on Presidential Campaign Activities, In re Application of, 361 F.Supp. 1270 (D.D.C. 1973), 469

United Transp. Union v. State Bar of Mich., 401 U.S. 576, 91 S.Ct. 1076, 28 L.Ed.2d 339 (1971), 559

Upjohn Co. v. United States, 449 U.S. 383, 101 S.Ct. 677, 66 L.Ed.2d 584 (1981), 142, 144, 145, 148, 339

Ursery, United States v., 518 U.S. 267, 116 S.Ct. 2135, 135 L.Ed.2d 549 (1996), 62

Uy v. Bronx Municipal Hosp. Center, 182 F.3d 152 (2nd Cir.1999), 593

Vadner, United States v., 160 F.3d 263 (5th Cir.1998), 650

Valdez v. Winans, 738 F.2d 1087 (10th Cir. 1984), 492

Valentine v. Chrestensen, 316 U.S. 52, 62 S.Ct. 920, 86 L.Ed. 1262 (1942), 498, 501

Vanguard Production, Inc. v. Martin, 894 F.2d 375 (10th Cir.1990), 347

Van Jackson v. Check 'N Go of Illinois, 114 F.Supp.2d 731 (N.D.Ill.2000), 259

Venegas v. Mitchell, 495 U.S. 82, 110 S.Ct. 1679, 109 L.Ed.2d 74 (1990), 593

Vereins–Und Westbank, AG v. Carter, 691 F.Supp. 704 (S.D.N.Y.1988), 70, 347

Violet v. Brown, 1996 WL 686508 (Vet.App. 1996), 262

Virginia Elec. & Power Co. v. Sun Shipbuilding & Dry Dock Co., 539 F.2d 357 (4th Cir.1976), 622

Virginia State Bd. v. Virginia Citizens Consumer Council, 425 U.S. 748, 96 S.Ct. 1817, 48 L.Ed.2d 346 (1976), 498

Virgin Islands v. Weatherwax, 77 F.3d 1425 (3rd Cir.1996), 388

Virgin Islands Housing Authority v. David, 823 F.2d 764 (3rd Cir.1987), 408

Virzi v. Grand Trunk Warehouse and Cold Storage Co., 571 F.Supp. 507 (E.D.Mich. 1983), 326, 327, 328

Vizcaino v. Microsoft Corp., 290 F.3d 1043 (9th Cir.2002), 590

von Bulow, In re, 828 F.2d 94 (2nd Cir.1987), 202

Von Wiegen, Matter of, 481 N.Y.S.2d 40, 470 N.E.2d 838 (N.Y.1984), 506

Waggoner v. Snow, Becker, Kroll, Klaris & Krauss, 991 F.2d 1501 (9th Cir.1993), 298

Wagshal v. Foster, 28 F.3d 1249 (D.C.Cir. 1994), 657

Walker, Matter of, 254 N.W.2d 452 (S.D. 1977), 52

Wallman, In re, 260 A.D.2d 148, 696 N.Y.S.2d 164 (N.Y.A.D. 1 Dept.1999), 533

Wal–Mart Stores, State ex rel. v. Kortum, 251 Neb. 805, 559 N.W.2d 496 (Neb.1997), 236

Walsh, United States v., 699 F.Supp. 469 (D.N.J.1988), 55

Wamsley, Matter of, 725 N.E.2d 75 (Ind. 2000), 511

Washington Legal Foundation v. Massachusetts Bar Foundation, 993 F.2d 962 (1st Cir.1993), 575

Washington Legal Foundation v. Texas Equal Access to Justice Foundation, 270 F.3d 180 (5th Cir.2001), 576

Washington State Physicians Ins. Exchange & Ass'n v. Fisons Corp., 122 Wash.2d 299, 858 P.2d 1054 (Wash.1993), 413

Washington, United States ex rel. Green v., 917 F.Supp. 1238 (N.D.Ill.1996), 490

Weaver v. Bonner, 309 F.3d 1312 (11th Cir. 2002), 642

W.E. Bassett Co. v. H. C. Cook Co., 201 F.Supp. 821 (D.Conn.1961), 246

Webb's Fabulous Pharmacies, Inc. v. Beckwith, 449 U.S. 155, 101 S.Ct. 446, 66 L.Ed.2d 358 (1980), 576

Weeks v. Independent School Dist. No. I–89, 230 F.3d 1201 (10th Cir.2000), 308

Weibrecht v. Southern Illinois Transfer, Inc., 241 F.3d 875 (7th Cir.2001), 309

Welch & Forbes v. Cendant Corp. (In re Cendant Corp. Prides Litigation), 243 F.3d 722 (3rd Cir.2001), 590

Wellmore Coal Corp. v. Harman Mining Corp., 264 Va. 279, 568 S.E.2d 671 (Va. 2002), 605

Wells Fargo Bank v. Superior Court (Boltwood), 91 Cal.Rptr.2d 716, 990 P.2d 591 (Cal.2000), 149

Wemark v. State, 602 N.W.2d 810 (Iowa 1999), 428

Wendy, United States v., 575 F.2d 1025 (2nd Cir.1978), 568

Wesp v. Everson, 33 P.3d 191 (Colo.2001), 140

Westbrook, Commonwealth v., 484 Pa. 534, 400 A.2d 160 (Pa.1979), 247

Westinghouse Elec. Corp. v. Kerr–McGee Corp., 580 F.2d 1311 (7th Cir.1978), 181, 182

West Virginia State Police Crime Laboratory, Matter of, 190 W.Va. 321, 438 S.E.2d 501 (W.Va.1993), 489

"We The People" Paralegal Services, L.L.C. v. Watley, 766 So.2d 744 (La.App. 2 Cir. 2000), 529

Wheat v. United States, 486 U.S. 153, 108 S.Ct. 1692, 100 L.Ed.2d 140 (1988), 196

White v. McBride, 937 S.W.2d 796 (Tenn. 1996), 100

White, United States v., 743 F.2d 488 (7th Cir.1984), 170

White, United States v., 401 U.S. 745, 91 S.Ct. 1122, 28 L.Ed.2d 453 (1971), 458

Whitehouse v. United States Dist. Court, 53 F.3d 1349 (1st Cir.1995), 477

Wieder v. Skala, 593 N.Y.S.2d 752, 609 N.E.2d 105 (N.Y.1992), 536

Wigoda, In re, 77 Ill.2d 154, 32 Ill.Dec. 341, 395 N.E.2d 571 (Ill.1979), 35

Wiley v. County of San Diego, 79 Cal.Rptr.2d 672, 966 P.2d 983 (Cal.1998), 67

Wilkinson, In re, 805 So.2d 142 (La.2002), 532

Will, United States v., 449 U.S. 200, 101 S.Ct. 471, 66 L.Ed.2d 392 (1980), 623

Williams, In re, 221 Minn. 554, 23 N.W.2d 4 (Minn.1946), 429

Williams, United States v., 504 U.S. 36, 112 S.Ct. 1735, 118 L.Ed.2d 352 (1992), 317, 474

Williams v. Williams, 554 Pa. 465, 721 A.2d 1072 (Pa.1998), 649

Williamson v. Vardeman, 674 F.2d 1211 (8th Cir.1982), 568

Wilson, People v., 953 P.2d 1292 (Colo.1998), 552

Wilson, State ex rel. Counsel for Discipline of Nebraska Supreme Court v., 262 Neb. 653, 634 N.W.2d 467 (Neb.2001), 121

Wilson v. Wilson, 984 S.W.2d 898 (Tenn. 1998), 200

Wilson P. Abraham Const. Corp. v. Armco Steel Corp., 559 F.2d 250 (5th Cir.1977), 238

Winkler v. Keane, 7 F.3d 304 (2nd Cir.1993), 108

Winskunas v. Birnbaum, 23 F.3d 1264 (7th Cir.1994), 72

Wisconsin v. Hotline Industries, 236 F.3d 363 (7th Cir.2000), 589

Witness Before Special Grand Jury 2000–2, In re, 288 F.3d 289 (7th Cir.2002), 147

Wolf v. Mitchell, Silberberg & Knupp, 90 Cal.Rptr.2d 792 (Cal.App. 2 Dist.1999), 299

Wolfram, In re, 174 Ariz. 49, 847 P.2d 94 (Ariz.1993), 48

Wood v. McGrath, North, Mullin & Kratz, P.C., 256 Neb. 109, 589 N.W.2d 103 (Neb. 1999), 66

Woodall, United States v., 438 F.2d 1317 (5th Cir.1970), 135

Woodruff v. Tomlin, 616 F.2d 924 (6th Cir. 1980), 66, 71

Worldspan, L.P. v. Sabre Group Holdings, Inc., 5 F.Supp.2d 1356 (N.D.Ga.1998), 186

Wouters v. Algemene Raad van de Nederlandse Orde van Advocaten, 2002 WL 29971, [2002] All. E.R. (EC) 193 (ECJ 2002), 613

Wright v. Williams, 47 Cal.App.3d 802, 121 Cal.Rptr. 194 (Cal.App. 2 Dist.1975), 522

W.T. Grant Co. v. Haines, 531 F.2d 671 (2nd Cir.1976), 312

Wunsch, United States v., 84 F.3d 1110 (9th Cir.1996), 400

Wunschel Law Firm, P.C. v. Clabaugh, 291 N.W.2d 331 (Iowa 1980), 108

Yarbrough v. Superior Court, 216 Cal.Rptr. 425, 702 P.2d 583 (Cal.1985), 569

Yengo, In re, 84 N.J. 111, 417 A.2d 533 (N.J.1980), 78

Young v. United States ex rel. Vuitton et Fils S.A., 481 U.S. 787, 107 S.Ct. 2124, 95 L.Ed.2d 740 (1987), 200

Youngblood, Petition of, 895 S.W.2d 322 (Tenn.1995), 228

Zahrey v. Coffey, 221 F.3d 342 (2nd Cir. 2000), 475

Zang, Matter of, 154 Ariz. 134, 741 P.2d 267 (Ariz.1987), 510

Zarabia v. Bradshaw, 185 Ariz. 1, 912 P.2d 5 (Ariz.1996), 569

Zauderer v. Office of Disciplinary Counsel, 471 U.S. 626, 105 S.Ct. 2265, 85 L.Ed.2d 652 (1985), 508, 509, 510, 511

Zbiegien, In re, 433 N.W.2d 871 (Minn.1988), 38

Ziegelheim v. Apollo, 128 N.J. 250, 607 A.2d 1298 (N.J.1992), 66

Zielinski v. Schmalbeck, 269 Ill.App.3d 572, 207 Ill.Dec. 89, 646 N.E.2d 655 (Ill.App. 4 Dist.1995), 40

Zimmerman v. Mahaska Bottling Co., 270 Kan. 810, 19 P.3d 784 (Kan.2001), 241

Zolin, United States v., 491 U.S. 554, 109 S.Ct. 2619, 105 L.Ed.2d 469 (1989), 152

Zuck v. Alabama, 588 F.2d 436 (5th Cir. 1979), 175

Zurich Ins. Co. v. Knotts, 52 S.W.3d 555 (Ky.2001), 462

*

TABLE OF STATUTES

ABA CANONS OF PROFESSIONAL ETHICS

Canon	This Work Page
4	120
4	122
4	362
4	659
7	548
9	362
11	208
20	466
27	496
32	16
34	526
34	528

ABA MODEL CODE OF JUDICIAL CONDUCT

Canon	This Work Page
1	663
2	623
2A	623
2A	661
2A	663
2B	628
2B	650
2B	651
2B	659
2B	661
2B	664
2C	662
3A(4)	662
3B	653
3B(4)	655
3B(5)	655
3B(6)	656
3B(7)	660
3B(7)	661
3B(7)	662
3B(7)(b)	661
3B(7)(d)	274
3B(9)	657
3B(9)	658
3B(9)	660
3C(2)	642
3C(2)	643
3C(2)	656
3C(5)	651
3C, Comment 1	642
3C, Comment 2	643
3D(1)	646
3D(2)	59
3D(3)	647
3E	620
3E	622
3E	628

ABA MODEL CODE OF JUDICIAL CONDUCT

Canon	This Work Page
3E(1)	273
3E(1)	623
3E(1)(a)	659
3E(1)(b)	627
3E(1)(c)	622
3E(1)(c)	623
3E(1)(c)	624
3E(1)(c)	625
3E(1)(d)	624
3E(1)(d)	625
3E(1)(d)(ii)	626
3E(1)(e)	625
3E(2)	624
3E(2)	625
3E, Comment 1	273
3F	622
3F	634
3F	635
4A	660
4A, Comment 1	660
4B	660
4C(1)	659
4C(2)	659
4C(3)	659
4C(3)(a)	659
4C(3)(b)	659
4D	621
4D(1)(b)	620
4D(4)	623
4D(5)(c)	620
4D(5)(e)	620
4D(5)(f)	621
4G	660
5	640
5A(1)(b)	641
5A(1)(e)	642
5A(2)	642
5A(3)(a)	637
5A(3)(d)	637
5A(3)(d)(ii)	637
5B(2)	643
5B(2)(b)	643
5C(1)(a)	642
5C(2)	642
5C(2)	643
5C(4)	642
5C(5)	642

ABA DEFENSE FUNCTION STANDARDS

No.	This Work Page
4–3.4	202

xxxiii

ABA DEFENSE FUNCTION STANDARDS

No.	This Work Page
4–3.5(c)	196
4–4.3(c)	312
4–5.2	375
4–6.1(b)	320
4–7.6	389
4–7.7	447
4–8.5	491

ABA FORMAL OPINION

No.	This Work Page
00–417	334
00–418	204
00–420	98
00–420	123
01–1	165
01–3	177
01–421	227
01–422	461
01–423	617
01–424	536
02–425	123
02–426	212
02–427	127
85–352	337
87–353	415
87–353	449
88–356	243
90–357	250
90–358	86
91–361	181
91–361	298
92–362	306
92–362	307
92–363	332
92–364	212
92–365	182
92–366	353
92–366	354
92–367	176
92–368	396
92–369	557
93–370	415
93–371	333
93–372	185
93–373	109
93–374	530
93–375	332
93–375	356
93–376	410
93–377	187
93–379	109
93–379	533
94–380	149
94–380	300
94–381	552
94–382	396
94–383	57
94–383	333
94–384	58

ABA FORMAL OPINION

No.	This Work Page
94–385	480
94–386	402
94–387	329
94–388	249
94–389	110
95–390	179
95–395	238
95–396	304
95–397	327
96–3	175
96–399	572
96–401	77
96–402	458
96–403	226
96–404	283
96–404	284
97–2	287
97–405	176
97–406	175
97–407	176
97–408	310
98–410	292
98–411	136
98–412	416
99–413	136
99–414	550
99–415	236
95	313
250	120
266	555
287	414
287	415
287	449
314	295
314	328
314	337
335	357
337	460
337	461
338	123
340	253
341	449
342	262
342	265
342	266
342	268
342	269
343	270
346	358
348	575

ABA INFORMAL OPINION

No.	This Work Page
84–1505	402
87–1523	164
1273	48
1309	270
1418	247
1457	550

ABA INFORMAL OPINION

No.	This Work Page
1474	270
1486	249

ABA MODEL CODE OF PROFESSIONAL RESPONSIBILITY—DISCIPLINARY RULES

DR	This Work Page
1–102(a)	534
1–102(A)(4)	393
1–102(A)(4)	394
1–102(A)(5)	199
1–102(D)	331
1–102(D)	393
2–101	501
2–101(A)	501
2–101(B)	511
2–103	514
2–103(D)(4)(a)	559
2–103(D)(4)(e)	561
2–106(A)	108
2–108(A)	552
4–101(A)	134
4–101(B)(3)	208
4–101(C)(3)	295
4–101(C)(3)	352
4–101(C)(4)	362
5–102(B)	479
5–103(B)	584
5–105(A)	160
5–105(D)	247
6–102	75
6–102(A)	75
7–102(A)	408
7–102(A)(1)	199
7–102(A)(3)	327
7–102(A)(3)	328
7–102(A)(4)	439
7–102(A)(5)	327
7–102(A)(5)	393
7–102(A)(6)	439
7–102(B)(1)	449
7–102(B)(2)	58
7–104	316
7–104	580
7–104(A)(1)	308
7–104(A)(1)	580
7–104(A)(2)	311
7–105(A)	332
7–107	466
7–107	467
7–109	458
7–109(B)	439
9–101(B)	262
9–101(B)	265

ABA MODEL CODE OF PROFESSIONAL RESPONSIBILITY—ETHICAL CONSIDERATIONS

EC	This Work Page
2–2	495

ABA MODEL CODE OF PROFESSIONAL RESPONSIBILITY—ETHICAL CONSIDERATIONS

EC	This Work Page
2–2 to 2–5	506
2–23	120
2–26	88
3–5	597
5–18	290
7–1	30
7–3	277
7–27	327
7–27	328

ABA MODEL RULES FOR LAWYER DISCIPLINARY ENFORCEMENT

Rule	This Work Page
11	59
23	52

ABA MODEL RULES OF PROFESSIONAL CONDUCT

Rule	This Work Page
1.0	161
1.0(c)	247
1.0(e)	161
1.0(e)	175
1.0(e)	635
1.0(f)	433
1.0(i)	433
1.0(k)	86
1.0(k)	240
1.0(k)	256
1.0(k)	266
1.0, Comment 2	249
1.0, Comment 3	249
1.0, Comment 6	161
1.0, Comment 7	161
1.0, Comments 8—10	86
1.0, Comments 8—10	240
1.0, Comments 8—10	266
1.1	48
1.1	103
1.1	246
1.1	518
1.1	519
1.1	532
1.1, Comment 1	519
1.1, Comments 1—4	519
1.1, Comment 2	519
1.2	93
1.2(a)	92
1.2(a)	93
1.2(a)	118
1.2(a)	224
1.2(a)	288
1.2(a)	319
1.2(a)	375
1.2(a)	440

ABA MODEL RULES OF PROFESSIONAL CONDUCT

Rule	This Work Page
1.2(a)	441
1.2(b)	89
1.2(c)	91
1.2(c)	92
1.2(c)	229
1.2(c)	320
1.2(d)	280
1.2(d)	281
1.2(d)	282
1.2(d)	353
1.2(d)	416
1.2(d)	430
1.2(d)	436
1.2, Comment 1	92
1.2, Comment 2	92
1.2, Comment 2	93
1.2, Comments 6—8	91
1.2, Comment 9	280
1.2, Comment 9	281
1.2, Comment 10	156
1.2, Comment 10	221
1.2, Comment 10	280
1.2, Comment 10	281
1.2, Comment 10	354
1.3	48
1.4	93
1.4	320
1.4	321
1.4	346
1.4	431
1.4	441
1.4	446
1.4(a)(2)	93
1.4(a)(2)	320
1.4(a)(3)	550
1.4(b)	123
1.4, Comment 2	321
1.4, Comment 3	93
1.4, Comment 3	396
1.4, Comment 7	431
1.5	204
1.5	205
1.5	208
1.5	526
1.5	533
1.5(a)	97
1.5(a)	102
1.5(a)	204
1.5(a)	212
1.5(a)	531
1.5(b)	91
1.5(b)	92
1.5(b)	96
1.5(b)	97
1.5(c)	91
1.5(c)	96
1.5(d)(1)	108
1.5(d)(2)	108
1.5(d)(2)	199
1.5(d)(2)	482
1.5(e)	525

ABA MODEL RULES OF PROFESSIONAL CONDUCT

Rule	This Work Page
1.5(e)	526
1.5(e)	527
1.5(e)	530
1.5(e)	556
1.5(e)(1)	526
1.5(e)(2)	527
1.5, Comment 1	98
1.5, Comment 5	102
1.5, Comment 5	104
1.5, Comment 6	108
1.5, Comment 7	526
1.5, Comment 9	380
1.6	57
1.6	58
1.6	92
1.6	127
1.6	149
1.6	153
1.6	154
1.6	155
1.6	177
1.6	221
1.6	228
1.6	258
1.6	268
1.6	269
1.6	285
1.6	352
1.6	354
1.6	362
1.6	366
1.6	367
1.6	396
1.6	410
1.6	420
1.6(a)	134
1.6(a)	135
1.6(a)	416
1.6(a)	456
1.6(a)	487
1.6(a)	551
1.6(b)	155
1.6(b)	295
1.6(b)	352
1.6(b)	365
1.6(b)(1)	121
1.6(b)(1)	153
1.6(b)(1)	154
1.6(b)(1)	288
1.6(b)(1)	295
1.6(b)(1)	429
1.6(b)(1)	492
1.6(b)(2)	136
1.6(b)(2)	352
1.6(b)(3)	120
1.6(b)(3)	154
1.6(b)(3)	362
1.6(b)(3)	535
1.6(b)(3)	536
1.6(b)(5)	420

ABA MODEL RULES OF PROFESSIONAL CONDUCT

Rule	This Work Page
1.6(b)(6)	420
1.6, Comment 2	136
1.6, Comment 4	136
1.6, Comment 6	154
1.6, Comment 7	136
1.6, Comment 11	134
1.6, Comment 12	154
1.6, Comment 12	536
1.6, Comment 13	154
1.6, Comment 13	295
1.6, Comment 14	156
1.6, Comment 15	156
1.6, Comment 16	137
1.6, Comment 16	156
1.6, Comment 17	156
1.7	86
1.7	92
1.7	161
1.7	162
1.7	164
1.7	166
1.7	182
1.7	243
1.7	245
1.7	305
1.7(a)	160
1.7(a)	176
1.7(a)	217
1.7(a)	231
1.7(a)(1)	173
1.7(a)(1)	175
1.7(a)(1)	177
1.7(a)(1)	184
1.7(a)(1)	218
1.7(a)(2)	175
1.7(a)(2)	198
1.7(a)(2)	204
1.7(a)(2)	215
1.7(a)(2)	217
1.7(a)(2)	218
1.7(a)(2)	226
1.7(a)(2)	231
1.7(a)(2)	255
1.7(a)(2)	581
1.7(b)	161
1.7(b)	212
1.7(b)	214
1.7(b)(1)—(b)(3)	164
1.7(b)(3)	169
1.7(b)(4)	162
1.7, Comment 3	233
1.7, Comment 5	183
1.7, Comment 6	160
1.7, Comment 6	175
1.7, Comment 8	160
1.7, Comment 8	176
1.7, Comment 9	187
1.7, Comment 11	203
1.7, Comment 11	255
1.7, Comment 15	170
1.7, Comments 15—17	165

ABA MODEL RULES OF PROFESSIONAL CONDUCT

Rule	This Work Page
1.7, Comment 18	161
1.7, Comment 18	175
1.7, Comment 19	168
1.7, Comment 20	162
1.7, Comment 21	163
1.7, Comment 22	186
1.7, Comment 24	188
1.7, Comment 25	240
1.7, Comment 27	300
1.7, Comments 28—33	166
1.7, Comment 30	168
1.7, Comment 31	168
1.7, Comment 34	179
1.7, Comment 34	181
1.7, Comment 35	179
1.7, Comment 35	293
1.8(a)	127
1.8(a)	204
1.8(a)	205
1.8(a)	206
1.8(a)	207
1.8(a)	615
1.8(a)(2)	212
1.8(b)	208
1.8(b)	209
1.8(c)	210
1.8(c)	211
1.8(c)	212
1.8(d)	201
1.8(d)	202
1.8(e)	584
1.8(e)	585
1.8(e)(1)	584
1.8(f)	217
1.8(f)	218
1.8(f)	223
1.8(f)	226
1.8(g)	335
1.8(g)	582
1.8(h)	122
1.8(h)	123
1.8(h)	229
1.8(h)(1)	75
1.8(h)(1)	76
1.8(h)(1)	77
1.8(h)(2)	76
1.8(i)	126
1.8(i)	255
1.8(j)	203
1.8(j)	204
1.8(j)	213
1.8(j)	214
1.8(j)	215
1.8(j)	245
1.8(k)	215
1.8(k)	245
1.8, Comment 1	207
1.8, Comment 5	209
1.8, Comment 6	210
1.8, Comment 7	212
1.8, Comment 8	211
1.8, Comment 9	201

ABA MODEL RULES OF PROFESSIONAL CONDUCT

Rule	This Work Page
1.8, Comment 10	584
1.8, Comment 13	335
1.8, Comments 17—19	214
1.8, Comment 18	215
1.8, Comment 19	215
1.8, Comment 20	215
1.9	86
1.9	92
1.9	182
1.9	184
1.9	231
1.9	232
1.9	233
1.9	235
1.9	238
1.9	240
1.9	243
1.9	245
1.9	261
1.9	262
1.9	265
1.9	267
1.9	269
1.9	381
1.9	552
1.9(a)	231
1.9(a)	258
1.9(b)	250
1.9(b)	251
1.9(c)	239
1.9(c)	262
1.9(c)	334
1.9(c)	487
1.9(c)	536
1.9, Comment 1	262
1.9, Comment 2	232
1.9, Comment 8	415
1.10	86
1.10	243
1.10	247
1.10	250
1.10	256
1.10	259
1.10(a)	160
1.10(a)	233
1.10(a)	245
1.10(a)	246
1.10(a)	249
1.10(a)	255
1.10(b)	251
1.10(b)	381
1.10(d)	245
1.10, Comment 1	247
1.10, Comment 1	249
1.10, Comment 3	246
1.10, Comment 4	240
1.10, Comment 4	242
1.11	55
1.11	245
1.11	256
1.11	261

ABA MODEL RULES OF PROFESSIONAL CONDUCT

Rule	This Work Page
1.11	262
1.11	262
1.11	263
1.11	264
1.11	265
1.11	267
1.11	272
1.11(a)	250
1.11(a)	264
1.11(a)	266
1.11(a)(1)	261
1.11(b)	265
1.11(b)	266
1.11(c)	267
1.11(d)	268
1.11(d)(2)	272
1.11(d)(2)(ii)	271
1.11, Comment 2	269
1.11, Comment 3	265
1.11, Comment 3	272
1.11, Comment 4	267
1.12	256
1.12	272
1.12	273
1.12	274
1.12	382
1.12	627
1.12(a)	272
1.12(a)	273
1.12(a)	381
1.12(a)	628
1.12(b)	272
1.12(c)	250
1.12(c)	274
1.12(c)	381
1.12, Comment 1	272
1.12, Comment 3	272
1.13	181
1.13	294
1.13	295
1.13(a)	291
1.13(a)	337
1.13(b)	291
1.13(b)	293
1.13(b)	294
1.13(b)	352
1.13(b)	492
1.13(c)	294
1.13(c)	295
1.13(c)	352
1.13(c)	365
1.13(d)	311
1.13(d)	313
1.13(e)	181
1.13(e)	311
1.13(e)	313
1.13, Comment 3	291
1.13, Comment 5	295
1.13, Comment 6	176
1.13, Comment 6	180
1.13, Comment 6	270
1.13, Comment 6	366

ABA MODEL RULES OF PROFESSIONAL CONDUCT

Rule	This Work Page
1.13, Comment 7	181
1.13, Comment 8	181
1.13, Comment 10	302
1.13, Comment 11	302
1.14	223
1.14	283
1.14	284
1.14	285
1.14, Comment 6	283
1.14, Comment 7	283
1.14, Comment 8	283
1.14, Comment 9	284
1.14, Comment 10	284
1.15	113
1.15(a)	115
1.15(a)	127
1.15(b)	115
1.15(d)	115
1.15(e)	115
1.15, Comment 3	380
1.16	221
1.16	568
1.16(a)	119
1.16(a)	353
1.16(a)(1)	117
1.16(a)(2)	117
1.16(b)(1)	117
1.16(b)(3)	118
1.16(b)(4)	118
1.16(b)(6)	119
1.16(c)	119
1.16(d)	118
1.16, Comments 4—6	118
1.16, Comment 6	283
1.17	555
1.17	556
1.17(c)	556
1.17, Comment 7	556
1.17, Comment 8	556
1.17, Comment 14	556
1.18	85
1.18	86
1.18	256
1.18(b)	86
1.18(c)	86
1.18(d)	86
1.18(d)(2)	86
1.18(d)(2)(i)	86
1.18, Comment 3	85
1.18, Comment 4	86
1.18, Comment 5	86
1.18, Comment 7	86
1.18, Comment 8	86
1.18, Comment 9	85
2.1	92
2.1	337
2.1	379
2.1	446
2.1, Comment 5	379
2.2	166
2.2	380

ABA MODEL RULES OF PROFESSIONAL CONDUCT

Rule	This Work Page
2.3	339
2.3	346
2.3	350
2.3	357
2.3(c)	340
2.4	380
2.4	382
2.4(a)	380
2.4(b)	380
2.4, Comment 1	380
2.4, Comment 2	381
2.4, Comment 3	380
3.1	91
3.1	93
3.1	329
3.1	370
3.1	376
3.1	379
3.1	382
3.1, Comment 2	91
3.1, Comment 2	372
3.1, Comment 2	377
3.2	377
3.3	327
3.3	329
3.3	488
3.3	536
3.3(a)(1)	389
3.3(a)(1)	390
3.3(a)(1)	408
3.3(a)(1)	410
3.3(a)(1)	416
3.3(a)(1)	438
3.3(a)(1)	439
3.3(a)(2)	281
3.3(a)(2)	402
3.3(a)(2)	404
3.3(a)(3)	410
3.3(a)(3)	416
3.3(a)(3)	436
3.3(a)(3)	437
3.3(a)(3)	438
3.3(a)(3)	450
3.3(a)(3)	475
3.3(b)	410
3.3(b)	416
3.3(b)	437
3.3(b)	450
3.3(b)	456
3.3(c)	437
3.3(c)	456
3.3(c)	492
3.3(d)	410
3.3, Comment 1	410
3.3, Comment 1	411
3.3, Comment 2	405
3.3, Comment 4	403
3.3, Comment 4	405
3.3, Comments 5—8	436
3.3, Comments 5—8	437
3.3, Comments 7—12	449
3.3, Comment 10	450

ABA MODEL RULES OF PROFESSIONAL CONDUCT

Rule	This Work Page
3.3, Comment 11	450
3.3, Comment 12	456
3.3, Comment 13	437
3.3, Comment 14	410
3.3, Comment 15	437
3.3, Comment 15	450
3.4	411
3.4(a)	378
3.4(a)	430
3.4(b)	457
3.4(b)	477
3.4(b)	586
3.4(c)	402
3.4(e)	390
3.4(e)	464
3.4(f)	378
3.4, Comment 2	426
3.4, Comment 2	429
3.4, Comment 2	430
3.4, Comment 3	457
3.4, Comment 3	458
3.4, Comment 3	586
3.5	454
3.5(a)	456
3.5(a)	620
3.5(c)	455
3.5(d)	398
3.5, Comment 5	400
3.6	466
3.6	467
3.6	468
3.6	470
3.6	471
3.6	472
3.6(a)	469
3.6(b)(2)	468
3.6(b)(2)	472
3.6(c)	468
3.6(c)	471
3.6(c)	472
3.6(d)	470
3.7	462
3.7	479
3.7(a)	245
3.7(a)	461
3.7(a)	462
3.7(a)(3)	462
3.7(b)	245
3.7(b)	250
3.7(b)	462
3.7(b)	463
3.7, Comment 1	463
3.7, Comment 5	463
3.8	317
3.8	474
3.8	485
3.8	491
3.8(a)	473
3.8(d)	330
3.8(d)	474
3.8(e)	317
3.8(e)	472

ABA MODEL RULES OF PROFESSIONAL CONDUCT

Rule	This Work Page
3.8(e)	477
3.8(e)	479
3.8(f)	317
3.8(f)	466
3.8(f)	470
3.9	189
3.9	355
3.9, Comment 3	355
4.1	322
4.1	324
4.1	327
4.1	331
4.1	393
4.1(a)	331
4.1(a)	390
4.1(a)	393
4.1(b)	155
4.1(b)	353
4.1(b)	416
4.1, Comment 2	323
4.1, Comment 2	324
4.1, Comment 3	156
4.1, Comments	324
4.2	303
4.2	305
4.2	306
4.2	307
4.2	308
4.2	309
4.2	310
4.2	311
4.2	312
4.2	313
4.2	314
4.2	315
4.2	316
4.2	317
4.2	321
4.2	393
4.2	515
4.2	580
4.2	581
4.2	583
4.2, Comment 4	307
4.2, Comment 5	310
4.2, Comment 7	308
4.3	289
4.3	311
4.3	312
4.3	395
4.3, Comment 1	311
4.4	389
4.4	396
4.4(a)	459
4.4(a)	487
4.4(b)	138
4.4(b)	397
4.4, Comment 2	138
4.4, Comment 2	396
4.4, Comment 3	396
5.1	77

ABA MODEL RULES OF PROFESSIONAL CONDUCT

Rule	This Work Page
5.1	243
5.1	532
5.1(a)	533
5.1(b)	533
5.2(a)	533
5.2(b)	533
5.3	77
5.3	243
5.3	532
5.3	616
5.3(b)	533
5.3, Comment 8	616
5.4	77
5.4	598
5.4	612
5.4	616
5.4	617
5.4(a)	529
5.4(a)	530
5.4(a)	556
5.4(a)(4)	530
5.4(b)	598
5.4, Comment 2	610
5.4, Comment 5	616
5.4(d)	610
5.5(a)	598
5.5(a)	599
5.5(a)	610
5.5(b)	598
5.5(c)	609
5.5(d)	609
5.5, Comment 2	596
5.6	554
5.6(a)	552
5.6(a)	553
5.6(a)	554
5.6(a)	555
5.6(a)	556
5.6(b)	333
5.6(b)	334
5.6, Comment 1	552
5.7, Comments	615
5.8	612
6.1	565
6.1	567
6.2	567
6.2(a)	569
6.2(b)	568
6.2, Comment 1	88
6.2, Comment 2	569
6.3	188
6.4	188
6.5	87
6.5(a)(1)	87
6.5, Comment 1	87
6.5, Comment 3	87
6.5, Comment 4	87
7.1	501
7.1	502
7.1	522
7.1, Comment 3	511

ABA MODEL RULES OF PROFESSIONAL CONDUCT

Rule	This Work Page
7.1, Comment 3	522
7.2	501
7.2	502
7.2	613
7.2(b)	528
7.2(b)(2)	530
7.2(b)(2)	560
7.2(b)(3)	556
7.2(b)(4)	513
7.2(b)(4)	528
7.2, Comment 1	495
7.2, Comment 4	579
7.2, Comment 8	528
7.3	502
7.3	505
7.3	506
7.3	507
7.3	514
7.3	515
7.3	550
7.3(a)	506
7.3(a)	507
7.3(a)	548
7.3(b)	506
7.3(b)(1)	507
7.3(c)	506
7.3(c)	508
7.3(d)	560
7.3, Comment 6	560
7.3, Comment 8	560
7.4	519
7.4(a)	523
7.4(d)	521
7.5	511
7.5, Comment 1	511
7.6	651
7.6, Comment 2	651
8.1	35
8.1	37
8.1(b)	39
8.1, Comment 3	39
8.2(a)	470
8.2(a)	645
8.2(b)	637
8.2, Comment 1	646
8.3	52
8.3	56
8.3	59
8.3(a)	58
8.3(a)	333
8.3(b)	59
8.3(b)	646
8.3(c)	58
8.3, Comment 3	58
8.4	47
8.4	533
8.4	618
8.4(a)	47
8.4(a)	472
8.4(b)	34
8.4(b)	48

ABA MODEL RULES OF PROFESSIONAL CONDUCT

Rule	This Work Page
8.4(b)	49
8.4(b)	63
8.4(b)	209
8.4(b)	456
8.4(c)	34
8.4(c)	50
8.4(c)	63
8.4(c)	211
8.4(c)	214
8.4(c)	313
8.4(c)	322
8.4(c)	329
8.4(c)	393
8.4(c)	395
8.4(c)	416
8.4(c)	456
8.4(c)	459
8.4(c)	469
8.4(c)	531
8.4(d)	50
8.4(d)	51
8.4(d)	211
8.4(d)	388
8.4(d)	456
8.4(d)	477
8.4(d)	532
8.4(e)	266
8.4(e)	271
8.4(f)	620
8.4, Comment 2	34
8.4, Comment 2	37
8.4, Comment 3	388
8.4, Comment 3	540
8.5	13
8.5	54
8.5	55
8.5	609
8.5(a)	54
8.5(b)	54
8.5(b)(2)	54
8.5(b)(2)	55
8.5, Comment 5	54
8.5, Comment 6	55

ABA PROSECUTION FUNCTION STANDARDS

No.	This Work Page
3–1.1	476
3–1.2(c)	491
3–2.7	313
3–3.1	476
3–3.2(b)	436
3–3.8	476
3–3.9(d)	475
3–4.1(a)	320
3–4.1(c)	330

ABA STANDARDS FOR IMPOSING LAWYER SANCTIONS

No.	This Work Page
2.8	61
4.41(c)	61
4.42(b)	61
4.43	61
4.44	61
9.22	61
9.32	61

ABA STANDARDS RELATING TO JUDICIAL DISCIPLINE AND DISABILITY RETIREMENT

Sec.	This Work Page
Pt. 10	666

RESTATEMENT 2nd AGENCY

Sec.	This Work Page
388, Comment c	208

RESTATEMENT 3rd LAW GOVERNING LAWYERS

Sec.	This Work Page
2, Comment d	33
3	608
3, Comment e	609
4, Comment c	597
4, Comment d	601
4, Comment e	602
5, Comment b	47
5, Comment c	47
6	81
6, Comment g	77
6, Comment i	169
14	90
15	85
18(1)(a)	91
18(1)(a)	100
21, Comment e	319
21, Comment e	321
22	93
22	319
22	440
22, Comment c	319
23	94
24	283
26	93
27, Comment d	321
30	322
30(3)	93
32	119
32(1)	118
32, Comment b	118
34, Comment c	103
36(2)	584
36(2)	585

RESTATEMENT 3rd LAW GOVERNING LAWYERS

Sec.	This Work Page
36, Comment b	126
36, Comment c	584
36, Comment c	585
37, Comment b	74
42(1)	120
43	124
43(2)	125
43, Comment c	125
43, Comment d	125
44, Comment e	115
47(2)	527
51	68
51(2)	346
51(3)	69
51(4)	70
51(4)	299
51, Comment h	70
52(1)	65
52(2)	72
53, Comment b	72
53, Comment b	74
53, Comment d	67
54, Comment b	75
57, Comment c	472
60	209
60(1)(b)	136
60, Comment j	209
60, Comment l	167
63	134
65, Comment b	121
66	295
66(1)	154
66(2)	154
66(3)	154
66(3)	295
66, Comment g	299
67	155
67	157
67	354
67	355
68	128
69, Comment g	418
70	129
72, Comment e	598
74	146
74	366
75	150
75, Comment d	151
76	150
76, Comment f	151
77, Comment d	139
79	134
79, Comment f	135
79, Comment h	137
82	152
84	149
85	149
87	132
89	133
89, Comment d	133
93	152

RESTATEMENT 3rd LAW GOVERNING LAWYERS

Sec.	This Work Page
94	379
95, Comment b	339
95, Comment c	340
96(1)(a)	291
98	348
98, Comment c	324
99	304
99, Comment b	307
99, Comment e	307
100(2)	308
100, Comment g	309
101	310
103	311
103, Comment e	312
106, Comment b	461
106, Comment c	389
108, Comment e	464
109	469
110	370
111, Comment c	404
114, Comment b	645
115(1)	457
115, Comment b	457
119	426
119(a)	426
120, Comment h	450
120, Comment i	450
121	159
122(1)	161
122(2)	163
122, Comment d	185
122, Comment f	163
123	246
123, Comment d(iii)	248
123, Comment d(v)	247
123, Comment e	249
123, Comment f	242
123, Comment g	255
124(2)	259
125, Comment g	246
125, Comment g, Illus. 7	246
126	207
126, Comment a	208
126, Comment b	207
126, Comment c	208
127(1)	211
127(2)	210
127, Comment g	212
128, Comment c	165
128, Comment d(i)	335
130, Comment c	167
132	233
132, Comment b	231
132, Comment g(ii)	239
132, Comment g(ii)	487
132, Comment i	237
134, Comment a	217
134, Comment f	217
134, Comment f	218
134, Comment f	221
134, Comment f	223
134, Comment f	227

RESTATEMENT 3rd LAW GOVERNING LAWYERS

Sec.	This Work Page
134, Comment f	229
135	232

RESTATEMENT 3rd TORTS

Sec.	This Work Page
552	348

TABLE OF AUTHORITIES

References are to Pages.

A.B.A. Center for Professional Responsibility, Standing Committee on Professional Discipline, 1995 Survey on Lawyer Discipline Systems (1997), 60

A.B.A. Commission on Advertising, Lawyer Advertising at the Crossroads: Professional Policy Considerations (1995), 502

A.B.A. Commission on Billable Hours Report (2002), 109, 111

A.B.A. Commission on Multijurisdictional Practice (Aug.2002), 609

A.B.A. Section of Litigation, Ethical Guidelines for Settlement Negotiations (2002), 322

A.B.A. Special Committee on Public Interest Practice, Implementing the Lawyer's Public Interest Obligation 1–7 (June, 1977), 565

A.B.A. Standards Relating to Judicial Discipline and Disability Retirement, Part 10 (1977), 666

A.B.A. Task Force on Law Schools and the Profession: Narrowing the Gap, Legal Education and Professional Development— An Educational Continuum (1992), 10

A.B.A. Task Force on the Model Definition of the Practice of Law, Draft Definition (Sept. 18, 2002), 597

A.B.A. Working Group on Civil Justice, Blueprint for Improving the Civil Justice System 12 (ABA 1992), 24

Alschuler, Courtroom Misconduct by Prosecutors and Trial Judges, 50 Tex.L.Rev. 629 (1972), 654

Armstrong & Possley, Illinois Courts May End Secrecy, Chicago Tribune (Feb. 3, 1999), 489

Armstrong & Possley, Trial & Error: How Prosecutors Sacrifice Justice to Win, Chicago Tribune (Jan. 10–14, 1999), 488

Association of American Law Schools Special Committee on Problems of Substance Abuse in the Law Schools, 44 J.Legal Educ. 35 (1994), 51

Association of the Bar of the City of New York Committee on Professional and Judicial Ethics Formal Opinion 2001–3 (2001), 177, 306

Association of the Bar of the City of New York, Formal Opinion No. 1997–2, 52 Record of the Association of the Bar of the City of New York 430 (1997), 287

Association of the Bar of the City of New York Formal Opinion 1996–3 (Apr. 2, 1996), 175

Axelrod, The Evolution of Cooperation (1984), 325

Begley, The Memory of September 11 Is Seared in Your Mind: But Is It Really True?, Wall Street Journal (Sept. 13, 2002), 390

Binder & Price, Legal Interviewing and Counseling: A Client-Centered Approach (1977), 280

Blodgett, "I Don't Think That Ladies Should be Lawyers," 72 A.B.A. Journal, (Dec. 1986), 655

Blodgett, Time and Money: A Look at Today's Lawyer, ABA Journal, p. 47 (Sept. 1, 1986), 3

Bloom, (ed.), Lawyers, Clients & Ethics 1–5 (Council on Legal Education for Professional Responsibility, Inc., 1974), 277

Bloom, The Law Office Search: An Emerging Problem and Some Suggested Solutions, 69 Georgetown L.J. 1 (1980), 478

Bloom, The Trouble With Lawyers 1–35 (1969), 117

Bok, "A Flawed System": Report to the [Harvard] Board of Overseers, 85 HARVARD Magazine 38 (May–June 1983), 3

Boswell, The Life of Johnson, 47 (Hill Edition 1887), 287

Braithwaite, Who Judges the Judges? 161–165 (1971), 648

Brewer III & Bickel II, Etiquette of the Advocate?, Texas Lawyer 20 (Mar. 21, 1994), 24, 400

Brickey, Forfeiture of Attorneys' Fees: The Impact of RICO and CCE Forfeitures on the Right to Counsel, 72 Virginia L.Rev. 493 (1986), 482

Brickman, Horowitz & O'Connell, Rethinking Contingency Fees (1994), 108

Brickman & Rotunda, When Witnesses Are Told What to Say, Washington Post (Jan. 13, 1998), 435

Brownell, Legal Aid in the United States (1951), 573

Bryan, The Clients' Security Fund Ten Years Later, 55 A.B.A.J. 757 (1969), 117

xlv

Business Planning and Professional Responsibility—Problem 1, The Practical Lawyer 18 (Jan.1962), 338

Butler, Racially-Based Jury Nullification: Black Power in the Criminal Justice System, 105 Yale L.J. 677 (1995), 490

Cahn, Inconsistent Stories, 81 Georgetown L.J. 2475 (1993), 279

Chicago Council of Lawyers, Report on Code of Professional Responsibility 20 (1972), 104

Choper, Consequences of Supreme Court Decisions Upholding Individual Constitutional Rights, 83 Michigan L. Rev. 1 (1984), 501

Christensen, The Unauthorized Practice of Law: Do Good Fences Really Make Good Neighbors—or Even Good Sense?, A.B.F.Res.J. 159 (1980), 602

Clermont & Currivan, Improving on the Contingent Fee, 63 Cornell L.Rev. 529 (1978), 112

Cohn, Judicial Discipline in Illinois—a Commentary on the Judge Elward Decision, 59 Chi. Bar Rec. 200 (1978), 641

Corneel, Ethical Guidelines for Tax Practice, 28 Tax.L.Rev. 1 (1972), 338

Curran, The Lawyer Statistical Report 19-21 (1985), 300

Curran, The Legal Needs of the Public: The Final Report of a National Survey 238 (A.B.F., Chicago, 1977), 25

Curran & Carson, The 1991 Lawyer Statistical Report (1994), 2

Cutler, The Role of the Private Law Firm, 33 Bus. Lawyer 1549 (Mar.1978), 363

Davis, Corporate Law Departments—A New Look at the "New Look," 18 Business Lawyer 569 (January, 1963), 300

Dershowitz, Preventive Disbarment: The Numbers Are Against It, 58 A.B.A.J. 815 (1972), 52

Developments in the Law: The Paths of Civil Litigation, 113 Harvard L. Rev. 1827 (2000), 580

Eichenwald, Anderson Guilty in Effort to Block Inquiry on Enron, New York Times (June 16, 2002), 431

Elam, The Role of a Lawyer Isn't to Police Clients, USA Today, at 10A (Feb. 15, 1983), 362

Ellmann, The Ethic of Care as an Ethic for Lawyers, 81 Georgetown L.J. 2665 (1993), 22

Farron, Llewelyn & Middleton, Public Perception of the Legal Profession: Attitudinal Surveys as a Basis for Change, 20 J. Legal Profession 79 (1995–96), 26

FitzGibbon & Glazer, Legal Opinions: What Opinions in Financial Transactions Say and What They Mean (1992), 341

Frankel, The Adversary Judge, 53 Tex.L.Rev. 465 (1976), 485

Frankel, The Search for Truth: An Umpireal View, 123 U.Pa.L.Rev. 1031 (1975), 653

Freedman, Must You Be the Devil's Advocate?, Legal Times (August 23, 1993), 89

Freedman, Perjury: The Lawyer's Trilemma, 1 Litigation 26 (No. 1, Winter 1975), 451

Freedman, The Professional Responsibility of the Prosecuting Attorney, 55 Georgetown L.J. 1030 (1967), 476

Fuller, The Morality of Law 5–6 (Rev.Ed. 1969), 15

Galen, Prepaid Plans a Boon for the Bar, National L.J., p. 1 (Jan. 30, 1989), 561

Gibeaut, "Yes, I'm Sure That's Him": Eyewitness Reliability Under Question By Experts, Courts, 85 A.B.A. Journal 26 (Oct. 1999), 489

Gilligan, In a Different Voice: Psychological Theory and Women's Development (1982), 22

Gilson & Mnookin, Sharing Among the Human Capitalists: An Economic Inquiry into the Corporate Law Firm and How Partners Split Profits, 37 Stanford L.Rev. 313 (1985), 555

Glazer, It's Time to Streamline Opinion Letters, Business Lawyer Today (1999), 341

Grady, Some Ethical Questions About Percentage Fees, 2 Litigation 20 (Summer, 1976), 105

Hanaway, Corporate Law Departments—A New Look, 17 Business Lawyer 595 (April, 1962), 300

Hansen, Expertise on Trial: Testimony on Reliability of Eyewitness Identification Stalls on General Acceptance, ABA Journal (Dec.2002), 390

Hansen, Post–Trial Interview Limits Criticized, ABA Journal (April, 1994), 455

Heinz & Laumann, Chicago Lawyers: The Social Structure of the Bar (1982), 11, 301

Hillman, Hillman on Lawyer Mobility: The Law and Ethics of Partner Withdrawals and Law Firm Breakups § 1.3 (1994), 545

Hillman, Law Firm Breakups: The Law and Ethics of Grabbing and Leaving 143–45 (1990), 555

Hobbs & Hobbs, The Ethical Management of Assets for Elder Clients: A Context, Role, and Law Approach, 62 Fordham L.Rev. 1411 (1994), 282

Hoffman, A Course of Legal Study 754 (2d Ed.1846), 287

Jackson, The American Bar Center: A Testimony to Our Faith in the Rule of Law, 40 A.B.A.J. 19 (1954), 286

Jensen, Ethics Row Looms on [Law Firm] Affiliates, Nat'l L.J. 1 (Feb. 20, 1989), 614

Judicial Immunity Insurance Available, 23 Judges Journal 2 (Summer, 1984), 656

Keeton, Trial Tactics and Methods § 1–3 (2d ed.1973), 377

Kohlberg, The Philosophy of Moral Development: Moral Stages and the Idea of Justice 17–19 (1981), 17

Kornhauser, Sowing Client Discord, Reaping Political Fallout, 13 Legal Times of Washington 1 (June 25, 1990), 188

Landers, Attorney Fee Forfeiture: Can It Be Justified? Yes, 1 Crim.Justice 8 (Spring, 1986), 482

Lefkowitz, The Attorney–Client Relationship and the Corporation, 26 Record of the Association of the Bar of the City of New York 697 (No. 8, Nov.1971), 293

Lerman, Lying to Clients, 138 U. Pennsylvania L. Rev. 659 (1990), 110

Lerman, Unethical Billing Practices, 50 Rutgers L. Rev. 2151 (1998), 110

Llewellyn, The Bramble Bush: Of Our Law and Its Study 142 (1960), 25

Lorne, The Corporate and Securities Adviser, The Public Interest, and Professional Ethics, 76 Mich.L.Rev. 425 (1978), 291, 343

Love, The Revised ABA Model Rules of Professional Conduct: Summary of the Work of Ethics 2000, 3 Geo.J.Legal Ethics 441 (2002), 380

Luban, Paternalism and the Legal Profession, Wisconsin L.Rev. 454 (1981), 285

Lubet, Beyond Reproach: Ethical Restrictions on the Extrajudicial Activities of State and Federal Judges 44 (1984), 660

Mailer, The Executioner's Song 490 (1979), 285

Mallen & Smith, Legal Malpractice (5th ed. 2000), 65, 92

Mann, Defending White Collar Crime (1985), 431

Manson, Helping Lawyers Who Need Help, 9 ALI–ABA CLE Review, (1978), 62

Marks, et al., The Lawyer, The Public and Professional Responsibility 288–292 (1972), 564

Mayer, The Lawyers 3, 161–62 (1967), 26, 120

Miller, Confidentiality, Protective Orders, and Public Access to the Courts, 105 Harvard L. Rev. 427 (1991), 334

Miller, Plain Speaking: An Oral Biography of Harry S. Truman (1974), 272

Miller, Rumpole and the Equal Opportunity Harasser (or Judge Bork's Revenge), 20 J. Legal Profession 165 (1995–96), 25

Mindes, Lawyer Specialty Certification: The Monopoly Game, 61 A.B.A. Journal 42 (1975), 524

Morgan, Appropriate Limits on Participation by a Former Agency Official in Matters Before an Agency, Duke L.J. 1 (1980), 266

Morgan, Economic Reality Facing Twenty-First Century Lawyers, 69 U.Wash.L.Rev. 625 (1994), 11

Morgan, Practicing Law in the Interests of Justice in the Twenty-First Century, 70 Fordham L. Rev. 1793 (2002), 11

Morgan, Screening the Disqualified Lawyer: The Wrong Solution to the Wrong Problem, 10 U.Ark. at Little Rock L.J. 37 (1987–88), 257

Morgan, Suing a Current Client, 9 Georgetown J. Legal Ethics 1157 (1996), 178

Morgan, The Evolving Concept of Professional Responsibility, 90 Harv.L.Rev. 702 (1977), 24, 169

Morgan, Thinking About Lawyers as Counselors, 42 Florida L. Rev. 429 (1990), 280

Morgan, Toward Abandoning Organized Professionalism, 30 Hofstra L. Rev. 947 (2002), 24

Morgan, Whose Lawyer Are You Anyway?, 23 Wm. Mitchell L. Rev. 11 (1997), 217

Morris, Race & Crime: What Evidence Is There That Race Influences Results in the Criminal Justice System, 72 Judicature 111 (1988), 490

Morris, The Legal Profession in America on the Eve of the Revolution, in Harry W. Jones, Ed., Political Separation and Legal Continuity 4–11 (1976), 4

Moya, The Doors Stay Shut on Discipline, Nat'l L.J., p. 1 (Dec. 8, 1980), 61

Muris & McChesney, Advertising and the Price and Quality of Legal Services: The Case for Legal Clinics, American Bar Foundation Research J. 179 (1979), 501

Murphy, The Brandeis/Frankfurter Connection: The Secret Political Activities of Two Supreme Court Justices (1982), 660

Note, Professional Responsibility—Conflicts of Interest Between Legal Aid Lawyers, 37 Mo.L.Rev. 346 (1972), 247

Nowak & Rotunda, Constitutional Law § 16.44 (6th ed.2000), 36

O'Connell, Ending Insult to Injury: No-Fault Insurance for Products and Services 4–6 (Univ. of Illinois Press 1975), 387

O'Sullivan, Professional Discipline for Law Firms? A Response to Professor Schneyer's Proposal, 16 Georgetown J. Legal Ethics 1 (2002), 62

Performance Testing: A Valuable New Dimension or a Waste of Time and Money?, The Bar Examiner, p. 12 (November 1983), 44

Perkins, Criminal Law 499 (2d ed.1969), 429

Pierre & Lydersen, Illinois Death Row Emptied: Citing 'Demon of Error,' Ryan Commutes Sentences, Washington Post (Jan. 12, 2003), 489

Plotkin & Mazoral, Judicial Malpractice: Pulliam Is Not the Answer, 20 Trial 24 (Dec. 1984), 656

Podgers, Public: "Shyster" OK—If He's on Your Side, 67 A.B.A. J. 695 (1981), 24

Postema, Moral Responsibility in Professional Ethics, 55 N.Y.U.L.Rev. 63 (1980), 19

Pound, The Lawyer from Antiquity to Modern Times 5 (1953), 23, 24

Professional Responsibility: Report of the Joint Conference, 44 A.B.A.J. 1159 (1958), 277

Rehnquist, Sense and Nonsense About Judicial Ethics, 28 Record of Assoc. of the Bar of the City of New York 694 (1973), 630

Report and Recommendations of the Joint Illinois State Bar Association—Chicago Bar Association Committee on Rules of Judicial Conduct (April, 1974), 651

Report of the Special Study Committee on Professional Responsibility, Comments and Recommendations on the Lawyer's Duties in Representing Husband and Wife, 28 Real Property, Probate and Trust Journal 765 (1994), 167

Report of the Task Force on Law Schools and the Profession: Narrowing the Gap, "Legal Education and Professional Development—An Educational Continuum" (1992), 43

Report of the Trustee Concerning Fraud and Other Misconduct in the Management of * * * O.P.M. Leasing Service, Inc., Reorganization No. 81–B–10533 (BRL) (April 25, 1983), 352

Reuben & Ring, Judges Have Rights Too, 220, p. 641

Rhode, Gender and the Profession: The No-Problem Problem, 30 Hofstra L. Rev. 1001 (2002), 111, 542

Rhode, In the Interests of Justice: Reforming the Legal Profession (2000), 280

Rhode, Moral Character as a Professional Credential, 94 Yale L.J. 491 (1985), 33

Rhode, Why the ABA Bothers: A Functional Perspective on Professional Codes, 59 Texas L. Rev. 689 (1981), 24

Rotunda, A Few Modest Proposals to Reform the Law Governing Federal Judicial Salaries, 12 The Professional Lawyer 1 (ABA, Fall 2000), 3

Rotunda, Book Review, 89 Harv.L.Rev. 622 (1976), 377

Rotunda, Conflicts Problems When Representing Members of Corporate Families, 72 Notre Dame L. Rev. 655 (1997), 179, 180

Rotunda, Judges as Ambulance Chasers, 8 The Professional Lawyer 14 (ABA, No. 8, 1997), 526

Rotunda, Judicial Comments on Pending Cases: The Ethical Restrictions and the Sanctions—A Case Study of the Microsoft Litigation, 2001 U.Ill.L.Rev. 611 (2001), 658

Rotunda, Law, Lawyers, and Managers, in C. Walton, ed., The Ethics of Corporate Conduct 127, 142–43 (American Assembly 1977), 302, 379

Rotunda, Moving from Billable Hours to Fixed-Fees: Task-Based Fees and Legal Ethics, 47 U. Kansas L. Rev. 1 (1999), 112

Rotunda, Professionalism, Legal Advertising, and Free Speech in the Wake of Florida Bar v. Went For It, Inc., 49 Arkansas L. Rev. 703 (1997), 502

Rotunda, Rubbish About Recusal, Wall Street Journal (Dec. 13, 2000), 627

Rotunda, The Lawyer's Duty To Report Another Lawyer's Unethical Violations in the Wake of Himmel, 1988 U. Illinois L. Rev. 977 (1988), 57

Rotunda, The Legal Profession and the Public Image of Lawyers, 23 Journal of the Legal Profession 51 (1999), 24

Rotunda & Nowak, Treatise on Constitutional Law: Substance and Procedure § 20.44 (3d ed.1999), 36

Rubin, A Causerie on Lawyers' Ethics in Negotiation, 35 La.L.Rev. 577 (1975), 324

Rudolph & Maher, The Attorney Subpoena: You Are Hereby Commanded to Betray Your Client, 1 Crim.Justice 15 (Spring 1986), 479

Ryan, Costly Counsel, Wall St.J., p. 1, col. 1 (April 13, 1978, midwest ed.), 300

Samborn, Anti–Lawyer Attitude Up, But NLJ/West Poll Also Shows More People Are Using Attorneys, National Law Journal (Aug. 9, 1993), 25

Sandburg, The Lawyers Know Too Much (1951), 25

Schiltz, "On Being a Happy, Healthy, and Ethical Member of an Unhappy, Unhealthy, and Unethical Profession," 52 Vand. l. Rev. 871 (1999), 111, 542, 544

Schneyer, Professional Discipline for Law Firms, 77 Cornell L.Rev. 1 (1991), 62

Schneyer, Professionalism as Bar Politics: The Making of the Model Rules of Professional Conduct, 14 Law & Social Inquiry 677 (1989), 24

Shaffer & Cochran, Jr., Lawyers, Clients and Moral Responsibility (1994), 280

Sharswood, Professional Ethics 33–35 (1854), 287

Shaw, Preface to The Doctor's Dilemma, 9 (1911), 23

Simon, The Practice of Justice (1998), 280

Smith, Justice and the Poor (1919), 573

Sommer, Emerging Responsibilities of the Securities Lawyer, Fed.Sec.L.Rep. ¶79,631 (Jan.1974), 357

Sorenson, Bar Ethics: Guardian of the Profession, Trial Magazine 15 (March–April, 1975), 559

Spiegel, Lawyering and Client Decision–Making: Informed Consent and the Legal Professional, 128 U.Pa.L.Rev. 41 (1979), 94

Spiegel, The New Model Rules of Professional Conduct: Lawyer–Client Decision–Making and the Role of Rules in Structuring Lawyer–Client Dialogue, A.B.F.Res.J. 1003 (1980), 94

Steele & Nimmer, Lawyers, Clients and Professional Regulation, A.B.F.Res.J. 917 (1976), 47

Stephens, Taking Stock On the Bench: Federal Appeals Court Judges With Conflicts of Interest, Washington Post (Sept. 13, 1999), 625

Stevens, Democracy and the Legal Profession: Cautionary Notes, 3 Learning and the Law 18 (No. 3, 1976), 7

Stevens, Why Lawyers Are Depressed, Anxious, Bored Insomniacs, Wall Street Journal (Midwest ed. June 12, 1995), 24

Symposium, Legal Billing: Seeking Alternatives to the Hourly Rate, Judicature, pp. 186–202 (Jan.–Feb.1994), 109

Taylor, Sleazy in Seattle, The American Lawyer (April, 1994), 413

Taylor & Strafer, Attorney Fee Forfeiture: Can It Be Justified? No. 1 Crim.Justice 9 (Spring, 1986), 482

Third Circuit Task Force on the Selection of Class Counsel (2002), 580

Thode, The Ethical Standard for the Advocate, 29 Ins. Counsel J. 33 (1962), 404

Toulmin, Legal Practice in Europe, International Financial Law Review (August, 1989), 610

Uviller, The Virtuous Prosecutor in Quest of an Ethical Standard: Guidance from the ABA, 71 Mich.L.Rev. 1145 (1973), 475

Wall Street Journal (Nov. 30, 1991), 51

Wasserstrom, Lawyers as Professionals: Some Moral Issues, 5 Human Rights 1 (1975), 18

Watson, The Watergate Lawyer Syndrome: An Educational Deficiency Disease, 26 J.Legal Ed., 441 (1974), 29

West, Race Matters (1993), 490

Wetlaufer, The Ethics of Lying in Negotiations, 75 Iowa L.Rev. 1219 (1990), 326

White, Machiavelli and the Bar: Ethical Limits on Lying in Negotiation, A.B.F. Research J. 926, 927 (1980), 324, 326

Wigmore, Introduction xxiv, in O. Carter, Ethics of the Legal Profession (1915), 23

Williston, Life and Law: An Autobiography 271–72 (1940), 406

Windt, Insurance Claims and Disputes; Representation of Insurance Companies and Insureds 191 (1982), 224

Wolfram, Modern Legal Ethics 840 (1986), 617

Wyzanski, A Trial Judge's Freedom and Responsibility, 65 Harv.L.Rev. 1281 (1952), 653

Zitrin & Langford, The Moral Compass of the American Lawyer, Chap. 9 (1999), 334

Zonana, Bribery and Slush Spur Ethics Courses at Business Schools: Would You Have Gone Along With Equity Funding Deal? Many Students Say Yes, Wall Street J., p. 1, col. 4 (July 8, 1975), 275

*

PROBLEMS AND MATERIALS

PROFESSIONAL RESPONSIBILITY

*

CHAPTER I

THE LEGAL PROFESSION: BACKGROUND AND FUNDAMENTAL ISSUES

A. INTRODUCTION

DOONESBURY   by Garry Trudeau

* Copyright, 1975, G. B. Trudeau. Distributed by Universal Press Syndicate.

The Doonesbury humor is still biting, but in this case Garry Trudeau proved a poor prophet. The study of professional responsibility has proved to be more than "just another defunct fad." It has survived and prospered and seems likely to continue to do so. At least three reasons may account for the continuing interest.

First, the subject of the course in professional responsibility is the legal profession itself. Law students may use the substance of their torts course periodically, but they will use the substance of professional responsibility daily. This course is about lawyers as they engage in the practice of law. Whatever the theoretical interest of the subject matter, its practical content is extremely high.

Second, at the time Trudeau produced the Doonesbury cartoon, the ABA Model Code of Professional Responsibility was only five years old. Many people believed that the Code, the product of several years work by a distinguished commission, had resolved all questions that were worth considering.

Almost as soon as significant numbers of people began to look seriously at the Code, however, they realized it had answered many questions badly and left others unresolved altogether. The work of the ABA Commission on Evaluation of Professional Standards, commonly called the Kutak Commission after its chair, the late Robert J. Kutak, produced the ABA Model Rules of Professional Conduct and demonstrated that there were many issues left to debate and discuss. The debate on the appropriate content of the standards, and the work of articulating them in enforceable rules, has continued to this day.

Third, while much of the work in professional responsibility has focused on the legal rules applicable to an attorney's behavior, it has become increasingly clear that the course in "legal ethics" offers an unusually good opportunity to apply the insights of history, sociology, economics and philosophy to fundamental legal questions.

What such study reveals is that, far from being a unitary profession with a long and consistent tradition grounded in fundamental philosophical ideals, the legal profession is a rich, complex, and often perverse mixture of traditions, roles and standards. Understanding the insights and distinctions suggested by history and philosophy will not automatically resolve practical problems, but it may help a lawyer better understand the questions presented and better see relationships between issues that otherwise might be obscured.

B. DEVELOPMENT OF THE AMERICAN LEGAL PROFESSION

The United States has about 1,000,000 lawyers. That is roughly three times the number of lawyers practicing in 1970. Roughly 40,000 new lawyers are admitted to the bar each year from ABA accredited schools, and at least 15,000 leave the practice annually due to death, retirement, or simply because they don't like the work.[1]

Not everyone takes a sanguine view of the profession's growth. The rapid growth in the last quarter of the 20th century led Harvard President Derek Bok, for example, to assert:

> The net result of these trends is a massive diversion of exceptional talent into pursuits that often add little to the growth of the economy, the pursuit of culture, or the enhancement of the human spirit. I cannot press this point too strongly. * * * [T]he supply of exceptional people is limited. Yet far too many of these rare individuals are becoming lawyers at a time when the country cries out for more talented business executives, more enlightened

1. The actual number of active lawyers is surprisingly hard to determine. Traditionally, the most carefully documented statistics on the American legal profession have been from the American Bar Foundation, but the most recent of those studies is now a decade out of date. See Barbara A. Curran & Clara N. Carson, The 1991 Lawyer Statistical Report (1994). U.S. Census Bureau, 2001 Statistical Abstract of the United States, p. 380, puts the number of lawyers and judges at 926,000, a figure lower than the ABF projections. The problem in making any such estimate is the difficulty knowing how many licensed lawyers are no longer engaged in a law-related activity.

public servants, more inventive engineers, more able high-school principals and teachers.

* * * A nation's values and problems are mirrored in the ways in which it uses its ablest people. In Japan, a country only half our size, 30 percent more engineers graduate each year than in all the United States. But Japan boasts a total of less than 15,000 lawyers, while American universities graduate 35,000 *every year*. It would be hard to claim that these differences have no practical consequences. As the Japanese put it, "Engineers make the pie grow larger; lawyers only decide how to carve it up."[2]

QUESTIONS

1.   Do you agree with President Bok's analysis? Apart from any given lawyer's economic interest in slowing the growth of the legal profession, can one objectively say that there are too many lawyers? What standard would you use to make such an assessment? For example, can you say that all persons with a need for a lawyer now get help at prices they can afford?

2.   While we hear about much higher incomes, the average American lawyer probably earns about $90,000 per year.[3] Is such an income level characteristic of a profession that is overcrowded? Does the income data tend to answer President Bok's concerns, or does it tend to reinforce them?

Whatever one's answers to these questions, it is clear that the legal profession and the role of the lawyer in our society is significantly different

---

2.   Derek Bok, "A Flawed System": Report to the [Harvard] Board of Overseers, 85 HARVARD Magazine 38, 41 (May–June 1983).

3.   Again surprisingly, there is little reliable data on the incomes of lawyers as a whole. One study found the average income of lawyers to be about $100,000 and the median income to be $64,448. Nancy Blodgett, Time and Money: A Look at Today's Lawyer, ABA Journal, Sept. 1, 1986, p. 47. The same study found that about 45% of American lawyers in 1986 earned between $35,000 and $75,000 per year. Another 35% earned between $75,000 and $250,000 annually. About 16% earned less than $35,000 per year, and about 4% earned over $250,000.

More recently, Bureau of Labor Statistics, 2000 National Occupational Employment and Wage Estimates, p. 211, reported that the median earnings of all lawyers is $88,280, while 25% earn more than $130,000 and 25% earn less than $60,700.

What gets most attention, of course, are the very high earnings of many big firm partners and corporate legal officers. A survey of the 100 largest U.S. law firms found the median profits per partner at those firms in 1997 to be $587,000. Supplement to The American Lawyer, July/August 1998, p. 92. In 1999, 17 of the 20 top-grossing firms in the Washington, DC, metropolitan area had average profits per partner of at least $500,000. Ronald D. Rotunda, A Few Modest Proposals to Reform the Law Governing Federal Judicial Salaries, 12 The Professional Lawyer 1 (ABA, Fall 2000).

today than at most times in the nation's history. The following two excerpts help put our present situation into context.

Richard B. Morris,* The Legal Profession in America on the Eve of the Revolution, in Harry W. Jones, Ed., Political Separation and Legal Continuity
4–11, 18–19 (1976).**

If the Revolutionary era was a legal-and constitution-minded age dominated by lawyers, the period of seventeenth-century settlement was the miraculous era of law without lawyers, a time when law was shaped by theologians, politicians, farmers, fishermen, and merchants. This general-ization applies to all the colonies settled before the Stuart Restoration, but it is conspicuously appropriate to the Puritan colonies wherein the clergy played an exceptional role in lawmaking and where laymen universally acted as judges. Not a single lawyer came to Plymouth on the *Mayflower*. Massachusetts Bay, settled a decade later, did have some legally-trained men among its first arrivals, but not one among them had then been practicing law in England. The first educated attorney venturing to prac-tice in that colony was Thomas Lechford, whose activities dating from 1637 or thereabouts, were limited, since he was disbarred shortly thereafter for tampering with a jury. While lawyers were not technically prevented from practice, Article XXVI of the Body of Liberties, the initial law code adopted in 1641, while permitting attorneys to plead causes other than their own, disallowed all fees or rewards, thus, for a time at least, withholding inducements to practice as a respectable means of livelihood. Indeed, many of John Cotton's fellow Puritans, both in England and in America at that time, would have agreed with his characterization of lawyers as unconscio-nable advocates who "bolster out a bad case by quirks of writ and tricks and quillets of law."

Early hostility to the profession of the law was by no means confined to reformist New England. It was manifest as well in the tobacco colonies. A Maryland act of 1674 recited the allegation that the "good people of this Province are much burthened" by lawyers taking and exacting "excessive fees." Curbs continued into the eighteenth century. In 1707, Maryland's legislature set rules for controlling the admission of attorneys on the basis of the alleged "corruption, ignorance and extortion" of several of them and set such ceilings on fees that leading attorneys withdrew in protest from practice for a short time. The limitation on fees continued in force as late as 1729. In Virginia so deep-seated was anti-lawyer prejudice that a statute of 1645 virtually disbarred paid attorneys. Its repeal a decade later failed to end discrimination against the legal profession. In 1657 the court heavily fined a lawyer for appearing in court on behalf of a client, and the situation

---

* At the time this article was written, the author was Gouverneur Morris Professor of History Emeritus at Columbia University.

was not stabilized until 1680, when attorneys were permitted to practice under rigid restrictions and after obtaining a license from the governor. * * *

Whether the low repute of the lawyers stemmed from their relatively obscure social origins in this early period, from their lack of professionalism, or from their tendency to regard law as a minor part of the multiple enterprises in which they were engaged, their early conduct failed to evoke good will. In short, courts dominated by laymen informed by a few basic lawbooks such as Dalton's *Country Justice*, as in the contemporary English county seats, and litigated by attorneys in fact, who were agents with powers of attorney (including among them numerous wives of absent litigants), provided the substance of justice without the benefit of a professional bar. * * *

* * * Somewhere between the Stuart Restoration and that systematic imperial machinery set up following the Glorious Revolution, one finds that the socio-economic structure of the colonies underwent a transformation. In the North a merchant-capitalist system was evolving based upon rapidly expanding transatlantic and intercolonial trade. In the South, a plantation economy emerged, based on the production for export of the great staples, tobacco and rice, and spawning a slave-holding and property-conscious society. That emergent business society was less egalitarian than at the time of settlement and determined to protect its interests against a variety of threats—whether from the constrictive trade laws of Parliament, from challenges to land titles, or from depreciating currencies. Everywhere the propertied class now exerted an influence toward security and stability, while the rapid expansion of business and the utilization of more sophisticated instruments in transatlantic trade necessitated a resort to the more technical legal system of the mother country.

Somewhere, then, around 1690 we find the legal profession establishing a foothold in the colonies. While the roster of trained legal specialists expanded dramatically over the next three decades, nonspecialists without professional training were descending on the courts in hordes. A host of parasitic pettifoggers, encouraged by the practice of filing writs by sheriffs and their deputies, easily outnumbered the trained members of the bar. Shoemakers, wigmakers, and masons procured deputations from the sheriffs and stirred up petty and contemptible litigation. It seems almost incredible that the colonial folk of the eighteenth century would manifest a litigious spirit even more intense than their forbears, but the theologian-statesman Cotton Mather was prompted in 1719 to found, in addition to a variety of organizations for effective lobbying and for suppressing vice, a Society of Peacemakers, which aimed to "divert Law-suits" and promote arbitration. If Mather achieved any success, it was not perceptible to the later generation of lawyers which claimed John Adams. Rather did Adams, whose own town attained such notoriety that "as litigious as Braintree" became proverbial, feel impelled to declaim against "the dirty dabblers in the law" who were taking bread out of the mouths of respectable lawyers.

Efforts to limit the legal profession to qualified attorneys mark the entire pre-Revolutionary era, along with enjoining sheriffs and their deputies from filing writs or giving legal advice. Even earlier, in the first few decades of the eighteenth century we find the legal profession asserting its claims to a monopoly over litigation. In New York a bar association has been unearthed as early as 1710, and one scholar insists that it functioned continuously thereafter, certainly in a rather formal sense by the year 1756. In Massachusetts an embryo bar association can be traced back at least to the year 1759. Even John Adams found its meeting "delightful." Aside from affording their members a chance for sociability, such associations, in effect guilds, were concerned about limiting the number of practitioners, restricting clerkships, barring the disqualified and, in later years, proposing legislative reforms.

To a rising and ambitious lawyer like Adams, the restrictive measures that had been taken by the bar of his province did not seem a sufficient deterrent, and he was led to bemoan the threatening number of his juniors seeking admission to practice. "They swarm and multiply," he complained with characteristic exaggeration. Still, the standards that were drawn up in Massachusetts were rather rigid. The Essex County bar in 1769 prescribed three years of clerking before admission to the inferior courts, another two years of practice in the lower courts before being admitted to the Superior Court as an attorney, and another two years more in practice before the Superior Court as a prerequisite to the status of barrister that they were desperately intent on establishing. Not only did they attempt to transplant those distinctions in the legal profession found in contemporary England, but in 1762 they further introduced the pageantry of the common law courts by requiring judges and lawyers to wear austere judicial gowns and wigs, a practice emulated in New York two years later.

In New York also, the lawyers raised the bars. An agreement entered into in 1756 by the "gentlemen of the Law" provided that they would cease taking any clerks for a period of fourteen years, the only exception being that each subscriber could take one of his own sons. Furthermore, at the end of that period, when clerkships were reopened, the lawyers stipulated that clerks must possess college degrees and that attorneys could take only one clerk at a time. The lawyer was to exact a £200 fee from his clerk, who would be required to serve for a minimum of five years. It was this monopolistic agreement which stood in the way of young John Jay's plans to study law. His father, a prosperous New York merchant, considered sending his son to London or Bristol to clerk in a law office there. He found out that in Bristol a five-year clerkship was required and the payment of a fee of from £200 to £300. If there was no alternative, Jay's father even thought of enrolling his son at the Inns of Court. Fortunately for Jay, in January of 1764 the members of the New York City bar relaxed their rules. Under the new agreement, an attorney could take a second clerk, but only after his first clerk had served for three years, thus insuring that no attorney would have more than two clerks at one time. Benjamin Kissam agreed to take John Jay on under these terms, but in fact Kissam had taken Lindley Murray as his clerk only a year before. Strictly speaking,

Kissam should have waited until the end of 1764 before admitting another clerk to his office. Somehow these technicalities were waived; no one seems to have protested, and the first Chief Justice of the United States Supreme Court finally won his chance to climb the ladder of the legal profession.

————

Robert Stevens,* Democracy and the Legal Profession: Cautionary Notes

3 Learning and the Law 18 (No. 3, 1976).**

Law was not a profession [then] open to the masses, and during the 1780s and 1790s in most states an effort was made to keep it as narrow as possible. Each state except for Virginia—and that for peculiar reasons— retained a period of apprenticeship. This period was reduced if the young lawyer attended college, but there were still only half a dozen colleges in the new states. (For instance, Massachusetts had a five-year apprenticeship at that time, but only three years for Harvard or Yale graduates.)

* * * We still don't know what happened to lawyers [from 1820 to 1860] * * * . But what we can say, categorically, is that if the profession was heavily anglicized until 1820, after 1820 the old English notions of the professions slowly collapsed.

The differences between the American and English systems of legal training were made dramatically evident. In America, there was an obvious decline of formal structures; the bar associations had largely evaporated, as had the apprenticeship system. Legal education in the United States had fallen into a decline. The legal profession was "wide open." Such training as there was in law was almost invariably picked up on the job.

What does appear to have emerged from the impact of these forces is that, by the mid-nineteenth century, the lawyer had a different function in America from his counterpart in England. He became the man who greased the wheels of society—what today might be referred to, depending on one's perspective, as the "leading citizen," "hired gun," or "the multi-purpose social science decision maker." Whichever perspective you have, however, there is no question that the concept of the lawyer and the function he served in America after the Civil War bore little resemblance to his English counterparts.

What happened after 1870, both in the society as a whole and in the legal profession, was a process of institutionalization. It followed the years of Civil War, of rapid growth in population and of westward expansion. It was a time when great corporations were born, when great law firms grew and when universities came of age.

* At the time this article was written, the author was Provost at Tulane University.

** Copyright © 1976 by the American Bar Association. Reprinted by permission.

Significantly, the development of legal education—or, more accurately, of the resurgence of law schools—preceded that of the legal profession. Dwight at Columbia in the late 1860s, and Langdell, who became dean of Harvard Law School in 1870, were the two who set the pattern for the kind of legal education which we think of today.

What Langdell did was to take the erratic law training as it was being practiced in the law offices and systematize it. Building on the earlier work of Story at Harvard, he completed the process of taking law training out of the law offices and placed it firmly inside the universities. Academic law became respectable, as it never had been under the English system—or during the Jacksonian period. * * *

Langdell had a vision of academic respectability, and he was remarkably successful as a role model. Other universities began developing law schools, as did various private entrepreneurs. At the same time, under pressure from the ABA, states gradually reintroduced a period of apprenticeship.

Indeed, by 1900 most states had returned to the three-year apprenticeship requirement, and bar exams had begun to reappear in the 1890s. Yet legal education still remained voluntary. "The principle of supply and demand works" remarked the Englishman Bryce upon his visit to Harvard during this time. "No one is obliged to attend these courses to obtain admission and the [bar] examinations are generally too lax to require elaborate preparation. But the instruction is found so valuable, so helpful for professional success, that young men throng the lecture halls, willingly spending two or three years in the scientific study of law, which they might have spent in the chambers of a practicing lawyer."

Basically, anyone who wanted to be a lawyer could hang out his shingle, and there were very few requirements for doing so, except limited apprenticeship in some states. So the vast majority of lawyers at the turn of the century—80 to 90 percent—never saw the inside of a university, whether it was a law school or a college. Most of them had to take a bar exam, but, unlike the situation today, the market was the primary determinant of whether they would be successful.

Meanwhile, Harvard Law School continued to grow and to train the elite lawyers—at least those whose parents had money. In 1900 a young man went to Harvard Law School if he wanted to practice with one of the large Boston or New York firms. But in addition, there were a plethora of other law schools—part-time and full-time, one year, two year and three year—while apprenticeship remained the normal method of entry to the profession.

In the last 70 years, we have seen the apprenticeship method go the way of the dodo and formal, institutionalized legal education become compulsory.

What happened was not really the academic lawyer's fault. It was the American Bar Association's. I don't mean to say that the academic lawyer was entirely innocent in the implementation of this retrograde step, but it was the ABA which was the primary mover in making law school compulsory. It wanted to make law school compulsory because it wanted to contribute to "raising standards."

"Raising standards" is purposely vague. What it meant in this case undoubtedly included concern over the large number of illiterate and dishonest lawyers. A significant number of lawyers in 1900 had not finished high school and heretofore the ABA's effort to raise standards was in part a genuine effort to protect the public.

The developments, however, also represented an effort on the part of many practitioners to restrict numbers. The move was, to some extent, an anticompetitive device, and it was also undoubtedly—although I think that some recent studies overstate this—an effort to discriminate against certain groups. It was an effort to keep blacks and immigrant groups—especially Jews—out of the legal profession.

The first state to make law school compulsory was West Virginia which, in 1928, required one year of law school. It was not difficult to see where these pressures were coming from. West Virginia argued the need to inculcate "The Spirit of American Government." A New York delegate to the ABA put it more bluntly: "The need to have lawyers able to read, write and talk the English language—not Bohemian, not Gaelic, not Yiddish, but English." That was the beginning of compulsory legal education and prior college training in the United States—the debates of the House of Delegates in the 1930s and 1940s make it clear that the same sentiment motivated the ABA when it tried to drive out some law schools—and the depression provided a powerful stimulus to "raising standards."

Gradually, between 1929 and 1942 each state, partly for anticompetitive reasons and partly in a genuine effort to raise standards, followed the lead of West Virginia—and the suggestions of the American Bar Association. In 1920 there had still been a certain flexibility: many law schools only had two-year programs and only two or three law schools required an undergraduate degree. Increasingly, lawyers had gone to law school and most of the leading universities had law schools—but not because they were required to. At that time virtually every state allowed, as an alternative, three years of apprenticeship; and the majority of American lawyers had still not been to law school.

By 1950 attendance at law school was compulsory, and during the 1950s law school entrance requirements included two, and later three years of college. It was all part of the movement to "improve standards," although for reasons both good and bad. Moreover, in the post-Second World War years, the number of lawyers who had attended law school for the first time outran the number who had not.

The transition from compulsory apprenticeship to compulsory legal education was accomplished in three steps. First, law schools had become an alternative to apprenticeship; second, they had gradually driven out apprenticeship, and finally, they had become anxious to tighten standards and cut back on the number of accredited schools, thereby further limiting access to a legal education. * * *

The question of access to the legal profession, especially for minorities, is directly tied to the accreditation process. For example, when a new, small, low cost law school opens which has a sizable minority student population, is that school serving a minority group or exploiting it? The line between serving and exploiting is an extremely difficult one, but, in effect, there is always an inherent danger in a self-regulating profession to reproduce itself in the same colors and tones.

———

Changes in the Bar Over the Past Twenty–Five Years

The above articles were written in 1976 at the time of the bicentennial of the nation and the centennial of the founding of the American Bar Association. Few lawyers in 1976 could have predicted the changes in professional life that were about to come.

The profession in 1976 was beginning a rate of growth that has not abated and that so concerned President Bok a few years later. The number of lawyers admitted to the bar in 1975 was 34,930, for example; that was almost double the number admitted in 1970.[4] In 2001, nearly 48,000 were admitted to the bar by examination.[5]

The demographics of the legal profession had begun to change as well. Less than 7,000 women were in law school in 1970; the figure rose to over 40,000 by 1980.[6] During the same decade, the number of African–Americans in law school rose from less than 4000 to almost 15,000.[7] By the year 2001, 62,476 or 49% of U.S. law students were women and 26,257 or 20.6% were members of minority groups.[8]

The rules governing the practice of law were likewise on the brink of change in 1976. Before 1975, most lawyers adhered to schedules that established minimum levels for fees for their services.[9] Lawyers were also potentially subject to professional discipline if they allowed their legal talents to be praised even in a positive news story.[10] As you will see in these materials, professional standards on both points have changed markedly.

4. ABA Task Force on Law Schools and the Profession: Narrowing the Gap, Legal Education and Professional Development—An Educational Continuum (hereafter Task Force) (1992) at 14.

5. 71 The Bar Examiner (Issue 2, May, 2002), at p. 15 (table of "Admission to the Bar by Jurisdiction"). Nearly 6000 other lawyers were admitted by motion.

6. Task Force at 18.

7. Id. at 25.

8. ABA Consultant on Legal Education, Annual Report 2001–02, at p. 11.

9. The Supreme Court held that these fee schedules violated the antitrust laws in Goldfarb v. Virginia State Bar, 421 U.S. 773, 95 S.Ct. 2004, 44 L.Ed.2d 572 (1975), discussed in Problem 5, infra.

10. Cf., Belli v. State Bar, 519 P.2d 575 (Cal.1974) (the court censured Melvin Belli, a well-known tort lawyer, for appearing in an advertisement for scotch in which his legal talent was praised).

Further, while some legal practitioners have always been more prominent or successful than others, the profession has probably become even
more stratified today than it was before. Professors Heinz and Laumann
concluded their landmark study of Chicago lawyers this way:

> [M]uch of the differentiation within the legal profession is
> secondary to one fundamental distinction—the distinction between
> lawyers who represent large organizations (corporations, labor
> unions, or government) and those who represent individuals. The
> two kinds of law practice are the two hemispheres of the profes-
> sion. Most lawyers reside exclusively in one hemisphere or the
> other and seldom, if ever, cross the equator.
>
> Lawyers who serve major corporations and other large organi-
> zations differ systematically from those who work for individuals
> and small businesses whether we look at the social origins of the
> lawyers, the prestige of the law schools they attended, their social
> or political values, their networks of friends and professional
> associates, or several other social variables.[11]

In the mid–1990s, the principal concern of lawyers was whether they
would continue to have a job. As the economy raced ahead in the late–
1990s, those concerns abated, but they returned with the recession early in
the 21st century. As the ethics rules have allowed more competition, there
unquestionably will be increased pressure for the efficient delivery of legal
services at ever lower prices in the years to come.[12]

What will such pressures do to the idea of a unified legal profession?
What will it do to lawyers' ability and willingness to deliver pro bono
service? Can lawyers' professional standards survive the economic pressures lawyers will face? Will the profession itself survive if its standards do
not exceed those of the economic marketplace? You will discuss these
questions and others as you work through the materials of this course.

C. The Development of Standards of Professional Conduct

For at least 150 years, American lawyers have tried to describe proper
professional behavior. The earliest such standards were statements of
moral principles that had no legal effect. Throughout most of the 19th
Century, such principles were developed and published by lawyers who
were also teaching law.

In 1836, for example, Baltimore lawyer David Hoffman closed his two
volume *A Course of Legal Study* with "Fifty Resolutions" to which he

11. John P. Heinz & Edward O. Laumann, Chicago Lawyers: The Social Structure of the Bar, pp. 319–20 (1982).

12. See, e.g., Thomas D. Morgan, Economic Reality Facing Twenty–First Century
Lawyers, 69 U. Washington L. Rev. 625
(1994); Thomas D. Morgan, Practicing Law
in the Interests of Justice in the Twenty–
First Century, 70 Fordham L. Rev. 1793
(2002).

urged lawyers to adhere. Those resolutions, in turn, appear to have been an important influence on the writing of George Sharswood, whose *A Compend of Lectures on the Aims and Duties of the Profession of the Law* was published in Philadelphia in 1854.

Sharswood's standards are usually cited as the source of the Code of Ethics adopted by the State of Alabama in 1887. It was the Alabama Code, in turn, that formed the basis for the American Bar Association's first statement of ethical principles, the Canons of Professional Ethics, published in 1908.

The ABA Canons remained the national professional model for over sixty years, although over that time its original thirty-two Canons were supplemented by fifteen others. You will find the ABA Canons in the Standards Supplement to this book. In many states, however, lawyers were subject to professional discipline for offenses not much more specific than "conduct unbecoming a lawyer."

Thus, in 1969, the ABA adopted its Model Code of Professional Responsibility. That Code, adopted almost universally by state supreme courts around the country, was a set of principles designed to be more specific and more amenable to disciplinary enforcement. The Code became "law" in the same sense that the Rules of Civil Procedure become law when a court adopts them.

The nine "Canons" in the Code were "axiomatic norms," i.e., general propositions serving as little more than chapter headings for the rest of the text. The "Disciplinary Rules" were "mandatory in character," that is, violations would subject the attorney to discipline up to and including disbarment. The Ethical Considerations, on the other hand, were "aspirational in character" and were said to be an unenforceable but hopeful statement of the profession's consensus about proper lawyer behavior.

The decade of the 1970s ushered in a period of great ferment in the field of legal ethics. The Supreme Court handed down some important cases and there was vigorous debate about ethical propositions that to that point had been little challenged.

Thus, in 1983, the ABA adopted yet another version of its statement of professional standards. The 1983 ABA Model Rules of Professional Conduct were structured in a "Restatement" format. They had black-letter rules that were followed by explanatory "Comments" and notes ("Code Comparisons") comparing the Model Rules to the Model Code. The Comments were meant to have authoritative status; the Code Comparisons did not.

In 2002, the ABA adopted extensive revisions to the 1983 Model Rules of Professional Conduct, although it changed neither the basic format nor the name of the new document. That leaves room for confusion whether the Model Rules being cited are those from 1983 (as amended over the years) or 2002. All references to Rule numbers or Comment numbers in these materials are to the Model Rules as amended in 2002 unless otherwise indicated. From time to time, however, the materials refer either to

the "1983 Model Rules" or "the Model Rules prior to the 2002 amendments," primarily in the context of showing how the new rules differ from
the old.

ABA Model Rules, whether prior to or after 2002, have only the status
of proposed law. They are a "model," and the ABA must lobby state and
federal courts to enact these Rules as positive law. The ABA has been quite
successful in its lobbying efforts, but one will find more nonuniform
versions of the Model Rules than existed during the heyday of the Model
Code. In fact, a few jurisdictions still follow the format of the Model Code
although the substance is usually similar to the Model Rules. It is important to understand that none of the ABA documents is legally binding on
anyone. That is, they are models that must be adopted or rejected by
individual state supreme courts before they have any legal effect.

To make your life even more interesting, as of 2002, over forty-two
jurisdictions had revised their own rules to follow the 1983 Model Rules in
substantial part. Others had amended their Model Code to adopt important
1983 Model Rules ideas. As of the end of 2002, no states had adopted the
Model Rules as amended in 2002, but several had established committees to
review the changes and many state supreme courts are likely to adopt them
in due course.

The current ABA Model Rules, the 1983 Model Rules, as amended, the
ABA Model Code of Professional Responsibility, and even the ABA Canons
of Ethics, are reprinted in the Standards Supplement to this book. In this
text, we ask primarily how the Model Rules approach the practical ethical
issues lawyers confront. Keep in mind, however, that the "code of ethics"
that will be legally binding on you will be the one adopted by the supreme
court of the state or states in which you are licensed.[13] It may or may not
correspond exactly to the ABA model from which it is derived.[14]

At least four other sources of authority and advice will also be
important to your analysis of legal ethics issues. First are court decisions,
whether in cases seeking discipline of lawyers, cases seeking malpractice
damages, contempt proceedings, criminal cases, or the like.

Second, the ABA and state and local bar associations often issue ethics
opinions. These are advisory opinions that respond to a specific question or
an assumed state of facts. Although these opinions are not formally binding

---

13. Lawyers licensed in more than one
state are subject to discipline in each of them
and may face problems of conflicting professional standards. Situations in which disclosure of information is required by some
states but prohibited by others can prove
particularly difficult. At least in principle, a
state supreme court may impose discipline on
lawyers it has licensed wherever the conduct
takes place. ABA Model Rule 8.5, discussed in
Problem 2 *infra*, is an attempt to try to
establish a common choice of law rule with
which to deal with this problem.

14. In the Standards Supplement, Ap-
pendices A, B, & C to the Model Rules consist
of charts that map out the important varia-
tions among state ethics rules that govern
client confidences, lawyer screening, and
when fee agreements must be in writing.

on any lawyer, they are influential with the courts, which often cite them as evidence of the law.

Third, in 2000, the American Law Institute finished fourteen years of work on the Restatement Third, The Law Governing Lawyers.[15] Like other ALI Restatements, this one is not legally binding, but courts often cite it as reliably describing the law. The topics addressed in the Restatement go beyond subjects of lawyer discipline to cover issues such as the attorney-client privilege, lawyer malpractice, liens to secure legal fees, and the like. These materials will often refer to the Restatement to articulate a particular legal rule, to explain the rationale for a principle of law set forth in the Model Rules, or to suggest the body of tort or agency law on which some provision of the Model Rules is based.

Finally, federal agencies have begun to issue regulations that regulate the work of lawyers who appear before them. They have always had procedural rules, of course, governing practice before the agency, but early in 2003, for example, in response to a series of corporate scandals, the Securities and Exchange Commission issued important new regulations dictating how lawyers for publicly-held companies must respond to possible wrongdoing by or within those companies.[16]

D. SOME CONTRIBUTIONS FROM MORAL PHILOSOPHY TO THE STUDY OF LEGAL ETHICS

Ethics is a traditional field for philosophers. The dilemma for any course such as this one is how to acknowledge philosophical traditions while recognizing that most questions of modern legal ethics are debated in more traditional legal terms. The most helpful approach seems to be to look at some distinctions that have been important in the philosophical tradition and that can also be useful to us.

1. THE ETHICS OF DUTY VERSUS THE ETHICS OF ASPIRATION

The task of ethical analysis might be understood as one of defining a minimum standard below which conduct may not fall, establishing standards of ideal behavior toward which individuals should aim but cannot realistically expect to reach, or giving "practical advice" that is somewhere in between. Professor Lon Fuller suggested a distinction between what he called the "morality of duty" and the "morality of aspiration."

---

15. There is no Restatement, First or Second, of The Law Governing Lawyers. This Restatement is called "Third" because the American Law Institute is now drafting the third wave of Restatements on various subjects. Although we do not normally think of a "third" unless there is a "first" or "second", there are exceptions. Napoleon III was Emperor of France although there was never a Napoleon II who was Emperor.

16. See 17 CFR Part 205, issued Jan. 29, 2003. Earlier, the Internal Revenue Service issued new regulations affecting lawyers who advise issuers of "potentially abusive tax shelters." 26 CFR Part 301 (effective Jan. 1, 2003).

Lon Fuller, The Morality of Law

5–6, 9–10 (Rev. Ed. 1969).

The morality of aspiration is most plainly exemplified in Greek philosophy. It is the morality of the Good Life, of excellence, of the fullest realization of human powers. In a morality of aspiration there may be overtones of a notion approaching that of duty. But these overtones are usually muted, as they are in Plato and Aristotle. Those thinkers recognized, of course, that a man might fail to realize his fullest capabilities. As a citizen or as an official, he might be found wanting. But in such a case he was condemned for failure, not for being recreant to duty; for shortcoming, not for wrongdoing. Generally with the Greeks instead of ideas of right and wrong, of moral claim and moral duty, we have rather the conception of proper and fitting conduct, conduct such as beseems a human being functioning at his best.

Where the morality of aspiration starts at the top of human achievement, the morality of duty starts at the bottom. It lays down the basic rules without which an ordered society is impossible, or without which an ordered society directed toward certain specific goals must fail of its mark. It is the morality of the Old Testament and the Ten Commandments. It speaks in terms of "thou shalt not," and, less frequently, of "thou shalt." It does not condemn men for failing to embrace opportunities for the fullest realization of their powers. Instead, it condemns them for failing to respect the basic requirements of social living. * * *

As we consider the whole range of moral issues, we may conveniently imagine a kind of scale or yardstick which begins at the bottom with the most obvious demands of social living and extends upward to the highest reaches of human aspiration. Somewhere along this scale there is an invisible pointer that marks the dividing line where the pressure of duty leaves off and the challenge of excellence begins. The whole field of moral argument is dominated by a great undeclared war over the location of this pointer. There are those who struggle to push it upward; others work to pull it down. Those whom we regard as being unpleasantly—or at least, inconveniently—moralistic are forever trying to inch the pointer upward so as to expand the area of duty. Instead of inviting us to join them in realizing a pattern of life they consider worthy of human nature, they try to bludgeon us into a belief we are duty bound to embrace this pattern. All of us have probably been subjected to some variation of this technique at one time or another. Too long an exposure to it may leave in the victim a lifelong distaste for the whole notion of moral duty.

The ABA Model Code of Professional Responsibility was an explicit attempt to create propositions based on the morality of duty. Its Disciplinary Rules are exactly the kinds of minimum standards that can be enforced in disciplinary proceedings. The ABA Model Rules of Professional Conduct continue that approach. Contrast that with the following provision from the ABA Canons of Professional Ethics, which the Model Code replaced.

American Bar Association, Canons of Professional Ethics

Canon 32 (1908)

The Lawyer's Duty in Its Last Analysis

No client, corporate or individual, however powerful, nor any cause, civil or political, however important, is entitled to receive nor should any lawyer render any service or advice involving disloyalty to the law whose ministers we are, or disrespect of the judicial office, which we are bound to uphold, or corruption of any person or persons exercising a public office or private trust, or deception or betrayal of the public. When rendering any such improper service or advice, the lawyer invites and merits stern and just condemnation. Correspondingly, he advances the honor of his profession and the best interests of his client when he renders service or gives advice tending to impress upon the client and his undertaking exact compliance with the strictest principles of moral law. * * * But above all a lawyer will find his highest honor in a deserved reputation for fidelity to private trust and to public duty, as an honest man and as a patriotic and loyal citizen.[17]

QUESTIONS

1. Which approach to ethics seems more appropriate? Could a lawyer ever be prosecuted for violating most of former Canon 32? Does that mean that it was inappropriate to include it in a code of conduct for lawyers? Would lawyers' conduct likely be elevated more by minimum standards or by ethical aspirations?

2. Notice as you look at the ABA Model Code of Professional Responsibility that the Ethical Considerations that it contains are nominally aspirational provisions of the sort described by Fuller. Do the ECs qualify as aspirational in any real sense? Could they be rewritten so as to assert principles that elevate a lawyer's thinking about behavior in particular situations?

3. The ABA Model Rules abandoned the use of separate "Ethical Considerations." Does that make the Model Rules less aspirational than the Model Code? Is the current ABA and state bar concern about "professionalism" a new shorthand for an attempt to revive aspirational standards? Do you agree that restoration of such standards would be desirable?

---

17. The sexist language of Canon 32 is jarring to present-day ears, but the terms "he" and "his" did accurately describe the vast majority of members of the bar when Canon 32 was in force.

2.   Moral People versus Moral Actions

Is there a difference between what we want a lawyer to do and the kind of person we want a lawyer to be? Should the law demand only that a lawyer comply with applicable rules of professional conduct, or should it be concerned that a lawyer be a person who will seek to act morally in each of life's situations?

Many people assume that personal and professional standards are congruent. That is, if someone has good moral sense, his or her behavior will necessarily comply with professional standards. But professional ethics are not synonymous with moral conduct. It is not "immoral" for a lawyer to form a law partnership with a non-lawyer, for example, but it would violate current professional standards in almost every jurisdiction.

Confusing concepts of personal character and professional conduct has even caused some to assert that legal ethics cannot be taught. If one assumed—and if the assumption were correct—that a law student has largely formed his or her moral character before coming to school, the question would naturally be whether there is anything left to teach in a course such as this one. To the extent one sees differences between personal ethics and professional standards, however, and to the extent that personal moral development continues to occur all through life, there is a lot left to examine in a professional responsibility course.

Furthermore, if the definition of an ethical lawyer consists only of a capacity to follow rules, one might understandably worry about the future of the profession. Real life ethical problems rarely come up in forms that are easily resolvable by simple norms.

Indeed, most important moral choices require a person to make important judgments when no one else is looking. Thus, there must inevitably be a concern for the quality of a lawyer's moral decisionmaking in the countless situations when a lawyer is unlikely to get caught. The source of good decisions in those settings is what we usually call a person's "character".

Psychologist Lawrence Kohlberg is usually credited with identifying six stages of moral development.[18] Adherence to rules such as those imposed on lawyers by state supreme courts is only Kohlberg's first stage and represents no more than the moral development achieved by a small child who knows wrongdoing is associated with punishment.

In the second stage of moral growth, a person basically says "I will be good to you if you are good to me," while in the third stage a person conforms behavior to something he thinks others will approve. Neither is the morality of aspiration, but both forms of moral thought are certainly familiar to lawyers.

---

18. See, e.g., Lawrence Kohlberg, The Philosophy of Moral Development: Moral Stages and the Idea of Justice 17–19 (1981).

Stages four and five of Kohlberg's moral development require conforming acts to what is required by the social order and the social contract respectively. Stage four requires respect for authority, and would be seen in legal ethics as respect for courts and other legal institutions. Stage five recognizes greater possibilities of change in the social order and is what Kohlberg identifies as the "official" morality of democracy.

Finally, in the sixth and highest stage of moral development, a person looks to "universal ethical principles." These principles ultimately must be self-chosen, but they must appeal to "logical comprehensiveness, universality, and consistency."

In Kohlberg's view, a mature person—certainly a mature lawyer—should be engaged in a lifelong effort to identify and conform behavior to universal ethical principles. As is true when dealing with any field of substantive law, of course, lawyers must also conform their behavior to rules applicable to their conduct. Problems such as the ones in this book should help you analyze how lawyers should decide what constitutes appropriate behavior in concrete and problematic situations. Ideally, you and other lawyers can conform your conduct *both* to law and to "universal ethical principles."

----

3. ROLE ETHICS VERSUS COMMON ETHICAL STANDARDS

Can a good person be a good lawyer? Can a good lawyer be a good person? Is behavior that would be morally unacceptable for persons in general permitted or even required of persons who have assumed the mantle of attorney? The nature of the debate on these issues is suggested in the following contrasting excerpts:

Richard Wasserstrom, Lawyers as Professionals: Some Moral Issues
5 Human Rights 1 (1975).

[O]ne central feature of the professions in general and of law in particular is that there is a special, complicated relationship between the professional, and the client or patient. For each of the parties in this relationship, but especially for the professional, the behavior that is involved is to a very significant degree, what I call, role-differentiated behavior. And this is significant because it is the nature of role-differentiated behavior that it often makes it both appropriate and desirable for the person in a particular role to put to one side considerations of various sorts—and especially various moral considerations—that would otherwise be relevant if not decisive. Some illustrations will help to make clear what I mean * * * .

Being a parent is, in probably every human culture, to be involved in role-differentiated behavior. In our own culture, and once again in most, if not all, human cultures, as a parent one is entitled, if not obligated, to prefer the interests of one's own children over those of children generally. * * * In short, the role-differentiated character of the situation alters the relevant moral point of view enormously.

A similar situation is presented by the case of the scientist. For a number of years there has been debate and controversy within the scientific community over the question of whether scientists should participate in the development and elaboration of atomic theory, especially as those theoretical advances could then be translated into development of atomic weapons that would become a part of the arsenal of existing nation states. The dominant view, although it was not the unanimous one, in the scientific community was that the role of the scientist was to expand the limits of human knowledge. Atomic power was a force which had previously not been utilizable by human beings. The job of the scientist was, among other things, to develop ways and means by which that could now be done. And it was simply no part of one's role as a scientist to forego inquiry, or divert one's scientific explorations because of the fact that the fruits of the investigation could be or would be put to improper, immoral, or even catastrophic uses. The moral issues concerning whether and when to develop and use nuclear weapons were to be decided by others; by citizens and statesmen; they were not the concern of the scientist *qua* scientist. * * *

All of this is significant just because to be a professional is to be enmeshed in role-differentiated behavior of precisely this sort. One's role as a doctor, psychiatrist, or lawyer, alters one's moral universe in a fashion analogous to that described above. Of special significance here is the fact that the professional *qua* professional has a client or patient whose interests must be represented, attended to, or looked after by the professional. And that means that the role of the professional (like that of the parent) is to prefer in a variety of ways the interests of the client or patient over those of individuals generally.

Gerald Postema, Moral Responsibility in Professional Ethics
55 N.Y.U.L.Rev. 63 (1980).

Maintaining a hermetically sealed professional personality promises to minimize internal conflicts, to shift responsibility for professional "knavery" to broader institutional shoulders, and to enable a person to act consistently within each role he assumes. But for this strategy to succeed, the underlying values and concerns of important professional roles, and the characteristic activities they require, must themselves be easily segregated and compartmentalized. However, since there is good reason to doubt they can be easily segregated, [this] strategy risks a dangerous simplification of moral reality. Furthermore, in compartmentalizing moral responses one blocks the cross-fertilization of moral experience necessary for personal and professional growth. * * * I contend that a sense of responsibility and sound practical judgment depend not only on the quality of one's professional training, but also on one's ability to draw on the resources of a broader moral experience. This, in turn, requires that one seek to achieve a fully integrated moral personality. Because this is not possible under the present conception of the lawyer's role, as exemplified by the Code of Professional Responsibility, that conception must be abandoned, to be replaced by a conception that better allows the lawyer to bring his full moral sensibilities to play in his professional role.

————

QUESTIONS

1.   Are you convinced that a scientist has no moral responsibility for the uses made of his or her discoveries? Why? Can scientist *A* rest comfortably knowing that if she had not learned how to make nuclear weapons someone else would have? Can lawyer *A* make a comparable argument about the work she does?

2.   Is Professor Postema correct that role ethics contemplates a "hermetically sealed professional personality"? On the other hand, does Professor Wasserstrom deal here with the tough issue of how far from ordinary norms role identity might allow one to stray?

3.   In his provocative book The Practice of Justice: A Theory of Lawyers' Ethics (1998), Professor William Simon argues that much of the anxiety that lawyers experience arises from the fact they are required to do what they know to be morally questionable things (e.g., not reveal information that could help others avoid harm) in order to serve an arguably larger good (e.g., encourage people to tell their lawyers the truth and get good legal advice). Does that explanation ring true to you?

Do you agree with Professor Simon that an even greater problem for thoughtful lawyers arises when they start to question whether the theoretical long-term future good is in fact worth the significant, concrete, immediate price that must be paid to achieve it?

————

4.   CONSEQUENTIAL VERSUS DEONTOLOGICAL STANDARDS

In thinking about universal principles, philosophers sometimes ask whether the ethical analysis is based on achieving a good result (consequentialism) or whether the analysis values given behavior as an end in itself (deontological).

The consequential approach is best illustrated for most lawyers by utilitarianism. The utilitarian asks how particular conduct affects people's happiness and well being. If more total well being will be generated by one course of conduct than another, then that course of conduct is morally preferable.

Utilitarianism is not a clearly sound approach; a policy that harmed all African–Americans but benefitted all other racial groups in the United

States might be preferred by a utilitarian, for example, because African–Americans constitute a minority of U.S. citizens. Yet lawyers act as utilitarians most of the time in evaluating legal rules. In most substantive fields of law, we ask how a rule seems to "work" and whether people are "better off" as a result of one rule than they would be under some other rule.

Utilitarianism, in turn, can be divided into two categories—act utilitarianism and rule utilitarianism. The first asks which behavior will lead to more happiness or well being in a particular situation. The second takes the view that there is value in establishing appropriate standards of behavior for particular classes of cases. Thus, one would not ask how best to produce maximum welfare in a unique case, but what principle or course of conduct is most appropriate for a class of similar cases.

Deontological approaches, on the other hand, tend to be based on a set of first principles, such as "responsibility" or "equal rights." Where the first principles come from and how they are justified present problems for deontological theories, but for many people the truths either are revealed by religious faith or are obvious. A deontological approach subordinates goals such as maximizing happiness or welfare to such first principles.

Deontological approaches, in turn, can also be subdivided into two categories. The first is based on "duty" and says that there are particular general principles of moral responsibility that can be derived logically and applied universally; "act in a manner that you would have others act toward you" might be an example. A moral person acting from this perspective would say that behavior is right or wrong, without regard to particular effects produced by the behavior in a given situation. A person who says it is God's will that he or she behave in a given manner, for example, would not be impressed by the argument that the consequence of that behavior in a given case would not serve the utilitarian goal of maximizing happiness in the society.

Another important deontological approach is based on "rights," a term with which lawyers are certainly comfortable. This approach would assert, for example, that individuals have certain human rights that lawyers should help preserve and protect. This position sees particular behavior of lawyers as appropriate quite without regard to what the effect would be on the general happiness or well being of the rest of society produced by asserting the rights.

Can you comfortably fit your own approach to ethical decision-making into one of these general categories? Do you sometimes subordinate your selection of a basis for making ethical decision to your preference for a preconceived outcome?

———

5.   The Ethic of Care

An important alternative line of argument suggests that both adhering to standards of conduct such as those prescribed by the courts and seeking to identify universal moral principles to govern one's behavior may actually reduce the moral quality of a lawyer's actions. Drawing particularly on the insights of feminist writers such as Carol Gilligan,[19] this view stresses enhancing the quality of the *relationship* between the lawyer and "all those affected by a given situation," not on analyzing the inherent propriety of particular conduct of the lawyer.[20]

At minimum, this represents an important change of perspective on legal ethics and suggests, for example, that neutrality and objectivity are simply not possible for lawyers and clients. Even objectively accurate trial testimony may be impossible because witnesses come from different backgrounds and social settings and express themselves in ways different from those in which lawyers and judges often seek to pigeonhole their answers.

Ultimately, this view holds that the governing ethical concept should be the positive personal relationship the lawyer and client have. There will always be conflicts of interest between lawyers and clients; the task must be to manage them in ways that seem to work for both. Clients are often unsure of what they want and lawyers are often unsure what is possible; thus, one cannot always say that either lawyer or client should "control" the relationship. Issues can be best evaluated by a pragmatic assessment of the concrete contexts out of which they arise.

The basic focus of the ethic of care is on the lawyer's acting as a healer who takes a comprehensive view of her situation and seeks to make everyone—not necessarily just her client—better off. That makes it an attractive alternative for many to the rhetoric of individual rights that pervades so much of legal analysis.

Ask yourself, however, whether such an approach will always be helpful to a lawyer faced with tough issues affecting the interests of many people. Might one need some universal principles—perhaps even some rules—to know what values and interests should best be recognized and advanced? Without such principles, might a lawyer revert to unexamined prejudices or even to the lawyer's own self–interest in formulating approaches to difficult situations?

––––––––

6.   PERSONAL VERSUS SOCIAL ETHICS

Up to now, we have largely assumed that ethical issues are limited to choices about personal loyalties and integrity. In a larger sense, however,

19.   The key book is Carol Gilligan, In a Different Voice: Psychological Theory and Women's Development (1982). Gilligan criticized Kohlberg, for example, because he primarily used male subjects in his empirical work.

20.   Among the best descriptions of this approach is Stephen Ellmann, The Ethic of Care as an Ethic for Lawyers, 81 Georgetown L.J. 2665 (1993).

one should include a sense of the lawyer as a political and social actor within the realm of legal ethics.

It surely is appropriate, for example, to think of Thurgood Marshall's choices of how to invest his professional time and talent as "ethical" decisions. Every day, thousands of lawyers make similar ethical choices—for good or ill—about how they try to influence the ways in which legal authority is brought to bear on the allocation of power within society and on political choices the society makes.

Keep these issues in mind as you explore the technical issues of legal ethics. Do ethical rules adequately address is likely to require legal assistance, obtain it, or both? Are some persons or interests—perhaps those of the poor or powerless—more deserving of legal assistance than others? Should lawyers be compelled to represent persons or interests that would otherwise go unrepresented?

E. THE MATTER OF PROFESSIONALISM

In 1986, the ABA appointed a "Commission on Professionalism." Its report called for the profession's return to a common set of institutional values based on Roscoe Pound's definition of a profession as "a common calling in the spirit of a public service—no less a public service because it may incidentally be a means of livelihood."[21]

George Bernard Shaw was less glowing in his view of professions, describing them as "conspiracies against the laity."[22] There is some truth to Shaw's cynicism, but just as one can be too naive about professionalism, one can be too dismissive as well. "There is much more to it than rules of ethics. There is a whole atmosphere of life's behavior."[23] And this atmosphere exists whether or not the constable is watching.

In the Middle Ages, it was said that there were four professions: the military, who professed peace; the medical doctors, who professed health; the clergy, who professed God; and lawyers, who professed justice.[24] A risk

---

21. Roscoe Pound, The Lawyer from Antiquity to Modern Times 5 (1953).

22. George Bernard Shaw, Preface to The Doctor's Dilemma, 9 (1911), reprinted in, 1 Bernard Shaw, Complete Plays with Prefaces (1962). Shaw was specifically talking about medical doctors, but he made clear that his complaint that the medical profession is "a conspiracy to hide its won shortcomings," is true "of all professions." Id. He also complained:

"The only evidence that can decide a case of malpractice is expert evidence: that is, the evidence of other doctors; and every doctor will allow a colleague to decimate a whole countryside sooner

than violate the bond of professional etiquet[te] by giving him away."

Id. at 8.

Cf. Hizey v. Carpenter, 830 P.2d 646 (Wash.1992), which held that a lawyer's violations of professional ethical standards—which are drafted to protect clients from the lawyer's improper actions—are never admissible as evidence of a lawyer's duty of care.

23. John H. Wigmore, Introduction xxiv, in, O. Carter, Ethics of the Legal Profession (1915).

24. Roscoe Pound included in the category of "professions," the "callings"—a word that he used—of ministry, medicine, law, and of labeling the practice of law or other occupations as a "profession" is that this label is then used to justify restraints of trade that would otherwise not be accepted.[25] The most fruitful use of the term "professional" today probably would describe individuals, not groups. Some lawyers act like professionals, and some do not.[26] But even as applied to individuals, the term has an uncertain meaning.

Society places a dual role on lawyers. Citizens want lawyers to be understanding and socially responsible, but the same people freely admit that, when they have a problem, they want a lawyer who will play hardball.[27] Psychologists are not surprised that these contradictory expectations lead lawyers to be confused and depressed. As one New York Gestalt psychologist explains: "Nobody ever says they want a nice lawyer. They say, 'I want a barracuda. I want a real throat-slitter.' So lawyers have these qualities dumped on them."[28] Lawyers, in short, take on society's distaste for what society's members ask lawyers to do.

While lawyers wax eloquently about professionalism, the general public is not so sure.[29] Artists often capture the public mood. A print in London is titled, *The Law Suit*. In the center is a cow, representing the law suit. On the right is the plaintiff, pulling the cow's head. On the left is the defendant, tugging at the tail. And in the center? In the center is the barrister, milking the law suit for all that it is worth.

Poets as well as artists have their fingers on the public pulse. Carl Sandburg has this to say about lawyers:

> When the lawyers are through
> What is there left, Bob?
> Can a mouse nibble at it
> And find enough to fasten a tooth in?
>
> Why is there always a secret singing

teaching. Roscoe Pound, The Lawyer from Antiquity to Modern Times: With Particular Reference to the Development of Bar Associations in the United States 5 (West Pub. Co. & ABA, 1953).

25. *See* Thomas D. Morgan, The Evolving Concept of Professional Responsibility, 90 Harvard L. Rev. 702 (1977); Thomas D. Morgan, Toward Abandoning Organized Professionalism, 30 Hofstra L. Rev. 947 (2002); Deborah L. Rhode, Why the ABA Bothers: A Functional Perspective on Professional Codes, 59 Texas L. Rev. 689 (1981); Ted Schneyer, Professionalism as Bar Politics: The Making of the Model Rules of Professional Conduct, 14 Law & Social Inquiry 677 (1989).

26. ABA Working Group on Civil Justice, Blueprint for Improving the Civil Justice System 12 (ABA 1992):

"Professionalism lies not so much in following certain rules as in the development of personal attitudes and a manner of deportment that leads to appropriate professional relationships and courtesy in manner and creed."

27. William A. Brewer III & John W. Bickel II, Etiquette of the Advocate?, Texas Lawyer, March 21, 1994, at 20, 21 col. 4; James Podgers, Public: "Shyster" OK—If He's on Your Side, 67 A.B.A. J. 695 (1981).

28. Amy Stevens, Why Lawyers Are Depressed, Anxious, Bored Insomniacs, Wall Street Journal, June 12, 1995, at B1, col. 3 & B6, col. 5 (Midwest ed.).

29. Ronald D. Rotunda, The Legal Profession and the Public Image of Lawyers, 23 Journal of the Legal Profession 51 (1999).

> When a lawyer cashes in?
> Why does a hearse horse snicker
> Hauling a lawyer away?[30]

Sandburg's perception of lawyers is hardly new. Nowadays, ethnic jokes are no longer politically correct, but jokes about lawyers are always in good taste. Needless to say, the jokes are hardly flattering, and they reflect the view of lawyers in the popular culture.[31]

It is hardly surprising that lawyers would like to be more well-liked. So also would car mechanics, tax collectors, undertakers, medical doctors, policemen, politicians, cheerleaders, movie stars, grandparents, and just about everyone else. However, lawyers may never be widely loved as long as we are really doing our jobs. Proponents of professionalism sometimes say that lawyers should be less aggressive, nicer to their opponents, and compromise more, but deep in their hearts they also know that if Rosa Parks objects to a law forcing her to sit at the back of the bus, the last thing she needs is a lawyer who will only find her a seat in the middle of the bus.[32]

Oddly enough, empirical evidence demonstrates that the primary way some people learn about lawyers is through watching *fictionalized* portrayals of lawyers, ranging from *Rumpole of the Bailey*[33] to *L.A. Law.*[34] When people were asked to name the lawyer that they most admired, frequently cited names were Perry Mason and Matlock. Indeed, because Matlock fought for justice, many of the people who watched *Matlock* thought more highly of lawyers.

There is further reason for hope. Empirical studies have also shown that people who use lawyers, whether in this country [35] or abroad,[36] have a

30. Karl Llewellyn, The Bramble Bush: Of Our Law and Its Study 142 (1960), quoting Carl Sandburg, The Lawyers Know Too Much (1951).

31. *E.g.*—Two people searching for grave rubbings were walking in the famous cemetery in the crowded Wall Street area. One noticed a tombstone that read: "Here lies a lawyer and an honest man." He said to his companion, "This cemetery must really be crowded; they're burying them two to a grave." Or, there was the lawyer who was questioned about part of his bill. "What is this $75 charge for?" asked the client. The lawyer replied: "That's when I was walking downtown, saw you on the other side of the street, crossed over to say hello, and found out that it wasn't you."

32. Because lawyers have been instrumental in securing civil liberties for racial minorities, it should be no surprise that in some polls, African–Americans view lawyers more favorably than do whites; 51% of African-Americans say that their overall impression of lawyers is "good," but only 26% of whites come to that conclusion. Randall Samborn, Anti–Lawyer Attitude Up, But NLJ/ West Poll Also Shows More People Are Using Attorneys, National Law Journal, Aug. 9, 1993, at 1, col. 1.

33. *Cf.* Douglas S. Miller, Rumpole and the Equal Opportunity Harasser (or Judge Bork's Revenge), 20 J. Legal Profession 165 (1995–96).

34. Lawyer Advertising at the Crossroads at 66.

35. Barbara Curran, The Legal Needs of the Public: The Final Report of a National Survey 238, *passim* (American Bar Foundation, Chicago, 1977) (surveys showing that people who have used lawyers are more positive about them then people who have not used lawyers).

36. Sue Farron, Margaret Llewelyn & Kath Middleton, Public Perception of the Lehigher opinion of them than people who have never used them. Familiarity can breed respect.

Several years ago, Justice Harry Blackmun said that if he had his life to live over again, he would like to be a medical doctor. At the time he was a U.S. Supreme Court Justice. One would think that he was at the pinnacle of his career. Why would anyone want to trade that to become a doctor. One person who heard this story suggested, "People often want to be doctors so that they can help people."[37]

But lawyers help people too. Granted, unlike engineers, we construct no bridges. Unlike doctors, we mend no bones. Unlike architects we design no buildings. Unlike artists, we paint no portraits. There is little that we do that the human hand can touch. But—if we are doing our jobs properly—we take on other people's burdens, we relieve stress, we pursue justice. We enable mankind to live a more peaceful and just life. We take the veneer of civilization and we make it a little thicker.[38]

As you work your way through these materials, ask yourself whether law is still a profession with common core values. Is it united by any more than a set of regulatory provisions? If there are still core values, what do they include? Is the "spirit of a public service" among the values? If not, should the lack of that or other core values be a cause for concern?

F. AN INTRODUCTORY PROBLEM

ACHIEVING JUSTICE FOR THE INNOCENT CLIENT

Before going on to the next Chapter, some recurring questions in legal ethics may be illustrated by a Problem—organized like many you will discuss in this book—whose discussion requires only the materials of this Chapter:

FACTS

A lawyer knows that her client is innocent of the murder with which he is charged, but she also knows that the prosecutor has a convincing eyewitness who will not be shaken and who will testify that he saw the client commit the crime. The lawyer knows that she can obtain a forged hotel register from a city several hundred miles away that will "prove" that her client was in the other city

---

gal Profession: Attitudinal Surveys as a Basis for Change, 20 J. Legal Profession 79, 87 (1995–96): "... those who have no experience of legal services have a poor perception of them." But, when the "measure of satisfaction was measured for users, the [satisfaction] scores increased."

37. We should not be surprised that medical doctors rate more highly in the public opinion polls than lawyers do, because doctors only "represent" the patient. There is no doctor fighting zealously for the disease. On the other hand, our legal system gives everyone their day in court, and some litigants are viewed less favorably than ugly diseases. Lawyers are the messengers who are blamed for the bad message.

38. *Cf.* Martin Mayer, The Lawyers 3 (1967).

at the time of the event; the lawyer firmly believes that she will not be caught if she engages in this fraud. If you were the lawyer, what would you do?

QUESTIONS

1.   How do you instinctively react to this problem? What do you think you would do if you had to respond almost without thinking?

a.   What is the level of maturity of your thinking in terms of Kohlberg's six stages? Are you moved more by a fear of punishment if you get caught falsifying evidence than you are by your desire to "do the right thing?"

b.   Is your choice of what to do affected by your status as a lawyer? That is, would a morally sensitive layperson tend to think differently about the right way to act than you as a lawyer would?

2.   How would a utilitarian respond to this situation?

a.   How would a situation-oriented act utilitarian respond? Might he or she argue that the lawyer should obtain the false document and introduce it into evidence? Could a client's potential execution for a crime we know he did not commit ever be outweighed by any legitimate happiness of others about the client's conviction?

b.   On the other hand, might a rule utilitarian reach the opposite result? Fraud might seem to serve justice in this case, but reliance on such behavior generally in litigation would tend to reduce the amount of justice done in the world. Would a regular practice of fraud thus lower confidence in the system and the degree of well being and satisfaction of litigants generally?

3.   Would a deontological analysis change the answer you might give?

a.   Imagine that you approach the issue through the lens of duty. Might you conclude that you have a duty not to assist in a lie because lying is immoral? If the result of adhering to such a moral standard might be the sending of an innocent client to the electric chair, should this standard of morality control?[39]

b.   On the other hand, if you were a deontological "rights-based" lawyer, what would you argue? Might you say that the client has a right not to be convicted unjustly? Reasoning from that position, might you argue that you have both the right and obligation to do everything possible on your client's behalf to see that such a conviction does not occur?

---

39.   If the client's life were not at stake, should the answer be different? Would that be because no one is a deontologist in all cases or because opposition to the death penalty can also be a deontological principle?

4.   Where would the ethics of care lead the lawyer?

a.   Might it lead her to seek a negotiated disposition of the charge so as not to put her client through the trauma of a trial?

b.   If the source of the lawyer's knowledge that her client is innocent were legally protected against disclosure, as well as embarrassing to her client, should she nevertheless give it to the prosecutor in an effort to have the charges dropped and obviate the need for her own fraud?

5.   And how might a socially-conscious lawyer deal with the case?

a.   Should it be relevant whether this was a street crime? How about whether violence is seen to be a serious problem in the city for citizens of all races and economic strata?

b.   Should it matter to you if the accused had previously been guilty of frequent acts of domestic violence and the victim in this case was his wife? Would such facts increase or reduce the justification for producing the fraudulent document to save an innocent man? Should they have any impact at all?

6.   What does the concept of professionalism add to your analysis?

a.   Would your desire to act professionally cause you to be less vigorous in your efforts on behalf of your client? Would it make you more determined to win by any available means?

b.   Would professionalism concerns make you more sensitive to the consequences of your action on the public? Would it make you more polite in your dealings with professional colleagues, whether on your side or acting as the prosecution?

————

You can see from the above Problem that simply articulating distinctions highlighted by moral philosophy will not lead to easy answers or eliminate the moral dilemmas a lawyer faces in practice. Indeed, philosophical distinctions may make apparently simple questions even harder.

On the other hand, the Problem should reveal that top of the head responses, or even uncritical applications of the Model Rules to a problem are also not enough. It may also show that when two people disagree about conclusions in the area of legal ethics, they are often disagreeing about the premises underlying their moral reasoning.

G.   A WORD ON THE ORGANIZATION OF THIS BOOK

Most of the problems that follow are adapted from actual cases collected from ethics opinions, disciplinary proceedings, news articles, and the authors' professional experiences. Of course, all names are hypothetical and facts have been altered to protect the persons involved or to make a question more interesting. Yet most of these problems were faced by real people. They should suggest that an attorney in a concrete situation must sometimes act when no course is wholly satisfactory.

They should also suggest that some situations may present professional dilemmas that are not at first apparent. Professor of psychiatry and law Andrew Watson properly accused law schools of developing analytic barriers to students' reliance on their personal moral reactions to situations.[40] But you will see that lawyers can be disciplined for conduct that may trigger little righteous indignation; developing *sensitivity* to ethical ambiguity is an important objective of these materials.

Each of the problems presented here is designed to require you to think. Initially, many may seem to set you adrift on a sea of ambiguity. To help you stay afloat, each problem begins with an introduction to put it in context. After presentation of the facts of each problem, the remaining materials present four main topics in legal ethics that the authors believe the problem raises. Each topic, in turn, asks a series of black-letter questions that are intended to provide the structure for a logically-ordered discussion.[41] Each black-letter question, in turn, is followed by cases, ethics opinions, and even other questions designed both to help you answer the questions and to help you see why some of those questions have puzzled so many lawyers for so long.

Further, with respect to each of the following problems it should be helpful to ask yourself questions such as the following:

1. Is the conduct in question a violation of one or more standards of the ABA Model Rules? What should be the penalty, if any, for the misconduct?

2. Is the conduct properly subject to criticism even if not inconsistent with the Model Rules? By what standard do you judge the moral character of the conduct?

3. Should the lawyer have taken particular action even though the failure to take action would not subject the lawyer to discipline?

4. How could the lawyer have served the client well and still have been professionally responsible?

Another useful way to approach these problems is to recognize that in an important sense, any rules of professional conduct attempt to accommodate at least five interests. The interests are those of (1) the lawyers as individuals, (2) lawyers in their relationships with each other, (3) the lawyers' clients, (4) non-clients with whom the lawyers deal, and (5) institutions of the legal system through which the lawyers work. Look for these interests as they appear and conflict in particular problems. Should

---

40. Andrew Watson, The Watergate Lawyer Syndrome: An Educational Deficiency Disease, 26 J. Legal Ed., 441, 442 (1974).

41. You saw examples of the black-letter question format in the Introductory Problem, supra.

the client's interest always be preferred above all others? Do the Model Rules ever give a lawyer's personal interest ethical precedence over legitimate public concerns?

In addition to this book, there is a separate supplement of Selected Standards on Professional Responsibility that is updated annually. That Supplement includes not only the ABA Model Rules of Professional Conduct and its predecessors, but the ABA Model Code of Judicial Conduct (which has also been adopted by many state Supreme Courts), and other statutes and guides to professional conduct that have proved influential in determining the legal profession's standards. You should begin an analysis of each problem by looking at the ABA Model Rules, but do not assume that they are the only sources of relevant authority.

Finally, be on your guard against two simplistic approaches that initially may be tempting when you read these problems.

First, it will usually not be enough to say, "I would tell the client to get another lawyer." That may, of course, be a part of the answer in some cases, but it is easier for a law student to turn down a hypothetical client than for a practicing lawyer to insult someone who may be a long-time client and a good friend. Save classroom "resignations" for situations in which you believe you would have the courage and necessity to do so in practice. Do not use withdrawal as a substitute for addressing tough questions.

Second, do more than simply decide that you will always stay "well within" ethical boundaries; in some situations the territory between two ethical frontiers may be very narrow. Ethical Consideration 7–1 of the ABA Model Code of Professional Responsibility, for example, said that one of the prime professional obligations of a lawyer was to "represent [a] client *zealously* within the bounds of the law, which includes Disciplinary Rules and enforceable professional regulations." The lawyer cannot always merely decide to forego a certain tactic. The lawyer must serve his or her client *well* and still be professionally responsible.

After you have completed this course you should be in a better position to evaluate the comments expressed at the outset of this Chapter by the Doonesbury characters. Is a course in Professional Responsibility a naive attempt to teach "right and wrong" to adults with fixed moral views? More cynically, is it only "trendy lip service to our better selves"? Or, do you find that the study of professional responsibility is based on a recognition that (1) ethical issues are as important to a lawyer as any other aspect of his or her professional life; (2) like any other area of law, the *law* of professional responsibility may be learned; and (3) *ethical* questions present analytic problems as challenging and difficult as any a law student or lawyer will face?

CHAPTER II

REGULATION OF THE LEGAL PROFESSION

As we saw in Chapter I, both entry into the legal profession and the conduct of lawyers once admitted are regulated by the highest court of each state. Although in a few states, the supreme courts have ceded limited authority over lawyers to the state legislatures, in most states, lawyer governance continues to be the exclusive province of the court.

To exercise their authority, the courts have established admission and disciplinary machinery. While most bar associations are voluntary, some jurisdictions require that lawyers join an official bar organization, which is then called an "integrated" or "unified" bar.* The responsibilities of such an official bar association typically include a role in bar admission and enforcement of conduct standards.

Even in states that have no official bar association, the courts often turn to the voluntary bar for assistance in staffing the disciplinary system. Under all systems, the courts often fund the disciplinary system by taxing lawyers in the form of mandatory dues and fees.**

State supreme courts regulate the right to practice law even if the lawyer is solely an office counselor and never appears in court. Federal courts separately regulate admission to practice before them, but a lawyer need not be admitted to a federal court unless he or she will be litigating there. Federal courts usually defer to state admission standards, and admission before a federal court is often close to automatic, although lately, some federal courts have been interested in asserting a more active role.

---

* In Lathrop v. Donohue, 367 U.S. 820, 81 S.Ct. 1826, 6 L.Ed.2d 1191 (1961), the Supreme Court, with no majority opinion, upheld such a bar against an attack based on freedom of association.

** The Supreme Court considered the uses to which mandatory dues may properly be applied in Keller v. State Bar of California, 496 U.S. 1, 110 S.Ct. 2228, 110 L.Ed.2d 1 (1990). The bar argued that it was a state agency and that its public responsibilities included taking positions on law-related issues such as abortion and gun control. The Court held that even an official bar functions more like a labor union than a government office. Thus mandatory dues may only be used to finance activities of common benefit to bar members to which there would be a risk of "free riders" if all lawyers were not required to share the burden. These activities included recommending bar admission standards, conducting bar discipline, and recommending changes in bar codes of conduct, but not taking positions on broader public questions. See also, Morrow v. State Bar of California, 188 F.3d 1174 (9th Cir.1999), cert. denied 528 U.S. 1156, 120 S.Ct. 1162, 145 L.Ed.2d 1073 (2000) (constitutional to require membership in bar association that takes positions on public issues if dissenting members can get refund of portion of dues that go to support that function).

In the problems that follow, consider questions such as:

a. Why do courts regulate admission to the bar and the professional behavior of attorneys? Should they be concerned about specific conduct, discerning a lawyer's moral character, or both?

b. What should be the relative roles of the courts, both state and federal, legislatures, bar associations, individual lawyers, and even lay persons in these processes?

c. What is the range of sanctions that lawyers face for a violation of professional standards? Are public sanctions such as disbarment necessarily of more concern to lawyers than private sanctions such as malpractice liability?

PROBLEM 1

ADMISSION TO THE BAR

Your first "case" as a law graduate will be your application for admission to the bar. In effect, it will be filed as a original action before your state's supreme court. The remedy you seek will be an order placing you on the roll of attorneys licensed to appear before that supreme court and all the state's inferior courts. Typically, the state supreme court will delegate to the bar examiners the task of reviewing the applications, the character and fitness reports, and the examination results. The examiners will then submit the list of approved candidates to the court for ratification. Your approval, in turn, will get you a license that will allow you to give legal advice and engage in whatever other acts the state defines as the practice of law. This problem examines what you will be required to demonstrate to the state supreme court to justify the grant of that license. In particular, it considers the "character and fitness" requirement and your duty of candor in representations you make in seeking bar admission. Finally, it looks at the education and knowledge required for bar admission and finally some other standards state and federal courts have imposed on candidates for their bar.

FACTS

You have been in practice for a few years in the city where you went to law school. Gerry Smith, a third year law student, has come to you for help. "I have been accused of cheating on the final exam in my advanced tax class," he tells you. "I did it. I had not had time to study, and I wanted to get a good grade. The exam proctor will testify that he thought he saw me cheat, but I have denied everything. I'm afraid of what this could do to my chances of being admitted to the bar. Please help me."

In addition, Smith has told you, "I changed my name when I was a freshman in college. My name then was Patrick Saville. Under that name, I was convicted of a misdemeanor for possession of marijuana. Do I have to report something like that? Will the bar ever catch me?"

You are an old friend of the law school dean. The dean has offered not to charge Smith and force him to a hearing on the charge of cheating if Smith agrees to accept a failing grade in the course. He can make up the course in summer school (for which he will have to pay tuition), and that will let him graduate in time to take the bar with the rest of his class. The dean also offers to agree not to disclose the incident to the character and fitness committee of the bar. Smith is happy to be able to get off so lightly.

QUESTIONS

A.   CHARACTER AND FITNESS FOR ADMISSION TO THE BAR

1.   Every American jurisdiction requires that applicants for admission to the bar have the necessary "character and fitness" to practice law. What is the point of the requirement?

a.   Restatement Third, The Law Governing Lawyers § 2, Comment *d*, explains the requirement this way:

"A license to practice law confers great power on lawyers to do good or wrong. Lawyers practice an occupation that is complex and often, particularly to nonlawyers, mysterious. Clients and others are vulnerable to wrongdoing by corrupt lawyers. Hence, as far back as the first bars in medieval England efforts have been made to screen candidates for the bar with respect to their character. * * * The central inquiry concerns the present ability and disposition of the applicant to practice law competently and honestly."

b.   Professor Deborah Rhode goes on:

"The first [purpose] is shielding clients from potential abuses, such as misrepresentation, misappropriation of funds, or betrayal of confidences. * * * A second concern involves safeguarding the administration of justice from those who might subvert it through subornation of perjury, misrepresentation, bribery, or the like.

" * * * [A] less frequently articulated rationale for character screening rests on the bar's own interest in maintaining a professional community and public image. * * * An overriding objective of any organized profession is to enhance its members' social standing, and the bar is scarcely an exception."[1]

---

1.   Deborah L. Rhode, Moral Character   508–10 (1985).
as a Professional Credential, 94 Yale L.J. 491,

2. Does Gerald Smith's cheating in law school demonstrate that he lacks "good moral character"?

a. Should we be as concerned about the subsequent denial of guilt as about the original act of cheating?

b. Should Smith's drug conviction be conclusive evidence of a lack of "character and fitness"? Would your answer be different if he had been convicted of a drug-related felony?[2]

c. Does cheating involve "dishonesty, fraud, deceit, or misrepresentation" so as to justify disciplining a licensed lawyer for violation of Model Rule 8.4(c)? Should marijuana possession be held to be "a criminal act that reflects adversely on the lawyer's honesty, trustworthiness, or fitness as a lawyer in other respects"? See Model Rule 8.4(b) and Comment 2.

d. If a practicing lawyer in your state would not be suspended or disbarred for a charge of marijuana possession, must Smith be admitted to practice? Hallinan v. Committee of Bar Examiners, 421 P.2d 76 (Cal.1966), said the test for discipline and bar admission is the same, namely whether the individual "is a fit and proper person to be permitted to practice law." Most observers agree, however, that, in practice, the bar admissions authorities are more likely to deny a person a license to practice law than to take it away.

3. Should dishonesty in the handling of money defeat a person's bar admission?

a. In re Mustafa, 631 A.2d 45 (D.C.1993), involved the chief justice of a law school's moot court program who embezzled over $2000 from the moot court account to pay emergency expenses of his sister. He repaid the money and the school fully supported his bar admission, but only a year had passed since the misconduct, so the court denied admission. See also, Application of Majorek, 508 N.W.2d 275 (Neb.1993), denying admission of an applicant who embezzled $300 of law student association funds and shoplifted a pack of cigarettes among other offenses.

b. In re Krule, 741 N.E.2d 259 (Ill.2000), denied admission to a man who had pled guilty to felony theft (insurance fraud) in 1988, years *before* going to law school. The applicant, while "a mature adult and a licensed [insurance] professional," had organized a group that arranged for excessive or not-performed treatment of accident victims and then submitted their claims to insurance companies. The court said the applicant had not been candid about his criminal history when he applied to law school (he also did not tell the law school about three previous misdemeanor charges resulting in two guilty pleas), and he was still less than forthcoming about it. He had been generous with his volunteer time in recent years, but the court, over the dissent of one justice, found that work insufficient to support a finding that he had the requisite character to be a lawyer.

---

2. Current practice in most states does not automatically deny bar admission to convicted felons. See, e.g., In re Polin, 630 A.2d 1140 (D.C.1993) (applicant admitted after serving time for conspiracy to distribute cocaine).

c. Should an applicant to the bar be denied admission for borrowing money for his education and then filing for bankruptcy three days before law school graduation? Does such action show a lack of sensitivity to his "moral responsibility to his creditors * * * [and] a lack of the moral values" required of a lawyer? Some states have held that it does, while acknowledging the applicants' legal right to file bankruptcy.[3]

d. Why might these kinds of offenses be of particular concern to bar admission authorities? Are lawyers so frequently entrusted with the handling of client funds that honesty in the handling of money should be a significant concern?

4. Should there be a statute of limitations on how long prior incidents can affect current bar admission decisions?

a. Note that some of Smith's problems occurred when he was a freshman in college, years before his graduation from law school. Should that make a difference? Hallinan v. Committee of Bar Examiners, supra, said that "adolescent misbehavior" was not sufficient to disqualify the applicant.[4] Would you want to know how old Smith–Saville was at the time of the alleged college incidents before you turned him in? Is it your business to ask, or is the seeking of such information up to others? Look at ABA Model Rule 8.1.

b. Matter of Prager, 661 N.E.2d 84 (Mass.1996), involved an applicant who was in his late 40s. For about six years in the 1970s, he had headed a "large-scale international marijuana smuggling operation." After indictment for his crimes, he fled the country and lived as a fugitive for several years in England and the Caribbean. He pled guilty in connection with his return to the country, and as a condition of his probation, he provided care in his home to terminal AIDS patients. He also attended the University of Maine law school, served on the law review, and after graduation summa cum laude, clerked for a justice of the Maine Supreme Court. The question was whether he was sufficiently rehabilitated after all that to be permitted to sit for the Massachusetts bar examination. The court held he was not. His flight to avoid prosecution had "undermined the integrity of the judicial process" and his admission without the passage of at least five more years, "would reflect poorly on the integrity of the bar." Do you agree?[5]

3. Florida Board of Bar Examiners v. G.W.L., 364 So.2d 454 (Fla.1978) ("he exercised his legal right to be freed of debt by bankruptcy well before the first installments on his debt became due, with absolutely no regard for his moral responsibility to his creditors."); In re Gahan, 279 N.W.2d 826 (Minn.1979); Application of Taylor, 647 P.2d 462 (Ore.1982). But see Matter of Anonymous, 549 N.E.2d 472 (N.Y.1989); In re C.R.W., 481 S.E.2d 511 (Ga.1997).

4. An interesting analogy can be drawn to the problem of an attorney's reinstatement after disbarment. As a general rule, almost no matter how serious the original offense, the attorney may be reinstated upon a showing of rehabilitation and present fitness. See, e.g., In re Hiss, 333 N.E.2d 429 (Mass.1975); In re Wigoda, 395 N.E.2d 571 (Ill.1979).

5. Frasher v. West Virginia Board of Law Examiners, 408 S.E.2d 675 (W.Va.1991), even held that a record of three convictions for driving under the influence was enough to deny an applicant admission to the bar. The result initially seems harsh, but it represents

5.   Historically, the principal concern about the character and fitness requirement has been its potential to deny bar admission based on political beliefs rather than character. In the 1950s, for example, it was the principal basis for denying members of the communist party admission to the bar.[6] Is there a risk of that misuse of the requirement today?

a.   Converse v. Nebraska State Bar Commission, 602 N.W.2d 500 (Neb.1999), involved an applicant who had engaged in bizarre but non-criminal behavior while in law school. The student wrote to the state supreme court and prominent federal judges to criticize his appellate advocacy teacher. When he got in trouble for displaying a photograph of a "nude female's backside" on his law school carrel, he raised a First Amendment charge. Later, he sold T-shirts with a "nude caricature of [his law school Dean] shown sitting astride * * * a very large hot dog" with a caption "Astride the Peter Principle." The court denied him admission to the bar, saying the "threshold question we must answer is whether conduct arguably protected by the First Amendment can be considered by the Commission during an investigation into an applicant's moral character and fitness to practice law. We answer this question in the affirmative." 602 N.W.2d at 505. The court declared: "abusive, disruptive, hostile, intemperate, intimidating, irresponsible, threatening, or turbulent behavior is a proper basis for the denial of admission to the bar." 602 N.W.2d at 508. Do you agree?

b.   In re Hale, 723 N.E.2d 206 (Ill.1999), cert. denied sub nom. Hale v. Committee on Character and Fitness of the Illinois Bar, 530 U.S. 1261 (2000), involved Matthew Hale, an outspoken white supremacist who founded a "church" to espouse those beliefs. The Illinois character and fitness panel held that, in lawyer regulation, " 'fundamental truths' of equality and nondiscrimination 'must be preferred over the values found in the First Amendment.' " Thus, the panel asserted, if Hale were admitted to

an important part of a continuing struggle with the problem of lawyer alcoholism and drug abuse that we will see again in Problem 2.

6. Important constitutional cases on bar admissions include, Konigsberg v. State Bar, 353 U.S. 252, 77 S.Ct. 722, 1 L.Ed.2d 810 (1957) (Konigsberg I); Schware v. Board of Bar Examiners, 353 U.S. 232, 77 S.Ct. 752, 1 L.Ed.2d 796 (1957) (one cannot be denied admission merely because he is a member of the Communist Party); Konigsberg v. State Bar (Konigsberg II), 366 U.S. 36, 81 S.Ct. 997, 6 L.Ed.2d 105 (1961) (the Bar can refuse admission because applicant obstructs the investigation—e.g., refuses to say whether he is or is not a knowing member of the Communist Party); In re Anastaplo, 366 U.S. 82, 81 S.Ct. 978, 6 L.Ed.2d 135 (1961); Baird v. State Bar of Arizona, 401 U.S. 1, 91 S.Ct. 702, 27 L.Ed.2d 639 (1971) (applicant may not be denied bar admission for failure to state whether she has ever been a member of an organization that "advocates overthrow of the United States by force or violence"); Application of Stolar, 401 U.S. 23, 91 S.Ct. 713, 27 L.Ed.2d 657 (1971); Law Students Civil Rights Research Council, Inc. v. Wadmond, 401 U.S. 154, 91 S.Ct. 720, 27 L.Ed.2d 749 (1971) (one can be refused admission if, with scienter, he is a knowing member of the Communist Party with intent to further its illegal goals). See generally, 4 Ronald D. Rotunda & John E. Nowak, Treatise on Constitutional Law: Substance and Procedure § 20.44 (3d ed.1999). John E. Nowak & Ronald D. Rotunda, Constitutional Law § 16.44 (6th ed.2000).

the Bar, he would be "on a collision course with the Rules of Professional Conduct." The Illinois Supreme Court refused to review the character and fitness panel's opinion, thus affirming its denial of admission, and the U.S. Supreme Court denied certiorari. Would you have admitted Hale to the bar?

He is certainly an unattractive fellow, but in the sole dissent, Justice Heiple, said: "The Committee seems to hold that it may deny petitioner's application for admission to the bar without finding that petitioner has engaged in any specific conduct that would have violated a disciplinary rule if petitioner were already a lawyer." Should a lawyer who violated no law but preached racial hatred *after* bar admission be subject to disbarment? Is Rule 8.4, Comment [2] controlling on that issue?[7]

c. In re Roots, 762 A.2d 1161 (R.I.2000), denied admission to someone with a long criminal record ranging from shoplifting to resisting arrest to violating probation. The applicant had a cache of weapons and had published articles manifesting "explicit racial and ethnic bias as well as contempt and disdain for the federal government." The court may have thought this was another Matthew Hale. The court expressly refused to ground its decision on the applicant's political views alone, but taken with the explicit criminal offenses and lack of candor with the character and fitness committee, it found the applicant had not demonstrated that he deserved bar admission.

d. Do you agree with the results in these cases? Are courts likely to be good predictors of which people are "good enough" to be a lawyer?

B. CANDOR IN THE BAR APPLICATION PROCESS

1. How candid must bar applicants like Smith/Saville and their supporters be in the application process?

a. It is often said that an applicant is more likely to be denied admission for covering up his or her past than for what that past contains.

b. In Attorney Grievance Commission v. Myers, 635 A.2d 1315 (Md. 1994), for example, a lawyer was disbarred for lying on his bar application about the number of traffic tickets he had even though the driving record itself would not have justified denial of admission. Cf. Rule 8.1. Is such an approach by admission authorities reasonable? Is it likely to be inevitable?

c. In Radtke v. Board of Bar Examiners, 601 N.W.2d 642 (Wis.1999), the applicant said that he had left an earlier position as a history lecturer because of "low pay" and denied that he had been warned of professional discipline. Apparently, he had been charged with plagiarism of a history article and left his department as part of a negotiated settlement. His lack of candor, more than the plagiarism itself, seems to have motivated the court's denial of his admission.

---

7. Shortly before publication of these materials, Hale was indicted in Chicago for "plotting to kill a federal judge and obstruct-ing justice." Washington Post, Jan. 9, 2003, p. A–2.

d. In re Zbiegien, 433 N.W.2d 871 (Minn.1988), on the other hand, rewarded honesty. A bar applicant admitted he had plagiarized several pages of a paper in a products liability seminar, but said that he had been under great stress because of work pressures and injuries that his wife had suffered. Petitioner was given an "F" in the course but permitted to graduate. He reported the incident in his application for admission to the bar, and, while the court held that a single incident of misconduct could be the basis for denial of bar admission, the applicant had been punished for the misconduct and now showed remorse. Thus, the court admitted him to the bar.

e. But candor is not always rewarded. In Application of Taylor, 647 P.2d 462 (Ore.1982), the applicant had been arrested for shoplifting but the trial court dismissed the charges when the defendant denied he had intended to steal the item. Before the bar committee, however, the applicant made a clean breast of things and admitted that he really had intended to steal. Rather than commend his current honesty, the committee denied him admission for his misleading testimony in the criminal case.

Are you troubled by this result? Relieved that the dishonesty came out in time? What is its message to bar applicants about how safe it is to volunteer incriminating information?

2. How much should a state supreme court be able to ask a candidate for bar admission about his or her history of mental illness?

a. Is such an illness a "disability" within the meaning of the Americans with Disabilities Act? Suits challenging such questions have been filed and the ABA, being concerned that such inquiries may prevent law students from getting mental health assistance, has urged states to limit inquiry to "specific, targeted questions about the applicant's behavior, conduct or any current impairment of the applicant's ability to practice law."

b. Questions 25, 26 & 27 in the Character and Fitness questionnaire prepared by the National Conference of Bar Examiners now ask:

"25. Within the past five years, have you been diagnosed with or have you been treated for bi-polar disorder, schizophrenia, paranoia, or any other psychotic disorder?

"If you answered yes, complete Forms 7 and 8. * * *

"26. A. Do you currently have any condition or impairment (including, but not limited to, substance abuse, alcohol abuse, or a mental, emotional, or nervous disorder or condition) which in any way currently affects, or if untreated could affect, your ability to practice law in a competent and professional manner?

"B. If your answer to Question 26(A) is affirmative, are the limitations caused by your mental health condition or substance abuse problem reduced or ameliorated because you receive ongoing treatment (with or without medication) or because you participate in a monitoring program?

"If your answer to Question 26(A) or (B) is yes, complete Forms 7 and 8. * * * As used in Question 26, 'currently' means recently enough so that the condition could reasonably have an impact on your ability to function as a lawyer.

"27. Within the past five years, have you ever raised the issue of consumption of drugs or alcohol or the issue of a mental, emotional, nervous, or behavioral disorder or condition as a defense, mitigation, or explanation for your actions in the course of any administrative or judicial proceeding or investigation; any inquiry or other proceeding; or any proposed termination by an educational institution, employer, government agency, professional organization, or licensing authority?

"If you answered yes, furnish a thorough explanation * * * ."

c.   Do you think those questions ask any more than is appropriate and necessary to decide whether an applicant should be admitted to the bar?

3.   Would you favor a policy of fingerprinting all applicants for admission to the bar, a procedure that might tend to expose people like Gerry Smith in this Problem who had tried to change their identity?

a.   In Cantor v. Supreme Court of Pennsylvania, 353 F.Supp. 1307 (E.D.Pa.1973), affirmed without opinion 487 F.2d 1394 (3d Cir.1973), the court upheld as constitutional and not violating any right of privacy a state requirement that lawyers provide their social security number to the Court Administrator. In dictum the court approved a fingerprinting requirement.

b.   Why should lawyers have to submit to procedures such as fingerprinting that are not required of the public generally? When Georgia instituted a policy of fingerprinting applicants, 100 law graduates reportedly withdrew their applications. 53 Bar Examiner 20 (Aug. 1984).

4.   If you are Smith's lawyer (or just his friend who happens to be a lawyer), what are your own obligations to the bar admission authorities in connection with Smith's bar application?

a.   Look at Model Rule 8.1(b). Must you report what Smith admitted to you about his guilt in the cheating case? Must you report what you know about Smith's change of name and past criminal record?

b.   Look at Comment [3] to Model Rule 8.1. Why should your responsibilities change when you undertake to represent Gerry Smith? Is the public interest in having all the facts before bar admission authorities any less?

5.   What should be the obligation of law schools and their deans in cooperating with investigations conducted by bar admission officials?

a.   Was it proper for the law school to enter into a "plea bargain" with Smith under which Smith agreed to accept a law school sanction for cheating and the school agreed not to report the matter to the bar? You might want to think again about this question after reading about the *Himmel* case in Problem 2.

b. Zielinski v. Schmalbeck, 646 N.E.2d 655 (Ill.App.1995), involved a dean's potential liability for telling the character and fitness committee about a student. The student was accused by another student of sexually harassing her. A professor who knew both students believed the charge and, on his recommendation, the dean informed bar admission authorities. The plaintiff sued the professor and dean under § 1983 of the Civil Rights Act of 1871. The court held that the constitutional right to practice law if bar admission requirements are met does not prohibit character and fitness investigations. The dean's report was subject to absolute immunity from civil liability, and neither the professor nor the dean had acted under color of state law so as to implicate the Civil Rights Act.

c. Law schools' reluctance to get involved, however, may be partly explained by Rothman v. Emory University, 828 F.Supp. 537 (N.D.Ill.1993). There, a law school dean had submitted a critical letter about an applicant to the Board of Law Examiners reporting the applicant's "chronic hostili-ty" toward other students and the faculty. The applicant was admitted to the Bar, and then sued the law school, alleging that his demeanor was the result of "chronic epilepsy" and that the negative report constituted a violation of the Americans with Disabilities Act. Although the negative report to the Bar was absolutely privileged as a matter of state libel law, the court said that reports to the Bar about most students are positive and that such reports are "services" and "privileges" that one may not deny on the basis of an applicant's disability. The court refused to dismiss the ADA claim.

d. What obligations do you think law schools and individual profes-sors should have in making reports to bar admission authorities? If they fail to be candid, are future clients of problem lawyers likely to be affected? On the other hand, might law school personnel make uninformed or idiosyncratic comments that absolute immunity would only encourage?

C. EDUCATIONAL AND KNOWLEDGE STANDARDS FOR ADMISSION TO THE BAR

1. Why does almost every jurisdiction require lawyers to grad-uate from a law school before being able to take the bar examina-tion? Is a formal education the best way to learn what lawyers need to know?

a. Abraham Lincoln never went to law school. Like many 19th century lawyers, he learned what he needed to know from books and from working in a law office. Other 19th century law students supplemented their experiential learning with lectures given by local practitioners such as David Hoffman in Baltimore and George Sharswood in Philadelphia, both seen as among the definers of modern legal ethics. Even early university law schools such as those at Harvard and Yale were initially staffed primarily by practitioner-lecturers.

b. Yet today, it is rare to find a lawyer who has not attended law school. Indeed, one common requirement for bar admission is graduation from an law school accredited by the American Bar Association.[1]

2. If you were defining the standards for law school accreditation, what standards would you impose? What do you believe are the essential features of a good law school education?

a. Would you say that no law school may graduate a student who has not been enrolled in classes totaling 56,000 minutes of instruction time extending over at least six semesters, for example? ABA Standards for Approval of Law Schools, Standard 304(b). Why should a student who can sit through the right number of minutes over five semesters not be permitted to graduate?

b. Would you say that if a student is employed more than 20 hours per week, the law school may not award the student more than 12 hours credit in the semester? ABA Standard 304(f).

c. Would you say that a law school must have a system of faculty tenure to be good enough that its graduates may become lawyers? ABA Standard 405(b) makes that a condition of accreditation.

3. Should graduates of schools that take a different approach to legal education be denied the right to sit for the bar examination in their states?

a. In Massachusetts School of Law at Andover, Inc. v. American Bar Association, 107 F.3d 1026 (3d Cir.1997), the ABA denied accreditation to a new law school, which then sued the Association on antitrust grounds, asking for a waiver of the accreditation standards. The school asserted that some of the standards had more to do with enhancing faculty salaries and increasing law school tuition than with assuring a quality legal education. The school proposed to offer a less expensive educational program, but— because its students could not take the bar exam in most states—it alleged that the ABA accreditation standards significantly damaged its ability to attract students. The court did not opine on whether requiring ABA accreditation was wise. It held only that the opinions expressed in an ABA inspection report are entitled to First Amendment protection and that any damage the law school suffered arose from the requirement of state law that required bar applicants to have attended an ABA-accredited school. The act of seeking such state action is itself immune from antitrust liability under the *Noerr-Pennington*[2] doctrine, so the court granted summary

1. California is one major state that departs from this requirement, but it has an additional "baby bar" requirement for students at unaccredited law schools. At the end of their first year, students at such schools must pass the special examination or not receive credit for further law study. The requirement has also survived a charge that it invidiously discriminates between students at accredited and unaccredited schools. Lupert v. California State Bar, 761 F.2d 1325 (9th Cir.1985).

2. The Noerr–Pennington doctrine refers to two related cases, Eastern R.R. Presidents Conference v. Noerr Motor Freight, Inc., 365 U.S. 127, 81 S.Ct. 523, 5 L.Ed.2d 464 (1961), and United Mine Workers of America v. Pennington, 381 U.S. 657, 85 S.Ct. 1585, 14 L.Ed.2d 626 (1965), where the judgment in favor of the ABA.[3]

b.   In re Brooks, 11 S.W.3d 25 (Ky.2000), involved a requirement that a bar applicant graduate from a law school providing an education that is the "substantial equivalent" of one provided by ABA-approved law schools in Kentucky. The applicant had graduated from the Nashville School of Law in Tennessee and the Kentucky bar had sent an inspector to that school to determine what kind of education it provided. The Kentucky court found "no full-time faculty at Nashville [and] no seminars or small class experience." The library was small and there was no "adequate computer facility which would permit students to do legal research." This was not the "substantial equivalent" of a legal education in Kentucky. Dissenting Justice Graves had little good to say about ABA accreditation and said that none of the court's criticism of the law school addressed whether the applicant had learned enough to be a good lawyer.

c.   Efforts at accreditation of the Concord University School of Law, and applications for bar admission by its graduates, should provide interesting tests of the force of ABA standards. Concord is an Internet-based law school operated by Kaplan Educational Centers. Students receive video lectures via their home computers, library materials are available on line, and students take exams on-line. Almost certainly, this method of study violates ABA standards such as those on hours of class time, numbers of days in which classes are held, and numbers of days in which students are present. There may also be problems of internet security: e.g., how can one be sure that the person who takes the examination is the same person who is enrolled?

d.   What do you think of such alternative ways to study law? What important parts of your present law school experience might you miss if you attended law school on-line or under less than first-class conditions?

4.   The requirement of attending an ABA-accredited law school is particularly burdensome on foreign lawyers seeking to practice in the United States. How should states deal with applications from lawyers trained outside the United States?

a.   Gail Collins–Bazant was a Canadian citizen who had graduated from the University of Saskatchewan Law School. Pursuant to Canadian practice, she had served a year's clerkship before being admitted to the bar in two provinces. For five years, she was in private practice in Saskatchewan, and for eight more, she was a prosecutor in Newfoundland. In 1997,

Court held, on First Amendment grounds, that the Sherman and Clayton Acts do not extend to those who exercise their First Amendment right to petition the government in either a legislative or administrative setting, despite the fact that they are seeking the enactment of laws or regulations with anticompetitive effects.

3. While this case was going on, the U.S. Justice Department had sued the ABA alleging that the gathering of salary data and basing accreditation in part on adequacy of professorial salaries and the share of tuition revenue the law school was allowed to keep constituted violations of the antitrust laws. Rather than conduct the antitrust fight on two fronts, the ABA agreed to change some of its accreditation standards and procedures. See 60 Fed. Reg. 39,421 (1995) (text of consent decree).

she moved to Nebraska and applied for admission to the Nebraska bar without examination, even though she had not graduated from an ABA-accredited law school. The court rejected her argument that the North American Free Trade Agreement (NAFTA) required waiver of that requirement. In re Application of Gail Elizabeth Collins, 561 N.W.2d 209 (Neb. 1997).

b.   The next year, Ms. Collins–Bazant was back in court seeking permission to take the bar examination. The court acknowledged that many states do not create an exception to the requirement of graduation from an ABA-accredited law school for graduates of foreign schools, in part because they cannot evaluate those schools. However, this applicant had studied at a law school giving common law training in English; she had substantial professional experience, and she was making an effort to learn American law. Thus, while the court recognized that it was making it easier for a Canadian law graduate to get admitted to the bar of Nebraska than for a U.S. graduate of an unaccredited law school, it allowed the applicant to sit for the bar exam. In re Application of Gail Collins–Bazant, 578 N.W.2d 38 (Neb.1998).

c.   In Jia v. Board of Bar Examiners, 696 N.E.2d 131 (Mass.1998), the foreign lawyer was not as lucky. The court refused to let a lawyer trained in China sit for the Massachusetts bar exam even though he had earned two advanced degrees from Tulane and already had been admitted to practice by Louisiana and New York.

5.   Should the taking of particular law school courses be a prerequisite to becoming a lawyer?

a.   Rule 13 of the Rules on Admission to the Bar of Indiana requires 14 specific courses totaling at least 54 semester hours of a student's law study. South Carolina Supreme Court Rule 5A mandates courses in 14 specific fields for admission to the bar.

b.   The Report of the Task Force on Law Schools and the Profession: Narrowing the Gap, "Legal Education and Professional Development—An Educational Continuum" (1992), often called the MacCrate Report after its chair, former ABA President Robert MacCrate, eschewed a regulatory objective, but urged law schools to produce lawyers with specific "skills and values." Do you think that all law students should have to take clinical or other skills courses?

c.   The ABA requires all schools to provide instruction in Professional Responsibility and a majority of states require their lawyers to have passed the Multistate Professional Responsibility Exam (MPRE).[4] Do you agree

---

4. For many years, the MPRE only tested issues of legal ethics in which the same answer was given by the ABA Model Rules and the ABA Model Code. Thus, many important areas of law—e.g., most aspects of lawyer advertising—could not be tested at all. Now, the MPRE tests "what is widely termed the 'law of lawyering.'" Bar admission standards, malpractice issues, the organization of law firms, the formation of the lawyer-client relationship, and so forth are all fair game for the examiners. As a result, *all* of the problems in this book are relevant to the MPRE, not just some of them.

that no lawyer should be admitted to the bar unless she has taken such a course?

6.   Of course, the principal requirement for successful admission to the bar in most states is passage of a bar examination. Why should applicants be required to pass another examination after they have already completed a three year legal education at an accredited school?[5]

a.   What should the bar exam examine? Could a uniform bar examination be used nationwide? Is the law really so different from state to state that each should use a different test? Development of the Multistate Bar Examination (MBE) has been a move in the direction of uniformity, but it is rarely the only test used by a state and what constitutes a passing score varies from state to state.

b.   California has developed what it calls a "performance test." Would it be possible to develop a reliable test of the practical ability to serve a client, for example, instead of solely the applicant's legal knowledge?[6]

c.   Should an applicant have an unlimited number of chances to take the bar examination? Is a failure to provide such opportunities unfair to individuals or groups? Jones v. Board of Commissioners of Alabama State Bar, 737 F.2d 996 (11th Cir.1984), upheld a limit of five-times to take the bar; there is a thoughtful dissent.

7.   The American with Disabilities Act (ADA) affects the bar examination process in important ways. How should bar examiners be required to accommodate applicants who have disabilities?

a.   D'Amico v. New York State Board of Law Examiners, 813 F.Supp. 217 (W.D.N.Y.1993), involved an applicant who was near-sighted and suffered visual fatigue when reading for extended periods. She was given a separate testing room, extra light, a large print exam, and 50% more time than other applicants but she still failed the exam. In this decision, the federal court ordered the state to give her four days to complete the exam that other applicants were required to complete in two days.

b.   In re Rubenstein, 637 A.2d 1131 (Del.1994), involved an applicant who had failed the bar exam three times. Only then was she diagnosed as learning disabled. She passed the essay portion of the exam on her fourth try after being given an extra hour for each three hour block of essays but no extra time for the multiple choice part, the MBE. This case says that the board of bar examiners should have granted her 50% more time than other students to take the multistate portion of the exam as well. The court did not require her to retake that examination but instead ordered her admission "forthwith."

5. Wisconsin has long been the only state to grant a "diploma privilege" to graduates of in-state law schools.

6. See, e.g., Performance Testing: A Valuable New Dimension or a Waste of Time and Money?, The Bar Examiner, November 1983, p. 12.

c.   In Bartlett v. New York State Bd. of Law Examiners, 226 F.3d 69 (2d Cir.2000), the applicant failed the bar exam four times and said it was a result of dyslexia and other learning disabilities. The court upheld a finding that the applicant was disabled by reading difficulties, that her ability to work quickly was impaired, and consequently that she was entitled to extra accommodation in taking the bar exam. Judge Cabranes, in dissent, however, argued that the ADA requires reasonable accommodations by employers. By extending it to require accommodating disability in taking the bar examination, the majority may make it possible for the applicant to qualify artificially for a license to do a job that she then cannot perform effectively.

d.   What approach would you take to tough cases such as these that try to accommodate genuine disabilities of applicants with genuine client needs for high-quality, reliable lawyer performance?

D.   OTHER ATTEMPTS AT STATE AND FEDERAL LIMITS ON BAR ADMISSION

1.   Should there anything wrong with a state requiring bar applicants to be United States citizens and state residents?

a.   A state may not require a bar applicant to be a U.S. citizen. In re Griffiths, 413 U.S. 717, 93 S.Ct. 2851, 37 L.Ed.2d 910 (1973), held that such a requirement denies aliens the Fourteenth Amendment guarantee of equal protection of the law.

b.   Similarly, the U.S. Supreme Court has struck down states' efforts to limit bar admission to the state's own residents citing the Privileges and Immunities clause. Supreme Court of New Hampshire v. Piper, 470 U.S. 274, 105 S.Ct. 1272, 84 L.Ed.2d 205 (1985).

c.   However, Tolchin v. Supreme Court of New Jersey, 111 F.3d 1099 (3d Cir.1997), dismissed a challenge to the requirement that New Jersey lawyers have a "bona fide office" in the state and attend CLE programs there. Tolchin was admitted to practice in New Jersey, but he lived and practiced in New York and did not want to take a "skills and methods" course required of newly-admitted New Jersey lawyers. The Third Circuit rejected his claims that New Jersey's requirements violated the dormant commerce clause, the privileges & immunities clause, and his right to equal protection. A state may protect its citizens against lawyers who, although licensed in the state, practice there only occasionally and therefore may not be up to date on New Jersey law and practice. Further, the law not only barred out of state residents, it also barred state residents who did not have a regular office from which to practice. In short, the court concluded that even if there were some economic protectionism inherent in the rules, there was not enough to make the rules unconstitutional.

2.   Should federal courts have the right to limit admission of lawyers already certified by a state as qualified to practice law?

a.   As a practical matter, admission to the highest court of a state will ordinarily be sufficient to qualify for admission to the federal courts of that state. See, e.g., United States District Courts for the Southern and Eastern

Districts of New York, Local Civil Rule 1.3, contained in the Standards Supplement.

b. However, some courts have tried to justify different rules for federal litigators. See Brown v. McGarr, 583 F.Supp. 734 (N.D.Ill.1984) (upholding special rules for membership in a federal trial bar).

PROBLEM 2

LAWYER DISCIPLINE AND THE DISABLED LAWYER

Admitting an applicant to the bar is only the first time a state supreme court may evaluate that person's conduct. For as long as the lawyer is a member of its bar, the court retains jurisdiction to sanction that lawyer for violations of the court's rules of professional conduct. This problem examines professional discipline in the context of the requirement that a lawyer represent each client competently and diligently. It then considers the serious problem of lawyer disability, primarily in the context of alcohol and drug abuse. Next, it asks which courts have jurisdiction to discipline a lawyer for particular misconduct, and finally, it looks at each lawyer's duty to report the misconduct of other lawyers.

FACTS

Morris Andrews has been watching his contemporary and good friend Harold Black slowly lose his battle with a drinking problem. Andrews knows from long association that Black was once an able lawyer but that a series of personal crises have stimulated a case of alcoholism that has greatly reduced his effectiveness. In a recent case, Andrews' client had a less-than-even chance of winning, but won easily because Black seemed unable to represent his own client effectively.

Andrews resolved to go to Black and encourage him to withdraw from practice until he had gotten himself together. Black took the suggestion as an officious insult. "I represent my clients better than you do," Black said. "At least I don't take on more work than I can handle. You never finish anything. All your cases are on the back burner and you only appear in court to get continuances. I lay off the bottle when I have a big case, and as for that recent one when you beat me, you were just lucky."

Andrews did not consider Black's outburst wholly responsive to the main issue, but he did have to admit that Black was right about his caseload. Indeed, Andrews made a mental note to settle some of his minor cases so as to spend more time on the rest. But he was still left uncertain about what, if anything, to do about Black.

QUESTIONS

A. CONDUCT THAT CAN SUBJECT A LAWYER TO PROFESSIONAL DISCIPLINE

1. Where does a lawyer look to see what can justify professional discipline?

a. In a state that has adopted the ABA Model Rules, professional discipline is imposed for violations of Rule 8.4. Rule 8.4(a) incorporates by reference the other Model Rules.

b. The remaining parts of Rule 8.4 are what Restatement Third, The Law Governing Lawyers § 5, Comment *c*, calls the "catch all" provisions. Notice that the term "appearance of impropriety" as a ground for discipline does not appear in the Model Rules, although courts and commentators sometimes still use that phrase in justifying imposing discipline.

2. What should be the purposes and functions of the lawyer discipline process? Should it be only to punish dishonesty or other "serious" wrongdoing? Should the purposes of the process include responding to what clients see to be problems with their lawyers, even if the concerns seem minor to lawyers themselves?

a. Two American Bar Foundation researchers have suggested that the process has three functions: "(1) to identify and remove from the profession all seriously deviant members (the 'cleansing' function), (2) to deter normative deviance and maximize compliance with norms among attorneys (the deterrence function), and (3) to maintain a level of response to deviance sufficient to forestall public dissatisfaction (the public image function)."[1]

b. Restatement Third, The Law Governing Lawyers § 5, Comment *b*, explains that

"Professional duties defined in lawyer codes are mainly concerned with lawyer functions performed by a lawyer in the course of representing a client and causing harm to the client, to a legal institution such as a court, or to a third person. Those duties extend further, however, and include some lawyer acts that, even if not directly involving the practice of law, draw into question the ability or willingness of the lawyer to abide by professional responsibilities."

c. Do you agree with these analyses and explanations? How many lawyers do you think would have to be disciplined before the bar would be completely "cleansed" of deviant members? Might the effectiveness of "deterrence" depend, in turn, in part on the likelihood of getting caught?

d. Would "public image" be improved by highly-publicized discipline in cases that had come to public attention and confidential treatment of other instances of lawyer misconduct? Does enhancing lawyers' public image seem to you to be an appropriate *purpose* of professional discipline, as opposed to being a consequence of any effective system?

1. Eric Steele and Raymond Nimmer, Lawyers, Clients and Professional Regula- tion, 1976 A.B.F.Res.J. 917, 999–1014.

3. Applying these ideas to the facts of this Problem, does using the discipline process to pursue Andrews and Black seem desirable?

a. Are Andrews and Black "bad people"? Indeed, is Andrews' problem that too many people have found him to be a good lawyer? As a practical matter, does Andrews have the luxury of determining the amount of work in the office at any one time? Might turning a client away today cause that client (and perhaps a friend of that client) not to come back tomorrow?

b. Surely, however, representing clients "competently" and "diligently" are among the most important ethical responsibilities of a lawyer. See Model Rules 1.1 and 1.3. Has Morris Andrews violated those rules by taking on more work than he can handle expeditiously and effectively?

c. Do we have evidence that Andrews has "neglected" his clients' work? ABA Informal Opinion 1273, November 20, 1973, asserted that:

> "Neglect involves indifference and a consistent failure to carry out the obligations which the lawyer has assumed to his client or a conscious disregard for the responsibility owed to the client. * * * Neglect usually involves more than a single act or omission. Neglect cannot be found if the acts or omissions complained of were inadvertent or the result of an error of judgment made in good faith."

Is the standard set by that definition appropriate for interpreting Model Rule 1.3? Do you suppose clients care how many other cases a lawyer has neglected? May Andrews rely on Opinion 1273 to continue with business as usual? Has Model Rule 1.3 effectively overruled Informal Opinion 1273?

d. Disciplinary authorities have pursued incompetence, negligence and neglect as violations of both Model Rules 1.1 & 1.3. In re Wolfram, 847 P.2d 94 (Ariz.1993), for example, imposed an 18–month suspension from practice on a lawyer whose acts of neglect constituted providing inadequate assistance of counsel in a criminal case.

e. Iowa Supreme Court Board of Professional Ethics and Conduct v. Hill, 576 N.W.2d 91 (Iowa 1998), revoked the license of a lawyer who tried to handle an interstate adoption when he knew or should have known he was incompetent to do it. He said that he had "heard of" the interstate compact governing such adoptions but did not know its provisions and did not comply with it. Nor did he know that he had engaged in the unauthorized practice of law in Missouri as part of the adoption process. The Iowa Supreme Court found that a lawyer this incapable of competent practice "does not possess the attributes required of a lawyer licensed to practice in this state."

4. Under Model Rule 8.4(b), what criminal acts should be held to "reflect adversely on the lawyer's honesty, trustworthiness or fitness as a lawyer in other respects."

a. Some of the conduct sanctioned under that rule borders on the unbelievable. In re Bloom, 745 P.2d 61 (Cal.1987), for example, was a case of a lawyer who got deeply involved in his client's illegal sale of explosives to Libya. He leased a plane for his client, and filed false documents with the U.S. Customs Service. His defense was that his client told him that the sale was a top secret government operation and that to try to verify that fact would violate national security. The court found the lawyer's good-faith-belief defense not credible.

b. Attorney Grievance Commission v. Protokowicz, 619 A.2d 100 (Md.1993), was even more bizarre. A divorce lawyer was convicted of helping his former client break into the home of the client's estranged wife. When a feline resident of the home came into the kitchen, the lawyer put it into the microwave oven. You can guess the rest. The court suspended the lawyer for not less than one year for both breaking into the house and cooking the cat.

c. In People v. Musick, 960 P.2d 89 (Colo.1998), a lawyer was suspended for a year and a day on the basis of three incidents of physical assault on the woman he was living with. The Hearing Board concluded that he was a good lawyer and that his temper was unlikely to affect dealings with his clients. However, on review, the Court held that even if the assaults were never prosecuted criminally, the conduct was *malum in se* and reflected adversely on his ability to practice law.

d. In The Florida Bar v. Brown, 790 So.2d 1081 (Fla.2001), an attorney assisted his corporate client in making political contributions by soliciting $500 contributions from law firm employees that were to be reimbursed through billing inflated hours in legal matters. The client's officers were convicted of felony violations of state campaign finance laws, but the attorney claimed that he did not know of the laws that banned his conduct. "Our legal system depends on attorneys who appropriately question requests from clients that should arose suspicion," the court wrote. Even if the lawyer did not purposefully evade the law, his acts assisted a client in conduct the lawyer "should have known was criminal or fraudulent." The court imposed a 90–day suspension.

5. Should an attorney be subject to professional discipline for behavior not in his or her capacity as an attorney? What might lead state supreme courts to sanction lawyer misconduct even when the lawyer was not acting as a lawyer at the time?

a. The issues clearly can arise under Model Rule 8.4(b). In Matter of Rowe, 604 N.E.2d 728 (N.Y.1992), for example, the lawyer had killed his wife and three children but was found not guilty by reason of mental disease. He was now cured and wanted to resume practice. The court, however, would not let him do so. It justified disbarment primarily on grounds of public perception. It would "undermine public confidence in the bar" to have a killer practicing law, regardless of his lack of legal responsibility for the acts. Do you agree? Is concern about the bar's public image a sufficient basis on which to deny an otherwise qualified person the right to practice law?

b. In re Boudreau, 815 So.2d 76 (La.2002), involved a lawyer importing sexually-explicit child pornography from Europe, a crime for which he served 21 months in prison. In this action, the state supreme court disbarred Boudreau even though he had no prior disciplinary record. The court found that even the purchase of magazines constituted participation in the sexual exploitation of children, and analogized the conduct to making unwanted sexual demands on clients. Regardless of revulsion at the content of the magazines, do you agree that buying them reflects adversely on the lawyer's "honesty, trustworthiness or fitness as a lawyer in other respects."

c.   Model Rule 8.4(c) also prohibits a lawyer's engaging "in conduct involving dishonesty, fraud, deceit or misrepresentation," whether or not in a representational setting. In re Fornari, 599 N.Y.S.2d 545 (App.Div.1993), suspended a lawyer for one year for filing fraudulent documents in making a claim with his homeowner's insurer. He submitted bills for work other than that caused by a storm, for example, and altered the figures on other bills, allegedly to speed up payment he legally was due.

d.   In re Scruggs, 475 N.W.2d 160 (Wis.1991), suspended the lawyer for resume fraud. He had taken another student's transcript and inserted his own name and biographical information on it. He also said he had attended American University when he had actually attended American Technological University. Do you agree that these kinds of misrepresentations should cost a lawyer his or her license? Why or why not? See also In re Lamberis, 443 N.E.2d 549 (Ill.1982) (censure imposed for lawyer's plagiarism in work on an LL.M. degree); In re Lamb, 776 P.2d 765 (Cal.1989) (lawyer disbarred for 5 years for taking bar exam for her husband).

e.   Matter of Diggs, 544 S.E.2d 628 (S.C.2001), suspended a lawyer for 90 days for filing a form saying he had attended a CLE seminar when, in fact, he arrived near the end of the program. Does this case send an important message to lawyers? Does you suppose it mean that lawyers might also have to pay attention to the speakers at CLE programs?

6.   What conduct should be sufficient to violate the Model Rule 8.4(d) prohibition of "conduct that is prejudicial to the administration of justice"?

a.   In Grievance Administrator v. Fried, 570 N.W.2d 262 (Mich.1997) (per curiam), two judges had close relatives who practiced in the county. When parties wanted a reassignment from one or the other of the judges, local lawyers told clients to hire the relevant relative as co-counsel to force the judge's recusal. Disciplinary panels had dismissed the charges, saying this tactic was no different than hiring a lawyer known to have been found persuasive by a particular judge, but the Michigan Supreme Court disagreed. It is one thing to affect a result by having a judge find the lawyer's arguments persuasive, and quite another for a lawyer to traffic in the ability to force recusal. "The alleged conduct surely exposes the legal profession and the courts to contempt and ridicule—no reasonable person would approve a system in which one can obtain a more lenient judge (and, presumably, a more lenient sentence) in a criminal case by paying $1,000 to a judge's relative. The alleged conduct is contrary to justice, ethics, honesty, and good morals. It is wrong." The court relied on Rule 8.4(d) ("prejudicial to the administration of justice"). "On the other hand," the court said, "the rules do not prohibit a lawyer from taking a case that might lead to a recusal." The court returned the matter to the disciplinary panels for trial to determine if the co-counsel designation served "principally to obtain the recusal" with the lawyer engaging in "de minimis activity."

b. Matter of Karahalis, 706 N.E.2d 655 (Mass.1999), involved a lawyer whose uncle was in a federal prison far from his family. He was told that payment of $12,000 to a Congressman could get the uncle moved nearer to home, so the lawyer made the payment. He cooperated with the prosecution of the Congressman, but the bribery was a serious enough offense that the court suspended the lawyer for four years. Cf. Florida Bar v. Karahalis, 780 So.2d 27 (Fla.2001) (Florida gave the Massachusetts disciplinary findings preclusive effect so the respondent was disbarred in Florida as well).

c. In Iowa Supreme Court Board of Professional Ethics and Conduct v. Lane, 642 N.W.2d 296 (Iowa 2002), Lane had represented a client in a federal suit under the Americans with Disabilities Act. He submitted a lengthy post-trial brief to the court, and in his fee application certified that he had spent 80 hours writing the brief. The district judge noticed style oddities in the brief and made several requests for Lane to submit a list of sources used. Lane eventually provided a list of over 200 sources, but failed to call attention to any one. Through independent research, the district judge discovered that over 18 pages of Lane's brief had been copied verbatim, with footnotes, from a treatise on employment discrimination law. The Iowa Supreme Court suspended Lane for six months, finding that billing for plagiarized work and repeated evasion of the court's inquiries constituted a deliberate attempt to perpetrate a fraud upon the court.

d. If Harold Black were to assert his privilege against self-incrimination in a discipline proceeding against him, should that assertion be deemed "prejudicial to the administration of justice" under Rule 8.4(d)? Spevack v. Klein, 385 U.S. 511, 87 S.Ct. 625, 17 L.Ed.2d 574 (1967), said no, holding that a state may not disbar an attorney for taking the fifth amendment.

B. AGGRAVATING AND MITIGATING FACTORS IN DISCIPLINE CASES; THE PROBLEM OF ALCOHOL & DRUG ABUSE

1. Think about yourself and your law school colleagues. Are alcoholism and drug abuse serious problems among lawyers?

a. There is evidence suggesting that the problem of lawyers' drug and alcohol abuse is significant. A State of Washington study, for example, reported that 18% of all lawyers and 25% of those in practice over 20 years have a problem with drugs or alcohol. See Wall Street Journal, Nov. 30, 1991, at B1. A study by the Association of American Law Schools Special Committee on Problems of Substance Abuse in the Law Schools, 44 J. Legal Educ. 35, 41 (1994), found that nearly two-thirds of law students admitted using at least one illegal drug during their lifetime. Over 20% had used marijuana, and nearly 5% had used cocaine during the previous year.

b.   Nowadays, we often think of alcoholism as a disease, not a character flaw. Should Harold Black be disciplined for conduct made more likely by a disease over which he possibly lacked full control? Can we justify the discipline as a way to prevent future misconduct arising from such a condition? If that logic were followed to its conclusion, would it follow that all lawyers should have to pass psychological predisposition tests before admission to practice so as to increase the public's protection?[2]

2.   Should Black's alcoholism be a factor that affects the nature of his discipline?

a.   In re Kelley, 801 P.2d 1126 (Cal.1990), involved a lawyer who was brought into the discipline system after her second conviction for drunk driving. Nominally, this was because she had violated the probation imposed in the first drunk driving case, but it also seems to have been part of California's effort to identify lawyers with an alcohol problem *before* they injure a client. Her professional discipline in this case consisted primarily of three years probation on condition that she abstain from alcohol. Three justices were troubled at what could become an arbitrary use of discipline to coerce behavior that only *might* get worse. Indeed, might sanctions imposed to try to prevent harm rather than punish actual conduct constitute a violation of the Americans with Disabilities Act? Recall the relation of that law to bar admission issues discussed in Problem 1.

b.   On the other hand, courts have sometimes cited alcoholism as mitigation of the sanction for lawyer misconduct. In Matter of Walker, 254 N.W.2d 452 (S.D.1977), for example, there was proof that alcoholism had been the causative factor in the lawyer's conduct. Proof the lawyer was now a recovering alcoholic, although not excusing the misconduct, led the court to allow the lawyer to keep his license. Cf. Petition of Johnson, 322 N.W.2d 616 (Minn.1982) (suggests criteria for when proof of recovery should lead to such a result).

c.   Rule 23 of the ABA Model Rules for Lawyer Disciplinary Enforcement (1989) provides for placing lawyers on an indefinite period of "disability inactive status" in case of their mental or physical incapacity. Proceedings are to be conducted in the manner of a discipline case, but they are to be confidential. Provisions are made to notify clients and the public if a lawyer is placed on disability status. Is such a procedure and disposition too severe for a condition such as alcoholism? Is it both necessary for protection of the public and more humane than disbarment? Is it necessary to have the leverage of tough sanctions, if only as a threat to coerce the lawyer into getting help?[3]

2.   Cf. Alan M. Dershowitz, Preventive Disbarment: The Numbers Are Against It, 58 A.B.A.J. 815 (1972).

3.   The impaired attorney has been one of the particular concerns of the American Bar Association in the last few years, and Model Rule 8.3 was amended in August 1991 to provide that lawyers need not report to discipline authorities any information they learn as part of a lawyers' assistance program (often called an "L.A.P.") designed to help lawyer–abusers recover from addiction.

3. Should other kinds of mental disease affect a lawyer's level of discipline?

a. In Conduct of Loew, 642 P.2d 1171 (Ore.1982), for example, the lawyer's defense was that he was a victim of "burn-out syndrome." His psychiatrist testified that professionals commonly take on too much work and then psychologically evade it by "procrastination and self-denial." Should this be a good defense? Would recognition of such a defense give adequate protection to clients? This court was sufficiently impressed by the defense that it did not disbar the lawyer, although it did suspend him for 30 days.

b. People v. Lujan, 890 P.2d 109 (Colo.1995), involved a lawyer who had received a head injury four years earlier that she said had given her a "compulsion to shop." The manifestation of that compulsion was her charging her personal expenses to her firm's credit card and fabricating justifications for the charges. The court accepted her story in mitigation and noted she was on medication for her condition. Because the lawyer was already on disability inactive status, she would have to apply to the court before resuming any active practice of law.

c. Florida Bar v. Clement, 662 So.2d 690 (Fla.1995), raised the issue whether the Americans with Disabilities Act (ADA) protects a lawyer with bi-polar disorder (often called manic-depression) against disbarment. The lawyer engaged in complex financial deals with little attention to whether he was using client funds improperly. The psychiatric testimony was that the disease kept him from knowing right from wrong. The court held that, even if that were true, the ADA did not void the requirement that an impaired individual must be "qualified" to practice his profession. Thus, the ADA did not prevent this lawyer's disbarment.

d. Attorney Grievance Commission of Maryland v. Vanderlinde, 773 A.2d 463 (Md.2001), rejected respondent's plea for mitigation of a disbarment sanction for embezzling money while working in a non-legal position. The respondent said that she had been depressed at the time, and she tried to analogize her disability to alcoholism. The Commission found that depression should not mitigate the consequences of a lawyer's intentional dishonest conduct unless the depression was the "root cause" of the actions. Specifically, the Commission said that an attorney would have to establish that she had such a serious and debilitating mental condition that she could not complete the least of her day-to-day activities in a normal fashion. The evidence of mental impairment in this case was insufficient to meet that standard.

e. How would you have treated the lawyers' claims in these cases? Is there any way to find an appropriate accommodation of the lawyer's condition and the clients' legitimate expectation that their lawyers will be able to represent them effectively?

C.   INTERSTATE DISCIPLINE: JURISDICTIONS THAT MAY SANCTION AND THE LAW THEY APPLY

1.   What jurisdictions may impose professional discipline on a lawyer?

a.   In our Problem, Black and Andrews are practicing in the same jurisdiction. Does the analysis change if Black were admitted in State #1 but lost his case against Andrews in State #2? Assume that Black was admitted in State #2 only for purposes of that particular case. Look at Model Rule 8.5(a). Notice that, basically, any state in which the lawyer is licensed may discipline a lawyer for misconduct wherever it occurs, and even a state to which the lawyer travels for temporary practice may try the lawyer for conduct occurring there.

b.   In the Matter of Spraker, 744 N.E.2d 415 (Ind.2001), shows how Rule 8.5 can work. Discipline was imposed on an Indiana lawyer for conduct that occurred in Illinois but was illegal in both states. Spraker represented clients attempting to obtain permanent residency in the United States. There was evidence that he had failed to properly submit forms to the INS on more than 50 occasions. Indeed, several forms contained misstatements and lies about the clients. However, Spraker's clients all resided in Illinois where the alleged misconduct took place. The Supreme Court of Indiana found it had jurisdiction over Spraker's discipline because of his Indiana license. The court even allowed the hearing to be held in Illinois, given the sensitivity of many of Spraker's former clients to crossing state borders when they were still illegal residents. The court suspended Mr. Spraker from practice for two years.

2.   Does each jurisdiction simply apply its own standards to evaluate the conduct? If a lawyer is licensed in one state and negotiates a contract in another, which state's rules should govern her professional conduct?

a.   Look at Model Rule 8.5(b). Suppose a lawyer licensed in Florida negotiates a commercial transaction with a New Jersey resident and learns that the lawyer's client has lied about certain important facts. New Jersey ethics rules require its lawyers to disclose facts necessary to prevent a fraud and New Jersey clients may have come to expect such conduct from lawyers with whom they deal. Florida ethics law, on the other hand, requires its lawyers *not* to disclose such facts. The lawyer's principal office is in Miami but the negotiations occurred in Newark. What is the lawyer to do about disclosure?

b.   Must the lawyer assume the risk that a court will later say she followed the rules of the wrong state? How would a lawyer prove he or she had complied with Rule 8.5(b)(2)'s safe harbor for "reasonable belief" that the "predominant effect of the conduct" will be in a particular jurisdiction? Does Comment [5] to Model Rule 8.5 provide much help in answering that question?

3.   What is the effect of lawyer discipline in one state on a lawyer's status in other states where the lawyer is admitted to practice law?

a.   Should whatever sanction is imposed by the first state to try a lawyer be binding in all other states as well? What does Comment [6] to Model Rule 8.5 say about that?

b.   It is often easier to state such principles than to make them stick. In Matter of Iulo, 766 A.2d 335 (Pa.2001), New Jersey had permanently disbarred the lawyer in 1989 for misapplying client funds. In 1996, Pennsylvania allowed the applicant to sit for the bar, and later admitted him, after being informed of the New Jersey action. In 1999, the Pennsylvania Office of Disciplinary Counsel sought to have the lawyer subjected to reciprocal disbarment based on the New Jersey action. The Pennsylvania Supreme Court said no. Pennsylvania seeks to rehabilitate lawyers, the court said, while New Jersey seeks to exclude them from practice. Principles of reciprocal discipline may require honoring factual findings made elsewhere but they do not require identical sanctions. The court said that "imposition of reciprocal discipline in this instance would be a grave injustice." Do you agree? If Pennsylvania were to adopt the 2002 amendment to Model Rule 8.5, would cases like this be decided differently?

c.   In re Rufus Cook, 49 F.3d 263 (7th Cir.1995), was a case where the federal district court had held a lawyer in contempt for keeping more class action proceeds than the court found belonged to him. The Illinois Attorney Registration and Discipline Commission, to whom the case was referred, refused to take any disciplinary action unless the federal judge agreed to testify before it. In the Seventh Circuit opinion, Judge Easterbrook roundly criticized the state agency for trying to look behind the federal court's findings regarding the misconduct. He argued that the attorney could not relitigate in state disciplinary proceedings the factual findings a federal trial court had determined. Then, the Seventh Circuit imposed a two-year suspension. How would such a case come out under Model Rule 8.5(b)(2)?

4.   Should federal courts create their own disciplinary standards or apply the state disciplinary standards of the state in which they are sitting?

a.   United States v. Walsh, 699 F.Supp. 469 (D.N.J.1988), considered New Jersey amendments to Model Rule 1.11 on disqualification of former government lawyers. In practice, many federal courts adopt, as a matter of "dynamic conformity," the ethics rules of the states in which they sit; a few courts adopt their own ethics rules. In this case, the court held that the Model Rules as adopted by the ABA were controlling in that federal court, not the Rules as adopted by New Jersey, the state in which the court is located.

b.   In re Hoare, 155 F.3d 937 (8th Cir.1998), dealt with reciprocal discipline in a federal court based on state discipline. The federal court required that a lawyer disciplined in state court show by clear and convincing evidence that identical discipline should not be imposed by the federal system. The Eight Circuit upheld that standard and the disbarment of a lawyer for driving while intoxicated, killing another driver in a collision, and refusing a blood alcohol test.

c.   In re Kramer, 282 F.3d 721 (9th Cir.2002), adopted a more elaborate test before a federal court could impose reciprocal discipline. New York had disbarred a lawyer named Kramer after a full hearing for misconduct in two separate cases. Initially, based only upon notice of the New York disbarment, the Central District of California imposed reciprocal discipline. Relying on an old U.S. Supreme Court case, Selling v. Radford, 243 U.S. 46 (1917), the Ninth Circuit found that Kramer had not received due process before imposition of the reciprocal discipline. The district court then issued an order to show cause why discipline should not be imposed, held a hearing at which Kramer bore the burden of presenting evidence that he should not be disbarred, and then disbarred Kramer again. This time, the Ninth Circuit upheld the sanction, finding that Kramer had the burden of proving one of three "*Selling* factors," *i.e.*, that (1) he was deprived of due process in the first proceeding, (2) the evidence of misconduct was insufficient in the first proceeding, or (3) grave injustice would result if reciprocal discipline were imposed. Because Kramer did not show that any of the *Selling* factors applied, and because the court had afforded Kramer a hearing, the court held that reciprocal discipline was appropriate.

D.   THE DUTY TO REPORT ANOTHER LAWYER'S MISCONDUCT; THE DISCIPLINE PROCESS ITSELF

1.   Should the bar discipline a lawyer for failure to report another lawyer?

a.   Model Rule 8.3 addresses a lawyer's duty to report misconduct of another lawyer or judge. This requirement tends to be one of the most underenforced rules of professional conduct.

b.   The first and, thus far, apparently the only case ever to discipline a lawyer *solely* for the failure to report is In Re James H. Himmel, 533 N.E.2d 790 (Ill.1988).

Himmel represented Tammy Forsberg, a client who had been injured in a motorcycle accident. Earlier, Forsberg had retained a different lawyer to represent her in her personal injury action. That lawyer had negotiated a settlement of $35,000 on Forsberg's behalf, received the settlement check, endorsed it, and converted the funds. Forsberg then retained Himmel to get her share back. He negotiated an arrangement whereby the first lawyer would pay her $75,000 if she would not report him to the authorities for possible criminal or disciplinary sanction. The court noted: "Forsberg told respondent that she simply wanted her money back and specifically instructed respondent to take no other action. Because of respondent's efforts, Forsberg collected another $10,400 from Casey. Respondent received no fee in this case."

Ultimately, Forsberg had to go to court to enforce even this agreement, and the jury awarded her $100,000. The court said that "the client had contacted the Commission prior to retaining respondent and, therefore, the Commission did have knowledge of the alleged misconduct.'' In April 1985, the Commission petitioned to have Casey suspended from practicing law because of his conversion of client funds and his conduct in matters unrelated to Forsberg's claim. The court subsequently disbarred Casey on consent on November 5, 1985.

The Illinois Attorney Registration and Discipline Commission then pursued Himmel for his failure to report Casey himself, and the Illinois Supreme Court suspended Himmel from practice for a year. The court asserted:

"Common sense would dictate that if a lawyer has a duty * * * [to report], the actions of a client would not relieve the attorney of his own duty. * * *

"As to respondent's argument that he did not report Casey's misconduct because his client directed him not to do so, we again note respondent's failure to suggest any legal support for such a defense. A lawyer, as an officer of the court, is duty-bound to uphold the rules in the Code. * * * A lawyer may not choose to circumvent the rules by simply asserting that his client asked him to do so. * * *"

Finally, the Court found that the information was not protected by the attorney-client privilege because the client's mother and fiancé had been present when the client talked to the lawyer.[4]

c. What do you think of this result? What do you think of the reasoning? The Illinois Disciplinary Commission did not seek any discipline against Casey's lawyer, who defended him in the suit that Forsberg brought. Surely that lawyer also had unprivileged information, such as the allegations in Forsberg's complaint, and the jury verdict finding Casey liable. Should the Commission have brought a disciplinary action against Casey's lawyer too?[5]

2. How soon must the lawyer make a report against a fellow lawyer? How sure should a lawyer be before reporting?

a. If there is a civil or criminal action pending involving the same conduct, disciplinary authorities often prefer that the lawyer wait until that action is completed. If the information comes in earlier, disciplinary authorities often suspend or abate their own inquiry so as to be able to work with a complete record and avoid duplicative investigation.

b. How would waiting tend to affect the threat of discipline being used as leverage in the civil case? See ABA Formal Opinion 94–383 (July 5, 1994), expressing a concern that the threat to file a discipline charge might

4. You will learn more about the attorney-client privilege and protection of confidential information in Problem 7. For this problem, assume that the privilege ruling is correct but that Rule 1.6 provides protection for information that is broader than the evidentiary privilege.

5. See Ronald D. Rotunda, The Lawyer's Duty To Report Another Lawyer's Unethical Violations in the Wake of Himmel, 1988 U. Illinois L. Rev. 977 (1988).

be used to get an advantage in a civil case and urging the postponing of reporting until the conclusion of that case. Do you agree? Might the dynamics work the other way? Would the coercive power of the threatened charge exist *before* reporting and be dissipated thereafter?[6]

c.   Doe v. Federal Grievance Committee, 847 F.2d 57 (2d Cir.1988), considered how certain the lawyer should have to be before reporting in the context of DR 7–102(B)(2) that requires reporting information "clearly establishing" that someone has committed fraud on tribunal. The court held a lawyer must have "actual knowledge" before a failure to report is actionable under that rule. Do Rule 8.3(a) and Comment 3 affirm or reject that test? Must the lawyer have "substantial" evidence or merely *some* evidence of a "substantial" offense?

d.   Might there be a cost to overreporting? Might reporting become vindictive or a tactical ploy in litigation? Is that at least part of the message of Comment 3 to Rule 8.3? Would it be better to have Black and Andrews call each other's law partners and have their firms impose informal sanctions?

3.   **Must Andrews report Black even if he learned of Black's failings because of his work for client who does not want him to report?**

a.   In our Problem, might Andrews' knowledge about Black be said to be "confidential" and thereby protected against disclosure by Rule 8.3(c)? Would Andrews' client want it known that he won largely because Black was an alcoholic? Is that the kind of information Rule 1.6 was meant to protect? Should the concept of confidentiality be read broadly or narrowly for this purpose?

b.   In the *Himmel* case, supra, did Rule 1.6's confidentiality obligations prohibit Himmel from reporting the other lawyer, even if the information was not protected by the attorney-client evidentiary privilege? Should Rule 1.6 give Forsberg, the client, the right to tell her lawyer not to disclose Casey's errors to the Disciplinary Commission?

c.   In re Ethics Advisory Panel Opinion, 627 A.2d 317 (R.I.1993), is a careful discussion of the tension between the duty to preserve client confidences and the duty to report misconduct by other lawyers. The court did not follow *Himmel* and concluded that a lawyer must secure client consent in order to report another lawyer's misconduct if he learned about that misconduct from a client.

d.   Should *Himmel* be limited to its facts? The court said: "By the terms of the agreement, Forsberg agreed not to initiate any criminal, civil, or attorney disciplinary action against Casey. This agreement was executed on April 11, 1983. Respondent stood to gain $17,000 or more if Casey honored the agreement." The court acknowledged that, because of his

6. Cf. ABA Formal Opinion 94–384 (July 5, 1994), advising that a lawyer who is made the subject of a disciplinary charge filed by the opponent in connection with a pending case is not required to withdraw from representation of the client in that case.

efforts, Forsberg collected an additional $10,400 from Casey. Respondent himself received no fee in this case, but the case arguably involved selling out the public interest for a potentially increased recovery. Did the Illinois supreme court seem to place any such limit on its holding?

e. In Skolnick v. Altheimer & Gray, 730 N.E.2d 4 (Ill.2000), the issue was whether the duty to report a lawyer prevails over the duty to obey a protective order. A law firm associate and the firm itself had accused a partner of creating and filing a false document in a case. The Attorney Registration and Disciplinary Commission (ARDC) filed a charge but later dismissed it for lack of evidence. Thereafter, the accused lawyer sued the firm and its associate for defamation that allegedly damaged his practice. The parties conducted discovery under a protective order, and the associate allegedly turned up information now proving the lawyer's fraud. She wanted to use it in a counterclaim and to send it to the ARDC. The Illinois Supreme Court held that the duty to report to the ARDC is absolute and transcends protective orders; indeed, it held that the protective order should not even apply to the counterclaim.

4. If a judge were to observe Black's impaired state or Andrews' inability to keep up with his caseload, would the judge's obligation to report be any different than that of a lawyer?

a. The Illinois Disciplinary Commission did not seek any discipline against the judge who presided in the case that Forsberg brought against Casey. Should the judge be liable? See ABA Model Code of Judicial Conduct, Canon 3D(2), which parallels Rule 8.3. May a judge assume that an attorney will report all misconduct in a case? Might lawyers, in turn, rely on the judge?

b. Are lawyers required to report the misconduct of judges? Look at Model Rule 8.3(b).

5. If Black or Andrews or one of their clients makes a complaint to a disciplinary agency, what will happen?

a. A complainant has no personal right to have his or her complaint actively pursued by disciplinary authorities. Doyle v. Oklahoma Bar Association, 998 F.2d 1559 (10th Cir.1993), found the claim of such a right to be frivolous. Do you agree? Is the system of professional discipline simply a private preserve of lawyers in which clients have no role? Was the court acknowledging that so many acts of lawyers could merit professional discipline that disciplinary authorities must exercise substantial discretion and only pursue the most serious offenders?

b. If a complaint about a lawyer is made to a disciplinary agency, procedures vary from state-to-state, but those described in Rule 11 of the ABA Model Rules for Lawyer Disciplinary Enforcement are representative. A state's "disciplinary counsel," operating under the authority of the jurisdiction's highest court, is required to evaluate all complaints filed by clients or others about a lawyer. If the conduct would not violate the state disciplinary rules even if true, the complaint is dismissed. For example, it is on this basis that disagreements over fees are often dismissed if they do not allege fraud or overreaching.

However, if the facts alleged would constitute a violation of the rules of professional conduct, the disciplinary counsel is required to investigate whether or not the facts are true. Ordinarily, at least by that point, the lawyer is offered a chance to respond to the complaint. If a non-serious violation is found or admitted, the disciplinary counsel may impose a private sanction such as an admonition and the case is closed. However, if the alleged violation is serious, or if the lawyer does not consent to the private sanction, the disciplinary counsel is expected to file a formal charge to which the lawyer must file an answer.

The matter is then set for trial before a hearing panel composed of other lawyers, typically working as volunteers, that either dismisses the matter or recommends a sanction. The lawyer may then appeal a sanction to a review board, again composed of fellow lawyers. If that board also recommends a sanction, the lawyer may appeal to the licensing court. It is the court decisions in several such cases that you will read about throughout this book.

c.   The discipline procedures are impressive, but observers are not always impressed by the results. The ABA reports that in 1995 over 116,000 complaints were made to state lawyer discipline agencies; that was about 1 for every 9 lawyers in the country. Of those complaints, however, almost 50,000 were dismissed for failure to allege a violation of the disciplinary rules. Of the 66,000 remaining complaints, 49,000 more were dismissed after investigation. Often in such cases, the complainant was not even told what happened as a result of the complaint.

Indeed, only about 5,700 (under 5%) of complaints received actually led to formal disciplinary charges, and only about half of those, 2,900 lawyers, led to convictions after trial. Of those convicted, about 25% were disbarred, 50% suspended, and 25% publicly reprimanded.[7]

d.   Should this data be seen as suggesting that lawyers in the discipline process are too forgiving? The ABA Model Rules for Lawyer Disciplinary Enforcement now provide for one-third public members on both the hearing panels and disciplinary board. Do you agree with that approach? On the other hand, does it represent a decline in self-regulation by the bar?

e.   Another controversial feature of the present discipline process is that, at least until formal charges are filed, the entire process is usually confidential. Potential clients cannot determine, for example, whether a lawyer they are considering retaining has been the subject of numerous complaints, none of which were among the 5% in which charges were filed.

There has been no rush to open the process to the public. Opponents of openness "say their biggest fear is the specter of sensationalist newspaper publicity about a flimsy allegation of misconduct. If the allegation ultimate-

---

7. The statistics are taken from ABA Center for Professional Responsibility, Standing Committee on Professional Discipline, 1995 Survey on Lawyer Discipline Systems (1997). We have rounded the data because the ABA data itself is incomplete and to claim more precision than the data justifies would itself be misleading.

ly is disproved, they are convinced, then news of the vindication would be banished to the back pages of the paper, doing little to offset the stigma of the original publicity." Proponents "say they see no reason for protecting lawyers' privacy in disciplinary proceedings when no similar protective measures exist for laymen charged with crime."[8] With which of these positions do you agree?

6. Assuming disciplinary charges were filed, what sanctions should be imposed on Andrews and Black for the conduct discussed in this Problem?

a. In 1986, the ABA House of Delegates approved the "Standards for Imposing Lawyer Sanctions." Various courts have referred to these new Standards for guidance. The Standards propose that a court, in imposing a sanction after a finding of lawyer misconduct, should consider four factors:

(a) the duty violated;

(b) the lawyer's mental state;

(c) the actual or potential injury caused by the lawyer's misconduct; and

(d) the existence of aggravating or mitigating factors.

b. If a lawyer "engages in a pattern of neglect with respect to client matters and causes serious or potentially serious injury to a client," the Standards state that disbarment is generally appropriate. Standard 4.41(c). If the lawyer's pattern of neglect causes injury or potential injury that is not serious, the Standards recommend suspension. Standard 4.42(b). If the lawyer is merely negligent, does not act with reasonable diligence, and causes injury or potential injury to a client, the Standards recommend only a reprimand. Standard 4.43. If such a lawyer causes little or no actual or potential injury, the Standards recommend admonition. Standard 4.44. A reprimand is a public censure and an admonition is private.[9]

c. In addition to the sanctions of disbarment, suspension, reprimand, admonition, or probation (which allows the lawyer to practice law under specified conditions), the Standards allow "restitution, assessment of costs, limitation upon practice, appointment of a receiver, requirement that the lawyer take the bar examination or professional responsibility examination, requirement that the lawyer attend continuing education courses," or other sanctions that the disciplinary authority may deem appropriate.[10] Standard 2.8.

d. Should the law permit a lawyer to resign from a state bar when charged with a disciplinable offense? Should an admission of guilt be a

---

8. Frank Moya, The Doors Stay Shut on Discipline, Nat'l L.J., Dec. 8, 1980, at pp. 1, 11 and 12.

9. A lawyer's physical or mental disability or impairment are to be mitigating factors, while aggravating factors include the lawyer's refusal to acknowledge the wrongful nature of his conduct, the vulnerability of the victim, the lawyer's substantial experience in the practice of law, and his or her indifference to making restitution. Standards 9.22, 9.32.

10. One commentator has suggested that "corrective actions" replace sanctions. Such actions might include counseling a lawyer to reduce his case load, not to accept cases in certain areas, and to establish new prerequisite to resignation? Why or why not? Is it important to know how easy it is for an attorney who has resigned to apply for readmission to the bar?[11]

e.   Is there any reason to impose professional sanctions only on individual lawyers? Should Black's and Andrews' law firms be subject to sanctions as well? Might imposition of sanctions on law firms create a better incentive for firms to police their own policies and the practices of their individual members?[12]

New York was the first jurisdiction to authorize discipline of a "law firm." Sections 1200.3, 1200.5 and 1200.24(e) of the New York Code of Professional Responsibility make a law firm subject to discipline, basically for failure to supervise subordinates properly or to have good systems for avoiding conflicts. While it may be unlikely that a law firm will be "disbarred" pursuant to this rule, lesser sanctions are certainly possible.

7.   Should lawyer discipline be considered the equivalent of a criminal sanction and should lawyers be entitled to the constitutional guarantees inherent in a criminal process?

a.   Supreme Court cases like Montana Dept. of Revenue v. Kurth Ranch, 511 U.S. 767, 114 S.Ct. 1937, 128 L.Ed.2d 767 (1994), and United States v. Halper, 490 U.S. 435, 109 S.Ct. 1892, 104 L.Ed.2d 487 (1989), have asked whether a civil penalty is so severe that later criminal prosecution would create a sanction disproportionate to the offense. United States v. Ursery, 518 U.S. 267, 116 S.Ct. 2135, 135 L.Ed.2d 549 (1996), said that in reviewing a double jeopardy claim, a court must ask whether the civil sanction had a purpose other than punitive.

b.   People v. Artman, 553 N.W.2d 673 (Mich.App.1996), reasoned that lawyer discipline "is not to punish for wrongdoing, but to protect the public, the courts, and the legal profession." Thus, it found there is no double jeopardy.

Similarly, In re Segal, 719 N.E.2d 480 (Mass.1999), involved a lawyer *acquitted* of making false statements to a federally-insured bank but later charged by the bar for the same conduct. The lawyer was doing residential closings for a bank that had a policy against lending to people who financed their down payment with a second mortgage. When a buyer said he had just signed a second mortgage, the lawyer said "I can't hear that" and "I am not supposed to know that." The criminal court had decided that closing loans in such circumstances did not involve making a false statement to his bank client, but this court concluded that it constituted dealing dishonestly with respect to what he knew to be his client's wishes. The court then imposed a two year suspension.

---

office procedures. Patricia Manson, Helping Lawyers Who Need Help, 9 ALI–ABA CLE Review, Feb. 10, 1978, at 6.

11. Cf. Court Rejects a Nixon Bid to Resign from State Bar, N.Y.Times, Sept. 20, 1975, p. 1.

12. See Ted Schneyer, Professional Discipline for Law Firms, 77 Cornell L.Rev. 1 (1991); Julie Rose O'Sullivan, Professional Discipline for Law Firms? A Response to Professor Schneyer's Proposal, 16 Georgetown J. Legal Ethics 1 (2002).

c. In re Harris, 49 P.3d 778 (Ore.2002), reasoned further that because attorney discipline cases are not traditionally viewed as criminal proceedings, a lawyer charged with a discipline offense has no right to court-appointed counsel to defend him.

d. A lawyer can be disciplined based on testimony given under a grant of immunity from criminal prosecution, for example. See In re Daley, 549 F.2d 469 (7th Cir.1977), cert. denied 434 U.S. 829, 98 S.Ct. 110, 54 L.Ed.2d 89 (1977), where the court held that—while discipline proceedings were called "quasi-criminal" in In re Ruffalo, 390 U.S. 544, 88 S.Ct. 1222, 20 L.Ed.2d 117 (1968), for purposes of requiring fair notice of the charges—the criminal label should not be extended to the grant of immunity. The state could use the lawyer's compelled testimony in the criminal case against him in the later discipline proceeding.[13]

e. Even a presidential pardon may not eliminate a lawyer's exposure to professional discipline. In re Abrams, 689 A.2d 6 (D.C.1997) (en banc), involved one of President Reagan's aides who had pled guilty to two misdemeanor charges of "unlawfully [withholding] material information" from Congress in the Iran–Contra investigation. Within days after the Bar hearing, President Bush (who had lost his bid for reelection) gave Mr. Abrams a full pardon. In a lengthy opinion citing mostly post-Civil War cases, a panel of the D.C. Court of Appeals had held that a pardon makes an offender "as it were, a new man." Thus, the panel held, the President's "act of grace" had rendered it powerless to impose professional discipline for Abrams' acts. 662 A.2d 867 (D.C.1995). On rehearing, however, the full D.C. Court of Appeals reversed the panel by a 5 to 4 vote. Even a Presidential pardon cannot wipe out the fact that false testimony was given, the majority said. It can protect the lawyer against criminal prosecution but not from public censure under the lawyer discipline process.

Are you troubled by this result? Should it be significant that Abrams was charged with DC's counterpart to Model Rule 8.4(c), "conduct involving dishonesty, fraud, deceit or misrepresentation," rather than Rule 8.4(b) that requires a "criminal act"?

———

PROBLEM 3

REGULATING LAWYERS OUTSIDE OF THE
FORMAL DISCIPLINARY SYSTEM

We looked at professional discipline in Problem 2. Here, we look at additional sanctions that lawyers may face. Actions for professional mal-

---

13. Accord, Anonymous Attorneys v. Bar Association of Erie County, 362 N.E.2d 592 (N.Y.1977); In re Schwarz, 282 N.E.2d 689 (Ill.1972), cert. denied 409 U.S. 1047, 93 S.Ct. 527, 34 L.Ed.2d 499 (1972).

practice may seek damages against a lawyer for wrongs characterized in at least three ways—as a tort committed by the lawyer against the client, as a breach of the contract the client made for the lawyer's services, or as a breach of fiduciary duties that the lawyer owes to the client. Sometimes all of these theories work equally well; sometimes the theory matters, as when the statute of limitations may have run on one or more claims or when the remedy affects the amount of damages, as when the client may seek punitive damages in tort but not in contract. In this Problem, we look first at the standard of care and conduct used in malpractice cases. Next, we examine what goes into determining whether that standard has been violated. Then we consider remedies for professional malpractice and attempts to contract away those remedies. Finally, we look at a range of sanctions other than professional malpractice that a lawyer may face for his or her professional misconduct.

FACTS

Sarah Field is a young lawyer with a great future. She has attracted several clients with a wide range of interests and problems. Her outstanding record before juries is the envy of the local bar. Sometimes, however, she is not as careful as she might be.

Field is active in local politics. At a party picnic, an acquaintance of hers, Mary Moore, took her aside and told Field, "My doctor really messed me up two years ago. He performed supposedly minor surgery but cut the wrong things and now I can never have children." Field put her arm around Moore and said, "That's terrible. I know how to handle doctors like that. Leave everything to me." When Field got back to her office, she wrote a nasty letter to the doctor demanding that he "fully compensate my client." By return mail, she received a settlement offer of $250,000. Moore, the client, said she was delighted and Field was impressed at how intimidated the doctor seemed to be by her letter. Field did not have Moore examined by an independent physician. Had she done so, both would have learned that Moore's injuries were much worse than she believed. Instead, Field recommended that Moore accept the settlement, which she did. Now, Moore has learned the full extent of her injuries, and she realizes how inadequate her settlement really was.

Field does very little tax work. One of her wealthy clients heard that income can be made taxable to her children, instead of herself, by the use of certain trusts. She asked Field to see that the trusts were properly prepared. Field researched the problem as well as her small office library would permit and discussed the issues over coffee with a CPA from down the hall. The client later learned that Field's handiwork was not good enough to accomplish her objectives, and a large tax deficiency was assessed. "Don't blame me," Field said defensively, "If you wanted tax advice you should have called a specialist. I told you I was not positive of the tax consequences.''

In yet another incident, this time a criminal trial in which she was appointed counsel, Field had gone on a vacation and failed to appear when the case was called. The case was reset for the following morning. Field's office reached her and she quickly returned. The next day, although she was physically present for the trial, she was not prepared and did a terrible job. The client was convicted and sentenced to a long prison term.

QUESTIONS

A.   THE STANDARD OF CARE AND CONDUCT IN A MALPRACTICE ACTION

1. By what standard should a lawyer be judged in a malpractice case?

a.   A leading treatise on lawyer malpractice says:

"[T]he essential elements of a cause of action for professional negligence are:

"(1) The employment of the attorney or other basis for imposing a duty;

"(2) the failure of the attorney to exercise ordinary skill and knowledge; and

"(3) that such negligence was the proximate cause of damage to the plaintiff.''

1 Ronald E. Mallen & Jeffrey M. Smith, Legal Malpractice § 8.13 (5th ed. 2000).

b.   Restatement Third, The Law Governing Lawyers § 52(1) is even more succinct: "[A] lawyer who owes a duty of care must exercise the competence and diligence normally exercised by lawyers in similar circumstances.''

c.   Lawyers sometimes try to comfort themselves by citing Lucas v. Hamm, 364 P.2d 685 (Cal.1961), which said the rule against perpetuities is so difficult that violation of it is not inevitably malpractice. But in reality, *Lucas* is little help. Horne v. Peckham, 158 Cal.Rptr. 714 (Ct.App.1979), made clear that the *Lucas* situation was unusual if not unique. "An attorney's obligation is not satisfied by simply determining that the law on a particular subject is doubtful or debatable [because] an attorney has a duty to *avoid* involving his client in murky areas of law if research reveals alternative courses of conduct. At least he should inform his client of uncertainties and let the client make the decision.'' 158 Cal.Rptr. at 721.

2. Did Sarah Field commit malpractice by recommending the inadequate settlement to the victim of medical malpractice?

a.   Traditional doctrine used to say that a client could not sue in such a case because she would not have settled unless she were happy with the result. Later cases, however, such as Lowman v. Karp, 476 N.W.2d 428 (Mich.App.1991), Ziegelheim v. Apollo, 607 A.2d 1298 (N.J.1992), and Grayson v. Wofsey, Rosen, Kweskin & Kuriansky, 646 A.2d 195 (Conn. 1994), reason that clients tend to follow their lawyers' advice and do not have independent bases on which to evaluate a settlement. Therefore recommending an inadequate settlement may indeed constitute malpractice.

b.   Muhammad v. Strassburger, McKenna, Messer, Shilobod and Gutnick, 587 A.2d 1346 (Pa.1991) held that, while a settlement did not completely bar a later action for malpractice, the action would only lie if the client proved that her lawyer had fraudulently induced her to settle as opposed to negligently giving her inadequate information. Might the Pennsylvania rule be justified by a concern that settlements often represent less than the party might have gotten at trial? Might it also reflect a desire to have settlements be the end of litigation, not the start of another round of it? Would the Pennsylvania rule adequately protect the client in this Problem?

c.   In McMahon v. Shea, 688 A.2d 1179 (Pa.1997), a husband agreed to a divorce settlement that "incorporated" the terms of a separation agreement into the divorce decree but did not "merge" the agreements. When the husband wanted to be excused from alimony payments upon his former wife's remarriage, he learned why the distinction made a difference. The Pennsylvania Supreme Court held its decision in *Muhammad* did not bar a malpractice action against a firm that did not advise its client of this consequence of the settlement terms.

d.   Woodruff v. Tomlin, 616 F.2d 924 (6th Cir.1980) (en banc), cert. denied 449 U.S. 888, 101 S.Ct. 246, 66 L.Ed.2d 114 (1980), relied on the typical rule that there is no malpractice liability for an honest exercise of professional judgment such as whether to call a particular person as a witness. However, *Woodruff* said, that rule does not protect a lawyer's decision not to interview a potentially material witness as Field had failed to do in this case. Without interviewing the witness, the lawyer would have no basis on which to make a judgment about the witness' importance, so the failure to interview may indeed be malpractice.

e.   Wood v. McGrath, North, Mullin & Kratz, P.C., 589 N.W.2d 103 (Neb.1999), also upheld a claim against lawyers for recommending an inadequate settlement. The lawyers allegedly failed to tell the wife in a divorce action that the law was unsettled but that she might be entitled to a share of her husband's unvested stock options, and capital gain taxes might not have to be deducted from the share to which she was entitled. The lawyers said their overall advice about the merits of the settlement was sound, but the Court held the client could not decide whether to settle without adequate information about the legal questions presented.

3. Should Field have been obliged to refer the tax case to a specialist?

a. In Horne v. Peckham, supra, the client had asked Attorney to draft a Clifford Trust in order to shelter income from federal taxes. Attorney testified that he told the client: "I had no knowledge of tax matters. I had no expertise in tax matters; that if somebody else could figure out what needed to be done, I could draft the documents." Attorney consulted with the client's accountant and a two volume set of American Jurisprudence on federal taxation. When the trust failed to qualify for favorable tax treatment the client sued and the jury awarded damages of $64,983.31. The appellate court affirmed the judgment and upheld a jury instruction that it "is the duty of an attorney who is a general practitioner to refer his client to a specialist or recommend the assistance of a specialist if under the circumstances a reasonably careful and skillful practitioner would do so." If Attorney did not refer the case or seek a specialist's help, it was his duty to have the knowledge and skill possessed and used by specialists in the same locality and under the same circumstances. Why didn't Rule 1.2(c) protect the lawyer, who warned the client, after all, that he "had no knowledge of tax matters."

b. Battle v. Thornton, 646 A.2d 315 (D.C.1994), on the other hand, held that in a jurisdiction that does not certify specialties, the malpractice standard is the ordinary lawyer, not persons who concentrate their practice in a given area of the law and usually handle a given kind of case.

c. With which rule do you agree? Does the California rule encourage making legal services more expensive?

4. Should Field be liable to the criminal defendant whose defense she handled badly?

a. The majority rule on this subject may surprise you. Ordinarily, an element of a suit for lawyer malpractice is that a convicted criminal defendant must prove himself actually innocent of the charges against him, not just that a better lawyer might have obtained a not guilty verdict.

Wiley v. County of San Diego, 966 P.2d 983 (Cal.1998), for example, found that "the clear majority of courts that have considered the question * * * require proof of actual innocence" and explained:

"[A] guilty defendant's conviction and sentence are the direct consequence of his own perfidy. The fact that nonnegligent counsel 'could have done better' may warrant postconviction relief, but it does not translate into civil damages, which are intended to make the plaintiff whole. While a conviction predicated on incompetence may be erroneous, it is not unjust. * * * Only an innocent person wrongly convicted due to inadequate representation has suffered a compensable injury * * * ." 966 P.2d at 987.

b. Restatement Third, The Law Governing Lawyers § 53, Comment d, acknowledged cases like Wiley but proposed a less restrictive rule, saying:

"Although most jurisdictions addressing the issue have stricter rules, under this Section, it is not necessary to prove that the convicted defendant was in fact innocent. As required by most jurisdictions addressing the issue, it is necessary for a former criminal defendant seeking damages for malpractice causing a conviction to have had that conviction set aside, when process for that relief on the grounds asserted in the malpractice action was available.''

c. Levine v. Kling, 123 F.3d 580 (7th Cir.1997), also acknowledged the usual rule but, in dictum, distinguished a situation in which a client might have done a prohibited act but nevertheless might have a complete legal defense to the criminal charge.

"We used the awkward term 'guilty in law' to distinguish the case in which the defendant is guilty in fact but has a sound legal defense, such as double jeopardy, from a case in which he is both guilty in fact and has no sound legal defense yet might, because of the heavy burden of proof on the prosecution, have obtained an acquittal if he had had a skillful lawyer. Only in the second case is the malpractice suit against the less-than-skillful lawyer barred.'' 123 F.3d at 582.

d. Which of these approaches makes most sense to you? Might you propose still another approach to the malpractice of criminal defense lawyers?

e. Why do you suppose the cases are so cautious about allowing malpractice actions after criminal cases? Is there a reason to treat criminal and civil clients differently as regards attorney malpractice? Might it be harder to find lawyers willing to act as criminal defense counsel, for example, if the law permitted more such suits?[1]

5. Might Field ever be held liable to professional malpractice to persons other than her clients?

a. A lawyer's liability for malpractice to someone who is not her client is a controversial and evolving area of lawyer liability. Restatement Third, The Law Governing Lawyers § 51 suggests four situations in which liability may be found.

b. First, a lawyer may be liable to a prospective client for revealing confidential information communicated to the lawyer or, for example, if the

---

1. Whether appointed counsel should ever be subject to a malpractice action has also been a controversial issue. Ferri v. Ackerman, 444 U.S. 193, 100 S.Ct. 402, 62 L.Ed.2d 355 (1979), said that federal law does not require immunity of appointed counsel in federal cases from state malpractice claim. See also, Mossow v. United States, 987 F.2d 1365 (8th Cir.1993) (government can be sued for malpractice of military lawyer); Barner v. Leeds, 13 P.3d 704 (Cal.2000) (public defender liable for malpractice when negligent omission is not a discretionary act); Schreiber v. Rowe, 814 So.2d 396 (Fla.2002) (public defender not immune from suit, but suit barred because defendant did not show actual innocence). However, Dziubak v. Mott, 503 N.W.2d 771 (Minn.1993), held that a public defender is immune from suit; public defenders may not turn down cases, and the public treasury cannot afford to defend malpractice cases. Moreover, immunity may encourage private lawyers to accept court appointments. See also Polk County v. Dodson, 454 U.S. 312, 102 S.Ct. 445, 70 L.Ed.2d 509 (1981) (state public defender does not act "under color of state law" so as to be liable for malpractice under 42 U.S.C. § 1983).

lawyer fails to tell the prospective client that the statute of limitations on his claim will soon run out. E.g., Miller v. Metzinger, 154 Cal.Rptr. 22 (Ct.App.1979).

c. Second, a lawyer may also be liable to beneficiaries named in a client's will if, due to the lawyer's negligence, the will does not carry out the testator's intention. See, e.g., Lucas v. Hamm, 364 P.2d 685 (Cal.1961).

Blair v. Ing, 21 P.3d 452 (Hawaii 2001), for example, found that beneficiaries of a trust had standing to sue the draftsman whose negligence had cost the trust $200,000 in increased taxes. The plaintiffs were the intended beneficiaries of the lawyer-client relationship, the court said, and they could make the lawyer restore the trust corpus to the level it would have been but for the negligence. But see, Miller v. Mooney, 725 N.E.2d 545 (Mass.2000) (will beneficiaries cannot sue lawyer because they were neither clients of the lawyer, nor third party beneficiaries of a contract with the lawyer, nor persons entitled to be told how the testator was leaving her money).

d. Third, a lawyer may be liable to a non–client to whom the lawyer expressly assumes an obligation to investigate facts and accurately report them to the non-client. See, e.g., Greycas, Inc. v. Proud, 826 F.2d 1560 (7th Cir.1987), cert. denied 484 U.S. 1043, 108 S.Ct. 775, 98 L.Ed.2d 862 (1988) (lawyer who agreed to investigate state of client's title to property being posted as security for loan held liable to the lender when failed to investigate and inaccurately reported the state of the client's title).[2]

In Paradigm Insurance Co. v. Langerman Law Offices, P.A., 24 P.3d 593 (Ariz.2001), the issue was whether an insurance company that retains a lawyer to defend the insured may sue that lawyer for malpractice. The insurance company had paid a settlement on behalf of the insured doctor after the defendant lawyer had mistakenly concluded the doctor was not covered under the hospital's malpractice insurance. Relying on § 51(3) of the Restatement, the court held that the fact that the lawyer-defendant in this case had earlier represented the doctor (not the doctor's insurance company), did not defeat the insurance company's claims. The court explained that when an insurance company hires a lawyer to represent the insured, the lawyer's obligation to the insured (to defeat the claim) and to the insurer were the same; there was no conflict of interest. It would be unjust, the court said, for the lawyer to have no malpractice liability to the insurer that hired him, assigned the case to him, and paid his fees.

However, courts are reluctant to extend liability just because a third party takes it upon himself to rely on someone else's lawyer. MacMillan v. Scheffy, 787 A.2d 867 (N.H.2001), for example, held that a real estate buyer has no malpractice claim where a seller's lawyer failed to include an agreed-upon restrictive covenant in the deed. The lawyer admitted that he considered the buyers the beneficiaries of his drafting, but the court found he had made no express undertaking to benefit them. Further, the court

2. You will see more about this role of the lawyer as evaluator in Problem 21, infra.

said that real estate transactions are "adversarial in nature" and declined to impose a duty on a seller's lawyer to benefit the seller's adversary.

e. Fourth, under Restatement § 51(4), and Comment *h*, a lawyer who aids a trustee-like fiduciary to breach an obligation to the intended beneficiary of the fiduciary's duty may be liable to that beneficiary. See, e.g., Fickett v. Superior Court, 558 P.2d 988 (Ariz.App.1976).

In Guardianship of Karan, 38 P.3d 396 (Wash.Ct.App.2002), the plaintiff was the successor guardian of a minor, Amanda, who was the beneficiary of her father's life insurance policy. When Amanda's father died, her mother hired the defendant-lawyer to represent the mother in a petition in which she asked to be named the guardian of Amanda's estate. The lawyer obtained an order for Amanda's mother to establish and manage an account in Amanda's name, but he failed to include statutorily-required safeguards requiring the mother to post a bond or to place the funds in a blocked account. By the time the plaintiff was substituted as Amanda's guardian, her mother had spent most of the $50,000 left to Amanda and was judgment proof. When the plaintiff sued the lawyer for legal malpractice, the lawyer argued that only Amanda's mother, his client, could bring a malpractice claim. The court rejected that defense, pointing to several factors in the case: the lawyer performed the work for Amanda's benefit; it was reasonably foreseeable that a failure to obtain the required safeguards would make depletion of the estate more likely; Amanda suffered harm as a result; the failure to implement the safeguards caused Amanda's injury; if the court refuses to impose a duty on lawyers to act in the interests of the beneficiaries who are minors, similarly situated individuals will be harmed in the future; and imposing such a duty will not create any undue burden on lawyers because the beneficiary's interest is not in conflict with any legitimate request of any guardian.

f. In some states, notably New York and Texas, in spite of the cited cases, the theory of liability to non–clients is significantly qualified by the requirement of privity between lawyer and client in order to maintain a malpractice action. The privity limitation is derived from a leading tort case, Ultramares v. Touche, 174 N.E. 441 (N.Y.1931), in which Judge Cardozo had feared giving professionals unlimited liability to investors who relied on their opinions. Compare, e.g., Security Pacific Business Credit, Inc. v. Peat Marwick Main & Co., 597 N.E.2d 1080 (N.Y.1992) (continuing to follow *Ultramares*), with Vereins–Und Westbank, AG v. Carter, 691 F.Supp. 704 (S.D.N.Y.1988) (holding lawyer liable on opinion letter).

Do you see any good reason to retain the privity requirement today?

B. PROVING A MALPRACTICE CASE

1. How is the trier of fact supposed to know what skill and knowledge a lawyer would ordinarily employ in the circumstances presented in this problem?

a. A plaintiff must ordinarily present expert testimony about the duty of care in a suit for professional malpractice. This rule applies even in a bench trial because the standard of care must be presented on the record with a chance for cross examination rather than left to the subjective standard of the judge.

b.   Sometimes the court excuses expert testimony, however, where the issue is so simple or the lack of skill so obvious as to be within the range of ordinary experience of lay people. In Schmitz v. Crotty, 528 N.W.2d 112 (Iowa 1995), for example, while completing death tax returns begun by another lawyer, the successor lawyer did not recognize that the same land was being reported more than once, thus increasing the taxes due. The court found the negligence so obvious that it did not require an expert to explain it to the trier of fact.

2. If a client sues Sarah Field for malpractice, should the state's Rules of Professional Conduct be determinative of the standards of care and conduct?

a.   Are violations of professional conduct rules like the violations of law underlying the tort doctrine of negligence per se? For example, if the speed limit is 40 m.p.h., and the driver is traveling at 50 m.p.h, the normal rule is that driver's speeding is negligent. He cannot argue he was not driving too fast; he can only argue causation and damages.

b.   The 1983 Model Rules, Scope ¶ 18, disclaimed that use of professional standards. It said in part: "Violation of a Rule should not give rise to a cause of action nor should it create any presumption that a legal duty has been breached. * * * [N]othing in the Rules should be deemed to augment any substantive legal duty of lawyers or the extra-disciplinary consequences of violating such a duty." What effect do you believe a court should give to that disclaimer?

c.   Most courts at least allow expert witnesses to cite the professional rules as evidence of the standards to which most lawyers adhere in the situations they face. E.g., Woodruff v. Tomlin, 616 F.2d 924 (6th Cir.1980) (en banc), cert. denied 449 U.S. 888, 101 S.Ct. 246, 66 L.Ed.2d 114 (1980) (Model Code is "some evidence of the standards required of lawyers"); Mirabito v. Liccardo, 5 Cal.Rptr.2d 571 (Ct.App.1992) (disciplinary standards may be the subject of experts' testimony and cited to the jury); Mayol v. Summers, Watson & Kimpel, 585 N.E.2d 1176 (Ill.App.1992) (rules may be treated as analogous to a statute); Allen v. Lefkoff, Duncan, Grimes & Dermer, P.C., 453 S.E.2d 719 (Ga.1995) (a lawyer's violation of state ethics rules is a "circumstance that can be considered along with other facts and circumstances"); Maritrans GP, Inc. v. Pepper, Hamilton & Scheetz, 602 A.2d 1277 (Pa.1992) (violation of state ethics rule does not *preclude* finding of malpractice; rule may state a principle of fiduciary duty, for example, that will be enforced in a malpractice case even if the rule is not itself enforced).

However, Hizey v. Carpenter, 830 P.2d 646 (Wash.1992), held that violation of a disciplinary rule is not only not enough to show malpractice, the language of the rule may not even form the basis of a jury instruction. See also, Lazy Seven Coal Sales, Inc. v. Stone & Hinds, P.C., 813 S.W.2d

400 (Tenn.1991); Mergler v. Crystal Properties Associates, Ltd., 583 N.Y.S.2d 229 (App.Div.1992).

d. Restatement Third, The Law Governing Lawyers § 52(2) concluded from the plethora of cases that proof of violation of a professional rule (a) "does not give rise to an implied cause of action" for negligence or breach of fiduciary duty, (b) "does not preclude other proof concerning the duty of care * * * or the fiduciary duty," but (c) "may be considered by a trier of fact as an aid in understanding and applying" the applicable standard of care or conduct.

e. The Model Rules, in what is now Scope ¶ 20, have now deleted the disclaimer and substituted: "Nevertheless, since the Rules do establish standards of conduct by lawyers, a lawyer's violation of a Rule may be evidence of breach of the applicable standard of conduct."

f. What approach should the courts take as to the relevance of professional standards in lawyer malpractice cases? Do the standards to which you are expected to adhere persuasively describe the conduct expected of a "reasonable lawyer"?

Should violation of an ethics rule drafted for the protection of clients be treated, like exceeding the speed limit in a tort case, as negligence per se? What does it mean to say that a violation "may be considered by the trier of fact"? Should the jury take the violation seriously or not?

3. How should courts deal with the problem of causation? Should a client be able to recover damages if the client would have lost the case no matter what the lawyer had done?

a. The traditional requirement of proof of what a non-negligent lawyer could have obtained for the client is often called the "suit-within-a-suit." Restatement Third, The Law Governing Lawyers § 53, Comment *b*, explains:

> "All the issues that would have been litigated in the previous action are litigated between the plaintiff and the plaintiff's former lawyer, with the latter taking the place and bearing the burdens that properly would have fallen on the defendant in the original action. * * * Similar principles apply when a former civil defendant contends that, but for the misconduct of the defendant's former lawyer, the defendant would have secured a better result at trial."

b. In Winskunas v. Birnbaum, 23 F.3d 1264 (7th Cir.1994), for example, the court found there was no evidence the plaintiff could have won his suit, so there was no basis for saying that his lawyer's failure to appeal caused his loss. Similarly, in Pickens, Barnes & Abernathy v. Heasley, 328 N.W.2d 524 (Iowa 1983), the court said the trial court erred in refusing to instruct the jury that any favorable judgment in the original suit might not have been collectable.

Similarly, in this Problem, Field might try to defend against Moore's malpractice claim by showing that Moore did not have very strong case as to the doctor's negligence or that Moore herself had been negligent in waiting too long to seek medical help.

c. What do you think of this requirement? Should a lawyer be able to use a client's confidence in the lawyer against the client, for example, to prove the client's contributory negligence?

In Arnav Industries Inc. Retirement Trust v. Brown, Raysman, Millstein, Felder & Steiner, LLP., 751 N.E.2d 936 (N.Y.2001), the defendant law firm had revised a settlement agreement for the plaintiff client and had represented that the revised version only corrected a typographical error from the original settlement. In fact, the new version also misstated the total amount due, a mistake that was costly to the plaintiff. Given the firm's representation that there was only one change, the plaintiff signed the revised document without reading it. The court held that the plaintiff's failure to read the contract did not defeat a malpractice claim, reasoning that the plaintiff had justifiably relied on its attorney's representations.[3]

d. Other courts have been concerned that a case-within-a-case requirement inadequately explores how a matter would really have proceeded if handled properly by the first lawyer.

In Conklin v. Hannoch Weisman, 678 A.2d 1060 (N.J.1996), for example, the plaintiffs had sold property subject to a purchase money mortgage. They alleged that their lawyer had not sufficiently explained to them the effect of a subordination agreement whereby the defaulting buyer's other creditors got paid but the sellers ultimately did not. The jury had been given a traditional proximate cause instruction and had found the lawyer's advice inadequate but not the cause of the client's loss because they would have sold the property anyway. The court reversed and said that, on retrial, the jury should be told that the lawyers' malpractice need only be a "substantial factor" in bringing about the plaintiff's loss. The fact that a client goes ahead with a deal in the face of advice about risks can negate causation, but the fact that the client did not ask about the consequences of the approach the lawyer had chosen did not excuse the lawyers' obligation to tell the client about those consequences.

What do you think of moderating the causation requirement in this way? Does the "substantial factor" test take a more realistic view of the nature of causation? Does it give a jury too much room to speculate about what caused a plaintiff's loss?

C. MALPRACTICE REMEDIES; ADVANCE WAIVERS OF A LAWYER'S MALPRACTICE

1. What remedies should be available to redress Sarah Field's professional malpractice?

3. In Clark v. Rowe, 701 N.E.2d 624 (Mass.1998), however, a lawyer was allowed to assert comparative negligence as a defense where the client, an experienced real estate investor, was found 70% responsible for the loss in the refinancing of a mortgage loan.

a.   The range of possible remedies is substantial. Typically, the client's damages are what the client would have obtained by way of trial or settlement if the lawyer had handled the matter non-negligently. But malpractice can take other forms; a lawyer who negligently discloses a client's trade secret, for example, might be liable for damage to the client's business resulting from the disclosure. See Restatement Third, The Law Governing Lawyers § 53, Comment *b*.

b.   Patrick v. Ronald Williams, P.A., 402 S.E.2d 452 (N.C.App.1991), held that a lawyer may be sued for punitive damages if the conduct amounts to gross negligence. The court found that the lawyer had failed to estimate the value of his clients' claim, failed to tell the clients about an offer of settlement, failed to tell them judgment had been entered until six months had passed, and lost their rights under the uninsured motorist provisions of their insurance policy by failing to appeal a trial court order. Those facts were extreme, but even the specter of exposure to punitive damages in a world that is often hostile to lawyers is sobering.

c.   Campagnola v. Mulholland, Minion & Roe, 555 N.E.2d 611 (N.Y. 1990), added another wrinkle to the question of damages. Because the lawyer did not comply with the policy provisions, the client lost her $100,000 uninsured motorist coverage. The lawyer asserted that this sum should be reduced by the portion of the judgment she would have had to pay as the lawyer's contingent fee. In a sharply divided 4–3 decision, the New York Court of Appeals said her contract to pay fees was not part of the measure of what she had lost. Judge Kaye wrote in a concurring opinion that the plaintiff would be required to pay fees to bring this malpractice case, so not deducting fees for the first case from the damage award was necessary to make her whole.

2.   In the case of a breach of fiduciary duty, should the court excuse the client from paying all or part of the lawyer's fee even if the client can show no actual damages?

a.   Hendry v. Pelland, 73 F.3d 397 (D.C.Cir.1996), is one of the increasing number of claims for fee forfeiture, even in the absence of economic harm to the client. The law firm had represented all five members of a family selling a parcel of land. All the clients had somewhat different wishes about the terms of sale. While finding no intentional misconduct that would support punitive damages, or even any actual damage suffered by family members, the court found that representation of all five was a conflict of interest. Because a conflict of interest is a breach of fiduciary duty, the court required the law firm to disgorge all fees it had earned in the case.

What do you think of this result? Is there much that lawyers do that cannot be pled as a breach of fiduciary duty? Does the punishment exceed the crime if the court imposes fee forfeiture when the lawyer's action has cause no harm to the client?

b.   Restatement Third, The Law Governing Lawyers § 37, Comment *b*, acknowledges this theory of relief but makes clear:

"Forfeiture of fees * * * is not justified in each instance in which a lawyer violates a legal duty, nor is total forfeiture always appropriate. Some violations are inadvertent or do not significantly harm the client. Some can be adequately dealt with by [other remedies] or by a partial forfeiture. Denying the lawyer all compensation would sometimes be an excessive sanction, giving a windfall to the client. The remedy of this Section should hence be applied with discretion."

c.   Burrow v. Arce, 997 S.W.2d 229 (Tex.1999), relied on § 37 of the Restatement to hold that the remedy of fee forfeiture indeed does not require proof a client suffered actual damage from the lawyer's conduct. Moreover, the court went on to hold that the amount of any forfeiture should be set by the trial judge, not the jury.

3.   In the future, in order to reduce her malpractice liability, should Field add a clause to her standard retainer agreement pursuant to which the client waives any malpractice claims against Field?

a.   Look at Model Rule 1.8(h)(1). Under what conditions, if any, might Field offer such an option to her client? DR 6–102 of the ABA Model Code of Professional Responsibility would not have allowed such a clause under any circumstances. Do you agree that the client should be able to consent to such a clause if he or she is independently represented in doing so?

b.   Why would any client agree to such an arrangement? Suppose that, in return, Field would charge the client less per hour than a specialist. A client has a right to buy a Yugo instead of a Mercedes; should the client have the right to buy lower quality legal services?

c.   What client would seek independent legal counsel about whether to sign such a clause? In the case of a corporate client, might the independent advice come from the company's in-house lawyer? When might a corporate client be willing to sign such a clause?

d.   Instead of limiting the lawyer's liability for malpractice, might a lawyer be able to require arbitration of all claims against the lawyer? Restatement Third, The Law Governing Lawyers § 54, Comment *b*, makes clear:

"[A] lawyer and client may properly take certain measures that may have the effect of narrowing or otherwise affecting the lawyer's liability * * *. A client and lawyer may agree in advance * * * to arbitrate claims for legal malpractice, provided that the client receives proper notice of the scope and effect of the agreement and if the relevant jurisdiction's law applicable to providers of professional services renders such agreements enforceable."

e.   Oregon State Bar Legal Ethics Committee Formal Opinion 2001–165 explored whether a lawyer retained to investigate one of its corporate client's employees for possible malfeasance may put an indemnity provision in the engagement agreement in case the employee (a non-client) sues the lawyer. The Committee found that DR 6–102(A) did not prohibit the lawyer from having the client indemnify him against independent civil claims by third parties arising out of the services performed, but the client could not indemnify the lawyer against a malpractice suit brought by the client based on the handling of the investigation.

f.   Should Rule 1.8(h)(1) be amended to make advance waivers harder to obtain? Would any such changes in the rule simply make it harder for clients to do something they believe it is in their interest to do?

4.   Does a lawyer have a duty to tell a client about the lawyer's own malpractice in the client's case?

a.   Matter of Tallon, 447 N.Y.S.2d 50 (App.Div.1982), held that a lawyer must inform the client, withdraw, and advise the client to get independent legal advice about whether or not to sue. Cf. ABA Model Rule 1.8(h)(2) and California Rules of Professional Conduct Rule 3–400 (lawyer may not settle malpractice claim with lawyer's client without advising in writing that client get independent representation).

b.   In re Blackwelder, 615 N.E.2d 106 (Ind.1993), involved a lawyer whose clients had sought to reopen a default judgment entered against them. The lawyer missed the filing deadline for doing so, and he proposed to handle their bankruptcy free in exchange for a release from malpractice liability. The court found that the clients had not been advised in writing to get independent counsel before signing the malpractice release and it publicly reprimanded the lawyer.

c.   N.Y. State Bar Association Committee on Professional Ethics, Opinion 734 (2000) discussed whether a Legal Aid Society is bound by the ethical duty applicable to other attorneys to disclose their lawyer's malpractice to their clients. The opinion states that the Society is obliged to keep their clients reasonably informed about their cases and therefore has a duty to disclose any significant error or omission. The Society can then continue representing the client only after getting that client's informed consent and a showing that "a disinterested lawyer would believe that the representation of the client would not be adversely affected thereby."

d.   Should a lawyer have any duty to tell a client about the possible malpractice of a former lawyer? Suppose one learned in the course of representing a client that a former lawyer had missed a statute of limitations, forfeiting the client's right to file a suit? Should there be a tacit understanding among lawyers that we will not speak negatively about a fellow professional? Might a lawyer properly be accused of barratry, i.e. stirring up litigation, if the prior malpractice were mentioned? Should we take exactly the opposite view?

5.   Should law firms be permitted to shield each of the lawyers from vicarious liability for the malpractice of other lawyers in the firm?

a.   Depending on state statute, the usual vehicle for trying to do that is the Limited Liability Company (LLC) or the Limited Liability Partnership (LLP). Each is a form of law firm organization that purports to say that lawyers are liable for their own malpractice but not for that of their partners and associates.

b. ABA Formal Opinion 96–401 (Aug. 2, 1996) ruled that it does not violate the Model Rules for a lawyer to be part of a limited liability partnership. Model Rule 1.8(h)(1) on limiting liability for one's own malpractice does not address vicarious liability, and no other Model Rule requires a lawyer to be liable for his or her partner's malpractice. However, limited liability companies, like other law firms, must comply with Model Rules 5.1 and 5.3 on the duty to supervise and Rule 5.4 on participation of non-lawyers in the organization.

c. Whether liability is direct or vicarious is a recurring issue in the LLC cases. Sanders, Bruin, Coll & Worley, P.A. v. McKay Oil Corp., 943 P.2d 104 (N.M.1997), involved an LLC that voted to terminate representation of a client six weeks before a major arbitration, allegedly because of illness of the partner who was to handle the litigation. The client considered the termination to be malpractice, and the question was whether liability was limited to the firm's assets or could be asserted against each shareholder in the LLC. The court held each lawyer liable. While shareholders in an LLC cannot be held vicariously liable, the court said, in this case the liability was for each shareholder's individual act of voting.

d. Indeed, in Gosselin v. Webb, 242 F.3d 412 (1st Cir.2001), a group of lawyers shared office space but were not legally partners at all. The District Court therefore had held they could not be vicariously liable for each other's conduct, but the First Circuit reversed. The lawyers practiced under a common trade name and the negligent lawyer represented that he was "with" a firm. Those acts of holding out as a partnership, the court held, are sufficient to make lawyers vicariously liable for each other's acts.

e. Do you have any strong feelings about the propriety of lawyers' seeking to limit their liability for the malpractice of their partners? Might the limitations tend to reduce partners' efforts to improve the "culture" of high professional standards in a firm? Does the fact that most law firms carry high levels of malpractice insurance tend to make questions of personal liability of less concern than they would otherwise be?

D. OTHER SIGNIFICANT CONSEQUENCES OF NEGLIGENCE OR MISCONDUCT BY LAWYERS

1. What sanctions might Field expect for missing the first trial date in the criminal case? Even if her client cannot successfully sue for malpractice, should she have other concerns?

a. For a situation such as Field's criminal case, Restatement Third, The Law Governing Lawyers § 6, Comment *g* says:

> "[A] lawyer functioning as an advocate in a proceeding may be subject to remedies through contempt orders * * * where necessary and appropriate to * * * prevent significant impairment of the proceedings * * * . Included in such relief may be an appropriate sanction directed toward repairing or punishing harm that the lawyer's contemptuous conduct caused to the lawyer's own client."

b. In re Yengo, 417 A.2d 533 (N.J.1980), cert.denied 449 U.S. 1124, 101 S.Ct. 941, 67 L.Ed.2d 110 (1981), involved a trial before a judge who had emphasized to the defense attorneys the need for regular attendance and said that before any tardiness or absence the attorney should secure her prior approval. After an attorney failed to appear for several days of trial, the judge tried to reach the attorney by phone. The judge talked to the attorney's daughter who said that he was in Bermuda on vacation. When the attorney finally appeared before the judge, he explained that he was in Bermuda on business and had no opportunity to obtain the judge's prior approval. The judge summarily held the attorney in contempt and fined him $500. The state supreme court affirmed.[4]

2. Should the criminal defendant be able to cite Field's poor representation as a basis of reversing the conviction?

a. The leading case on "ineffective assistance of counsel" is Strickland v. Washington, 466 U.S. 668, 104 S.Ct. 2052, 80 L.Ed.2d 674 (1984). Even in a death penalty case, the Court held, to justify a issuance of a writ of habeas corpus, a court must find that the lawyer's acts or omissions were not only "outside the wide range of professionally competent assistance" but also that the ineffectiveness caused "actual prejudice." "It is not enough for the defendant to show that the errors had some conceivable effect on the outcome of the proceedings." 466 U.S. at 693, 104 S.Ct. at 2067, 80 L.Ed.2d at 697. "The defendant must show that there is a reasonable probability that, but for counsel's unprofessional errors, the result of the proceeding would have been different. A reasonable probability is a probability sufficient to undermine confidence in the outcome." 466 U.S. at 694, 104 S.Ct. at 2068, 80 L.Ed.2d at 698.

b. Frazer v. United States, 18 F.3d 778 (9th Cir.1994), illustrates that convictions are sometimes overturned on this basis. The defendant was charged with bank robbery. He waived his right to a jury trial and was convicted based on stipulated facts. The defendant alleged the lawyer had called him a very offensive, racially-derogatory name and warned that if he insisted on going to trial the lawyer would promise to be "very ineffective." The court found that from such statements, prejudice could be presumed.

c. Cottle v. State, 733 So.2d 963 (Fla.1999), held that it is ineffective assistance of counsel to fail to tell a criminal client about a plea offer from the prosecutor and fail to give the client the right to decide whether to accept it. The client is not required to show that the trial judge would have confirmed the agreement. See also, People v. Curry, 687 N.E.2d 877 (Ill.1997).

d. Roe v. Flores–Ortega, 528 U.S. 470, 120 S.Ct. 1029, 145 L.Ed.2d 985 (2000), addressed the failure to appeal in a criminal setting. The defendant pled guilty to second-degree murder and, when he was sentenced, he was told he had 60 days to appeal. The public defender made a note to file the appeal but then failed to do so. The defendant's later efforts

---

4. See also, Matter of Mix, 901 F.2d 1431 (7th Cir.1990) (lawyer censured for seemingly doing as little as he could get away with in appeal on behalf of appointed client).

to appeal were rejected as untimely but, on habeas corpus, the Ninth Circuit found the lawyer's failure to file had been without the defendant's consent and thus constituted per se ineffective assistance of counsel.

The Supreme Court held that under the "objective standard of reasonableness" element of *Strickland*, there is no automatic obligation to appeal, but there is a constitutionally-based duty to consult when "there is reason to think either (1) that a rational defendant would want to appeal, or (2) that this particular defendant reasonably demonstrated to counsel that he was interested in appealing." After a guilty plea, an appeal may be less likely, but the court must ask, for example, whether the defendant was denied the bargained-for sentence. Under the "prejudice" element of *Strickland*, the defendant must show that, but for the lawyer's conduct, he would have appealed. Justices Souter, Stevens, Breyer & Ginsburg concurred, but said that a failure of counsel to consult with the defendant about an appeal will "almost always" be ineffective assistance.

e.   In Glover v. United States, 531 U.S. 198, 121 S.Ct. 696, 148 L.Ed.2d 604 (2001), counsel failed to get charges "grouped" under the Sentencing Guidelines, thus increasing the defendant's sentence by 6 to 21 months. The Seventh Circuit had refused to find inadequate assistance because it considered the sentence increase so small as not to constitute "prejudice" under *Strickland*, but the Supreme Court rejected that analysis. Even a 6 month additional sentence must be taken into account, the Court said, in making the overall judgment whether the lawyer's assistance was inadequate.

f.   Burdine v. Johnson, 262 F.3d 336 (5th Cir.2001) (en banc), cert. den. sub nom., Cockrell v. Burdine, 535 U.S. 1120, 122 S.Ct. 2347, 153 L.Ed.2d 174 (2002), considered the availability of post-conviction relief where the lawyer slept through large parts of the trial for capital murder. The en banc 5th Circuit granted relief. It found that a lawyer's unconsciousness during critical portions of the trial rendered counsel "in effect, absent" and thus denied effective assistance. The court distinguished an unconscious attorney, who is essentially absent from the proceedings, from a drunk or impaired attorney, who may be capable of giving some assistance. Thus, the court was willing to presume prejudice and overturn the original conviction.

3.   Might lawyers ever find themselves charged criminally as accomplices of their clients?

a.   It happens more often that lawyers like to think. See, e.g., United States v. Morris, 988 F.2d 1335 (4th Cir.1993), where the government charged a lawyer with conspiracy to distribute drugs based in part on real estate work he did in closing the purchase of a house where crack cocaine was manufactured.

b.   United States v. Cueto, 151 F.3d 620 (7th Cir.1998), affirmed an obstruction of justice conviction against a lawyer who (1) charged an FBI investigator with soliciting a bribe, (2) filed false motions that attacked the operations of the FBI and U.S. Attorney, and (3) urged the defendants to file several motions, including one to disqualify the district judge. The opinion describes a complex set of events. The National Association of Criminal Defense Lawyers filed a brief on behalf of the defendant who said he was just doing his job and only committed, if anything, a victimless crime, but the court disagreed. "We refuse to accept the notion that lawyers may do anything, including violating the law, to zealously advocate their clients' interests and then avoid criminal prosecution by claiming that they were 'just doing their job'." 151 F.3d at 634.

c.   In re American Honda Motor Co. Dealerships Relations Litigation, 958 F.Supp. 1045 (D.Md.1997), held a law firm potentially liable under RICO for aiding and abetting an alleged illegal kickback scheme to American Honda executives from some of its dealers. Lawyers from the firm served as company directors and handled all dealer complaints about the kickbacks. In one case, they allegedly told an executive his ownership interest in a dealership was "acceptable as long as he did not tell anyone." In another case, they allegedly urged others to give incomplete or inaccurate testimony and "allegations of obstruction of justice abound." Without defending any of the alleged conduct, one can observe that not all the acts alleged are completely different from conduct that lawyers would defend as aggressive defense or counseling. The point is that an overly-aggressive lawyer can well find himself or herself in the dock with the client.

d.   Durie v. State, 751 So.2d 685 (Fla.App.2000), again illustrates that the too-clever lawyer can be charged criminally. Durie's two clients were hurt in a bar fight. They sued the bar and collected for their injuries. Medicaid had paid the medical expenses of one of them and placed a lien on the proceeds of the lawsuit. So, Durie had the settlement paid primarily to the victim not subject to the lien, and that client then made a "gift" to the other client. A jury called this Medicaid fraud and convicted the lawyer of grand theft. The court affirmed, holding that "while an attorney must do the best job he can for his client, he cannot engage in dishonest or fraudulent conduct." It is one thing to minimize lien claims and quite another to affirmatively misrepresent what the settlement arrangement was.

4.   Should lawyers be held to be debt collectors, able to pursue a client's creditors only in ways sanctioned by the federal Fair Debt Collection Act?

a.   In Heintz v. Jenkins, 514 U.S. 291, 115 S.Ct. 1489, 131 L.Ed.2d 395 (1995), a unanimous Supreme Court held that lawyers who collect consumer debts through litigation may be sued under the Fair Debt Collection Practices Act for engaging in abusive and unfair practices. Depending on the nature of their practice, lawyers can come within the statutory description of persons who "regularly collect or attempt to collect [consumer] debts," and there is no basis to exclude them from the Act's coverage.[5]

---

5. On remand, the Seventh Circuit affirmed a finding that the lawyer did not know of the invalidity of the debt and thus had insufficient intent to be in violation of the Act. Jenkins v. Heintz, 124 F.3d 824 (7th Cir.1997).

b. Bartlett v. Heibl, 128 F.3d 497 (7th Cir.1997), held that a lawyer's letter threatening suit within a week—but giving 30 days to contest the debt—was confusing and therefore violated the Fair Debt Collection Practices Act even though the debtor conceded he had not read the letter. A letter can be confusing and thus violate the Act, Judge Posner wrote, even though the debtor was not in fact confused by it.

See also, Romea v. Heiberger & Associates, 163 F.3d 111 (2d Cir.1998), where the landlord's law firm sent three-day rent demand notices that New York law requires before a summary eviction proceeding. The Second Circuit held that the Fair Debt Collection Practices Act applies to such letters and thus reinstated the tenant's complaint against the law firm.

5. What other kinds of remedies and sanctions for improper conduct might lawyers face?

a. While professional malpractice is the most common civil claim against a lawyer, it is far from the only one. Disqualification of the lawyer from participation in a case is another common remedy that we will see primarily in Chapter 4. Indeed, Restatement Third, The Law Governing Lawyers § 6 lists thirteen remedies available to a client or non-client to redress a lawyer's conduct.

b. A court may void transactions made in violation of the lawyer's professional obligations, for example. See, e.g., Abstract & Title Corp. of Florida v. Cochran, 414 So.2d 284 (Fla.App.1982) (lawyer's right of first refusal on client's property set aside); Spaulding v. Zimmerman, 116 N.W.2d 704 (Minn.1962) (tort settlement with minor set aside where lawyer for defendant did not disclose what he knew of the seriousness of plaintiff's injury).

c. Shartzer v. Israels, 59 Cal.Rptr.2d 296 (Ct.App.1996), opinion modified, 67 Cal.Rptr.2d 42 (Ct.App.1997), found a lawyer liable to a witness for the other side for invasion of privacy. In a sexual battery prosecution, the defense counsel subpoenaed the complaining witness' confidential mental health records as California law permits. The doctor was supposed to send the records to the court to be reviewed for relevance before defense counsel received them. In this case, however, the records were sent directly to the defense counsel who did not send them to the court. He read them, gave them to the defense expert, and used them in cross-examining the witness before the jury. The court held that the mere reading of the confidential records under these circumstances rendered the lawyer liable to the complainant and there was no litigation privilege defense. See also, Bakker v. McKinnon, 152 F.3d 1007 (8th Cir.1998) (patients' lawyer requested credit reports about dentist and his adult daughters from a local credit bureau when federal law allows only persons with a legitimate "business need" to request such reports; actual and punitive damages assessed).

d. Latham v. Castillo, 972 S.W.2d 66 (Tex.1998), upheld a state Deceptive Trade Practices Act claim where the lawyer affirmatively misrepresented to his clients that he had filed a medical malpractice claim on their behalf.

e.   The bottom line of the cases in this Problem is that being a lawyer is a risky business. The issues you will see in the remainder of this book raise not only questions about potential disciplinary sanctions, but also questions of civil liability and even whether you will be able to stay out of jail. Ethical issues raise important questions of right and wrong, but the law governing lawyers also has teeth.

———

CHAPTER III

FUNDAMENTALS OF THE LAWYER–CLIENT RELATIONSHIP

A good lawyer-client relationship works on many levels. Ideally, a lawyer and client like each other and trust each other to communicate with candor and act with integrity. Ideally, the lawyer will act as a client's friend, telling the hard truth when necessary but consistently providing reliable support. Ultimately, however, the relationship between lawyer and client is based on law. Many of the legal elements will seem *sui generis*, but they are made up of familiar elements—agency law, contracts, and requirements of the ABA Model Rules.

The lawyer-client legal relationship can best be seen as a mixture of status and contract. That is, some elements of the relationship are the subject of a contract between lawyer and client that is basically like any other service contract. Other obligations, however, are inherent in the status of a lawyer as a fiduciary and are not entirely subject to amendment by lawyer and client.

Throughout this chapter, ask yourself which matters should be limited only by issues of informed consent of the client and which require a more absolute and general prohibition. Think about questions such as the following:

a. How is the lawyer-client relationship formed? At what point do preliminary discussions produce enforceable obligations? What does it mean to call the relationship thus formed a "fiduciary" relationship?

b. What is a lawyer required/authorized to do on behalf of a client? May lawyer and client define and limit the scope and objectives of the representation? What are the lawyer's rights and obligations if they fail to do so?

c. What legal protection is afforded to communications between lawyer and client? What obligations does that protection impose on the lawyer?

d. What is the impact of the financial relation between lawyer and client on the lawyer's obligations? May the lawyer refuse to provide legal services until the fee is paid, for example? Should the lawyer's obligation to protect confidential information of the client be suspended in a fee dispute?

e. What are the lawyer's obligations to protect client property in the lawyer's possession? Should failure to keep accurate financial records be grounds for the lawyer's disbarment?

PROBLEM 4

UNDERTAKING TO REPRESENT A CLIENT

If you join a large law firm, you will find, at first, that work for existing clients appears as if by magic on your desk. Each of the firm's clients, however, was once a prospective client, and the client and firm each had to decide whether to commit to the relationship. Obviously, a firm cannot turn down all prospective clients and remain in operation, but neither is the decision to take on a client automatic. Once representation begins, a lawyer assumes duties not easily shed and cases sometimes assume a life of their own. This problem puts you first in the role of dealing with a prospective client. Then you will make the decision whether to undertake a representation and work through the matter of documenting that relationship. Finally, you will think about decision-making within the lawyer-client relationship.

FACTS

You are a lawyer in a private firm. Morris Cannell, an elderly man whom you had never met before, came to you and complained about the handling of his investment account by a local broker. Cannell told you that the broker invested over $200,000 of Cannell's pension money in speculative stocks and the account's value has now been reduced to less than $20,000. Cannell claimed that the broker not only took excessive risks with his money, he also bought and sold the stocks frequently, with the result that the broker made a lot in commissions while the client's retirement savings almost vanished.

As Cannell talked, he became more animated and more candid. "I knew what he was doing," he said, "and I suppose I could have stopped him at any time. But I guess I got greedy and wanted to turn my nest egg into millions just like I thought all my friends were doing." Cannell was very bitter and told you in no uncertain terms, "I want you to throw the book at my broker. He showed me no mercy and I don't want you to show any to him."

In researching the problem before deciding whether to take the case, you concluded that your best arguments would be that the broker engaged in illegal churning (excessive buying and selling), and that he violated federal rules relating to an investor's suitability (what stocks are suitable to meet a given investor's objectives, here safety and income). With respect to both arguments you planned to allude to Cannell's age and relative lack of sophistication.

When you told Cannell the results of your analysis, however, he was angry and wanted you to do more. "He must have a license," Cannell said. "Do everything you can to get him suspended. See what you can do to tie up his bank accounts. If you won't do it, show me what to do and I'll do it myself.''

The statute of limitations was about to run on all state and federal claims, and you told Cannell you would only represent him if he agreed to raise no more than the churning and suitability issues. You refused to seek suspension of the broker's license or to try to harass him financially, and you refused to give Cannell the behind-the-scenes help to take those steps himself. Cannell reluctantly agreed to your terms and signed your engagement letter. You entered an appearance as Cannell's attorney and filed suit on his behalf.

After extensive discovery, the broker's lawyer made what to you seemed a fair settlement offer. Knowing that your client was still angry, you did not want to have him throw away the opportunity to conclude the case and you accepted the offer on the spot.

QUESTIONS

A. THE LAWYER'S DUTIES TO A PROSPECTIVE CLIENT

1. Before you had agreed to represent Mr. Cannell, was he legally a stranger?

a. Lawyers often like to think that until they agree to represent a client, they owe no duties to the person across their desk. However, that simply is not true. Until adoption of the new ABA Model Rules, no professional rule described the relationship in detail, but as Restatement Third, The Law Governing Lawyers § 15 reports, the law has long been clear on at least three points:

(1) Communications from a prospective client are legally privileged and protected by the lawyer's duty of confidentiality as if they were communications from an actual client;

(2) If the lawyer takes possession of documents or other property of a prospective client, the lawyer must protect those items as if they were documents or property of a client; and

(3) If the lawyer gives advice to a prospective client, for example, by saying "you have no claim and it is not worth your while to retain a lawyer," the lawyer may be responsible to the prospective client for malpractice if that advice is wrong.

b. New ABA Model Rule 1.18 confirms these principles; see especially, Comments [3] & [9]. The term used to describe Mr. Cannell, both in Restatement § 15 and Model Rules 1.18, is "prospective client." As you see, such persons are legally far from strangers.

2. Suppose that shortly after Mr. Cannell had left your office, you learned that someone else in your firm had already agreed to represent Mr. Cannell's broker in the matter? May you or your firm continue to represent the broker?

a.   As you will learn from Model Rule 1.7, you clearly would have to decline to represent Mr. Cannell, because a law firm may not represent both sides in the same litigated case. Again, as you will learn in later Problems, the fact that a lawyer has learned confidential information from an *actual* client typically means that neither that lawyer—nor anyone else in that lawyer's firm—may oppose that client in the same or a substantially related matter. See Model Rules 1.9 and 1.10.

b.   You will also have no doubt after reading Model Rule 1.18 (b), (c) & (d), that ordinarily you personally could have no involvement whatsoever in the broker's defense. Do you suppose that on the facts in this Problem, Mr. Cannell would be likely to consent to your involvement?

c.   Under what conditions may others in your firm be involved in the broker's representation? What does it mean to have avoided "exposure to more disqualifying information than was reasonably necessary to determine whether to represent the prospective client?" Model Rule 1.18, Comments [4] & [5] may be helpful in suggesting ways to conduct an initial interview so as to minimize the likelihood of later disqualification. See also, ABA Formal Opinion 90–358 (1990).

d.   Model Rule 1.18(d)(2)(i) would also require that you be "timely screened" from participation in the broker's defense. You will see screening possibilities in later Problems as well. You will find "screened" defined in Model Rule 1.0(k) and Comments [8]–[10]. See also, Model Rule 1.18, Comment [7].

e.   Why are you required to notify Mr. Cannell about the fact you have been screened? Is he likely to be pleased to hear from you? What does "timely" notice require? Look at Model Rule 1.18, Comment [8]. Is the notice required to be given before the time Mr. Cannell would normally learn what firm is going to represent the broker?

f.   Clark Capital Management Group, Inc. v. Annuity Investors Life Insurance Co., 149 F.Supp.2d 193 (E.D.Pa.2001), a pre-Rule 1.18 opinion, roughly illustrates how the Rule 1.18(d)(2) process might work. The defendant in this trademark infringement suit sought to disqualify plaintiff's counsel based on telephone conversations between the defendant's attorney and attorney Biemer, a member of plaintiff's law firm, during which the defendant's attorney had discussed possibly retaining that firm to act as co-counsel for the defendant. These calls occurred prior to the time the plaintiff retained the law firm. The attorneys never reached any agreement concerning representation, but the defendant's attorney said that he revealed confidential client information to Biemer that he had a reasonable expectation that Biemer would keep confidential. The court found, however, that the plaintiff's expectation of confidentiality was unreasonable: no actual offer had been made to, or accepted by, Biemer. Indeed, both the defendant's lawyer and Biemer had recognized Biemer's need to perform a conflict check before consenting to represent him, so the defendant could not be a former client of Biemer's firm. Furthermore, Biemer was not working on the case because the firm had already screened him from any involvement with it, and the likelihood that confidential information would reach the trial attorneys was minimal.

3.   Imagine that, instead of meeting Mr. Cannell in your office, you had talked to him during the pro bono work that you do at a local legal services agency. Suppose that Mr. Cannell did not want to hire you; he simply wanted to be given some basic advice and told how to file a claim against the broker himself. Under those circumstances, would Mr. Cannell have been a prospective client or an actual client?

a.   Would you have been permitted to provide advice to Mr. Cannell at all in that context without your usual conflicts review? Look at Model Rule 6.5 and its Comment [1].   *No*

b.   Now, suppose that when you get back to your office, you again find that—although you did not know it earlier—your firm represents the broker. Has your discussion with Mr. Cannell in the legal services context disqualified your firm from continuing that representation? Look at Model Rule 6.5, Comments [3] & [4].   *No, only if you knew*

c.   Indeed, does Model Rule 6.5 prevent you from representing the broker yourself? At what time is the lawyer's "knowledge" of a conflict disqualifying under Model Rule 6.5(a)(1)? Whatever your answer to that question, does anything in Model Rule 6.5 require that you be screened from future involvement in the matter?

d.   Are you satisfied that legal services clients are adequately protected by Model Rule 6.5? Is the Rule structured as it is to help assure that private lawyers will be available to staff "hot line" services? Should we be concerned that if we give middle class and poor clients "second class" service, we may discourage them from seeking needed legal help altogether?

4.   Now imagine that your discussion with Mr. Cannell occurred on-line in a chat room for people interested in investing. Would you be comfortable that you knew how your obligations to Mr. Cannell would later be characterized? Are lawyers wise to "troll" for clients in such places?

a.   Association of the Bar of the City of New York, Formal Opinion 2001–1, considered the case of an unsolicited e-mail from a prospective client in response to a law firm's web site invitation to contact the firm. The opinion assumes that the e-mail contained confidential information about the prospective client concerning a dispute with one of the firm's existing clients. Using a web site to invite communications with the firm does not constitute an invitation to burden the firm with confidential information, the Opinion says, any more than would an advertisement in a telephone directory. Thus, the firm should not be barred from continuing to represent the firm's current client in opposition to the prospective client. That said, however, prospective clients should not be forced to suffer more than necessary for mistakenly thinking they could communicate in confidence with the firm. Especially given the lack of a warning on the web site, the firm must treat the information from the prospective client as confidential and not use it to advantage the firm's client in the dispute.

b.   DC Bar Association Opinion No. 316 (2002), in turn, deals with chat rooms. It reports that several exist at which lawyers give real-time, online advice and invite inquirers to contact the lawyers for further advice.[1] After reviewing the possible ineffectiveness of disclaimers that no lawyer-client relationship is formed with such inquirers, the Opinion recognizes a tension between the desirability of educating the public about their legal rights and the danger of inviting reliance on a lawyer-client relationship that the lawyer wants to avoid. The Opinion advises lawyers to make clear from the outset that they are providing only legal "information," not legal advice. It also suggests running a conflicts check before agreeing to consider client-specific information. However, the Opinion does not condemn chat rooms and notes that they someday may become useful ways to deliver legal services to poor and middle class persons who today often go unserved.

B.   THE DECISION TO REPRESENT A CLIENT

1.   Did you have an obligation to accept Cannell as your client?

a.   ABA Model Code of Professional Responsibility, EC 2–26, stated the traditional view that:

> "A lawyer is under no obligation to act as advisor or advocate for every person who may wish to become his client; but in furtherance of the objective of the bar to make legal services fully available, a lawyer should not lightly decline proffered employment. The fulfillment of this objective requires acceptance by a lawyer of his share of tendered employment which may be unattractive both to him and the bar generally."

b.   The Model Rules contain no comparable statement; the nearest analogue is Model Rule 6.2, Comment [1], dealing with the duty to accept court appointments to represent indigent clients.

2.   Is it fair to say that a lawyer makes an implicit moral decision every time the lawyer undertakes to use his or her talent and training in support of a cause?

a.   Given the fact that every client's right to have a lawyer does not necessarily translate into a personal obligation on every lawyer to undertake every proffered representation, do you agree with Professor Monroe Freedman when he says:

> "[A] lawyer's decision to represent a client may commit that lawyer to zealously furthering the interests of one whom the lawyer or others in the community believe to be morally repugnant. For that reason, the question of whether to represent a particular client can present the lawyer with an important moral decision—a decision for

---

1.   We will explore the "solicitation" implications of doing so later in Problem 31.

which the lawyer can properly be held morally accountable, in the sense of being under a burden of public justification.

"That would not be so if each lawyer were ethically bound to represent every client seeking the lawyer's services. If there were no choice, there would be no responsibility. Under both rule and practice, however, lawyers have always been free to choose whether to represent particular clients. * * * [Indeed,] the Comment to Rule 6.2 of the ABA Model Rules of Professional Conduct says * * * that a lawyer ordinarily is 'not obliged to accept a client whose character or cause the lawyer regards as repugnant.' "[2]

b. Is Model Rule 1.2(b) disingenuous, then, when it says that in accepting a representation, a lawyer does not "endorse" the "client's political economic, social or moral views or activities"?

3. Even assuming that there is no obligation to accept every client, should there be legal limits on the grounds a lawyer may rely upon to reject a case?

a. Until recently, the lawyer's right to decline a case for any reason—or no reason—has been virtually absolute, except perhaps when appointed by a court.

In Stropnicky v. Nathanson, 19 M.D.L.R. 39 (M.C.A.D. 1997), however, the Massachusetts Commission Against Discrimination found that a law firm that specialized in representing women in divorce cases violated the state's antidiscrimination law by refusing to represent a man in such a case. The firm was known as expert in obtaining awards for women who had put their husbands through professional school, and the prospective male client had done the same thing for his wife.

b. Is *Stropnicky* correctly decided? Should lawyers be permitted to devote their time and talent to representing only women? Is that different from electing to represent only corporations? Suppose the law firm wanted to represent only abused women with children? Would your answer be the different if the lawyers wanted to represent only white women? Only men? What is the basis for the distinctions you would draw?

4. Was your client's anger at the broker something you might properly have given greater weight in deciding whether to take the case?

a. Suppose you believed that your client's claim had modest merit, but that the main reason the client wanted to sue was to make the broker's life miserable. Is your time and effort something you are willing to sell simply to help a client settle a grudge? Remember that Cannell has admitted to you privately that "I knew what he was doing and I could have stopped him at any time, but I guess I got greedy."

2. Monroe Freedman, Must You Be the Devil's Advocate?, Legal Times, August 23, 1993.

b. Is there something else you should worry about in accepting Cannell's request that you represent him? He has already shown himself willing to sue one professional—the broker. Who might you worry he would choose to sue next if he were unhappy with your work? Is that appropriate to think about as you decide whether to represent Cannell?

C.   DOCUMENTING THE DECISION TO UNDERTAKE A REPRESENTATION

1.   When did Mr. Cannell become your client?

The magic moment at which someone becomes your client is an important issue in many cases seeking to define your obligations. Restatement Third, The Law Governing Lawyers § 14 says:

"A relationship of client and lawyer arises when:

"(1) a person manifests to a lawyer the person's intent that the lawyer provide legal services for the person; and either

"(a) the lawyer manifests to the person consent to do so; or

"(b) the lawyer fails to manifest lack of consent to do so, and the lawyer knows or reasonably should know that the person reasonably relies on the lawyer to provide the services * * *."

2.   Who should bear the risk of ambiguity about whether the lawyer-client relation has been formed?

a. In Togstad v. Vesely, Otto, Miller & Keefe, 291 N.W.2d 686 (Minn.1980), Mrs. Togstad consulted an attorney about a possible medical malpractice claim. The attorney said he did not believe she had a case but that he would "discuss this with his partner." The attorney did not send a bill and Mrs. Togstad waited a full year before talking to another attorney. By then, the statute of limitations had run. The first law firm was held liable to the Togstads for $649,500, the amount the jury found she would have won if the medical malpractice case had been timely filed. The informal advice the lawyer had given Mrs. Togstad about her lack of a case was both inaccurate and inadequate. At minimum, the lawyer should have told Mrs. Togstad about the statute of limitations.

b. In DeVaux v. American Home Assurance Co., 444 N.E.2d 355 (Mass.1983), the purported client wrote the firm asking for help. The lawyer's secretary misfiled the letter so that no attorney ever saw it. The client also called the office several times but her calls were not returned. The court, in denying summary judgment for the law firm, concluded that a jury might reasonably find that an attorney-client relationship was formed. Does that help clarify whether the test is whether the lawyer believed the relation had been formed or whether a reasonable client would so conclude?

3. Do limits on the scope of the representation require client consent?

a. A lawyer who fails to get such consent may later be accused of malpractice.

In Nichols v. Keller, 19 Cal.Rptr.2d 601 (Ct.App.1993), for example, the client was a construction worker who had been hit in the head by a piece of steel while on the job. He signed a retainer asking the lawyer to file a worker's compensation on his behalf. Later, Nichols learned he could have filed a third-party claim as well, and he sued the lawyer for not telling him. The Court held that when a lawyer takes on a case, the client may not know the range of remedies that is possible. It is not enough to present a retainer agreement for the worker's compensation case without discussing with the client what other remedies may be possible and either bringing those actions as well or advising the client that he may get other counsel to do so.

b. Could you properly have taken the case without getting the agreement you did to limit the issues raised? Look at Model Rule 3.1, and Comment [2], dealing with what issues you could raise in litigation.[3] What do Model Rule 1.2(c), and Comments [6]–[8] say about such limitations?   *Yes*

c. Were you wise to reach the agreement to limit the issues you would assert at the outset of the representation, as opposed to later? Typically, an agreement between lawyer and client made after representation has begun may be avoided by the client unless both the substance of the agreement and the manner of reaching it are shown by the lawyer to have been fair and reasonable to the client. Terzis v. Estate of Whalen, 489 A.2d 608 (N.H.1985) (attempt to revise fee agreement); Restatement Third, The Law Governing Lawyers § 18(1)(a).

4. What matters will you want to address in any engagement letter with your client?

a. At the outset of any representation, a lawyer should prepare an "engagement letter" that will be transmitted to, and typically counter-signed by, the client. At least the following items should typically appear in a good engagement letter.[4]

(1) Who the client is (and sometimes who is *not* the client). This is particularly important in the case of a corporation with multiple subsidiaries, but it can also be important where, for example, the law firm agrees to represent a husband in drafting a will but will not be representing the wife.

(2) The fee for the representation, or the basis of the fee, and an outline of expenses for which the client will be responsible. See Model Rule

---

3. We will see this issue again in Problem 29 when we consider possible limits on the proper zeal of a prosecutor. Cf. Bill Johnson's Restaurants, Inc. v. NLRB, 461 U.S. 731, 742–43, 103 S.Ct. 2161, 2170, 76 L.Ed.2d 277, 289 (1983) (In light of "the First Amendment right of access to the courts," the "filing and prosecution of a well-founded lawsuit may not be enjoined as an unfair labor practice, even if it would not have been commenced but for plaintiff's desire to retaliate against the defendant for exercising rights protected by the [National Labor Relations] Act.").

4. We will take up the substantive content of various of these items in later Problems.

1.5(b) & (c). It is also helpful to specify when bills will be rendered, how promptly they must be paid, and whether interest will be charged for late payments.

(3) The scope of the representation, i.e., what the lawyer is undertaking to do and not to do. See Model Rules 1.2(c) and 1.5(b). This Problem illustrates the negotiation of such matters with a prospective client, but the point is important in any case to avoid malpractice liability for matters the firm never thought it was supposed to undertake and to establish what work is covered by the fee.

(4) Conflicts of interest the lawyer may have and sufficient information to let the client give informed consent if it is willing waive the conflicts. See Model Rule 1.7 and 1.9.

(5) Any departures from the usual assumptions about handling confidential information, such as a possible agreement to share information between spouses who come in for joint estate planning. See Model Rule 1.6.

(6) Undertakings the client will be asked to make in connection with the representation, such as an agreement to be candid with the lawyer about the relevant facts.[5]

b.   Similarly, if a lawyer decides not to represent a client, a wise lawyer will send a letter documenting that fact so as to avoid a later claim that the prospective client reasonably believed the lawyer had undertaken the representation.

D.   DECISION-MAKING DURING REPRESENTATION—ISSUES THE LAWYER IS TO DECIDE AND ISSUES RESERVED TO THE CLIENT

1.   Should you have to get permission from your client to say what you plan to say in the pleading about his lack of financial sophistication?

a.   Look at Model Rules 1.6 and 2.1. Is your client reasonably entitled to be interested in what you say about him in a public document?

b.   Assume that you explain the pleading to Cannell and he says, "I'm paying you to represent me; I don't want you to say that." Your firm has a reputation as a tough litigator, and you are reluctant to abandon your best argument. May you, notwithstanding client objection, make the argument? Are Model Rule 1.2(a), and its Comments [1] & [2], helpful on this issue?

2.   May the client require you to make an argument that, although not frivolous, seems to you to be a loser that will weaken the case?

a.   Suppose Mr. Cannell has a theory that the broker's firm had registered its name incorrectly, for example. You explain the weakness of that argument, but the client insists that you use it anyway and you have

---

5. More suggestions for engagement letters, file control and the like, may be found in Ronald E. Mallen & Jeffrey M. Smith, Legal Malpractice, Chapter 2 (5th ed. 2000).

to admit that doing so would not violate Model Rule 3.1. If you may make the argument, must you do so? *No, same as a.)*

b. Is making such an argument a matter of "objectives" or "means" as those terms are used in Model Rule 1.2? Does Comment [2] to Rule 1.2 provide much help about how such disagreements are to be resolved?

c. Notice that Rule 1.2 expects that the "communication" required by Rule 1.4 will ordinarily be sufficient for the lawyer and client to reach agreement about most important issues. Look at new Rule 1.4(a)(2) and Comment [3]. What is the lawyer supposed to do if the disagreement about use of the argument cannot be resolved?

3. May a lawyer accept what the lawyer thinks is a good settlement of a civil case?

a. Look at Model Rule 1.2(a). Who has the authority to decide whether or not to settle a civil case? The answer can create tension between lawyer and client. *Client*

b. In Auvil v. Grafton Homes, Inc., 92 F.3d 226 (4th Cir.1996), the lawyers had agreed upon a settlement to recommend to their clients. Each then told the other he had received approval from his client, but Auvil later denied he had given that authority. As a result, the court held that Grafton Homes could not hold Auvil to the agreement. Giving a lawyer authority to conduct settlement negotiations, the court said, <u>does not create apparent authority to consummate the agreement</u>. Some additional act of client consent to the settlement or waiver of the right to approve the settlement is required. See also Restatement Third, The Law Governing Lawyers § 22 (authority reserved to client); § 26 (lawyer's actual authority); § 30(3) (lawyer's liability to third person for [unauthorized] conduct on behalf of client).

c. In re Lewis, 463 S.E.2d 862 (Ga.1995), in turn, suspended a lawyer for 18 months for requiring the client to give the lawyer blanket authority to settle. <u>The client always has the right to decide on settlement,</u> the Court said, and a contingent fee agreement cannot be used as a vehicle to waive that right so as to let the lawyer make decisions in a way that will maximize the lawyer's fee.

4. Is Model Rule 1.2(a) wise to also give the client exclusive authority to decide what plea to enter in a criminal case?

a. Giving a defendant authority analogous to that seemed questionable in People v. Bloom, 48 Cal.3d 1194, 259 Cal.Rptr. 669, 774 P.2d 698 (1989). By the time of the penalty phase of his murder trial, Bloom demanded to address the jury directly and ask that they sentence him to death. Both the trial judge and the defense counsel tried to talk Bloom out of his decision, but he insisted and the jury gave him his wish. Ultimately, so did the Supreme Court of California, which said:

> "Given the importance which the decisions of both this court and the United States Supreme Court have attached to an accused's ability to control his or her own destiny and to make fundamental decisions

Seamless Web

affecting trial of the action, and given this court's recognition that it is not irrational to prefer the death penalty to life imprisonment without parole, it would be incongruous to hold that a trial court lacked power to grant a mid-trial motion for self-representation in a capital case merely because the accused stated an intention to seek a death verdict. While we do not suggest that trial courts must or even should grant such mid-trial motions, we do not find the trial court's ruling on the motion in this case to be violative of defendant's rights or contrary to any fundamental public policy."

Do you agree? Does this decision take deference to client wishes beyond all reasonable limits? Is it really allowing the client to choose death with what to him may seem relative dignity?

b. On the other hand, would a court be required to ignore efforts of lawyers to prevent the defendant's attempt to commit suicide? Might the Court in *Bloom* have believed simply that a defendant must be bound by what he has elected to do so that he cannot later rely upon his own bad judgment as a basis for a new trial?

5. What values are really at stake in the question of who controls the litigation?

a. Do you agree with the commentator who argued: "Unless the client chooses to delegate decision-making authority to the lawyer, the client should be presumed to have control over all aspects of his case. [Client control increases] the moral force and acceptability of the decisions made by the system, in that each party has had the opportunity 'to choose his strategy, plot his fate, and rise or fall by his own choices.' * * * When the lawyer, as a representative, acts without authority, he violates the clients integrity by presenting the client falsely to others."[6] If all key decisions have to be made by the client, what is the professional role of the lawyer?

b. Does it follow that the client should be able to control your decisions about trial strategy? How about your decisions to show common courtesy? Suppose that after you file the complaint, defense counsel asks you for a short delay to allow him extra time to file an answer. May the client forbid you to grant any delays on the ground that he is anxious to move the case along? Suppose the client is simply so angry at the broker that he does not want to give any quarter?

c. Restatement Third, The Law Governing Lawyers § 23 identifies only two matters that are beyond the reach of client direction. The lawyer may alone decide "to refuse to * * * [act in a way] that the lawyer reasonably believes to be unlawful," and "to take actions * * * that the

---

6. Mark Spiegel, Lawyering and Client Decision–Making: Informed Consent and the Legal Professional, 128 U. Pennsylvania L. Rev. 41, 73–76 (1979). See also Mark Spiegel, The New Model Rules of Professional Con- duct: Lawyer–Client Decision–Making and the Role of Rules in Structuring Lawyer– Client Dialogue, 1980 Amer. Bar Foundation Res. J. 1003.

lawyer reasonably believes to be required by law or an order of a tribunal.''
Do you agree that lawyers require no more inherent discretion than that?

d. Suppose Mr. Cannell had been investing the $200,000 as trustee
for his grandchildren. Would that change your obligation to follow the
client's directions? Suppose a trustee asked you to settle the case on terms
that would enrich himself, but not benefit the trust?

The point is that a client's authority to direct a lawyer depends in part
on restrictions the law imposes on the client's conduct. If in your own
practice, you knowingly accept a direction the client does not have legal
authority to give, you may be liable to the party to whom the client owed
duties. As you will see later in Problem 22, many lawyers paid substantial
sums in damages to the receiver of their savings and loan clients for
accepting direction from officers of those clients to do things the officers
were not authorized by law to have the clients do. E.g., F.D.I.C. v. Mmahat,
907 F.2d 546 (5th Cir.1990)(general counsel for a now-defunct savings and
loan, and his law firm, found liable for legal malpractice through a jury
verdict for $35 million); F.D.I.C. v. O'Melveny & Myers, 969 F.2d 744 (9th
Cir.1992), rev'd on other grounds sub nom. O'Melveny & Myers v. F.D.I.C.,
512 U.S. 79, 114 S.Ct. 2048, 129 L.Ed.2d 67 (1994).

―――――

PROBLEM 5

BILLING FOR LEGAL SERVICES

Noble as it might seem to pretend otherwise, the ability to earn a
substantial fee is a major part of many lawyers' decisions to take some
cases and reject others. How lawyers charge for their work, however, has
varied over the years. For a long time, lawyers charged fixed fees for
routine work. Indeed, not that many years ago, local bar associations
published schedules of minimum fees for particular services and lawyers in
that area adhered to them.

Goldfarb v. Virginia State Bar, 421 U.S. 773, 95 S.Ct. 2004, 44 L.Ed.2d
572 (1975), however, changed all that. The Supreme Court of the United
States intervened in the world of the previously state-regulated legal
profession and held that such "minimum fee schedules" violate the antitrust laws. Since *Goldfarb,* other bases for setting fees have assumed more
importance. Fees based on hourly rates, for example, have dominated life in
most firms in recent years, while contingent fees continue to predominate
in personal injury cases. This Problem first asks when a fee agreement
must be reached, then what limit the law imposes on the size of a lawyer's
fee. We then consider specialized rules applicable to contingent fees, and
finally, problems surrounding hourly rate fees as well.

FACTS

A well-known local psychiatrist has a contract claim for about
$100,000 against a local firm. The matter appears to be of average

complexity. She has brought her case to attorney Paul T. Novak. "I'll take your case," Novak says. "My fee will be only 44 per cent of the amount recovered." Shocked, the psychiatrist says that she has never heard of even psychiatrists charging such high fees. "One-third is average," Novak tells her. "I am giving you a bargain. I am only charging you one-third more than the going rate and I am at least twice as good as the average lawyer."

Novak also has agreed to represent a plaintiff in a personal injury suit for a "discount" contingent fee of one-third of the amount recovered. The other side has offered, before Novak begins work, to pay his client $15,000. Based on what he knows about the case, Novak believes the actual damages that a jury would award would be more like $60,000, but it would take him about 200 hours of work to recover that amount, and, of course, the client might possibly not recover anything at all. Novak has concluded that it is best to recommend to the client that he accept the $15,000 immediately so that Novak can pocket a $5,000 fee with little effort and go on to the next case.

When a prospective client asked Novak about his willingness to charge a fee on an hourly-rate basis, Novak simply laughed and said he would never agree to charge fees on any basis other than one that let him share in any good result. Novak added that other lawyers charge hourly fees and the prospective client could always go there.

QUESTIONS

A. THE FEE AGREEMENT BETWEEN LAWYER AND CLIENT

1. Must a lawyer's fee agreement be in writing?

a. Notice that Model Rule 1.5(c) requires a written agreement in the case of a contingent fee but Model Rule 1.5(b) declares only that a written agreement is "preferable." Does that distinction make sense to you?

Starkey, Kelly, Blaney & White v. Estate of Nicolaysen, 796 A.2d 238 (N.J.2002), dealt with the Rule 1.5(c) requirement that a contingent fee agreement be in writing. The law firm represented an elderly couple who were attempting to sell their farm. The firm had represented the couple over several years, and the parties initially entered into an oral contingent fee agreement that entitled the attorney to 30% of any purchase price obtained in excess of the price in an earlier contract. The firm did not reduce the agreement to writing for two-and-a-half years, however, and when it did, the percentage was reduced to 20%. The couple died before the farm was sold, and when the attorneys sought payment from the couple's estate, the beneficiaries refused to recognize the fee agreement. They argued it was invalid because the attorneys had waited too long to formalize it. The Supreme Court of New Jersey agreed, and refused to uphold the contract. The Court found, however, that the attorneys satisfied the requirements for *quantum meruit* recovery by showing (1) that legal services had been performed in good faith, and (2) that the clients had accepted the services, (3) with expectation of payment for the services, (4) and the value of the services could be ascertained.

b.   Should the law require all fee agreements to be in writing? DC Rule of Professional Conduct 1.5(b), for example, requires a writing in all cases where the lawyer has not regularly represented the client before.

c.   Might the requirement turn instead on how large the bill is likely to be? California Business & Professions Code § 6148 requires a writing when it is "reasonably foreseeable" that fees and expenses in a matter will exceed $1000.

d.   Would Novak be wise to rely on an oral agreement to be paid an hourly fee? Regardless of any formal requirement, would you want to put the agreement in writing for your own protection and possible use in later efforts to collect the fee?

2.   The 2002 revision of Model Rule 1.5(a) added a requirement that expenses charged by a lawyer be made a part of the fee agreement. Why might it be important to spell out responsibility for those expenses?

a.   Would it shock you to know that some lawyers view their copy machine as a profit center in their practice, charging 25 cents or more per page copied? One lawyer once called the firm's photocopy machine a "silent partner." Should a firm charge the client $1 per page faxed, even for local calls? Can you think of other ways in which a client might feel cheated if not told in advance how a lawyer planned to bill expenses?

b.   Does this requirement in Model Rule 1.5(a) now make it presumptively unreasonable for a lawyer to fly first-class? Assume that the bill to the client accurately lists all expenses, such as "first class round trip, L.A. to NYC, $1,688." Is it inherently unreasonable for a lawyer to order an expensive wine with dinner? In short, what constitutes an "unreasonable amount for expenses" in violation of Model Rule 1.5(a)?

c.   Do the eight factors listed in Model Rule 1.5(a) help you answer that question? Those factors were originally intended to define what constitutes an unreasonable fee; one can argue they are not of much help with respect to expenses.

Columbus Bar Association v. Brooks, 721 N.E.2d 23 (Ohio 1999), suspended a lawyer for two years, all but six months stayed, for various violations, including collecting a one-third contingent fee but then also charging an hourly rate for the lawyer's secretary and paralegal as additional expenses. The court found that, unless clearly agreed otherwise in writing, secretarial and legal assistant expenses are general overhead, not separately billable: "by collecting for secretarial and law clerk expenses, in addition to filing fees, deposition fees, and his thirty-three percent of the settlement, respondent did not adhere to his written contract with the Jacksons and thereby charged a clearly excessive fee in violation of DR 2–106(A)."

d. Does Comment [1] to Rule 1.5 give more help in understanding what costs are reasonable? Does it limit the lawyer to simply passing through out-of-pocket costs? Should it be limited in that way?

ABA Formal Opinion 00–420 (2000) considered whether a firm may add a surcharge in billing for the services of a contract attorney that it hires to work on a case. Absent a separate agreement, the Opinion says, if the firm treats the work as an expense item (over and above its fee), the firm must bill only what it actually paid for the contract lawyer's services. If the contract lawyer is billed as just another lawyer whose work makes up the fee for the matter, on the other hand, the firm may bill any reasonable rate for the services just as it does for one of its associates.

3. Should a lawyer be permitted to charge a client a "nonrefundable retainer"? That is, may the lawyer say that her entire fee is payable before any work is begun and is not refundable even if the work turns out to take little time or if the client later fires the lawyer?

a. Matter of Cooperman, 633 N.E.2d 1069 (N.Y.1994), ruled that many non–refundable fees are invalid. Cooperman in effect told his clients, "Once I enter an appearance in this case, even if you fire me, I will not have to return any part of the fee." In at least three cases, the clients fired him before he did much work. Non-refundable fees violate the fiduciary relationship between lawyer and client, the Court of Appeals argued; they inhibit the client's right to terminate the lawyer. Thus, the court affirmed the lawyer's two-year suspension from practice.[1] But the court said: "Minimum fee arrangements and general retainers that provide for fees, not laden with the nonrefundability impediment irrespective of any services, will continue to be valid and not subject in and of themselves to professional discipline."

b. Do you agree that the issue is that simple? Suppose a lawyer incurs real opportunity costs by taking a case? What if the client tells the lawyer he wants her to set aside the month of May to try a matter. She agrees to do so for a "non-refundable" fee of $25,000, her typical monthly billing, and turns down work she would otherwise do in May. On April 30, the client fires the lawyer. Is it clear the lawyer should not be able to keep all or most of the fee?

c. Consider Raymark Industries, Inc. v. Butera, Beausang, Cohen & Brennan, 1997 WL 746125 (E.D.Pa.1997), aff'd 193 F.3d 210 (3d Cir. 1999), where a client adopted an aggressive strategy for defense of asbestos cases

---

1. Kelly v. MD Buyline, Inc., 2 F.Supp.2d 420 (S.D.N.Y.1998), distinguished *Cooperman* as only involving single-case, or "special" retainers; a non-refundability retainer is permissible if it is for a fixed amount to be available for a defined period. "[G]eneral retainer agreements provide that the attorney will be available for a period of time, whereas in 'special' retainer agreements the attorney is hired to handle a specific case or matter." The court concluded that a three-year retainer agreement was a *general* retainer agreement and, thus, was enforceable, despite the client's claim that agreement was a nonrefundable *special* retainer agreement that violated New York public policy.

against it, including filing suits against opposing counsel. To control overall costs, it retained firms at fixed fees of $1 million each, non-refundable. When ten weeks into work for the client, the law firm demanded time to investigate before filing a suit accusing another law firm of wrongdoing, the client fired the firm and demanded its million dollars back. The court said the firm could keep it. The fee agreement had been proposed by a sophisticated client, and while that client can terminate the relationship at any time, the law firm had performed properly and may keep its fee.[2]

d. On the other hand, the point of the *Cooperman* rule is suggested by Federal Savings & Loan Insurance Corp. v. Angell, Holmes & Lea, 838 F.2d 395 (9th Cir.1988), cert. denied sub nom. Van Voorhis & Skaggs v. FSLIC, 488 U.S. 848, 109 S.Ct. 127, 102 L.Ed.2d 100 (1988). The savings and loan paid its counsel a large fee that purported to be nonrefundable. Three weeks later, the client went into receivership. The FSLIC fired the lawyer and asked for return of the retainer. Because a client is always free to fire its lawyer, the firm had to return all but a reasonable fee for work done before termination. Put into that context, where the lawyer has no opportunity cost, does the rule make more sense?[3]

4. Should a lawyer be able to increase her fees during the course of the representation?

a. Severson & Werson v. Bolinger, 1 Cal.Rptr.2d 531 (Ct.App.1991), says the issue turns on the understanding of a reasonable client. The firm's standard contract said the client would pay the firm's "regular hourly rates" and the client had been told orally what those rates were. The court held that under these circumstances, the firm could not increase the rates it charged the client "without notice."

b. The court left open the option of giving notice of an increase and then imposing it if the client did not object. But what if the client objects? Should a client have a right to insist that a lawyer's rates be frozen for the many years it may take to complete a matter? Remember that, as discussed in Problem 4, a lawyer and client may revise their agreement as to scope of work and fees after the representation has begun, but at that point the lawyer assumes a greater burden of showing the agreement to be fair and

---

2. See also, National Credit Union Administration Board v. Johnson, 133 F.3d 1097 (8th Cir.1998) (lawyer not necessarily required to refund a non-refundable retainer paid by a credit union right before it was taken over by the government).

In re Sather, 3 P.3d 403 (Colo.2000), raised the question how a lawyer must account for a non-refundable retainer. This lawyer did not put the retainer into his trust account, arguing it had been fully earned upon accepting the retainer. A lawyer is entitled to a fee only after doing work to earn it, the court says. "Engagement retainers" may be justified if the lawyer turns down other work or otherwise benefits the client, but even flat fees must be put into a trust account, the court said, because otherwise the client might be deterred from discharging the lawyer. See also, Matter of Dawson, 8 P.3d 856 (N.M.2000), to the same effect.

3. See also, In re Gastineau, 857 P.2d 136 (Ore.1993) (non-refundable flat-fee not per se improper, but result in a prohibited unreasonable fee where the lawyer did not do the necessary legal work); In re Hirschfeld, 960 P.2d 640 (Ariz.1998) (failure to return unearned portions of non-refundable retainers rendered fees unreasonable).

reasonable. See Restatement Third, The Law Governing Lawyers § 18(1)(a) (post-contract modifications must be "fair and reasonable to the client").

B.   The requirement that a lawyer charge only a "reasonable" fee

1.   Is the fee Novak proposes to charge the psychiatrist unreasonable?

a.   Should any fee negotiated at arms length between the lawyer and a competent adult ever be held to be unreasonable?

In re Fordham, 668 N.E.2d 816 (Mass.1996), involved the public censure of a prominent lawyer who charged a client $50,000 to defend the client's son's drunken driving case. The evidence showed that other lawyers would have taken the case for between $3,000 and $10,000. The lawyer billed at his large firm's regular hourly rates and the son was acquitted, but the client balked at paying such a large amount. The court found the hours the firm spent on the case were disproportionate to its difficulty and saw fit to publicly embarrass the lawyer through discipline.

See also Matter of Hanna, 362 S.E.2d 632 (S.C.1987), where the lawyer charged 40% to collect the no-fault benefits under a client's auto policy. The benefits were "no-fault," so there really was no contingency. The court found the fee excessive and publicly reprimanded the lawyer conditioned upon his restitution.

b.   On the other hand, might one argue that any fee arrangement presents an inherent conflict of interest because it creates a way for an unscrupulous lawyer to put his or her interest ahead of the client's? Indeed, might the process of agreeing upon a fee itself be inherently "unethical" because it is the one time in the lawyer-client relationship that the lawyer and client are adversaries?

2.   Are there important reasons for limiting freedom of contract between lawyer and client? What might the reasons be?

a.   In American Home Assurance Co. v. Golomb, 606 N.E.2d 793 (Ill.App.1992), a lawyer in a medical malpractice case had his clients sign an agreement purporting to pay a contingent fee of 40% and to "hold the lawyer harmless" from any reduction of fees required by an Illinois statute limiting fees in such cases. The court held the fee contract void and encouraging an illegal act and it denied the lawyer all fees for the representation, even on a quantum meruit basis.

b.   White v. McBride, 937 S.W.2d 796 (Tenn.1996), involved a contract to charge a 1/3 contingent fee to help a surviving spouse collect what was due to him from his wife's estate. The client had an inventory of the wife's assets and there was very little to do. The court held that the lawyer's continuing effort to collect the unreasonable fee showed his conduct was not inadvertent, so he lost his right to collect a fee on a quantum meruit basis as well.

c.   In re Green, 11 P.3d 1078 (Colo.2000), found a fee excessive when it was based on time the *lawyer* spent faxing documents, calling the clerk's office, and other tasks that would usually be done by an assistant. "There is no reason or excuse for charging a client," the court said, "for one's own inefficiencies."

3. Might a local bar association simply adopt a schedule of fees that lawyers would be required to charge for particular services?

a. Goldfarb v. Virginia State Bar, 421 U.S. 773, 95 S.Ct. 2004, 44 L.Ed.2d 572 (1975), established that such a fee schedule would violate the antitrust law. The *Goldfarb* plaintiffs needed a title examination to secure title insurance and only a member of the Virginia State Bar could legally perform that service. Their lawyer "quoted them the precise fee suggested in a minimum fee schedule published by respondent Fairfax County Bar Association," and no other lawyer would charge them less than that rate. The bar association was "a purely voluntary association of attorneys" with "no formal enforcement powers." In principle, the state disciplinary agency could have charged lawyers with improperly soliciting clients if they regularly charged less than the prescribed fee, but it had never done so. Petitioners argued that the use of such a minimum fee schedule constituted price fixing in violation of § 1 of the Sherman Act, and the Supreme Court unanimously agreed.

The County Bar had argued that lawyers were members of a "learned profession," not engaged in "trade or commerce," and thus not subject to the Sherman Act. But the Court answered that the "public service aspect of professional practice [is not] controlling in determining whether § 1 includes professions. * * * Whatever else it may be, the examination of a land title is a service; the exchange of such a service for money is 'commerce' in the most common usage of that word. It is no disparagement of the practice of law as a profession to acknowledge that it has this business aspect * * *." 421 U.S. at 787–88, 95 S.Ct. at 2013, 44 L.Ed.2d at 585.

The Court acknowledged that a "purely advisory fee schedule issued to provide guidelines, or an exchange of price information without a showing of an actual restraint on trade, would present us with a different question," but in this case "the desire of attorneys to comply with announced professional norms; the motivation to conform was reinforced by the assurance that other lawyers would not compete by underbidding." 421 U.S. at 781–82, 95 S.Ct. at 2010, 44 L.Ed.2d at 581.

Finally, the Court distinguished situations where a state agency sets the prices for services:

"In Parker v. Brown, 317 U.S. 341, 63 S.Ct. 307, 87 L.Ed. 315 (1943), the Court held that an anticompetitive marketing program 'which derived its authority and efficacy from the legislative command of the state' was not a violation of the Sherman Act because the Act was intended to regulate private practices and not to prohibit a State from imposing a restraint as an act of government. Respondent State Bar and respondent County Bar both seek to avail themselves of this so-called state action exemption.

" * * * [However, h]ere we need not inquire further into the state action question because it cannot fairly be said that the State of Virginia through its Supreme Court Rules. required the anticompetitive activities of either respondent." 421 U.S. at 788–90, 95 S.Ct. at 2014–15, 44 L.Ed.2d at 585–86.

b.   Should *Goldfarb* also prohibit lawyers from agreeing to maximum fees? For example, might a local voluntary bar association, in an effort to deal with complaints that lawyers make too much money, publish a schedule of maximum fees in routine cases? See, e.g., Arizona v. Maricopa County Medical Society, 457 U.S. 332, 102 S.Ct. 2466, 73 L.Ed.2d 48 (1982) (schedule of maximum rates to be reimbursed by insurance companies held per se illegal).

c.   After *Goldfarb*, could lawyers seek to take advantage of the "state action" exemption by lobbying their state supreme court or legislature to enact into law the minimum fee schedule that *Goldfarb* held violated the Sherman Act? Lawyers did not respond to *Goldfarb* in that way. Why might they have been reluctant to do so?

d.   After *Goldfarb*, could bar associations publish reports explaining what fees would tend to produce different levels of lawyer income, taking into account normal overhead? Should they be permitted to do so?

4. How would you apply the factors in Model Rule 1.5(a) to the fee Novak has charged the psychiatrist?

a.   Is the case likely to take extraordinary skill, for example? Has the doctor set unusual time limitations on the lawyer's work? Do Novak's reputation and experience justify a higher than normal fee?

b.   Rule 4–200(B)(11) of the Rules of Professional Conduct of the State Bar of California provides that, among the factors that may be considered in determining the reasonableness of the fee is the "informed consent of the client to the fee." Should that factor be added to the ABA Model Rules as well?

5. May a lawyer properly consider the client's ability to pay in setting a "reasonable" fee? Assume the lawyer would be charging some clients more than others for the same kind of work. Should that be improper?

a.   May wealthy clients be charged an otherwise "unreasonable" fee in order to subsidize work done without compensation? Even if we do not explicitly tolerate such overcharging, is that the practical effect of charging some clients more than others for the same kind of work?

b.   Look at Model Rule 1.5, Comment [5]. What does the Comment mean when it says that "it is proper to define the extent of services in light of the client's ability to pay?" Does it shock you to think that a lawyer might agree to do less for a poor client than she would for a more prosperous one? In any event, must that Comment be read in light of

Model Rule 1.1 that requires a lawyer to deliver at least "competent" representation in any case?

6. At what point in the case should one judge the reasonableness of a fee?

a. If a case turns out to be resolved more easily than expected, should a client be able to have a large fee reduced? Restatement Third, The Law Governing Lawyers § 34, Comment *c*, says:

> "Although reasonableness is usually assessed as of the time the contract was entered into, later events might be relevant. * * * [E]vents not known or contemplated when the contract was made can render the contract unreasonably favorable to the lawyer or, occasionally, to the client. Compare Restatement Second, Contracts §§ 152–154 and 261–265 (doctrines of mistake, supervening impracticality, supervening frustration). To determine what events client and lawyer contemplated, their contract must be construed in light of its goals and circumstances and in light of the possibilities discussed with the client * * *. Events within [the contemplated] range of risks, such as a high recovery, do not make unreasonable a contract that was reasonable when made."

b. Do you agree that this standard captures the proper considerations in evaluating a fee after the work is done? Do you believe the standard will be easy to apply in concrete cases?

7. Should a trial judge be permitted to raise *sua sponte* whether an excessive fee is being charged by counsel?

a. Gagnon v. Shoblom, 565 N.E.2d 775 (Mass.1991), gave the usual answer. A truck driver had severely injured the plaintiff when he crashed into the plaintiff's trailer. The plaintiff signed a 33% contingent fee agreement and after extensive discovery, there was a settlement for $2.9 million. The trial judge thought a fee of $975,000 was too large for the case, and, although the plaintiff had not complained, the judge lowered the fee to $695,000. The Massachusetts Supreme Court held that a trial judge has no such general authority to lower a fee on his own motion.

b. United States v. Strawser, 800 F.2d 704 (7th Cir.1986), cert. denied sub nom. Anderson v. United States, 480 U.S. 906, 107 S.Ct. 1350, 94 L.Ed.2d 521 (1987), on the other hand, involved a situation where the criminal defendant's payment of an excessive fee in Case 1 meant that the defendant was indigent and needed appointed counsel in Case 2. On those facts, the court said, it was proper to order part of the excessive fee in Case 1 refunded.

c. In re A.H. Robins, 86 F.3d 364 (4th Cir.1996), upheld the district court's imposition of a limit on contingent fees to 10% as it applied to distribution of certain amounts still remaining in the trust. The 29 lawyers had already received over $90 million in fees, and even the new limitation allowed them to receive another $20 million for no additional work. However, it did deny them the full additional $66 million that they had requested.

C.   SPECIAL RULES APPLICABLE TO CONTINGENT FEES

1.   In England, the contingent fee was traditionally considered inherently unethical as a violation of the rule against champerty that prohibited supporting a lawsuit in exchange for a share in the expected recovery.[4] Should the same be true in this country?

a.   The contingent fee is sometimes called a "poor-person's fee." Should a contingent fee be improper if the client can afford to pay an hourly rate? Why might a corporation or wealthy individual prefer a contingent fee in some cases?

b.   The Chicago Council of Lawyers has suggested "that the contingent fee 'problem' is a symptom, rather than a cause of a much wider problem—the unequal access to the courts for the poor and near poor."[5] Thus, the Council favors dealing with that "wider problem." Do you agree? In what ways might a system of prepaid legal insurance, for example, radically change the calculation as to the proper time to charge a contingent fee? Would that be a change for the better? Should that affect the bar's position on prepaid insurance?[6]

c.   Should a lawyer have to advise a client that he or she may choose between a contingent fee and a non-contingent fee? What is now Model Rule 1.5, Comment [5] used to say:

> "When there is doubt whether a contingent fee is consistent with the client's best interest, the lawyer should offer the client alternative bases for the fee and explain their implications."

The 2002 revisions deleted that sentence. Does that mean that lawyers may insist on contingent fees even if they are not in their client's best interests? Would a lawyer who did so be breaching his or her fiduciary obligations to the client?

Drafters of the change were told that some lawyers—like Novak in our Problem—only charge contingent fees. Does that justify the deletion? In such a situation, would it simply make sense for the lawyer to say, "In this circumstance, where there is strict liability and only a minor dispute over damages, it may make more sense for you to pay a lawyer an hourly fee. I only work for contingent fees, but I can recommend others who charge hourly or fixed fees."

2.   May Novak claim a $5,000 fee in the personal injury suit if the case is settled before he begins work?

a.   What if Novak says that the reason the defendant quickly offered to settle is because he knew that Novak now represented the plaintiff? Is it enough to say that Novak needs to make a few big fees, as here, to make up

---

4. England no longer prohibits all contingent fees, although their use is still less frequent than in the United States.

5. Chicago Council of Lawyers, Report on Code of Professional Responsibility 20 (1972).

6. Issues relating to prepaid legal insurance will be taken up in Problem 34 of these materials.

for the losing cases on which he realizes nothing? Judge John Grady has written a provocative article that takes that argument head on:[7]

"I propose to analyze the typical automobile accident case * * * [that] accounts for the vast majority of personal injury claims. * * * I think it should take a competent lawyer no more than 15 hours to prepare this type of case for trial. * * * The trial itself should not take more than * * * about ten hours in court and five hours spent before and after court sessions at the office, including any time required for post-trial motions. * * *

"Let us assume that the lawyer has taken the case on a one-third contingent basis, which is typical. If plaintiff's injury was not very serious—assume he sustained soft tissue injuries with modest special damages—we might have a verdict of $4,500. This would certainly be in the low range of cases that would be thought worth trying to a jury verdict. On such a verdict, the lawyer would receive a fee of $1,500, which, divided by his 30 hours of effort, results in compensation at the rate of $50 per hour. * * *

"What causes me to question the propriety of the ever-increasing fee in proportion to the size of the verdict is this: there is little, if any, relationship between the efforts of the lawyer and the size of the verdict, once we assume a verdict in favor of the plaintiff. The size of the verdict is determined by the nature and extent of the plaintiff's injury and resulting damages. Conceding that some lawyers are more brilliant and more eloquent than others, we flatter ourselves unduly if we think the performance of counsel is a large factor in the size of the verdict. * * * To illustrate the point, the identical collision can cause a whiplash injury or result in an amputation of a leg. * * * But even though the same amount of work is involved, the whiplash verdict might be $4,500, for a fee of $50 per hour, while the amputation verdict might be $200,000, providing a fee of more than $6,000 per hour. * * *

"Another fortuitous circumstance affecting the fee is the number of claimants the lawyer represents in a particular case. Assume that a father, mother and two children are struck at an intersection and all of them sustain injuries. The liability evidence is the same for all. Frequently, they will have the same doctor, who simply brings four sets of records to court instead of one. His testimony takes longer, and I admit that there is some additional work required of the lawyer. However, in the typical case of four plaintiffs, the additional work is not at all proportionate to the additional fees the lawyer will realize when he charges each of the plaintiffs the same percentage, which— make no mistake about it—is what he ordinarily does. * * *

7. John F. Grady, Some Ethical Questions About Percentage Fees, 2 Litigation 20 (Summer, 1976). Copyright 1976 by the American Bar Association. Used with permission.

"Thus far, I have been raising questions about the propriety of the fees charged in cases tried to verdict. As we all know, however, * * * [r]oughly 90 percent of the cases filed are settled before trial commences. * * * The ethical questions presented in the settled cases are, I think, even more serious than those presented by the cases which are tried. In the case of the $45,000 settlement, for example, how can a $15,000 fee be justified? Such a fee amounts to $1,000 an hour, assuming the lawyer has completed his trial preparation and settles just as the trial is about to start. But it might not happen that way. The case may be settled before suit is even filed, or shortly after it is filed, or midway through discovery. In any of those situations (and, again, confining ourselves to the simple automobile accident case), the lawyer will spend less than 15 hours. * * *

" * * * Surely there is much to be said for providing a means to permit indigent persons to engage counsel to press meritorious suits. * * * [But t]he problem, it seems to me, is that we have regarded the 'one-third contingent fee' arrangement as applicable to all cases involving personal injuries, without paying enough attention to the facts of the particular case and the needs of the particular client. * * *

"One sometimes hears the argument that the attorney is entitled to collect his 'third' in easy cases to make up for all the 'losers' he handles. This explanation does not withstand analysis. Putting aside for a moment the question of whether one client can properly be surcharged to compensate for the deficiencies in another client's case, the fact of the matter is that there just are not very many 'losers.' As we have seen, at least 95 percent of the total claims handled by lawyers are settled before trial, and many of these settlements involve very little work on the part of the lawyer. * * *

"I think we must start determining our fee charges in personal injury cases on the same basis we determine fees in any other kind of litigation. * * * Specifically, I think the lawyer must consider at least these three questions in each case:

"1. Is there a genuine and substantial question on liability, or is the only real question the amount of damages?

"2. Is the case likely to be settled or tried to verdict?

"3. Is the amount of the recovery likely to be small or large—for example, is it a soft tissue injury or does it involve the death of the family breadwinner?

"Until the lawyer knows the answers to these questions, he has insufficient basis for determining whether a percentage fee is proper and, if proper, what percentage would be fair."

b. Do you agree with Judge Grady? Should clients simply shop around for the best lawyer at the lowest price? When we discuss advertising of legal services in Problem 31, you will see that it is easier to shop around now than when Judge Grady wrote his article. However, based on what you have observed about law practice, do you think clients are likely to be offered a wide range of contingent fee percentages?

Note also that Judge Grady says, "there is little, if any, relationship between the efforts of the lawyer and the size of the verdict, once we assume a verdict in favor of the plaintiff." Is that an heroic assumption? When the client has a 90% chance of winning, he doesn't get 10 throws of the dice with the jury, only one. Is Judge Grady's point that most cases are settled and never get to the jury, so that genuinely injured plaintiffs can reasonably assume they will win at least something?

c. One court has established and enforced a schedule of maximum fees in medical malpractice cases. The schedule provides for 30% on the first $250,000 recovered, 25% on the next $250,000; 20% on the next $500,000, 15% on the next $250,000, and 10% thereafter. An attorney's fee at or below these sums is conclusively deemed "reasonable." Any sum in excess of these figures is by definition "unconscionable" unless approved by the court.[8] Would you favor such an approach?

d. Levine v. Bayne, Snell & Krause, Ltd., 40 S.W.3d 92 (Tex.2001), decided an interesting question about how to determine the amount on which a contingent fee should be calculated. The Levines had agreed to pay a fee of one-third of "any amount received" from against the Smiths for defects in their house. Because of the defects, the Levines had stopped making contract payments to the Smiths, so the Smiths filed a counter-claim. At the end of the day, the Levines recovered about $240,000 and the Smiths about $160,000, leaving a net to the Levines of about $80,000. The question became whether the Levines owed a contingent fee based on $240,000 or $80,000. The court saw that the Levines had gotten $240,000 worth of benefit because they now owned the house free of the mortgage, but it said the better interpretation of the words "any amount received" was to base the fee on the net, or $80,000. The burden was said to be on lawyers to write their contracts more clearly if they intended any other result.

e. Note that Novak wanted to recommend the prompt settlement offer of $15,000 before he had really begun work on the case. Was that proper? Suppose the law required personal injury lawyers to ask the defendant to make an offer of settlement very early. If the offer were accepted, the plaintiff's lawyer would have to bill based on hours worked and the total fee could be no more than 10% of the recovery. If the initial offer were rejected, the contingent fee could be charged on only so much of the ultimate recovery as exceeded the initial offer.

Would you favor such a plan? What would it do to the dynamics of settlement negotiations? Would it tend to reduce the number of lawyers who would serve injured clients? Would it tend to reduce the amount of lawyer advertising as the expected return to the lawyer from getting each

8. N.Y. Judicial Law § 474a (McKinney 1983). Cf. California Business & Professions Code § 6146 (maximum percentage fees in cases against health care providers) and § 6147.5 (maximum fees in recovery of claims between merchants).

new client in the office was decreased? See Lester Brickman, Michael Horowitz & Jeffrey O'Connell, Rethinking Contingency Fees (1994).[9]

3. Are there kinds of cases in which a contingent fee should not be proper?

a. May a lawyer charge a contingent fee in a domestic relations case? Look at Model Rule 1.5(d)(1). What is the basis for such a prohibition? Is Model Rule 1.5, Comment [6] helpful in explaining the rationale?

Connecticut Bar Ethics Opinion 87–17 (1988), takes the position that a lawyer may take a contingent fee in a action to partition ownership of a house owned by an unmarried couple. The court said that the rule against charging a contingent fee in domestic relations matters does not apply where the couple is not married. Do you agree with the distinction? In a time when unmarried relationships are common, might one ask whether the policies behind the rule, e.g., not discouraging parties from reconciling, should apply to such cases too?

b. Should the law allow a contingent fee in a criminal case? Look at Rule 1.5(d)(2). What reasons might support such a prohibition?

Winkler v. Keane, 7 F.3d 304 (2d Cir.1993), considered whether a defense lawyer's charge of a contingent fee in a criminal case should be per se grounds for reversal of the conviction. The state accused the defendant of killing his father. The fee agreement provided that if the lawyer secured an acquittal so that the defendant could inherit from his father, the lawyer would get an extra $25,000. The New York Court of Appeals accepted the defendant's contention that the basis for prohibiting contingent fees in criminal cases is the law's concern that such a fee arrangement might discourage the lawyer from working out a guilty plea in an appropriate case, seeking a charge on a lesser included offense, or the like. That court had held, however, that while charging the contingent fee might be grounds for professional discipline of the lawyer, it was not per se grounds for reversal. For that, the defendant must show actual prejudice. In this case, it found no actual prejudice, and the Second Circuit agreed.

4. Would it be wise to prohibit the use of contingent fees in other kinds of cases?

a. Should contingent fee arrangements for defense counsel in civil cases be banned?

Wunschel Law Firm, P. C. v. Clabaugh, 291 N.W.2d 331 (Iowa 1980), was a defamation action. The defendant agreed with defense counsel that

9. In this connection, see Committee on Legal Ethics v. Gallaher, 376 S.E.2d 346 (W.Va.1988). The court found, in the facts of this case, that a 50% contingent fee was excessive for recovering personal injury damages where the lawyer advised acceptance of the first real offer the insurance company made: "If an attorney's fee is grossly disproportionate to the services rendered and is charged to a client who lacks full information about all of the relevant circumstances, the fee is 'clearly excessive' within the meaning of Disciplinary Rule 2–106(A), even though the client has consented to such fee." The court ordered restitution to the personal injury plaintiff of an amount sufficient to reduce the fee to one-third.

the law firm would defend him for a fee that would be one-third of the difference between the prayer in the petition and the amount actually awarded. Defendant was offered the alternative of paying a fee of $50 per hour. The court held that such a contingent defense fee is void and unenforceable as a matter of public policy. The court reasoned that such a fee would be based on "pure speculation" because "it provides for determination of the fee by factors having no logical relationship to the value of the services." Do you agree?

In Formal Opinion 93–373 (1993), however, the ABA Standing Committee on Ethics and Professional Responsibility expressly rejected that view and held that contingent fees for defense counsel in civil cases do not violate the Model Rules provided that the amount saved is "reasonably ascertainable," the total amount of the fee is reasonable, and the client's consent to the arrangement was "fully informed".

b. Has the time come to allow something like contingent fees in corporate transactions? Should counsel in takeover fights receive a "premium" if they successfully complete or defeat the takeover attempt, for example? Might counsel for an entertainer take a percentage of the value of the contracts she negotiated?

c. Do such fee arrangements bring a lawyer dangerously close to engaging in "business"? Is that something about which we should be concerned? Does the practice sound better if the lawyer calls it "value billing" and consistently sets the fee on the basis of how much the client has benefitted from the lawyer's efforts? See, e.g., ABA Commission on Billable Hours Report (2002); Symposium, Legal Billing: Seeking Alternatives to the Hourly Rate, Judicature, Jan.–Feb.1994, pp. 186–202.

D. THE ALTERNATIVE OF THE HOURLY-RATE FEE

1. At least a generation of lawyers has experienced the hourly rate fee as dominant in the life at most large firms, and many smaller firms as well. Does hourly rate billing harmonize the interests of lawyers and clients?

a. What abuses might be inherent in hourly billing? Might firms have an incentive to file every possible motion, for example, and have their associates research legal theories more than they would if they were billing on a contingent fee basis?

b. Can even more flagrant questions of abuse arise when firms bill by the hour? Suppose a lawyer has to fly to a meeting for Client A, for example, but works on the airplane on a matter for Client B. May the lawyer bill the same hour twice, once to each client? The practice of hourly rate billing is full of such issues, and ABA Formal Opinion 93–379 (December 6, 1993) addressed them as follows:

" * * * [I]t is helpful to consider these questions, not from the perspective of what a client could be forced to pay, but rather from the perspective of what the lawyer actually earned. A lawyer who spends four hours of time on behalf of three clients has not earned twelve billable hours. A lawyer who flies for six hours for one client, while working for five hours on behalf of another, has not earned eleven billable hours. A lawyer who is able to reuse old work product has not re-earned the hours previously billed and compensated when the work product was first generated. * * * [If] it turns out that the lawyer is particularly efficient in accomplishing a given result, it nonetheless will not be permissible to charge the client for more hours than were actually expended on the matter. * * * [T]he economies associated with the result must inure to the benefit of the client, not give rise to an opportunity to bill a client for phantom hours."[10]

Have all lawyers and firms taken the ABA's directions to heart? You will have no doubt that they have not after reading Lisa G. Lerman, Lying to Clients, 138 U. Pennsylvania L. Rev. 659 (1990), and Lisa G. Lerman, Unethical Billing Practices, 50 Rutgers L. Rev. 2151 (1998).

   c. Clients are increasingly hiring independent specialists to "audit" their lawyers bills. In Glenn K. Jackson, Inc. v. Roe, 273 F.3d 1192 (9th Cir.2001), for example, the plaintiff law firm was hired by an insurance company to represent its insureds against workers' compensation claims. In its engagement letter, the firm had agreed to let the insurer to hire a legal auditor to verify the firm's bills. The auditor found that over $200,000 of the nearly $800,000 charged should be disallowed, and the law firm filed this action against the auditors for breach of fiduciary duty, interference with contract, fraud, deceit, defamation, unfair competition, and false advertising. The district court dismissed all of the plaintiff's claims and the 9th Circuit agreed, finding that the audit firm owed no duty to the law firm. The law firm was a sophisticated party that agreed to be audited, and if auditing firms were held liable to third parties, it would encourage the auditors to be less candid in rendering opinions. Quite apart from the result itself, however, the case illustrates how much "fat" auditors can often find in the bills of even reputable law firms.

   2. What collateral effects may the charging of hourly fees have had on the practice of law? Should those effects concern you?

   a. Dean Patrick J. Schiltz reports:

       " 'Conventional wisdom just a few decades ago was that lawyers could not reasonably expect to charge for more than 1200 to 1500 hours per year.' Thirty years ago, most partners billed between 1200 and 1400 hours per year and most associates between 1400 and 1600 hours. As late as the mid–1980s, even associates in large New York firms were often not expected to bill more that 1800 hours annually.

---

10. When invited to extend a similar analysis to contingent fees, however, the ABA Standing Committee on Ethics and Professional Responsibility said only that "the charging of a contingent fee * * * does not violate ethical standards as long as the fee is appropriate in the circumstances and reasonable in amount, and as long as the client has been fully advised of the availability of alternative fee arrangements." ABA Formal Opinion 94–389 (Dec. 5, 1994).

Today, many firms would consider these ranges acceptable only for partners or associates who had died midway through the year."

b.   It may seem that lawyers of an earlier day just did not know how to work hard, but Dean Schiltz points out that:

"you will end up billing only about two hours for every three hours that you spend at 'work.' And thus, to bill 2000 hours per year, you will have to spend about sixty hours per week at the office, and take no more than two weeks of vacation/sick time/personal leave. If it takes you, say, forty-five minutes to get to work, and another forty-five minutes to get home, billing 2000 hours per year will mean leaving home at 7:45 a.m., working at the office from 8:30 a.m. until 6:30 p.m., and then arriving home at 7:15 p.m.—and doing this six days per week, every week. That makes for long days, and for long weeks. And you will have to work these hours not just for a month or two, but year after year after year."[11]

c.   Professor Deborah L. Rhode, Chair of the ABA Commission on Women and the Legal Profession, writes that women are particularly disadvantaged by current law firm expectations.

"[I]ncreasing billable hour quotas have pushed working hours to new and often excessive limits. Lawyers remain perpetually on call—tethered to the workplace through cell phones, emails, faxes, and beepers. 'Face time' is taken as a proxy for commitment, ambition, and reliability under pressure. The result is a 'rat race equilibrium' in which most lawyers feel that they would be better off with shorter or more flexible schedules, but find themselves within institutional structures that offer no such alternatives.* * * Particularly in large firms, unmarried associates report finding it 'difficult to have a cat, much less a family.' As one lawyer responded to a bar survey on quality of life: 'This is not a life.' "[12]

3.   What alternatives to hourly rate and contingent fees might better align lawyer incentives with client interests and also produce an appropriate return for lawyer efforts?

a.   The ABA Commission on Billable Hours Report (2002) found a move toward fixed fees for recurring, routine tasks (sometimes called "commodity" work) because clients want the burden of doing the work efficiently placed entirely on the law firm. Billable Hours Report p. 25. Can you see any collateral effects to such a development?

b.   The Report also suggests that lawyer productivity might be measured in terms of revenue generated for the firm, in whatever form, and not on hours worked. Billable Hours Report, p. 28. Would you prefer to work under such a system?

11.   Patrick J. Schiltz, "On Being a Happy, Healthy, and Ethical Member of an Unhappy, Unhealthy, and Unethical Profession," 52 Vand. L. Rev. 871 (1999).

12.   Deborah L. Rhode, Gender and the Profession: The No–Problem Problem, 30 Hofstra L. Rev. 1001 (2002).

c. Fixed fees make it easier for corporate counsel to conduct auctions in which firms compete to offer the lowest prices for the right to do defined packages of work, say defense of sets of 100 personal injury cases. Billable Hours Report, p. 33. Does that represent a move in a direction you would favor?

d. Does the move toward fixed fees seem appropriate for services that are not routine and that require work by experienced experts? Are fees likely ultimately to be set at some combination of fixed fee for routine services, hourly rate where complexity of the case is hard to predict, and a contingent element where intensity of the lawyer's efforts may make a difference.[13]

———

PROBLEM 6

HANDLING CLIENT PROPERTY AND WITHDRAWING FROM REPRESENTATION

Issues of the relationship between lawyer and client are in some ways best seen when the going gets tough. The client may be unhappy because things are going more slowly or less well than hoped. The lawyer may be unhappy because the client demands more services than expected and pays less promptly than promised. Some clients are "high maintenance." This problem examines some of the issues that can arise in such contexts. It first considers the lawyer's duty to protect and account for a client's property. It then examines the circumstances under which a lawyer may withdraw from representing the client. Then, it considers how lawyers should deal with clients who fail to pay the lawyer's fee. Finally, it considers the lawyer's possible right to a lien on client property and papers.

FACTS

In a recent suit to recover a valuable ring that the defendant had wrongfully withheld, a jury awarded Elizabeth Jackson's client the ring and $100,000 punitive damages. The fee contract between Jackson and her client provided that Jackson would get 40% of all punitive damages. "That was because we thought the punitive damages would be low," the client complained after the verdict was announced. "On a big recovery such as this, 40% is unfair," the client said. "I'll pay you 25% and not a penny more." The defendant satisfied the judgment by giving Jackson the ring and a check for $100,000 payable to Jackson and the client. Jackson promptly deposited the full amount of the check into her client

13. See, e.g., Kevin M. Clermont & John D. Currivan, Improving on the Contingent Fee, 63 Cornell L. Rev. 529 (1978); Ronald D. Rotunda, Moving from Billable Hours to Fixed–Fees: Task–Based Fees and Legal Ethics, 47 U. Kansas L. Rev. 1 (1999).

trust account and put the ring on her finger. She told the client, "Until we get this fee dispute worked out, I'm not giving you a nickel."

Jackson is a well-known and very busy litigator and she doesn't have time for difficult clients. When one client told her that she was not returning his phone calls quickly enough, she told him to get another lawyer, filed a notice of withdrawal with the court before which the matter was pending, and did no more work on the matter.

In another case, Jackson represented a local business person in a dispute over title to real estate. She anticipated a hard time collecting her fee, so she took a security interest in the real estate that was the subject of the suit. When the case was over and the client was slow to pay, Jackson filed suit to collect her fee out of the proceeds of an involuntary sale of the real estate. She also refused to send her client a copy of the judgment entered in the underlying case that the client needed to reassure his bank that the suit was indeed over.

QUESTIONS

A. HANDLING CLIENT PROPERTY

1. Why is it important that lawyers pay attention to their handling of client property?

a. A lawyer has a fiduciary relationship with a client. "Fiduciary" is a title also applied to trustees and guardians, people who manage the property of others. In that sense, then, the trustworthy management of a client's property is one of the most fundamental duties of a lawyer.

b. Violation of fiduciary standards with respect to client property is also one of the most certain ways for a lawyer to be disbarred. That is only partly because of the seriousness of the offense of stealing from a client. It is also in part because proof of a violation of accounting rules is typically much more straightforward than proof of failing to be forthcoming in disclosure of information, of less than competent representation of a client, or even of a conflict of interest. Disciplinary authorities have limited resources and tend to use them in cases where the results will be most certain.

c. It is thus critically important that you as a lawyer know the rules for management of client property. Large firms will have a whole staff devoted to preserving and accounting for such property, but ultimately the ones with their licenses on the line will be the lawyers for whom the staff work. Those lawyers need to know the rules as well.

2. Did Jackson violate Model Rule 1.15 by depositing the $100,000 settlement check into her trust account?

a. A lawyer may sign the lawyer's own name on a settlement check made out to the lawyer, but the lawyer may sign the client's name on a settlement check only if she has actual authority to do so. Sometimes such authority is given, but too often the need for such authority is overlooked.

b.   In Advisory Committee on Professional Ethics Docket No. 22–95, 677 A.2d 1100 (N.J.1996), a lawyer doing debt collection work for an institutional creditor was permitted to accept the creditor's suggestion that the lawyer endorse checks as they arrive, deduct the lawyer's contingent fee, and transmit the balance to the creditor. The court found that it was reasonable for the client to give this authority because debt collection is a big business with so many small transactions that any other system would be unnecessarily complex.

c.   Without such authority, on the other hand, signing the client's name on a check may not only be a disciplinary violation, it may also constitute the crime of conversion. See, e.g., Sampson v. State Bar, 524 P.2d 139 (Cal.1974) (endorsement of clients' names to checks without authorization of clients, accepting false acknowledgments and failing to secure clients' authorization for payment of settlement funds to doctor may properly be the subject of disciplinary action).

3.   How must an attorney keep his or her office accounts? Is it important that each client's funds go into separate accounts or only that the lawyers keep individual records of each client's funds?

a.   The California and New York rules found in the Standards Supplement are good examples of more detailed provisions than the ABA has heretofore provided. Their basic purpose is to require the lawyer to establish records that an auditor can then review. In February 1993, the ABA House of Delegates adopted a "Model Financial Recordkeeping Rule" much like the state rules. Its status is unclear, however, and it has never been made a part of the Model Rules of Professional Conduct.

b.   Columbus Bar Association v. Zauderer, 687 N.E.2d 410 (Ohio 1997), involved a lawyer who collected a lot of money for his clients. His problem arose when he started to allocate expenses of the cases. Without prior agreement with his clients, he accrued many of his litigation-related expenses in a "General" category and then created a formula to assign them to individual cases. Some claimants complained, and the Bar charged him with failure to keep adequate records. The Ohio Supreme Court agreed and suspended Zauderer for a year.

c.   The Florida Bar v. Bailey, 803 So.2d 683 (Fla.2001), shows that even living legends are not immune from trouble under these rules. The accusations against F. Lee Bailey, a celebrated criminal defense lawyer, arose out of his representation of an alleged drug smuggler. Bailey arranged a plea agreement by which his client pled guilty and forfeited all of his assets to the U.S. government in the hopes of receiving a lighter sentence. The defendant was French and owned a significant amount of property in France. To maintain the properties and cover the expenses of their liquidation, Bailey took control of a block of stock owned by the defendant. After selling the stock, Bailey was to return the proceeds to the government; the higher the amount Bailey was able to remit to the government, the less the defendant's sentence would be. The Florida Bar charged Bailey with commingling the defendant's assets with his own during the liquidation process. The evidence showed that he had borrowed against his client's money to fund his own investments and used the client's money for his own profit instead of remitting the maximum amount to the government, as was in the client's best interest. Although the court acknowledge that Bailey had been a member of the bar in two states for over 40 years and was admitted to practice before several federal courts, it found that his acts warranted his permanent disbarment in Florida.

4. When the client asked for his money, should lawyer Jackson have paid over the full $75,000 that the client thought was due? Would it have been proper for Jackson to pay the client only what Jackson thought was due?

a. Look at Model Rule 1.15(d). How much is Jackson required to pay over to the client?

b. What should she do with the portion of the fee that the client agrees Jackson is due? May she keep it in the trust account? Would that be consistent with Model Rule 1.15(a) and (b)?

c. What must she do with the amount of the fee that remains in dispute?

d. Suppose a creditor of the client asserts a lien on the client's share of the judgment. May the lawyer ignore that lien? Take a look at Model Rule 1.15(e). A lawyer who pays settlement proceeds over to the client in knowing disregard of a creditor's lien may become directly liable to the lien holder and basically required to pay twice. Kaiser Foundation Health Plan Inc. v. Aguiluz, 54 Cal.Rptr.2d 665 (Ct.App.1996).

5. Was it proper for Jackson to wear the client's ring while it was in her possession?

a. Restatement Third, The Law Governing Lawyers § 44, Comment *e*, makes clear:

> "This Section requires a lawyer to use reasonable measures for safekeeping such objects, for example, by placing them in a safe-deposit box or office safe. The reasonableness of measures depends on the circumstances, including the market value of the property, its special value to the client * * *, and special difficulties that would be required to replace it if known to the lawyer * * * ."

b. The Florida Bar v. Grosso, 760 So.2d 940 (Fla.2000) (per curiam), illustrates how a lawyer might fail to protect client property. When the court sentenced the lawyer's client to probation, it provided that he could not have a gun. The lawyer agreed to keep the client's gun collection for him and put the guns in his garage. Florida weather being humid, when the lawyer returned the guns a year later, they were rusty, pitted and parts were missing. The court suspended the lawyer for 90 days for not protecting the client's gun collection.

6. Should the bar subject a lawyer to discipline for the dishonesty of her office staff or associated lawyers? Have no doubt; it happens.

a.   Office of Disciplinary Counsel v. Ball, 618 N.E.2d 159 (Ohio 1993), involved a lawyer who gave responsibility for most of his probate practice to his secretary. She took in money and wrote checks on his trust accounts. Ultimately, she got behind and diverted funds from some accounts to others. The lawyer said he knew nothing about this. Even if that were true, the court said, the lawyer failed in his duty of supervision. The court suspended him from practice for 6 months.

If the lawyer did adequately supervise his secretary, but she stole the money anyway, should the lawyer be subject to discipline? Will the lawyer be liable to the clients to repay the money?

b.   Duggins v. Guardianship of Washington, 632 So.2d 420 (Miss. 1993), involved a lawyer retained to pursue a medical malpractice action on behalf of a child. He associated himself with a second lawyer who was to try the case. The second lawyer ultimately settled the case without telling the client or Duggins, and ran off with most of the money. The question was Duggins' liability to the clients. The court held that under these circumstances, the lawyers were partners or joint venturers with respect to the case. Thus, Duggins was liable for all damage caused by the second lawyer, plus punitive damages, even though he had no moral culpability for what had occurred.

c.   Is there good reason for taking this kind of strict liability approach to the problem? The *Duggins* court asserted that "an agreement, preferably in writing, with the client concerning the division of legal representation may prevent the liability of one attorney for any errors committed by the other," but if "the division of responsibility is not clearly spelled out, the client's consent to the association does not prevent vicarious liability between or among counsel when the attorneys share the representation and legal fees." Does that make strict liability in the absence of an agreement more palatable?

7. Should an attorney's trust account be subject to random audits, i.e. "spot checks"? Should lawyers collectively have to reimburse clients victimized by the acts of other lawyers?

a.   Traditional doctrine requires that there be no audit unless there is probable cause to believe that the accounts have not been properly maintained. Do you believe audits should be conducted without probable cause to believe a particular lawyer is in violation of the legal requirements? In February 1992, the ABA House of Delegates approved proposals for disciplinary reform that called for random audits. Proponents believe that these audits will catch some lawyers who commingle funds and deter others.

b.   Some lawyers have tried to resist audit of their trust accounts, citing attorney-client privilege or their own expectation of privacy. Those defenses have generally not prevailed. E.g. In re Kennedy, 442 A.2d 79 (Del.1982) (spot check system), cert. denied, 467 U.S. 1205, 104 S.Ct. 2388,

81 L.Ed.2d 346 (1984); Doyle v. State Bar of California, 648 P.2d 942 (Cal.1982) (subpoena system).

c. Even where the audit determines that the lawyer has stolen from his or her law firm instead of from a client, disbarment of the lawyer may follow. See, e.g., In re Siegel, 627 A.2d 156 (N.J.1993). See also, In re Busby, 855 P.2d 156 (Ore.1993) (lawyer suspended for four months for lying to his firm about the fees he was paid and pocketing the difference).

d. Suppose the lawyer who had converted client funds were now judgment proof. What remedies, if any, might you pursue on the client's behalf? Most states have established a Client Security Fund to reimburse clients victimized by their attorneys.[1] Should all members of the bar be assessed to provide the corpus of such a fund? Should the existence of the fund be kept quiet so as to prevent the lawyers' assessments from becoming as high as doctors' malpractice premiums?

B.   WITHDRAWAL WHEN THE CLIENT BECOMES TOO DIFFICULT

1. Should a lawyer ever be _required_ to terminate a representation?

a. Where "the lawyer's physical or mental condition materially impairs the lawyer's ability to represent the client," for example, Model Rule 1.16(a)(2) makes withdrawal mandatory.

How would this rule apply to the client who calls the lawyer at all hours of the night, interrupts the lawyer if they accidentally meet at a restaurant, etc.? May the lawyer say the client has become so much of a pain in the neck that it affects the lawyer mentally?

b. Withdrawal is also required by Model Rule 1.16(a)(1) where continued representation will violate another Model Rule. As you go through this course, watch for situations that might trigger such a requirement. Conflicts of interest create such situations, for example, as may situations involving uncorrected client fraud.

2. We know a lawyer has significant discretion whether to undertake representation of a client, but once having done so, does the lawyer have less ability to terminate that representation over the client's objection?

a. Model Rule 1.16(b)(1) authorizes a lawyer to withdraw from representation at any time if the withdrawal affects no material interests of the client adversely. If the client does not want the lawyer to withdraw, can the client's material interests ever be said _not_ to be adversely affected? Should

---

1. See, e.g., John W. Bryan, The Clients' Security Fund Ten Years Later, 55 A.B.A.J. 757 (1969); Murray T. Bloom, The Trouble With Lawyers 1–35 (1969). Beard v. North Carolina State Bar, 320 N.C. 126, 357 S.E.2d 694 (1987), upheld a system by which the state supreme court requires each lawyer to pay $50 each year into the client security fund. See also, Clients' Security Fund of State v. Grandeau, 526 N.E.2d 270 (N.Y. 1988) (upholds suit by New York Fund against the partner of defaulting lawyer on a theory of vicarious liability).

withdrawal be seen to be a breach of the lawyer's duty of loyalty to the client unless the lawyer has a reason for withdrawal other than being tired of the client's case? If the lawyer does withdraw, who should pay for the cost of bringing a new lawyer up to speed?

b.   On the other hand, ordinarily the client may discharge the lawyer at any time and for any reason, having an obligation only to pay for work done to that time. See, e.g., Model Rule 1.16(b)(3). Thus, Restatement Third, The Law Governing Lawyers § 32(1), Comment *b* says bluntly: "A client may always discharge a lawyer, regardless of cause and regardless of any agreement between them." Why should a client have more right than a lawyer to walk away from what is otherwise a binding contract between them? Are Comments [4]–[6] to Model Rule 1.16 at all helpful in answering that question?

c.   In Gilles v. Wiley, Malehorn & Sirota, 783 A.2d 756 (N.J.App.2001), the lawyer had agreed to represent the plaintiff in a medical malpractice case. The first medical expert consulted by the lawyer said that the plaintiff's doctor had not acted negligently, but a later expert gave an opinion more favorable to the plaintiff. After getting the second opinion, the lawyer held the case for six more months and only about three weeks before the statute of limitations expired, he sent his client (the plaintiff in this case) a letter terminating the representation. In the letter, the defendant explained that his firm had moved away from medical malpractice claims because they were not very profitable, and he advised the plaintiff to find another lawyer because her claim faced a two-year statute of limitations. The plaintiff ultimately did not find another lawyer until after the statute of limitations had expired. On these facts, the court denied summary judgment for the defendant in a malpractice action against the lawyer. The lawyer's late withdrawal had a material adverse effect on the plaintiff's interests, and the lawyer did not take reasonable measures to protect her interests. At the very least, the lawyer could have prepared a pro se complaint for the plaintiff to file while she sought representation elsewhere.

3.   Should a lawyer be permitted to withdraw under Model Rule 1.16(b)(4) whenever the client insists on taking action "with which the lawyer has a fundamental disagreement"?

a.   Is it the lawyer or the client that has authority to define the objectives of representation under Model Rule 1.2(a)? Can that authority be real if a lawyer who disagrees with client decisions may simply resign?

b.   The "fundamental disagreement" language replaced a standard permitting a lawyer to withdraw in the face of any decision the lawyer found "imprudent." Was that ground even more favorable to lawyer withdrawal?

c.   Is the answer that Model Rule 1.16(d) requires a lawyer to take "reasonably practicable" steps "to protect a client's interest?" Are you satisfied that such a cautionary requirement overcomes the consequences of a lawyer's election to withdraw?

4.   Should a lawyer be permitted to withdraw from a case that has become financially unprofitable for the lawyer to pursue?

a.   In Smith v. R.J. Reynolds, 630 A.2d 820 (N.J.Super.App.Div.1993), a firm had agreed to charge a contingent fee to represent a smoker in a damage claim against R.J. Reynolds. As discovery went on, however, the firm had expended over $1 million in out-of-pocket costs and $5 million in lawyer time. The prospect of much more expense remained before the case would come to trial, but the plaintiffs wanted to go to trial to establish a "principle." The lawyers, in turn, said that "there comes a time when we can't afford to operate on the fuel of just principle * * * when the finances are such that it becomes an unreasonable burden." 630 A.2d at 825.

b.   Should the court let the lawyers off the hook? In this case, the Appellate Division concluded that if the litigation had been paid for at hourly rates, all would agree the time had come to call it quits. Because a contingent fee contract gives the client has no incentive to drop the matter, the court ordered the trial judge to determine the likelihood of success in the case, the likely recovery, if any, and then make the assessment that new Model Rule 1.16(b)(6) contemplates. But see Haines v. Liggett Group, 814 F.Supp. 414 (D.N.J.1993), a related case in which the court said the firm had made a deal with the client and had to live with it.

c.   Restatement Third, The Law Governing Lawyers § 32 identifies no ground comparable to Model Rule 1.16(b)(6). Should courts permit withdrawal on financial grounds? Would failure to do so harm future clients by making it hard to get lawyers to take cases with uncertain costs and outcomes? See, e.g., Fidelity National Title Insurance Co. v. Intercounty National Title Insurance Co., 310 F.3d 537 (7th Cir.2002) (business firms "have no right to free legal aid in civil suits").

5.   What role should courts play in reviewing attempted withdrawal?

a.   If a matter from which the lawyer seeks to withdraw is pending before a tribunal, the rules of that tribunal will ordinarily require the tribunal's permission to withdraw. See Model Rule 1.16(c).

b.   Can you imagine circumstances in which a court will not permit a lawyer to withdraw even where withdrawal would be required under Model Rule 1.16(a)? Keep that question in mind when you look at Problem 27, for example, on what to do when a client lies in court testimony.

c.   As an alternative to withdrawal, should Jackson be able to turn to the Court for help in seeing that the client pays the fee in advance? Journalist Martin Mayer writes that:

> " * * * criminal practice is the one branch of the law where lawyers collect their fees in advance. Not long ago, an older New York lawyer with little experience in the criminal courts had a client who had been picked up in another county for drunk driving, and for whom a conviction at precisely this moment would be extremely inconvenient. He wanted a postponement, but knew of no excuse a judge would have to accept, so he consulted with the

young assistant district attorney who would be on duty that day. The DA heard the reason for the postponement, which was a good one, and said. 'That's all right. You just tell the judge that you haven't been able to get hold of your witness, Mr. Green.' "

"But I don't have any witness, Mr. Green."

The DA looked incredulously at the older lawyer's white hairs and said, "Don't you *know*? It means you haven't been paid. Any judge will give you an adjournment on that."

In Washington, D.C., these matters are handled with greater formality: a lawyer still waiting for his fee comes into court and demands an adjournment "pursuant to Rule I of this Court."[2]

Should a Judge assist an attorney to collect a fee in this way? Is it only professional courtesy to do so? Is there anything else the judge might do to assist the lawyer other than grant a delay? What is the professionally responsible way for both lawyer and judge to handle this situation?

C. LIMITATIONS ON A LAWYER'S EFFORTS TO COLLECT A FEE

1. Should a lawyer be permitted to sue a client to collect a fee?

a. ABA Formal Opinion 250 (1943) upheld suits against clients, but without enthusiasm. Do you agree with the committee's view that "Ours is a learned profession, not a mere money-getting trade"? Does it follow that "suits to collect fees should be avoided"? See ABA Model Code of Professional Responsibility, EC 2–23.

b. Any legal prohibition on suits to collect legal fees is now ancient history, see Restatement Third, The Law Governing Lawyers § 42(1), although such suits often backfire against lawyers when clients use them as an occasion to counterclaim with a suit for professional malpractice.

2. Should a lawyer be bound by the obligation to preserve client confidences and secrets in establishing the elements of the lawyer's claim?

a. As you will see in later problems, a lawyer's duty to keep information about a client confidential is very strict. However, look at Model Rule 1.6(b)(3). What principle, if any, would justify sacrificing the client's interest in confidentiality in favor of furthering the lawyer's interest in getting paid?[3]

---

2. Martin Mayer, The Lawyers 161–62 (1967) (emphasis in original).

3. For a long time the bar has protected its right to use confidential information when necessary to collect the fee, even while stating that the ethical privilege is broad and a lawyer should not breach it to prevent third parties from suffering substantial financial loss. An old ABA Opinion 250 (1943) conclud-

ed that Canon 4 of the former ABA Model Code of Professional Responsibility did not prevent a lawyer from disclosing confidential information in order to the attach client's property to collect his fee. See also, Nakasian v. Incontrade, Inc., 409 F.Supp. 1220, 1224 (S.D.N.Y.1976) (in order to collect fee, lawyer may attach the funds of his clients, even

b. Model Rule 1.6(b)(1) creates an exception to the obligation of confidentiality when disclosure is required to avoid "reasonably certain death or substantial bodily harm," but not when failure to disclose will cause third parties to be victims of securities fraud. Does it make sense to allow disclosure to be sure the lawyer gets paid, but not to protect innocent victims of the client's fraud?

c. Restatement Third, The Law Governing Lawyers § 65, Comment *b*, argues

> "Without this exception, a lawyer could be deprived of important evidence to prove a rightful claim. Clients would thus sometimes be immune from honest claims for legal fees. Moreover, at least some disclosures necessary to establish a fee will not involve information that a client would find embarrassing or prejudicial, other than in defeating the client's position in the dispute."

Are you convinced by this argument? By failing to pay the lawyer's fee, might the client be said to have breached the contract that underlies the lawyer's confidentiality obligation?[4]

3. In order to "encourage" the client's payment, may the lawyer threaten to reveal more client confidences than necessary to prove the lawyer's case?

a. In re Disciplinary Proceeding Against Boelter, 985 P.2d 328 (Wash. 1999), suspended a lawyer for six months for his threats to reveal confidential client information in order to collect a fee. The lawyer had told the client that failure to pay means "you forego the attorney-client privilege and I would be forced to reveal that you lied on your statements to the IRS and to the bank as to your financial condition. This would entail disclosure of the tapes of our conversations about your hidden assets. There is a federal statute, 18 U.S.C. § 1001, which provides for up to one year in jail for such perjury. The choice is yours." Fair warning about the firm's limited ability to disclose confidential information is permissible, the court said, but the "tape" was a fabrication and the fees being claimed were excessive. These actions justified the lawyer's six-month suspension.

b. In State ex rel. Counsel for Discipline of Nebraska Supreme Court v. Lopez Wilson, 634 N.W.2d 467 (Neb.2001), the lawyer had represented a client in obtaining a visa and in divorce proceedings. However, when the lawyer learned that the client was engaged in an intimate relationship with the lawyer's ex-wife, he withdrew and threatened both to tell the INS that the client's job status had changed and to re-open the prior divorce proceedings unless the client paid him for services that the lawyer had

where the attachment is facilitated by confidential information possessed by the lawyer).

4. D.C. Bar Legal Ethics Committee, Opinion No. 298 (2000) says that a lawyer may use a collection agency to collect legal fees as long as the ethical standards of the agency is consistent with the lawyer's ethical standards and the lawyer only discloses the minimal information about the representation necessary to collect the fee. The Opinion advised that the ethics rules prohibit the outright sale of client accounts receivable to a collection agency.

provided free of charge. In upholding a two year suspension, the court stated that Canon 4 of the Model Code of Professional Responsibility allowed limited disclosure of client confidences in a suit to collect a legal fee, but it did not permit "violent threats" to disclose such information more generally.

4. Should a fee dispute between attorney and client be subject to mandatory arbitration at the request of the client?

a. Anderson v. Elliott, 555 A.2d 1042 (Me.1989), cert. denied 493 U.S. 978, 110 S.Ct. 504, 107 L.Ed.2d 507 (1989), upheld the Maine requirement that lawyers submit to client-initiated mandatory arbitration of fee claims. The lawyer had argued that arbitration denied him his constitutional right to a jury trial, but the court held that the right must be read in the context of the court's supervisory power over attorneys.

b. In Guralnick v. New Jersey Supreme Court, 747 F.Supp. 1109 (D.N.J.1990), aff'd 961 F.2d 209 (3d Cir.1992), lawyers argued that a New Jersey system of fee arbitration that only a client may initiate unconstitutionally denied them due process, violated their Thirteenth Amendment rights and violated the antitrust laws as well. In a thoughtful opinion, the Court rejected all such challenges.

c. A. Fred Miller, P.C. v. Purvis, 921 P.2d 610 (Alaska 1996), examined mandatory fee arbitration and held that the lack of judicial review of an arbitration award did not deny due process. The court agreed that judicial review on the merits might be desirable in an arbitration process, but the lack of it does not violate the Constitution. Part of the purpose of arbitration is to achieve a quick, binding review of a dispute. Judicial review would put a burden on clients that the Constitution does not require be imposed. See also, Nodvin v. State Bar of Georgia, 544 S.E.2d 142 (Ga.2001) (upholds state's fee arbitration procedure).

5. Should a lawyer's engagement letter be able to specify that non–fee complaints the client has about the lawyer must be submitted to arbitration as well?

a. A lawyer's suit for unpaid fees will often trigger a malpractice claim from the client who hopes to reach a compromise of the fee amount. As you may remember, Model Rule 1.8(h) forbids limiting the lawyer's liability for malpractice or settling a malpractice claim without advising the client of the need for independent counsel. The question thus is whether an arbitration requirement in a lawyer's engagement letter violates either or both prohibitions.

b. California State Bar Standing Committee on Professional Responsibility and Conduct, Formal Opinion 1989–116, concluded that public policy favors arbitration and that a lawyer dealing with a new client has no fiduciary obligation that would prohibit using such a clause in the retainer. Because arbitration goes to remedy and not liability, the committee reasoned, it does not constitute limiting liability for malpractice. When dealing with an existing client, however, the committee said that the lawyer has a fiduciary duty to fully explain the provision and its legal consequences.

c.   ABA Formal Opinion 02–425 (2002), reached the same result. First, the Committee said that an arbitration clause, by itself, does not violate Rule 1.8(h). The Committee acknowledged that an attorney has a fiduciary duty under Rule 1.4(b) "to advise clients of the possible adverse consequences as well as the benefits that may arise from the execution of an agreement," and because a client potentially waives significant rights by agreeing to mandatory arbitration, the attorney has a duty to explain the potential consequences of that "to the extent reasonably necessary to permit the client to make [an] informed decision about the contract." However, the Opinion reasoned that because the arbitration clause only defines the forum in which the disgruntled client must proceed, it does not limit the lawyer's liability for malpractice.

6.   In the absence of agreement, what rights should a lawyer have if the client terminates the relationship the day before trial, or under other circumstances where significant time has been invested but no results achieved on which to calculate a contingent or percentage fee?

a.   The usual rule permits the lawyer a quantum meruit recovery. In the case of a contingent fee, the first lawyer can usually recover only if the second lawyer wins the case, i.e., if the plaintiff ultimately prevails. E.g., Plaza Shoe Store Inc. v. Hermel, Inc., 636 S.W.2d 53 (Mo.1982) (en banc).

b.   Gagne v. Vaccaro, 766 A.2d 416 (Conn.2001), involved a lawyer who had not entered into a written contingent fee agreement with his client. Then, a second lawyer, who replaced the first one, successfully pursued the matter and collected a contingent fee. Now, the first lawyer wanted a fair share of the fee earned. The court held he could get a quantum meruit payment. The lack of a written agreement was not enough to deny him all fees, and where he had acted loyally and his work had contributed to the final outcome, quantum meruit recovery was appropriate.

7.   May a lawyer charge interest or a "late payment penalty" on overdue accounts? May a lawyer accept Master Card in payment of his fees and simply leave all collection problems up to the credit card company?

a.   These used to be serious questions, but the ABA upheld both charging interest and accepting credit cards in ABA Formal Opinion 338 (November 16, 1974) and reconfirmed that result in ABA Formal Opinion 00–420 (2000).

b.   Contrast Lustig v. Horn, 732 N.E.2d 613 (Ill.App.2000), which considered a firm's charge of 1% of its fee for late payment, plus additional attorney's fees if the fee had to be collected in court. The court refused to allow the charges. They not only put the firm in a position of "prosecuting" its own client, but they could be used "to silence a client" who wanted to protest an improper fee.

c.   DC Bar Legal Ethics Committee Opinion No. 310 (2001) re-examined when a lawyer may charge interest on past due fees. It says that even where the original fee agreement made no provision for interest, if the client gets behind in payments, the lawyer may condition further representation on the client's willingness to pay interest in the future. The opinion acknowledges that any such situation involves a conflict of interest between lawyer and client, but it says that every fee arrangement creates such a conflict. Any such change in the fee arrangement will be subject to "strict scrutiny," the opinion says, but it is not absolutely prohibited.

D. ATTORNEYS' LIENS AND OTHER SECURITY INTERESTS

1. Should a lawyer be permitted to retain a client's property and papers until the lawyer's fee is paid?

a. In Sage Realty Corp. v. Proskauer Rose Goetz & Mendelsohn L.L.P., 689 N.E.2d 879 (N.Y.1997), a client who had paid over a million dollars in fees in a large financing transaction decided to switch lawyers. It asked the firm for its file, now totaling so many volumes that the index alone ran 58 pages. The firm turned over the closing documents, client-supplied papers and correspondence with third parties, but not its own internal work product. Citing what is now § 43 of the Restatement Third, The Law Governing Lawyers, the New York Court of Appeals held that the client is presumptively entitled to all its papers, save for limited exceptions. The court did not require the firm to disclose documents that might violate its duty of nondisclosure owed to a third party, or duties otherwise imposed by law, or firm documents intended for internal law office review and use (such as "documents containing a firm attorney's general or other assessment of the client, or tentative preliminary impressions of the legal or factual issues presented in the representation, recorded primarily for the purpose of giving internal direction to facilitate performance of the legal services entailed in that representation."). The court said that the firm may ordinarily charge the client for the function of assembling and delivering the documents to the client.

b. In many states, California being a major exception, an attorney has a "retaining lien" that gives the lawyer a possessory interest in the client's papers and funds in the attorney's possession.[5] On the other hand, Restatement Third, The Law Governing Lawyers § 43, rejects the availability of such a lien on the ground that "[a] broad retaining lien could impose pressure on a client disproportionate to the size or validity of the lawyer's fee claim." With which position do you agree?

c. The significance of the retaining lien is greatest when the client really needs the papers, for example, where new counsel for a murder defendant needs the files to prepare for trial. To the relief of most

---

5. The retaining lien does not apply to property simply given to the lawyer for safekeeping. See Akers v. Akers, 46 N.W.2d 87 (Minn.1951) (evidence sustained finding that property was originally left with attorney for purpose of placing it beyond reach of defendant Akers and not for security for payment of attorney's fees). Similarly, a lawyer may not take excess funds deposited by the client for payment of court reporter charges and apply them to payment of the lawyer's unpaid fees. See State ex rel. Oklahoma Bar Association v. Cummings, 863 P.2d 1164 (Okl.1993).

observers, Pomerantz v. Schandler, 704 F.2d 681 (2d Cir.1983) (per curiam), found an exception to the attorney's lien, in the court's discretion, when the client had an urgent need for papers to defend a criminal case and lacked the means to pay the lawyer's fee.

d.   However, that exception is not broad. The whole purpose of a retaining lien is to put pressure on the client to pay the lawyer's bill. An "attorney's lien cannot otherwise be disregarded merely because the pressure it is supposed to exert becomes effective." 704 F.2d 681, 683.

e.   Thus, the Restatement recognizes that "[a] client who fails to pay for the lawyer's work in preparing particular documents * * * ordinarily is not entitled to receive those documents." Restatement Third, The Law Governing Lawyers § 43, Comment c.

2.   In order to guarantee payment of a lawyer's fee, should the lawyer be able to assert a lien on sums recovered on behalf of the client?

a.   Most states give the attorney a right to assert a "charging lien" that gives the lawyer a right to have the recovery in a case applied to payment of his or her fees. Restatement Third, The Law Governing Lawyers § 43, Comment d, explains that many states "recognize a charging lien without a contract" between the lawyer and client, but Restatement § 43(2) provides that there should be a contract in order to safeguard the client.

b.   The attorney must give notice to the person paying the judgment or settlement. Once such notice is given, the person paying the judgment or settlement is liable for the attorney's fees if that person pays the entire judgment or settlement directly to the attorney's client. See Restatement Third, The Law Governing Lawyers § 43, Comment e.

c.   People v. Philip Morris, Inc., 759 N.E.2d 906 (Ill.2001), shows that huge sums can turn on the application of these principles. This case arose out of several states' lawsuits against the tobacco industry. The Illinois Attorney General selected an Illinois Special Counsel (ISC) and agreed that its compensation would be 10% of the total recovery to the State of Illinois. Subsequently, the state and the tobacco defendants entered into the Master Settlement Agreement (MSA) pursuant to which Illinois would receive an estimated $9 billion, i.e., $360 million annually for 25 years from the tobacco defendants. Section 17 of the MSA also created an arbitration panel to award attorneys' fees. That panel awarded the ISC $121 million (about 1.3% of the recovery), also to be paid over 25 years. The ISC (which was not precluded by the panel from seeking additional fees) then served notice of its attorney's lien of 10%, based on the fee agreement with the Attorney General. The circuit court ordered that 10% of all settlement payments be deposited into an escrow account pending a decision on the merits of the lien petition, and the Illinois Supreme Court held that, pursuant to the Attorneys Lien Act, a lawyer may assert a lien if the lawyer was hired by a client to assert a claim and the lawyer serves notice, in writing, upon the party against whom the client has the claim. Further, the court held that an attorneys' lien proceeding is not a claim against the state and thus need not be asserted before the state's court of claims. The funds recovered are not "state funds" until after "ISC's attorney fees are paid and the funds go into the state treasury."

d. Bell & Marra v. Sullivan, 6 P.3d 965 (Mont.2000), gives an important warning to lawyers. When the client refused to settle on terms the lawyer thought wise and also refused to sign a new fee agreement, the firm withdrew from the representation. After new lawyers successfully concluded the case for the client, the first firm asserted an attorneys lien. The court held that the firm's unjustified withdrawal from the matter forfeited its right to any of the ultimate fee.

e. Should a lawyer be able to demand that a settlement check be made out solely to him so as to be able to enforce his charging lien? See Hafter v. Farkas, 498 F.2d 587 (2d Cir.1974) (per curiam), holding no, but permitting the check to be made out to *both* lawyer and client.

3. May the engagement letter with a client give the lawyer a security interest in the property that is the subject matter of the litigation?

a. Look at Model Rule 1.8(i). Why might such a security interest be suspect? Restatement Third, The Law Governing Lawyers § 36, Comment *b*, traces the prohibition to common law fears of champerty and maintenance, i.e., that wealthy lawyers would buy claims and clog the courts with litigation. If that were the only rationale, would you favor repeal of Model Rule 1.8(i)?

b. However, the same Comment continues:

"The justification for the rule in its present form is that a lawyer's ownership gives the lawyer an economic basis for claiming to control the prosecution and settlement of the claim and provides an incentive for the lawyer to relegate the client to a subordinate position. * * * The rule also prevents a lawyer from disguising an unreasonably large fee, violative of § 34, by buying part of the claim for a low price."

Does that give you more confidence that Model Rule 1.8(i) has a place in modern law?[6]

4. Is Model Rule 1.8(i) the only Rule governing the lawyer taking an interest in the client's property?

6. The Comment continues: "The prohibition * * * is limited to matters in litigation. Thus, * * * a lawyer may acquire an ownership or other proprietary interest in a client's patent when retained to file a patent application, while * * * the lawyer could not acquire such an interest if retained to bring a patent-infringement suit. The difference in treatment is largely historical." In other words, in litigation, the lawyer cannot use the contingent fee to become part owner of the property such that he can prevent settlement. Assuming the fee is otherwise reasonable, he can become a 10% owner of a patent as a charge for filing the patent. If there is litigation, if the lawyer is not an owner of the patent, he can charge 10% of the value of the patent as his contingent fee, but he cannot become a 10% owner of the patent because that would make him a co-plaintiff.

a. Hawk v. State Bar of California, 754 P.2d 1096 (Cal.1988), says that when a lawyer takes any interest in property of the client as security for payment of the lawyer's fee, the arrangement is a business transaction with the client subject to the California equivalent of Model Rule 1.8(a). The court implies that in some cases the arrangement could properly be entered into as a way of helping the client afford necessary legal services. If the lawyer ignores the conflict of interest concerns and does not comply with the safeguards of the cited rules, however, he or she will be subject to discipline, and in this case, the court suspended Attorney Hawk for 6 months and put him on probation for 4 years.

b. Similarly, in Petit–Clair v. Nelson, 782 A.2d 960 (N.J.App.2001), Nelson had retained attorney Petit–Clair to represent the Nelsons' two corporations. During the course of the representation, the Nelsons gave the lawyer a mortgage on their personal residence as security for payment of the legal fees. Subsequently, they did not pay their bill and the lawyer sought to foreclose on the obligation. However, the court said, a lawyer negotiating a security interests adverse to his client is entering into a business transaction with that client. Thus, the lawyer must establish both that 1) the terms of the agreement were fair and reasonable, and 2) the lawyer advised the client that it would be desirable to seek outside counsel to review the agreement. Because the lawyer had not so advised the client, the lawyer could not enforce the mortgage.

c. ABA Formal Opinion 02–427 (May 31, 2002) says that "there is nothing inherently unethical in a lawyer asking a client to provide security for payment of fees." Such a transaction is subject to the standards in Model Rule 1.8(a), however, and if the lawyer takes possession of the security, the lawyer must safeguard it as provided in Model Rule 1.15(a). Further, if property is transferred to the lawyer as payment of the fee, the lawyer may retain only so much of the proceeds as represents a reasonable fee. Any excess value must be treated as property belonging to the client.

———

PROBLEM 7

THE DUTY OF CONFIDENTIALITY

The ability to talk freely and confidentially is one of the central elements defining the relationship between lawyer and client. However, the lawyer's confidentiality obligation, found in Rule 1.6, is made up of three quite different bodies of law:

1. The attorney-client privilege, a part of the law of evidence.

2. Work product immunity, which arises out of discovery rules and the law of civil procedure.

3. The professional duty of confidentiality, which derives from the obligations of trustees, agents, and other fiduciaries.

The first three topics in this problem try to help you keep those concepts straight. You will see that the scope and character of each of the protections can vary considerably in a given case. The fourth topic examines how confidentiality protection can be lost and suggests the care a lawyer must take against that eventuality.

FACTS

Your long-time client, John Carter, recently came to your office to tell you that he expects to be sued by the person who bought his house. When expressly asked by his prospective buyer prior to the sale, he told the buyer that the house had a dry basement. He has admitted to you, however, that although the basement had never flooded in the five years he had lived there, Carter had been warned by a prior owner that the basement regularly flooded after a heavy rain. There was such a rain this year, and some of the buyer's expensive electronic equipment suffered major damage.

Shortly before his death, you were able to interview the prior owner of the house, who confirmed to you what he had told Carter about the tendency to flood. You have notes of that interview in which you comment on the former owner's likely credibility at trial. Later, at a party at a friend's home, Carter's banker let slip that Carter is in bad financial condition. You mentally filed that away as important to your settlement posture in case Carter were sued.

The buyer has now filed suit against Carter. The buyer has subpoenaed your notes of your interview with the prior owner. Someone else has asked you informally if the rumors that Carter has suffered financial reverses are true.

QUESTIONS

A. INFORMATION PROTECTED BY THE ATTORNEY-CLIENT PRIVILEGE

1. Protecting information covered by the attorney-client privilege is one of a lawyer's most basic obligations. How will you know such information when you see it?

a. Restatement Third, The Law Governing Lawyers § 68 says that the attorney-client privilege protects "(1) a communication, (2) made between privileged persons,[1] (3) in confidence, (4) for the purpose of obtaining or providing legal assistance for the client."

---

1. "Privileged persons" are "the client (including a prospective client), the client's lawyer, agents of either who facilitate com- munication between them, and agents of the lawyer who facilitate the representation." Re-

b. Proposed Federal Rule 503[2] goes into more detail about when the privilege protects or does not protect:

"*(a) Definitions.* As used in this rule:

"(1) A 'client' is a person, public officer, or corporation, association, or other organization or entity, either public or private, who is rendered professional legal services by a lawyer, or who consults a lawyer with a view to obtaining professional legal services from him.

"(2) A 'lawyer' is a person authorized, or reasonably believed by the client to be authorized, to practice law in any state or nation.

"(3) A 'representative of the lawyer' is one employed to assist the lawyer in the rendition of professional legal services.

"(4) A communication is 'confidential' if not intended to be disclosed to third persons other than those to whom disclosure is in furtherance of the rendition of professional legal services to the client or those reasonably necessary for the transmission of the communication.

"*(b) General Rule of Privilege.* A client has a privilege to refuse to disclose and to prevent any other person from disclosing confidential communications made for the purpose of facilitating the rendition of professional legal services to the client, (1) between himself or his representative and his lawyer or his lawyer's representative, or (2) between his lawyer and the lawyer's representative, or (3) by him or his lawyer to a lawyer representing another in a matter of common interest, or (4) between representatives of the client or between the client and a representative of the client, or (5) between lawyers representing the client.

"*(c) Who May Claim the Privilege.* The privilege may be claimed by the client, his guardian or conservator, the personal representative of a deceased client, or the successor, trustee, or similar representative of a corporation, association, or other organization, whether or not in existence. The person who was the lawyer at the time of the communication may claim the privilege but only on behalf of the client. His authority to do so is presumed in the absence of evidence to the contrary.

"*(d) Exceptions.* There is no privilege under this rule:

"*(1) Furtherance of crime or fraud.* If the services of the lawyer were sought or obtained to enable or aid anyone to commit

statement Third, The Law Governing Lawyers § 70.

2. When the Federal Rules of Evidence were approved by Congress, none of the 13 rules dealing with privileges, including Proposed Rule 503 were enacted, see Fed. Rules of Evidence, Pub.L. 93–595 (Jan. 2, 1975). The reasons for non-enactment did not reflect on the merits of Proposed Rule 503, which is, in general, a fair summary of the law of most states.

or plan to commit what the client knew or reasonably should have known to be a crime or fraud; or

"(2) Claimants through same deceased client. As to a communication relevant to an issue between parties who claim through the same deceased client, regardless of whether the claims are by testate or intestate succession or by *inter vivos* transactions; or

"(3) Breach of duty by lawyer or client. As to a communication relevant to an issue of breach of duty by the lawyer to his client or by the client to his lawyer; or

"(4) Document attested by lawyer. As to a communication relevant to an issue concerning an attested document to which the lawyer is an attesting witness; or

"(5) Joint clients. As to a communication relevant to a matter of common interest between two or more clients if the communication was made by any of them to a lawyer retained or consulted in common, when offered in an action between any of the clients."

2.   Should the privilege be held to apply in the following situations?

a.   In D'Alessio v. Gilberg, 617 N.Y.S.2d 484 (App.Div.1994), the question was the privileged character of the client's identity. A client who had caused a hit-and-run accident consulted a lawyer about the accident. The victim wanted to sue the client but did not know his name, so he asked a court to compel the lawyer to reveal it. Should the lawyer have to do so? The identity of a client is normally not privileged; it is the first thing the lawyer discloses when entering an appearance in a case. But, in this situation, no appearance had been entered and revealing the client's identity could have caused the client both to be prosecuted criminally and to be sued. Thus, the court held the identity privileged.

b.   In People v. Gionis, 892 P.2d 1199 (Cal.1995), the state accused Gionis of brutally assaulting his ex-wife with whom he was in the midst of a bitter custody battle. Attorney Leuck was a friend of the couple. Gionis asked him to come to the house when he had been served with divorce papers. Leuck agreed although he expressly said he would not represent either side in the divorce because he was a friend of both. While together, Gionis told Leuck "how easy it would be" to hire someone to "really take care of" his wife. When the state called Leuck to testify to that statement at Gionis' trial, Gionis objected that the conversation was privileged. A majority of the California Supreme Court held that where the attorney tells the alleged "client" that the attorney will *not* represent him, communications with the lawyer are not privileged.

c.   In Commonwealth v. Mrozek, 657 A.2d 997 (Pa.Super.Ct.1995), a potential client called the lawyer's office to ask the receptionist for an appointment because "I've just committed a homicide." The statement to the receptionist (a non-lawyer) was held to be privileged because she was an employee of the lawyer whose job it was to communicate with clients and potential clients.

d.   In re Grand Jury Subpoenas Dated March 9, 2001, 179 F.Supp.2d 270 (S.D.N.Y.2001), sought production of documents related to the effort by lawyers for Marc Rich and Pincus Green to get them a presidential pardon. Since 1983, Rich and Green had been living abroad and had refused to come to the United States to face criminal charges. Prosecutors in the Southern District of New York had refused to drop the charges, so the defendants' lawyers developed a network of contacts with then-President Clinton who pardoned the two men in early 2001. In this case, the Justice Department sought production of documents as part of its investigation of circumstances surrounding the pardon. The court held that materials related to procuring Rich's pardon were not privileged because the attorneys were acting as lobbyists, not lawyers, once the decision to seek a pardon was made. Because lobbying could legally be done by non-lawyers, the lawyers' communications were not for the purpose of rendering legal assistance to Rich. Needless to say, this opinion has worried many lawyers who do things for clients, e.g., lobbying, that non-lawyers could also legally do.

3.   With all this in mind, go back to the facts in our problem. May the other lawyer force you, Carter's lawyer, to testify that your client, John Carter, admitted to you that he had lied to the buyer of his home about the tendency of the basement to flood?

a.   Why should the law protect against disclosure, communications with a lawyer that were solely designed to help the client avoid the consequences of his wrongful conduct? Professor Wigmore says:

> "In order to promote freedom of consultation of legal advisers by clients, the apprehension of compelled disclosure by the legal advisers must be removed; hence the law must prohibit such disclosure except on the client's consent." 8 Wigmore, Evidence § 2291 at 545 (McNaughton rev. 1961).

Are you convinced?

b.   Because the exercise of the attorney-client privilege so clearly conflicts with the search for truth, commentators and courts have long held that the privilege "ought to be strictly confined within the narrowest possible limits consistent with the logic of its principle." 8 Wigmore, supra § 2291, at 554. Thus:

(1) While Carter cannot be forced to testify about the content of his conversation with you, the fact that he talked to you about what he knew will not prevent Carter himself from being forced to testify as to the underlying facts about his knowledge of the tendency to flood.

(2) Similarly, the attorney-client privilege will not prevent you from being compelled to produce your notes of the statement by the former owner. Do you see why?

(3) Likewise, the privilege will not protect against your being forced to reveal what you heard about your client from the banker. Again, when you look at the factors required before a statement is protected by the attorney-client privilege, you should see several reasons this is so.

(4) If Carter had told you that he planned to lie to the buyer *before* he did so, would the statement have been privileged? Look again at the crime-fraud exception in Proposed Federal Rule of Evidence 503(d)(1), supra.

c.   The point of this discussion is that lawyers often glibly cite the "privilege" when it either doesn't apply or they are relying on some other doctrine. The attorney-client privilege would protect only one kind of material in this Problem against testimony from the lawyer. If the lawyer is not to talk to the client's opponent about other facts in the Problem, it must be on the basis of some other principles.

B.   INFORMATION PROTECTED BY WORK PRODUCT IMMUNITY

1.   What constitutes a lawyer's "work product" and what are the consequences of so designating it?

a.   Restatement Third, The Law Governing Lawyers § 87 says:

"(1) Work product consists of tangible material or its intangible equivalent in unwritten or oral form, other than underlying facts, prepared by a lawyer for litigation then in progress or in reasonable anticipation of future litigation.

"(2) Opinion work product consists of the opinions or mental impressions of a lawyer; all other work product is ordinary work product.

"(3) Except for material which by applicable law is not so protected, work product is immune from discovery or other compelled disclosure * * * ."

b.   Work product immunity is the legacy of Hickman v. Taylor, 329 U.S. 495, 67 S.Ct. 385, 91 L.Ed. 451 (1947). Construing the proper scope of discovery, the Court wrote: "Not even the most liberal of discovery theories can justify unwarranted inquiries into the files and the mental impressions of an attorney." The Court went on to say that where one side had information other than mental impressions that was "essential to the preparation of [the other side's] case," it could be discovered "and production might be justified where the witnesses are no longer available or can be reached only with difficulty." The doctrine is now embodied in Federal Rules of Civil Procedure, Rule 26(b)(3).

c.   In re Sealed Case, 146 F.3d 881 (D.C.Cir.1998), involved materials prepared in anticipation of litigation that had not yet been filed. The Republican National Committee had founded a think tank and loaned it $2.5 million. The Washington Post raised a question whether federal election laws applied to it, and the Democratic National Committee filed suit alleging that they did. In between the news story and the lawsuit, lawyers prepared various memoranda and the question was whether work product protection applied to them. The court held that it did. The test is whether litigation could reasonably have been anticipated; the lack of a specific case at the time the documents were prepared did not deny the protection.

d. Likewise, United States v. Adlman, 134 F.3d 1194 (2d Cir.1998), held that a study that a CPA prepared for a tax attorney predicting how the IRS would view a proposed transaction qualified as prepared "in anticipation of litigation." A document prepared "because of" the prospect of litigation would tend to show legal strategy expected to be employed and be exactly the kind of document *Hickman* intended to protect. Do you agree? Was Judge Kearse right in her dissent that planning lawyers will now claim work product immunity for a wide variety of documents, saying that litigation about the validity of the transaction was always a possibility?

2. Is any of the information in this Problem protected by work product immunity?

a. What about the interview with the former owner? Did you interview him in anticipation of litigation? Does it matter whether the anticipated litigation was this particular lawsuit?

b. Should the fact that the former owner is now dead mean that the notes you took will be discoverable? As we will see *infra*, a witness' death does not affect the character of the notes as work product. However, under Federal Rule 26(b)(3), a "party seeking discovery [may show it] has substantial need of the materials in preparation of the party's case and that the party is unable without undue hardship to obtain the substantial equivalent of the material by other means."

3. Does it matter whether the notes of the discussion with the now-deceased former owner are considered ordinary or opinion work product?

a. Look again at the language of Hickman v. Taylor quoted above; "ordinary" work product may be obtained in discovery upon a showing of "substantial need." However, according to Restatement Third, The Law Governing Lawyers § 89:

"[O]pinion work product is immune from discovery or other compelled disclosure unless * * * extraordinary circumstances justify disclosure."

b. Should the fact that the former owner is now dead constitute such "extraordinary circumstances" that compelled disclosure is justified? Comment *d* to Restatement § 89 says that "the concept of 'extraordinary circumstances' has never been intelligibly defined. It apparently signifies unwillingness on the part of tribunals to put the work-product immunity on quite the same footing as the attorney-client privilege."

c. How should the concept apply in this Problem? If you make sure to comment in your notes about the witness' credibility, why should the notes not be absolutely immune from discovery?

C. THE LAWYER'S PROFESSIONAL OBLIGATION OF CONFIDENTIALITY

1. May you respond to the informal inquiry about your client's financial situation? Is the chance information learned at a party something the lawyer must keep confidential unless ordered by a court to disclose it?

a.   Is the information about your client's financial situation covered by either the attorney-client privilege or work product immunity? Why or why not?

b.   Look at Model Rule 1.6(a). Does the information you received from the banker qualify as "relating to the representation"? Remember, you have said yourself that the information may affect your settlement posture.

c.   Look at ABA Model Code of Professional Responsibility, DR 4–101(A). Is the information learned at the party a "confidence" of the client as defined there? Is it a "secret"? Would it tend to embarrass the client? Was it learned as part of the "professional relationship"?

2.   What does it mean to say that the information is protected against disclosure by these rules? Does it mean any more than that the lawyer may not volunteer the information to others?

a.   In Matter of Goebel, 703 N.E.2d 1045 (Ind.1998), the lawyer represented a criminal defendant while the lawyer's partner was handling an unrelated guardianship. By chance, the husband of the guardianship client was to be a prosecution witness in the criminal case. The criminal client asked the guardianship client's address. To prove he didn't know, the lawyer showed the criminal client an envelope returned because it had the wrong address. However, even the wrong address was enough to help the criminal client find the prosecution witness and kill him. The court said that the incorrect address was "information relating to the representation" of the guardianship client. Thus the Court publicly reprimanded and admonished the lawyer for revealing it.

b.   If you were called to testify about what you heard at the party about Carter's financial situation, would you be required to reveal the information? It is important to see that one of the important distinctions between information that is "privileged" and information that is protected only by the obligation of "confidentiality" is that a lawyer may be required to testify about the latter. See, e.g., Restatement Third, The Law Governing Lawyers § 63.

c.   Should the lawyer have to resist the order to testify rather than simply comply? Take a look at Model Rule 1.6, Comment [11]. Does the approach outlined there make sense to you?

D.   HOW LEGAL PROTECTION AGAINST DISCLOSURE CAN BE LOST

1.   Should disclosure of privileged information outside the confidential relationship forfeit the attorney-client privilege?

a.   If the client, by mistake or otherwise, tells an outsider—even a trusted friend—the content of your confidential conversations with him, the attorney-client privilege as to those conversations will be lost for all time. That means you can be required to testify about the discussions as well. Restatement Third, The Law Governing Lawyers § 79.

b.   Suppose your revelation of privileged information is made in settlement negotiations, i.e., you say "I have told my client to be willing to accept $50,000." Typically, such a revelation—whether by lawyer or client—will result in waiver of the privilege. See, e.g., United States v. Martin, 773 F.2d 579 (4th Cir.1985) (attempt to settle tax case).

c.   Further, if a lawyer reveals some privileged information, often the privilege will be lost at least for all information needed to put the privileged material into context. See, e.g., United States v. Woodall, 438 F.2d 1317 (5th Cir.1970) (en banc). Indeed, the waiver may be construed even more broadly. See Restatement Third, The Law Governing Lawyers § 79, Comment *f* (subject matter waiver).

d.   Would such a revelation violate your professional obligation of confidentiality? Look at Model Rule 1.6(a). A lawyer may make disclosures that are "impliedly authorized to carry out the representation," but the fact that disclosure does not violate the obligation of confidentiality has no necessary effect on whether it forfeits the attorney-client privilege.

2.   Should the privilege be lost as to later private litigation if a company voluntarily turns documents over documents to a government agency in an effort to demonstrate there has been no violation of law?

a.   In re Columbia/HCA Healthcare Corporation Billing Practices Litigation, 293 F.3d 289 (6th Cir.2002), involved the defendant's turn over of privileged matter to the Justice Department and the Health Care Finance Administration pursuant to an agreement that the disclosure did not "constitute a waiver of any applicable privilege or claim under the work product doctrine." The court acknowledged that recognizing confidentiality even after such a turnover would tend to make it easier for the government to obtain needed information. It concluded, however, that the same principle of practicality would permit confidential turnover of information in a private case, and that is clearly not the law. Thus, the court affirmed a holding that disclosure to the government constituted a waiver of both the attorney-client privilege and work product protection in a later private action.

b.   McKesson HBOC, Inc. v. Adler, 562 S.E.2d 809 (Ga.Ct.App.2002), however, drew a distinction between privilege and work product on this issue. Adler, a shareholder, sued McKesson HBOC for filing false financial statements in connection with an upcoming merger. As part of its informal investigation of the merger, the SEC had received internal reports from McKesson pursuant to a confidentiality agreement. Now, Adler sought discovery of the reports given to the SEC, but the court found McKesson had a valid work-product claim. First, the court noted, while disclosure of information to a third party may forfeit the privilege, work-product protection is different and designed to protect the efforts of lawyers working in the adversary system. McKesson's insistence on a confidentiality agreement showed that it intended to protect the information. Finally, the party seeking work-product information must show a substantial need for the reports, and an undue burden of obtaining the information through other means. The court found that Adler had shown neither.

3. What if you, the lawyer, want ethics advice from a lawyer in another firm about your own obligations in a particular matter? May you discuss the issues in the matter with the other lawyer without violating your duty of confidentiality and forfeiting the privilege?

a. ABA Formal Opinion 98–411 (1998) acknowledged that such consultations, made typically without fee and without intending to create an additional lawyer-client relationship, are often useful and in the interest of the client. However, the Opinion tells the lawyer to (1) do so in hypothetical terms, (2) get permission from the client if the consultation might put the client at risk, (3) not consult a lawyer who might represent the adverse party, and (4) obtain assurances of confidentiality for the information.

b. The Ethics Opinion does not resolve the issue of waiver of the attorney-client privilege issue, of course, although the exclusive use of hypothetical facts in the consultation should be helpful in that regard. Cf. Model Rule 1.6, Comment [4].

c. Notice that the Model Rules now specifically allow a lawyer to use confidential information as reasonably necessary to seek legal advice about the lawyer's compliance with ethics requirements. See Model Rule 1.6(b)(2) & Comment [7].

4. How much affirmative effort must a lawyer undertake to preserve the confidentiality of communications with clients and others?

a. It is important that lawyers carefully maintain the confidentiality of their oral and written communications with clients. See Restatement Third, The Law Governing Lawyers § 60(1)(b): "[T]he lawyer must take steps reasonable in the circumstances to protect confidential client information against impermissible use or disclosure." See also, Model Rule 1.6, Comment [2].

b. Illinois State Bar Opinion 90–7 (1990) notes that if a communication is capable of being overheard, even though not intended to be, the privilege can be lost. The Opinion argues that talking with a client over a cordless telephone such as a car phone might forfeit the privilege because such conversations can be overheard by someone with a radio receiver. A lawyer is not required to ask whether the client is using a cordless or mobile phone, the Opinion said, but if it sounds like the client may be doing so, the lawyer should warn that the privilege may be lost.

See also, New York State Bar Association Opinion 641 (Feb. 16, 1993) (lawyers obeying recycling laws must be careful to assure papers with client confidences cannot be read by others).

c. ABA Formal Opinion 99–413 (March 10, 1999) discusses the use of unencrypted email and concludes that its use neither violates the duty of confidentiality nor waives the privilege unless the client insists on, or unusual circumstances require, heightened security. E-mail communications are legally protected against interception, the Opinion said, so lawyer and client have a reasonable expectation of privacy. Further, the risk of interception is no greater than that inherent in land-line phones. Several state bar opinions come to the same conclusion. Could lawyers effectively carry on their practice in modern times if the rule were different? See new ABA Model Rule 1.6, Comment [16]: a lawyer need not "use special security measures if the method of communication affords a reasonable expectation of privacy."

5. What, then, should happen if a lawyer or client inadvertently reveals confidential client information? Suppose, for example, the lawyer's secretary mistakenly faxes a highly confidential memo to opposing counsel instead of to the client?

a. Restatement Third, The Law Governing Lawyers § 79, Comment *h*, says that "waiver does not result if the client or other disclosing person took precautions reasonable in the circumstances to guard against such disclosure." See, e.g., In re Reorganization of Electric Mutual Liability Insurance Co. (Bermuda), 681 N.E.2d 838 (Mass.1997) (if the client could show that adequate protective steps were taken to preserve the confidentiality of the information, the disclosure would be presumed not to have been voluntary).

b. United States v. Gangi, 1 F.Supp.2d 256 (S.D.N.Y.1998), involved a government strategy memorandum in a securities and bank fraud case that was mistakenly handed to a magistrate judge in open court in Arizona in the belief it was a copy of the indictment. In fact, however, it contained highly confidential wiretap material and information about witnesses. It bore the legend "This Document Contains Grand Jury Material" but it was not otherwise marked confidential or privileged. The judge had turned the document over to defense counsel, it got into the hands of other corporate officers, and for three weeks it was in the public court file. Only when the case was moved to New York did the Government realize the mistake and ask that all copies of the document be returned. Under these circumstances, Judge Chin ruled, the privilege was waived, although he did permit redacting a limited amount of sensitive information. See also, S.E.C. v. Cassano, 189 F.R.D. 83 (S.D.N.Y.1999) (erroneously disclosed 100–page trial memo cannot regain its character as attorney-client privileged and protected as work product).

c. In Amgen v. Hoechst Marion Roussel, Inc., 190 F.R.D. 287 (D.Mass. 2000), the defense counsel inadvertently produced a box of over 3200 pages of privileged material among boxes with 70,000 pages of unprivileged material. The opinion distinguishes three ways courts have approached such situations—the "never waived" rule that requires giving the documents back, the "strict accountability" rule that treats all such situations as waivers, and a third or middle ground that looks at (1) reasonableness of precautions taken, (2) time taken to discover the error, (3) scope of the production, (4) extent of the disclosure, and (5) the interests of fairness in the situation. In this case, the defendant didn't realize what had happened until the plaintiff called the situation to its attention and little could be done to avoid damage. The court treated the privilege as waived, saying it would be unjust to reward counsel's "gross negligence."

d. In State Compensation Insurance Fund v. WPS, Inc., 82 Cal. Rptr.2d 799 (Ct.App.1999), the California Court of Appeals told counsel that when they receive inadvertently disclosed documents, they should refrain from examining them more than necessary in order to confirm they are privileged. They should then immediately notify the sender that they have the material, work out how to return the material and protect their privileged character. If a lawyer fails to give the required notice, the court said, she may be sanctioned up to and including disqualification. Do you agree that the court should place the obligation on the recipient of the documents?

e. In re Nitla S.A. de C.V., 92 S.W.3d 419 (Tex.2002), was a case where arguably the trial court, not the lawyer, made the improper disclosure. Nitla S.A., a Mexican pharmaceutical company, sued Bank of America (BOA) for alleged misappropriation of millions of dollars Nitla had deposited. Nitla sought to discover certain documents from BOA, but the bank claimed the documents were privileged. The trial court found that BOA had no valid claim of privilege, granted Nitla's motion to compel disclosure, and gave Nitla the documents. BOA told the court it intended to appeal the motion and asked both the court and Nitla to stay review of the documents pending appeal, but Nitla's counsel began review of the documents nonetheless. Subsequently, the court of appeals upheld BOA's privilege claim, and Nitla's counsel returned the documents, but BOA then sought to disqualify that counsel, contending that BOA was irreparably harmed by Nitla's access to privileged documents. The Supreme Court of Texas held that the trial court did not abuse its discretion in refusing to disqualify Nitla's counsel. Although BOA argued that the documents identified additional witnesses for Nitla to depose, the court found that BOA did not identify actual harm that resulted from Nitla's access to the documents. Furthermore, any harm to BOA could be remedied in a less severe way, such as by quashing the depositions of the additional witnesses.[3]

f. Model Rule 4.4(b), Comment [2], says: "[T]his Rule requires the lawyer to promptly notify the sender in order to permit that person to take protective measures. Whether the lawyer is required to take additional steps, such as returning the original document, is a matter of law beyond the scope of these Rules, as is the question of whether the privileged status of a document has been waived." Has the ABA been as helpful as anyone reasonably can be on this issue? Has it instead abdicated its role in helping to resolve some difficult questions?

---

3. Contrast a lower court Texas case a year earlier: In re Bank of America, N.A., 45 S.W.3d 238 (Tex.App.2001). The court ruled that the trial court's physical turnover of defense documents to plaintiff was substantively wrong and did not cause the documents to lose their character as privileged and work product. The other side now knew their contents but could not use or refer to them at trial. The court concluded: "plaintiff's counsel should be disqualified after extensively reviewing and digesting approximately 135 pages of defendant's privileged information, obtained through no wrongdoing."

6. Should the attorney-client privilege, work product immunity, or the lawyer's duty of confidentiality be lost by the passage of time or by the client's death?

a. Restatement Third, The Law Governing Lawyers § 77, after noting that lawyers may sometimes testify to privileged conversations in order to explain the terms of a will or otherwise carry out the wishes of the deceased client, says in Comment *d*:

> "It would be desirable that a tribunal be empowered to withhold the privilege of a person then deceased as to a communication that bears on a litigated issue of pivotal significance. The tribunal could balance the interest in confidentiality against any exceptional need for the communication. The tribunal also could consider limiting the proof or sealing the record to limit disclosure. Permitting such disclosure would do little to inhibit clients from confiding in their lawyers."

Do you agree with this attempt to balance the competing interests in cases where the confidential communications could help do justice in a pending matter? Do you agree that such a rule would have little effect on the willingness of clients to entrust information to their lawyers?

b. Matter of John Doe Grand Jury Investigation, 562 N.E.2d 69 (Mass.1990), gave the usual answer on some tough facts. The case involved whether the late Charles Stuart had been responsible for the deaths of Carol and Christopher Stuart. Charles Stuart had talked with his lawyer for two hours on the day before his death, and the prosecutor guessed that he had admitted the crime to the lawyer. If so, the state could both stop looking for a suspect for the murders and be sure not to charge someone else for them. The court held, however, that the privilege did not end with Charles' death and no amount of interest in knowing the truth could justify making the lawyer testify. Do you agree? If the prosecutor gave Stuart criminal immunity, he could have been forced to testify. Now, Stuart was dead. Should the court treat that as the functional equivalent of immunity in order to find the truth?

c. What rule would you apply in a case like State v. Macumber, 544 P.2d 1084 (Ariz.1976)? The defendant had been convicted of two murders and was serving a life term. At trial, his lawyer tried to call two other lawyers who were prepared to testify that their now-deceased client had confessed to them that he, not Macumber, had committed the murders. The court excluded the testimony. Communications with a lawyer are privileged, the court said, and that privilege does not end with death. Is the Restatement wrong to suggest that sometimes the need to do justice to the living should prevail over the interests of the dead?[4]

---

4. We will see this issue later when we get to Problem 30, *infra*. At least part of the problem in *Macumber* may have been doubts about the truth of such confessions. One can give a relatively costless gift to a friend by making a deathbed confession to a crime the friend committed.

d.   Swidler & Berlin v. United States, 524 U.S. 399, 118 S.Ct. 2081, 141 L.Ed.2d 379 (1998), was the celebrated case testing whether the Office of Independent Counsel could obtain notes of conversations between Vincent Foster (a White House lawyer) and his lawyer shortly before Mr. Foster's suicide. The D.C. Circuit had found that, while cases often say the attorney-client privilege survives death, it is usually said in the context of finding an exception to the rule to assist in construction of a will, the so-called testamentary exception. Thus, the court said, it is reasonable to make another exception for communications significant to a criminal prosecution since the client's own criminal liability obviously expires when he does. Further, the court held, post-death reputation is not sufficiently important to most people to make them not be candid with their lawyer even if the privilege would not survive them. See In re Sealed Case, 124 F.3d 230 (D.C.Cir.1997).

The U.S. Supreme Court (6 to 3) reversed. Writing for the Court and upholding survival of the privilege, Chief Justice Rehnquist said:

> "While the arguments against the survival of the privilege are by no means frivolous, they are based in large part on speculation—thoughtful speculation, but speculation nonetheless—as to whether posthumous termination of the privilege would diminish a client's willingness to confide in an attorney. In an area where empirical information would be useful, it is scant and inconclusive." 524 U.S. at 410, 118 S.Ct. at 2088, 141 L.Ed.2d at 388.

Do you agree that the problem is a lack of empirical evidence? Do you suppose there is solid evidence demonstrating the value of the attorney-client privilege in the first place? Might it be that most of our views about the privilege are closely tied to almost instinctive ideas of what justice requires?

e.   In Wesp v. Everson, 33 P.3d 191 (Colo.2001), Wesp sought tort damages against her mother and stepfather, Cheryl and Frank Brewer, based on charges that Frank had sexually abused her. After criminal charges were filed against Frank, both Brewers wrote letters to family and friends and committed suicide. Wesp sought to depose Brewer's defense attorney in the criminal action to find out what Brewer had told him. She argued that the suicide letters mentioned a joint meeting between Cheryl and Frank Brewer and Frank's defense attorney and constituted a waiver of the privilege with respect to the subject matter of all meetings with the lawyer. The court agreed that the meeting with both Brewers was not privileged because Cheryl, who was not represented by that lawyer, was present. However, the fact of that meeting could not operate as a waiver to the privilege in private meetings that Frank had with his lawyer. The court relied on *Swidler & Berlin* to hold that the privilege survives the death of the client and declined either to create a "manifest injustice" basis to invade the privilege or to expand the "testamentary exception" to tort cases such as this one. Do you agree with this result?

———

PROBLEM 8

CONFIDENTIALITY AND THE ORGANIZATION AS A CLIENT

A corporation is not a "person" that has a privilege against self-incrimination.[1] One can therefore argue that a corporation should also not have an attorney-client privilege. However, the law has not developed that way. Business corporations and other organization clients have the protection of the attorney-client privilege, work product immunity, and the lawyer's professional duty of confidentiality. Yet the fact that a client is an organization rather than an individual raises some additional important issues that are considered in this problem. The problem closes with some critically important issues of limits on the duty of confidentiality when it collides with important interests of third parties.

FACTS

Your client, the Western Chemical Company, produces some of the country's best known chemical fertilizers. The availability of those fertilizers is among the reasons American agriculture is the world's most productive. But fertilizers are composed of materials that are highly toxic. If even small quantities of those materials seep into a region's drinking water, for example, deaths from cancer over a ten year period can be expected to rise by at least 5%. Thus, companies like Western Chemical are required to file detailed reports to the EPA about the quantities of such materials they have on hand, when and how they are converted into fertilizer, and the disposition of any unused materials. Filing an intentionally inaccurate report is a federal crime.

An employee in one of Western Chemical Company's regional offices sent a letter to company management claiming that, when a plant manager recently found he could not account for 10,000 pounds of a phosphate compound, the manager falsely reported the material had been sold to another company at a large profit. Western Chemical asked your firm to interview employees of its regional offices to determine whether the incident occurred and whether it was part of a larger pattern of deception.

As a result of your investigation, you concluded that the incident reported to the company probably happened. Indeed, you learned that a former assistant general counsel of Western Chemical had written a confidential memorandum authorizing the plant manager to file inaccurate reports "if you think you won't get caught." You also learned that the company's auditors did not discover that the purported sale of the compound was erroneous. Thus, they certified a report of company earnings that exceeded

---

1. McPhaul v. United States, 364 U.S. 372, 81 S.Ct. 138, 5 L.Ed.2d 136 (1960).

analysts' estimates and earned large bonuses for company managers.

Recently, International Chemicals offered to purchase Western Chemical. International's own general counsel has asked you for a copy of the report of your investigation, but the former officers of Western Chemical have refused to permit you to turn it over. Of course, the EPA would also like to see—but has not subpoenaed—a copy of your report and any supporting documentation, which would include the memorandum that purported to authorize deceptive reporting.

QUESTIONS

A. Privilege and confidentiality rules when the client is an organization

1. Will the results of your internal investigation be protected by the attorney-client privilege or work product immunity?

a. By far the leading case on the corporate attorney-client privilege is still Upjohn Co. v. United States, 449 U.S. 383, 101 S.Ct. 677, 66 L.Ed.2d 584 (1981).

Upjohn makes and sells pharmaceuticals all over the world. In January 1976, accountants doing an audit of one of Upjohn's foreign subsidiaries found that the subsidiary made payments to or for the benefit of foreign government officials in order to secure government business. Such payments were very likely a violation of U.S. law, and Upjohn's general counsel launched an investigation. Upjohn managers were directed to treat the situation as highly confidential and to cooperate fully in the investigation. Some received questionnaires that they returned to the general counsel; others were interviewed in person by inside or outside counsel.

In March 1976, the company voluntarily submitted a preliminary report to the Securities and Exchange Commission on Form 8–K disclosing certain questionable payments. A copy of the report was simultaneously submitted to the Internal Revenue Service, which immediately began an investigation to determine the tax consequences of the payments. Agents conducting the investigation were given lists by Upjohn of all those interviewed and all who had responded to the questionnaire, but in November 1976, the Service issued a summons to Upjohn demanding all of its internal files relating to the general counsel's investigation. Upjohn said those files and reports were protected both by the attorney-client privilege and as work product.

The Court of Appeals ordered disclosure, finding that the investigation ranged far beyond senior management officials, that only interviews with the corporate "control group" could be protected by the attorney-client privilege, and that work product immunity did not protect corporations at all. The Supreme Court reversed, saying:

"The attorney-client privilege is the oldest of the privileges for confidential communications known to the common law. Its purpose is to encourage full and frank communication between attorneys and their clients and thereby promote broader public interests in the observance of law and administration of justice. The privilege recognizes that sound legal advice or advocacy serves public ends and that such advice or advocacy depends upon the lawyer's being fully informed by the client. * * *

" * * * [Limiting protection to communications from a control group] overlooks the fact that the privilege exists to protect not only the giving of professional advice to those who can act on it but also the giving of information to the lawyer to enable him to give sound and informed advice. The first step in the resolution of any legal problem is ascertaining the factual background and sifting through the facts with an eye to the legally relevant. * * *

" * * * Middle-level—and indeed lower-level—employees can, by actions within the scope of their employment, embroil the corporation in serious legal difficulties, and it is only natural that these employees would have the relevant information needed by corporate counsel if he is adequately to advise the client with respect to such actual or potential difficulties. * * *

"The narrow scope given the attorney-client privilege by the court below not only makes it difficult for corporate attorneys to formulate sound advice when their client is faced with a specific legal problem but also threatens to limit the valuable efforts of corporate counsel to ensure their client's compliance with the law. * * *

"The communications at issue were made by Upjohn employees to counsel for Upjohn acting as such, at the direction of corporate superiors in order to secure legal advice from counsel. * * * Information, not available from upper-echelon management, was needed to supply a basis for legal advice concerning compliance with securities and tax laws, foreign laws, currency regulations, duties to shareholders, and potential litigation in each of these areas. The communications concerned matters within the scope of the employees' corporate duties, and the employees themselves were sufficiently aware that they were being questioned in order that the corporation could obtain legal advice. * * * Consistent with the underlying purposes of the attorney-client privilege, these communications must be protected against compelled disclosure.

" * * * Here the Government was free to question the employees who communicated with Thomas and outside counsel. * * * While it would probably be more convenient for the Government to secure the results of petitioner's internal investigation by simply subpoenaing the questionnaires and notes taken by petitioner's attorneys, such considerations of convenience do not overcome the policies served by the attorney-client privilege. * * * "[2]

b.   *Upjohn* is also still the leading case on lawyer work product in the corporate setting.

"The Government concedes, wisely, that the Court of Appeals erred and that the work-product doctrine does apply to IRS summonses. This doctrine was announced by the Court over 30 years ago in Hickman v. Taylor, 329 U.S. 495 (1947). * * * The 'strong public policy' underlying the work-product doctrine * * * has been substantially incorporated in Federal Rule of Civil Procedure 26(b)(3).

[handwritten margin note: Gov't Claims Strong showing]

" * * * While conceding the applicability of the work-product doctrine, the Government asserts that it has made a sufficient showing of necessity to overcome its protections. * * *

"The Government stresses that interviewees are scattered across the globe and that Upjohn has forbidden its employees to answer questions it considers irrelevant. * * * [However,] forcing an attorney to disclose notes and memoranda of witnesses' oral statements is particularly disfavored because it tends to reveal the attorney's mental processes.

"Rule 26 * * * permits disclosure of documents and tangible things constituting attorney work product upon a showing of substantial need and inability to obtain the equivalent without undue hardship. * * * Rule 26 goes on, however, to state that '[i]n ordering discovery of such materials when the required showing has been made, the court shall protect against disclosure of mental impressions, conclusions, opinions or legal theories of an attorney or other representative of a party concerning the litigation.' Although this language does not specifically refer to memoranda based on oral statements of witnesses, the *Hickman* court stressed the danger that compelled disclosure of such memoranda would reveal the attorney's mental processes. It is clear that this is the sort of material the draftsmen of the Rule had in mind as deserving special protection.

"While we are not prepared at this juncture to say that such material is always protected by the work-product rule, we think a far stronger showing of necessity and unavailability by other means than was made by the Government or applied by the Magistrate in this case would be necessary to compel disclosure. * * * "

2.   Do you agree with the Court's concern that corporations must have the ability to get candid legal advice in order to help them comply with the law?

a.   Does the complexity of many modern corporate organizations mean that, without protection of the privilege, it would be impossible for manage-

---

2. Chief Justice Burger filed an opinion   judgment.
concurring in part and concurring in the

ment to try to identify instances of non-compliance with the law as Upjohn tried to do? Might it instead be likely that corporations would conduct compliance audits whether or not they were privileged simply because failing to comply with the law could subject them to massive liability?[3]

b. Payton v. New Jersey Turnpike Authority, 691 A.2d 321 (N.J. 1997), examined application of the privilege to an investigation of alleged sexual harassment. Under federal law, an employer is required to conduct a prompt, thorough investigation of such charges, and both lawyers and non-lawyers participated in that investigation in this case. The plaintiff wanted to see what the investigation turned up. The court acknowledged that assuring confidentiality is an important way to encourage complete and accurate reporting, but it declined to deny the plaintiff all access to what the defendant had discovered. The presence of lawyers among the investigators did not privilege all documents, the Court said. Indeed, by asserting the fact of the investigation as a defense to the plaintiff's claim, the defendant was found to have waived its privilege except as to documents giving what could fairly be called legal advice or conclusions. The court thus ordered the trial judge to conduct a document by document review of the materials and even to redact privileged material if possible, rather than denying access to a document altogether.

3. We know that *Upjohn* rejected the "control group" test. Does that mean there are no limits on what individuals' communications within a corporation should be protected?

a. In Samaritan Foundation v. Goodfarb, 862 P.2d 870 (Ariz.1993), a paralegal had interviewed operating room personnel in preparation for defense of a medical malpractice case, and the plaintiff wanted summaries of the interviews. The court asked whether the interviews were conducted "to assist the lawyer in assessing or responding to the legal consequences of [the employee's own] conduct for the corporate client." The court ordered the notes disclosed because, although the personnel were witnesses to acts alleged to be negligent, their own acts were not alleged to be negligent.

b. United States v. Ackert, 169 F.3d 136 (2d Cir.1999), refused to apply the privilege to conversations between a corporation's in-house tax counsel and a legally-trained outside investment banker who had explained the logic underlying a tax-advantaged investment proposal the banker's company was touting. When the IRS wanted to question the investment banker, the company argued that he had been assisting its legal evaluation of the proposal even if not giving it legal advice. The court rejected the contention. What the corporation's lawyer told management would be privileged, but not what an outside investment banker told the lawyer.[4]

---

3. Some courts have recognized a related "self-evaluative" privilege protecting internal reports done by non-lawyers. See, e.g., Bredice v. Doctors Hospital, Inc., 50 F.R.D. 249 (D.D.C.1970), aff'd 479 F.2d 920 (D.C.Cir.1973). But as suggested in Federal Trade Commission v. TRW, Inc., 628 F.2d 207 (D.C.Cir.1980), the concept has met with limited success in the courts.

4. *But see* Boca Investerings Partnership v. United States, 31 F.Supp.2d 9 (D.D.C. 1998) (communications between corporate management and a lawyer working in a tradi-

c.   However, Satcom International Group PLC v. Orbcomm International Partners, L.P., 49 F.Supp.2d 331 (S.D.N.Y.1999), held the entire meeting of a corporation's Executive Committee was privileged because its general counsel was present. The meeting had been called solely to discuss termination of a contract with the plaintiff, so legal issues were central to the discussions. The fact that the participants also discussed possible business consequences of the action did not render the meeting unprivileged.

4.   Suppose that another, or even the principal, target of the investigation is a leading figure in the organization. How should these rules apply when the organizational setting is the government, for example, and one possible client is a prominent government official?

a.   In re Grand Jury Subpoena Duces Tecum, 112 F.3d 910 (8th Cir.1997), cert. denied sub nom. Office of the President v. Office of Independent Counsel, 521 U.S. 1105, 117 S.Ct. 2482, 138 L.Ed.2d 991 (1997), involved the grand jury assisting Independent Counsel Kenneth Starr. It had subpoenaed "all documents created during meetings attended by any attorney from the Office of Counsel to the President and Hillary Rodham Clinton (regardless whether any other person was present)." The White House said nine sets of notes met that description but refused to produce them citing the attorney-client privilege and work product. Mrs. Clinton was permitted to intervene. Citing Restatement Third, The Law Governing Lawyers [§ 74], the court said the government may assert an attorney-client privilege. However, it said United States v. Nixon, 418 U.S. 683, 94 S.Ct. 3090, 41 L.Ed.2d 1039 (1974), makes clear that the White House cannot easily resist a subpoena, particularly one from a federal grand jury. If a government official wants advice about possible criminal liability for past acts, the court said, he or she should get it from a private lawyer, not a government employee. Further, although White House lawyers attended meetings that Ms. Clinton had with her personal lawyer, the court found no common interest that would extend the privilege to notes taken by the government attorneys. The fact that Ms. Clinton's problems might have political ramifications was not enough to create a cognizable governmental interest in having White House lawyers there. And while Ms. Clinton might herself face litigation in Whitewater-related matters, there was no reason to believe the White House had the same problem because the Office of the White House cannot be indicted. Thus, the government lawyers' notes did not have work product immunity either.[5]

tional business role who gave legal advice concerning a particular corporate transaction held privileged).

5.   While part of the White House resistance was based on Ms. Clinton's alleged status as a White House official, albeit an unpaid one, that argument cut both ways. The Eighth Circuit held that lawyers in the White House do not have a governmental attorney-client privilege to withhold relevant information from the Independent Counsel (who stands in the shoes of the Attorney General), in light of 28 U.S.C.A. § 535(b), which provides:

"Any information, allegation, or complaint received in a department or agency of the

b. In re Lindsey, 158 F.3d 1263 (D.C.Cir.1998), involved a Deputy White House Counsel talking to President Clinton and outside counsel for the President in connection with a grand jury investigation of the President's alleged criminal conduct. The attorney-client privilege for White House Counsel communications, the court said, ran only to the government. The government, in turn, had no legitimate interest in covering up criminal conduct, and government lawyers are not hired "to protect wrongdoers from public exposure." Even the possibility the lawyer's testimony might be used against the President in an impeachment context was not enough to make it privileged, the court said. The President can retain a personal lawyer. He did, and to the extent the White House lawyer was used as an "intermediary" between the President and his private counsel, the privilege did apply.[6] Judge Tatel, dissenting in part, agreed that personal legal advice that Mr. Lindsey gave to President Clinton was not privileged, but argued that official legal advice that any White House counsel gave a sitting President should be privileged, lest no President know what would later be considered confidential.

c. In re Witness Before the Special Grand Jury 2000–2, 288 F.3d 289 (7th Cir.2002), involved conversations between Roger Bickel, then-Chief Legal Counsel to Illinois Secretary of State George Ryan, and Mr. Ryan. Ryan consulted with Bickel on both official and non-official matters, then and later when Ryan was Governor of Illinois. Meanwhile, federal prosecutors had begun investigating the Secretary of State's office for evidence of an alleged bribery scheme, and the grand jury hearing the bribery case subpoenaed him. Bickel and Governor Ryan resisted the subpoena, arguing that Bickel's conversations in the Secretary of State's office were privileged, but the Seventh Circuit ordered Bickel to testify. The court did more than say that a state official does not enjoy a personal attorney-client privilege with a state-employed attorney. It said that federal courts recognize no attorney-client privilege at all for government officials in a criminal case, even if the officials and the lawyers had been discussing official state business. A government lawyer has an overarching duty to act in the public interest, the court said, and thus is unlike a lawyer for an individual or corporation. In addition, the government lawyer's client, the state, may not be held criminally liable for its actions. Thus, the law recognizes the attorney-client privilege in this context is not necessary to foster open communications. Finally, the court noted, no attorney-client privilege exists for Federal Government officials in such cases (citing cases like *Lindsey*), and it declined to create such a privilege for state officials.

---

executive branch of the Government relating to violations of Title 18 involving Government officers and employees shall be expeditiously reported to the Attorney General by the head of the department or agency."
Later, In re Lindsey, 158 F.3d 1263 (D.C.Cir. 1998), came to the same conclusion.

6. Accord, In re Grand Jury Subpoena Duces Tecum, 112 F.3d 910 (8th Cir.1997), cert. denied sub nom. Office of the President v. Office of Independent Counsel, 521 U.S. 1105, 117 S.Ct. 2482, 138 L.Ed.2d 991 (1997).

5. Is a law firm an organization that may assert an attorney-client privilege?

a. United States v. Rowe, 96 F.3d 1294 (9th Cir.1996) applied the attorney-client privilege to internal investigations by associates assigned by a law firm of how one of the firm's lawyer's handled client funds. That lawyer was ultimately investigated by a grand jury that issued a subpoena to have the associates testify about their report to the firm's senior partner. The trial judge held that the associates were not in a lawyer-client relationship with the senior partner and that the fact finding did not qualify as "professional legal services." The Ninth Circuit disagreed on both counts. The associates were effectively in-house counsel and fact finding is an important part of lawyering, the court said. The court could not force the associates to testify.

b. Nesse v. Shaw Pittman, 206 F.R.D. 325 (D.D.C.2002), involved a malpractice case against the firm in which the plaintiff sought notes made by the firm's general counsel in his internal investigation of the conduct of firm members. Citing *Upjohn*, the court held such notes privileged and said they do not lose their protection when the general counsel discusses the findings with firm management. Notes taken by another member of the management committee in separate discussions with some of the same people, however, were found not privileged. The firm management committee is composed of lawyers, of course, but the court says that when they act as managers of the firm, the primary purpose of their activity is not legal representation. Thus, neither privilege nor work product protects the documents from discovery. Clearly, the case is likely to cause well-advised firms to have internal investigations conducted only by duly-appointed "counsel" to the firm.

c. Do these cases suggest that it will be wise for law firms to designate a lawyer within the firm as its general counsel, responsible for legal issues affecting the firm as an organization? Many well-advised firms are doing exactly that.

6. In this Problem, the former managers of Western Chemical—the ones who hired you to conduct the internal investigation—do not want you to turn your report over to new management. Who should control the privilege here?

a. An individual client to whom you owe a duty of confidentiality is typically the only one who can tell you when the protection should be waived. When the client is an organization, ordinarily whomever is in charge of the organization at the moment controls the waiver. Thus, the basic rule is that neither the privilege nor the duty of confidentiality prevents successor corporate management from learning the content of discussions of former management with corporate counsel.

b. A trustee in bankruptcy may waive the privilege in the face of former management's opposition to revelation of their discussions with counsel. Commodity Futures Trading Commission v. Weintraub, 471 U.S. 343, 105 S.Ct. 1986, 85 L.Ed.2d 372 (1985).

c. In re Grand Jury Subpoena, 274 F.3d 563 (1st Cir.2001), involved a novel interplay of personal and corporate privilege claims. Oldco Corporation entered into a plea agreement, agreed to cooperate with the government's ongoing investigation of its former officers, and thus expressly waived its attorney-client and work product privileges. Subsequently, the government issued a subpoena to Oldco's parent demanding the production of documents relating to a program run by Oldco in an earlier period in which it had been a closely held corporation run by Roe and Moe, with Lawyer as Oldco's counsel. Roe, Moe, and Lawyer resisted the subpoena, saying that in representing Oldco, Lawyer had really been representing Roe and Moe. Although Roe and Moe persuaded the court that Lawyer had represented them in their individual capacities, the court held that "a corporation may unilaterally waive the attorney-client privilege with respect to any communications made by a corporate officer in his corporate capacity, notwithstanding the existence of an individual attorney-client relationship between him and the corporation's counsel." Roe and Moe could assert attorney-client and work product privileges with regards to individual acts and liabilities, but not with regards to discussions involving the corporation.

7. Suppose the client is a trustee, a person with fiduciary obligations to others? Is the trust an "organization" like those we have been considering in this Problem? Even if it is for some purposes, who controls waiver of the privilege? For example, should a beneficiary of the trust be entitled to know what transpired in the discussion between lawyer and trustee?

a. ABA Formal Opinion 94–380 says that ordinarily the answer is no; a trustee or other fiduciary is entitled to consult a lawyer and Rule 1.6 has no exception where persons with fiduciary duties are involved. See, e.g., Wells Fargo Bank v. Superior Court (Boltwood), 990 P.2d 591 (Cal.2000) (trust beneficiaries have no right to see trustee-attorney communications about administration of the trust; trustee may have duties to the beneficiaries, but the lawyer does not).

b. Restatement Third, The Law Governing Lawyers § 84, notes an important exception. The beneficiary can get access to communications between a trustee and a lawyer where (1) the trustee is charged with a breach of fiduciary duty, (2) the communication is relevant to the claimed breach, and (3) the lawyer was retained to advise the trustee concerning the administration of the trust (as opposed to being hired later to defend the trustee).[7]

---

7. An analogous issue is presented when shareholders seek access to attorney-corporate communications in order to prosecute a derivative suit, i.e., a suit brought in the name of the corporation. The leading case authorizing their access is Garner v. Wolfinbarger, 430 F.2d 1093 (5th Cir.1970), cert.denied sub nom. Garner v. First American Life Ins. Co., 401 U.S. 974, 91 S.Ct. 1191, 28 L.Ed.2d 323 (1971). See Restatement Third, The Law Governing Lawyers § 85.

B. THE COMMON INTEREST PRIVILEGE AMONG MULTIPLE ORGANIZATIONS

1. What effect is there on assertion of the attorney-client privilege when organizations or individuals take a "we're all in this together" approach to the use of counsel?

a. Remember from Problem 7 that, ordinarily, if your client talks with a lawyer in a setting where a third party is present, the discussion is not privileged at all.

b. Suppose the EPA has begun an investigation of several area fertilizer producers. You have been asked to represent Western Chemical in discussions with lawyers for Colorado Chemical, a nearby producer, about data each company has and possible positions to take during the investigation. Should the EPA be able to treat those discussions as unprivileged and question all participants in common-interest discussions about the content of their talks?

c. Ordinarily, defendants with a common interest may hold joint discussions at which they and the various lawyers talk freely with each other about matters relevant to their common interest. Any client who is part of that discussion or similar information exchange may assert the privilege just as it could if the client had been talking to its lawyer alone. See Restatement Third, The Law Governing Lawyers § 76.[8]

2. What happens when the former friends have a falling out? If Colorado Chemical wants to take confidential minutes of the talks with Western Chemical to the EPA, may it freely do so?

a. Ordinarily, the answer is no. Colorado Chemical may waive the common interest privilege and disclose what it and its attorney discussed, but the privilege continues to apply to what you and your client, Western Chemical, said.

b. In Hunydee v. United States, 355 F.2d 183 (9th Cir.1965), for example, at a joint conference attended by two defendants (husband and wife) and their separate attorneys, the husband agreed to plead guilty of income tax evasion and "take the blame." But he went to trial, and the Government, over objection, had the wife and her attorney testify to what was said at this joint conference. The court held that it was error to admit the testimony. The joint conference was privileged to the extent it concerned a common issue and was intended to facilitate representation in possible subsequent proceedings.

c. On the other hand, if Colorado Chemical learns in the course of the discussions that Western Chemical has polluted Colorado Chemical's land, it may file a suit for damages and use against Western whatever may have been disclosed. Unless the parties have agreed otherwise in advance, the common interest privilege does not protect information disclosed by the

---

8. Very similar principles apply under the "joint defense" privilege, i.e., when two or more clients share the same lawyer. See Restatement Third, The Law Governing Lawyers § 75.

participants in "subsequent adverse proceedings" between them. See Restatement Third, The Law Governing Lawyers § 76, Comment *f*.

d. In re Regents of University of California, 101 F.3d 1386 (Fed.Cir. 1996), cert. denied, 520 U.S. 1193, 117 S.Ct. 1484, 137 L.Ed.2d 695 (1997), was patent litigation between Genetech, Eli Lilly and UC Berkeley about recombinant DNA technology. Genetech and Lilly settled the claims between them, and Genetech then wanted to depose Lilly lawyers about discussions concerning prior art that the Lilly lawyers had with University officials earlier in the proceeding. The University had patented the process that the Lilly lawyers helped Lilly license. Both Lilly and the University had an interest in having the patent upheld, the Court reasoned, and the prior art discussions could affect the patent's validity. Thus, the University could assert a common-interest privilege with respect to the discussions between them and they were not subject to discovery by Genetech.

3. If a single lawyer represents more than one defendant, she is likely to get confidential information from each. Does information from multiple defendants or shared in multi-lawyer conferences constitute "privileged" or "confidential" information of all of the client(s)?

a. Assume now that you represent *both* Western Chemical and Colorado Chemical. Each has told you things they would not tell the EPA. Do you need permission before you use the information to try to get a better deal for both clients? Is a secret still a secret once it is told to others?

b. McCormick stated the principle as:

"When two or more persons, each having an interest in some problem or situation, jointly consult an attorney, their confidential communications with the attorney, though known to each other, will of course be privileged in a controversy of either or both of the clients with the outside world, that is, with parties claiming adversely to both or either of those within the original charmed circle. But it will often happen that the two original clients will fall out among themselves and become engaged in a controversy in which the communications at their joint consultation with the lawyer may be vitally material. In such a controversy it is clear that the privilege is inapplicable."[9]

c. Furthermore, if one client tells the common lawyer something relevant to the other client[s] in the joint representation, under traditional doctrine, unless the clients have agreed otherwise, the lawyer must disclose that information to the other clients even if the disclosing client would prefer that it be kept confidential. See Restatement Third, The Law Governing Lawyers § 75, Comment *d*: "Courts sometimes refer to this as a presumed intent that there should be no confidentiality between co-clients."

___

9. McCormick on Evidence (E. Cleary, 3d ed. 1984), § 91, at 219 (footnote omitted).

d.   The net effect of all this is to suggest that the decision of multiple defendants to adopt a common defense is not risk free. The Commentary to Proposed (but not enacted) Rule 503 of the Federal Rules of Evidence, discussed in Problem 7, was also cautious. It said that in the "joint defense" or "pooled information" situation, the "better view" is not that one of the various clients "could prevent another from disclosing what the other had himself said," but rather that "if all resist disclosure, none will occur."

C.   CONFIDENTIALITY AND RISKS TO PUBLIC HEALTH AND SAFETY

1.   Is the memorandum from the former Assistant General Counsel that purports to authorize the false reporting protected by the attorney-client privilege or as work product?

a.   You may remember from Problem 7 that the privilege does not extend to discussions in furtherance of an intended, unlawful end. The traditional common law view required that the communication be in furtherance of a crime or fraud before the privilege was lost. See Proposed Federal Rule of Evidence 503(d)(1).

b.   Restatement Third, The Law Governing Lawyers § 82 states the rule this way:

> "The attorney-client privilege does not apply to a communication occurring when a client:
>
> > "(a) consults a lawyer for the purpose, later accomplished, of obtaining assistance to engage in a crime or fraud or aiding a third person to do so, or
> >
> > "(b) regardless of the client's purpose at the time of consultation, uses the lawyer's advice or other services to engage in or assist a crime or fraud."[10]

c.   In re BankAmerica Corp. Securities Litigation, 270 F.3d 639 (8th Cir.2001), cert. den. 535 U.S. 970, 122 S.Ct. 1437 (2002), summarizes what a party must show to rely on the crime-fraud exception. Under United States v. Zolin, 491 U.S. 554, 109 S.Ct. 2619, 105 L.Ed.2d 469 (1989), the party must make a threshold showing that "the legal advice was obtained in furtherance of the fraudulent activity and was closely related to it." To do this, it must make a specific showing that a given communication was made in furtherance of the client's alleged crime or fraud. Indeed, the party seeking discovery must make this showing separately for each document or communication. If the threshold is met, the district court has discretion to conduct an in camera review of the allegedly privileged documents.

d.   United States v. Richard Roe Inc., 68 F.3d 38 (2d Cir.1995), involved a subpoena for legal records that the Government argued "collec-

---

10.   The corresponding work product exception is § 93: "Work-product immunity does not apply to materials prepared when a client consults a lawyer for the purpose, later accomplished, of obtaining assistance to engage in a crime or fraud or to aid a third person to do so or uses the materials for such a purpose."

tively have the real potential of being relevant evidence of activity in furtherance of a crime." The court quashed the subpoena. The claim was much too general and a "relevant evidence" test would leave virtually nothing protected. The crime-fraud exception "applies only when the court determines that the client communication or attorney work product in question was *itself* in furtherance of the crime or fraud." Further, there must be "probable cause to believe that the particular communication with counsel * * * was intended in some way to facilitate or to conceal the criminal activity." 68 F.3d at 40.

e. American Tobacco Co. v. State of Florida, 697 So.2d 1249 (Fla.App. 1997) was part of the series of state cases against the tobacco industry. The case held confidential company documents in lawyers' files that allegedly showed tobacco companies knew of health risks of smoking were all within the crime-fraud exception and hence discoverable. There was evidence that the companies hid health risks from the public and used their lawyers to do so, the court said. Evidence that the lawyers may have knowingly participated in a client fraud was held sufficient to overcome the privilege.

f. In re Sealed Case, 107 F.3d 46 (D.C.Cir.1997), involved a corporation that allegedly had made an illegal campaign contribution even after its officers had received a briefing and a legal memorandum explaining what the election laws do and do not permit. The D.C. Circuit held that the fact a client violates the law after talking with a lawyer does not place the communication within the crime-fraud exception and thus subject to disclosure. Nor was the file memorandum that counsel prepared upon learning of the illegal contributions unprivileged. Otherwise, the court said, corporations could not freely consult "a lawyer for the purpose of achieving law compliance." While the memorandum might show client *scienter*, it did not show the lawyer had assisted the client in committing any alleged crime.

2. Putting aside attorney-client privilege and work product issues, would your duty of confidentiality under pre-2002 Model Rule 1.6 prevent your voluntarily turning the memorandum over to the EPA?

a. Remember that your report and the memorandum clearly show that the company does not account for its chemicals well but not what has happened to the chemicals. On the other hand, if the chemicals really have been illegally dumped and in fact get into the region's drinking water, the effects over the next decade could be catastrophic.

b. Even assuming the worst, is your client *about to* commit a crime (as opposed to having done so)? Are any deaths resulting from the client's acts "imminent," as opposed to made more likely to occur in the future?

c. As an aside, you should note that Model Rule 1.6(b)(1), prior to its 2002 amendments, never really stated the law applicable in most jurisdictions. Take a look at Appendix A, "Ethics Rules on Client Confidences," that comes after the Model Rules in the Standards Supplement. Notice how many states permit—or even require—a lawyer to make disclosure in a situation like the one in this Problem.

d. Does Model Rule 1.6(b)(1) increase your authority to disclose over what it was prior to 2002?[11] Does the new rule say that what you are disclosing must be an act of the client, for example? Does it say that only a criminal act may be disclosed? Must the conduct occur in the future or only have future effects? Does the new rule require that the adverse effects occur within any particular temporal period? Look at Model Rule 1.6, Comment [6], to see that these changes were indeed intended.

3. Do you welcome this clearer authority to disclose? Are lawyers often more comfortable trying to avoid the issue of harm to third parties by in effect saying to them, "I am too ethical to ever protect you against the evil my client may do?"

a. Assuming that you want to voluntarily disclose the report and memorandum to the EPA, is there anything you should be required to do before disclosure? Look at Model Rule 1.6, Comment [12]. Do you agree that "Where practicable, the lawyer should first seek to persuade the client to take suitable action to obviate the need for disclosure"?[12]

b. Why does Rule 1.6 add this caveat? Is it typically better that the client do the right thing than that its lawyer be put in the position of tattling on the client? Might the discussion with the client itself get the client focused on the problem and obviate the need for disclosure at all?

c. Should the lawyer be subject to discipline—or liability—for a failure to disclose what could be disclosed consistent with Rule 1.6(b)(1)? What does Comment [13] to new Model Rule 1.6 say about that?

d. Section 66(3) of the Restatement Third (the counterpart to new Comment [13]) expressly disclaimed any lawyer responsibility to persons injured by the conduct whose effects the lawyer might have mitigated, at least responsibility "solely by reason of such [a failure to warn]." Can you defend that position on any basis other than lawyer self interest? Might it turn out to be difficult in many cases for a lawyer to assess the risks correctly before the harm occurs and then impossible later to explain the ambiguity the lawyer faced to a jury that is looking for deep pockets?

e. Might authority to disclose come from a source other than Model Rule 1.6(b)(1)? Suppose the EPA asserts that you knew about the false reporting before the reports were filed and joins you as a defendant. Would that allow you to reveal your report? Take a look at new Model Rule

11. Model Rule 1.6(b)(1) is taken directly from Restatement Third, The Law Governing Lawyers § 66(1) "A lawyer may use or disclose confidential client information when the lawyer reasonably believes such use or disclosure is necessary to prevent reasonably certain death or serious bodily harm to a person."

12. This too comes directly from Restatement Third, The Law Governing Lawyers § 66(2).

"Before using or disclosing information pursuant to this Section, the lawyer must, if feasible, make a good faith effort to persuade the client either not to act or, if the client or another person has already acted, to warn the victim or take other action to prevent the harm and, if relevant, to advise the client of the lawyer's ability to use or disclose pursuant to this Section and the consequences thereof."

1.6(b)(3). To what other situations might the lawyer's "self-protection" exception apply?

D. CONFIDENTIALITY AND CLIENT FRAUD—AN INTRODUCTION[13]

1. When International Chemicals proposed to buy Western Chemical and wanted to see the report of your investigation of the company, would any privilege or other obligation prevent your disclosing it to International if Western would prefer that you not do so?

a. As you remember, the crime-fraud exception to the attorney-client privilege and work product immunity applies to fraud as well as crime. Non-disclosure may not always be fraudulent, but when it is, neither the privilege nor work product immunity will bar disclosure.

b. Indeed, take a look at Model Rule 4.1(b). Does that provision mandate disclosure in a case like the one in this Problem? Is such disclosure "prohibited by Rule 1.6"?

c. Do you find an exception permitting disclosure in Model Rule 1.6(b)? The ABA House of Delegates has more than once rejected any proposed authority of a lawyer to reveal information to prevent or rectify a fraudulent act of the client, even one "that the lawyer reasonably believes is likely to result * * * in substantial injury to the financial interests or property of another."

d. Restatement Third, The Law Governing Lawyers § 67, on the other hand, says that lawyers already have the authority to disclose in such cases, at least if "the client has employed or is employing the lawyer's services in the matter in which the crime or fraud is committed." See also, state rules on this issue in Appendix A, "Ethics Rules on Client Confidences," that comes after the Model Rules in the Standards Supplement.

2. If the lack of Model Rule 1.6 authority leads you to conclude you would not disclose the report to International, the content of which could significantly affect what International believes Western Chemical is worth, what might you do?

a. Consider the view of Washington lawyer Lloyd Cutler:

"When outside corporate counsel give advice that management rejects, what is counsel's duty? Must they inform the outside directors? If the advice is that the Corporation has a duty to disclose a past or continuing offense to investors or to the authorities, or to terminate a practice that may violate the law, we think they must. If the outside directors decline to act, should outside counsel resign? We think they should. Is mere resignation sufficient, or must they also inform the authorities about a past or continuing offense? If the continuing act or omission is a criminal

---

13. This section is described as only an introduction because the issues are revisited   in greater detail later in Problem 22.

offense, the [Code of Professional Responsibility] says they have a right if not a duty to disclose, but I think this is outmoded and unrealistic in at least one important current context. The Code was written to fit the lawyer whose human client tells him of an intent to commit a bodily assault. It does not appear to fit the lawyer who advises a corporate client that it is committing a continuing but unchallenged violation of an environmental or other regulation backed by criminal penalties, where the client decides not to desist because compliance is beyond the state of the art or beyond the client's resources, or even because the cost of correction is greater than the potential fine if detected. The lawyer has a clear duty to advise the client that the continuing violation should be terminated and perhaps even to resign if it is not terminated. But it would severely limit the willingness of companies to seek legal advice about complex compliance issues if the lawyer has the right to inform the authorities that his advice has been rejected. * * *

"In my own view, a law firm's willingness to carry its advice to the highest corporate level and to resign if all else fails is a more potent enforcement weapon than the threat that the firm may inform. Directors will rarely act contrary to firm legal advice, and they will certainly think again if their lawyers show a willingness to resign when their advice is declined. They will think again not only because of the potential public consequences if the resignation becomes generally known, but also because most managements genuinely respect the judgment and character of their counsel, and are bound to be impressed by the courage and conviction that a decision to resign involves. Unhappily, resignation on principle went out of style in public life a long time ago. But in the private relationships between corporations and their lawyers, it is a potential that should always be preserved." Lloyd Cutler, The Role of the Private Law Firm, 33 Business Lawyer 1549, 1556–57 (Mar. 1978).

b.   In light of Mr. Cutler's comments, look again at the advice given lawyers by the pre–2002 revisions of Model Rule 1.6, Comments [15], [16] & [17]. Those three Comments were all grouped under a heading titled, "Withdrawal." After the 2002 revisions, the three Comments were not substantively changed but they were grouped into one new Comment [14]. Under Comment [14] may you (must you) now send a notice of withdrawal to others with whom you have dealt in the matter saying, e.g., "I have withdrawn from this matter for ethical reasons"? In doing so, would you be "flying a red flag" and thus prejudicing your client's interests? Do the Comments thus permit, or even require, a form of "disclosure" that the Rule itself seems not to permit?

c.   In addition to Rule 1.6, Comment [14], other provisions that deal with a "noisy withdrawal" can be found in Model Rule 1.2, Comment [10] and Model Rule 4.1, Comment [3].

3. Should a lawyer face civil liability for a failure to warn a third party about a potential or completed client fraud?

a.   Restatement Third, The Law Governing Lawyers § 67 tries to give lawyers some comfort in that regard:

> "(4) A lawyer who * * * takes action or decides not to take action permitted under this Section is not, solely by reason of such action or inaction, subject to professional discipline, liable for damages to the lawyer's client or any third person, or barred from recovery against a client or third person by an affirmative defense based solely thereon."

What do you think of this disclaimer? Should courts give effect to it? Why or why not?

b.   In the mid–90s, creation of a private remedy against lawyers who allegedly assisted their clients to commit securities fraud was dealt a significant blow in Central Bank of Denver, N.A. v. First Interstate Bank of Denver, N.A., 511 U.S. 164, 114 S.Ct. 1439, 128 L.Ed.2d 119 (1994). The issue was liability of professionals who did not themselves make misrepresentations to investors but who "aided and abetted" clients who violated § 10(b) of the Securities Exchange Act of 1934. The Supreme Court held that lawyers and others who themselves violate § 10(b) can be held accountable, but "aiding and abetting" a violation is not enough. But see Newby v. Enron Corp., 235 F.Supp.2d 549 (S.D.Tex.2002) (claim for primary liability held stated against lawyers and other professionals).

c.   Now, in the wake of recent accounting scandals affecting once-prominent corporations, the greatest risk of lawyer sanction for non-disclosure is likely to come from the Securities and Exchange Commission. Congress required the SEC to

> "establish rules, in the public interest, setting forth minimum standards of professional conduct for attorneys appearing and practicing before the Commission in any way in the representation of public companies, including a rule requiring an attorney to report evidence of a material violation of securities law or breach of fiduciary duty or similar violation by the company or any agent thereof to the chief legal counsel or the chief executive officer of the company (or the equivalent thereof), and if the counsel or officer does not appropriately respond to the evidence (adopting, as necessary, appropriate remedial measures or sanctions with respect to the violation), requiring the attorney to report the evidence to the audit committee of the board of directors or to another committee of the board of directors comprised solely of directors not employed directly or indirectly by the company, or to the board of directors."

The new SEC Rules can be found in 17 CFR Part 205 (2003).

CHAPTER IV

THE REQUIREMENT OF LOYALTY TO THE CLIENT

The Biblical injunction against serving inconsistent masters has long been a fundamental principle of fiduciary duty. Because lawyers have a fiduciary relationship with their clients, the principle applies with full force in the Model Rules. For a lawyer, interests possibly conflicting with the client's interest may be the interest of another client, a former client, a third party, or even the lawyer's own self-interest.

Each client of a lawyer expects full loyalty, yet it is as usual for a lawyer to represent many clients as for a doctor to treat many patients. Indeed, in some cases, several clients may believe they want a common attorney. Moreover, the lawyer's partners will all have clients, thus extending the possible conflicts, because the Model Rules often impute the conflicts of one lawyer to others in the same firm.

Lawyers are usually not happy to discover a conflict of interest; they face economic pressures that discourage them from turning away business. But the law of legal ethics sets limits beyond which lawyers may not go without client consent. Those limits are the subject of this Chapter, and you are likely to find that the questions you examine here will be the ethical issues that most frequently arise in your practice. In the problems that follow, consider questions such as:

a. How can a lawyer recognize, anticipate, and avoid conflicts of interest?

b. When will your personal interests, as opposed to those of your other clients, raise questions about the zealousness of your representation?

c. Do rules about conflicts of interest ever serve to increase, unnecessarily, the cost of legal services? Might they prevent clients from legitimately choosing to save the cost of the extra lawyer?

d. If a lawyer determines that he or she is in a conflict situation, how should the lawyer deal with it? Is it enough to obtain consent of all the affected persons? When must the lawyer refuse to take the case? When must she withdraw?

e. To what extent do conflict of interest rules represent ends in themselves, and to what extent do they further other objectives such as the obligation to preserve client confidences?

PROBLEM 9

REPRESENTING MULTIPLE PARTIES
DEALING WITH EACH OTHER

Probably the most basic kind of conflict of interest is that between two clients, simultaneously represented by a single lawyer, when everything gained by one of them will be at the other's expense. It might seem never appropriate to have a single lawyer represent both parties to such a "zero-sum game," but many real-life situations make such representation tempting, and starting our analysis of conflicts of interest there is helpful in identifying the factors that will be important throughout this Chapter.

FACTS

Mr. and Mrs. Wilson have been married for 12 years. They have children ages 10, 8, and 6. They both realize that their marriage has not been going well for the past four years, and while they consider each other friends, they no longer wish to remain married. They have come to attorney Wayne Green's office and have asked Green to help them secure a divorce.

The Wilsons tell Green they have agreed that Mr. Wilson will be the custodial parent of the 8–year-old son and Mrs. Wilson will be custodial parent of the two daughters. Each will have liberal rights of contact with the children living with the other. Mrs. Wilson wants $1000 a month child support, and Mr. Wilson considers that a bargain.

Neither of the Wilsons wants a separate attorney called into the case because of the added expense. "We both trust you," they say. "Why create problems when there aren't any now?"

QUESTIONS

A. DETERMINING WHETHER A LAWYER HAS A CONFLICT OF INTEREST

1. **Will the simultaneous representation of both Wilsons involve attorney Green in a conflict of interest?**

a. Restatement Third, The Law Governing Lawyers § 121 describes the basic rule prohibiting a lawyer's conflict of interest.

"Unless all affected [persons give informed consent] * * *, a lawyer may not represent a client if the representation would involve a conflict of interest. A conflict of interest is involved if there is substantial risk that the lawyer's representation of the client would be materially and adversely affected by the lawyer's own interests or by the lawyer's duties to another current client, a former client, or a third person."

b. The most nearly corresponding provision in the ABA Model Rules is Model Rule 1.7(a):

"Except [with informed consent] * * *, a lawyer shall not represent a client if the representation involves a concurrent conflict of interest. A concurrent conflict of interest exists if:

"(1) the representation of one client will be directly adverse to another client; or

"(2) there is a significant risk that the representation of one or more clients will be materially limited by the lawyer's responsibilities to another client, a former client or a third person or by a personal interest of the lawyer."

c. Under these definitions, are the representations of Mr. Wilson and Mrs. Wilson each "directly adverse" to the other? What "material limits" on the representation of Mr. or Mrs. Wilson is Green likely to experience?

d. The Wilsons have told Green that they have worked everything out. Do you agree that they have done so? Are there practical problems Green should foresee in helping two people achieve even an amicable dissolution of an unwanted legal relationship? What might be some of those practical problems?

2. What concerns underlie the rules governing conflicts of interest?

a. Comments [6] and [8] to Model Rule 1.7 provide a start toward answering that question. Is the inability of Wayne Green to push hard for one client at the expense of the other a serious problem? If Mr. Wilson is willing to pay only $1000 a month, for example, may Green, on behalf of Mrs. Wilson, ask for $1500?

b. Both the Restatement and Model Rule provisions replaced ABA Model Code of Professional Responsibility DR 5–105(A) that provided:

"A lawyer shall decline proffered employment if the exercise of his independent professional judgment in behalf of a client will be or is likely to be adversely affected by the acceptance of the proffered employment, or if it would be likely to involve him is representing differing interests * * * ."

c. Was the concept of "independent professional judgment" in DR 5–105(A) a useful one for defining the fundamental concern underlying conflict of interest regulation? On the other hand, is the effect on lawyer "judgment" the real concern?

3. Should Green be able to avoid the conflict problem by representing Mr. Wilson himself while having his law partner represent Mrs. Wilson?

a. It is important to understand that ABA Model Rule 1.10(a) usually "imputes" a single lawyer's conflicts to all other lawyers in the firm. That would be true even if Mrs. Wilson were to consult Green's partner who worked out of an office in another city. It would be true even if the two lawyers never talk to each other except with their clients present. It is true even if Mr. and Mrs. Wilson have no material secrets from each other about this matter.

b.   What concerns or assumptions about attorney behavior underlie such imputation? Do you agree with those assumptions? Does it follow that imputation should be automatic?

c.   Whatever your view of that, imputation is well-settled law that you should presume applies throughout most of the issues in the Chapter. We will explore the more important implications of the concept later, primarily in Problem 15.

B.   WAIVER OF A CONFLICT OF INTEREST; THE REQUIREMENT OF INFORMED CONSENT

1.   Is the short answer to conflicts issues that clients may waive the conflicts whenever the rules get in the way of what the clients want to do?

a.   A moment's reflection reveals that the conclusion that a conflict exists does not mean Green is prohibited from undertaking the common representation. It simply means that whether he may do so is for the Wilsons to decide, not for Green alone.

b.   Restatement Third, The Law Governing Lawyers § 122(1) says:

"A lawyer may represent a client notwithstanding a conflict of interest prohibited by § 121 if each affected client or former client gives informed consent to the lawyer's representation. Informed consent requires that the client or former client have reasonably adequate information about the material risks of such representation to that client or former client."

The corresponding provision in the ABA Model Rules is Rule 1.7(b).

2.   What kind of information should Green provide the Wilsons about the "material risks" of his representing them both?

a.   Does Model Rule 1.7, Comment [18] give a complete answer to that question? As you can see from that Comment, even discussion of the effects of the conflict on "loyalty, confidentiality and the attorney-client privilege and the advantages and risks involved" is quite a list of topics.

b.   Also look at Model Rule 1.0 on Terminology. The need for "informed consent" appears throughout the Model Rules, so a definition is provided in Model Rule 1.0(e) and lengthy Comments [6] & [7] to that Rule provide more guidance than you will find in Rule 1.7 itself.

c.   What disadvantages should Green mention? May he contrast them with the potential cost saving if he represents them both? Do you suppose Green will be telling the Wilsons something they do not already know? If they already know or should know, for example, that Green will not keep any of Mr. Wilson's secrets from Mrs. Wilson, is Green's reminder still useful?

3. Should the Model Rules require that any client consent to a conflict be in be in writing?

a. California Rule of Professional Conduct 3–310 imposes such a requirement. Model Rule 1.7, prior to 2002, did not.

b. Look at the requirement now imposed by Model Rule 1.7(b)(4). What does it mean to have consent "confirmed in writing"?

c. Comment [20] to new Model Rule 1.7 provides the answer. Do you agree that it should be sufficient to send a client a letter that the client does not need to acknowledge? Will a failure to challenge the accuracy of the representations that the lawyer makes about consent constitute agreement with the representations?

d. As a matter of prudence, of course, most lawyers will discuss conflicts in their engagement letter that they will have the client countersign. If they have fully recorded the advice they gave about the advantages and disadvantages of waiving the conflict, any subsequent dispute will more likely be resolved in their favor. Of course, any advice they forget to mention in the letter may seem never to have been said.

4. For how long should a conflict waiver be effective? Suppose that in the course of the representation, the lawyer learns facts that make the conflict more severe than first appeared. Must she secure a new waiver?

a. In re Cohen, 853 P.2d 286 (Ore.1993), illustrates how a relatively simple situation can quickly get out of hand. Wife accused Husband of beating their daughter. Husband faced criminal charges and both parents faced the possibility the child would be taken from them. The lawyer agreed to represent Husband in the criminal case and to represent both parents in the custody matter. Later, Wife called the lawyer and told him Husband was not going to counseling. A presentence report was to the same effect and also said that Wife was often calling the police about Husband. Wife said she still wanted lawyer to jointly represent them so they could "act as a team." In imposing discipline on the lawyer, the court found that he had neither adequately explained the potential conflict at the outset nor dealt with the actual conflict later.

b. In re Houston, 985 P.2d 752 (N.M.1999), was another case of the lawyer going too far trying to represent everyone in a family. The wife went to the lawyer who advised her to report to police that her husband had beaten her and molested her daughter. The lawyer then defended the husband against the wife's charges; the wife consented to this but the lawyer did not tell her that she would have to testify at the trial. Finally, he represented both husband and wife in a divorce and secured a court decree giving the husband unsupervised visitation rights that the wife found unsatisfactory. For this web of conflicts, the court required the lawyer to submit to 18 months of supervised probation.

5. Should a client be permitted to revoke consent and then require that the lawyer not represent either of the clients?

a. Look at Comment [21] to Model Rule 1.7. Clearly, either of the clients may terminate his or her own representation for any (or no) reason. The subject of this Comment is whether the client can thereby preclude the lawyer from representing the other client.

b. Comment [21] is derived from Restatement Third, The Law Governing Lawyers § 122, Comment *f.* Two examples that the Restatement offers illustrate the distinction. Illustration 4 says:

> "Client A and Client B validly consent to be represented by Lawyer in operating a restaurant in a city. After an amicable and profitable collaboration, Client A reasonably concludes that Lawyer has begun to take positions against Client A and consistently favoring the interests of Client B in business. Reasonably concerned that Lawyer is no longer properly serving the interests of both Clients, Client A withdraws consent. Withdrawal of consent is effective and justified. Lawyer may not thereafter continue representing either Client A or Client B in a matter adverse to the other and substantially related to the Lawyer's former representation of the clients."

Contrast Illustration 6:

> "Clients A and B validly consent to Lawyer representing them jointly as co-defendants in a breach-of-contract action. On the eve of trial and after months of pretrial discovery on the part of all parties, Client A withdraws consent to the joint representation for reasons not justified by the conduct of Lawyer or Client B and insists that Lawyer cease representing Client B. At this point it would be difficult and expensive for Client B to find separate representation for the impending trial. Client A's withdrawal of consent is ineffective to prevent the continuing representation of B in the absence of compelling considerations such as harmful disloyalty by Lawyer."

c. Could a lawyer eliminate this issue by drafting the consent more carefully? For example, could the clients' consent provide that either Client A or Client B may revoke consent at any time, for any reason, but that if either A or B does that, the Lawyer may continue to represent the other client? Are there fiduciary obligations inherent in such situations that should override such private agreements?[1]

C. CONFLICTS FOR WHICH CONSENT IS NOT EFFECTIVE

1. Should there be some conflicts that a client may not waive?

a. Restatement Third, The Law Governing Lawyers § 122(2) says:

> "(2) Notwithstanding the informed consent of each affected client or former client, a lawyer may not represent a client if:
>
> "(a) the representation is prohibited by law;

---

1. We will return to an issue much like this, the issue of advance consent, in Problem 10.

"(b) one client will assert a claim against the other in the same litigation; or

"(c) in the circumstances, it is not reasonably likely that the lawyer will be able to provide adequate representation to one or more of the clients."

The corresponding Model Rule provisions are Model Rule 1.7(b)(1)–(b)(3).

b. The first two subsections are easy enough to understand. What about the third? When should the law provide that competent and fully-informed adults should not be able to waive a conflict?

c. Is the rule really trying to identify situations in which a reasonable party would not grant consent if he were fully-informed? Does the Rule instead assume that sometimes the system of justice has an interest in the way parties are represented that makes some conflicts not subject to waiver?

2. When should Rule 1.7 not allow a client to waive a conflict?

a. In re Michelman, 616 N.Y.S.2d 409 (App.Div.1994), leave to appeal denied 84 N.Y.2d 811 (1994), considered the problem of representing both a biological mother and adoptive parents in a private adoption. The adoptive parents were already the lawyer's clients and a medical doctor referred the biological mother to the lawyer, who prepared the necessary papers and explained the process to her. Assuming that all the participants consented to the common representation, do you see any problem with it? What about a biological mother's possible right to revoke consent to the adoption? Because it is easy to foresee that an effort to revoke consent might occur, ABA Informal Opinion 87–1523 (1987) had said the situation presented an non-consentable conflict. This court agreed, and under the circumstances of the case, suspended the lawyer for three years.

b. In Fiandaca v. Cunningham, 827 F.2d 825 (1st Cir.1987), New Hampshire Legal Assistance (NHLA) represented women prison inmates who claimed that their prison facilities were overcrowded. The state offered to move some of the female inmates to another facility that mentally retarded patients currently used as a hospital. The NHLA, which represented these patients in another case challenging conditions at that facility, rejected the state's offer because if would adversely affect the mentally retarded clients if the hospital were converted into a women's prison. The court held that it was error for the trial court to certify NHLA as class counsel. When a lawyer must decline a settlement offer in one case in order to benefit the lawyer's clients in another case, there is a fatal conflict of interest requiring NHLA's disqualification from continuing to act for the prisoners.

c. Baldasarre v. Butler, 625 A.2d 458 (N.J.1993), involved a lawyer who represented the sellers in a real estate transaction, while knowing that the buyer, his other client, had arranged immediately to sell the property to someone else at a large profit. Needless to say, the sellers believed their lawyer should have told them that the ultimate buyer wanted the property and should have helped them get the higher price. The New Jersey

Supreme Court said there was no way the lawyer could have acted loyally to both clients in such a situation and held that a lawyer may not represent both buyer and seller in a commercial real estate deal, even with the consent of each.

Do you agree with this result? Is this simply a case where no valid consent could be obtained because the lawyer could not fully inform the original sellers of the buyer's plans?

d. Association of the Bar of the City of New York Committee on Professional and Judicial Ethics, Formal Opinion 2001–1, on the other hand, was more sympathetic to joint representation. It concluded that, particularly if the lawyer regularly represents each of the parties, each client has an almost fundamental right not to be required to get new counsel. In short, a single law firm could represent two clients negotiating a major merger. The key issue in each case should be whether a "disinterested lawyer" would conclude that the lawyer cannot adequately represent each client. That, in turn, will require a focus on the nature of the conflicts, the ability to preserve confidential information of each client, the ability of the lawyer to explain and the client to understand the reasonably foreseeable risks of the conflict, and whether the lawyer has a closer or longer-standing relationship with one of the clients than the other.

e. Are Comments [15]–[17] to Model Rule 1.7 helpful in determining whether the clients may waive a conflict? Do they persuade you which of the above cases and opinions are correct?

3. Should courts and the disciplinary authorities treat Green's representation of Mr. & Mrs. Wilson as a non-consentable conflict?

a. Even an uncontested divorce is filed in most states in the form of litigation between the husband and wife? May a lawyer represent both the plaintiff and defendant in a litigated case? Does the fact that the court will have to approve the Wilsons' divorce mean that there could be no harm from Green's representing them both?

b. The Reporter's Note to Restatement Third, The Law Governing Lawyers § 128, Comment c says:

"The question of representing opposing clients in hearings on uncontested marital dissolution has arisen frequently. Some courts have permitted use of only one lawyer in some of those situations. While the divorce proceeding is still a nominally contested litigation in most jurisdictions, in some remedial contexts, courts will confirm a negotiated property settlement where both parties consented to the simultaneous representation and the settlement appears fair. See, e.g., Klemm v. Superior Court, 142 Cal.Rptr. 509 (Ct.App. 1977) (while parties may not waive conflict in contented litigation, they may do so in an uncontested dissolution); * * * . [However, several] jurisdictions treat joint representation of spouses in a dissolution action as a nonconsentable conflict in all instances."

c. Might Green handle the representation jointly through negotiation of the property settlement, but have the Wilsons hire another lawyer to represent one of the parties at the divorce hearing while Mr. Green represents the other? Is there any public interest in requiring that the process be bifurcated in that way? If Mr. Green represents one of the parties, how will he choose which one? If a new lawyer represents the other party, is that lawyer required to accept the property settlement as given, or should he or she independently evaluate it?

4. Should consent be more likely to be possible in business planning matters and other non-litigation settings that are less contentious than a divorce?

a. Assume, for example, that the parties who have come to Green are three individuals who wish to set up a close corporation. He has met none of them before. Is it possible that he can represent them all effectively?

b. Before the ABA House of Delegates deleted Model Rule 2.2 in the 2002 revisions, that Rule addressed this situation, calling the lawyer an "intermediary between clients." It permitted the lawyer to undertake such representation if:

"(1) the lawyer consults with each client concerning the implications of the common representation, including the advantages and risks involved, and the effect on the attorney-client privileges, and obtains each client's consent to the common representation;

"(2) the lawyer reasonably believes that the matter can be resolved on terms compatible with the clients' best interests, that each client will be able to make adequately informed decisions in the matter and that there is little risk of material prejudice to the interest of any of the clients if the contemplated resolution is unsuccessful; and

"(3) the lawyer reasonably believes that the common representation can be undertaken impartially and without improper effect on other responsibilities the lawyer has to any of the clients."

c. At the time the ABA Commission revised the Model Rules, the drafters concluded that these principles were already inherent in Model Rule 1.7. Do you agree?

d. While the ABA has repealed Model Rule 2.2, some of its ideas are reflected in Comments [28]–[33] to Model Rule 1.7. What would you conclude from those Comments about the ability of the parties to consent to using a single lawyer in establishing a business?

5. Could Green represent both Mr. and Mrs. Wilson if, instead of seeking a divorce, they had come to Green for estate planning advice?

a. An ABA report analyzed the issue as follows:

"From an ethical standpoint, the risk is that, in counseling the couple as a unit for tax and planning purposes, neither individual will receive the representation a single individual might receive under the same circumstances. Yet family needs, tax incentives, and the very nature of marriage often make separate counseling unnecessary, and indeed, inappropriate."[2]

b.   Under that analysis, should a lawyer normally obtain a conflicts waiver before beginning estate planning for the couple? May the lawyer properly "view the couple as unified in goals and interests until shown otherwise"?[3]

c.   Restatement Third, The Law Governing Lawyers § 130, Comment *c*, cautions: "A lawyer is not required to suggest or assume discord where none exists, but when a conflict is reasonably apparent or foreseeable, the lawyer may proceed with multiple representation only after all affected clients have consented as provided in § 122." Do you agree with the Restatement approach?

6.   What are Green's obligations to Mr. Wilson if, during estate planning, Mrs. Wilson privately discloses confidential information to Green but not to her spouse?

a.   Confronted with the choice between both hiring the same lawyer or each hiring a lawyer from separate law firms, which option do you believe most couples would choose, at least when they were together in a lawyer's office? However, what should Green do if, the day after both wills are signed, Mrs. Wilson comes back to the lawyer's office and says, "I want to change my will and don't want my husband to know"? Does your answer depend on whether Mr. Wilson is leaving all his property to his wife in the expectation she is doing the same for him?

b.   A v. B. v. Hill Wallack, 726 A.2d 924 (N.J.1999), presented a very similar question. Husband and Wife sought estate planning advice. Because of a mistake in conflicts checking, the firm had already accepted another woman's paternity action against Husband. Husband did not object to the firm's handling that case against him, and DNA tests showed he was the father of the woman's child. At that point, the firm wanted to tell Wife that, because she was leaving the residue of her estate to Husband, part of that estate could wind up going to his illegitimate child. Husband did not want the firm to tell her that he had fathered the child. In this paternity action, the mother's former law firm, which contemporaneously represented the father and his wife in planning their estates, sought to disclose to the wife the existence of the father's illegitimate child. The court said that a lawyer for co-clients should reach an agreement *in advance* with co-clients about how confidential information of each will be handled. Citing an earlier version of what is now Restatement Third, The Law Governing Lawyers § 60, Comment *l*, however, the court held that, in the absence of such an agreement, the lawyer has the "discretion" to tell each client the secrets of the other that may adversely affect that client's interest. It

2.   Report of the Special Study Committee on Professional Responsibility, Comments and Recommendations on the Lawyer's Duties in Representing Husband and Wife, 28 Real Property, Probate and Trust Journal 765, 770 (1994).

3.   Id. at 779.

authorized the firm to tell Wife the existence but not the identity of the child.

c. Armed with this opinion, what should a lawyer do in the future? The Restatement section on which the *Wallack* court relied makes clear that "[s]haring of information among the co-clients with respect to the matter involved in the representation is normal and typically expected. * * * Moreover, the common lawyer is required to keep each of the co-clients informed of all information reasonably necessary for the co-client to make decisions in connection with the matter." When the lawyer gets information that one client wants to keep secret from the other, however, there is a conflict of interest between the clients that the lawyer cannot ignore. That is the context of the Restatement passage that the *Wallack* court quotes: "In the course of withdrawal [because of the conflict], the lawyer has discretion to warn the affected co-client that a matter seriously and adversely affecting that person's interests has come to light, which the other co-client refuses to permit the lawyer to disclose."

d. D.C. Bar Legal Ethics Committee Opinion No. 296 (2000) addresses the question saying that a lawyer may not reveal a secret of one joint client to another. A lawyer who undertakes dual representation has a duty to clarify, at the outset of the representation, "the impact of such representation on the lawyer's duty to maintain client confidences and to keep each client reasonably informed, and obtain each client's informed consent to the arrangement." In the absence of such an agreement, when one joint client discloses confidential information that a lawyer would have a duty to disclose to the other in order to keep that client reasonably informed, the lawyer must seek consent to disclose such information from the disclosing client. According to the Committee, if the lawyer is unable to obtain consent, a conflict of interest arises and the lawyer must withdraw from the case. After withdrawal, the lawyer may not represent either client in the matter without the consent of the other.

e. The Model Rules now address this issue in Comments [30] and [31] to Rule 1.7. How do they direct Green to proceed? How do they say the lawyer should have acted in the *Wallack* case?

f. If the lawyer knows, before undertaking the representation, that one of the clients is withholding relevant information from the other, may the lawyer take the case at all? Look at Comment [19] to Model Rule 1.7. Might he take the case with the informed consent of the other client? Does the inability to make full disclosure render informed consent impossible?

7. Are the Model Rules too quick to find conflicts and prohibit consent?

a. In spite of the obvious problems associated with Mr. and Mrs. Wilson using the same lawyer for their divorce, might it nonetheless be reasonable for them to desire that arrangement? Is their desire for noncontentious resolution of the matter a legitimate concern? Should the ethics rules require two lawyers if one will do?

b. Do you agree with the following view?

"[H]aving more than one lawyer to accomplish the parties' objectives may be an unnecessary and wasteful luxury. Individuals entering upon a contractual relationship, for example, might find it significantly less expensive and less disruptive to hire a single lawyer to draft a contract incorporating the business consensus of both sides than to have two lawyers, each trying to exact the marginal pound of flesh for his client. So, too, in many cases of uncontested divorce, the presence of combatant lawyers may re-open wounds better left closed and exacerbate problems rather than solve them.

"The response to this argument from many lawyers is that a situation which appears nonlitigious at the moment may develop into a contested situation in the future. This is not an unreasonable concern * * *. But having two lawyers from the outset in every case is expensive insurance against the unknown. Moreover, in many situations where things go badly, both sides can simply bring in separate counsel. The only person hurt by such a procedure would be the first lawyer who will now represent neither party. That the lawyer might not like this result is understandable. That his unhappiness should rise to the level of an ethical precept is less clear."[4]

c. What do these considerations suggest about how readily courts should construe Model Rule 1.7(b)(3) to prohibit joint representation?

D. REMEDIES OTHER THAN PROFESSIONAL DISCIPLINE FOR A CONFLICT OF INTEREST VIOLATION

1. Should a judge enforce the rule against representing conflicting interests by ordering the representation terminated, or should judges leave enforcement to the lawyer discipline process?

a. In litigated matters, a court faced with a conflict of interest will most often order the lawyer disqualified from representing any or all of the clients in the matter. Restatement Third, The Law Governing Lawyers § 6, Comment *i* explains:

"Disqualification draws on the inherent power of courts to regulate the conduct of lawyers * * * as well as the related inherent power of judges to regulate the course of proceedings before them * * *. Disqualification, where appropriate, ensures that the case is well presented in court, that confidential information of present or former clients is not misused, and that a client's substantial interest in a lawyer's loyalty is protected."[5]

---

4. Thomas D. Morgan, The Evolving Concept of Professional Responsibility, 90 Harvard L.Rev. 702, 727–28 (1977). Copyright © 1977 by the Harvard Law Review Association.

5. The Supreme Court has held that denial of a disqualification motion in a civil case is *not* an appealable final decision under 28 U.S.C.A. § 1291. Firestone Tire & Rubber Co. v. Risjord, 449 U.S. 368, 101 S.Ct. 669, 66 L.Ed.2d 571 (1981). Likewise, the granting of

b. In non-litigation matters, some courts will issue an injunction against the continued representation and thereby achieve the practical effect of a disqualification. See Maritrans GP, Inc. v. Pepper, Hamilton & Scheetz, 602 A.2d 1277 (Pa.1992).

c. Yet, as Panduit Corp. v. All States Plastic Mfg. Co., 744 F.2d 1564, 1576–77 (Fed.Cir.1984), warns: "Judges must exercise caution not to paint with a broad brush under the misguided belief that coming down on the side of disqualification raises the standard of legal ethics and the public's respect. The opposite effects are just as likely—encouragement of vexatious tactics and increased cynicism by the public."

d. If a judge concludes that failing to disqualify would make a trial unfair, should the judge refuse to disqualify because the moving party seems to have bad motives? The 2002 revisions to the Model Rules eliminated former Comment 15 to Rule 1.7, which had said that opposing counsel may "properly raise the question" of disqualification if the "conflict is such as clearly to call in question the fair or efficient administration of justice," but such an objection "should be viewed with caution," because "it can be misused as a technique of harassment."

Do you agree that it was a good idea to delete that Comment? Should a court grant a disqualification motion that will protect the trial process, because doing so will encourage parties to bring an important issue to the attention of the court? Should the moving party's subjective motive be relevant at all?

e. Throughout this Chapter, watch for this tension between rigorous enforcement of professional standards and the desire to prevent opportunistic efforts by the parties to impose additional costs on each other by seeking to disqualify their lawyers.

2. What other remedies should be available to sanction a lawyer who represented conflicting interests?

a. If either of the clients has been disadvantaged by the conflict, a malpractice remedy is often available. See, e.g., Hughes v. Consol–Pennsylvania Coal Co., 945 F.2d 594, 617 & n. 3 (3d Cir.1991) (client called for advice whether transaction was fair; lawyer did not disclose he represented the other side; therefore trial court erred by failing to uphold the jury verdict on malpractice); Milbank, Tweed, Hadley & McCloy v. Boon, 13

a disqualification motion in a criminal case is not immediately appealable. Flanagan v. United States, 465 U.S. 259, 104 S.Ct. 1051, 79 L.Ed.2d 288 (1984). The same result has been reached with respect to the grant of a motion to disqualify in a civil case, Richardson–Merrell, Inc. v. Koller, 472 U.S. 424, 105 S.Ct. 2757, 86 L.Ed.2d 340 (1985), and the denial of a motion to disqualify in a criminal case, United States v. White, 743 F.2d 488 (7th Cir.1984).

However, a few courts of appeal have agreed to review lower court decisions when the losing party has sought a writ of mandamus. E.g., In re American Airlines, Inc., 972 F.2d 605 (5th Cir.1992); Matter of Sandahl, 980 F.2d 1118 (7th Cir.1992). The Seventh Circuit has concluded that mandamus is appropriate if the trial judge applied an incorrect legal rule; it continues to defer to the trial judge on questions of fact. Do you think the law/fact distinction is likely to be easily applied in disqualification cases?

F.3d 537 (2d Cir.1994) ($2 million in damages awarded for acting adversely to client in same transaction).

b.   Even in the absence of economic harm to the clients, some courts deny lawyers part of all of their fees as a sanction for the breach of fiduciary duty inherent in a lawyer's conflict of interest.

In Hendry v. Pelland, 73 F.3d 397 (D.C.Cir.1996), for example, the law firm had represented all five members of a family selling a parcel of land. All the clients had somewhat different views about acceptable terms for the sale. While finding no intentional misconduct that would support punitive damages, or even any actual damage suffered by family members, the court ruled that representation of all five family members was a conflict of interest that required the law firm to disgorge all fees it had earned in the case. See also, Burrow v. Arce, 997 S.W.2d 229, 240 (Tex.1999): "a client need not prove actual damages in order to obtain forfeiture of an attorney's fee for the attorney's breach of fiduciary duty to the client."

c.   In Electro–Wire Products, Inc. v. Sirote & Permutt, P.C. (In re Prince), 40 F.3d 356 (11th Cir.1994), before the husband's Chapter 11 proceeding began, the law firm had done estate planning for husband and wife and had represented the husband's corporation. The firm filed an affidavit, however, declaring that it had "not formerly represented the Debtor." In fact, during the estate planning for the family, the husband (debtor) had transferred $600,000 to his wife's name. The court found that the law firm's representation of the debtor in bankruptcy thus could not have truly been "disinterested," as the statute requires, and it denied the firm all fees it otherwise would have earned for the bankruptcy work.

d.   United States v. Gellene, 182 F.3d 578 (7th Cir.1999), held that failure to disclose a conflict of interest can sometimes be a crime. Gellene, a partner in the New York firm Milbank, Tweed, Hadley & McCloy, represented the debtor in a Chapter 11 bankruptcy. He swore to a declaration identifying the firm's connection to all other parties in interest, but failed to disclose that the firm also represented the senior secured creditor. He admitted bad judgment but denied a fraudulent intent. The jury found otherwise. The court sentenced Gellene to 15 months in the penitentiary and imposed a $15,000 fine, the sentence being increased because Gellene, as a lawyer, had abused a "position of trust."

e.   Should each of these remedies be exclusive, or should all be available simultaneously in appropriate cases?

———

PROBLEM 10

THE DUTY OF LOYALTY

Problem 9 involved representation of clients with opposing positions in the same case. More commonly, a lawyer is asked to represent one client against another whom the lawyer represents in a different case. Literally any of the clients that a lawyer represents in any matter might coincidentally become the opponent of another of the lawyer's clients. The growth of multistate and multinational law firms with hundreds of lawyers, each of whose conflicts is imputed to the other, means the possibility that one of a law firm's clients will oppose another is enormous. This Problem first explores how firms deal with the problem of "direct adversity," then how one determines who is "currently" a client of a law firm, then whether the firm may simply terminate a client so as to eliminate the conflict, and finally, how lawyers are to deal with situations in which two clients, in two factually unrelated cases, differ on how they believe a court should rule on a point of law.

FACTS

You represent the First National Bank in its commercial lending work. The bank had made a large mortgage loan to International Bolts Co., a parts manufacturer, for construction of a new plant. The loan has now gone into default, and the bank has directed you to commence foreclosure proceedings.

International Bolts has occasionally hired you over the last few years to write opinion letters on labor law matters. You do not now happen to be drafting any opinion for that company. You have never represented International Bolts in connection with this loan, but when you mention to the President of International Bolts that you will soon be handling the foreclosure of his plant, he is personally offended. "I really would not like you to be the one that does that to us," he says, "after all we've been through together."

Meanwhile, a neighbor has consulted you with respect to a "prepayment penalty" in the residential mortgage loan he has with the Second National Bank. Second National is not one of your clients, and you agree with the neighbor that "prepayment penalties" seem not to be in consumers' best interests. Thus, as a favor to your neighbor, you have agreed to file a declaratory judgment action challenging the validity of such agreements under state and federal law.

You have informed the Second National Bank of the impending suit, and you later receive a call from the President of your client, the First National Bank, who says: "I've heard about your proposed law suit against the Second National Bank. We do not want the law of prepayment penalties changed." Then the President tells you: "You owe it to us to withdraw from representing the plaintiff in the pending suit." First National Bank has nothing to do with the proposed lawsuit against Second National Bank, which has never been one of your client's, but First National Bank is concerned about the holding that may emerge from your prospective lawsuit.

QUESTIONS

A.   TAKING A CASE AGAINST A CURRENT CLIENT

1.   Is International Bolts' demand that you not represent the First National Bank in the foreclosure proceeding more than simply a question of keeping good relations with a sometimes client? Does International Bolts have a legal right to keep you out of the case?

a.   Look at Model Rule 1.7(a)(1). Must you take International Bolts' objection seriously?[1] As a matter of good business, you may not want to offend International Bolts, but would you be acting "unethically" if you were willing to to so?

b.   What is the purpose of Model Rule 1.7(a)(1)? Does the concern about protecting clients' confidences help justify it? Remember that in many instances, like the one in this Problem, there will be no substantive factual or legal relationship between the cases at all and thus no significant likelihood of misuse of any confidential information.

2.   Does the overarching concern go to the lawyer's loyalty to the client rather than protection of the client's confidences?

a.   Early cases like Grievance Committee v. Rottner, 203 A.2d 82 (Conn.1964), focused on loyalty. This case established the rule against a firm's handling an unrelated law suit against a current client. A law firm had accepted an assault and battery case for O'Brien against Twible. At the same time, the firm was representing Twible in a collection matter against a third party. The cases were not at all related but the court explained:

> "When a client engages the services of a lawyer in a given piece of business he is entitled to feel that, until that business is finally disposed of in some manner, he has the undivided loyalty of the one upon whom he looks as his advocate and his champion. If, as in this case, he is sued and his home attached by his own attorney, who is representing him in another matter, all feeling of loyalty is necessarily destroyed, and the profession is exposed to the charge that it is interested only in money." 203 A.2d at 84.

b.   Cinema 5, Ltd. v. Cinerama, Inc., 528 F.2d 1384 (2d Cir.1976), applied this principle where attorney Fleischmann was a partner in two different law firms, one in New York City and one in Buffalo. Cinerama hired the Buffalo firm to represent it in an antitrust action that upstate New York theater operators filed. Later, several plaintiffs retained the New York City firm to sue several companies, including Cinerama, for alleged attempts to take over theater companies in New York City. Thus, one law firm was suing Cinerama while the other law firm was suing Cinerama. They were connected by a common partner, so the court treated it as an

---

1. In re Dresser Industries, 972 F.2d 540 (5th Cir.1992), holds that the principle against filing suit for one client against another current client is a national standard that federal courts must use in ruling on disqualification motions, even in the face of contrary state law.

instance of a law firm representing a client in one case while suing it in a different case.

The firm appealed the district court disqualification, saying that two different cases in completely different markets were involved. The Second Circuit assumed the two lawsuits were not related and responded:

> "The 'substantial relationship' test is indeed the one that we have customarily applied in determining whether a lawyer may accept employment against a former client. * * * However, in this case, suit is not against a former client, but an existing one. One firm in which attorney Fleischmann is a partner is suing an actively represented client of another firm in which attorney Fleischmann is a partner. The propriety of this conduct must be measured not so much against the similarities in litigation, as against the duty of undivided loyalty which an attorney owes to each of his clients.

> "A lawyer's duty to his client is that of a fiduciary or trustee. * * * When Cinerama retained Mr. Fleischmann as its attorney in the Western District litigation, it was entitled to feel that at least until that litigation was at an end, it had his undivided loyalty as its advocate and champion, * * * and could rely upon his 'undivided allegiance and faithful, devoted service.' * * * Because 'no man can serve two masters', Matthew 6:24; * * * it had the right to expect also that he would 'accept no retainer to do anything that might be adverse to his client's interests.' * * * Needless to say, when Mr. Fleischmann and his New York City partners undertook to represent Cinema 5, Ltd., they owed it the same fiduciary duty of undivided loyalty and allegiance. * * *

> "Whether such adverse representation, without more, requires disqualification in every case, is a matter we need not now decide. We do hold, however, that the 'substantial relationship' test does not set a sufficiently high standard by which the necessity for disqualification should be determined. That test may properly be applied only where the representation of a former client has been terminated and the parameters of such relationship have been fixed. Where the relationship is a continuing one, adverse representation is prima facie improper, * * * and the attorney must be prepared to show, at the very least, that there will be no actual or *apparent* conflict in loyalties or diminution in the vigor of his representation. We think that appellants have failed to meet this heavy burden * * *. [T]he record shows that after learning of the conflict which had developed, the Jaeckle firm, through Mr. Fleischmann, offered to withdraw its representation of Cinerama in the Western District actions. However, that offer was not accepted, and Mr. Fleischmann continued, albeit reluctantly, to have one foot in each camp."

Thus, the court affirmed the disqualification order.

3. In addition to the issue of loyalty, should there be a concern that the lawyer might represent Client A less vigorously so as not to offend Client B?

a. In Zuck v. Alabama, 588 F.2d 436 (5th Cir.1979), a law firm represented a defendant in a criminal case while also representing the prosecutor sued in his personal capacity in an unrelated civil matter. The prosecutor was not the real party in interest in the criminal case: he was not the state. Yet, "the defense attorneys were subject to the encumbrance that the prosecutor might take umbrage at a vigorous defense of Zuck and dispense with the services of their firm." In other words, the defense lawyer might be cautious about offending the prosecutor, his civil client, such as by charging prosecutorial misconduct. This constituted an actual conflict of interest rendering the criminal trial unfair in the absence of the criminal defendant's knowing and intelligent waiver. The court also said that although a witness apparently informed the defendant that his attorneys were also representing the prosecutor, that did not establish that the defendant waived his right to conflict-free representation absent a showing that the defendant was aware of the consequences of proceeding to trial with such counsel or that he knew that he had a right to have other counsel. See Rule 1.0(e)("informed consent") and Rule 1.7, Comments [6] & [18].

b. ABA Formal Opinion 97–406 (Apr. 19, 1997) considered the case where one lawyer (Lawyer 1) represents another lawyer (Lawyer 2). For example, Lawyer 2 might be a defendant in a malpractice case. At the same time, Lawyer 1 simultaneously represents clients who oppose parties who are represented by Lawyer 2 in different, unrelated cases. The Committee said that the issue should be analyzed under what is now Model Rule 1.7(a)(2), not 1.7(a)(1). The Opinion advised that there is a conflict if there is reason to believe that one or the other of the representations "may be materially limited" by duties the lawyer owes the other client. In the view of the Opinion, six issues affect the determination of this issue: (1) the relative importance of the matters to the represented lawyer, (2) the relative sizes of the fees expected by the representing lawyer, (3) the relative importance of the clients' matters to each lawyer and client, (4) the sensitivity of each matter, (5) the similarity of the subject matter of the two cases, and (6) the nature of the relationship of the lawyers with each other and with their clients. If the lawyer concludes that her representation would not be affected by the relationship with the other lawyer, she may seek client consent to her continued representation. However, if a reasonably objective observer would conclude that her representation would be adversely affected, she may not even ask for client consent.[2]

---

2. Association of the Bar of the City of New York Formal Opinion 1996–3 (Apr. 2, 1996) says that the concerns about letting one firm [Firm A] represent another law firm [Firm B] as a client when Firm B represents clients in other cases that Firm A opposes are that (1) Firm A will learn things about Firm B that can be used adversely to Firm B's clients in the other matters, and (2) Firm A will tend to pull its punches in the unrelated matters so as to preserve the good will of Firm B. The opinion concludes that no bright

4. Should the concern about lawyer loyalty extend to more than instances of filing suit against another client?

a. The ABA Standing Committee on Ethics and Professional Responsibility has explored the suit against a present client issue in several other contexts. ABA Formal Opinion 97–407 (May 13, 1997), for example, asked whether a lawyer who serves as an expert witness in a matter is deemed to have a lawyer-client relationship with the party for which he or she testifies so as to prevent that lawyer from acting contrary to the interest of that client in another matter. The Committee said "no" if the lawyer is only testifying on the party's behalf, but "yes" if the lawyer is also consulting with lawyers for that party. However, if the lawyer's duty of confidentiality to other clients would be affected, consent of those other clients would be required before the lawyer could act as an expert at all.

b. May a lawyer cross-examine an opponent's expert witness whom the lawyer concurrently represents in unrelated matters? ABA Formal Opinion 92–367 (Oct. 16, 1992) concluded that the cross-examination would "ordinarily" present a conflict under Rule 1.7(a). The opinion reasoned that vigorous cross-examination would violate the lawyer's duty of loyalty to one client, the expert, while failure to cross-examine vigorously would violate the duty to zealously represent the lawyer's other client. Furthermore, the lawyer might know confidential information about the expert that would be relevant to the cross-examination but that the lawyer would be forbidden to use. The opinion suggests that a lawyer from another firm could be retained to conduct the cross-examination, and that the first lawyer could continue to conduct the rest of the defense. Do you agree that such a solution should suffice? Cf. Rule 1.7, Comment [8].

c. ABA Formal Opinion 97–405 (Apr. 19, 1997) found it "fairly clear" that, under Model Rule 1.7(a), a lawyer who currently represents a government entity in some kinds of work may not represent a private client against that entity, even in an unrelated matter. The question then became whether the lawyer for one government entity, say a school board, may represent a private client against a different government entity in the same jurisdiction, say the city government. The Committee said that the identity of a government client is "to some extent a matter of common sense and sensibility," and at bottom it is a matter of functional considerations of how the government works. If the same City Attorney represents both entities, for example, they would be more likely considered a single client for purposes of Rule 1.7(a). Ideally, lawyer and governmental client will reach agreement on that at the outset of the representation of the government entity.[3] See Model Rule 1.13, Comment [6].

line test can be formulated as to when the representation represents a conflict of interest. If a lawyer in a big firm closes a residential real estate transaction for a lawyer in another firm whose out-of-state office is litigating against a different office of the first firm, there may be no conflict at all. If a solo practitioner represents a small firm lawyer in a divorce case, taking even unrelated cases against each other might be a non-consentable conflict. Somewhere between those extremes, the clients in the unrelated matters should be notified and be given the chance to consent or get other counsel.

3. A particularly difficult form of conflict can arise in the patent field where a law

5.   May a lawyer avoid creating conflicts by limiting the scope of the representation?

a.   In Sumitomo v. J.P. Morgan & Co., 2000 WL 145747 (S.D.N.Y. 2000), the Paul Weiss firm had represented Sumitomo in investigating an employee who was responsible for losses from copper trading. Later, Sumitomo received demands for payment from banks with respect to transactions of which it was unaware. Paul Weiss realized that it represented some of those banks and told Sumitomo it could not evaluate or litigate the bank claims on Sumitomo's behalf. Paul Weiss represented Sumitomo in filing suit against J.P. Morgan, but Chase Manhattan, a Paul Weiss client in other matters, refused to waive the conflict, so Sumitomo had another firm represent it in filing suit against Chase. The judge consolidated the two cases for pretrial discovery, and Chase moved to disqualify Paul Weiss from suing J.P. Morgan because the two cases were allegedly one. The court refused to disqualify. "Chase is a huge financial institution," the court said. It is not an individual that would feel a betrayal of trust. Further, there was no reason to believe Paul Weiss would go easy on Chase out of a desire to keep its good will. Thus, the court found no reason to disqualify Paul Weiss.

b.   Association of the Bar of the City of New York Committee on Professional and Judicial Ethics Formal Opinion 2001–3 (2001), also addressed this issue. The opinion approved of having another firm bring the case against the client the principal firm cannot sue, and referred to negotiations in multi-party business deals where the technique might also be used. The practice may not be used as a sham in which the otherwise-conflicted firm becomes a behind-the-scenes manager of the matter which she has undertaken not to pursue, and the firm may not take actions that hurt the firm's other client, but with those caveats, the presence of one or two avoided areas of conflict does not mean the lawyer is disqualified altogether.

c.   Does this make sense to you? Can you think of other situations in which limiting the scope of representation might allow a lawyer to avoid violating Model Rule 1.7(a)(1)?

6.   Might excessive concern about loyalty to the lawyer's current clients lead to injustice to clients who are trying to find a capable lawyer to represent them?

a.   In Flatt v. Superior Court (Daniel), 885 P.2d 950 (Cal.1994), for example, a prospective client came to a law firm wanting to sue a prior lawyer. The prospective client disclosed confidential information and the

firm has two clients seeking related patents. Under the rules of the Patent and Trademark Office, 37 C.F.R. § 1.56, a lawyer for an applicant must disclose all "prior art" in the applicant's field. At the time of consideration of the applications, however, they are each confidential and information about each would be protected by Rule 1.6. Even ac-

knowledging the impossible situation the law firm had found itself in, failure to disclose the application of one client in the application of the other was expressly found to be "inequitable conduct" that rendered the issued patent invalid and unenforceable. Molins PLC v. Textron, Inc., 48 F.3d 1172 (Fed.Cir.1995).

person with whom he talked told him that he "definitely" had a good malpractice claim. A week later, the firm called the prospective client back and declined the representation because it represented the prior lawyer in an unrelated matter. The firm did not tell the prospective client about the statute of limitations for his claim or recommend that he get other counsel. The California Supreme Court declared that this handling of the conflict was proper. Giving the prospective client information about protecting his interests would have been disloyal to the existing client, the Court said. Do you agree?

b. However, courts do temper the rule with realism. Commercial Union Insurance Co. v. Marco International Corp., 75 F.Supp.2d 108 (S.D.N.Y.1999), for example, involved a law firm that was claims counsel for Commercial Union in a suit determining coverage of a policy. In a different action involving the same policy, the firm had been retained by Commercial Union to sue in the name of Marco but on behalf of the insurer as subrogee to recover sums the insurer had paid Marco for a loss. The question was whether Marco was a current client for purposes of the present suit. The court took what it called a "flexible" approach and refused to disqualify the firm. Marco had no "material pecuniary or other interest" in the other case, paid no fees and had no control over the prosecution or settlement of that action. There would be no reason, "beyond empty formalism," to find the present action to be a prohibited suit against a current client.[4]

B. ASCERTAINING WHO IS A CURRENT CLIENT

1. Assume it is well established that a lawyer may not represent someone in litigation against a current client without both parties' consent. Is International Bolts a current client? At this moment you are not doing any work for International Bolts, and the company may never call again.

a. In IBM v. Levin, 579 F.2d 271 (3d Cir.1978), IBM sought to disqualify a law firm, CBM, for representing a client in a suit against IBM. The trial court disqualified CBM and the court of appeals affirmed. The trial "court found as a fact that at all relevant times CBM had an on-going attorney-client relationship with both IBM and the plaintiffs. This assessment of the relationship seems entirely reasonable to us. Although CBM had no specific assignment from IBM on hand on the day that [CBM filed] the antitrust complaint [against IBM] and even though CBM performed services for IBM on a fee for services basis rather than pursuant to a retainer arrangement, the pattern of repeated retainers, both before and after the filing of the complaint, supports the finding of a continuous relationship." 579 F.2d at 281.

---

4. For more about the history of the rule and possibly tempering its application with reason, see Thomas D. Morgan, Suing a Current Client, 9 Georgetown J. Legal Ethics 1157 (1996).

b. Should a law firm be able to avoid the inference of continued representation by writing a letter to each client terminating the relationship at the end of a given matter? Why do you suppose firms are loath to do that? Is the approach in IBM v. Levin simply recognizing a relationship the firm hopes the client believes still exists?

2. Should every division and wholly-owned subsidiary of a present client be considered to be a client of the lawyer for conflict purposes?

a. A division within one corporation typically is treated as part of the client itself. In Image Technical Services v. Eastman Kodak Co., 820 F.Supp. 1212 (N.D.Cal.1993), for example, the law firm prepared plaintiffs' briefs in a Supreme Court antitrust case against Kodak. At the same time, the firm's Hong Kong office represented a division of Kodak that was doing completely unrelated work in China and other international markets. The law firm had obtained oral consent from the division representative with whom the firm worked, but it had not sought consent from the Kodak general counsel. The court disqualified the law firm from all further participation in the case. Furthermore, when the plaintiff, using different counsel, won the case on remand to the trial court, the first firm applied for the statutory attorneys' fees due the prevailing plaintiff for the period it had participated in the Supreme Court case. The 9th Circuit held, however, that to award attorney fees under the Clayton Act for the law firm's representation of the plaintiff case prior to its disqualification would reward its work while it had a conflict of interest. Image Technical Service v. Eastman Kodak Co., 136 F.3d 1354 (9th Cir.1998).

b. ABA Formal Opinion 95–390 (Jan. 25, 1995), analyzed conflicts of interest in the corporate family context beyond corporate division cases. The Opinion said that the world of corporate family relationships is too varied to adopt a bright-line rule forbidding a law firm that represents a parent corporation, for example, from bringing suit against the parent's subsidiary. The lawyer must ask whether (1) the subsidiary and parent are in effect operated as one entity, (2) there has been an agreement to treat the whole corporate family as the client, or (3) the lawyer's obligations to the parent will materially limit pursuit of the claim against the subsidiary.[5] See also, Illinois State Bar Association Opinion 95–15 (May 17, 1996) (economic impact on related corporation is not, by itself, enough to render representation "directly adverse" to the related corporation). See also ABA Model Rule 1.7, Comment [34] & [35] ("Organizational Clients").

c. In United States v. ASCAP, 129 F.Supp.2d 327 (S.D.N.Y.2001), a composer claimed that ASCAP had failed to pay him the royalties he was due for use of music he had composed. ASCAP's regular counsel defended this suit and the composer moved to disqualify that firm, arguing that he was a member of ASCAP and thus that the lawyers represented him as well. The court held that even though ASCAP is an unincorporated

---

5. See, e.g., Ronald D. Rotunda, Conflicts Problems When Representing Members   of Corporate Families, 72 Notre Dame L. Rev. 655 (1997).

association, it is an "organization" for ethics purposes. ASCAP lawyers do not represent the members personally and thus the court denied disqualification.

d.   Brown & Williamson v. Pataki, 152 F.Supp.2d 276 (S.D.N.Y.2001), refused to disqualify Covington & Burling because it represented New York state's welfare department in efforts to get federal funding while simultaneously representing clients who were suing the state trying to overturn the state's prohibition on selling cigarettes to New York residents by mail order. The court said that determining who the client was in a case involving the government was a difficult matter, and the agency signing the contract with the firm was not controlling. Nor could the whole state executive branch be deemed the client. But there was no relationship between this case and what the firm did for the state in other matters; the firm would not cross-examine people it was advising in other matters, for example, so both representations could continue. See also, Model Rule 1.13, Comment [6] ("Government Agency").

e.   JPMorgan Chase Bank v. Liberty Mutual Insurance Company, 189 F.Supp.2d 20 (S.D.N.Y.2002), involved Davis Polk & Wardwell, which had long represented The Chubb Corporation, a large financial holding company, handling securities filings and financing on its behalf. Late in 2001, Davis Polk also took on representation of J.P. Morgan Chase in claims on surety bonds issued by various insurance companies to guarantee obligations of Enron Corporation. One of the defendants in those cases, Federal Insurance Company, was Chubb's primary subsidiary. Thus, Davis Polk was representing Chubb on various matters while suing a Chubb subsidiary. The court disqualified Davis Polk from representing J.P. Morgan in the claims against Federal. The court observed that Federal accounted for 90% of Chubb's net income, the two companies shared identical corporate headquarters, an identical board of directors, and identical general counsel. Furthermore, the prejudice to the bank from having to substitute new counsel was relatively modest.[6]

3.   Should a lawyer for a business partnership or trade association be treated as the lawyer for each of the members individually?

a.   Most courts hold that it depends on the facts. A specific undertaking to represent the partnership and not to represent the individual members will ordinarily be enforced, whether the partnership is an "entity" under state law or an "aggregate" of the individual partners. See, e.g., Greate Bay Hotel & Casino, Inc. v. Atlantic City, 624 A.2d 102 (N.J.Super.1993) (a lawyer for a business trust represents the trust as an "entity"

---

6.   See also Discotrade Ltd. v. Wyeth–Ayerst International, Inc., 200 F.Supp.2d 355 (S.D.N.Y.2002) (Dorsey & Whitney disqualified from representing plaintiff because it also represented the defendant's sister corporation in unrelated matters. All of the directors of the sister companies were the same, they shared the same President, computer system, and financial management, and the same in-house legal department served them all.) The case is discussed in Ronald D. Rotunda, Conflict Problems When Representing Members of Corporate Families, 72 Notre Dame L. Rev. 655 (1997).

and thus is not barred from suing a member of the trust in an unrelated matter); Responsible Citizens v. Superior Court (Askins), 20 Cal.Rptr.2d 756 (Ct.App.1993) (lawyer who represents partnership may sue individual partner in unrelated proceeding).

b. ABA Formal Opinion 91–361 (July 12, 1991) concludes that the Model Rules treat partnerships as entities and that their representation is governed by Rule 1.13. One or more individual members of a partnership may separately retain the partnership lawyer, as provided in Rule 1.13(e), but representation of an individual partner is not automatic. The Opinion concludes that lawyers should make clear to the individual partners at the outset of the representation whom the lawyers represent so as to avoid misunderstandings later. See Comment [34] to Model Rule 1.7, and Comments [7] and [8] to Model Rule 1.13.

c. In Westinghouse Electric Corp. v. Kerr–McGee Corp., 580 F.2d 1311 (7th Cir.1978), cert. denied 439 U.S. 955, 99 S.Ct. 353, 58 L.Ed.2d 346 (1978), Kirkland & Ellis filed an antitrust action on behalf of its client, Westinghouse, against various corporations alleging price fixing violations in the uranium industry. Meanwhile the American Petroleum Institute ("AmPI") had retained Kirkland to oppose legislative proposals introduced in Congress to cause energy companies to divest uranium companies that they owned. On the same day that Kirkland's Chicago office filed the antitrust suit, Kirkland's Washington, D.C. office, representing AmPI, released a report that developed the opposite thesis and took an affirmative position on the subject of existing competition in the oil-uranium industry. AmPI was not a defendant in the antitrust suit, but three AmPI *members* were defendants.

It turned out that individual members of AmPI had given Kirkland & Ellis' Washington office confidential information on their uranium assets in order to aid the firm in opposing the threatened legislation. Moreover, the General Counsel of AmPI and Kirkland & Ellis had promised the members that the information would be held confidential. The Seventh Circuit held that "the attorney is held to obligations to the client which go far beyond those of an agent and beyond the principles of agency * * *. [AmPI members] each entertained a reasonable belief that it was submitting confidential information regarding its involvement in the uranium industry to a law firm which had solicited the information upon a representation that the firm was acting in the undivided interest of each company." 580 F.2d at 1321.

Do you agree? Should *Westinghouse* be read to say any more than that when information is supplied on a promise of confidentiality, a court will see that the promise is honored? Could the lawyers have avoided this problem if they had not promised confidentiality and had clarified their role? Rule 1.13, Comments [7].

d. D.C. Bar Legal Ethics Committee, Opinion 305 (2001), concludes that representation of a trade association as an entity does not create an attorney-client relationship between the lawyer and members of the association. However, there are circumstances in which representing a client adverse to a member of the association might create a conflict of interest. If the member reasonably believes that it is being individually represented by the lawyer, the member is, regardless of an express agreement, a de facto client of the lawyer. Factors to look at when inquiring as to what a reasonable belief by the member is include whether the member disclosed confidential information to the association's lawyer, whether the member had separate representation, whether the lawyer had ever previously represented the member individually, and whether the member relied on the lawyer's representation of his individual interest.

See also, ABA Formal Opinion 92–365 (July 6, 1992) (law firm that represents a trade association ordinarily may file an unrelated action against a member of the association with whom the lawyer has formed no attorney-client relationship unless the representation would impair the lawyer's representation of the association itself).

Do these opinions reject *Westinghouse* or apply it?

C.   FIRING A CURRENT CLIENT; THE HOT POTATO RULE

1. If you find that a conflict develops between two clients, may you avoid the problem by "firing" one of the clients and continuing to represent the other?

a. At the end of *Cinema 5*, supra, the Second Circuit noted that attorney Fleischmann offered to withdraw from representation of Cinerama in the Western District actions, but Cinerama refused and pressed forward on its disqualification motion. The court did not treat Cinerama's refusal to permit withdrawal as a waiver of its conflict claim. Why not? We know that at least part of the justification for disqualification is the breach of fiduciary duty of loyalty inherent in a conflict of interest. If Fleischmann were permitted to withdraw from further representation of Cinerama without penalty, would he be seeking to profit from his breach of loyalty?

b. Unified Sewerage Agency of Washington County, Oregon v. Jelco, Inc., 646 F.2d 1339, 1345 n. 4 (9th Cir.1981), recognized the problem of choosing to represent one client against another and noted that a challenged attorney may not convert a *present* client governed by Rule 1.7 into a *former* client governed by Rule 1.9 merely "by choosing when to cease to represent the disfavored client."

c. In Picker International, Inc. v. Varian Associates, Inc., 670 F.Supp. 1363 (N.D.Ohio 1987), affirmed 869 F.2d 578 (Fed.Cir.1989), a large national law firm merged with a firm in another city, and when the client lists were compared, it turned out that the merging firms represented clients who were opponents in current litigation. The merged firm was suing *B* on behalf of *A* (a long-time client of the acquiring firm), while representing *B* (the acquired firm's client) on various other matters. The firm sought to withdraw from representation of *B*, and to continue to represent the long time client of the big firm. The court held that the firm could not do that without consent of all affected clients. Failing consent, the new firm must withdraw from *all* representation of all parties in the case of *A v. B.* The court said: "A firm may not drop a client like a hot potato, especially if it is in order to keep a far more lucrative client." In the case law this principle is often called the "hot potato" rule. The law of conflicts develops from a metaphor of the kitchen.

d.   Stratagem Development Corp. v. Heron International N.V., 756 F.Supp. 789 (S.D.N.Y.1991), further found that the law of New York gives a lawyer the same duty of loyalty to a wholly-owned subsidiary as to the parent corporation. Thus, this court also held that a firm may not cease representation of the subsidiary, i.e., drop the client like a "hot potato," in order to file an unrelated action against the parent.

2.   Should the "hot potato" rule ever recognize exceptions?

a.   The law of ethics does not have the certainty of Euclidian geometry, and the hot potato rule has not been applied in all cases. In Pennwalt Corp. v. Plough, Inc., 85 F.R.D. 264 (D.Del.1980), the law firm had represented Pennwalt for decades. In 1978, the firm began to defend Scholl against antitrust charges. In April 1979, Schering–Plough acquired Scholl as a wholly owned subsidiary. Because Plough was already a wholly-owned subsidiary of Schering–Plough, Scholl and Plough then became sister corporations. In May, 1979, the law firm filed suit against Plough on behalf of its longtime client Pennwalt. Upon learning a week or two later that it represented Scholl in one case and simultaneously represented Pennwalt against Scholl's parent, the firm sought to withdraw from representing Scholl. After the court granted that motion, Plough moved to disqualify the firm from the second case. The court agreed that counsel may not eliminate a conflict "merely by choosing to represent the more favored client and withdrawing its representation of the other." However, in this case the firm's conflict was inadvertent: the merger activities of the client created the problem. "Scholl is a corporate entity distinct from Plough and Schering–Plough,"and it was highly unlikely that as of the date of the law firm's representation there was any misuse of confidential information or adverse effect on its exercise of independent judgment. Thus, the court did not mandate disqualification. See Comment [5] to Model Rule 1.7, which takes this case into account.

b.   In Gould Inc. v. Mitsui Mining & Smelting Co., 738 F.Supp. 1121 (N.D.Ohio 1990), the Jones Day law firm was representing Gould in suing various defendants who had allegedly misappropriated Gould trade secrets. One of these defendants was Pechiney. In 1989, Pechiney acquired IG Technologies (IGT), a company that Jones Day represented in an unrelated matter. Thus, Jones Day found itself in a conflict between Gould and IGT's parent. In response to a motion to disqualify Jones Day from representing Gould against Pechiney, the court reasoned that, because of the "explosion of merger activity by corporations during the past fifteen years" it is appropriate to adopt a "less mechanical approach" and "balanc[e] the various interests." In this case, there was "no demonstration that Pechiney has been prejudiced by the law firm's representation of Gould." Further, disqualification would cost Gould a great deal of time and money, and significantly delay progress in this case. Finally, "the conflict was created by Pechiney's acquisition of IGT several years after the instant case was commenced, not by an affirmative act of Jones, Day." However, the court held, the conflict "must not endure." Hence, the law firm had to discontinue its representation of either Gould or IGT, and erect a "screen" around the lawyers who had worked for the party whom the firm dropped.[7]

c.   D.C. Bar Opinion 272 (May 1997) considered a situation in which Client 1, a long-time client to whom Law Firm gave occasional advice, brought an administrative proceeding using another lawyer against Client 2, whom Law Firm was now representing before the agency in an unrelated matter. Client 1 refused to waive the conflict and Law Firm wanted to know whether it could continue representing Client 2. The Opinion said that Law Firm may do so. The Opinion agreed that what is now Model Rule 1.7(a)(1) was implicated, not Model Rule 1.9, but it said that Law Firm could withdraw from representation of Client 1 because withdrawal would have no material adverse effect on that client.

d.   Similarly, in Pioneer–Standard Electronics, Inc. v. Cap Gemini America, Inc., 2002 WL 553460 (N.D.Ohio 2002), plaintiff Pioneer–Standard, sought to disqualify defendant's counsel, Shearman & Sterling, arguing that the firm currently represented it. Shearman & Sterling's relationship with Pioneer–Standard began when Shearman merged with a German firm that had been handling Pioneer–Standard regulatory matters before the European Commission. After the merger, Shearman & Sterling billed approximately ten hours to Pioneer–Standard on those matters. Although the court found that Pioneer–Standard was a current client of Shearman & Sterling, it refused disqualification. It acknowledged the existence of the hot potato rule but found that there should be no disqualification if the matters "were unrelated and posed no likelihood of passing confidential information." The European regulatory matters did not generate confidential information that could be used against Pioneer–Standard in this case, there was no other prejudice to Pioneer–Standard from the continued representation, the foreign matter was limited to registering a commercial transaction of plaintiff, it consumed few hours of counsel's time, and the case was wholly unrelated to the instant litigation.

e.   By contrast, GATX/Airlog Co. v. Evergreen International Airlines, 8 F.Supp.2d 1182 (N.D.Cal.1998), disqualified the law firm. Evergreen was sued by GATX in a case that involved Boeing 747s converted for cargo use. Evergreen's law firm (MBP) had raised defenses that would be applicable against any Evergreen customer. Bank of New York (BNY) had financed one of the airplanes and had become its beneficial (but not record) owner, and it turned out that BNY was a client of the firm in unrelated matters. Well into the case, BNY filed suit against Evergreen itself, so only after doing a great deal of work on the case did MBP find itself opposing a current client. The court held that MBP should have anticipated that BNY might file such a suit. Its failure to get consent from BNY earlier required

---

7.   You will see more about "screening" in Problems 15 & 16, infra.

its disqualification in not only the BNY matter but all of the related litigation it was handling on behalf of Evergreen.

3. What about waivers of possible future conflicts? Should clients be able to agree at the outset of the representation that, if a conflict later arises, the lawyer may represent one of the clients against the other? Should law firms make an advance waiver of conflicts part of the boilerplate in their retainer agreements?

a. Restatement (Third) The Law Governing Lawyers § 122, Comment *d*, says:

> "A client's open-ended agreement to consent to all conflicts normally should be ineffective unless the client possesses sophistication in the matter in question and has had the opportunity to receive independent legal advice about the consent. * * *

> "On the other hand, particularly in a continuing client-lawyer relationship in which the lawyer is expected to act on behalf of the client without a new engagement for each matter, the gains to both lawyer and client from a system of advance consent to defined future conflicts might be substantial. A client might, for example, give informed consent in advance to types of conflicts that are familiar to the client. Such an agreement could effectively protect the client's interest while assuring that the lawyer did not undertake a potentially disqualifying representation."

b. ABA Formal Opinion 93–372 (Apr. 16, 1993) also expressed caution. It is more difficult for the client to waive a lawyer's duty to respect the client's confidences than the lawyer's duty of loyalty because—at the time that the lawyer asks the client to waive confidentiality—the client would not normally know how significant that piece of information would be in the future. Yet, even the client's ability to waive the duty of loyalty has limits. It would be "unlikely," the Opinion advised, that a prospective waiver that "did not identify either the potential opposing party or at least a class of potentially conflicting clients would survive scrutiny." The Opinion concluded:

> "[O]ne principle seems certain: no lawyer can rely with ethical certainty on a prospective waiver of objection to future adverse representations simply because the client has executed a written document to that effect. No lawyer should assume that without more, the 'coast is clear' for undertaking any and all future conflicting engagements that come within the general terms of the waiver document. Even though one might think that the very purpose of a prospective waiver is to eliminate the need to return to the client to secure a 'present' second waiver when what was once an inchoate matter ripens into an immediate conflict, there is no doubt that in many cases that is what will be ethically required."

See also, DC Bar Legal Ethics Committee Opinion No. 309 (2001) (advance waivers permissible, at least where specific and given by sophisticated clients who have advice of counsel).

c.   Worldspan, L.P. v. Sabre Group Holdings, Inc., 5 F.Supp.2d 1356 (N.D.Ga.1998), gave pause to firms who hope rely on advance waivers of conflicts. The law firm was counsel to Worldspan in state tax matters in Georgia and Tennessee. In this case, it agreed to represent the defendants in an unrelated matter filed by Worldspan. The firm relied on its standard engagement letter that Worldspan had signed six years earlier on the advice of experienced, independent counsel. The letter's stated that "we will not be precluded from representing clients who may have interests adverse to Worldspan" that are not substantially related and do not involve the use of adverse information. The court held that this six-year-old waiver was ineffective to constitute an informed prospective consent to the current representation; its language was not specific enough to cover representing an adverse party in a lawsuit filed by Worldspan, even where the letter expressly named that adverse party as an existing client of the law firm. In a portion of the opinion on reconsideration, the court also found the tax work more closely related to the current litigation than the law firm had believed.

d.   However, General Cigar Holdings, Inc. v. Altadis, S.A., 144 F.Supp.2d 1334 (S.D.Fla.2001), honored a broad advance waiver. Latham & Watkins, counsel to General Cigar in an antitrust suit against Altadis, continued to represent General Cigar, Altadis, and other tobacco companies in an action to challenge state advertising restrictions in Massachusetts. When accepting the Massachusetts engagement, the firm obtained a signed waiver from each client waiving any objection to current or future representation of one against the other in some other matter. None of the lawyers handling the antitrust suit had worked on the Massachusetts case, nor did firm members have access to other confidential information about Altadis. The court found Altadis' advance consent was valid. It was made by informed and sophisticated parties who knew of the firm's standing relationship with General Cigar, even though they did not know of the planned antitrust litigation. The court also found that the antitrust/trademark claims in the instant suit were not substantially related to the free speech/advertising claims in the other case. Finally, the court concluded that representation of the plaintiff in the instant case would not impair the firm's substantive representation of Altadis in any other matter.

e.   What do you think of the use of advance consent to conflicts? The ABA Model Rules address advance consent in Comment [22] to Model Rule 1.7. Is that Comment likely to lead to more consistent results in this area?

D.   THE PROBLEM OF POSITIONAL CONFLICTS

1.   What duty of loyalty, if any, do you have not to take a legal position on prepayment penalties that is inconsistent with the interest of a regular client like the First National Bank? Is there a

technical conflict of interest that would obligate you not to take this case?

a. Should a lawyer be permitted to assert a legal position in one case that—if accepted by the court—may conflict with the legal position of another client in a different case that another lawyer in the same firm advances? We know that lawyers often take inconsistent legal positions in the *same* case. A lawyer for an alleged debtor pleads, for example, "My client did not borrow the money (it was a gift), but even if he did borrow it, he already has repaid the debt." Is the problem of inconsistency *between* cases different?

b. Does the permissibility of positional conflicts depend on whether interpretations of fact or of law are involved? Might you represent Client Y in one case arguing that facts justify a finding of negligence, but defend Client Z in another case on identical facts saying that the conduct showed due care? Should the propriety of the conduct be different if, as in this Problem, you plan to try to change a controlling legal standard?

2. Should it matter whether your inconsistent positions are taken before the same court? What if your law firm takes inconsistent positions in different forums?

a. Before the 2002 amendments, Comment [9] to Model Rule 1.7 said:

"[I]t is ordinarily not improper to assert such [inconsistent] positions in cases pending in different trial courts, but it may be improper to do so in cases pending at the same time in an appellate court."

Do you agree that the trial-appellate and different-appellate-court distinctions are useful ways to decide when a positional conflict is proper or improper?

b. ABA Formal Opinion 93–377 (October 16, 1993) cast doubt on the trial-appellate court distinction. It analyzed the so-called "positional conflicts" issue as follows:

"[I]f the two matters are being litigated in the same jurisdiction, and there is a substantial risk that the law firm's representation of one client will create a legal precedent, even if not binding, which is likely materially to undercut the legal position being urged on behalf of the other client, the lawyer should either refuse to accept the second representation or (if otherwise permissible) withdraw from the first, unless both clients consent after full disclosure of the potential ramifications of the lawyer continuing to handle both matters. * * *

"[Even if the matters are being litigated in different jurisdictions,] if the lawyer concludes that the issue is of such importance and that its determination in one case is likely to have a significant impact on its determination in the second case, thus impairing the lawyer's effectiveness—or if the lawyer concludes that, because of the dual representation, there will be an inclination by the firm either to 'soft pedal' the issue or to alter the firm's arguments on behalf of one or both clients, thus again impairing the lawyer's effectiveness—the lawyer should not accept the second representation."

c. By contrast, California State Bar Standing Committee on Professional Responsibility and Conduct, Formal Opinion No. 1989–108 (1989), says that "To devise a rule that could be applied uniformly to 'issues conflicts' threatens the ability of lawyers to carry out their roles in the legal system." What do you think the California committee meant by this comment?

d. Comment [24] to Model Rule 1.7 tries to take a more nuanced approach to positional conflicts. Do you agree that it provides good guidance to lawyers trying to conduct a complex practice in a manner consistent with appropriate professional standards?

3. Would Model Rule 6.3 impose different obligations if you were a member of a legal service organization's board of directors that wanted to take a position contrary to one of your paying clients?

a. John Erlenborn, a former member of Congress, was appointed by the President to the Board of the Legal Services Corporation ("LSC"). He was also a partner in a major law firm that represented growers in disputes over farm workers' conditions; the farm workers were often represented by LSC-funded lawyers. The American Farm Bureau Federation, a private lobbying group representing agricultural interests, began a campaign to persuade the firm's agricultural clients (the Farm Bureau was not one of the firm's clients) to object to what the Farm Bureau characterized as Erlenborn's conflict of interest, i.e., he took positions as an LSC board member that the Farm Bureau claimed were harmful to farm interests.

Erlenborn offered to recuse himself from any decisions of the LSC board that directly involved reform legislation that the Farm Bureau supported, or that involved agricultural activities that could have an impact on his firm's clients, but the Farm Bureau's objections (including its objection to Erlenborn's proposed congressional testimony on the reform legislation) continued until Erlenborn resigned from the LSC board. The ABA President-elect said that there was no conflict of interests that required Erlenborn's resignation.[8] Do you agree? Was Erlenborn ethically required to resign from the LSC board, or was he simply bending over backwards to please some firm clients?

b. Suppose that the legal services agency agrees with your bank client and opposes regulations prohibiting prepayment penalties because it believes such regulations will raise the cost of credit to unacceptable levels. May you lobby on the agency's behalf against the regulatory proposals. Must you inform the agency that you also represent the First National Bank who will be pleased by its position? Look at Model Rule 6.4.

---

8. Anne Kornhauser, Sowing Client Discord, Reaping Political Fallout, 13 Legal Times of Washington 1, 15–16 (June 25, 1990).

c. Assume that you fully inform the legal services agency and the bank of your representation of each. Does Model Rule 3.9 require you to voluntarily disclose to the regulatory body that in appearing on behalf of the legal services agency you also further the interests of the First National Bank?

4. Even if the ethics rules allow you to represent the consumer against the bank, are there other problems you might face?

a. Could your banking client force you out of the case indirectly? Could it insist that, although it is not now a party, it wants you to file an amicus brief on its behalf? If you agreed and withdrew from representing your neighbor, could your neighbor force you to withdraw from the case altogether? Of course you could ask your regular client, the First National Bank, to relieve you of any further obligations to represent it in paying matters, but that would make your pro bono activities on behalf of your neighbor a lot more costly.

b. If you want to take this case and in fact do so, must you warn your neighbor that one of your best clients is opposed to your attacking the prepayment penalty? Even if no technical conflict of interest exists, why might the neighbor consider this information relevant?

PROBLEM 11

CONFLICTS OF INTEREST IN CRIMINAL LITIGATION

Criminal cases present some of the most interesting conflicts of interest questions. We require that a client's decision to waive a conflict be informed and unconstrained, yet criminal defendants often make that decision in a setting where the consent to common representation is seen as a sign of loyalty to fellow defendants, or an unwillingness to make a deal with prosecutors. In most cases, we assume there is little public stake in a decision whether to consent to a conflict of interest. In criminal cases, however, courts have a duty to protect defendants' constitutional right to a fair trial. Finally, criminal cases can sometimes make or break the careers of prosecutors and defense counsel. They can create personal incentives for those lawyers to represent their clients differently than they might in another setting. All those issues are presented in this Problem.

FACTS

Barbara Bentley regularly represents Bitter Creek, Inc, the defendant in a case charging price fixing, a criminal violation of the federal antitrust laws. Chuck Carson, manager of the widget division at Bitter Creek is accused of conspiring with Mary Morton, his counterpart at Widgetech, Inc., a major competitor. In Bentley's first interview with Carson, Carson told Bentley he was unrepresented and asked her to represent him. Carson told Bentley that Mary Morton also needed a lawyer and thought it would be best if Bentley would represent her as well. Widgetech, Inc., has in–house counsel and Bentley already has been meeting with him to share information and develop a joint defense.

Bentley confirmed Morton's interest in retaining her and she has now entered an appearance on behalf of Bitter Creek, Carson and Morton. The United States Attorney is interested in demonstrating his commitment to consumers because he plans to run for Governor next year. Thus, he is determined to obtain convictions, although he does not care who takes the fall. He proposes to Bentley that she get Carson and Morton to plead guilty to charges for which he will recommend no jail time. In exchange, he will drop the felony charge against Bitter Creek. Because this will reduce the chance of subsequent treble damage actions against the corporation, Bentley finds the proposal attractive. She recommends that Carson and Morton accept it, accurately telling them that if they were found guilty after a trial, their sentences could be more severe.

Bentley sees herself as an extraordinary lawyer, and she plans to write an article about her handling of the Bitter Creek case under the title, "There's Nothing I Won't Do To See That At Least One of My Clients Goes Free."

QUESTIONS

A. LIMITS ON ONE LAWYER'S REPRESENTING CO-DEFENDANTS IN A CRIMINAL CASE

1. Why might the courts consider it particularly important that criminal defendants be warned about possible conflicts of interest?

a. For federal criminal cases like the one in this problem, Rule 44(c), Federal Rules of Criminal Procedure provides:

"(c) JOINT REPRESENTATION. Whenever two or more defendants have been jointly charged pursuant to Rule 8(b) or have been joined for trial pursuant to Rule 13, and are represented by the same retained or assigned counsel or by retained or assigned counsel who are associated in the practice of law, the court shall promptly inquire with respect to such joint representation and shall personally advise each defendant of his right to the effective assistance of counsel, including separate representation. Unless it appears that there is good cause to believe no conflict of interest is likely to arise, the court shall take such measures as may be appropriate to protect each defendant's right to counsel."

b. Holloway v. Arkansas, 435 U.S. 475, 98 S.Ct. 1173, 55 L.Ed.2d 426 (1978), raised the question of a lawyer's conflicts of interest to a constitutional dimension. It said that a state criminal conviction must be reversed if a trial judge requires joint representation in a criminal case after a defendant's timely objection. The joint representation is presumed prejudicial. "Joint representation of conflicting interests is suspect because of what it tends to prevent the attorney from doing." 435 U.S. at 489–90, 98 S.Ct. at 1181, 55 L.Ed.2d at 438.

c. *Holloway* illustrated some of the problems inherent in joint representation. In that case, the conflict may have precluded defense counsel "from exploring possible plea negotiations and the possibility of an agreement to testify for the prosecution, provided a lesser charge or a favorable sentencing recommendation would be acceptable. [A] conflict may also prevent an attorney from challenging the admission of evidence prejudicial to one client but perhaps favorable to another, or from arguing at the sentencing hearing the relative involvement and culpability of his clients in order to minimize the culpability of one by emphasizing that of another." 435 U.S. at 490, 98 S.Ct. at 1181, 55 L.Ed.2d at 438.

2.   How does the concern about conflicts relate to the constitutional guarantee of effective assistance of counsel?

a.   The constitutional concern about lawyer conflicts of interest is linked directly to the Sixth Amendment concern for the effective assistance of counsel. *Holloway* was so based, and it, in turn, must be read in light of later cases.

b.   Cuyler v. Sullivan, 446 U.S. 335, 100 S.Ct. 1708, 64 L.Ed.2d 333 (1980), dealt with the situation in which no party lodges an objection to multiple representation. If there is no objection and absent special circumstances, the trial court may assume that multiple representations do not result in a conflict or that the clients knowingly accepts such risk of a conflict. If the court knows or reasonably should know that a particular conflict of interest exists, however, it must initiate an inquiry into the propriety of multiple representation. If the court does not know of the conflict, the lack of an inquiry is not constitutionally significant. In order to establish a Sixth Amendment violation from multiple representation that was not the subject of an objection at trial, a defendant must demonstrate that the conflict of interest actually adversely affected the adequacy of his lawyer's performance. Adverse effect is presumed, but the mere possibility of prejudice arising from a conflict of interest is not sufficient to impugn a criminal conviction.

c.   The leading case dealing with claims of ineffective assistance of counsel in general is Strickland v. Washington, 466 U.S. 668, 104 S.Ct. 2052, 80 L.Ed.2d 674 (1984). *Strickland* created a high hurdle for the criminal defendant. To justify a reversal, the defendant must show that [1] the lawyer's acts or omissions were "outside the wide range of professionally competent assistance," 466 U.S. at 690, 104 S.Ct. at 2067, 80 L.Ed.2d at 695, and [2] the ineffectiveness must have caused actual prejudice. "It is not enough for the defendant to show that the errors had some conceivable effect on the outcome of the proceedings." 466 U.S. at 693, 104 S.Ct. at 2067, 80 L.Ed.2d at 697.

d. *Strickland* distinguished its test from *Cuyler*'s.

"In Cuyler v. Sullivan, the Court held that prejudice is presumed when counsel is burdened by an actual conflict of interest. In those circumstances, counsel breaches the duty of loyalty, perhaps the most basic of counsel's duties. Moreover, it is difficult to measure the precise effect on the defense of representation corrupted by conflicting interests. Given the obligation of counsel to avoid conflicts of interest and the ability of trial courts to make early inquiry in certain situations likely to give rise to conflicts, it is reasonable for the criminal justice system to maintain a fairly rigid rule of presumed prejudice for conflicts of interest. Even so, * * * [p]rejudice is presumed only if the defendant demonstrates that counsel 'actively represented conflicting interests' and that 'an actual conflict of interest adversely affected his lawyer's performance.' "

466 U.S. at 692, 104 S.Ct. at 2067, 80 L.Ed.2d at 696.

e. In Burger v. Kemp, 483 U.S. 776, 107 S.Ct. 3114, 97 L.Ed.2d 638 (1987), one lawyer had represented one defendant while the lawyer's partner represented the co-defendant in a separate proceeding. The Court (5 to 4) explained that *Holloway* had rejected a per se approach and required a showing that the conflict had an adverse effect on the lawyer's performance. The two partners in *Burger* did talk about trial strategy, but there were separate trials, reducing any incentive of one lawyer to change tactics for the benefit of the other client. There was no argument that any conflict prevented counsel from negotiating a plea bargain because the prosecutor refused to bargain, and even if there was an actual conflict of interest, the majority concluded that it did not harm the lawyer's advocacy.

f. In Mickens v. Taylor, 535 U.S. 162, 122 S.Ct. 1237, 152 L.Ed.2d 291 (2002), after Mickens was sentenced to death for murder, he discovered that his court-appointed attorney had been representing the victim on other criminal charges at the time the victim was murdered, a fact that the lawyer had not disclosed to the defendant. The trial court judge, who had appointed the lawyer in both instances, apparently failed to realize what had happened and did not inquire whether the situation presented a conflict of interest. Following Cuyler v. Sullivan, the Supreme Court upheld Mickens' conviction and sentence.

Writing for the 5–member majority, Justice Scalia emphasized that a defendant must show that a conflict of interest had an actual effect on the lawyer's performance. The Court noted that *Cuyler,* although calling for an inquiry where the trial court has notice of a conflict, only presumes prejudice to the defendant where an effect on the representation is shown. Justice Kennedy, concurring, said the particular facts of the case indicated that Mickens' attorney did not believe he had a continuing duty to his former client, the murder victim, and the lawyer in question did not pursue an unreasonable trial strategy. The four dissenting justices disputed the belief that defense counsel might not have handled the case differently absent a conflict. Justice Stevens said Mickens' attorney passed up several opportunities to present negative character evidence about the victim. Justice Souter read *Cuyler* and *Holloway* to impose a duty to inquire into a possible conflict of interest in such cases, and argued the trial judge had such a duty to inquire in this case, because the same judge had made the appointment of counsel for both killer and victim.[1]

3. Was Bentley's independent judgment on behalf of each client likely to have been compromised in this case?

a. Notice that the Federal Rules of Criminal Procedure require the court to "take such measures as may be appropriate to protect each defendant's right to counsel." What kind of inquiry should the judge conduct to assure the effective assistance of counsel for Carson and Morton?

b. Lettley v. State, 746 A.2d 392 (Md.2000), presented one of the ultimate problems of loyalty to two clients. A client told trial counsel in a murder case that he and not the current defendant had committed the crime. The lawyer asked to withdraw, reasoning that she could neither reveal who had made this confession nor effectively represent the current client without using the information, such as by seeking to show that the other person looked like the defendant. The trial judge refused to let the lawyer withdraw because, the judge argued, no new lawyer would have known the information and could have provided better representation. But the Maryland Supreme Court reversed. The problem was divided loyalties, it said. Defense counsel would feel constrained in such things as cross-examination; the conflict was serious enough to constitute ineffective assistance of counsel permitting the defendant a new trial.

c. In Thomas v. State, 551 S.E.2d 254 (S.C.2001), the same lawyer represented both petitioner and her husband after both were arrested and indicted for drug trafficking. Each client had waived the possible conflict of interest. The prosecutor then offered a plea bargain to the couple's attorney that would allow husband and wife to each accept responsibility for half of the drugs seized and serve a reduced jail sentence, or one spouse to accept responsibility for all of the drugs and serve the 25–year statutory minimum sentence. The attorney advised both clients to accept some responsibility in order to obtain the lesser sentence, but the petitioner took responsibility for the entire amount. In this case, the court granted the petitioner post-conviction relief on the grounds that she had been denied effective assistance of counsel. The court stated that, once the plea agreement was offered, the initial conflicts waiver was not sufficient to let the lawyer represent both clients, because any action in either spouse's best interest would unavoidably harm the other. A plea bargain of the sort offered was unexpected and neither client could be deemed to have initially waived a conflict of the type actually faced.

---

1. See also, State ex rel. S.G., 791 A.2d 285 (N.J.App.2002) (refusing to disqualify retained defense counsel in a murder trial who had previously represented the victim in unrelated incidents).

   d.   United States v. Schwarz, 283 F.3d 76 (2d Cir.2002), involved one of the police officers convicted of brutally assaulting Abner Louima while he was in police custody. The district court sentenced the police officer (Schwarz) to over 15 years in prison for the crime. At trial, a lawyer named Worth represented Schwarz; the Policeman's Benevolent Association (PBA) had retained Worth to represent Schwarz. Then, the PBA retained Worth's firm at $5 million per year to represent its members in all disciplinary and criminal proceedings. Before trial, the government objected to Worth representing Schwarz while Schwarz's firm represented co-defendants as well as the PBA itself, but after careful and specific warnings by the court of the risks of such multiple representation, Schwarz waived the conflict and the trial went ahead. The Second Circuit reversed the conviction, finding that the conflict could not be waived. Louima had also filed a civil suit against the PBA. A lawyer with no loyalties to PBA might have blamed the assault on one of the other officers, but that strategy would have hurt the civil case in which the lawyer's law firm was representing the PBA, which may have explained the lawyer's failure to present exculpatory evidence that could have changed the outcome at trial. What the case makes abundantly clear is that a trial judge cannot take a conflict waiver as the last word on who will represent a criminal defendant.

   e.   In People v. Morales, 768 N.E.2d 84 (Ill.App.Ct.2002), Morales was convicted of a drug-related murder and related offenses, and sentenced to life in prison. The prosecution's theory of the case was that Morales sold drugs on behalf of another individual, Hernandez. The prosecution alleged that Morales murdered the victim whom Hernandez had sent to collect money from Morales. Morales' appeal was based on ineffective assistance of counsel. Specifically, Morales argued that his lawyer suffered from a conflict of interest because he was representing Hernandez in a federal drug proceeding at the same time he defended Morales on the murder charges. Despite the fact that Morales orally consented to the concurrent representation before the trial judge, the appellate court found that Morales' consent was not knowing and voluntary. It held that the trial court should have made further inquiries to determine whether Morales actually understood the potential consequences of the conflict.

   4.   Should it be a conflict of interest for a lawyer to defend a client when the lawyer is personally and simultaneously facing charges filed by the same prosecutor?

   a.   In Government of Virgin Islands v. Zepp, 748 F.2d 125 (3d Cir. 1984), defense counsel not only faced potential criminal liability on the same charges for which defendant was tried; defense counsel was also a potential prosecution witness. The defendant was convicted for possession of cocaine and destruction of evidence. Defense counsel, in order to avoid being called as a witness and thereby being disqualified, had stipulated that he (who was alone with the defendant in her house at a time when the toilet was heard to flush several times) did not personally flush any toilets; subsequently the cocaine giving rise to the prosecution was discovered in the house's septic tank. The appellate court reversed the conviction and concluded: "Trial counsel's interest in testifying [via the stipulation] on his own behalf impaired the exercise of independent professional judgment on behalf of the client," because "[p]lastic bags of cocaine do not fall off of trees into septic tanks."

    b. In Campbell v. Rice, 265 F.3d 878 (9th Cir.2001), the appellant had been convicted on several counts of burglary. In seeking habeas corpus, he argued that his lawyer had an impermissible conflict in that the same office that was prosecuting the lawyer on drug charges also was prosecuting the appellant. Although the prosecutor had brought the situation to the attention of the trial judge in a brief conference, the judge allowed the trial to continue. The Ninth Circuit found that habeas corpus was appropriate. The lawyer might have felt pressure to refrain from antagonizing the prosecutor (e.g., by filing a motion alleging prosecutorial misconduct), even when it might be in the best interest of her client to do so. Furthermore, the appellate court found the trial court's inquiry into the conflict had been "insufficiently searching and specific." The court had neither asked the attorney whether she could effectively continue the representation, nor sufficiently determined that appellant understood and waived the conflict.

    c. In United States v. Fulton, 5 F.3d 605 (2d Cir.1993), a prosecution for importation of heroin, one lawyer represented four co–defendants. One of the defendants had told the DEA that the lawyer was himself personally involved in the heroin sales. The U.S. Attorney informed the court, and the Second Circuit held that where a defense lawyer is accused of being involved in the same or closely related criminal conduct, the conflict is per se unwaivable and thus continued representation constitutes ineffective assistance of counsel.

    d. Rubin v. Gee, 292 F.3d 396 (4th Cir.2002), involved a conflict that justified habeas corpus relief. Rubin was convicted of first degree murder. When she called her lawyers after the crime, they had her admitted to a hospital under a false name and then helped her escape detection while she withdrew $105,000 to pay their fee. The lawyers' desire to collect their fee, "caused them to counsel Rubin to act in an unnecessarily suspicious fashion when they caused her to delay her surrender to the police for 24 hours." They also hid the evidence of the crime at their law office and only then turned the client over to the police. Other lawyers acted for Rubin at trial, but the original lawyers continued to represent her. The Fourth Circuit, per Judge Wilkinson, found this conduct rendered the lawyers "almost accessories after the fact," and their efforts to help Rubin escape detection allowed the prosecutors to refute her claim of self-defense. The lawyers' desire to collect a large fee undercut their efforts to defend their client, the court found. They did not even testify at trial to help Rubin explain why her conduct was not inconsistent with a plea of self-defense. This conflict denied Rubin effective assistance of counsel. Judge Motz dissented, agreeing that the lawyers had acted badly but observing they were not the counsel at trial whose conduct is the test of ineffectiveness.

B. THE POSSIBLE PUBLIC INTEREST IN OBJECTING TO MULTIPLE REPRESENTATION

1. Should a court ever grant a prosecution motion to require that defendants have separate counsel?

a. Deputy Assistant Attorney General Joe Sims announced that the Department of Justice Antitrust Division would aggressively seek to stop multiple representation by seeking relief from the court having supervisory power over the grand jury. "[T]hese conflicts—where both the corporation and potentially culpable employees are represented by a single counsel—are so inherently serious that there should be a presumption against such multiple representation during a criminal investigation." He continued

> "[T]he target corporation all too often sees its best interest served by keeping witnesses in 'friendly' hands and limiting the cooperation of its employees. Such an attitude will inevitably lead to bad advice for the individual if he does not have independent counsel. [M]erely informing the employee of the existence of the potential conflict and seeking a waiver from him [does not] satisfactorily deal with this problem. For example, it is frequently in the interest of one or more low level employees in a corporation to seek immunity by offering evidence against higher level employees or the corporation itself. In this situation, even if there has been a waiver, it is impossible for a single lawyer to give each of his clients effective legal representation."[2]

b. Do you agree with Mr. Sims? What if it is in fact in the best interests of all defendants to keep each other in "friendly" hands rather than risk the chance that one of the parties will plead guilty and implicate the others? Do public policy and professional responsibility forbid, or require, the attorney to seek knowing waivers of the conflicts and participate in a "We're all in this together" arrangement? See ABA Standards Relating to the Defense Function, § 4–3.5(c), in the Standards Supplement, advising that, except for preliminary matters such as applications for bail, the "potential for conflict of interest in representing multiple defendants is so grave" that lawyers should not do it. And, if they do, they should secure informed consent on the record after questioning by the judge.

c. In Wheat v. United States, 486 U.S. 153, 108 S.Ct. 1692, 100 L.Ed.2d 140 (1988), the Supreme Court (5 to 4) held that the district court was within its discretion in rejecting defendant's waiver of his right to conflict-free counsel and in refusing to permit defendant's proposed substitution of attorneys. Two days before trial, defendant asked to be represented by the lawyer who was representing others charged in a series of cases against an alleged drug conspiracy. The government objected on the grounds that defendants in some cases would be witnesses in others. If the same lawyer represented them all, he would be restricted in his cross-

---

2. Bureau of National Affairs, Antitrust & Trade Reg.Rptr., No. 819, June 23, 1977, at p. A–13.

examination of his clients when they were witnesses and would lay the predicate for a later claim of ineffective assistance of counsel.[3]

The Court upheld the district court's power to limit the joint representation: "Federal courts have an independent interest in ensuring that criminal trials are conducted within the ethical standards of the profession and that legal proceedings appear fair to all who observe them. Both the American Bar Association's Model Code of Professional Responsibility and its Model Rules of Professional Conduct * * * impose limitations on multiple representation of clients * * *. DR 5–105(C); Rule 1.7. * * * Not only the interest of a criminal defendant but the institutional interest in the rendition of just verdicts in criminal cases may be jeopardized by unregulated multiple representation. * * * The District Court must recognize a presumption in favor of petitioner's counsel of choice, but that presumption may be overcome not only by a demonstration of actual conflict but by a showing of a serious potential for conflict." 486 U.S. at 160, 108 S.Ct. at 1698, 100 L.Ed.2d at 149. The District Court must be given substantial latitude in refusing waivers of conflicts because, even if the defendant waives any conflicts, experience shows that the defendant will later still claim ineffective assistance of counsel.

2. Might the power to disqualify counsel to "protect the interest" of the accused make it easier for the government to get a conviction?

a. United States v. Locascio, 6 F.3d 924 (2d Cir.1993), cert. denied 511 U.S. 1070, 114 S.Ct. 1645, 128 L.Ed.2d 365 (1994), involved the prosecution of alleged mob boss John Gotti. Bruce Cutler had very effectively represented Gotti in previous criminal trials. The Government did not want him to do so again. This time, he had been caught on tapes of conversations with Gotti that the Government intended to introduce at trial to show the planning of illegal acts. Thus, even if Cutler would not be called to testify, he was said to be in a position analogous to an "unsworn witness" who would be forced to defend his own conduct before the jury. Further, Cutler had once represented a Gotti associate, Michael Coiro, who had now turned government witness. He would thus be impaired in cross-examining Coiro. Over Gotti's objection, the court intervened to "protect" Gotti from Mr. Cutler's conflicts. The Second Circuit affirmed. Do you suppose the late Mr. Gotti was pleased by the court's concern for his welfare?

b. Freund v. Butterworth, 165 F.3d 839 (11th Cir.1999) (en banc), analyzed when a conflict of interest will constitute ineffective assistance of counsel. The defendant was convicted in Florida state court of a gruesome first degree murder. His lawyers had previously represented his separately-tried co-defendant, apparently a career criminal, against charges of aggravated assault and diazepam possession. The present defendant alleged that

---

3. See also, Burden v. Zant, 510 U.S. 132, 114 S.Ct. 654, 126 L.Ed.2d 611 (1994) (remanding for factual findings to see if pre- trial counsel's representation of a prosecution witness who had been granted immunity created an actual conflict affecting the result).

(1) the law firm knew confidential information about him that he was afraid it would use against him in the present case, and (2) members of the firm had used drugs with him and engaged in other illegal activity. The evidence that Freund had killed the victim was overwhelming, and his insanity defense, based on the idea the co-defendant had rendered him a "robot," was unsuccessful.

The Eleventh Circuit majority held that *Cuyler v. Sullivan* applied to such conflicts, but said there had to be a showing of actual "inconsistent interests" or "specific instances in the record" where the defendant's interests were impaired. The defendant had to show either that the prior representation was substantially related to the present one or that counsel had learned particular confidential information in the prior representation that was relevant to the present case. In some cases, even proof of both elements would be insufficient to show ineffective assistance. The court found the cases involved here were not substantially related and that no confidential information had been learned relevant to the present case. The Court affirmed the conviction, but Judge Tjoflat and three other judges dissented. They argued that the lawyer could have blamed the co-defendant for the murder but did not. He could have plea bargained for Freund in exchange for testimony against the co-defendant but he did not. Instead, the lawyer only relied on an insanity defense that was a long-shot and did little to damage the co-defendant.

C.   CONFLICTS OF INTEREST FACED BY PROSECUTORS

1. Of what relevance is it that the prosecutor in this problem is highly motivated to get convictions that will tend to further his political ambitions? Could a prosecutor's personal motives ever constitute a conflict of interest with his or her duties as a public prosecutor?

a.   In People v. Superior Court (Greer), 561 P.2d 1164 (Cal.1977), the court upheld the trial court's decision to disqualify the district attorney from prosecuting a murder case. The unusual conflict was based on the fact that the victim's mother was employed in the prosecutor's office. Moreover, the mother was scheduled to be a material witness for the prosecution, and if the defendant were convicted, the mother would stand to gain custody of her grandchild. Evidence surrounding the arrest of the criminal defendant suggested that the arrest had been used to aid the victim's mother in gaining such custody. The court concluded that a "district attorney may thus prosecute vigorously, but both the accused and the public have a legitimate expectation that his zeal, as reflected in his tactics at trial, will be born of objective and impartial consideration of each individual case." 561 P.2d at 1172.[4] See Model Rule 1.7(a)(2) ("personal interest of the lawyer").

---

4. For discussion of the subsequent California statute modifying the standard for prosecutor disqualification see People v. Conner, 666 P.2d 5 (Cal.1983): "'The motion [to recuse] shall not be granted unless it is shown by the evidence that a conflict of inter-

b.   In re Complaint of Rook, 556 P.2d 1351 (Ore.1976) (per curiam), involved a state district attorney accused of refusing to plea bargain with 15 criminal defendants on the same basis as previously offered to another criminal defendant so long as the 15 were represented by either of two attorneys. After the two attorneys withdrew as counsel and another attorney represented the 15, the district attorney allowed the 15 to accept the plea bargain that he had earlier offered another defendant. When the district attorney was asked to explain his position, he is reported to have said that one of the unacceptable defense attorneys was involved in "organized crime" and that he was upset with the other for saying "bad things" about him. The state Supreme Court publicly reprimanded the district attorney. The court found a violation of DR 1–102(A)(5), based on a state statute which provided, inter alia, that "[s]imilarly situated defendants should be afforded equal plea bargaining opportunities." It also found that the district attorney was motivated in his conduct not only by frustration but also by "animosity and a desire to punish" that supported the finding of a violation of DR 7–102(A)(1) as well.

c.   In Lewis v. Superior Court, 62 Cal.Rptr.2d 331 (Ct.App.1997), the defendant was the auditor-controller of Orange County whose alleged negligent supervision of the county treasurer's investment of county funds contributed to the County's need to seek bankruptcy protection. The bankruptcy resulted in drastic budget cuts in the prosecutor's office, deletion of staff lines, cancellation of pay raises, and the like. In short, the prosecutor apparently took the case personally and even called a county supervisor to try to persuade him not to vote to pay for the auditor-controller's defense. The court ordered the entire county prosecutor's office disqualified from handling the case.

2.   Would conflicts problems be created if the prosecution function were "privatized"?

a.   In People ex rel. Clancy v. Superior Court (Ebel), 705 P.2d 347 (Cal.1985), cert. denied sub nom., City of Corona v. Superior Court, 475 U.S. 1121, 106 S.Ct. 1638, 90 L.Ed.2d 184 (1986), a city had hired a private attorney to bring abatement proceedings against an adult book store. The fee arrangement with the lawyer provided that his fee would double if he won the case. The court pointed to the "prosecutor's duty of neutrality" which stems from the fact that "he is a representative of the sovereign" and "has the vast power of the government available to him." Giving the prosecutor a contingent fee compromised the duty of fairness and neutrality inherent in the role of prosecutor, the court said, and the private attorney was disqualified.

Do you agree with this result? Should Model Rule 1.5(d)(2) be revised so that they are not limited to the case of "a contingent fee for representing a *defendant* in a criminal case"? (emphasis added).

est exists such as would render it unlikely that the defendant would receive a fair trial." This standard differs from that enunciated by us in *Greer*." 666 P.2d 5, 8, (Cal.1983).

b. In *Young v. United States ex rel. Vuitton et Fils S.A.*, 481 U.S. 787, 107 S.Ct. 2124, 95 L.Ed.2d 740 (1987), the District Court had issued an injunction against violation of Vuitton's trademark. When Vuitton learned that defendants were violating its trademark, Vuitton's counsel asked the District Court to appoint him as special prosecutor to bring a charge of criminal contempt against defendants. The court did so. The Supreme Court reversed the contempt conviction, holding that such a case constitutes an actual conflict of interest because the special prosecutor also represented the private party who would be the beneficiary of the court order allegedly violated. While the trial court has inherent authority to appoint someone to enforce its order, the matter must be referred first to the public prosecutor. If he refused to prosecute, the court should appoint someone not connected to the civil plaintiff. Only in that way can the court avoid the "potential for private interest to influence the discharge of public duty".[5] 481 U.S. at 805, 107 S.Ct. at 2136–37, 95 L.Ed.2d at 757.

c. *People v. Eubanks*, 927 P.2d 310 (Cal.1996) involved defendants who were charged with stealing trade secrets in the computer industry. When Borland International went through one of its executive's e-mail, it found he had sent confidential messages to an executive of Symantec, a competitor. This situation was significant to Borland but possibly less so to the local District Attorney, so Borland offered to contribute up to $10,000 to pay for the work of experts necessary to build the criminal case. The district attorney hired the expert who sent his bill to that office, but the D.A. accepted reimbursement from Borland, justifying his actions by explaining that victims often cooperate with prosecutors in the preparation of cases. The California Supreme Court disagreed. Even though the prosecutor was not lining his own pockets, no private citizen may direct the exercise of prosecutorial discretion, and such private contributions would inevitably influence whether given defendants are or are not prosecuted. The court affirmed the trial court's order forcing recusal of the entire D.A.'s office.

d. *Hambarian v. Superior Court*, 44 P.3d 102 (Cal.2002), involved the audit of a local trash collection business in the city of Orange, California. The city was suspicious that Hambarian had artificially inflated its costs in an effort to overcharge the city millions of dollars in excess trash fees. The Orange police department launched an investigation, but transferred the case to the major fraud unit of the county district attorney's office because

5. *Federal Trade Commission v. American National Cellular*, 868 F.2d 315 (9th Cir. 1989), considered what effect *Vuitton* should have on the FTC practice of having its attorneys act as special prosecutors to punish TRO violations in its cases. The court found *Vuitton* not controlling where a government lawyer rather than a private attorney was acting as special prosecutor. However, the court said that appearances are important. The U.S. Attorney's office should be in control of the contempt matter, although it may then delegate prosecution to the agency attorney.

See also, *Crowe v. Smith*, 151 F.3d 217, 231–33 (5th Cir.1998) (improper to appoint opposing counsel in RICO case to prosecute attorney sanction matters). But see, *Wilson v. Wilson*, 984 S.W.2d 898 (Tenn.1998) (not inherently improper to have beneficiary of order prosecute charge of contempt).

it lacked the expertise to handle a complex accounting matter. The district attorney retained a private certified public accountant, Franzen, to review Hambarian's books. Over the course of two years, the city paid Franzen over $450,000 to conduct his investigation. Citing *Eubanks*, Hambarian argued that the court should disqualify the prosecutor because it accepted the efforts of an expert witness who was compensated by the victim, in this case the city. The California Supreme Court disagreed and distinguished *Eubanks*. First, this district attorney did not suffer under any severe budgetary constraints, and had not asked the city to pay Franzen. In addition, the city had done its own investigation as part of a civil suit against Hambarian. Further, the victim was not a private party. Thus the prosecutor and the victim/city had a common interest to represent the citizens of Orange and obtain refunds from the defendant. Finally, the court noted that Franzen, the accountant, did not have a supervisory role in the investigation and cross-examination could easily reveal any bias.

e.   Commonwealth v. Ellis, 708 N.E.2d 644 (Mass.1999), involved criminal insurance fraud. The defendant moved to dismiss on the ground that the state statute created a fund out of which prosecution of such cases was financed. Only insurance companies paid into the fund and they arguably underwrote cases that interested them as private entities. "A prosecutor's discretionary choices must be unaffected by private interests," the Massachusetts Supreme Court held, but "routine cooperation from a victim of crime is * * * often necessary and should be encouraged." The fund here was industry-wide and spent on cases prosecutors independently determined had merit. There was no risk that individual companies would be influencing how prosecutorial resources would be employed.

D.   CONFLICTS OF INTEREST OF DEFENSE COUNSEL; PUBLICATION RIGHTS AND SOCIAL ENTANGLEMENTS

1.   To what extent, if any, may a defense attorney personally and financially benefit from the publicity surrounding a major trial? May a criminal lawyer write a book about her trials, or a particular case that she defended?

a.   Look at Model Rule 1.8(d). What purpose does a rule serve? Does Comment [9] to Model Rule 1.8 help provide an answer?

b.   People v. Corona, 145 Cal.Rptr. 894 (Ct.App.1978), held that by entering into a literary rights contract with the accused prior to trial, he "was forced to choose between his own pocketbook and the best interests of his client, the accused." The lawyer's financial stake in the literary rights encouraged him to insist on a lengthy and sensational trial, rather than invoke various defenses that might abort or change the nature of the trial.

Compare United States v. Hearst, 638 F.2d 1190 (9th Cir.1980), where a hearing was ordered in which Patty Hearst would be required to show that the conflict in fact affected her lawyer's judgment whether to seek a continuance and a change of venue, and whether to have the defendant testify. It would not be necessary, however, for her to show that the conflict actually changed the result in the case.

c.   Beets v. Scott, 65 F.3d 1258 (5th Cir.1995) (en banc), reversed an earlier decision that had found ineffective assistance of counsel where the defendant had given media rights to the son of his lawyer as payment of attorney's fee. The lawyer thought giving the rights to the son would avoid the Rule 1.8(d) problem. The court rejected that ruse out-of-hand, but then had to ask whether it should reverse the conviction. Over a vigorous dissent by Judge King, it held that the *Strickland* "actual prejudice" test of ineffective assistance had to be applied, not Cuyler v. Sullivan's willingness to reverse in cases of attorney breach of loyalty. Beets received a fair trial, the court said; enforcement of state ethics rules was up to the state.

d.   Rule 1.8(d) only applies to defense counsel. Why? Should there be similar limits on prosecutors writing their memoirs?

2.   Should a client be able to waive the protection of Rule 1.8(d)? Is this rule only to protect the defendant's private interest or is there a public interest involved?

a.   The California Supreme Court in Maxwell v. Superior Court of Los Angeles County, 639 P.2d 248 (Cal.1982), allowed waiver by relying on California Rule 5–101 allowing lawyers to enter into business relations adverse to a client if the client consents. The defendant, charged with capital crimes, signed a contract with his attorneys in which the attorneys promised to act competently but also warned the defendant of the possible conflicts and prejudice which the publication agreement would create: "It declares that counsel may wish to (1) create damaging publicity to enhance exploitation value, (2) avoid mental defenses because, if successful, they might suggest petitioner's incapacity to make the contract, and (3) see him convicted and even sentenced to death for publicity value." The court did not require disqualification of defense counsel but it also did not deny the possibility of later discipline of the attorney.

Do you agree with this result? Is there a systemic interest (an interest in the interest of justice) in seeing that defendants get a fair trial? If the latter interest is relevant, should it be improper for a court to accept the defendant's "waiver" of the conflict?

b.   May a criminal defense lawyer secure literary rights *after* the conclusion of the legal matter? See ABA Defense Function Standard § 4–3.4, in the Standards Supplement. Why should we draw this distinction? Might publication of a lawyer's memoirs waive the attorney-client privilege of the clients regardless of when the contract is made? See, e.g., In re von Bulow, 828 F.2d 94 (2d Cir.1987) (privilege waived as to matters specifically revealed in book; no broader subject matter waiver as to undisclosed communications not mentioned in the book).

3.   If defense counsel has an active social life, will that create conflicts?

a.   Hernandez v. State, 750 So.2d 50 (Fla.Ct.App.1999) (motion on rehearing en banc), involved a lawyer who had an affair with the client's wife. A panel of the court originally concluded this was per se ineffective assistance of counsel. The lawyer could not truly have wanted the defendant acquitted so as to return home. The full court, however, saw the case differently. The conflict of interest was only "potential," not actual, the court said. Suggestion of an effect on the defense was simply "informed speculation;" indeed, the defendant was acquitted of the most serious charge against him. The defendant's unqualified endorsement of the results achieved by the same lawyer in a concurrent Federal prosecution also undercut defendant's argument. See also, Hernandez v. Spears, 2002 WL 1205058 (S.D.Fla.2002), denying habeas corpus and saying it would be possible for a lawyer to provide an effective defense even though his success would let the defendant return home and possibly bring an end to the affair. Do you agree? Does Model Rule 1.8(j) cover this situation? Would any other rule apply?

b. In Commonwealth v. Croken, 733 N.E.2d 1005 (Mass.2000), appointed defense counsel was in a "close relationship" with an assistant district attorney who later became his wife. The court found no "actual" conflict requiring automatic reversal of the conviction, but it found that defense counsel should have disclosed the relationship to his client and obtained informed consent. The court required an evidentiary hearing into the adequacy of the defense. Does this result make sense to you? Does Comment [11] to Model Rule 1.7 regulate this situation? If there is no actual conflict of interest, why should defense counsel have to disclose his or her social life to a client?

PROBLEM 12

CONFLICTS BETWEEN CLIENT INTERESTS AND
THE LAWYER'S PERSONAL INTEREST

A lawyer who represents a client must put the client's interest ahead of the lawyer's own. That is easy to say, harder to assure, and proving that the requirement has been met can be harder still. This problem presents some situations in which a lawyer might profit as a result of a professional relationship in ways that go beyond collecting normal legal fees. We first ask under what conditions a lawyer may properly collect a fee in a form that makes the lawyer a business associate of the client. Next, we ask whether a lawyer may use confidential client information to engage in business transactions with third parties. Then we look at whether a lawyer may accept a client's gift, and finally, at what happens when the lawyer and client fall in love.

FACTS

Attorney Joan Doe went to high school with James Johnson, a local engineer. Johnson asked Doe to help him set up a small business. He had very little money, and the capital he had raised from a few local investors was not enough to pay much of a legal fee. Johnson asked if he could pay the fee over an extended period of time, with interest. Instead, Doe suggested that Johnson pay her by giving her 10 percent of the stock in the new corporation as payment for all the work necessary to establish it and carry it through the first year. Doe thought the business looked like a good, relatively cheap investment opportunity, and after Johnson agreed to the arrangement, Doe drafted the articles of incorporation, by-laws and a shareholders' agreement.

Johnson's company is doing very well. Doe has learned from him that the company will be building a new plant in an industrial park near town. The plans for the industrial park are a secret to all but a few people, and Doe realizes that property in proximity to the park is likely to increase in value. She knows of such a nearby parcel that is for sale, and, after concluding that Johnson probably does not plan to buy it, she has now done so.

After his company had made its first million dollars, Johnson was thrilled. "Joan", he said, "you have been my lawyer these three years and I could not have succeeded without you. Please draw up the papers to transfer the title to my year-old Mercedes Benz to yourself." The car is worth $75,000. Doe was stunned and does not know how to reply to Johnson's generous direction.

Now, Doe and Johnson have fallen in love. Marriage seems in their future, but meanwhile, they are together whenever they are not both at work.

QUESTIONS

A. ACCEPTING PAYMENT IN THE FORM OF STOCK; BUSINESS TRANSACTIONS WITH A CLIENT

1. Does the law prohibit lawyers from taking all or part of their fee in the form of stock in the client's business?

a. ABA Formal Opinion 00–418 (July 7, 2000) makes clear that Model Rule 1.8(a) treats such fees as business transactions with a client. They are also subject to Rule 1.5(a)'s requirement that the total fee be reasonable. The stock should be valued at the time it is acquired and its reasonableness should be determined at that time. The Opinion also notes other conflicts that can arise, e.g., problems under Rule 1.8(j) if the company's only asset is a cause of action, and under Rule 1.7(a)(2) if the stock is a major asset of the lawyer.

b. Utah State Bar Advisory Opinion 98–13 (1998) agrees that Rules 1.5, 1.7(a)(2), and 1.8(a) are all implicated when a lawyer takes stock in payment of a fee. It says the lawyer should be especially concerned if the stock will be publicly traded or if the client might want restrictions on its trading. Both will affect determination of the stock's value and the latter could constitute a conflict of interest. In any event, Rule 1.8(a) requires that a stock transaction be fair and reasonable and the terms discussed specially with the client, not simply be reasonable in value as required by Rule 1.5.[1]

2. Why do the courts view business dealing with clients with suspicion? Can you imagine ways in which the lawyer might take advantage of the client?

a. In Beery v. State Bar of California, 739 P.2d 1289 (Cal.1987), a lawyer had represented a client in a personal injury suit and had been asked to write his will. The client wanted advice on what to do with his settlement proceeds and the lawyer advised him to invest it in a satellite venture that the lawyer said was a "good investment." The lawyer did not tell the client that the venture was in trouble, that it could borrow no money commercially, and that the lawyer was a principal in the venture. The client trusted the lawyer, invested, and lost $35,000. The court, rejecting the argument that the nondisclosures were technical or minor, suspended the lawyer from practice for two years, plus a three year period of probation.

b. In Matter of Pappas, 768 P.2d 1161 (Ariz.1988), a CPA/lawyer marketed tax shelters to people he said he considered accounting clients. He became general partner in one of the deals that went bad. The court held that the business transactions violated what is now ABA Model Rule 1.8(a), rejected the argument that he was not acting as a lawyer in the transactions, and suspended him from practice for five years.

c. Cotton v. Kronenberg, 44 P.3d 878 (Wash.App.2002), involved the defense of Cotton against serious charges of child rape. Cotton signed two fee agreements with lawyer Kronenberg. The first provided that Cotton would pay Kronenberg an hourly fee of $140. The second, signed three days later, required Cotton to pay for the services up-front and estimated the cost at between $10,000 and $30,000. In satisfaction of the fee, Cotton deeded real property to Kronenberg, but even before the trial began, the court disqualified Kronenberg because it found he had improperly contacted some of the prosecution's witnesses. Nevertheless, Kronenberg kept Cotton's land, and eventually sold it for about $42,000. Cotton sought a full refund, arguing that the fee agreement was void because Kronenberg had breached his fiduciary duty to Cotton. The court agreed. It found that taking the land in payment was a business transaction with the client under Rule 1.8(a), the land-for-services transaction was not fair and reasonable to the client, these facts supported a finding of breach of fiduciary duty, and they justified forfeiture of Kronenberg's entire fee.

3. On the other hand, are all business transactions with clients similarly suspect? Might Model Rule 1.8(a) become a trap for the unwary?

---

1. Two more opinions providing helpful analysis of these issues are D.C. Bar Legal Ethics Committee, Opinion 300 (July 25, 2000), and N.Y. Comm. on Professional. and Judicial Ethics, Formal Opinion 2000–3 (2000).

a. In Passante v. McWilliam, 62 Cal.Rptr.2d 298 (Ct.App.1997), a client invented baseball cards imprinted with a hologram to prevent counterfeiting. The company flourished, but early in its history it lacked $100,000 to buy an order of paper without which it would have failed. The lawyer stepped up to the plate and went to bat for the client, lending it the desperately-needed $100,000. In gratitude, the company gave him 3% of the common stock. The lawyer never sought repayment of the $100,000 loan, but when the 3% share became worth $33 million, he asked for the shares. The court, however, said he could not have them. If they were a gift from the company, he had no contractual right to the shares. Further, as a business deal, he had not complied with the professional rules. His apparent home run became simply a long out.

b. In re Kirsh, 973 F.2d 1454 (9th Cir.1992), involved a lawyer's loan to his client and close friend. The lawyer knew the friend was in financial trouble, lent him $40,000, and took some real property as security. He took the client's word that the title was good. It was not, the client filed for bankruptcy, and the lawyer alleged that he had been defrauded and thus that the debt should not be discharged. While lawyers ordinarily should not engage in business transactions with clients, the court said, the purpose of that rule is to protect clients against overreaching. In this case, the terms of the loan were fair and the lawyer was the victim, but the court said the rule regulating business transactions is a shield for the client and the lawyer may not avoid it. Moreover, the client had not committed a fraud, the court held, because a lawyer who knows how to search a title could not reasonably rely on a client's representation about that title.

c. In Committee on Professional Ethics v. Mershon, 316 N.W.2d 895 (Iowa 1982), a farmer owned 100 acres of farmland adjacent to a country club near the city. He was interested in developing the land for residential purposes and hired an engineer to prepare a preliminary plat and market study. The farmer and engineer then came to the lawyer for advice, telling the lawyer that the farmer did not have enough cash to pay for the engineering and legal work. The land was conveyed to a corporation, and based on the value of the land and the usual cost of the professional work, the farmer got 40% of the stock, the engineer 40%, and the lawyer 20%. Development of the parcel depended on the ability to get financing, and when none of the three individuals was willing to give a personal guarantee of the loan, the bank would not lend the money and the project never went forward. Mershon, the lawyer, believed that this meant that he and the engineer must turn in their stock. The lawyer did so, but the engineer did not, and after the farmer's death, his children had to litigate their rights with the engineer.

The question in this case, however, was whether these facts revealed a violation of what is now Model Rule 1.8(a). The Iowa Supreme Court found that they did.

> " * * * Miller [the farmer and land owner] and Mershon plainly had differing interests in at least two aspects of the transaction. One was the issue of giving respondent [Mershon] a present interest in the

corporation in anticipation of future legal services. * * * Because respondent's fee was tied to the amount of his stock in the corporation, he and Miller [the farmer] had differing interests concerning the extent of respondent's stock ownership. Another differing interest involved making respondent a debtor of the corporation to assure that the services would be performed. Because Miller's interest was aligned wholly with the corporation, he and respondent had differing interests with respect to respondent's promissory note. * * *

"The fighting issue * * * was whether respondent made full disclosure to Miller within the meaning of the [ethics rule] before Miller entered the transaction. If full disclosure means only that respondent made Miller fully aware of the nature and terms of the transaction, this requirement was satisfied. * * * Full disclosure, however, means more than this.

"Because of the fiduciary relationship which exists, the attorney has the burden of showing that the transaction 'was in all respects fairly and equitably conducted; that he fully and faithfully discharged all his duties to his client * * * by active diligence to see that his client was fully informed of the nature and effect of the transaction proposed and of his own rights and interests in the subject matter involved, and by seeing to it that his client either has independent advice in the matter or else receives from the attorney such advice as the latter would have been expected to give had the transaction been one between his client and a stranger.' * * *

Even though it found the lawyer had been "forthright and honest and gained no profit from the transaction," the court found that he had violated what is now Model Rule 1.8(a).

d.   Do you agree with the results in these cases? Why don't we make fairness of the transaction a complete defense? Restatement Third, The Law Governing Lawyers § 126, Comment *b*, says the rationale for the strict rule is that "[p]roving fraud or actual overreaching might be difficult." Do you agree? Could that difficulty be overcome by putting the burden of proving fairness on the lawyer?

4.   Must a lawyer comply with the terms of Model Rule 1.8(a) when she buys a car from her car dealer client? Does a lawyer who owns a restaurant have to abide by Model Rule 1.8(a) whenever a client comes in for a meal?

a.   Look at Comment [1] to Model Rule 1.8. Does it resolve both questions? Restatement § 126 also makes clear that Rule 1.8(a) does not prohibit "standard commercial transactions in the regular course of business of the client, involving a product or service as to which the lawyer does not render legal services." Comment *c* explains that these are transactions "regularly entered into between the [lawyer or] client and the general public, typically in which the terms and conditions are the same for all customers."

b.   Comment *c* warns, however, that "where a lawyer engages in the sale of goods or services ancillary to the practice of law, for example, the sale of title insurance, the requirements of this Section do apply." Do you see a good reason for such an exception to the rule?

c.   Comment *a* to Restatement § 126 also says that "ordinary client-lawyer fee agreements providing, for example, for hourly, lump-sum, or contingent fees" are not business transactions with the client. Do you agree that this statement is literally true? Is it enough to say simply that fee agreements are business transactions that are found in almost every lawyer-client relationship and that are specially addressed in Model Rule 1.5?

B.   USING CONFIDENTIAL CLIENT INFORMATION TO MAKE PRIVATE INVESTMENTS

1.   May Doe, without Johnson's consent, invest in the parcel near the industrial park? As we have posed the problem, Johnson does not want to buy the property himself.

a.   ABA Canons of Professional Ethics (1908), Canon 11, made clear that: "The lawyer should refrain from any action whereby for his personal benefit or gain he abuses or takes advantage of the confidence reposed in him by his client." This provision was held to prohibit a lawyer from using confidential client information for the lawyer's benefit, even if the lawyer did not reveal the information to third parties and even if the client did not suffer detriment. See, e.g., Healy v. Gray, 168 N.W. 222 (Iowa 1918).

b.   Model Code of Professional Responsibility DR 4–101(B)(3) was equally definitive that absent informed client consent, a lawyer may not "knowingly * * * [u]se a confidence or secret of his client for the advantage *of himself* or of a third person." (Emphasis added).

c.   Model Rule 1.8(b) instead says that, without the client's informed consent, a lawyer "shall not use information relating to representation of a client *to the disadvantage of the client*" unless the client consents. (Emphasis added).

2.   Do you agree with the Model Rules' limitation of the prohibition? Is possible disadvantage of the client the only concern that underlies the rule?

a.   The source of the earlier ethics rule is agency law. A lawyer is an agent of the client; the client is the principal. The typical agency rule is that an agent (whether a lawyer, or other agent) may not use secret information of a principal without securing the principal's consent. The remedy in agency law is for the agent to disgorge the profit to the principal. See, Restatement Second, Agency § 388, Comment *c* :

> "[If] a corporation has decided to operate an enterprise at a place where land values will be increased because of such operation, a corporate officer who takes advantage of his special knowledge to buy land in the vicinity is accountable for the profits he makes,

even though such purchases have no adverse effect upon the enterprise."

b. One draft of Restatement Third, The Law Governing Lawyers, Tentative Draft No. 3 (1990), followed Model Rule 1.8(b). However, following the law of agency, the final Restatement provides in § 60 that, unless the client consents, "a lawyer who uses confidential information of a client for the lawyer's pecuniary gain other than in the practice of law must account to the client for any profits made."

c. Comment *j* to this section of the Restatement explains that this duty exists "regardless of lack of risk of prejudice to the affected client." The Comment goes on to say that the

> "sole remedy of the client for breach of duty is restitutionary relief in the form of disgorgement of profit (see Restatement, Second, Agency § 388, Comment *c*). The lawyer codes differ over whether such self-enriching use or disclosure constitutes a disciplinary violation in the absence of prejudice to the client."

3. Do you agree that the only remedy for a violation of this principle should be a suit for disgorgement? Why should professional discipline not be a possible sanction?

a. Look at Comment [5] to ABA Model Rule 1.8. Does it give a satisfactory explanation of why discipline for use of the information should be unavailable? Indeed, does it attempt to give any explanation at all?

b. United States v. O'Hagan, 521 U.S. 642, 117 S.Ct. 2199, 138 L.Ed.2d 724 (1997), addressed the securities law consequences of insider trading in securities of a client. Grand Metropolitan PLC (Grand Met), a London corporation, retained Dorsey & Whitney in Minneapolis, in an effort to acquire Pillsbury, a large publicly-traded company. O'Hagan, a Dorsey & Whitney partner not working on the matter, purchased call option contracts and shares of Pillsbury stock on the open market. When Grand Met announced its takeover plans, Pillsbury stock rose from $39 to $60 and O'Hagan made over $4.3 million. The SEC prosecuted him criminally for securities fraud under the so-called "misappropriation theory," i.e., it said he defrauded both his law firm and its client, persons to whom he owed a fiduciary duty, by taking their information and using it to benefit himself. Writing for a six-person majority, Justice Ginsburg sustained the application of the misappropriation theory to Rule 10b–5 cases. Use of the information is inherently "deceptive," the Court said, and the fraud is "consummated" when the confidential information is used "in connection with the purchase or sale of [a] security."

c. Where does that ruling leave the lawyer for purposes of professional discipline? If a lawyer engages in illegal insider trading in a client's stock, but the trading does not directly injure the client, is the lawyer immune from professional discipline? Should Model Rule 8.4(b) trump Rule 1.8(b) in such a case?

C. ACCEPTING UNSOLICITED GIFTS FROM HAPPY CLIENTS

1. May Doe follow Johnson's direction to prepare the documents necessary to give herself title to the Mercedes Benz?

a. Does your answer turn on fact that a Mercedes Benz is more valuable than a Yugo? What does Model Rule 1.8(c) tell you are the relevant issues for Doe to consider?

b. Although it is unusual in not finding an ethics violation, In re Barrick, 429 N.E.2d 842 (Ill.1981), is a typical case of the type Model Rule 1.8(c) had in mind. A widow had told her business manager that she wanted to leave her attorney a lifetime annuity amounting to his annual retainer ($12,000 per year). The manager relayed this information to the attorney, who advised her to select another lawyer to draft the will. The widow objected; she said that she did not want others to know her business. She was "adamant." The attorney drafted the new will as requested, eventually received the legacy, and the Attorney Registration and Disciplinary Commission brought a disciplinary charge. The state supreme court upheld the lawyer's conduct in the special circumstances of this case: "[A]lthough undue influence might [be] presumed, the evidence established that there was none. There was no overreaching by the respondent. On the contrary, he urged his client to employ another attorney until she would hear no more about it. Exactly how far to press the point was a matter of judgment, and we will not snipe at the respondent's." 429 N.E.2d at 846.

c. Would all ethical questions vanish if Johnson had simply thrown Doe the keys to the car and no paperwork were involved? Of course, the car title has to be transferred for the gift to be effective, so Johnson cannot avoid the language of Rule 1.8(c) referring to an instrument. But why should preparation of an instrument be relevant? Does it make sense that a gift without an instrument would present fewer ethical issues?

d. Restatement Third, The Law Governing Lawyers § 127(2), tells lawyers that they "may not *accept*" (emphasis added) a substantial gift from a client, whether or not preparation of an instrument is required. The different statement of the rule may be explained by Comment [6] to Model Rule 1.8, which says that a lawyer may accept a substantial gift, but the gift "may be voidable by the client under the doctrine of undue influence, which treats client gifts as presumptively fraudulent." In short, the Restatement is addressing a variety of sources of law, while the lawyer will only be disciplined if preparation of an instrument was involved.

2. Is it proper for Doe to admire the car and let Johnson know she would like to have it?

a. Before the 2002 amendments, Model Rule 1.8(c) did not prohibit Doe from "soliciting" a substantial gift. Do you agree the change to prohibit such solicitation was an improvement? Does Comment [6] to Model Rule 1.8 supply a persuasive explanation of why solicitation of a substantial gift from a client should subject a lawyer to discipline?

b. Morrissey v. Virginia State Bar, 448 S.E.2d 615 (Va.1994), helps illustrate the concern, albeit in an very unusual situation. As part of a plea agreement in a rape case, the defendant agreed to pay the victim $25,000 damages and to give a $25,000 gift to charities selected by the prosecutor. (The prosecutor originally wanted the $25,000 to fund a "prosecutor's corner" show on a local TV station.) The prosecutor did not disclose the charitable gift portion of the agreement to the victim or the court. The court found that, in soliciting this arrangement, the prosecutor had misled the victim of the crime into accepting this resolution of the case and had concealed the terms of the gift from the court, both in violation of what are now Model Rules 8.4(c) and (d). The court suspended the prosecutor from practice for 6 months.

3. Why does Model Rule 1.8(c) have an exception for gifts to relatives and others in a "familial relationship" with the lawyer?

a. Is the exception self-evident? Would any other rule mean that if the lawyer's spouse is also a client, the spouse could never throw the lawyer a birthday party?

b. On the other hand, is it really a good idea for lawyers to represent their relatives as this rule clearly tolerates? What problems can you see if you draft your mother's will, for example, and she gives you a gift that is larger than the one she gives your sister? Restatement Third, The Law Governing Lawyers § 127(1) provides that the lawyer may not prepare an instrument effecting a gift unless the lawyer is a relative or in a similar position *and* the "gift is not significantly disproportionate to those given other donees similarly related to the donor." Do you think this is a more appropriate statement of the rule than that found in Model Rule 1.8(c)?

4. Is a lawyer's appointment as a compensated executor of a client's estate, or to a similar fiduciary position, a "gift" from the client within the meaning of Model Rule 1.8(c)?

a. The executor of an estate collects the decedent's assets and, after payment of bills owed by the estate, distributes the assets to the beneficiaries designated in the decedent's will. Being an executor takes work, and the executor typically may be paid a fee. Sometimes, the fee is specified by statute; sometimes, it must be approved by a court. In either case, the fee can be significant. A family member who is designated executor, on the other hand, will often waive the fee and leave more to distribute to the beneficiaries.

b. In addition, an executor ordinarily consults a lawyer who receives a fee as well. Law firms have been accused of trying to be appointed executor, lawyer for the executor, or both, of their clients' estates. Should the lawyer or law firm that drafts the will be able to accept such an appointment? Is an appointment the equivalent of receiving a substantial bequest from a client? Why or why not?

c. Comment [8] to Model Rule 1.8 tries to give an authoritative answer to such questions. The first sentence is definitive. On the other hand, does the remainder of this Comment give adequate guidance to a lawyer about what the lawyer must tell a client about the client's options? Could a lawyer's appointment as executor ever *not* create a conflict of interest for the lawyer that requires her to secure client consent under Model Rule 1.7(b)? When does the possibility of a "lucrative fiduciary position" ever not "materially limit" the lawyer's likely advice?

d.   ABA Formal Opinion 02–426 (May 31, 2002) addresses such issues as well. It says that the lawyer/fiduciary's law firm may represent the lawyer in administration of the estate, but the combined fee for acting and fiduciary and lawyer must be reasonable under Model Rule 1.5(a). Now is your mind at ease? If the fee is "reasonable" under Model Rule 1.5(a), do all the other ethics issues go away?

5.   Suppose that in our problem, Johnson, before giving any gift to Doe, his lawyer, seeks the advice of a different lawyer as Model Rule 1.8, Comment [7] advises. What should that lawyer do for Johnson?

a.   The new lawyer should obviously be concerned that Doe is not exercising any coercion or undue influence. Is there anything else? Should the recommendations of Comment [7] be lifted into the Rule, so that substantial gifts under Rule 1.8(c) are treated the same as business transactions under Rule 1.8(a)(2)?

b.   Consider Restatement Third, The Law Governing Lawyers § 127, Comment *g*. It advises that even if outside counsel is involved in reviewing a gift, the gift "remains subject to invalidation if the circumstances warrant under the law of fraud, duress, undue influence, or mistake." Do you agree that a court should always be able to look behind a gift if it is challenged on these grounds?

D.   INTIMATE RELATIONSHIPS BETWEEN LAWYERS AND CLIENTS

1.   Should Doe's license to practice be put at risk if Doe and Johnson enter into a consensual relationship involving physical intimacy? Why might we be concerned about such a relationship between lawyer and client?

a.   ABA Formal Opinion 92–364 (July 6, 1992) wrestled with this issue, concentrating on (1) potential abuse of the fiduciary relationship between the lawyer and a vulnerable client, (2) loss of emotional distance from the client required for good professional judgment, (3) potential conflicts of interest between lawyer and client, and (4) confusion between which communications were made in a professional relationship and which were personal. The Opinion concluded:

> "[B]ecause of the danger of impairment to the lawyer's representation associated with a sexual relationship between lawyers and client, the lawyer would be well advised to refrain from such a relationship. If such a sexual relationship occurs and the impairment is not avoided, the lawyer will have violated ethical obligations to the client. * * *

"The client's consent to sexual relations alone will rarely be sufficient to eliminate this danger. In many cases, the client's ability to give meaningful consent is vitiated by the lawyer's potential undue influence and/or the emotional vulnerability of the client."

b. How do those considerations apply to the facts of this Problem? Is James Johnson, the client, likely weak or vulnerable, for example? On the other hand, are Joan Doe's possible loss of emotional distance, potential conflicts of interest, and possible compromise of confidentiality all likely to be legitimate concerns?

2. Did ethical standards prior to the adoption of Model Rule 1.8(j) prohibit relationships between lawyers and clients?

a. Reported cases involving sex with clients have abounded; the issue began when the legal profession began. Indeed, the ABA adopted new Model Rule 1.8(j) in large part because, in some cases, lawyers were exonerated because of the lack of specific prohibition in the Model Rules, even though lawyers are fiduciaries who are always required not to over-reach their clients. Some cases have seen the problem of lawyers who appear to take advantage of their clients; other cases have been less concerned about the seriousness of the issue.

b. Suppressed v. Suppressed, 565 N.E.2d 101 (Ill.Ct.App.1990), for example, involved a divorce client who testified that her lawyer had twice taken her to an apartment where he had her inhale something that disoriented her and then had sexual relations with her. She filed a charge with the Illinois Attorney Registration and Disciplinary Commission, but it dismissed the matter. A malpractice action alleging breach of fiduciary duty was also dismissed. This Illinois appellate court said that a lawyer's only fiduciary obligation to a client is not to make sex a quid pro quo for legal services. The client felt coerced into sex, the court acknowledged, but that alone was not enough. Further, the client only suffered emotional harm, not "quantifiable" injury. Are you shocked by this result?[2]

c. Drucker's Case, 577 A.2d 1198 (N.H.1990), in contrast to *Suppressed*, involved a lawyer who knew his divorce client was under psychiatric care and emotionally fragile. The lawyer initiated, then ended their affair, but the client had fallen in love with him and her husband found her diary describing her feelings, thus prejudicing her in the divorce case. In spite of the lack of a specific prohibition of the relationship, the court found

2. In re Rinella, 677 N.E.2d 909 (Ill. 1997), finally said such charges are serious even in Illinois. Even without a disciplinary rule specifically on pressuring a client into a sexual relationship, the Illinois Supreme Court held that it constituted a conflict of interest in that the women believed they had to submit to get quality legal representation. The conduct was also prejudicial to the administration of justice and the court ruled that the lawyer should be suspended for three years. Doe v. Roe, 681 N.E.2d 640 (Ill.Ct.App.1997), appeal denied, 686 N.E.2d 1160 (Ill.1997), went even farther. Rejecting much of the analysis in *Suppressed*, the court held that a lawyer in a divorce case who coerces the client into a sexual relationship breaches a fiduciary duty to the client and emotional distress may be considered as an element of damages.

that the lawyer had taken advantage of his client and suspended him for two years.

d.   In Lawyer Disciplinary Board v. Artimez, 540 S.E.2d 156 (W.Va. 2000), a lawyer for the victim of an auto accident started a sexual relationship with the client's wife. She later left her husband and, at that point, the lawyer asked his partner to represent the husband in the accident case. Of course, he lied to both the client and his partner about the reason why. After the husband discovered the sexual relationship, he sued the lawyer for malpractice and threatened to file ethics charges against him. The lawyer agreed to take a lesser legal fee in exchange for the client's agreement not to tell the disciplinary authorities, but ultimately, the client went to the authorities anyway. The investigative panel found the sexual relationship violated Rule 1.7(b), while lying about it violated Rule 8.4(c). The West Virginia Supreme Court, however, found that no ethics rule specifically forbids a sexual relationship with the wife of a client, so the conduct could not lead to discipline. The court further concluded that the lawyer's initial lie about his inappropriate sexual relationship concerned a matter that did not constitute an ethical violation per se and, thus, "we are hard-pressed to find that his failure to be forthcoming with his law partner about this matter violated Rule 8.4(c)." The court "appreciate[d] his recognition of his irreconcilable conflicting personal interests" in asking his partner to take over Mr. Cook's case. Only the effort to get the husband not to file ethics charges resulted in discipline for the lawyer, and the court limited that to a public reprimand.

e.   Gaspard v. Beadle, 36 S.W.3d 229 (Tex.App.2001), involved a lawyer who undertook a real estate matter for a couple. The wife then filed for divorce and began a sexual relationship with the lawyer. The lawyer also represented her individually in a matter collateral to the divorce. He did not bill her while the relationship continued, but after it ended, he sent a bill for all the work done. A jury found him guilty of fraud and intentional infliction of emotional distress for his conduct, but this court reversed. A man's giving the impression that he loves a woman is not actionable fraud, the court said. Further, failing to send a legal bill until a sexual relationship with a client ended amounted only to the kind of "occasional malicious and abusive" conduct that society must tolerate, not the "extreme and outrageous conduct" that could give rise to a cause of action.

Is it any wonder that the ABA thought a specific regulatory rule was required?

3.   Does Model Rule 1.8(j) deal adequately with the issues that sexual relationships present?

a.   Does Model Rule 1.8(j) reach relationships with clients' spouses of the kind found in *Artimez*, for example? Should such conduct be prohibited? Might some other rule reach it? Look at Comments [17]–[19] to Model Rule 1.8. Do they explain the rule sufficiently and suggest appropriate additional areas of caution?

b.   Should intercourse with a client be the only prohibited conduct? In re Heilprin, 482 N.W.2d 908 (Wis.1992), for example, disbarred the lawyer for asking women clients "sexually explicit and suggestive * * * questions." The court had earlier suspended the lawyer after he had been exposing himself to clients. Should acts that fall short of intimate physical contact raise discipline issues? Should the court discipline a lawyer who makes explicit and suggestive remarks to his secretary or another person who is not a client or client's spouse?

c.   Is it important to create an exception for pre-existing sexual relationships? Is that exception necessary so that a lawyer may represent his or her spouse? Should the rule not allow the exception because the spouse or paramour probably should have a different lawyer anyway? Note that even if the lawyer complies with Rule 1.8(j), Rule 1.7(a)(2) is still relevant. See Comment [18] to Model Rule 1.8.

d.   Should the prohibition extend to relationships between lawyers and officials of the lawyers' corporate clients? Look at Comment [19] to Model Rule 1.8. Are such relationships likely to present the same problems as those with individual clients? Might Comment [19] take the prohibition too far?

e.   If one lawyer in a firm enters into a sexual relationship with a client, should the lawyer be able to refer the client to another lawyer in the firm? Notice that Model Rule 1.8(k), confirmed in Comment [20], expressly does not impute the Model Rule 1.8(j) prohibition throughout a law firm. Can you see any good reason for not doing so?

PROBLEM 13

REPRESENTING THE INSURED AND THE INSURER

In a simple model of lawyer-client relations, the client pays the lawyer's fees. However, things do not always work out that way. Sometimes, a third party pays the fee; indeed, the lawyer might look to that third party for fees in multiple cases. Such a situation arises when a company pays its employees' legal fees in matters arising out of their work, or a parent pays the legal fees of a child who gets into trouble. It arises most often when insurance companies pay lawyers pursuant to contractual obligations to pay the legal fees of policyholders who face liability claims. In such cases, the lawyers typically never expect to see the policyholders again, but they devoutly hope that the insurance company will repeatedly retain them. That arrangement may create an incentive to serve, not the client, but the source of the fee. In this Problem, we explore the nature of a lawyer's relationship with an insurance company and its insured, the duty to protect confidential information of the insured, the right of the insurer to approve a settlement, and whether the insurance company may impose limits on efforts to be made in defense of the client's case.

FACTS

Terry Tenant is the son-in-law of Larry Landlord. Tenant rented an apartment in one of Landlord's apartment complexes. Landlord has a liability insurance policy with the All–Mutual Company covering all accidents in the apartment complex up to $100,000. One cold evening in January 1993, Tenant injured himself when he slipped on some ice just outside the main entrance. Landlord saw the accident and rushed to help Tenant, but Tenant said that he would "be all right." Thus, Landlord did not report the accident to All–Mutual. Unknown to Landlord, Tenant took several weeks off from work claiming back injuries. In June 1993, Tenant sued Landlord, his father-in-law, for $175,000 for his alleged pain and suffering and expenses in connection with the resulting back injury.

All–Mutual's liability insurance policy has several standard clauses. First, a "Notice of Accident" clause requires the insured to notify the carrier promptly of any accident for which it will expect coverage; failure to so notify is said to be a waiver of coverage. Second, the policy requires All–Mutual to provide and pay for a lawyer to defend the insured from any claim arising under the policy and to pay any claim within the monetary limits of the policy. Third, the policy requires the insured to cooperate with All–Mutual in defending against any claims.

After Tenant filed suit, Landlord notified All–Mutual, and All–Mutual retained Sara Henderson to investigate and prepare the defense. All–Mutual also wrote Landlord that it "was not waiving any defenses under the policy." Henderson interviewed Landlord and Tenant but was unable to find any other witnesses who had a clear recollection of the accident. Landlord's and Tenant's version of the events were almost identical and very favorable to Tenant. Henderson, on the other hand, has wondered how Tenant could be so careful and suffer such severe injuries, and yet have an immediate reaction that he would "be all right." Moreover, because Landlord and his son-in-law seem to be on good terms, she has wondered why Tenant neither told Landlord of the alleged "serious complications" nor, at least prior to filing, that Tenant was going to bring a lawsuit.

Tenant has offered to settle for $50,000, and Landlord has told Henderson that he would prefer All–Mutual's agreeing to that amount rather than going to trial and placing Landlord at risk for the $75,000 in excess of policy coverage.

Henderson believes that Landlord's failure to notify All–Mutual about the accident at the time it happened has so hampered factual development of the case that All–Mutual should deny coverage under its prompt notice clause. She has not told either Landlord or All–Mutual of her opinion. She also believes that Landlord is not cooperating, although she also has not said this to

Landlord or All–Mutual either. During one interview Landlord told Henderson: "Just between you and me, my son-in-law and I remain the best of friends, but I wouldn't want All–Mutual to know that."

Henderson has sent Tenant's settlement offer to Landlord and All–Mutual. All–Mutual has asked for her advice on whether it should accept the offer.

QUESTIONS

A. A LAWYER'S CLIENT(S) WHEN RETAINED BY AN INSURER TO REPRESENT AN INSURED

1. Whom does Sara Henderson represent when she is retained by an insurance company under circumstances like the one in this problem?

a. You might be surprised to learn that whether Henderson represents only Landlord, the insured, or whether she also represent All–Mutual, the insurance company, is a hotly-disputed issue. Henderson clearly represents Landlord. He is the named defendant in the case and the person for whom Henderson will enter her appearance as defense counsel. However, insurance companies tend to argue that they, too, are clients of the lawyers they retain on behalf of their policyholders.

b. Initially, it might seen important to identify whom Henderson represents in order to determine whether this is a third-party payer situation to which Model Rule 1.8(f) applies. Furthermore, if All–Mutual is also held to be Henderson's client, Rule 1.7(a) would come into play because Henderson would be representing two clients in the same matter.

However, even if All–Mutual were held to be Henderson's client, Rule 1.8(f) would still apply because Henderson would still be "accept[ing] compensation for representing a client [Landlord] from one other than the client [All–Mutual]". Alternatively, even if All–Mutual is not Henderson's client, the concerns of Model Rule 1.7(a)(2) are clearly still present.

c. For reasons such as these, Restatement Third, The Law Governing Lawyers § 134, Comment *a*, takes the position that whether the lawyer has one client or two is a matter of insurance law, not the law governing lawyers. Comment *f* then goes on to say that "it is clear in an insurance situation that a lawyer designated to defend the insured has a client-lawyer relationship with the insured. The insurer is not, simply by the fact that it designates the lawyer, a client of the lawyer."[1]

2. Are the problems of obtaining consent different depending on whether the insurance company is characterized as a client?

---

1. For a further development of these issues, see Thomas D. Morgan, Whose Lawyer Are You Anyway?, 23 Wm. Mitchell L. Rev. 11 (1997).

a. Look at Model Rule 1.8(f). To get informed consent under that provision, must Sara Henderson explain to Landlord the advantages and disadvantages of having her be Landlord's lawyer? What disadvantages should she be required to mention? Should she be required to tell the client the amount of all payments she received or anticipated from All–Mutual over the past year as an indication of her financial dependence on the company?

b. Suppose the law said that there are two clients and thus that Model Rule 1.7(a)(2) governs the situation. Would Henderson have to get informed consent from All–Mutual as well? Would the fact that All–Mutual retained Henderson constitute consent to the joint representation? Do we say in any other situation that the fact of retention alone constitutes consent to a conflict of interest?

c. May the lawyer assume that the insurance policy, which both parties signed when insurance was obtained, constitutes whatever consent is necessary to waive whatever conflicts of interest may be presented? Would the usual conversation between insurance agent and the insured guarantee the kind of informed consent the Model Rules demand?

3. You remember from Problem 10 that a lawyer ordinarily must secure client consent to file suit against a current client. Would Henderson be barred from representing a client in an unrelated case suing the insurance company that retains her in other cases to represent its policyholders?

a. In re Anonymous Member of South Carolina Bar, 432 S.E.2d 467 (S.C.1993), said that Model Rule 1.7(a)(1) forbids a lawyer to help a client collect under the uninsured motorist coverage of his own policy if the lawyer is retained by the insurance company to represent its policyholders in other cases. Do you agree that this result is required based on what you have learned?

b. Regardless of the answer under Rule 1.7(a)(1), if one analyzes the situation under Rule 1.7(a)(2), is it not clear that representation of the client may be affected by the lawyer's own financial interests, i.e., her desire that the insurance company continue to refer cases to her? Remember that Rule 1.7(a)(2) contemplates that the disqualifying interest could be created by a third person, not just another client.

4. Suppose that, when Landlord gets on the witness stand, he tells a story more favorable to Tenant than he had told Henderson earlier. May Henderson seek to impeach Landlord's story and thus help reduce the amount the insurance company will have to pay?

a. Restatement Third, The Law Governing Lawyers § 134, Comment *f*, says:

"With respect to events or information that create a conflict of interest between insured and insurer, the lawyer must proceed in the best interests of the insured, consistent with the lawyer's duty not to assist client fraud (see § 94) * * *. If the designated lawyer finds it impossible so to proceed, the lawyer must withdraw from representation of both clients * * * ."

Is withdrawal a practical alternative when the surprise testimony occurs in the middle of a trial?

b. In Montanez v. Irizarry–Rodriguez, 641 A.2d 1079 (N.J.Super.App.Div.1994), Wife was suing Husband for injuries suffered in an auto accident. In pre-trial interviews with the lawyer appointed by the insurer, Husband said he had been driving safely but a tire had blown out. On the witness stand, however, he said that the blowout occurred after the accident and that he had not driven safely. At that point, the defense lawyer demanded the right to treat his client as a "hostile witness" so as to try to minimize the sum the insurer would have to pay Wife. The court held that impeachment of one's own client was improper. If the insurer later wanted to sue the client for non-cooperation, it could do so, but the lawyer represented the insured, not the insurer, in the action before the court.[2]

B. A LAWYER'S OBLIGATION TO PROTECT CONFIDENTIAL INFORMATION OF THE INSURED

1. What must a lawyer do when he or she learns embarrassing or incriminating information about the insured that the insurance company would want to know?

a. Perhaps the leading case on defense counsel handling of confidential information is Parsons v. Continental National American Group, 550 P.2d 94 (Ariz.1976). Fourteen-year-old Michael Smithey had brutally assaulted a neighbor. A CNA claims representative investigated the incident and wrote a detailed letter to his company on his investigation of Michael's background. The letter concluded:

> "In view of this information gathered and in discussion with the boy's father's attorney, Mr. Howard Watts, and with the boy's parents, I am reasonably convinced that the boy was not in control of his senses at the time of this incident. It is, therefore, my suggestion that, and unless instructed otherwise, I will proceed to commence settlement negotiations with the claimant's attorney so that this matter may be disposed of as soon as possible."

However, counsel retained by CNA to defend Michael told CNA:

> "I have secured a rather complete and confidential file on the minor insured who is now in the Paso Robles School for Boys, a maximum-security institution with facilities for psychiatric treatment, and he will be kept there indefinitely and certainly for at least six months * * *. The * * * file shows that the boy is fully aware of his acts and that he knew what he was doing was wrong.

2. Lurking within this question is what a lawyer must do when even a client to whom the lawyer clearly owes a duty of loyalty gives perjured testimony. You will see that issue in more detail in Problem 27.

It follows, therefore, that the assault he committed on claimants can only be a deliberate act on his part."

This was important information because the insurance policy specifically excluded liability for intentional acts. Thus, after receiving the lawyer's report, CNA sent a reservation of rights letter to the boy's parents saying that it would investigate and defend the case, but that it did not waive this possible defense against payment of any judgment.

b.   Later, in preparing for trial, the defense attorney interviewed Michael and wrote to CNA: "His own story makes it obvious that his acts were willful and criminal." At trial, the lawyer offered no defense, and a $50,000 judgment was entered against Michael. When the plaintiffs tried to have the trial court order CNA to pay them the amount of its policy, CNA successfully claimed that the intentional act exclusion applied. The CNA defense was handled by the same law firm and attorney that had previously represented the insured in the underlying action.

c.   Do you think the defense attorney acted properly? Where did he go wrong, if at all? What should be the consequence of the attorney's conduct?

d.   The Arizona Supreme Court held that CNA was estopped to deny coverage and thus had to pay the judgment. The court found that CNA "took advantage of the fiduciary relationship between its agent (the attorney) and Michael Smithey." The court explained:

> "The attorneys, retained by CNA, represented Michael Smithey at the personal liability trial, and, as a result, obtained privileged and confidential information from Michael's confidential file at the Paso Robles School for Boys * * * [because of] the attorney-client relationship. Both the A.B.A. Committee on Ethics and Professional Responsibility and the State Bar of Arizona * * * have held that an attorney that represented the insured at the request of the insurer owes undivided fidelity to the insured, and, therefore, may not reveal any information or conclusions derived therefrom to the insurer that may be detrimental to the insured in any subsequent action. * * *

> "The attorney in the instant case should have notified CNA that he could no longer represent them when he obtained any information (as a result of his attorney-client relationship with Michael) that could possibly be detrimental to Michael's interests under the coverage of the policy. * * *

> "The attorney in the present case continued to act as Michael's attorney while he was actively working against Michael's interests. When an attorney who is an insurance company's agent uses the confidential relationship between an attorney and a client to gather information so as to deny the insured coverage under the policy in the garnishment proceeding we hold that such conduct constitutes a waiver of any policy defense, and is so contrary to public policy that the insurance company is estopped as a matter of law from disclaiming liability under an exclusionary clause in the policy."

2.   Given the authority of *Parsons*, what should Henderson tell All–Mutual with respect to the prompt notice clause?

a.   Would it constitute disloyalty to the insured to report to the company that five months had passed between the accident and the insured's report? Would that be information be obvious to the company if it looked at dates in the insured's own report of the accident?

b.   Remember that all information "relating to the representation" is protected by Model Rule 1.6. Most insurance policies, however, give the insured a contractual duty to cooperate with the insurer in preparing the defense. Should there be a distinction between a lawyer's disclosure of "innocent" information given under the duty of cooperation and the disclosure of more sensitive information that the lawyer learns in the course of preparing the defense?

c.   Rhode Island Ethics Opinion 98–10 (Apr. 1998) declared that an insured has the right to see all communications from the lawyer to the insurance company about the progress of the case. Does that approach protect all relevant interests? Remember that such reports might, for example, include the lawyer's assessment of how credible a witness the client would be. That is something the lawyer and company might not want the insured to see, but it might be very relevant to the company as it decides how much liability exposure the case presents.

3.   Where would telling the company about the "I wouldn't want All–Mutual to know" comment fit into this analysis? Would such a report constitute a breach of Henderson's duty of confidentiality?

a.   Are you at all troubled by the suggestion that Henderson could not tell All–Mutual about the possibility of collusion between Landlord and Tenant here? Would a failure to report it constitute participation by Henderson in a possible fraud by the insured?

b.   Restatement Third, The Law Governing Lawyers § 134, Comment *f*, advises that when there is a question of the insured's right to policy coverage, the lawyer for the insured "may not reveal adverse confidential client information of the insured to the insurer concerning that question without explicit informed consent of the insured. That follows whether or not the lawyer also represents the insurer as co-client and whether or not the insurer has asserted a 'reservation of rights' with respect to its defense of the insured." The Comment continues that the lawyer must proceed in the insured's best interest, "consistent with the lawyer's duty not to assist client fraud," and if that is impossible, "the lawyer must withdraw from representation of both clients * * * ."

c.   If Henderson obtains "sensitive" information about the insured's coverage, should she withdraw from the representation under Rule 1.16? Could she do so without signaling to the company that there was a possible policy or coverage defense? Would such signaling be appropriate? Cf. Model Rule 1.2, Comment [10].

4. The Problem says that All–Mutual is defending the insured under a "reservation of rights" of the kind in *Parsons*. Does that in itself create a conflict of interest for a lawyer?

a. The reservation of rights is a statement that the insurance company is not waiving any policy defenses it may have against bearing the ultimate liability. Traditionally, the insurer's duty to defend and its duty to pay a damage award are separate duties. That is, a policy may provide coverage of defense costs even though the company would have a valid defense against paying the ultimate judgment. Thus, defense of the plaintiff's claim and the gathering of evidence as to policy coverage tend to go on simultaneously for some period.

b. The point at which a reservation of rights is asserted is usually seen as a time when the insured and the insurer have a conflict of interest. The usual rule is that two different lawyers must be involved, i.e., one to give the insurer an opinion on policy defenses or policy coverage and one to defend the insured.

c. In Allstate Insurance Co. v. Keller, 149 N.E.2d 482 (Ill.Ct.App. 1958), for example, the attorneys assigned to represent the insured deposed the insured to gather evidence that he was not the driver of the vehicle at the time of the accident. They did not explain to the insured that the purpose of the deposition was to strengthen the insurer's claim of lack of coverage. The court agreed that the insured's initial false statements that he was the driver were a breach of the cooperation clause, but it held the defense was waived. After the insured's assigned attorneys "became aware of a conflict of interest between their client, the defendant [insured], and their employer, the plaintiff [insurer]," they had to disclose this information and its significance to the insured. Failure to deal with this conflict in a way that assured the insured had loyal, independent representation, resulted in loss of the policy defense.

d. Similarly, in Employers Casualty Company v. Tilley, 496 S.W.2d 552 (Tex.1973), the insured had claimed that his failure to report an accident promptly, as the policy required, was because he had not known about it until he was sued. A lawyer was assigned to defend him, pursuant to a reservation of the company's rights. All the while he was preparing the defense, however, the lawyer was apparently also gathering evidence of just when Tilley or his employees first knew of the accident. The court held that "[a]n attorney employed by an insurer to represent the insured simply cannot take up the cudgels of the insurer against the insured." 496 S.W.2d at 560. The insured was found to have been prejudiced by the lawyer's dual role, so the insurer was "estopped as a matter of law" from asserting its policy defense.

e. No matter what the courts say about who the client is in situations like this, is it realistic to presume that the attorney faces no conflict of loyalties? Concern about this conflict has led some courts to say an insured himself must be entitled to select the lawyer who will represent him (at the insurer's expense) on the liability issues when the insurer has raised a policy defense. See, e.g., CHI of Alaska, Inc. v. Employers Reinsurance

Corp., 844 P.2d 1113 (Alaska 1993). In any event, a case like this may be one in which Henderson must treat possible policy defenses as someone else's problem.

5. Move the questions to a context other than insurance company cases. If parents pay a lawyer to represent their child accused of a hit and run accident, for example, must the lawyer secure the child's consent before disclosing information to the parents?

a. The answer is almost surely yes, and because the parents may not understand that, the lawyer should make it clear at the outset of the representation.

b. Illinois State Bar Association Advisory Opinion on Professional Conduct, Opinion 00–02 (2000) advised that a lawyer may not release a psychiatric report of his mentally disabled adult client to the adult client's parents. Because the mentally disabled adult is the lawyer's client, not the parent, even under Model Rule 1.14 such disclosure would violate a lawyer's duty to preserve his client's confidential information.

c. Might a lawyer paid by a legal aid office to represent an indigent client face issues very similar to those in this problem? What should the lawyer do about verifying the client's eligibility for free assistance, for example? Should the legal aid lawyer and the insurance defense lawyer resolve such questions in exactly the same way? What differences might there be?

C. A LAWYER'S DUTY AT THE TIME OF A SETTLEMENT OFFER IN A THIRD-PARTY PAYMENT CASE

1. How should Henderson react to the settlement offer? Does Rule 1.8(f) offer concrete guidance on the question?

a. Do you see the conflict of interest? The insured would normally want to settle any case at a figure within policy limits because that would assure he will not have to bear liability in excess of those limits; the insurer, on the other hand, faced with an offer for the full amount of the policy, has relatively little to lose by going to trial.

b. In such cases, as a matter of substantive law in many states, if the insurance company rejects a reasonable offer within policy limits, it must bear any sum—even in excess of policy limits—that the court ultimately awards. E.g., Crisci v. Security Insurance Co., 426 P.2d 173, 176 (Cal.1967) ("when 'there is great risk of a recovery beyond the policy limits so that the most reasonable manner of disposing of the claim is a settlement which can be made within those limits, a consideration in good faith of the insured's interest requires the insurer to settle the claim.' ").

c. Under these circumstances, can there be any doubt that the lawyer must at least tell the insurance company of the settlement offer? See Restatement Third, The Law Governing Lawyers § 134, Comment *f*, saying that telling the company of the offer is not a breach of duty to the insured.

2. What is the lawyer to do if the insurer wants to settle the case but the insured does not?

a. You remember that Model Rule 1.2(a) gives the "client," i.e., the insured, the absolute right to decide whether to settle a matter. On the other hand, it is standard insurance law and often a part of the standard insurance contract that an "insurance company is free to exercise its own judgment as to whether to enter into a settlement. It can, therefore, absent an express policy provision to the contrary, settle a case despite the insured's request that it not do so."[3]

b. Professional malpractice policies, however, are sometimes written differently than the garden variety liability policy. The professional may want to protect her reputation and avoid any implication that she was incompetent. Thus the insured may want the insurer to fight, not settle. Consequently "[p]rofessional liability policies usually contain a *settlement clause* permitting the insured to refuse to consent to a settlement, and expressly limiting the insurer's liability in the event of a subsequent excess judgment."[4] What should the lawyer do with a settlement offer when representing a professional under such an arrangement?

3. Suppose there is no clause reserving the right of the insured to settle the case; must the lawyer nevertheless obtain the insured's permission to settle? Must the lawyer inform the insured about the offer of settlement even if the insured legally has no veto power?

a. The Illinois Supreme Court said yes to both questions in Rogers v. Robson, Masters, Ryan, Brumund & Belom, 407 N.E.2d 47 (Ill.1980). Plaintiff was a doctor who had an insurance policy that provided that the insurer did *not* have to secure the written consent of the insured before the insurer made settlement of any claim or suit. The doctor was sued for medical malpractice and the lawyers assigned by the insurer to defend the case negotiated a settlement with the victim. The insurer accepted the settlement, paid $1250, and the lawyers effected dismissal of the action. The doctor had "repeatedly informed" one of the law partners that he would not consent to settlement and the doctor was never advised that the insurer intended to settle. The Illinois Supreme Court held that these facts gave rise to a cause of action. Saying that the doctor and the insurance company were both the lawyers' clients, the court said that the doctor—

> "was entitled to a full disclosure of the intent to settle the litigation without his consent and contrary to his express instructions. Defendants' duty to make such disclosure stemmed from their attorney-client relationship with plaintiff and was not affected by the extent of the insurer's authority to settle without

3. Allan D. Windt, Insurance Claims and Disputes; Representation of Insurance Companies and Insureds 191 (1982). See also, Mitchum v. Hudgens, 533 So.2d 194 (Ala. 1988) (insurance contract may give the insurance company the right to settle a case with-

in the policy limits, even over the objection of the insured); Feliberty v. Damon, 527 N.E.2d 261 (N.Y.1988).

4. Windt, supra, at 191 n. 22.

plaintiff's consent. * * * Nor need we reach the question whether plaintiff can prove damages which are the proximate result of the breach of the duty to make a full disclosure of the conflict between the defendants' two clients." 407 N.E.2d at 48.

Do you agree with this analysis? What is the "conflict between the defendants' two clients" in a case like this? What should the lawyer do if the insured does not want to settle? Should the lawyer advise the insured that, if he forbids the insurance company to make the settlement, he may be deemed to have breached the policy terms and wind up paying the legal fees and final judgment himself?

b. Lysick v. Walcom, 65 Cal.Rptr. 406 (Ct.App.1968), also illustrates the importance of these issues. The insurer was prepared to concede liability and initially authorized the lawyer to settle for up to $9500, policy limits being $10,000. The plaintiff proposed to settle for $12,500, and the estate of the insured had expressed a willingness to contribute $2,500 over the policy limits. However, because the lawyer lacked the authority to pay full policy limits and was hesitant about seeking more authority from the insurer, he failed to tell the insured's estate about the offer. Nor did he tell the insured's estate when he rejected the offer on its behalf. The action went to trial and resulted in a judgment in favor of plaintiff for $225,000. The court held:

> "[When the attorney for the insured] became aware of a conflict of interest between his two clients concerning the settlement offer made by plaintiffs[,] [h]e could have then terminated his relationship to the estate, but chose to continue to act as attorney for both clients. Accordingly, by so continuing to act, he impliedly agreed to use such skill, prudence and diligence in the representation of the estate as lawyers of ordinary skill and capacity commonly possess in the performance of like tasks. Moreover, since he was representing two parties with divergent interests, insofar as the settlement of the case was concerned, defendant labored under the duty of disclosing all facts and circumstances which, in the judgment of a lawyer of ordinary skill and capacity, were necessary to enable each of his clients to make free and intelligent decisions regarding the subject matter of the representation. * * *

> " * * * By continuing to act as counsel for the estate, while entertaining the belief that his primary obligation in the matter of settlement was to the insurer, defendant violated the legal and ethical concepts which delineated his duties to the estate." 65 Cal.Rptr. at 416.

The court concluded that, assuming proximate cause, the attorney would be personally liable for the amount of the judgment in excess of policy limits.

c. Is the implication, then, that Henderson should advise acceptance of the settlement in this Problem? Will that protect her against personal liability? Does she inevitably have a personal stake in whatever she recommends that itself creates a conflict of interest under Model Rule 1.7(a)(2)?

d. ABA Formal Opinion 96–403 (Aug. 2, 1996) tried to straighten out the seeming conflict between ethics law and insurance law that a lawyer faces when the insurance contract has given the insurance company the right to control the defense and settlement of a case. The ABA Committee refused to take sides in the debate as to whether the lawyer has one client or two, but it made clear that the lawyer must communicate with the insured to inform him or her about the limited nature of the representation and the lawyer's intent to take direction from the insurance company. The Opinion says that lawyer does not need formal consent from the insured before the lawyer may take direction from the company, but if the insured objects and wants to control the defense—thereby assuming the risk of a loss of insurance coverage—the lawyer must honor that demand.

D.   DEFINING THE APPROPRIATE LEVEL OF EFFORT WHEN AN INSURER PAYS FOR THE DEFENSE

1. Suppose the insurance company faces a maximum liability of $10,000 under the policy. Litigation costs could well be that much or more, in addition to the amount of the liability. In order to reduce the cost of litigation, may the insurer direct the lawyer to take no more than, say, two depositions in the case?

a. Look at Model Rule 1.8(f). Does it forbid the lawyer to honor such a direction by the insurer? Is a prohibition against accepting direction by others something that is generally in the interest of clients? Might it be in the interest of lawyers? Does such a prohibition serve the interest of policyholders in cases such as the one in this problem?

b. Utah State Bar Ethics Advisory Committee Opinion 02–03 (2002), found that an attorney's agreement to abide by an insurer's case management guidelines is not per se unethical. Instead, it required evaluation of such agreements on a case by case basis, finding that they were illegal only if the agreement in fact caused the attorney to act contrary to the interest of his client, the insured. The Committee emphasized that an attorney may not contract around general ethical obligations under the state rules of professional conduct and suggested that the attorney tell the insured any restrictions on the representation, how the case would be handled especially regarding settlement, the insured's responsibility for adverse verdicts in excess of the policy coverage, and the insured's other rights. Further, the Opinion says, within the defined terms of the representation, the attorney must continue to exercise independent professional judgment on behalf of the insured client.

c. Is the concern in such cases the same one people have about the incentives of their HMOs? That is, should we be afraid insurance companies will put a concern about profits ahead of protection of their policyholders? Don't accept the analogy too quickly. An HMO will not get sick if care is inadequate. If foreseeable liability is within policy limits in an automobile accident case, on the other hand, and the company will pay the whole award, is there any reason the insurance company should not be permitted to make a tradeoff between the cost and value of specific litigation tactics? If the company were willing to pay the full amount of the claim, could it decide to put on no defense at all? However, does the *Rogers* case, above, suggest that lawyers can never be wholly confident they can ignore the insured's non–economic interest in vigorously fighting a claim?

d. Restatement Third, The Law Governing Lawyers § 134, Comment *f*, advises that the lawyer "may not follow directions of the insurer if doing so would put the insured at significantly increased risk of liability in excess of the policy coverage." The Illustration to the Comment says that the lawyer may accept the insurer's direction not to double the number of depositions at a cost of $5,000 even if taking them would "somewhat increase" the insured's chances of winning. In this Illustration, the claims against the insured are within the policy coverage, the insurance contract "confers authority on Insurer to make such decisions," and the lawyer believes that he can forgo these depositions "without violating the duty of competent representation" that he owes the insured.

2. How should a lawyer respond to an insurance company's demand that it show its files to an "auditor" retained by the insurance company to review the lawyer's compliance with insurance company guidelines?

a. State ethics committees, unsurprisingly, express the view that to give auditors that information would be to expose confidential client information and interfere with the lawyer's professional judgment. Alabama State Bar Formal Opinion RO–98–02 (1998), for example, says that lawyers should not turn over information to such a reviewer if by doing so they will compromise privilege or work product protection, or waive the protection of confidential client information. Maryland Ethics Docket 99–7 (1999) reaches the same result, and cites opinions from Florida, South Carolina, Louisiana, Washington and Kentucky to the same effect.

b. Do you agree with these opinions? Of course, enforcing these ethical dictates in a world in which the insurance company will refuse to refer cases to lawyers who decline to cooperate is likely to prove more difficult than asserting the principles involved. Restatement § 134, Comment *f*, concludes that referral of progress reports, case evaluations, and settlement offers to the insurer should not cause them to lose their privileged character even if the insurer is not treated as a client. Does that make it easier to justify letting the insurance company auditor see such documents?

c. ABA Formal Opinion 01–421 (Feb. 16, 2001) is the probable culmination of opinions on acceding to demands that lawyers submit their records to outside auditors. A lawyer may disclose information to the insurance company itself, the opinion says, if the lawyer reasonably believes it will advance the interest of the insured, i.e., by helping the company decide when to settle, assuring the company that all is being handled properly, etc. However, the lawyer may not disclose information that may reveal the client's motives or other sensitive insights, nor disclose information to third party auditors, without the insured's consent. In seeking consent, the lawyer may have to explain to the insured that a failure to consent could result in denial of insurance coverage and that disclosure to an auditor could result in loss of the attorney-client privilege. Finally, the Opinion says that a lawyer may only comply with insurance company litigation guidelines where they do not materially impair the lawyer's own independent professional judgment on behalf of the client.

d.   United States v. Legal Services, 100 F.Supp.2d 42 (D.D.C.2000), enforced a subpoena from the inspector general's office of the Legal Services Corporation for similar information from local legal aid organizations. The LSC was concerned that organizations were overstating the number of cases handled, so it required data by case number, subject matter and client names. The court rejected a blanket assertion of privilege, saying client names were typically not privileged. In addition, it held that the LSC's statutory authority to audit trumped Rule 1.6's requirement of confidentiality.

3.   If states try to enforce restrictions on directions to lawyers that insurance companies retain to represent their insureds, are the companies likely to respond by having their own in-house lawyers represent the policyholders? Should the law permit that response?

a.   Gardner v. North Carolina State Bar, 341 S.E.2d 517 (N.C.1986), said insurance companies may not move to such a practice. Nor may an insurance company's in-house attorney appear as counsel of record for the insured in the prosecution of a subrogation claim for property damage. North Carolina law (like the law of many states) bans corporations (although typically not professional legal corporations) from performing legal services for another. "Since a corporation cannot practice law directly, it cannot do so indirectly by employing lawyers to practice for it." 341 S.E.2d at 521.[5]

b.   In re Allstate Insurance Co., 722 S.W.2d 947 (Mo.1987) (en banc), however, went the other way. It specifically refused to follow *Gardner* and concluded that the insurance company may either hire independent lawyers or use its own employee-lawyers instead. "An insurer has a very substantial interest in litigation involving its insured, and is entitled to retain counsel of its own choosing to protect its interest." 722 S.W.2d at 950. If the insurer can hire an independent contractor it can act through its employee. Any danger of conflict of interest is minimized because the insurance company uses its employee-lawyers "only when there is no question of coverage, and when the claim is within policy limits."

c.   In re Petition of Youngblood, 895 S.W.2d 322 (Tenn.1995), involved review of an ethics opinion that had opposed an insurance company's using

5. We will look at the unauthorized practice implications of a corporation practicing law when we get to Problem 38, infra.

an in-house lawyer to represent the insured. The court agreed that an insurance company may not tell the insured that the in-house lawyer is practicing independently, and the lawyer's loyalty in any given defense must be to the insured alone. However, the court ruled that it was proper for the insurance company to use employed attorneys as an economical way to assure experienced counsel for policyholders.[6]

4. Should the lawyer be concerned about potential malpractice liability to the insurer, the insured, or both, if the lawyer accedes to the company's limited-effort demand?

a. Might the lawyer simply ask the insurer and insured to waive in advance any right to sue for any malpractice that results from adhering to the insurance company's direction? Be careful! What about Rule 1.8(h)? Does Rule 1.2(c) save the day for the lawyer? Which "client's" consent must the lawyer secure?

b. Should the insurance company, in turn, be liable for malpractice committed by the lawyer it retains to defend the insured? Should it matter how much direction the company exercised over the lawyer? State Farm Mutual Automobile Insurance Co. v. Traver, 980 S.W.2d 625 (Tex.1998), said there could be no vicarious liability. The lawyer is an independent contractor retained to defend the insured who is the lawyer's client, not an agent of the insurer. However, if the insured claims the insurance company intruded on the lawyer-client relationship, failed to defend in good faith, or undermined the defense, that would constitute a direct action against the insurance company that could proceed.

c. May the insurance company sue the lawyer for malpractice, even if the insurer is not treated as a client of the lawyer? Restatement Third, The Law Governing Lawyers, says yes. "Because and to the extent that the insurer is directly concerned in the matter financially, the insurer should be accorded standing to assert a claim for appropriate relief from the lawyer" if the lawyer's professional negligence or other wrongful act caused the damage. Restatement § 134, Comment *f.* Do you agree that such an analysis of the relationship between the insurance company and the lawyer is accurate?[7]

---

6. But see, American Insurance Ass'n v. Kentucky Bar Ass'n, 917 S.W.2d 568 (Ky. 1996) (forbids use of in-house lawyers, citing the ancient maxim for construction of legal rules, "If it ain't broke don't fix it").

7. Cases have split as to whether an insurance company may sue for malpractice of the lawyers it retains to defend its insureds.

Atlanta International Ins. Co. v. Bell, 475 N.W.2d 294 (Mich.1991), used a doctrine of equitable subrogation to permit it to do so.

Unigard Insurance Group v. O'Flaherty & Belgum, 45 Cal.Rptr.2d 565 (Ct.App.1995), found the insurer and insured were both the lawyer's clients in order to reach the same result. See also, National Union Insurance Co. v. Dowd & Dowd, P.C., 2 F.Supp.2d 1013 (N.D.Ill.1998) (same result; excess insurer stood in the shoes of the insured); GEICO v. Forbes, 1999 WL 371625 (E.D.Pa.1999) (so holding will not reduce the loyalty the lawyer must have to the insured, and it gives the

PROBLEM 14

THE LAWYER AND HER FORMER CLIENT

So far, we have seen problems involving conflicts among prospective clients, current clients, conflicts with the lawyer's own interest, and conflicts created by the involvement of a third party. Now, we look at how the lawyer's duties to a former client might be affected by a current representation and present a threat to the former client, the current client, or both. Lawyers and law firms often have long lives. That means they have a great many former clients, and it would impossibly limit the choice of counsel available to current clients to say lawyers that are as prohibited from opposing a former client as they are from opposing a current one. We will ask, then, how broadly the prohibition of opposing a former client extends, what makes matters the same or substantially related, whether non-lawyers face similar prohibitions, and what may be done with the work product of a lawyer who is not permitted to continue in a case.

FACTS

Martha Heath has a wide reputation for her success in handling medical malpractice cases for plaintiffs. She is in great demand and is rightfully feared by doctor defendants.

Recently, Linda Parker came to Heath with a claim against Dr. Charles Abraham. Heath investigated the facts, found they seemed sound, and proceeded to go to work on the matter. Until she had worked on the case for about 90 days, Heath had not recalled that about five years earlier she had represented Dr. Abraham in the routine adoption of his wife's children.

Heath might have forgotten Dr. Abraham but he had not forgotten her. "How could you of all people—my own lawyer—sue me?" he said. More to the point, he had his malpractice defense counsel move to disqualify Martha Heath from handling Parker's claim.

QUESTIONS

A. MATTERS AS TO WHICH DISQUALIFICATION IS REQUIRED

1. Does a lawyer owe the same duty of loyalty to a former client as to a current one? What standard defines when a lawyer

right to sue to the only person who has an incentive to pursue it).

However, Jones Lang Wootton USA v. LeBoeuf, Lamb, Greene & MacRae, 674 N.Y.S.2d 280 (App.Div.1998), said no. Under New York law, the insurer could not have sued its insured for being required to pay the judgment, so the insurer may not stand in the client's shoes to pursue the claim. See also Fireman's Fund Insurance Co. v. McDonald, Hecht & Solberg, 36 Cal.Rptr.2d 424 (Ct.App.1994) (California law does not recognize equitable subrogation).

may undertake a matter that is contrary to the interest of a former client?

a.   Judge Weinfeld developed the basic standard limiting such representation in the leading case of T. C. Theatre Corp. v. Warner Brothers Pictures, Inc., 113 F.Supp. 265, 268–69 (S.D.N.Y.1953):

> " * * * I hold that the former client need show no more than that matters embraced within the pending suit wherein his former attorney appears on behalf of his adversary are *substantially related* to the matters or cause of action wherein the attorney previously represented him, the former client. The Court will assume that during the course of the former representation confidences were disclosed to the attorney bearing on the subject matter of the representation. It will not inquire into their nature and extent. Only in this manner can the lawyer's duty of absolute fidelity be enforced and the spirit of the rule relating to privileged communications be maintained." (emphasis added).

b.   The Model Rules now incorporate Judge Weinfeld's test in ABA Model Rule 1.9(a). It is to Rule 1.9, not Rule 1.7(a), to which lawyers look to determine their obligations to a former client.[1]

c.   Restatement Third, The Law Governing Lawyers § 132, Comment *b*, says that the former client rule:

> "accommodates four policies. First, absent the rule, a lawyer's incentive to serve a present client might cause the lawyer to compromise the lawyer's continuing duties to the former client. Specifically, the lawyer might use confidential information of the former client contrary to that client's interest * * * . The second policy consideration is the converse of the first. The lawyer's obligations to the former client might constrain the lawyer in representing the present client effectively, for example, by limiting the questions the lawyer could ask the former client in testimony. Third, at the time the lawyer represented the former client, the lawyer should have no incentive to lay the basis for subsequent representation against that client, such as by drafting provisions in a contract that could later be construed against the former client. Fourth, and pointing the other way, because much law practice is transactional, clients often retain lawyers for services only on specific cases or issues. A rule that would transform each engagement into a lifetime commitment would make lawyers reluctant to take new, relatively modest matters."

Would those policies help a judge in deciding Dr. Abraham's motion to disqualify Martha Heath?

---

1. You will see a reference to "former client" in Model Rule 1.7(a)(2). That refers to the effect of the lawyer's obligations under Model Rule 1.9 to a former client on the interest of a current client of the lawyer.

2.   Does the term "matter" refer only to litigated cases?

a.   Notice that Judge Weinfeld makes clear that "matters" are not limited to "causes of action." Comment [2] to Model Rule 1.9 also makes clear that the term "matter" covers more than lawsuits. Do you agree that a lawyer should be barred from seeking to rescind a contract drafted for a former client, for example? Is the rationale offered by the Restatement, supra, convincing in explaining why the rule might extend that far?

b.   In Berry v. Saline Memorial Hospital, 907 S.W.2d 736 (Ark.1995), a lawyer in the plaintiff's firm had been a director of the defendant hospital. The problem was not that he thus knew confidential information about this case; it was that he knew generally the hospital's policies and practices that were also at issue in the matter. The lawyer-director owed a continuing duty of loyalty to the hospital, the court held, and his firm was thus disqualified from taking the case.[2]

c.   In Townsend v. Townsend, 474 S.E.2d 424 (S.C.1996), a lawyer tried to represent a father who was trying to reduce his child support payments. Earlier, the lawyer had served as guardian ad litem for the child. The court conceded that a guardian ad litem is an officer of the court and does not technically represent the child. However, as guardian, the lawyer needed to have the confidence of the child and the family and may have received confidential information that would justify invoking Rule 1.9's bar.

d.   Fields–D'Arpino v. Restaurant Associates, Inc., 39 F.Supp.2d 412 (S.D.N.Y.1999), asked whether an act of "informal mediation" constituted a "matter" for purposes of Rule 1.9. The plaintiff complained that the defendant was discriminating against her because of her pregnancy. A lawyer from the outside law firm representing the defendant held a meeting of the parties to try to resolve the dispute short of litigation. Even after the filing of an administrative complaint, the lawyer tried to mediate the dispute, and now the question was whether the firm could represent the defendant in the subsequent litigation. The court held it could not. All parties to a mediation must have the assurance it will be confidential. That could not be assured if the mediator's firm now represented one of the parties, so disqualification was required.[3]

B.   DETERMINING WHEN MATTERS ARE THE "SAME OR SUBSTANTIALLY RELATED"

1.   In the middle of her representation of Dr. Abraham in the adoption matter, could Heath have withdrawn and taken the side of Mrs. Abraham's former husband in seeking to resist the Doctor's adoption of his and his former wife's children?

2.   Conflicts created by a lawyer's "fiduciary or other legal obligation to a nonclient" are the subject of Restatement Third, The Law Governing Lawyers § 135.

3.   See also McKenzie Construction v. St. Croix Storage Corp., 961 F.Supp. 857 (D.Vi.1997) holding that a lawyer who had been an unsuccessful mediator in a case could not become of counsel to the firm representing one of the parties without disqualifying that firm from work on the case. The court cited Poly Software International, Inc. v. Su, 880 F.Supp. 1487 (D.Utah 1995), and Cho v. Superior Court, 45 Cal.Rptr.2d 863 (Ct.App. 1995). We focus more directly on limitations on former mediators in Problem 16.

a. Something as blatant as side switching in the *same* case, rarely arises in practice. Far more often, what happens is that Heath would resign from one firm and move to a new firm that has been representing Mrs. Abraham's former husband. Remember that even if the lawyer who changes firms never works an hour on the case while at the new firm, the fact that he or she would be disqualified from doing so can disqualify everyone at the new firm. See Model Rule 1.10(a).

b. The harder problem for lawyers is deciding when two matters are "substantially related" within the meaning of Model Rule 1.9. Restatement Third, The Law Governing Lawyers § 132 says:

"* * * The current matter is substantially related to the earlier matter if:

"(1) the current matter involves the work the lawyer performed for the former client; or

"(2) there is a substantial risk that representation of the present client will involve the use of information acquired in the course of representing the former client, unless that information has become generally known."

Comment [3] to Model Rule 1.7 expands on this definition and provides examples. Can you begin to identify some recurring types of issues lawyers will face?

c. One type of substantially related matter consists of later developments in an earlier matter. In Damron v. Herzog, 67 F.3d 211 (9th Cir.1995), cert. denied 516 U.S. 1117, 116 S.Ct. 922, 133 L.Ed.2d 851 (1996), for example, Lawyer had represented Seller in sale of his business. Nine years later, Lawyer represented Buyer and told him to stop making payments for the company because Seller had not complied with the terms of the deal. The court held that such advice breached Lawyer's continuing "ethical duty of loyalty to his former client" and constituted a basis for a malpractice action even though there was no showing that confidential information of the former client was disclosed to Buyer, the lawyer's current client.

In Sullivan County Regional Refuse Disposal District v. Town of Acworth, 686 A.2d 755 (N.H.1996), the lawyer who had previously helped set up a multi-town garbage disposal district was prohibited from helping one of the member towns to withdraw. No confidential information of the district was at issue, and the agreement was a public document, but the case involved construction of language drafted while the lawyer was principal counsel for the district. For him to now advocate a particular interpretation of the agreement was said to be contrary to his duty of loyalty to the rest of the towns in the district.

d. Tekni–Plex Inc. v. Meyner & Landis, 674 N.E.2d 663 (N.Y.1996), involved a firm that had represented both a corporation and its sole shareholder in the sale of the company to Buyer. Later, Buyer (acting in the name of the corporation) claimed that the Sellers' covenants about compliance with environmental requirements were false, and the law firm sought to represent the former sole shareholder of the corporation in defending those claims. However, the New York Court of Appeals held the law firm disqualified from opposing its former corporate client in the matter, even on behalf of the other client with whom he had worked. The court ruled that the current management controlled the attorney-client privilege with regard to communications arising out of pre-merger operations, including any pre-merger communications between the predecessor entity and the law firm relating to the company's environmental compliance. For that law firm to oppose the former corporate client would risk using the privileged information against that client.

See also, Detter v. Schreiber, 610 N.W.2d 13 (Neb.2000) (lawyer who represented two clients forming a corporation may not represent one against the other when they have a falling out).

2.   Should the current medical malpractice case and the former adoption proceeding discussed in this Problem be held to be "substantially related" matters?

a.   The legal issues in the two cases are not likely to be the same. If they had been, some cases would say they could be considered substantially related even though the facts differ. See, e.g., Government of India v. Cook Industries, Inc., 569 F.2d 737 (2d Cir.1978) (cases substantially related because both involved short-weight shipping of grain, albeit in different factual settings); State v. Barnett, 965 P.2d 323 (N.M.App.1998) (defendant in a burglary recognized prosecutor as former Public Defender who represented him when he pled guilty to charges of a different burglary three years earlier: "Defendant had a right to disqualify the prosecuting attorney because she previously represented him in a substantially related matter").

b.   The touchstone in most cases is whether the lawyer received relevant confidential information in the prior representation. In making this determination, courts often apply factors such as those articulated in H.F. Ahmanson & Co. v. Salomon Bros., Inc., 280 Cal.Rptr. 614 (Ct.App. 1991): (1) the factual similarity of the cases, (2) their legal similarity, and (3) the extent of the lawyer's involvement in the cases. The fact that firm members testify they do not presently remember anything about the prior representation is ordinarily *not* a relevant factor.

c.   Marten v. Yellow Freight System, Inc., 1996 WL 568840 (D.Kan. 1996), involved a lawyer who had given an employment discrimination seminar to management personnel of a company. Later, she tried to represent employees in an employment dispute with the company. The court assumed that the previous seminar constituted "representation" of the company, but it found the current work was not substantially related to the seminar. Even though it involved the same area of law, the lawyer had not received confidential information about company policies in the course of giving a seminar on the general state of the law and thus should not now be disqualified.

d.   National Medical Enterprises v. Godbey, 924 S.W.2d 123 (Tex. 1996), on the other hand, disqualified a law firm in a damage suit against a chain of psychiatric hospitals because one of its lateral hires had previously represented one of the hospitals' administrators in a criminal case arising out of the same facts. The lawyer in question had never represented the hospital itself, but he had expressly promised to keep confidential the corporate information he had learned while representing the administrator. In addition, the information turned up by the firm in the tort case could lead to the filing of new criminal charges against the administrator who was clearly a former client.

e. Cardona v. General Motors Corp., 939 F.Supp. 351 and 942 F.Supp. 968 (D.N.J.1996) involved firms who specialized in so-called "lemon law" cases involving allegedly defective cars. The small firm that represented hundreds of lemon law plaintiffs hired a lawyer who had defended hundreds of lemon law cases on behalf of General Motors. To GM, that disloyalty violated Rule 1.9 even though the plaintiffs in the cases the lawyer would work on now were all different from the parties in the cases he had defended. The court agreed that while every car and every "lemon" was different, there was a factual nexus running through the cases that made it very likely confidential knowledge of General Motors' approach to the cases would be important in the lawyer's new job. The court held that the cases were substantially related and ordered disqualification.

3. Suppose Heath knows no crucial secrets (e.g. that Abraham operates while intoxicated), but she does have general impressions of Abraham's personality and specific knowledge of his financial situation. Could that make the cases "substantially related"?

a. In Chugach Electric Association v. United States District Court, 370 F.2d 441 (9th Cir.1966), cert.denied 389 U.S. 820, 88 S.Ct. 40, 19 L.Ed.2d 71 (1967), the attorney was general counsel and later a consultant to Chugach. The Board of Directors of the Company was divided on many issues and when a minority of the Board gained control and became a majority, the attorney resigned. The attorney later represented the trustee in bankruptcy of a coal company and sued Chugach claiming an antitrust conspiracy because of alleged agreements and overt acts occurring after the attorney severed any connection with Chugach. The court disqualified the attorney. "The problem here is not limited to the question whether [the attorney] was connected with petitioner as its counsel at the time agreements were reached and overt acts taken, but includes the question whether, as attorney, he was in a position to acquire knowledge casting light on the purpose of later acts and agreements. * * * A likelihood here exists which cannot be disregarded that [the attorney's] knowledge of private matters gained in confidence would provide him with greater insight and understanding of the significance of subsequent events in an antitrust context and offer a promising source of discovery." Id. at 443.

b. In Franzoni v. Hart Schaffner & Marx, 726 N.E.2d 719 (Ill.Ct.App. 2000), plaintiff's counsel in an age discrimination and retaliatory discharge case had served for 14 years as the defendant's in-house counsel. Some years earlier, on behalf of the company, the lawyer had negotiated a settlement with Plaintiff of another case and had worked on over 580 employment-related matters for all divisions of the company. The court found the lawyer was "privy to the secrets and confidences of [the company]" as it related to cases like the current one. Further, executives he might be required to depose or cross-examine were persons with whom he had worked while at the company. Thus, the lawyer was disqualified.

c. In Mitchell v. Metropolitan Life Ins. Co., 2002 WL 441194 (S.D.N.Y.2002), plaintiffs sued their former employer for gender-based employment discrimination. Fleishman, a partner at one of two firms hired by the plaintiffs, had previously worked at a different firm and defended MetLife in a variety of products liability suits over a period of several years. The court disqualified Fleishman's current firm. First, the scope of Fleishman's prior representation of MetLife exposed her to matters that would be at issue in the instant case. For instance, Fleishman defended MetLife against claims for unfair selling practices and interviewed several employees in the company's sales division. The plaintiffs in this case worked in that division and lodged their discrimination complaints against supervisors whom Fleishman had interviewed. Thus, the matters were substantially related even though the legal issues were much different. Fleishman learned "confidential" information that is "substantially related to disputed factual issues material to the resolution of the present action."

d. However, Unified Sewerage Agency v. Jelco Inc., 646 F.2d 1339 (9th Cir.1981), refused to disqualify a law firm even though it had earlier gained general "information and insights from Jelco about such things as Jelco's institutional attitudes towards negotiation and settlement and Jelco's method of doing business." 646 F.2d at 1349. The law firm did "not have access to any specific information that would help [it] prevail against Jelco (other than general information concerning the personality of a client, which is always helpful in later suits against that client)." 646 F.2d at 1351. The court also found that the party seeking disqualification had earlier consented and thus waived its rights.

e. State ex rel. Wal–Mart Stores v. Kortum, 559 N.W.2d 496 (Neb. 1997), was a suit for damages from a fall in the store's parking lot. The lawyer had previously defended the store in a claim for a fall inside the store and in so doing had received access to Wal–Mart's policies and general defense strategy. The court said the fact the pleadings in the two cases were similar was not controlling. Similarly, the Wal–Mart procedures were common knowledge and the policies manuals were discoverable. Thus, neither represented truly confidential information. The court concluded that the cases were not substantially related. See also, ABA Formal Opinion 99–415 (Sept. 8, 1999) ("general knowledge of the strategies, policies, or personnel of the former employer" not sufficient to justify disqualification).

4. Should cases be deemed "substantially related" if, although the factual issues in two or more cases are closely related, the problem of confidentiality is not presented?

a. Allegaert v. Perot, 565 F.2d 246 (2d Cir.1977), was a bankruptcy case. Law Firm had earlier represented a joint venture consisting of

Company A and Company B. Company B was now bankrupt. Law Firm wanted to represent Company A in the bankruptcy proceeding but the trustee for Company B was opposed. Law Firm was obviously closely involved with the factual issues relating to the joint venture, the court held, but there was no reasonable expectation that the facts it learned would be kept confidential from Company *A*. Thus the "substantial relation" test was not met. "[B]efore the substantial relationship test is even implicated, it must be shown that the attorney was in a position where he *could* have received information which his former client might reasonably have assumed the attorney would withhold from his present client." 565 F.2d at 250 (emphasis in original).

   b. Strasbourger Pearson Tulcin Wolff, Inc. v. Wiz Technology, 82 Cal.Rptr.2d 326 (Ct.App.1999), reached the same result. The Stroock firm was counsel to Strasbourger, the underwriter for Wiz's public stock offering. It was also counsel to Coopers & Lybrand, Wiz's auditors. When Strasbourger sued Wiz for allegedly selling unregistered stock, Wiz tried to disqualify Stroock on the ground that it had learned confidential information while representing the underwriter and auditor and that Wiz had paid Stroock's fees. The court rejected that analysis. It is standard practice for the issuer to pay the underwriter's legal fees, the court said, but that does not make the issuer a client. Further, Stroock's due diligence work was done for Strasbourger, not Wiz, and what it learned there and in work for Coopers & Lybrand did not involve information Stroock was required to keep confidential from either of them. Disqualification thus was not appropriate.

   c. Restatement Third, The Law Governing Lawyers § 132, Comment *i*, created the concept of an "accommodation client" to deal with cases like these in which the lawyer clearly represented one client but agreed to act for the benefit of another as well in a setting in which confidentiality between the clients was not expected. The lawyer, as an accommodation to the existing client, will represent another "typically for a limited purpose in order to avoid duplication of services and consequent higher fees." When the interests of the two later differ, the Comment says, the lawyer may not continue to represent both, but she may continue to represent the original client even contrary to the interest of the client that had been "accommodated." The typical circumstances that warrant the inference that the "accommodation client" understood and consented, at least impliedly, to the lawyer's continuing to represent the regular client are that "the lawyer has represented the regular client on for a long period of time before undertaking representation of the other client, that the representation was to be of limited scope and duration, and that the lawyer was not expected to keep confidential from the regular client any information provided to the lawyer by the other client."

   d. In re Rite Aid Corp. Securities Litigation, 139 F.Supp.2d 649 (E.D.Pa.2001), applied the accommodation client principle in a securities action filed against the Rite Aid Corporation and some of its directors and officers. Ballard Spahr, long-time company counsel, represented all of the defendants, including Grass, the former CEO, from the time the suit commenced. Grass then resigned from Rite–Aid, and other director-defendants retained other lawyers to represent them, but Ballard Spahr continued to represent the corporation. When new corporate management directed the firm to attempt to settle with the plaintiffs, a settlement agreement was reached under which the plaintiffs preserved their claims against Grass. In this motion, Grass sought to disqualify Ballard Spahr from settling with the rest of the defendants, arguing that the firm had taken a position adverse to his interests as a client without obtaining consent. The court denied the motion. First, the court said, from the beginning, the corporation had been the primary client and Grass's interests were secondary. Furthermore, Grass left the company after the litigation had started; the conflict of interest was created by his act. Next, the court held that representing Grass was simply an accommodation and that Ballard Spahr had agreed with Rite–Aid that, if a conflict arose between Rite–Aid and Grass, it would continue to represent Rite–Aid. The court held that by using the corporation's counsel at all, Grass effectively consented to this provision of the engagement.

C. OTHER SITUATIONS IN WHICH MODEL RULE 1.9 MAY REQUIRE DISQUALIFICATION

1. **Assume that Martha Heath had not represented Dr. Abraham in any earlier malpractice case, but she had represented a codefendant in such a case. Should that bar her from taking the current case against Dr. Abraham?**

a. Does Rule 1.9 apply to the co-defendant situation? See Wilson P. Abraham Const. Corp. v. Armco Steel Corp., 559 F.2d 250 (5th Cir.1977), and Kevlik v. Goldstein, 724 F.2d 844 (1st Cir.1984), holding that the lawyer must be disqualified because confidences are shared in such a common defense.

b. In GTE North Inc. v. Apache Products Co., 914 F.Supp. 1575 (N.D.Ill.1996), there had been a "joint investigation agreement" (JIA) under which separately represented firms shared the costs of determining responsibility for waste at a Superfund site. Later, counsel for one potential defendant undertook representation of a claimant suing a different defendant who had been part of the JIA for the same site. The court found that each JIA member was an "implied client" of the firm and consequently ordered disqualification.

c. ABA Ethics Opinion 95–395 (July 24, 1995) asked whether a lawyer who had once represented one member of a joint insurance-defense consortium might take on a related case against one of the other insurer-members. Relevant confidential information learned from the prior client clearly could not be disclosed, the Committee said, and the lawyer could not act contrary to the interest of his own former client. If the lawyer knows no relevant confidences, and if the new case is not contrary to the interests of the prior client, or if the prior client waives its rights, there is no per se prohibition, but the new client should know these limitations and be told of any implications they may have for the lawyer's role in the present case.

d. Colorpix Systems of America v. Broan Mfg. Co., 131 F.Supp.2d 331 (D.Conn.2001), applied a similar analysis to determine when representation of a parent company in a prior case would bar later representation against a subsidiary. The plaintiffs alleged two fires were caused by defective bathroom exhaust fans made by Broan. The plaintiff's law firm had represented Broan's parent company, Nortek, in an earlier case of the same kind. First, the court noted that Broan shared the same legal department with Nortek, and Broan and Nortek had developed a common strategy for defending cases such as these. Then, in order to determine whether Broan had been a "vicarious client" of R & C in the prior case (and thus could be said to be a former client in this case), the court asked (1) whether the current litigation will have a financial impact on the former client, Nortek; (2) the importance that the former client has attached to the current litigation against its subsidiary in terms of supervision; and (3) whether the affiliated companies share an "identity of interest." In this case, Broan accounted for a substantial share of Nortek's business, Nortek's general counsel had supervised Broan's defense in the present action, and Broan and Nortek share an "identity of interest" because they share a legal department and business philosophy. Thus, disqualification was required.

2. Suppose that, while doing discovery in her earlier representation of Dr. Abraham's co-defendant, Heath had learned something about a different patient of that doctor—the patient's tendency to alcoholism, for example. Could Heath use that information in a suit against that other patient on behalf of a current client?

a. Look at Model Rule 1.9(c). Notice that, quite apart from whether two matters are the same or substantially related, a lawyer may not use or reveal information acquired in a prior representation contrary to the interest of the former client unless the information has become generally known.

b. The point being made in the current question is that the former client—the doctor—has a duty to protect the confidentiality of his patients' medical information. While defending him, Martha Heath learned information about his prior cases subject to that confidentiality obligation. Thus, it would be contrary to the interest and obligation of the former client to have the information used by Heath in a current case.

c. Restatement Third, The Law Governing Lawyers § 132, Comment *g(ii)*, Illustration 7 explains:

> "Lawyer has represented Hospital in several medical-malpractice cases. In the course of preparing to defend one such case, Lawyer reviewed the confidential medical file of Patient who was not a party in the action. From the file, Lawyer learned that Patient had been convicted of a narcotics offense in another jurisdiction. Patient is now a material witness for the defense in an unrelated case that Lawyer has

filed on behalf of Plaintiff. Adequate representation of Plaintiff would require Lawyer to cross-examine Patient about the narcotics conviction in an effort to undermine Patient's credibility. Lawyer may not reveal information about Patient that Hospital has an obligation to keep confidential. That limitation in turn may preclude effective representation of Plaintiff in the pending case."

    d.   Does recognition of this obligation make sense to you?

    3. Suppose Heath recently filed a class action on behalf of all the residents of her city against a local department store alleging systematic overcharging of interest on past due accounts. Would Heath now be prohibited from representing the department store suing a customer who happened to be a member of the former class for failure to pay a department store bill?

    a.   Because of the many members of a represented class and the lack of confidential information acquired by the class action lawyer about any one of them, typically a lawyer is not barred from proceeding in a later action against such a former class member. See ABA Model Rule 1.7, Comment [25].

    b.   Fuchs v. Schick, 2002 WL 538842 (S.D.N.Y.2002), was an exception to that principle because of its exceptional facts. Fuchs sued Schick for selling partnership units in a Marriott hotel venture at a price that exceeded the market value for the units. The lawyer that Fuchs wanted to represent him had previously represented Schick when he was a plaintiff in a similar class action suit against Marriott. In that suit, Schick had served as the head of a committee of plaintiffs and, as such, had conversations with lawyers for the class regarding the purchase and sale of the partnership units. That prior relationship with those lawyers led the court to reject the motion of Fuchs' counsel to be admitted pro hac vice. Schick had not been a passive class member, the court said, and thus it was fair to say that his former counsel, who secured secret information from Schick in that earlier case would now be appearing against him in a substantially related matter.

    4. Suppose that, instead of a lawyer who has represented the plaintiff changing firms, it is that lawyer's non-lawyer assistant, e.g., a secretary or paralegal, who does so. Does Model Rule 1.9 have anything to say about that situation?

    a.   Rule 1.9 only talks of lawyers, but Model Rule 1.10, Comment [4] says that people like paralegals ordinarily must be screened. The leading case on the issue is Herron v. Jones, 637 S.W.2d 569 (Ark.1982), holding that disqualification of the new firm is required unless the secretary is "walled off" or "screened" from work on the case for the new firm.[4]

---

4. Although requirements that someone be "screened" are usually applied to lawyers, and the ABA Model Rules' definition of "screened" speaks of the isolation of a "lawyer," the requirements for such a "screen" described in new ABA Model Rule 1.0(k) and Comments [8]–[10] to Rule 1.0 would presumably apply to the screening of non-lawyers as well.

b.   In re Complex Asbestos Litigation, 283 Cal.Rptr. 732 (Ct.App. 1991), upheld the disqualification of a law firm representing plaintiffs in asbestos claims because it had hired a paralegal who had worked for one of the defense firms on similar cases. The danger of misuse of defense confidences was too great given the lack of screening from participation in asbestos matters.

c.   In re American Home Products, 985 S.W.2d 68 (Tex.1998), concerned disqualification of a law firm that had hired a legal assistant who had worked for counsel for one of the defendants in the Norplant litigation. She billed 72.5 hours interviewing potential witnesses, meeting with counsel, investigating plaintiffs, and writing memoranda about how witnesses might be used. Counsel for the plaintiffs then hired her, and the defendant moved to disqualify that firm. The Texas Supreme Court ordered disqualification. It was not improper to hire an opposing firm's legal assistant, but it was improper not to screen her. Indeed, where she was assigned to work on the very case she had researched for the other side, disqualification was required. The court did not automatically disqualify plaintiffs' co-counsel, but it might have done so if co-counsel had jointly prepared the case for trial or otherwise could be presumed to have shared the legal assistant's tainted information. But see, Phoenix Founders, Inc. v. Marshall, 887 S.W.2d 831 (Tex.1994) (firm not disqualified where paralegal had worked only 0.6 hours looking for a pleading and had been screened at the new firm).

d.   However, Zimmerman v. Mahaska Bottling Co., 19 P.3d 784 (Kan. 2001), rejects the usual rule that a secretary that moves from one law firm to another may be screened at all. In this case, the secretary had not worked for anyone connected with the case, although lawyers at the former firm had talked about it in front of her. The court concluded that the secretary acquired material and confidential information regarding the personal injury suit while working for plaintiff's lawyers, and thus the court disqualified the defendants' firm where the secretary began working after leaving plaintiff's firm. If the secretary had been a lawyer moving from one firm to the other, she would have been disqualified in spite of screening, the court said, and there was no reason to treat non-lawyers differently. The court observed: "a majority of courts have rejected screening because of the uncertainty regarding the effectiveness of the screen, the monetary incentive involved in breaching the screen, the fear of disclosing privileged information in the course of proving an effective screen, and the possibility of accidental disclosures."

See also, First Miami Securities, Inc. v. Sylvia, 780 So.2d 250 (Fla.App. 2001) (holding that screening is not a valid alternative if the legal secretary has "actual knowledge" of material confidences instead of merely being "exposed" to this information, and then remanding for a hearing).

5.   Bring the facts closer to home. Suppose you, a law student, worked on a case for Firm A between your first and second years in law school but work for opposing counsel, Firm B, the next summer. Should that disqualify Firm B from continuing in the

case? Must you be screened from participation in the matter that you worked on at Firm A?

a. Allen v. Academic Games Leagues of America, Inc., 831 F.Supp. 785 (C.D.Cal.1993), was a suit for trademark and copyright infringement brought by a maker of educational games. While a law student, Wright had been a competitor, had served on the plaintiff's advisory committee, and had even tried to help settle this lawsuit. Once he became a lawyer, he went to work for the firm that represented the defendant and participated actively in that defense. Because Wright had been a law student at the earlier time, the plaintiff was not his "former client", the court held, but Wright had a duty to protect the plaintiff's confidential information. To prevent a violation of that duty, his law firm was disqualified from continuing to represent the defendant.

b. In Actel v. Quicklogic, 1996 WL 297045 (N.D.Cal.1996), an associate in the firm representing the plaintiff had worked a split-summer for the firm defending a case while he was in law school. When interviewed by the plaintiff's firm, he said he had no memory of working on the case. Later he said that he remembered nothing substantive about the case, but his time records showed he spent two hours working on a memorandum and "reading the case file." The court found these facts raised a presumption that the student, now a lawyer, had received and shared confidential information. Given that his new firm neither screened the lawyer nor overcame the presumption of shared confidential information, the court disqualified the plaintiff's firm.

c. Do these cases give you pause? Why should law firms be able to screen law students and lawyers who obtained their disqualifying information before becoming lawyers? Notice that Comment [4] to Model Rule 1.10 expressly adopts this rule.

Restatement Third, The Law Governing Lawyers § 123, Comment f, says that law clerks "typically have limited responsibilities and thus might acquire little sensitive information. Absent special circumstances, they should be considered nonlawyer employees for the purposes" of imputing their knowledge to others in the law firm. On the other hand, "[p]ersons who have completed their legal education and are awaiting admission to practice at the time of providing services to a client of a law firm typically have duties comparable to admitted lawyers and accordingly should ordinarily be treated as lawyers for purposes of imputation."

d. Do you agree with this approach to law student conflicts? Would any other rule make it too risky for firms, particularly large firms, to hire students during law school? Should placement concerns be relevant where issues of ethical conduct are at stake?

6. What about "lawyer-temporaries" engaged by a law firm for a limited period of time, either directly or through a placement agency. Should they be treated as any other lawyers for purposes of imputing disqualification?

a.   Functionally, a "temp" looks a lot like a law student or other non-lawyer. Temps may work on a single matter or on several different matters. Sometimes, they may simultaneously work on matters for other firms. Firms typically hire temporaries to meet short–term staffing needs or to supply special expertise on a particular matter. On the other hand, they are not non-lawyers; they are licensed to practice law.

b.   ABA Formal Opinion 88–356 (Dec. 16, 1988) said that Model Rules 1.7 and 1.9 govern such lawyers. For example, under Rule 1.7, a temporary lawyer may not personally work simultaneously on matters for clients of different firms if the work for each is directly adverse to the other.

c.   Are temporary lawyers "associated" with a firm for purposes of the *imputed* disqualification sections of Rule 1.10? The Opinion concluded that the answer must be determined by a functional analysis of the facts and circumstances involved.

> "Ultimately, whether a temporary lawyer is treated as being 'associated with a firm' while working on a matter for the firm depends on whether the nature of the relationship is such that the temporary lawyer has access to information relating to the representation of firm clients other than the client on whose matters the lawyer is working and the consequent risk of improper disclosure or misuse of information relating to representation of other clients of the firm."

d.   What do these examples suggest to you about the general duty of a law firm to supervise the handling of confidential information by its professional and support employees? Look at Model Rules 5.1 & 5.3.

D.   ACCESS TO THE WORK PRODUCT OF DISQUALIFIED COUNSEL

1. If Dr. Abraham's motion were granted and Heath were disqualified, should substituted counsel have access to Heath's work product?

a.   Should the rule depend on why the lawyer was disqualified? For example, if the court disqualifies the lawyer because the lawyer knew material confidences, and transferring the work product would transfer the confidences, then the rule should bar the transfer. But if the work product was not tainted by the confidential information, why should new counsel not be entitled to it?

b.   In First Wisconsin Mortgage Trust v. First Wisconsin Corp., 584 F.2d 201 (7th Cir.1978) (en banc), the majority held that there is no per se rule against subsequent counsel's use of work product developed by disqualified counsel. Thus, unless there is evidence of "improper advantage" having been secured, "such as the use of confidential information," it is an abuse of discretion for the trial court to prevent the turning over of the work product. The work product at issue in that case was an analysis of loan files conducted by a team of 15 lawyers for more than a year prior to the ultimate disqualification of the firm. The majority thought the loan file summaries to be "the result of routine lawyer work of a type which any competent lawyer, by spending the substantial time which would be required, could accomplish just as well as did [the disqualified counsel]." 584 F.2d at 204. Accord, IBM Corp. v. Levin, 579 F.2d 271 (3d Cir.1978).

c. In re EPIC Holdings, Inc., 28 S.W.3d 511 (Tex.2000), was a case in which the court had earlier disqualified the plaintiff's first firm. Some of that firm's members had been at the firm that had incorporated the defendant company and thus they could have received relevant confidential information. Now, the disqualified firm sought to prevent plaintiff's new counsel from using the former counsel's work product. The firm was afraid that defendant could later accuse it of turning over confidential information and wanted to assure it had a defense to that charge. The Texas Supreme Court refused to prohibit use of all such work product. First, "when an attorney is disqualified, successor counsel is presumptively entitled to obtain the pleadings, discovery, correspondence and all other materials in the public record or exchanged by the parties." As for other material, the court created a rebuttable presumption that the work product contained confidential information. There were three dissents.

2. How can the new lawyer demonstrate that no confidential information is included in the material being used?

a. Is the theoretical ability to use the work product merely a mirage? The dissent in *First Wisconsin* accused the majority of "attempting to draw fine ethical lines based upon the specific content of the objectionable material," an approach "which has been repeatedly condemned. * * * [T]he majority further compounds its error by intimating that once the defendants have disclaimed the use of confidential information, the former client is the one who must point to the confidences used in the work." In camera inspection of the work product, the dissenters argued, would be "both unworkable and a dangerous departure from long-accepted ethical guidelines." 584 F.2d at 211–13.

b. Similar arguments were made by the dissenters in *EPIC Holdings*. The majority, however, outlined standards for determining whether the material contained or reflected confidential information of the defendant. The subject matter of the work product is relevant, e.g., factual information or legal research, the court said. So is its nature, i.e., lawyer notes or deposition transcripts. The trial judge should inspect the materials in camera if the answer is not obvious.

c. Who has the better of the argument on this issue? The right to such work product will not be worth fighting about if the litigation costs outweigh the cost of redoing the work. Thus, the client may wind up paying twice for discovery of the information.

PROBLEM 15

IMPUTED DISQUALIFICATION

Ever since Problem 9, we have assumed that if one lawyer in a law firm has a conflict of interest, every lawyer in the firm is treated as having such a conflict. Thus, if one lawyer in a firm formerly represented the plaintiff in a law suit, another lawyer in the firm may not now represent the defendant even if the respective lawyers worked in offices in different cities. Not all conflicts are imputed,[5] but many are, and that obviously creates a very important limit on the operation of law firms. In this Problem we look at particular issues that arise in administration of the principle. We first ask how the principle applies in firms and organizations other than traditional firms. Next, we ask to how many firms in any single case the reach of the rule might extend. We then ask whether the same principle should impute conflicts among family members who practice law in different firms, and finally, we ask whether "screening" the conflicted lawyer should be sufficient to overcome the force of the rule.

FACTS

Charles & Burls (C & B) is a prestigious, 200–person Wall Street firm with a national clientele. It represents World Wide Container Corp. in many matters, one of which is a suit by National Gasket Co. against World Wide for contribution in a products liability case. The case is to be tried in New Orleans, and C & B is cooperating with Willis & Xeres (W & X), the law firm that World Wide uses as local counsel in New Orleans.

Willis of W & X is the only lawyer in that firm actively working on the case. His only role is to file papers, motions, and other pleadings forwarded to him by C & B. National Gasket has now moved to disqualify both C & B and W & X from acting as World Wide's lawyers because Xeres (while he had been in a solo practice before forming W & X) had represented National Gasket in various product liability matters arising out of the same facts that led to the present suit. Xeres learned confidential information that, if disclosed, would be useful to World Wide's defense of the present suit. C & B has never represented National Gasket.

QUESTIONS

A.   IMPUTATION OF CONFLICTS THROUGHOUT A LAW FIRM

1.   May Willis continue to act as local counsel for World Wide?

a.   Look at Model Rule 1.10(a). We know from Problem 14 that Xeres could not represent World Wide because of his previous representation of National Gasket in a matter substantially related to the present matter. What reasons justify a sweeping disqualification of everyone in Xeres' firm?

---

5. Note that the general imputation rule, Rule 1.10(a), imputes only Rules 1.7 and 1.9. Rule 1.8(k) makes clear that all of that Rule is imputed except Rule 1.8(j), dealing with sexual relations with a client. Rule 3.7(b) makes clear that the provisions of Rule 3.7(a) are not imputed unless the lawyer is also covered under Rules 1.7 or 1.9. And Rule 1.10(d) recognizes that Rule 1.11 has special rules for imputation involving former government lawyers.

b. Should disqualification turn on whether Willis has learned any relevant confidential information from Xeres? Could Xeres properly disclose any such information to Willis, whether or not the firm was involved in this lawsuit? Remember that Xeres learned the information while working somewhere else. Why shouldn't the law simply assume that Xeres will comply with his duties of loyalty and confidentiality and let the other W & X lawyers work on the case?

c. W.E. Bassett Co. v. H.C. Cook Co., 201 F.Supp. 821 (D.Conn.1961), aff'd per curiam 302 F.2d 268 (2d Cir.1962), was one of the early cases establishing the clear and sweeping imputation rule. Lawyer X had represented the plaintiff in a lengthy case. X then joined a firm—one member of which had once represented and advised a corporate defendant on some important issues in the same controversy. The lawyers in X's new firm agreed that X would continue to represent the plaintiff corporation in the matter, but without any participation by X's new partners in either the work or the fees. But when the district court learned of this plan, it *sua sponte* held a hearing on the disqualification of X. The court found X's partners and X "made every effort to comply with Canons 6 and 37 [of the 1908 ABA Canons of Ethics as amended] as they honestly interpreted them," but the circumstances "will inevitably lead to suspicion and distrust in them in the minds of the defendants and the opportunity for misunderstanding on the part of the public. * * * " 201 F.Supp. at 825. Thus, the court required X to cease all further participation in the case.

2. Should conflicts that are "personal" to a given lawyer be imputed throughout a firm?

a. Look at new ABA Model Rule 1.10(a) and Comment [3]. Note that, ordinarily, the Rules do not impute "personal" interest conflicts. Assume that Lawyer A in a criminal defense firm objects to defending persons charged with rape because of strongly held moral or political beliefs. His objection is such that he could not do a competent job. Clearly, Lawyer A may not take that case because to do so would violate Rule 1.1. But if the law firm excuses Lawyer A from working on such cases, should Lawyer A's disqualification be imputed to other members of the firm?

b. Restatement Third, The Law Governing Lawyers § 123 and § 125, Comment *g*, were written when Model Rule 1.10(a) did not have the "personal interest" exception. Thus, they restated the law as imputing such conflicts but suggested that the rule should not apply where "the personal interest conflict [of Lawyer A] was not known to the [other] lawyer handling the matter and could not have been determined by use of a reasonable conflict-checking system." Comment *g* also says that one should not impute "idiosyncratic" personal interests. For example, if Lawyer has "strong philosophical or political aversion" to the objectives of Landlord, Lawyer B in the same firm can represent Landlord as "as long as Lawyer A has no part in the representation and no supervisory or other control over Lawyer B * * * ." Restatement § 125, Comment *g*, Illustration 7.

   c. Should personal interest conflicts be imputed to others in the firm? Should it matter whether the lawyer with the strong beliefs is a new associate or the firm's influential senior partner?

3. How should courts approach the question of imputation outside the traditional law firm setting?

   a. How should one define "firm" for purposes of Rule 1.10? See Rule 1.10, Comment [1] and Rule 1.0(c). For example, should strict imputation be required if opposing parties are both clients of a legal aid office? That is, if one legal aid lawyer represents the plaintiff, may another represent the defendant? See Rule 1.10, Comment [1]. Some argue that, unlike a private law firm, a "government-financed organization of lawyers does not receive any compensation directly from its clients; therefore, a legal aid attorney has no economic interest in a client represented by a colleague in the same office." In addition, the "attorneys in a legal aid service are not associated for the practice of law in the same sense that private law firm members are associated. Legal aid operates solely as a nonprofit, public benefit organization."[1]

   b. Should that distinction be controlling? What problems are raised if the legal aid lawyers are part of a single office? Flores v. Flores, 598 P.2d 893 (Alaska 1979), said that a state must supply private counsel to one party where the legal services agency's internal procedures were inadequate to guarantee confidentiality to both. See also Restatement Third, The Law Governing Lawyers § 123, Comment *d(v)*, to the same effect.

   c. Does the same analysis apply to dual representation by a Public Defender's Office? The Chief Public Defender of a state asked for an ABA Ethics Opinion as to whether the Public Defender Department could represent two criminal defendants in the same case with conflicting interests. Public Defender office in City 1 had 16 lawyers and Public Defender office in City 2 had 5 lawyers. The Committee ruled that there was a conflict. If one public defender in City 1 is disqualified, then all those in City 1 are disqualified; and since the Public Defender Department is "subject to the common control" of the Chief Public Defender, both offices in City 1 and City 2 are disqualified. The Ethics Committee offered no reason and merely cited DR 5–105(D). ABA Informal Opinion 1418 (1978). Accord, Commonwealth v. Westbrook, 400 A.2d 160 (Pa.1979) (members of public defender's office are members of the "same firm" for conflict of interest purposes). This Opinion and the case are decades old. Are they relevant under the law today?

   d. In United States v. Reynoso, 6 F.Supp.2d 269 (S.D.N.Y.1998), the Federal Defender Division of the Legal Aid Society assigned Lawyer #1 to represent Reynoso. Four years earlier, another lawyer (Lawyer #2), while in private practice and now also in the Federal Defender Division, had represented Vasquez in another trial. Vasquez was now a potential govern-

---

   1. Note, Professional Responsibility— Conflicts of Interest Between Legal Aid Law- yers, 37 Mo.L.Rev. 346, 349 (1972).

ment witness against Reynoso. The government argued that Lawyer #2 should be disqualified from cross-examining his former client about the very matter that was the subject of the former representation. The court agreed. The government argued that Lawyer #2's disqualification should be imputed to Lawyer #1, but the court disagreed and refused to impute disqualification within the Federal Defender Division. The lawyers had no common financial interest in the cases, they did not talk about the cases, and the files in the earlier case had been sent to storage. The Federal Defender Division should not be treated as a private law firm.

e. Which result do you think reflects a better understanding of the purposes of imputing the disqualification of one lawyer to other lawyers in an organization?

4. How should disqualification be imputed within a prosecutor's office?

a. State ex rel. Eidson v. Edwards, 793 S.W.2d 1 (Tex.Crim.App. 1990), considered whether an entire prosecutor's office should be disqualified because a new assistant prosecutor had previously represented the defendant. Indeed, the new prosecutor had interviewed the defendant, potential witnesses, and acted as lead defense counsel at the preliminary hearing. The court held, however, that prosecutors' offices are different from private law firms. The former defense lawyer obviously could not try the case, but his disqualification would not be imputed to the office.

b. Turbin v. Arizona Superior Court, 797 P.2d 734 (Ariz.Ct.App.1990) reached the opposite result. There, too, the lawyer had interviewed the defendant and witnesses and had negotiated with the prosecutor before withdrawing and joining the prosecutor's staff. There, too, it was conceded that he discussed the case with no one while at the prosecutor's office, but this court believed that the appearance of impropriety required that the whole office be disqualified when the lawyer had been this involved in the defendant's representation. See also, Matter of Ockrassa, 799 P.2d 1350 (Ariz.1990), imposing discipline on a lawyer who moved from the defense to the prosecutor's office.

c. However, Restatement Third, The Law Governing Lawyers § 123, Comment *d(iii)*, says that "if the [prosecutor's] office is operated so as to avoid material risk that confidential information will be inadequately safeguarded," imputation should not be inevitable. And State ex rel. Romley v. Superior Court, 908 P.2d 37 (Ariz.Ct.App.1995), held that if the disqualified prosecutor is screened from participation in a matter, the court need not disqualify the whole Maricopa County prosecutor's office.

d. With which of these approaches do you agree? Are courts justifiably concerned that states not wind up in a situation in which no persons will be available to prosecute criminal defendants if courts impose strict imputation?

5. **Should there be imputation among private lawyers who share office space but not fees?**

a. In Great Britain, chambers of barristers are not partnerships. Each barrister is an independent lawyer, and it is possible for one barrister in the chambers to be prosecuting a case that another is defending. America has not copied the barrister model, but there are many instances of lawyers who are not partners sharing offices, sharing a library, and even sharing secretarial staff. If one lawyer is disqualified, should another lawyer in the same office suite be disqualified, even though they are not partners?

b. ABA Informal Opinion 1486 (1982) say it all depends. There should be no imputation if the lawyers "exercise reasonable care" to protect confidences of the clients. See also, Rule 1.0, Comment [2]. Restatement Third, The Law Governing Lawyers § 123, Comment *e*, is to the same effect. How would you organize such an office to assure that confidential information is appropriately protected? How should lawyers make clear to the world that they are not in the same firm, only in the same office.

B. PERSONS AND FIRMS TO WHICH IMPUTATION WILL EXTEND

1. If the court disqualifies the firm of W & X and all of its partners and associates, may C & B simply get new local counsel? Will the disqualification of W & X require that C & B be disqualified as well?

a. What reasons would justify such a result? Willis is presumed to know what Xeres knows, so should that presumption extend to C & B, the firm with which Willis regularly talks?

b. Is that result required by Model Rule 1.10(a), Comment [1]? Should W & X and C & B be considered one firm for purposes of the imputation rules? Rule 1.0, Comment [3] recognizes that some corporations are "affiliated" with other corporations. Should a law firm ever be treated as "affiliated" with another firm?

c. ABA Formal Opinion 94–388 (Dec. 5, 1994) issued some useful warnings as it considered issues of "affiliations" between firms that are initiated and advertised to give a national scope to relatively small local firms. The Opinion notes that when firms suggest they are affiliated, they risk misleading a client into believing a small firm has more resources at its disposal than it really has. In addition, if two firms hold themselves out as a single firm, e.g., use a common name, they have long been held to be one for conflict purposes. While the Opinion refused to draw bright lines as to when relationships would require firms to be treated as one, it said it should be relevant whether the law firms have a "close and regular, continuing and semi-permanent" relationship.

d. Mustang Enterprises, Inc. v. Plug–In Storage Systems, Inc., 874 F.Supp. 881 (N.D.Ill.1995), expressly held that firms in different cities who hold themselves out as "affiliated" will be held to be one firm for conflicts purposes, just as lawyers who are "of counsel" to a firm regularly have their conflicts imputed to the firm.[2]

2. If Xeres' confidential knowledge about National Gasket is imputed to Sandra Jones, an associate at W & X, and then Jones leaves to join a second firm, what does Model Rule 1.9(b) say about whether her new firm will also be disqualified?

a. American Can Co. v. Citrus Feed Co., 436 F.2d 1125 (5th Cir.1971), is the leading case on the point. The Fifth Circuit noted that: "All authorities agree that all members of a partnership are barred from participating in a case from which one partner is disqualified. * * * [O]nce a partner is thus vicariously disqualified for a particular case, the subsequent dissolution of the partnership cannot cure his ineligibility to act as counsel in that case. * * * However, new partners of a vicariously disqualified partner, to whom knowledge has been imputed during a former partnership, are not necessarily disqualified: they need show only that the vicariously disqualified partner's knowledge was imputed, not actual." The court was concerned that "imputation and consequent disqualification could continue *ad infinitum*," and that such a result is not needed "to maintain public confidence in the bar." 436 F.2d at 1129.

b. Essex Chemical Corp. v. Hartford Accident and Indemnity Co., 993 F.Supp. 241 (D.N.J.1998), involved an action filed by Essex seeking a declaration of insurance coverage for certain environmental claims. In 1988, Essex had retained Skadden Arps to fight off a takeover, and in that work, Skadden had learned confidential information about Essex. In this case, filed in 1993, Skadden appeared for Home Insurance, one of the defendants. The court found the confidences previously acquired were sufficient to disqualify Skadden, and in an earlier opinion, 975 F.Supp. 650 (D.N.J.1997), the Magistrate Judge had also disqualified the firms representing all the other defendants who were party to a joint defense agreement in the case. But the district court found the last step went too far. Citing *American Can*, it said sharing of the confidences with other firms

---

2. An "of counsel" designation is normally used to indicate that the person will assist in the legal matter but is not a partner attorney or an associate/employee in the firm. See ABA Opinion 90–357 (May 10, 1990), which states in part that the use of the title "of counsel" on letterheads, law lists, professional cards, notices, office signs and the like is "a holding out to the world at large about some general and continuing relationship between the lawyers and the law firms in question. A different use of the same term occurs when a lawyer (or firm) is designated as of counsel in filings in a particular case: in such circumstances there is no general holding out as to a continuing relationship, or as to a relationship that applies to anything but the individual case." A lawyer may be "of coun-sel" to more than one firm, and a firm may be "of counsel" to another firm. The Opinion concluded:

"There can be no doubt that an of counsel lawyer (or firm) is 'associated in' and has an 'association with' the firm (or firms) to which the lawyer is of counsel, for purposes of both the general imputation of disqualification pursuant to Rule 1.10 of the Model Rules and the imputation of disqualifications resulting from former government service under Rules 1.11(a) and 1.12(c); and is a lawyer *in* the firm for purposes of Rule 3.7(b), regarding the circumstances in which, when a lawyer is to be a witness in a proceeding, the lawyer's colleague may nonetheless represent the client in that proceeding."

was not to be presumed and ordered a hearing on the real nature of the joint defense work.

Do you agree with this analysis? Is it consistent with Model Rule 1.9(b)? Dicta in *American Can* says that the subsequent dissolution of the partnership cannot cure the conflict of the *vicariously* disqualified lawyer. Rule 1.9(b) rejects that conclusion. Which approach is preferable?

c. Adams v. Aerojet–General Corporation, 104 Cal.Rptr.2d 116 (Cal. Ct.App.2001), confirms that California law reaches the same result as Model Rule 1.9(b). Plaintiff's lawyer in an environmental case had formerly been at a firm that represented the defendant on environmental issues. The trial court disqualified the lawyer, presuming that he had learned the confidential information the firm had received. The Court of Appeals rejected such an automatic rule: a firm-switching attorney is not automatically disqualified, on the basis of imputed knowledge, from a case involving a client of a former law firm. The court remanded and concluded that the lawyer whose disqualification is sought should carry the burden of proving that he had no exposure to confidential information relevant to the current action while he was a member of the former firm. The trial court must review the lawyer's billing records or other evidence of what information he may have received.

d. In Frazier v. Superior Court, 118 Cal.Rptr.2d 129 (Cal.Ct.App. 2002), Frazier's insurer hired one firm, Murchison & Cumming (M & C) to defend it, and another, Hartley & Hartley (H & H) to defend Frazier individually. Subsequently, M & C became aware that the plaintiffs in the case had previously approached an attorney at a different M & C office about handling the claim. Although M & C never took the plaintiffs' case, it withdrew from representing the insurer, and the plaintiffs wanted to disqualify H & H as well based on the plaintiffs' prior contact with M & C. The court refused to make "double imputation" of the insights about the plaintiffs' case possibly obtained by one attorney at M & C, first to another attorney at M & C, and from there to lawyers at H & H. Because there was no evidence that attorneys at H & H had access to any confidential information obtained by the M & C attorney who initially met with the plaintiffs, the lawyers' certification that no confidential information had passed between them was sufficient to avoid disqualification.

3. Now suppose Xeres resigns from the firm of W & X. Will Willis still be disqualified from representing World Wide? *No*

a. What factual determination does Rule 1.10(b) require be made? Who should have the burden of proof on the question of what information was disclosed by Xeres before he left the firm? Would a hearing on that question ever consist of more than testimony about who told what to whom at W & X, testimony that the other side could neither challenge nor rebut?

b. Should the extent of imputation depend in part on how large a part the disqualified lawyer played in the earlier matter? In Silver Chrysler Plymouth, Inc. v. Chrysler Motors Corp., 518 F.2d 751 (2d Cir.1975), the court considered whether an attorney was disqualified from representing

1.9 know about this case, but did not accept it.
— So rule is not Silver Chrysler

an automobile dealer by reason of once having been an associate in the firm that represented the manufacturer. At that firm, he conceded he had worked on Chrysler matters. The court concluded, however, that the "cases and the Canons on which they are based are intended to protect the confidences of former clients when an attorney has been in a position to learn them." The court held that the attorney had rebutted the presumption that he had received significant confidential material when he was associated with the 80–member firm. The attorney's involvement—

> "was, at most, limited to brief, informal discussions on a procedural matter or research on a specific point of law. * * * [W]e do not believe that there is any basis for distinguishing between partners and associates on the basis of title alone—both are members of the bar and bound by the same Code of Professional Responsibility. But there is reason to differentiate for disqualification purposes between lawyers who become heavily involved in the facts of a particular matter and those who enter briefly on the periphery for a limited and specific purpose related solely to legal questions. In large firms at least, the former are normally the more seasoned lawyers and the latter the more junior." Id. at 756–57.

While purporting not to make a distinction between partners and associates, is the *Silver* case in effect making such a distinction? While neither the Model Rules not the Model Code distinguish between partners and associates, should they? Would a bright line test be appropriate?

c.   These issues are further illustrated by Novo Terapeutisk Laboratorium A/S v. Baxter Travenol Laboratories, Inc., 607 F.2d 186 (7th Cir.1979) (en banc). During July 1976, while at the Hume law firm, Attorney Cook spent 2 1/4 hours reviewing legal authorities and conferring with Baxter attorneys, during which time he received confidential information relating to a patent infringement matter. In December 1976, Cook left the Hume firm and took the Baxter account with him. In February 1977, plaintiff Novo filed a patent infringement action (substantially related to the July conference) against Baxter, and in August 1977, the Hume firm filed an appearance on behalf of Novo. The court readily agreed that on these facts Cook could not represent Novo, but that was not the issue; Cook was at a new firm and was still counsel for Baxter. The question was whether Cook's disqualification should be imputed to the other members of the Hume firm. "It is reasonable to presume that members of a law firm freely share their client's confidences with one another," but the circumstances of this case demonstrated that such a presumption need not be irrebuttable. Since Cook received the confidences, "he is in a position to know exactly what confidences he may have shared with others in his firm." He said he did not share any and the remaining members of the Hume firm submitted affidavits confirming that they did not receive any confidential information from Cook. The court thus refused to disqualify the Hume firm.

4.   In deciding these cases, should courts give weight to the fact that lawyers' movement from one position to another is very common these days?

a. City of Cleveland v. Cleveland Electric Illuminating Co., 440 F.Supp. 193, 211 (N.D.Ohio 1976), aff'd without published opinion 573 F.2d 1310 (6th Cir.1977), noted: "Imputing to an attorney in the private practice all confidential information obtained, or presumed to have been obtained, by other members of his law firm may severely limit the scope of the private attorney's future career and the effective operation of his firm, as well as the individual's right to legal counsel of choice." 440 F.Supp. at 210.[3]

b. Court of Appeals opinions following *Silver Chrysler Plymouth* include Gas–A–Tron of Arizona v. Union Oil Co. of California, 534 F.2d 1322 (9th Cir.1976) (per curiam), cert. denied 429 U.S. 861, 97 S.Ct. 164, 50 L.Ed.2d 139 (1976), and Schloetter v. Railoc of Indiana, Inc., 546 F.2d 706 (7th Cir.1976). In the latter, the court suggested:

> "a different result in *Gas–A–Tron* or *Silver Chrysler* might have severely restricted mobility within the legal profession. For law firms would be understandably reluctant to hire a young lawyer who had previously worked at a large firm if it were to mean full automatic disqualification from any case involving a party represented by the young lawyer's former employer." Id. at 712 n. 11.

c. What role do you think facilitation of lawyer mobility should play in conflicts analysis? Do you agree with Reardon v. Marlayne, 416 A.2d 852, 860 (N.J.1980), that "problems in the job market and mobility are not solved by loosening ethical standards required of the profession"?

C.   IMPUTATION WITHIN LAWYERS' FAMILIES

1. Assuming that Willis & Xeres may not represent World Wide in the case brought by National Gasket, may W & X suggest that World Wide go to the firm across the street in which Xeres' wife practices?

a. Why might there be reason for concern if Xeres' wife represents a client that her husband was prohibited from representing? If we presume that lawyers in a firm share confidential information, for example, what should we presume about lawyers in a marriage?

b. ABA Formal Opinion 340 (Sep. 23, 1975) addressed such questions and concluded:

> "It is not necessarily improper for husband-and-wife lawyers who are practicing in different offices or firms to represent differing inter-

---

3. The court also asserted a narrow, but now rarely followed test. "The * * * rule in the private practice of law should therefore limit the imputation of confidential disclosures, actual or presumed, to only those lawyers practicing in the attorney's area of concentration. Absent direct proof to the contrary, the attorney would not be deemed to have shared confidential information relating to matters and services exclusively within the sphere of representation of another department or section of his firm. This * * * rule is more acutely dramatized in the large, departmentalized law firm characteristically more prevalent in an era of evolving legal specialization." 440 F.Supp. at 211. Should such a rule be taken more seriously than most courts have done?

ests. No disciplinary rule expressly requires a lawyer to decline employment if a husband, wife, son, daughter, brother, father, or other close relative represents the opposing party in negotiation or litigation. Likewise, it is not necessarily improper for a law firm having a married partner or associate to represent clients whose interests are opposed to those of other clients represented by another law firm with which the married lawyer's spouse is associated as a lawyer.

" * * * We cannot assume that a lawyer who is married to another lawyer necessarily will violate any particular disciplinary rule, such as those that protect a client's confidences, that proscribe neglect of a client's interest, and that forbid representation of differing interests. Yet it also must be recognized that the relationship of husband and wife is so close that the possibility of an inadvertent breach of a confidence or the unavoidable receipt of information concerning the client by the spouse other than the one who represents the client (for example, information contained in a telephoned message left for the lawyer at home) is substantial. * * *

" * * * [T]he possibility of a violation of DR 5–101, in particular, is real and must be carefully considered in each instance. If the interest of one of the marriage partners as attorney for an opposing party creates a financial or personal interest that reasonably might affect the ability of a lawyer to represent fully his or her client with undivided loyalty and free exercise of professional judgment, the employment must be declined. We cannot assume, however, that certain facts, such as a fee being contingent or varying according to results obtained, necessarily will involve a violation of DR 5–101(A). In some instances the interest of one spouse in the other's income resulting from a particular fee may be such that professional judgment may be affected, while in other situations it may not be; the existence of such interest is a fact determination to be made in each individual case. Wherever one spouse is disqualified under DR 5–101(A), the entire firm is disqualified under DR 5–105(D).

"In any event, * * * the lawyer should advise the client of all circumstances that might cause one to question the undivided loyalty of the law firm and let the client make the decision as to its employment. If the client prefers not to employ a law firm containing a lawyer whose spouse is associated with a firm representing an opposing party, that decision should be respected."

c. Do you agree with the analysis in this Opinion? If the representation is not expressly improper, why does the opinion require disclosure of the situation to the client?

2. Should we presume that Xeres' wife would share whatever relevant information she learned from Xeres with others in her firm?

a. Why should we assume she will treat this information differently from other relevant information she learns? If we assume such sharing as to all other information and thus disqualify law firms under Model Rule 1.10(a), why shouldn't all lawyers in the wife's firm be disqualified as well?

b.   Model Rule 1.7, Comment [11], says the conflict is "personal," and thus "ordinarily is not imputed." Restatement § 123, Comment *g*, agrees that "in general, the law does not impute conflicts" because of family relationships, but the husband and wife may not "personally represent" clients adverse to each other. If there is any logic to the analogy between imputation within a family and imputation within a law firm, is there a good reason not to say that the law firms of the wife and husband are disqualified as well?

c.   Is the problem one of knowing where we can arbitrarily terminate the logic of imputation? Should it be relevant that there are many two-lawyer marriages today and that without some limit on imputation, most couples could not get jobs in the same geographic area? See Restatement Third, The Law Governing Lawyers § 123, Comment *g*, offering this rationale for the failure to require broader imputation.

d.   Notice that, before 2002, the Model Rules addressed imputation within families in Model Rule 1.8(i). Now, the subject is treated in ABA Model Rule 1.7, Comment [11]. Has the substance of the rules changed as well?

3.   Does the concern that spouses might intentionally or inadvertently share confidential information apply with the same force to other relationships?

a.   Is a child as likely to share confidential information with a parent in another law firm, for example? How about a brother with a sister? Are persons in familial relationships other than marriage likely to get each other's phone messages or share fees earned in a matter?

b.   What then has caused the rules to lump all such relationships into the same rule? Might we be concerned that a parent might pull her punches so as not to embarrass her child who is representing the other side? Would that same concern arise if siblings were the opposing lawyers?

c.   Note that Model Rule 1.7, Comment [11], like the case law, refers to lawyers related by "blood or marriage." What if lawyers are living together but not joined by benefit of clergy? Does any Rule cover that? How about Model Rule 1.7(a)(2) ("a personal interest of the lawyer"). Suppose that, instead of being married, the opposing lawyers had gone to dinner together several times? Would it be fair to have a strict rule governing those who marry and no rule for the rest?

d.   Restatement Third, The Law Governing Lawyers § 123, Comment *g*, says: "Conflicts arising out of relationships in which financial resources are pooled and living quarters shared in circumstances closely approximating marriage should be treated in the same way as spousal conflicts." Do you agree? Should lawyers in such relationships be required to inform their clients of their relationship and to obtain informed consent to continued representation of the parties? How much privacy should lawyers have to give up to avoid a charge of conflict of interest?

e. State Bar of Arizona, Opinion 2001–10 (2001), addressed whether cohabiting couples who opposed each other in a criminal case should be subject to the same rules as married couples and said yes. The same problem of inadvertently getting confidential information can arise, the Opinion says, as can the same loss of professional distance. Thus, where a prosecutor and public defender live together, the Opinion holds, they may not take cases against each other without the consent of their respective clients. See also, People v. Jackson, 213 Cal.Rptr. 521 (Ct.App.1985), setting aside the defendant's conviction because neither the prosecutor nor the appointed defense counsel disclosed the fact that they were dating each other before the trial and they continued to meet on a "regular basis" for movie and dinner dates throughout duration of the criminal proceedings against the defendant.

D. The use of "screening" to avoid imputation

1. Does ABA Model Rule 1.10 recognize the availability of screening to avoid imputation in the case of lawyers like Xeres who have moved from one private firm to another?

a. The Model Rules certainly recognize screening in other contexts. Rule 1.11 provides for screening the former government lawyer, Rule 1.12 permits screening of former judges and law clerks, and Rule 1.18 allows screening the lawyer who talked to a prospective client.

b. Model Rule 1.0(k) defines screening by saying that to be " 'screened' denotes the isolation of a lawyer form any participation in a matter through the timely imposition of procedures within a firm that are reasonably adequate under the circumstances to protect information that the isolated lawyer is obligated to protect under these Rules or other law."

c. For many years, however, most courts have rejected any notion that a law firm could build a screen—once called a "Chinese Wall"—around someone disqualified on the basis of knowing significant confidential information that would traditionally be imputed to other lawyers in the firm. See, e.g., Fund of Funds, Ltd. v. Arthur Andersen & Co., 567 F.2d 225, 229 n. 10 (2d Cir.1977).

d. One commentator has argued that imputed disqualification based on an irrebuttable presumption of shared confidential information "is required by three realities of life in the modern law firm."

"First is the relative informality of information exchange within most law firms [because] people tend to specialize their work within firms and tend to consult others in the firm who can give them necessary help on areas outside their expertise.

"Second is the powerful economic incentive to use information that will help the firm win a case on behalf of a current client. * * * Indeed, a highly-regarded American Bar Foundation study of Chicago lawyers suggests that the fear of losing clients creates the single most important pressure to engage in less-than-clearly ethical behavior today.

"Third and perhaps most important is the fact that no one outside a firm—indeed often leadership inside a firm—can ever be sure what has transpired behind the law firm's closed doors."

The proper question, therefore, is "not whether one can screen the disqualified lawyer from contact with others in the firm—but whether the lawyer realistically should be said to have received enough of the former client's information that the court's protection is required."[4]

e. We saw in Problem 14 that many courts have permitted screening of non-lawyers who have moved from one firm to another. Does it make sense to you to say that non-lawyers may be screened even in states where lawyers may not? Is the distinction based on the idea that non-lawyers do not learn anything about the cases on which they work? Is that consistent with your own experience? Might the distinction be based on the fact that non-lawyers do not share in law firm profits? But isn't that true of many lawyers in a firm? In short, does the distinction make any sense at all?

2. Are the concerns about screening now out of date? Should courts recognize screening more broadly? Specifically, should they allow screening of the lawyer who moves from one firm to another and who would otherwise disqualify all the lawyers in the new firm from representing a particular client?

a. The ABA drafts a model rule, but it is the courts who adopt the rules with legal force. If courts want to allow screening, it is a simple matter for the state supreme court to approve a rule that does so. Should courts create case law allowing screening in some cases when the court rules do not allow it in all cases?

b. A number of cases have now said, in dictum or otherwise, that screening of lawyers is permissible. Schiessle v. Stephens, 717 F.2d 417 (7th Cir.1983), for example, involved MK, who while a partner in the Antonow firm, had been in charge of representing one of the defendants in the *Schiessle* litigation. MK then left the Antonow firm and became a partner in the Ross firm, which was co-counsel for the plaintiff. The Seventh Circuit concluded that a substantial relationship existed between the matters. The court even concluded that MK was "actually privy" to and shared confidential information involving the case while at the Antonow firm. Thus, the trial court had to determine whether a "specific institutional mechanism" had been implemented to insulate effectively against confidential information flowing from the "infected" attorney to any other member of his present firm.

"Such a determination can be based on objective and verifiable evidence presented to the trial court and must be made on a case-by-case basis. Factors appropriate for consideration by the trial court might include, but are not limited to, the size and structural divisions of the law firm involved, the likelihood of contact between the 'infected' attorney and the specific attorneys responsible

4. Thomas D. Morgan, Screening the Disqualified Lawyer: The Wrong Solution to the Wrong Problem, 10 U. Ark. (Little Rock) L. J.37, 48 (1987–88).

for the present representation, the existence of rules which prevent the 'infected' attorney from access to the present litigation or which prevent him from sharing in the fees derived from such litigation." 717 F.2d at 420.

Having provided this guidance, the court found the screening ineffective in the case before it and upheld the disqualification.

c. Nemours Foundation v. Gilbane, Aetna, Federal Insurance Co., 632 F.Supp. 418 (D.Del.1986), on the other hand, upheld the use of screening of Lawyer, who had been an associate at Firm A that represented Client. At the direction of lead counsel, Lawyer had prepared books of documents for use in a "mini-trial" to be conducted as part of settlement negotiations. After the mini-trial, Lawyer was hired by Firm B, the firm that represented Opponent in the litigation, to work on completely different matters. At Firm B, Lawyer was totally "screened" from the litigation between Client and Opponent. No one at Firm B could talk to Lawyer about the case, and Lawyer was permitted to see no files. Citing what it saw as the policies underlying Rule 1.6, the court held that the "cone of silence" created around Lawyer by Firm B was sufficient to avoid disqualification. Lawyer had been an associate at Firm A and had not been intimately involved in the case. The court refused to adopt a per se rule, reasoning that, "Attorney mobility, especially among young associates, would be severely restricted if a per se rule against a 'cone of silence' were adopted." 632 F.Supp. at 429.

d. In Manning v. Waring, Cox, James, Sklar & Allen, 849 F.2d 222 (6th Cir.1988), bondholders had sued the underwriter ("Bank") when a bond issue went into default. Bond counsel ("Counsel") was named a third party defendant. "Lawyer" had been a chief attorney for Bank in its defense of the bondholders' case and in Bank's action over against Counsel. Then the law firm representing Counsel hired Lawyer for work not in the litigation side of that firm's practice. The court, again anxious not to impede lawyer mobility, remanded for factual findings but held that imputed disqualification can be avoided if the law firm bears the burden of showing "objective and verifiable evidence" of effective screening. Factors such as the "size and structural divisions" of the firm, "rules" that prevent the "infected" lawyer from having access to files in the case, and whether the infected attorney will share in fees from the case all should be considered by the lower court.

e. In Cromley v. Lockport Board of Education, 17 F.3d 1059 (7th Cir.1994), a lawyer in the firm representing a teacher who alleged she had been denied administrative positions moved to the firm representing the school board. The court found the same matter was involved and asked whether the presumption of shared confidences had been rebutted (citing *Schiessle v. Stephens*). The court found an effective screening procedure had been established, and that it was done at the time the lawyer was hired. The screen denied the lawyer access to the relevant files (which were kept in a different city), admonished the lawyer not to discuss the case, and denied him any share in the fees derived from the case.[5]

3. What do you think? Have these courts helped bring realism to the world of imputed disqualification? Have they created unnecessary uncertainty in a rule that was previously clear?

a. Some jurisdictions (e.g., Pennsylvania and Illinois) have rejected the prohibition of Model Rule 1.10 and have adopted ethics rules that allow screening in limited circumstances. Those states are identified in Appendix B, "Chart on Lawyer Screening," found in the Standards Supplement.

b. Van Jackson v. Check 'N Go of Illinois, 114 F.Supp.2d 731 (N.D.Ill. 2000), illustrates that when the state rule permits screening, the screen must be opaque before a court will accept it. A lawyer who had represented plaintiffs in cases involving "payday lenders" now moved to a four-person firm defending such cases. Although he was not personally named as counsel at the new firm, the court disqualified that firm. In a four-person firm, the effectiveness of screening is suspect at best, the court said, and this firm had offered no evidence of how effective screening had been achieved. The new firm had recruited the lawyer in the midst of a pending case, so it could not argue the motion to disqualify was simply a strategic ploy.

c. In an attempt to articulate a position that reflects both the traditional skepticism about screening and the cases that have permitted it, Restatement Third, The Law Governing Lawyers § 124(2) adopts the Model Rules position with respect to screening in most cases, but adopts a *Nemours* exception. It provides that screening is available, but only with respect to former-client conflicts and then only when

" * * * there is no substantial risk that confidential information of the former client will be used with material adverse effect on the former client because:

"(a) any confidential client information * * * is unlikely to be significant in the subsequent matter;

"(b) the personally prohibited lawyer is subject to screening measures adequate to eliminate participation by that lawyer in the representation; and

---

5. Other cases have been more restrictive. State ex rel. Freezer Services, Inc. v. Mullen, 458 N.W.2d 245 (Neb.1990), for example, involved a merger of the law firm representing the plaintiff with the firm representing the defendant. The new firm wished to continue to represent the defendant and to screen the lawyer who had handled the plaintiff's case. The court held the firm must be disqualified. When a lawyer who has been 'intimately involved' with one side of a case joins the firm on the other side, no amount of screening can give the first client a secure feeling that its confidential information will be safe. Courts have also rejected screening as a remedy in Lansing–Delaware Water District v. Oak Lane Park, Inc., 808 P.2d 1369 (Kan.1991); United States v. Davis, 780 F.Supp. 21 (D.D.C.1991); and Henriksen v. Great American Savings & Loan, 14 Cal. Rptr.2d 184 (Ct.App.1992). See also, Kala v. Aluminum Smelting & Refining Co., 688 N.E.2d 258 (Ohio 1998) (screening imposed when lawyer arrived at firm, but job negotiations with opposing counsel at time he was representing client deemed so egregiously disloyal that screen not permitted to avoid the new firm's disqualification).

"(c) timely and adequate notice of the screening has been provided to all affected clients."

d. What do you think of this approach? Do the standards appropriately balance the competing interests? Do they unwisely capitulate to the interests of large law firms who want to be able to take on more cases? How is the court to determine if the information is "unlikely to be significant" in the case?

e. In Kassis v. Teacher's Insurance and Annuity Association, 717 N.E.2d 674 (N.Y.1999), the New York Court of Appeals cited the Restatement when it disqualified a lawyer, imputed the disqualification to the law firm, and rejected screening as a cure for the disqualification. An associate had conducted five depositions and represented the plaintiff in two mediation sessions but then moved to the firm representing the defendant. Relying on the Restatement rule, the Court said that imputation was not per se required, nor should disqualification be imposed mechanically. However, to avoid disqualification the lawyer must show the information previously acquired is "unlikely to be significant or material in the litigation." In this case, the information was so significant that even effective screening would be "inconsequential" in avoiding disqualification.

PROBLEM 16

SPECIAL PROBLEMS OF GOVERNMENT LAWYERS

Government lawyers have long been seen to have responsibilities beyond those of lawyers in private practice. Some have worried, for example, that the lawyers might be tempted use their public position to benefit a future private employer. Others fear that former private clients might get special treatment—whether favorable or unfavorable—from their former lawyer. Concerns such as these have produced the rules governing government lawyers that this problem explores. First, we look at the limits on the conduct of former government lawyers under the Model Rules and the corresponding federal criminal statute. Then, we examine limits on the practice of former private lawyers while in government. Third, we consider the special screening rules applicable to government lawyers, and finally, we look at the rules applicable to former judges, arbitrators, mediators and analogous third-party neutrals.

FACTS

Harold Smithers was a commissioner with the Federal Trade Commission for several years until 10 months ago when his term expired. Prior to his appointment as a commissioner he had spent about 15 years—over half of his professional life—on the staff of the F.T.C.

Smithers retired from the Government at the end of his term and became a partner in the well-respected firm of Able & Baker in Washington, D.C. Smithers became familiar with Able & Baker because it engages in a great deal of F.T.C. work and has a reputation for excellence. In fact, for the last year, the firm has been representing the subject of a major investigation before the F.T.C. Although he disagreed with the strategy that Able & Baker was using in that case, he carefully avoided discussing that case while he was quietly negotiating with Able & Baker about his future employment at the firm.

Now that Smithers has moved to Able & Baker, P.D. Quick, Chief Executive Officer of Quick, Inc., has come from California to seek Able & Baker's help. The Commission staff has threatened to file an action in United States District Court seeking a preliminary injunction pending institution of a proceeding before the Commission alleging consumer fraud by Quick, Inc. The fraud is minor, but Quick is personally worried about it and wants to end the matter as soon as possible.

Neither Quick nor Quick, Inc., had ever before consulted with Able & Baker about this matter. P.D. Quick, during his initial conference with Smithers, mentioned in passing that the reason he decided to come to Able & Baker was because Smithers was there and a recent article about Smithers in Forbes Magazine (published as he was leaving the F.T.C.) said that Smithers had been one of the most influential and hardworking members in the history of the Commission. The article quoted one F.T.C. staff member who said that "even today when Smithers calls me on the phone, I instinctively straighten my tie and call him 'Sir!'"

The actual drafting of papers to be filed with the Commission staff will be handled by another partner of Able & Baker, but Smithers has been asked by the client and the active partner to give "a topside look" at the client's problems and to sign the important papers that will be filed with the Commission. Smithers also has agreed to call several staff members and a current commissioner or two who "owe their jobs to me." This last remark was made in an off-hand way in the presence of P.D. Quick who appeared pleased.

[handwritten marginal note: Violating 8.4 (e) p.108]

QUESTIONS

A. THE RULES APPLICABLE TO FORMER GOVERNMENT LAWYERS

1. What legal standards govern Smithers' return to private life?

a. Because Smithers is a lawyer, he is subject to ABA Model Rule 1.11. He is not subject to Model Rule 1.9, except as Model Rule 1.11(a)(1) expressly subjects him to Model Rule 1.9(c).[1]

b.   The content of Model Rule 1.11, in turn, can be traced to ABA Formal Opinion 342 (Nov. 24, 1975), which interpreted ABA Model Code of Professional Responsibility DR 9–101(B).

"The policy considerations underlying DR 9–101(B) have been thought to be the following: the treachery of switching sides; the safe-guarding of confidential governmental information from future use against the government; the need to discourage government lawyers from handling particular assignments in such a way as to encourage their own future employment in regard to those particular matters after leaving government service; and the professional benefit derived from avoiding the appearance of evil.

"There are, however, weighty policy considerations in support of the view that a special disciplinary rule relating only to former government lawyers should not broadly limit the lawyer's employment after he leaves government service. Some of the underlying considerations favoring a construction of the rule in a manner not to restrict unduly the lawyer's future employment are the following: the ability of government to recruit young professionals and competent lawyers should not be interfered with by imposition of harsh restraints upon future practice nor should too great a sacrifice be demanded of the lawyers willing to enter government service; the rule serves no worthwhile public interest if it becomes a mere tool enabling a litigant to improve his prospects by depriving his opponent of competent counsel; and the rule should not be permitted to interfere needlessly with the right of litigants to obtain competent counsel of their own choosing, particularly in specialized areas requiring special, technical training and experience. * * *

"As used in DR 9–101(B), 'substantial responsibility' envisages a much closer and more direct relationship than that of a mere perfunctory approval or disapproval of the matter in question. It contemplates a responsibility requiring the official to become personally involved to an important, material degree, in the investigative or deliberative processes regarding the transactions or facts in question. Thus, being the chief official in some vast office or organization does not *ipso facto* give that government official or employee the 'substantial responsibility' contemplated by the rule in regard to all the minutiae of facts lodged within that office. Yet it is not necessary that the public

---

1. Before the 2002 revisions of the Model Rules, there was some precedent for applying both Model Rules 1.9 and 1.11 to former government lawyers, e.g., Violet v. Brown, 9 Vet.App. 530 (Ct.Vet.App.1996). ABA Formal Opinion 97–409 (Aug. 2, 1997), on the other hand, said that Rule 1.11, not Rule 1.9, governs the conflict of interest obligations of a former government lawyer. Because Rule 1.9(c), prohibiting use and disclosure of a former client's confidential information, has no counterpart in Rule 1.11, however, the ABA Opinion said it was applicable to a former government lawyer as well. Now, Model Rule 1.11 alone is intended to govern the conduct of former government lawyers. See Comment [1] to Model Rule 1.9.

employee or official shall have personally and in a substantial manner investigated or passed upon the particular matter, for it is sufficient that he had such a heavy responsibility for the matter in question that it is unlikely he did not become personally and substantially involved in the investigative or deliberate processes regarding that matter. * * *

"The extension by DR 5–105(D) of disqualification to all affiliated lawyers is to prevent circumvention by a lawyer of the Disciplinary Rules. Past government employment creates an unusual situation in which inflexible application of DR 5–105(D) would actually thwart the policy considerations underlying DR 9–101(B). * * *

" * * * The purposes of limiting the mandate to matters in which the former public employee had a substantial responsibility are to inhibit government recruitment as little as possible and enhance the opportunity for all litigants to obtain competent counsel of their own choosing, particularly in specialized areas. An inflexible extension of disqualification throughout an entire firm would thwart those purposes. So long as the individual lawyer is held to be disqualified and is screened from any direct or indirect participation in the matter, the problem of his switching sides is not present; by contrast, an inflexible extension of disqualification throughout the firm often would result in real hardship to a client if complete withdrawal of representation was mandated, because substantial work may have been completed regarding specific litigation prior to the time the government employee joined the partnership, or the client may have relied in the past on representation by the firm."

c. In addition to Model Rule 1.11, it is important to recognize that current and former government employees, including lawyers, are often subject to special ethics legislation. In this Problem, because Smithers is a former *federal* official, he is subject to the *criminal* provisions in 18 U.S.C.A. § 207(a)(1):

"Any person who is an officer or employee * * * of the executive branch of the United States * * * and who, after the termination of his or her service or employment * * * makes, with the intent to influence, any communication to or appearance before any officer or employee of * * * the United States * * * in connection with a particular matter—

"(A) in which the United States * * * is a party or has a direct and substantial interest,

"(B) in which the person participated personally and substantially as such officer or employee, and

"(C) which involved a specific party or specific parties at the time of such participation, shall be punished [by up to 5 years imprisonment, a $50,000 fine, or both]."

2. How do these rules apply in concrete cases like Smithers'?

a. In re Sofaer, 728 A.2d 625 (D.C.1999), was a celebrated case in which Abraham Sofaer was accused of a violation of Rule 1.11(a). While serving as Legal Advisor (functionally the General Counsel) to the State Department, he was found to have taken part in "legal activities flowing from the government's efforts to address" the Pan Am 103 bombing incident that the U.S. government alleged was ordered by the Libyan government. After leaving the State Department, Libya retained Sofaer at a fee of $250,000 per month to represent it in connection with civil and criminal litigation arising out of that incident. When charged with a violation of Rule 1.11(a), Sofaer responded that his involvement in the matter at the State Department had not been "personal and substantial." Indeed, while he was there, suspicion was substantially focused on other possible perpetrators. Amici curiae added that if Sofaer were found guilty, no lawyer could safely move in and out of government. However, the court found the violation of Rule 1.11 was clear and ordered an informal admonition.

b. D.C. Bar Legal Ethics Committee Opinion No. 297 (2000) explored whether a former government lawyer may represent a private party in a negotiated rulemaking in which the lawyer had participated while in government. The Opinion said that doing so would not violate either Rule 1.11 or 18 U.S.C. § 207. A negotiated rulemaking does involve specific participants, the Opinion says, but it deals with formation of general policy and thus is not the kind of "matter" involving particular parties to which conflicts rules apply.

c. Outdoor Advertising Association of Ga., Inc. v. Garden Club of Ga., Inc., 527 S.E.2d 856 (Ga.2000), considered the limits on subsequent employment of a former state attorney general. The case involved permits for trimming trees to make billboards easier to see from the highway. Earlier, Michael Bowers was Georgia Attorney General and his office was counsel of record for the state Department of Transportation. The litigation was handled by a Deputy who never consulted with Bowers, and Bowers made no court appearances although an Opinion was issued from his office about some of the relevant legal issues. Thus, the court found that Bowers had no "substantial responsibility" for the earlier matters and was not disqualified now. Otherwise, he would be disqualified from 16,000 cases in which his office was involved while he was in office.

d. E.E.O.C. v. Exxon Corporation, 202 F.3d 755 (5th Cir.2000), was a case alleging that Exxon's failure to let alcoholics pilot oil tankers violates the Americans with Disabilities Act. Part of Exxon's defense was that its policy grew out of a requirement placed on it by the federal government as part of settling criminal charges arising out the Exxon Valdez oil spill. In support of its defense, Exxon hired two former Justice Department lawyers, now in private practice, as expert witnesses to testify about the events leading up to the earlier settlement. The Justice Department asserted that their testimony would violate federal ethics standards, but the district judge permitted the testimony insofar as it was limited to publicly-known information. The Fifth Circuit affirmed. Being an expert witness is not the same as representing a party, the court said, so it is not forbidden by either the Federal statute or the ABA Model Rules. The court went on to say that there was also no violation of the Texas Ethics Rules (the jurisdiction where this action arose) or the DC Bar Rules (the jurisdiction where the lawyers were admitted).

3.   ABA Model Rule 1.9 only prohibits representation that is "materially adverse" to the former client. Is Rule 1.11 so limited? How about 18 U.S.C. § 207?

a.   What reasons might forbid a lawyer who has left government from taking a case that *furthers* the government's objectives? Does it seem that government lawyers are likely to be in a position to bring cases while in government whose results they could later exploit? Do you agree that government lawyers have access to information that private lawyers would not have or could not obtain through discovery?

b.   ABA Model Rule 1.11(b) and Comment [3] are derived from General Motors Corp. v. City of New York, 501 F.2d 639 (2d Cir.1974). While a lawyer for the U.S. Government in 1956, *L* filed and signed an antitrust complaint against General Motors. Subsequently, in 1972 while he was in private practice, he agreed to represent New York City in another, similar antitrust claim on a contingent fee basis.[2] The court disqualified the lawyer. It concluded that his prior responsibility for the case was "substantial;" that his contingent fee arrangement with the City constituted private employment; that the City's antitrust suit was sufficiently similar to the federal case so as to constitute the same "matter" for purposes of DR 9–101(B); that it was irrelevant that the lawyer had not "switched sides" but had continued to litigate against G.M.; and that the lawyer's representation of the City would constitute the "appearance of impropriety."

c.   Do you think the court reached the right result? Cf. Armstrong v. McAlpin, 625 F.2d 433 (2d Cir.1980) (en banc), vac'd 449 U.S. 1106, 101 S.Ct. 911, 66 L.Ed.2d 835 (1981), where the court assumed this construction of DR 9–101(B) but accepted the screening approach described in ABA Formal Opinion 342, supra.

d.   Look at 18 U.S.C. § 207(a) in the Standards Supplement, the main federal statute dealing with the revolving door. Does that statute also prohibit a lawyer's involvement in certain matters even when the lawyer's position is consistent with that of the government, the former client?

4.   Is Smithers barred from all activity within his own law firm in the case involving Quick, Inc.? May Smithers talk to Quick, for example, about what the F.T.C. is likely to do? May he give tactical advice to his partners who are handling the Quick matter?

2.   It might seem there would be a statute of limitations on the bar to subsequent representation of a private party in such a case. If Smithers had personally worked on a case 15 years ago, for example, early in his career at the F.T.C., it might seem he should now be free to work on the matter in private practice. As the *General Motors* case shows, however, that is not current law.

a. Do the federal statute, the Model Rules and the Model Code all provide the same answer? Why might the federal statute forbid only contacts with current agency officials?

b. Consider P.D. Quick's view of the situation. If Smithers cannot work on the matter, why should Quick travel all the way from California to hire Smithers when there are plenty of good lawyers in California? Does Model Rule 8.4(e) have any effect on what Smithers can say about his ability to help Quick?

c. The legislative history of § 207 shows that Congress meant to have questions about imputation within a law firm, and any right of the government to waive the disqualification, governed by the Bar's own rules of ethics.[3] ABA Formal Opinion 342 (1975), quoted above, of course said that application of the usual rules of imputation of disqualification within a firm would "actually thwart the policy considerations underlying [Model Rule 1.11]"? See also Armstrong v. McAlpin, 625 F.2d 433 (2d Cir.1980) (en banc), vacated on other grounds 449 U.S. 1106, 101 S.Ct. 911, 66 L.Ed.2d 835 (1981).

d. Thus, ABA Model Rule 1.11(b) clearly provides that imputation can be avoided by timely "screening" of the former government lawyer. Remember, the requirements for an effective screen are set forth in new ABA Model Rule 1.0(k) and Comments [8]–[10] to Model Rule 1.0.

e. Problem 15 discussed the courts' debates over whether to permit screening devices when a lawyer moves from one private firm to another. Are you confident that the required screening devices will be more effective in cases involving former government lawyers? Might it be easier to keep track of cases on which a former SEC employee may not work, for example, than to do so in the case of a private litigator whose cases might have involved any number of different clients? On the other hand, what dangers of intentional or inadvertent "breaches in the Wall" can you see?

5.   If a matter came to the Commission the week after Smithers left the agency, would there be any limits on Smithers' ability to contact his friends back at the agency?

a. Would there be any bar to his work on the matter under ABA Model Rule 1.11(a)? Remember that Smithers was not personally and substantially involved with work on the matter.

b. Look at 18 U.S.C.A. § 207(c) in the Standards Supplement. What purpose is served by a one-year "cooling-off" provision?

c. United States v. Nofziger, 878 F.2d 442 (D.C.Cir.1989), reversed the conviction of President Reagan's assistant, Lynn Nofziger, who had been convicted under 18 U.S.C.A. § 207(c). On behalf of clients of his lobbying firm, he had sent a letter to Edwin Meese, then Counselor to the President, urging that the Army be encouraged to give a contract to Wedtech, a minority-owned firm in the South Bronx. He also sent a copy of

3. See Thomas D. Morgan, Appropriate Limits on Participation by a Former Agency Official in Matters Before an Agency, 1980 Duke L.J. 1, 11.

a letter to a Meese deputy urging use of civilian crews on noncombatant Navy ships. Finally, he met with National Security Council staff members to urge continued production on the A–10 aircraft for which Congress had cut off funds. Nofziger argued that the Government had not proved that he knew these were issues in which the agencies he had contacted already had a "direct and substantial interest." Judges Buckley and Williams found such a knowledge requirement arguably in the statute and concluded that where there is ambiguity in a criminal statute the defendant should prevail. Judge Edwards in dissent found no such ambiguity.

6. Suppose that while working at the FTC, Smithers learned some shocking information about the business practices of several companies. May he undertake to represent persons injured by the companies whose practices he had studied?

a. Take a look at ABA Model Rule 1.11(c). Why should the law prevent Smithers from working on behalf of companies whose injuries he is especially well suited to redress?

b. Does Comment [4] to Model Rule 1.11 explain the underlying policies to your satisfaction? Does the rule prohibiting Smithers' use of confidential government information give too great protection to wrong-doers that the agency simply lacks the resources to pursue?

7. Should the special ethics requirements applicable to government lawyers reach lawyers who are not government employees but who are retained to represent the government in particular matters?

a. Houghton v. Department of Health, 962 P.2d 58 (Utah 1998), for example, involved cases challenging the State's authority to impose Medicaid liens on personal injury judgments to recover payments the state had made for medical care. This disqualification motion involved two lawyers who had previously represented the State in seeking to recover such payments but were now challenging the system. The court applied Rule 1.9 to the issue, not Rule 1.11. The present cases did not involve use of factual information used in representation of the State, the court said, and the State had not cited any other disadvantage to it caused by the fact these lawyers rather than others represented the plaintiffs in this case. Thus, the court refused to disqualify them.

b. P.J.S. v. Pennsylvania State Ethics Commission, 723 A.2d 174 (Pa.1999), involved a lawyer who served as part time City Solicitor while maintaining a private law practice. When a citizen filed suit against the city, the mayor, and the police chief, the city's insurer retained the Solicitor's private firm to defend them. The State Ethics Commission alleged that this constituted a conflict of interest, but the lawyer argued he was not a city official subject to the Commission's jurisdiction. A part-time City Solicitor is both a city official subject to state ethics laws, the Pennsylvania Supreme Court said, and a lawyer subject to the court's jurisdiction. Invocation of the Ethics Commission's jurisdiction was proper and not an invasion of the court's authority to regulate lawyers.

8.   Assume Smithers had been a Member of Congress instead of an FTC Commissioner. What limitations on his law practice would Smithers face when he retired from Congress?

a.   Suppose Smithers had been chairman of a subcommittee charged with oversight of the F.T.C., and P.D. Quick wants Smithers to persuade his old subcommittee to approve a proposed law that would permit a practice being investigated by the F.T.C. Would former-Congressman Smithers be under the same ethical restraints as ex-Commissioner Smithers?

b.   Take a look at 18 U.S.C.A. § 207(e)(1) in the Standards Supplement. Why should the scope and duration of the rules differ depending on the branch of government in which the former official served?

c.   If former–Congressman Smithers had been joined at Able & Baker by the Chief Counsel of the House subcommittee, would the Chief Counsel have been subject to the same limitations? See 18 U.S.C.A. § 207(e)(3).

B.   THE FORMER PRIVATE LAWYER WHO ENTERS GOVERNMENT SERVICE

1.   Consider the other direction of the revolving door. What must a lawyer consider when he or she enters government service?

a.   Must a government official recuse herself every time something comes up involving a former private client? Does the lawyer continue to owe the former client duties under ABA Model Rules 1.6 and 1.9(a)? In what ways does new ABA Model Rule 1.11(d) differ from Rule 1.9(a)?

b.   ABA Model Rule 1.11(d) is also based on ABA Formal Opinion 342, supra, which said:

> "When the Disciplinary Rules of Canons 4 and 5 mandate the disqualification of a government lawyer who has come from private practice, his governmental department or division cannot practicably be rendered incapable of handling even the specific matter. Clearly, if DR 5–105(D) were so construed, the government's ability to function would be unreasonably impaired. * * * The relationships among lawyers within a government agency are different from those among partners and associates of a law firm. The salaried government employee does not have the financial interest in the success of departmental representation that is inherent in private practice. * * * The channeling of advocacy toward a just result as opposed to vindication of a particular claim [also] lessens the temptation to circumvent the disciplinary rules through the action of associates. Accordingly, we construe DR 5–105(D) to be inapplicable to other government lawyers associated with a particular government lawyer who is himself disqualified * * * . Although vicarious disqualification of a government department is not necessary or wise, the individual lawyer should be screened from any direct or indirect participation in the matter, and discussion with his colleagues concerning the relevant transaction or set of transactions is prohibited by those rules."

c.   In analyzing these issues, DC Bar Legal Ethics Committee Opinion No. 308 (2001), concluded that the lawyer's first constraint stems from the duty of confidentiality. Rule 1.6 says that (1) the lawyer must be vigilant not to reveal any protected information obtained from the former client, and (2) the lawyer may not knowingly "use" protected information "to the disadvantage of the client." Thus, even though not all uses of a former client's confidences involve revealing them to others, the second part of Rule 1.6 does not allow use either.

The second constraint stems from Rule 1.9. The test to determine if a lawyer may work on a matter while in government is "whether the lawyer was so involved in the matter that the subsequent representation can be justly regarded as a changing of sides in the matter in question." If the answer is yes, the lawyer may not continue without written consent from both sides. If written consent is not obtained, the lawyer may not work for the government in the matter.

d.   For the reasons stated in ABA Formal Opinion 342, the principles of imputed disqualification do not apply to lawyers who practice in a government agency with the lawyer who is disqualified. However, D.C. Opinion No. 308, supra, says that voluntary screening measures in the agency should be considered. See also, ABA Model Rule 1.11, Comment [2].

2.   What conflicts might a government lawyer expect to find in advising multiple agency clients?

a.   State Bar of California Formal Opinion No. 2001–156 (2001), discusses when a conflict of interest arises under California Rule 3–310(C) where a city attorney offers legal advice to different constituent sub-entities or to officials of a city whose positions differ on a subject.

The Opinion recognizes that application of the Rules of Professional Conduct must consider factors peculiar to the governmental context. It says the courts have developed a two-part test to determine potential conflicts of interest arising from an attorney advising different bodies or officials within a city government: (1) An attorney for a governmental entity such as a city usually has only one client, the entity itself, and (2) A constituent sub-entity or official may become an independent client of the entity's attorney only if the sub-entity or official possesses authority to act independently of the main entity and if the entity's attorney is asked to represent the constituent sub-entity or official in its independent capacity.

Therefore, no conflict of interest arises when there is a disagreement between a government entity and its subordinate constituents, or between subordinate constituents of the entity. However, a conflict of interest may arise if a constituent or official has an independent right of action that would require the attorney to choose between conflicting duties. In the case of a city council and a mayor seeking legal advice from the city attorney, but taking different positions, no conflict of interest exists because the attorney represents neither the city council nor the mayor; the lawyer represents only the municipal corporation as an indivisible unit. Further, because neither of these sub-entities of the municipal corporation can function independently, the attorney may not represent either in its independent capacity. See ABA Model Rule 1.13, Comment [6].

b.   Military legal offices regularly also represent multiple clients and multiple interests. Except in cases of military necessity, the ABA Standing Committee on Ethics and Professional Responsibility says, "representation of opposing sides by lawyers working in the same military office and sharing common secretarial and filing facilities should be avoided." ABA Informal Opinion 1474 (1982) (citing Formal Opinion 343 and Informal Opinion 1309).

3.   Should legislative branch officials be subject to limits such as those imposed on officials in the executive branch?

a.   Assume that Smithers becomes a Congressman in addition to being a practicing lawyer. Because Smithers is familiar with the problems of the First Savings Bank, which is also one of his constituents, he decides that he will introduce a bill in Congress to cut back the powers of the Federal Reserve Board and other federal agencies to investigate alleged inappropriate credit behavior of banks. Is there anything wrong with introducing such a bill if the lawyer does not charge First Savings Bank for this service?

b.   Office of Disciplinary Counsel v. Eilberg, 441 A.2d 1193 (Pa.1982), suspended a lawyer/Congressman from the practice of law for violating 18 U.S.C.A. § 203(a), a federal law prohibiting a member of Congress from receiving compensation for representing a client before a federal agency. The lawyer had set up a "dual practice," i.e., the lawyer's law partners set up a separate entity to receive compensation for representing clients before federal agencies. But the lawyer/Congressman encouraged prospective clients to hire the "other" firm to represent the clients, and, in one case the lawyer/Congressman (apparently because of an accounting error) received a portion of the profits from the representation before a federal agency. The court said that it need not rule on the ethics of the "dual practice" law firm, but said it is ethically "dubious," even though it did not technically violate section 18 U.S.C.A. § 203(a).

c.   In Two Thirty Nine Joint Venture v. Joe, 60 S.W.3d 896 (Tex.App. 2001), the plaintiff, a real estate development venture was represented by the law firm in which the defendant was a partner. The firm helped the plaintiff negotiate a contract to sell land for an apartment complex. When the contract was near completion, the city council met and declared a moratorium on the building of any more apartment complexes. The defendant, as a member of the city council, voted for the moratorium, and the plaintiff's contract for sale of the land fell through. The plaintiff argued that by his vote, the defendant and his law firm breached their fiduciary duty to the plaintiff. The defendants argued that the partner was protected by legislative immunity for such votes. The court held that the lawyer's action on the city council created an impermissible conflict of interest about which the firm had to tell the plaintiffs. The court observed that most cases involving a conflict of interest are those where an attorney acts as a public official in decisions furthering his client's interest. It held, however, that a conflict between the attorney's public and private duties arises where the attorney acts adversely to the interest of a private client as well. Had it known of the pending moratorium, the court reasoned, the plaintiff might have taken steps to prevent its land from being subject to it.

C. NEGOTIATING FOR POST-GOVERNMENT EMPLOYMENT WHILE STILL IN GOVERNMENT

1. Did Smithers do anything wrong when he was negotiating for employment prior to his retirement from the F.T.C.? How may a lawyer in government service look for a job on the outside?

a. May the lawyer contact firms that regularly deal with the lawyer's agency? Look at ABA Model Rule 1.11(d)(2)(ii). Might those be the very firms that would find the lawyer's experience valuable?

b. Federal employees are also subject to 18 U.S.C. § 208(a) that provides:

> "[W]hoever, being an officer or employee of the executive branch of the United States Government * * * participates personally and substantially as a Government officer or employee * * * in a * * * particular matter in which to his knowledge, * * * any person or organization with whom he is negotiating or has any arrangement concerning prospective employment, has a financial interest [may be imprisoned up to 5 years, pay a $50,000 fine, or both]."

c. Section 208, however, creates an exception where the government employee makes a full advance disclosure of all relevant facts to the "Government official responsible for appointment to his or her position" and receives a written determination "that the interest is not so substantial as to be deemed likely to affect the integrity of the services" the employee will render in the matter.

To whom would Smithers write such a letter? Do you suppose the President of the United States spends a lot of time making the determinations required by such notifications?

2. Smithers told P.D. Quick that several commissioners "owe their jobs to me." Is there anything wrong with saying that? How about saying it to law firms with whom he is negotiating employment?

a. Assuming that this statement is factually correct and well known, what is the comment trying to imply? Does the comment violate Model Rule 8.4(e)?

b. Would it be unrealistic to require people like Smithers never to use the access they obtained while working for the government? President Truman is said to have—

> "had strong feelings about using one's official position, *past or present*, for gain. He was extremely fond of General Omar Bradley, the fellow Missourian who at one time during Mr. Truman's administration was Chief of Staff. After Bradley retired, he took a job as chairman of the board of the Bulova Watch Company, and

one day in discussing General Bradley Mr. Truman said, 'I hold it against him, taking that job. They weren't hiring him; what they thought they were doing was buying some influence in the Pentagon, and I don't care at all for that sort of thing, and I can't understand how General Bradley could bring himself to do it.' Being an admirer of General Bradley, I said, no doubt apologetically, 'He probably felt he needed the money.' And Mr. Truman said, 'Nobody ever needs money that bad.' "[4]

c.   When President Kennedy appointed Arthur Goldberg to the Cabinet as Secretary of Labor, Goldberg promised never to practice labor law again, although that field of law had been his specialty. Goldberg always kept that promise. Would such a prophylactic rule—preventing a former government employee from using the benefits of his former position while in private practice—tend to discourage many good persons from entering government service?

D.   CONFLICTS OF THE FORMER JUDGE OR THIRD PARTY NEUTRAL

1.   Where does one find the limits on the activities of a former judge?

a.   Notice that former government officials who have served as judges are subject, not to ABA Model Rule 1.11, but to Model Rule 1.12. That rule also now governs private arbitrators, mediators and other third-party neutrals.

b.   What values are we trying to protect by imposing limits on later private work by judges and other neutrals? None of the former adjudicators governed by Model Rule 1.12(a) "represented" anyone in their prior role. None of them has any duty of "loyalty" to the parties who appeared before them. Nor is information that comes out at trial "confidential" in any meaningful sense. What, if anything, is left to worry about?

c.   Do you get any insight into a possible rationale from the judges whom Comment [1] to Model Rule 1.12 says are not reached by the rule? Does Comment [3] provide an independent rationale for the rule itself, or only for the screening requirement?

2.   What does Model Rule 1.12(b) tell us about how judges should accomplish a transition back to practice?

a.   Isn't it likely that almost *all* the major firms in a given area are likely to be counsel, or potentially counsel, in cases before the judge while he is looking for post-judicial employment. Does Model Rule 1.12(b) mean that the judge may not talk to any of them?

b.   Comment 3 to Model Rule 1.11 states that Model Rule 1.11(d)(2) is designed to "prevent a lawyer from exploiting public office for the advan-

---

4. Merle Miller, Plain Speaking: An Oral Biography of Harry S. Truman (1974) at 201–02, n. † (emphasis added).

tage of another client." That is not literally applicable to the judge, but does the same concern underlie Model Rule 1.12(b)?

3. If the Judge does not comply with the requirements of Model Rule 1.12, what remedies or sanctions might the judge expect?

a. Pepsico, Inc. v. McMillen, 764 F.2d 458 (7th Cir.1985), involved a judge who had become eligible to take senior status. He contacted a "head hunter" who agreed to contact Chicago firms to see if any would want the judge to become affiliated with them. Inadvertently, and contrary to the judge's instructions, the head hunter contacted firms representing both the plaintiff and defendant in a pending antitrust case. Neither expressed an interest in hiring the judge, although the plaintiff's firm left the matter a bit more open than did the other. The judge did not go to work for either firm. Defendants sought a writ of mandamus to disqualify the judge. The Court of Appeals was careful to stress that there was no intentional impropriety committed in the case, but it ordered the judge recused to avoid any "appearance of partiality" in the matter before him. See Model Rule 1.12(b).

b. How might the judge in *Pepsico* have avoided disqualification? Look at Commentary [1] following Canon 3E(1) of the ABA Model Code of Judicial Conduct, found in the Standards Supplement to these materials.

c. Kentucky Bar Association v. Bates, 26 S.W.3d 788 (Ky.2000), is another in the "what was he thinking" line of cases. A part-time judge also practiced law as permitted by ABA Model Code of Judicial Conduct, Application of the Code of Judicial Conduct § C. On behalf of one of his private divorce clients, he filed a petition seeking a divorce; five days later, he filed another petition, also on behalf of this client, seeking an Emergency Protective Order against the wife, alleging an immediate danger of domestic violence. Purportedly because no other judge was handy, the lawyer not only drafted the order on behalf of his client but signed it in his capacity as a judge. The next day, another judge signed the protective order. The court found a violation of Rule 1.12(a) in that the lawyer had acted as counsel in a matter on which he had acted as a judge. It issued a public reprimand.

4. Are the rationales for Model Rules 1.12(a) and 1.12(b) the same?

a. One can readily understand why under Model Rule 1.12(b) a judge may not negotiate for employment with law firms representing parties whose cases have not yet been decided; the opportunity for bribery is obvious.

b. Does a similar opportunity for dishonesty exist where a former judge, who decided a case long ago, represents the winner in seeking to get the loser to comply with the earlier order? Such representation would clearly be prohibited by Model Rule 1.12(a). Why? Is it realistic to expect that the other party would consent to such representation? What might legitimately concern the other party about the former judge's involvement?

c. Does the screening authorized by Model Rule 1.12 (c) provide adequate protection for the values implicit in Model Rule 1.12 generally? If one were concerned that a party might try to reward a judge for a favorable verdict by later hiring the judge's firm, does the prohibition on the judge's directly collecting a fee for the matter remove all concern?

5. Is it wise to try to deal with all forms of third-party neutrals in a single rule? Might our concerns about later involvement by a mediator, for example, be different than those about a former arbitrator or judge?

a. Mediators often necessarily learn each side's bargaining positions that would never come out at a trial, for example. See ABA Model Code of Judicial Conduct, Canon 3B(7)(d). Should the rule at least treat persons who have obtained such confidential information differently from those who have not?

b. In Cho v. Superior Court, 45 Cal.Rptr.2d 863 (Ct.App.1995), for example, a judge who had presided over settlement discussions in a case had left the bench and joined the defendant's law firm. Faced with these facts, the court ordered the former judge's entire firm disqualified. Quoting Poly Software International, Inc. v. Su, 880 F.Supp. 1487 (D.Utah 1995), the court said: "[A]lthough mediators function in some ways as neutral coordinators of dispute resolution, they also assume the role of a confidant, and it is that aspect of their role that distinguishes them from adjudicators." 45 Cal.Rptr.2d at 868.

c. The court in *Cho* said that screening under Model Rule 1.12 is proper for former adjudicators who only see what each side shows the other, but in the case of former mediators, disqualification of the entire firm is required. Do you agree? Should Model Rule 1.12 draw this distinction?

CHAPTER V

ADVISING CLIENTS

A news story reported a class discussion in a business school:

> "What should your role as a manager be when a subordinate comes to you reporting a product safety defect?" [Professor James Wilson of the University of Pittsburgh] asks. "Is your primary motivation to make a good widget or a good profit?"
>
> "I'd get another opinion," ventures one candidate for a master's in business administration.*

The lawyer for this widget producer should not be surprised if the manager comes to her for the other opinion. What should the lawyer say?

Lawyers usually spend more time counseling and trying to stay out of court than they do trying cases. As you concern yourself with the lawyer's obligations in giving advice to clients, consider questions such as these:

a. What is the standard for determining the best interest of the client? Is the client by definition the best judge of his or her interest? Does the lawyer have a right—an obligation—to offer an opinion about what course of action would be in the client's best interest? Should a lawyer ever try to pressure a client into taking one course of action rather than another?

b. What special questions are presented when the client is not an individual? When the client is a corporation, for example, who really speaks for the client? Is it the Board of Directors? The managers? The common stockholders? If the client is the fictional corporate entity, what does that mean when the flesh and blood persons are at odds and the lawyer is in the middle?

c. Does a lawyer ever owe obligations to persons or entities other than the client? Does the lawyer owe the same obligation to a third party that the client owes to that party? May the lawyer voluntarily assume an obligation to report accurate information on which third parties may rely? Why might a lawyer do so even where the report might not reflect entirely favorably on the lawyer's client?

d. Does a lawyer have a right—an obligation—to warn third parties about potential wrongdoing by the lawyer's client? On what theory would such a right or obligation rest? Should the lawyer with knowledge of

---

* Victor Zonana, Bribery and Slush Spur Ethics Courses at Business Schools: Would You Have Gone Along With Equity Funding Deal? Many Students Say Yes, Wall Street J., July 8, 1975, p. 1, col. 4.

potential wrongdoing have a different right or obligation of disclosure than a non-lawyer would have?

———

PROBLEM 17

THE LAWYER FOR AN INDIVIDUAL CLIENT

Clients have the almost infinite range of characteristics human beings can have. Some seek to protect their wealth, others hope to expand their influence, still others want to avoid being hurt by someone else. This book tries to introduce you to a variety of such clients, but as we introduce you to the lawyer's advisor role, you have a new client who is confused and frustrated by a legal system that she believes has not served her or her family well. This problem first asks the difference between a lawyer's acting as an advisor and acting as an advocate; indeed, it asks whether a lawyer may have both roles in the same matter. Then, it explores what limits there are on the advice a lawyer may give and the projects a lawyer may assist. Next, it examines how the lawyer's role might differ if the lawyer concludes that the client lacks normal mental ability. Finally, it asks the lawyer's options if the client's conduct seems likely to endanger others.

FACTS

Marilyn Anderson came to you for legal help. "They have taken away my children," she told you bitterly. "I have a right to them, don't I? I am a good mother, but the welfare department has put my babies in a foster home."

You were moved by Mrs. Anderson's sincerity and agreed to take the case. In the course of your subsequent investigation, however, you discovered that Mrs. Anderson had not told you all the facts. The children, Mary, age 7, and Billy, age 3, were removed from the home based on a finding of both neglect and abuse. Social workers at Mary's school became suspicious when the little girl appeared bruised and malnourished after several days' absence. The social workers' questioning of Mary revealed that Mrs. Anderson sometimes hit the children and sent them to bed hungry. Mrs. Anderson also often left the home for hours at a time leaving no adult to care for them.

But that was only the beginning of the story. Mrs. Anderson herself told you that her husband, John, has frequent violent episodes during which Mrs. Anderson sometimes leaves the house and the children because she literally fears for her life. John has a job, but he is paid in cash and the family cannot rely on how much will be left in the pay envelope after he gets home. Mrs. Anderson had been employed as a hospital aide before Mary was born, but she has enjoyed staying home with her children.

A particular irritant in the Andersons' relationship has been the situation of Mrs. Anderson's mother. She is alert and lives in her own house, but she is lonely. Marilyn wants to invite her to come to live with the family, but whenever she suggests it, John flies into a violent rage.

You wonder whether or not Marilyn Anderson should win the upcoming custody hearing. Although you sympathize with her situation, you hesitate to use all the skill and resources at your command to overwhelm the overworked counsel for the Department of Children and Family Services. If you do restore custody to Mrs. Anderson, you worry about the children's future.[1]

QUESTIONS

A. THE DIFFERENCE BETWEEN ADVICE AND ADVOCACY

1. In this Problem, is Marilyn Anderson asking you only to advocate for the return of her children? Is she also seeking your experience and judgment about how to deal with her situation?

a. In 1952, the ABA and the Association of American Law Schools established a Joint Conference on Professional Responsibility, among whose conclusions were that:

"The most effective realization of the law's aims often takes place in the attorney's office, where litigation is forestalled by anticipating its outcome, where the lawyer's quiet counsel takes the place of public force. Contrary to popular belief, the compliance with the law thus brought about is not generally lip serving and narrow, for by reminding him of its long-run costs the lawyer often deters his client from a course of conduct technically permissible under existing law, though inconsistent with its underlying spirit and purpose.

"Although the lawyer serves the administration of justice indispensably both as an advocate and as office counselor, the demands imposed on him by these two roles must be sharply distinguished. * * * [R]esolution of doubts in one direction [in favor of the client] becomes inappropriate when the lawyer acts as counselor. * * *"[2]

b. Later, Model Code of Professional Responsibility Ethical Consideration 7–3 picked up that theme, saying:

"A lawyer may serve simultaneously as both advocate and adviser, but the two roles are essentially different. In asserting a position on behalf of his client, an advocate for the most part deals with past conduct and must take the facts as he finds them. By contrast, a

---

1. This problem is adapted with permission from one discussed in Murray Teigh Bloom (ed.), Lawyers, Clients & Ethics (Council on Legal Education for Professional Responsibility, Inc. 1974) 1–5.

2. Professional Responsibility: Report of the Joint Conference, 44 A.B.A.J. 1159, 1161 (1958).

lawyer serving as adviser primarily assists his client in determining the course of future conduct and relationships. While serving as advocate, a lawyer should resolve in favor of his client doubts as to the bounds of the law. In serving a client as adviser, a lawyer in appropriate circumstances should give his professional opinion as to what the ultimate decisions of the courts would likely be as to the applicable law.''

c. Is this distinction self-righteous and naive? Is a client always entitled to a lawyer who makes a pit bull seem docile? Is the distinction instead capturing an important reality about how lawyers best serve their clients' interests?

d. Is there a difference between Marilyn Anderson's short-term and long-term interests? Which should be more important as you decide how to proceed yourself and what to advise her to do? Might the answer to that question vary from client to client?

2. Are you confident that you know what the dynamics of this family really are? Are you obliged to accept what your client tells you as true? Should you assume that most clients will lie about things that embarrass them, at least until they come to trust you?

a. Professor Naomi Cahn suggests that almost all events are likely to be come to the lawyer in the form of "inconsistent stories."

"A woman, Darlene Adams, has come into my office, saying that she wants to leave the man she has been living with because he has beaten her up. In the initial interview, she states that the most recent time this happened was yesterday, when she was leaving the apartment with a female friend to go out to the movies. Mr. Ponds pleaded with her not to go; when she refused, he called her a whore and threatened to call Child Protective Services. He then slapped her face and pulled out a clump of hair. Her face stung for several hours, and her scalp still hurt when she came to see me. * * * She wants Mr. Ponds to leave the apartment and to stay away from her; she also wants custody of their child.

"At the interview, I take a picture of the bald spot on her head. Ms. Adams then tells me that the friend with whom she was going to the movies came with her to my office and would be happy to talk to me about what happened. When I interview the friend, Ms. Campbell, she tells me that she and Ms. Adams had talked to each other earlier in the day, and that Ms. Adams had told her that the situation at home was tense. When Ms. Campbell came over, the two of them decided to go to a movie, taking along young Ben. As they were leaving, Ms. Adams walked past Mr. Ponds, who then reached out towards her head. After Ms. Adams pulled away from him, he was left holding some hair. The friend did not see Mr. Ponds slap Ms. Adams. * * * I begin to prepare the papers and I ask Ms. Adams to return in two days, so that she can review and sign them.

"Two days later, Ms. Adams calls to say that she has decided not to go through with any legal action. Mr. Ponds has told her that he loves her, and has been especially nice to her. * * * She says that he really has not hurt her all that much * * *. * * *

"I have recognized, after reflection on these experiences * * * the following layers of inconsistent stories: the two different stories my client tells on different days, the discrepancies between my client's perceptions and those of her witness, the differences between what my client wants and what I think she needs, and the variation between my client's desire to stay and the oft-asked question, 'Why doesn't she leave?' Underlying these different stories include the stories my client tells me and what she tells herself. Once we file the papers, there will be another set of inconsistent stories: differences between my client's language and 'courtroom' language, dissimilarities between my client's story and her desired remedies, which differ from the judge's story and stock of remedies, which further differ from the definitions of what her 'case' actually is."

"The issues of whose story is told and of how the story will be related are complex. A lawyer envisions several tellings of the story; the client envisions several tellings as well. Each has (in)complete information about what will happen within the legal system, and about what 'actually happened.' Different approaches by lawyers and clients and a more fluid ethical system will allow for some better attorney-client relationships and some better retellings. Some stories will also 'seem' truer than others. But the conflicts will remain, conflicts between stories within the same 'case,' conflicts over what constitutes the 'case,' and conflicts between and within outsider groups seeking to tell their own stories. * * * So long as we have a legal system that values consistent stories, we must confront, and challenge, the possibility of constructing a true story of a case. Examining how inconsistent stories are left out of traditional legal ethics makes visible their presence and their significance, and provides an opportunity to accept and use them."[3]

b. Bring these insights to bear on our Problem. How do you know that Mary, the young daughter, told the social workers the truth about her mother's hitting her? How do you know the social workers accurately reported what Mary said? How do you know that Marilyn Anderson's account of her husband's conduct is reliable? How should you as a lawyer go about determining the facts you need to know?

3.   Do you have sufficient skills to handle this case effectively?

a. Is your law school training preparing you to be a social worker? Are you confident of your skills as a family therapist? May you simply say that you will limit your practice to giving legal advice and not worry about the context in which the client's legal problem arises?

---

3. Naomi R. Cahn, Inconsistent Stories,   permission.
81 Georgetown L.J. 2475 (1993). Used with

b. Is that a cop-out? Can you deal effectively with the legal problems without addressing the context? Might you get a restraining order against John Anderson's domestic violence, for example? Might you get an order requiring that a regular part of his pay be sent to a bank account to which only Mary would have access?

c. In short, rather than being overwhelmed by what you don't know and can't fix, might you concentrate your efforts on steps that only deal with part of the problem but that are steps that only a lawyer knows how to take?

4. What possible "styles" of client counseling might you adopt in your dealings with Ms. Anderson?

a. Any categorization of counseling styles is obviously arbitrary, but that has not stopped commentators from trying to do it. Professors David Binder and Susan Price, for example, have been identified with "client-centered" counseling in which the lawyer's primary role is to help the client understand what the client wants and how to achieve it.[4]

b. By contrast, Professor William Simon takes a more directive view that urges lawyers to move clients toward results that are just, not simply favorable to one's own clients.[5]

c. Professors Thomas Shaffer and Robert Cochran advocate a counseling of moral discourse and treating of the client as one would treat a good friend, being supportive but willing to urge moral considerations as well as merely legal advice.[6]

d. Professor Deborah Rhode, in turn, advocates "contextual counseling" that might use different techniques when asserting the rights of a rich corporation, for example, than when defending a poor individual.[7]

e. Does any one of those approaches seem intuitively better to you than the others? Whatever your initial view, keep these kinds of alternatives in mind as you think about what you would do in counseling Marilyn Anderson and other clients you will meet in this Chapter.

B. Limits on the Advice a Lawyer May Give

1. Look at Model Rule 1.2(d) and Comments [9] & [10] to Rule 1.2. Do you agree that there should be no exceptions to the rule that a lawyer may not "counsel or assist" a client to commit a crime or fraud?

4. Their leading book on the subject is David Binder & Susan Price, Legal Interviewing and Counseling: A Client–Centered Approach (1977).

5. See, e.g., William Simon, The Practice of Justice (1998).

6. See, e.g., Thomas Shaffer & Robert F. Cochran, Jr., Lawyers, Clients and Moral Responsibility (1994). See also, Thomas D. Morgan, Thinking About Lawyers as Counselors, 42 Florida L. Rev. 429 (1990).

7. See, e.g., Deborah L. Rhode, In the Interests of Justice: Reforming the Legal Profession (2000).

a. People v. Chappell, 927 P.2d 829 (Colo.1996), was a discipline case in which the lawyer represented the wife in a custody dispute. Both parents were forbidden to take the child out of state. When the lawyer for the mother learned that the court-appointed evaluator was going to recommend giving the father custody of both the living and her unborn child, the lawyer "advised her [the client] as an attorney to stay, but as a mother to run" and told her of a network of safehouses that might take her in. At the lawyer's request, a friend of the client came into the client's home and moved her belongings into a storage locker to which the lawyer kept the key. When the lawyer came to the next hearing and the court asked where her client was, the lawyer told the court that the client's location was privileged. Only at a later hearing did the lawyer admit the client had fled the state. The court ruled that the lawyer had violated Rule 1.2(d) by counseling the client to commit a crime, and Rule 3.3(a)(2) by not revealing the client's action to the trial judge. The court was incensed, and the lawyer was disbarred.

b. Iowa Supreme Court Board of Professional Ethics & Conduct v. Hughes, 557 N.W.2d 890 (Iowa 1996), imposed a public reprimand on a lawyer who advised his client to ignore a court order to undergo substance abuse testing at the client's expense. The lawyer believed such an order was beyond the authority of the court. The client disregarded the advice and underwent the testing, but the trial judge referred the lawyer's conduct to the disciplinary committee. The Iowa Supreme Court assumed without deciding that a lawyer could counsel a client to ignore a void order, i.e., the order of a court with no jurisdiction over the matter, but in a case like this one, when the client's interests "conflict with a lawful court order, the lawyer's duty to uphold the law is paramount." 557 N.W.2d at 894.

c. Do you agree with the results in these cases? Can you imagine ever counseling a client to flee the jurisdiction or violate a court order? What if you believed your client's life would be in danger if she did not flee, for example? What if violation of a court order were the only way to make the order ripe for appellate review?

2. Is it obvious what it means to "counsel or assist" wrongdoing?

a. Would you be "counseling" wrongdoing if you gave the client honest information about whether it was likely that a violation of law would be prosecuted, for example? Does Comment [9] to Model Rule 1.2 answer that question to your satisfaction?

b. Would you be "assisting" wrongdoing if a client charged with murder asked you which South American countries have no extradition treaties with the United States? Look at Comments [9] & [10] to Model Rule 1.2.

c. Should the lawyer offer such information, even if not asked, as a way of providing the client full service? Must the lawyer refuse to answer questions that a dishonest client might use to avoid the consequences of past misconduct or plan future misdeeds? Must the lawyer ask the murder defendant for his passport and hold it lest the client try to flee?

3. Assume that Marilyn Anderson's mother owns her own house and a few stocks but has no other source of income. If she were to become ill, the house could be seized to reimburse Medicaid authorities for her care. What would you think of encouraging her to give her house to Ms. Anderson as a way of avoiding that result?

a. Assume that, as long as she did not make clear she had given her house to a relative, Marilyn's mother could also qualify for welfare because she would be without assets and unable to work. She might then even pay part of her benefits to Marilyn as "rent."

b. Would it be appropriate for you to suggest this approach to Marilyn's mother and offer to draft the documents necessary to transfer the property to Marilyn?[8] Would it be important for you to have Marilyn promise to care for her mother or otherwise show some consideration for the transfer?

c. Section 217 of the 1996 Health Insurance Portability and Accountability Act, 42 U.S.C. § 1320a–7b, purported to deal with the practice described in this question by making it a crime to dispose of assets to qualify for Medicaid. Thus, the law was nicknamed the "Granny Goes to Jail Act." The provision was then reinforced by § 4734 of the Balanced Budget Act of 1997 that also made it a crime to take a fee for counseling someone how to manipulate assets in prohibited ways.[9]

d. If you—the lawyer—fail to give such asset-management advice, will you be violating Model Rule 1.1's obligation to act "competently"? Will you be committing malpractice? If you *do* give the advice, will you be violating Model Rule 1.2(d)? Which rule should control?

4. Would you be more uncomfortable, or less, about helping a wealthy client buy an expensive house in Florida or set up a trust in the Cook Islands that would exempt those assets from being seized by creditors if the client ever went bankrupt?

a. Would you justify the conduct by saying that the wealthy are such deep-pocket targets of frivolous litigation that any action is justified to defend them against such injustice?

---

8. Lest you think this proposal is hypothetical, the ethics of "asset management" of elderly clients is an every day issue faced by "elder law" attorneys around the nation. See, e.g., Steven H. Hobbs & Fay Wilson Hobbs, The Ethical Management of Assets for Elder Clients: A Context, Role, and Law Approach, 62 Fordham L.Rev. 1411 (1994).

9. N.Y. State Bar Association v. Reno, 999 F.Supp. 710 (N.D.N.Y.1998), was a suit to enjoin the Attorney General's enforcement of the prohibition. The Justice Department had already notified Congress it would not enforce the provision and said an injunction was not necessary, but the court found that even the existence of the statutory prohibition was enough to cause self-censorship by lawyers who had taken an oath to abide by the law. Because the government was unlikely to defend the constitutionality of the statute, the court found the plaintiffs were likely to succeed on the merits and granted a preliminary injunction.

b.   Is the answer to such questions simply that if conduct is permitted under a technically-defensible interpretation of the law, all moral questions vanish? Do you suppose that lawyers for companies accused of misleading investors about their financial condition can rest easy that the public will be comfortable with that answer?

C.   THE CLIENT SUFFERING FROM DIMINISHED CAPACITY

1.   Would your answer about following Marilyn Anderson's directions differ if you had concluded that she had less than normal intelligence and was immature for her age?

a.   Look at Model Rule 1.14 and Restatement Third, The Law Governing Lawyers § 24. When should you conclude that your client has "diminished capacity"? Are you competent to tell? Does Comment [6] to Model Rule 1.14 give you helpful guidance? Should you be held to be guilty of malpractice if you treat your client as sovereign when she really is impaired?

b.   If your client was legally incompetent, did she have the capacity to retain you? Can she consent to your continuing to act as counsel? Does such a client have the capacity to fire you? Look at Model Rule 1.16, Comment [6]. Might a client have the capacity to make the decisions to retain and terminate you without having the capacity to make all decisions about the objectives and conduct of the representation?

2.   May or must you ever seek to have a guardian appointed to act on an apparently incompetent client's behalf? What if the client objects to having a guardian?

a.   Look at Model Rule 1.14, Comments [7] and [8]. May you testify at the client's competency hearing? In doing so, should you be permitted to reveal what the client told you in confidence? What if the incoherence of those confidential conversations is your best evidence of the client's need of a guardian's assistance?

b.   ABA Formal Opinion 96–404 (Aug. 2, 1996) acknowledges that if a client's "ability to communicate, to comprehend and assess information, and to make reasoned decisions is partially or completely diminished," Rule 1.14's admonition to "maintain a normal lawyer-client relationship" with the client "may be difficult or impossible." Indeed, in some states, the agency relationship between lawyer and client may be dissolved by the client-principal's incompetence. Further, lawyer withdrawal in such circumstances may be impossible without "material adverse effect" on the client's interests. The Opinion thus counsels that a lawyer should take the "least restrictive action under the circumstances;" appointment of a guardian should only be chosen "if other, less drastic, solutions are [not] available." Further, even if a guardian is needed for some purposes, something less than a general guardianship should be sought if possible. While the lawyer may file the petition for guardianship, it must be because the lawyer concludes it is necessary, not because someone else (such as a family member) requests it. Finally, if the lawyer is asked to recommend a guardian, any expectation the lawyer may have of future employment by the guardian must be disclosed to the appointing court, as must any different preference for a guardian that the client might have expressed.

c.   Matter of M.R., 638 A.2d 1274 (N.J.1994), involved a moderately-retarded 21–year old woman with Down's syndrome who was said to be "generally incompetent" and in need of a guardian. The question before the court was whether M.R. could decide whether she wanted her father or her mother to be that guardian. Part of the court's analysis involved whether appointed counsel should advocate M.R.'s preference to have her father as guardian or should make an independent report to the court about M.R.'s best interest. The court drew a distinction between a court-appointed lawyer and a court-appointed guardian ad litem. The latter is to make an investigation and report. Citing Model Rule 1.14, however, the court said that counsel appointed to represent M.R. must try to maintain "a normal client-lawyer relationship" with her. The lawyer must advocate what the client wants, short of things "patently absurd or that pose an undue risk of harm to the client." 638 A.2d at 1285. Do you agree?

d.   L.A. County Bar Association, Formal Opinion 504 (2000) discusses an attorney's duty with regard to confidential information of a minor client's on-going sexual abuse. The opinion says the attorney has a duty to keep such information confidential if, after discussing the matter with the minor, the attorney reasonably believes that the client is competent to make a decision on the matter. What the attorney thinks is in the best interest of the client is not controlling. Indeed, even if the attorney feels that the minor is not competent to make such a decision, the attorney may not substitute her own decision for that of the client but may seek other appropriate measures such as having a guardian ad litem appointed and disclosing the information to that guardian.

3.   Should special rules apply if immediate action must be taken on behalf of a person—typically not a current client of the lawyer—who seems to lack the ability to make the necessary decisions to provide for his or her own welfare?

a.   In response to ABA Formal Opinion 96–404, supra, the ABA House of Delegates amended the Comments to Rule 1.14 in February 1997 to add what are now Comments [9] & [10] on "Emergency Legal Assistance." The core idea of Comment [9] is that "where the health, safety or a financial interest of a person under a disability is threatened with imminent and irreparable harm, a lawyer may take legal action on behalf of such a person even though the person is unable to establish a client-lawyer relationship or make or express considered judgments about the matter, when the disabled person or another acting in good faith on that person's behalf has consulted the lawyer."

b.   Comment [10] goes on to say that the lawyer should protect the confidences of the disabled person, should not act in this capacity if the person has another lawyer, and normally should not charge a fee for the services rendered.

c. How would you exercise the authority and responsibility given by these Comments? Might you seek to find and involve family members of the person, for example? Might you see if they belong to a church or other religious or social community whose members might help them? Might the lack of such a support network be part of why you now find the person in crisis?

4. If there were grounds to believe that your client were about to make a fatal mistake, would you have an obligation to disregard the client's expressed preference and substitute your own judgment of what was best for the client?

a. Convicted killer Gary Gilmore is reported to have said that he "had to" die for a crime he had committed two centuries ago in England, and that he would still be in existence after his death. His attorneys thought that Gilmore's references to eighteenth century England would have made a difference to psychiatrists if they had heard it. The lawyers said, "we feel duty bound to go ahead with the appeal." Gilmore sent a letter to the attorneys saying: "butt out" and "you're fired." The attorneys then filed a notice of appeal in their own names saying that it was "in the best interest" of Gilmore, who was eventually executed.[10]

Were the lawyers right to ignore the client's call for his own death? One commentator has argued: "If the client expresses ends which, due to imprudence or excessive moralism, seem self-destructive, it is the lawyer's job to question the client's competence where it may need questioning * * * . When, on the other hand, the client is able to make his or her ends plausible to the lawyer, the check which he means to provide must give way."[11]

Do you agree? Should the client have to convince the lawyer before the lawyer has to give the client his own way?

b. Massachusetts Bar Association Opinion 01–2 (2001) addresses revealing a client's intention to commit suicide. Because neither suicide nor attempted suicide is a crime in Massachusetts, its Rule 1.6 did not supply a basis for disclosure. The opinion thus is based on Rule 1.14. It says that if a lawyer reasonably believes the client's suicide threat is real and that the client is suffering from a mental disorder or disability that prevents him from making a rational decision about whether to continue living, the lawyer may notify family members, adult protective agencies, the police, or the client's doctors in an attempt to prevent the suicide. The opinion does not give a blanket authority to disclose even the client's wish to die. Presumably, if the client were in great pain from a terminal disease, for example, but not unduly depressed or otherwise mentally impaired, Rule 1.14 would not authorize disclose of the client's plans.

Do you agree? What would you do if you were the one told of the client's intention to end his or her life?

---

10. Norman Mailer, The Executioner's Song 490, 513–14 (1979).

11. David Luban, Paternalism and the Legal Profession, 1981 Wisconsin L. Rev. 454, 493.

D.   THE CLIENT WHO IS LIKELY TO ENDANGER OTHERS

1.   Should the interest of your client be the only interest relevant to you? Might a lawyer properly consider the interests of others, including the public interest, in rendering advice to a client?

a.   In his address at the laying of the cornerstone of the American Bar Center in 1954, Justice Robert Jackson said:

> "We believe in an independent Bar, free not only from govern-ment control, but intellectually independent of client control. In the client-and-attorney relation the client is not a master, the lawyer is not a mere hired hand—he is an officer of the court, with a duty of independent judgment in the performance of his profes-sional service and under a duty to serve all sorts and conditions of men."[12]

b.   Do you agree? Should lawyers be "intellectually independent of client control"? If a lawyer acts with "independence," is the client getting what the client properly thinks he or she is paying for? Putting aside his rhetorical excess, is Justice Jackson really saying that no client is an island and no client's act should be seen as without consequences that a lawyer must consider in giving sound advice?

2.   May a lawyer properly refuse to pursue a legally-sound but unjust cause?

a.   California Business and Professional Code § 6068(h) provides that it is a lawyer's duty:

> "Never to reject, for any consideration personal to himself, the cause of the defenseless or the oppressed."

Does this section apply to the lawyer for Marilyn Anderson? Is she the one who is oppressed and defenseless, or is it her children?

b.   The question of pursuing an unjust cause often seems not to trouble lawyers today. Our instincts seem to be to look to positive law, not natural law or "justice" in some other sense. But to many, the problem of what causes to champion has been one of the fundamental moral issues facing the legal profession.

c.   David Hoffman, the Baltimore lawyer who in 1836 was one of the first to organize and espouse legal ethics principles, for example, considered the situation of the client who owes a just debt, suit to collect which is barred by the Statute of Limitations. His conclusion would surprise many modern lawyers.

> "I will never plead the Statute of Limitations, when based on the *mere efflux of time;* for if my client is conscious he owes the

---

12. Robert H. Jackson, The American Bar Center: A Testimony to Our Faith in the Rule of Law, 40 A.B.A.J. 19, 21 (1954).

debt; and has no other defence than the *legal bar*, he shall never make me a partner in his knavery."[13]

Is that idea archaic? Would a lawyer who lived out his own morality in this way have to answer in malpractice to his client?

d. Or consider George Sharswood, whose lectures laid the groundwork for the Alabama Code of Ethics of 1887, and in 1908, for the American Bar Association Canons of Ethics:

> "Counsel * * * have an undoubted right, and are duty bound, to refuse to be concerned for a plaintiff in the legal pursuit of a demand which offends his sense of what is just and right. The courts are open to the party in person to prosecute his own claim, and plead his own cause; and although * * * he ought to examine and be well satisfied before he refuses to a suitor the benefit of his professional skill and learning, yet * * * it would be on his part an immoral act to afford that assistance, when his conscience told him that the client was aiming to perpetrate a wrong through the means of some advantage the law may have afforded him."[14]

Is that shocking to you? Does a lawyer bear a moral responsibility for accepting an unjust cause? Is Sharswood right that it is only plaintiffs' cases to which that responsibility attaches (because defendants don't have a choice whether or not to be sued)? Does Model Rule 1.2(b) contradict this view of the lawyer's role?

e. In an even earlier time, James Boswell once reported that Dr. Johnson's solution to supporting a cause he knew to be bad was:

> "Sir, you do not know it to be good or bad till the Judge determines it. I have said that you are to state facts fairly; so that your thinking, or what you call knowing, a cause to be bad, must be from reasoning, must be from supposing your arguments to be weak and inclusive. But, Sir, that is not enough. An argument which does not convince yourself, may convince the Judge to whom you urge it: and if it does convince him, why, then, Sir, you are wrong and he is right."[15]

Do you agree with Dr. Johnson, or was Johnson engaged in ethical sophistry?

3. How do these considerations apply when a lawyer knows about child abuse?

a. Association of the Bar of the City of New York, Formal Opinion No. 1997–2, 52 Record of the Association of the Bar of the City of New York 430 (1997), written in the context of a lawyer for a social services agency, acknowledges that children ordinarily have the right to have their communications with a lawyer kept confidential. The Opinion even suggests that a

---

13. David Hoffman, A Course of Legal Study 754 (2d Ed.1846).

14. George Sharswood, Professional Ethics 33–35 (1854).

15. James Boswell, The Life of Johnson, vol. 2, p. 47 (Hill Edition 1887).

lawyer might not be required to disclose some intentions of the child to kill or maim himself. If the lawyer observes physical evidence of child abuse, however, the Opinion points out that the visual observation would not be privileged. Indeed, even communications of the child may be disclosed (1) if disclosure is "required by law," (2) to save the life of the child, or (3) where the child is too young to have the capacity to make decisions.

b. Utah Bar Opinion 97–12 (Jan.1998) addressed the situation of a lawyer whose client revealed himself to be a child abuser. The Opinion says the state law requiring "any person" who suspects child abuse to report it does not apply to such cases. Under Rule 1.6(b)(1), the lawyer may disclose the client's intent to commit future abuse, but a client's confession to a lawyer about past conduct is privileged and may not be disclosed.

c. Do you agree with these opinions? As a parent, might you have a different view than you have as a lawyer?

4. Is your duty different now that you have agreed to take the case and are considering withdrawal than it would have been had you not yet decided whether to represent Mrs. Anderson?

a. In re Rose Lee Ann L., 718 N.E.2d 623 (Ill.Ct.App.1999), is a situation with elements of the facts of this Problem. The state's attorney had asked for adjudication of the wardship of a child. The public guardian had been appointed to advocate that the parents have that role. That lawyer concluded, however, that his clients, both minors, "may present a serious risk of bodily harm to the * * * defenseless child." He asked for permission to withdraw and for advice about what a lawyer is to do in such a situation. The court refused to render an advisory opinion about the subject in general, but said that if a lawyer could not comply with Rule 1.2(a), i.e., not accept his client's decisions about the objectives of the representation, the lawyer should be replaced.

Do you agree with this result? Was the court implicitly saying that the next lawyer must blind his or her eyes to the interests of the child? What would you do if you were that next lawyer?

b. In re Pressly, 628 A.2d 927 (Vt.1993), involved a client who had a restraining order against her husband and custody of the children, subject to the husband's visitation rights. Later, she told the lawyer she wanted the husband to have only supervised visitation. When asked why, she said she thought he had sexually abused their daughter but she explicitly told the lawyer not to tell her husband of her suspicions. When the lawyer told opposing counsel the wife wanted supervised visitation, however, opposing counsel asked if it was because of suspected sexual abuse. The lawyer confirmed that abuse was suspected and asked opposing counsel not to tell the husband. Opposing counsel did tell the husband, and the wife was shocked and furious at her lawyer. The Vermont supreme court said the confirmation that abuse was suspected—contrary to the client's express direction not to reveal it—justified a public reprimand of the lawyer.

How would you have responded to opposing counsel's question in *Pressly*? Was the lawyer's mistake accepting the client's original direction without discussion or qualification? A client can always fire her lawyer, of course, so the client necessarily has the last word. Might the lawyer best take the client's direction as the beginning of a conversation with the client, however, rather than as an order to be carried out blindly?

5. What creative ways can you see to deal with Marilyn Anderson's situation?

a. Think back to Anderson's mother. What would you think of having Marilyn and the children move in with her? She could watch the children while Marilyn went back to work. In exchange, Marilyn would make sure her mother was in good health. She could start proceedings to divorce John and request child support. Do you have some better ideas?

b. Suppose that at the custody hearing the social worker from the Department of Children and Family Services appeared without counsel. You were still representing Mrs. Anderson, but Mrs. Anderson's children were unrepresented by counsel. Might you suggest that counsel be appointed for the children even though you surmise that, if that suggestion is implemented, your chances of winning will be substantially lessened?

c. Do you have an ethical obligation to Mrs. Anderson to oppose appointment of such counsel? Does Model Rule 4.3 provide a good analogy that helps you decide what to do? If counsel were appointed, would that lessen your own ethical burden and allow you to use all the tricks in your bag on Mrs. Anderson's behalf?

———

PROBLEM 18

ADVISING THE BUSINESS CORPORATION

It is one thing to advise an individual whom the lawyer can address face to face. When the client is a business corporation, however, the lawyer can only counsel the client's agents. Those agents, in turn, are likely to believe themselves limited by the authority of others, so the lawyer's task of giving wise counsel becomes immeasurably more complex. This Problem explores who the lawyer's ultimate client is when the lawyer represents an organization and from whom the lawyer is to accept direction. Next, it asks when a lawyer may or must disclose wrongdoing either inside or outside the organization. It then examines whether a lawyer may personally be liable to persons hurt by client conduct that the lawyer did not prevent, and finally, it considers whether the role of inside counsel as to these issues differs from that of a lawyer in an outside firm.

FACTS

You have long been are outside counsel to Sleepware, Inc., a clothing manufacturer. The company makes a line of children's pajamas that is a big seller. Recent tests have shown, however, that the pajama fabric can catch fire if a match is held against it for a few seconds.

Sleepware's Vice President for pajamas wants to keep selling the pajamas. Regulations of the Consumer Product Safety Commission prohibit sale of products known to cause burns to children, but the Vice President believes that the CPSC is unlikely to recognize the potential injuries the pajamas will cause.

Further, the Vice President points out that, although children wearing pajamas sometimes play with matches, experts he has consulted say that not more than one in 50,000 children would hold the matches on their pajamas long enough for it to catch fire. The experts admit that if the pajamas burn, the child's injuries could be expected to be severe, but a management consulting firm has estimated that civil damages would not exceed $250,000 per victim. Sleepware sells 200,000 of these pajamas each year, the Vice President tells you proudly, and it makes a profit of $2,000,000 on this product. Thus, even under a worst-case scenario, he has calculated that it will be $1 million more profitable to sell the pajamas than not to sell them.

You have not been asked for advice about whether to market this product; you only learned about the flammability while working on an unrelated matter. Indeed, the Vice President is annoyed that you have raised the issue with him. "The President will retire soon," he tells you, "and I am his natural successor. My enemies in the company would love to embarrass me with this."

QUESTIONS

A.   THE CLIENT TO WHOM A CORPORATE LAWYER OWES PRIMARY LOYALTY

1. Is your client in this Problem Sleepware's Vice President for Pajamas?

a. Describing the corporate lawyer's client has proved harder for some lawyers than for rule drafters. It is tempting to think, for example, that the clients are the persons to whom most of the lawyer's advice is given and from whom confidential information is received. Other lawyers sometimes think of their clients as shareholders generally, or perhaps the largest shareholder—the one who influences decisions the corporate managers will make.

b. To try to minimize confusion on the issue, Model Code of Professional Responsibility, Ethical Consideration 5–18 said:

> "A lawyer employed or retained by a corporation or similar entity owes his allegiance to the entity and not to a stockholder, director, officer, employee, representative, or other person connected with the entity."

c. That statement of the rule was and is accurate, but to acknowledge that corporations and other organizations only act through living people, the rule has been transformed in Model Rule 1.13(a) to say:

> "A lawyer employed or retained by an organization represents the organization acting through its duly authorized constituents."

d. The principle was further refined in Restatement Third, The Law Governing Lawyers § 96(1)(a) to say:

> "When a lawyer is employed or retained to represent an organization, the lawyer represents the interests of the organization as defined by its responsible agents acting pursuant to the organization's decision making procedures."

2. How do these definitions apply in real life? Do they all point the same way in particular cases?

a. Do you suppose the interest of the entity is always self-evident? Might the employees want higher pay and secure jobs, for example, while the shareholders might want to change the company's direction in search of faster growth? Might the bondholders have objectives that differ from both the employees and the shareholders?

b. Might it be best to see the board of directors as having the last word on defining the goals of a corporate client? Is it realistic to believe they represent all affected constituencies in the corporation? Is it enough that they are at the top of the corporate decision-making pyramid? This view would have the lawyer look to the board for authoritative guidance on difficult issues. As one writer put it:

> "That answer is certainly the one suggested by most corporate laws. * * * If the view is taken that the board of directors *cannot* be accepted as representing the corporation * * * then we are indeed in a difficult position * * * ."[1]

Do you agree that the answer is that simple?

c. Should a lawyer mentally stand outside the corporation and see the "entity" as the objectives and purposes that are shared by most of the people who have invested in and managed the corporation? Those people will each have many different private interests, of course, but the lawyer for the corporation would not only not represent those private interests, he or she would often have to see that they are subordinated to the purposes they have in common.

Look at the first two sentences of Comment [3] to Model Rule 1.13. Do they eliminate such an affirmative role for the corporate lawyer, except in matters serious enough to require action under Model Rule 1.13(b)? Do you think the line between poor business decisions and illegal conduct is always as clear as the Comment suggests?

1. Simon Lorne, The Corporate and Securities Adviser, The Public Interest, and Professional Ethics, 76 Michigan L.Rev. 425, 436–37 (1978) (emphasis in original). See also id. at 477–79.

3. Might you as Sleepware's counsel become a director of Sleepware? Are the duties of corporate counsel and director both duties to the corporate entity and thus sufficiently close that the roles would be compatible?

a. ABA Formal Opinion 98–410 (Feb. 27, 1998) concluded that the dual relationship is not per se improper, but problems of conflicts of interest and preservation of privilege might arise. First, the Opinion says, at the outset of the dual relationship, the lawyer should advise the company—preferably in writing—of both kinds of problems, and should independently satisfy herself that problems are unlikely to become serious. At least four types of conflicts may arise in such situations: (1) acting as counsel as to a decision the lawyer opposed as a director, (2) opining on past board action in which the lawyer participated as a director, (3) voting on corporate action affecting the lawyer's firm, and (4) representing the corporation in litigation that may involve a conflict of interest. Further, when the client seeks legal advice as opposed to business judgment, the lawyer should take precautions to make a record as to what kind of advice is being given so as to be sure the privilege is preserved.

b. A long-time corporate lawyer further explained the concerns:

"Let me give you some examples of the everyday problems. * * *

"The most difficult situation arises when an attorney is himself a witness to events involving a corporation in which he has a financial interest as a stockholder-director as well as being counsel. His questioning is continually interrupted by assertions of privilege because of the attorney-client relationship. Once again all parties must wade through a morass to determine whether the privilege is being misused.

"Another set of problems exists when an attorney is called upon to advise a client as to the client's exercise of his privilege against self-incrimination. Sometimes it is apparent that the business dealings of the attorney involved were perhaps more incriminating than the acts of his client involving the same set of circumstances. How can such an attorney be expected to impartially advise his client as to the wisdom of the exercise of the privilege against self-incrimination, when the attorney's own incrimination may possibly be involved? * * *

"The attorney in such position potentially may be involved in the conflict of interest that may emerge within his mind when he weighs advice. For that task, he wears two hats. He is a businessman quite often with a personal business stake in the decisions of the company. However, he is more than likely to be called on for legal advice by the company. Can it not be said that determinations made by such an attorney, when asked for legal advice, are necessarily colored by the personal interest which he has as a substantial stockholder, option-owner, salaried official, or otherwise? To put it more simply, the question is whether we should permit the continuing growth of such conflicts in the practice of law by which the lawyer-confidant merges with the interested businessman."[2]

c. Does Comment [35] to Model Rule 1.7 adequately describe the potential concerns about a lawyer also serving as a director of a client? Does it give inadequate recognition to the good a lawyer could potentially do as a director?

4. Today, of course, large corporations are often composed of several divisions and subsidiaries. Who is the lawyer's client in those situations?

a. Suppose, for example, Sleepware produces hats through an existing subsidiary. It wants to acquire a new firm in the same industry, but to do so it must divest itself of the present sub. Is it clear whose interests Sleepware's corporate counsel must represent in structuring the sale of the subsidiary firm? Would it matter to you whether the subsidiary was wholly-owned or whether it still had other shareholders as well? See, e.g., F.T.C. v. Exxon Corp., 636 F.2d 1336 (D.C.Cir.1980) (separate counsel required for divested subsidiary because former parent might structure sale so as to see that it did not survive as a viable competitor).

b. Suppose instead that the corporate subsidiary is a regulated entity that has duties to interests other than those of the parent. Lincoln Savings, for example, was a wholly–owned subsidiary of ACC, the holding company that Charles Keating used to make other investments. The government asserted that, because the Federal Deposit Insurance Corporation must make good the losses of an insured savings and loan, the law firm representing Lincoln could not accept direction from ACC's officers, at least once Lincoln was in financial trouble. ACC would bear the entire loss of equity from its failure, but the interest of the Lincoln "entity" included the interest of Lincoln's insurer, the F.D.I.C., as well. See, In re American Continental Corporation/Lincoln Savings and Loan Securities Litigation, 794 F.Supp. 1424 (D.Ariz.1992), which held, in ruling on a motion for summary judgment, that there were valid claims stated against Lincoln's attorneys and accountants.

B. REPORTING CORPORATE MISCONDUCT WITHIN AND OUTSIDE THE CLIENT ORGANIZATION

1. What steps are you required to take in the situation presented in our Problem? Is the Vice President's instruction to drop the matter something you must or may accept as final? When does a lawyer's obligation shift from taking orders to taking action?

a. Look at Model Rule 1.13(b). There was no corresponding provision in the Model Code, but does Rule 1.13(b) make sense? Might it provide

2. Hon. Louis J. Lefkowitz, The Attorney–Client Relationship and the Corporation, 26 Record of the Association of the Bar of the City of New York 697 (No.8, Nov.1971).

appropriate guidance for lawyers in states that have not yet adopted the Model Rules?

b.   Is the sale of the pajamas "a violation of a legal obligation to the organization"? Is it "a violation of law which reasonably might be imputed to the organization"? Is it "likely to result in substantial injury to the organization"?

c.   On the "substantial injury" issue, is the Vice President's judgment the only relevant one? Are his "experts'" estimates of the rate of injury and the management consultant's estimate of the likely jury award convincing to you? Indeed, is reevaluation of critical factual assumptions such as these often one of the most helpful services a lawyer can perform for a client?

2.   If you conclude that the conditions specified in Model Rule 1.13 are met, are you required to take action? What action?

a.   Look closely at Model Rule 1.13(b). Are the three steps described there each formal up-the-line requirements or simply examples of steps the lawyer might take?

b.   Assuming that the Vice President will not reconsider and does not want a second opinion, is this a matter you would take to the President of Sleepware? If the President tells you to take the issue no farther, should you accept that as binding? Can you answer that question without knowing the reasons for the President's direction?

c.   If you take the matter to Sleepware's Board of Directors, what will be your appropriate role? Must you be an advocate against the continued sale of the product? Is such advocacy an appropriate role for outside counsel? Whatever happened to the idea that the client is the principal and the lawyer only the agent?

3.   If your advice to discontinue sales of the pajamas is ignored by the Board of Directors, may you report the situation to the shareholders?

a.   Look at Model Rule 1.13(b) & (c). Shareholders ordinarily do not have authority to "act on behalf of" a corporation. Nor may they ordinarily countermand decisions of the Board of Directors. This leads many to suggest that the lawyer may not tell the shareholders what is going on.

b.   However, shareholders typically have authority to defeat directors when they come up for re-election. If the shareholders cannot be informed about director wrongdoing, how are they to exercise the authority they do have?

4.   May you report the corporate client to a public enforcement agency such as the Consumer Product Safety Commission?

a.   Look again at Model Rule 1.13 (b) & (c). They don't say anything about disclosure outside the organization. Should they?

b.   The present form of Model Rule 1.13 is no accident. Look at Model Rule 1.13(c) as proposed by the Kutak Commission and reprinted as a footnote to Model Rule 1.13 in the Standards Supplement. That proposal would have allowed disclosure outside the organization "that the lawyer reasonably believes to be in the best interest of the organization" if the lawyer reasonably believed that "the highest authority in the organization has acted to further the personal or financial interests of members of that authority which are in conflict with the interests of the organization." Would you have favored at least this limited right of disclosure?

5. Does the corporate lawyer have to look to Model Rule 1.13 to find authority to disclose the dangerous character of the product? How about looking to Model Rule 1.6(b)?

a. ABA Formal Opinion 314 (Apr. 27, 1965) implied that a lawyer *must* disclose even the confidences of his clients if "the facts in the attorney's possession indicate beyond reasonable doubt that a crime will be committed." Did the text of ABA Model Code of Professional Responsibility DR 4–101(C)(3) support that interpretation? Did the term "may" in that rule mean "must"? Should violation of a CPSC regulation be treated as the *equivalent* of a crime?

b. Notice that the Model Rules are more restrictive. Should the permission to withdraw in Rule 1.13(c) negate the lawyer's right to disclose under Rule 1.6(b)(1)? Does Comment [5] to Rule 1.13 settle the issue? Surely, there is no doubt that the sale of these pajamas will result in "reasonably certain * * * substantial bodily harm."

c. What does Restatement Third, The Law Governing Lawyers § 66 tell you about the circumstances in which even confidential information about a dangerous product may be disclosed? Does it require criminal conduct, for example? Does it require that the death or injury be "imminent"? Do you welcome the latitude it gives to make disclosure in cases such as this one?[3]

C. LAWYER LIABILITY FOR FAILURE TO TAKE APPROPRIATE ACTION

1. If you assume that disclosure of the danger to children is permitted in this case, could you be held liable to anyone for a failure to disclose?

a. Comment [13] to Model Rule 1.6 advises: "A lawyer's decision not to disclose as permitted by paragraph (b) does not violate this Rule."

b. Restatement § 66(3) says even more clearly:

"A lawyer who takes action or decides not to take action permitted under this Section is not, solely by reason of such action or inaction, subject to professional discipline, liable for damages to the lawyer's client or any third person, or barred from recovery against a client or third person."

3. As you may know, the lawyer's right or obligation to reveal the unwillingness of a corporate board to stop illegal or fraudulent conduct is controversial today. We will return to this issue in Problem 22, infra.

c. Is that the end of the matter? Is there any information a lawyer should be *required* to disclose?

In State v. Hansen, 862 P.2d 117 (Wash.1993), a lawyer had gotten a call from a prospective client, recently out of prison, who said of the participants in his criminal trial, "I am going to get a gun and blow them all away, the prosecutor, the judge and the public defender." The lawyer did not take the case but he did call the prosecutor and the judge. The police arrested Hansen, the prospective client, and he was convicted of intimidating a judge. He claimed the remarks for which he was convicted had been privileged. Not surprisingly, the court found that the comments were within the crime-fraud exception, and the court went on that "attorneys, as officers of the court, have a duty to warn of true threats to harm members of the judiciary communicated to them by clients or by third parties." 862 P.2d at 122.

Do you agree? Should the "duty" in this passage be seen as more than a rhetorical flourish?

2. If you might be liable to anyone for a failure to disclose, might one possible plaintiff be your client, the corporation itself?

a. Might its claim be that you did not protect it from the wrongdoing of its management and directors? Similar charges were faced by law firms being sued for not taking sufficiently tough steps to prevent the failure of their savings and loan clients.

b. In FDIC v. Mmahat, 907 F.2d 546 (5th Cir.1990), cert. denied 499 U.S. 936, 111 S.Ct. 1387, 113 L.Ed.2d 444 (1991), for example, a lawyer had been general counsel of a savings and loan association for over 20 years. Indeed, he served as chairman of the Board of Directors of the institution for six of those years. When the Garn–St Germain Act of 1982 allowed S & Ls to lend more freely, the association did so. Even if a loan would violate the FHLBB's "loans to one borrower" regulations, the lawyer did not seek to prevent its making the loan. The judgment recovered by the FDIC against the lawyer was $35 million.[4]

c. FDIC v. O'Melveny & Myers, 969 F.2d 744 (9th Cir.1992), rev'd on other grounds sub nom. O'Melveny & Myers v. FDIC, 512 U.S. 79, 114 S.Ct. 2048, 129 L.Ed.2d 67 (1994), was a suit against a law firm that had helped a bank create real estate syndications that were sold to large investors. The firm wrote much of the private placement memorandum and purported to do a due diligence review of the relevant facts. Much of the success of the deal depended on the financial health of the bank. The bank's auditors had said the bank had little or no net worth, but the law firm apparently did not talk to them. The investors did not bring the lawsuit; they had complained earlier and the FDIC had given them their

---

4. As usual in such cases, even though Mmahat had been the only lawyer in the firm involved, all lawyers in the firm were liable for his acts. To the chagrin of the lawyers, however, because the cause of the losses was found to be Mmahat's dishonesty, the firm's malpractice carrier was excused from liability by the terms of its policy. The lawyers apparently had to come up with the money themselves.

money back. Thus, the suit here was a claim by the bank's receiver to recover funds it had to repay the investors. The law firm argued that the client had deceived it and that the firm did not have to protect the client against its own wrong. The court rejected such a bright line test. "It is an attorney's duty to protect the client in every possible way," the court said. "No California cases advise us of an exception to the general rule that a lawyer has to act competently to avoid public harm when he learns that his is a dishonest client." 969 F.2d at 748. Thus, summary judgment for the law firm was reversed.[5]

d. FDIC v. Clark, 978 F.2d 1541 (10th Cir.1992), gave lawyers even more reason for concern. The law firm had represented the bank in many matters since its opening. Unknown to the law firm, several bank officers initiated a "heist money scheme" in which they used $2 million in bank money to buy $9 million in stolen money. To do this, they created loan files to non-existent borrowers and forged checks on non–existent accounts. Ultimately, they were caught, but the FDIC argued that the lawyers were slow to act when they first heard the charges. The bank officers had told the lawyers that it was all a misunderstanding and not to worry about it. The law firm so advised the bank's board without making an investigation of its own. The court, citing *O'Melveny & Myers*, affirmed that a jury could find that inaction under these circumstances was a sufficient basis for imposing liability. The jury was properly instructed, and a lawyer may not necessarily rely on the client's officers' assertions about their lack of wrongdoing.

e. Conceding that these cases were more about a failure to inquire than a failure to disclose, given the cases, would you feel comfortable simply taking the Vice President's assurance that selling the pajamas raised no issues worth examining further?[6]

5. The Supreme Court decision in the case, 512 U.S. 79, 114 S.Ct. 2048, 129 L.Ed.2d 67 (1994), was largely an anticlimax. The firm said that the FDIC itself should be deemed to know what company management knew, and thus that the law firm had nothing to discover or "inform" anyone about. The FDIC tried the case on the theory that federal law, not state law, governed the question of what knowledge would be imputed to it. In its opinion, the Supreme Court said there is no general federal common law and no statute that creates a federal rule of decision on the question of what management knowledge should be imputed to the FDIC. Thus, the case was remanded for decision of that point under state law. On remand, the Court of Appeals expressed surprise that the Supreme Court had thought it decided the case on federal instead of state law, and reached the same result expressly as an inter-

pretation of California law. FDIC v. O'Melveny & Myers, 61 F.3d 17 (9th Cir.1995).

6. But see, FDIC v. Ferguson, 982 F.2d 404 (10th Cir.1991), holding that the proportion of the loss for which the lawyer can be held liable can be reduced by extent of the contributory acts of the bank client's officials. Cf. Reves v. Ernst & Young, 507 U.S. 170, 113 S.Ct. 1163, 122 L.Ed.2d 525 (1993), holding that for purposes of RICO liability, professionals such as lawyers may not be sued unless they actually took part in the management of the client. See also, F.D.I.C. v. Cocke, 7 F.3d 396 (4th Cir.1993) (statute of limitations in suits against lawyers for savings and loan associations is a matter of state law). See also, Kansas Public Employees Retirement System v. Kutak Rock, 44 P.3d 407 (Kan.2002) (law firm does not have duty to warn client about doubtful financial wisdom of a transaction).

3.   Might you be subject to a direct suit by the shareholders of the corporation for a decline in the value of their stock?

a.   The theory that lawyers represent the entity has served to insulate some corporate lawyers from suits by individual shareholders. TJD Dissolution Corp. v. Savoie Supply Co., 460 N.W.2d 59 (Minn.App.1990), for example, was a malpractice action in which a corporate shareholder sued the corporation's lawyer for losses the shareholder personally suffered in a deal that the lawyer had worked out for a buyout of the corporation by other shareholders. The shareholder argued that the lawyer owed a duty of care to each shareholder, but the court disagreed. The lawyer clearly represented only the corporation and the interests of the shareholders were in conflict. The lawyer had advised the plaintiff shareholder to get separate counsel and did not owe him any duty individually. See also, Skarbrevik v. Cohen, England & Whitfield, 282 Cal.Rptr. 627 (Cal.Ct.App.1991).

b.   Waggoner v. Snow, Becker, Kroll, Klaris & Krauss, 991 F.2d 1501 (9th Cir.1993), was a particularly interesting case dealing with corporate counsel's dealings with the major shareholder. When the company was in financial trouble, Waggoner, the CEO and major shareholder, agreed to sign guarantees in exchange for voting control of the corporation while his guarantees were in effect. Corporate counsel said that could be arranged, drew up the papers and had Waggoner sign them. Later, the Board fired Waggoner, and he tried to remove them using what he thought was his voting control. It turned out, however, that corporate counsel's work had not successfully delivered control to Waggoner, so Waggoner both lost his job and remained liable on the guarantees. He sued the corporate counsel for malpractice. The court found that corporate counsel had made clear he represented only the corporation and had not assumed any personal duties to Waggoner. It affirmed summary judgment for the lawyer.

c.   The same principle often applies to partnerships, i.e., a lawyer who purports only to represent the partnership often has civil liability only to the partnership as an entity. Hopper v. Frank, 16 F.3d 92 (5th Cir.1994), for example, reached that result and quoted with approval, ABA Formal Opinion 91–361 (July 12, 1991):

> "[A] lawyer who represents a partnership represents the entity rather than the individual partners unless the specific circumstances show otherwise. * * * This analysis may include such factors as whether the lawyer affirmatively assumed a duty of representation to the individual partner, whether the partner was separately represented by other counsel when the partnership was created or in connection with its affairs, whether the lawyer had represented an individual partner before undertaking to represent the partnership, and whether there was evidence of reliance by the individual partner on the lawyer as his or her separate counsel * * *." Id. at 95–96.

e.   But see Granewich v. Harding, 985 P.2d 788 (Ore.1999) (corporation's lawyers held liable to minority shareholder "squeezed out" by controlling shareholder; lawyers held to be co-conspirators with the controlling shareholder in a breach of fiduciary duty); Arpadi v. First MSP

Corporation, 628 N.E.2d 1335 (Ohio 1994) (under Ohio law a lawyer for a partnership represents the partners, not the entity, so even each limited partner has a right of action against the lawyer.)

4. Might you be held liable in civil damages to consumers hurt by sale of the pajamas?

a. In this regard, lawyers have long feared the precedent of Tarasoff v. Regents of the University of California, 551 P.2d 334 (Cal.1976), vacating 529 P.2d 553 (Cal.1974). There, the court held that a psychotherapist who knew of a planned murder and did not warn the victim was subject to a tort cause of action.

> "When a therapist determines, or pursuant to the standards of the profession should determine, that his patient presents a serious danger of violence to another, he incurs an obligation to use reasonable care to protect the intended victim against such danger. The discharge of this duty may require the therapist to take one or more of various steps, depending upon the nature of the case. Thus it may call for him to warn the intended victim or others likely to apprise the victim of the danger, to notify the police, or to take whatever other steps are reasonably necessary under the circumstances." 551 P.2d at 340.

b. Should the *Tarasoff* rule be extended to apply to lawyers? Restatement Third, The Law Governing Lawyers § 66, Comment *g*, warns:

> "Critical facts may be unclear, emotions may be high, and little time may be available in which the lawyer much decide on an appropriate course of action. Subsequent re-examination of the reasonableness of a lawyer's action in the light of later developments would be unwarranted; reasonableness of the lawyer's belief at the time and in the circumstances in which the lawyer acts is alone controlling."

Are you convinced? Could you have made the same argument for the therapist in *Tarasoff*?

c. Crawford & Lewis v. Boatmen's Trust Co., 1 S.W.3d 417 (Ark. 1999), illustrates that a similar question of liability can arise in the context of trust administration. There were two trustees, a bank and an individual who was also the residuary beneficiary. The individual trustee wanted to use trust assets to help himself buy a house. The bank resisted that move as self-dealing but the individual went ahead with the purchase and the lawyer for the trust represented him at the closing. Later, the individual sold the house to someone who took bankruptcy before finishing paying for the house. When the law firm filed a petition for fees, its assistance in a breach of the trustee's fiduciary duty was found both to justify denying additional fees and disgorgement of the fees already paid. Most of the firm's efforts were on behalf of the individual trustee, not the trust itself, and the trust was not required to pay for those efforts.

d. See also, Restatement Third, The Law Governing Lawyers § 51(4) (liability to non-client for client's breach of fiduciary duty); Wolf v. Mitchell, Silberberg & Knupp, 90 Cal.Rptr.2d 792 (Cal.Ct.App.1999) (residuary beneficiary of trust permitted to sue the trustee's lawyer for assisting the trustee to use trust assets to pay his gambling debts and otherwise engage in self-dealing). But see ABA Formal Opinion 94–380 (May 9, 1994) (lawyer's duties run only to fiduciary, not the beneficiary); Comment [27] to Model Rule 1.7 (lawyers should make clear to whom the lawyer owes duties when representing fiduciary). See generally, Robert Tuttle, The Fiduciary's Fiduciary: Legal Ethics in Fiduciary Representation, 1994 U. Illinois L. Rev. 889.

D. SOME SPECIAL PROBLEMS OF COUNSEL EMPLOYED BY THE CORPORATION

1. Would you expect to see the number of lawyers employed by corporations to be increasing or decreasing?

a. Corporate counsel, sometimes known as in-house or inside counsel, represent one of the fastest growing segments of the bar. In 1980, for example, the number of lawyers employed as such by private industry was 54,626, or just over 10% of the 542,205 lawyers in the country. That was a 40% increase from 39,000 such lawyers in 1970. By 1988, the number was 66,627.[7]

b. This trend may well continue, in part because of the rising fees charged by outside counsel. For example, the Chairman of the Board of I.B.M. once said that its general counsel "is the only department head to whom we've given an unlimited budget—and he's already exceeded it." Many corporations, in an effort to cut costs, push for settlements, try to use arbitrators, and expand their inside corporate legal staff. The average hourly cost of work of inside counsel has been said to be approximately half that of outside counsel.[8]

2. Is the trend to increase the work done by inside corporate counsel desirable?

a. Several years ago, an author wrote that a lawyer sometimes chooses the life of "salaried employment" in a corporate law department because he may be "just happier in a job where someone else has the ultimate responsibility." And—unlike a private practice—the salaried lawyer's job has "aspects of dependence."[9]

b. In reply, another defended the professionalism of house counsel and contended that "a lawyer is a lawyer whether he charges fees or receives a salary. A salary corrupts no more than does a fee. * * *"[10]

c. Who is correct? Do you think it is true today that corporate counsel lack "ultimate responsibility" and "independence"? Might the lack of need

---

7. See Barbara A. Curran, et al., The Lawyer Statistical Report 19–21 (1985), and the 1988 supplement thereto, published in 1991.

8. John Ryan, Costly Counsel, Wall St. J., April 13, 1978, at 1, col. 1. (midwest ed.); Wall St.J.,, April 26, 1984, at 1, col. 6 (midwest ed.)(major bank's outside legal costs up to 250% more than inside legal costs).

9. William L. Hanaway, Corporate Law Departments—A New Look, 17 Business Lawyer 595, 599 (April, 1962).

10. Stephen E. Davis, Corporate Law Departments—A New Look at the "New Look," 18 Business Lawyer 569, 570 (January, 1963).

to measure their contribution in terms of billable hours give them even more independence than outside counsel experience?

3. One of the major functions of the corporate general counsel is the selection and supervision of outside counsel. How might that affect the freedom felt by outside counsel to tell the officers of the corporation what they might not want to hear?

a. Might the growing alternative of going inside, and possibly getting an answer more supportive of what management wants to do, tend to make outside firms less "independent"? See, e.g., John P. Heinz & Edward O. Laumann, Chicago Lawyers: The Social Structure of the Bar 365–373 (1982).

b. Might low-level inside counsel fear the consequences of pointing out embarrassing problems even more? Should such lawyers have whistle-blower protection when they bring such issues to the attention of the general counsel and corporate management? When we return to this question in Problem 33, we will see that they increasingly do have such protection.

c. In connection with the possible differences in pressures bearing on in-house and outside counsel consider the following:

"Do we ask too much of inside counsel? Should the Code of Professional Responsibility draw distinctions between the independence of judgment expected of outside counsel and the independence of judgment expected of inside counsel? * * * For example, the law could require that the responsibility of inside counsel be normally satisfied by reporting to outside counsel and accepting his judgment as to the proper course of action in close cases and ambiguous situations. By expecting too much of inside counsel we may receive nothing. By requiring less we are more likely to obtain all that we can realistically require. Yet we ought not, by relaxing rules, to encourage wrong behavior. We should continue to require in-house counsel to be responsible for the exercise of independent judgment. However, in close or ambiguous situations, in-house counsel ought not to be satisfied with relying solely on its own judgments. In-house counsel should be required particularly in these close cases to inform outside counsel who is subject to different pressures, and then rely on the latter's advice. * * *

"One should not overdraw the differences between outside and inside counsel. The associate of a law firm is also subject to similar pressures because disagreement with the ethical judgment of his partners could require withdrawal from the firm. The Code does not provide in such instances for a discreet withdrawal from a particular matter any more than it provides for discreet withdrawal on the part of in-house counsel. Even a large firm may be under economic pressures because a large percentage of its business may come from a very few corporate clients. While this line, which distinguishes the differing pressures on in-house and outside counsel may not be a bright one, it still provides a useful starting point."[11]

4. Should judicial concerns about the perceived lack of independence of corporate counsel affect the outcome of cases?

a. In re Oracle Securities Litigation, 829 F.Supp. 1176 (N.D.Cal. 1993), involved both a class action and a derivative suit. The court was asked to approve settlement of both and each was contingent on approval of the other. The court found the class settlement fair to those who bought or sold the stock, but the settlement of the derivative action produced few benefits to the company. Further, the court said, the company's directors lacked the requisite independence to settle the derivative action and did not consult independent counsel. Legal advice about the settlement had come from the in–house general counsel. In-house lawyers have to live with management, the court suggested, and thus "are inevitably subservient to the interests of the defendant directors and officers whom they serve." Id. at 1188. Thus, the court required the corporation to hire outside counsel to advise the directors on the issue.

Do you think the court's assessment of in–house counsel is fair? Does it make sense to always require expensive outside assessments of what will sometimes be meritless suits?

b. By contrast, in Bell Atlantic Corp. v. Bolger, 2 F.3d 1304 (3d Cir.1993), the court approved settlement of a derivative action in which a single law firm represented both the corporation and the directors. The action alleged the directors were guilty of mismanagement, but not fraud. There was a convergence of individual and corporate interests in this case, the court found. It takes allegations of intentional wrongdoing or self-dealing, the court suggested, to make separate representation mandatory.

c. Comments [10] & [11] to Model Rule 1.13 attempt to state the law in this area clearly. Do you agree that they do so?

PROBLEM 19

CONTACT WITH REPRESENTED AND UNREPRESENTED PERSONS

Lawyers frequently contact others on behalf of clients. Typically, the contacts are to obtain or deliver information. Sometimes, they are to suggest solutions to contentious problems. It might initially seem odd that all such contacts would be regulated, but concerns that lawyers might mislead an opposing party or interfere with that party's relationship with its own lawyer have carried the day. This Problem first considers the regulation of such contacts in general. Next, it applies the rule to contacts

---

11. Ronald D. Rotunda, Law, Lawyers, and Managers, in C. Walton, ed., The Ethics of Corporate Conduct 127, 135–36 (American Assembly 1977).

with corporate employees. Then, it explores the standards governing contacts with officers and employees of the lawyer's own client. Finally, it considers the rule in a criminal context, asking whether police questioning should be considered contact by agents of the prosecuting attorney and examining whether federal prosecutors should be governed by national standards rather than by the standards in the states in which the prosecutors have law licenses.

FACTS

Speedy Corp. has a fleet of trucks and couriers to deliver packages throughout the city. The company has made a standing offer to return the shipper's fee for any package not delivered within one hour. There is reason to believe that this policy causes Speedy's drivers and couriers to take dangerous chances.

One rainy Tuesday, President Mary Speedy was standing across the street from the company headquarters. Barry Winters, an employee in the accounting department of Speedy Corp. happened to be standing beside her. Just then, a Speedy delivery truck came out of the headquarters building at a high rate of speed. It hit an elderly man, causing him serious injuries.

Before filing the complaint, Louis Shabazz, lawyer for the injured man, interviewed Barry Winters and the truck driver and took their statements about how the accident happened. Barbara Bentley, lawyer for Speedy Corp., was not told of those interviews or invited to be present. Now, Shabazz has called Mary Speedy and asked to interview her as well; Speedy, in turn, has called Bentley who has told Speedy to decline to be interviewed in any setting other than a formal deposition.

Bentley herself now wants to investigate to find out what the facts surrounding the accident are. She wants to prepare for litigation and to formulate recommendations for possible changes of the one-hour guarantee. Indeed, she fears a grand jury may be convened to determine whether Speedy's guarantee of one-hour service might support a charge of criminal negligence. Bentley wants to talk to present and former employees of Speedy, both officers and nonofficers, who might know how the policy has affected safety. Shabazz, of course, would like to talk to the same people.

QUESTIONS

A.   CONTACT WITH A REPRESENTED OPPONENT IN GENERAL

1.   Attorney Shabazz just wants to question witnesses to an accident. What rules regulate his questioning?

a.   ABA Model Rule 4.2 is the principal authority:

"In representing a client, a lawyer shall not communicate about the subject matter of the representation with a person the lawyer knows to be represented by another lawyer in the matter, unless the lawyer has the consent of the other lawyer or is authorized to do so by law or court order."

Read that rule again; every part of it is significant.

b. ABA Formal Opinion 95–396 (July 28, 1995), for example, says that the ban on contact applies (1) in both criminal and civil cases, (2) to represented persons and not just parties, (3) less clearly in the investigation phase of criminal cases prior to an arrest or charge, (4) only when the lawyer should know the other person is represented, (5) only to contacts related to the subject matter of the case, (6) even though the represented person initiates the contact, (7) until the representation of the person is in fact terminated, and (8) to contacts made by a lawyer's investigators, not just the lawyer personally.

c. Restatement Third, The Law Governing Lawyers § 99 states the rule as:

"(1) A lawyer representing a client in a matter may not communicate about the subject of the representation with a nonclient whom the lawyer knows to be represented in the matter by another lawyer or with a representative of an organizational nonclient so represented as defined in § 100, unless:

"(a) the communication is with a public officer or agency to the extent stated in § 101;

"(b) the lawyer is a party and represents no other client in the matter;

"(c) the communication is authorized by law;

"(d) the communication reasonably responds to an emergency; or

"(e) the other lawyer consents.

"(2) Subsection (1) does not prohibit the lawyer from assisting the client in otherwise proper communication by the lawyer's client with a represented nonclient."

2. Does the rule against ex parte contact with a represented party make sense to you? Whom does the rule seek to protect? Is the concern that a persuasive lawyer will cause the represented person to take action disadvantageous to himself without realizing what is going on?

a. In Attorney Grievance Commission v. Kent, 653 A.2d 909 (Md. 1995), a defendant, represented by counsel, had pled guilty and agreed to testify against Kent's client in exchange for a reduced sentence. Lawyer Kent persuaded him to deny responsibility for the crime, to fire his separate counsel and to let Kent take over his case. Kent's original client was thus acquitted for lack of a cooperating witness, but because the witness had already pled guilty and did not then cooperate, he was sentenced to two life terms. Kent asserted that all he had done was zealously defend his original client, but the court found his conduct violated both Rules 1.7 and 4.2. Kent was disbarred for his role in contacting and misleading the second defendant.[1]

b. Utah State Bar Ethics Advisory Opinion 98–07 (1998) examined whether a lawyer for the plaintiff in an accident may contact the adjuster for the defendant's insurance company directly. The Opinion said that, in the period before the case is referred to a lawyer for defense, the answer is clearly yes. However, after the insurance company has hired a lawyer for the defendant, the question is whether the insurance company is also a represented party and thus contact with it is prohibited except through counsel. The Opinion said that at a minimum, the insurance company has a "direct interest in the results of any litigation or settlement." Thus, the Opinion concluded, it may only be contacted through counsel unless the plaintiff's lawyer knows that the insurance company does not consider itself to be represented by counsel in the matter.

c. In re News America Publishing, Inc., 974 S.W.2d 97 (Tex.App. 1998), was a mandamus proceeding to disqualify plaintiffs' counsel. One of the co-defendants, who had been represented by counsel, had written plaintiffs' counsel a letter stating that he had decided to fire his lawyer and that "I am no longer represented by any attorney in this matter." The plaintiffs' firm met with him, dismissed him from the case, and listed him as a witness on plaintiffs' behalf. It turned out that the person had not yet fired his lawyer, and the question was whether Rule 4.2 forbade the conversation with plaintiffs' counsel until the first lawyer clearly knew he had been fired and the co-defendants thus knew what had happened. The court said that plaintiffs' counsel had indeed violated the anti-contact rule. Clients can always fire their lawyers, the court said, but plaintiff's counsel cannot encourage them to waive the protection of Rule 4.2. Until plaintiffs' counsel confirmed defense counsel had withdrawn from the case, it was improper to talk to the defendant without permission. In order to eliminate any advantage plaintiffs might have gained from the secret decision to go over to the plaintiffs, the court disqualified plaintiffs' counsel.

d. However, State v. Harper, 995 P.2d 1143 (Okla.2000), involved an insurance defense lawyer who had dealt only with the plaintiff's lawyer until the plaintiff told the company she was going to fire her lawyer that very day. The defense lawyer thus took a statement directly from her, telling her she could have an attorney present if she wished. Later, it turned out that she had not formally fired her first lawyer after all. The court found no evidence the defense lawyer knew the true facts and held that, in the absence of such knowledge, there is no violation of Rule 4.2.[2]

1. See also, Matter of Alcantara, 676 A.2d 1030 (N.J.1995), reprimanding a lawyer for asking represented co-defendants not to testify against his client, and United States v. Santiago–Lugo, 162 F.R.D. 11 (D.P.R.1995), censuring a lawyer and barring use of any the notes made while interviewing the client's co-defendants ex parte.

2. Oregon State Bar Opinion, Formal Opinion 2001–164 (2001) reaches what may

3. Might the anti-contact rule be based in part on the desire of lawyers to control their clients, i.e., that the clients not be able to work things out without their lawyer's help? Might it even reflect the concern of lawyers who want to be sure they spend the maximum number of billable hours being involved in the pre–trial process?

a.   ABA Formal Opinion 92–362 (July 6, 1992), for example, states that a lawyer who has made an offer to opposing counsel may neither call the opposing party to see if the offer has been communicated nor send the opposing party a copy of the offer. Is such a rule likely to be in the interest of the opposing party? Is it likely to be in the interest of the opposing party's lawyer alone?

b.   Cleveland Bar Association v. Rossi, 690 N.E.2d 501 (Ohio 1998), illustrates how strict the rule against direct contact with an opposing party can be. A claimant under a will hired a lawyer to see if the inventory compiled by the executor was undervalued. The executor's lawyer could not be reached because he had changed offices and his phone had been disconnected. Time to object to the inventory was running, so the claimant's lawyer called the executor directly and determined that the estate did indeed have more assets than previously thought. For that contact, he received a public reprimand, and two dissenting justices would have suspended him, saying that the lawyer could do no more than ask the executor to have his attorney call the lawyer.

c.   In re Grievance Proceeding, 2002 WL 31106389 (D.Conn.2002), on the other hand, says that while Rule 4.2 prohibits direct contact with an individual client, there is no reason to apply the same principle to contact with the general counsel of a corporate client, even if the client is represented in the matter by an outside firm. Do you agree?

4. May represented clients talk to each other without going through their lawyers?

a.   State Bar of California, Formal Opinion 1993–131 (1993) gives the standard answer that the clients *may* talk; indeed, it says that failure to encourage such talks may forfeit opportunities to terminate disputes short of trial. The opinion also says the lawyers for each client may advise the clients before they get together, but the communications must be those of the clients, not the lawyers acting out the lawyers' "scripts" for them.

b.   Association of the Bar of the City of New York Committee on Professional and Judicial Ethics Formal Opinion 2002–3 withdraws a 1991 opinion and says a lawyer may even advise a client what to say in the meeting between the clients. Opposing such coaching is "at odds with modern authority," the Committee says, citing both the Restatement

be an obvious conclusion that a lawyer may visit the web site of a represented person so long as there is no interaction with the site, such as sending a message with the expecta-tion of receiving a personal response. Going to a company's website, for example, and reading what is said there to the public does not violate Rule 4.2.

Third, The Law Governing Lawyers § 99, Comment *k*, and Comment [4] to Model Rule 4.2.

c. ABA Formal Opinion 92–362, supra, says that a lawyer for a client making a settlement offer may advise his client that the other attorney may not have communicated the offer and suggest that the lawyer's client convey the information directly.

d. In Holdren v. General Motors Corp., 13 F.Supp.2d 1192 (D.Kan. 1998), on the other hand, plaintiff's counsel urged his client to talk about the case with other GM employees, including managers, who might offer favorable testimony at trial, and to get affidavits from them. The court recognized that clients may talk to each other without violating Rule 4.2, but it said plaintiff's counsel had "circumvented" Rule 4.2 in violation of Rule 8.4(a) by "encouraging" his client to obtain the affidavits. The court acknowledged that there was "no evidence" that the lawyer "knowingly or deliberately" violated the no-contact rule, but it enjoined further efforts to get affidavits and required the plaintiff to turn over names of persons contacted and any evidence obtained thereby, so the court could determine which persons were protected against contact under the rule.

5. If a lawyer is a party to the litigation, should Model Rule 4.2 bar that lawyer's contact with the opposing party?

a. D.C. Bar Ethics Opinion 258 (Sept. 20, 1995) says the lawyer's ability to overreach is no less because he is a party. Thus, the no-contact rule controls, and a lawyer appearing pro se may not contact the other side directly if the opposing party is represented by counsel, even though a pro se layperson could contact the other side directly. See also, Runsvold v. Idaho State Bar, 925 P.2d 1118 (Idaho 1996) (upholds private reprimand to pro se lawyer for writing and sending court papers directly to represented ex-wife instead of to her lawyer).

b. Restatement Third, The Law Governing Lawyers § 99, Comment *e*, on the other hand, says that a "lawyer representing his or her own interests pro se may communicate with an opposing represented nonclient on the same basis as other principals. * * * A lawyer representing both a client and the lawyer's own interests in the same matter is subject to the anti-contact rule * * * ."

c. Which of those positions makes more sense to you?

B. SPECIAL ISSUES WHEN DEALING WITH OFFICERS AND EMPLOYEES OF AN ORGANIZATION

1. After considering all the above issues, does Shabazz still have an answer about his right to interview Mary Speedy, Barry Winters and the truck driver? You can assume that none of them has yet hired personal counsel to represent them in connection with the accident.

a. It is relatively easy to proscribe contacts with individuals. When the opposing "person" is a corporation or other organization, however, the question becomes when contact with particular living people will be considered prohibited contact with the organization. One might imagine a rule, for example, that said that because all employees are agents of the corporation, each of them is off limits to contact. On the other hand, such a rule might be broader than necessary to protect the interests the rule is legitimately designed to protect.

b. In Niesig v. Team I, 558 N.E.2d 1030 (N.Y.1990), a personal injury lawyer for a plaintiff wished to interview a corporate defendant's employees who had witnessed an accident that occurred at a construction site. The court noted that when a corporation is a party to a lawsuit, the entity is the only party. "The issue therefore distills to which corporate employees should be deemed parties for purposes of DR 7–104(A)(1), and that choice is one of policy. The broader the definition of 'party' in the interests of fairness to the corporation, the greater the cost in terms of foreclosing vital informal access to facts." 558 N.E.2d at 1033. The court noted that there should be a public policy of reducing litigation costs by allowing plaintiffs to use informal, off the record, private interviews rather than costly depositions or interviews attended by the adversary counsel, and the corporation has ample opportunity to interview its own employees, gather facts, and counsel them so that they do not make improvident disclosures. The court thus concluded that "parties" for purposes of New York DR 7–104(A)(1) should include only "corporate employees whose acts or omissions in the matter under inquiry are binding on the corporation (in effect, the corporation's 'alter egos') or imputed to the corporation for purposes of its liability, or employees implementing the advice of counsel." All other employees may be interviewed informally.

c. Restatement Third, The Law Governing Lawyers § 100(2) is consistent with *Nieseg* and says that opposing counsel may *not* contact current corporate employees and agents without the other lawyer's permission:

"(a) if the employee or other agent supervises, directs, or regularly consults with the lawyer concerning the matter or if the agent has power to compromise or settle the matter;

"(b) if the acts or omissions of the employee or other agent may be imputed to the organization for purposes of civil or criminal liability in the matter; or

"(c) if a statement of the employee or other agent, under applicable rules of evidence, would have the effect of binding the organization with respect to proof of the matter."

Do those standards help you decide whom Shabazz may interview without asking Bentley? See also, Model Rule 4.2, Comment [7].

d. In Weeks v. Independent School District No. I–89, 230 F.3d 1201 (10th Cir.2000), plaintiff's counsel represented a bus driver suing for overtime pay. She talked ex parte to the school district's operations supervisor and her client's immediate supervisor, whom she characterized as "low-level supervisory employees." The 10th Circuit found that the supervisors had "speaking authority" whose testimony would "bind" the school district; thus, communication was prohibited by Rule 4.2. As a sanction for the interviews, plaintiff's counsel was disqualified from continuing to represent the plaintiff.

e.   Weibrecht v. Southern Illinois Transfer, Inc., 241 F.3d 875 (7th Cir.2001), involved a barge accident tried in federal court. Apparently at his lawyer's suggestion, two days before a scheduled deposition of Bader, the barge operator at the time of the accident, the plaintiff called Bader and told him the lawsuit was simply designed to make the company a safer place to work. The plaintiff's lawyer then also called Bader and left a message. The barge owner said these contacts had violated Rule 4.2, but the lawyer said that § 60 of the FELA, which applied here, preempted Rule 4.2 and prohibited any effort to prevent voluntary statements about the cause of an accident. The court found § 60 and Rule 4.2 were not inconsistent, and that Bader, as barge captain, was an employee whose acts or omissions could have been held against his employer. Thus, Rule 4.2 was indeed violated and the case was remanded for imposition of sanctions.

f.   In Messing, Rudavsky & Weliky, P.C. v. President and Fellows of Harvard College, 764 N.E.2d 825 (Mass.2002), on the other hand, a law firm represented a former employee of Harvard College in her gender discrimination suit against the College. While investigating its client's claim, the firm conducted informal interviews with five of the client's co-workers in the Harvard University police department, and the Superior Court granted Harvard's motion to sanction the firm for violating Rule 4.2. The Massachusetts Supreme Court, however, citing *Niesig* and the Restatement, held that Rule 4.2 only prohibits lawyers from contacting "employees who exercise managerial responsibility in the matter, who are alleged to have committed the wrongful acts at issue in the litigation, or who have authority on behalf of the corporation to make decisions about the course of the litigation." 764 N.E.2d at 833. Thus, the court denied Harvard's motion for sanctions, finding that the employees interviewed did not have "supervisory authority over the events at issue in the litigation."

2.   Should the prohibition against contacting corporate employees apply to former employees? Are they still part of the "person" that opposing counsel is forbidden to contact? Would the same concerns that underlie Rule 4.2 apply to contact with former employees as well?

a.   Restatement Third, The Law Governing Lawyers § 100, Comment *g*, says:

> "Contact with a former employee or agent ordinarily is permitted, even if the person had formerly been within a category of those with whom contact is prohibited. * * * [However,] a former employee who, as the lawyer knows, continues regularly to consult about the matter with the lawyer for the ex-employer [may not be contacted] * * *."

b.   In Camden v. Maryland, 910 F.Supp. 1115 (D.Md.1996), the plaintiff had filed a discrimination case against a university; the university affirmative action officer was a non-lawyer who later left the school with some bad feelings and subsequently talked to the plaintiff's lawyer about the case. The court recognized that lawyers may contact most former employees of a represented firm, but said contact is prohibited with former employees who had "been extensively exposed to relevant trade secrets, confidential client information, or similar confidential information of another party interested in the matter." The defendant's former in-house manager of the case was thus someone the plaintiff's lawyer could not interview ex parte, and the lawyer who did so was disqualified.

c. G–I Holdings, Inc. v. Baron & Budd, 199 F.R.D. 529 (S.D.N.Y. 2001), involved former employees of the defendant whose work had exposed them to privileged information and whom plaintiff's investigators wanted to interview. Because both the interviewers and former employees were lay persons who might inadvertently disclose the privileged information, the court issued a protective order under which the interviews could only continue if either (1) notice and the right of defendants' counsel to be present were given or (2) the interviews were conducted in the presence of a special master who would determine whether any privileged information was being disclosed.

3. Should somewhat different considerations apply when the issue is contact with officers or employees of a government agency?

a. ABA Formal Opinion 97–408 (Aug. 2, 1997) considered the application of Model Rule 4.2 to contact by the lawyer for a private party in a dispute with a government agency. The Opinion finds that the terms of Model Rule 4.2 would cover such contacts, but the Opinion argues that Rule 4.2 has "an important exception based on the constitutional right to petition and the derivative public policy of ensuring a citizen's right of access to government decisions makers." Rule 4.2 "permits a lawyer representing a private party in a controversy with the government to communicate about the matter with government officials who have authority to take or recommend action in the matter, provided that the sole purpose of the lawyer's communication is to address a policy issue, including settling the controversy." In such cases, "the lawyer must give government counsel reasonable advance notice of his intent to communicate with such officials in order to afford them an opportunity to seek advice of counsel before deciding whether to entertain the communication."

b. Does this approach make sense to you? Do you find any reference to it in Model Rule 4.2, Comment [5], after its amendment in 2002?

c. Compare Restatement Third, The Law Governing Lawyers § 101, which says that (1) the fact that the government agency has a general counsel's office does not ordinarily bar contact with employees or officials of that agency, but (2) Rule 4.2 does apply to negotiation or litigation of a specific claim against the agency, except with respect to issues of general policy.

C. Interviewing client employees and other unrepresented persons

1. Now turn your attention to Barbara Bentley and her defense of Speedy Corp. Should we be equally concerned that she

might overreach in interviews of unrepresented persons like Winters and the truck driver?

a. The Florida Bar v. Buckle, 771 So.2d 1131 (Fla.2000), involved a criminal defense lawyer's telephone calls and letter to an unrepresented complaining witness. In an attempt to get her to drop the criminal complaint, he called her at home and sent her religious materials that the discipline referee found "objectively humiliating and intimidating." The court found the letter "essentially threatens to take away her job, her children and to expose her to ridicule, contempt, and hatred." The lawyer even threatened to raise questions about a prior murder in the complainant's family. This kind of intimidation, the court found, is "patently unfair and prejudicial to the administration of justice," but the only sanction it merited was a public reprimand.

b. How should professional rules be drafted to guard against such overreaching? Before the 2002 amendments, ABA Model Rule 4.3 said only:

> "In dealing on behalf of a client with a person who is not represented by counsel, a lawyer shall not state that the lawyer is disinterested. When the lawyer knows or reasonably should know that the unrepresented person misunderstands the lawyer's role in the matter, the lawyer shall make reasonable efforts to correct the misunderstanding."

Did that rule address all important concerns?

c. Model Code of Professional Responsibility DR 7–104(A)(2) had said that a lawyer may not

> "Give advice to a person who is not represented by a lawyer, other than the advice to secure counsel, if the interests of such person are or have a reasonable possibility of being in conflict with the interests of his client."

d. Now, 2002 ABA Model Rule 4.3 has moved that Model Code language from where it had been in Comment [1] into the black letter rule. Is that an important change? Compare Restatement Third, The Law Governing Lawyers § 103.

2. How should Bentley handle her interviews with her client's officers and employees?

a. Should she take a "we're all in this together" approach? Should she instead advise the truck driver, for example, to obtain independent counsel? How about the Vice President in charge of the truck maintenance facility? The Board members who approved the on-time delivery guarantee? Look beyond Model Rule 4.3; does Model Rule 1.13(d) provide important direction as well?

b. Might Bentley become the lawyer for each of the corporate officers, directors and employees personally? At minimum, that would make them all "represented persons" and invoke the protection of Rule 4.2. Model Rule 1.13(e) would seem to permit such representation, but what problems could you see arising if Bentley chose that course?

c. W.T. Grant Co. v. Haines, 531 F.2d 671 (2d Cir.1976), involved a corporation's antitrust action against one of its former employees and others. The employee moved to disqualify the corporation's law firm, alleging it had violated [Model Rule 4.3] when corporate attorneys had earlier interviewed the employee. When this interview took place, counsel correctly identified the character and nature of their representation, but he did not disclose that earlier that morning a lawsuit had been filed naming the employee as a defendant. The court found no violation. The employee had expressed a desire to be interviewed to help "clear the air." He was said to be sophisticated, "neither a callow youth nor a befuddled widow." As for not giving advice to unrepresented persons with interests opposed to the client's, the court said that the question was "close," but that even assuming a violation, disqualification of counsel was inappropriate and would unduly delay the proceedings. This is an old case; do you think a court should be as restrained about enforcing Rule 4.3 today?

d. United States v. Talao, 222 F.3d 1133 (9th Cir.2000), was a criminal action alleging that an employer had required workers to kickback a portion of their wages and had falsely reported their wages and hours to the U.S. Labor Department. Defense counsel wanted to talk to the defendant's bookkeeper about her upcoming grand jury testimony, but the bookkeeper asked the Assistant U.S. Attorney to keep him away from her because she felt he pressured her to lie. She told the attorney that she did not want him to represent her. The bookkeeper then explained her employer's scheme to the prosecutors, the grand jury returned an indictment, and the defendants moved to dismiss it as the product of an improper violation of Rule 4.2 (Cal.Rule 2–100). The district court agreed that the prosecutor had violated the Rule, but refused to dismiss the indictment, and proposed instead to instruct the jury that it could consider the violation in assessing the witness' credibility. On pre-trial appeal, the 9th Circuit found no ethical violation and thus that no remedial instruction was needed. When a corporate employee comes forward to disclose corporate misconduct, the Court said, there is a conflict between the corporation and the employee and the corporation's lawyer cannot continue to represent both. Thus, Rule 4.2 cannot be used to prevent prosecutor contact with that employee. Otherwise, the Court said, "subornation of perjury" could be "cloaked by an ethical rule." Do you agree?

3. If Bentley is interviewing a witness who is an employee of her corporate client—but who is not her client—and the witness starts giving incriminating information that is helpful to Bentley's corporate client, must Bentley give *Miranda* warnings?

a. Consider ABA Standards Relating to the Administration of Criminal Justice, The Defense Function, Standard 4–4.3(c): "It is not necessary for defense counsel or defense counsel's investigator, in interviewing a prospective witness, to caution the witness concerning possible self-incrimination and the need for counsel."

b. Restatement Third, The Law Governing Lawyers § 103, Comment *e* suggests the dilemma the situation presents:

"Failing to clarify the lawyer's role and the client's interests may redound to the disadvantage of the organization if the lawyer, even if unwittingly, thereby undertakes concurrent representation of both the organization and the constituent. * * * Among other consequences, the lawyer may be required to withdraw from representing both clients because of the conflict. * * * [However, t]he absence of a warning in such a situation will often be in the interests of the client organization in assuring that the flow of information and decisionmaking is not impaired by needless warnings to constituents with important responsibilities or information. * * * "

c. Do you agree that the lawyer's duty of loyalty to her client may require that she take advantage of the ignorance of the person she is interviewing? Look again at ABA Model Rules 1.13(d) & (e). What should Bentley do? How serious is the risk she will be held to be the employee's personal lawyer?

4. What limits are there on how Shabazz—the opposing counsel—may conduct his interviews of Winters and other eyewitnesses who are neither represented themselves nor treated as represented by corporate counsel?

a. May he take potential witnesses to lunch, for example, and seek to develop a good rapport with them so that they will be more forthcoming in their conversations with him?

b. May he imply that he is conducting an investigation on behalf of a government traffic safety agency, i.e., must he say that he represents the witnesses' employer's potential opponent in litigation? Remember Model Rule 8.4(c).

D. THE POSSIBILITY THAT SPECIAL RULES APPLY TO FEDERAL PROSECUTORS

1. Now suppose the police want to interview the same group of company employees. Must they refrain from such interviews without permission of Bentley, the corporate counsel?

a. Look at ABA Prosecution Function Standard 3–2.7:

"(a) The prosecutor should provide legal advice to the police concerning police functions and duties in criminal matters.

"(b) The prosecutor should cooperate with police in providing the services of the prosecutor's staff to aid in training police in the performance of their function in accordance with law."

Does this provision in effect make police the agents of the prosecuting attorney for purposes of Model Rule 4.2 when they conduct questioning?

b. Long before adoption of Model Rule 4.2, in Formal Opinion 95 (May 3, 1933), the ABA Ethics Committee had said:

"The law officer is, of course, responsible for the acts of those in his department who are under his supervision and control. Opinion 85. * * *

"It would be unavailing to contend that the police officers or detectives are not under the supervision and control of the law officer, but rather are under the supervision and control of the municipality."

Do you agree? Is this Opinion realistic today?

c.   Consider United States v. Thomas, 474 F.2d 110 (10th Cir.1973), cert. denied 412 U.S. 932, 93 S.Ct. 2758, 37 L.Ed.2d 160 (1973), where the court held that, even though the defendant had waived his *Miranda* rights:

"[O]nce a criminal defendant has either retained an attorney or had an attorney appointed for him by the court, any statement obtained by interview from such defendant may not be offered in evidence unless the accused's attorney was notified of the interview which produced the statement and was given a reasonable opportunity to be present. To hold otherwise we think would be to overlook conduct which violated both the letter and the spirit of the canons of ethics. This is obviously not something which the defendant alone can waive.

"A violation of the canon of ethics as here concerned need not be remedied by a reversal of the case wherein it is violated. This does not necessarily present a constitutional question, but this is an ethical and administrative one relating to attorneys practicing before the United States courts. * * * The enforcement officials are agents of the prosecuting party, and in the event use is made of information secured by interviews of the nature which here took place, short of its introduction in evidence, the problem will be dealt with in the proper case." 474 F.2d at 112.

Should the *Thomas* analysis be applied in a typical state system where the state's attorney, usually a county officer, has no direct control over the police, typically a city agency?

d.   State v. Miller, 600 N.W.2d 457 (Minn.1999), involved interviewing corporate employees during a surprise search of the corporate offices that prosecutors had coordinated. The employees were not under arrest and were told that law enforcement officials were "simply gathering information." Miller, whose statement was involved in this case, had faxed the search warrant to his attorney when it was served, so investigators knew he had counsel. Indeed, the lawyer appeared at the office, demanded that the interview be terminated, but was denied entry because Miller had not expressly asked for the right to consult him. The Minnesota Supreme Court made clear that Rule 4.2 provides more protection than *Miranda* rights. Even assuming that the interview was not unconstitutional, the court held that the prosecutor's involvement in keeping the lawyer out of the interview room violated Rule 4.2, and the appropriate sanction for that violation was suppression of the statement.

2.   How should this principle apply when the lawyers involved are U.S. Attorneys supervising FBI and other federal agents in drug and antiterrorism investigations?

a. United States v. Ryans, 903 F.2d 731 (10th Cir.1990), involved the secret recording of the conversation between the target of an antitrust investigation, known to be represented by his regular lawyer, and a cooperating witness at a time prior to indictment and while the target was not in custody. The court reported that "it is now well settled that [Model Rule 4.2] applies to criminal as well as civil litigation", and that it applies to agents of public prosecutors " 'when they act as the alter ego of the prosecuting attorneys.' " *Id.,* at 735. Three circuits, the 5th, 7th and 10th have said that the principle does or may apply to pre-indictment interviews when the defendant is in custody. United States v. Hammad, 846 F.2d 854 (2d Cir.1988), applied [Model Rule 4.2] to noncustodial, pre-indictment investigations as well, but refused to require exclusion of the evidence obtained. This court agreed that what is now Model Rule 4.2 does not apply "before the initiation of criminal proceedings."

b. Does that make sense to you? If a disciplinary rule should be enforced at all, why shouldn't it be enforced at the trial? Does experience with the conflict of interest rules suggest that such direct enforcement would convert disciplinary rules into mere trial tactics? Should the court enforce the ethics rule only when its violation affects the fact-finding process? For example, should the court enforce at trial, court rules governing client confidences but not rules regulating lawyer advertising? On which side of that line would a violation of Rule 4.2 fall?

c. In United States v. Ofshe, 817 F.2d 1508 (11th Cir.1987), the defendant faced drug charges. He retained one lawyer (Black) to prepare for trial and another (Glass) to negotiate with the government about a plea. Glass later found himself accused in Chicago's "Operation Greylord" corruption cases and wanted to do what he could to win favorable treatment for himself. Chicago Assistant U.S. Attorney (and well-known author) Scott Turow had Glass wear a body bug to his meeting with Ofshe, his Florida client. Agents monitoring the tape "were given very strict guidelines to instruct Glass not to violate any attorney-client privilege;" instead, Ofshe and Glass discussed other criminal plans. Ofshe argued that this use of defense counsel as informer justified dismissing the indictment against him. The court held that, absent prejudice, the remedy is not warranted. Not only was no useful information developed by the bug, but the Florida U.S. Attorney's office was given none of what was developed. Finally, although Glass did not provide effective assistance of counsel to Ofshe, his co-counsel did, so there was no harm done.

What do you think of this analysis? Should a prosecutor ever be able to use a suspect's lawyer as an informant? Does this practice make Barbara Bentley look like a model of ethical virtue by comparison?

3. Does the federal government have a legitimate interest in having its lawyers not subject to all of the strictures of Model Rule 4.2?

a. Following the lead of former Attorney General Richard Thornburgh, Attorney General Janet Reno promulgated what is now called the Reno Memorandum. See Communications with Represented Persons, 28

C.F.R. Part 77 (1994). In the comments accompanying this rule, the Attorney General emphasized that the Department of Justice "has long maintained, and continues to maintain, that it has authority to exempt its attorneys from the application of DR 7–104 and Model Rule 4.2 and their state counterparts." 59 Fed. Reg. 39910–11 (Aug. 4, 1994).

b.   28 C.F.R. § 77.6 listed various exceptions to the no-contact rule. For example, there was an exception for discovery by legal process (such as during a grand jury testimony); or when the "represented party initiates the communication directly with the attorney for the government or through an intermediary" and the party knowingly waives his or her right and a federal judge or magistrate concludes that the waiver is knowing and voluntary; or when there is a waiver of *Miranda* rights at the time of arrest; or when there is an investigation of "additional, different or ongoing crimes or civil violations," including "undercover or covert" operations; or when the government attorney believes in "good faith" that the communication is necessary to prevent against the "risk of injury or death" to any person.

c.   United States v. Lopez, 4 F.3d 1455 (9th Cir.1993), was a particularly interesting example of these issues. Lopez was charged with a drug offense and feared his children were being abused while he was in prison. He wanted to discuss cooperation with the government. However, his lawyer had a reputation for refusing to negotiate cooperation. Thus, Lopez tried to deal with the government through the lawyer for a co-defendant, and after obtaining permission of a magistrate judge, the U.S. Attorney's office negotiated a deal with him—later rejected by both defendants— through that lawyer. When he heard about the negotiations behind his back, Lopez' preferred lawyer withdrew, and substitute counsel moved to dismiss the indictment based on government misconduct. The District Court agreed that—even where the defendant initiated the contact—it was so improper for the U.S. Attorney's office to meet with him in the absence of his lawyer that the indictment must be dismissed. The Ninth Circuit opinion was contemptuous of the Justice Department position that it was exempt from California Rule 2–100 [Model Rule 4.2] and equally critical of the U.S. Attorney's claim that the contact with Lopez had been "authorized by law," but it concluded that dismissing the indictment went too far. In a concurring opinion, Judge Fletcher opined that both defense counsel's unwillingness to negotiate on Lopez' behalf and the magistrate judge's failure to apprehend the complete picture of what was going on had been big parts of the problem and thus there was plenty of blame to go around.

d.   How would you have decided the *Lopez* case? Do criminal defendants sometimes need protection from their own lawyers? Should it be improper for a prosecutor to talk with a defendant who voluntarily seeks such a meeting? The new "or court order" language added to ABA Model Rule 4.2 in 2002 is intended to make clear that in cases like *Lopez*, both state and federal prosecutors may take the defendant before a magistrate judge who can evaluate the sincerity of the defendant's wish to talk to the prosecutors and authorize such discussions in appropriate cases. Do the

Lopez facts suggest, however, that magistrate judges may not always make decisions in such cases that reviewing courts will conclude were appropriate?

4. As a matter of policy, should the Attorney General be able to exempt federal prosecutors from the operation of Model Rule 4.2 as it applies in the states that have licensed the prosecutors?

a. United States v. Colorado Supreme Court, 87 F.3d 1161 (10th Cir.1996), was one of the first direct Justice Department challenges to the applicability of state ethics rules to federal prosecutors. The rule at issue was what is now Rule 3.8(e) that forbade a prosecutor's requiring a lawyer to testify before a grand jury or in any other setting if the evidence could be obtained from another source. The District Court held that because no federal prosecutor had been disciplined by the state there was no case or controversy, but the Tenth Circuit said the mere threat of discipline was enough to give the court jurisdiction. The Rule 3.8 requirements also raised a threat to the grand jury process sufficient to require a hearing in the district court. The court then remanded for further proceedings.

Earlier, in a 5–4 decision written by Justice Scalia, United States v. Williams, 504 U.S. 36, 112 S.Ct. 1735, 118 L.Ed.2d 352 (1992), had held that grand juries were independent of the judicial branch and traditional judicial regulation did not apply to their operation. Thus, usual court rules did not apply and federal prosecutors need not present exculpatory evidence to a grand jury. In light of *Williams*, on remand, the district court held that Rule 3.8(f) was invalid as applied to federal prosecutors practicing before a grand jury, but valid in other settings. United States v. Colorado Supreme Court, 988 F.Supp. 1368 (D.Colo.1998). The 10th Circuit affirmed, 189 F.3d 1281 (10th Cir.1999).

b. Matter of Howes, 940 P.2d 159 (N.M.1997) (per curiam), was the first state case to impose discipline on a federal prosecutor who complied with the Justice Department regulations on ex parte contact. When Howes was an Assistant U.S. Attorney (AUSA) in the District of Columbia, he was a member of only the New Mexico bar. Following office policy, Howes permitted a D.C. police detective to talk to a represented criminal defendant in the absence of his appointed counsel as long as the defendant initiated the contact. Howes later knew such conversations were being held and did not notify the defendant's lawyer, and that lawyer moved to dismiss the indictment for prosecutorial misconduct. The motion was denied, but the matter was sent to the D.C. Board of Professional Responsibility, which said its rules did not apply to an AUSA. Therefore, New Mexico took up the case. In upholding a sanction of public censure, the court held that neither a superior's direction nor office policy can excuse a lawyer's violation of clear ethical standards. The Reno Memorandum was found not to have been promulgated under valid statutory authority, and the supremacy clause was held not independently to protect a federal prosecutor from state professional discipline for his official acts.

c. United States ex rel O'Keefe v. McDonnell Douglas Corp., 132 F.3d 1252 (8th Cir.1998), examined the legal authority of the Attorney General to issue the Reno Guidelines. The case was a civil action under the False Claims Act and government agents made contacts with various of the defendant's employees. The defendant sought a protective order against such contacts. The 8th Circuit found the Reno Guidelines were not something the Attorney General had authority to issue either under 5 U.S.C. § 301, the "housekeeping statute," or other law defining her role. Thus, the District Court's order prohibiting contact with a defendant's current employees was proper and would be enforced.

d.   This issue has now been resolved by federal legislation that has expressly made federal lawyers subject to state ethics rules. Called the McDade Act, the law took effect in April 1999 and is found at 28 U.S.C.A. § 530B. Do you agree that the issue has been resolved correctly?

PROBLEM 20

THE ETHICS OF NEGOTIATION

Negotiation may be the quintessential activity of a lawyer. Reaching agreement on a sale of an asset or formation of a contractual relationship can provide protection for and benefits to the lawyer's client. Indeed, year in and year out, even where relationships sour and litigation results, over 90% of the parties to filed cases resolve their differences by negotiation before trial. Is negotiation an ethical wasteland where the lawyer has no standards of conduct? Is it a world where literally anything goes? This Problem suggests the answer is no. It considers first where the lawyer gets authority to negotiate and the boundaries of that authority. Next, it looks at the duty to tell the truth in negotiations and any limits to that duty. Then, it asks whether lawyers ever have to volunteer information in order to avoid a misapprehension by the other side. Finally, it examines limits on what negotiated results parties and their lawyers may reach.

FACTS

James Young, age 19, was in a traffic accident. The driver of the other car suffered personal injuries and has paid medical bills of $18,000. There was $7,000 in property damage to the other car. Young was unhurt, but his car suffered $5,000 damage.

At the scene of the accident, the investigating officer charged Young with drunk driving. Young denied it and told the officer that he had nothing alcoholic to drink the entire day. He told you, however, that he had three large drinks within an hour of the accident. By chance, the arresting officer had failed to bring along his kit to test for blood alcohol, so there is no scientific evidence on that issue.

Young's criminal trial is coming up next week. Conviction of drunk driving would probably mean that Young would pay a large fine and lose his driving privileges for a year. You have plea negotiations scheduled with the prosecutor this afternoon. Settlement discussions about the potential civil claims are also expected soon.

You have not talked at all with Young about what kind of plea he might be willing to enter, but you have authority from his insurance company to pay up to a total of $20,000 for the combined personal injuries suffered by the other driver and the property damage incurred by the owner of the other car.

QUESTIONS

A. AUTHORITY TO PARTICIPATE IN AND CONSUMMATE NEGOTIATIONS

1. What gives you the authority to conduct negotiations on behalf of James Young? Is the authority to negotiate inherent in a lawyer's role as a client's representative?

a. The answer is not as clear as one might imagine. Restatement Third, The Law Governing Lawyers § 21, Comment *e*, says:

"A lawyer has authority to take any lawful measure within the scope of representation that is reasonably calculated to advance a client's objectives as defined by the client, unless there is a contrary agreement or instruction and unless a decision is reserved [by law] to the client."

b. Thoughtful lawyers acknowledge that they have only as much authority to conduct negotiations as their client gives them. What does ABA Model Rule 1.2(a), for example, say about who ultimately has the legal authority to settle a matter?

c. Restatement Third, The Law Governing Lawyers § 22 reinforces Rule 1.2(a):

"(1) As between client and lawyer, * * * the following and comparable decisions are reserved to the client except when the client has validly authorized the lawyer to make the particular decision: whether and on what terms to settle a claim; how a criminal defendant should plead; * * *

"(3) Regardless of any contrary contract with a lawyer, a client may revoke a lawyer's authority to make the decisions described in Subsection (1)."

2. Why is even the commencement of negotiations something the lawyer should not take lightly?

a. Comment *c* to Restatement § 22 continues:

"In the absence of a contrary agreement or instruction, a lawyer normally has authority to initiate or engage in settlement discussions, although not to conclude them * * * ."

b.   Is even starting to negotiate something the lawyer must discuss with the client pursuant to Model Rule 1.4? Is talking about settlement of a case a "means by which the client's objectives are to be accomplished" within the meaning of Model Rule 1.4(a)(2), for example?

c.   Can a lawyer intelligently even make a first offer or respond to one from the other side without knowing what the client is currently prepared to accept? Negotiators often talk about trying to find ways to "create value," i.e., to identify ways to engage in sufficient "trade" of issues that both parties feel themselves better off as a result of the negotiations. In short, most negotiations involve a range of potential outcomes and the optimal result will vary with the personal values placed on them by the parties.

d.   Is obtaining authority to negotiate and determining the range of acceptable settlement terms a one-time event? Does Model Rule 1.4 create a continuing obligation on the lawyer? Is negotiation often an evolving process in which settlement authority that seemed reasonable at one time may require revision as new opportunities for agreement open up while others seem less likely?

3.   Do lawyers in a criminal case have an obligation to consider plea bargaining?

a.   ABA Standards Relating to the Administration of Criminal Justice, The Prosecution Function, Standard 3–4.1(a) says:

"The prosecutor should make known a general policy or willingness to consult with defense counsel concerning disposition of charges by plea."

b.   ABA Standards Relating to the Administration of Criminal Justice, The Defense Function, Standard 4–6.1(b), says in turn:

"Defense counsel may engage in plea discussions with the prosecutor. Under no circumstances should defense counsel recommend to a defendant acceptance of a plea unless appropriate investigation and study of the case has been completed, including an analysis of controlling law and the evidence likely to be introduced at trial."

c.   In re Stanton, 682 A.2d 655 (D.C.1996), is an interesting case of a lawyer who was suspended and whose reinstatement was delayed for several years for his refusal to assist clients in plea bargaining because he believes "attorney-assisted guilty pleas are unconstitutional." The lawyer argued that, under Rule 1.2(c), he and his client could agree in advance to limit the scope of his representation and he would plan to do so if readmitted. He would also only represent clients who truly wanted to plead guilty, as opposed to those whose plea he negotiates as part of a settlement package. The court ruled that this attitude reflects an "inability to draw workable distinctions between his philosophical beliefs and his ethical obligations," and thus sufficiently draws into question his willingness to "seek a client's lawful objectives" as to deny readmission. Do you agree? The dissenting justice suggested that the plea bargaining process is indeed broken and that a lawyer's personal philosophical views should not be held to support a finding of a lack of character.

d. Imagine that in this Problem, for example, the prosecutor might be willing to forego most sanctions if Young will plead guilty to some misdemeanor. Young, in turn, might be willing to accept almost any offense that will not involve jail time or a fine in excess of $1,000. Could you negotiate competently on your client's behalf without knowing the relative importance of such alternatives to your client? Can you know those objectives without communicating with your client as Model Rule 1.4 requires?

4. Should a lawyer be required to tell the client about all settlement offers received from the other side?

a. Restatement § 21, Comment *e*, says:

"A lawyer must ordinarily report promptly to the client a settlement offer in a civil action or a proposed plea bargain in a criminal prosecution."

b. Model Rule 1.4, Comment [2] goes on:

"[A] lawyer who receives from opposing counsel in a civil controversy or a proffered plea bargain in a criminal case must promptly inform the client of its substance unless the client has previously indicated that the proposal will be acceptable or unacceptable or has authorized the lawyer to accept or reject the offer."

c. Is this requirement realistic? Might a lawyer ever want to say: "That offer is so bad I would not dignify it by taking it back to my client"? Why might we not want to let lawyers make such statements without at least having learned from the client just what kinds of settlement offers would be acceptable?

d. Think back to Problem 19. Might requiring a lawyer to convey all offers to his or her client be a necessary corollary to Rule 4.2's prohibition of direct contact with that lawyer's client?

5. Should the client be bound by a settlement that the lawyer was not authorized by the client by make? Put another way, may a lawyer assume the lawyer for the other side has authority to make the settlement being proposed?

a. The law's answer may surprise you. Restatement § 27, Comment *d*, says:

"Generally, a client is not bound by a settlement that the client has not authorized a lawyer to make by express, implied, or apparent authority (and that is not validated by later ratification under § 26(3)). * * * When a lawyer purports to enter a settlement binding on the client but lacks authority to do so, the burden of inconvenience resulting if the client repudiates the settlement is properly with the opposing party, who should know that settlements are normally subject to approval by the client and who has no manifested contrary indication from the client. The opposing party can protect itself by obtaining clarification of the lawyer's authority."

b.   In Luethke v. Suhr, 650 N.W.2d 220 (Neb.2002), for example, the parties' lawyers thought they had reached a settlement agreement, but when the defendants tried to enforce it, the plaintiff said he had not authorized his lawyer to settle. The plaintiff was developmentally disabled, and his lawyer had not been able to reach him before agreeing to the settlement. The defense lawyer knew those circumstances but had been assured there would be no problem getting the plaintiff's agreement. In affirming a finding that the plaintiff's lawyer could not bind her client, the court said, "The ordinary employment or retainer of a lawyer * * * does not of itself give the lawyer the implied or apparent authority to bind the client by a settlement or compromise of the claim; and, in the absence of express authority, knowledge, or consent, the lawyer cannot do so." 650 N.W.2d at 225.

c.   A lawyer who affirmatively misrepresents his or her settlement authority to a non-client is subject to liability for damages proximately caused by that misrepresentation. Restatement Third, The Law Governing Lawyers § 30.[1]

B.   THE DUTY OF HONESTY IN NEGOTIATIONS

1.   When you start to discuss this case with the prosecutor, or the opposing counsel in the civil case, may you assert that Young had nothing alcoholic to drink on the day of the accident?

a.   Remember that this is the story that Young has told everyone but you, and if you fail to take that position, you might seem to undercut Young's credibility.

b.   As you will see in Problem 27, you clearly could not encourage Young to testify in the upcoming criminal trial that he had not drunk any alcoholic beverage. Is any distinction between perjury in a trial and deception in negotiation supported by Model Rules 4.1 and 8.4(c)? Should such a distinction be drawn? Should the answer that governs the trial setting be controlling in a negotiation setting as well?

c.   May your negotiating position in the civil and criminal cases be that, whether or not your client had drunk anything alcoholic before the accident, he was not intoxicated at the time the accident occurred? Is that a different question than what he had to drink? Is that something you in fact *know* is untrue?

d.   May you assert that neither the police nor the plaintiff can prove that Young was intoxicated? Are statements about facts and statements about strength of the evidence different as a practical matter? Are they— should they be—different as a matter of ethics?

e.   May you tell your civil adversary that your client will testify that the other car was traveling at an excessive rate of speed and "came out of

---

1. Many of these issues are also discussed in a useful report of the ABA Section of Litigation, Ethical Guidelines for Settlement Negotiations (2002).

nowhere" to cause the accident? May you say that if you know that your client really does not remember the accident very well, but you hope that the other side may factor into its own estimate of the worth of the case the risk that your client would tell such a story?

2. Are all lies created equal? Might some lies be tolerated, some even encouraged, while other lies are forbidden?

a. Look at Comment [2] to Model Rule 4.1. Do you agree that:

"Under generally accepted conventions in negotiation, certain types of statements ordinarily are not taken as statements of material fact. Estimates of price or value placed on the subject of a transaction and a party's intentions as to an acceptable settlement of a claim are ordinarily in this category * * * ."

b. What about misrepresenting one's attitude? Is it proper to fake anger during negotiations, for example? Is it proper to delay making or responding to an offer so as not to let the other side get the sense that your client is in a hurry to dispose of the case by settlement? Does the duty to bargain in good faith prohibit such behavior?

c. May a lawyer lie about the client's alternatives? Might a lawyer arrange for a "telephone call" in the middle of the negotiation for a piece of property, for example, so that she can leave the room and pretend to have received a better offer? May the lawyer say she has to "seek permission from the client to go any higher" when in fact the client has already approved the suggested settlement figure as within the attorney's discretion?

d. The late Federal Judge Alvin B. Rubin took a strong stand on the issue of honesty in negotiations:

" * * * Most lawyers say it would be improper to prepare a false document to deceive an adversary or to make a factual statement known to be untrue with the intention of deceiving him. * * *

"Interesting answers are obtained [, however,] if lawyers are asked whether it is proper to make false statements that concern negotiating strategy rather than the facts in litigation. Counsel for a plaintiff appears quite comfortable in stating, when representing a plaintiff, 'My client won't take a penny less than $25,000,' when in fact he knows that the client will happily settle for less; counsel for the defendant appears to have no qualms in representing that he has no authority to settle, or that a given figure exceeds his authority, when these are untrue statements. Many say that, as a matter of strategy, when they attend a pre-trial conference with a judge known to press settlements, they disclaim any settlement authority both to the judge and adversary although in fact they do have settlement instructions; estimable members of the bar support the thesis that a lawyer may not misrepresent a fact in controversy but may misrepresent matters that pertain to his authority or negotiating strategy because this is expected by the adversary.

"To most practitioners it appears that anything sanctioned by the rules of the game is appropriate. From this point of view, negotiations are merely, as the social scientists have viewed it, a form of game; observance of the expected rules, not professional ethics, is the guiding precept. But gamesmanship is not ethics."[2]

e.   Consider a largely opposing view. Professor James J. White writes of the "paradoxical nature of the negotiator's responsibility":

"On the one hand the negotiator must be fair and truthful; on the other he must mislead his opponent. Like the poker player, a negotiator hopes that his opponent will overestimate the value of his hand. Like the poker player, in a variety of ways he must facilitate his opponent's inaccurate assessment. The critical difference between those who are successful negotiators and those who are not lies in this capacity both to mislead and not to be misled."[3]

f.   With which of these writers do you agree? Can both be right?

3.   Is the obligation to be truthful higher for lawyers than for non-lawyers?

a.   Look closely at Model Rule 4.1 and its Comments. Does it prohibit any more than "false" statements of "material" fact? May the lawyer lie about where John was going on the day of the accident, for example? May he say John was going to church services when he really was going to shoot pool? Is the issue of where he was going "material" to the legal issues in the case? Would it be disloyal to the client to suggest that he is other than a choir boy?

b.   If a non–lawyer knowingly made a false statement of material fact, wouldn't the non–lawyer be guilty of fraud? Does Model Rule 4.1 demand any more of lawyers? Put another way, if a statement would not constitute the tort of fraud or intentional misrepresentation, would it violate Model Rule 4.1? Look especially at Model Rule 4.1, Comment [2]. Is there any statement for which a lawyer would be subject to professional discipline but not liability for damages?

c.   Restatement Third, The Law Governing Lawyers § 98, Comment *c*, suggests that Model Rule 4.1 has two functions. First, it shows that lawyers at least have the same obligations of truthfulness as do persons generally, i.e., lawyers are not specially privileged to make material misstatements of fact. Second, to prove a violation of Model Rule 4.1, it is not necessary to show either reliance on the misstatement or actual damages as a tort suit would require.

2.   Alvin B. Rubin, A Causerie on Lawyers' Ethics in Negotiation, 35 Louisiana L.Rev. 577, 585–86 (1975).

3.   James J. White, Machiavelli and the Bar: Ethical Limits on Lying in Negotiation, 1980 A.B.F. Research J. 926, 927.

d.   Should the law be otherwise? Should the law require lawyers to be more honest than it requires non-lawyers to be? On the other hand, might one to say that because people are more on their guard when dealing with a lawyer, the obligation of a lawyer to tell the truth should be less?

e.   In any event, it is worth knowing that even this apparently minimal rule can have teeth. Fire Insurance Exchange v. Bell, 643 N.E.2d 310 (Ind.1994), involved a lawyer's client who had been burned in a fire at his grandfather's home. The lawyers retained by the homeowner's insurer (one of the state's most prominent firms) offered to pay policy limits, which they represented to be $100,000. Although the injuries would have justified a higher verdict against the plaintiff's grandfather, the plaintiff's lawyer recommended taking the settlement as the only money the plaintiff would be likely to collect. Only later did the lawyer learn that the policy limits were in fact $300,000, not $100,000. This action was brought against the defense lawyers for misrepresentation. The defendants basically argued that no one can reasonably rely on what a lawyer says in "adversarial settlement negotiations." But the court answered: "[t]he reliability and trustworthiness of lawyers' representations is an integral component of the fair and efficient administration of justice." 643 N.E.2d at 312. Even though the plaintiff's counsel could have gotten discovery of the policy and learned the policy limits himself, he was entitled to rely on what opposing counsel told him about this material matter.

5.   Is deception and withholding of information inevitably good negotiating strategy?

a.   Is negotiation inevitably a zero–sum game in which anything one side receives is at the expense of the other? Suppose Ann has a candy bar and Bill has a pen. Ann needs something with which to write and Bill is hungry. Will Ann and Bill each be better off trying to figure out how to trick the other out of what the other has? Might the first to acknowledge the possibility of a fair trade improve the lot of both of them?

b.   Some students of negotiating strategy have used computer simulations to explore approaches to negotiation and have evaluated them in terms of benefits to each negotiator. One successful strategy is known as tit-for-tat.[4] As a negotiator, you would be wise to break the process down into a series of small "deals", not just one large one. As to the first deal, you would begin by being open and honest in your negotiating. If your opposing number responded in the same way, you would reward her by again being open and honest. If your opponent ever deceives you or takes advantage of your honesty, however, you must punish her by non–cooperative behavior as to the next issue. The point is that neither side needs to trust the other or sacrifice its own interests. It simply will turn out to be better for all sides to make honesty and cooperation pay.

c.   Even assuming that is true, however, is every negotiating situation one that has multiple steps? Is every situation one that both sides can win? Might even negotiations that "increase the size of the pie" have a stage in

4.   See Robert Axelrod, The Evolution of Cooperation (1984).

which the pie gets divided? At that stage, what would good negotiators do? Might they agree on a solution that mimics the situation in which one party gets to cut the pie and the other chooses the first piece?[5]

6.   Is it a mistake to think of negotiation as a single type of phenomenon?

a.   Consider again the argument of Professor White:

"One who conceives of negotiation as an alternative to a lawsuit has only scratched the surface. Negotiation is also the process by which one deals with the opposing side in war, with terrorists, with labor or management in a labor agreement, with buyers and sellers of goods, services, and real estate, with lessors, with governmental agencies, and with one's clients, acquaintances, and family. * * * Surely society would tolerate and indeed expect different forms of behavior on the one hand from one assigned to negotiate with terrorists and on the other from one who is negotiating with the citizens on behalf of a government agency. * * * Performance that is standard in one negotiating arena may be gauche, conceivably unethical, in another."[6]

b.   Do you agree with Professor White? Would you have a right to mislead management in a labor negotiation about your union client's willingness to strike?

c.   Might you even have a *duty* to mislead a hostage-taker about whether he will be granted amnesty if he lets his hostages go? What ethical values lead you to your conclusions?

C.   THE DUTY TO VOLUNTEER INFORMATION OR CORRECT A MISAPPREHENSION

1.   Should you as a lawyer ever be required to disclose facts affirmatively in a negotiation? May you simply say it is the duty of the other side to ask you to confirm its assumptions, not your obligation to volunteer that it is acting under a misapprehension?

a.   Virzi v. Grand Trunk Warehouse and Cold Storage Co., 571 F.Supp. 507 (E.D.Mich.1983), raises this question in a particularly interesting form. The plaintiff in a personal injury case had died from causes unrelated to the lawsuit prior to a pre-trial conference and settlement negotiation. Plaintiff's attorney failed to inform opposing counsel and the court of the plaintiff's death throughout those negotiations, but defendant's

---

5. Many observers remain unconvinced that honesty is the best policy if the only measure is to be "profit and effectiveness." See, e.g., Gerald B. Wetlaufer, The Ethics of Lying in Negotiations, 75 Iowa L. Rev. 1219, 1230 (1990): "In those bargaining situations which are at least in part distributive, a category which includes virtually all negotiations, lying is a coherent and often effective strategy." Professor Wetlaufer argues that "lying in negotiations is instrumentally effective and that most such lies are ethically impermissible." Id. at 1221.

6. James J. White, Machiavelli and the Bar: Ethical Limits on Lying in Negotiation, 1980 A.B.F. Research J. 926, 927.

attorney at no time asked plaintiff's attorney if plaintiff was still alive and available for trial. A personal representative had even been appointed to administer the plaintiff's estate, but the lawyer did not move to substitute parties. When the defendant later learned what had happened, it moved to set aside the settlement. The court relied, *inter alia*, on DR 7–102(A)(3) & (5), EC 7–27 of the ABA Model Code of Professional Responsibility; Model Rules 3.3 & 4.1, and on Judge Rubin's article, to grant that relief, saying that zealous representation

> "does not justify a withholding of essential information, such as the death of the client, when the settlement of the case is based largely upon the defense attorney's assessment of the impact the plaintiff would make upon a jury because of his appearance at depositions. Plaintiff's attorney clearly had a duty to disclose the death of his client both to the Court and to opposing counsel prior to negotiating the final agreement." 571 F.Supp. at 512.

b. ABA Formal Opinion 95–397 (Sept. 18, 1995), addressed the same question and explained why disclosure of the client's death is required. Upon the client's death, the Opinion said, the agency relationship ends and the lawyer has no client. The failure to disclose is "tantamount to making a 'false statement of material fact'" to the opponent and to any tribunal. The lawyer "must inform her adversary of the death of her client in the first communication with the adversary after she has learned of that fact."

c. Most later cases are consistent with this result. In Kentucky Bar Ass'n v. Geisler, 938 S.W.2d 578 (Ky.1997), the client was a pedestrian hit by a car. The lawyer told the defense lawyer that the client was too ill to be deposed. After the client's death, she wrote to defense counsel and asked for an offer of settlement. The defense first learned of the client's death when the plaintiff's administrator endorsed the settlement check. Citing ABA Opinion 95–397 and *Virzi*, the court condemned her silence about the client's death in the letter opening settlement talks and ordered a public reprimand. See also, Matter of Forrest, 730 A.2d 340 (N.J.1999) (discussing settlement while saying a deceased client was "unavailable" for an arbitration hearing and delaying court-ordered medical examination justified lawyer's six month suspension).

2. Should each round of settlement discussions have to begin with questions by each side designed to trigger this kind of disclosure? Would a general obligation on lawyers to disclose relevant changes in circumstances be a better approach?

a. Kath v. Western Media, Inc., 684 P.2d 98 (Wyo.1984), involved several individuals and a corporation, all of whom had been represented by a single lawyer in an earlier proceeding. The former co-defendants were now suing each other and part of the question related to the role their attorney had played in the prior action. The former attorney had given a deposition in which he purported not to have known that some of the co-defendants planned to sue the others after his conclusion of the first case. Later, however, counsel for those persons benefitted by that lie by the prior lawyer, learned of the prior lawyer's deception. The question was whether, in the course of settling the current case, the new lawyer was obliged to disclose what he knew of the lies in the prior lawyer's deposition. Citing *Virzi*, DR 7–102(A)(3), EC 7–27, Model Rule 3.3 and Judge Rubin's article, the court held that the lawyer did have a "duty of candor and fairness to disclose [the deception] to opposing counsel and the court." 684 P.2d at 102. The settlement was set aside and the case reopened.

b. Davin v. Daham, 746 A.2d 1034 (N.J.Super.App.Div.2000), imposed an obligation of candor on a lawyer negotiating a lease. The lawyer represented the owner of a shopping center that, unknown to the new lessees, was about to go into foreclosure. The lessees incurred costs getting the new space ready for use, only to be evicted by the company that bought the property at the foreclosure sale. The court held that the lessees' lawyer may have been guilty of malpractice for not searching the title. However, the court also held that the lessor's lawyer may be liable as well. A lawyer "has a duty to represent his or her client effectively and vigorously," the court said, but also "to act fairly, and in good faith." The lessor's lawyer at least had a duty to tell his client to disclose the impending foreclosure; if the client refused, the lawyer had a duty to withdraw. 746 A.2d at 1045. "Jaffe was in a difficult position," the court said. "However, the practice of law is not easy. Attorneys are frequently faced with difficult decisions. They must make the right decision." Id. at 1046.

3. Might some courts properly be concerned about requiring lawyers to be candid?

a. State v. Mark Marks, P.A., 698 So.2d 533 (Fla.1997), involved a Florida criminal statute that prohibited the filing "incomplete" claims with insurance companies in an attempt to obtain payment. It expressly forbade lawyers from helping clients file such claims, apparently out of concern for insurance fraud. The court found the term "incomplete" unconstitutionally vague as applied to lawyers who had failed to include medical records that cast doubt on their clients' injuries in claims that they filed. The state argued that the law only forbade withholding information with an "intent" to defraud, but the court held that even the intent requirement did not cure the vagueness. Lawyers often are required to withhold unfavorable information, the court said, and this statute did not clearly tell them what they were required to disclose.

b. ABA Formal Opinion 314 (Apr. 27, 1965) considered the lawyer's obligation in settling a tax claim with the IRS:

"Negotiation and settlement procedures of the tax system do not carry with them the guarantee that a correct tax result necessarily occurs. The latter happens, if at all, solely by reason of chance in settlement of tax controversies just as it might happen with regard to other civil disputes. In the absence of either judicial determination or of a hypothetical exchange of files by adversaries, counsel will always urge in aid of settlement of a controversy the strong points of his case and minimize the weak; this is in keeping with Canon 15 [of the ABA Canons of Ethics of 1908, as amended], which does require 'warm zeal' on behalf of the client. Nor does the absolute duty not to make false assertions of fact require the disclosure of weaknesses in the client's case and in no event does it require the disclosure of his confidences, unless the facts in the attorney's possession indicate beyond reasonable doubt that a crime will be committed. A wrong, or indeed sometimes an unjust, tax result in the settlement of a controversy is not a crime."

Do you agree? Are these insights peculiar to negotiations with the IRS? Do they represent a realistic understanding of many kinds of negotiations?

c. ABA Formal Opinion 94–387 (Sept. 26, 1994) also narrowly interpreted the duty to disclose. It ruled that "where the lawyer knows that her client's claim may not be susceptible of judicial enforcement because the stature of limitations has run, * * * the ethics rules do not preclude a lawyer's nonetheless negotiating over the claim without informing the opposing party of this potentially fatal defect." However, the lawyer must "be careful not to make any affirmative misrepresentations about the facts showing that the claim is time-barred, or suggest that she plans to do something to enforce the claim (e.g., file suit) that she has no intention of doing. See Rule 4.1." According to the Opinion, there is also no violation of Rule 3.1 [frivolous suits] or Rule 3.3 [candor to tribunal] to file a time–barred claim in court "so long as this does not violate the law of the relevant jurisdiction," such as would be the case if the limitations defect were jurisdictional. Normally, the Opinion noted, the statute of limitations is an affirmative defense that the opposing party must assert. Finally, there is no basis in the ethical rules to hold a government lawyer to a higher or different standard.

Committee member Richard McFarlain filed a dissent. He regarded this Opinion much "as Julia Child would regard a fly in her soup;" it is "unneeded, unwanted, and too much to swallow." In his view, Rule 8.4(c), prohibiting deceit, prohibits lawyers from engaging in this activity.

With which of these views do you agree?

4. Should the rules about negotiation be different in criminal cases? How candid should a prosecutor have to be about the strength of the evidence?

a. In Fambo v. Smith, 433 F.Supp. 590 (W.D.N.Y.1977), aff'd 565 F.2d 233 (2d Cir.1977), the court refused to disturb a guilty plea but held that the prosecutor *did* have a duty to disclose to the defendant, who was charged with possession of explosives, that the dynamite (which formed the basis of one of the counts) had been destroyed prior to the defendant's arrest (and replaced with sawdust). However, the court then found that under the circumstances the error was harmless and the defendant's plea bargain was voluntary, fair and reasonable.

b. In People v. Jones, 375 N.E.2d 41 (N.Y.1978), cert. denied 439 U.S. 846, 99 S.Ct. 145, 58 L.Ed.2d 148 (1978), the court held that the defendant was not denied due process when the District Attorney did not disclose during plea negotiations that the complaining witness had died. Under Brady v. Maryland, 373 U.S. 83, 83 S.Ct. 1194, 10 L.Ed.2d 215 (1963), the prosecutor is under a constitutional duty to respond to defendant's request that he disclose material evidence favorable to the accused, either as to guilt or punishment. The death of the state's critical witness did not fit within *Brady,* the court reasoned, because while it affected the prosecutor's practical ability to prove the case, it did not cast doubt on the defendant's guilt.

Do you agree? Should either Model Rule 3.8(d) or ABA Standard Relating to the Prosecution Function 3–4.1(c) change the result in this case? Do the cited provisions merely incorporate the *Brady* rule?

c. Kyles v. Whitley, 514 U.S. 419, 115 S.Ct. 1555, 131 L.Ed.2d 490 (1995), continued to explore what evidence a prosecutor must reveal to satisfy the *Brady* obligation. This prosecutor had failed to turn over inconsistent statements from its key witness. The Court held the *Brady* test is not whether having access to the withheld material would have meant there was not enough evidence to convict; it was whether the evidence, taken as a whole and not piece by piece, would have made a different result "reasonably probable." By a 5–4 vote, the Court found this evidence met that standard.

d. In United States v. Ruiz, 536 U.S. 622, 122 S.Ct. 2450, 153 L.Ed.2d 586 (2002), however, a unanimous Supreme Court made clear that in negotiating a plea bargain, the government need not tell a criminal defendant impeachment information about its witnesses that it would have to disclose if the case went to trial. After immigration agents found 30 kilos of marijuana in Ruiz's luggage, the government offered a "fast track" plea bargain in which Ruiz would waive trial in exchange for a two-level sentence reduction. The government agreed to tell Ruiz any exculpatory information it had, but she was required to waive receiving information about informants or in support of affirmative defenses she might raise. The 9th Circuit held that defendants are entitled to such information before entering a plea and the required waiver was thus unconstitutional. Justice Breyer said for the Court that such "impeachment" information might go to the fairness of a trial but not to whether a guilty plea was voluntary. Full disclosure of matters such as informant identity, the Court said, "could seriously interfere with the Government's interest in securing those guilty pleas that are factually justified, desired by defendants, and help to secure the efficient administration of justice." 536 U.S. at 631, 122 S.Ct. at 2456, 153 L.Ed.2d at 596–97.

5. In the plea-bargaining negotiations with the prosecutor, may criminal defense counsel assert that he or she "knows" the client is innocent? Is the case for stretching the truth stronger in criminal defense work?

a. Why? Is it because potential sanctions are more severe than in most civil litigation? Is it because "everyone expects" counsel for criminal defendants to be dishonest?

b. Timothy McVeigh was tried and convicted of the bombing of an Oklahoma City federal building, a bombing described as one of the worst terrorist acts in the country's history. Shortly before the trial, the media obtained what was described as McVeigh's "confession" to his lawyer. One of McVeigh's lawyers, Stephen Jones, explained the "confession" by saying that it was an intentionally false document prepared by the defense to show to potential witnesses to see if they would stick to their stories. Is it consistent with Rule 4.1 to "lie" to potential witnesses to see if they are telling the truth?

c.   Is there a difference between lying to deceive someone into changing their position and lying to see how they would honestly react to a set of facts? Would this distinction help justify sending "testers" of different races, none of whom really wants to buy a house, to a real estate agency to see if they receive discriminatory treatment? Might others understandably say that a lie is a lie, and Rule 4.1 condemns them all?

d.   You will see this issue again in Problem 24. One of the important cases there is Conduct of Gatti, 8 P.3d 966 (Ore.2000). In preparing a plaintiff's case, Lawyer Gatti called State Farm Insurance pretending to be a chiropractor who wanted to work as a claim reviewer. He asked them detailed questions about their protocols and guidelines, hoping in fact to develop facts to support a lawsuit, which he later filed, alleging fraud by State Farm. Gatti defended his conduct by saying that government lawyers use deception all the time in undercover operations that seek to "root out evil." He, too, was trying to root out evil in the insurance industry. Even the U.S. Attorney intervened in the case to assert the importance of the government's ability to do undercover work. The Oregon Fair Housing Council and other groups that use testers to develop discrimination cases took the same position.

What do you think of Gatti's defense? Is Model Rule 4.1(a) too absolute? Gatti was, after all, trying to get people to talk who would not have done so if he had told them the truth. However, the Oregon Supreme Court held that there were no exceptions to the rule against misrepresentation. Until the Rules were formally amended, the prohibition applied to all lawyers in all cases.[7]

e.   Would the lawyer have a similar duty of candor when making representations to a federal regulatory agency on behalf of a financial institution client? Matter of Peter M. Fishbein * * * and Kaye, Scholer, Fierman, Hays & Handler, OTS AP–92–19 (1992), attracted lawyers' atten-

---

7. In response to public reaction to *Gatti*, the Oregon Supreme Court has amended its Code of Professional Responsibility DR 1–102 to add a (D) that says:

"[I]t shall not be professional misconduct for a lawyer to advise clients or others about or to supervise lawful covert activity in the investigation of violations of civil or criminal law or constitutional rights, provided the lawyer's conduct is otherwise in compliance with these disciplinary rules. 'Covert activity,' as used in this rule, means an effort to obtain information on unlawful activity through the use of misrepresentations or other subterfuge. 'Covert activity' may be commenced by a lawyer or involve a lawyer as an adviser or supervisor only when the lawyer in good faith believes there is a reasonable possibility that unlawful activity has taken place, is taking place or will take place in the foreseeable future."

tion to these issues. Lincoln Savings' semi-annual routine regulatory examination in 1986 turned up signs that the institution was in trouble. The regulators wanted more information and Charles Keating allegedly knew the future of his organization was at stake. He hired the Kaye Scholer firm to protect him from the regulators and Peter Fishbein, a litigator, took over the defense. Fishbein allegedly treated the situation as adversary litigation, resisted document requests, and did not volunteer negative information. OTS charged that Kaye Scholer had thus become the alter ego of the client. Lincoln was obliged to make information available, OTS argued, so the law firm could not assume that the secrecy that would be proper in litigation was proper in this situation. The regulations required disclosure to protect third parties such as the depositors. If Lincoln Savings had to disclose this information pursuant to regulation, Lincoln's lawyers had no right to refuse to disclose. After a "freeze" of the law firm's assets, Kaye Scholer agreed to pay the government $42 million. What would you have done if you were in Mr. Fishbein's position? At the very least, can we say that lawyers should not assume they can do things for their clients that the clients could not legally do themselves.[8]

D. Possible limits on the results that can be reached in negotiations

1. **Should there be any limit on what parties to a negotiation may agree? May a lawyer agree, for example, that in exchange for a generous financial payment to the lawyer's client, neither the lawyer not the client will file criminal charges against the opposing lawyer for conduct that would justify such charges?**

a. ABA Model Code of Professional Responsibility, DR 7–105(A) seemed to say "no" when it asserted:

> "A lawyer shall not present, participate in presenting, or threaten to present criminal charges solely to obtain an advantage in a civil matter."

See also, California State Bar Rule 5–100(A):

> "A member shall not threaten to present criminal, administrative, or disciplinary charges to obtain an advantage in a civil action."

b. You will not find a comparable provision in the ABA Model Rules, and ABA Formal Opinion 92–363 (July 6, 1992) has now revisited whether such conduct is still prohibited. Applying the Model Rules, the Opinion found that a lawyer *may* use the possibility of bringing criminal charges in negotiations in a civil case if both the civil case and criminal violation are well founded in fact and law, the lawyer does not suggest improper influence over the criminal process, and the threat would not constitute extortion under state law. The lawyer may even agree not to file criminal

---

8. The ABA's Formal Opinion commenting on these issues is 93–375 (Aug. 6,   1993).

charges as an element of settling a civil claim if that agreement would not violate a provision of law that required reporting of crimes.

Do you agree? Is the ABA getting more realistic? Does the opinion simply represent a further decline in lawyers' ethical standards?

c.   Does it follow that a lawyer should be permitted to agree not to file disciplinary charges against an opposing lawyer in order to induce settlement of a civil case? ABA Formal Opinion 94–383 (July 5, 1994) saw that as a different issue. Just as In re Himmel, 533 N.E.2d 790 (Ill.1988), cited in Problem 2, held that a lawyer may not bargain away a duty to report a lawyer's disciplinary violation in order to get a better settlement for a client, Opinion 94–383 says that a lawyer may not agree to fail to report any matter the lawyer is required to report by Model Rule 8.3(a). Even as to matters sufficiently minor as to not require reporting, a threat to report may possibly be "prejudicial to the administration of justice" because it might introduce extraneous calculations into the decision to settle. Do you agree?

2.   In the course of defending James Young, you have discovered that the city often has problems with its alcohol detection kits. That is information the city would prefer be kept quiet. Assume the city proposes to drop all charges against Young in exchange for your agreement never to defend another drunk driving case. Do the Model Rules permit you to get Young off the hook on that basis?

a.   Look at Model Rule 5.6(b). What rationale justifies that rule? Why should a rule require a lawyer to sacrifice the interests of a current client, Young, to protect the interests of a hypothetical future drunk driving defendant?

b.   ABA Formal Opinion 93–371 (Apr. 16, 1993), directly addressed only proposed "global settlements" on behalf of both present and future claimants. Yet it is also relevant to this problem because it identified three important policies underlying Model Rule 5.6(b):

"First, permitting such agreements restricts the access of the public to lawyers who, by virtue of their background and experience, might be the very best available talent to represent these individuals. Second, the use of such agreements may provide clients with rewards that bear less relationship to the merits of their claims than they do to the desire of the defendant to 'buy off' plaintiff's counsel. Third, the offering of such restrictive agreements places the plaintiff's lawyer in a situation where there is conflict between the interests of present clients and those of future clients. While the Model Rules generally require that the client's interests be put first, forcing a lawyer to give up future representations may be asking too much, particularly in light of the strong countervailing policy favoring the public's unfettered choice of counsel."

c.   Yet Feldman v. Minars, 658 N.Y.S.2d 614 (App.Div.1997), enforced an agreement like the one in this question even though the court conceded that the agreement violates New York DR 2–108(B) [and Model Rule 5.6(b)], and that many courts in other jurisdictions have held such agreements as non-enforceable for violating public policy. But *Feldman* asserted that the rule makes no sense because, if the legal claim is legitimate, then the market will supply another lawyer to take the next case. Thus, it directed the trial court to disqualify the lawyer from acting in violation of his agreement.

Do you agree with the court? Are lawyers always fungible? If the fact that future clients could not have you on their side meant nothing to the defendant, would it have bothered to bargain and pay for that result in the first place?

3. Suppose that in investigating Young's case you learn that his car had a serious steering defect that could have involved him in an even more serious accident. You realize that thousands of other drivers have cars with the same defect that the manufacturer has not acknowledged. May you negotiate a handsome settlement for Young that includes a provision that you will keep what you know confidential and not use it on behalf of any future client?

a. Do you see why people might be troubled by such "secret settlements"? While their very secrecy makes it difficult to determine how great a social problem they present, a pattern of such settlements clearly could allow dangerous conditions to go uncorrected for many years.[9]

b. It has been difficult to reach an agreement that secret settlements should be prohibited. Judges tend to see such settlements, if at all, in the context of resolution of particular cases whose significance they may not appreciate. Defendants argue, in turn, that the settlements are an important way to protect trade secrets that liberal discovery rules put at risk, so the public interest favors protecting confidentiality though such settlements.[10]

c. ABA Formal Opinion 00–417 (Apr. 7, 2000) considered settlements containing the condition that a lawyer not use any information learned against the defendant in the future. A settlement term that prohibited a lawyer from, *e.g.*, using the same expert witness or subpoenaing certain records on behalf of the new client that the lawyer had previously subpoenaed on behalf of the former client would, the Opinion said, "[a]s a practical matter" effectively bar the lawyer from future representations in violation of Rule 5.6(b), because the lawyer's inability to use that information might materially limit her representation of a future client.

The Opinion noted that "the subsequent use of information relating to the representation of a former client is treated quite liberally as compared to restrictions regarding disclosure of client information." Rule 1.9(c)

---

9. This issue is discussed in, e.g., Richard Zitrin & Carol M. Langford, The Moral Compass of the American Lawyer, Chap. 9 (1999).

10. Such agreements are defended vigorously in Arthur R. Miller, Confidentiality, Protective Orders, and Public Access to the Courts, 105 Harvard L. Rev. 427 (1991).

restrains only use that is *disadvantageous* to the former client and does not apply when the information has become generally known or when other exceptions apply. "As long as the lawyer does not disclose information relating to the representation of the former client to a third party, the lawyer may use that information in subsequent representations, subject to the limited restrictions of Rule 1.9(c)(1)."

d. Los Angeles County Bar Association Professional Responsibility and Ethics Committee, Formal Opinion 505 (2000), on the other hand, says that a lawyer, in negotiating an engagement, may ethically agree to waive certain of the lawyer's fees if the client agrees to waive a confidentiality clause in any settlement. If the client later accepts a settlement containing such a non-disclosure agreement, however, the client would have to pay the higher fees. The committee found that such a provision would not prevent the client's ability to accept a favorable settlement with a confidentiality clause, nor would it require the consent of the lawyer to a secret settlement. Therefore, because the a provision would not prevent the client from settling the matter on the terms the client chose, it should not be against public policy.

Do you agree that this Opinion has found a way out of the dilemma presented by secret settlements? Does the approach really address the significant issues at all?

4. In this Problem, the insurance company has authorized you to pay $20,000 to settle a total of $25,000 in claims. May counsel for Young's opponents negotiate a settlement that would pay the other driver $18,000 for his personal injuries and then tell his other client, the car owner, that there is only $2,000 left to pay for the property damage?

a. If the driver and owner were represented by separate counsel, how would the settlement talks have proceeded? Would they be likely to have involved a race to settle, i.e, for one or the other plaintiffs to have sought to settle first for a disproportionate share of the sum offered?

b. Take a look at ABA Model Rule 1.8(g). Why should the result be different when a single lawyer represents both plaintiffs. Should a lawyer who represents two clients be able to settle on behalf of the most deserving first, without giving the less deserving a right to veto that settlement?

c. Restatement Third, The Law Governing Lawyers § 128, Comment *d(i)*, suggests that any such situation presents a conflict of interest and that Model Rule 1.8(g) should be seen as a requirement of informed consent that simply takes a particular form in the context of an aggregate settlement. See also, Comment [13] to Model Rule 1.8.

d. Does that make sense to you? Then, what is the justification for a "writing signed by the client" in this context whereas a consent "confirmed in writing" suffices for most conflicts?

PROBLEM 21

THE LAWYER AS EVALUATOR

We have said a lot about confidentiality and about loyalty to a client's interest. We have also explored the requirement of honesty in negotiations. The lawyer's role as an evaluator involves each of these lawyer obligations. When the lawyer acts as an evaluator, the lawyer undertakes to vouch for facts or legal conclusions to a third party in an effort to assist the client to complete a transaction or resolve a disagreement. This Problem looks first at the traditional legal opinion a lawyer might address to a client. It then examines what, if anything, changes when the addressee of the opinion is a third party to whom the lawyer does not otherwise owe duties. Next, it looks at reports made to a client's auditor, and finally asks what consequences flow from an inaccurate opinion.

FACTS

Luther Klose is president of the Klose Corporation, a privately-held family enterprise. All of the stockholders are also officers of the corporation and receive benefits from the corporation both in the form of dividends and in the form of salary. In order to keep the overall tax liability at a minimum, the shareholders would prefer that as much money as possible be paid as salary that is deductible to the corporation, rather than as dividends that are not. Mr. Klose would like you, the corporation's outside attorney, to write him an opinion letter explaining that a new salary schedule to be inaugurated by the company properly represents greater responsibilities of the shareholder officers and thus is bona fide and not adopted with intent to circumvent the tax laws.

Klose Corporation is also seeking a large loan from the local bank. Given the Klose Corporation's local reputation for taking aggressive tax positions, the bank wants to be aware of any foreseen tax difficulties that might materially affect the Klose Corporation's ability to repay its loan. Mr. Klose, at the suggestion of the bank, has asked you to write a letter to the bank giving your legal opinion that all of the major tax deductions that the Klose Corporation took in the last three years are reasonable under the tax laws and that, if the Internal Revenue Service disallows any of these major deductions, the taxpayer is likely to prevail in litigation.

Now, the company's auditor has asked for information on "all actual or potential legal problems that might materially affect the Klose Corporation." You know that Klose Corporation has sold a large stock of defective goods, but no customer has yet discovered the defects. When the defects are discovered it may be difficult to trace them back to your client, but if the tracing is made, the company may be liable for up to half its net worth in damages.

QUESTIONS

A.   DUTIES TO A CLIENT WHO ASKS FOR A LEGAL OPINION

1. Does Mr. Klose have a right to "purchase" the opinion letter he wants from you concerning the reasonableness of his salary?

a. Think back to Model Rule 2.1. What obligation might you have to tell a client something he does not want to hear? To what extent, if any, must you "audit" the client to assure yourself that the duties of the officers are in fact as your opinion will assume them to be?

b. To whom does your duty run in this situation. Even when your client is a privately-held corporation, does your professional duty of loyalty run solely to Mr. Klose? Remember Model Rule 1.13(a).

2. Does the fact that this Problem involves a tax opinion increase or decrease the lawyer's responsibilities? Can one say that anything is fair where avoiding taxes is concerned?

a. ABA Formal Opinion 314 (Apr. 27, 1965), dealing with the lawyer's duty of candor in dealing with the IRS, said:

> "The Internal Revenue Service is neither a true tribunal, nor even a quasi-judicial institution. * * * [F]ew will contend that the service provides any truly dispassionate and unbiased consideration to the taxpayer. * * *

> "It by no means follows that a lawyer is relieved of all ethical responsibility when he practices before this agency. * * *

> "[A] lawyer who is asked to advise his client in the course of the preparation of the client's tax returns may freely urge the statement of positions most favorable to the client just as long as there is reasonable basis for those positions. Thus where the lawyer believes there is a reasonable basis for a position that a particular transaction does not result in taxable income, or that certain expenditures are properly deductible as expenses, the lawyer has no duty to advise that riders be attached to the client's tax return explaining the circumstances surrounding the transaction or the expenditures."

b. However, the ABA later found it had to modify Opinion 314 in Formal Opinion 85–352 (1985). The ABA Standing Committee on Ethics and Professional Responsibility reported that it was "informed that the standard of 'reasonable basis' [to support a position] has been construed by many lawyers to support the use of any colorable claim on a tax return to justify exploitation of the lottery of the tax return audit selection process." To correct the record, the Standing Committee offered this guidance:

> "[A] lawyer may advise reporting a position on a return even where the lawyer believes the position probably will not prevail, there is no 'substantial authority' in support of the position, and there will be no disclosure of the position in the return. However, the position to be asserted must be one which the lawyer in good faith believes is

warranted in existing law or can be supported by a good faith argument for an extension, modification or reversal of existing law. This requires that there is some realistic possibility of success if the matter is litigated. In addition, in his role as advisor, the lawyer should refer to potential penalties and other legal consequences should the client take the position advised."

Does that help? Now is your responsibility clear?

c.   May your opinion fail to discuss relevant facts that you know are inconsistent with your client's position on the tax questions? With respect to what must be disclosed on a tax return, one tax practitioner reports that:

> "The consensus of opinion appears to be that the smaller the amount involved and the greater the likelihood that the taxpayer will ultimately prevail, the less is the obligation to disclose the weakness. On the other hand, where the amount involved is large and the taxpayer's ultimate chance of success substantially less than even, most Bostonians feel some disclosure is required. Rarely however, will the disclosure be a large red flag. Usually it will be a relatively inconspicuous reference to a fact—just enough to preclude any claim of fraud, but not enough to stimulate further inquiry by any but the most astute of agents."[1]

Is this position is morally defensible? Is it a practical compromise based on how likely one is to face sanctions if caught defending an indefensible position?

3.   Suppose you conclude and say in your opinion that the ultimate tax liability will depend to a great extent on the intent of the taxpayer. May you help Klose "manufacture" intent? Does your answer depend on whether you personally believe that Klose has the proper legal intent and you are merely helping him preserve and articulate it?

a.   How may you properly counsel creation of proof of intent? May you prepare minutes of meetings that never occurred in which the participants recite their intent? Does it matter whether these minutes are eventually approved ("ratified") by the participants?

b.   One might argue that the lawyer is not justified in "drawing a misleading minute" in order to develop intent for tax consideration, but that "having made the decision in his own mind that the action the client proposes is justified under the law, he is entitled to set out in the minutes the considerations that led him to that conclusion, and when he has done that he probably has gone as far as he can."[2] Do you agree?

---

1. Frederic G. Corneel, Ethical Guidelines for Tax Practice, 28 Tax L. Rev. 1, 10 (1972). Mr. Corneel, in addition to his own research and experience, relied in this article on a survey of Boston lawyers and practitioners engaged in tax practice.

2. Business Planning and Professional Responsibility—Problem 1, 8 The Practical Lawyer 18, 33 (Jan.1962).

4. Would you let a client purchase your ratification of its officials' socially beneficial objectives in the guise of a legal opinion?

a. Suppose the president of the corporate client wants the company to make a significant charitable contribution to engender goodwill or for other positive reasons, but also wants to nip in the bud a shareholder suit second guessing the president's judgment.

b. May you tell the client that certain legal considerations make it proper to make the contribution when your real reason for the conclusion is based on non-legal considerations? Assume that the legal justification is at least arguable but that you need to be less than candid about the client's primary motivation. Medical doctors, some people claim, are sometimes justified in lying to their patients. May juris doctors ever lie to the clients for the clients' own good? How about to make the lawyer feel good?

B. DUTIES IN PREPARATION OF A LEGAL OPINION FOR DELIVERY TO A THIRD PARTY

1. Look at Model Rule 2.3. Did it add something not in the Model Code? Was it an important addition? Do you suppose lawyers were "evaluators" even before adoption of the Rule?

a. Restatement Third, The Law Governing Lawyers § 95, Comment *b,* suggests that the role is familiar and reasonable.

> "For example, a lawyer for a corporation entering into a contract with a third person may address an opinion letter to the third person as to the authority of the officers of the corporate client to bind the corporation to the contract. In a real-estate transaction, a title opinion rendered by the lawyer for the seller may be addressed to the purchaser or a financial institution lending funds to the purchaser to be secured by the property. In such instances, the * * * client's interest is advanced by making it possible for the third person to proceed with the transaction on the basis of the evaluation."

b. In connection with the bank loan described in this problem, what does Rule 2.3 require of you? Why must you "consult" with the client before agreeing to give the opinion? Why isn't the fact the client asked you to prepare the evaluation enough?

2. What circumstances would ever make you conclude that the evaluation was incompatible with other aspects of your relationship with the client?

a. Think about the attorney-client privilege; does it apply when one is conducting an internal investigation, the results of which may be available to others? Look again at Upjohn Co. v. United States, 449 U.S. 383, 101 S.Ct. 677, 66 L.Ed.2d 584 (1981), that you saw in Problem 8. The protection that will be granted to communications with inside and outside corporate counsel is broad in cases where no public disclosure is planned, but the result may be different where the lawyer's conclusions are intended to be made available outside of the corporation. See also Model Rule 2.3(c).

b. Then again, suppose you learn something in the course of your investigation that is harmful to your client, e.g., that its factory is too close to the properly line under applicable zoning regulations. Might the client wisely decide not to seek the loan rather than publicly reveal its problem?

c. Both such possibilities might suggest to you that, while rendering third-party opinions is a significant part of many transactional lawyers' work, the decision to give such an opinion should not be made lightly.

3. Can you just cover up embarrassing facts, i.e., ignore them in your opinion? What relationship do you assume vis-a-vis the non-clients to whom your opinion will be addressed?

a. Restatement Third, The Law Governing Lawyers § 95, Comment *c*, says:

> " * * *Unless otherwise required or permitted by the terms under which the evaluation is given, the lawyer's duty is to provide a fair and objective opinion. * * * By statements in the evaluation, the lawyer may undertake to exercise a higher or lesser standard of care. * * *

> " * * * [However, t]he third-person recipient of a lawyer's evaluation does not thereby become the client of the lawyer, and the lawyer does not thereby undertake all duties owed to a client, such as confidentiality or avoidance of conflicting interests * * * ."

b. Is your obligation of accuracy greater, less or the same as one you would assume in giving an opinion to your own client? Restatement § 95, Comment *c*, continues:

> "In all events, unless stated or agreed otherwise, a lawyer's evaluation does not entail a guarantee by the lawyer that facts stated in it are accurate. In some circumstances, such as when the lawyer purports to be making a report of a factual investigation undertaken by the lawyer, a reasonable reader of the report would assume that the lawyer is reporting facts known by the lawyer to be accurate. A lawyer normally may rely on facts provided by corporate officers and other agents of a client that the lawyer reasonably believes to be appropriate sources for such facts without further investigation or specific disclosure, unless the recipient of the opinion objects or the version of the facts provided or other circumstances indicate that further verification is required."

c. Might you simply base your opinion on an assumed set of facts? Comment *c* answers:

> "A lawyer may not without express disclosure rely for purposes of a legal opinion or other evaluation report on a fact or factual assumption that the lawyer knows to be inaccurate or, in the case of a factual representation, to have been provided under circumstances making reliance unwarranted."

d. Because what are called "third party opinions", i.e., opinions to be relied upon by persons other than the lawyer's client, have become such a central part of commercial dealing, several bar association groups have developed standard definitions for the usual representations that lawyers make.[3]

e. In 1998, the ABA Business Law Section's Committee on Legal Opinions published its own "Legal Opinion Principles" that summarize the emerging consensus in this area. Among the principles declared are that:

(i) "The matters usually addressed in opinion letters, the meaning of the language normally used, and the scope and nature of the work counsel is expected to perform are based (whether or not so stated) on the customary practice of lawyers who regularly give * * * opinions of the kind involved." An opinion giver may vary any of the customary practice, but must do so expressly.

(ii) "The opinions contained in an opinion letter are expressions of professional judgment regarding the legal matters addressed and not guarantees that a court will reach any particular result."

(iii) " * * *[A]n opinion recipient ordinarily need not take any action to verify the opinions it contains."

(iv) Opinions may and customarily do "specify the jurisdiction(s) whose law they are intended to cover and sometimes limit their coverage to specified * * * [laws] of the named jurisdiction(s)."

(v) "Customary practice permits [an opinion author to rely 'in large measure on factual information obtained from others, particularly company officials'] * * * unless the factual information * * * appears irregular on its face or has been provided by an inappropriate source."

(vi) "An opinion should not be based on a factual representation that is tantamount to the legal conclusion being expressed."

(vii) "An opinion letter speaks as of its date. An opinion giver has no obligation to update an opinion letter for subsequent events or legal developments."[4]

C. SPECIAL PROBLEMS RESPONDING TO AN AUDITOR'S REQUEST FOR INFORMATION

1. What are your responsibilities in replying to the independent auditors of the Klose Corporation who have required the company to get a letter from you evaluating various legal claims that have been or are likely to be asserted against the company?

3. These definitions are collected and analyzed in Scott FitzGibbon and Donald W. Glazer, Legal Opinions: What Opinions in Financial Transactions Say and What They Mean (1992).

4. For background and more detail about these principles, see Donald W. Glazer, It's Time to Streamline Opinion Letters, Business Lawyer Today, Nov/Dec 1999, at p. 32, 35.

a. Such letters are routinely required at the time of any corporation's certified audit. Auditors want to be confident there will be no surprises that will render their conclusions misleading, and—to be realistic—they want someone at whom to point a finger if surprises do arise.

b. As courts began to hold accountants liable in damage actions if they did not maintain independence from and verify the representations of the corporate clients whose books were being audited, the auditors sought "comfort" from the corporation's lawyers. The auditors asked the lawyers to verify the corporation's contingent liabilities.

> "When the legal profession became fully aware of the implications of such requests for information regarding contingent liabilities, the die was cast. By then the accounting profession had come to view responses to these inquiries as essential to an audit, and a failure to receive the appropriate response was viewed as a limitation on the scope of the audit, necessitating a disclaimer of opinion or, depending on the circumstances, other qualification, which could render the financial statements effectively unaudited. That, in turn, had a serious impact on the client—which often was required to pay its auditors and its attorneys to debate the question—since it was required to file audited financial statements under the 1934 Act or, in the case of any new registration of securities, the 1933 Act.

> "For a number of reasons, however, the lawyers could not readily submit to such an inquiry. First, the lawyer has the ethical obligation * * * to [preserve the confidentiality of client information]. Accompanying that ethical obligation is the legal obligation, imposed under slightly varying conditions, to maintain the attorney-client privilege. While each of those barriers to disclosure might technically be overcome by the client's consent, there was significant doubt about whether consent coerced in this fashion could be valid, particularly when—as was usually the case—the client was not fully cognizant that such disclosure might destroy the confidentiality privilege for all purposes. Moreover, most law firms, and in particular the larger ones, reasonably feared liability for a failure to recognize the full consequences of facts coming to the attention of their lawyers in a context other than request by the client for advice. For example, a lawyer involved in litigating one case might easily become aware, through discovery, of facts that could constitute the basis for another action by a different party against the client.

> "Finally, of course—and to this difficulty clients were most sensitive—disclosure of a contingent liability could often lead to removal of its contingent aspect. While a publicly held company might properly be required to disclose some potential liabilities to existing or potential shareholders, the analysis of whether or not disclosure was, in fact, required could often be a close question of judgment. Since it was obviously not in the interest of all shareholders to increase the claim's potential by disclosure, lawyers were understandably reluctant to substitute their judgment for that of their clients. And since the lawyers

themselves received no economic benefit from nondisclosure, ran no risk from disclosure, but did run a risk in nondisclosure, one could reasonably expect that a disclosure decision made by lawyers would have an overly conservative bias not necessarily in the public interest."[5]

c. The sensitivity of the information lawyers possess led to a formal agreement between the legal and accounting professions. The ABA and the American Institute of Certified Public Accountants reached a compromise and both groups issued coordinated statements.[6] The [statements] distinguished between "litigation which is pending or which a third party has manifested to the client a present intention to commence," and "other contingencies of a legal nature or having legal aspects."

As to the first category, "unquestionably the lawyer representing the client in a litigation matter may be the best source for a description of the claim or claims asserted, the client's position (e.g. denial, contest, etc.) and the client's possible exposure in the litigation. * * * "As to the second category, the Statement found that "it is not in the public interest for the lawyer to be required to respond to general inquiries from auditors concerning possible claims."

Paragraph (3) of the Statement stated that the lawyer's response to the auditors request for disclosure of the loss contingencies of the client may be limited "to items which are considered individually or collectively material to the presentation of the client's financial statements."

Paragraph (5) then provided:

"(5) *Loss Contingencies. When properly requested by the client,[7] it is appropriate for the lawyer to furnish to the auditor information concerning the following matters if the lawyer has been engaged by the client to represent or advise the client professionally with respect thereto and he has devoted substantive attention to them in the form of legal representation or consultation:*

---

5. Simon Lorne, The Corporate and Securities Adviser, The Public Interest, and Professional Ethics, 76 Michigan L. Rev. 425, 448–49 (1978) (footnote omitted).

6. The American Institute of Certified Public Accountants (AICPA), which is the principal organization of practicing accountants, issued Statement on Auditing Standards (SAS) No. 12, Inquiry of a Client's Lawyer Concerning Litigation, Claims and Assessments (1976), which coordinates with the ABA Statement of Policy Regarding Lawyers' Responses to Auditors' Requests for Information * * * [an edited version of which] is reprinted here. The text of each statement

may be found in 31 Business Lawyer 1709 (1976).

While Chairman of the Securities and Exchange Commission, Roderick M. Hills called this ABA/AICPA agreement "a major step forward," but others have thought the compromise "as resting, in the final analysis, upon a mutual abdication of purported responsibilities. As such it is only a matter of time before its frailty is exposed." Lorne, supra n. 4, at 449–50. For a frail document, the agreement has remained in force for a long time.

7. Emphasis added.

"(a) overtly threatened or pending litigation, whether or not specified by the client;

"(b) *a contractually assumed obligation* which the client has specifically identified and upon which the client has specifically requested, in the inquiry letter or a supplement thereto, comment to the auditor;

"(c) *an unasserted possible claim or assessment* which the client has specifically identified and upon which the client has specifically requested, in the inquiry letter or a supplement thereto, comment to the auditor.

"With respect to clause (a), overtly threatened litigation means that a potential claimant has manifested to the client an awareness of and present intention to assert a possible claim or assessment unless the likelihood of litigation (or of settlement when litigation would normally be avoided) is considered remote. With respect to clause (c), where there has been no manifestation by a potential claimant of an awareness of and present intention to assert a possible claim or assessment, * * * the client should request the lawyer to furnish information to the auditor only if the client has determined that it is probable that a possible claim will be asserted, that there is a reasonable possibility that the outcome (assuming such assertion) will be unfavorable, and that the resulting liability would be material to the financial condition of the client. Examples of such situations might (depending in each case upon the particular circumstances) include the following: (i) a catastrophe, accident or other similar physical occurrence in which the client's involvement is open and notorious, or (ii) an investigation by a government agency where enforcement proceedings have been instituted or where the likelihood that they will not be instituted is remote, under circumstances where assertion of one or more private claims for redress would normally be expected, or (iii) a public disclosure by the client acknowledging (and thus focusing attention upon) the existence of one or more probable claims arising out of an event or circumstance. * * *

"The information that lawyers may properly give to the auditor concerning the foregoing matters would include (to the extent appropriate) an identification of the proceedings or matter, the stage of proceedings, the claim(s) asserted, and the position taken by the client.

"In view of the inherent uncertainties the lawyer should normally refrain from expressing judgments as to outcome except in those relatively few clear cases where it appears to the lawyer that an unfavorable outcome is either 'probable' or 'remote;' for purposes of any such judgment it is appropriate to use the following meanings:

"(i) **probable.**—an unfavorable outcome for the client is probable if the prospects of the claimant not succeeding are judged to be extremely doubtful and the prospects for success by the client in its defense are judged to be slight.

"(ii) **remote**—an unfavorable outcome is remote if the prospects for the client not succeeding in its defense are judged to be extremely doubtful and the prospects of success by the claimant are judged to be slight. * * * No inference should be drawn, from the absence of such a judgment, that the client will not prevail.

"The lawyer also may be asked to estimate, in dollar terms, the potential amount of loss or range of loss in the event that an unfavorable outcome is not viewed to be 'remote.' In such a case, the amount or range of potential loss will normally be an inherently impossible to ascertain, with any degree of certainty, as the outcome of the litigation. Therefore, it is appropriate for the lawyer to provide an estimate of the amount or range of potential loss (if the outcome should be unfavorable) only if he believes that the probability of inaccuracy of the estimate of the amount or range of potential loss is slight. * * * The lawyer should not be asked, nor need the lawyer undertake, to furnish information to the auditor concerning loss contingencies except as contemplated by this Paragraph 5."

Paragraph (6) provided that the lawyer may not "knowingly" participate in any violation by his client "of the disclosure requirements of the securities laws" and that "[i]ndependent of the scope of his response to the auditor's request for information" the "lawyer also may be required under the Code of Professional Responsibility to resign his engagement if his advice concerning disclosures is disregarded by the client." While the lawyer is under a duty to consult with the client concerning the question of disclosure, there is no requirement that the attorney inform the auditor.

2. How do these standards apply to the situation in this Problem?

a.   If the IRS had challenged the accounting treatment of the Klose Corporation's salaries, for example, would you be required to disclose that to the auditors? Look at Paragraph 5(a) of the Statement of Policy. The challenge would almost certainly constitute "overtly threatened or pending litigation."

b.   How would you describe the client's chance of successfully resisting the IRS claim? Do the terms "probable" and "remote" used in the Statement of Policy leave a large range of possibilities as to which neither term accurately applies?

c.   Must you disclose, in your letter to the auditor, the possible litigation regarding the product defect? Would the Statement of Policy call that an "unasserted possible claim or assessment"? Would you expect your client to "specifically identify" and request comment upon that heretofore undiscovered risk?

3. What should a lawyer do if an auditor demands more information than the Statement of Policy contemplates?

a.   It is not uncommon in today's environment of multi-million dollar suits against accounting firms for auditors to demand that companies ask their lawyers for more information than the Statement of Policy would give them.

b. What exposure would your law firm incur trying to respond to a demand for "all actual or potential legal problems that might materially affect the Klose Corporation"? Could you ever respond to that question in a way that would assure you would not be later surprised by a claim that you had not anticipated? Would it tend to turn your firm into an insurer of the client's financial health?

c. Might the lawyer try to resist the auditor's demands? Might it seek to negotiate a more proscribed scope of disclosure? Would such an effort imply the company has something to hide? Needless to say, these are the kinds of concerns that have caused Rules 1.4 and 2.3 to require consultation between lawyer and client before any such response is given to the auditors.

D.   LAWYER LIABILITY FOR AN INACCURATE OPINION

1. Mr. Klose wants you to write him a letter that will make him feel good about his decision to raise the salaries of his family members. Might you potentially be liable to your client, the Klose Corporation, for an opinion that the client wanted you to render but that turned out to be inaccurate?

a. It is tempting for lawyers to tell their clients what they want to hear. In a world in which clients can fire lawyers at will and a dozen new lawyers stand ready to pursue the client's business, it might seem that lawyers could not behave otherwise.

b. Remember, however, that the lawyer's corporate client is not Mr. Klose; it is the Klose Corporation. If the company should be sold or go into bankruptcy, do you suppose the bankruptcy trustee or the new owner will be impressed that your opinion was solicited by Mr. Klose rather than based on your firm's independent professional judgment?

c. If the law firm did not use reasonable care in rendering an opinion, even one solicited by the client's management, the client will very likely have a malpractice claim against the lawyer. See, e.g., FDIC v. O'Melveny & Myers, 969 F.2d 744 (9th Cir.1992), rev'd on other grounds, 512 U.S. 79, 114 S.Ct. 2048, 129 L.Ed.2d 67 (1994), aff'd on remand, 61 F.3d 17 (9th Cir.1995) (firm held liable for failing to discover that its client was in poor financial health); FDIC v. Clark, 978 F.2d 1541 (10th Cir.1992) (firm failed to discover that bank officers were diverting bank funds to their own use), both discussed in Problem 18.

2. Should the bank to whom you have written a third-party opinion have recourse against you if your report is inaccurate or misleading?

a. Restatement Third, The Law Governing Lawyers § 51(2) makes clear that lawyers may be held liable to a nonclient "when and to the extent that: (a) the lawyer or (with the lawyer's acquiescence) the lawyer's client invites the nonclient to rely on the lawyer's opinion or provision of other legal services, and the nonclient so relies * * * ." Numerous cases confirm that basis for lawyer liability.

b. In Greycas, Inc. v. Proud, 826 F.2d 1560 (7th Cir.1987), cert. denied 484 U.S. 1043, 108 S.Ct. 775, 98 L.Ed.2d 862 (1988), a borrower had sought to raise money from a finance company on the strength of a security interest in certain farm machinery. The lender, Greycas, agreed to put up the money if the borrower would supply the borrower's lawyer's opinion that there were no prior liens on the assets. Lawyer Proud, who was the borrower's brother-in-law, wrote a letter saying that he had "conducted a U.C.C., tax, and judgment search" and that Greycas had the only perfected security interest. In fact, Proud had made no such inquiry, the assets were encumbered, and when the borrower defaulted, Greycas was left with no security.

Under these circumstances, the court held, the lawyer was liable to Greycas for the amount of the loan. The lawyer argued that he owed no duty to someone not his client. The court agreed with that general proposition, and indeed called it "an undesirable novelty to hold that every bit of sharp dealing by a lawyer gives rise to prima facie tort liability to the opposing party in the lawsuit or negotiation." 826 F.2d at 1563. The court also assumed that Greycas could not be said to have become Proud's client. However, the court said that Proud supplied information to Greycas knowing that it was to be relied upon by Greycas. Whether the suit was treated as one for negligent misrepresentation or professional malpractice, it stated a cause of action and the lawyer was liable.[8]

c. Kirkland Construction Co. v. James, 658 N.E.2d 699 (Mass.App.Ct. 1995), involved a client who wanted work done to renovate its retail space. The contractor wanted assurances that the client could pay for the work, and an associate with the client's law firm wrote a letter full of such assurances. When the client did not pay, the court found a valid cause of action against the law firm because the firm "knew and intended that Kirkland would rely on the representations in its letters and Kirkland so relied." 658 N.E.2d at 701.

d. In Rubin & Cohen v. Schottenstein, Zox & Dunn, 143 F.3d 263 (6th Cir.1998) (en banc), a group of potential investors had met with company officials about putting money into the company in exchange for bonds and stock. The officials told the investors to call the company's lawyers for confirmation of the company's financial soundness and its relationship with its bank lender. The lawyers told the investors all was well and that there was no need to call the bank as part of their due diligence. However, the investment constituted a default under the company's financing agreement with the bank, the bank froze all company funds, the company filed for bankruptcy and the investors lost their money. A

8. Accord, Vanguard Production Inc. v. Martin, 894 F.2d 375 (10th Cir.1990) (title opinion used in selling oil & gas leases); Vereins–Und Westbank, AG v. Carter, 691 F.Supp. 704 (S.D.N.Y.1988) (lawyer's letter to support issuance of surety bond).

panel of the 6th circuit had held that the lawyers could not be held liable to persons not their clients, but this en banc opinion reversed that result. It held that, under both the securities laws [Rule 10b–5] and the common law, while a lawyer does not have an "independent duty to volunteer information about the financial condition of the client, he assumes a duty to provide complete and non-misleading information with respect to subjects on which he undertakes to speak." 143 F.3d at 268.

e. In Orshoski v. Krieger, 2001 WL 1388037 (Ohio Ct.App.2001), a couple had built a pre-fabricated home in violation of a subdivision covenant. Before building, they asked their real estate agent whether their plans would violate the covenant. The real estate agent asked the developer who asked the lawyer who had drafted the covenant, and the lawyer said the house would not be in violation. A court later held the covenant indeed was violated, and the issue became whether a third party, not the client of the lawyer, could recover economic damages resulting from such a negligent misrepresentation. The court held, based on § 552 of the Restatement 3rd of Torts, that in limited situations a third party may bring suit for negligent misrepresentation against a lawyer (as opposed to a case for legal malpractice). The plaintiff in such an action must show, "that the defendant [attorney] knew that its report of opinion is intended to be used for a particular purpose, that the plaintiff relied on that statement in furtherance of the purpose, that the defendant understands the reliance, that the report of opinion contains a misrepresentation, and the plaintiff suffers damage as a result of reliance on the misrepresentation." In this case, the court found all of these requirements well pleaded and reinstated the complaint.

f. Hansen v. Anderson, Wilmarth & Van Der Maaten, 630 N.W.2d 818 (Iowa 2001), involved a claim by a law firm against another lawyer, Kennedy, for making false representations during the course of a transaction. The Anderson firm had represented the purported buyer of a company, and Kennedy had represented the purported seller. After the sale was completed, however, a third party showed that it in fact owned the company. The buyer thus sued its own law firm for malpractice, and that firm sought indemnification from Kennedy, alleging that it had justifiably relied on Kennedy's intentionally false representations regarding the ownership of the company. The court found the claim stated a cause of action, saying that the question was whether lawyers on opposite sides of a transaction owe one another a duty to refrain from making intentional misrepresentations. Relying on Restatement Third, The Law Governing Lawyers § 98, the court held that they do. Thus, the Anderson firm could sustain a claim for indemnification, even though it was not Kennedy's client. Kennedy's false representations, if proven, were intentional, not negligent, and "once the lawyer undertakes to provide information, that lawyer has a duty to provide the information truthfully." 630 N.W.2d at 825.

3. Should you be liable to investors in an offering of securities if your investigation is inadequate or if you fail to prevent fraudulent conduct by your client?

a. Central Bank of Denver, N.A. v. First Interstate Bank of Denver, N.A., 511 U.S. 164, 114 S.Ct. 1439, 128 L.Ed.2d 119 (1994), is the leading case limiting lawyers' financial exposure under § 10(b) of the Securities Exchange Act of 1934. Municipal bonds issued in 1986 to finance public improvements related to a residential and commercial project near Colorado Springs required that the appraised value of the land exceed 160% of the amount of the bonds. Central Bank was the indenture trustee; it delayed getting an independent 1988 appraisal, allegedly thinking it might show land values had been declining. When the bonds went into default, the issuer and underwriter were alleged to be primarily liable under § 10(b), and Central Bank was alleged to be secondarily liable for aiding and abetting the violation. The Supreme Court held that there is no "aiding and abetting" liability under § 10(b). Because many lawyers, accountants, and other professionals would be sued under such an "aiding and abetting" theory, the decision appears to have limited this form of exposure. Does this rule give lawyers more protection than they deserve?

b. However, in Mehaffy, Rider, Windholz & Wilson v. Central Bank Denver, N.A., 892 P.2d 230 (Colo.1995), a Town Development Authority had issued bonds whose validity had been challenged in a lawsuit; that made Central Bank unwilling to buy the bonds without an opinion that the lawsuit had no merit. Therefore, the law firm for the Authority rendered such an opinion to induce potential purchasers to buy the bonds. Ultimately, the lawsuit was found meritorious, and the bonds went into default. The case makes clear that a lawyer who renders an opinion that the lawyer knows will be used to induce a non-client to purchase bonds can be held liable to those non-clients for any negligent, material misstatements of fact. On the other hand, the court said the lawyer would not be liable to such non-clients for legal malpractice.

c. In re Enron Corporation Securities, Derivative & ERISA Litigation, 235 F.Supp.2d 549 (S.D.Tex.2002), held that "professionals, including lawyers and accountants, when they take the affirmative step of speaking out, whether individually or as essentially an author or co-author in a statement or report, whether identified or not, about their client's financial condition, do have a duty to third parties not in privity not to knowingly or with severe recklessness issue materially misleading statements on which they intend or have reason to expect that those third parties will rely." 235 F.Supp.2d at 610. The court worried, however, about "opening the professional liability floodgates to any and every potential investor or foreseeable user of the allegedly misleading information who might obtain and rely on the statement." Thus, the court limited the class of plaintiffs to persons "the attorneys or accountants allegedly intended, or might reasonably have expected, to rely on their material misrepresentations." Id. at 610–11.

The court found that the pending "complaint goes into great detail to demonstrate that Vinson & Elkins did not remain silent, but chose not once, but frequently, to make statements to the public about Enron's business and financial situation. * * * Moreover in light of its alleged voluntary, essential, material, and deep involvement as a primary violator in the ongoing Ponzi scheme, Vinson & Elkins was not merely a drafter, but essentially a co-author of the documents it created for public consumption concealing its own and other participants' actions." 235 F.Supp.2d at 705.

4. Assume that all you do is pass document prepared by the client on to the investors, i.e., you do not render an opinion yourself. If you know that the documents are materially inaccurate, are you liable for making a false representation to the investors?

a.   In Schatz v. Rosenberg, 943 F.2d 485 (4th Cir.1991), cert. denied sub nom. Schatz v. Weinberg & Green, 503 U.S. 936, 112 S.Ct. 1475, 117 L.Ed.2d 619 (1992), the client was obliged to give the sellers of a business a current financial statement at the closing to show he would be able to pay off notes that he had personally guaranteed. An earlier financial statement had been accurate, but the new one concealed serious losses. The purchaser's lawyers did not prepare the financial statement but they delivered it to the sellers at closing, allegedly knowing that the client was in fact bankrupt. The Fourth Circuit held that the lawyers were not liable to the sellers under the federal securities laws for not disclosing that the documents were false. "Silence, absent a duty to disclose, does not violate section 10(b) and Rule 10b–5," the court said. There is no securities law liability for a "failure to blow the whistle" unless the defendant has a duty to do so. 943 F.2d at 490. As a matter of federal securities law, the court held, the lawyers had no duty to disclose information about clients to third party purchasers in the absence of a fiduciary relationship between the lawyer and the third party. The Court assumed that the lawyer may have had a duty of disclosure under the Maryland Rules of Professional Conduct but said: "Courts have consistently refused to use ethical codes to define standards of civil liability for lawyers." Id. at 492. Do you agree with this result?

b.   Is the *Schatz* court at least correct in suggesting that professional discipline might be preferable to civil liability as a way to enforce Rule 2.3? On the other hand, are violations of Rule 2.3 so likely to cause financial losses to recipients of the erroneous information that professional discipline would be inadequate to deal with the wrong? Further, is discipline likely to be a lesser deterrent for most lawyers than malpractice liability would be?

PROBLEM 22

OBLIGATIONS WHEN THE CLIENT
MAY BE ENGAGED IN FRAUD

A series of financial collapses at major companies has greeted the new century. Each of the companies that collapsed had many lawyers, and at first glance, each of the companies seemed to have engaged in transactions and practices that lawyers might have prevented. On the other hand, circumstances are not always what they appear. To the lawyers, individual steps in the company's decline might have seemed innocent, even mundane. As you work through this problem, keep asking yourself when a client has crossed the line from risk taking to dishonesty, from brash optimism to fraud. We look first at the lawyer's general duty not to assist a client's crime or fraud, and then at the special world of securities lawyers. We next examine special duties imposed on lawyers for publicly traded companies by the SEC, and finally, we consider possibly analogous issues faced by government employees.

FACTS

International Energy, Inc., a publicly-held company listed on the New York Stock Exchange, has done most of its recent financing through bank loans. It is about to sell a new issue of securities. The company, to induce the bank to lend and the public to invest, has written a glowing account of its prospects.

The strength of the company has been based on its reputation for vigorous research, which thus far has resulted in a series of patents for energy saving devices. The new product, production of which will be financed by the loan, will be another patented device. All of the company reports suggest glowing prospects for its performance. The company's auditors have declared International Energy to be in outstanding financial health. The current draft of your firm's opinion letter indicates no knowledge of material facts inconsistent with that optimism.

You had lunch today with your good friend, the director of research and development at International Energy, Inc. "A great company is in real trouble," he told you. "When our former president retired, a sense of integrity retired as well." Your friend and his scientist colleagues have great concern that the device described in the documents given investors has not been sufficiently tested and that its reliability and performance have been overrated.

In addition, the engineer told you that the production facility for the new product was recently purchased from a shell corporation owned by the company's new president. He said the price paid by the company was outrageously high. The auditors did not catch the problem and thus their audit did not footnote the fact that the purchase was from a corporate officer. As a result, the balance sheet of the corporation looks significantly better than it would if the facility were carried at its true value.

QUESTIONS

A. DISCLOSURE OF A CLIENT'S INTENDED CRIME OR FRAUD

1. Has your lunch given you indigestion? What will you do with the information you now have?

a. May your firm's opinion letter that will accompany the new issue of securities reflect what the director of research and development has told you? Must it do so?

b. How sure are you that what your friend has told you is true? Do you really *know* that the new product is unreliable? Might your friend, the engineer, be understandably depressed? Is that possibility enough to let you ignore what he has told you?

c. How will you go about finding out what is really going on at International Energy, Inc.? Will you ask questions in any event as part of your due diligence before completing your opinion letter?

d. What kinds of questions will you now ask? If your client's officers are dishonest, will you be confident they will give you reliable answers? Could you tell the client's auditors the information you have received and rely on them to ask the necessary questions?

2. What is the legal status of what you have learned from the director of research and development? What legal right or obligation do you have to reveal it to others?

a. Is the information protected by the attorney-client privilege? Was it communicated in confidence? Was it communicated for the purpose of seeking legal advice? Did it involve the client's possible crime or fraud?

b. Does the information "relate to the representation" within the meaning of ABA Model Rule 1.6? Would disclosure of the information to other members of corporate management violate Model Rule 1.6? Might such disclosure be required by Model Rule 1.13(b)?

c. Could you disclose the information to persons or entities outside the corporation? Look at Model Rules 1.6(b) and 1.13(c). Do either of those sections permit disclosure of a client's financial fraud?

d. Look at the proposed drafts of Model Rules 1.6(b)(2) and 1.13(c) set out in footnotes to those rules in the Standards Supplement. Would you have voted for those proposals? Why or why not? If they had been adopted, would they have permitted disclosure outside the corporation in a situation like the one in this Problem?

e. ABA Model Code of Professional Responsibility DR 4–101(C)(3) permitted a lawyer to disclose "the intention of his client to commit a crime and the information necessary to prevent the crime." That provision allowed a lawyer to disclosure confidential client information necessary to prevent the client from committing fraud in obtaining a bank loan, for example. Do you agree with the ABA Model Rules of Professional Conduct's rejection of that approach?[1]

---

1. In Report of the Trustee Concerning Fraud and Other Misconduct in the Management of * * * O.P.M. Leasing Service, Inc., Reorganization No. 81–B–10533 (BRL) (April 25, 1983), the Trustee condemned the ABA House of Delegates for rejecting draft Rule 1.6: "[T]he ABA House of Delegates, the organization's policy-making body, rejected the proposed rule and voted instead for a rule that would make it unethical for lawyers to divulge client secrets in order to protect third parties from an ongoing fraud. * * * The

f. As you remember from Problem 8, many states never made the transition from the permitted disclosure of the Model Code to the more restrictive approach of the Model Rules. What did your state do? You can see the wide variety of state approaches to disclosure of a client's intent to commit a fraud in Appendix A to the Model Rules in the Standards Supplement.

3. Is confidentiality the only relevant issue that you face? What other obligations do you have under the Model Rules that you need to take into account?

a. Take a look at ABA Model Rule 1.2(d): "A lawyer shall not counsel a client to engage, or assist a client, in conduct that the lawyer knows is criminal or fraudulent."

b. Model Rule 4.1(b) continues: "In the course of representing a client a lawyer shall not knowingly fail to disclose a material fact when disclosure is necessary to avoid assisting a criminal or fraudulent act by a client, unless disclosure is prohibited by Rule 1.6."

c. Where does this combination of obligations leave you? Remember Model Rule 1.16(a): "[A] lawyer shall not represent a client or, where representation has commenced, shall withdraw from the representation of a client if: (1) the representation will result in violation of the rules of professional conduct or other law."

4. What is the significance of the fact that the information you have relates in part to the security of bank loans the company has already received? Are a lawyer's rights and responsibilities different when dealing with a client's (and perhaps the lawyer's) past statements?

a. Think of the opinions your firm has rendered that have been transmitted to the bank. In them, you have opined that the appropriate corporate resolutions were adopted and powers granted. You may even have opined that you know of no material facts that have been misstated or omitted from the documents that the bank has received. If preparing those opinions was part of your role, what should you do now that you have had your lunch with the chief engineer?

b. Suppose, instead, that you gave advice to the company about how to structure the financing transaction but did not render an opinion to any third parties. May you assume that therefore the bank will not rely on anything you did? Does it mean you need do nothing to correct misstatements that you now believe were made?

c. ABA Formal Opinion 92–366 (Aug. 8, 1992) assumes that a lawyer for a small manufacturing firm has given an opinion that its client's accounts receivable represent legal obligations of the purchasers of the goods. Later, the lawyer finds that many of the accounts are fictional and that the client is in financial trouble. The Opinion says that under Model Rule 1.6, the lawyer must withdraw from all future dealings involving this loan, and may or, in some cases, must disavow the prior opinion. Otherwise, the lawyer would be "assisting" the client to get future extensions of credit, for example.

d. ABA Formal Opinion 92–366 was controversial, and there was a vigorous dissent, but Comment [10] to Model Rule 1.2 now provides:

" * * * A lawyer may not continue assisting a client in conduct that the lawyer originally supposed was legally proper but then discovers is criminal or fraudulent. The lawyer must, therefore, withdraw from the representation of the client in the matter. See Rule 1.16(a). In some cases, withdrawal alone might be insufficient. If may be necessary for the lawyer to give notice of the fact of withdrawal and to disaffirm any opinion, document, affirmation or the like. In extreme cases, substantive law may require a lawyer to disclose information relating to the representation to avoid being deemed to have assisted the client's crime or fraud. See Rule 4.1."

e. Do you agree that withdrawal is the best approach to the situation you face? It might get you off the hook, but will it help either your corporate client or its past lenders and potential investors?

5. Does the Restatement Third, The Law Governing Lawyers provide help in sorting out a lawyer's duties under the circumstances of this Problem?

a. Section 67 of the Restatement reflects the law in a majority of jurisdictions when it says:

"(1) A lawyer may use or disclose confidential client information when the lawyer reasonably believes that its use or disclosure is necessary to prevent a crime or fraud, and:

"(a) the crime or fraud threatens substantial financial loss;

"(b) the loss has not yet occurred;

"(c) the lawyer's client intends to commit the crime or fraud either personally or through a third person; and

"(d) the client has employed or is employing the lawyer's services in the matter in which the crime or fraud is committed.

"(2) If a crime or fraud described in Subsection (1) has already occurred, a lawyer may use or disclose confidential client information when the lawyer reasonably believes its use or disclosure is necessary to prevent, rectify, or mitigate the loss."

b. The Section goes on to describe what a lawyer must do before making such disclosure to verify the facts and give the client an opportunity to clear its own name.

"(3) Before using or disclosing information under this Section, the lawyer must, if feasible, make a good-faith effort to persuade the client not to act. If the client or another person has already acted, the lawyer must, if feasible, advise the client to warn the victim or to take other action to prevent, rectify, or mitigate the loss. The lawyer must, if feasible, also advise the client of the lawyer's ability to use or disclose information as provided in this Section and the consequences thereof."

c. Is this statement of the lawyer's options adequate? Why may a lawyer disclose only information about issues in which the lawyer's services were employed, for example? Should the primary issue be the protection of investors and others in the corporation or is the only proper concern the lawyer's ability to defend herself against possible liability?

d. Restatement Section 67 goes on to deal with the question of lawyer liability to the client for an improper disclosure or to others for a failure to disclose:

"(4) A lawyer who takes action or decides not to take action permitted under this Section is not, solely by reason of such action or inaction, subject to professional discipline, liable for damages to the lawyer's client or any third person, or barred from recovery against a client or third person."

Do you think courts will give effect to this provision? Should they do so? Do you agree that the lawyer is in such a difficult position in these cases that civil liability is inappropriate?

6. Should a lawyer have the same duties in a non-financial context? Might a lawyer's right or obligation to withdraw or disclose depend on the kind of matter involved and the lawyer's role in the matter?

a. Suppose your firm is doing work with the Department of Energy to get the client's new device approved for sale. Suppose further that if the DOE had the device tested at an independent laboratory it would be likely to find the device unreliable and thus ruin the likelihood of the loan being made. May you argue to Department of Energy officials that it should not require such outside testing?

b. Look at Model Rule 3.9 on the "Advocate in Nonadjudicative Proceedings." Does it appear to say that representations to the DOE must have the same level of integrity and candor as representations to a court? Does that mean any more than that you may not help the company invent records of non-existent outside tests to try to persuade the DOE to approve the product?

c. What is the significance of Comment [3] to Model Rule 3.9 saying that the Rule does not "apply to the representation of a client in connection with an investigation or examination of the client's affairs"? If the rule does not apply in that setting, to what matters does it apply?

d. In re American Continental Corporation/Lincoln Savings and Loan Securities Litigation, 794 F.Supp. 1424 (D.Ariz.1992), involved a regulatory investigation of a savings and loan association in which the court, refusing to grant summary judgment approving the conduct of the law firm, observed:

"During the regulatory compliance audit * * * the law firm found multiple regulatory violations. There is evidence that Jones Day knew that Lincoln had backdated files, destroyed appraisals, removed appraisals from files, told appraisers not to issue written reports when their oral valuations were too low, and violated affiliated transaction regulations. * * *

"There is evidence that Jones Day instructed ACC in how to rectify deficiencies so that they would not be apparent to FHLBB examiners. * * *

"Jones Day contends that it may not be held liable for counseling its client. The line between maintaining a client's confidence and violating the securities law is brighter than Jones Day suggests, however. Attorneys must inform a client in a clear and direct manner when its conduct violates the law. If the client continues the objectionable activity, the lawyer must withdraw 'if the representation will result in violation of the rules of professional conduct or other law.' Ethical Rule 1.16. * * * An attorney may not continue to provide services to corporate clients when the attorney knows the client is engaged in a course of conduct designed to deceive others, and where it is obvious that the attorney's compliant legal services may be a substantial factor in permitting the deceit to continue. * * *"

e. ABA Formal Opinion 93–375 (Aug. 6, 1993), was the ABA's reflection on a lawyer's duty to disclose adverse information in the context of a bank examination. The opinion says that while the lawyer may not lie to the examiners, the lawyer is not affirmatively obliged to warn about problems at the bank or otherwise reveal confidential client information. The bank itself may have disclosure obligations, however, and if the lawyer reasonably believes the bank is engaged in fraud, the lawyer *must* take steps to avoid assisting it to do so, including, in some cases, withdrawing from the representation.

B. THE SPECIAL OBLIGATIONS OF A SECURITIES LAWYER

1. What changes when the lawyer represents an issuer of publicly-traded securities? What kind of inquiry about the relevant facts must the lawyer make?

a. While he was a SEC Commissioner, A.A. Sommer argued:

"[T]he registration statement has always been a lawyer's document and with very, very rare exceptions the attorney has been the field marshal who coordinated the activities of others engaged in the registration process, wrote (or at least rewrote) most of the statement, made the judgments with regard to the inclusion or exclusion of information on the grounds of materiality, compliance with registration form requirements, necessities of avoiding omission of disclosure necessary to make those matters stated not misleading. * * *

"[T]he professional judgment of the attorney is often the 'passkey' to securities transactions. * * * If he judges that certain information must be included in a registration statement, it gets included (unless the client seeks other counsel or the attorney crumbles under the weight of client pressure); if he concludes it need not be included, it doesn't get included. * * *

"I would suggest that in securities matters (other than those where advocacy is clearly proper) the attorney will have to function in a manner more akin to that of the auditor than to that of the advocate. * * * "[2]

b. Do you agree with Mr. Sommer that—at least as to documents the lawyer bears primary responsibility for preparing for disclosure to third parties—the lawyer should act as an auditor rather than an advocate? Indeed, is that the underlying assumption about opinions issued pursuant to Model Rule 2.3? Should the fact that, unlike in the usual Rule 2.3 opinion situation, the lawyer does not know the individual recipients of disclosure documents make the lawyer less obliged to make complete and accurate disclosure? Should it increase the lawyer's obligation to be thorough and candid?

2. May the securities lawyer accept her client's representations about matters to be disclosed? Must the lawyer independently investigate the client?

a. ABA Formal Opinion 335 (Feb. 2, 1974) addressed that issue in the context of a securities lawyer certifying that the conditions exist in which it is proper to sell unregistered securities. The Opinion says:

"It is, of course, important that the lawyer competently and carefully consider what facts are relevant to the giving of the requested opinion and make a reasonable inquiry to obtain such of those facts as are not within his personal knowledge. Depending upon the circumstances, the lawyer may or may not need to go beyond directing questions to his client and checking the answers by reviewing such appropriate documents as are available. * * *

"[T]he lawyer should, in the first instance, make inquiry of his client as to the relevant facts and receive answers. If any of the alleged facts, or the alleged facts taken as a whole, are incomplete in a material respect; or are suspect; or are inconsistent; or either on their face or on the basis of other known facts are open to question, the lawyer should make further inquiry. The extent of this inquiry will depend in each case upon the circumstances; for example, it would be less where the lawyer's past relationship with the client is sufficient to give him a basis for trusting the client's probity than where the client

---

2. A.A. Sommer, Emerging Responsibilities of the Securities Lawyer, [1973–1974 Transfer Binder] Fed.Sec.L.Rep. ¶ 79,631 (Jan., 1974).

has recently engaged the lawyer, and less where the lawyer's inquiries are answered fully than when there appears a reluctance to disclose information.

"Where the lawyer concludes that further inquiry of a reasonable nature would not give him sufficient confidence as to all the relevant facts, or for any other reason he does not make the appropriate further inquiries, he should refuse to give an opinion. However, assuming that the alleged facts are not incomplete in a material respect, or suspect, or in any way inherently inconsistent, or on their face or on the basis of other known facts open to question, the lawyer may properly assume that the facts as related to him by his client, and checked by him by reviewing such appropriate documents as are available, are accurate. * * *

"If the lawyer has some reason to believe that one or more of the statements of fact furnished him as a basis for the opinion may not be correct, he should make a determination as to whether to refuse to give an opinion or whether to attempt to verify one or more of the relevant facts. * * *

"A properly drafted opinion will recite clearly the sources of the attorney's knowledge of the facts. Where verification is otherwise called for, an attorney should make appropriate verification and should not rely on the use of such phrases as 'based upon the facts as you have given them to me' or 'apart from what you have told me, I have not inquired as to the facts.'

"The essence of this opinion * * * is that, while a lawyer should make adequate preparation including inquiry into the relevant facts that is consistent with the above guidelines, and while he should not accept as true that which he should not reasonably believe to be true, he does not have the responsibility to 'audit' the affairs of his client or to assume, without reasonable cause, that a client's statement of the facts cannot be relied upon."

Does this opinion impose a higher standard on attorneys than do the Model Rules? Does it provide good counsel to *any* attorney asked to sign an opinion?

b.   Describing the lawyer's duties in connection with a related kind of issue—the lawyer's declaration that a promoter's tax shelter is likely to receive favorable treatment by the IRS—ABA Formal Opinion 346 (Jan 29, 1982) said bluntly:

"The lawyer who accepts as true the facts which the promoter tells him, when the lawyer should know that a further inquiry would disclose that these facts are untrue, * * * gives a false opinion. * * * [L]awyers cannot 'escape criminal liability on a plea of ignorance when they have shut their eyes to what was plainly to be seen.' United States v. Benjamin * * *. Recklessly and consciously disregarding information strongly indicating that material facts expressed in the tax shelter opinion are false or misleading involves dishonesty. * * * We equate the minimum extent of the knowledge required for the lawyer's conduct to have violated these disciplinary rules with the knowledge required to sustain a Rule 10b–5 recovery, see Ernst & Ernst v. Hochfelder, 425 U.S. 185 (1976), rather than the lesser negligence standard.

"But even if the lawyer lacks the knowledge required to sustain a recovery under the *Hochfelder* standard, the lawyer's conduct nevertheless may involve gross incompetence, or indifference, inadequate preparation under the circumstances, and consistent failure to perform obligations to the client. If so, the lawyer will have violated DR 6–101(A). A.B.A. Informal Opinion 1273 (1973)."

c. In SEC v. Frank, 388 F.2d 486 (2d Cir.1968), the defendant, an attorney, appealed from a district court's temporary injunction ordering him to refrain from "drafting or causing to be drafted any offering circular, prospectus or other document or writing containing any untrue statements of material facts, or omissions to state material facts necessary in order to make the statements made in the light of the circumstances under which they were made, not misleading, concerning Nylo–Thane Plastics Corp.'s principal product * * *." The court, per Judge Friendly, while reversing and ordering an evidentiary hearing, stated:

"Although Frank makes much of this being the first instance in which the Commission has obtained an injunction against an attorney for participation in the preparation of an allegedly misleading offering circular or prospectus, we find this unimpressive. As this court said in United States v. Benjamin, 328 F.2d 854, 863 (2 Cir.), cert. denied, 377 U.S. 953, 84 S.Ct. 1631, 12 L.Ed.2d 497 (1964), 'In our complex society the accountant's certificate and the lawyer's opinion can be instruments for inflicting pecuniary loss more potent than the chisel or the crowbar.' A lawyer has no privilege to assist in circulating a statement with regard to securities which he knows to be false simply because his client has furnished it to him. At the other extreme it would be unreasonable to hold a lawyer who was putting his client's description of a chemical process into understandable English to be guilty of fraud simply because of his failure to detect discrepancies between their description and technical reports available to him in a physical sense but beyond his ability to understand. The instant case lies between these extremes. * * * [A] lawyer, no more than others, can escape liability for fraud by closing his eyes to what he saw and could readily understand. Whether the fraud sections of the securities laws go beyond this and require a lawyer passing on an offering circular to run down possible infirmities in his client's story of which he has been put on notice, and if so what efforts are required of him, is a closer question on which it is important that the court be seized of the precise facts, including the extent, as the SEC claimed with respect to Frank, to which his role went beyond a lawyer's normal one * * *." 388 F.2d at 488–89.

3.   Should the SEC have authority to discipline lawyers whose conduct results in inadequate disclosures or other violations of the securities laws?

a.   Remember that, up to now, we have assumed that lawyers were regulated by the state supreme courts that license them. No lawyer needs a license to practice before the SEC. Even if everyone would agree that an SEC administrative law judge may regulate the conduct of lawyers at a hearing, does it follow that the SEC should be able to sanction lawyers who draft registration materials issued by regulated companies?

b.   In SEC v. Universal Major Industries Corp., 546 F.2d 1044 (2d Cir.1976), cert. denied 434 U.S. 834, 98 S.Ct. 120, 54 L.Ed.2d 95 (1977), the agency pursued a lawyer it believed had violated Section 5 of the Securities and Exchange Act of 1933, 15 U.S.C.A. § 77e, by aiding and abetting his client's selling over three million shares of unregistered stock. The lawyer advised UMI that the stock could be sold as a private offering exempt from registration only under certain conditions. When UMI failed to comply with the conditions, the lawyer instructed the client to register the securities. UMI hired a second lawyer to process the registration, but he never did. Later, the company's stock transfer agent required an opinion letter from the first lawyer stating that various stock transfers were legal. The first lawyer sent a letter stating that he had no opinion, but "I rely on the opinion of [the second lawyer] * * * ." He enclosed that opinion which said that because the first sales had been illegal, resales would not compound the problem. The opinion was wrong, and the district court rejected the first lawyer's "obvious attempt to avoid a personal commitment in [his own] letters." The District Court enjoined the lawyer from "doing business while he is in violation of SEC rules," and the Court of Appeals affirmed that result.

c.   Then, SEC v. National Student Marketing Corp., 457 F.Supp. 682 (D.D.C.1978), sought an injunction against lawyers at Lord, Bissel & Brook and others involved in a merger of National Student Marketing Corp. with Interstate National Corporation and the immediate sale of newly-acquired NSMC stock by former Interstate principals. The court explained:

> "These transactions are alleged to have occurred despite the prior receipt by the defendants of information which revealed that NSMC's interim financial statements, used in securing shareholder approval of the merger and available to the public generally, were grossly inaccurate and failed to show the true condition of the corporation. The information was included in a comfort letter prepared by NSMC's accountants." 457 F.Supp. at 687.

The court concluded that the defendant-attorneys had indeed aided and abetted violations of the securities laws by going ahead with the closing in the face of this information. When information is "obvious[ly]" material:

> "the attorneys' responsibilities to their corporate client required them to take steps to ensure that the information should be disclosed to the shareholders. * * * [A]t the very least, they [the lawyers] were re-

quired to speak out at the closing concerning the obvious materiality of the information and the concomitant requirement that the merger not be closed until the adjustments were disclosed and approval of the merger was again obtained from the Interstate shareholders. Their silence was not only a breach of this duty to speak, but in addition lent the appearance of legitimacy to the closing. The combination of these factors clearly provided substantial assistance to the closing of the merger." Id. at 713.

However, in spite of the finding of clear illegality, the court denied the SEC's request for injunctive relief because "the Court is confident that [the defendants] will take appropriate steps to ensure that their professional conduct in the future comports with the law." Id. at 717.

d. Later, In re Carter & Johnson, Exchange Act Release No. 17,597 (1981), involved lawyers who represented a telephone leasing company from 1973 until it went out of business in 1975. During 1974, the company concealed its cash flow problems from the public, by drawing down its line of credit. The lawyers knew of the problems, but prepared a press release and materials filed with the SEC that said nothing of the impending end of its access to credit and its need to end business operations. The company's president failed to heed the lawyers' advice to disclose, but the lawyers themselves did not disclose. Rather than sanction the lawyers, however, in a legal environment in which the norms governing securities lawyers had not been "firmly and unambiguously established," the Commission simply announced that in the future:

> "When a lawyer with significant responsibilities in the effectuation of a company's compliance with the disclosure requirements of the federal securities laws becomes aware that his client is engaged in substantial and continuing failure to satisfy those disclosure requirements, his continued participation violates professional standards unless he takes prompt steps to end the client's noncompliance."

e. The current version of the SEC rule is 17 CFR 201.102(e). In part because of a running dispute with the ABA about whether federal agencies may discipline lawyers, the SEC has not brought any Rule 102(e) complaints against lawyers since *Carter & Johnson*, although In re Gutfreund, Exchange Act Release No. 31 (1992), reiterated the Commission's belief that the duties set out in *Carter & Johnson* remained in force and could even be construed to require disclosure of client misconduct "to [state] regulatory authorities."[3]

---

3. Checkosky and Aldrich v. S.E.C., 139 F.3d 221 (D.C.Cir.1998), involved accountants but dealt with the same "improper professional conduct" provision of SEC Rule 102(e) that applies to lawyers. The decision, which came after earlier SEC efforts to artic- ulate and defend the Rule, held the Commission had offered "no clear and coherent standard" for what would constitute a violation of Rule 102(e) and thus dismissed the charges against the defendants.

4. If the client will not disclose what the lawyer believes should be disclosed, is the lawyer limited to withdrawing from the representation? May the lawyer do more?

a. In Meyerhofer v. Empire Fire & Marine Insurance Co., 497 F.2d 1190 (2d Cir.1974), cert. denied 419 U.S. 998, 95 S.Ct. 314, 42 L.Ed.2d 272 (1974), lawyer Goldberg had been working on a registration statement and expressed concern to the partners in his firm that the company had failed to disclose adequately certain features of the compensation arrangements between the company and the law firm, as well as other matters. After Goldberg insisted on a full and complete disclosure and the partners disagreed, he resigned from the firm. That same day he appeared before the SEC and placed before it the relevant information on the nondisclosure.

Later, another law firm sued on behalf of the purchasers of the common stock alleging that the registration statement and prospectus were materially false and misleading. One of the named defendants was Goldberg. After consulting his own attorney and a Special Counsel to the SEC's Division of Enforcement, Goldberg, in an attempt to avoid the charges, gave the plaintiffs' firm a copy of the affidavit with exhibits that he had earlier given to the SEC. The other defendants, relying on Canons 4 and 9, moved to disqualify the plaintiffs' lawyers and to enjoin Goldberg from disclosing any confidential information.

The district court granted the motions but the Second Circuit reversed.

"There is no proof—not even a suggestion—that Goldberg had revealed any information, confidential or otherwise, that might have caused the instigation of the suit. To the contrary, it was not until after the suit was commenced that Goldberg learned that he was in jeopardy. * * * The cost in money of simply defending such an action might be very substantial. The damage to his professional reputation which might be occasioned by the mere pendency of such a charge was an even greater cause for concern. Under these circumstances Goldberg had the right to make appropriate disclosure with respect to his role in the public offering [citing DR 4–101(C)(4)]." 139 F.2d at 1194–95.

b. Do you agree that Model Rule 1.6 would permit disclosure in a case like *Meyerhofer* today? Look at Model Rule 1.6(b)(3).

5. What would you do if your client were about to violate the securities laws?

a. Compare John Elam, The Role of a Lawyer Isn't to Police Clients, USA Today, Feb. 15, 1983, at 10A, with Ronald D. Rotunda, id. Elam states:

"It's a fallacy to make the lawyer a watchman or policeman over his client; that would be a mortal blow to the traditional attorney-client privilege. The true function of a lawyer is to counsel a client on proper conduct. A lawyer cannot give sound and informed advice unless the lawyer obtains *all* the facts. The client must be able to feel free to communicate all of the facts without fear of disclosure. * * * Attempting to make lawyers the self-appointed consciences of their corporate clients has the same inherent evil—of discouraging the free exchange of information."

Rotunda answers:

"[It should be the law] that the lawyer 'may reveal' client information in order to prevent the client from committing a criminal or fraudulent act likely to result in 'substantial' financial injury to another, or to rectify the consequences of the client's criminal or fraudulent act, where the lawyer's services had been used to further the scheme. [It is wrong to] discipline—and even disbar—a lawyer who would speak out to prevent the fraud. * * * Client confidentiality is important, to be sure, when the client has confessed *past crimes*. But what public policy justifies allowing the client to misuse his lawyer in order to commit *future crimes*? [Ethical rules] allow a lawyer to breach his client's confidences if necessary to collect a fee. If lawyers can breach confidentiality to protect themselves, they should have the same right to protect the public."

b.   With which of these comments do you agree?[4]

C.   SPECIFIC ABA AND SEC RESPONSES TO A SERIES OF CORPORATE FAILURES

1.   **Should the SEC and other federal agencies be obliged to respect the confidentiality requirements of the Model Rules? Why should the desire to protect the public against securities fraud require a compromise of lawyers' ethical standards when the desire to protect the public against, say, bank robbers does not?**

a.   Whatever the theoretical answers to those questions, the collapse of Enron and the accounting "corrections" at WorldCom and other high-profile companies led Congress to adopt the Sarbanes–Oxley Act of 2002. Section 307 of that Act required the SEC to—

---

4.   Compare Lloyd N. Cutler, The Role of the Private Law Firm, 33 Bus. Lawyer 1549, 1556–57 (Mar. 1978), quoted in Problem 8, supra.

"establish rules, in the public interest, setting forth minimum standards of professional conduct for attorneys appearing and practicing before the Commission in any way in the representation of public companies, including a rule requiring an attorney to report evidence of a material violation of securities law or breach of fiduciary duty or similar violation by the company or any agent thereof to the chief legal counsel or the chief executive officer of the company (or the equivalent thereof), and if the counsel or officer does not appropriately respond to the evidence (adopting, as necessary, appropriate remedial measures or sanctions with respect to the violation), requiring the attorney to report the evidence to the audit committee of the board of directors or to another committee of the board of directors comprised solely of directors not employed directly or indirectly by the company, or to the board of directors."

b. On January 29, 2003, the SEC issued the Final Rule mandated by Section 307. It may be found at 17 CFR Part 205. An ABA Task Force on Corporate Responsibility has been working separately from but parallel to the SEC considering possible changes in the ABA Model Rules that might help prevent unanticipated corporate failures in the future.

2. If you had been writing the new SEC regulations, how would you have drafted the circumstances that should trigger a lawyer's duty to act?

a. The SEC initially had to define the attorneys to which the regulation applied at all. Attorneys "appearing and practicing before the Commission" were defined to include anyone "providing advice * * * regarding any document that the attorney has notice will be filed with * * to the Commission" or providing advice that information need not be filed with the Commission.

b. The attorney's duty to act is triggered when he or she "becomes aware" of "evidence" of a client's "material violation" of federal or state securities law, a material breach of fiduciary duty by an officer or agent of the client, or a "similar" violation of any other federal or state law.

c. The "evidence" required is "credible evidence, based upon which it would be unreasonable, under the circumstances, for a prudent and competent attorney not to conclude that it is reasonably likely that a material violation has occurred, is ongoing, or is about to occur."

3. What would you then require the lawyer to do?

a. The attorney who becomes aware of "evidence of a material violation" is required to "report such evidence to the [client's] chief legal officer" (CLO). It you are a "subordinate attorney," i.e., one who works "under the supervision or direction of another attorney," it is sufficient to report the evidence to your superior. It then becomes the supervisor's responsibility to report the information to the client's CLO. 17 CFR §§ 205.3(b)(1), 205.4 & 205.5.

b. Upon getting the report, the CLO must "cause such inquiry into the evidence of a material violation as he or she reasonable believes is appropriate to determine whether" there has been or will be such a violation. Whether the CLO concludes that no such violation has or will occur, or concludes that the reporting attorney was right and takes steps to correct the violation, the CLO must report the conclusion back to the reporting attorney "and advise the reporting attorney of the basis for such determination." 17 CFR § 205.3(b)(2).

c. Unless the reporting attorney "reasonably believes" that the [CLO] has provided an appropriate response within a reasonable time, the attorney must report the evidence of a material violation to the "audit committee of the [client's] board of directors," a different committee composed solely of independent directors, or the full board of directors. 17 CFR § 205.3(b)(3).

d. Alternatively, if the client has established a qualified legal compliance committee (QLCC) composed solely of independent directors and given authority to investigate and report to the full board about evidence of the client's possible material violations of the law, the attorney may make the initial report directly to that QLCC and have no further obligation to evaluate what they do to investigate or correct the situation. 17 CFR § 205.3(c).

4. When, if ever, should a lawyer be required to disclose the wrongdoing to persons or agencies outside the client organization?

a. Given the failure of the ABA House of Delegates to expand lawyer discretion under Model Rule 1.6(b) to disclose a client's intended crime or fraud, Model Rule 1.13(c) is now clear that the lawyer's option is simply to resign. A draft report of the ABA Task Force, on the other hand, proposed making disclosure outside the corporation, not just permitted, but mandatory "in order to prevent client conduct known to the lawyer to involve a crime, including violations of federal securities laws and regulations, in furtherance of which the client has used or is using the lawyer's services, and which is reasonably certain to result in substantial injury to the financial interests or property of another."

b. Would you favor that requirement? Would it be better to make disclosure discretionary, provided that if the discretion were exercised unreasonably the lawyer could be subject to discipline? Would it be best to say that, whether or not the lawyer discloses, the lawyer should not be able to be second-guessed?

c. At the same time it published the regulations required by the Sarbanes–Oxley law, the SEC issued a proposed rule that would also say that if the response from the CLO is insufficient or not received within a reasonable time, the lawyer must withdraw from the representation and inform the SEC of that action. Under one alternative, the client, not the lawyer, would be required to notify the SEC of the lawyer's action.[5] The report would then presumably trigger an investigation by the SEC.

d. Would such an obligation give lawyers leverage with which to require clients to do what the lawyers believe is required? Given the requirement of lawyer withdrawal and then reporting to the SEC, do you suppose many clients would fail to change their conduct so as to avoid reaching that point?

D. SPECIAL ISSUES OF DISCLOSURE BY A GOVERNMENT LAWYER

1. Are the issues of "whistle blowing" by a government lawyer comparable to those we have seen in a corporate context?

a. Should the client of a government lawyer be said to be the "public"? Would that mean that a government lawyer has no enforceable duty of confidentiality comparable to that owed a private client? Does Model Rule 1.6 give any indication that it does not protect confidential information of government agency clients?

b. Further, lest there be any doubt, Restatement Third, The Law Governing Lawyers § 74 provides: "Unless applicable law otherwise provides, the attorney-client privilege extends to a communication of a governmental organization * * * ."

c. Are government agencies "organization" clients? Look at Comment [6] to Rule 1.13. Do you agree that "a different balance may be appropriate between maintaining confidentiality and assuring that the wrongful act is prevented or rectified, for public business is involved."

---

5. Release No. 33–8186 (Jan. 29, 2003), proposing addition of a 17 CFR § 205.3(d). Because of the personal hardship of withdrawal on a lawyer who works as inside counsel, the proposed rule would require inside counsel to tell the CLO that the response was insufficient, but it would not require that counsel to resign from the company.

2. To whom should the government lawyer turn with information about what he or she believe is improper behavior in government?

a. Crandon v. State, 897 P.2d 92 (Kan.1995), cert. denied 516 U.S. 1113, 116 S.Ct. 913, 133 L.Ed.2d 844 (1996), upheld the firing of the general counsel of a state agency. The lawyer had reported to the Federal Deposit Insurance Corporation that she believed the Deputy Commissioner of the state banking commission had received loans from banks she regulated. If true, that would have violated both state and federal law. However, she did not take her concerns to the agency Commissioner, whom she believed knew of the issue from other sources and had believed there was no violation. He only learned from the FDIC about her reports of illegality. The court found that the plaintiff, an "at will" employee, was dismissed because she had gone behind the Commissioner's back. "[A]lthough plaintiff may have acted in utmost good faith, she used poor judgment and did not take steps available to her that a reasonably prudent attorney would have taken prior to reporting" her concerns outside the agency. 897 P.2d at 103.

b. Consider Conduct of Lackey, 37 P.3d 172 (Ore.2002), where the respondent had worked as the full-time Judge Advocate for the Oregon National Guard. In 1991, a reservist was appointed as Lackey's superior, and Lackey objected that because the new superior was only in the reserves, his appointment was illegal. Lackey refused to follow that lawyer's orders and complained about the "illegal" appointment to senior officers and oversight committees. A later investigation determined that Lackey's position was technically correct, but recommended his termination as full-time Judge Advocate. An arrangement was reached whereby Lackey resigned and kept his retirement rights. Shortly thereafter, Lackey disclosed to local reporters the circumstances surrounding a recent internal audit that had revealed that senior Oregon National Guardsmen had erroneously received over $38,000 in overpayments. In that regard, Lackey had prepared a memo recommending that certain officers be sanctioned for negligence, but Lackey's superiors decided to impose a less severe sanction. Lackey argued that a public policy exception to Rule 1.6 allowed lawyers to expose illegal actions by public officials, but finding that Lackey's leak to the news media about the audit and a second personnel matter were primarily an act of revenge, the Oregon Supreme Court suspended Lackey for 1 year.

c. Do you agree with the results in these cases? Do they make going through channels more important than reaching the right result? Do they illustrate that whistleblowing may have complex motives? Can you come up with an approach that would protect legitimate concerns about confidentiality of government information without inhibiting appropriate disclosure of wrongdoing by government officials?

CHAPTER VI

ETHICAL PROBLEMS IN LITIGATION

Civil and criminal litigation present the most dramatic problems of legal ethics—problems that have attracted a great deal of public attention. The lawyers who face these issues do not always think of themselves as litigators. Because the issues that any lawyer confronts ultimately may be resolved in a courtroom, many problems presented in this chapter may be faced whatever the nature of a lawyer's practice. As you analyze these problems ask yourself such questions as:

a. How far may an attorney go to suppress the truth in representing a client in litigation? How far *must* he or she go? May or must the lawyer refrain from disclosing relevant information to the trier of fact, for example? May or must the lawyer allow the client to offer perjured testimony to further the client's interest?

b. To what extent may or must a lawyer adopt the client's values and objectives? Is the lawyer solely the client's advocate and never a judge of the client's position?

c. How is the role of the lawyer as litigator different from the role of the lawyer as counselor? May a lawyer defend what he or she could not recommend?

Remember as well that the reputation of a lawyer is his or her most important asset. A litigator may appear before the same judge or agency with some frequency. If hindsight shows that she was too clever by half in one case, she may develop a reputation that will haunt her and her clients in other cases. The extent to which a lawyer should take into consideration the effect on her future clients of the way she represents the present client is a recurring issue of professional responsibility.

———

PROBLEM 23

THE DECISION TO FILE A CIVIL SUIT

To the inexperienced, it may seem that the decision to file a civil suit is hardly a difficult one. Your client feels wronged and the courts are available to vindicate him. A moment's reflection, however, suggests how simplistic that view is. Litigation is expensive; while one side may prevail on paper, there may be no real winner. Sometimes, parties may use litigation as a tactic, perhaps a delaying tactic, rather than an instrument for reaching a particular result. This problem looks first at the minimum standards governing the filing of a civil action. Next, it examines the tactical use of litigation as an instrument of delay. It then considers a possible obligation to counsel the client about alternative forms of dispute resolution, and finally, it asks what the sanctions might be for abusive use of the litigation process.

FACTS

Your client is a producer of a large assortment of California wines. Many of its wines do not "travel well" from California to their destination and have a short bottle life. In order to enable the wines to travel better and maintain their quality for a longer period of time, your client uses a unique process that places a small amount of a chemical substance into each bottle. Recent testing of that substance suggests that when large amounts of the substance are consumed by rats, a statistically significant number of rats contract cancer of the throat. Under the so-called Delaney Amendment to the Food and Drug Act,[1] if the Food and Drug Administration determines that any substance consumed in any amount by man or animal causes cancer, the FDA must ban the substance.

Some reputable scientists fully support the very conservative approach taken by the Delaney Amendment; others do not. Your client tells you that it is imperative that the FDA delay banning his wines, because he believes he would likely go bankrupt if he could not sell the thousands of cases he has already shipped out. The Food & Drug laws do not provide for any compensation for your client, and the chances of Congress passing a private bill for your client are remote. Moreover, he tells you that the shelf life of his wine is only six months (that is, within six months, over 95% of the wine he has shipped will have been sold to consumers by the liquor stores and removed from the shelves). The new wines that he is producing will not contain substances that may be carcinogenic.

You plan to file suit attacking the factual basis for the FDA order in this case and the constitutionality of the Delaney Amendment. You know that court dockets are so crowded that such a suit is likely to delay the effectiveness of the FDA's order banning the wines. Several years ago, your circuit upheld the law against just such a constitutional attack.

---

1. 21 U.S.C.A. § 348(c)(3)(A). It was under this law that cyclamates were banned from soft drinks in the early 1970s. The section provides, in part: "That no additive shall be deemed to be safe if it is found to induce cancer when ingested by man or animal. . . ."

QUESTIONS

A. ETHICAL STANDARDS GOVERNING THE FILING OF A CIVIL ACTION

1. Do the Model Rules tell you whether or not it is proper to file suit in this case? Is the fact that the delay obtained by such a suit might serve to save the client from bankruptcy the only relevant concern?

a. Does Model Rule 3.1 clearly answer this question? Is it ever "obvious" that a position is taken "merely to harass or maliciously injure" the opponent? Is there any proposition of law that cannot be the subject of a good faith proposal for at least a change in the law?

b. Matter of Capoccia, 709 N.Y.S.2d 640 (App.Div.2000) (per curiam), involved a lawyer who represented debtors in consumer collection cases. He had prepared a list of defenses and counterclaims that the courts in over 70 prior cases had uniformly rejected, but he continued to file them anyway. "A common finding in many of these decisions sanctioning or warning respondent was that he had intentionally engaged in a course of conduct whereby he barraged the court system with meritless and 'canned' defenses and counterclaims as a tactic to force settlements." On that record, the court found, first, that the determinations of courts in prior actions that the lawyer had engaged in frivolous conduct had a collateral estoppel effect, and second, that the lawyer's conduct violated various disciplinary rules, including "knowingly advancing a claim or defense that is unwarranted under existing law which could not be supported by a good-faith argument for an extension, modification or reversal of existing law." The court did say that the respondent, at a later time, could present any arguments for mitigation.

c. Does that case confirm for you that Model Rule 3.1 has teeth? Does it suggest instead that it takes so much to violate the rule that it is not a significant deterrent to frivolous law suits? See also, Restatement Third, The Law Governing Lawyers § 110 (frivolous advocacy).

2. What other rules might impose discipline for the filing of frivolous litigation?

a. In federal court, Rule 11 of the Federal Rules of Civil Procedure, has a much greater impact on the filing of civil actions than does Model Rule 3.1. Many states have adopted a similar rule to govern state proceedings.

b. Rule 11, as amended in 1993, is not a traditional standard of professional discipline because courts enforce it in the course of litigation, while disciplinary authorities enforce their state versions of Model Rule 3.1. Federal Rule 11 certainly offers the most important practical sanction if a lawyer fails to verify the factual basis of a representation made to a federal court. Rule 11 provides:

Rule 11. Signing of Pleadings, Motions, and Other Papers; Representations to Court; Sanctions

(a) Signature. Every pleading, written motion, and other paper shall be signed by at least one attorney of record in the attorney's individual name, or, if the party is not represented by an attorney, shall be signed by the party. * * *

(b) Representations to Court. By presenting to the court (whether by signing, filing, submitting, or later advocating) a pleading, written motion or other paper, an attorney or unrepresented party is certifying that to the best of the person's knowledge, information, and belief, formed after an inquiry reasonable under the circumstances,—

(1) it is not being presented for any improper purpose, such as to harass or to cause unnecessary delay or needless increase in the cost of litigation;

(2) the claims, defenses, and other legal contentions therein are warranted by existing law or by a nonfrivolous argument for the extension, modification, or reversal of existing law or the establishment of new law;

(3) the allegations and other factual contentions have evidentiary support or, if specifically so identified, are likely to have evidentiary support after a reasonable opportunity for further investigation or discovery; and

(4) the denials of factual contentions are warranted on the evidence or, if specifically so identified, are reasonably based on a lack of information or belief.

(c) Sanctions. If, after notice and a reasonable opportunity to respond, the court determines that subdivision (b) has been violated, the court may, subject to the conditions stated below, impose an appropriate sanction upon the attorneys, law firms, or parties that have violated subdivision (b) or are responsible for the violation.

(1) How Initiated.

(A) By Motion. A motion for sanctions under this rule * * * shall not be filed with or presented to the court unless, within 21 days after service of the motion * * *, the challenged paper, claim, defense, contention, allegation, or denial is not withdrawn or appropriately corrected. If warranted, the court may award to the party prevailing on the motion the reasonable expenses and attorney's fees incurred in presenting or opposing the motion. Absent exceptional circumstances, a law firm shall be held jointly responsible for violations committed by its partners, associates, and employees.

(B) On Court's Initiative. On its own initiative, the court may enter an order describing the specific conduct that appears to violate subdivision (b) and directing an attorney, law firm, or party to show cause why it has not violated subdivision (b) with respect thereto.

(2) Nature of sanction: Limitations. A sanction imposed for violation of this rule shall be limited to what is sufficient to deter repetition of such conduct or comparable conduct by others similarly situated. Subject to the limitations in subparagraphs (A) and (B), the sanction may consist of, or include, directives of a nonmonetary nature, an order to pay a penalty into court, or, if imposed on motion and warranted for effective deterrence, an order directing payment to the movant of some or all of the reasonable attorneys' fees and other expenses incurred as a direct result of the violation.

Cf. Model Rule 3.1, Comment 2.[2]

c. Prior to its amendment in 1993, Rule 11 had a Procrustean quality that neither gave lawyers a chance to correct a pleading prior to sanctions being imposed nor gave the trial court discretion not to impose a sanction. Cross & Cross Properties v. Everett Allied Co., 886 F.2d 497 (2d Cir.1989), for example, imposed Rule 11 sanctions for a single improper count in a complaint, although all other counts in the complaint were well pleaded. Cooter & Gell v. Hartmarx Corp., 496 U.S. 384, 110 S.Ct. 2447, 110 L.Ed.2d 359 (1990), imposed sanctions even though the plaintiff had withdrawn the offending complaint.

d. In Garr v. U.S. Healthcare, 22 F.3d 1274 (3d Cir.1994), also decided under former Rule 11, Lawyer A had filed a class action alleging that U.S. Healthcare had issued false and misleading statements about its financial health. Lawyers B & C read about the case and filed identical complaints, changing only the names of their clients and the number of shares owned. Lawyers B & C had only read the first complaint and seen that it seemed to be verified by a Wall Street Journal story. The Court held 2 to 1 that such a copycat filing violates Rule 11 *even if the complaint turns out to be meritorious.* Does this make sense to you? What interest does the court have in sanctioning a meritorious complaint?

e. Some lawyers report that judges suggest or threaten them with Rule 11 sanctions. For example, the judge might say, with respect to a motion, "If I rule against you, I may decide to impose Rule 11 sanctions." The lawyer then may withdraw the motion. There is no appeal because

---

2. Consider also, 28 U.S.C.A. § 1927, which provides:

Any attorney or other person * * * who so multiplies the proceedings in any case unreasonably and vexatiously may be required by the court to satisfy personally the excess costs, expenses, and attorneys' fees reasonably incurred because of such conduct.

California Bar Formal Opinion 1997–151 (July 1997), considered whether a motion for sanctions filed against both lawyer and client

created a conflict of interest between them. The Opinion says that a conflict clearly is presented if they plan to file different answers to the charges, i.e., blame each other for the misconduct. Ordinarily, however, the lawyer will defend the client and herself without a problem. Who pays sanctions, in turn, should be addressed in the retainer agreement and applied accordingly unless the Court orders one or the other to bear them alone.

nothing was decided, but the judge has affected the proceeding in a way that the appeals process cannot affect. Is that fair? However unfair it may seem to a given lawyer at the moment, might it reasonably seem to be a practical way for judges to manage unruly lawyers?

3. Does the current version of Rule 11 appropriately balance the interests of forcing lawyers to do their homework before they file a document against the danger of turning sanctions issues into collateral litigation that ultimately delays justice in the case?

a. In re Keegan Management Co. Securities Litigation, 78 F.3d 431 (9th Cir.1996), was a suit alleging that sellers of Nutri/System weight loss centers had not disclosed gall bladder problems that the system could cause. Ultimately, the district court found insufficient connection between weight loss and gall bladder damage and granted summary judgment for the defendant. At the same time, on its own motion, the court imposed Rule 11 sanctions on the plaintiff's lawyers for failure to do adequate inquiry into the facts. In evaluating the lawyers' conduct, the district court considered only what they knew when they filed their complaint, not the confirming evidence learned afterwards. The Ninth Circuit in effect rejected the theory of *Garr*, and said that if the facts turn out to be non-frivolous, there is no Rule 11 violation, regardless of the quality of the lawyer's original investigation.

b. In Sussman v. Bank of Israel, 56 F.3d 450 (2d Cir.1995), cert. denied, 516 U.S. 916, 116 S.Ct. 305, 133 L.Ed.2d 210 (1995), the United States resident directors of an Israeli bank brought suit against another bank, after that bank had brought suit against these directors in an Israeli court. Lewin was the plaintiffs' lawyer in the New York suit, and the plaintiffs alleged, in this New York action, that the other bank had deceived them in an attempt to cover up yet another financial scandal. Before filing the New York action, the plaintiffs wrote to several prominent Israeli officials threatening to embarrass them by the lawsuit, and therefore urging a pre-filing settlement. That ploy failed, but after they filed suit and the U.S. court dismissed it on forum non conveniens, the defendants sought sanctions alleging that these U.S. directors had filed suit to embarrass and coerce, not to reach the truth. The court held that, where the underlying claims in the suit were not frivolous, the plaintiffs' desire to embarrass, taken alone, could not be a basis for sanctions.

c. Bullard v. Chrysler Corp., 925 F.Supp. 1180 (E.D.Tex.1996), found a Rule 11 violation in a lawyer's motion to withdraw. Lawyer Tracy was one of three lawyers representing the plaintiff in a products liability case. He asserted that a conflict of interest had arisen. In the course of the hearing, however, the Court found Tracy had withdrawn because Chrysler told him that they would refuse to settle any case he was involved in against Chrysler if he did not withdraw from this one. The Court said Chrysler had filed nothing to this effect for which the Court could impose sanctions, but it did sanction Tracy for withdrawing to protect his own economic future and then not being candid with the Court about the real reasons for his motion.[3]

d.   In Massengale v. Ray, 267 F.3d 1298 (11th Cir.2001), both litigants represented themselves. After the court repeatedly dismissed plaintiff's claims, the court granted the defendant's motion for Rule 11 sanctions. But the Eleventh Circuit found that Rule 11 sanctions could not include an award for attorney's fees to a litigant who had proceeded pro se. The purpose of Rule 11 is to discourage dilatory or abusive tactics, the court said, but a pro se litigant, by definition, could not have incurred any attorney's fees and thus could not recover an award under Rule 11.[4] If the purpose behind Rule 11 is to save the court's time, should the court excuse an offender from Rule 11 sanctions just because the abused party did not have a lawyer?

4.   Are the same answers about what is frivolous appropriate when one is selecting issues to raise on appeal?[5] Should it matter whether the appeal is of a criminal conviction instead of a verdict in a civil case?

a.   In Anders v. California, 386 U.S. 738, 87 S.Ct. 1396, 18 L.Ed.2d 493 (1967), the Court held that appointed counsel in a criminal case may not withdraw a nonfrivolous appeal. The Court required counsel appointed in appeals of criminal cases of indigents to file what is now called an *Anders* Brief. If the appointed lawyer, after conscientious examination, finds the criminal defendant's case to be wholly frivolous he should advise the court and request permission to withdraw. However, he must then supply a brief referring to anything in the record that might arguably support an appeal. The lawyer should furnish the defendant with a copy of the brief with enough time to raise any points that the indigent chooses. Then, the court (not counsel) should proceed, after full examination of all proceedings, to decide whether the case is wholly frivolous, grant the lawyer's request to withdraw if it finds the claims to be frivolous, and

---

3.   In Cunningham v. Hamilton County, Ohio, 527 U.S. 198, 119 S.Ct. 1915, 144 L.Ed.2d 184 (1999), the Court unanimously held that an order imposing sanctions on a lawyer for discovery abuse pursuant to the Federal Rule of Civil Procedure is not a "final" decision and not immediately appealable under either the final judgment rule or the collateral order doctrine, even if the court has disqualified the lawyer from representing the party in the case. The Court noted that if an immediate appeal were permitted, that would undermine the purpose of Rule 37(a), Federal Rules of Civil Procedure, which was designed to protect courts and opposing parties from delaying or harassing tactics during discovery. On the other hand, one could just as well argue that, if the sanctioned lawyer's conduct

is that bad, an immediate appeal would not take the appellate court much time.

4.   But see Laborde v. Aronson, 112 Cal. Rptr.2d 119 (Cal.Ct.App.2001) (where a lawyer represents himself, sanctions can include an award for the lawyer's time spent on his own behalf).

5.   Each Circuit is required to have a "criminal justice plan" for providing counsel to indigent defendants. The Fourth Circuit plan required counsel to file petitions for certiorari on behalf of indigent defendants regardless of whether there were non-frivolous claims to raise. In Austin v. United States, 513 U.S. 5, 115 S.Ct. 380, 130 L.Ed.2d 219 (1994), the Supreme Court required that the plan be amended so as not to require filing the frivolous claims.

afford assistance of counsel to argue the appeal for the indigent if it finds some legal issues to be nonfrivolous.

b. Later, Jones v. Barnes, 463 U.S. 745, 103 S.Ct. 3308, 77 L.Ed.2d 987 (1983), held that the indigent has no constitutional right to compel appointed counsel to press all nonfrivolous issues requested by the client "if counsel, as a matter of professional judgment, decides not to present those points." Both the Court and the dissent in *Barnes* cited Model Rule 1.2(a) and Defense Function Standard 4–5.2. Who has the better argument? Is a client usually competent to specify errors worthy of appeal? Is giving the client the sense that he or she is in control as important as the inherent force of the arguments raised?[6] If a client who can afford a lawyer can insist on focusing on a particular nonfrivolous issue (although it may not be wise to do so), should the indigent have fewer rights?

c. Smith v. Robbins, 528 U.S. 259, 120 S.Ct. 746, 145 L.Ed.2d 756 (2000), considered how much appointed counsel must do to comply with *Anders*. Robbins defended himself at trial. On appeal, his appointed counsel filed a no-merits brief, which briefly outlined the facts surrounding the trial and presented no possible grounds for appeal. Robbins then filed a brief of his own, which the California courts rejected. In a federal habeas corpus proceeding, the District Court held that, in these circumstances, the *Anders* brief amounted to ineffective assistance of counsel. The Court of Appeals affirmed, but the U.S. Supreme Court reversed by a 5 to 4 vote, holding that the California procedure is adequate to protect a defendant's right to the effective assistance of counsel. Justice Thomas, writing for the Court, said that although California's procedure does not comply in all respects with *Anders*, under the procedure, appellate counsel allows the defendant to file a supplemental brief and the lawyer remains available to brief any issue requested by the appellate court. The *Anders* language about the lawyer's noting any points that might support an appeal was meant as an example of acceptable procedure, the Court said, not as the minimum procedure tolerable. The California procedure allows "adequate and effective" appellate review, and the Supreme Court should not impose a single procedure on the states.

Justices Stevens, Souter, Ginsburg and Breyer dissented, arguing that the Court has now effectively overruled *Anders* and that, while frivolous litigation is a problem, denying defendants an appeal by a "committed representative" who will engage in a "partisan scrutiny of the record" is much more serious. "Without the assurance that assigned counsel has done his best as a partisan, his substantial equality to a lawyer retained at a defendant's expense cannot be assumed."[7] Do you agree with the dissenters? Can *Anders* and *Robbins* both be right?

---

6. On sanctions for a frivolous civil appeal, see Cooter & Gell v. Hartmarx, 496 U.S. 384, 110 S.Ct. 2447, 110 L.Ed.2d 359 (1990), and Hilmon Co. (V.I.) Inc. v. Hyatt International, 899 F.2d 250 (3d Cir.1990).

7. In Hughes v. Booker, 220 F.3d 346 (5th Cir.2000), appointed appellate counsel had followed Mississippi procedure and found "no substantial issue evidencing reversible error." The defendant had a right to file a brief of his own, and counsel had asked the

5. States also have counterparts to Federal Rule 11. Should Model Rule 3.1 be changed to incorporate any Rule 11 elements?

a. In Jandrt ex rel. Brueggeman v. Jerome Foods, Inc., 597 N.W.2d 744 (Wis.1999), several employees of a company bore children with birth defects. The law firm noted the coincidence and filed suit alleging a causal connection. However, when the firm later interviewed experts in birth defects, they said the medical science was inconclusive and an epidemiologist's study would be needed to provide proof of causation. The firm decided the study would be too expensive and voluntarily dismissed the case. A sharply divided Wisconsin Supreme Court concluded that the firm had done sufficient scientific research to justify filing the case, particularly because a law was about to take effect limiting such suits, but it waited too long to dismiss the case. Thus, the court awarded the defendant several hundred thousand dollars in attorney's fees for the time between filing and dismissal.

b. Givens v. Mullikin, 75 S.W.3d 383 (Tenn.2002), explored who besides the lawyer may be liable under state law for sanctions for a lawyer's conduct. Givens' suit stemmed from a car accident. Allstate, Mullikin's insurer, hired a lawyer to defend Mullikin. Now, Givens seeks to hold Allstate liable for that lawyer's alleged misconduct during the course of the lawyer's representation of Mullikin. Specifically, Givens says that the defendant's lawyer harassed her by requiring an exorbitant number of interrogatories and deposing her more than necessary. The court recognized that the lawyer was an independent contractor, not an agent of the insurer. Nonetheless, it allowed the claim to proceed against Allstate. The court held that both the insurer and the insured face liability for misconduct of an attorney when they have control over and direct the actions of the attorney. In this case, although Allstate had no legal right to control the representation of the insured, it had hired the attorney. Furthermore, Allstate hired the offending attorney after another firm had already completed discovery, giving rise to the inference that Allstate wanted a new firm to harass Givens. However, the court found that the insured himself was not liable, because he had no personal input at all into directing the defense.

c. What do you think about these cases? Do they give you a sense that sanctions litigation can become an industry of its own? Note that in the *Givens* case, Givens' lawyer could have asked for sanctions against Mullikin's lawyer earlier, asserting that the lawyer allegedly asked too many interrogatories or deposed her more than necessary. What is the advantage of creating a separate remedy against the insurance company that retained the lawyer to represent the insured?

Mississippi Supreme Court to review the record itself. Nevertheless, the 5th Circuit found this insufficient even under *Robbins*. In California, the court reasoned, the state court *must* independently review the record; in this case it had only been asked to do so. Perhaps that is a persuasive distinction, or it may suggest that some Courts of Appeal are uncomfortable with the *Robbins* holding.

B. THE ETHICAL STATUS OF DELAY AS A LITIGATION TACTIC

1. Does Model Rule 3.2 establish a different ethical standard for the use of litigation to resolve differences? Is its key principle that a lawyer must "expedite" resolution of the dispute? Is the Rule focused only on the inefficient use of court time that delay engenders?

a. What does Rule 3.2 mean when it says that a lawyer need only expedite litigation when "consistent with the interests of the client"? Look at the last sentence of the Comment. If one cannot use delay to "realize financial or other benefit," what other "interests of the client" would justify it? If the delay is "nonfrivolous" and thus not subject to Rule 11 sanctions, does that mean the lawyer has complied with the requirements of Model Rule 3.2?

b. May one never consider the benefits of delay that arise from filing a motion? Must the motion be justified only in terms of its probability of success? May the benefits of delay be considered if there is *some* possibility of success, i.e., the motion is not filed *solely* for purposes of delay? Because the Comment refers to "otherwise improper delay," may the lawyer file a nonfrivolous motion with delay as its dominant purpose? Note that in the Model Rules revisions of 2002, the ABA removed from Rule 3.1, Comment 2, the statement that an action is frivolous if the "client desires to have the action taken primarily for the purpose of harassing or maliciously injuring a person."

c. If your motion is not baseless, and if your client desires delay—if, in other words, you *may* delay on behalf of your client—then *must* you delay? Are you required to use every tool in your bag to further your client's interest? May you refuse to file the motion in order to protect your long-term relationship with the FDA, for example? Suppose you conclude that if you pull your punches in this case, the FDA may be pleased and more likely to give the benefit of the doubt to your *other* clients, and to this one on other cases?

d. One manual of trial practice states that the "duty of supporting the client's cause is sometimes so forcefully stated as to support the argument that as a trial lawyer you are obliged to assert every legal claim or defense available, except those you reject on tactical grounds relating to the immediate case. But the aim of the trial system to achieve justice, the interests of future clients, and your legitimate interest in your own reputation and future effectiveness at the bar compel moderation of that extreme view." Robert Keeton, Trial Tactics and Methods § 1–3 (2d ed. 1973). See also, Ronald D. Rotunda, Book Review, 89 Harvard L.Rev. 622, 628–29 (1976). Do you agree?

2. What obligation do you have to make witnesses available for trial and for deposition by the opposing party?

a. Assume that prior to any FDA hearing to determine whether or not to issue a ban against your client's wine additive, you knew that the first and most important witness that the FDA would seek to call would be the chief research chemist for your client. The chemist prefers not to testify because his testimony would greatly damage his employer, your client. Would it be proper for you to recommend that the chemist be hospitalized for tests and possible surgery on his recently discovered knee injury that, while not life-threatening nor terribly painful, limits his workday? Would you be let off the ethical hook if the company doctor initiated the suggestion that the knee needs treatment? Is it merely a rationalization to say that by creating the delay you would eliminate the possibility that the zealously loyal chemist might commit perjury?

b. May you advise a witness who is not your client not to talk to the other party? Suppose that the witness does not want to "become involved." Look at Model Rules 3.4(a) & (f).

In North Carolina State Bar v. Graves, 274 S.E.2d 396 (N.C.App.1981), the court upheld the discipline of an attorney who attempted to influence a witness who was not his client to refuse to testify or, in the alternative, to plead the Fifth Amendment. Although the witness had a constitutional right to plead the Fifth Amendment, the court held it is still a criminal act for someone "with corrupt motive to induce a witness to exercise that privilege."

In People v. Kenelly, 648 P.2d 1065 (Colo.1982), the Colorado courts suspended an attorney because he drew up a contract under which his client settled a civil case against X, and, in exchange, agreed to evade a subpoena in X's upcoming criminal trial. Accord, In the Matter of Lutz, 607 P.2d 1078 (Idaho 1980).[8]

c. To cope with the knee problem, might you simply ask the FDA staff for a delay in the hearings? Remember, in six months the case will be moot as far as your client is concerned, although it would still be a real issue to the FDA and possibly other wine producers. Is the only ethical issue your motive for delaying the expected testimony of the research chemist?

d. In Chevron Chemical Co. v. Deloitte & Touche, 501 N.W.2d 15 (Wis.1993), the lawyer represented that a witness would be unavailable for six weeks due to surgery; in fact, he had hernia surgery and would have been available in less than a week. For this and other misconduct, a judgment against the defendant notwithstanding the verdict was imposed and the case remanded to assess damages. Do you agree that a severe sanction was justified for the misconduct? Do you suppose the professional discipline process would have been produced a sanction that was nearly this quick and sure?

8. See also, Snyder v. State Bar, 555 P.2d 1104 (Cal.1976) (attorney disbarred, inter alia, for advising clients not to be available for depositions); Florida Bar v. Machin, 635 So.2d 938 (Fla.1994) (lawyer suspended for offering to establish a trust fund for the child of a murder victim if the victim's family agreed not to testify at the client's sentencing hearing). Cf. Taylor v. Commonwealth, 233 S.W. 895 (Ky.1921) (attorney disbarred when he was party to an arrangement under which a witness was paid to leave the jurisdiction and not return).

e. Should the appropriateness of delay in litigation vary depending on the type of legal proceeding involved? Consider Ronald D. Rotunda, Law, Lawyers, and Managers, in Clarence Walton, ed., The Ethics of Corporate Conduct 142–43 (1977):

> "[D]elay is a knife that cuts both ways. Some corporate lawyers have charged that environmentalists and other public-interest litigants have used delay to bog down the regulatory system, to prevent needed rate increases, to prohibit or delay power plant expansion, to obstruct programs for highway construction, and to delay or modify housing developments."

Is delay permissible when invoked in service of the public interest?

f. What about delay in criminal cases? Should filing appeals and habeas corpus petitions for purposes of delay be a permissible strategy in a death penalty case, for example? Is it often the *only* strategy?

3. In the dispute with the FDA, are you giving your client advice in your capacity as a lawyer in litigation or your capacity as a lawyer advising a client more generally?

a. Look at Model Rule 2.1 governing the lawyer as advisor. Now look again at Model Rule 3.1. If the lawyer may advance any nonfrivolous claim without being likely to suffer professional discipline, does that mean the lawyer acting under Rule 2.1 should advise the client to go ahead and take any position that is not completely frivolous?

b. Does it trouble you that, under the assumptions in this problem, your delay will allow tainted wine to be sold *in the future?* That is, what you do here may expose consumers to the risk of getting cancer, not simply help allocate losses after an event has occurred.

c. Indeed, might selling the wine expose your client to unwanted publicity or even litigation if what it has done becomes public knowledge? Might you then be liable to your client for a failure to warn it about the adverse consequences of pressing its legal rights to the limit? See, e.g., Restatement Third, The Law Governing Lawyers § 94 (Advising and Assisting a Client—In General).

d. Rather than seek delay, should you suggest that your client—before the FDA's expected order becomes effective—immediately sell his stock of tainted wine to a foreign wholesaler, assuming foreign law and scientific understanding are different and that the wine can be resold abroad? Will you sleep better knowing that only people you are unlikely to meet will have their cancer risk increased?

C. CONSIDERATION OF **ADR** ALTERNATIVES

1. What is your obligation to propose non-litigation alternatives to your client, the wine producer?

a. The buzzword in modern times is Alternative Dispute Resolution, or ADR. In the 2002 revisions to the Model Rules of Professional Conduct, the ABA added a new sentence to Model Rule 2.1, Comment [5], that now provides: "[W]hen a matter is likely to involve litigation, it may be necessary under Rule 1.4 to inform the client of forms of dispute resolution that might constitute reasonable alternatives to litigation."

b.   What alternatives to litigation might the Comment have in mind? Is negotiation an alternative to litigation, or is negotiation always done in the shadow of litigation, i.e., whether or not litigation is actually filed, does the right to litigate make the alternative of negotiation more compelling?

c.   The Model Rules explicitly give their approval to ADR in particular instances. Rule 1.5, Comment [9], for example, requires lawyers to comply with any system of mandatory arbitration or mediation of fee disputes. Another clause in that same sentence urges lawyers to submit to arbitration or mediation "even when it is voluntary." Further, if the lawyer and client have a dispute as who owns funds in the lawyer's trust fund account, Rule 1.15, Comment [3], advises the lawyer to suggest means, "such as arbitration," for resolving the dispute promptly.

2.   Why are there special rules restricting lawyers who act as third party neutrals that do not apply to non-lawyers who occupy the same role?

a.   In the 2002 amendments, the ABA added a new provision dealing specifically with ADR—Rule 2.4, "Lawyer Serving as Third–Party Neutral." Rule 2.4 defines a "third-party neutral" as a person who acts as a "mediator, arbitrator, conciliator or evaluator," to assist two or more persons who are not the lawyer's clients. See ABA Model Rule 2.4(a) and Comment [1].

b.   At the same time the ABA created Model Rule 2.4, it eliminated Model Rule 2.2, which had governed the lawyer as "Intermediary." Model Rule 2.2 had defined an intermediary as a lawyer who represented two or more clients with "potentially conflicting interests," typically a dispute between them. In contrast, under Rule 2.4, the lawyer explicitly does not represent any clients.

c.   Model Rule 2.4 does not, of course, regulate the conduct of third party neutrals who are not lawyers. Why are people who use a third party neutral more likely to be confused by the neutral's role if the neutral is a lawyer? Look at Comment [3] to Model Rule 2.4(b). Are you convinced?

d.   Should Rule 2.4(b) require more than an explanation that the lawyer does not represent either of the disputing parties? Does the suggestion in Comment [3] that the lawyer tell parties that the attorney-client privilege is inapplicable sound suspiciously like the giving of legal advice? Is anything wrong with that? The ABA Ethics 2000 Commission rejected a proposal that would have prohibited third-party neutrals from giving legal advice to the parties.[9] Does that mean the third-party neutral should be permitted to help the parties draft a settlement agreement, for example?

9.   Margaret Colgate Love, The Revised ABA Model Rules of Professional Conduct: Summary of the Work of Ethics 2000, 15 Geo.J.Legal Ethics 441, 462 (2002).

e. Does it make sense to leave the rules governing third-party neutrals to standards-setting bodies more focused on current thinking about ADR processes? Comment [2] to Model Rule 2.4 suggests that most regulation of ADR neutrals will come from such other sources.

3. Does it seem likely that you can help your client, the wine producer, in this case by suggesting the use of a third-party neutral?

a. Many states today require or make available the alternative of mediation. A mediator who has the confidence of both sides may determine the relative intensity of their preferences for items in dispute—immediate cash vs. particular assets, for example—and propose trades that will make both sides feel better off. Further, in some contexts, for example a divorce, some outcomes may be possible as a result of mediation—e.g., the future religious training made available to children—that would be more difficult to get a court to order.

b. Arbitration is yet another form of ADR. When might it be most effectively employed? The relative lack of discovery in many arbitration settings, and the limited rights to appeal an arbitration ruling to a court help account for the reputation of arbitration as a relatively quick way to get a decision in a matter.

c. Might arbitration work particularly well when the subject matter of the dispute is complex and specialized? If the question is whether a medical technician has the skills to do a particular job, for example, might it be better to get an answer directly from a panel of doctors than from a lay jury who hears from doctor-witnesses with opposing views?

d. Can mediation or arbitration work in the case of the wine producer? At least to date, the alternative seems unlikely. In disputes with the government, the FDA and similar agencies do not have a reputation of favoring mediation or arbitration over litigation, although there is some evidence that policy could be changing.

4. If a lawyer has been a third-party neutral in a matter, may that lawyer or one of his partners later represent a client in a related matter?

a. Assume that after the FDA required the recall of wine from retailers' shelves, one of the retailers wanted your client to reimburse it for its loss. Alpha was the arbitrator who decided that dispute. Now, your client has another dispute with the retailer that is tangentially related to the earlier one. In the new dispute, the retailer has hired Beta who has recently become Alpha's law partner. Your client did not give any information to Alpha during the arbitration that you expected he would keep secret from the retailer. Do you have any grounds to object to Beta's representing the wine retailer in the controversy?

b. Look at Model Rule 1.12 (a) and (c). How related should two disputes have to be before Rule 1.12(a) would prohibit Alpha's own representation of the retailer in the second dispute? Remember that Alpha did not represent either party to the arbitration so Model Rules 1.9 and 1.10

are not controlling? What is the rationale for excluding Alpha from involvement in later stages of the same "matter"? What will the Alpha Beta firm have to do to screen Alpha so that Beta may continue to represent the retailer even if Alpha is disqualified?

c.   If Beta had represented the retailer on various other matters over the years, should Alpha have been ineligible to serve as arbitrator if he were Beta's partner at the time that he was selected to be the arbitrator of the dispute? Does either Model Rule 1.12 or 2.4 authoritatively answer the question? How would you answer it? How would you explain your answer?

D.   OTHER SANCTIONS FOR LITIGATION MISCONDUCT

1.   Do courts have powers to sanction lawyers beyond Rule 11 and its state-law equivalents?

a.   Earlier in this Problem, we saw that lawyers may be sanctioned for violations of Model Rule 3.1 and Rule 11 of the Federal Rules of Civil Procedure. Other sources of sanction authority are available as well.

b.   Chambers v. NASCO, Inc., 501 U.S. 32, 111 S.Ct. 2123, 115 L.Ed.2d 27 (1991), held that a federal court has inherent power to award attorneys' fees to a party whom the court concludes has been engaging in harassing litigation. Chambers had agreed to sell his television station to NASCO, but then changed his mind. The Court found that he tried to prevent the sale by fraudulently trying to deprive the federal court of jurisdiction and by other tactics of "delay, oppression and harassment." Rule 11 would have allowed sanctions for frivolous pleadings, of which there were several, but not for the other wrongs. The Supreme Court held that a district judge has inherent power to manage the proceedings and may award attorneys' fees to sanction bad faith and oppressive conduct, even if it is not covered by Rule 11.

The Chief Justice and Justices Kennedy, Scalia and Souter dissented, suggesting the Court had granted carte blanche to judges to sanction lawyers. Are you equally concerned?

c.   United States v. Eisen, 974 F.2d 246 (2d Cir.1992), provides an important reminder that a lawyer may be found guilty of criminal and tortious conduct—here, mail fraud and RICO violations—for allegedly professional activities. The Government convicted the lawyers of conspiring with private investigators and others in a scheme of contriving phony traffic accidents and then filing claims with insurance companies. The opinion looked at several issues. For example, it held that the "fortuity" that a witness' testimony as "influenced turned out to be truthful" is not a defense to the bribery of the witness because: "The essence of bribery is the intent to influence improperly the conduct of another by bestowing a benefit, [so] there is no requirement that the intended result be accomplished." 974 F.2d at 256. The lawyers' "misrepresentations in pleadings and pretrial submissions were made in the hope of fraudulently inducing a settlement before trial. And in cases that went to trial, fraudulent representations concerning the claims were directed at the civil defendants and their insurers in an effort to induce settlement before verdict. In fact, several of the lawsuits listed in the indictment were settled. Even in cases decided by a jury, defendants' misconduct was intended to defraud their adversaries." Id. at 253. The bottom line was that Rule 11 and the Model Rules may be the least of a lawyer's worries in some cases.

2.   Should courts have the power to sanction a lawyer for filing a lawsuit that is nonfrivolous, but would not be filed but for the plaintiff's desire to hurt or somehow impose costs on the defendant? Should litigants have a Constitutional right to impose burdens on their enemies?

a. Dove Audio Inc. v. Rosenfeld, Meyer & Susman, 54 Cal.Rptr.2d 830 (Ct.App.1996), involved statements that Audrey Hepburn's lawyer made in a letter seeking to get celebrities to join in a complaint against a recording company that had allegedly reneged on its promises to make gifts to the celebrities' favorite charities. The recording company sued the lawyer's firm for defamation, but the Court dismissed the suit, finding that statements relating to litigation were privileged against a charge of defamation. More interesting, the Court held that the lawyer had his own claim for damages (over $27,000) from the recording company filing the action. California has an anti-SLAPP [strategic lawsuit against public participation] statute that permits the award of attorney's fees against someone who uses litigation to try to prevent someone else from asserting first amendment rights.

b. These SLAPP statutes can raise their own first amendment problems. The First Amendment guarantees a right to petition the government for redress of grievances. A lawsuit is a classic petition, and if it is not frivolous, i.e., is not "baseless," ordinarily it would be protected conduct. Granted, the plaintiff may harbor ill will towards the defendant, but the law does not require litigants to like each other; indeed, they often grow to dislike each other immensely.

See, e.g., Bill Johnson's Restaurants, Inc. v. N.L.R.B., 461 U.S. 731, 742–43, 103 S.Ct. 2161, 2170, 76 L.Ed.2d 277, 289 (1983), where the Court said that, in light of "the First Amendment right of access to the courts," the "filing and prosecution of a well-founded lawsuit may not be enjoined as an unfair labor practice, even if it would not have been commenced but for plaintiff's desire to retaliate against the defendant for exercising rights protected by the [National Labor Relations] Act."

c. The First Amendment even applies if the lawsuits are ultimately unsuccessful. In BE & K Construction Co. v. National Labor Relations Board, 536 U.S. 516, 122 S.Ct. 2390, 153 L.Ed.2d 499 (2002), unions had lobbied and filed health and safety charges against a non-union contractor who had secured a large contract. The contractor retaliated by filing secondary-boycott and antitrust claims against the unions, all of which were either dismissed or voluntarily withdrawn with prejudice. Then, the unions complained to the NLRB, which found that the contractor's suits were "unmeritorious" and the employer had a bad motive: it had filed the suits in order to retaliate against union members who were engaged in conduct that the NLRA protects. The NLRB and the Sixth Circuit agreed that the employer had engaged in an unfair labor practice, but the Supreme Court reversed.

Justice O'Connor wrote for the Court that lawsuits could not constitute an unfair labor practice unless they were "sham litigation," that is, both (1) subjectively brought with a bad motive and (2) "objectively baseless," which these were not. The NLRB may not "burden an unsuccessful but reasonably based suit" even though it "was brought with a retaliatory purpose." Mere ill will is not enough because "ill will is not uncommon in litigation." The right to petition, said the Court, is one of "the most precious of the liberties safeguarded by the Bill of Rights,"and the "right of access to the courts" is "one aspect of the right of petition." "As long as a plaintiff's *purpose* is to stop conduct he reasonably believes is illegal, petitioning is genuine both objectively and subjectively." 536 U.S. at 534, 122 S.Ct. at 2401, 153 L.Ed.2d at 516 (emphasis added).

The Court made clear, however, that it was not undercutting the right of lower courts to impose "common litigation sanctions," e.g Rule 11 "We do not decide whether the Board may declare unlawful any unsuccessful but reasonably based suits that would not have been filed but for a motive to impose the costs of the litigation process, regardless of the outcome, in retaliation for NLRA protected activity, [and] nothing in our holding today should be read to question the validity of common litigation sanctions imposed by courts themselves—such as those authorized under Rule 11 of the Federal Rules of Civil Procedure—or the validity of statutory provisions that merely authorize the imposition of attorney's fees on a losing plaintiff." 536 U.S. at 537, 122 S.Ct. at 2402, 153 L.Ed.2d at 517.

Justice Scalia, joined by Justice Thomas, concurring, said the implication of the decision is that the Court will conclude that the NLRB will "prohibit only lawsuits that are *both* objectively baseless *and* subjectively intended to abuse process." Id., 153 L.Ed.2d at 519 (emphasis in original).

Justice Breyer, joined by Justices Stevens, Souter, & Ginsburg, concurring in part and in the judgment, read the majority's ruling narrowly, as covering only cases where the NLRB "rests its finding of 'retaliatory motive' almost exclusively upon the simple fact that the employer filed a reasonably based but unsuccessful lawsuit and the employer did not like the union. The Court expressly leaves open other circumstances in which the evidence of 'retaliation' or antiunion motive might be stronger or different, showing, for example, an employer, indifferent to outcome, who intends the reasonably based but unsuccessful lawsuit simply to impose litigation costs on the union." 536 U.S. at 539, 122 S.Ct. at 2403, 153 L.Ed.2d at 520.

3. What are other limitations should be imposed on a court's power to sanction lawyers for what the court regards as improper litigation conduct?

a. In re Tutu Wells Contamination Litigation, 120 F.3d 368 (3d Cir.1997), imposed limitations on the court's power to sanction a law firm for discovery violations. The case involved an alleged release of petrochemicals into the water supply of eastern St. Thomas. The trial Court found that the defense firm suppressed certain engineering tests of affected soil and water. The Court suspended three lawyers from practice before it and ordered Exxon and its law firm to pay a total of $1 million to train jail inmates, construct a halfway house, and renovate the criminal justice complex, as well as pay sums to the plaintiffs damaged by the release. The Third Circuit upheld the sums for the plaintiffs but found that the Court had no authority to order payments to benefit the island's penal system, a purpose having nothing whatsoever to do with the case.

b.   Mackler Productions, Inc. v. Cohen, 146 F.3d 126 (2d Cir.1998), required procedural protections when a court imposes large sanctions against a lawyer. In this case, the court ordered $45,000 in compensatory sanctions, and $10,000 in punitive sanctions, payable to the court. The Second Circuit held that a large punitive sanction such as this one required the protection of criminal process. The compensatory sanction did not require such process, but it did require notice of the threatened sanction and an opportunity to be heard. Crowe v. Smith, 151 F.3d 217 (5th Cir.1998), reached the same result.

c.   Guardianship of Melissa W., 118 Cal.Rptr.2d 42 (Cal.Ct.App.2002), was a complicated case in which the court ordered Melissa, a 16 year-old minor, into her father's custody after her mother died. Melissa's grandparents appealed the custody determination, and while the appeal was pending, the court stayed the order so that Melissa could finish the year at her current school. At the same time, however, the grandparents signed a consent form that allowed Melissa to marry her 19 year-old boyfriend in the Bahamas. Although the grandparents lacked authority to sign the consent as Melissa's guardians, the grandparents' attorney accompanied Melissa to the Bahamas and served as a witness in the ceremony. The marriage emancipated Melissa, but the grandparents did not inform the court of the marriage and continued to pursue their appeal of the original order. Upon discovering the Bahamian marriage, the court imposed sanctions equal to the father's costs on appeal upon both the grandparents and their attorney. The court reasoned that the attorney had assisted the grandparents in violating a court order by facilitating Melissa's marriage. Because Melissa's marriage, if valid, had rendered the custody determination moot, the court, in addition, leveled sanctions of over $13,000 against both counsel and the grandparents for prosecuting a frivolous appeal. The court also referred the matter to the State Bar for investigation.

4.   Should there be a remedy against the government for a wrongful or vexatious criminal prosecution?

a.   United States v. Gilbert, 198 F.3d 1293 (11th Cir.1999), considered the criminal law counterpart to Rule 11. The jury convicted Gilbert of fraudulently concealing assets in bankruptcy, but the court reversed his conviction because the statute of limitations had run. The defendant then sued for attorneys' fees under the 1997 Hyde Amendment, 18 U.S.C. § 3006A, which allows such fees if the prosecution was "vexatious, frivolous or in bad faith." The court determined that the decision as to when the statute of limitations began to run had been a matter of first impression in the circuit and that the government was entitled to take the position it did. Thus, the statute did not justify any fee award.

b.   United States v. Adkinson, 247 F.3d 1289 (11th Cir.2001), on the other hand, found that the government, with full knowledge, asserted a position that recent and controlling precedent had foreclosed. That conduct constituted "vexatious", "frivolous," and "bad faith" prosecution that entitled the defendant to Hyde Amendment fees.

c.   Should the fact the government fails to prove its case be enough to demonstrate that the proceeding was vexatious? In United States v. Sherburne, 249 F.3d 1121 (9th Cir.2001), the government had prosecuted thirteen defendants for alleged abuses in the funding and construction of a housing development. The prosecution charged over fifty offenses and the court failed to convict on any of them. In a subsequent related hearing the trial court awarded attorney's fees pursuant to the Hyde Amendment to some, but not all, of the defendants, finding that the government's prosecution had been "vexatious." The Ninth Circuit found that the use of a solely objective standard to measure "vexatiousness" was incorrect, and that the correct standard involved both subjective and objective characteristics. The test should be whether "the prosecution was unwarranted because it was intended to harass and [was] without sufficient foundation." The court stated that to use a solely objective standard would put too much of a burden on the prosecution and would lead to judicial second-guessing. Do you agree?

————

PROBLEM 24

LITIGATION TACTICS

Some of the public's favorite stories involve lawyers uncovering deception or perhaps acting as deceivers in order to uncover deception. Early television lawyer Perry Mason was adept at goading the guilty party into confessing in open court (with Mason sometimes suggesting that he knew more than he did) just before Mason's client was about to be convicted at the end of each episode. This Problem explores when we should admire a lawyer's imagination and when we should condemn it. We first look at the line between creative lawyering and deception, wonder if the line is bright or equivocal, and then explore the role of deception in the search for truth. Next, we ask when a lawyer may use confidential information inadvertently disclosed by an opponent, and finally, whether and how judges might better enforce standards of civility among litigators.

FACTS

Hugh Martin, one of the most famous insurance defense lawyers in San Francisco, defends clients of many of the largest insurance companies in the United States. His firm's office overlooks the bay and occupies an entire floor of the Transamerica building. Yet despite his luxurious office and income to match, Martin cuts a different figure in court. He dresses in baggy tweed jackets with elbow patches, his shirts have badly frayed sleeves, and his unpolished shoes have very worn heels and soles. While he is a dapper figure outside of the courtroom with his custom suits and handmade cigars, he justifies his shabby attire and country lawyer act in the halls of justice as an effort to win sympathy from the juries while helping insurance companies avoid large tort judgments.

Martin confides to his young associates that they should avoid choosing younger jurors because of their "social worker, do-gooder mentality." He also advises: "Try to pick a jury with racial and class differences; by exploiting and encouraging dissension you create disunity; a disunified jury rarely grants large awards."

In one lecture to new associates in his firm he explained:

"You have to use your ingenuity and use all the tricks of the trade to win for the defense in a large tort claim. If you see that you can exploit an opposing witness' emotional weakness to make him seem uncertain about a fact, don't hesitate to do so even if the fact is true. The client doesn't pay for justice. It pays for victory."

In a case that Martin likes to brag about, he defended a manufacturing concern charged with the negligent death of the wife of a middle-aged worker. All during the trial Martin had his attractive secretary sit in the courtroom. Then, according to plan, Martin had this secretary—just before closing arguments, during a short break in the proceedings when the plaintiff's lawyer's back was turned—ask the plaintiff-widower the time; she smiled at his response, patted him on the head, and then left. The three older members of the jury looked with icy stares at the plaintiff and five hours later the jury rendered judgment for the defense. One or more of the jurors mistakenly assumed that Martin's secretary was the plaintiff's new wife.

Martin justifies these and similar practices (he calls them "tricks") as necessary to counteract what he considers the unfair advantage of the plaintiff's lawyer in winning verdicts because of sympathy and other reasons not connected with the merits of the case.[1]

QUESTIONS

A. The Ambiguous Line Between Creative Lawyering and Deception

1. Which of Hugh Martin's litigating "tricks" are proper, if any? Are some in a gray area? Should Martin be subject to criti-

---

1. This problem is adapted, with permission, from the discussion of a somewhat analogous situation in Ending Insult to Injury: No–Fault Insurance for Products and Services 4–6 (Univ. of Illinois Press 1975) by Professor Jeffrey O'Connell.

cism for wearing different clothes in court than he wears to the office, for example?

a. Should regulation of Martin's wardrobe be the responsibility of the judges before whom he appears? Courts sometimes do try to regulate the clothing of lawyers who appear before them. In State v. Cherryhomes, 840 P.2d 1261 (N.M.App.1992), for example, the lawyer appeared in a dress shirt with a bandanna at his neck. A local court rule required that he wear a necktie. He argued that a bandanna was a form of tie, but he was fined for contempt. The Court of Appeals affirmed. A lawyer's dress is not a form of "speech", the court ruled, and the judge's interpretation of the local rule controlled. Do you agree?

b. In Berner v. Delahanty, 129 F.3d 20 (1st Cir.1997), a court required a lawyer to take off a political advocacy button when he was in the courtroom. The button said "No on 1" and referred to an upcoming referendum issue. The First Circuit held that the prohibition of all advocacy buttons did not discriminate on the basis of content and was appropriate to preserving an atmosphere of impartiality in the courtroom.

2. Is there anything improper about Martin's approach to jury selection? When, if ever, does a lawyer have a duty to the justice system to pick only jurors who will be fair to both sides?

a. Georgia v. McCollum, 505 U.S. 42, 112 S.Ct. 2348, 120 L.Ed.2d 33 (1992), held that it is unconstitutional for either prosecutor or defense counsel to exercise peremptory challenges based on race. J.E.B. v. Alabama ex rel. T.B., 511 U.S. 127, 114 S.Ct. 1419, 128 L.Ed.2d 89 (1994), reached the same result as to sex-based challenges, and Edmonson v. Leesville Concrete Co., 500 U.S. 614, 111 S.Ct. 2077, 114 L.Ed.2d 660 (1991), came to the same conclusion in a civil case involving only private litigants.

United States v. Omoruyi, 7 F.3d 880 (9th Cir.1993), held that a prosecutor's statement indicating that he exercised peremptory challenges against two unmarried female prospective jurors because he was concerned they would be attracted to a "good-looking" male defendant was an admission of purposeful gender discrimination in violation of the defendant's right to equal protection.

b. Given all this authority, is there any possible justification for the last sentence in Comment [3] to ABA Model Rule 8.4? Should unconstitutional conduct by a litigator constitute virtually a per se violation of Model Rule 8.4(d)?

c. What should the result be in a medical malpractice case if the defense lawyer exercises a peremptory challenge against a potential juror (a Jehovah's Witness or a Christian Scientist) for religious reasons? Assume that the lawyer believes that the juror may be prejudiced against the defendant medical doctor. See State v. Davis, 504 N.W.2d 767 (Minn.1993) (holding that religiously–motivated peremptory challenge against Jehovah's Witness is not unconstitutional).

d. In Virgin Islands v. Weatherwax, 77 F.3d 1425 (3d Cir.1996), the white defendant was accused of killing a black man. Black persons made up a majority of potential jurors, and the jury selected had nine blacks and three whites. One day during the trial, defense counsel saw that a white juror had taken a newspaper with a story prejudicial to the defendant into the jury room in violation of a court order. Counsel failed to call it to the judge's attention, however, because he did not want a white juror dismissed. Ultimately, the jury convicted the defendant of second degree murder and he appealed his lawyer's failure to challenge the juror misconduct. By a 2–1 vote, the Third Circuit refused to second-guess the lawyer's decision. This was a tactical matter within the "exclusive province of the lawyer," the Court held, and the failure to act did not constitute ineffective assistance of counsel. Do you agree? Is taking race into account in this circumstance consistent with *McCollum*?

3. When Martin cross-examines a truthful witness, may he properly try to get that witness to express uncertainty about something that Martin knows to be true?

a. Read ABA Model Rule 3.3(a)(1). If a lawyer may not "make a false statement of fact or law to a tribunal," why should Martin be permitted to try to impeach the reliability of testimony that he knows to be accurate? What understanding of "justice" would warrant Martin's approach? Is Martin right that the client is not paying for justice? Should that end the ethical discussion?

b. Read ABA Model Rule 4.4 and ABA Standard Relating to the Defense Function 4–7.6, both found in the Standards Supplement. What seems to be their primary concern? Should the proper issue for a lawyer be whether the witness is "embarrassed" or "humiliated unnecessarily"? Should the issue instead be whether the lawyer is misleading the trier of fact?

c. How would you draft a rule that prohibits vigorous cross-examination of a truthful witness and yet preserves the essence of the adversary system? If the lawyer had to go easy on witnesses that were telling the truth, would that send the jury too clear a signal about whom they should believe? Would that be a bad thing? Are the times when the adversary system is too adversarial for its own good?

d. Restatement Third, The Law Governing Lawyers § 106, Comment *c*, tries to defend the present rule by saying:

> "A particularly difficult problem is presented when a lawyer has an opportunity to cross-examine a witness with respect to testimony that the lawyer knows to be truthful, including harsh implied criticism of the witness's testimony, character, or capacity for truth-telling. Even if legally permissible, a lawyer would presumably do so only where that would not cause the lawyer to lose credibility with the tribunal or alienate the factfinder. Moreover, a lawyer is never required to conduct such examination, and the lawyer may withdraw if the lawyer's client insists on such a course of action in a setting in which the lawyer considers it imprudent or repugnant."

e. Is a lawyer "never required to conduct such examination" when the best hope for the client is to persuade the jury that the nervous witness with bad eyesight is wrong, even though the lawyer knows that he is right in this instance?

4. What other "tricks" of Martin's would raise ethical issues in this Problem?

a. Would it be proper for Martin to have a low income employee sit at the counsel table instead of a company manager to make the company appear nearly broke? Look at Model Rule 3.4(e).

b. Were you offended by the incident where Martin's secretary implied that she had a relationship with the plaintiff? What, if anything, made the incident ethically improper? Should we worry about trial tactics at all? Is the point of the adversary system that a lawyer may rely on opposing counsel's guile to counterbalance his or her own?

c. In deciding which of Martin's "tricks" are unethical, should the test be a bright line or should it vary depending on whether a case is before a jury, for example? Would one argue that wearing shabby clothes during a settlement conference is improper? Is the test whether the lawyer's *motive* was to mislead? Is the test whether in a given case a juror or lawyer was in fact misled?

B. USING DECEPTION IN THE SEARCH FOR TRUTH

1. May a lawyer ever use deception as part of uncovering a mistaken eye-witness identification?

a. ABA Model Rule 3.3(a)(1) provides that a lawyer shall not knowingly "make a false statement of fact or law to a tribunal." Model Rule 4.1(a), the rule as applied to third persons (not tribunals), is similar, except that it adds the word "material."

b. Does "never" mean "never"? Is there a place for deception in the search for truth? What if the purpose of the deception is to uncover an honest, but significant mistake in identification? Commentators tell us that some of the most persuasive testimony is eye witness identification, but sometimes that testimony is simply mistaken. Witnesses "tend to incorporate post-identification feedback into their recollections of events," and "witnesses to a crime in which the perpetrator displays a weapon tend to focus their attention on the weapon, not the perpetrator."[3]

---

3. Mark Hansen, Expertise on Trial: Testimony on Reliability of Eyewitness Identification Stalls on General Acceptance, ABA Journal, Dec. 2002, at 22.

Further, what one remembers may not be true. For example, there were no television pictures of the first airplane hitting the World Trade Center on September 11, 2001, yet 77% of New Yorkers surveyed, and 73% of people nationwide recall that they saw such coverage. Memories "suffused with emotion are barely more likely to be true than memories of last Tuesday's lunch." The September 11 memory studies "confirm that eyewitness recall is fallible." Sharon Begley, The Memory of September 11 Is Seared in Your Mind: But Is It Really True?, Wall Street Journal, Sept. 13, 2002, at B1, col. 1.

c. Consider the lawyer's strategy in United States v. Thoreen, 653 F.2d 1332 (9th Cir.1981), cert. denied 455 U.S. 938, 102 S.Ct. 1428, 71 L.Ed.2d 648 (1982). The court tells us:

"In February 1980, Thoreen represented Sibbett, a commercial fisher, during Sibbett's nonjury trial * * * for criminal contempt for three violations of a preliminary injunction against salmon fishing. In preparing for trial, Thoreen hoped that the government agent who had cited Sibbett could not identify him. He decided to test the witness's identification.

"He placed next to him at counsel table Clark Mason, who resembled Sibbett and had Mason dressed in outdoor clothing—denims, heavy shoes, a plaid shirt, and a jacket-vest.

"Sibbett wore a business suit, large round glasses, and sat behind the rail in a row normally reserved for the press.

"Thoreen neither asked the court's permission for, nor notified it or government counsel of, the substitution.

"On Thoreen's motion at the start of the trial, the court ordered all witnesses excluded from the courtroom. Mason remained at the counsel table.

"Throughout the trial, Thoreen made and allowed to go uncorrected numerous misrepresentations. He gestured to Mason as though he was his client and gave Mason a yellow legal pad on which to take notes. The two conferred. Thoreen did not correct the court when it expressly referred to Mason as the defendant and caused the record to show identification of Mason as Sibbett.

"Because of the conduct, two government witnesses misidentified Mason as Sibbett. Following the government's case, Thoreen called Mason as a witness and disclosed the substitution. * * *

[The court let the government recall the government agent who then made the proper identification. Sibbett was convicted, and the Judge held Thoreen in contempt.]

"Thoreen's principal defense is that his conduct was a good faith tactic in aid of cross-examination and falls within the protected realm of zealous advocacy. He argues that as defense counsel he has no obligation to ascertain or present the truth and may seek to confuse witnesses with misleading questions, gestures, or appearances. * * *

"While we agree that defense counsel should represent his client vigorously, regardless of counsel's view of guilt or innocence, we conclude that Thoreen's conduct falls outside this protected behavior.

"Vigorous advocacy by defense counsel may properly entail impeaching or confusing a witness, even if counsel thinks the witness is truthful, and refraining from presenting evidence even if he knows the truth. When we review this conduct and find that the line between vigorous advocacy and actual obstruction is close, our doubts should be resolved in favor of the former. * * *

"Thoreen's view of appropriate cross-examination, which encompasses his substitution, crossed over the line from zealous advocacy to actual obstruction because, as we discuss later, it impeded the court's search for truth, resulted in delays, and violated a court custom and rule. Moreover, this conduct harms rather than enhances an attorney's effectiveness as an advocate.

" 'It is fundamental that in relations with the court, defense counsel must be scrupulously candid and truthful in representation of any matter before the court. This is not only a basic ethical requirement, but it is essential if the lawyer is to be effective in the role of advocate, for if the lawyer's reputation for veracity is suspect, he or she will lack the confidence of the court when it is needed most to the serve the client.' [4] * * *

"The record shows that Sibbett's identification was not an issue, contradicting the need to attack credibility."

The court upheld the finding of contempt but did not indicate what sanction was imposed.[5]

d. Do you agree that Thoreen's conduct crossed the line and was impermissible deception? How else was he to establish reasonable doubt about the government's identification? In a later portion of the opinion, the court suggests:

"If identification is at issue, an attorney could test a witness's credibility by notifying the court and counsel that it is and by seeking the court's permission to (1) seat two or more persons at counsel table without identifying the defendant * * *; (2) have no one at counsel table; (3) hold an in-court lineup."

Would you as defense counsel have chosen any of those alternatives? Is our problem with Thoreen's conduct that it was designed to mislead the trier of fact, not aid the search for truth? What if Thoreen did not trust the judge and did not seek the court's permission for that reason? Would that change the behavior we should expect of him?

4. The court was quoting American Bar Association Standards for Criminal Justice, The Defense Function 4.9 (1980).

5. By a 4 to 3 vote, the Illinois Supreme Court followed *Thoreen* on similar facts. People v. Simac, 641 N.E.2d 416 (Ill.1994), as did the Massachusetts Supreme Court in Matter of Gross, 759 N.E.2d 288 (Mass.2001). Attorney Gross represented a woman on drunk driving charges. Even though his client had admitted at the accident scene that she had been driving the car, Gross chose to present an alibi witness to testify that the defendant had been at home watching television. Upon discovering that the alibi witness also looked like the defendant, and believing that the accident victim could probably not identify the driver, Gross had the alibi witness impersonate the defendant in court. A police investigator present in the courtroom realized that the alibi witness was not the real defendant and that the defendant was present as a spectator. Even after the court questioned Gross as to the identity of the woman he had presented as the defendant, Gross continued to contend that she was his client. The district attorney reported this conduct to the state Board of Bar Overseers, and the Massachusetts Supreme Court upheld an 18-month suspension of Gross.

2. May a lawyer use deception as part of law enforcement or other investigatory functions?

a. A different use of deception in a search for truth is found in Conduct of Gatti, 8 P.3d 966 (Ore.2000). Lawyer Gatti knew that a company, CMR, did reviews for State Farm Insurance of how badly hurt claimants were. He believed State Farm had CMR deny benefits using a formula rather than relying on doctors' professional judgment of the injuries. State Farm denied the claim of Gatti's client, and the lawyer suspected that State Farm based its denial on a CMR report. The lawyer then called both the doctor who had conducted the review for CMR, and the director of operations for CMR. He said—or at least wanted them to believe—that he was a chiropractor who wanted to work as a claim reviewer for CMR. He asked them detailed questions about their protocols and guidelines, hoping in fact to develop facts to support a lawsuit, which he later filed, alleging fraud by CMR and State Farm.

The Oregon Supreme Court found that lawyer Gatti violated DR 1–102(A)(4) and DR 7–102(A)(5) [Model Rules 8.4(c) and 4.1]. "A misrepresentation may be a lie, a half-truth, or even silence," the Court said, and a "material fact consists of information that, if disclosed, would have influenced the recipient's conduct." This lawyer's conduct clearly met that definition. The court, in this attorney discipline case, imposed a public reprimand.

The lawyer defended his conduct by saying that government lawyers use deception all the time in undercover operations that seek to "root out evil." He, too, was trying to root out evil in the insurance industry. Even the U.S. Attorney intervened in the case to assert the importance of the government's ability to do undercover work, as did the Oregon Fair Housing Council and other groups that use testers to develop discrimination cases. However, the court held that there were no exceptions (not even a law enforcement exception) to the rule against misrepresentation. Until the Rules are formally amended, it said, the prohibition applies to all lawyers in all cases. As you might imagine, this case has joined Rule 4.2 as Exhibit A in the Justice Department's campaign against its lawyers being subject to state ethics rules while engaged in customary law enforcement operations.

b. What do you think of Gatti's defense? Is Model Rule 4.1(a) too absolute? Gatti was, after all, trying to get people to talk honestly who would not have talked at all if he had told them the truth.

c. In response to the public reaction to *Gatti*, the Oregon Supreme Court amended its Code of Professional Responsibility DR 1–102 to add a (D) that says:

"Notwithstanding DR 1–102(A)(1), (A)(3) and (A)(4) and DR 7–102(A)(5), it shall not be professional misconduct for a lawyer to advise clients or others about or to supervise lawful covert activity in the investigation of violations of civil or criminal law or constitutional rights, provided the lawyer's conduct is otherwise in compliance with these disciplinary rules. 'Covert activity,' as used in this rule, means an effort to obtain information on unlawful activity through the use of misrepresentations or other subterfuge. 'Covert activity' may be commenced by a lawyer or involve a lawyer as an adviser or supervisor only when the lawyer in good faith believes there is a reasonable possibility that unlawful activity has taken place, is taking place or will take place in the foreseeable future."

Would you recommend that your state adopt a similar provision?

d. United States v. Parker, 165 F.Supp.2d 431 (W.D.N.Y.2001), both distinguished and refused to follow *Gatti*: "As *Gatti* does not involve a government attorney's supervision of agents engaged in a formal criminal investigation, it is inapplicable on its facts. Moreover, the court's determination that DR 1–102(A)(3) forbids the use of undercover investigative techniques by attorneys in civil matters is contrary to caselaw in this circuit. [Gidatex, S.r.L. v. Campaniello Imports, Ltd., 82 F.Supp.2d 119, 122 (S.D.N.Y.1999)] (holding that DR 1–104(A)(4) prohibiting circumvention of Disciplinary Rules through 'dishonesty, fraud, deceit, or misrepresentation' not applicable to undercover investigation hired by private counsel to elicit statements from persons approached by investigators). In *Gidatex*, there was no indication that the investigators, who had been engaged by private attorneys, posing as interior decorators, caused the interviewed sales clerks to make 'any statements they otherwise would not have made.' 'The policy interests behind forbidding misrepresentations by attorneys are to protect parties from being tricked into making statements in the absence of their counsel and to protect clients from misrepresentations by their own attorney.' Accordingly, *Gatti* is neither controlling nor persuasive authority supporting Defendants' request for suppression of evidence." 165 F.Supp.2d at 477–78.

e. Utah State Bar Ethics Opinion 02–05 (2002) advised lawyers that it is not a violation of the rules of professional conduct for an attorney who works for a federal agency to perform covert investigations for the purpose of gathering relevant information about a suspect. The Committee likened the situation presented to the use of testers to gather evidence in discrimination cases. The Committee noted that misrepresentation was proscribed by the state rules of professional conduct, and that other courts, such as in *Gatti*, had declined to find an exception for lawyers advising federal officials. This Committee argued, however, that the rules had to be applied with reference to the purposes of legal representation. It declined to defend such conduct by a private attorney, however, and stated that private misconduct could not be cured simply by its association with a covert operation.[6]

---

6. On the other hand, In re Ositis, 40 P.3d 500 (Ore.2002), reaffirmed *Gatti* and reprimanded a lawyer who directed an investigator to pose as a journalist to interview someone he thought was an animal rights advocate who might "raid" his client's medical research breeding business. The court expressly reserved comment on whether the conduct would violate its newly amended rule.

f. How would you resolve the conflicting concerns inherent in the use of deception in the search for truth? Have any of the opinions resolved the issues to your satisfaction?

3. May a lawyer use deception to catch a criminal?

a. In re Pautler, 47 P.3d 1175 (Colo.2002), is a dramatic case about the place of deception in seeking an otherwise important objective. A man named William Neal, who had already brutally murdered several people, attacked and kidnaped a woman and then told her to tell the police how to contact him. On the phone, Neal described his gruesome crimes in detail for over three-and-a-half hours, but the police did not know where he was and he demanded to talk to a defense lawyer before turning himself in.

Chief Deputy District Attorney Mark Pautler, who was with the police, spoke to Neal on the phone and posed as a public defender. Pautler did not advise Neal about his rights, but he promised to meet Neal when he turned himself in. Later, when the real public defender met Neal and listened to a tape recording of the earlier conversation, he recognized Pautler's voice and realized that Pautler had impersonated someone other than a prosecutor. The court convicted Neal and imposed the death penalty.

b. Would you have given Pautler a medal for saving Colorado from a serial killer or would you have considered him deceitful and an embarrassment to the bar?

The Colorado Supreme Court took the latter view, suspending him from practice for three months, which was stayed for twelve months of probation. The court acknowledged that Pautler was motivated by a strong desire to protect other potential victims, but it said that no imminent public harm exception existed to the ethical principle that a lawyer may not engage in deceptive conduct, Rule 8.4(c). Further, Paulter had violated Rule 4.3, which provides that, in dealing on behalf of a client with a person not represented by counsel, the attorney is required to state that he is representing a client and could not state or imply that he was disinterested. The court also emphasized that Pautler did not attempt to contact a real public defender after failing to reach Neal's preferred attorney and that he showed no "remorse" for his use of deceit to help get a violent killer off the streets.

Are you impressed by the Court's adherence to principle? Do you wonder if some people lose all common sense when they put on a black robe?

C. Using an opponent's inadvertently disclosed confidential information

1. May a lawyer take advantage of a confidential fax sent inadvertently to her from her adversary in litigation?

a. Remember from Problem 8 that, under the rules of evidence, some courts hold that the inadvertent disclosure of confidential information forfeits the attorney-client evidentiary privilege, even if the lawyer acted "reasonably." Other courts are more forgiving before finding that the evidentiary privileged is treated as waived. What about the broader ethical obligation in Model Rule 1.6? If a lawyer receives material that was sent to her mistakenly by the opposing lawyer, may she use it? May she use it to argue that the opposing lawyer has "waived" the privilege? *Must* she use, or try to use, the information as part of her duty to fight zealously for her client? The question for the recipient of the information becomes whether to say "there but for the Grace of God go I," or to press the advantage on behalf of the recipient's own client.

b. ABA Formal Opinion 92–368 (Nov. 10, 1992), came down in favor of letting the lawyer who made the mistake off the hook. It held that as a matter of ethical responsibility, a lawyer who gets misdirected material from an opponent [a fax, an email] should refrain from reading it, notify the sending lawyer, and either return or destroy the material as the sending lawyer directs.

D.C. Bar Opinion No. 256 (May 16, 1995), on the other hand, criticized Opinion 92–368 and offered a compromise. It said that if a lawyer receives an inadvertently disclosed document and knows it was mistakenly sent before reading it, the lawyer must return the document to the sender. If the lawyer reads the document before learning of the mistake, however, the lawyer may both retain the document and use it.

Which approach do you prefer? Do you think many lawyers will know a document has been inadvertently sent before reading it?

c. The ABA Model Rules of Professional Conduct was silent on these issues until 2002 when subsection (b) was added to Model Rule 4.4 requiring that a lawyer who receives an inadvertently sent document to "promptly notify the sender." Is that response sufficient?

Look at Comment [2] to Rule 4.4. What "protective measures" might the sender be expected to seek?

Look as well at Comment [3]. What "professional judgment" is involved in deciding whether to return the document unread? Is the citation in Comment [3] to Model Rule 1.4 an implicit acknowledgment that what to do with the document is something the lawyer in most cases should talk over with the client?

2. May (must) the lawyer use the information that a whistle-blower from the opposing party intentionally sent?

a. ABA Formal Opinion 94–382 (July 5, 1994) considered the situation where the sender intended to send the material to the lawyer but the sender had no authority to do so. The sender might be a whistle-blower, a disgruntled employee (whether or not the discontent is justified), or someone seeking to rectify what he or she considered to be improper or unjust conduct, for example, the failure to disclose documents pursuant to a valid subpoena.

The Opinion referred to In re Shell Oil Refinery, 143 F.R.D. 105 (E.D.La.1992), which required the party receiving the materials not to make use of them, to identify and return them, and to have no further contact with the disclosing persons. On the other hand, the Committee also noted (but did not find convincing) a number of state ethics opinions that concluded that "the receiving lawyer has no obligation to disclose to a court or an adverse party that she possesses the adverse party's privileged or confidential information and that the receiving lawyer may use such materials." The Opinion rejected an "absolute rule that would prohibit a receiving lawyer from reviewing or using such materials under all circumstances." The receiving lawyer, for example, may have a legitimate claim that the documents should have been produced during discovery, or the person sending the documents may be acting under the authority of a whistle-blowing statute, such as 5 U.S.C.A. § 1221, et seq. Thus, the Opinion recommended that the lawyer's actions include:

> "(a) refraining from reviewing materials which are probably privileged or confidential, any further than is necessary to determine how appropriately to proceed; (b) notifying the adverse party or the party's lawyer that the receiving lawyer possesses the documents, (c) following the instructions of the adverse party's lawyer, or (d), in the case of a dispute, refraining from using the materials until a definitive resolution of the proper disposition of the materials is obtained from a court."

Does this advice make sense to you?

b. Courts are not always solicitous of party's rights to secrecy. In Castano v. American Tobacco Co., 896 F.Supp. 590 (E.D.La.1995), for example, a former paralegal working on cases about whether nicotine is addictive allegedly stole a large number of confidential documents, gave them to a California library, and put them on the Internet. The question was whether the defendant could at least have the documents' legal privilege restored so they could not be used in later litigation. The court held that because the documents, by now, were in the public domain and no showing had been made that plaintiffs' counsel had been involved in their taking or dissemination, an order to retrieve the documents would not issue, and a ruling on privilege would be reserved until trial.[7]

c. On the other hand, in Lipin v. Bender, 644 N.E.2d 1300 (N.Y. 1994), the plaintiff had stolen privileged documents that defense counsel had brought to a hearing. Plaintiff's counsel had then copied and used the stolen documents against the defendant. The court was unforgiving. It dismissed the complaint to sanction the plaintiff for this extreme and obvious misconduct.

d. Do you agree that "stolen papers" cases present different issues than those raised by "inadvertent disclosure" situations? However, does Model Rule 4.4(b) suggest an approach that should work in both situations?

---

7. Cf. American Tobacco Co. v. State, 697 So.2d 1249 (Fla.App.1997) (similar documents held not privileged because of the crime-fraud exception, i.e., they related to covering up known health risks of smoking).

D.   JUDICIAL EFFORTS TO ENFORCE CIVILITY

1.   Should courts attempt to require "civility" of litigators who appear before them?

a.   "Civility" is the modern buzzword in litigation, with efforts to require civility both frequent and increasing. For example, Dondi Properties Corporation v. Commerce Savings & Loan Association, 121 F.R.D. 284 (N.D.Tex.1988)(en banc), promulgated a code of civility for civil litigation. The Texas Code was designed to end "unnecessary contention and sharp practices between lawyers."

See also, the Proposed Seventh Circuit Standards for Professional Conduct and the Northampton County Bar Association Guide to Conduct and Etiquette at the Bar, both contained in the Standards Supplement.

b.   Should the ABA Model Rules require new civility standards? Are such standards unnecessary or even counterproductive? Look at Model Rule 3.5(d). Might some prohibited conduct be already disallowed as "conduct intended to disrupt a tribunal?"

2.   What should courts do, if anything, to impose or encourage civility?

a.   Cook v. American Steamship Co., 134 F.3d 771 (6th Cir.1998) involved one lawyer who physically assaulted opposing counsel, resulting in the court declaring a mistrial. Relying on the right to sanction a lawyer who "multiplies the proceedings * * * vexatiously," the Court affirmed a sanction that required the lawyer to pay his opponent's costs of conducting the additional trial. Of course, a physical assault is already a crime. Should the court have simply referred the case to the local prosecutor?

b.   In Lee v. American Eagle Airlines, 93 F.Supp.2d 1322 (S.D.Fla. 2000), the court cut plaintiff's counsel's fee award as a sanction for lack of civility in the courtroom. "Let's kick some ass," counsel called out as the trial for employment discrimination got underway. In another incident, counsel told a defense lawyer she had only been assigned to work on the case because she was African–American. On another occasion, counsel said to the court reporter, "What are you here for, just to look pretty?" In addition, counsel accused the judge of bias and laughed and looked up at the ceiling in response to rulings. Ultimately, the court halved the lawyers' rates for pre trial work and gave them nothing for their time in trial. It also sent a copy of the order to the Florida Bar for possible disciplinary action.

c.   In Florida Bar v. Martocci, 791 So.2d 1074 (Fla.2001), during a divorce proceeding, the lawyer had harassed the opposing side, repeatedly telling the opposing client that she was "crazy" and a "nut case," telling opposing counsel that she should "go back to Puerto Rico," and threatening to beat up the opponent's father in open court. The court found the lawyer's conduct crossed the line from "zealous advocacy" to "unethical misconduct." The court ordered that the lawyer be publicly reprimanded, put on probation for 2 years, and evaluated for possible anger management assistance.

d. In Office of Disciplinary Counsel v. Breiner, 969 P.2d 1285 (Hawaii 1999), the respondent repeatedly violated the trial court's admonitions not to be argumentative in his opening statement, to be respectful in cross-examining witnesses, and not to make "disrespectful and disruptive outbursts" before the jury. In addition to upholding findings of contempt, the court suspended the lawyer for six months.

e. In Pounders v. Watson, 521 U.S. 982, 117 S.Ct. 2359, 138 L.Ed.2d 976 (1997), the trial court held the lawyer in summary contempt for failing to obey the trial court's order not to make reference in front of the jury to the possible sentence the defendant faced. The Ninth Circuit reversed, saying a lawyer could not be sentenced for summary contempt without a hearing to determine whether the violation was willful, but the U.S. Supreme Court agreed with the trial court, holding that where the contempt occurs in open court and prompt action is required to avoid "demoralization of the court's authority," summary action is proper even if the conduct is not inherently disruptive of the proceeding. Justices Stevens and Breyer dissented.

3. What should a court do about abusive conduct that occurs in depositions, out of sight of the jury or a judicial officer who might regulate it?

a. In Paramount Communications, Inc. v. QVC Network, Inc., 637 A.2d 34 (Del.1994), the Delaware Supreme Court sua sponte criticized remarks of Texas lawyer Joseph Jamail towards opposing counsel during a deposition. At one point in the record, Mr. Jamail instructed his witness not to answer a question and then said: "He's not going to answer that. Certify it. I'm going to shut it down if you don't go to your next question." The other lawyer said, "No. Joe, Joe". Mr. Jamail responded, "Don't 'Joe' me, a————. You can ask some questions, but get off of that. I'm tired of you. You could gag a maggot off a meat wagon." The Court did not discipline Mr. Jamail, who did not otherwise appear in the case, was not a member of the Delaware bar, and was not admitted pro hac vice. However, the Court said that his conduct "relates to a serious issue of professionalism involving deposition practices in Delaware trial courts." Do you agree?[8]

b. In re Estiverne, 741 So.2d 649 (La.1999), the conduct was even wilder. After Lawyer A accused Lawyer B of misconduct during a deposition, Lawyer B suggested "stepping outside and settling the matter man to man." After the deposition, Lawyer A stepped out, returned with a gun and threatened to kill Lawyer B. Lawyer A explained that Lawyer B held a black belt in karate while Lawyer A was less physically fit. The court found

---

8. Hall v. Clifton Precision, 150 F.R.D. 525 (E.D.Pa.1993), also involved deposition conduct. Plaintiff's counsel insisted that, while his client was being deposed by defense counsel, the plaintiff could confer with his counsel about his answers. The Court held that to be improper. A client may confer with counsel about whether a privilege can be asserted, but otherwise, the lawyer taking the deposition is entitled to the witness' answers uncorrupted by suggestions of counsel.

threatening a legal colleague with a gun was less egregious than killing him, but it still suspended Lawyer A for a year and a day—a sanction that required the lawyer to file a petition for readmission.

c. Matter of Golden, 496 S.E.2d 619 (S.C.1998), imposed a public reprimand on a lawyer whose deposition conduct involved "sarcasm and maliciousness," "unnecessary combativeness," "gratuitous threatening and intimidation," and "unequivocal bad manners." At one point in the deposition, for example, he called the female opposing party a "meanspirited, vicious witch" and said he wanted to be "locked in a room naked with you with a sharp knife," explaining that he wanted to kill the woman.

d. Do these cases help explain why Model Rule 3.5 now has Comment [5]?

4.   What should a court do about other disruptive conduct that occurs out of the courtroom setting?

a. In Hirschfeld v. Superior Court, 908 P.2d 22 (Ariz.Ct.App.1995), the lawyer who represented the father in a child custody dispute believed the mother was not living up to a joint custody agreement. During an overnight recess in the proceedings, the lawyer followed the mother and kept calling out and asking her in a loud voice to tell him where she had hidden the child. The judge's office had to summon help from the sheriff to protect the mother from further harassment. This court affirmed holding the lawyer in contempt: "the court has the right and the duty to protect litigants, witnesses, attorneys and jurors from misbehavior and harassment while they are in or near the courtroom, whether they are arriving, waiting, or departing."

b. In United States v. Wunsch, 84 F.3d 1110 (9th Cir.1996), however, a male criminal defense lawyer had written a letter to the female Assistant U.S. Attorney with an attachment stating in large, bold type: "MALE LAWYERS PLAY BY THE RULES, DISCOVER TRUTH AND RESTORE ORDER. FEMALE LAWYERS ARE OUTSIDE THE LAW, CLOUD TRUTH AND DESTROY ORDER." The District Court had ordered the lawyer to apologize, but the Ninth Circuit reversed. Although the Court acknowledged cases in which a *pattern* of sexist speech was sanctioned, it found that this single incident neither impugned the "integrity of the court" nor interfered with the "administration of justice."

The court held that California Business & Professions Code § 6068(f)—requiring an attorney to "abstain from all offensive personality"—was unconstitutionally vague. The Court expressed concern about the First Amendment problems in sanctioning lawyer for speech, even uncouth speech.

c. Do you agree? See also, e.g., Brewer & Bickel, Etiquette of the Advocate?, Texas Lawyer 20, 21 (Mar. 21, 1994), which is to the same effect. These litigators argue that the courts' efforts to sanction such loose and non-definable concepts as "civility" will be counter-productive and will chill lawyers's legitimate behavior. Clients "are bound to be adversely affected as they witness their lawyers tiptoeing toward compromise with opposing counsel as 'cooperatively' as possible."

d.   Do you believe effective advocacy demands boorish behavior by lawyers? Is "speech" simply the use of words or is it a form of "action" that can constitute intimidation? Should lawyers more disposed to winning on the merits than by making their opponents' lives hellish have to learn to live with crude and callous conduct, or does failing to sanction such conduct tend to encourage more of it in the future?

e.   Do courts already have so much to do so that, on a scale of evil, "boorishness" does not rank terribly high? Judges sometimes make callous or gratuitous remarks about lawyers in their opinions. Should judges be reluctant to cast the first stone when they are not always without fault themselves?

PROBLEM 25

DISCLOSURE OF LAW OR FACTS FAVORABLE TO THE OTHER SIDE

Confidentiality is the watchword for much of what a lawyer does. Litigators in particular assert work product immunity, as well as the attorney-client privilege and their ethical duty of confidentiality, as bases for non-disclosure. Some advocates may be surprised to learn that the confidentiality obligation has important exceptions. Indeed, in some situations, lawyers are required to volunteer information they might prefer remain undisclosed. This Problem begins by discussing the duty to reveal adverse legal authority. It then examines when factual information must be disclosed. Next, it explores the lawyer's duty when discovery responses have been incomplete or inaccurate. And lastly, if examines the lawyer's duty where the court is mistaken about publicly-available information in a way that is favorable to the lawyer's client.

FACTS

You have prepared your case fully, and you consider it a sure winner on the motion for summary judgment. However, hours before the argument on that motion, you discovered several cases with dicta directly against you. Two of the cases have holdings that by analogy are against you. You have concluded that the likelihood is great that the judge would rule against your client on the summary judgment motion if she knew of the cases you have discovered. Your opponent (perhaps because he is less prepared than you) has not referred to these cases.

Now, you have come across a witness who can supply a *factual* piece of evidence harmful to your client's case. You conclude that if you make a motion for summary judgment you would win because opposing counsel has not been able to present an affidavit on a vital point. However your secretly-discovered witness could supply the essential link in the opposition's evidentiary chain. The opposing party has not contacted this witness, and you assume no one else knows of his existence.

3.3(a)(3)– As you are reviewing the deposition testimony that you have attached to your motion for summary judgment, you realize that one of your best witnesses testified about a fact important to your case in a way that you know is false. You don't know whether she was lying or simply mistaken, and the other side clearly has not discovered the inaccuracy.

In another case, you represent a convicted client who stands before the judge to be sentenced. The court clerk indicates to the court that the defendant has no record. The court thereupon says to the defendant—who stands silent—"Since you have no criminal record, I will only put you on probation." You know, either by independent investigation or from what your client has told you, that he in fact has a criminal record and the clerk's information is incorrect. The judge turns to you and says, "Anything to add, counsel?"

QUESTIONS

A. CANDOR ABOUT ADVERSE LEGAL AUTHORITY

1. Must you cite all relevant cases to the court, even those not favorable to your position? What are the limits, if any, on that obligation?

a. Look at ABA Model Rule 3.3(a)(2). What does this rule imply the courts expect of a lawyer? May you simply put contrary cases in a footnote in your brief without in any way explaining their relevance?[1] Do you have to highlight the contrary authority?

b. In Katris v. Immigration and Naturalization Service, 562 F.2d 866 (2d Cir.1977), the attorney for petitioner failed to cite a particular Second Circuit case and several cases from other circuits because, he said "these decisions were adverse to his position here and that he did not agree with them." The attorney had represented one of the parties in the adverse Second Circuit case. The court concluded the lawyer had misled the Court and taxed costs against the attorney personally.

c. ABA Informal Opinion 84–1505 (Mar. 5, 1984) reaffirmed the disclosure obligation. A plaintiff's lawyer had successfully beaten the defendant's motion to dismiss in a case of first impression interpreting a recently enacted statute. Based on earlier analogous cases, the trial court's ruling

---

1. ABA Formal Opinion 94–386 (Aug. 6, 1994) suggests *limits* on what a lawyer may cite. The Opinion says that a lawyer who cites unpublished opinions, in violation of court rules against such citations, violates Model Rule 3.4(c).

had been correct. Later, however, during the pendency of the action, plaintiff's lawyer learned that an appellate court elsewhere in the state had recently interpreted the statute in a way that was arguably contrary to the trial court's ruling. He asked the ABA Standing Committee on Ethics and Professional Responsibility whether he was obliged to disclose the new appellate opinion to the trial court. Even though one could have interpreted the appellate ruling in a way not "directly adverse to the position of the client," another reading was clearly adverse. The trial court would certainly be benefitted in this case of first impression by having information about the appellate decision, so the ABA Committee concluded that the plaintiff's lawyer had a duty to reveal the information to the court.

d.   In re Thonert, 733 N.E.2d 932 (Ind.2000), involved a client who wanted to withdraw his guilty plea. The lawyer argued that the trial judge had a duty to ask whether the client understood his rights at the time of the plea, in spite of the fact the client had seen a videotape explaining those rights. The lawyer's position was directly contrary to a decision by the same Indiana Supreme Court a year earlier in a case argued by the same lawyer. He neither cited that decision nor argued that the result should be changed or distinguished. For the failure to do so—and for taking a fee from the client without disclosing what a long shot the argument was—the court formally admonished the lawyer.

e.   In Tyler v. State of Alaska, 47 P.3d 1095 (Alaska Ct.App.2001), Tyler, the defendant, appealed his felony DWI conviction by asserting that one of his two prior convictions had been invalid. Although Tyler had conceded his guilt in the instant case, he contended that invalidation of the prior offenses would make felony prosecution inappropriate. Tyler's attorney, Cyrus, however, failed to cite a case of the Alaska Supreme Court that had decided against Tyler's theory in a felony DWI case. The court fined Cyrus $250 for violating his ethical duty to cite directly adverse authority. First, the court found that Cyrus was aware of the prior case, because he had participated in it as defense counsel. Although Cyrus argued that he did not cite the case because he believed it was distinguishable, the court stated that the attorney was under a duty to cite any case that would reasonably be considered to "cast substantial doubt" on the argument being made and thus be important to the judge hearing the case. It was irrelevant, the court said, whether the omitted case would completely control the decision.

2.   Do these cases make sense to you? What is the rationale underlying this rule? Does the rule simply serve to penalize a lawyer who engages in more effort in uncovering the relevant case law? Why should one lawyer have the obligation to do his or her opponent's homework?

a.   One statement of the rationale is found in Comment [4] to Model Rule 3.3. It says: "A lawyer is not required to make a disinterested exposition of the law, but must recognize the existence of pertinent legal authorities. * * * The underlying concept is that legal argument is a discussion seeking to determine the legal premises properly applicable to the case."

b.   Restatement Third, The Law Governing Lawyers § 111, Comment *c*, says that failure to disclose adverse legal authority

"may have the same effect as a misstatement of the law. It deprives the court of useful information and serves no interest of the client other than obtaining a result not provided for by the law. It is sometimes argued that the rule requires the advocate to act against the client's interest * * * . However, the advocate's role is to present the client's case within the framework of the law, which requires common terms of legal reference with the court and opposing counsel."

c.   Another analyst put the explanation this way:

"[T]here is no obligation to the client to withhold knowledge of the applicable law. The obligation is to present the applicable law to the court. This, of course, is not to say that the lawyer need not do his best to distinguish, or even obtain an overruling of the prior law. The obligation is to represent the client fully in obtaining a determination of the law, but to extend it to a concealment of the law would be to distort our judicial process which relies upon stare decisis as a cornerstone. An allied question is whether or not the advocate is required to advance new theories, which may be controlling, on behalf of the other party to the lawsuit, as an aid to the court. I agree with those who say 'no'. This inaction does not mislead the court in deciding disputed points of law which are before the court. A contrary position involves an abandonment of the adversary system in regard to the decisional process."[2]

d.   Do these explanations put to rest any reservations you might have about the rule? Are most briefs and oral arguments you have observed simply a "discussion seeking to determine the legal premises properly applicable to the case"? Is the law so clear that "common terms of legal reference" will inevitably be found if all cases are cited to the court?

e.   Indeed, does a conclusion about what constitutes "legal authority that is directly adverse" require the lawyer to develop a theory of the case that competes with the lawyer's own? Might the result of that effort be to suggest a theory to the other side that it had not realized might be possible? In short, might this rule indeed require a lawyer to do the other side's work for it?

3.   How does the obligation that Model Rule 3.3(a)(2) imposes relate to Rule 11 of the Federal Rules of Civil Procedure?

a.   Rule 11 of the Federal Rules of Civil Procedure was discussed in Problem 23. In Rodgers v. Lincoln Towing Service, Inc., 771 F.2d 194 (7th Cir.1985), the Seventh Circuit approved Rule 11 sanctions that the trial

---

2. E. Wayne Thode, The Ethical Standard for the Advocate, 29 Ins. Counsel J. 33,   39–40 (1962) (footnotes omitted).

court had imposed, because the plaintiff's lawyer had insisted that a particular U.S. Supreme Court case was applicable "despite clear authority in this Circuit to the contrary." Counsel did not "even attempt to construct an argument regarding why" the case should apply. Counsel had "refused to recognize or to grapple with the established law of the Supreme Court and of this Circuit. * * *." Accord, DeSisto College, Inc. v. Line, 888 F.2d 755 (11th Cir.1989), cert. denied 495 U.S. 952, 110 S.Ct. 2219, 109 L.Ed.2d 544 (1990); Jorgenson v. Volusia County, 846 F.2d 1350 (11th Cir.1988) (counsel had argued the same point in an earlier case and lost but did not tell the trial court in this case).

b. In Golden Eagle Distributing Corp. v. Burroughs Corp., 801 F.2d 1531 (9th Cir.1986), on the other hand, a law firm had moved for summary judgment on a matter. The trial court both denied the motion and then, sua sponte, imposed sanctions against the firm. The judge, relying on Model Rule 3.3, Comments 2 & 4, ruled that the firm's positions in its summary judgment motion papers were legally and factually supportable, but that the firm had engaged in misleading conduct because it "should have stated that a position it was taking was grounded in a 'good faith argument for the extension, modification, or reversal of existing law,' rather than implying that its position was warranted by existing law." The Ninth Circuit reversed. The language of Rule 11 does not require counsel to differentiate between a position supported by existing law from one that would extend it, the court said. It is "not always easy to decide whether an argument is based on established law or is an argument for the extension of existing law." In fact, whether "the case being litigated is or is not materially the same as earlier precedent is frequently the very issue which prompted the litigation in the first place."

c. With which of these decisions do you agree? Is Federal Rule 11 an appropriate tool to use to sanction a lack of candor? Might its use threaten to create collateral litigation in every case about whether one lawyer or another was sufficiently forthcoming?

B. CANDOR ABOUT ADVERSE FACTS

1. Do the Rules treat disclosure of the newly discovered witness differently from the disclosure of adverse legal authority? Why?

a. Must a lawyer reveal a witness when opposing counsel has neither sought the witness nor asked questions in discovery that would lead to the witness? Must the lawyer reveal the witness to the court in order to further the search for truth? *May* a lawyer reveal the witness to the court? Listen to Samuel Williston:

"The case was tried before Chief Justice Knowlton. I opened the case at some length and I also made the preliminary part of the final argument. The Chief Justice decided promptly in favor of [my client,] the defendant, and since the decision was upon the facts, there was no opportunity for the plaintiffs to carry the case further. The handsomely bound volumes of interrogatories were only useful as waste paper. The plaintiffs either did not have so full a file of their correspondence with the defendant as we did, or it had not been so carefully examined by their counsel, for we had letters in our file that would have been useful to them. They did not demand their production and we did not feel bound to disclose them. In the course of his remarks the Chief Justice stated as one reason for his decision a supposed fact which I knew to be unfounded. I had in front of me a letter that showed his error. Though I have no doubt of the propriety of my behavior in keeping silent, I was somewhat uncomfortable at the time.

"One of the troublesome ethical questions which a young trial lawyer is confronted with is the extent to which he is bound to disclose to the court facts which are injurious to his client's case. The answer is not doubtful. The lawyer must decide when he takes a case whether it is a suitable one for him to undertake and after this decision is made, he is not justified in turning against his client by exposing injurious evidence entrusted to him."[1]

Professor Williston reports that he was "uncomfortable at the time" with his ethical decision. Are you satisfied that he was being "professional" in suppressing his discomfort?

b. People v. Cassas, 646 N.E.2d 449 (N.Y.1995), makes clear that a lawyer does not have a right to make a unilateral decision not to protect the client's rights. The defendant shot his wife to death at their home. The next morning, the lawyer brought the defendant to the nearest police precinct, said the defendant had committed the crime, and told the police where to find the body and the gun. Those statements were all put before the jury. The Court found the statements were not authorized by the defendant and ordered a new trial.

2. Should the law impose a higher standard than that to which Professor Williston was held?

a. Federal Rule of Civil Procedure 26, as amended in 2000, for example, provides that:

(a) Required Disclosures; Methods to Discover Additional Matter.

(1) Initial Disclosures. Except in categories of proceedings specified in Rule 26(a)(1)(E), or to the extent otherwise stipulated or directed by order, a party must, without awaiting a discovery request, provide to other parties:

(A) the name and, if known, the address and telephone number of each individual likely to have discoverable information that the disclosing party may use to support its claims or defenses, unless solely for impeachment, identifying the subjects of the information;

(B) a copy of, or a description by category and location of, all documents, data compilations, and tangible things that are

---

1. Samuel Williston, Life and Law: An Autobiography 271–72 (1940). In a similar case, New York County Lawyers' Association Opinion No. 309 (1933) ruled, without discus-sion, that it is "not professionally improper" for the attorney not to volunteer this witness to the court.

in the possession, custody, or control of the party and that the disclosing party may use to support its claims or defenses, unless solely for impeachment;

(**C**) a computation of any category of damages claimed by the disclosing party, making available for inspection and copying as under Rule 34 the documents or other evidentiary material, not privileged or protected from disclosure, on which such computation is based, including materials bearing on the nature and extent of injuries suffered; and

(**D**) for inspection and copying as under Rule 34 any insurance agreement under which any person carrying on an insurance business may be liable to satisfy part or all of a judgment which may be entered in the action or to indemnify or reimburse for payments made to satisfy the judgment.

(**E**) The following caregories of proceedings are exempt from initial disclosure under Rule 26(a)(1):

(**i**) an action for review on an administrative record;

(**ii**) a petition for habeas corpus or other proceeding to challenge a criminal conviction or sentence;

(**iii**) an action brought without counsel by a person in custody of the United States, a state, or a state subdivision;

(**iv**) an action to enforce or quash an administrative summons or subpoena;

(**v**) an action by the United States to recover benefit payments;

(**vi**) an action by the United States to collect on a student loan guaranteed by the United States;

(**vii**) a proceeding ancillary to proceedings in other courts; and

(**viii**) an action to enforce an arbitration award.

* * * A party must make its initial disclosures based on the information then reasonably available to it and is not excused from making its disclosures because it has not fully completed its investigation of the case or because it challenges the sufficiency of another party's disclosures or because another party has not made its disclosures.

* * *

(**e**) **Supplementation of Disclosures and Responses.** A party who has made a disclosure under subdivision (a) or responded to a request for discovery with a disclosure or response is under a duty to supplement or correct the disclosure or response to include information thereafter acquired if ordered by the court or in the following circumstances:

(**1**) A party is under a duty to supplement at appropriate intervals its disclosures under subdivision (a) if the party learns that in some material respect the information disclosed is incomplete or incorrect and if the additional or corrective information has not otherwise been made known to the other parties during the discovery process or in writing. * * *

(2) A party is under a duty seasonally to amend a prior response to an interrogatory, request for production, or request for admission if the party learns that the response is in some material respect incomplete or incorrect and if the additional or corrective information has not otherwise been made known to the other parties during the discovery process or in writing.

b. If Federal Rule 26 were applicable in the circumstances of this problem, what would it compel you to do about disclosure of the newly-discovered witness?

3. When should a court conclude that a lawyer deceived it by not volunteering factual information?

a. In Toledo Bar Association v. Fell, 364 N.E.2d 872 (Ohio 1977) (per curiam) the lawyer had filed a workers' compensation claim for permanent disability of his client, but his client died before the hearing on the claim. The attorney did not volunteer this information to the Industrial Commission because he knew it routinely denied permanent disability claims in such cases. Assuming the claim was originally filed in good faith, what discipline, if any, is justified by this nondisclosure? The Ohio Supreme Court indefinitely suspended the attorney. Would you have done the same?[2]

b. The court in *Fell* relied on several provisions then in the Model Code of Professional Responsibility, the predecessor of the present Model Rules of Professional Conduct. One rule, DR 7–102(A), said simply that a lawyer shall not "conceal or knowingly fail to disclose that which he is required by law to reveal." What provision in the present Model Rules comes closest to saying the same thing? Is it Model Rule 3.3(a)(1)? When the lawyer's client dies, under the law of agency, the lawyer no longer has a client; the agency is terminated by death. Is it easy to see that the lawyer should have told the court that he no longer had a client in the case?

c. If the lawyer must volunteer this adverse fact, what other facts must the lawyer volunteer? Should the lawyer volunteer that one of his major witnesses is ill and may not be able to testify, thereby undercutting the settlement value of his case?

d. Virgin Islands Housing Authority v. David, 823 F.2d 764 (3d Cir.1987), reminds lawyers that they must state accurately what happened below when they make an argument on appeal. Tenant had clearly lost in the territorial court on the issue whether an administrative hearing had been denied the tenant before his eviction. The Housing Authority had not appeared at the hearing in the District Court, however, and so was not in a position to correct the record when the tenant's lawyer flatly denied that any finding on the issue had been made below. Thus, the District Court had mistakenly reversed the judgment of eviction. The Third Circuit reversed the District Court and then directed it to consider imposing sanctions on the tenant's lawyer for lying about the events in the territorial court. Given these prior cases, what sanctions should the court impose?

2. If this result sounds familiar, it may be because we looked at a similar answer in Problem 20 to the question of the duty to disclose adverse facts in negotiation.

4. What sanction should a lawyer expect if a court concludes that the lawyer has deceived it by affirmatively misrepresenting facts?

a.   In *Fell*, the lawyer did not affirmatively make a misstatement to the court, yet it indefinitely suspended the attorney. By contrast, In re Jeffers, 3 Cal. State Bar Ct. Rptr. 211, 1994 WL 715918 (Cal.Bar Ct.1994), imposed a two-year probation on an attorney who, among other things, affirmatively made misstatements to the court about his client's death. The lawyer told the court at a September 1990 mandatory settlement conference that he had last communicated with his client just before this conference and that the client had indicated that he was not responsible for the accident and wanted the matter to go to trial. The lawyer did not tell the court that the client had died on June 21. The lawyer then said that he could not presently communicate with client because the "client's brain was not functioning," but he presented no medical verification of this fact. The court asked the lawyer how he could personally know of his client's brain incapacity if there had been no medical verification. "After a long pause," the lawyer admitted to the court that his client had died months earlier.

b.   In Office of Disciplinary Counsel v. Hazelkorn, 480 N.E.2d 1116 (Ohio 1985), the defendant, whose real name was Foster, gave his name as Frantz when he was arrested. The lawyer knew that his client had given a false identity but represented him in the bond hearing as if his name were Frantz. If defendant had used his real name, the prosecutor and court would have realized that he had an extensive record; instead, they accepted a no-contest plea and sentenced him to a fine. When he failed to pay the fine, a contempt citation and then an arrest warrant were issued. He was arrested, and the judge learned of the original misinformation. When the court determined that the lawyer had known all along about his client's deception to the court, the court indefinitely suspended the lawyer from practice. Why the indefinite suspension in *Hazelkorn* and the probation in *Jeffers*? Courts typically do not discuss cases in other jurisdictions and they do not explain why the sanctions differ.

c.   State v. Casby, 348 N.W.2d 736 (Minn.1984), upheld a misdemeanor criminal conviction of an attorney for misleading the court. The state prosecuted the lawyer's client for speeding and littering. It did not know that he had been driving after revocation of his license, because he identified himself using his brother's name when the police arrested him. At his arraignment and pretrial hearing, the client continued the deception. Later he pled guilty, still using the name of his brother. There was an issue whether the attorney knew the real name of her client, but the court found that she did. The lawyer asserted that, even if she knew the client's name, she was precluded by the attorney-client privilege and the professional obligation to keep the client's secrets from disclosing the deception he was perpetrating on the court. The court held that the lawyer had gone far beyond *passively* protecting confidential information. She had undertaken plea negotiations and written letters in which she referred to her client using the brother's name. At minimum, she should have withdrawn, but the court went on to say that it believed she could and should properly have revealed her client's true identity.

d. Attorney Grievance Commission of Maryland v. Rohrback, 591 A.2d 488 (Md.1991), involved a client who told his lawyer that he had given a false name to the arresting officer. The court said that the lawyer was under no obligation to correct that prior misstatement. When the bondsman arrived, the lawyer gave him the client's real name, but the client used the false name at the bond hearing. That, says the court, was all right too because the client, not the lawyer, gave the false name. Where the lawyer went wrong was in using the false name with the pre-sentence investigator for whom the name was critical because the client was a repeat offender. Thus, the court suspended the lawyer for 45 days. Do you agree? Does Rule 3.3(a)(3) support the court's analysis of the lawyer's duties?

5. Do different rules of candor apply to a lawyer's application for a temporary restraining order? Why do the Model Rules draw this distinction?

a. Assume that your recently discovered witness has evidence adverse to your position at the ex parte hearing on your application for a TRO. Must you ask the witness the questions that will put the disadvantageous testimony to the court?

b. Take a look at Model Rule 3.3(d). Why do the Rules create this distinct obligation for ex parte matters? Does Comment [14] to Model Rule 3.3 answer the question to your satisfaction?

c. What should qualify as an ex parte matter for purpose of applying Rule 3.3(d)? Should a prosecutor's appearance before a grand jury be subject to its requirements, for example? You can imagine that prosecutors and defense counsel differ as to the degree of candor a prosecutor should be required to express to a grand jury. At the moment, prevailing thought is that grand jury processes are *sui generis* and that Rule 3.3(d) does *not* apply to them. Do you agree with that the wisdom of that conclusion?

C. CANDOR ABOUT INCOMPLETE OR INACCURATE DISCOVERY RESPONSES

1. What should a lawyer do if, as in this Problem, she discovers that the client or a material witness has given false testimony in a deposition?

a. Look at Rule 3.3(a)(1), Rule 3.3(a)(3) and Rule 3.3(b)? Must a lawyer reveal the truth if doing so will injure the client? ABA Formal Opinion 93–376 (Aug. 6, 1993) made clear that a lie in response to a deposition question or a discovery request is "perjury" and the requirement of current Model Rule 3.3(a)(3) controls. As provided in Comment [1] to Model Rule 3.3, the lawyer has an obligation to correct the record in spite of the usual operation of Model Rule 1.6.

b. Nissenson v. Bradley, 738 N.E.2d 586 (Ill.Ct.App.2000), was a medical malpractice case in which the plaintiff replaced his first lawyer with another. The complaint attached what purported to be a medical certification that the doctor's conduct violated the standard of care, but when the second lawyer contacted the doctor, he learned that the doctor had never written it and also disagreed with its conclusions. Nevertheless, the second lawyer did not withdraw the report and continued to try to settle the case. The trial court found that the lawyer's failure to withdraw the "at minimum inaccurate" report after learning of its inaccuracy constituted contempt of court and the appellate court affirmed. Even though he did not file the false report initially, a lawyer has a continuing duty to correct inaccurate material information that his side has brought forth.

c. In re Case of Feld, 737 A.2d 656 (N.H.1999), involved dishonest testimony in a civil suit. The court found that, in a hotly contested matter, the lawyer heard his client testify at his deposition to facts the lawyer knew were not true. Indeed, the lawyer interrupted after certain questions and said his client did not have the information, a fact he also knew was untrue. The lawyer argued that, in the heat of battle, both sides probably violated the rules. The court did not accept that as a defense, found that the lawyer violated Rule 3.4, but limited his sanction to public censure. Is the ethics rule any different if the witness offers surprise testimony at a deposition in the lawyer's office rather than testimony in open court before the judge and jury? See Model Rule 3.3, Comment [1].

d. Jones v. Clinton, 36 F.Supp.2d 1118 (E.D.Ark.1999), confirms the client's duty not to dissemble in a deposition. Judge Wright held President Clinton in contempt for providing misleading answers in his deposition in the Paula Jones case. Judge Wright noted she had ruled that Ms. Jones, in discovery, was entitled to "information regarding any individuals with whom the President had sexual relations and who were during the relevant time frame state or federal employees." In spite of those rulings, Judge Wright found that "the President responded to plaintiff's questions by giving false, misleading and evasive answers that were designed to obstruct the judicial process." The two answers that Judge Wright found no reasonable person could believe were truthful were whether the President had ever been alone with Monica Lewinsky and whether he had ever had sexual relations with her. Judge Wright also referred the matter to the Arkansas bar for possible disciplinary action because President Clinton, the deponent, was also a lawyer. The bar later imposed discipline.[3]

In the *Jones* case, the President's counsel, Robert Bennett, later notified Judge Wright that he had, unknowingly, submitted false evidence during the course of the President's deposition. The judge noted, 36 F.Supp.2d at 1130 n. 15:

> "Indeed, even though the President's testimony at his civil deposition was entirely consistent with Ms. Lewinsky's affidavit denying 'sexual relations' between herself and the President, *the President's attorney later notified this Court pursuant to his professional responsibility* that portions of Ms. Lewinsky's affidavit were reported to be 'misleading and not true' and that this Court should not rely on Ms. Lewinsky's affidavit or remarks of counsel characterizing that affidavit. See Letter of September 30, 1998. *The President's testimony* at his deposition that Ms. Lewinsky's denial in her affidavit of a 'sexual relationship' between them was 'abso-

---

3. Neal v. Clinton, No. CIV 2000–5677 (Pulaski Cty, AR, Cir.Ct.2001), is the case imposing a negotiated sanction of a five year suspension and a $25,000 fine on President Clinton. The "Agreed Order of Discipline" and related documents can be found at: http://www.oicray.com/, under "News: January 19, 2001."

lutely true' *likewise was 'misleading and not true.'*" (emphasis added).

2. Should the courts impose the same standards on compliance with discovery requests?

a. Should stonewalling by a plaintiff in the face of defendant's discovery requests justify dismissal of the case? It did in Penthouse International, Limited v. Playboy Enterprises, Inc., 86 F.R.D. 396, 406–07 (S.D.N.Y.1980), affirmed 663 F.2d 371 (2d Cir.1981). On appeal the Second Circuit noted: "Penthouse deliberately disobeyed Judge Griesa's March 22, 1978, order to produce in full all of its financial statements for the relevant periods relating to gross income, net income and circulation revenue, including its balance sheets, and profit and loss statements, as had been requested by Playboy's Rule 34 demand * * *. The fact that the March 22 order was oral rather than written, and that it was not entered pursuant to a formal written Rule 37(a) motion, does not deprive it of any of its binding force and effect."

b. Pumphrey v. K.W. Thompson Tool Co., 62 F.3d 1128 (9th Cir. 1995), cert. denied 516 U.S. 1158, 116 S.Ct. 1042, 134 L.Ed.2d 189 (1996), was a wrongful death case. When the decedent dropped a handgun and it went off, he was killed. The defendant gun manufacturer introduced videotaped evidence in which guns dropped from various heights and in various ways did not fire. However, the court later learned that the defendant had not produced in discovery a video showing times the gun *did* fire. That failure was held to be a fraud upon the court, and it set aside the verdict.

c. In re E.I. DuPont De Nemours & Co. (Benlate Litigation), 99 F.3d 363 (11th Cir.1996), cert. denied sub nom., E.I. du Pont de Nemours & Co. v. Bush Ranch, Inc., 522 U.S. 906, 118 S.Ct. 263, 139 L.Ed.2d 190 (1997), involved a situation where the court found that a corporation did not disclose important raw test data about its herbicide product prior to a lengthy trial. The plaintiffs only learned about the data over 18 months later, when another case revealed its existence. Plaintiffs persuaded the judge in the first case to impose a sanction of $6.8 million representing plaintiffs' cost of trial preparation, plus an equal amount to represent wasted time of the Court, plus $101 million in sanctions for other trial misconduct. The Eleventh Circuit reversed the order, finding the sanctions "punitive" rather than civil in nature. The conduct was wrongful but the defendant was entitled to a new hearing with process appropriate for imposition of a criminal sanction.

d. In Shepherd v. American Broadcasting Companies, 62 F.3d 1469 (D.C.Cir.1995), two graphic artists sued ABC for race and sex discrimination. During discovery, they alleged that ABC had altered a document describing a meeting plaintiffs had attended. ABC denied the charge, but the District Court credited the plaintiffs and entered a default judgment against ABC. The D.C.Circuit agreed that courts have inherent power to punish discovery abuse but said that the punishment must be tailored to the crime. The law favors resolution of cases on the merits, the Court said, so discovery abuse must be shown by "clear and convincing evidence," not just a preponderance of the evidence, and in this case the proof was insufficient. See also, Washington State Physicians Ins. Exch. & Association v. Fisons Corp., 858 P.2d 1054 (Wash.1993).[4]

3. Should courts be advised to direct sanctions at counsel rather than punish the client when the counsel is the cause of the failure to turn over evidence?

a. In Litton Systems, Inc. v. AT & T, 700 F.2d 785 (2d Cir.1983), the court upheld the jury verdict for Litton but also upheld the trial court's finding that Litton's attorneys had engaged in a "pattern of intentional concealment of evidence" relating to certain documents. Thus, the Second Circuit upheld the trial court's decision to deny Litton recovery of all costs and attorneys' fees to which it would otherwise be entitled. These fees had been expected to run "well into the eight figure range." Litton Systems, Inc. v. AT & T, 91 F.R.D. 574, 578 (S.D.N.Y.1981).

b. In The Florida Bar v. Burkich–Burrell, 659 So.2d 1082 (Fla.1995), the lawyer represented her husband, the plaintiff, in a suit for personal injuries suffered in an auto accident. One of the interrogatories asked if the plaintiff had been injured before, and if so, for the names of doctors who had treated him. He had been previously injured but did not disclose any the requested information. The lawyer tried to blame the omission on a paralegal working in her office, but the Court didn't buy it. The court suspended the lawyer for 30 days.

c. In Cleveland Hair Clinic, Inc. v. Puig, 200 F.3d 1063 (7th Cir.2000), the plaintiff wanted to get out of the federal court and file in state court instead. The defendant wanted to stay in federal court, so the plaintiff's plan was to make it appear that another lawyer had filed a different case in the state system. The lawyer told the federal judge that he was not involved in the state matter, when in fact he had worked closely with the other lawyer. Ultimately, the trial judge imposed sanctions and attorney's fees exceeding $250,000! The Court of Appeals said that the high amount "strikes us as a bit much" but refused to set it aside as an abuse of discretion.

4. Should similar litigation sanctions be imposed on government lawyers who are working for the public interest?

a. Do you believe government lawyers, who often make salaries far below those paid to private counsel, should be at risk of personal liability for litigation sanctions? Might it be relevant that there is authority holding that making the government itself liable for sanctions would violate principles of sovereign immunity? E.g., United States v. Horn, 29 F.3d 754 (1st Cir.1994). Thus, if anyone on the government side may be sanctioned, it will likely be the lawyer.

---

4. The *Fisons* case is discussed in Taylor, Sleazy in Seattle, The American Lawyer, April 1994, p. 5 (describing the trial court's failure to impose sanctions on a firm that withheld a "smoking gun" document in spite of its representation that it had produced all relevant documents).

b. In Chilcutt v. United States, 4 F.3d 1313 (5th Cir.1993), cert. denied sub nom. Means v. Wortham, 513 U.S. 979, 115 S.Ct. 460, 130 L.Ed.2d 367 (1994), discovery abuse indeed resulted in imposition of sanctions on government counsel. The lawyer argued that it was a violation of separation of powers for a federal judge to discipline an executive branch official, but the Court held that the Federal Rules of Civil Procedure override Justice Department regulations governing lawyers. The District Court could even bar the government from reimbursing the lawyer for a sanction imposed upon the lawyer personally.

c. United States v. Shaffer Equip. Co., 158 F.R.D. 80 (S.D.W.Va. 1994), also imposed discovery sanctions on government lawyers personally. The Court ordered the lawyers to pay a total of $4500 into the E.P.A. Superfund for trying to cover up their expert witness' misrepresentation of his credentials.

D.   CANDOR AS TO FACTUAL MATTERS THAT ARE NOT EASILY VERIFIABLE

1.   Is the third item not disclosed to the court in this Problem—the prior criminal record of your client—a factual matter or a legal matter, i.e., is it more analogous to the situation in Part A or Part B of the Problem?

a. Is it the duty of defense counsel to correct the court clerk who mistakenly informed the judge that the client had no previous record? In ABA Formal Opinion 287 (June 27, 1953), the Ethics Committee ruling on this question split three ways. The Committee included Henry S. Drinker, later author of *Legal Ethics*, and William B. Jones, later a district judge in the District of Columbia. The majority concluded:

> "If the court asks the lawyer whether the clerk's statement is correct, the lawyer is not bound by fidelity to the client to tell the court what he knows to be an untruth, and should ask the court to excuse him from answering the question, and retire from the case, though this would doubtless put the court on further inquiry as to the truth.

> "Even, however, if the court does not directly ask the lawyer this question, such an inquiry may well be implied from the circumstances, including the lawyer's previous relations with the court. The situation is analogous to that discussed in our Opinion 280 where counsel knows of an essential decision not cited by his opponent and where his silence might reasonably be regarded by the Court as an implied representation by him that he knew of no such authority. If, under all the circumstances, the lawyer believes that the court relies on him as corroborating the correctness of the statement by the clerk or by the client that the client has no criminal record, the lawyer's duty of candor and fairness to the court requires him, in our opinion, to advise the court not to rely on counsel's personal knowledge as to the facts of the client's record. * * * The indignation of the court * * * on learning that

the lawyer had deliberately permitted him, where no privileged communication is involved, to rely on what the lawyer knew to be a misapprehension of the true facts, would be something that the lawyer could not appease on the basis of loyalty to the client. No client may demand or expect of his lawyer, in the furtherance of his cause, disloyalty to the law whose minister he is (Canon 32) or 'any manner of fraud or chicane' (Canon 15).

"If the lawyer is quite clear that the court does not rely on him as corroborating, by his silence, the statement of the clerk or of his client, the lawyer is not, in our opinion, bound to speak out."

The dissenting opinion argued that the lawyer may in no event "stand idly by in open court and permit the court to be deceived at a time when the lawyer knows that the court is relying upon an untrue statement."[5]

b. The ABA Committee on Ethics and Professional Responsibility again revisited this issue after adoption of the Model Rules and concluded that, on the assumption that the client has engaged in no fraud or perjury, the ABA Committee "could offer no better guidance under the Model Rules" than that offered by the authors of Formal Opinion 287. ABA Formal Opinion 87–353 (Apr. 20, 1987). California Formal Opinion 1986–87 is to the same effect.

c. Do you agree with this analysis? Is the proposed course of conduct workable? If the judge turns to you and asks, "Anything to add, counsel?" what do you say? Do you just hem and haw?

2. Does it help in figuring out what to say about the criminal record to analyze the distinction drawn between candor regarding adverse law and nondisclosure of adverse facts?

a. Is the distinction best grounded in the law of what constitutes confidential client information? That is, while one may correctly view disclosure of contrary legal authority as detrimental to the client, is it properly thought of as the client's confidential information? On the other hand, is all "information relating to the representation" properly viewed as confidential? But cf., Comment [8] to Model Rule 1.9 (information that is "generally known" may be used in a later case on behalf of another client).

b. ABA Formal Opinion 93–370 (Feb. 5, 1993) addressed whether a court should be able to ask a lawyer to be candid about the limits of the lawyer's settlement authority. The Opinion recognized that settlement discussions are an important part of modern trial management but concluded that a lawyer should not tell a judge the extent of settlement authority the client has given. Further, because such authority would be a material fact about which the lawyer could not lie if asked, a judge should not inquire into the authority.

5. ABA Formal Opinion 287 also considered what the lawyer should do if the lawyer knows that the client will lie about his or her previous record, or the lawyer discovers later that the client had lied. These issues are considered in Problem 27, *infra*.

Is asking about the client's criminal record the same as asking the lawyer's settlement authority? If asked either question, should a lawyer tell the judge, "Don't ask me about that?" Or, "I am not permitted to answer that question?" Is there any way at all to deflect a judge's question gracefully?

c.   ABA Formal Opinion 98–412 (Sept. 9, 1998) dealt with the obligation of a lawyer who learns that his client has violated a court order prohibiting the transfer of assets. The Opinion says that the lawyer must disclose the fact to the Court (1) if necessary to avoid or correct a misrepresentation made by the lawyer to the Court, or (2) to avoid assisting the client in a fraud upon the Court. If the lawyer has made misstatements to the court, the correction is required by Rule 3.3(a)(1). If the client made the misstatement, what is now Rule 3.3(a)(3) requires the correction. If no misrepresentation has been made, the Opinion says, the lawyer is not required to report a violation of a court order if the violation is unlikely to have a material effect on the resolution of the case. However, if failure to report the violation would imply that all was well, a lawyer must correct that misapprehension.[6]

Are the governing principles all becoming clear to you? How, for example, is the lawyer supposed to know if failure to report the violation implies that all is well?

d.   In any event, lawyers should be aware that resolving these issues in a way the court thinks was improper can result in significant sanctions for a lawyer.

In re Cardwell, 50 P.3d 897 (Colo.2002), involved violations of state rules corresponding to Model Rule 3.3(a)(1)(3), and also Rule 1.2(d), Rule 4.1(b) & Rule 8.4(c). In this case, the attorney misrepresented to the court in a prosecution for driving under the influence (DUI) that his client had no previous alcohol driving offenses. The lawyer's misrepresentation resulted in the trial court accepting a plea agreement, finding the client guilty of a reduced offense of "driving while ability impaired," and imposing a suspended sentence that was not legal for a second-time offender. For his efforts, the lawyer received a three-year suspension with 18 months stayed.

PROBLEM 26

HANDLING PHYSICAL EVIDENCE

Information "relating to the representation" comes in a variety of forms. The lawyer is required by Model Rule 1.6(a) to hold most of it in

----

6. The Opinion also says that if the client discharges the lawyer before the client misconduct, but the lawyer knows that the misconduct is planned, the lawyer has neither the duty nor the right to disclose those plans, even to successor counsel, without the client's consent. Is that advice consistent with Model Rule 3.3(b)?

confidence. Yet some kinds of confidential material *may* be disclosed, while others are the subject of required disclosure. In this Problem, we first examine the name of the client, normally something a lawyer discloses to anyone with whom the lawyer deals. Next, we look at physical evidence of a crime that has come into the lawyer's possession. Then, we ask whether there is a difference between concealing information and simply not disclosing it. Finally, we consider how a lawyer may advise a client on whether and when it may or should destroy documents or other potential evidence of its conduct.

FACTS

Neil Hammer, a person whom you have never advised before, has come into your office, set a gun and a bag of money on your desk, and said, "I have just used this gun to rob a bank, and I killed a guard in the process. Help me; I don't want to get caught. What should I do?"

Only yesterday, J.B. Wallace, president of the Wallace Corporation, came into your office. The Wall Street Journal had reported that the Justice Department is investigating a firm in Wallace's industry for possible price-fixing. A Wall Street Journal reporter had asked for an interview with Mr. Wallace about industry pricing practices and Mr. Wallace asked you to help him prepare for the interview. He told you that in order to help you evaluate any allegation involving him and price-fixing, you could listen to the secret tape recordings of all discussions in his office for the last three years. He keeps these tapes at his home and plans to use them to help write his memoirs. You have learned that the Department is about to file a criminal antitrust action against the corporation and perhaps Mr. Wallace personally.

The local police have contacted you about reports that a man with a gun was seen entering your office. You are thinking about how to respond.

 QUESTIONS

A. CONFIDENTIALITY OF A CLIENT'S IDENTITY

1. What will you say when the police ask you who came to your office at the time a witness saw Hammer enter? Are the names of your clients confidential? How about the names of your prospective clients?

a. Client identity is not normally confidential. After all, if lawyers did not tell courts and other lawyers whom they represented, the lawyers could get little done for those clients. Hence, the traditional rule is that no privilege attaches either to the fact that someone has consulted a lawyer or to the general subject of the representation. The general evidentiary rule is that the identity of the client, the amount of the fee, the identification of payment by case file name, and the general purpose of the work performed are usually not protected from disclosure by the attorney-client privilege, because such information ordinarily reveals no confidential professional communications between attorney and client.

On the other hand, what if there are situations in which the fact one had consulted a lawyer is itself be incriminating or embarrassing? Suppose you are a divorce lawyer. During an Internal Revenue Service audit of your tax records, the investigator discovers a $25,000 cash deposit that you made into your client trust account marked "retainer." The client has not yet told his wife he is considering a divorce. If the investigator asks you whose money it is, may you reply without asking the client's permission to do so?

b.   Baird v. Koerner, 279 F.2d 623 (9th Cir.1960), is the leading case on the attorney-client privilege and client identity. The client or clients consulted a lawyer for legal advice as to what to do about unpaid taxes. Paying the taxes stops the accrual of interest; also there are clients who would like to clear their consciences by paying the money owed, but do not want to confess to tax fraud. The lawyer, on behalf of these undisclosed clients, paid the additional income tax. The IRS wanted to know the clients identity, but the court concluded that the privilege protected their identity against disclosure.

If the unidentified client or clients in *Baird* had hired a non-lawyer to deliver the money to the IRS, would there be any evidentiary privilege protecting the non-lawyer from disclosing the identity of the principal? Why should the fact that the money was transmitted by a lawyer change that result?

c.   Restatement Third, The Law Governing Lawyers § 69, Comment *g*, concludes that the privileged character of client identity, under the law of evidence, cannot be described categorically but should be determined based on the extent to which the testimony or other information sought would, "directly or by reasonable inference, reveal the *content* of a privileged communication" (emphasis added). The evidentiary privilege, the Restatement continues, does not protect clients or lawyers "against revealing a lawyer's knowledge about a client solely on the grounds that doing so would incriminate the client or otherwise prejudice the client's interests."

d.   In a criminal setting, some cases have called the *Baird* rule the "last link" doctrine: if the fact of consultation would itself be sufficient to tie the client to a crime, the lawyer should not have to disclose the client's identity. See, e.g., In re Grand Jury Proceedings 88–9, Cherney, 899 F.2d 1039, 1043 (11th Cir.1990):

> "the 'last link' doctrine is only applicable to rare situations 'where the disclosure of fee information would give the identity of a previously undisclosed client/suspect.' In essence, the last link doctrine extends the protection of the attorney-client privilege to nonprivileged information—the identity of the client—when 'disclosure of that identity would disclose *other*, privileged communications (e.g., motive or strategy) and when the incriminating nature of the privileged communications has

created in the client a reasonable expectation that the information would be kept confidential.' "

2.   Would you have ruled the client identity privileged in the following cases?

a.   Baltes v. Doe I, 57 U.S.L.W. 2268 (Fla.Cir.Ct. 1988) (No. CL–88–1145–AD), was a celebrated case in which a client told a lawyer that he had been the driver in a highly-publicized hit-and-run accident. Without disclosing the client's identity, the lawyer tried to plea bargain on his behalf. The victim's survivors filed a civil action against the unknown driver and tried to compel the lawyer to disclose his identity. The trial court held that, under these circumstances, the client's identity was privileged. The client ultimately turned himself in before a higher court heard the appeal.

b.   Dietz v. Doe, 935 P.2d 611 (Wash.1997), is another example of the *Baltes* issue. A hit-and-run accident killed a man, and later attorney Ritchie acknowledged in the newspaper that he represented that unknown man. When the deceased's family sought the client's name, however, Ritchie refused to reveal it. The court held that, while the identity of a client may be privileged in some cases, the fact of an attorney-client relationship between Ritchie and the driver may not be presumed. Nor may the court presume that the driver sought Ritchie's legal advice (as opposed to simply making a phone call on his behalf to get information), or that the client has not waived the privilege. On remand, the trial judge must inquire about all three issues.

c.   Matter of Nackson, 555 A.2d 1101 (N.J.1989), considered whether an attorney may refuse to disclose the whereabouts of a client who jumped bail and consulted the lawyer about a fugitive warrant for his arrest. The client wanted to return to the jurisdiction only if his lawyer could work out a plea agreement in advance. Citing *Baltes*, the court held that the privilege can protect against disclosure of client whereabouts; it offered as an example, matrimonial cases where the attorney need not disclose the whereabouts of a wife who feared injury from her husband. The privilege is not absolute, the court said, but prosecutors must first use all other reasonable ways of learning the defendant's whereabouts. Even then, before ordering disclosure, the lower court must "balance" the need to know against the client's right to confidentiality. However, the court did not calibrate the scales and tell us how to weigh the competing interests. The court made no reference to the last link doctrine.

Should the court have simply denied the applicability of the evidentiary privilege on the grounds that the purpose of keeping the client's whereabouts secret was to assist the client to avoid lawful process in a proceeding pending at the time the lawyer gave his advice? See In re Doe, 456 N.Y.S.2d 312 (1982) (bail-jumper's counsel required to reveal his client's whereabouts to a grand jury).

d.   In re Grand Jury Subpoena, 204 F.3d 516 (4th Cir.2000), was an effort to get a lawyer to reveal his client's identity. The government filed a petition of forfeiture of property used as an open air drug market. The property was titled in the name "Daniel C. Quispehuman," a name likely to be a straw owner. The lawyer said that he would be representing the owner of the property whom he said was not Quispehuman, but he refused to reveal the client's real name because, he argued, its disclosure would reveal the client's confidential communication—his motive or purpose for seeking legal advice. The court agreed that a lawyer sometimes may avoid identifying a client who has not sought to get involved in a matter, but once the client authorized the attorney to disclose the client's motives or purposes in retaining the attorney (to deal with the allegations regarding drug-trafficking on his property), those motives or purposes were no longer confidential, and thus the client's identity was not within the attorney-client evidentiary privilege based on a theory that disclosure would reveal those motives or purposes. The court specifically rejected the "last link" doctrine as giving too much protection to clients.

3. Must you appeal a court order making you reveal your client's identity?

No.

a.   Suppose you refuse to disclose the client's identity to the investigator. The IRS, in turn, asserts a claim against you for back taxes on the $25,000, asserting that it is unreported income. Are you still obliged not to disclose the name of the client? Look at Model Rule 1.6(b)(5).[1]

b.   Suppose, in order to test a lower court order, you must appeal it. Must you go to jail before revealing the client's identity? Does Model Rule 1.6(b)(6) adopt the position of two judges in People v. Kor, 277 P.2d 94 (Cal.Ct.App.1954), who stated that the attorney, rather than having testified, "should have chosen to go to jail and take his chances of release by a higher court"? 277 P.2d at 101. Is such self-sacrifice necessary or realistic?

c.   These cases deal with the evidentiary privilege. The requirement of Model Rule 1.6 applies to more types of information. Assume that the court orders you to tell the grand jury the name of the client who owns property in your trust account that is arguably subject to forfeiture because it was used for drug trafficking. You leave the grand jury room and a reporter asks you, "Did you disclose the name of your client?" You respond that you obeyed the court order. The reporter then says, "What is the name?" Can you answer that question, knowing that the evidentiary privilege was held not to apply to the information?

B.   TAKING POSSESSION OF PHYSICAL EVIDENCE FOR TESTING OR SAFEKEEPING

1. May you take Hammer's gun for safekeeping? Is the gun privileged against discovery if Hammer turns it over to you?

1.   26 U.S.C.A. § 6050I, adopted as part of the war on drugs, requires cash transactions in excess of $10,000 to be reported to the Internal Revenue Service on its Form 8300. On its face, the requirement applies to everyone, but lawyers have argued that transactions with them should be exempt from the requirement. So far, the I.R.S. considers lawyers subject to the law, but criminal defense lawyers complain that reporting will render Baird v. Koerner a nullity. This issue is discussed further in Problem 29, *infra*.

a. The leading case on that issue is In re Richard R. Ryder, 263 F.Supp. 360 (E.D.Va.) (per curiam), aff'd per curiam 381 F.2d 713 (4th Cir.1967) (per curiam). The issue before the district court was whether to remove Richard R. Ryder, a former assistant U.S. Attorney, from practice before that court.

"On August 24, 1966 a man armed with a sawed-off shotgun robbed the Varina Branch of the Bank of Virginia of $7,583. Included in the currency taken were $10 bills known as 'bait money,' the serial numbers of which had been recorded.

"On August 26, 1966, [after a bank robbery], Charles Richard Cook rented safety deposit box 14 at a branch of the Richmond National Bank. Later in the day Cook was interviewed at his home by agents of the Federal Bureau of Investigation, who obtained $348 from him. Cook telephoned Ryder, who had represented him in civil litigation. * * *

"Later that afternoon Ryder telephoned one of the agents and asked whether any of the bills obtained from Cook had been identified as a part of the money taken in the bank robbery. The agent told him that some bills had been identified. * * *

"The next morning, * * * Ryder conferred with Cook again. He urged Cook to tell the truth, and Cook answered that a man, whose name he would not divulge, offered him $500 on the day of the robbery to put a package in a bank lockbox. Ryder did not believe this story. Ryder told Cook that if the government could trace the money in the box to him, it would be almost conclusive evidence of his guilt. He knew that Cook was under surveillance and he suspected that Cook might try to dispose of the money.

"That afternoon Ryder telephoned a former officer of the Richmond Bar Association to discuss his course of action. * * *

"The lawyers discussed and rejected alternatives, including having a third party get the money. At the conclusion of the conversation Ryder was advised 'Don't do it surreptitiously and do be sure that you let your client know that it is going back to the rightful owners.' * * *

"Ryder did not follow the advice he had received on Saturday. He did not let his client know the money was going back to the rightful owners. He testified about his omission:

'I prepared [the power of attorney] myself and told Mr. Cook to sign it. In the power of attorney, I did not specifically say that Mr. Cook authorized me to deliver that money to the appropriate authorities at any time because for a number of reasons. One, in representing a man under these circumstances, you've got to keep the man's confidence, but I also put in that power of attorney that Mr. Cook authorized me to dispose of that money as I saw fit, and the reason for that being that I was going to turn the money over to the proper authorities at whatever time I deemed that it wouldn't hurt Mr. Cook.'

"Ryder took the power of attorney which Cook had signed to the Richmond National Bank. He rented box 13 in his name with his office address, presented the power of attorney, entered Cook's box, took both boxes into a booth, where he found a bag of money and a sawed-off shotgun in Cook's box. * * * He transferred the contents of Cook's box to his own and returned the boxes to the vault. He left the bank, and neither he nor Cook returned. * * * Within a half-hour after he left the bank, he talked to a retired judge and distinguished professor of law. * * * Ryder testified that he told about the shotgun. The judge also testified that Ryder certainly would not have been under the impression that he—the judge—thought that [Ryder] was guilty of unethical conduct. That same day Ryder talked with other prominent persons [and] was advised that a lawyer could not receive the property and if he had received it he could not retain possession of it. * * *

"On September 12, 1966, F.B.I. agents procured search warrants for Cook's and Ryder's safety deposit boxes in the Richmond National Bank. They found Cook's box empty. In Ryder's box they discovered $5,920 of the $7,583 taken in the bank robbery and the sawed-off shotgun used in the robbery. * * *

"We reject the argument that Ryder's conduct was no more than the exercise of the attorney-client privilege. * * *

"It was Ryder, not his client, who took the initiative in transferring the incriminating possession of the stolen money and the shotgun from Cook. Ryder's conduct went far beyond the receipt and retention of a confidential communication from his client. * * *

"The money in Cook's box belonged to the Bank of Virginia. The law did not authorize Cook to conceal this money or withhold it from the bank. His larceny was a continuing offense. Cook had no title or property interest in the money that he lawfully could pass to Ryder. * * * No canon of ethics or law permitted to Ryder to conceal from the Bank of Virginia its money to gain his client's acquittal.

"Cook's possession of the sawed-off shotgun was illegal. Ryder could not lawfully receive the gun from Cook to assist Cook to avoid conviction of robbery. Cook had never mentioned the shotgun to Ryder. When Ryder discovered it in Cook's box, he took possession of it to hinder the government in the prosecution of its case, and he intended not to reveal it pending trial unless the government discovered it and a court compelled its production. No statute or canon of ethics authorized Ryder to take possession of the gun for this purpose. * * *

"Ryder's action is not justified because he thought he was acting in the best interests of his client. To allow the individual lawyer's belief to determine the standards of professional conduct will in time reduce the ethics of the profession to the practices of the most unscrupulous. Moreover, Ryder knew that the law against concealing stolen property and the law forbidding receipt and possession of a sawed-off shotgun contain no exemptions for a lawyer who takes possession with the intent of protecting a criminal from the consequences of his crime. * * *

"[However,] Ryder intended to return the bank's money after his client was tried. He consulted reputable persons before and after he placed the property in his lockbox, although he did not precisely follow their advice. Were it not for these facts, we would deem proper his permanent exclusion from practice before this court. In view of the mitigating circumstances, he will be suspended from practice in this court for eighteen months * * * ."

The Fourth Circuit affirmed and called the suspension "lenient in the circumstances." It then "suspend[ed] Ryder from practice before * * * [the Court of Appeals] for the duration of his suspension from the District Court."

Are you equally incensed by Mr. Ryder's conduct? What is it about his behavior that most troubles you?

b. Compare State v. Olwell, 394 P.2d 681 (Wash.1964). Olwell was a lawyer who refused to honor a coroner's subpoena for the knife allegedly used by his client in a murder. He asserted both the attorney-client privilege and the client's privilege against self-incrimination. He was found in contempt and appealed. The court held:

"The attorney should not be a depository for criminal evidence (such as a knife, other weapons, stolen property, etc.), which in itself has little, if any material value for the purposes of aiding counsel in the preparation of the defense of his client's case. Such evidence given the attorney during legal consultation for information purposes and used by the attorney in preparing the defense of his client's case, whether or not the case ever goes to trial, could clearly be withheld for a reasonable period of time. It follows that the attorney, after a reasonable period of time, should, as an officer of the court, on his own motion turn the same over to the prosecution.

" * * * [T]he state [in order to protect the attorney-client privilege], when attempting to introduce such evidence at the trial, should take extreme precautions to make certain that the source of the evidence is not disclosed in the presence of the jury and prejudicial error is not committed." 394 P.2d at 684–85.

The court also found the self-incrimination privilege inapplicable because it must be asserted by the client alone. Is the decision consistent with *Ryder*? Does the procedure suggested by the court protect all the relevant interests?

2. May you take bag of money for safekeeping? What if you are concerned that the would spend it instead of returning it to its rightful owners?

a. The money belongs to the bank while the gun presumably belongs to Hammer. In *Ryder*, the court noted that Ryder "knew that Cook was under surveillance and he suspected that Cook might try to dispose of the money." Does that make Ryder's holding on to the money less reprehensible, or more?

b. Consider In re January 1976 Grand Jury, 534 F.2d 719 (7th Cir.1976). The attorney refused to comply with a grand jury's subpoena duces tecum to turn over moneys received by him from clients suspected of bank robbery. The Court of Appeals affirmed the contempt order, and Judge Tone, joined by Judge Bauer, argued:

"We must assume for purposes of this appeal that shortly after robbing a savings and loan association, the robbers delivered money stolen in the robbery to appellant. If that occurred, the money was delivered either for safekeeping, with or without appellant's knowledge that it was stolen, or as an attorney's fee.

"If it was the latter, the robbers voluntarily relinquished the money and with it any arguable claim that might have arisen from their possession or constructive possession. As Judge Pell points out, the payment of a fee is not a privileged communication. The money itself is non-testimonial and no plausible argument is left for resisting the subpoena.

"If the money was not given as a fee but for safekeeping, the delivery of the money was an act in furtherance of the crime, regardless of whether appellant knew it was stolen. The delivery of the money was not assertive conduct and therefore was not a privileged communication, and, as we just observed, the money itself is non-testimonial. The attorney is simply a witness to a criminal act. The fact that he is also a participant in the act, presumably without knowledge of its criminal quality, is irrelevant since he is not asserting his own privilege against self incrimination. There is no authority or reason, based on any constitutional provision or the attorney-client privilege, for shielding from judicial inquiry either the fruits of the robbery or the fact of the later criminal act of turning over the money to appellant. Accordingly, it is immaterial that in responding to the subpoena appellant will be making an assertion about who turned over the money and when.

"Finally, the proceedings have not yet reached the point at which we must decide whether, when the robbers have chosen to make appellant a witness to their crime, they may invoke the Sixth Amendment [right to effective assistance of counsel] to bar his eyewitness testimony at trial, although, for me, to ask that question is almost to answer it." 534 F.2d at 730–31 (concurring opinion).

3. What principles can you derive from these cases? Is a client's statement to the lawyer linking the gun to the crime a privileged communication?

a.   Morrell v. State, 575 P.2d 1200 (Alaska 1978), upheld the decision of the trial court to admit incriminating evidence of a kidnaping plan that the defendant had allegedly written. A friend of the defendant turned over the plan to defense counsel, who then aided the friend in turning the evidence over to the police. Defense counsel then withdrew from the case. After examining the cases discussed in the text the Alaska supreme court held, at 575 P.2d at 1210–12:

> "From the foregoing cases emerges the rule that a criminal defense attorney must turn over to the prosecution real evidence that the attorney obtains from his client. Further, if the evidence is obtained from a non-client third party who is not acting for the client, then the privilege to refuse to testify concerning the manner in which the evidence was obtained is inapplicable. * * *

> "We believe that [defense counsel] would have been obligated to see that the evidence reached the prosecutor in this case even if he had obtained the evidence from Morrell. His obligation was even clearer because he acquired the evidence from [a third party], who made the decision to turn the evidence over to [defense counsel] without consulting Morrell and therefore was not acting as Morrell's agent.

> "[Defense counsel] could have properly turned the evidence over to the police himself and would have been obliged to do so if [the third party] had refused to accept the return of the evidence.

> "[Finally, while] statutes which address the concealing of evidence are generally construed to require an affirmative act of concealment in addition to the failure to disclose information to the authorities, taking possession of evidence from a non-client third party and holding the evidence in a place not accessible to investigating authorities would seem to fall within the statute's ambit. Thus, we have concluded that Cline breached no ethical obligation to his client which may have rendered his legal services to Morrell ineffective."

Do the earlier cases in this Problem support the Court's conclusion?

b.   Consider the court's analysis in People v. Meredith, 631 P.2d 46 (Cal.1981). The defendant told his lawyer the location of the robbery-murder victim's wallet. The lawyer then had his investigator remove it. The court held that the client's disclosure was privileged and telling the investigator the location did not destroy the privilege. On the other hand, removing the wallet did destroy it. When defense counsel removes or alters evidence, he necessarily deprives the prosecution of the opportunity to observe that evidence in its original condition or location. The lawyer's decision to remove evidence is therefore tactical; if he leaves the evidence where he discovered it, his observations derived from privileged communications are insulated from revelation. If he removes the evidence to examine or test it, "the original location and condition of that evidence loses the protection of the privilege." 631 P.2d at 54.

c. *People v. Superior Court (Fairbank)*, 237 Cal.Rptr. 158 (Ct.App. 1987) held that, if a lawyer takes possession of stolen property, the lawyer must inform the court of the action. "The court, exercising care to shield privileged communications and defense strategies from prosecution view, must then take appropriate action to ensure that the prosecution has timely access to physical evidence possessed by the defense and timely information about alteration of any evidence." 237 Cal.Rptr. at 163. Nothing turns on whether the prosecution "needs" the evidence.[1]

d. Restatement Third, The Law Governing Lawyers, tries to sum up these cases in § 119, which says that with respect to physical evidence of a client crime, a lawyer

"(1) may, when reasonably necessary for purposes of the representation, take possession of the evidence and retain it for the time reasonably necessary to examine it and subject it to tests that do not alter or destroy material characteristics of the evidence; but

"(2) following possession under Subsection (1), the lawyer must notify prosecuting authorities of the lawyer's possession of the evidence or turn the evidence over to them."

Comment *a* to § 119 then provides that the rules on turning over physical evidence of client crime apply to "contraband, weapons, and similar implements used in an offense. It also includes such materials as documents and material in electronically retrievable form used by the client to plan the offense, documents used in the course of a mail-fraud violation, or transaction documents evidencing a crime."

e. See also, Comment [2] to ABA Model Rule 3.4 that also summarizes these principles. Do you agree that courts should sometimes require defense counsel to turn over evidence that will help convict their clients?

C. NONDISCLOSURE OF PHYSICAL EVIDENCE

1. Is failure to disclose facts different from affirmatively concealing them? Are there times a lawyer simply must keep quiet about information others would consider significant to them?

a. A news story that was highly publicized at the time it was reported said:

---

1. See also *Commonwealth v. Stenhach*, 514 A.2d 114 (Pa.Super.1986), leave to appeal denied 534 A.2d 769 (Pa.1987), where the court affirmed the rule that physical evidence of a crime in possession of criminal defense attorneys who acquired the evidence at client's direction was not subject to the attorney-client privilege, but reversed the criminal conviction of lawyers for failure to turn over physical evidence because, the court held, statutes prohibiting hindering prosecution and tampering with evidence were unconstitutionally vague or overbroad as applied to lawyers engaged in representation of criminal defendants.

The good faith of an attorney who advises his client to invoke the Fifth Amendment in response to a subpoena in a civil case protects the lawyer from being held in contempt. *Maness v. Meyers*, 419 U.S. 449, 468, 95 S.Ct. 584, 596, 42 L.Ed.2d 574, 589 (1975). Should the same principle apply here?

"An Onondaga County grand jury this afternoon [February 7, 1975] cleared a lawyer, Frank H. Armani, of criminal wrongdoing in failing to disclose that his client in a murder case had told him where he had hidden two bodies. * * *

"Mr. [Francois] Belge and Mr. Armani were lawyers for Robert Garrow, who was found guilty of murder after a trial in Hamilton County last summer.

"During the trial Mr. Belge revealed that he and Mr. Armani had discovered the two bodies after having been told of their whereabouts by Mr. Garrow, but that they did not tell authorities. * * *

"Mr. Armani's attorney, Elliot A. Taikoff of New York City, said later that his client had been 'very troubled' over his role in the matter and had received advice from a 'very high-ranking judge in this state.' He refused to name the judge, but said he had testified before the grand jury."[2]

Was the grand jury's decision consistent with that of the *Ryder* court? Were the situations analytically different?

b.   In considering the *Belge* case, N.Y. State Bar Committee on Professional Ethics Opinion No. 479 (Mar. 6, 1978), advised: "the lawyer was under an injunction not to disclose to the authorities his knowledge of the two prior murders, and was duty-bound not to reveal to the authorities the location of the bodies." The Opinion also concluded that the attorney acted properly by using the information, with his client's consent, in engaging in plea bargaining, and in destroying photographs the lawyer took of the bodies and records the lawyer made of his conversation with the client.

Do you agree that the restrictions on the lawyer were that great? Could Mr. Belge have told the police about the location of the bodies—so that they could receive a decent burial—by calling the police anonymously and not revealing either his name or the name of his client?

c.   In Clutchette v. Rushen, 770 F.2d 1469 (9th Cir.1985), cert. denied 475 U.S. 1088, 106 S.Ct. 1474, 89 L.Ed.2d 729 (1986), the Government accused the defendant of shooting a man in the defendant's car. The police were having a hard time proving their case until the defendant's wife voluntarily turned over some receipts to them. She had been acting as an investigator for her husband's defense lawyer, and the lawyer had sent her to Los Angeles to get (and arguably to destroy) the receipts that showed that her husband had arranged for the car to be reupholstered shortly after the murder. With the help of the receipts, the police found the former seat covers and matched the blood type to the victim's. The court held that the wife's surrender of the receipts was not a violation of the defendant's attorney-client privilege. If the attorney had not done anything to retrieve

2. New York Times, Feb. 8, 1975, p. 54, col. 5. See also, People v. Belge, 372 N.Y.S.2d 798, 803 (Co.Ct.1975) (indictment on same facts dismissed on "grounds of a privileged communication and in the interests of justice * * *").

the receipts, he would not have had to tell the police about them. Having taken the receipts into his possession, however, through the wife-investigator, they were fair game for police discovery. Further, because the police made no overt act to get the receipts, there was even less reason to find a deprivation of Sixth Amendment rights.

d.   In Wemark v. State, 602 N.W.2d 810 (Iowa 1999), the defendant told his lawyers that he had hidden the murder weapon, a knife

> "in a pile of automotive parts under the basement steps of the house, which law enforcement authorities failed to detect during their extensive search of the home. Defense counsel were immediately concerned they had an ethical obligation to disclose the location of the knife to the prosecution. They considered nondisclosure to be the same as concealment and an interference with police investigation. * * * [D]efense counsel concluded they had three options to pursue once Wemark informed them of the location of the knife. The first option was to wait for the State to search the house again and find the knife. Yet, defense counsel believed it was unlikely law enforcement would search the home a second time. The second option was to have Wemark inform Dr. Taylor of the location of the knife during the scheduled interview. Defense counsel knew Dr. Taylor would then notify the prosecutor. The third option was to engage the services of an attorney to relay the location of the knife to the prosecutor without disclosing the source of the information." 602 N.W.2d at 813.

What do you think of the lawyers' analysis of their options? Were they right that they faced an ethical dilemma? Is nondisclosure the "same as concealment"?

e.   The lawyers chose the second option. "They hoped Dr. Taylor might bolster the defense of diminished responsibility. Defense counsel informed Wemark of the ethical dilemma and the three options. They urged him to keep the appointment with Dr. Taylor and to disclose the location of the knife during the course of the examination." Id. They knew the doctor would then tell the prosecutor and the lawyers would not have to do so.

Would you have chosen the same alternative? Why or why not? In this opinion, the court said that the lawyers did not have an ethical dilemma after all. They could not "actively participate in hiding" the knife, but "if defense counsel leaves the evidence alone, the only matter possessed is the communication which remains insulated from disclosure by the attorney-client privilege." Id. at 817. Thus, the lawyers did not have to disclose the location of the weapon, but the client had effective assistance of counsel anyway because disclosure to the doctor was a "tactical choice," and any error was harmless because the evidence of guilt was overwhelming.

Are you convinced that the court analyzed the lawyers' obligations correctly?

2.   Suppose you, like Mr. Belge, have a client who claims that he killed several women and buried their bodies in a secluded

place. This time, however, when you check out his story, one of the victims is not yet dead. May you tell the police her location?

a. Look at ABA Model Rule 1.6(b)(1), a provision that was not in effect at the time of the *Belge* case. Do you agree with the disclosure authority given to you by that rule? Should you disguise your voice when you disclose the information about the victims to the police so they cannot connect you to your client?

b. Under the auspices of the Roscoe Pound–American Trial Lawyers Foundation, a special Commission prepared its own proposed ethics rules called The American Lawyer's Code of Conduct.[3] The Commission applied its proposed Code to this hypothetical as follows:

> [S]he is seriously injured and unable to help herself or to get help. The lawyer calls an ambulance for her, but takes care not to be personally identified. The lawyer has *committed a disciplinary violation* * * *.[4]

c. Do you agree that loyalty to the client requires this result? What logic would lead otherwise sensible lawyers to such a conclusion?

D. DESTROYING, OR FAILING TO RETAIN, PHYSICAL OR DOCUMENTARY EVIDENCE

1. What if Hammer's fingerprints were on the gun that he put on your desk? Could you advise him to wipe off the fingerprints?

a. Does Hammer's right not to incriminate himself allow him to wipe the gun clean? Would you, his lawyer, have a right to do it for him? Does even the privilege against self-incrimination give a client authority to try to cover up evidence of a crime?

b. If Hammer does not wipe off his fingerprints, should you tell him the consequences of leaving his prints there? Should you send the gun to the police with the fingerprints on it?

c. Cases have routinely held that a party may be charged with a "conspiracy to obstruct the due administration of justice in a proceeding which [is not pending but which] becomes pending in the future. * * * "[5] In general, it is an obstruction of justice "to stifle, suppress or destroy evidence knowing that it *may* be wanted in a judicial proceeding or is being sought by investigating officers. * * * "[6] How should that construction of the law affect the lawyer's ethical responsibilities in a case like this? See also Rule 3.4, Comment [2].

3. The proposal was intended to compete with the ABA Model Rules. It provides interesting contrast to the Model Rules on several issues, but no state has yet adopted it and it has not proved to be influential.

4. The American Lawyer's Code of Conduct, Illustrative Case 1(g) (Revised Draft, 1982) (emphasis added).

5. United States v. Perlstein, 126 F.2d 789, 796 (3d Cir.1942), cert. denied 316 U.S. 678, 62 S.Ct. 1106, 86 L.Ed. 1752 (1942); see also, e.g., In re Williams, 23 N.W.2d 4, 9 (Minn.1946) (per curiam).

6. Rollin M. Perkins, Criminal Law 499 (2d ed.1969) (emphasis added).

2.   Turning to your second client, Mr. Wallace, may you properly counsel him to destroy the incriminating tape recordings? Does it matter whether or not suit has already been filed?[7]

a.   No law compelled Wallace to make the tape recording. Will Wallace be obstructing justice if he destroys these tapes so that they are not later subpoenaed?

b.   Assume that the Justice Department is not yet involved but that Mr. Wallace is afraid the Wall Street Journal reporter may come across information that indicates the secret taping device has been set up in the office. May you advise the president to destroy the tapes, using as your reason the embarrassment that would be caused if his business associates knew he had secretly taped and retained tapes of private conversations?[8] Look at Rule 3.4(a) and Comment [2].

3.   After Mr. Wallace has told you of his taping system and you have listened to the relevant conversations, should you tell Mr. Wallace that the tapes are damaging and are likely to be subpoenaed by the government?

a.   May you tell Wallace this bad news if you privately expect him to destroy the incriminating material which has not yet been subpoenaed? Can you do anything about that? How does Model Rule 1.2(d) require you to act? How about Model Rule 3.4(a)?

b.   Could the attorney in *Belge*, supra, ethically have destroyed the photographs of the dead girls' bodies if his client had taken them? If the attorney had taken them? If they were subject to subpoena? Might they be protected by the work product immunity and not subject to disclosure in any event?

7.   There is an important question presented whether you represent the corporation as an entity, the president of the corporation, or both, and whether or not representing both the president and the corporation would be a conflict of interest. For now, assume that you just represent Wallace, because that is the focus of this question.

8.   Cf. Wall Street J., Apr. 7, 1975, at 7, col. 1–2 ("Official at ITT Unit Destroyed Letters After Journal Questioned Some Practices"):

"A retired official of International Telephone & Telegraph Corp. subsidiary disclosed in testimony before a Senate subcommittee that last summer, while he was still with the company, he destroyed certain letters in his file after the Wall Street Journal began questioning the unit's competitive practices.

" 'I was scared,' John James told the Senate subcommittee on Antitrust and Monopoly, which is investigating the effectiveness of voluntary industry standards. 'I have been associated with code and standard-making activities for many years, and this was the first time in all of that experience that I had anybody question the propriety of the way I conducted myself in connection with this type of work,' he said. *.* *

"After reviewing the testimony, an arm of the [American Society of Mechanical Engineers] came up with a conclusion that appears in the current issue of Mechanical Engineering. It commends Mr. James on this testimony and says the society's Professional Practice Committee 'finds no improper or unethical conduct in his action.' "

Would this conclusion have been the same if a lawyer had been the one who destroyed the letters?

c. To prevent Wallace from destroying the evidence, may you refuse to tell him that the material in the files is damaging? May you refuse to return the materials to him if you believe that he will then destroy them? Remember Rule 1.4, and Comment [7]. Would you do this to protect Mr. Wallace? Would you do it to protect yourself?

4. May you tell Mr. Wallace that if he destroys the tapes, he may well be involved in an obstruction of justice but that the next time he engages in a regular housecleaning of the files he ought to destroy these tapes and any transcripts of them?

a. Is it the rule be that a client must keep all *incriminating* material even though businesses routinely dispose of countless other documents every day?

b. If you suspect that the government may soon subpoena materials, may you send around an e-mail to your client advising it that there is no need to keep these materials and that if there is no real need to keep them, the client should destroy them? If Mr. Wallace has a document retention policy but has not followed it (e.g., the policy says to destroy documents after they are four years old if no one has accessed them for two years, but the client just keeps the documents for years), may you advise him to destroy those documents when the newspapers report that the government may want to subpoena them?

c. In 2002, when the Enron Corporation fell into bankruptcy after its stock collapsed amid charges of fraud, attention turned to Enron's auditors, Arthur Andersen. After an Andersen lawyer emailed Anderson employees reminding them of a policy that, after an audit, they should not keep documents that were not necessary to back up the audit, the employees engaged in extensive shredding of documents. Later, the Federal Government indicted Arthur Andersen for obstruction of justice. On June 15, 2002, the jury found Arthur Andersen guilty. "Soon afterward, Andersen informed the government that it would cease auditing public companies as soon as the end of August, effectively ending the life of the 89–year-old firm."[9]

Did the lawyer serve her client well?

d. Consider the following viewpoints of various lawyers, all discussed in Kenneth Mann, Defending White Collar Crime (1985):

One lawyer:

9. Kurt Eichenwald, Anderson Guilty in Effort to Block Inquiry on Enron, New York Times, June 16, 2002 at § 1, pp. 1, 22. The story went on: "The jury verdict, reached in the 10th day of deliberations, reflected a narrow reading of the events last fall that led to Andersen's indictment. In interviews, jurors said that they reached their decision because an Andersen lawyer had ordered critical deletions to an internal memorandum, rather than because of the firm's wholesale destruction of Enron-related documents. At bottom, then, the guilty verdict against Andersen—on a charge brought because of the shredding of thousands of records and deletion of tens of thousands of e-mail messages—was ultimately reached because of the removal of a few words from a single memorandum." Id.

"My job is to keep the client out of jail. Some of my clients have ended up in jail not because of the crime for which they were being investigated, but because they lied, or burned documents, or altered them in the course of the investigation. So I tell them right off the bat that if they want to stay out of jail, let me know what's there, and keep hands off." (p. 121).

Another lawyer:

"There are many cases in which one would surmise that documents summoned from the client existed at the time the summons was issued. My function in this procedure is a very limited one. I, of course, do not want the client convicted of [an] obstruction of justice charge, and I do warn him of the dire consequences of such a happening. But in the end it is the client's choice. I have no doubt that clients destroy documents. Have I ever known of such an occurrence? No. But you put two and two together. You couldn't convict anyone on such circumstantial evidence, but you can draw your own conclusion." (p. 110).

Yet another lawyer:

"The person faced with the tragedy of a criminal prosecution should not be told by an attorney how to handle the evidence that can lead to a conviction. As long as the attorney does not involve himself directly, it is the client's choice." (Id.)

Which of this positions comes closest to your own?

———

PROBLEM 27

THE CLIENT WHO INTENDS TO COMMIT PERJURY

Now we turn to perhaps the classic, most mooted problem in legal ethics. Surely every law student has been asked, "How can you defend someone you know is guilty?" It is one thing to answer that the prosecution must be put to its proof, but sometimes your client will want to present a defense. Indeed, sometimes he may wants to take the witness stand to deny his guilt even though you and he knows he is guilty. This Problem initially explores what it means to "know" a client plans to lie. What is a lawyer's duty when the client offers to produce a witness who will be willing to lie on the client's behalf? Does the criminal defendant have a right to testify in his or her own defense? Then, the Problem asks what the lawyer is to do when the defendant actually gives false testimony.

FACTS

William Smith is a defendant in a robbery prosecution. Smith is also one of the many criminal defendants represented by M. Maynard Hawley. Smith said to Hawley that he would like to be called as a witness in order to present an alibi defense. After Hawley reminded him that he had never mentioned an alibi defense before, Smith said that his girl friend had agreed now to lie for him and testify that he was at her house at the time of the robbery. Smith told Hawley that he would like to take the stand to confirm his girl friend's story.

Hawley told Smith, "I cannot be a party to any perjurious testimony." Smith retorted: "I have a right to take the stand and testify," but Hawley was reluctant to let Smith do so. Smith assured Hawley: "The last thing I would want you to do is to be unethical. Put me on the stand; I will have to tell the truth."

Hawley put Smith on the stand. Contrary to Smith's earlier pledge, he lied.

QUESTIONS

A. KNOWING WHEN A LAWYER KNOWS SOMETHING

1. Does an attorney ever really "know" that a witness will commit perjury?

a. When the Model Rules talk about "knowing," do they mean "know pragmatically" or "know absolutely"? How does Model Rule 1.0(f) define what it means to "know" something. If you think that you only "reasonably believe"—Rule 1.0(i)—something, is there a risk that a disciplinary panel, or a judge or jury in a later malpractice case, will decide that you really did "know" the information?

b. At some point, surely the lawyer cannot close her eyes to what she "knows." The client may confide in the lawyer that he intends to lie. Or, the lawyer may know because the client's testimony keeps changing in order to accommodate new evidence. The lawyer may know that the client seeks to deny the existence of a document that the lawyer (but not the opposing side) knows exists. At some point, in short, the lawyer does not "suspect" or "infer" but "knows" within the meaning of Rule 1.0(f).

c. In Patsy's Brand, Inc. v. I.O.B. Realty, 2002 WL 59434 (S.D.N.Y. 2002), the court introduced its opinion by stating this case "arises from this Court's *sua sponte* issuance of an order requiring Pennie & Edmonds, the attorneys for the principal defendants, to show cause why it should not be sanctioned for permitting its client to submit a false affidavit." The court did "not dispute counsel's assertion that they acted with subjective good faith." But, the court concluded that, "rather than risk offending and possibly losing a client, counsel simply closed their eyes to the overwhelming evidence that statements in the client's affidavit were not true."

The underlying dispute centered around the trademark rights to use of the name "Patsy's" in marketing spaghetti sauce. A principal of the defendant in an infringement suit submitted an affidavit stating that he had created the Patsy's name before the plaintiff registered its mark. The man further stated that he had taken the mark to a printer at that time and submitted a sample jar label to the court. The plaintiff, however, showed that the label the defendant submitted was created long after the defendant asserted, based on a bar code on the label and the printer's own records. Defense counsel then withdrew from representation and was replaced by Pennie & Edmonds, a firm specializing in trademark law. Although the plaintiff had already proven the falsity of the defendant's affidavit in court, Pennie & Edmonds allowed its client to submit a new affidavit that contained substantially the same statements as the first. The firm argued that it was required to rely on its clients' assertions about the date the mark was created. The court, however, found that no reasonable attorney ("a lawyer of even modest intelligence"), much less one knowledgeable in trademark law, could believe the statements in the affidavits.[1]

2. In preparing Smith's testimony, if Smith tells Hawley a story that appears untruthful, may Hawley explain to him the weaknesses that the prosecutor would see in his story?

a. If Smith then revises his story to eliminate these weaknesses, may Hawley counsel him as to whether the new story is more plausible? May Hawley advise him that the new story would be even more plausible if Smith would change it slightly again? Would Hawley in effect be advising his client as to the best method of telling a lie? At some point, is Hawley suborning perjury?

b. In Resolution Trust Corp. v. Bright, 6 F.3d 336 (5th Cir.1993), the district judge disbarred two lawyers from practice in his court for trying to get a witness to sign an affidavit that described how certain events had occurred. The witness had said she had no knowledge about some of the things they wanted her to say and she refused to sign the affidavit. The Fifth Circuit reversed. It described the conduct as follows:

> "With respect to some of the statements in the affidavit, the attorneys were not content to accept Erhart's initial refusal to revise her changes. In an effort to have Erhart see things their way, Lovato and Graber described their understanding of how certain events transpired at Bright Banc, presented Erhart with independent evidence to support this interpretation of events, and aggressively challenged some of Erhart's assumptions about Bright and Reeder. After making their case for further revisions, Lovato and Graber asked Erhart whether she believed them and whether she was now convinced that their version of certain events was

---

1. Ultimately, the court adopted what many might consider to be a light sanction: "Given Pennie & Edmonds' reputation and its candor in these proceedings, the Court is persuaded that little sanction beyond the publication of this Opinion is required to prevent repetition of similar conduct. Thus all that the Court will require is that a partner of the firm submit to the Court an affidavit stating that a copy of this Opinion has been delivered to each of the lawyers in the firm with a memorandum that states that it is firm policy that its partners and associates adhere to the highest ethical standards and that if a lawyer's adherence to those standards results in the loss of a client, large or small, the lawyer will not suffer any adverse consequence."

correct. Erhart, unconvinced, declined to alter the initial changes she had made to the draft affidavit. When it was clear to the attorneys that Erhart would not sign a statement agreeing with the attorneys' version of some of the disputed events at Bright Banc, they incorporated Erhart's handwritten changes into a new draft affidavit. Erhart read this draft and made a few changes which were then included in a third draft. Erhart read and approved this version of the affidavit, signed it and left the offices of Hopkins & Sutter."

The witness, Erhart, initially described the lawyers' conduct as "almost like browbeating me" but later said that the lawyers "were doing their job, just like everybody else." The Fifth Circuit reversed the trial court, rejected its conclusion that the lawyers were "making or urging the making of 'false' statements," and concluded: "The attorneys' sometimes laborious interviews with Erhart were conducted with the goal of eliciting an accurate and favorable affidavit from a key witness in the underlying case." Are you convinced of that?

c.   State ex rel. Abner v. Elliott, 706 N.E.2d 765 (Ohio 1999) (per curiam), involved asbestos workers who had been given instructions about the answers to give in their depositions. Plaintiffs said the instructions were just helpful advice; defendants said they were improper "coaching." The trial court found that a deposition preparation document constituted evidence of improper coaching of prospective deponents.

The document, entitled "Preparing For Your Deposition," starts off by telling plaintiffs what they will need to say to make the defendant "want to offer you a settlement." The document states: "try to remember how close you were [to these products at the place where you worked]. The more often you were around [them], the better for your case." This witness preparation statement advises that the defendants and their attorneys "have NO RECORDS to tell them what products were used on a particular job." And, "never mention" the existence of this witness preparation document. It also instructs: "You will be asked if you ever saw any WARNING labels on containers of asbestos. It is important to maintain that you NEVER saw any labels on asbestos products that said WARNING or DANGER."[2]

The Court upheld the trial court's order that plaintiffs turn the "advice" documents over to the defendants in discovery or face adverse jury instructions about them.

d.   In re Hingle, 717 So.2d 636 (La.1998), disbarred a lawyer for arranging to have his clients assume debts owed by an employee in exchange for the employee's favorable testimony. The lawyer told the

---

2.   Lester Brickman & Ronald D. Rotunda, When Witnesses Are Told What to Say, Washington Post, January 13, 1998, at A–15. See also, G–I Holdings, Inc. v. Baron & Budd, 179 F.Supp.2d 233, 242 (S.D.N.Y.2001), which said that: "Baron & Budd conducted regular in-house training sessions concerning the giving of misleading and false deposition testimony and issued various memoranda instructing employees how to prepare clients for giving testimony without regard to its truth."

district attorney "[i]f you as prosecutors can offer immunity to a witness to get him to cooperate, why can't I offer him money?" Are you persuaded by the lawyer's analogy?[3]

B.   THE DECISION TO CALL A WITNESS WHO MAY TESTIFY FALSELY

1. Must the lawyer refuse to call Smith's girl friend if he knows she will commit perjury on his client's behalf?

a. The general rule is clear: Lawyers, like anyone else, have a duty not to suborn perjury, which is a criminal offense. See, e.g., Model Rule 3.3(a)(3), and Comments [5]–[8] thereto; Harris v. New York, 401 U.S. 222, 91 S.Ct. 643, 28 L.Ed.2d 1 (1971) (a criminal defendant's privilege to testify in his own behalf does not include a right to commit perjury).

Further, lawyers may not aid and abet a client's perjury. See ABA Model Rule 1.2(d). Complying with those principles, however, has been difficult for some litigators.

b. In Louisiana State Bar Association v. Thierry, 366 So.2d 1305 (La.1978), a grand jury indicted Thierry (a lawyer) for having Henry Joshua testify falsely as an alibi witness for Thierry's client in a robbery prosecution. Thierry was found guilty of suborning the perjury of Joshua and sentenced to three years. Thierry's main defense "appears to be that in his enthusiasm he acted zealously in the interest of his client as well as out of naivete or ignorance * * *." He argued that "a more experienced lawyer would perhaps have considered the impropriety of his conduct and 'have seen [it] as a stop sign,' but respondent demonstrated a 'lack of caution.'" The state Supreme Court ordered Thierry disbarred. "So basic to the criminal justice system of this country is the sanctity of the oath of witnesses and the integrity of lawyers that these principles cannot be unknown to or violated by, the least learned or experienced in the profession of law." 366 So.2d at 1307.

c. In Breezevale v. Dickinson, 759 A.2d 627 (D.C.2000), the lawyer learned that the client's case was apparently based on lies. The night before a deposition in which the client's records custodian was going to be asked about key documents, the witness told the lawyer the documents had been forged. She said she didn't want to lie, and the lawyer told her to tell the truth. Before her deposition testimony reached those issues, the client demanded that the lawyer and witness walk away from the deposition, but the lawyer said he had no basis for doing so. Thus, the fact of the forgery came out at the deposition and the case ultimately settled for a much lower

3. We will look at prosecutors' practice of granting immunity in Problem 29. Note that statutes authorize the immunity, the courts technically grant it on application of the prosecutor, and the court fully discloses to the jury that the prosecutor's witness has immunity from prosecution. ABA Standards Relating to the Administration of Justice, The Prosecution Function, Standard 3–3.2(b) states explicitly that there must be "no attempt to conceal the fact of reimbursement." The Court said in Kastigar v. United States, 406 U.S. 441, 446, 92 S.Ct. 1653, 32 L.Ed.2d 212 (1972): "many offenses are of such a character that the only persons capable of giving useful testimony are those implicated in the crime."

amount. At that point, the client sued the firm for malpractice, arguing that the employee was lying and that the documents were real. The jury in the malpractice case found that the documents were indeed forged but that it was malpractice to have let the witness testify truthfully without at least vigorously trying to prevent her from testifying at all.

The trial judge set aside that malpractice verdict, saying that if the documents were forged (as he too found they were), the plaintiff could not use the failure to introduce forged documents as the basis for the underlying claim. Thus, the lawyer's conduct could not have caused the plaintiff's loss. He also ordered plaintiff to pay defendant's attorneys fees in the malpractice case, finding that the case had been filed in bad faith and in reliance on the forged documents. The D.C. Court of Appeals reversed, saying that the jury could have found that the firm did not do enough to try to protect its dishonest client: there was a jury question whether the forged documents caused the plaintiff's low settlement of its suit or whether the law firm's failure to postpone the deposition of employee and notify the plaintiff earlier was the cause. The court remanded the case, but also said that sanctions against the plaintiff were possible on remand.

2.   What do the Model Rules instruct a lawyer to do when the client wants to call an alibi witness whom the lawyer knows will lie on the stand?

a.   Look at Model Rule 3.3(a)(3), (b), & (c). Look also at the related Comments [5]–[8], [13], & [15]. How are you to proceed?

b.   The Model Rules build on some of the prior case law. People v. Schultheis, 638 P.2d 8 (Colo.1981), examined the procedures a lawyer should follow when confronted with a client who insists that the lawyer call an alibi witness who will testify perjuriously. The court declared:

"A lawyer who presents a witness knowing that the witness intends to commit perjury thereby engages in the subornation of perjury. We will not permit the truth-finding process to be deflected by the presentation of false evidence by an officer of the court. Therefore, we hold that a lawyer may not offer testimony of a witness which he knows is false, fraudulent, or perjured." 638 P.2d at 11.

The court said further that if the lawyer cannot persuade the client to stop insisting that the lawyer offer false testimony, the lawyer should request permission to withdraw based on an irreconcilable conflict. This motion should not elaborate further. If the trial court denies the motion to withdraw, the lawyer must continue to represent the defendant but still not offer the false testimony of the witness. Because of the possibility of post conviction challenges, the lawyer "should proceed with a request for a record out of the presence of the trial judge and the prosecutor if the court denies the motion to withdraw." 638 P.2d at 14.

c.   In Tibbs v. United States, 628 A.2d 638 (D.C.App.1993), the defendant was convicted of armed robbery. He said the victim had identified the wrong man. At his first trial (which ended in a hung jury), his wife provided him with an alibi. At the second trial, his lawyer did not call her: the wife had told the lawyer before the second trial that she would not testify because "her testimony [at the first trial] was not true and [the defendant] knew this." The defendant said that the lawyer's failure to call her was ineffective assistance of counsel, but the court held that a lawyer may not call a witness who would testify falsely and that, "as a matter of law," the failure to do so cannot be ineffective assistance.

3. What if the lawyer discovers that his witness lied under oath, but the lawyer has an argument that the factual misrepresentation is not "material"?

a. May the lawyer refuse to disclose to the court if it is likely that the factual matter is not "material"? What if it is merely arguable that the factual matter is not "material"? What if the issue is whether the failure to disclose an adverse case precedent is not really material?

b. Model Rule 3.3(a)(1) used to say that the lawyer shall not knowingly make "a false statement of material fact...." The 2002 revisions deleted the word "material." Now, Rule 3.3(a)(3) prohibits the lawyer from offering any evidence that the lawyer "knows" to be false. There is no requirement of materiality. Yet the next sentence requires the lawyer to take remedial measures if the lawyer learns that the witness has offered "material evidence" that is false. So, what is the relevance of materiality?

c. In United States v. Shaffer Equipment Co., 11 F.3d 450 (4th Cir.1993), EPA's on–site coordinator lied to the Court about his academic and professional record. When the Government lawyers discovered this inconvenient fact, they did not tell the court. When the trial court found out about it, the court dismissed the case as a sanction. The Fourth Circuit remanded so the trial court could determine if a lesser sanction was appropriate. In the meantime, the government lawyers argued that the falsity (the witness, for example, falsely claimed to have a college degree) was not "material." The Fourth Circuit rejected that argument: "the significance of impeaching the principal EPA witness, who was largely responsible for developing the record, renders impeachment information material." 11 F.3d at 460–61.

d. Florida Bar v. Cox, 794 So.2d 1278 (Fla.2001), suspended a prosecutor for a year for having an informant use a false name during trial. The state charged the defendant with solicitation of a minor to engage in a sexual act. The US Customs Service had used an informant to pose as a 13 year old girl on the Internet. Before trial, the magistrate ordered the prosecution to provide the informant's real name to the defense, but instead, it gave her pseudonym and used it during the trial. Midway through the trial, it came out that the informant had a previous criminal history. Because the prosecution's strategy had prevented the defense from discrediting the witness or even seeking a mistrial, the court found that the prosecutor's failure to give the defendant the informant's real name was intentional misconduct. The referee recommended that the lawyer receive a public reprimand and be placed on probation, but the court found the presumptive sanction should have been disbarment. The court said that prosecutors have heightened responsibilities to assure that justice is served. However, because this was apparently an isolated incident by a prosecutor with an otherwise good record, the court suspended her with the requirement that rehabilitation be proven prior to reinstatement.

4. Is there any justification for using perjury if the lie comes from government witnesses and its purpose is to trap criminals?

a. In re Friedman, 392 N.E.2d 1333 (Ill.1979), was a lawyer discipline case that arose because the government introduced false testimony to catch a lawyer who was suborning perjury. The respondent, an attorney in the criminal division of the Cook County State's Attorney office, learned that the defense lawyer had solicited a police officer to commit perjury. The respondent instructed the officer to agree in order to apprehend the briber. After the officer testified falsely under oath that a witness was unavailable, the defense lawyer gave the officer $50, and the state indicted the defense lawyer for bribery. Although the assistant State's Attorney allowed the false testimony to be introduced solely for the purpose of developing evidence to be used in a subsequent prosecution, a disciplinary action was brought against him.

Two justices found a violation of Illinois DR 7–102(A)(4), (6), & DR 7–109(B), which correspond to Model Rule 3.3(a)(1). They said: "The integrity of the courtroom is so vital to the health of our legal system that no violation of that integrity, no matter what its motivation, can be condoned or ignored." 392 N.E.2d at 1335. These Justices refused to impose any sanctions, however, because respondent had acted without the guidance of settled opinion, and because of the belief of many lawyers that respondent's conduct in the circumstances of this case was proper. Two justices went further and found the respondent guilty of prejudicing the administration of justice. Two justices found that the respondent did not violate any ethical proscriptions at all.

What do you think? How else could the prosecutor have trapped the crooked lawyer? If the police officer had not testified falsely pursuant to the deal, the prosecutor might not have been able to convict the lawyer, who would simply have denied that he had offered a bribe.

b. What if the prosecutor wants to run a "sting" operation against a judge or group of judges? Not too long after *Friedman*, a federal prosecution of Chicago state court corruption began in what was called "Operation Greylord." See, e.g., United States v. Maloney, 71 F.3d 645 (7th Cir.1995), cert. denied, 519 U.S. 927, 117 S.Ct. 295, 136 L.Ed.2d 214 (1996); Bracy v. Gramley, 520 U.S. 899, 117 S.Ct. 1793, 138 L.Ed.2d 97 (1997). In some of these cases, contrived disputes were filed to see if judges would accept bribes to help assure particular results. In several of the cases resulting from Operation Greylord, defendant judges relied on *Friedman* for the proposition that "before injecting a contrived case into the court system and thereby conducting its undercover project in the Illinois courts, the government was required to notify appropriate court officials."

In United States v. Murphy, 768 F.2d 1518, 1528–29 (7th Cir.1985), the court answered:

"Bribery, like a wholesale transaction in drugs, is a secret act. * * * Because the crime leaves no complaining witness, active participation by the agents may be necessary to establish an effective case. The agents' acts merely appear criminal; they are not, because they are performed without the state of mind necessary to support a conviction. The agents who made up and testified about the Operation Greylord 'cases' did so without criminal intent. They were decoys, and the Greylord cases made it easier to separate the honest judges from the dishonest ones. It may be necessary to offer bait to trap a criminal. * * * In the pursuit of crime the Government is not confined to behavior suitable for the drawing room. It may use decoys, and provide the essential tools of the offense. * * * The FBI and the prosecutors behaved honorably in establishing and running Operation Greylord. They assure us that they notified the Presiding Judge of the Circuit Court's Criminal Division, the State's Attorney of Cook County, the Attorney General of Illinois, and the Governor of Illinois. Such notice may not be necessary, and certainly a criminal defendant is in no position to complain of the absence of such notice (for he has no personal right to protect the dignity of the Cook County courts) * * * ."

Do you agree that exceptional circumstances may require exceptions from the rule against using testimony that is objectively untrue?

c. After *Murphy,* federal courts did not suppress such testimony, but should the state courts discipline any lawyers (e.g., FBI agents who were lawyers) who "lied" to the judge by pretending that they were filing real cases or not disclosing that they were decoys and not offering a bribe in a real case? At the time of Operation Greylord, there were those who argued that these federal investigators should be disciplined but the matter was never tested in the courts.

C.   THE DECISION TO CALL THE DEFENDANT WHO MAY COMMIT PERJURY

1.   May a lawyer decide whether or not a client in a criminal case will take the witness stand to testify in his or her own defense?

a.   Look at ABA Model Rule 1.2(a). Is there any question who has the right to make that decision? See also, Restatement Third, The Law Governing Lawyers § 22, to the same effect.

b.   That right of the client has a constitutional dimension. Rock v. Arkansas, 483 U.S. 44, 107 S.Ct. 2704, 97 L.Ed.2d 37 (1987), held that criminal defendants have a right to testify as a result of the due process clause of the Fourteenth Amendment, the compulsory process clause of the Sixth Amendment, and the Fifth Amendment's privilege against self-incrimination. This right to present relevant evidence has limitations, the Court said, but any restrictions must not be "arbitrary or disproportionate." Thus, the Court ruled (5 to 4) that Arkansas' per se rule excluding all hypnotically refreshed testimony impermissibly infringed on the criminal defendant's right to testify on her own behalf.

c. Nichols v. Butler, 953 F.2d 1550 (11th Cir.1992) (en banc), is a good example of how not to proceed. The court found ineffective assistance of counsel where the lawyer threatened to withdraw in the middle of trial if the defendant elected to testify. The facts of the case did not relate to any claim that the defendant would testify falsely. In addition, the majority noted that there was substantial evidence that the defendant was not guilty, that defendant's trial lawyer was simply concerned that defendant's "prior felony record and serious drug problem might be exposed to the jury and severely damage him." The lawyer told defendant that if he chose to testify, counsel would seek to withdraw from his case. The counsel did not inform defendant that he had a right to testify and that "even if counsel sought to withdraw from the case after the first day of trial, the trial court could have refused the request."

d. On the other hand, in many cases, courts have not granted defendants new trials where their lawyers decided to keep them off the witness stand, sometimes without regard to whether the defendant understood that the decision whether or not to testify was his to make. See, e.g., Ortega v. O'Leary, 843 F.2d 258 (7th Cir.1988), cert. denied 488 U.S. 841, 109 S.Ct. 110, 102 L.Ed.2d 85 (1988) (state trial court's refusal to allow petitioner to testify was improper but did not warrant habeas corpus relief on grounds of harmless error); United States v. Edwards, 897 F.2d 445 (9th Cir.1990) (defendant's silence at trial effectively waived his right to testify on his own behalf, despite the defendant's contention that his attorney refused to allow him to testify and that the defendant was unaware that he had right to testify; the defense lawyer "testified that he made the decision not to call Edwards [the defendant] without consulting Edwards, and that he conveyed the decision to the trial judge in chambers, out of the presence of Edwards"); Brown v. Artuz, 124 F.3d 73 (2d Cir.1997) (the lawyer did not tell the client of his right to testify, but this failure was harmless error, so the court affirmed the conviction).

Do you agree with the results in these cases? Is the duty to explain the client's normal right to take the witness stand inherent in the lawyer's obligation under Model Rule 1.4? How else can the client make the decision reserved to the client by Model Rule 1.2(a)? Are the cases simply saying that, even if the lawyer has not complied with his or her professional obligations, that failure does not determine the constitutional issue of effective assistance of counsel?

2. Does it follow that a lawyer must sit by and do nothing if the criminal defendant wants to testify falsely?

a. The most definitive word from the Supreme Court about whether a criminal defendant has a right to lie on the witness stand, or a right to seek the aid of his lawyer in lying, is found in Nix v. Whiteside, 475 U.S. 157, 106 S.Ct. 988, 89 L.Ed.2d 123 (1986). In 1977, Whiteside had gone to Calvin Love's apartment to buy marijuana. Love was in bed and an argument arose during which Whiteside stabbed Love to death. Whiteside told his lawyer, Gary Robinson, that he had seen Love reach under his pillow, apparently to grab a gun.

"Until shortly before trial, Whiteside consistently stated to Robinson that he had not actually seen a gun, but that he was convinced that Love had a gun in his hand. About a week before trial, during preparation for direct examination, Whiteside for the first time told Robinson and his associate Donna Paulsen that he had seen something 'metallic' in Love's hand. When asked about this, Whiteside responded that

" '[I]n Howard Cook's case there was a gun. If I don't say I saw a gun I'm dead.'

"Robinson told Whiteside that such testimony would be perjury and repeated that it was not necessary to prove that a gun was available but only that Whiteside reasonably believed that he was in danger. On Whiteside's insisting that he would testify that he saw 'something metallic' Robinson told him, according to Robinson's testimony,

'[W]e could not allow him to [testify falsely] because that would be perjury, and as officers of the court we would be suborning perjury if we allowed him to do it; * * * I advised him that if he did do that it would be my duty to advise the Court of what he was doing and that I felt he was committing perjury; also, that I probably would be allowed to attempt to impeach that particular testimony.'

"Robinson also indicated he would seek to withdraw from the representation if Whiteside insisted on committing perjury.

"Whiteside testified in his own defense at trial and stated that he 'knew' that Love had a gun and that he believed Love was reaching for a gun and he had acted swiftly in self defense. On cross examination, he admitted that he had not actually seen a gun in Love's hand. Robinson presented evidence that Love had been seen with a sawed-off shotgun on other occasions, that the police search of the apartment may have been careless, and that the victim's family had removed everything from the apartment shortly after the crime. Robinson presented this evidence to show a basis for Whiteside's asserted fear that Love had a gun." 475 U.S. at 160–62, 106 S.Ct. at 991–92, 89 L.Ed.2d at 131.

The jury convicted Whiteside of second-degree murder. Whiteside moved for a new trial, claiming he had been denied effective assistance of counsel by Robinson's advice not to say he had actually seen a gun in Love's hand. The trial court denied the motion, and the Iowa Supreme Court affirmed Whiteside's conviction.

Whiteside applied for a writ of habeas corpus, which the district court denied but the Eighth Circuit granted. The court accepted the finding that Whiteside intended to perjure himself on the witness stand, but "the court reasoned that an intent to commit perjury, communicated to counsel, does not alter a defendant's right to effective assistance of counsel and that Robinson's admonition to Whiteside that he would inform the court of Whiteside's perjury constituted a threat to violate the attorney's duty to preserve client confidences."

The Supreme Court reversed, with several opinions but no dissent. Chief Justice Burger wrote for the Court, joined by Justices White, Powell, Rehnquist, and O'Connor. The Court began by noting that the "right of an accused to testify is of relatively recent origin." By the end of the 19th century, statutes had abolished the rule that the accused was disqualified by virtue of his or her interest as a party to the case. Then the Court turned to the merits:

"[We have] recognized counsel's duty of loyalty and his 'overarching duty to advocate the defendant's cause.' Plainly, that duty is limited to legitimate, lawful conduct compatible with the very nature of a trial as a search for truth. Although counsel must take all reasonable lawful means to attain the objectives of the client, counsel is precluded from taking steps or in any way assisting the client in presenting false evidence or otherwise violating the law. * * *

"Both the Model Code of Professional Conduct and the Model Rules of Professional Conduct also adopt the specific exception from the attorney-client privilege for disclosure of perjury that his client intends to commit or has committed. DR 4–101(C)(3) (intention of client to commit a crime); Rule 3.3 (lawyer has duty to disclose falsity of evidence even if disclosure compromises client confidences). Indeed, both the Model Code and the Model Rules do not merely *authorize* disclosure by counsel of client perjury; they *require* such disclosure. See Rule 3.3(a)(4); DR 7–102(B)(1).

"These standards confirm that the legal profession has accepted that an attorney's ethical duty to advance the interests of his client is limited by an equally solemn duty to comply with the law and standards of professional conduct; it specifically ensures that the client may not use false evidence. This special duty of an attorney to prevent and disclose frauds upon the court derives from the recognition that perjury is as much a crime as tampering with witnesses or jurors by way of promises and threats, and undermines the administration of justice. * * *

"It is universally agreed that at a minimum the attorney's first duty when confronted with a proposal for perjurious testimony is to attempt to dissuade the client from the unlawful course of conduct. * * *. The Commentary [to the Model Rules] * * * also suggests that an attorney's revelation of his client's perjury to the court is a professionally responsible and acceptable response to the conduct of a client who has actually given perjured testimony. Similarly, the Model Rules and the commentary, as well as the Code of Professional Responsibility adopted in Iowa expressly permit withdrawal from representation as an appropriate response of an attorney when the client threatens to commit perjury. Model Rules of Professional Conduct, Rule 1.16(a)(1), Rule 1.6, Comment [14, 15] (1983); Code of Professional Responsibility, DR 2–110(B), (C) (1980). Withdrawal of counsel when this situation arises at trial gives rise to many difficult questions including possible mistrial and claims of double jeopardy.

"The essence of the brief *amicus* of the American Bar Association reviewing practices long accepted by ethical lawyers, is that under no circumstance may a lawyer either advocate or passively tolerate a client's giving false testimony. This, of course, is consistent with the governance of trial conduct in what we have long called 'a search for truth.' The suggestion sometimes made that 'a lawyer must believe his client not judge him' in no sense means a lawyer can honorably be a party to or in any way give aid to presenting known perjury.

"Considering Robinson's representation of respondent in light of these accepted norms of professional conduct, we discern no failure to adhere to reasonable professional standards that would in any sense make out a deprivation of the Sixth Amendment right to counsel. Whether Robinson's conduct is seen as a successful attempt to dissuade his client from committing the crime of perjury, or whether seen as a 'threat' to withdraw from representation and disclose the illegal scheme, Robinson's representation of Whiteside falls well within accepted standards of professional conduct and the range of reasonable professional conduct acceptable under *Strickland*. * * *

"Whatever the scope of a constitutional right to testify, it is elementary that such a right does not extend to testifying *falsely*. * * * In Harris [v. New York,] we held the defendant could be impeached by prior contrary statements which had been ruled inadmissible under Miranda v. Arizona, 384 U.S. 436, 86 S.Ct. 1602, 16 L.Ed.2d 694 (1966). *Harris* and other cases make it crystal clear that there is no right whatever—constitutional or otherwise—for a defendant to use false evidence. * * *

"Robinson's admonitions to his client can in no sense be said to have forced respondent into an *impermissible* choice between his right to counsel and his right to testify as he proposed for there was no *permissible* choice to testify falsely. * * * The crime of perjury in this setting is indistinguishable in substance from the crime of threatening or tampering with a witness or a juror. A defendant who informed his counsel that he was arranging to bribe or threaten witnesses or members of the jury would have no 'right' to insist on counsel's assistance or silence. Counsel would not be limited to advising against that conduct. * * * We hold that, as a matter of law, counsel's conduct complained of here cannot establish the prejudice required for relief under the second strand of the *Strickland* inquiry. * * * If a 'conflict' between a client's proposal and counsel's ethical obligation gives rise to a presumption that counsel's assistance was prejudicially ineffective, every guilty criminal's conviction would be suspect if the defendant had sought to obtain an acquittal by illegal means. Can anyone doubt what practices and problems would be spawned by such a rule and what volumes of litigation it would generate?

"Whiteside's attorney treated Whiteside's proposed perjury in accord with professional standards, and since Whiteside's truthful testimony could not have prejudiced the result of his trial, the Court of Appeals was in error to direct the issuance of a writ of habeas corpus and must be reversed." 475 U.S. at 166–76, 106 S.Ct. at 994–99, 89 L.Ed.2d at 134–41.

b. Justice Brennan, concurring in the judgment and joined by no other justice, argued that the "Court's essay regarding what constitutes the correct response to a criminal defendant's suggestion that he will perjure himself is pure discourse without force of law." The issue "is a thorny one" that is not "presented by this case." He advised: "Lawyers, judges, bar associations, students and others should understand that the problem has not now been 'decided.' " 475 U.S. at 176–77, 106 S.Ct. at 999, 89 L.Ed.2d at 141.

c. Justice Blackmun, joined by Justices Brennan, Marshall and Stevens, concurred in the judgment:

"How a defense attorney ought to act when faced with a client who intends to commit perjury at trial has long been a controversial issue. But I do not believe that a federal habeas corpus case challenging a state criminal conviction is an appropriate vehicle for attempting to resolve this thorny problem. When a defendant argues that he was denied effective assistance of counsel because his lawyer dissuaded him from committing perjury, the only question properly presented to this Court is whether the lawyer's actions deprived the defendant of the fair trial which the Sixth Amendment is meant to guarantee. Since I believe that the respondent in this case suffered no injury justifying federal habeas relief, I concur in the Court's judgment. * * *

"[T]he Double Jeopardy Clause bars the reprosecution of [criminal defendants acquitted on the basis of their perjured testimony], although on occasion they can be prosecuted for perjury. But the privilege every criminal defendant has to testify in his own defense 'cannot be construed to include the right to commit perjury.' * * *

" * * * [T]he lawyer's interest in not presenting perjured testimony was entirely consistent with Whiteside's best interest. If Whiteside had lied on the stand, he would have risked a future perjury prosecution. Moreover, his testimony would have been contradicted by the testimony of other eyewitnesses and by the fact that no gun was ever found. In light of that impeachment, the jury might have concluded that Whiteside lied as well about his lack of premeditation and thus might have convicted him of first-degree murder. And if the judge believed that Whiteside had lied, he could have taken Whiteside's perjury into account in setting the sentence. In the face of these dangers, an attorney could reasonably conclude that dissuading his client from committing perjury was in the client's best interest and comported with standards of professional responsibility. * * *

"* * * But the American Bar Association's implicit suggestion in its brief *amicus curiae* that the Court find that the Association's Model Rules of Professional Conduct should govern an attorney's responsibilities is addressed to the wrong audience. It is for the States to decide how attorneys should conduct themselves in state criminal proceedings, and this Court's responsibility extends only to ensuring that the restrictions a State enacts do not infringe a defendant's federal constitutional rights. * * *

d.   Justice Stevens also filed an opinion concurring in the judgment, and said that, in his view, the "much more difficult question" is what must or may the lawyer do if "his client has given testimony that the lawyer does not believe."

3.   If the lawyer knows the client wants to testify falsely, how should the lawyer proceed? Given Nix v. Whiteside, how should the lawyer to counsel the client pursuant to Model Rules 1.4 and 2.1?

a.   In United States v. Teague, 953 F.2d 1525 (11th Cir.1992) (en banc), the defense lawyer advised the client not to testify and the client took the advice. Then he argued that this advice violated his constitutional right. The court was unwilling to go that far. It agreed that the decision whether or not to testify is for the defendant to make, but the lawyer's professional advice on the question is a part of the effective assistance of counsel, not a denial of it.

b.   United States v. Scott, 909 F.2d 488 (11th Cir.1990), showed how a trial court should *not* proceed. When the lawyer moved to withdraw, the judge told the defendant that if he were to have counsel, he would have to agree not to testify; otherwise, he would have to proceed pro se. He chose the pro se alternative and the Court of Appeals reversed the conviction. It recognized that the proper way of dealing with client perjury was unclear, but it relied on an alleged lack of evidence that the defendant would have lied if he were represented. Basically, it said the trial judge's approach of requiring the defendant to act pro se from the outset solved a problem that might not have arisen.

c.   In United States v. Litchfield, 959 F.2d 1514 (10th Cir.1992), on the other hand, defense counsel held an ex parte conference with the judge during the trial. He told the judge that he had advised the client he should testify but the lawyer now feared the client would not be truthful. The judge told the lawyer it was for the jury to decide what was true and untrue, so the trial went on normally, the defendant took the stand, and he was convicted. The Court of Appeals held that the lawyer's alerting the judge about his concerns, by itself, did not deny the defendant effective assistance of counsel. Under the Model Rules, is it correct to conclude that a lawyer has to alert the judge to his concerns if the client insists on testifying falsely?

d. State v. Berrysmith, 944 P.2d 397 (Wash.App.1997), involved a lawyer who believed his client was about to commit perjury, so he sought and received permission to withdraw. The case was then continued beyond the Speedy Trial Act date to let the new lawyer prepare. The client was convicted and then argued that he was denied a speedy trial because the judge did not have sufficient evidence to permit the first lawyer to withdraw. The Court found that the client had significantly changed the story he had told his lawyer and that this gave rise to a reasonable belief the client intended to lie. Thus, the request to withdraw was proper, as was the delay to give new counsel time to prepare.

4. Should the lawyer advise his client, who wants to testify falsely, that he should give his testimony in the form of a narrative?

a. Rule 3.3(b) of D.C. Rules of Professional Conduct provides that a lawyer for an accused in a criminal case who plans to lie should first "make a good faith effort to dissuade the client from presenting the false evidence." If unsuccessful, "the lawyer shall seek leave of the tribunal to withdraw." However, if withdrawal is not permitted: "the lawyer may put the client on the stand to testify in a narrative fashion, but the lawyer shall not examine the client in such manner as to elicit testimony which the lawyer knows to be false, and shall not argue the probative value of the client's testimony in closing argument."[6]

b. What do you think about this "narrative" approach? It was once the heart of Proposed Standard 4–7.7 of the ABA Standards Relating to the Defense Function, but the majority opinion in Nix v. Whiteside expressly acknowledged the debate about it in a footnote:

"In the evolution of the contemporary standards promulgated by the American Bar Association, an early draft reflects a compromise suggesting that when the disclosure of intended perjury is made during the course of trial, when withdrawal of counsel would raise difficult questions of a mistrial holding, counsel had the option to let the defendant take the stand but decline to affirmatively assist the presentation of perjury by traditional direct examination. Instead, counsel would stand mute while the defendant undertook to present the false version in narrative form in his own words unaided by any direct examination. This conduct was thought to be a signal at least to the presiding judge that the attorney considered the testimony to be false and was seeking to disassociate himself from that course. Additionally, counsel would not be permitted to discuss the known false testimony in closing arguments. * * * Most courts treating the subject rejected this approach and insisted on a more rigorous standard, [but t]he Eighth Circuit in this case and the Ninth Circuit have expressed approval of the 'free narrative' standards.

6. By contrast, Florida Bar Rule 3.3(4) prohibits all false testimony whether or not in a narrative form.

"The Rule finally promulgated in the current Model Rules of Professional Conduct rejects any participation or passive role whatever by counsel in allowing perjury to be presented without challenge." 475 U.S. at 170 n.6, 106 S.Ct. at 996 n.6, 89 L.Ed.2d at 136 n.6.

c. The Court referred to Lowery v. Cardwell, 575 F.2d 727 (9th Cir.1978), which approved narrative testimony in principle but found it inappropriate in a trial where the judge is the fact finder. In the midst of a trial, the court went on, if defense counsel is surprised by a client's perjury, counsel need not withdraw because that course is not feasible. Instead, the lawyer should not "advance" the perjury. Judge Hufstedler, concurring, said: "No matter how commendable may have been counsel's motives, his interest in saving himself from potential violation of the canons was adverse to his client, and the end product was his abandonment of a diligent defense." Id. at 732. See also, Matter of Goodwin, 305 S.E.2d 578 (S.C.1983); State v. Robinson, 224 S.E.2d 174 (N.C.1976).

d. In State v. Fosnight, 679 P.2d 174 (Kan.1984), defense counsel requested permission to withdraw but the trial court refused. Before the jury, counsel asked his client whether he wished to "tell the court some things today" and then stood aside while the defendant told his story. The court held that the attorney's actions were not grounds for reversal. The request to withdraw was made in chambers during a natural break in the proceeding; it did not itself call the jury's attention to any problem. The use of narrative testimony was similarly not prejudicial. The court distinguished *Lowery* on the ground that was a bench trial and there the defense counsel had affirmatively told the judge of the intention of his client to testify falsely.

e. However, the lawyer in United States v. Long, 857 F.2d 436 (8th Cir.1988), asked to approach the bench at the close of the government's case. He told the judge he was concerned about the truth of what his client might testify. The lawyer told the court that he had advised his client not to take the stand and he offered to withdraw. The trial judge then told the defendant that he could testify on his own behalf but that his lawyer could not assist him to testify falsely. The judge said that the defendant could give narrative testimony but that if he lied, his lawyer "may have other obligations at that point." The client did not testify and the jury convicted.

The Eighth Circuit (the court that had been reversed in Nix v. Whiteside) argued that there were three key distinctions that made this case different from *Nix*. In *Nix*, the court found that the client would have testified falsely, but in this case the lawyer only believed that he would. There must be "a firm, factual basis" for the belief before the lawyer may raise a red flag. Second, in *Nix*, the client did testify and simply did so truthfully; here the client did not testify at all. Third, here the lawyer told the trial judge about his concerns, while in *Nix* there was no discussion beyond that between lawyer and client. Thus, the court concluded that *Nix* did not control this case. It ordered an evidentiary hearing to see whether prejudice arising from the lawyer's action amounted to ineffective assistance of counsel.

Do you agree with this result? Should we be more troubled than some courts have been by the use of narrative testimony? What is the court to do if the opposing counsel makes the obvious evidentiary objection. A lawyer is supposed to ask non-leading questions to which the other lawyer may object; the lawyer is not supposed to say "tell us your side of the story"?

D. WHAT TO DO WHEN THE CLIENT DOES GIVE FALSE TESTIMONY

1. When Smith took the stand and broke his promise to be truthful, what should Hawley have done? Should Hawley have tried to withdraw from the representation in the middle of the trial?

a. If the client knows that the lawyer will urge him not to testify if he plans to testify falsely, we can expect savvy, street-smart defendants (who are ready to lie under oath) to lie to their lawyers when they are not under oath.

b. Did the ABA Model Code of Professional Responsibility provide helpful guidance on this point? Look at DR 7–102(B)(1), for example:

> "A lawyer who receives information clearly establishing that [h]is client has, in the course of the representation, perpetrated a fraud upon a person or tribunal shall promptly call upon his client to rectify the same, and if his client refuses or is unable to do so, he shall reveal the fraud to the affected person or tribunal, except when the information is protected as a privileged communication."

Did that rule give the lawyer clear guidance? Did it instead create as many questions as answers for the lawyer? Is a client's admission to past perjury privileged, for example? What may the lawyer do if the client has not admitted anything, but the lawyer knows testimony was perjured based on earlier privileged discussions the lawyer had with the client?

c. Look at Comments [7]–[12] to ABA Model Rule 3.3 as they existed prior to the 2002 amendments. They go into some detail about alternative ways to deal with the problem of perjury by a criminal defendant, but are you satisfied that they give a clear roadmap of what the lawyer is to do?

d. After the adoption of the Model Rules and the Supreme Court's decision in Nix v. Whiteside, the ABA Standing Committee on Ethics and Professional Responsibility issued Formal Opinion 87–353 (Apr. 20, 1987). The opinion reviewed and superseded Formal Opinion 287 (June 27, 1953) (discussed in Problem 25), and Formal Opinion 341 (Sep. 30, 1975). The Committee wrote:

> "It is now mandatory * * * for a lawyer, who knows the client has committed perjury, to disclose this knowledge to the tribunal if the lawyer cannot persuade the client to rectify the perjury.

> " * * * Rule 3.3(a)(2) and (4) complement each other.[7] While (a)(4), itself, does not expressly require disclosure by the lawyer to

---

7. Ed. Note: The Committee is using the pre–2002 numbering of the Model Rules.

the tribunal of the client's false testimony after the lawyer has offered it and learns of its falsity, such disclosure will be the only 'reasonable remedial [measure]' the lawyer will be able to take if the client is unwilling to rectify the perjury. The Comment to Rule 3.3 states that disclosure of the client's perjury to the tribunal would be required of the lawyer by (a)(4) in this situation.

"Although Rule 3.3(a)(2), unlike 3.3(a)(4), does not specifically refer to perjury or false evidence, it would require an irrational reading of the language: 'a criminal or fraudulent act by the client,' to exclude false testimony by the client."[8]

Do you agree that the cited rules are this clear and that the obligation is this simple?

e. What do Model Rules 3.3(a)(3) and 3.3(b) mean by the term "reasonable remedial measures"? Do Comments [10], [11] & [15] to Model Rule 3.3 help you answer that question? These comments were added or extensively rewritten as part of the 2002 amendments to the Model Rules. Do they still leave hard questions not satisfactorily answered?[9]

f. People v. DePallo, 754 N.E.2d 751 (N.Y.2001), affirmed the defendant's conviction on several counts of murder and robbery, and rejected his claim that he had been denied the effective assistance of counsel. At trial, the defendant's lawyer told his client not to testify, but said that if he did testify, he must do so truthfully. The defendant elected to testify and the lawyer elicited the testimony in narrative form. During cross-examination of the defendant, the lawyer made numerous objections. Thereafter, the lawyer disclosed to the court ex parte in chambers that his client had given perjured testimony. In closing argument, the lawyer did not refer to the defendant's testimony.

The New York Court of Appeals held that the lawyer was correct in first attempting to dissuade his client from perjuring himself or from even testifying at all. The lawyer also acted properly in notifying the court of the defendant's actions because the intent to commit a crime was not protected by the attorney-client privilege. The court also rejected the defendant's argument that the New York Code of Professional Responsibility required the lawyer to withdraw from the representation. Withdrawal would not have achieved anything and could have facilitated the introduction of the perjured testimony.

These two sections are now Model Rules 3.3(a)(3) and 3.3(b).

8. On the question of the criminal defendant who *intends* to lie, the Committee concluded that the lawyer could not call that client as a witness. The Committee continued: "[I]f the lawyer does not offer the client's testimony, and, on inquiry by the court into whether the client has been fully advised as to the client's right to testify, the client states a desire to testify, but is being prevented by the lawyer from testifying, the lawyer may have no other choice than to disclose to the court the client's intention to testify falsely."

9. Restatement Third, The Law Governing Lawyers, examines these issues in § 120, Comments *h* and *i*, but the answers are no more precise than those in the Model Rules.

Do you agree that this case represents about all the lawyer could do in a difficult situation? Would you have done anything different than this lawyer did?

2.   What do you think of the argument that the Model Rules approach to client perjury is utterly wrong, i.e., that the right to testify is meaningless if the defendant cannot tell the story he wants to tell, even if that story is false?

a.   Professor Monroe Freedman has often articulated the argument that the lawyer's duty is to call the client, ask the relevant questions, let the client tell his own story even if the story is fabricated, and then rely on the client's story in his summation to the jury. He says that any other approach ignores what he calls the lawyer's "trilemma":[10]

"[T]he attorney functions in an adversary system of justice which imposes three conflicting obligations upon the advocate. The difficulties presented by these obligations are particularly acute in the criminal defense area because of the presumption of innocence, the burden on the state to prove its case beyond reasonable doubt, and the right to put the prosecution to its proof.

"First, the ABA Standards Relating to the Defense Function requires the lawyer to determine all relevant facts known to the accused * * *. The lawyer who is ignorant of any potentially relevant fact 'incapacitates himself to serve his client effectively,' because 'an adequate defense cannot be framed if the lawyer does not know what is likely to develop at trial.'

"Second, the lawyer must hold in strictest confidence the disclosures made by the client in the course of the professional relationship. * * * [C]ounsel is required to establish a relationship of trust and confidence, to explain the necessity of full disclosure of all facts, and to explain to the client the obligation of confidentiality which makes privileged the accused's disclosures.

"Third, * * * the lawyer is an officer of the court, and his or her conduct before the court 'should be characterized by candor.'

"As soon as one begins to think about those responsibilities, it becomes apparent that the conscientious attorney is faced with what we may call a trilemma—that is, the lawyer is required to know everything, to keep it in confidence, and to reveal it to the court. * * *

"In my opinion, the attorney's obligation [when the client wants to lie] would be to advise the client that the proposed testimony is unlawful, but to proceed in the normal fashion in presenting the testimony and arguing the case to the jury if the client makes the decision to go forward. Any other course would be a betrayal of the assurances of confidentiality given by the attorney to induce the client to reveal everything, however damaging it might appear.

---

10. The version of the argument quoted here comes from Monroe H. Freedman, Per-   jury: The Lawyer's Trilemma, 1 Litigation 26 (No. 1, Winter 1975).

"A frequent objection to the position that the attorney must go along with the client's decision to commit perjury is that the lawyer would be guilty of subornation of perjury. Subornation, however, consists of willfully procuring perjury, which is not the case when the attorney indicates to the client that the client's proposed course of conduct would be unlawful, but then accepts the client's decision. Beyond that, there is a point of view which has been expressed to me by a number of experienced attorneys, that the criminal defendant has a 'right to tell his story.' What that suggests is that it is simply too much to expect of a human being, caught up in the criminal process and facing loss of liberty and the horrors of imprisonment, not to attempt to lie to avoid that penalty. * * *

"I agree that * * * the case involving collateral witnesses is not at all as clear as that involving the client alone. [However,] * * * a spouse or parent would be acting under the same human compulsion as a defendant, and I find it difficult to imagine myself denouncing my client's spouse or parent as a perjurer, and, thereby, denouncing my client as well. I do not know, however, how much wider that circle of close identity might be drawn."

b.   What do you think of Professor Freedman's position? Is any other position consistent with the desire to leave a convicted defendant with the sense that he had a fair trial? Is giving the defendant a sense that he did everything he could as important as giving the jury only honest evidence upon which to base their verdict?

c.   The implications of Professor Freedman's position are provocative, if disturbing. Professor Freedman was one of the reporters for the Proposed American Lawyer's Code of Conduct (Rev.Draft, 1982), prepared under the auspices of the Roscoe Pound–American Trial Lawyers Foundation. That Code proposed to solve the problem of client perjury by protecting client confidences completely. Consider some of its Illustrative Cases:

Illustrative Case 1(j). "A lawyer learns from a client during the trial of a civil or criminal case that the client intends to give testimony that the lawyer knows to be false. The lawyer reasonably believes that a request for leave to withdraw would be denied and/or would be understood by the judge and by opposing counsel as an indication that the testimony is false. The lawyer does not seek leave to withdraw, presents the client's testimony in the ordinary manner, and refers to it in summation as evidence of the case. The lawyer has not committed a disciplinary violation."

Illustrative Case 3(e). "A lawyer is conducting the defense of a criminal prosecution. The judge calls the lawyer to the bench and asks her whether the defendant is guilty. The lawyer knows that the defendant is guilty, and reasonably believes that an equivocal answer will be taken by the judge as an admission of guilt. The lawyer assures the judge that the defendant is innocent. The lawyer has not committed a disciplinary violation."

Illustrative Case 3(f): "The same facts as in 3(e), but the lawyer replies to the judge, 'I'm sorry, your Honor, but it would be improper for me to answer that question.' The lawyer has committed a disciplinary violation."

What do you think? Would you want to try cases in a system that was tolerant of the fact that defendants' testimony is untrue? What do you think juries believe about such testimony today?

d. Does the use of narrative testimony avoid the "trilemma" about which Professor Freedman writes? As you might expect, Professor Freedman writes:

"It is difficult to imagine a more unprofessional and irresponsible proposal. * * *

"[E]xperienced trial attorneys have often noted that jurors assume that the defendant's lawyer knows the truth about the case, and that the jury will frequently judge the defendant by drawing inferences from the attorney's conduct in the case. There is, of course, only one inference that can be drawn if the defendant's own attorney turns his or her back on the defendant at the most critical point in the trial, and then, in closing argument, sums up the case with no reference whatsoever to the fact that the defendant has testified or to the evidence presented in that testimony. Ironically, the Standards reject any solution that would involve informing the judge, but then propose a solution that, as a practical matter, succeeds in informing not only the judge but the jury as well."

e. Does Professor Freedman convince you that the Supreme Court was wrong in *Nix*? Do you agree that the rights of the defendant require tolerating more that a client wants to do? Is the fact that a lawyer would be aiding and abetting perjury if he or she were to knowingly elicit false testimony from the client and argue that the perjury is true, enough to make the Freedman argument ultimately unsatisfying?

———

PROBLEM 28

THE VERDICT THAT MAY BE TAINTED

Lawyers don't like to lose, and win or lose, they like to know how jurors reacted to their presentation. Lawyers often ask jurors, after the verdict, why they voted the way they did. Jurors have no obligation to respond but they often do, and in this and other settings, lawyers sometimes want to preserve an accurate record of what was said. Hence, this Problem first explores the propriety of a lawyer contacting jurors after trial to find out where a lawyer went wrong. It then moves to the rules restricting the contact of jurors before or during trial, and the restrictions relating to the payment of experts and fact witnesses. Following that, the

Problem explores the ethics of the lawyer secretly tape recording a conversation, and lastly, it looks at the rules governing when a lawyer may testify about what she has heard and observed.

FACTS

Marian Talley represented the defendant in a products liability case in which the jury returned an unexpectedly large verdict against her client. After the verdict, Talley sought to determine what had gone wrong. She asked a juror to come to her office and he did so. He was completely cooperative and said, "Most of the jurors initially voted to find no liability, or at least to set a much lower damage figure. One juror held out, however, and we finally came around to his position. That juror later confided to me, after the foreman announced the verdict, that he worked for a competitor of your client and would be paid handsomely for making the verdict come out as it did. It was too late to do anything, and I don't want to get involved, but it is good to get this off my chest."

Talley was angered by this explanation of the verdict and she asked the former juror to put the story in an affidavit. The juror said that he would prefer not to do so, but he told Talley where the supposed payoff was to be made. The juror threatened to deny everything if he were ever asked about the incident in court. At that point Talley activated a secret tape recording device that she always carried with her for occasions in which she needed to preserve what was said in a conversation. Talley skillfully got the former juror to repeat most of the story, and Talley left satisfied that she had gotten the information on the tape.

Using the information supplied by the former juror, Talley went to the place established for the payoff and saw a fat envelope handed to the allegedly dishonest juror by an executive of the juror's employer. She has moved for a new trial and plans to authenticate the tape recording of the former juror's disclosures and testify about her own observations of the payoff at the hearing on her motion. She had asked one of the firm's investigators to accompany her, but he never showed up (it turns out he got sick), so she is the only witness to the transfer of the envelope.

QUESTIONS

A. THE ETHICS OF CONTACTING JURORS AFTER TRIAL

1. Was it proper for Talley to talk to the juror and investigate the jury's deliberative process?

a. Look at Model Rule 3.5. Are you surprised by any of the restrictions placed on contacting jurors? Do you think they unduly restrict lawyers' ability to get the kind of information Talley was seeking?

b. Rapp v. Hawaii Supreme Court, 916 F.Supp. 1525 (D.Haw.1996), held that restrictions on post-trial contact with jurors violate free speech rights of the lawyers, the litigants and the jurors. Rapp, a lawyer, had been a pro se plaintiff in a state case. The jurors voted in his favor and he wanted to thank the jurors and learn how they had reacted to aspects of his advocacy. Alleging a fear of discipline if he contacted jurors, he filed this federal court action to have Rule 3.5 held unconstitutional. The court held that by allowing only contact with jurors that was "permitted by law," Rule 3.5(c) placed a vague and over broad limitation on First Amendment rights. Do you agree with this decision? Does the court seem to have been "solving" a non-existent problem?

c. In Commission for Lawyer Discipline v. Benton, 980 S.W.2d 425 (Tex.1998), the plaintiff's lawyer in a personal injury action in which the jury had awarded no damages wrote to all the jurors: "I was so angry with your verdict that I could not talk with you after the trial. I could not believe that 12 allegedly good people from Cameron County, who swore to return a verdict based on the evidence, could find [as you did]. * * * Your cold and unfair conduct does not matter now. Judge Hester * * * decided that your verdict was obviously unjust and granted * * * a new trial." The Texas Commission for Lawyer Discipline found that by sending this letter, the lawyer had violated the Texas version of Rule 3.5. It put the lawyer on probation. The Court of Appeals reversed, finding the Rule itself unconstitutional, but a badly split Texas Supreme Court found the Rule did not violate the lawyer's right of free speech, was not unconstitutionally overbroad, and was not unconstitutionally vague in prohibiting communications calculated to influence a juror's actions in future jury service.

Would the lawyer's letter in *Benton* have violated Model Rule 3.5(c)? Should a lawyer have been able to write such a letter to the judge after a trial without being held in contempt of court? Should the standard for what a lawyer may say to a juror be any less restrictive?

d. Is the concern that jurors will be harassed by the news media less serious than that they will be harassed by lawyers? Conversely, should jurors be able to sell stories about their deliberations to the highest bidder? See, e.g., Hansen, Post–Trial Interview Limits Criticized, ABA Journal, April 1994, at p. 26 (limits imposed on interviews of "Crazy Eddie" fraud trial jurors). Would you see greater constitutional issues raised if restrictions such as those in Model Rule 3.5 were placed on reporters?

2. Now that Talley believes that a juror violated his oath, what should she do?

a. Rule 606(b) of the Federal Rules of Evidence provides that "a juror may testify on the question whether extraneous prejudicial information was improperly brought to the jury's attention or whether any outside influence was improperly brought to bear upon any juror." Many state laws similarly make it possible to impeach a jury's verdict by showing that one or more of the jurors have been corrupted and that the integrity of the verdict is in doubt. Does that possibility, in turn, create a duty on a lawyer to bring the issue to the attention of the court?

b. Do the Model Rules give Talley such a professional obligation? Look at Model Rule 3.3(b) and Comment [12]. Do you have any doubt about what Talley is required to do?

c. Talley is undoubtedly glad she did not learn it was her client who had tried to bribe a juror. Suppose it had been her client who committed that crime. What would Talley's obligation be? Is she required to reveal information that clearly relates to the representation and thus that would be confidential under Model Rule 1.6(a)? Look at Model Rule 3.3(c).

B.   CONTACTING JURORS BEFORE TRIAL; COMPENSATION OF WITNESSES

1.   Would it be improper for Talley's opponent to try to bribe one or more of the jurors before the trial?

a. Do not ponder long whether or not a lawyer may bribe a juror. That is clearly illegal under the law of all jurisdictions.

b. Is it similarly prohibited by the Model Rules? Look at Model Rule 3.5(a). Remember also Model Rules 8.4(b), 8.4 (c) & 8.4 (d). Everywhere Talley's opponent turns, it is clear that he or she is in big trouble.

2.   Can we just stop there and feel self-righteous? Does the complex mix of people in a modern society mean that investigating the characteristics of individual jurors must be of greater concern than ever to the honorable trial lawyer as well?

a. Consider one report of how juries really work:

"In an unusual post-trial move, the lawyer for Eric Menendez invited seven sympathetic female jurors to her office where they told reporters on Saturday that a battle between men and women on Mr. Menendez's jury doomed the chances for a verdict.[1] * * *

" 'It was hostile in there,' said one juror * * *. 'There were insults, sexual comments. * * *

"Another juror * * * said, 'We were called ignorant asses and empty headed and "those women." We had one juror who would put on his sunglasses and be balancing his checkbook and cutting out coupons when the women were talking.' * * *

"A vote on the first day of deliberations indicated the jury was split, the female jurors said, with six women for manslaughter convictions and six men for first-degree murder. Ultimately, five men voted for first-degree murder, one for second-degree. The women voted for voluntary manslaughter."[2]

b. Would Talley or any other lawyer be violating the Model Rules if she interviewed jurors before the trial outside the presence of the judge?

1. The state prosecuted Eric and Lyle Menendez for killing their parents in order to inherit a substantial fortune. They ultimately admitted the killing but claimed self-defense, asserting that they had been molested by their father for many years and were afraid he would kill them to prevent them from disclosing his acts.

2. New York Times, Jan. 13, 1994, Sec. A. p. 13, col. 1.

Should a lawyer be permitted to have private investigators do background checks on potential jurors? Should prosecutors have the information as well as defense counsel; should they be able to use police officers to investigate the jurors?

c.   Given the Supreme Court's limitations on the use of peremptory challenges to strike jurors based on general categories of race and sex,[3] do lawyers need more freedom to investigate so as to be able to challenge for cause and to defend their peremptory strikes? Should judges give lawyers less information in order to limit the lawyers' ability to exclude jurors for reasons that do not relate to their impartiality?

3.   If there is to be a prohibition on pre-trial communication or contact with jurors, how broadly should the rule be stated?

a.   Restatement Third, The Law Governing Lawyers § 115(1) says that, "except as allowed by law," a lawyer may not "communicate with * * * a person known by the lawyer to be a member of a jury pool from which the jury will be drawn." Comment *b* to § 115 explains: "The rules concerning jury trial undertake to ensure that no juror will have a predisposition toward either party. Prohibition of pretrial communication with prospective jurors both prevents improper influence and avoids the necessity of inquiry concerning such contacts."

Are you convinced that the entire jury pool should be off-limits to lawyer contact? Would a prohibition directed at any smaller group of jurors adequately protect the interest in seeing that none of the jurors are tainted?

b.   Might part of the justification for the restrictions be to protect the privacy of jurors? In the O.J. Simpson case, prospective jurors were forced to answer a court questionnaire over 50 pages in length about their religion, political attitudes, and life experiences. Should we be concerned about lawyers intruding into the jurors' personal lives without at least the minimal protection given by court review of the process?

4.   Is it proper to pay a witness for the time it takes to prepare and give testimony?

a.   Look at Model Rule 3.4(b) and Comment [3]. A lawyer clearly may not pay a witness for the content of his or her testimony, i.e., only pay the witness if he or she testifies in a particular way. It is routine, however, to pay expert witnesses for the time they spend preparing and testifying in a case.[4]

---

3. Georgia v. McCollum, 505 U.S. 42, 112 S.Ct. 2348, 120 L.Ed.2d 33 (1992) (unconstitutional for either prosecutor or defense counsel to exercise peremptory challenges based on racial stereotypes); J.E.B. v. Alabama ex rel. T.B., 511 U.S. 127, 114 S.Ct. 1419, 128 L.Ed.2d 89 (1994) (same result regarding sex–based challenges). These issues were discussed earlier in Problem 24.

4. However, an expert witness may not be paid a fee contingent on their testimony or the success of the client in the matter. See, e.g., Person v. Association of the Bar of the City of New York, 554 F.2d 534 (2d Cir.), cert. denied 434 U.S. 924, 98 S.Ct. 403, 54 L.Ed.2d 282 (1977), discussed in Problem 36, infra.

b. Should it be proper for Martin to pay a fact-witness (not an expert) for his time when he testifies and prepares for the testimony? ABA Formal Opinion 96–402 (Aug. 2, 1996) concluded that it is indeed proper to pay fact witnesses who have to devote substantial time to a case. Comment [3] to Model Rule 3.4 does not literally permit such payments, the Opinion conceded, but ABA Model Code of Professional Responsibility DR 7–109 did allow paying fact witnesses for the "loss of time in attending or testifying." The amount of any compensation paid must be reasonable, the Opinion says, so as not to suggest payment for the content of the testimony. But even retired people who do not forego salary while they are testifying may be paid for the value of their time, not just in testifying but in preparing for testimony as well.

c. What do you think of this Opinion? Do you think the distinction between paying for time and paying for testimony will be easily maintained? On the other hand, could a company pay a current employee her regular salary for time spent working on and testifying in the case? Is the payment to a former employee or other outside witness significantly different?

C. Secret tape recording

1. Was it professionally responsible for Talley to tape record the conversation when it became clear that the juror would not commit his testimony to paper or repeat it to any other person? How should Talley be able to preserve accurate evidence of what was said?

a. Talley's secret recording may not be a violation of state civil or criminal law. It is not a violation of federal law. Section 2511 of the Omnibus Crime Control and Safe Streets Act of 1968, 18 U.S.C.A. § 2511(2)(d), reads: "It shall not be unlawful under this Chapter for a person not acting under color of law to intercept a wire or oral communication where such person is a party to the communication * * * unless such communication is intercepted for the purpose of committing any criminal or tortious act * * * ."

See also, United States v. White, 401 U.S. 745, 91 S.Ct. 1122, 28 L.Ed.2d 453 (1971) (Sections 2510–2520 of the Omnibus Crime Control Act permit a participant to record a conversation secretly).

b. FCC regulations are applicable only if telephones are used; these require that there be an automatic tone warning device furnished, installed, and maintained by the telephone company before telephone conversations may be recorded. Failure of a person to use this device is not criminal, although it can subject one to loss of phone service. The law of evidence has been held not to prohibit the introduction of tapes obtained in violation of these FCC tariffs. Battaglia v. United States, 349 F.2d 556 (9th Cir.1965), cert. denied 382 U.S. 955, 86 S.Ct. 430, 15 L.Ed.2d 360 (1965).

c. State laws vary, but some states allow what is called "consensual" recording, i.e., one party to the conversation knows that it is being taped and does not object.

2.   If Talley's tape recording did violate state law, would her conduct also make her subject to professional discipline or other remedies?

a. Whatever the answer where the recording is legal, what if the recording is not legal? Look at ABA Model Rule 4.4(a). In this context, is tape recording a method of "obtaining evidence that violate[s] the legal rights" of the person being recorded?

b. Nissan Motor Co., Ltd. v. Nissan Computer Corp., 180 F.Supp.2d 1089 (C.D.Cal.2002), was a dispute over whether defense counsel could tape record conversations it had with plaintiff's counsel. Defense counsel allegedly believed the plaintiff's lawyers misrepresented what they had said in phone conversations and threatened to record those calls. Plaintiff's counsel objected to such recording, and the Court said that taping conversations with opposing counsel without consent violated California state law against wiretapping. More broadly, the court found that threatening to tape record conversations between counsel would violate Federal Rule of Civil Procedure, which mandates the "just, speedy, and inexpensive determination of every action." The court explained that inhibiting the ability of attorneys to freely communicate over the telephone would impair the progress of litigation by forcing the parties to put everything in writing, resulting in inevitable delays and complications. The court did not focus on the argument that using recording to reduce disagreement about what was actually said over the telephone might tend to reduce disputation and delay.

c. Whether or not a crime has been committed, however, might there may be a violation of Model Rule 8.4(c) if circumstances indicate the lawyer deceived the person into believing there would be no taping. For example, in Committee on Professional Ethics v. Mollman, 488 N.W.2d 168 (Iowa 1992), the lawyer had agreed to wear a concealed microphone to a meeting with his drug client in exchange for leniency in his own prosecution for drug possession. The Court held that for the lawyer to mislead his client in this way justified a 30–day suspension.

d. How else might a court deal with an attorney who engaged in secret tape recording? See, e.g., Parrott v. Wilson, 707 F.2d 1262 (11th Cir.1983), cert. denied 464 U.S. 936, 104 S.Ct. 344, 78 L.Ed.2d 311 (1983), holding that any alleged work product privilege involving clandestine tape recordings of witnesses was lost because such secret taping violated the attorney's ethical standards even though neither federal nor the relevant state law prohibited taping. Thus, the tapes had to be produced for discovery. Does this seem to you to be a sensible compromise? An arbitrary result?

3.   Should the ethical principle simply be that it is unprofessional for a lawyer to engage in tape recording, whether of a client or a third party?

a.   This is more than a theoretical inquiry. ABA Formal Opinion 337 (Aug. 10, 1974) told lawyers:

"With the exception noted in the last paragraph, the Committee concludes that no lawyer should record any conversation whether by tapes or other electronic device, without the consent or prior knowledge of all parties to the conversation.

"There may be extraordinary circumstances in which the Attorney General of the United States or the principal prosecuting attorney of a state or local government or law enforcement attorneys or officers acting under the direction of the Attorney General or such principal prosecuting attorneys might ethically make and use secret recordings if acting within strict statutory limitations conforming to constitutional requirements. This opinion does not address such exceptions which would necessarily require examination on a case by case basis. It should be stressed, however, that the mere fact that secret recordation in a particular instance is not illegal will not necessarily render the conduct of a public law enforcement officer in making such a recording ethical."

b.   Was the ABA Committee too sweeping in its conclusion? Does our society have a common moral revulsion against secret tape recording? Notice the date of the Opinion. It was written the same year that President Nixon (a lawyer) resigned from the Presidency. During the Watergate investigation it became public knowledge that he had secretly taped conversations to which he was a party. Many people objected to the secret taping along with a lot of other things President Nixon had done.

c.   Would you support a similar broad prohibition by the ethics committee of your state today? Why should private attorneys in criminal cases be placed under stricter ethical standards than the prosecutor? Should it be unethical for prosecutors to engage in secret tape recordings as well? Note that the Opinion does not bless such secret recordings, when it says: "the mere fact that secret recordation in a particular instance is not illegal will not necessarily render the conduct of a public law enforcement officer in making such a recording ethical."

4. Is the older ABA position on tape recording now outdated?

a.   Does the text of the Model Rules justify the ABA Opinion? The rules at the time, and the rules today, forbid deceitful conduct. Is it deceitful to secretly tape a conversation to which you are a party, if you do not make any representation about whether or not it is being taped?

b.   The Association of the Bar of the City of New York partly rejected ABA Formal Opinion No. 337 and held that, because prosecutors may surreptitiously record a conversation by placing a tape recorder on one of the parties to the conversation with only the consent of that party, criminal defense lawyers should be able to record their conversations with witnesses as well. Recording of conversations with the lawyer's own clients and recording in commercial or civil contexts remained prohibited. See A.B.C.N.Y. Inquiry No. 80–95 (1982).

c.   In Opinion No. 515 (1979), the New York State Bar Association added that a lawyer should be able to respond to a question initiated by a client and advise that client that the client himself may surreptitiously record a conversation where that recording is lawful. Counsel, however, may not do the recording. See also Texas Professional Ethics Committee Opinion No. 514 (May 24, 1995), to the same effect.

Does that distinction make sense to you?

d.   Restatement Third, The Law Governing Lawyers § 106, Comment *b*, says:

> "When secret recording is not prohibited by law, doing so is permissible for lawyers conducting investigations on behalf of their clients, but should be done only when a compelling need exists to obtain evidence otherwise unavailable in an equally reliable form. Such a need may exist more readily in a criminal-defense representation."

Do you agree that there should be a "compelling need" requirement to engage in secret tape recording? Why might criminal defense lawyers have a greater such need than other lawyers?

e.   Now, the ABA has explicitly overruled ABA Formal Opinion 337 in ABA Formal Opinion 01–422 (June 24, 2001). The new Opinion preserves the prohibition of recording in violation of state law. Nor may a lawyer falsely represent that a conversation is not being recorded. However, the Committee concluded: (1) that it is no longer universally accepted that nonconsensual taping of conversations is inherently deceitful, (2) that there are circumstances in which disclosure would defeat a legitimate and necessary activity, and (3) that Opinion 337 is no longer consistent with the Model Rules. However, the Committee found that it is inadvisable for a lawyer to record a conversation with his own client concerning the subject matter of the representation without the client's knowledge.

Has the Opinion touched on all the relevant issues to your satisfaction?

D.   THE LAWYER AS A WITNESS AT THE CLIENT'S TRIAL

1. Is any ethical problem presented if Talley testifies at the hearing on her motion for a new trial?

a.   Look at Model Rule 3.7(a). For whose protection were the restrictions on the lawyer's acting as a witness intended?

b.   Might one argue that a jury might not be able to distinguish between a lawyer's argument and her testimony? Does that mean the rule ought not apply when the advocate testifies in a bench trial? A hearing on a motion for new trial? A pro se litigant may both represent himself and testify even if he has a law license, so how can one argue that the two roles are inherently inconsistent?

c.   In United States v. Edwards, 154 F.3d 915 (9th Cir.1998), the police found a bag with cocaine, but there was no direct evidence to tie it to the defendant. In mid-trial, the prosecutor said that he had been inspecting the bag in the presence of two police officers and he found a receipt with the defendant's name on it in the lining at the bottom of the bag. A police officer testified at trial where the receipt was found. Even though the prosecutor never testified, the officer told how the receipt was found and used the prosecutor's name. The Court said that the fact his name was before the jury in connection with that evidence constituted prohibited "vouching" for evidence and required the prosecutor to withdraw. Because he failed to do so, the court reversed the conviction. Do the Model Rules support this analysis?

d.   In Zurich Insurance Company v. Knotts, 52 S.W.3d 555 (Ky.2001), the plaintiff sued an insurance company to obtain payment of a personal injury award against the insured. Plaintiff's lawyer had handled the claim throughout initial settlement negotiations and jury trial, and the plaintiff now says the insurance company acted in bad faith by not acting reasonably and promptly during the course of negotiations. The plaintiff's attorney filed a personal affidavit attesting to some of the practices of the defendant's counsel, although the attorney indicated no intention to actually testify at trial. The court held that filing the affidavit did not disqualify the attorney from continuing to represent the plaintiff. The court found it would be unduly prejudicial to disqualify counsel and any potential prejudice to the defendant could be mitigated by effective cross-examination. Disqualification is an extreme measure, and factors such as the attorney's level of expertise, familiarity with the claim, and the level of trust and confidence of the client in the attorney were all relevant considerations.

Do you agree with this result? Is it consistent with Model Rule 3.7(a) & (b)?

2.   Should a party be able to "waive" the protections of Model Rule 3.7?

a.   Which party would be the one to "waive" the protection? Would it be the party calling the witness or the party who might claim to be prejudiced by the testimony? Notice that Model Rule 3.7 does not provide for a waiver. Why not? Is the purpose of the rule to protect the parties or to protect the court and the fact-finding process?

b.   California does allow the client to "waive" the disqualification. The rule grew out of the decision in Comden v. Superior Court, 576 P.2d 971 (Cal.1978), cert. denied 439 U.S. 981, 99 S.Ct. 568, 58 L.Ed.2d 652 (1978). Plaintiff argued that disqualification of the firm created a "substantial hardship" because of the distinctive value of the services of the law firm. The lawyer argued that, although some of his work product could be transferred to new counsel, his "impressions and rapport with the people involved" could not be transferred. The court rejected these arguments and held that loss of expertise, interviews, research, and preliminary discussions of trial strategy do not constitute enough to support the substantial hardship exception also found in Model Rule 3.7(a)(3).

c.   California responded to *Comden* by amending its Rule [now Rule 5–210] to allow a lawyer to let the client decide how to balance the need for the lawyer against the possible problems created by the dual role. A lawyer could be both advocate and witness if the lawyer secures the "informed, written consent of the client" after fully advising the client and after giving the client a reasonable opportunity to seek the advice of independent counsel.

3. If the lawyer-witness is not herself the trial lawyer, are there any justifications for imputing the advocate-witness rules to other members of her firm who are trial counsel?

a. Look at ABA Model Rule 3.7(b) and Comments [1] & [5] that discuss the rationale for the Rule. The ABA Model Code of Professional Responsibility drew no distinction between trial counsel and other members of the lawyer's firm acting as a witness. It imputed disqualification of the advocate-witness to all lawyers in same firm.

b. Does Model Rule 3.7(b) represent more realism or simply a decline in ethical standards? If Talley's investigator in this Problem had not gotten sick at the last minute, could Talley have avoided the problem by having the investigator act as the witness? If so, why should there be any question about allowing other lawyers in the same law firm to conduct the trial while Talley is the one who testifies?

4. When is the lawyer required to be disqualified? Is it at the moment the lawyer is put on a witness list? Is it at some earlier time?

a. In Comden v. Superior Court, supra, the California Supreme Court upheld a trial court decision disqualifying a lawyer who could testify as to what was said in certain meetings involving the litigants. The plaintiffs argued that the disqualification order was premature because later discovery might make the attorney's testimony unnecessary. However, the court concluded that withdrawal is required whenever the attorney "ought" to testify. Contra, e.g., Connell v. Clairol, Inc., 440 F.Supp. 17, 19 n. 1 (N.D.Ga.1977) (the attorney's testimony must be "in fact, genuinely needed"). Which rule do you think is better?

b. In Taylor v. Grogan, 900 P.2d 60 (Colo.1995), cert.denied 516 U.S. 1094, 116 S.Ct. 816, 133 L.Ed.2d 761 (1996), the defendant called the plaintiff's lawyers for the limited purpose of testifying to facts underlying a statute of limitations defense. The question was whether calling those lawyers constituted a motion to disqualify the lawyers as well. The court held that it did not and that it had been error for the trial court to disqualify counsel.

c. Chappell v. Cosgrove, 916 P.2d 836 (N.M.1996), involved a lawyer who had been one of five persons at a meeting where the defendants allegedly agreed to construct a park. The plaintiff residents moved to disqualify him, alleging he was a potential witness. The court said that the test for disqualification is materiality of the testimony, the need for the lawyer to give it, and the prejudice if the lawyer does testify. Because there were several people at the meeting, the court concluded that the lawyer's testimony would be cumulative, not necessary, and therefore it did not order disqualification.

d. Restatement Third, The Law Governing Lawyers § 108, Comment *e*, however, says that the advocate-witness prohibition "is not affected by the character of the testimony as cumulative." Even cumulative testimony may be important, the Comment says, so the issue is whether "a reasonable lawyer, viewing the circumstances objectively, would conclude that failure of the lawyer to testify would have a substantially adverse affect on the client's cause."

e. If an attorney is disqualified from representing a client because the attorney will be a witness and the client then hires another law firm to handle the litigation, may the lawyer/witness help prepare the new lawyers? Why or why not, given the rationale that animates the Rule?

5. What should be defense counsel's response if the prosecutor in a criminal case tries to testify against the defendant? How can the prosecutor avoid the problem if it becomes necessary for her to testify?

a. People v. Donaldson, 113 Cal.Rptr.2d 548 (Cal.Ct.App.2001), granted a new trial based on ineffective assistance of counsel in a case of child endangerment. The prosecution had only one witness to the defendant's alleged acts; that witness testified at the preliminary hearing that she had actually seen the defendant holding a pillow over the defendant's daughter's face, but at trial, the witness seemed confused and said that she had never actually seen anything occur. The witness also said that the prosecutor had intimidated her and made her feel as though if she did not testify, she would be put under arrest. Then the prosecutor called herself as a witness to impeach the credibility of this key prosecution witness to give a narrative account of the conversations she had with the witness before the witness testified. The court held that, by calling herself as a witness she violated professional conduct rule generally prohibiting a lawyer from acting as both advocate and witness. The defense counsel then rendered ineffective assistance by failing to object when the prosecutor took the witness stand.

b. Might the prosecutor in *Donaldson* have violated some other rules as well? Look at Model Rule 3.4(e). Did the prosecutor "state a personal opinion as to * * * the credibility of a witness," for example? The court also found that in her closing argument, the prosecutor had improperly expressed personal belief in defendant's guilt.

PROBLEM 29

THE CRUSADING PROSECUTOR

The prosecutor, as a representative of the state, is a lawyer with special authority and special responsibilities. It should not be surprising, then, that some ethical standards of prosecutors are also sui generis. This Problem first considers the use of the media and other publicity as a tool in modern litigation in the context of a prosecutor's work. Next, it looks at the prosecutor's decision what to charge. Third, it asks when a prosecutor may subpoena the files or otherwise investigate a criminal defense lawyer. The Problem then examines restrictions on the leverage available to a modern prosecutor and broader questions about the ethical responsibilities of government lawyers.

FACTS

"Clean Gene" White is the crusading young State's Attorney of Springfield County, the home of the state legislature. He says he sees a public interest (and his detractors say a personal political benefit) in uncovering what he publicly has called a "lot of skeletons under the beds of some state legislators." Gene has started a "special prosecutions" branch of his office that is charged with discovering the misdeeds of legislators. Each week, on Monday, Gene holds a press conference to assert his belief in ethics, report on indictments just issued, allude to possible indictments, and answer questions put to him by the reporters covering his office.

Newspapers have begun to report rumors and rumors of rumors as to which persons are likely to be indicted; Gene has denied publicly that he or anyone in his office is responsible for the leaks and has said that he "denounces the rumor mill."

The special unit is responsible thus far for successfully prosecuting three cases: one consisting of forty-six unpaid parking tickets by the chairman of the motor vehicle committee (a "callous breach of the public trust," according to Gene); a second for failure to report a sale of race track stock on a legislator's ethics form; and a third against a House committee chairman for taking a $5,000 bribe to kill a bill.

Though his office normally exercises discretion not to prosecute persons found with minor amounts of marijuana, the office recently indicted a state official found with one marijuana cigarette in his car. This particular legislator is widely suspected of being in league with organized crime, although no admissible evidence has ever been found to support such a charge. Gene privately told one of his assistants to follow this legislator in an effort to uncover some wrongdoing. When the assistant reported the discovery of the marijuana cigarette, Gene said: "Prosecute. I know we normally don't in such cases, but I want to make it hot for this fellow."

QUESTIONS

A.   MEDIA RELATIONS IN MODERN LITIGATION

1. What limits do the Model Rules place on White's use of press conferences and other public statements to tell the public about his office's work?

a. ABA Model Rule 3.8(f) imposes specific trial publicity rules on the prosecutor, while Model Rule 3.6 imposes other publicity restrictions equally on both prosecutors and private lawyers. The history of the development of the modern day rules reflect the ABA responses to Supreme Court rulings in both free speech and fair trial cases. Canon 20 of the Canons of Professional Ethics (1908), in the Standards Supplement, provided:

> Newspaper publications by a lawyer as to a pending or anticipated litigation * * * [g]enerally * * * are to be condemned. * * * An ex parte reference to the facts should not go beyond quotation from the record and papers on file in the court; but even in extreme cases it is better to avoid any ex parte statement.

b. Sheppard v. Maxwell, 384 U.S. 333, 86 S.Ct. 1507, 16 L.Ed.2d 600 (1966), made clear that excessive pretrial and trial publicity could constitute a denial of due process of law. Marilyn Sheppard, wife of prominent Dr. Samuel Sheppard, was bludgeoned to death in their home. Dr. Sheppard was accused of the crime, although he said there had been an intruder in the home. From shortly after the murder, repeated news stories criticized Dr. Sheppard's alleged failure to cooperate with the police and accused prosecutors of letting Sheppard "get away with murder." The stories continued through jury selection and the trial, and the jurors saw much of it. With only Justice Black dissenting, the Court put primary blame for the "carnival atmosphere" on the trial judge. It said "the trial court might well have proscribed extrajudicial statements by any lawyer, party, witness, or court official which divulged prejudicial matters." 384 U.S. at 361, 86 S.Ct. at 1521, 16 L.Ed.2d at 619.

c. It was in the context of the *Sheppard* case that the ABA adopted DR 7–107 of the Model Code of Professional Responsibility. Take a look at it in the Standards Supplement. It permitted more pre-trial publicity than Canon 20 had, but it was quite specific about what lawyers could and could not say. Was the greater liberality of DR 7–107 a move in the right direction? A start down the slippery slope of declining professional standards? Was DR 7–107 too restrictive, in light of the First Amendment?

d. The Seventh Circuit held the latter was true. In Chicago Council of Lawyers v. Bauer, 522 F.2d 242, 249 (7th Cir.1975), cert. denied sub nom. Cunningham v. Chicago Council of Lawyers, 427 U.S. 912, 96 S.Ct. 3201, 49 L.Ed.2d 1204 (1976), the court said:

> "We are of the view that the rubric used in the rules under consideration, that lawyers' comments about pending or imminent litigation must be proscribed 'if there is a reasonable likelihood that such dissemination will interfere with a fair trial or otherwise prejudice the due administration of justice' is overbroad and therefore does not meet constitutional standards. Instead, we think a narrower and more restrictive standard * * * should apply: Only those comments that pose a 'serious and imminent threat' of

interference with the fair administration of justice can be constitutionally proscribed."[1]

e. Should the rules on pre-trial publicity in civil cases differ from those in criminal cases? The Court in *Bauer,* said yes:

"* * * [W]e should recognize that although we rightfully place a prime value on providing a system of impartial justice to settle civil disputes, we require even a greater insularity against the possibility of interference with fairness in criminal cases. Perhaps this is symbolically reflected in the Sixth Amendment's requirement of an 'impartial jury' in criminal cases whereas the Seventh Amendment guarantees only 'trial by jury' in civil cases. The point to be made is that the mere invocation of the phrase 'fair trial' does not as readily justify a restriction on speech when we are referring to civil trials." 522 F.2d at 257–58.

f. Later, the Fourth Circuit, in Hirschkop v. Snead, 594 F.2d 356 (4th Cir.1979) (per curiam), went even further. It upheld the constitutionality of Virginia DR 7–107 as applied to *criminal jury* trials, but invalidated it as applied to all other litigation, such as bench trials, presentencing hearings, disciplinary proceedings before a judge, civil cases, and matters pending before administrative agencies.

2. Is the present version of Model Rule 3.6 consistent with the First Amendment?

a. Gentile v. Nevada State Bar, 501 U.S. 1030, 111 S.Ct. 2720, 115 L.Ed.2d 888 (1991), was the first Supreme Court case in many years to test the rules on pre-trial statements to the press. In *Gentile,* drug evidence had disappeared from a safe deposit box that undercover police officers had rented. The state charged Gentile's client with taking the drugs. Gentile held a press conference on the day of the arraignment at which he said that a police officer had likely taken them and that the police were using his client as a scapegoat. The jury later acquitted his client and then the Nevada State Bar sought to discipline Gentile for creating a "substantial likelihood of material prejudice" by influencing the potential jury pool against the state. The Nevada Supreme Court affirmed a private reprimand.

The U.S. Supreme Court reversed in opinions authored by Chief Justice Rehnquist and Justice Kennedy. The Chief Justice persuaded a slim majority (White, O'Connor, Scalia & Souter) that lawyers' speech may be regulated by less than a "clear and present danger" standard, and that the "substantial likelihood of material prejudice" standard used by Nevada balanced relevant interests permissibly. However, Justice Kennedy persuaded an equally slim majority (Marshall, Blackmun, Stevens & O'Connor) that the specific Nevada rule was void for vagueness. The rule

---

1. The court also ruled that comments during the period between completion of trial and sentencing could "never be deemed a serious and imminent threat of interference with the fair administration of justice" and thus that the prohibition of comments "reasonably likely to affect the imposition of sentence" was invalid.

permitted a lawyer to announce the "general nature of the defense" but only to do so "without elaboration." That, said the Kennedy majority, was too vague to let Gentile know what he could and could not say. Instead of creating a safe harbor, Rule 3.6(c) created a "trap for the wary as well as the unwary."

b. In United States v. Bingham, 769 F.Supp. 1039 (N.D.Ill.1991), a district judge ordered the U.S. Attorney to consider prosecuting defense counsel who, on the eve of jury selection in a case involving street gangs, gave television interviews criticizing the judge, among other things, for planning to empanel an "anonymous jury," i.e., not reporting their names. The judge considered this statement to be a serious and imminent threat to the administration of justice and subject to discipline in spite of *Gentile*.

Do you agree with the judge's response? If the lawyer had objected to the anonymous jury in open court, could he then have repeated the objection to the media? See Model Rule 3.6(b)(2) ("state * * * information contained in a public record"). The *Bingham* opinion, at 769 F.Supp. at 1041, even quotes from a court rule that specifically says "the United States Attorney, or lawyer or law firm may quote from or refer without comment to public records of the court in the case." Do you agree that it is different to report something already said in court than to have the judge read your views for the first time in the newspaper?

c. In re Morrissey, 168 F.3d 134 (4th Cir.1999), involved criminal defense counsel who used the media as part of his effort to help his client fight drug charges. For example, he obtained a list of witnesses who testified before the state grand jury and interviewed one on videotape recanting his grand jury testimony. Morrissey knew that person would be called as a government witness in the federal case, and he said he was releasing the tape to send a message to other witnesses. Later, he said the prosecution was vindictive and the charges would have been laughed out of court if he had filed them when he was a prosecutor. The district judge, in a bench trial, convicted the attorney for criminal contempt for violating local version of Rule 3.6. The judge sentenced Morrissey to ninety days imprisonment and three years probation and also suspended him from practicing law in the Eastern District of Virginia for two years. The Fourth Circuit affirmed and rejected the First Amendment challenge the rule, which required a "reasonable likelihood" of material prejudice to a fair trial or the administration of justice.

d. In re Litz, 721 N.E.2d 258 (Ind.1999), the lawyer representing a woman in securing a reversal of her conviction for neglect of a dependent wrote a series of letters to area newspapers asserting, inter alia, that his client had spent the "last 18 months in jail for a crime she did not commit" and reporting that she had passed a lie detector test. The court found the letters made "a fair trial much less likely to occur" and "created a serious likelihood of materially prejudicing" the retrial. The court, however, limited the sanction to a public reprimand.

e. Iowa Supreme Court Board of Professional Ethics and Conduct v. Visser, 629 N.W.2d 376 (Iowa 2001), was a discipline case. The respondent lawyer had faxed a statement about a pending civil case to a reporter. The court found the statement misleading but ruled that the disciplinary board did not establish a violation of the state's counterpart to Rule 3.6(a) because, it said, his comments did not have "a substantial likelihood of materially" affecting the outcome of the proceeding. For example, the article, "which was the only one published in connection with the case, was published on November 6, 1998—almost two years before the trial." The court said that its interpretation of the rule was necessary so that it could "pass constitutional muster."[2] See also, Restatement Third, The Law Governing Lawyers § 109.

3.   Assuming that some restrictions on pre-trial comment are constitutional, on whom should such restrictions be imposed?

a.   Were you struck by the fact that in all of the above cases it was defense counsel, never prosecutors, who were accused of prejudicial publicity? Do you suppose the incidence of excessive publicity is as one-sided as these numbers suggest?

b.   Is the public interest often served by news stories about lawsuits? Think about suits filed by public interest groups, for example? Are some lawsuits filed more for the publicity they will generate than for the actual result expected at trial? Should that practice be discouraged? Should Federal Rule 11, discussed earlier in Problem 23, be relevant?

c.   Do the Model Rules recognize a different public disclosure interest in cases involving alleged public corruption?

When Archibald Cox, the first Watergate special prosecutor, moved to prevent the Senate Watergate Committee from granting testimonial immunity from prosecution to John Dean and Jeb Stuart Magruder on the grounds that their testimony in public would create prejudicial pre-trial publicity, Judge Sirica denied the motion and stated, inter alia:

> "It is apparent as well that a committee's legislative purpose may legitimately include the publication of information."[3]

It was the official position of the Senate Watergate Committee that:

> "the public had a right to know. * * * The full import of the hearings could only be achieved by observing the witnesses and hearing their testimony. * * * The committee believes that its position has proven correct and its public hearings awakened the public to the perils posed by the Watergate affair to the integrity of the electoral process and our democratic form of government.

2.   However, the court ruled that respondent's comments were a violation of the state's counterpart to Model Rule 8.4(c) (conduct involving misrepresentation) because his statements to the press that "one judge has already determined that [Heins] is unlikely to succeed on the merits of his far-fetched claims" was only partially true; the judge had not commented at all on a second suit which had different claims. The court then admonished the respondent for that violation.

3.   In re Application of United States Senate Select Committee on Presidential Campaign Activities, 361 F.Supp. 1270, 1281–82 (D.D.C.1973).

"Perhaps proof of the impact of the committee's hearings is found in the unprecedented public response to the firing of Special Prosecutor Cox on October 20, 1973. On that weekend alone, a half million telegrams came to the Congress. Hundreds of thousands of telegrams flowed in during the following days. The overwhelming sentiment of these telegrams was in opposition to the President's action. It is doubtful that public sentiment would have been so aroused by the President's action had the public not been sensitized to the issues involved through the committee's hearings."[4]

d. In re Sealed Case (Office of Independent Counsel Contempt Proceeding), 192 F.3d 995 (D.C.Cir.1999), involved alleged leaks of grand jury information from Independent Counsel Kenneth Starr's office. In an opinion not as widely publicized in the media as the original charge, the D.C. Circuit expressly found that the OIC had engaged in no violation of Rule 6(e), Federal Rules of Criminal Procedure. The Justice Department supported the OIC on this matter and argued that Rule 6(e) was not violated by a prosecutor's statement of opinion about someone's potential liability, even if some of the investigation upon which the conclusion was based was also taking place before a grand jury.

4. Did "Clean Gene" White violate Rule 3.6? If so, when?

a. Did White violate Rule 3.6 when he said that there are "a lot of skeletons under the beds of some state legislators"? When he held press conferences to report on indictments just issued? When he alluded to possible indictments? Should White not give any press conferences but let his press secretary perform that function? Look at Model Rule 3.6(d). Would it help if his press secretary were not a lawyer. See Model Rule 3.8(f).

b. Would White violate Rule 3.6 if he truthfully stated, "We have just filed a motion to force Judge Smith to recuse himself, because, as our motions states, 'the Judge's actions in this case show that he is soft on pubic corruption' "? Why or why not? Cf. Model Rule 8.2(a).

c. Would White violate Rule 3.6 if he truthfully said, "We have just indicted Kyle Jones, who often calls himself 'Kyle the Killer.' He was last seen heading south of Route 66. If you see him, call police, but do not try to apprehend, for he is considered armed and dangerous"? Why might any

---

4. The Final Report of the Select Committee on Presidential Campaign Activities, United States Senate, Report No. 93–981, 93d Cong., 2d Sess. (June, 1974) at xxxi–xxxii.

That a committee claims a need for publicity does not mean that types of publicity may not be distinguished. The Select Committee ruled for its public sessions:

"The committee followed a practice not typical of certain congressional hearings. It refrained from calling a witness in public session that it knew would refuse to testify on the assertion of the fifth amendment privilege against self-incrimination. * * * This policy was instituted * * * on the belief that no legislative purpose would be served by public exhibition of witnesses who claimed the privilege." Id. at xxxi.

reasonable rule have to allow prosecutors the latitude to make such statements?

d. Was Gene White acting properly in denouncing "the rumor mill"? If a commentator claims that a trial court once ruled in an unpublished opinion that one of White's assistants is "an over zealous prosecutor," may White respond truthfully, "The commentator is simply repeating a false charge that one of the suspects has made several times. The suspect is lying; the commentator should check his facts before he opens his mouth." Does Model Rule 3.6(c) protect such responses from prosecutors or only the responses of defense counsel?

5. Should the fact that Rule 3.6 allows certain kinds of trial publicity preclude other remedies against lawyers if they say that which Rule 3.6 allows?

a. In Buckley v. Fitzsimmons, 509 U.S. 259, 113 S.Ct. 2606, 125 L.Ed.2d 209 (1993), plaintiff filed a damage suit against a prosecutor for allegedly fabricating evidence of defendant's guilt and for announcing the defendant's arrest at a press conference that arguably prejudiced the later trial. The defendant spent about three years in jail and went through one mistrial before a third party confessed to the crime and the defendant was released. The Seventh Circuit held the conduct of the prosecutor subject to an absolute privilege because it was all part of normal preparation of a case. The Supreme Court reversed and instead applied a "functional test" looking to the function being performed rather than the role of the actor. "Comments to the media have no functional tie to the judicial process," the Court said. In some cases, such comments may serve an important public function, but that is not enough to cloak them in the absolute immunity that applies to statements made in the course of a trial. Do you agree?

b. Seidl v. Greentree Mortgage Company, 30 F.Supp.2d 1292 (D.Colo. 1998), involved publicity in a civil trial, this time over the Internet. Plaintiff's counsel in a suit charging Internet "spamming" (i.e., bulk e-mail advertising) had issued a press release about the case that she published on her web page. She argued that an attorney's absolute privilege against defamation liability for statements connected with the case protected her against the defendant's claim of libel. The court disagreed. It is one thing to say a lawyer cannot be sued for libel for what is in a complaint, but in this case the recipients of the press release had nothing to do with the case, so the release did not bear "some relation to the proceeding" and was not privileged.

c. Kennedy v. Zimmermann, 601 N.W.2d 61 (Iowa 1999), also shows that, while doing what the ethics rules do not prohibit serves to protect the lawyer from professional discipline, that does not necessarily create an immunity from liability under other law. Kennedy represented Richmond, who was an inmate, in a child custody matter. Kennedy was dating a different inmate at the same penitentiary. Richmond complained to Kennedy about her representation of him, and shortly thereafter, Kennedy's boyfriend assaulted Richmond. Richmond then hired Zimmerman to sue Kennedy, claiming she told her boyfriend what Richmond had said to her in confidence. The case attracted some media attention, and a reporter called Zimmerman about it. Zimmerman reported the allegations already published in the complaint, saying that Richardson claimed that "Kennedy's alleged actions were a 'breach of her ethical duties and negligent.' "

Thereupon, Kennedy sued Zimmerman for defamation. Zimmerman answered that what a lawyer says in the course of a judicial proceeding is absolutely privilege against a defamation claim. The court disagreed. The absolute privilege only applies to communications made in a judicial proceeding, the court said; it does not apply to interviews with reporters. The fact that the statement was not prohibited by the state's counterpart to Model Rule 3.6(b)(2) did not change the result.[5]

6.   Suppose White prosecutes the state legislator with a marijuana cigarette in his car. If publicity will help the legislator beat the charge, may the legislator's lawyer advise him of that? Does it make any difference whether the state legislator is a lawyer?

a.   Publicity adverse to White's special unit might deter the vigor of that unit's prosecution or lead the public to believe the prosecutions are based on politics rather than law. Look again at Model Rule 3.6. If the case has sufficient notoriety, publicity that is sufficiently adverse may even infect the pool from which the court selects the jurors.

b.   May the legislator himself call a press conference to give his side of the story? Cf. Rule 8.4(a). If the legislator does give a press conference, may his lawyer answer questions that reporters pose and that relate to the upcoming trial?

Does Rule 3.6(c) provide defense counsel with a necessary defense against statements from prosecutors and police officers? Why is Model Rule 3.8(f) not sufficient protection? Do Model Rules 3.6(c) and 3.8(f) threaten to turn pre-trial proceedings into successive rounds of public statements by defense counsel and motions for sanctions against prosecutors? Or, does this Rule merely reflect the axiom that one should fight fire with fire?

c.   In the background of all of these cases are not only the ethics rules but also the reluctance of state and federal courts to allow sweeping discovery of print and broadcast media. United States v. Cutler, 6 F.3d 67 (2d Cir.1993), involved John Gotti's lawyer, Bruce Cutler, who was quoted in several news stories commenting on the lack of merit of the government's case, all in apparent violation of a gag order imposed by the trial judge. When charged with a violation of the order, Cutler sought the notes of all the reporters who had quoted him, including their notes of statements made by others than Cutler. The Court held that Cutler was entitled to notes relating to his own statements, including portions of televised interviews that were not used, but that he was not entitled to notes of the reporters' conversations with government officials or others.

5. For more on a lawyer's privilege against defamation for statements made in litigation, see Restatement Third, The Law Governing Lawyers § 57, Comment c.

Later, United States v. Cutler, 58 F.3d 825 (2d Cir.1995), affirmed the lower court, holding that Cutler willfully violated the trial court's valid gag order and that his statements were reasonably likely to prejudice prospective jurors in the case. The court upheld Cutler's three year suspension from practice in the Eastern District of New York.[6]

d.   Also lurking in all of these cases are state and federal constitutional provisions that impose some free speech restrictions on the breadth of gag orders. Twohig v. Blackmer, 918 P.2d 332 (N.M.1996), for example, vacated a gag order at the request of defense counsel. The state had charged a Native American with vehicular homicide in the deaths of an Anglo mother and her three daughters. The government alleged that the defendant was driving drunk and on the wrong side of an interstate highway. The case got unprecedented media attention, most of it favorable to the prosecution. Two trials ended in hung juries, but the prosecutor promised to try again. Defense counsel appeared on radio talk shows and wrote a newspaper article saying enough was enough. At that point the trial judge imposed the gag order, which the State Supreme Court vacated because it did not lay out a factual foundation for finding "substantial likelihood of prejudice or clear and present danger to fair and impartial trial;" it did not contain any analysis of facts supporting the trial court's conclusion that a gag order was necessary; and it did not indicate that the court considered alternatives less restrictive of free speech than outright ban on all communication with the media.

B.   STANDARDS GOVERNING A PROSECUTOR'S DECISION WHETHER AND WHAT TO CHARGE

1.   May a prosecutor file a charge that he or she does not believe can be proved beyond a reasonable doubt? Suppose it would help encourage the defendant to enter a plea to an offense the defendant clearly committed?

a.   Look at Model Rule 3.8(a). Is this Rule too restrictive on prosecutors? Does it belong in an ethics code or in a code of criminal procedure? If the grand jury is willing to indict, should Rule 3.8(a) constrain the prosecutor?

b.   In United States v. Goodwin, 457 U.S. 368, 102 S.Ct. 2485, 73 L.Ed.2d 74 (1982), the government originally filed several misdemeanor charges against the defendant, but after he asked for a jury trial, the Government obtained an indictment that included a felony count. The defendant alleged prosecutorial vindictiveness and retaliatory intent that he argued should void the conviction. The Supreme Court disagreed. "Just as a prosecutor may forego legitimate charges * * *, a prosecutor may file

---

6. In re Cutler, 650 N.Y.S.2d 85 (App. Div.1996), was another round in Cutler's saga in which the state court suspended his New York license for six months for committing the federal criminal offense (which was reduced by the 3 months he was under federal house arrest and thus unable to practice). Effective June 12, 1997, the state court, without opinion, reinstated Mr. Cutler as a lawyer. Application of Cutler, 658 N.Y.S.2d 835 (Mem) (App.Div.1997).

additional charges if an initial expectation that a defendant would plead guilty to lesser charges proves unfounded." Thus, a presumption of vindictiveness was inappropriate and it found no actual vindictiveness in the circumstances of the case. See also Bordenkircher v. Hayes, 434 U.S. 357, 98 S.Ct. 663, 54 L.Ed.2d 604 (1978) (prosecutor, without violating due process, may threaten defendant with more severe charges, to which he is plainly subject, if defendant does not plead guilty to lesser charges).

2. How much exculpatory information should the prosecutor be required to give the grand jury in seeking an indictment?

a. In United States v. Williams, 504 U.S. 36, 112 S.Ct. 1735, 118 L.Ed.2d 352 (1992), the Government had charged the defendant with giving willfully false financial statements to a bank in order to get a large loan. At the time the prosecutor obtain the indictment, he allegedly had exculpatory information in his possession that he did not reveal to the grand jury. The Supreme Court rejected a claim that the indictment thus should have been dismissed. A grand jury sits to determine whether there is enough evidence to charge, Justice Scalia wrote for the Court; it does not sit to weigh conflicting evidence. Justices Stevens, Blackmun, O'Connor and Thomas dissented.

b. Even assuming that the Constitution does not require disclosure at the preindictment stage, what should the prosecutor's ethical duty be? If the prosecutor has a lot of exculpatory evidence, can the prosecutor still have probable cause to charge within the meaning of Model Rule 3.8? Can the prosecutor properly ignore portions of the evidence in his or her possession in making that determination?

c. Is it wise for the prosecutor to withhold exculpatory information from the grand jury? If the grand jury considers that information very persuasive, might it make more sense for the prosecutor to know that before the trial, because Rule 3.8(d) mandates its eventual disclosure it to the defense? Should an ethics rule be the way to enforce what many prosecutors regard as simply good policy?

3. What should the state's attorney's obligation be when she believes the police are lying?

a. In People v. Berrios, 270 N.E.2d 709 (N.Y.1971), the New York County District Attorney joined the defense in an effort to have the New York Court of Appeals shift the burden of proof to the state when the police alleged—in reply to a motion to suppress contraband drugs—that the defendant had abandoned the drugs. The district attorney had become very concerned that the police seemed to have a consistent story that the drugs had been abandoned.

The New York court rejected the joint request, quoting then Judge Warren Burger in Bush v. United States, 375 F.2d 602, 604 (D.C.Cir.1967): "[I]t would be a dismal reflection on society to say that when the guardians of its security are called to testify in court under oath, their testimony must be viewed with suspicion." Do you agree that the prosecutor should rely on Judge Burger's analysis and put the problem out of mind?[7]

b. Zahrey v. Coffey, 221 F.3d 342 (2d Cir.2000), was a civil case charging an Assistant U.S. Attorney with coercing or bribing witnesses into offering false evidence against the plaintiff, a police officer. The prosecutor allegedly agreed to drop serious charges, for example, if a defendant would testify against the officer. The trial judge dismissed the case, citing a prosecutor's immunity for official acts. The Second Circuit held that a prosecutor has only qualified immunity for acts in an investigative role. The plaintiff has a constitutional right "not to be deprived of liberty as a result of the fabrication of evidence by a government officer acting in an investigative capacity," the court said, and reinstated the case.

c. Idaho State Bar v. Warrick, 44 P.3d 1141 (Idaho 2002), explored the duty of a prosecutor to correct erroneous testimony of a government witness. Warrick served as the lead prosecutor in a drug trial. An assistant prosecutor in Warrick's office negotiated a plea bargain with one of the defendant's associates under which the individual received a substantially reduced sentence in exchange for his testimony in the trial. Warrick knew the agreement had been struck, although not the leniency of the sentence recommendation. During both direct and cross examination, the witness denied having a plea arrangement with the state and Warrick did not correct the witness. Later that day, the same judge presided over the witness's arraignment, and quickly realized that the witness had testified falsely earlier. Warrick met with the witness that evening and stated that he intended to recall the witness the next day to cure any defects in the testimony. However, the Professional Conduct Board, which initiated discipline, "found that he knew Spaulding's testimony was false at the time it was presented, and the Board's findings are supported by the record." Warrick, the court said, "knew it was false when the testimony was presented, and at that time he did not take any action to correct the testimony. Waiting until after the district judge and defense counsel learned the testimony was false was not reasonable," citing Rule 3.3(a)(3). The Professional Conduct Board imposed a 30 day suspension for this and another offense, and the state supreme court upheld the suspension.

4. Should a prosecutor be able to accept a plea to a reduced charge even though the prosecutor personally believes that the defendant is not guilty of the offense?

a. How about accepting the plea when she believes the defendant is guilty but that the jury might acquit, thus hurting the prosecutor's batting average? See ABA Prosecution Standard § 3–3.9(d).[8]

---

7. Judge Burger was perhaps more appropriately concerned about perjured testimony in his opinion in Nix v. Whiteside, in Problem 27, supra.

8. For a discussion of the prosecutor and selective prosecution, prejudgment of credibility, and conflict of interest in the light of the ABA Standards Relating to the Prosecution Function, see H. Richard Uviller, The Virtuous Prosecutor in Quest of an Ethical Standard: Guidance from the ABA, 71 Michigan L. Rev. 1145 (1973). For a different view,

b. The Model Rules of Professional Conduct do not deal with this issue, while the ABA Prosecution Standards explicitly do. These Standards "are not intended to be used as criteria for the judicial evaluation of alleged misconduct of the prosecutor to determine the validity of a conviction." Standard § 3–1.1. The Standards, however, do not provide for attorney discipline. Why would the ABA promulgate two type of rules—one that is supposed to be the framework for discipline and the other, "intended to be used as a guide to professional conduct and performance"? ABA Prosecution Standard § 3–3.1.

c. May a prosecutor negotiate the defendant's agreement to perform charitable work for a certain time in exchange for dropping all charges, i.e., could the prosecutor pretend the defendant was not guilty if the negotiated disposition conforms to rough justice? See ABA Prosecution Function Standards § 3–3.8.

5. May a prosecutor let a criminal defendant go free in exchange for testimony against someone the prosecutor believes poses a greater danger to society? Should anyone have a basis to complain about such conduct?

a. United States v. Singleton, 165 F.3d 1297 (10th Cir.1999) (en banc), cert. denied 527 U.S. 1024, 119 S.Ct. 2371, 144 L.Ed.2d 775 (1999), reversed an earlier panel decision that garnered a great deal of national publicity when it prohibited the government in a criminal case from offering immunity and leniency to a witness in exchange for his or her testimony. The three judge panel had ruled that this exchange constitutes payment for testimony, i.e., bribery. The en banc Tenth Circuit rejected that result because the anti-bribery statute refers to an individual offering the bribe. By contrast, an Assistant United States Attorney who offers a plea bargain is acting as the United States, not as an individual. Moreover, the court, not the prosecutor, actually grants the immunity. The statute cannot be meant to restrict the sovereign's prosecutorial powers and to prohibit that which other federal statutes authorize, the court said. Further, to so hold would upset generations of prosecutorial practice. Congress acts against a background of such practice; the statute could not have the meaning the panel found. Judges Kelly, Seymour and Ebel dissented, saying the statute is simple and means what it says. United States v. Lowery, 166 F.3d 1119 (11th Cir.1999), disagreed with the panel decision in *Singleton* and agreed with the en banc majority.

b. Asking the court to grant immunity to a witness in exchange for testimony is not done in the dark of night. It occurs in court and requires the judge's approval. On the other hand, in Disciplinary Proceedings Against Charles O. Bonet, 29 P.3d 1242 (Wash.2001), the agreement was not so open. The respondent had prosecuted a defendant on drug-related charges. One of the defendant's co-conspirators had been named to testify

see Monroe H. Freedman, The Professional   55 Georgetown L.J. 1030 (1967).
Responsibility of the Prosecuting Attorney,

on his behalf at trial, though he had made conflicting statements as to whether or not he actually planned to testify. The respondent allegedly told the potential witness that he would dismiss the criminal charges against him if he agreed to assert the Fifth Amendment and refrain from testifying for the defense. When the court asked the respondent made any such agreement, the respondent denied it, but the court found that the respondent had done so, and in so doing had offered an improper inducement to persuade a witness not to testify. The court found a violation of Rules 3.4(b) and 8.4(d): "a public or private attorney may not offer an inducement to a witness in order to influence that person to not testify at a trial * * * regardless of whether the offer or inducement influenced the witness's decision to testify or not testify." The witness' prior subjective intent not to testify was irrelevant because the inducement itself was improper.[9]

C. LIMITS ON PROSECUTORS INVESTIGATING DEFENSE ATTORNEYS

1. Should a prosecutor be permitted to subpoena office records of lawyers known to do criminal defense work? May prosecutors require defense counsel to appear before a grand jury? What if there is a reasonable concern that the defense lawyer may also be a criminal?

a. On October 1, 1985, the Massachusetts Supreme Judicial Court adopted a new disciplinary rule, Prosecution Function 15, which stated:

> It is unprofessional conduct for a prosecutor to subpoena an attorney to a grand jury without prior judicial approval in circumstances where the prosecutor seeks to compel the attorney-witness to provide evidence concerning a person who is represented by the attorney-witness.

United States v. Klubock, 639 F.Supp. 117 (D.Mass.1986), affirmed by an equally divided court 832 F.2d 664 (1st Cir.1987) (en banc), rejected a supremacy clause challenge to this Massachusetts rule as applied to federal prosecutors. Whitehouse v. U.S. District Court, 53 F.3d 1349 (1st Cir.1995), also upheld a rule requiring federal prosecutors to get advance judicial approval before issuing a subpoena to a lawyer. Model Rule 3.8(e) is the ABA version of the Massachusetts rule.

b. Is Rule 3.8(e) really a rule of procedure dressed up to look like an ethics rule? Critics of such rules often argue that the ABA and organized bars of defense lawyers have little success in getting courts to adopt particular evidence rules so they dress them up as rules governing lawyers. See Stern v. Supreme Judicial Court, 184 F.R.D. 10 (D.Mass.1999), holding that the Massachusetts federal court had the power to adopt what is now Rule 3.8(e).

---

9. Cf. North Carolina State Bar v. Graves, 274 S.E.2d 396 (N.C.App.1981), disciplining a lawyer who attempted to influence a witness (not his client) to not testify or plead the Fifth Amendment. The witness could plead the Fifth, but it is still a criminal act for someone "with corrupt motive to induce a witness to exercise that privilege."

2. Should lawyers have any more right than non–lawyers to resist a subpoena to produce records or appear for questioning?[10]

a.   Two lawyers who specialize in the defense of white collar criminal cases have argued that government subpoenas of attorneys are a serious interference with the attorney-client relationship and should not be issued without prior judicial approval:

> "Regardless of the type of information sought, * * * an attorney-subpoena has an obvious, unavoidable, and substantial impact on the attorney-client relationship. The fragile relationship of trust, built upon the understanding that what is said to the attorney is confidential and that the attorney's sole function is to serve as a zealous advocate for the client within the bounds of the law, is seriously strained whenever the government even attempts to have the attorney act as a witness against his client. As a practical matter, most clients simply do not understand the fine distinctions the courts have drawn between what is a privileged communication and what is not. [A client may] hold back critical information for fear that a future subpoena might be enforced. Nor can the client be absolutely sure that the attorney has actually invoked the privilege in response to all of the substantive questions asked in the secrecy of the grand jury room. The attorney, too, may decide to skimp on eliciting certain information from the client for fear he may have to divulge it in the future. * * * [O]nce the subpoena is served on the attorney, the attorney's own philosophical, emotional and financial concerns may color his professional judgment. Any advice he gives in this situation, whether it be to fight, to comply, or to compromise, may reasonably be seen by the client, or by others, as having been affected by those concerns. The resulting peril to the attorney-client relationship, and to the adversary system, is apparent. * * *

> "Finally, and perhaps most importantly, by using the subpoena the prosecutor can effectively exercise a veto power over the defendant's choice of counsel. Disciplinary Rule 5–102(B) of the Code of Professional Responsibility requires that an attorney withdraw from a case if 'it is apparent that [the attorney's] testimony is or may be prejudicial to his client.' The unrestrained power to issue a grand jury or trial subpoena, therefore, may substantially skew the adversary system—defendant's counsel serves at the pleasure of the prosecution. * * * "

---

10. Lawyers should understand that, contrary to the wishful thinking of some, neither the work product doctrine, the attorney client privilege, nor the Constitution absolutely prohibits a police search of a lawyer's office if there is probable cause to believe that the lawyer may be aiding in commission of a crime. See, e.g., Law Offices of Bernard D. Morley, P. C. v. MacFarlane, 647 P.2d 1215 (Colo.1982); Lackland Bloom, The Law Office Search: An Emerging Problem and Some Suggested Solutions, 69 Georgetown L.J. 1 (1980).

David S. Rudolph & Thomas K. Maher, The Attorney Subpoena: You Are Hereby Commanded to Betray Your Client, 1 Crim. Justice 15 (Spring 1986).

b. In re Grand Jury Subpoena Served Upon Doe, 781 F.2d 238 (2d Cir.1986) (en banc), cert. denied sub nom. Roe v. United States, 475 U.S. 1108, 106 S.Ct. 1515, 89 L.Ed.2d 914 (1986), involved a defendant who asserted that if the Government required his attorney to testify before the grand jury, the attorney would be disqualified from representing him in the later criminal case. The Government was investigating the "Colombo organized crime family and a faction of that enterprise known as the 'Anthony Colombo crew.'" The grand jury sought "to determine whether Colombo paid for, or otherwise arranged for, the legal representation of members of his crew. Evidence of such benefactor payments made to [Attorney] Slotnick might establish Colombo as the head of 'an enterprise' as that term is defined in the Racketeer Influenced and Corrupt Organizations Act (RICO)," 18 U.S.C.A. § 1961(4). The government had not attempted to show a compelling or reasonable "need" for the lawyer's information. In fact, it expressly asserted that there was no requirement that it demonstrate need, i.e., that it could not obtain the information from alternative sources.

The *en banc* Court agreed and held that in the "preindictment context" a requirement of such a showing of need "would unjustifiably impede the grand jury process." The possibility that the lawyer's testimony would disqualify him from later representing the defendant under the lawyer/witness rule was not sufficient to change the result. The majority said: "Before disqualification can ever be contemplated, the attorney's testimony must incriminate his client; the grand jury must indict; the government must go forward with the prosecution of the indictment; and ultimately, the attorney must be advised that he will be called as a trial witness against his client." After all, the attorney's grand jury testimony "may be exculpatory or neutral," or be otherwise inadmissible, or come within one of the exceptions to DR 5–102(B) or Model Rule 3.7. "The pretrial stage, not the grand jury stage, is the appropriate time to balance Colombo's interest in his right to counsel against the public interest in obtaining benefactor payment information, should the issue of disqualification arise."

c. In 1990, the ABA amended Rule 3.8(e) to require prosecutors to obtain prior judicial approval before subpoenaing defense counsel. In 1995, the ABA again amended Rule 3.8(e) so that it no longer requires prior judicial approval of subpoenas directed to lawyers but does place some roadblocks in a prosecutor's path. Is the new version of the rule likely to reduce the likelihood that the problems feared by defendants and defense counsel will arise?[11]

11. Cf. United States v. Mittelman, 999 F.2d 440 (9th Cir.1993), that involved a motion to suppress evidence seized in the search of a lawyer's office. The affidavit for the search warrant said the office was believed to contain evidence of conspiracy to commit bankruptcy fraud. The lawyer was subsequently charged with that crime along with the client. The Court found the search had exceeded the terms of the warrant, but said only evidence seized in "flagrant disregard" of those terms would be suppressed.

3. What should be the response of defense counsel who receives such a subpoena?

a. ABA Formal Opinion 94–385 (July 5, 1994) advises lawyers to resist such subpoenas, if issued. If the client whose files are subpoenaed by a government agency does not consent to disclosure, the lawyer must seek to limit the subpoena and resist disclosure "on any legitimately available grounds." However, such grounds are often unavailable.

b. In United States v. Saccoccia, 898 F.Supp. 53 (D.R.I.1995), the government wanted to depose the defendant's lawyers in a forfeiture proceeding to learn the location of certain assets. The compelled testimony had been deferred until the government won the underlying criminal cases. The question now was whether the attorney-client privilege barred the lawyer's testimony. The Court said no. Unless the information sought revealed lawyer-client communications concerning non-fee matters, the deposition could go forward.

c. In re Grand Jury Proceedings, 13 F.3d 1293 (9th Cir.1994), was a proceeding to force a lawyer to testify before a grand jury about what fees he had been paid by a particular client, the amount of any trust funds held by the lawyer for that client, and what the lawyer knew about the client's lifestyle, spending habits and sources of income. When the lawyer refused to talk, the court upheld the finding of contempt. The lawyer's Fifth Amendment rights were not at issue, it said, the facts did not relate to privileged information, and any Sixth Amendment challenge was premature.

d. In re Subpoena to Testify Before Grand Jury (Alexiou v. U.S.), 39 F.3d 973 (9th Cir.1994), cert. denied 514 U.S. 1097, 115 S.Ct. 1825, 131 L.Ed.2d 746 (1995), held that a lawyer must tell the Court which client paid him with a counterfeit bill. The client was not accused of counterfeiting and indeed may have received the bill from someone else. Thus, the name was held not to be privileged and its disclosure was required.

e. Conn v. Gabbert, 526 U.S. 286, 119 S.Ct. 1292, 143 L.Ed.2d 399 (1999), considered a challenge to a prosecutor's execution of a search warrant on a defense lawyer who represented Traci Baker, a former girlfriend of Lyle Menendez, one of two brothers who were murder defendants. The prosecutors thought that Baker may have been asked to testify falsely at the brothers' first trial. When Baker was called before the grand jury, she was told to bring with her any letters she had gotten from Menendez. She told investigators earlier that she had given them to her lawyer, so when the two arrived for the grand jury appearance, the prosecutors executed a search warrant on Gabbert as well. It turned up two pages of a three page letter from Menendez to Baker. Gabbert sued the prosecutors under 42 U.S.C. § 1983 (creating a private right of action for violation of constitutional rights). The Ninth Circuit held that the search was not entitled to qualified immunity. It said that "common sense" required a finding that Gabbert's constitutional rights had been violated.

Gabbert v. Conn, 131 F.3d 793 (9th Cir.1997). The Supreme Court unanimously reversed. The lawyer's own liberty interest was not violated, the Court said, nor was his client prejudiced by having her lawyer focusing on responding to the subpoena rather than assisting her to answer grand jury questions.

f.   In People v. Superior Court (Laff), 23 P.3d 563 (Cal.2001), prosecutors suspected two attorneys of possible automobile insurance fraud and, armed with a search warrant, seized documents from their homes and law offices even though the grand jury had not yet returned an indictment against the attorneys. The attorneys claimed that they had a right to a hearing to determine whether any of the documents were privileged. The court agreed that a lawyer who is a suspect—like any other lawyer—has a duty to protect confidential files. A court, in turn, has inherent and statutory authority to examine seized documents, rule upon the claims of privilege, and prohibit disclosure of documents that it finds to be privileged.

D.   FOCUSING ON THE FEES OF CRIMINAL DEFENSE COUNSEL

1.   May the Government seize the fees of privately retained defense counsel?

a.   Significant issues for criminal defense lawyers arise from issues relating to their fees. With the enactment of the Comprehensive Forfeiture Act of 1984, amending the Continuing Criminal Enterprise Statute (CCE), 21 U.S.C.A. §§ 848–853, and the Racketeer Influenced and Corrupt Organization Act (RICO), 18 U.S.C.A. §§ 1961–1968, title to income or property derived directly or indirectly from various criminal activities is subject to government forfeiture at the time the defendant committed the illegal acts. This "relation back" doctrine lets the Government argue that even property that is now in the hands of a third party can be seized by the government.

b.   Neither RICO nor CCE expressly mentions or exempts attorneys' fees. In a typical scenario, an indictment will allege that the defendant received 95% or more of his income as profits from narcotics trafficking, and that these assets are subject to forfeiture. The Government also then will serve notice to defendant's retained counsel that fees paid or promised to be paid are subject to forfeiture if the defendant is convicted. The Government then will claim that the attorney can retain fees already paid only if he establishes, in a post trial hearing, that "he is a bona fide purchaser for value of such property who at the time of purchase was reasonably without cause to believe that the property was subject to forfeiture." 18 U.S.C.A. § 1963(c), 21 U.S.C.A. § 853(c). The Government warning to the attorney that the fees are subject to forfeiture is designed to assure that the lawyer cannot establish that.

2.   How should a lawyer respond if the Government serves notice that his or her retainer may have been generated by the client's illegal activities (e.g., drug dealing), and therefore may be subject to forfeiture?

a. Some commentators argue that applying RICO and CCE forfeiture provisions to moneys paid to a defendant's retained counsel violate constitutional and ethical commands. Public defenders are "overwhelmed" and often have neither the staff nor experience necessary to handle a complex RICO or drug case. The forfeiture potential, it has also been argued, creates a prohibited contingency fee—see Model Rule 1.5(d)(2)—in that the lawyer only gets paid if the client avoids conviction of an offense subject to the forfeiture rule, but the "compelling objection" is that to "hold that a defendant may be deprived of the assets necessary to defend himself against criminal charges before those charges are proved is obnoxious to basic notions of due process as well as to the presumption of innocence."[12]

b. Other commentators have supported the forfeiture statutes. The purpose of forfeiture is "to separate convicted criminals from the economic power bases essential to continuation of their unlawful activities." The defendant who is indigent has only a right to appointed counsel, not to retained counsel of his choice; defendants whose assets are subject to forfeiture are no worse off. "An attorney's decision not to represent a defendant whose assets are threatened with forfeiture seems constitutionally indistinguishable from his decision not to represent a defendant whose assets have been seized as contraband or subjected to an IRS levy, or a defendant who has no assets at all." The lawyer has no ethical duty "to preserve forfeitable assets as a fee," though he does have a duty to "serve his client loyally."[13]

Another commentator noted: "[S]uppose a defendant is accused of stealing a car and pays a lawyer to defend against that charge by giving the car to the lawyer. Few would argue that the lawyer has a worthy claim to the car if the defendant is convicted and the jury finds that the car the lawyer received is the one that was stolen. Even fewer would champion the lawyer's right to keep the car if the lawyer had reason to know it was stolen. Suggest, however, that a lawyer who receives money generated by drug dealing or racketeering, is not entitled to keep that money for defending the drug dealer or racketeer, and an acrimonious debate ensues." Lawyers claim that they "must be immune from the hazards that others face when transacting business with drug dealers and racketeers."[14]

c. Lower courts had split on this issue. Most had interpreted the statutes to exempt attorneys fees, assuming that the payment was not a fraud or sham designed to protect illegal activities of the client. The Supreme Court resolved the issue in United States v. Monsanto, 491 U.S.

---

12. William W. Taylor & Richard G. Strafer, Attorney Fee Forfeiture: Can It Be Justified? 1 Crim. Justice 9, 43 (ABA Section of Criminal Justice, Spring 1986).

13. Kathleen F. Brickey, Forfeiture of Attorneys' Fees: The Impact of RICO and CCE Forfeitures on the Right to Counsel, 72 Virginia L.Rev. 493 (1986). In addition, Professor Brickey notes that the Justice Department's internal guidelines require the Gov-

ernment to describe with particularity the specific assets subject to forfeiture before they are transferred. Id. at 537–38. See U.S.Atty. Manual, § 9–111.530, reprinted in 38 Criminal L.Rep. 3001, 3006 (Oct. 2, 1985).

14. William J. Landers, Attorney Fee Forfeiture: Can It Be Justified? Yes, 1 Crim.Justice 8, 10 (ABA Section of Criminal Justice, Spring 1986).

600, 109 S.Ct. 2657, 105 L.Ed.2d 512 (1989). The Second Circuit had said that a pre-trial order may not freeze the defendant's assets intended to be paid as attorneys' fees, but by a 5 to 4 vote, the Supreme Court reversed. Writing for the majority, Justice White found first that the statutory language was "clear and unambiguous." All property of a defendant was subject to forfeiture; the statute did not say "crime does not pay, except for attorney's fees."

d. Caplin & Drysdale v. United States, 491 U.S. 617, 109 S.Ct. 2646, 105 L.Ed.2d 528 (1989), then considered whether forfeiture of the defendant's assets under such a statute was constitutional. The same majority (White, Rehnquist, O'Connor, Scalia & Kennedy) held that it was. The Sixth Amendment does not give "impecunious defendants" the right to "choose their own counsel;" it only gives them the right to be "adequately represented by attorneys appointed by the courts." Further, the government has a valid interest in getting the forfeited assets back to their rightful owners or having them go into a fund for law enforcement use. Any Fifth Amendment due process concern must await an instance of actual deprivation, e.g., a plea to a non-forfeiture offense induced by a lawyer interested only in preserving his fee.

Justice Blackmun, for himself and Justices Brennan, Marshall & Stevens, found no express statutory language requiring forfeiture of attorney's fees and urged a reading that would permit district courts latitude not to order it. On the constitutional issues, the dissenters asserted, "When the Government insists upon the right to choose the defendant's counsel for him * * * counsel is too readily perceived as the Government's agent rather than his own." 491 U.S. at 645, 109 S.Ct. at 2673, 105 L.Ed.2d at 554. The effectiveness of our "equal and adversarial" system is thus at risk because the power to seek disclosure gives the prosecutor a powerful club. This will, the dissenters predict, "decimate the private criminal-defense bar." They called on Congress to rewrite the statute and reverse the Court's construction of it. Congress has not done so.

e. United States v. Matta–Timmins, 81 F.Supp.2d 193 (D.Mass.2000), came at the fee forfeiture conflict question from a different direction. The Government indicted a lawyer's client for bank fraud, embezzlement and money laundering, and sought forfeiture of the proceeds of these acts. It notified defense counsel that money and property he had received from his client for use in meeting legal expenses could be the subject of forfeiture and of possible criminal charges. It then asserted that the threat of such forfeiture and charges created a conflict of interest that required the lawyer's disqualification. The court concluded that the defense counsel was not disqualified by the fact that he might be required to testify as to the source of funds; the lawyer also was not disqualified by the remote possibility that he might be subject to criminal or civil penalties for money laundering. If the defendant, after being apprized of all the facts, still wants the lawyer to represent her, the defendant's waiver of potential conflict was valid. The danger of any real conflict is remote, the court said, and will be addressed only if an actual conflict actually arises.

3.   The Internal Revenue Code, 26 U.S.C.A. § 6050I, requires lawyers to report the source of cash payments in excess of $10,000 even when the payments are made by clients. Do you believe that information should be privileged?

a.   One purpose of this law, of course, is to see that taxes are paid on the money. Another broader purpose may be to find out who is trying to conceal the fact they have hired lawyers. Cf. Baird v. Koerner, 279 F.2d 623 (9th Cir.1960), discussed in Problem 26. And, the Government may also be concerned that large cash payments may serve to launder ill-gotten goods. The IRS has announced that it will prosecute lawyers' failures to file the Form.

b.   In United States v. Ritchie, 15 F.3d 592 (6th Cir.1994), the lawyers moved to quash subpoenas asking the names of clients who had made the cash payments. The lawyer had reported the three payments but not the name of the client or the nature of the legal services. The lawyer said that he gave the IRS enough information to determine his own tax liability, and nothing else was relevant to legitimate IRS concern. Consistent with the majority of cases on the issues, however, the court refused to quash the subpoena and found no violation of the fifth or sixth amendments, the attorney-client privilege, or due process. See also Gerald B. Lefcourt P.C. v. United States, 125 F.3d 79 (2d Cir.1997).

In United States v. Sindel, 53 F.3d 874 (8th Cir.1995), however, Judge Arnold held that the common-law privilege could, when sufficiently strong, overcome the mandate of § 6050I. Thus, one client's identity remained protected from disclosure on Form 8300, but another client's identity was not so protected. Ralls v. United States, 52 F.3d 223 (9th Cir.1995), also held that if the question of who paid the lawyer's fee is so inextricably intertwined with the client's privileged communications, then the lawyer may not be forced to tell who paid that fee on the client's behalf.

See also, Office of Disciplinary Counsel v. Massey, 687 N.E.2d 734 (Ohio 1998) (lawyer suspended for six months for having a client pay in several units of cash, each less than $10,000, to try to evade the IRS reporting requirement); DeGuerin v. United States, 214 F.Supp.2d 726 (S.D.Tex.2002) (genuine issue of fact presented as to whether the clients' names were privileged).

4.   Does a prosecutor have any obligation to worry about fairness in deciding how much leverage to use against a criminal defendant? Should the prosecutor not use all the arrows in his quiver? Can one simply say the "war on crime" must be fought with any and all available weapons?

a.   Consider one prosecutor's advice on concealing motives:

"The voir dire is multi-purposed. In addition to selecting a sympathetic jury, you have a secondary purpose, that of endearing yourself and exhibiting your 'impartiality' and your objectivity to the jury.

"That is not a difficult task because you are on the side of right, you are on the side of the angels. The defense is defending a guilty man.

"Although your true purpose is to convict the guilty man who sits at the defense table, and to go for the jugular as viciously and rapidly as possible, do not allow the jury to perceive your attempt. Hide your claws. You must never forget your goal is total annihilation."[15]

This prosecutor has also opined:

"Man's greatest experience is the act of lovemaking.

"I sometimes wonder, if the moment when the jury foreman rises to utter those sweet words of verdict—'We the jury find the defendant guilty as charged'—is not as satisfactory an experience."[16]

Is such enthusiasm in a prosecutor admirable? Is it a sign of a society based on law and order? Is it quite a different sign?

b.   Kalina v. Fletcher, 522 U.S. 118, 118 S.Ct. 502, 139 L.Ed.2d 471 (1997), was a § 1983 action against a prosecutor who had allegedly made false statements in an affidavit used to obtain an arrest warrant. The prosecutor asserted a defense of absolute immunity, which the Supreme Court rejected. Such immunity is granted with respect to the prosecutor's functions as an advocate, but in this case she purported to act as a fact witness. The Court acknowledged many prosecutors routinely attest to facts in justifying the issuance of a warrant, but the Court found "no evidence the administration of justice is harmed where the * * * practice is not followed." There is a sharp line between advocacy and testimony as far as absolute immunity is concerned.

5.   Should Government lawyers have greater ethical obligations to do justice than lawyers in general have?

a.   Rule 3.8 places special rules on Government lawyers who are prosecutors. What of other Government lawyers, who represent the Government in civil cases? Do the Model Rules place any stricter obligations on them than on lawyers who represent private clients in civil cases?

b.   Freeport–McMoRan Oil & Gas Co. v. F.E.R.C., 962 F.2d 45 (D.C.Cir.1992) argued that Government lawyers have a special duty to be fair in *civil* litigation. The government knew certain orders had been superseded, but instead of conceding the point, it made the plaintiff challenge them in court.

Do you agree that courts should condemn such conduct? Do you believe that the government should press every advantage? If private lawyers, instead of government lawyers, had refused to concede the obvious point,

---

15.   Quoted in Marvin Frankel, The Adversary Judge, 53 Tex.L.Rev. 465, 471 (1976) (footnote omitted).

16.   Id.

would that not have been just as wrong? If so, does that suggest that the government lawyers in civil cases do not have a special duty, but have the same duty as private lawyers.

———

PROBLEM 30

THE DUTY TO SEE JUSTICE DONE

We frequently speak of lawyers as "officers of the court" and as having public duties as well as duties to their clients. This Problem examines how those assertions play out in the context of a case in which the lawyer believes someone has been wrongly imprisoned. Deciding what the lawyer should do proves harder than might first appear. The Problem asks the nature of the lawyer's legal obligations to various people involved where the lawyer sees an injustice may have been done. Is it plausible for lawyers to believe that the criminal process may have convicted the wrong person? Do lawyers have a moral obligation to respond to a likely injustice, and if so, how do they satisfy that obligation in a variety of difficult circumstances?

FACTS

Hamilton York was hired by a workers' compensation insurance carrier in the defense of a compensation claim brought by a woman who had been sexually assaulted in the course of her duties as a hotel night clerk. As a direct result of the assault, the woman suffered severe psychological shock that disabled her and prevented her from obtaining and holding gainful employment.

In the course of defending the substantial claim for compensation, the attorney was furnished psychological reports indicating that the claimant said she had been assaulted by "a Black man." The psychologist concluded that, as a result of her experience, whenever she encountered an African–American male, she became extremely fearful and withdrew into herself. Indeed, her psychological problems were such that if she even encountered a dark-skinned man walking down the street, she became terrified and would turn around and run. Further, she was unable to distinguish one African–American man from another. She considered all such men to be her attacker and this psychological situation had existed since the time of the attack.

In connection with the investigation of the facts underlying this compensation claim, York also learned that the victim had identified the first African–American she had seen in the lineup. At his criminal trial, the defendant, James Brooks, asserted an alibi that had been supported by two corroborating witnesses. However, the testimony of the victim had been so compelling that the jury apparently believed her. Brooks was convicted and sentenced to a life term in the penitentiary.

Some of this information, at least as to the general nature of the victim's disability, was available to both the prosecution and defense at the time of the criminal trial, but not to the extent it was developed later in the course of the workers' compensation negotiations. The psychologists' reports were furnished by the claimant's attorney to York with an explicit demand that their contents be revealed only to persons involved in settling the claim. The claim will soon be settled without a trial and the reports will not become a matter of public record.

York has never handled a criminal case in his professional career, and the facts he finds himself facing in this instance are the closest he has ever come to the criminal justice system. He believes an innocent man may be in the penitentiary for the rest of his life unless he acts, but Brooks is not his client and he does not know how to proceed.

QUESTIONS

A.   DUTIES OF A LAWYER WHO LEARNS AN INJUSTICE MAY HAVE BEEN DONE

1.   To whom does York, the workers' compensation attorney, owe duties in this situation? What kinds of duties?

a.   Does York owe a duty of confidentiality and a duty of loyalty to the hotel where the incident occurred and the insurance company who retained him? Does Rule 1.6(a) impose such a duty? How about Model Rule 1.9(c)? Must York secure the consent of either the hotel or the insurer before he may reveal what makes him believe there was an unjust conviction in the criminal case?

b.   If the hotel or the insurance company will not consent, perhaps out of fear that it will upset settlement negotiations in the workers' compensation case, should that end all analysis of York's obligations? Are there some client decisions that a lawyer simply must take as final?

2.   Might York have a duty to the rape victim not to make her psychiatric studies public?

a.   What would be the source of York's obligation, if any, to the victim? Restatement Third, The Law Governing Lawyers § 132, Comment *g(ii)*, for example, says that a "lawyer might have obligations to persons who were not the lawyer's clients but about whom information was revealed to the lawyer under circumstances obligating the lawyer not to use of disclose the information." Does this sound like the kind of case to which such a principle should apply?

b.   Does Model Rule 4.4(a) apply to this situation? Would the victim's lawyer's demand that the reports not be shown to others mean that York could say no more? Should York feel a moral if not a legal obligation not to further injure a person who has been severely traumatized?

3. Does York have any duty to the court that tried the case or to the man he believes is wrongly convicted?

a. Look at Model Rule 3.3. Is its requirement limited to revealing false evidence and fraud in the case York is now handling? Was the identification in this problem "dishonest" at all? The cited rules are disciplinary provisions, of course, but do they suggest a moral obligation to the court to disclose information necessary to overturn an unjust result?

b. Does York have any legal duty to Brooks, the man York believes was wrongly convicted? Does any provision of the Model Rules come close to creating such a duty? But does the absence of any affirmative duty to him suggest there is anything wrong with York's *assuming* an obligation to help? Put another way, should lawyers see discipline rules as *floors* on their conduct rather than as *ceilings*?

B. CONCERNS ABOUT THE RELIABILITY OF RESULTS IN OUR LEGAL SYSTEM

1. Can York rest easy in the knowledge that our justice system is highly reliable and that if there were reason to doubt the defendant's guilt, the jury most likely would have been told about it?

a. We know, based on DNA evidence, that innocent people can get convicted. By late 2002, DNA evidence alone "has accounted for 110 demonstrated and undeniable cases in which there was a conviction of the innocent. In every one of these cases DNA proved the innocence, but in every one of them something else convicted the defendant in the first place. We know what some of those things are. Faulty eyewitness identification, unreliable informant testimony, false confessions, faulty scientific testimony, poor crime scene work, inadequately funded public defender organizations, and occasionally misconduct by prosecutors or law enforcement have all been identified as contributors."[1]

b. On the one hand, do these exonerations prove that, at least in some cases, the system can be self-correcting? Furthermore, honest mistakes will slip into any system of justice.

c. However, cases abound in which prosecutors have been found to have suppressed materially exculpatory evidence, knowingly used false evidence at trial, or both. In some cases, such conduct has put the defendants on death row. See, e.g., Guerra v. Collins, 916 F.Supp. 620 (S.D.Tex.1995); People v. Jimerson, 652 N.E.2d 278 (Ill.1995); United States v. Boyd, 833 F.Supp. 1277 (N.D.Ill.1993); Bowen v. Maynard, 799 F.2d 593 (10th Cir.1986).[2]

---

1. The American Judicature Society, Restoring Confidence in the Criminal Justice System (2002). The American Judicature Society devoted an entire issue of its magazine to this problem. Wrongful Convictions of the Innocent, 86 Judicature, Sept.-Oct. 2002.

2. See also, Ken Armstrong & Maurice Possley, Trial & Error: How Prosecutors Sac-

d.   Furthermore, the misconduct is not limited to the prosecutor. In some cases, courts finds that police officers or crime lab personnel have falsified the evidence, requiring that verdicts be set aside. See, e.g., Matter of W.Va. State Police Crime Lab., 438 S.E.2d 501 (W.Va.1993), finding that the chief of the serology division of the crime lab had a "long history of falsifying evidence in criminal prosecutions."

2.   Doesn't a criminal defendant's right to counsel assure that no stone will be left unturned in providing a thorough defense?

a.   Unfortunately, sometimes the defendant's problem is not false evidence but defense counsel who do an inadequate job of discovering and presenting available information about the defendant's innocence. Then, when the result is later challenged in a petition for a writ of habeas corpus, it is hard for the defendants to secure reversal of convictions unless they can show that they were negatively prejudiced by that ineffective assistance of counsel.

b.   The standard now used by the Supreme Court is that the criminal defendant must show that the lawyer acted "outside the wide range of professionally competent assistance" and that the result was "actual prejudice" to the defendant. Strickland v. Washington, 466 U.S. 668, 104 S.Ct. 2052, 80 L.Ed.2d 674 (1984). In *Strickland*, the Court held that (1) the defense counsel's strategy at the sentencing hearing was reasonable, so the defendant was not denied effective assistance of counsel; and (2) even assuming the challenged conduct of counsel was unreasonable, the defendant suffered insufficient prejudice to warrant setting aside his death sentence.[3] See, e.g., Stephen Bright, Counsel for the Poor: The Death Sentence Not for the Worst Crime But for the Worst Lawyer, 103 Yale L.J. 1835 (1994).

c.   Court challenges to the adequacy of representation illustrate that the problem of inadequate counsel is concrete and substantial. In State v. Peart, 621 So.2d 780 (La.1993), for example, the state supreme court found that the funding of public defenders was so poor in some parts of the state

---

rifice Justice to Win, Chicago Tribune, Jan. 10–14, 1999 (five part series concluding that prosecutors are rewarded for convictions, not doing justice, and that even when they have been caught using false evidence or failing to disclose exculpatory information, they tend to get promoted to judgeships rather than being subjected to discipline). Following the series, Illinois Chief Justice Charles Freeman asked that prosecutors who commit misconduct be named in court opinions and that the facts be referred to the Attorney Registration and Disciplinary Commission for action. See Ken Armstrong & Maurice Possley, Illinois Courts May End Secrecy, Chicago Tribune, Feb. 3,1999. See also, John Gibeaut, "Yes, I'm

Sure That's Him": Eyewitness Reliability Under Question By Experts, Courts, 85 A.B.A. Journal 26 (Oct. 1999). In January, 2002, Illinois's outgoing Republican Gov. George Ryan commuted the death sentences of 167 people to life in prison after concluding that the capital punishment system was "haunted by the demon of error." Robert E. Pierre and Kari Lydersen, Illinois Death Row Emptied: Citing 'Demon of Error,' Ryan Commutes Sentences, Washington Post, Jan. 12, 2003, at A1.

3.   Justice O'Connor wrote the opinion for the Court. Justice Brennan concurred in part and dissented in part, and Justice Marshall dissented.

that it ruled that defendants had a rebuttable presumption that they had received inadequate assistance of counsel.[4]

d. In other cases, public defender programs have become so overwhelmed with clients that many say they cannot represent any of them effectively. See, e.g., In re Public Defender's Certification of Conflict and Motion to Withdraw Due to Excessive Caseload, 709 So.2d 101 (Fla.1998) (backlog in preparing appellate cases presents "a significant problem of constitutional magnitude"; courts ordered to appoint private lawyers and legislature encouraged to "examine the structure and funding of indigent representation in criminal cases"); United States ex rel. Green v. Washington, 917 F.Supp. 1238 (N.D.Ill.1996) (delay in appellate defender's filing of briefs on appeal violated due process and justified issuance of conditional writs of habeas corpus).

3. Is there a deeper issue than individual justice? Should it be relevant to York that the innocent man is an African–American?

a. Do you think our jury system may be more likely to believe the testimony of a white victim than an African–American accused? Is the convicted man likely to have fewer persons coming to his defense than he would if he were white?[5] Should that reinforce York's resolve to pursue justice in the man's case?

b. DNA tests led to the dismissal, in December of 2002, of five males who each served between 5 and 13 years in prison for rape and beating of a jogger in New York City's Central Park. This crime "exposed New York City's racial tensions and made national headlines." In 2001, a serial rapist said he alone attacked the 28–year-old woman as she jogged in Central Park on April 19, 1989. The prosecutor reinvestigated and DNA testing showed that semen samples from the scene belonged to Matias Reyes, the serial rapist, and "new forensic tests, more precise than those used a decade ago, failed to link the five convicted men to the rape." District Attorney Robert Morgenthau relied on that evidence "in recommending all convictions in the case be dropped. Prosecutors have said that they have no plans to retry any of the five." The primary evidence that had been used to convict the five defendants "had been confessions that the five, all black and Hispanic boys ranging in age from 14 to 16 at the time, had made to detectives."[6]

4. Cases rejecting such claims have usually only done so on jurisdictional grounds. See, e.g., Kennedy v. Carlson, 544 N.W.2d 1 (Minn.1996) (public defenders lack standing to assert interests of their future clients); Luckey v. Miller, 976 F.2d 673 (11th Cir.1992) (upholds federal court abstention from case that sought to reform the Georgia system of providing indigent defense).

5. For further background on these issues, see, e.g., Corneel West, Race Matters (1993); Paul Butler, Racially–Based Jury Nullification: Black Power in the Criminal Justice System, 105 Yale L.J. 677 (1995); Norval Morris, Race & Crime: What Evidence Is There That Race Influences Results in the Criminal Justice System, 72 Judicature 111 (1988).

6. Associated Press, Judge Vacates Rape Verdicts In Central Park Jogger Case, Wall Street Journal, Dec. 19, 2002.

c. Must our only response to such realities be that no system can be perfect? Is there any possible way to reduce the likelihood that such injustices will happen again?

C. THE OBLIGATION, IF ANY, TO RESPOND TO CONCERNS ABOUT AN INJUSTICE

1. Does anyone have an obligation to listen to York? Would the former prosecutor or defense counsel have such an obligation, for example? How about the trial judge?

a. Do the obligations of Model Rule 3.8 extend beyond the end of a case? Does ABA Standard Relating to the Prosecution Function 3–1.2(c) create a higher duty? It says only what many cases say, that the "duty of the prosecutor is to seek justice, not merely to convict." Should that platitude be given real meaning?

b. Imbler v. Pachtman, 424 U.S. 409, 96 S.Ct. 984, 47 L.Ed.2d 128 (1976), was a damage action under 42 U.S.C. § 1983 against a prosecutor who had allegedly knowingly suppressed favorable evidence and knowingly used false evidence against a defendant. The facts leading to the defendant's release had been turned up by and reported to the Governor after the conviction by the prosecutor who was now being sued. In upholding an absolute privilege against liability for a prosecutor's acts in the "judicial process," the Supreme Court said it did not want to discourage a prosecutor from reporting evidence of an unjust conviction. "[A]fter a conviction," the Court said, "the prosecutor is * * * bound by the ethics of his office to inform the appropriate authorities of after-acquired or other information that casts doubt upon the correctness of the conviction." 424 U.S. at 427 n. 25, 96 S.Ct. at 993 n. 25, 47 L.Ed.2d at 141 n. 25.

c. Would the former criminal defense counsel have any obligation to act on the new information? How long does the "zealous representation" obligation continue? Look at Standard 4–8.5 of the A.B.A. Standards Relating to the Defense Function? Does it suggest that former counsel, either trial or appellate, would have any duty to act?

d. Does the trial judge have a duty higher than the prosecutor or defense counsel's? Does the judge have any duty at all?

e. Lest you think that courts are always open to newly discovered evidence that an innocent person has been wrongly convicted, look at Herrera v. Collins, 506 U.S. 390, 113 S.Ct. 853, 122 L.Ed.2d 203 (1993), holding that even a defendant on death row has no automatic right to federal habeas corpus relief based on a claim of newly discovered evidence of actual innocence. In that case, the original conviction included two eyewitness identifications, numerous pieces of circumstantial evidence, and petitioner Herrera's handwritten letter impliedly admitting his guilt. Ten years after his conviction, he submitted affidavits tending to show that his now-dead brother had committed the murders.[7]

---

7. The courts are also sometimes suspicious of a defense based on the alleged confession of someone who cannot himself be convicted of a crime. See, e.g., Valdez v. Win-

2.   Suppose no one listened to York. Should he try to interest "60 Minutes"? Oprah? Geraldo?

a.   The news media's ability to raise questions and stimulate change has made it a serious venue for many accused and convicted people. The news media has often become the "court of last resort" in the United States today.

b.   Is that a positive development? Would a televised account of this story likely protect the assault victim, for example? Remember that she did not intentionally lie about what happened and her welfare and privacy are surely appropriate for the lawyer's moral concern.

D.   OTHER CONFLICTS BETWEEN PROFESSIONAL OBLIGATIONS AND DOING JUSTICE

1.   Suppose you learned that, in spite of the fact that you recently defeated a pollution charge against your client, it did indeed sometimes discharge toxic chemicals into a stream from which a nearby city gets its water supply.

a.   Suppose an employee of the client admits, after the trial and after the time for any appeal has passed, that he lied at the trial. Do you have any obligations under Rule 3.3(c)?

b.   Suppose you learn that the company no longer discharges the waste, but the toxic waste that was earlier discharged is still there and it will slowly harm people unless it is cleaned up? The company's accidently discharged the waste, and it is confident that it will not do it again, but it does not want to admit what it did.

c.   May you disclose this information if you believe that the toxic discharge will eventually, but inevitably, cause substantial bodily harm, even though accidental discharge is not a crime? Would Model Rule 1.6(b)(1) now apply to the situation? How about Model Rule 1.13(b)? Would you go to the E.P.A. if the company refused to make all necessary changes? Would you go back to court and confess error?

2.   How would you have acted if you learned that the plaintiff suing your client had a life-threatening condition of which that person was unaware?

a.   That was the situation presented in the well-known case of Spaulding v. Zimmerman, 263 Minn. 346, 116 N.W.2d 704 (Minn. 1962). David Spaulding, a teen aged boy, sustained injuries in an automobile accident. His injuries were diagnosed by his family physician, Dr. Cain, as

---

ans, 738 F.2d 1087 (10th Cir.1984) (confession of crime A by defendant in case B is not a basis for setting aside conviction of defendant in case A); State v. Macumber, 544 P.2d 1084 (Ariz.1976) (attorney-client privilege precludes use of confession by now-deceased person in trial of person accused of crime). But see People v. Burrows, 665 N.E.2d 1319 (Ill.1996) (conviction set aside when co-defendant admits she acted alone).

"a severe crushing injury of the chest with multiple rib fractures; a severe cerebral concussion, probably with petechial hemorrhages of the brain; and bilateral fractures of the clavicles. At Dr. Cain's suggestion, on January 3, 1957, David was examined by * * * an orthopedic specialist, who made X-ray studies of his chest. * * * Nothing in [that] report indicated the aorta aneurysm with which David was then suffering."

In the meantime, defense counsel also had a physical examination performed on David. The report from that doctor read as follows:

" 'The one feature of the case which bothers me more than any other part of the case is the fact that this boy of 20 years of age has an aneurysm, which means a dilatation of the aorta and the arch of the aorta. Whether this came out of this accident I cannot say with any degree of certainty and I have discussed it with the Roentgenologist and a couple of Internists. * * * Of course an aneurysm or dilatation of the aorta in a boy of this age is a serious matter as far as his life. This aneurysm may dilate further and it might rupture with further dilatation and this would cause his death.'

" 'It would be interesting also to know whether the X-ray of his lungs, taken immediately following the accident, shows this dilatation or not. If it was not present immediately following the accident and is now present, then we could be sure that it came out of the accident.' "

The day after the court called the case for trial, the parties settled for $6,500. David and his father did not know, and defense counsel did not tell them, how serious his injury really was. Two years later, David underwent a physical examination required for army reserve service. That exam fortuitously revealed the aneurysm, and after immediate surgery, David was cured.

Once David was no longer a minor, he filed suit to set aside the earlier settlement and seek additional damages for the aneurysm. In its opinion upholding reopening of the case, the court said:

" * * * The seriousness of this disability is indicated by [the defense doctor's] report indicating the imminent danger of death therefrom. This was known by counsel for both defendants but was not disclosed to the court at the time it was petitioned to approve the settlement. While no canon of ethics or legal obligation may have required them to inform the plaintiff or his counsel with respect thereto, or to advise the court therein, it did become obvious to them at the time that the settlement then made did not contemplate or take into consideration the disability described. * * * "

b. Are you struck by the court's simultaneous findings of (1) nondisclosure sufficient to reopen the settlement and (2) a lack of "ethical or legal obligation" to reveal the plaintiff's life-threatening condition to him? Are those findings consistent?

c.   If David had died, do you think the defense lawyers would have borne any legal or moral responsibility for his death? Why or why not?

d.   What would you have done if you were the defense lawyer in *Spaulding*? Might you have tried to work out an agreement to disclose the condition so long as the information could not be used against your client, for example? Do you suppose that would have been realistically possible in the context of negotiating a settlement?

e.   If you had been counsel for David and defense counsel had promised "life-saving information" in exchange for a waiver of some of his rights, would you have accepted the offer? Is genuine concern for the welfare of a non-client so rare among lawyers today that you would have suspected a trick?

3.   Suppose you have learned that the client whom you have just helped to defeat a charge of child molestation is indeed a pedophile and you have inadvertently helped put him back on the streets. May you ethically do anything?

a.   Assume that you learn that he has just become a camp director and that he disclosed neither the earlier charge nor the reality of his condition. Massachusetts Bar Association Ethics Opinion 90–2 (June 15, 1990), concluded that, in this circumstance, the lawyer may disclose the necessary information to the authorities "if the lawyer believes that the client's proclivities rise to the level where he is reasonably likely to commit a crime again against the children currently under his care."

b.   Would you welcome the authorization this Opinion gives you to report your former client? How certain do you have to be to "believe" that the client is "reasonably likely" to return to his old ways?

c.   If you had been the lawyer in this Problem, or the lawyer for the pedophile, would you just try to forget what you now know and reason that trials are never perfect? Would you see whether there are any openings in medical school or seek some other career confronting you with less stress-producing questions?

CHAPTER VII

THE DELIVERY OF LEGAL SERVICES

As discussed in the Introductory Chapter of these materials, the world of practicing lawyers has changed dramatically over the last quarter century. Ethical Consideration 2–2 of the ABA Model Code of Professional Responsibility reveals the official attitude toward lawyer behavior in 1977:

> "EC 2–2. The legal profession should assist laymen to recognize legal problems because such problems may not be self-revealing and often are not timely noticed. Therefore, lawyers acting under proper auspices should encourage and participate in educational and public relations programs concerning our legal system with particular reference to legal problems that frequently arise. Such educational programs should be motivated by a desire to benefit the public rather than to obtain publicity for particular lawyers. Examples of permissible activities include preparation of institutional advertisements and professional articles for lay publications and participation in seminars, lectures and civic programs. But a lawyer who participates in such activities should shun personal publicity."

Just over 25 years ago, the ethics rules saw lawyers as important providers of an essential public service, and making legal services broadly available to people who need them was the essence of professional activity. But these same rules required lawyers to "shun personal publicity." Even then, of course, reality fell short of aspiration, but the dominant ethical vision was clear.

As a result of events this Chapter will develop, Model Rule 7.2, Comment 1, exhibits a very different attitude:

> "To assist the public in obtaining legal services, lawyers should be allowed to make known their services not only through reputation but also through organized information campaigns in the form of advertising. Advertising involves an active quest for clients, contrary to the tradition that a lawyer should not seek clientele. However, the public's need to know about legal services can be fulfilled in part through advertising. This need is particularly acute in the case of persons of moderate means who have not made extensive use of legal services. The interest in expanding public information about legal services ought to prevail over considerations of tradition. * * * "

Changes in lawyer attitudes toward advertising represent just one window on the recent evolution of the legal profession. Lawyers now talk openly and aggressively about "marketing" services, stimulating client demand for those services, and seeking to take away clients currently served by other lawyers. Per-lawyer earnings, not reputation for public service, has become the standard by which many lawyers measure their firm. Lawyers now talk of making firms into "one-stop shopping" sources for both legal services and ancillary activities such as accounting, business consulting, investment banking, lobbying and real estate development.

This Chapter provides several such windows on current issues in the delivery of legal services. As you examine the materials in this Chapter, ask yourself such questions as:

a. Has law becoming a "commercial" activity? Is that inevitable? Desirable for lawyers? Desirable for clients? Does such a change make law less of a "profession"? Is there a difference between practicing a "profession" and being in a "trade or business"?

b. What role are the federal courts—as distinguished from state supreme courts—playing in transforming the profession? At whose expense are the rules being changed?

c. What is the nature of a law firm today? How does it come into being? How does it break up? What are the duties of its members to each other?

d. How can legal services be made widely available? Should the law require lawyers to volunteer their services to persons unable to pay for assistance? Should the law give lawyers an incentive to bring cases in the public interest by requiring defendants to pay the plaintiffs' legal fees?

e. Might alternatives to traditional law firms better provide legal services to persons not now receiving them? To what standards of conduct should those providers be expected to adhere?

––––––

PROBLEM 31

MARKETING PROFESSIONAL SERVICES

For many lawyers, reaching good results for clients is relatively easy. The big problem is getting clients to consult them in the first place. A lawyer without clients finds it hard to pay the bills, and lawyers can rarely produce services today for sale tomorrow. An hour spent with nothing to do is for the most part lost to a lawyer forever. For many years the organized bar, and state courts in their regulation of lawyers, forbade lawyer advertising. Canon 27 of the ABA Canons of Professional Ethics (1908) said simply: "It is unprofessional to solicit professional employment by circulars, advertisements, through touters or by personal communications or interviews not warranted by personal relations." A look at the Yellow Pages in any city shows that much has changed. Advertising is everywhere, and skill at "marketing" is now a requirement for promotion to partner at many law firms. This Problem first traces the constitutional analysis that led to the current rules about lawyer advertising. Next, it considers the distinction between advertising and in-person solicitation, and then it looks at what limits may or should be imposed on both advertising and solicitation.

FACTS

Jerry Harrold has just moved to a new community. He has published the following quarter-page advertisement in the local newspaper:

Introducing

JERRY HARROLD

Doctor of Law

Hi—

I'm Jerry Harrold and I'm a lawyer. I'm 34 years old and a native of this state. I was born in Rushville and have practiced law for the past six years in Capital City. I went to State Law School, was a member of the moot court team, and served my country for three years as a Judge Advocate in the Army. My doctor's degree in law is the professional degree a lawyer normally earns. I don't claim to be the best lawyer in the state, but some of my former clients have agreed to act as references. I'll be glad to supply their names to you so that you can check me out yourself.

I am unusual in one respect. I charge clients a flat rate of $95 per hour, win or lose, big case or small. That lets me cover my expenses and have a decent income, but most of my clients have found that it saves them a great deal in legal fees, particularly in routine matters like real estate and probate for which many lawyers charge a percentage of the sum involved in the transaction.

I look forward to meeting you soon.

                                                    Jerry

425 Center Street
Suite 518
Lewistown, Michigan 40608
332–4816

[C2593]

After practicing for a year or so, Jerry personally made a phone call to each of his current or former clients that was over 50 years of age. He said, "Everyone is worried about how they are going to pay for their retirement and provide for their loved ones after they're gone. Lawyers can help with some of those issues.

Why don't you stop by soon and have a routine legal checkup. I will only charge you for a one hour consultation, and it will help to put your mind at ease." If they expressed interest, he signed them up for an appointment. If they said they were not interested, he respected that decision.

At the end of last week, an airplane crash near Lewistown killed 45 people and badly injured 15 others. At least half of the victims lived near Lewistown, and Jerry plans to send a personal note to each of them or their survivors that expresses his deep personal sympathy for what the airline's negligence has forced them to bear. He plans to follow up with a personal visit where he plans to say, "It's up to you to decide whether to retain me, but if you wish to do so, I will be there for you."

QUESTIONS

A. The constitutional context of the regulation of lawyer marketing

1. What makes state-regulated lawyer advertising a matter for the federal courts?

a. The legal profession takes pride in regulating itself, but even lawyers live under the authority of the Constitution. For many years, the Constitution carefully protected political speech, but "commercial speech" was thought to be fair game for regulation. The leading case was Valentine v. Chrestensen, 316 U.S. 52, 62 S.Ct. 920, 86 L.Ed. 1262 (1942), which held that New York could regulate distribution of leaflets advertising a tour of a submarine even though regulating the distribution of political leaflets would have raised constitutional concerns.

b. By the mid–1970s, however, that distinction was breaking down. In Bigelow v. Virginia, 421 U.S. 809, 95 S.Ct. 2222, 44 L.Ed.2d 600 (1975), the Supreme Court said that Virginia could not punish a newspaper that published an advertisement for a New York abortion referral service. Similarly, Virginia Pharmacy Bd. v. Virginia Consumer Council, 425 U.S. 748, 96 S.Ct. 1817, 48 L.Ed.2d 346 (1976), held that a pharmacist's advertising of prescription drug prices was entitled to First Amendment protection, in part because of consumers' interest in receiving the information.

c. Thus, when John Bates and Van O'Steen left the Maricopa County Legal Aid Society to open what they called a "legal clinic" and sought to advertise their "very reasonable fees," the time was right for the Court to say that prohibition of such advertising violated Constitutional standards. In Bates v. State Bar of Arizona, 433 U.S. 350, 97 S.Ct. 2691, 53 L.Ed.2d 810 (1977), Justice Blackmun, writing for the Court, expressed doubt about the alleged state interest in maintenance of the prohibition:

"* * * [W]e find the postulated connection between advertising and the erosion of true professionalism to be severely strained. At its core, the argument presumes that attorneys must conceal from themselves and from their clients the real-life fact that lawyers earn their livelihood at the bar. We suspect that few attorneys engage in such self-deception. And rare is the client, moreover, even one of modest means, who enlists the aid of an attorney with the expectation that his services will be rendered free of charge. * * * If the commercial basis of the relationship is to be promptly disclosed on ethical grounds, once the client is in the office, it seems inconsistent to condemn the candid revelation of the same information before he arrives at that office.

"Moreover, the assertion that advertising will diminish the attorney's reputation in the community is open to question. Bankers and engineers advertise, and yet these professions are not regarded as undignified. In fact, * * * [s]tudies reveal that many persons do not obtain counsel even when they perceive a need because of the feared price of services or because of an inability to locate a competent attorney. Indeed, cynicism with regard to the profession may be created by the fact that it long has publicly eschewed advertising, while condoning the actions of the attorney who structures his social or civic associations so as to provide contacts with potential clients. * * *

"We are not persuaded that restrained professional advertising by lawyers inevitably will be misleading. Although many services performed by attorneys are indeed unique, it is doubtful that any attorney would or could advertise fixed prices for services of that type. The only services that lend themselves to advertising are the routine ones: the uncontested divorce, the simple adoption, the uncontested personal bankruptcy, the change of name, and the like—the very services advertised by appellants. * * *

" * * * Advertising [also] does not provide a complete foundation on which to select an attorney. But it seems peculiar to deny the consumer, on the ground that the information is incomplete, at least some of the relevant information needed to reach an informed decision. * * * [W]e view as dubious any justification that is based on the benefits of public ignorance. Although, of course, the bar retains the power to correct omissions that have the effect of presenting an inaccurate picture, the preferred remedy is more disclosure, rather than less. If the naiveté of the public will cause advertising by attorneys to be misleading, then it is the bar's role to assure that the populace is sufficiently informed as to enable it to place advertising in its proper perspective. * * *

" * * * The ban on advertising serves to increase the difficulty of discovering the lowest-cost seller of acceptable ability. As a result, to this extent attorneys are isolated from competition, and the incentive to price competitively is reduced. * * *

" * * * In the absence of advertising, an attorney must rely on his contacts with the community to generate a flow of business. In view of the time necessary to develop such contacts, the ban * * * serves to perpetuate the market position of established attorneys. Consideration of entry-barrier problems would urge that advertising be allowed so as to aid the new competitor in penetrating the market. * * *

" * * * We suspect that, with advertising, most lawyers will behave as they always have: they will abide by their solemn oaths to uphold the integrity and honor of their profession and of the legal system. For every attorney who overreaches through advertising, there will be thousands of others who will be candid and honest and straightforward. And, of course, it will be in the latters' interest, as in other cases of misconduct at the bar, to assist in weeding out those few who abuse their trust. * * *

"In holding that advertising by attorneys may not be subjected to blanket suppression, and that the advertisement at issue is protected, we, of course, do not hold that advertising by attorneys may not be regulated in any way. We mention some of the clearly permissible limitations on advertising not foreclosed by our holding.

"Advertising that is false, deceptive, or misleading of course is subject to restraint. * * * In fact, because the public lacks sophistication concerning legal services, misstatements that might be overlooked or deemed unimportant in other advertising may be found quite inappropriate in legal advertising. For example, advertising claims as to the quality of services—a matter we do not address today—are not susceptible to measurement or verification; accordingly, such claims may be so likely to be misleading as to warrant restriction. Similar objections might justify restraints on in-person solicitation. We do not foreclose the possibility that some limited supplementation, by way of warning or disclaimer or the like, might be required of even an advertisement of the kind ruled upon today so as to assure that the consumer is not mislead. In sum, we recognize that many of the problems in defining the boundary between deceptive and nondeceptive advertising remain to be resolved, and we expect that the bar will have a special role to play in assuring that advertising by attorneys flows both freely and cleanly.

"As with other varieties of speech, it follows as well that there may be reasonable restrictions on the time, place, and manner of advertising. * * * Advertising concerning transactions that are themselves illegal obviously may be suppressed. * * * And the special problems of advertising on the electronic broadcast media will warrant special consideration. * * *

"The constitutional issue in this case is only whether the State may prevent the publication in a newspaper of appellants' truthful advertisement concerning the availability and terms of routine legal services. We rule simply that the flow of such information may not be restrained, and we therefore hold the present application of the disciplinary rule against appellants to be violative of the First Amendment."[1]

---

1. The decision was 5 to 4. Justice Powell, a former ABA President, wrote the principal dissent; he believed the threat to professionalism from lawyer advertising was

2. What do lawyers have an inherent constitutional right to say in an advertisement after *Bates*? Does Jerry Harrold's ad deal with any subjects that could constitutionally be limited?

a. You can see the ABA's first response to *Bates* in DR 2–101of the ABA Model Code of Professional Responsibility. Extensively revised in light of *Bates*, DR 2–101(A) purported to prohibit any "false, fraudulent, misleading, deceptive, self-laudatory or unfair statement or claim." Then, however, DR 2–101(B) identified 25 safe harbors, i.e., specific things lawyers could say about themselves and their practice without violating DR 2–101(A).

b. Would Jerry Harrold have been subject to discipline for violating DR 2–101? Can you find the statements in his letter that fail to fit within the safe harbors of DR 2–101(B)?

c. Now look at ABA Model Rules 7.1 and 7.2 as they were before the 2002 amendments. How do they differ in approach from that taken in the Model Code? Do they differ in substance as well?

d. How would Jerry's letter fare under those Model Rules? For example, could the state discipline Jerry for saying flatly that he charges "$95 per hour, win or lose, big case or small"? Might the state be able to require him to add a disclaimer or say more about his charges, such as the fact that the client will also have to pay filing fees and other costs associated with the representation?

e. What is the significance, if any, of the changes made in the 2002 revisions of the Model Rules? Can you think of any cases that would come out differently under the new Model Rules?

3. Has the Court proved a good predictor of the nature and extent of lawyer advertising?

a. Data reported shortly after the *Bates* decision tended to confirm that advertising did lower fees for legal services. For example, the Bates & O'Steen clinic charged $195 for an uncontested divorce; a year later, clients could get such a divorce in Phoenix for as little as $125.[2]

b. Take a look in your current local telephone directory. Does most of the lawyer advertising that you see there describe the lawyer's availability for "routine" services like "the uncontested divorce, the simple adoption, the uncontested personal bankruptcy, the change of name, and the like"?

c. Think about the lawyer advertising that you see on television. Does most of it seem to facilitate the kind of price competition that the Court

substantial. In a separate dissent, Chief Justice Burger predicted that disciplinary authorities would be ill-equipped to regulate lawyer advertising as contemplated by the Court. Justice Rehnquist, in his dissent, said he thought *Valentine* had been decided correctly and he would not depart from it.

2. Jesse Choper, Consequences of Supreme Court Decisions Upholding Individual Constitutional Rights, 83 Michigan L. Rev. 1, 167 (1984). See also, Timothy Muris and Fred S. McChesney, Advertising and the Price and Quality of Legal Services: The Case for Legal Clinics, 1979 American Bar Foundation Research J. 179.

thought would follow from its decision? Indeed, at least on television, do you often see anything at all about lawyers' fees except for statements like: "No fee unless you recover"?

d.   Go to the internet and see what lawyer advertising you can find. If you were looking for a lawyer in another city to represent one of your family members, would you be satisfied that you were getting the amount and kind of information you needed to make a selection?

e.   Do you agree with the Court that advertising has no effect on lawyer professionalism? How about on the public perception of professionalism? A major empirical study found that lawyers' advertisements actually have had little effect on the general public's view of lawyers. ABA Commission on Advertising, Lawyer Advertising at the Crossroads: Professional Policy Considerations (1995).[3]

B. WHEN LAWYER ADVERTISING BECOMES IN-PERSON SOLICITATION

1. Is all lawyer marketing treated the same way? What is the distinction between lawyer advertising and in-person (or face-to-face) solicitation?

a.   While the ABA sets out principles applicable to all lawyer marketing in Model Rule 7.1, it draws a sharp distinction between lawyer advertising (Model Rule 7.2) and in-person solicitation (Model Rule 7.3). That distinction has its own important history.

b.   After the Court decided *Bates* in 1977, many lawyers worried there would be few practical limits on what lawyers could do to solicit clients. The next year, the Supreme Court considered the case of a lawyer, Albert Ohralik, whose conduct the Court concluded justified discipline. The case was Ohralik v. Ohio State Bar Association, 436 U.S. 447, 98 S.Ct. 1912, 56 L.Ed.2d 444 (1978).

One day when Ohralik was picking up his mail at the post office, he heard about an auto accident in which Carol McClintock, an 18–year old woman, had been injured. He called Carol's parents, who said their daughter was in the hospital. They told him that Carol had been driving the family car when she was hit by an uninsured motorist. Both Carol and her passenger, Wanda Holbert, were hospitalized. When Ohralik suggested to the McClintocks that they hire a lawyer, Mrs. McClintock said that such a decision would be up to Carol.

Then, Ohralik went to the hospital, where he found Carol lying in traction. After a brief conversation about her condition, Ohralik told Carol he would represent her and asked her to sign an agreement. Carol said she would have to discuss the matter with her parents. By the time he got to her parents' home, however, they said Carol had called to say Ohralik should "go ahead" with the representation. Two days later, Ohralik re-

---

3. The ABA report is discussed and evaluated in Ronald D. Rotunda, Professionalism, Legal Advertising, and Free Speech in the Wake of Florida Bar v. Went For It, Inc., 49 Arkansas L. Rev. 703 (1997).

turned to Carol's hospital room to have her sign a contract that provided he would receive one-third of her recovery.

In the meantime, Ohralik found Wanda Holbert's address and showed up at her home uninvited. He carried a concealed tape recorder and told Wanda that he had a "little tip" for her; the McClintocks' insurance policy contained an uninsured motorist clause which might net her a recovery of up to $12,500. He offered to represent her, as well as Carol, for a contingent fee of one-third of any recovery, and Wanda said "O.K."

Wanda's mother attempted to repudiate her daughter's oral assent the following day. She said that if they decided to sue they would consult their own lawyer, but Ohralik insisted that Wanda had entered into a binding contract. A month later Wanda ordered Ohralik to notify the insurance company that he was not her lawyer, because the company would not release a check to her until he did so. Carol also eventually fired Ohralik. Although another lawyer represented Carol in working out a settlement with the insurance company, she paid Ohralik one-third of her $12,500 recovery in settlement of his suit against her for breach of contract.

Both Carol and Wanda filed complaints with the lawyer discipline commission. The Ohio Supreme Court found that Ohralik's conduct was not constitutionally protected, and it increased the recommended sanction of a public reprimand to indefinite suspension.

Justice Powell, who was the principal dissenter the preceding year in *Bates*, wrote the Court's opinion in *Ohralik*:

> "Appellant contends that his solicitation of the two young women as clients is indistinguishable, for purposes of constitutional analysis, from the advertisement in *Bates*. * * * But in-person solicitation of professional employment by a lawyer does not stand on a par with truthful advertising about the availability and terms of routine legal services, let alone with forms of speech more traditionally within the concern of the First Amendment. * * *

> "In-person solicitation by a lawyer of remunerative employment is a business transaction in which speech is an essential but subordinate component. While this does not remove the speech from the protection of the First Amendment, as was held in *Bates* and *Virginia Pharmacy*, it lowers the level of appropriate judicial scrutiny.

> " * * * Unlike a public advertisement, which simply provides information and leaves the recipient free to act upon it or not, in-person solicitation may exert pressure and often demands an immediate response, without providing an opportunity for comparison or reflection. The aim and effect of in-person solicitation may be to provide a one-sided presentation and to encourage speedy and perhaps uninformed decision making; there is no opportunity for intervention or counter-education by agencies of the Bar, supervisory authorities, or persons close to the solicited individual. The admonition that 'the fitting remedy for evil counsels is good ones' is of little value when the circumstances provide no opportunity for any remedy at all. * * *

" * * * [N]either of the disciplinary rules here at issue prohibited appellant from communicating information to these young women about their legal rights and the prospects of obtaining a monetary recovery, or from recommending that they obtain counsel. [They] merely prohibited him from using the information as bait with which to obtain an agreement to represent them for a fee. * * *

" * * * While entitled to some constitutional protection, appellant's conduct is subject to regulation in furtherance of important state interests. * * *

"As is true with respect to advertising, see *Bates*, it appears that the ban on solicitation by lawyers originated as a rule of professional etiquette rather than as a strictly ethical rule. * * * But the fact that the original motivation behind the ban on solicitation today might be considered an insufficient justification for its perpetuation does not detract from the force of the other interests the ban continues to serve. * * *

"The substantive evils of solicitation have been stated over the years in sweeping terms: stirring up litigation, assertion of fraudulent claims, debasing the legal profession, and potential harm to the solicited client in the form of overreaching, overcharging, underrepresentation, and misrepresentation. * * *

"We need not discuss or evaluate each of these interests in detail as appellant has conceded that the State has a legitimate and indeed 'compelling' interest in preventing those aspects of solicitation that involve fraud, undue influence, intimidation, overreaching, and other forms of 'vexatious conduct.' * * *

"Appellant's concession that strong state interests justify regulation to prevent the evils he enumerates would end this case but for his insistence that none of those evils was found to be present in his acts of solicitation. * * * But appellant errs in assuming that the constitutional validity of the judgment below depends on proof that his conduct constituted actual overreaching or inflicted some specific injury on Wanda Holbert or Carol McClintock. * * * The rules prohibiting solicitation are prophylactic measures whose objective is the prevention of harm before it occurs. * * *

"The State's perception of the potential for harm in circumstances such as those presented in this case is well-founded. The detrimental aspects of face-to-face selling even of ordinary consumer products have been recognized and addressed by the Federal Trade Commission, and it hardly need be said that the potential for overreaching is significantly greater when a lawyer, a professional trained in the art of persuasion, personally solicits an unsophisticated, injured, or distressed lay person. * * * Although it is argued that personal solicitation is valuable because it may apprise a victim of misfortune of his or her legal rights, the very plight of that person not only makes him or her more vulnerable to influence but also may make advice all the more intrusive. Thus, under these adverse conditions the overtures of an uninvited lawyer may distress the solicited individual simply because of their obtrusiveness and the invasion of the individual's privacy, even when no other harm materializes. Under such circumstances, it is not unreasonable for the State to presume that in-person solicitation by lawyers more often than not will be injurious to the person solicited.

"The efficacy of the State's effort to prevent such harm to prospective clients would be substantially diminished if, having proved a solicitation in circumstances like those of this case, the State were required in addition to prove actual injury. * * * Often there is no witness other than the lawyer and the lay person whom he has solicited, rendering it difficult or impossible to obtain reliable proof of what actually took place. This would be especially true if the lay person were so distressed at the time of the solicitation that he or she could not recall specific details at a later date. If appellant's view were sustained, in-person solicitation would be virtually immune to effective oversight and regulation by the State or by the legal profession, in contravention of the State's strong interest in regulating members of the Bar in an effective, objective, and self-enforcing manner. It therefore is not unreasonable, or violative of the Constitution, for a State to respond with what in effect is a prophylactic rule."[3]

c. In a companion case, In re Primus, 436 U.S. 412, 98 S.Ct. 1893, 56 L.Ed.2d 417 (1978), Justice Powell again wrote for the Court. *Primus* gave constitutional protection to the conduct of a lawyer who first addressed a gathering of women about their legal rights resulting from their having been sterilized as a condition of receiving public medical assistance, and who then sent one of them a letter advising them that the ACLU was offering free legal assistance to women who had been involuntarily sterilized. The Court distinguished *Primus* from *Ohralik* on several grounds. First, it was important that the personal solicitation was in writing, which gave the recipient time for reflection. Second, the case had a political character and was a form of expression because it sought to redress an injustice done to many women. Third, the practicing lawyer who sent the letter was cooperating with the local branch of a nonprofit organization. The Court thus had two extreme cases. In one, it protected in-person contact; in the other, it did not. It left open where other cases would fall along this continuum.

d. Take a look at the modern-day ABA Model Rule 7.3. What you see is the product of a long series of changes, most of which responded to litigation that invalidated various restrictions that the ABA tried to impose on advertising and solicitation, first in the Model Code and later in the

---

3. The opinion was for a six-member majority. Justice Marshall concurred in the judgment, but said that even unsolicited contact from a lawyer can often provide important information and help to an accident victim whom the defendant or its insurer is already free to contact and with whom they may negotiate a settlement. Justice Rehnquist, also concurring in the judgment, continued to say that lawyer marketing was not constitutionally protected. Justice Brennan did not participate.

Model Rules. Model Rule 7.3 now limits "direct contact" with prospective clients only when pecuniary gain is a "significant motive." Indeed, the definition of direct contact now is limited to "in-person, live telephone or real-time electronic contact."

2. Do Jerry Harrold's phone calls proposing a "legal checkup" present issues under Model Rule 7.3(a)?

a. Should the fact the calls are all to clients or former clients make the contact less problematic? Might it make them more so?[4] If, in another month or so, Jerry were to call back those who turned him down the first time, would his conduct violate Model Rule 7.3(b)?

b. Is it proper for a lawyer to print color brochures extolling the law firm's virtues? Is there any question the lawyer's motive would be to bring more business to the law firm? Do the words "Advertising Material" have to appear on the brochure itself? Why does Model Rule 7.3(c) require that such a legend be printed on any envelope in which the lawyer mails a brochure, but not on the brochure the lawyer passes out at the local Rotary Club?

c. May a lawyer hold seminars or make public speeches about the law and legal problems? Is the analysis of proper motives in ABA Model Code of Professional Responsibility EC 2–2 to 2–5 still relevant? May a lawyer represent a person who comes for advice after attending one of these programs? Would you be troubled if the lawyer distributed his or her business card at the events?

3. When does permitted lawyer advertising become prohibited in-person solicitation? May Jerry Harrold send his proposed personal note to each of the victims of the plane crash?

a. Contact with persons believed to have a specific current need for legal service has come to be called "targeted direct mail." Should it be seen as more like advertising protected by *Bates* or subject to the greater regulation of in-person solicitation?

b. Matter of Von Wiegen, 470 N.E.2d 838 (N.Y.1984), saw targeted mailing as advertising. In-person solicitation "permits the exertion of subtle pressure and often demands an immediate response," the court said, while targeted direct mail gives the recipient time to reflect about—or indeed ignore—the offer of services and "the process of decision-making may actually be aided by information contained in the mailing." 470 N.E.2d at 841.

c. Not all states agreed, and the Court had to invalidate state rules that banned targeted direct mail. The leading case was Shapero v. Kentucky Bar Association, 486 U.S. 466, 108 S.Ct. 1916, 100 L.Ed.2d 475

---

4. A 1958 study of the ABA Special Committee on the Economics of Law Practice recommended trying to get all one's clients back to the office periodically for a "routine legal checkup" as a way of raising lawyers' incomes more nearly to the incomes of doctors. Should such a concern for the lawyer's income be improper in evaluating advertising for, and solicitation of, clients? Can such issues ever be wholly ignored?

(1988). Mr. Shapero had applied to the state Attorney General's Advertising Commission for approval of a letter he planned to send to persons against whom he believed foreclosure suits had been filed. The Commission did not find the letter false or misleading, but a Kentucky Supreme Court rule prohibited sending letters "precipitated by a specific event or occurrence involving or related to the addressee" rather than to the public generally. The United States Supreme Court held that the blanket ban was unconstitutional. The lawyer clearly could have published his truthful letter in a newspaper or mailed it in bulk throughout the community, the Court said. There is nothing about the constitutionality of advertising that requires that the method of distribution be inefficient. As for *Ohralik*'s concerns about "overwhelming" the targets of the letters, the Court said that whether or not letters are overwhelming has nothing to do with how randomly they are sent. Furthermore, no form of written communication presents the dangers of overreaching that *Ohralik* illustrated. "A letter, like a printed advertisement (but unlike a lawyer), can readily be put in a drawer to be considered later, ignored, or discarded." 486 U.S. at 475–76, 108 S.Ct. at 1923, 100 L.Ed.2d at 486. 108 S.Ct. at 1923. The fact that targeted direct mail could be the subject of abuses did not justify its complete ban.[5]

4. How does internet contact fit into this analysis? If a lawyer surfs the web looking for chat rooms, for example, and then seeks to get participants to consult the lawyer for legal services, how would new Model Rule 7.3(a) characterize the contact?

a.   Do you agree that "real-time electronic contact" presents the same concerns about solicitation that face-to-face contact presents? The lawyer providing truthful information in an electronic "chat room" is engaged in "real-time" contact, but no one has to respond. Anyone who wishes can even leave the chat-room; that is not considered impolite like hanging up the phone. Indeed, while in the chat-room, anyone may say that they do not want to be solicited and the lawyer would be required to stop by Model Rule 7.3(b)(1). So, why should the Model Rules seek to ban solicitation of prospective clients through this medium? Is "real-time electronic contact" more like a letter that one can throw away, like a prerecorded telephone call, or like a live telephone call that Rule 7.3 has long treated as direct contact?

b.   How would you characterize a law firm web site that provides interesting information the firm hopes will attract calls from potential clients? Would your answer be different if the law firm assigns a lawyer to be available for real-time interaction with persons who initiate visits to the web site?

5. Justice O'Connor, joined in dissent by Chief Justice Rehnquist and Justice Scalia, was willing to reconsider all of the attorney advertising cases. Justice O'Connor said that the cases were "built on defective premises and flawed reasoning." The entire analytical framework, she argued, "should be reexamined." She implicitly did so in *Florida Bar v. Went For It, Inc.*, *infra*.

c.   Should a lawyer's sending unsolicited e-mail to potential clients be treated as a form of newspaper advertising? Is it a form of targeted direct mail? How would the *Shapero* majority likely characterize such contacts? How are they characterized in new Model Rule 7.3(c)?

d.   D.C. Bar Legal Ethics Opinion No. 316 (July 2002) discussed the variety of ways lawyers operate in subject matter chat rooms on the internet. It reports one in which immigrants write questions, for example, and lawyers visiting the site write answers. The lawyers often invite the questioner to call for a brief, initially free, consultation. The Opinion recommends that lawyers give "legal information" on such web sites, but not "legal advice." The former "involves a discussion of legal principles, trends and considerations [such as] * * * one might give in a speech or newspaper article." The latter "involves offering recommendations tailored to the unique facts of a particular person's circumstances." Giving advice, the Opinion warns, may involve the lawyer in an attorney-client relationship with someone the lawyer does not know and create obligations greater than the lawyer means to assume. Do you agree?

C.   CONTINUING ISSUES IN THE FIELD OF LAWYER ADVERTISING

1.   Is it proper for a state to regulate advertising out of concern that it will increase litigation by encouraging people to bring suit who otherwise would not do so?

a.   The Court gave added content to the constitutional standards in *Bates* when it decided in Zauderer v. Office of Disciplinary Counsel, 471 U.S. 626, 105 S.Ct. 2265, 85 L.Ed.2d 652 (1985). Philip Zauderer put an advertisement in 36 Ohio newspapers offering to represent women injured by use of the Dalkon Shield Intrauterine Device (IUD). The ad included a drawing of the device and a question "Did you use this IUD?" Zauderer's ad said that his firm was representing other women in such cases and that the cases "are handled on a contingent fee basis of the amount recovered. If there is no recovery, no legal fees are owed by our clients."

b.   Ohio disciplinary counsel raised concern that such advertising constituted "stirring up litigation" but the U.S. Supreme Court answered:

"That our citizens have access to their civil courts is not an evil to be regretted; rather, it is an attribute of our system of justice in which we ought to take pride. The State is not entitled to interfere with that access by denying its citizens accurate information about their legal rights. Accordingly, it is not sufficient justification for the discipline imposed on appellant that his truthful and nondeceptive advertising had a tendency to or did in fact encourage others to file lawsuits." 471 U.S. at 643, 105 S.Ct. at 2277–78, 85 L.Ed. 2d at 667.

2.   Do illustrations in a lawyer's advertisement have the same constitutional protection as the text message? Might the illustrations be regulated if they are found to be "undignified"?

a.   The Court held the illustrations were protected speech.

"The use of illustrations or pictures in advertisements serves important communicative functions: it attracts the attention of the audience to the advertiser's message, and it may also serve to impart information directly. Accordingly, commercial illustrations are entitled to the First Amendment protections afforded verbal commercial speech: restrictions on the use of visual media of expression in advertising must survive scrutiny under the *Central Hudson* test."[6] 471 U.S. at 647, 105 S.Ct. at 2279–80, 85 L.Ed. 2d at 670.

b.   It also found that the state has no valid regulatory interest in preserving the dignity of the legal profession's image.

"[A]lthough the State undoubtedly has a substantial interest in ensuring that its attorneys behave with dignity and decorum in the courtroom, we are unsure that the State's desire that attorneys maintain their dignity in their communications with the public is an interest substantial enough to justify the abridgment of their First Amendment rights. * * * [T]he mere possibility that some members of the population might find advertising embarrassing or offensive cannot justify suppressing it. The same must hold true for advertising that some members of the bar might find beneath their dignity. * * * " 471 U.S. at 647–48, 105 S.Ct. at 2280, 85 L.Ed. 2d at 670.

3.   Should a state be able to require lawyers to tell clients they will have to pay litigation costs even if they lose their case?

a.   The Court in *Zauderer* distinguished requiring disclaimers from prohibiting speech altogether. It said:

"[There are] material differences between disclosure requirements and outright prohibitions on speech. In requiring attorneys who advertise their willingness to represent clients on a contingent-fee basis to state that the client may have to bear certain expenses even if he loses, Ohio has not attempted to prevent attorneys from conveying information to the public; it has only required them to provide somewhat more information than they might otherwise be inclined to present. * * *

"We do not suggest that disclosure requirements do not implicate the advertiser's First Amendment rights at all. We recognize that unjustified or unduly burdensome disclosure requirements might offend the First Amendment by chilling protected commercial speech. But we hold that an advertiser's rights are adequately protected as long as disclosure requirements are reasonably related to the State's interest in preventing deception of consumers. 471 U.S. at 650–51, 105 S.Ct. at 2281–82, 85 L.Ed. 2d at 672–73.

b.   Applying this standard, the Court said:

---

6.   The Court's reference was to Central Hudson Gas & Electric Corp. v. Public Service Commission, 447 U.S. 557, 100 S.Ct. 2343, 65 L.Ed.2d 341 (1980), which held that commercial speech could only be regulated in pursuit of a substantial government interest and by means narrowly tailored to protect that interest.

"The State's application to appellant of the requirement that an attorney advertising his availability on a contingent fee basis disclose that clients will have to pay costs even if their lawsuits are unsuccessful (assuming that to be the case) easily passes muster under this standard. * * * " 471 U.S. at 652, 105 S.Ct. at 2282, 85 L.Ed. 2d at 673.

4.   Do you agree that requiring a disclaimer could excessively "chill" protected speech?

a.   Tillman v. Miller, 133 F.3d 1402 (11th Cir.1998), declared the Georgia Workers' Compensation Truth in Advertising Act of 1995 unconstitutional. The Act required all lawyers and others involved in filing workers' compensation claims to put a large legend in their television ads saying that "willfully making a false * * * representation to obtain * * * benefits is a crime * * * ." The Court acknowledged that *Zauderer* permits a state to require disclaimers necessary to render an advertisement not false or misleading, but these ads were truthful. A state may not impose on a lawyer "the burden of the cost of educating the public about the criminal penalties for filing fraudulent claims." 113 F.3d at 1403–04.

b.   In Mason v. The Florida Bar, 208 F.3d 952 (11th Cir.2000), the state bar sought to discipline a lawyer who publicly advertised his rating in the Martindale–Hubbell Legal Directory. The Bar notified Mason that his advertisement must include a full explanation as to the meaning of the Martindale–Hubbell ratings and how the publication chooses the participating attorneys. This explanation must state "that the ratings and participation are based 'exclusively on * * * opinions expressed by * * * confidential sources' and that these publications do not undertake to rate all Florida attorneys." The lawyer's advertisement said that he was " 'AV' Rated, the Highest Rating Martindale–Hubbell National Law Directory." Specifically, the Bar objected to the phrase, "highest rating." The court held that the bar was not able to prove that the public would be misled by Mason's truthful advertisement. Moreover, "the Bar is not relieved of its burden to identify a genuine threat of danger simply because it requires a disclaimer, rather than a complete ban on Mason's speech."

5.   Should a lawyer be entitled to make claims as to her quality? Her won-lost record? How about publishing client testimonials?

a.   In Matter of Zang, 741 P.2d 267 (Ariz.1987), cert. denied 484 U.S. 1067, 108 S.Ct. 1030, 98 L.Ed.2d 994 (1988), two lawyers claimed to have "a personal injury law firm" with the capability to discover facts "essential to victory in the courtroom." Each of their advertisements emphasized their thorough preparation and use of investigators. The television ads showed Mr. Zang arguing before a jury. In fact, Mr. Zang had very little trial experience and "scrupulously avoided" taking a case to trial. If a trial were ever necessary, he would refer the case to another firm. He personally had never tried a personal injury case, and he conceded in the discipline proceeding that he did not feel competent to try one. He argued that the advertisements did not say that the lawyers were good at trial; they only said the lawyers were good at *preparing for* trial. The Court rejected the distinction and suspended the lawyers for 30 days. Instead, the court found the advertisement "flattering beyond the point of deception."

b. In Matter of Wamsley, 725 N.E.2d 75 (Ind.2000), the lawyer advertised on the back cover of the Indianapolis phone book, "Best Possible Settlement.... Least Amount of Time." The ad also said: "My reputation, experience, and integrity result in most of our cases being settled without filing a complaint or lengthy trial." The court found these statements implied something excessive about the quality of the lawyer's services and "likely created an unjustified expectation of such a result in any case the respondent agreed to handle." 725 N.E.2d at 77. The court publicly reprimanded and admonished the lawyer for his claims.

Do you think potential clients would be fooled by the advertisement? Did it merit discipline? Look at Rule 7.1, Comment 3. Would it ban this type of advertisement?

6. May a lawyer use a memorable trade name or internet web address such as "The Winning Team" or "suethebums.com"?

a. DR 2–101(B) of the ABA Model Code of Professional Responsibility provided:

"A lawyer in private practice shall not practice under a trade name * * * or a name containing names other than those of one or more of the lawyers [currently or formerly] in the firm * * * ."

b. Does ABA Model Rule of Professional Conduct 7.5 continue the same prohibition? Look at Comment [1] to Model Rule 7.5. What are now the relevant concerns with respect to the names law firms use? Do names like the ones suggested in this question raise concerns as to which regulation would be appropriate?

7. Does television advertising justify special regulation?

a. This issue became more significant after Committee on Professional Ethics v. Humphrey, 377 N.W.2d 643 (Iowa 1985). The Iowa Supreme Court had adopted strict limits on television advertising. Background sounds were forbidden, as were visible displays, more than a single nondramatic voice, and any self-laudatory statements. The U.S. Supreme Court remanded *Humphrey* to see if Iowa believed its rules could still stand in light of *Zauderer*, and on remand, the Iowa Supreme Court again said that they could. The problems with television advertising, it believed, are that:

"Both sight and sound are immediate and can be elusive because, for the listener or viewer at least, in a flash they are gone without a trace. Lost is the opportunity accorded to the reader of printed advertisements to pause, to restudy, and to thoughtfully consider." 377 N.W.2d at 646.

When an appeal from this decision was again taken to the U.S. Supreme Court, the Court surprised almost everyone by dismissing the appeal for lack of a substantial federal question, 475 U.S. 1114, 106 S.Ct. 1626, 90 L.Ed.2d 174 (1986). Do you agree that no substantial question was presented?[7] Had the Iowa court simply articulated concerns the U.S. Supreme Court had raised as early as *Bates* and *Ohralik*?

b.   Should Jerry Harrold be permitted to hire someone from the cast of Law and Order to say they wished they had someone like Jerry on their team? Might an attorney buy an ad on reruns of "L.A. Law" if she wanted to emphasize her sophisticated, tough trial style, or on "Entertainment Tonight" if she wanted to imply that she had high-profile celebrity clients? The court in *Humphrey* did not think so, saying: "Electronically conveyed image-building was not a part of the information package which has been described [by the U.S. Supreme Court] as needed by the public." 377 N.W.2d at 647. Is that correct? Are most lawyer ads that you see any more than image building?

c.   Office of Disciplinary Counsel v. Shane, 692 N.E.2d 571 (Ohio 1998), publicly reprimanded lawyers who used "not inaccurate" but self-laudatory claims of success in their television advertising. Former clients of the lawyers appeared before the camera saying such things as: "They really fought for me. * * * I never expected the large settlement they won for me," and "They fought for me and got me a very good judgment. * * * Take my word for it, they're the best." Do you agree that such testimonials "create unjustified expectations of similar outcomes in the future"?

d.   Do you think it was similarly wrong for Jerry Harrold in our Problem to offer to give potential clients the names of some of his past clients who might give personal testimonials about his services? What differences do you see between actually talking with a former client and seeing one on television?

D.   CONTINUING ISSUES OF IN-PERSON SOLICITATION BY LAWYERS

1.   Now, turn to the plane crash and Jerry's response to it. Is the concern that Jerry is too assertive in this context? Is the concern that the lawyer will make potential clients do something they would rather not do?

a.   In Edenfield v. Fane, 507 U.S. 761, 113 S.Ct. 1792, 123 L.Ed.2d 543 (1993), Florida had tried to regulate CPAs' personal solicitation of business clients. The plaintiff sued for the right to make unsolicited calls to such clients and to arrange appointments to explain his expertise and lower fees. The State said that the rule against such contacts was designed both to protect consumers of accounting services against overreaching and to assure the independence of financial audits. In an opinion by Justice Kennedy, the Court found the state interests "substantial in the abstract" but found that business clients were able to protect themselves against overreaching. Further, the concern about a lack of audit independence was said to be greater where businesses could *not* turn to newcomers like Fane because then the incumbent firm could get too close to management.

---

7.   The Court was divided on this issue. Justices White, Blackmun and Stevens would   have set the case for oral argument.

b. The state expressly relied on *Ohralik*, and the Court expressly distinguished it. The *Ohralik* "holding was narrow and depended upon certain 'unique features of in-person solicitation by lawyers' that were present in the circumstances of that case." CPAs, the Court observed, are not "trained in the art of persuasion" and clients being solicited for accounting work "are sophisticated and experienced business executives who understand well the services that a CPA offers." 507 U.S. at 774–75, 113 S.Ct. at 1802–03, 123 L.Ed.2d at 557–58.

c. Do you agree with the Court's concern that lawyers have qualities of intimidation against which clients need protection? Do you consider yourself intimidating? Are there any of your classmates against whom you think potential clients need protection?

2. What if the law firm sends "investigators" to the victims' homes to leave the attorney's business cards and encourage the signing of retainers?[8]

a. In Falanga v. State Bar of Georgia, 150 F.3d 1333 (11th Cir.1998), two lawyers challenged state restrictions on in-person, uninvited solicitation of professional employment. The lawyers tended to represent poor, uneducated persons in personal injury cases. The lawyers obtained names of potential clients by having law firm "public relations agents" contact doctors and chiropractors while other employees sifted through police reports. The lawyers then visited the potential clients and tried to persuade them to sign a retainer. The court found this conduct much more like that in *Ohralik* than that in *Edenfield*. The conduct fell "squarely within [the] category of 'ambulance chasing,'" and the Bar had anecdotal evidence the public did not like unsolicited, intrusive contact from these lawyers. Thus, the Court held the State had sufficiently justified its prohibitions on in-person solicitation, at least as applied to lawyers who approach "unsophisticated, injured, or distressed lay person[s]." 150 F.3d at 1347 (quoting both *Ohralik* and *Edenfield*).

b. Should your law firm be permitted to write to real estate agents asking the agents to recommend your law firm to their customers? The New York Court of Appeals drew the line at that. The lawyer might have an incentive to find good title so as to assure that the referring agent got his fee, the court said. The interest in preventing such conflicts of interests should permit regulation of letters to the agents. Greene v. Grievance Committee, 429 N.E.2d 390, 395 (N.Y.1981). Do you agree? Is it the letter that should be the subject of discipline? Would the later conflict of interest be so hard to prove that the bar must have a broad prophylactic rule?

c. Do you agree with the result in *Greene*? ABA Model Rule 7.2(b)(4) allows lawyers to refer clients to particular real estate agents pursuant to

---

8. Several courts have suspended attorneys who used such non-lawyer agents. Koden v. United States Department of Justice, 564 F.2d 228 (7th Cir.1977), and Goldman v. State Bar, 570 P.2d 463 (Cal.1977) (both decided before *Ohralik* and *Primus*), and In re Arnoff, 586 P.2d 960 (Cal.1978), and In re Teichner, 387 N.E.2d 265 (Ill.1979) (both decided later).

an understanding that the real estate agents will refer customers to the lawyers, so long as the agreement is not exclusive and the lawyers fully disclose what is going on. If such reciprocal arrangements are permitted, why should lawyers not be able to ask real estate agents to make the referrals unilaterally?

3.   Other circumstances in which lawyers engage in face-to-face solicitation of accident victims continue to amaze, but are all of them equally appropriate for discipline?

a.   In The Florida Bar v. Weinstein, 624 So.2d 261 (Fla.1993), for example, the lawyer tried to solicit a brain injury victim who was still in the hospital. In Texas State Bar v. Kilpatrick, 874 S.W.2d 656 (Tex.1994), the lawyer waited until the brain-damaged victim had been transported to a nursing home, but otherwise the solicitation—and the disbarment sanction—were the same.

b.   In Norris v. Alabama State Bar, 582 So.2d 1034 (Ala.1991), a young child had died after being left in a closed van in the hot sun by a day care center. Someone called the lawyer's office and told the receptionist that the family was "broke" and too poor to buy flowers for the funeral. The lawyer sent a wreath to the funeral home with his firm brochure attached and a letter inviting the family to contact him if he could be of any help. The story of his gesture got into the news and a disciplinary hearing followed. The Alabama Supreme Court acknowledged that DR 2–103 of its Code of Professional Responsibility did not precisely cover this situation, but said that Norris showed "indifference to the purpose and spirit of the rule." The Court rejected Norris' reliance on *Shapero* (the flowers did not go through the mail) and suspended him for two years.

Do you agree that this result would be required under Model Rule 7.3? Is this the result you would have reached?

c.   In Matter of Anis, 599 A.2d 1265 (N.J.1992), the court publicly reprimanded a lawyer for sending a letter to the father of a victim of the Lockerbie, Scotland bombing of a PanAm jet. The letter was not high pressure; it expressed condolences to the family and invited them to contact the lawyer. The court, however, found the sympathy "hollow" and the letter misleading about the lawyer's experience. Indeed, it said, the lawyer "could only have deepened the family's suffering." In an opinion replete with references to lawyers' low public image, the Court said the sanction was for "conduct that is patently offensive to the common sensibilities of the community because it intrudes upon the private grief of victims * * * and solicits representation of them at a moment of their extreme vulnerability." 599 A.2d at 1271.

Again, do you agree? Are you convinced the lawyer did something morally wrong? Was his conduct cruel and selfish? Professional and caring? Putting aside the possibly misleading content of the letter, was the conduct distinguishable from that in *Shapero*?

d.   Matter of Ravich, Koster, Tobin, Oleckna, Reitman & Greenstein, 715 A.2d 216 (N.J.1998), reprimanded members of a law firm a/k/a TEAM-

LAW who showed up outside a Red Cross shelter on the morning after at a gas line explosion that displaced many apartment residents. TEAMLAW rented an RV, taped copies of their newspaper ad to the RV's windows. and distributed toiletries to the victims after they were interviewed by the lawyers. The New Jersey Committee on Attorney Advertising said this conduct went too far. The New Jersey Supreme Court agreed. That close to the time of the explosion, victims were "in a state of mind not conducive to making reasoned judgment about such a weighty matter as legal representation." 715 A.2d at 221. The Court recognized that insurance agents were not similarly prevented from contacting the victims while they were confused and distraught, but it said the lawyers should have contented themselves with warning victims not to sign away their rights and not gone on to solicit future employment. Id. at 222.

Do you agree that such an approach is realistic? Is it even in the best interest of the clients? Remember Model Rule 4.2. Once the victims had retained a lawyer, they could have insisted that all communications from the insurance companies go through those lawyers.

e.   In Kentucky Bar Association v. Mandello, 32 S.W.3d 763 (Ky.2000), a lawyer had written a letter recommending that a woman call for legal help. The woman's husband had died while in the hospital and some nurses, in a social setting, had told the lawyer facts suggesting that the death was due to gross negligence. The court found the lawyer's letter misleading in that she did not volunteer that she was young and had no experience in medical malpractice cases. Further, the letter was a form of "advertising" and should have been submitted to the state Attorneys Advertising Commission for prior review. The court suspended the lawyer for six months for these mistakes.

Are you convinced that potential clients are better off as a result of decisions such as this? Might lawyers actually perform a public service by telling potential clients about the negligence of doctors and hospitals, for example? Is the requirement that the lawyer submit an advertisement to a state agency for prior review an unconstitutional prior restraint? Do the ABA Model Rules require prior review of lawyer advertising?

4.   The ABA responded to *Shapero* with the current version of Model Rule 7.3. However, Florida prohibited lawyers for potential plaintiffs from sending any targeted direct mail within 30 days of an accident. Does the Florida rule go too far? Should it be held to be constitutional?

a.   The U.S. Supreme Court considered the Florida rule in Florida Bar v. Went For It, Inc., 515 U.S. 618, 115 S.Ct. 2371, 132 L.Ed.2d 541 (1995). The rule prohibited plaintiffs' lawyers from using targeted direct mail to contact victims and their families within 30 days following an accident or disaster but it did not regulate similar contact by defense lawyers or insurance adjusters. The lawyers challenging the regulation relied on *Shapero*, but Justice O'Connor, the long-time dissenter in lawyer advertising cases, spoke for the Court and upheld the Florida rule. Chief Justice Rehnquist, and Justices Scalia, Thomas & Breyer, joined her opinion.

First, in this case, the state's "substantial interest" justifying the regulation was "the protection of potential clients' privacy." Second, the state showed that its regulation advanced that interest "in a direct and material way" by citing to a collection of newspaper editorials and a survey the Bar commissioned to study citizen attitudes. "Significantly, 27% of direct-mail recipients reported that their regard for the legal profession and for the judicial process as a whole was 'lower' as a result of receiving the direct mail." 515 U.S. at 627, 115 S.Ct. at 2377, 132 L.Ed.2d at 551. The Court thus concluded that a factual basis was present to justify regulation of post-accident contact.

The Court distinguished *Shapero* as a case that dealt with a broad ban on targeted direct mail. Thus, it was not authority for striking down a narrower ban directed at protecting the privacy of persons who have recently suffered a traumatic event. Further, the answer that recipients of mailings could just dispose of them was not sufficient; mailings sent to bereaved persons would inflict their pain when they were first seen, i.e., before they could be thrown away. Finally, the majority argued, the Florida regulation was a "reasonable fit" for the problem that the Bar had identified. It was "narrowly tailored to achieve the desired objective," even if not the "least restrictive means" of addressing the concern. There are other ways for lawyers to make their availability known to potential clients, e.g., television, newspapers, billboards, the Yellow Pages, or even non-targeted direct mail. 515 U.S. at 633–34, 115 S.Ct. at 2380, 132 L.Ed.2d at 555.

b.   Justice Kennedy led Justices Stevens, Souter and Ginsburg in an indignant dissent. The fact that advertising is "offensive" or "undignified" has not been enough before, the dissent noted, so to say that this result followed the earlier precedents was disingenuous. Further, the dissenters found the Bar's "proof" that a problem existed to be methodologically flawed and largely anecdotal. Finally, they found the "flat ban" on direct mail contact too broad because it applied no matter how serious the accident or disaster. They found the Bar's regulation self-serving and the Court's decision a "retreat" from constitutional guarantees. "[T]he State is doing nothing more * * * than manipulating the public's opinion [of lawyers] by suppressing speech that informs us how the legal system works. * * * This, of course, is censorship pure and simple." 515 U.S. at 639–40, 115 S.Ct. at 2383, 132 L.Ed.2d at 559.

c.   With which opinion do you agree? Note that the ABA has not added the Florida restriction to the Model Rules. Do you think it should do so?

5.   Do you think *Went For It, Inc.* stands alone or might it be a turning point in the Court's treatment of lawyer advertising and solicitation regulations?

a.   Ficker v. Curran, 119 F.3d 1150 (4th Cir.1997), considered a Maryland statute forbidding sending targeted direct mail to potential criminal defendants within 30 days of the date they are charged. The Court found that criminal defendants need representation most within the first 30 days and do not consider hearing from lawyers an invasion of privacy.

The rule denied access to lawyers during this critical period and thus it was unconstitutional.

b. Revo v. New Mexico Supreme Court Disciplinary Board, 106 F.3d 929 (10th Cir.1997), examined a New Mexico rule prohibiting all direct mail advertisements to personal injury victims and family members of wrongful death victims unless the lawyer has a prior personal, business or professional relationship with the person. The State argued that all such letters are "inherently misleading" and thus may be regulated because they falsely imply that lawyers who send the letters are tougher and more able than those who do not. However, the Tenth Circuit said that in making the 30–day ban in *Went For It* a permanent ban, the New Mexico prohibition was insufficiently tailored to address an identified problem and thus it, too, was unconstitutional. Do you agree?

c. In Los Angeles Police Department v. United Reporting Publishing Corp., 528 U.S. 32, 120 S.Ct. 483, 145 L.Ed.2d 451 (1999), the Supreme Court again dealt with a related issue. California has a statute permitting release of arrest records for a "scholarly, journalistic, political, or governmental purpose," but not for commercial use. Respondent, a publishing service that sold such information to lawyers and others who might want to send direct mail suggesting a need for their services, challenged the statute on its face. The Ninth Circuit had invalidated the law, saying that privacy interests could not justify the statute because the information was already released to the newspapers, and a letter from a lawyer could not be more intrusive than that. But in an opinion by Chief Justice Rehnquist, the Supreme Court reversed. The law does not inhibit anyone from "conveying information that the speaker already possesses," the Court said; it only limits access to information in the hands of the police.

The concurring justices noted that a lawyer can simply get the names from the newspapers when they are published there so the regulation has little practical effect. Justices Stevens and Kennedy dissented, however. The law denies access to accurate information to persons who want to use it for constitutionally-protected purposes, they said, and that makes it facially invalid.

Are the dissenters correct? Might the case again suggest the Supreme Court may be having second thoughts about having opened the door to lawyer advertising and solicitation?

PROBLEM 32

THE ETHICS OF REFERRAL TO A SPECIALIST

Your directory listing will say "lawyer." Your business card will call you a "member of the bar" of one or more jurisdictions. You will know, however, that you cannot competently provide all of the services that those titles suggest. No lawyer and few law firms stand ready to practice all the substantive areas of law that the modern world demands. Indeed, as a practical matter, most lawyers find it a full time job to keep their skills honed in enough areas to be able to sustain a satisfying practice. This Problem asks you to think about how lawyers should be able to describe the fields in which they practice and their level of expertise in those fields. It also explores when lawyers may take a case in some other field, and how they may distribute the financial rewards from the cases that come into their office so as to provide incentives to refer cases, when necessary, to practitioners better able to handle an unfamiliar matter.

FACTS

Hector Ramirez has represented the Peron family for several years in minor matters for which he has charged minimal fees. Young Joseph Peron was recently seriously injured when a telephone company truck went out of control and into a schoolyard. The Peron family wants to file suit and has come to Ramirez for help.

Ramirez realizes that he is a competent attorney and could handle this case without obvious errors. However, he also knows that he is not experienced in personal injury work, that the medical evidence necessary to prove the case correctly will be complex and that he may not be able to cross-examine the defense doctors effectively. Ramirez can see, on the other hand, that the fee this case would justify would be the largest he has ever earned and would support him while he did other, less-remunerative work.

Ramirez knows further that Joe Castro is a very successful "Certified Trial Specialist." He is experienced at handling personal injury cases and will take the Peron case very seriously. Best of all, Castro has offered to pay Ramirez one-third of his own one-third fee, or $10,000, whichever is less, as a "finder's fee" for sending the case to him. If Ramirez prefers, he and Castro will "jointly" handle the case on the same financial basis. Ramirez also has met another personal injury lawyer who might do an even better job than Castro but who is so ethical that he would be shocked at being asked to share his fee with Ramirez.

QUESTIONS

A.   A LAWYER'S DUTY WHEN A MATTER REQUIRES NEW SKILLS OR RAISES UNFAMILIAR ISSUES

1.   Does Ramirez have an ethical obligation not to handle this case entirely by himself?

a.   What are the elements of "competence" identified in ABA Model Rule of Professional Conduct 1.1? Assume that Ramirez will work hard on the matter and prepare to the best of his ability. Does Model Rule 1.1 require any more?

b.   Look at Comments [1]–[4] of Model Rule 1.1. Do they help you understand the level of legal knowledge and skill Ramirez must have before he decides not to send the Peron family to a different lawyer? Is the discussion in those Comments sufficient to guide the lawyer to an appropriate decision?

c.   What distinction is Comment [1] drawing between a case in which "the required proficiency is that of a general practitioner" and one in which "expertise in a particular field of law may be required?" On which side of that line does this case fall?

2.   If Ramirez believes that he can perform well enough that it is unlikely he could be successfully sued for malpractice, should that be the end of the issue of his "competence" to take on the matter?

a.   There is no doubt under Rule 1.1, Comment [2] that a lawyer may take a case "of a type with which the lawyer is unfamiliar." Indeed, the rule could not be otherwise. Everyone has a "first case" of any particular type. If one could not take cases with which he or she were initially unfamiliar, how could any lawyer ever get experience?

b.   Yet in our Problem, Ramirez is clearly not at ease with the freedom that minimum compliance with Model Rule 1.1 seems to give him. How would you feel in his shoes? Would you be satisfied that you would be giving your long-time clients, the Peron family, the kind of legal service they need and deserve?

B.   CALLING A LAWYER A "SPECIALIST" IN ONE OR MORE FIELDS OF PRACTICE

1.   Should the law be concerned about lawyers calling themselves specialists? Is there any question that good lawyers like Ramirez—or like you—will limit their practices primarily to litigation or to particular substantive fields?

a.   Virtually all lawyers specialize, of course, in the sense of concentrating their practice in particular areas of law. The principal question about specialization, then, is what a lawyer may tell the public about the nature of his or her practice. For many years, the answer was that the lawyer could say little or nothing, unless he or she was licensed to practice patent law or was a recognized proctor-in-admiralty, fields that had become de facto specialties because of special licensing requirements or accidents of history. See ABA Model Rule 7.4.

b.   Why might there be such concern about using the term "specialist"? What does the word "specialist" convey? Might many clients assume the term has the meaning that it has in the medical profession, i.e., someone who has had additional training and separate certification by his or her professional peers?

c.   Matter of Robbins, 469 S.E.2d 191 (Ga.1996), involved a lawyer who sent out a firm newsletter. One issue announced the return to the firm of another lawyer "with a specialty in personal injury and litigation." The newsletter went on, "Don't Forget, we specialize in automobile accidents, bicycle accidents, medical malpractice, workers' compensation and social security cases." The court found that Robbins practiced in the areas described and had "significant experience" handling such cases. Nevertheless, he could be disciplined for calling himself and his associate "specialists." Use of the term "specialist" is at least "potentially misleading," the court said. "Moreover, there is a reasonable possibility that a significant percentage of the public reading the term 'specialist' in a lawyer's advertisement, might be misled into thinking that an attorney has been 'certified' or 'designated' or has otherwise met objective standards established by a recognized organization." 469 S.E.2d at 193–94. The court ordered that Robbins receive a public reprimand administered in open court in his home county.

2.   Do you agree that the term "specialist" or "speciality" is misleading? In the belief that the term "specialist" suggests special expertise, states long forbade use of that designation unless lawyers had indeed met special conditions. What conditions should a state require?

a.   For many years, states most often imitated California's plan that was put it into operation in 1973. Today, to become a certified specialist, California requires that a lawyer:

(1) Have practiced in the speciality field for at least 25% of the lawyer's professional time during the preceding 3 years;

(2) Have performed designated tasks in the specialty field during the preceding 5 years;

(3) Have completed at least 45 hours of approved education in the specialty field during the preceding 3 years;

(4) Pass an independent examination in the specialty field; and

(5) Submit references who can attest to the lawyer's proficiency in the field.

Recertification is required every five years and comparable criteria are applied in the recertification decision.[1]

b.   Designation exclusively by state agencies changed as a result of Peel v. Attorney Registration and Disciplinary Commission, 496 U.S. 91, 110 S.Ct. 2281, 110 L.Ed.2d 83 (1990). Gary Peel's letterhead said that he had been "certified as a civil trial specialist by the National Board of Trial Advocacy," a group of judges, academics and practitioners established after Chief Justice Burger had complained about the general quality of U.S. trial practice. Standards required for certification included "specified experience as lead counsel in both jury and nonjury trials, participation in approved

---

1. The standards may be found at www.californiaspecialist.org.

programs of continuing legal education, a demonstration of writing skills, and the successful completion of a day-long examination. Certification expires in five years unless the lawyer again demonstrates his or her continuing qualification."

Illinois censured Peel for noting his NBTA certification on two grounds. First, it said the letterhead constituted an implied claim "as to the quality of [petitioner's] legal services." Second, the state feared that potential clients might think the NBTA was a state agency and that Peel's claim of specialty had state endorsement. The Supreme Court could not agree on a majority opinion, but five justices agreed that completely prohibiting Peel's reference to his certification was unconstitutional.

Justice Stevens, joined by Justices Brennan, Blackmun and Kennedy, found that Peel's claim of specialty certification was "true and verifiable" and there was no evidence anyone had been deceived by the claim. The idea of an implied claim of special quality, Justice Stevens said, "confuses the distinction between statements of opinion of quality and statements of objective facts that may support an inference of quality. A lawyer's certification by NBTA is a verifiable fact, as are the predicate requirements for that certification. * * * In this case, there is no evidence that a claim of NBTA certification suggests any greater degree of professional qualification than reasonably may be inferred from an evaluation of its rigorous requirements. Much like a trademark, the strength of a certification is measured by the quality of the organization for which it stands." 496 U.S. at 101–02, 110 S.Ct. at 2288, 110 L.Ed.2d at 95. Similarly, "there has been no finding that any person has associated certification with governmental action— state or federal—and there is no basis for belief that petitioner's representation generally would be so construed." 496 U.S. at 102–03, 110 S.Ct. at 2288–89, 110 L.Ed.2d at 96.

Justices Marshall and Brennan concurred in the judgment but found Peel's claim at least potentially misleading and thus subject to reasonable regulation short of the total ban that Illinois had imposed. Justice White, dissenting, agreed the claim was potentially misleading and would have required Peel to put explanations or disclaimers on his letterhead and with any other use of the speciality designation.

Dissenting Justices O'Connor, Scalia, and Chief Justice Rehnquist saw the case as "yet another example of the difficulties raised by rote application of the commercial speech doctrine in the context of state regulation of professional standards for attorneys." 496 U.S. at 119, 110 S.Ct. at 2297, 110 L.Ed.2d at 106–07. They found Peel's claims incapable of verification by "the ordinary consumer of legal services." Even disclaimers would not be sufficient, these dissenting justices wrote, because review of their adequacy would impose an excessive regulatory burden on the states.

c. In light of the *Peel* case, can new Model Rule 7.4(d) be constitutional? Is the unstated assumption that the ABA will "accredit" all private organizations like the NBTA that should be authorized to grant certification? Is there a certain arrogance in the ABA's assumption that the

Supreme Court will conclude that the ABA will always make accreditation decisions correctly?

3. May lawyers with a specialty designation affirmatively claim they will perform at a higher level of skill than would the average lawyer?

a. Do lawyers have a First Amendment right to say that they are better than other lawyers? Look back at Model Rule 7.1 and particularly Comment [3]. Does *Peel* affirm that designation as a specialist constitutes per se "factual substantiation" of such a comparison with others? When you sort out all the opinions, do you in fact find a majority of the justices taking that position?

b. Is the ability to claim special skill an unmixed blessing? If the state allows a lawyer to claim that he or she is a specialist in a particular area of law, courts might impose a higher standard of performance for determining malpractice liability. Cf. Wright v. Williams, 121 Cal.Rptr. 194, 199 (Ct. App.1975) ("a lawyer holding himself out to the public and the profession as specializing in an area of the law must exercise the skill, prudence and diligence exercised by other specialists of ordinary skill and capacity specializing in the same field").

4. Should only especially complex areas of law—e.g., bankruptcy and tax—be recognized as specialties, or should every area of law practice be a potential candidate?

a. The bar has never resolved that question in an entirely satisfactory way. In some states, the primary question surrounding specialty designation seems to be whether significant numbers of lawyers actually tend to limit their activities to the area. For example, trial practice is often a specialty so defined.

b. At least three kinds of collateral meanings have been given to specialization.

(i) "Certifying" specialists refers to designating certain people as having special skills and experience in an area.

(ii) "Licensing" specialists, on the other hand, might mean that only a specialist may practice in an area. In such a system, if trial practice were a "licensed" speciality, Ramirez would have no choice but to refer the Peron case to a trial specialist.

(iii) "Limiting" specialists, furthermore, would say that specialists may practice *only* their specialty. In such a system, a trial specialist like Castro might not, for example, be permitted to prepare a trust for his accident client to help assure proper management of the proceeds of a settlement.

c. Might you favor one of those versions of specialization over the others? Might some of them work better for more populous specialties like trial practice while others might work better for narrower fields such as international partnership taxation?

5.   What other descriptions of a lawyer's areas of practice do the Model Rules allow?

a.   May a lawyer say that her "practice is limited to" real estate law, for example, if in fact she will only take matters in that area? Does Model Rule 7.4(a) answer that question beyond all doubt? Would any public interest be served by preventing a lawyer from so informing the public? Should any qualification or disclaimer be required to accompany such a statement?[2]

b.   If a lawyer is presented with an award by a bona fide bar organization (e.g., the "Crystal Gavel" awarded by the State Bar Civil Practice Section for "outstanding contributions to the law of Civil Practice in 2002") should the lawyer be permitted to advertise that fact? If a lawyer belongs to the American Law Institute, or some other bona fide, prestigious private lawyers' group, may the lawyer note that on a business card? May the lawyer so distinguish herself from other lawyers even though the state does not recognize or certify specialities?

c.   May a lawyer say that she is "experienced" in a field of law, or has "15 years experience"? Is that a surreptitious claim of speciality? Is it an impermissible comparison with other lawyers? What should the claim of "experience" be held to require in this context? See, e.g., N.Y. State Bar Association Committee on Professional Ethics Opinion No. 487 (July 15, 1978), asserting that a representation of "experience" without "further qualification implies that the lawyer's experience over the stated period has been frequent rather than merely occasional, and substantial as distinguished from casual." So understood, should a claim of "experience" be seen as providing useful information to potential clients?

d.   In re Appeal of Hughes & Coleman, 60 S.W.3d 540 (Ky.2001), reviewed the Kentucky Bar Association's disapproval of one of the respondents' television advertisements that contained their claim to be "injury lawyers." The Kentucky Supreme Court found that decision was arbitrary because other lawyers had been allowed to call themselves "international lawyers" or even "a full-service business law firm." The bar association had argued that the respondent's ads implied the lawyers were specialists in the field of personal injury law, but the state supreme court found that the designation did not necessarily carry that implication and gave potential clients an accurate sense of the kinds of cases the firm handled.

6.   Is there reason to be concerned about division of the bar into specialties?

a.   Marvin Mindes argued that concern is appropriate. He cited what he saw going on in accounting and medicine.

---

2. Shortly after *Bates v. State Bar of Arizona*, the lawyer advertising case discussed in Problem 31, some states tried to limit disclosure of fields of practice to very precise categories, e.g., permitting "property law" but not "real estate." A unanimous Supreme Court, however, found such efforts unconstitutional because they furthered no substantial public purpose. In re R.M.J., 455 U.S. 191, 102 S.Ct. 929, 71 L.Ed.2d 64 (1982).

"The success of certified groups in achieving greater and greater control of their occupational territories might be attributed to competitive advantage through selling better services. But control is [often] achieved by anticompetitive devices, and success is often unrelated to either the quality of their services or the need for them. We have, for example, an over elaboration of accounting detail that serves neither uniformity of rules nor adequate disclosure, and there are systems that are unrelated to actual management needs. In medicine we see bizarre examples, such as unnecessary operations, * * * heroic measures to maintain comatose terminal life, and a wasteful overqualification of specialists for much of their work. * * *

"In the later stages of this process, the organized specialty will view its differences from other portions of the bar, and particularly from general practitioners, as considerably more important than its similarities. The specialty group will have completely convinced themselves, despite the fact that most of them were grandfathered in, that no one else has the judgment, wisdom, and skill to perform the simplest service within their domain. Of course, their mission and public responsibility will compel them to protect the public against uncertified practitioners.

"The main impact of certification on the bar comes from the fact that the choice of attorneys is so subjective that any self-protecting public or private bureaucrat will tend to use certification as a criterion rather than to take the chance of allowing—or making—an independent judgment. Thus certification does succeed, but at severe cost to the public, as well as to the excluded generalist or the lawyer who wishes to switch fields. First, as entry to the field is restricted, the price goes up, and many persons cannot afford the services. Second, the tendencies to differentiate the law and practice in the certified field and to overcomplicate and overextend tasks will be exacerbated. * * * *"[3]

b. Do have an answer to Mr. Mindes' concerns? Might those concerns help explain why an elaborate system of specialization has never really taken hold in the legal profession?

C. PAYMENT OF A "REFERRAL FEE" IN A CASE SUCH AS THIS

1. Do you suppose it is an accident that this problem describes solo practitioners and small firm lawyers? If Ramirez were a partner in a large firm, how would he be likely to handle the Peron family's case?

a. If Ramirez were in a law firm, don't you think he would probably go down the hall to the litigation department for the help he needed? All fees earned in the matter would stay in the firm, and "credit" for

---

3. Marvin Mindes, Lawyer Specialty   Journal 42 (1975).
Certification: The Monopoly Game, 61 A.B.A.

compensation purposes would be awarded within the firm on bases that are completely outside the scope of professional regulation. In most firms, Ramirez would get credit for "originating" the matter.

b. The propriety of paying or receiving a referral fee—what Model Rule 1.5(e) calls a "division of a fee between lawyers who are not in the same firm"—should be seen in this context. Indeed, as you look at Model Rule 1.5(e), you will see an acceptance of practices acknowledged as appropriate within law firms, e.g., securing access to specialists and rewards for bringing in business, something that "rainmakers" in the big firms do without thinking. Look also, however, at ways in which the relation of partners within a law firm may be different from that between solo practitioners like Ramirez and Castro in our Problem.

2. What has traditionally concerned lawyers about the payment of referral fees?

a. In a rebuttal to an American Trial Lawyers Association proposal defending use of above-the-table referral fees, the editors of a legal newspaper argued that the proposal "amounts to saying that a lawyer should be bribed to act ethically. For it happens to be the unambiguous rule * * * that lawyers not competent to handle cases should not handle them." The editorial continued, "if a lawyer can afford to forgo some percentage of his fee in favor of a lawyer who does no work on the case, then that lawyer * * * is charging too much." National Law Journal, Feb. 5, 1979, p. 18, col. 1. Can you suggest any responses to these arguments?

b. Even if prohibiting referral payments would discourage less experienced lawyers from sending clients to more experienced ones, might allowing referral payments tend to corrupt the judgment of the referring lawyer as to who the best qualified person is to handle the case? Might some lawyers simply refer cases to the highest bidder?

c. The fee arrangement in Ohio State Bar Association v. Kanter, 715 N.E.2d 1140 (Ohio 1999), illustrates a stark form of some of the concerns. Outside counsel for Glidden Company was found to have made regular payments of 30% of his legal fees to the inside counsel who referred the matters to him. "Kickbacks undermine the lawyer-client relationship and the relationship between in-house and outside counsel as well as the integrity and reputation or legal professionals," the court noted. 715 N.E.2d at 1141. "Yet kickbacks turn the careful selection of professionals into secret bidding contests and prevent attorneys from competing for legal employment in a fair and corruption-free environment." Id. at 1142.

Do you agree with the court's assessment of the arrangement in *Kanter*? Does it follow that all referral fee arrangements are subject to similar condemnation?

d. If referral fees were unregulated, might some lawyers use television advertising to attract clients but not assume the burden of representing any of them? Might the lawyers simply refer the cases to others, pay the cost of the advertising, and take the rest as profit? Should that be a cause for concern?

e. Would you be equally troubled if Ramirez acted as an "agent" for the Peron family in finding a lawyer? Suppose he did what lawyers often do in negotiating contracts for athletes? Would it be proper for Ramirez to interview tort lawyers, get "bids" on their taking the Peron child's case, and help the family decide which lawyer to retain? If so, why should it matter whether the Peron family paid Ramirez' fee or whether the winning lawyer paid it?

3. Look at Model Rule 1.5(e)(1) and Comment [7] to Rule 1.5. What do they mean when they require the lawyer to "assume joint responsibility for the representation"?

a. Does assumption of joint responsibility imply assumption of malpractice liability? Why is that thought to be an important requirement? Does it put the referral arrangement more nearly on terms equivalent to what happens in a law firm?[4]

b. Elane v. St. Bernard Hospital, 672 N.E.2d 820 (Ill.Ct.App.1996), tested the limits of a lawyer's taking "legal responsibility" for a referred case "as though he were the other lawyer's partner." After referring four cases to another lawyer, the referring lawyer became a judge. The lawyer to whom the cases were referred said that, as a judge, the plaintiff was prohibited from practicing law and could not help in any way with prosecution of the cases as a partner might do. Thus, it would be improper to pay her the 45% of the ultimate fee as the referral agreement had provided. The Court held that the Illinois counterpart to Model Rule 1.5(e) required only that the judge remain liable for the new lawyer's malpractice. It thus held that the Rule did not constitute a barrier to collection of the referral fee.[5]

c. New York State Bar Association Committee on Professional Ethics Opinion 745 (2001), considered whether a lawyer who is disqualified from a matter because of a conflict of interest may similarly collect a referral fee. It said that under New York Disciplinary Rule 2–107, each lawyer must assume joint responsibility for the representation. When a lawyer is disqualified due to a conflict of interest, he may not assume responsibility for the representation and so may not collect a fee. However, the Opinion says, if the case is one in which consent has properly been obtained to the conflict of interest, a referral fee can indeed be paid.

4. In order to make the referral proper, should the client have to be told what percentage of the fee the referring lawyer will receive?

a. Notice that such disclosure was not required under Model Rule 1.5 prior to 2002. Was that approach parallel to what a client would know in

4. Note that Rule 1.5(e) is not radical. It harkens back to an earlier era. Canon 34 of the ABA Canons of Professional Ethics, in the Standards Supplement stated simply: "No division of fees for legal services is proper, except with another lawyer, based upon a division of services *or* responsibility." (emphasis added).

5. The *Elane* case is criticized in Ronald D. Rotunda, Judges as Ambulance Chasers, 8 The Professional Lawyer 14 (ABA, No. 8, 1997).

dealing with a private firm? Does a law firm client usually know the intra-firm division of the fee?

b.   Restatement Third, The Law Governing Lawyers § 47(2) came out the other way and said that clients must consent to "the terms of the [fee] division," and new Model Rule 1.5(e)(2) now requires that the client agree to "the share each lawyer will receive." Why do you suppose this change was made? Do you agree with the additional requirement?

5.   Should the provisions of Model Rule 1.5(e) be controlling in a civil suit by one lawyer against the other?

a.   In Kaplan v. Pavalon & Gifford, 12 F.3d 87 (7th Cir.1993), an agreement to divide fees was found to be unenforceable unless it was made in accord with the state's version of Rule 1.5(e). Even though that rule only purports to create a disciplinary standard, the court said, it also articulates the state's policy about the need for consent and a writing before such contracts will be deemed proper. Thus, a lawyer who orally promised to pay a referral fee could avoid a contract that did not comply with the rule.

Do you agree? Were the requirements of Rule 1.5(e) drafted primarily for the protection of clients? Why, then, should lawyers be able to claim the protection of those provisions? If you had been trying to protect lawyers from each other, would you have drafted Rule 1.5(e) the same way? On the other hand, by refusing to enforce oral agreements, is the court making sure that agreements are put in writing so that the courts can better police them?

b.   In Chambers v. Kay, 56 P.3d 645 (Cal.2002), Chambers had acted as co-counsel with Kay in a sexual harassment case on behalf of Kay's client. When the lawyers had a disagreement, Kay removed Chambers from the case but promised to pay him a portion of the recovery. Neither lawyer, however, told the client about the fee arrangement or received her written consent to the referral as required by California Rule 2–200(A)(1). "Chambers, in effect seeks the aid of this court in dividing the fees of a client without satisfaction of the rule's written consent requirement," the court said. "We decline such aid." 56 P.3d at 654. The court concluded that both lawyers had violated Rule 2–200(A)(1) and Chambers did not deserve the aid of the court in avoiding a problem he had created for himself. Again, do you agree?

D.   ALTERNATIVES TO REFERRAL FEES DESIGNED TO ACHIEVE SIMILAR BENEFITS

1.   Might the referral issues be avoided if Ramirez "associated" with Castro in handling the case, i.e., created a joint venture in which each lawyer would contribute some services?

a.   Would Ramirez retain significant obligations in an association that he could avoid by referral? Might the fee allocation in an association relationship be different in amount than a traditional "finder's fee"?

b.   Would such an arrangement inevitably be a sham? To the contrary, might Ramirez serve an important function by remaining involved in the case as an active co-counsel or even by acting as lead counsel and hiring help for the trial itself? Do we sometimes overemphasize trial experience, given that only 5% or so of cases go to trial? Might the Peron family's confidence in Ramirez and his own desire to see them well served be among the most important factors in assuring that the Perons will get a satisfactory resolution of their case?

2.   Could Ramirez avoid all referral fee problems by saying to Castro, for example, "I'll send you this big case if you'll refer some good clients my way"?

a.   New Jersey Supreme Court Advisory Opinion No. 681 (July 17, 1995), considered a proposed affiliation between a New Jersey and a London firm whereby each would refer clients to the other and share fees in those cases. The Opinion condemned the arrangement. Even though it made business sense and might help clients of each firm find qualified counsel in the other country, it was found to violate what is now Model Rule 7.2(b). Do you agree that the arrangement is "giving * * * value to a person for recommending the lawyer's services"? Do you see any other reasonable objections to such an arrangement?

b.   Look at ABA Model Rule 7.2(b)(4) and Comment [8]. Those are a new provisions designed to recognize the existence of such informal "networks" among solo practitioners and small firms. Is the development of such networks a positive one for both lawyers and clients? Is it likely to allow lawyers to deliver "full service" to their clients without being absorbed into a larger law firm?

3.   Might payments analogous to referral fees be paid to non-lawyers, assuming that the client does not object? Would such arrangements always be corrupt or can you see ways in which they might be another way to deliver a range of services to clients?

a.   Even ABA Canon 34 (1908) required that the division of legal fees be with another lawyer. The prohibition derives from the practice of "ambulance chasers" finding injured persons and selling their cases to attorneys.

b.   The bar has traditionally condemned this method of acquiring cases. In re Cohn, 139 N.E.2d 301 (Ill.1956), concerned a lawyer's "investigator" who would find out about accidents, call upon the injured person, and recommend retaining the respondent. The Illinois Supreme Court found acceptance of cases from this source "reprehensible" and said it "deserves nothing but contempt in the eyes of judges, lawyers and the public generally." 139 N.E.2d at 303.

In his opinion specially concurring with respect to a petition for rehearing, Justice Bristow was unwilling to be wholly critical, saying: "Today, * * * [i]t is a veritable scramble between the claim agent and the 'chaser' to see which one can reach an injured claimant first. The net result of a timely arrival of the solicitor is that the claimant will eventually receive an amount that a court and jury deems adequate and just. * * * [S]olicitation of personal injury cases is the natural reflex or defensive response to the unfair methods of claim adjusters, just as naturally as the human organism elaborates its own antibodies to combat disease." 139 N.E.2d at 305–06.

With which opinion do you agree?

c. Illinois State Bar Association Committee on Professional Ethics, Opinion 01–05 (2002), asked whether a law firm could pay referral fees to non-lawyers by creating a subsidiary to handle only mediation cases. The law firm both rendered traditional legal services and conducted mediations. It proposed a plan under which it would create a subsidiary that would be owned by most or all of the law firm shareholders, share the same facilities and staff as the law firm, but generate profits only through lawyers' mediation activities. That second firm would then accept clients, some referred by an accounting firm, in return for a 20% referral fee. The committee found that creation of a mediation subsidiary controlled entirely by lawyers was a "sham designed only to circumvent the applicable rules." The committee found that state rules against fee-sharing with non-lawyers applied, and prohibited the proposed arrangement.

d. Do you agree that the issue is that simple? Is there reason to prohibit payment to a financial planner, for example, who refers a client to the lawyer to carry out provisions of the client's financial plan? Might referrals among professionals, each trying to meet part of a client's needs, properly be seen as different from the hospital orderly getting payments for distributing a lawyer's cards to victims of traffic accidents?

e. In "We the People" Paralegal Services, L.L.C. v. Watley, 766 So.2d 744 (La.App.2000), a firm of paralegals orally contracted with a law firm to perform paralegal services for a percentage of any legal fee recovered in the cases. When the law firm accepted the services but refused to pay, the paralegals sued. The court held that a contract to share fees with a non-lawyer is null and void, but the services being performed were not those of a "runner" or someone engaged in unauthorized practice. Thus, the paralegals were permitted to proceed on a theory of unjust enrichment, not for a percentage of the fees, but for the fair value of their services.

4. Should sharing legal fees with a recognized lawyer referral service be similarly prohibited? Should it be seen as a reasonable way to meet client needs?

a. In ACLU/Eastern Missouri Fund v. Miller, 803 S.W.2d 592 (Mo. 1991), an ACLU staff attorney had agreed that any attorney's fees recovered in actions he filed would be turned over to the ACLU. On behalf of two clients, Miller and a volunteer lawyer pursued and won a civil rights action against the city of St. Louis. The court awarded the client fees totaling $8090 for the work done by Miller, who by this time had resigned from the ACLU. The defendant paid the fees to Miller, who then refused to turn the fee over to the ACLU, asserting that to do so would violate the Missouri version of Model Rule 5.4(a). The court agreed with Miller, although there was a strong dissent arguing that Miller had been paid by the ACLU for his work and was now getting paid twice.

Do you agree with the court that the ACLU is the functional equivalent of an ambulance driver who puts a lawyer's card on a stretcher and wants to be paid for doing so? Would any significant principle of ethical conduct be violated by requiring Miller to keep the promise he made to the ACLU?[6]

b.   Richards v. SSM Health Care, 724 N.E.2d 975 (Ill.Ct.App.2000), involved sharing fees with a bar-sponsored non-profit lawyer referral service. The West Suburban Bar Association near Chicago charges potential clients $25 for a referral to a lawyer but demands that lawyers remit to it up to 25% of the fee they receive from referred clients. Lawyer Dahlgren refused to pay, citing the Illinois versions of Model Rules 1.5(e) and 5.4(a), and noting that the referral service did not agree to assume joint responsibility for the matter. The court rejected the argument. The controlling rule was what is now Model Rule 7.2(b)(2). Some 117 state and local bar associations are supported by percentage referral fees, the court noted. Referral services help potential clients make informed decisions, the court said, and public policy favors continuing financial support of their existence.

c.   Take a look at new Model Rule 5.4(a)(4). The ABA has clearly come down in favor of sharing fees with the organizations involved in these two cases. Do you agree that approach is the wisest one to take?

———

PROBLEM 33

ROLES AND RESPONSIBILITIES IN A MODERN LAW FIRM

While a majority of American lawyers do not work for large law firms, in popular culture and the minds of many students, such firms define where high-quality lawyering is done. Working at a major firm is often seen as both a way to learn how the best lawyers practice and a way to pay off student loans. Increasingly, however, lawyers are coming to question both ideas. This problem examines some issues about practice in modern firms. First it considers the obligations of supervisory lawyers as well as those they supervise. Next, it examines the rights of a lawyer who reports an ethical violation of someone else in the practice organization. Third, it asks whether lawyers are entitled to the same statutory and other legal rights to fair treatment in employment as are employees generally. Finally, it considers concerns expressed about life in many large law firms and some ideas about overcoming those concerns.

6. The ABA Standing Committee on Ethics and Professional Responsibility did not believe any such principle existed and rejected this reading of Model Rule 5.4(a) in its Formal Opinion 93–374 (June 7, 1993).

FACTS

Smart & Howe is one of the most successful new firms in its region of the country. It regularly reports one of the highest earnings per partner among firms under 300 lawyers in *The American Lawyer*'s annual surveys, and its starting salary of $150,000 per year is among the region's highest. So is its minimum annual billing requirement for associates of 2500 hours per year.

Sarah Smart is co-managing partner of Smart & Howe, and she is in charge of the firm's Real Estate Group. Smart assigns work to the sixteen associates who work with her, evaluates their work, and signs all legal opinions and other documents prepared by her Group in the name of the firm.

One of her associates, Arnie Able, has billed over 3500 hours in each of his first two years, over 50% more than any other associate in the Real Estate Group. Smart was surprised that Able could report such billings, because he seemed to leave at 5 o'clock most days and did not appear in the office on weekends. Clients had not complained, however, and Smart had appreciated the boost in her own compensation she got because she supervised such a productive associate. Indeed, when an elderly partner, Ted Truthful, confronted Smart with concrete evidence that Able was billing fictitious hours, Smart's only response was to try to force Truthful to retire and to deny him a promised pension.

Recently, Smart & Howe has noticed that associates stay with the firm an average of 2.8 years and then most move to less stressful work environments. Andy Howe, the other co-managing partner, has proposed creation of a part-time program under which associates could elect to be paid 80% of a normal salary for those of their age and experience, but would have a minimum annual billing requirement of only 2000 hours per year. Sarah Smart resists that idea, believing few associates would choose that alternative and saying, "We don't want to retain the kind of lawyer who will not give client needs the top priority in his or her life."

QUESTIONS

A.   THE OBLIGATIONS OF A SUPERVISORY LAWYER AND THOSE THEY SUPERVISE

1.   Is there any doubt that Arnie Able would be subject to discipline for billing hours he had never worked?

a.   How would you characterize his conduct for purposes of imposing discipline? Is billing more than on the basis agreed per se "unreasonable" under Model Rule 1.5(a)? Does it constitute "dishonesty" under Model Rule 8.4(c)?

b. In Matter of Haskell, 962 P.2d 813 (Wash.1998), the evidence showed that a lawyer had billed at his own hourly rate for work done by lower paid associates. He traveled first class in violation of his client's direction and billed for the higher fares, but he had his travel agent give him bills showing the tickets were for coach class. Finally, while he was having a cabin built for himself in Idaho, he had his secretary "bury" phone and blueprint charges for the work in bills sent to clients. The court suspended the lawyer from practice for two years.

2. What responsibility did Smart have to assure that Able did not engage in such dishonest billing?

a. Did Smart meet her responsibilities under Model Rule 5.1 in this case? Do those responsibilities flow from her role as co-managing partner or as head of the real estate group? Are her duties as a "supervisor" different from those she has as a firm manager?

b. As far as we know, Smart did not "order" the overbilling or even "ratify" it, but does that mean she is off the hook? Did she "know of the conduct at a time when its consequences [could] be avoided" but fail "to take reasonable remedial action"? Should she be deemed to have known of the overbilling even if she asserts now that she lacked actual knowledge of it?

c. Attorney Grievance Commission v. Ficker, 706 A.2d 1045 (Md. 1998), imposed an indefinite suspension on a lawyer, in part for a failure to supervise associates. The respondent had a high volume practice—750 to 850 cases per year—including many serious drunk driving cases. He had virtually no case management system and associates rarely stayed with him long enough to have any experience in his field of practice. The Court found that he regularly assigned cases to associates the day before trial. The lawyers typically would not have met the clients and they often had not even read the file. "Ficker essentially operated his practice like a taxicab company," the court found. "What he apparently, and inexcusably, failed to realize is that * * * legal services cannot routinely be dispensed on that basis with an acceptable degree of competence." 706 A.2d at 1054. The court found violations of the state version of Model Rules 1.1, 5.1, 5.3 and 8.4(d). The facts are extreme, but they show that the duty to supervise can have teeth.

d. Notice that Model Rule 5.3 imposes similar obligations on all lawyers—potentially even new lawyers—who supervise non-lawyer assistants. That rule also gets enforced.

In re Wilkinson, 805 So.2d 142 (La.2002), involved Wilkinson's employment of a law school graduate, Paul Stewart, who had taken the bar examination but not yet been admitted. When a client approached Wilkinson about handling an estate matter, Wilkinson referred her to Stewart. He explained that Stewart was not yet licensed, but said he could handle preliminary aspects of the case before he was admitted to the bar. Wilkinson also instructed Stewart not to give any legal advice to the client, but when the client needed to know what to do, Stewart did give the client advice that resulted in significant losses to the estate. Moreover, when Stewart left the firm, Wilkinson did not even look at the file for several months. The court held that Wilkinson had violated both Rules 5.1(b) and 5.3(b) as a result of his lack of supervision of Stewart. He received a 60–day suspension from practice as a result of that inattention.

3. Is Andy Howe, Sarah Smart's co-managing partner, equally responsible for Able's overbilling?

a. What does Model Rule 5.1(a) mean when it requires each partner in a law firm—and each lawyer with "comparable managerial authority"— to "make reasonable efforts to ensure that the firm has in effect measures giving reasonable assurance" that each lawyer in the firm is living up to applicable professional standards. Do firms have to hire "time sheet police" to prevent what Able did?

b. In re Wallman, 696 N.Y.S.2d 164 (App.Div.1999), involved a two partner firm in which one of the partners converted client funds from the firm's trust account. In this case, the court suspended the other partner for failing to catch and correct the problem. The court explained that each partner "should have been aware of how the firm escrow account was being handled."

c. Would it be enough for Howe to show that the firm's orientation video contains a two minute section in which Howe tells the new lawyers that the firm expects them to bill honestly? What more, if anything, should Model Rule 5.1(a) require? Would failure to put such a statement in the orientation program constitute a per se violation of Model Rule 5.1(a)?

4. Would Able's liability be different if overbilling was not his idea; he was just following orders?

a. Suppose Sarah Smart had said to Able, "That checklist that you took 40 hours to prepare lets you do complex real estate transactions in half the time it takes lawyers at other firms. There is no reason our current clients should pay less for our superior work; bill every client an extra 40 hours for preparation of the checklist as if we had prepared it just for them." Would following Smart's direction give Able a defense to discipline?

b. Is the answer given in Model Rule 5.2(a) completely clear? Is it clear whether billing clients for valuable work, but work that the firm has previously done, raises an "arguable question of professional duty" under Model Rules 1.5 and 8.4 and makes Able immune from discipline under Model Rule 5.2(b)?

c. Does it help you to know that ABA Formal Opinion 93–379 (Dec. 3, 1993) clearly says that billing for recycled work as if it had been done anew violates Model Rule 1.5? Should young associates be held to know the substance of all ABA ethics opinions? Should they be required to investigate the propriety of all directions, even if violating those directions might get them fired?

d. On the other hand, is there any principled basis for Model Rule 5.2(b) at all? Once a lawyer takes an oath to live up to professional standards, why should he or she be able to defend by saying "the devil made me do it"?

5. Regardless of individual discipline that might be imposed, should Smart & Howe be subject to professional discipline as a law firm for the conduct of Arnie Able?

a. Will Smart & Howe be liable if they are sued by clients who were overbilled? Wasn't the firm the principal beneficiary of Able's misconduct? If firms qua firms can be forced to bear civil liability, why don't we subject firms to professional discipline as well?

b. As you may remember from Problem 2, New York is the first jurisdiction to make a law firm itself subject to professional discipline. See N.Y. Code of Professional Responsibility § 1200.3(a) and DR 1–102(a). What form might discipline of a law firm take in a case like this? Could a law firm be disbarred, i.e., put out of business, for example? Might it be publicly censured?

B. THE RIGHTS OF A LAWYER WHO REFUSES TO VIOLATE THE LAW

1. If a lawyer refuses a direction to do something illegal, does that lawyer have any protection against being fired for his or her courage?

a. The issue seems first to have arisen in an action for wrongful discharge filed by an in-house corporate counsel. Herbster v. North American Company for Life and Health Insurance, 501 N.E.2d 343 (Ill.App.1986), cert.denied 484 U.S. 850, 108 S.Ct. 150, 98 L.Ed.2d 105 (1987), involved the chief legal officer of North American Insurance. He alleged he had been fired for refusing to destroy or remove documents that tended to show the company's fraud in its sale of flexible annuities and that were ordered to be turned over by a federal court in Alabama. The Illinois court assumed this allegation was true but still held the employee had no recourse for his discharge. The court conceded that "at will" employees typically can sue for retaliatory discharge if the discharge contravenes a clearly mandated public policy, but it said that lawyers are different. "The attorney is placed in the unique position of maintaining a close relationship with a client where the attorney receives * * * information that otherwise would not be divulged to intimate friends," the court said. 501 N.E.2d at 346. Because of the sensitive nature of this relationship, a private client always has the right to change lawyers for any reason. The court was unwilling to create an exception to that principle, even where the client wanted the lawyer to violate the law.

b. In Balla v. Gambro, Inc., 584 N.E.2d 104 (Ill.1991), Attorney Balla had threatened to reveal that his employer's kidney dialysis devices did not comply with FDA regulations and presented a danger to patients' lives. When he was fired for his insubordination, the Illinois Supreme Court reached the same result as *Herbster*. Its reasoning was ingenious. The lawyer was ethically *required* to report the employer's wrongdoing, the court said. Thus, to say the employer could not fire him for doing so would discourage the employer from consulting the lawyer about the issue in the first place and impose the cost of ethical compliance on the client instead of the lawyer. Further, "[s]ince the relationship between the plaintiff and the defendant company required an atmosphere of continued mutual trust, the breakdown of that trust allowed the defendant to discharge the plaintiff without liability." 584 N.E.2d at 111.

2. Do these results make sense to you? Should saying that a client may fire a lawyer for no reason be the same as saying that the client may fire the lawyer for a wrong reason, i.e., for a failure to violate the law?

a. Even if the lawyer's actions would rupture the trust relationship between the lawyer and the officers of the client, does it follow that the entity itself would not benefit from the lawyer's action? Furthermore, would the relief for wrongful discharge have to be reinstatement? Might damages suffice?

b. The California Supreme Court refused to follow the Illinois approach in General Dynamics v. Superior Court, 876 P.2d 487 (Cal.1994). This time, the lawyer allegedly had given his employer advice it did not want to hear about violations of the Fair Labor Standards Act and the alleged bugging of the office of the chief of security. Although it reaffirmed the general rule that a private client in a single case may fire its lawyer for any reason, the court believed that a lawyer working for a corporate employer was in a different position. The private lawyer with many clients can lose one without being unemployed; a fired in-house counsel, on the other hand, loses everything. Further, by "providing the employee with a remedy in tort damages for resisting socially damaging organizational conduct, the courts mitigate the otherwise considerable economic and cultural pressures on the individual employee to silently conform." 876 P.2d at 501. The court offered two qualifications. First, the values being protected by the lawyer must be grounded in the Rules of Professional Conduct or specific statutes. Second, "the in-house attorney who publicly exposes the client's secrets will usually find no sanctuary in the courts." Id. at 503.

c. In Kachmar v. SunGard Data Systems, Inc., 109 F.3d 173 (3d Cir.1997), the lawyer had objected to the company's handling of EEO matters and she alleged her dismissal was based on her "campaigning on women's issues." The Third Circuit reinstated her complaint, agreeing that the fact she was a lawyer did not cause her to lose the right to sue for retaliatory discharge. The company argued such a suit would require disclosure of confidential information beyond that permitted by Model Rule 1.6(b)(3). The court agreed that protection of material protected by the attorney-client privilege was an important consideration, but it left it up to the district judge to use protective orders, in camera review, and similar devices to protect such privileged material from public disclosure.

d. In Fox Searchlight Pictures, Inc. v. Paladino, 106 Cal.Rptr.2d 906 (Ct.App.2001), employer Fox sued Paladino, one of its former in-house attorneys, whom it knew intended to file a wrongful discharge action.

Paladino's lawyer had sent Fox a copy of her draft complaint and asked that, if it contained privileged information, Fox let the lawyer know before the complaint was filed. Fox responded with this suit alleging that Paladino improperly disclosed confidential company information when she explained her concerns to her lawyers in the first place. Indeed, Fox tried to disqualify her lawyers on the grounds that they had been exposed to the confidential information. This court refused to declare the disclosures improper, because Fox's view would effectively bar any suit by an in-house counsel against a former employer even if the lawyer represented herself. The court reiterated, however, that Paladino may not disclose the confidential information any more publicly than the litigation requires.

e.   Finally, ABA Formal Opinion 01–424 (Sept. 22, 2001) confirms that the Model Rules do not prohibit in-house lawyers from filing a suit for retaliatory discharge if the lawyers were discharged for complying with ethical obligations. The Opinion requires that in doing so, the lawyer not use information relating to the former representation that is protected by Model Rule 1.9(c) except as permitted by Model Rules 1.6(b)(3) and 3.3. The Opinion holds that a suit for retaliatory discharge is a "claim" within the meaning of Model Rule 1.6(b)(3), but it reminds lawyers that Comment [12] to Model Rule 1.6 requires disclosures "only to the extent that the lawyer reasonably believes * * * is necessary" and that "appropriate protective orders or other arrangements should be sought by the lawyer to the fullest extent practicable."

3.   The important question for most young lawyers is how all this should apply to an associate's discharge by a law firm for reporting an ethical violation. Is discharge by a law firm subject to the same principles as discharge by a corporate client?

a.   Again, the courts have not reached consensus on these issues. In Wieder v. Skala, 609 N.E.2d 105 (N.Y.1992), Weider had asked his own law firm to represent him in the purchase of an apartment. The associate the firm assigned to do the work did little or nothing, and when Weider inquired, he found that the associate had was known by the firm to be a "pathological liar" who had neglected several other clients' matters as well. Weider insisted that the associate be reported to the discipline commission, and for so insisting, Weider was fired. The New York Court of Appeals found that a law firm does not have the same freedom to dismiss a lawyer that a private client would have. "Associates are, to be sure, employees of the firm but they remain independent officers of the court responsible in a broader public sense for their professional obligations." The contract between an associate and the firm contains an implied term that the firm will not impair the associate's obligations to obey the "prevailing rules of conduct and ethical standards of the profession." Weider's suit for breach of contract was thus found to state a cause of action.

b.   In Lichtman v. Estrin, 723 N.Y.S.2d 185 (App.Div.2001), the lawyer alleged he was fired for making known his concerns about a partner's continuing to work after suspension or disbarment. Once again, the same "implied-in-law" contract term supported the lawyer's claim for breach of contract.

c.   Yet other cases come out the other way. Jacobson v. Knepper & Moga, P.C., 706 N.E.2d 491 (Ill.1998), involved a lawyer who concluded that some of his firm's practices violated venue provisions of the Fair Debt Collection Agency Act. He pointed it out to one of the firm's principal partners who promised things would change. They did not, so he protested a second and third time, after which he was fired. The Illinois Supreme Court agreed that the conduct discovered by the lawyer violated duties under the Rules of Professional Conduct but it said the lawyer should have reported it to disciplinary authorities. Such a report would have adequately protected "the public policy established by the collection statutes," and the court found it unnecessary to create a tort of retaliatory discharge to protect that policy. Chief Justice Freeman dissented, saying the opinion sent a clear message that it was more "economically advantageous to a lawyer to keep quiet" than to try to get his law firm to conform to proper professional conduct.

d.   Bohatch v. Butler & Binion, 977 S.W.2d 543 (Tex.1998), held that a law partner had no cause of action when the law firm expelled her from the partnership because she had, in good faith, accused another partner of overbilling a major client. "[A] partner can be expelled for accusing another partner [because that] may have a profound effect on the personal confidence and trust essential to the partner relationship," the court said. "Once such charges are made, partners may find it impossible to continue to work together to the * * * benefit of their clients." 977 S.W.2d at 546–47.

Justice Spector and Chief Justice Phillips dissented, saying that "retaliation against a partner who tries in good faith to correct or report perceived misconduct virtually assures that others will not take these appropriate steps in the future," and the result "sends an inappropriate signal to lawyers and to the public that the rules of professional responsibility are subordinate to a law firm's other interests." Id. at 561.

e.   Where do you come out on the issue of a law firm's right to fire or expel a lawyer for insisting that its other lawyers comply with their professional obligations? Is there any good explanation for how well-informed courts would come out so differently on the question? Are the competing values too absolute to be treated in a nuanced way?

C. SOME OTHER LEGAL RIGHTS OF LAWYERS AS COMPARED TO EMPLOYEES GENERALLY

1. Should all law firm partners have a right to be treated equally in terms of pay and responsibilities?

a. Quite the opposite is true at most firms. Law firms are sometimes said to categorize lawyers as "finders", "minders" and "grinders"; that is, some lawyers primarily bring in clients, others manage and supervise cases, while still others do most of the detail work. Often, firms distinguish sharply among these groups in terms of pay, the "finders" typically commanding the highest share of firm profits. "Minders" or "grinders"— even those who are called "partners" today—sometimes work on a salary and have no equity interest in the firm.

b. The question for law firms, then, is whether any of these realities should give rise to a cause of action for discrimination. What do you think?

2. Should a law firm incur legal liability for failing to give a new associate the job assignment discussed in the interview that made the firm attractive to the associate?

a. Stewart v. Jackson & Nash, 976 F.2d 86 (2d Cir.1992), upheld a cause of action for fraudulent inducement where a lawyer resigned from one firm and joined this one because the firm falsely asserted that it had a large environmental case and was building an environmental law department that the plaintiff would head. The firm's representations about its client base were "not future promises but representations of present fact," the court said. Even the promise to be promoted head of the department, if known to be false when made, would support a fraudulent inducement claim.

b. Geary v. Hunton & Williams, 684 N.Y.S.2d 207 (App.Div.1999), however, rejected a claim of fraudulent inducement premised on an alleged misrepresentation of the size of the firm's banking litigation practice. The Court said any damages from such a misrepresentation were "inherently speculative" because no one could know what the lawyer's experience would have been at some other firm.

c. In Slate v. Saxon, Marquoit, Bertoni & Todd, 999 P.2d 1152 (Ore.App.2000), the lawyer had worked for a firm while in law school and was allegedly promised a job by the firm as soon as he passed the Oregon bar examination. After he passed, the firm said it had no room for him. The court held that because a lawyer's employment with a firm is terminable at will, the lawyer can also be fired before he begins work. The offer could not have been a basis for reliance or substantial change of position by the lawyer. The dissent responded that the student performed his part of a unilateral contract and should be at least entitled to compensation for any opportunities foregone.

d.   If you can answer without a conflict of interest, what do you think the rule in these cases should be? Should Ted Truthful in our Problem, and other lawyers such as yourself, be presumed to be capable of practicing in some other setting if they are unhappy? Is that easier for young lawyers to do than for older or retired ones? Indeed, might one argue that in a tight employment market for lawyers, the assumption of easy lawyer mobility is increasingly open to question?

3.   Should federal anti-discrimination laws apply to law firms? Are issues about hiring and promotion of lawyers inherently too complex to be second-guessed by a judge or jury?

a.   A number of cases have held that hiring and promotion decisions of law firms can be reviewed under federal law. Lucido v. Cravath, Swaine & Moore, 425 F.Supp. 123 (S.D.N.Y.1977), for example, held that an associate may sue his law firm under Title VII of the Civil Rights Act of 1964 for discrimination on the basis of religion (Catholic) and national origin (Italian). Lucido alleged he was subjected to discrimination with respect to work assignments, training, rotation and outside work appointments, and that he was denied promotion to partner for the same unlawful reasons. Plaintiff's charges were found to state a cause of action.

b.   In Hishon v. King & Spalding, 467 U.S. 69, 104 S.Ct. 2229, 81 L.Ed.2d 59 (1984), a unanimous Supreme Court held that Title VII prohibits a law firm from discriminating on the basis of sex, race, religion, or national origin in deciding which associates to promote to partner. Even if elevation to partnership is a change in status from employee to employer, consideration for partnership is still a term, condition, or privilege of an associate's employment. Plaintiff's claim of sex discrimination thus stated a cause of action.[1]

c.   Should a firm be permitted to fire a lawyer because he has AIDS? Doe v. Kohn, Nast & Graf, P.C., 866 F.Supp. 190 (E.D.Pa.1994), held that a lawyer fired when he was discovered to be HIV positive has a cause of action under Section 12112 of the Americans with Disabilities Act.[2]

---

1.   There is a difference, of course, between alleging sex discrimination and proving it. In Ezold v. Wolf, Block, Schorr and Solis–Cohen, 983 F.2d 509 (3d Cir.1992), cert. denied 510 U.S. 826, 114 S.Ct. 88, 126 L.Ed.2d 56 (1993), the plaintiff alleged she had been denied partnership because of her sex. The court examined in great detail both her evaluations and those of males who made partner, and reversed a judgment in her favor, apparently concluding that the law firm reasonably thought the plaintiff was not capable of handling complex litigation. At minimum, the case illustrates that pleading a civil rights cause of action is a far cry from getting relief.

2.   See also Ozer v. Borquez, 940 P.2d 371 (Colo.1997) (no cause of action for lawyer

d. What do you think is likely to be the effect of these decisions? Might the existence of statutory grounds to resist termination at least tend to reduce the incidence of unfair treatment? Might they indirectly tend to keep lawyers on the job, who really should be terminated, because firms fear the consequences and cost of trying to terminate them?

e. Should a lawyer's violation of federal antidiscrimination law also constitute a basis for state professional discipline? California Rule 2–400 forbids lawyers' discrimination on the basis of race, sex, national origin, sexual orientation, religion, age or disability. D.C. Rule 9.1 forbids discrimination on all those bases plus color, marital status and family responsibility. The farthest the ABA has been willing to go is Model Rule 8.4, Comment [3]. Do you think the ABA has gone far enough? Indeed, does that Comment reach the conduct raised in this Problem at all?

4. May a partnership terminate partners when they are thought to be too old or insufficiently docile?

a. In EEOC v. Sidley & Austin, 315 F.3d 696 (7th Cir.2002), the EEOC tried to enforce a subpoena duces tecum issued to a law firm to investigate charges of age discrimination resulting from the firm's newly adopted retirement plan. The plan demoted 32 partners who were over the age of 40 to senior counsel status. Sidley responded that decisions of partnerships are outside the scope of EEOC review because everybody is an equal and no one is an employee. The EEOC responded that it was entitled to review independently whether Sidley was a partnership. The Seventh Circuit, in an opinion by Judge Posner, agreed that "[a]n individual who was classified as a partner-employer under state partnership law might be classified as an employee for * * * the purpose for which federal antidiscrimination law extends protection to employees but not employers." 315 F.3d at 702. This firm was alleged to be run by a powerful executive committee, the court said; partners were not all equal, and the EEOC needed access to the requested information so as to evaluate the nature of the organization and the EEOC's authority over its employment decisions.

b. Earlier, Bane v. Ferguson, 890 F.2d 11 (7th Cir.1989), had asked whether a retired law partner has a cause of action against his former law firm's management committee for allegedly negligent acts that caused the firm to dissolve, resulting in the termination of his retirement benefits. Judge Posner, for the Seventh Circuit, said no. A partner of a firm has a fiduciary duty to his partners, the court wrote, but none to his former partners. Furthermore, firms collapse for many reasons and the managers are not liable to their partners for that collapse. The court acknowledged that "[w]e are sorry about the financial blow" to the plaintiff, who was 72

dismissal because his companion had AIDS, but there is a cause of action for firm's invasion of privacy in giving unreasonable publicity to the lawyer's private life).

years old when he retired and, other than social security, apparently had no other source of income other than the pension (now lost) of less than $28,000 per year. However, the former partner should have protected himself through contract; "people should be encouraged to protect themselves through voluntary transactions rather than to look to tort law to repair the consequences of their improvidence." 890 F.2d at 15.

c. Barnhart v. Pickrel, Schaeffer & Ebeling Co., L.P.A., 12 F.3d 1382 (6th Cir.1993), was a suit for age discrimination. The firm said the lawyer was a chronic alcoholic who had not completed a course of treatment that the firm had required him to undergo. The court found the effect of alcoholism on his practice was well-documented and affirmed a grant of summary judgment for the firm.

d. Do you think the law should protect senior lawyers against their younger partners? On the other hand, is there any justification for older lawyers receiving high compensation simply because they have been around a long time? How would you recommend that firms handle issues of productivity and compensation to protect all lawyers in a firm?

5. Suppose it is the client rather than the law firm that demands discrimination? Remember that the courts have usually said that a client may terminate a lawyer for any reason.

a. In Plessinger v. Castleman & Haskell, 838 F.Supp. 448 (N.D.Cal. 1993), a fired associate sued his firm for age discrimination and the firm's client (Allstate Insurance) for tortious interference with business relations. The complaint alleged that Allstate had ordered the firm to fire him because it wanted younger lawyers working on its cases. Allstate asserted that it had an absolute right to counsel of its choice and thus that the claim must be dismissed. This Court disagreed, saying that state law would "not recognize a client's unlimited right to select among associates * * * where the selection criteria involves discrimination against a member of a protected class. To hold otherwise would allow * * * clients to demand that law firms not assign cases to women, racial minorities, or members of any other protected class * * *." Thus, Allstate's motion to dismiss was denied.

b. Do you agree with this result? Does it leave the usual assumption that a client may freely terminate a lawyer open to doubt? Is the principle that clients may fire their lawyers for reasons that they could not use to fire an employee, for example, a principle worth defending today?

D.   DOUBTS ABOUT LIFE IN THE MODERN LARGE LAW FIRM

1.   Were you shocked to read that Smart & Howe requires its lawyers to bill 2500 hours per year?

a.   Most firms for which you will work will require fewer hours, but some perspective on such requirements is useful. "Conventional wisdom just a few decades ago was that lawyers could not reasonably expect to charge for more than 1200 to 1500 hours per year."[3]

b.   Professor Deborah L. Rhode, Chair of the ABA Commission on Women and the Legal Profession, finds women particularly disadvantaged by current law firm expectations. "Women's opportunities are limited in three crucial ways," she says, "by traditional gender stereotypes; by inadequate access to mentors and informal networks of support; and by inflexible workplace structures."[4]

"Gender * * * characteristics traditionally associated with women are at odds with those traditionally associated with professional success, such as assertiveness, competitiveness, and business judgment. Some lawyers and clients still assume that women lack the aptitude for complex financial transactions or the combativeness for high-stakes litigation. Yet professional women also tend to be rated lower when they adopt 'masculine,' authoritative styles, particularly when the evaluators are men. * * * And what is assertive in a man often seems abrasive in a woman. * * *

" * * * Attorneys who assume that women with children are less committed or that women of color are less qualified will recall their errors more readily than their insights. They will note the times mothers leave early, not the times they stay late. * * *

"These assumptions can then become self-fulfilling prophecies. * * *

"[As for mentoring], [m]any men who endorse equal opportunity in principle fall short in practice; they end up supporting those who seem most similar in backgrounds, experiences, and values. * * * Even women who make real sacrifices to get a foot in the door find that a foot is all they get in. Working mothers short on time, interest, or innate ability have nonetheless learned to play golf, which makes it all the more aggravating when they still aren't invited to play. * * *

3.   Patrick J. Schiltz, "On Being a Happy, Healthy, and Ethical Member of an Unhappy, Unhealthy, and Unethical Profession," 52 Vanderbilt L. Rev. 871, 891 (1999).

4.   Deborah L. Rhode, Gender and the Profession: The No–Problem Problem, 30 Hofstra L. Rev. 1001, 1003–04 (2002).

"The result is that many female lawyers remain out of the loop of career development. They are not given enough challenging, high visibility assignments, nor are they included in social events that yield professional opportunities. Problems of exclusion are greatest for those who appear 'different' on other grounds as well as gender, such as race, ethnicity, disability, or sexual orientation. * * *

"A final obstacle involves workplace structures that fail to accommodate personal needs and commitments, particularly family responsibilities. * * *

"The most obvious ongoing failure is inhumane hours and a resistance to reduced or flexible schedules * * *. The problem is reinforced by the increasing pace and competition of legal life. Technological innovations have created expectations of instant responsiveness and total availability, while increasing billable hour quotas have pushed working hours to new and often excessive limits. Lawyers remain perpetually on call—tethered to the workplace through cell phones, emails, faxes, and beepers. 'Face time' is taken as a proxy for commitment, ambition, and reliability under pressure. The result is a 'rat race equilibrium' in which most lawyers feel that they would be better off with shorter or more flexible schedules, but find themselves within institutional structures that offer no such alternatives."[5]

c. Do these concerns reflect your own perceptions about much in law practice today? Are the problems one sees in practice limited to large firm associates? Will you ever rise far enough in a law firm to avoid these kinds of issues? Indeed, might the ability to always be reached by cell phone, for example, entrap the solo practitioner as much as the lawyer at a large firm?

d. Are these problems disproportionately faced by women? Are the perceptions and habits about which Professor Rhode writes unique to the legal profession? Does that make any of them matters of less appropriate concern?

2. In our Problem, Andy Howe has proposed that associates be given the option of working 80% of a full-time job for 80% of the pay. Is Sarah Smart right that not many lawyers would choose that option? Is Smart also right that the firm should be suspicious of the values of lawyers who would choose it?

a. Professor Rhode observes: "Even in workplaces that in theory offer these options, a wide gap persists between formal policies and actual practices. Although over 90% of surveyed law firms report policies permitting part-time schedules, only about 3% of lawyers actually use them. Most

---

5. Id. at 1004–08.

women surveyed believe, with good reason, that any reduction in hours or availability will carry a permanent price.[6]

b.   Dean Schiltz offers another suggestion about why part-time work seems rarely chosen:

"If all such lawyers making $160,000 per year sat down and asked themselves, 'What will make me a happier and healthier person: another $40,000 in income (which, after taxes, will mean another $25,000 or so in the bank) or 600 hours to do whatever I enjoy most?,' it is hard to believe that many of them would take the money.

"But many of them do take the money. * * * And they do so merely to be able to make seven or eight times the national median income instead of five or six times the national median income. Why? Are lawyers just greedy?

"Well, some are, but it is more complicated than that. For one thing, lawyers * * * don't sit down and think logically about why they are leading the lives they are leading any more than buffalo sit down and think logically about why they are stampeding. * * *

"More importantly, though, the flaw in my analysis is that it assumes that the reason lawyers push themselves to make so much money is the money itself. * * * What you need to understand, though, is that * * * [t]hey are doing it for a different reason.

"Big firm lawyers are, on the whole, a remarkably insecure and competitive group of people. Many of them have spent almost their entire lives competing to win games that other people have set up for them. First they competed to get into a prestigious college. Then they competed for college grades. Then they competed for LSAT scores. Then they competed to get into a prestigious law school. Then they competed for law school grades. Then they competed to make the law review. Then they competed for clerkships. Then they competed to get hired by a big law firm.

"Now that they're in a big law firm, what's going to happen? Are they going to stop competing? Are they going to stop comparing themselves to others? Of course not. They're going to keep competing—competing to bill more hours, to attract more clients, to win more cases, to do more deals. They're playing a game. And money is how the score is kept in that game. * * *

" * * * If a lawyer's life is dominated by the game—and if his success in the game is measured by money—then his life is dominated by money. For many, many lawyers, it's that simple."[7]

---

6. Id. at 1008.

7. Patrick J. Schiltz, "On Being a Happy, Healthy, and Ethical Member of an Unhappy, Unhealthy, and Unethical Profession," 52 Vanderbilt L. Rev. 871, 904–06 (1999).

c.   Do you agree with Dean Schiltz's analysis of lawyer motivation? Is "the game" what is motivating you? Should we care about such psychological explanations for lawyer behavior? Does the motivation potentially manifest itself in behavior that can have a real impact on clients and third parties?

————

PROBLEM 34

LEAVING ONE LAW FIRM AND FORMING ANOTHER

Lawyers once pictured themselves as wedded to their law firms for life. In recent years, however, those bonds have weakened. Whether because of unhappiness with pay, work assignments, hours at the office, or insensitive treatment by superiors, lawyers are leaving one firm to move to another setting. When they go, they often like to take as much familiar work with them as they can. Doing so usually increases their financial rewards at a new firm and reduces their dependence upon cases assigned by that firm. In this Problem, we look first at the law and ethics of departure from a law firm—what Professor Robert Hillman calls the "law and ethics of grabbing and leaving."[1] Second, we examine firms' efforts to limit such departures by restrictive agreements with their partners and associates. Third, we consider when lawyers might handle a departure by actually buying all or part of a law practice. Finally, we ask whether lawyers should be able to organize their practice so as to contract, for a fixed fee, to deliver legal services to all members of a defined group.

FACTS

Several years ago, Bill Bright and Larry Learned started the firm of Bright & Learned. It prospered and has grown to 425 lawyers. The two female partners and eight female associates who make up Bright & Learned's Estate Planning Group, however, view the firm as singularly unenlightened. None has been allowed to move into the litigation section of the firm, and many of the firm's partnership meetings are held in the all-male Thomas Jefferson Club. Further, although estate planning brings the firm substantial, steady revenue, the Group believe they have not been paid as well as they would be in a firm of their own.

The Group's lawyers believe that, if they leave together, they can bring with them most of the client families on whose estate plans they have worked during the past several years. Each lawyer will write a letter to the clients she knows best before she leaves Bright & Learned. The lawyers then plan to use these clients'

---

1. Robert W. Hillman, Hillman on Lawyer Mobility: The Law and Ethics of Partner Withdrawals and Law Firm Breakups § 1.3 (1994).

expressions of willingness to follow them to the new firm as a basis for getting loans to finance the new firm's start-up costs.

Before she became a lawyer, one of the Group's partners had been an officer of the local electrician's union. She hopes to present the union with a proposal under which, for a premium of $100 per union member per year, the Group's new firm will write wills and give periodic estate planning advice to persons in the immediate family of any of the union members.

When Bill Bright and Larry Learned came in one morning and found that their entire Estate Planning Group had disappeared, they were hurt and angry. As part of an effort to avoid a law suit, however, Bright & Learned offered to sell its former estate planning practice to the departing lawyers for an amount equal to the Group's prior two years' billings, payable in equal installments over the next five years.

QUESTIONS

A. THE LAW AND ETHICS OF DEPARTING FROM A LAW FIRM

1. What duties do law firm partners owe to each other? May some decide they would like to practice law somewhere else without violating their duties to the others?

a. Partners are traditionally said to owe each other the fiduciary duties of loyalty and care. Revised Uniform Partnership Act § 404. That includes the duty "to refrain from competing with the partnership and the other partners in the conduct of the partnership business before the dissolution of the partnership." Id. § 404(b)(3). The usual complaint of the original firm when partners leave with little warning is that the departing lawyers have breached their fiduciary duties.

b. How should courts approach that claim? Should partners be yoked together for life? Does the quoted prohibition imply that at all? Indeed, Revised Uniform Partnership Act § 601(1) recognizes that a partner becomes "dissociated" from the partnership upon "the partnership's having notice of the partner's express will to withdraw as a partner or on a later date specified by the partner." The critical issues on departure, then, are likely to be openness and fairness. After the desire to depart is known, the issues become payment of sums to which the departing partners are entitled and who will have ongoing relationship with the firm's clients.

c. In Dowd & Dowd, Ltd. v. Gleason, 693 N.E.2d 358 (Ill.1998), 58% of the firm's business was for a single client, a subsidiary of Allstate Insurance. The two departing lawyers contacted that client on December 31, the same day they notified the firm. That same day, the client sent a letter to the old firm requesting that its files be sent to the new one. The departing lawyers then hired others from the old firm to help work on the cases.

Lawyers who plan to leave a firm, the Court recognizes, "face a dilemma, caught between the fiduciary obligations they owe the other members of their firm * * * and the duty of being able to adequately represent clients who choose to follow them to their new place of employment * * *." 693 N.E.2d at 364. As a way of accommodating these competing pressures, the court says, lawyers "may make arrangements, prior to their departure, to obtain new office space * * * and other materials necessary for the practice of law." Id. However, "pretermination solicitation of clients by members of an existing firm for the benefit of a new firm rises to a breach of fiduciary duty." Id. at 366. Determining both the actual facts and what fiduciary duties partners owe each other under those circumstances, however, is not the stuff of summary judgment motions, so the case was remanded for trial.

2.   To whom do a law firm's clients belong? What rights should departing partners and associates have to try to cause clients to consult them at their new firm?

a.   Should clients properly be considered an "asset" of a law firm? Should it matter whether the clients originally came to Bright & Learned because of the firm's reputation, not that of the individual departing lawyers? Should it be relevant whether the clients now consider the individual women, not the firm, as their lawyers?

b.   Koehler v. Wales, 556 P.2d 233 (Wash.App.1976), suggests the traditional view that clients may hire or fire a lawyer at any time and their decisions to do so do not give rise to a cause of action by their lawyer. In this case, one lawyer had agreed to handle another's cases while the latter was out of the country; fee division was to be based on work performed. When the absent lawyer returned, some of her clients left with the "interim" lawyer, but the court refused to allow the absent lawyer damages for business interference. "The attorney-client relationship is personal and confidential, and the client's choice of attorneys in civil cases is near absolute," the court said. 556 P.2d at 236. "[W]e decline to recognize that plaintiff had any proprietary interest in her former law practice." Id. at 238.

c.   In Fred Siegel Co., L.P.A. v. Arter & Hadden, 707 N.E.2d 853 (Ohio 1999), KB had worked for Fred Siegel Co. for ten years when she resigned to join Arter & Hadden. Her expertise was real estate property assessments. She told Arter & Hadden who Fred Siegel's clients were and that she thought several would follow her. When she left, she took the cards she had in her Rolodex, and wrote letters to Siegel clients notifying them of her new association and closing, "When you need assistance or have questions, please contact me." Siegel responded, writing the same clients that it was still fully capable of serving them. Then Siegel filed suit against Arter & Hadden, claiming tortious interference with business relationships, and against KB for breach of fiduciary duty. The Court rejected the tortious interference claim, saying that the right of fair competition in Restatement of Torts § 768 trumped that theory when a contract is terminable at will.

However, the Court remanded the case to determine whether use of the names in her Rolodex was an improper use of the Siegel firm's trade secret.

d.   And in Meehan v. Shaughnessy, 535 N.E.2d 1255 (Mass.1989), two partners left to open a new office. They sued for fees due from their old partners, and the firm countersued for violation of fiduciary obligations and tortious interference with relations with clients. The two partners had decided in July to leave the firm at the end of December and had recruited four others to join them. During the summer and fall, they worked on getting office space and financing, and they kept up their caseload at the firm rather than letting people who would stay at the firm become familiar with the cases. During this period, they expressly denied plans to leave. They eventually gave the old firm 30 days notice, immediately called clients, and were able to get 142 out of 350 active cases shifted to the new firm. The court began by reminding lawyers that law partners owe fiduciary obligations to each other. The departing partners "used speed and preemptive" tactics and abused "their position of trust and confidence" in the firm. Then it remanded to let the old firm show its economic harm from the loss of clients, and it imposed on the departing lawyers the burden to prove that the clients would have come even if the lawyers had acted properly.

e.   In all such cases, ultimately the court must accommodate the legitimate interests of the old firm, the departing lawyers, and freedom of choice of the clients that each would like to serve. Which of the above decisions do you think best strikes that balance?

3.   Should there be any limits on the departing lawyers' contacts with firm clients in order to seek to persuade them to follow the lawyers to the new firm? How about on what the old firm may say to try to persuade them to stay?

a.   Original ABA Canon of Ethics 7 provided that "Efforts, direct or indirect, in any way to encroach upon the business of another lawyer, are unworthy of those who should be brethren at the Bar; * * *" Does that answer the question? Which lawyers' "business" do these clients represent?

b.   Have the Model Rules rejected the old approach? Take another look at Model Rule 7.3(a). With which lawyers should the clients be said to have a "prior professional relationship"? If a client asked the lawyer why she is leaving and where she may be reached, should the lawyer be permitted to give an honest and responsive answer?

c.   In one well-known case, associates in a law office decided to form their own firm. After telling their firm they planned to leave, they told 400 clients on whose cases they were working of their plans. They mailed forms to the clients that they could use to terminate the present firm and retain the new one as their counsel. Clients with about 1300 cases pending at the old firm moved the work to the new one. The old firm filed suit to enjoin the departing lawyers from "contacting and/or communicating with" persons who were its clients. If you were the trial court would you have entered the injunction?

The trial court enjoined the conduct, but the Superior Court reversed. Adler, Barish, Daniels, Levin & Creskoff v. Epstein, 382 A.2d 1226 (Pa.Super.1977). The communication was "not false, misleading or coercive," the court reasoned, citing *Bates* as to the importance of a free flow of information about the availability of legal services. Furthermore, while the first firm had expected additional fee generating business from these clients, "[b]ecause the law permits a client to seek and re-seek counsel of his choice, any expectation that a client would remain constant * * * is unrealistic." 382 A.2d at 1232. Finally, the court believed the clients would be best served by permitting contacts from the associates. "Many of the clients have dealt personally [with the departing lawyers]. * * * Having one's file transferred to a new associate [as proposed by the existing firm] will undoubtedly engender additional cost and time to the client." Id. Balancing the interests at stake, the court held the associates' contacts to be valuable to the clients, not a tort to enjoin.

However, the Pennsylvania Supreme Court disagreed, 393 A.2d 1175 (Pa.1978), cert. denied 442 U.S. 907, 99 S.Ct. 2817, 61 L.Ed.2d 272 (1979). Its first expressed concern was also for the clients. The departing lawyers were said to be

> "actively attempting to induce the clients to change law firms in the middle of their active cases. Appellees' concern for their line of credit and the success of their new law firm gave them an immediate, personally created financial interest in the clients' decisions. In this atmosphere, appellees' contacts posed too great a risk that clients would not have the opportunity to make a careful, informed decision." 393 A.2d at 1181.

The court's other concern was for the nature of relationships within law firms. The court reasoned that the lawyers'

> "contacts were possible because Adler Barish partners trusted appellees with the high responsibility of developing its clients' cases. From this position of trust and responsibility, appellees were able to gain knowledge of the details, and status, of each case to which appellees had been assigned. In the atmosphere surrounding appellees' departure, appellees' contacts unduly suggested a course of action for Adler Barish clients and unfairly prejudiced Adler Barish. No public interest is served in condoning use of confidential information which has these effects. Clients too easily may suffer in the end." Id. at 1185.

Thus, the injunction was reinstated.

d.   With which opinion do you agree? Which one is more nearly true to *Bates, Ohralik, Primus* and *Shapero* that you saw in Problem 31? Does the analysis of client interests in those cases apply to departing lawyer situations as well? Does this case demonstrate that the principles the U.S. Supreme Court has tried to establish in those cases will not always be easy to apply?

4. How, then, should lawyers proceed when leaving a law firm?

a. In the wake of *Adler Barish*, ABA Informal Opinion No. 1457 (Apr. 29, 1980), was an attempt to give practical advice to lawyers. It authorized sending the following letter:

"Dear [Client]:

"Effective [date], I became the resident partner in this city of the *XYZ* law firm, having withdrawn from the *ABC* law firm. My decision should not be construed as adversely reflecting in any way on my former firm. It is simply one of those things that sometimes happens in business and professional life.

"I want to be sure that there is no disadvantage to you, as the client, from my move. The decision as to how the matters I have worked on for you are handled and who handles them in the future will be completely yours, and whatever you decide will be determinative."

The ABA Committee made clear that—

"This opinion is limited to the facts presented: (a) the notice is mailed; (b) the notice is sent only to persons with whom the lawyer had an active lawyer-client relationship immediately before the change in the lawyer's professional association; (c) the notice is clearly related to open and pending matters for which the lawyer had direct professional responsibility to the client immediately before the change; (d) the notice is sent promptly after the change; (e) the notice does not urge the client to sever relationship with the lawyer's former firm and does not recommend the lawyer's employment (although it indicates the lawyer's willingness to continue his responsibility for the matters); (f) the notice makes clear that the client has the right to decide who will complete or continue the matters; and (g) the notice is brief, dignified, and not disparaging of the lawyer's former firm."[1]

Should *all* of the elements noted by the ABA Committee have to be present for the communication to be proper? Which, if any, might be unnecessary?

b. More recently, ABA Formal Opinion 99–414 (Sept. 8, 1999) declared that notice to affected clients is not only permissible, it is required. The departure of a lawyer who has played a significant role in the client's representation is information that may affect the "status" of a matter within the meaning of Model Rule 1.4(a)(3). Direct contact with the client does not violate Model Rule 7.3 unless the lawyer's work on a matter afforded little or no direct contact with that client. In any event, the departing lawyer "must not disparage the lawyer's former firm" and "should not urge the client to sever its relationship with the firm, but may indicate the lawyer's willingness and ability to continue her responsibility

---

1. Excerpted from Recent Ethics Opinions, as updated 1981, copyright American Bar Association.

for the matters upon which she currently is working," while making "clear that the client has the ultimate right to decide who will complete or continue the matters." The departing lawyer may also respond to questions about billing rates and available resources at the new firm. The Opinion notes, however, that joint notification by the lawyer and the old firm is preferred.

c. Do you think these Opinions represent realistic solutions to the issues surrounding departure from a law firm? What problems can you see that the Opinions might not address?

5. How much may a departing lawyer tell an existing firm to which the lawyer wants to move about the lawyer's practice and clients?

a. Up to now, our questions have assumed the departing lawyer is forming a new firm. At least as often, however, lawyers leave one firm to go to another existing firm. In considering whether to make such a lateral hire, a firm is likely to want to know what experience the lawyer has and what clients might want to come with him or her. As you can imagine, much of that information will be "confidential" and protected against disclosure by Model Rule 1.6(a).

b. New York State Bar Association Committee on Professional Ethics, Opinion 720 (Aug. 27, 1999) asked what information a departing lawyer may disclose for purposes of doing conflicts checks, i.e., determining whether the new lawyer will disqualify the hiring firm from continuing to act in some of its cases. The new lawyer may not simply transfer his old firm's information database to the new firm, the Opinion notes, because the clients of that firm have a right to have their information be kept confidential. The new firm "must seek the names of clients represented by the Moving Lawyer and, depending on the size of [the old firm], the names of all [that firm's] clients for a reasonable period of time. * * * If the information is * * * [confidential], then the Moving Lawyer may disclose only general information."

Is this Opinion too restrictive, i.e., can a hiring firm afford not to know the specific information? Would any other approach than the one required be inconsistent with the clients' legitimate interests? On the other hand, if the lawyer sought consent from the clients to disclose their names and matters, might that be considered a premature effort to inform them of the lawyer's impending departure?

c. Gibbs v. Breed, Abbott & Morgan, 710 N.Y.S.2d 578 (App.Div. 2000), raised a related issue. When the lawyers left Breed, Abbott, they told the new firm, Chadbourne & Parke, the names and billing rates of the other trust & estates lawyers at Breed, Abbott, several of whom were then recruited by Chadbourne. That information belonged to Breed, Abbott, the court agreed, and its disclosure was a breach of fiduciary duty to that firm. Do you agree?

B. EFFORTS BY LAW FIRMS TO INHIBIT THEIR LAWYERS' ABILITY TO LEAVE

1. Rather than relying on a suit for breach of fiduciary duty to inhibit departures, might a law firm simply put a covenant not to compete in its partnership and employment agreements that requires former partners and associates not to practice law in competition with the firm for a period of three years after leaving?

a. Look at Model Rule 5.6(a). Is it ambiguous about this point? Does Comment [1] to Model Rule 5.6 persuade you that the rule makes sense?

b. In Cohen v. Lord, Day & Lord, 550 N.E.2d 410 (N.Y.1989), the head of Lord, Day's tax department left that firm and joined another New York City firm. The Lord, Day partnership agreement provided that departing partners were entitled to a share of future partnership profits representing unpaid or unbilled fees. If the lawyer went into competition with Lord, Day, however, the agreement said there was to be no such right. Cohen requested his share of profits, the firm interposed the competition exception, and Cohen asserted its invalidity under DR 2–108(A) of the New York Code of Professional Responsibility [Model Rule 5.6(a)]. The court agreed the provision was invalid and thus unenforceable. "While a law firm has a legitimate interest in its own survival and economic well-being and in maintaining its clients," the court said, "it cannot protect those interests by contracting for the forfeiture of earned revenues * * * [and thereby restrict] the choices of the clients to retain and continue the withdrawing member as counsel." 550 N.E.2d at 413.

c. ABA Ethics Opinion 94–381 (May 9, 1994) said that a corporation may not require, and a lawyer may not accept, a term in an employment agreement that requires in-house lawyers who leave the corporation never to take a case against the it, even if the case is unrelated to work the lawyer did for the corporation. Model Rule 1.9 provides sufficient protection to the client, the Opinion says. Requiring any more protection violates Model Rule 5.6(a).[2]

2. How broadly should the rule reach? Should firms be able to impose restrictions designed to protect reasonable investment expectations of the firm?

a. Denburg v. Parker Chapin Flattau & Klimpl, 624 N.E.2d 995 (N.Y.1993), involved a firm that had contracted for larger space and believed it would take five years to pay off the debt and lease obligations. The provision in question required that if a partner withdrew and practiced in the private sector, he or she had to pay the firm 12.5% of the profits allocated to the partner in the preceding two years or 12.5% of the billings

---

2. See also People v. Wilson, 953 P.2d 1292 (Colo.1998) (lawyer publicly censured for making his associates sign a "Covenant not to Steal" clients if they leave the firm and to pay over 75% of any fee earned on cases the clients choose to send to the departing lawyer); D.C. Bar Ethics Committee, Opinion 194 (Nov. 15, 1988) (contract providing that if departing lawyer competes with the firm within a year of leaving the firm, lawyer loses rights to half of unearned fees, improperly limits both client's right to choose counsel freely and lawyer's right to practice).

to the firm's former clients who followed the lawyer to the new firm, whichever was greater. The lower courts had said the purpose of this requirement made it different from *Cohen*, but the Court of Appeals disagreed. Only lawyers who went into competition with the firm had to pay. Thus, it refused to enforce the agreement.

b. In Howard v. Babcock, 863 P.2d 150 (Cal.1993), on the other hand, the partnership agreement provided that a partner who withdrew and engaged in the same kind of practice in the same county would be entitled to return of his capital interest in the firm but no share in the next 12 months' receipts of the firm to which he would have been entitled but for the competition. The court said that California has a public policy in favor of competition and that only "reasonable" non-competition agreements will be upheld. But, it said, "[c]ommercial concerns are now openly recognized as important in the practice of law," and the decision to practice in competition with one's former partners does not have to be costless. An agreement like the one in this case is not a prohibition on competition. Rather, it can be seen as a "tax" or "liquidated damages" for the real costs the departure impose on the partners who remain in the firm. Thus, it does not violate California's version of Model Rule 5.6(a) to put reasonable limits on the absolute freedom of lawyers to practice somewhere else.

c. In Shuttleworth, Ruloff & Giordano, P.C. v. Nutter, 493 S.E.2d 364 (Va.1997), the firm again had leased new office space. The firm had required its partners and associates to sign personal guarantees of the lease and to pay their share of the rent for the eleven year term of the lease if they remained in the practice of law. The court held the agreement did not improperly burden the lawyers' right to practice in competition with the firm. The purpose of the provision was not anticompetitive; it was to be sure the rent was paid. Further, the duty to pay applied whatever kind of practice the lawyer undertook, not just if he or she did competitive work.

d. 8182 Maryland Associates, L.P. v. Sheehan, 14 S.W.3d 576 (Mo. 2000), asked who is liable on a law firm lease. The firm of Popkin & Stern and each of its 13 partners had signed a 10–year lease for office space. A year later, Sheehan withdrew from the partnership to become Assistant Chief Litigation Counsel of the SEC. Ultimately, the firm failed and the question was whether Sheehan was still liable for the rent. Even though he withdrew from the partnership before the lease default, the court held, Sheehan was still liable. See also, Pochopien v. Marshall, O'Toole, Gerstein, Murray & Borun, 733 N.E.2d 401 (Ill.Ct.App.2000), to the same effect.

e. Is one effect of these decisions likely to be that partners will be more concerned about withdrawal because they are more likely to be held liable for some of its collateral consequences? Is that an effect that should concern the courts? Why or why not?

3. How should courts interpret the "concerning benefits upon retirement" provision of Model Rule 5.6(a)?

a. In Neuman v. Akman, 715 A.2d 127 (D.C.1998), the firm's partnership agreement provided that lawyers who retired completely received their partnership share plus an "additional amount" out of the firm's future earnings based on their productivity over the years preceding retirement. A lawyer who went to work for another firm, however, got only a return of his or her partnership contribution. The lawyer argued based on *Cohen* that the distinction constituted a restriction on his right to practice law in violation of Model Rule 5.6(a), but the D.C. Court of Appeals disagreed. Nothing in the arrangement restricted Neuman's right to practice, the court said; it simply paid an additional amount to partners who really retired and had no outside professional income. That made the payment a "benefit upon retirement" that was fully consistent with Model Rule 5.6.

b.   And in Hoff v. Mayer, Brown & Platt, 772 N.E.2d 263 (Ill.App.Ct. 2002), the firm's retirement plan would have paid Hoff about $94,000 per year after his retirement at age 60 if he had ceased practicing law. Instead, he formed a new firm and, while the old firm returned his capital shares and fees earned before retirement, it did not send him retirement checks. This opinion joins those holding that while Model Rule 5.6(a) prohibits a law firm from financially penalizing a lawyer for going into competition with the firm, it does not forbid the firm's withholding bona fide retirement payments from lawyers who do not really retire.

c.   Donnelly v. Brown, Winick, Graves, Gross, Baskerville, Schoenebaum & Walker, P.L.C., 599 N.W.2d 677 (Iowa 1999), in turn, upheld a plan limiting benefits to lawyers who had ceased practice in the state. The lawyer had gone to work for another Iowa firm and tried to distinguish the *Neuman* case by saying that, if the lawyer could practice in another state, the plan could not really relate to retirement. But the court said that the "retirement plan" exception to Model Rule 5.6(a) can apply even where the lawyer is not fully retired. The court said that this plan only provided payments to lawyers over age 60 and paid them over a 10 year period, as one might expect in a retirement plan.

d.   Do these results make sense to you? What factors distinguish these cases from cases like *Cohen* that found the limitations on future practice unduly restrictive?

4.   Is the rule courts adopt as to lawyers' rights upon leaving a firm likely to affect how lawyers are treated while at the firm?

a.   Professor Robert Hillman suggests that if the law did less to restrain partners who left firms and tried to take their clients with them, the law firm might have an incentive to treat its lawyers more humanely to try to prevent such departures:

> "That some lawyers prosper from grabbing [business and leaving] while others suffer is likely evidence of market forces at work. A significant factor underlying the growth of grabbing and leaving is the inability of many firms to develop a method of compensation acceptable to their more mobile partners. Because there is now a market for lawyers who can carry a substantial 'portfolio' of clients to another firm, these lawyers have something to auction. Viewed from this perspective, the solution to the

problem of grabbing may lie more in the modification of business practices, particularly those pertaining to compensation, than in law reform.

"A laissez faire approach to the machinations of law partners is not without its drawbacks, however. One of the more important problems is that a hands off attitude fails to address the interests and values advanced in a more stable environment for law firms. An atmosphere conducive to grabbing encourages the hoarding of clients by lawyers within the same firm. At least a modicum of cooperation is required to maximize the value of a firm to both its lawyers and clients. Furthermore, firms need some sense of confidence concerning the client base in order, as businesses, to engage in long-term planning and commitments in such areas as hiring and promotion of associates and support staff * * * .

"It may be that another kind of market—a market for stable law firms—already exists and may develop further over time. * * * Those firms presently enjoying relative stability of membership are well positioned to capture gains in an environment of instability."[3]

b.   Do you agree with Professor Hillman? Without the covenants not to compete that Model Rule 5.6(a) seeks to inhibit, is simple humanity likely to be insufficient to cause lawyers to turn down lucrative opportunities to take their clients and move elsewhere?

C. BUYING A LAWYER'S OR LAW FIRM'S PRACTICE

1. Would any ethical problem have been presented if the women associates had bought their portion of the law practice from Bright & Learned?

a.   Look at ABA Model Rule 1.17? Why might such a rule have been adopted? Does it seem incongruous to think of a lawyer selling his or her practice?

b.   Quoting a New York County opinion, ABA Formal Opinion 266 (June 2, 1945) asserts: "Clients are not merchandise. Lawyers are not tradesmen. They have nothing to sell but personal service. An attempt, therefore, to barter in clients, would appear to be inconsistent with the best concepts of our professional status." Does that end the matter? Can you come up with reasons other than "professional status" to criticize sale of a practice?

c.   When a partner in a law firm retires, you have seen from cases cited above that the firm may pay that person retirement benefits. Might

---

3. Robert W. Hillman, Law Firm Breakups: The Law and Ethics of Grabbing and Leaving 143–45 (1990) (footnotes omitted). See also, Ronald J. Gilson & Robert H. Mnookin, Sharing Among the Human Capitalists: An Economic Inquiry into the Corporate Law Firm and How Partners Split Profits, 37 Stanford L.Rev. 313 (1985).

sale of a practice be the corresponding way for a solo practitioner to pay for his or her retirement? Does that make the rule make more sense?

2.   What problems can you see associated with a sale of client files?

a.   Should a lawyer be permitted to sell case files to someone the clients have never met? Do the relevant interests at stake have anything to do with whether the practice is sold? Would the ethical problems be any less if the retiring lawyer gave, not sold, the files to a new lawyer, for example? Are those concerns minimized in this Problem because the members of the estate planning group have been a part of the firm of Bright & Learned?

b.   How does Model Rule 1.17(c) address the problem of confidential client information? Does the Rule let the sale be completed before clients have had a right to decide whether they want the new lawyer to see their file? Do Comments [7] & [8] to Model Rule 1.17 adequately explain how the steps in the sale process are to be handled?

c.   May a lawyer properly recommend that his or her clients retain the lawyer who has bought the practice? Model Rule 7.2(b)(3) certainly seems to imply that such a recommendation is possible. Would the selling lawyer have a conflict of interest in making that recommendation? Is the selling lawyer required to reveal that conflict to the clients before they decide whether to let the purchaser take over their file?

d.   Think back to Model Rule 1.5(e). Remember that under that rule, the forwarding lawyer had to remain liable for the new lawyer's malpractice. Is there a corresponding requirement in Model Rule 1.17? Should there be?

3.   Are the terms of Model Rule 1.17 in fact applicable to the facts of this Problem?

a.   Does Model Rule 1.17 only apply to sale of a firm to a stranger? Does Comment [14] to Rule 1.17 answer that question adequately?

b.   If the estate planning portion of Bright & Learned's practice were sold, would that mean that no one at Bright & Learned may ever again engage in estate planning? What would be the justification for such a rule? Does it sound suspiciously inconsistent with Model Rule 5.6(a)?

c.   In short, would the rule work as well when a firm sells part of its practice to departing partners as it does when a single lawyer retires and sells the entire practice to one or more other lawyers? Do that mean we leave the law applicable to selling a practice to lawyers departing from a firm entirely subject to principles outside the Model Rules?

4.   Do the Model Rules treat the sale of a deceased lawyer's practice differently than sale of the practice of a lawyer who is retiring?

a.   Look at Model Rule 5.4(a). Does it give you much guidance about how to handle such a situation? If you were the executor for a deceased solo practitioner, how would you go about realizing the most you could for the lawyer's heirs and beneficiaries?

b. ABA Formal Opinion 92–369 (Dec. 7, 1992) recommended that lawyers, particularly solo practitioners, have a plan as to who will take over their files if they should die unexpectedly. The Opinion advised the successor lawyer to contact each client, and preserve each client's property and files until each client can decide whom to retain as a new lawyer. Do you agree?

c. On a cautionary note, in Sears, Roebuck & Co. v. Goldstone & Sudalter, P.C., 128 F.3d 10 (1st Cir.1997), the lawyer bought the practice of a deceased collection attorney. Some of the firm's assets included unbilled work and the new lawyer sent bills for that work to Sears, his largest client. After a while, Sears contested the bills and the lawyer had to admit he had no idea what work had actually been done by the former lawyer on the matters. This case held that the new lawyer's sending bills under such circumstances was both a breach of contract with the client and a violation of the state consumer protection statute.

D. ESTABLISHING A GROUP LEGAL SERVICES PLAN AS PART OF A LAW FIRM

1. What is a group legal services plan? Why would anyone want to receive legal services from a firm pursuant to such a plan?

a. Our Problem says that the new firm wants to set up a plan for serving members of a local union with which one of the lawyers was once associated. The concept of group legal services began with efforts of other labor unions to assure their members that lawyers would be available to handle their cases against companies that typically were already the clients of prominent law firms in each city.

b. Brotherhood of Railroad Trainmen v. Virginia ex rel. Virginia State Bar, 377 U.S. 1, 84 S.Ct. 1113, 12 L.Ed.2d 89 (1964), was a suit to enjoin a railway union's recommendations of lawyers who would handle worker injury cases for its members. The District Court had held that letting a lay organization like a labor union "channel" cases to particular lawyers was improper. The Supreme Court held it was protected by the First and Fourteenth Amendments. Justice Black wrote for the Court:

> "It cannot be seriously doubted that the First Amendment's guarantees of free speech, petition and assembly give railroad workers the right to gather together for the lawful purpose of helping and advising one another in asserting the rights Congress gave them in the Safety Appliance Act and the Federal Employers' Liability Act, statutory rights which would be vain and futile if the workers could not talk together freely as to the best course to follow. The right of members to consult with each other in a fraternal organization necessarily includes the right to select a spokesman from their number who could be expected to give the wisest counsel. * * * And the right of the workers personally or through a special department of their Brotherhood to advise concerning the need for legal assistance—and, most important-

ly, what lawyer a member could confidently rely on—is an inseparable part of this constitutionally guaranteed right to assist and advise each other. * * *

"Only last Term we had occasion to consider an earlier attempt by Virginia to enjoin the National Association for the Advancement of Colored People from advising prospective litigants to seek the assistance of particular attorneys. In fact, in that case, unlike this one, the attorneys were actually employed by the association which recommended them, and recommendations were made even to nonmembers. NAACP v. Button, [371 U.S. 415, 83 S.Ct. 328, 9 L.Ed.2d 405 (1963)]. We held that 'although the petitioner has amply shown that its activities fall within the First Amendment's protections, the State has failed to advance any substantial regulatory interest, in the form of substantive evils flowing from petitioner's activities, which can justify the broad prohibitions which it has imposed.' In the present case the State again has failed to show any appreciable public interest in preventing the Brotherhood from carrying out its plan to recommend the lawyers it selects to represent injured workers. The Brotherhood's activities fall just as clearly within the protection of the First Amendment. And the Constitution protects the associational rights of the members of the union precisely as it does those of the NAACP. * * *" 377 U.S. at 5–8, 84 S.Ct. at 1116–18, 12 L.Ed.2d at 93–94.

c.   Dissenting Justices Clark and Harlan were chagrined by what they saw as the Court's indifference to what they believed was a corrupt system. They wrote:

"By its decision today the Court overthrows state regulation of the legal profession and relegates the practice of law to the level of a commercial enterprise. * * * Local officials of the union call on each member suffering an injury and seek to secure employment of these approved attorneys in the prosecution of claims for damages arising therefrom. Moreover the union, through its president, not only controls the appointment and dismissal of the approved attorney but also has considerable influence over his fees and often controls the disposition of cases. Furthermore, from 1930 to at least 1959, the union had required these approved attorneys to pay to it a portion of their fees, usually 25%. Such an arrangement may even now be in effect through the ruse of reimbursement for investigatory services rendered by the union. This state of affairs degrades the profession, proselytes the approved attorneys to certain required attitudes and contravenes both the accepted ethics of the profession and the statutory and judicial rules of acceptable conduct. * * * 377 U.S. at 9, 84 S.Ct. at 1118, 12 L.Ed.2d at 95.[4]

---

4. Editors' Note: Justice Stewart took no part in the disposition of this case. Following this case, in United Mine Workers of America v. Illinois State Bar Ass'n, 389 U.S. 217, 88 S.Ct. 353, 19 L.Ed.2d 426 (1967), the Court upheld as constitutionally protected the practice of the United Mine Workers in employing a licensed attorney on a salaried basis to represent any of its members who wished to prosecute workmen's compensation

d.   With which opinion do you agree?

2.   Why do you suppose there was such concern about such plans, the legal equivalent of Health Maintenance Organizations ("HMO's")? Was it simply a fear of competition, i.e., unions steering a group of attractive clients to preferred lawyers and denying lawyers outside the plan a chance to get their business?

a.   One critic, Howard C. Sorenson, argued that:

"Under some proposals, groups of organizations such as labor unions, credit unions, farm organizations, corporations, banks and chambers of commerce could deliver legal services and benefits to their employees, members, or depositors. Unrestricted, these groups are placed in a position where they dominate the delivery, the rendition, and the exercise of judgment necessary to legal services. No longer is the attorney the dominant figure in upholding the rule of law. The lay intermediary becomes a significant factor, threatening the quality of service and the existence of the vast majority of small firms dependent upon middle income clientele.

"Quite possibly, the untoward effect will be the reduced availability of legal services to neighborhoods and country towns, which surveys show need legal services the most. * * * Change in our traditional delivery system must not do violence to the basic tenets that the legal profession stands upon. It is in the public interest that we as a profession promote and preserve the integrity, competence, confidentiality, and independence of judgment within our ranks. * * * "[5]

b.   Do you share Mr. Sorenson's concern? Do clients participate in a group legal services plan every time they buy auto insurance? As we saw in Problem 13, under most policies, the insurance company promises to select and provide a lawyer to defend the insured and to pay any judgments within policy limits. Even ABA Model Code of Professional Responsibility, DR 2–103(D)(4)(a), permitted insurance companies to do this? Why? Should it be important as a matter of legal ethics that in the insurance situation, the insurance company is obliged to pay the judgment?

claims before the Illinois Industrial Commission. Next, in United Transp. Union v. State Bar of Michigan, 401 U.S. 576, 91 S.Ct. 1076, 28 L.Ed.2d 339 (1971), the Union recommended selected attorneys to its members and their families in connection with suits for damages under the Federal Employers' Liability Act; it secured a commitment from those attorneys that the maximum fee charged would not exceed 25% of the recovery, and it recommended Chicago lawyers to represent Michigan claimants. The Court again reversed the state court, found the practice constitutionally protected, and concluded that the "common thread running through our decisions in *NAACP v. Button*, *Trainmen*, and *United Mine Workers* is that collective activity undertaken to obtain meaningful access to the courts is a fundamental right within the protection of the First Amendment." 401 U.S. at 585, 91 S.Ct. at 1082, 28 L.Ed.2d at 347.

5.   Howard C. Sorenson, Bar Ethics: Guardian of the Profession, Trial Magazine, March–April 1975, p. 15. The late Mr. Sorenson practiced law in Chicago.

3.   Do the risks that bothered Mr. Sorenson and Justices Clark and Harlan apply equally to the arrangement that the lawyers in this Problem plan to make with the electrician's union? Is the proposed plan consistent with the Model Rules?

a.   Look at ABA Model Rule 7.3(d). Does the exception for an "organization not owned or directed by the lawyer" suggest a prohibition on our new law firm's organizing such a plan? Look at Comment [6] to Model Rule 7.3. Doesn't it clearly speak of a "plan or arrangement which the * * * lawyer's firm is willing to offer"?

b.   Then what is the point of Model Rule 7.3(d)? Does it forbid lawyers in our new firm from talking with union members to help convince them the plan would be a good idea? Does Comment [8] to Model Rule 7.3 convince you of the need for this limitation?

c.   Is Model Rule 7.2(b)(2) addressing the same issue? Does a group legal services plan have some of the characteristics of a lawyer referral service? From the standpoint of the law firm, for example, will the union with which the firm is working send them clients?

4.   Will group legal services mean the end of the solo practitioner? Might the groups instead provide a flow of clients to such lawyers that will allow them once again to thrive?

a.   For many years, there has been relative slow growth in the number of union-sponsored prepaid legal plans. One development, however, has been the creation of "individual access" plans under which members pay a certain fee every month which usually grants them unlimited telephone consultation with "access" attorneys and then the right to deal with "referral" attorneys for more complex problems at a lower than normal hourly fee.

b.   Montgomery Ward, for example, introduced an individual access plan in 1985. In 1989, a customer paying just $6.75 a month would receive unlimited telephone consultation with an attorney, "who will write letters and make phone calls on the client's behalf. The plan also offers a laundry list of free services, including a 'simple' will, document review of up to six pages and a 24–hour emergency bail service." For referral work, the plan provided discounted contingency fees and guaranteed maximum rates of $50 per hour.

c.   Group legal services plans continue to operate. One writer reports:

"Every day of the week except Sunday, telemarketers call residents in 25 states, where regulations expressly permit telemarketing by non-lawyers." By early 1989, Montgomery Ward had a 2000–lawyer network in place for its prepaid individual access plan. Hyatt Legal Services, Amway Corp., and other companies are marketing their own prepaid individual access plans. Hyatt's plan has over 100,000 members. To check up on possibly incompetent or dishonest lawyers, most plans rely on customer complaints and questionnaires. The general counsel of one prepaid plan stated: 'The winners in this are clearly lawyers. This is probably the most positive economic movements for lawyers with the exception of the M[ergers] & A[cquisitions] craze in

New York.' The plans put 'money in the lawyer's pockets they would not have because people would not have used them.' "[3]

d.   Should the creators of legal services plans be liable for the malpractice of lawyers whom they provide? In Gonzalzles v. American Express Credit Corp., 733 N.E.2d 345 (Ill.App.Ct.2000), plaintiff joined a legal services referral plan operated by American Express. After the plan attorney allegedly failed to provide the plaintiff with adequate representation, the plaintiff sued American Express for negligent referral, breach of contract, and breach of its duty to provide him with "competent legal representation." The court rejected plaintiff's claims. There was no breach of contract, because defendants kept their only promise, which was to provide a lawyer licensed in Illinois at a specified price. There was no case for negligent referral, because a referral service is not responsible for services provided by the referred attorney. Further, American Express was not a licensed attorney and plaintiff did not retain it to perform legal services. Thus, the plaintiff had no cause of action against the plan provider.

e.   Might it be preferable to have unions and other organizations publish directories of lawyers with whom their members have sought help in the past? Might it be asking for trouble to have the directory report information about experiences the members have had with the lawyers?

In Flamm v. American Association of University Women, 201 F.3d 144 (2d Cir.2000), for example, the American Association of University Women (AAUW) had published a directory to help women select counsel for gender discrimination cases. The directory said that "[a]t least one plaintiff has described lawyer [Flamm] as an 'ambulance chaser' with interest only in 'slam dunk cases'." Flamm sued for defamation, and the court agreed that a jury should be able to decide whether the statement was defamatory. The statement was offered as more than an opinion, the court said, and Flamm was entitled to make this non-profit organization hire lawyers to defend their candor.

5.   Should a professionally proper plan be required to have an "opt-out" provision allowing a client to reject an attorney assigned by the plan?

a.   Look at ABA Model Code of Professional Responsibility DR 2–103(D)(4)(e). For many years an ability to change lawyers was considered essential for such a plan. Why might plan advocates resist that feature? Is it enough to say that the union member can always hire his or her own attorney?

b.   Does an indigent criminal defendant have to be represented by the public defender if the latter has a genuine conflict of interest? What if the defendant has a personality conflict with the assigned lawyer? Should the need for an opt-out feature in a group legal services plan be judged by the

---

3.   Galen, Prepaid Plans a Boon for the Bar, National L.J., Jan. 30, 1989, at p.1, 32–35.

same standard applied in the "right to counsel" settings that we saw in Problem 11?

PROBLEM 35

THE DUTY TO WORK FOR NO COMPENSATION

Although earlier Problems have introduced some issues about pro bono work, for the most part we have heretofore assumed that lawyers provide legal services to people who agree to pay for them. In this Problem, we acknowledge the obvious reality that many people in our society cannot afford the kinds of bills you will send your other clients. If such people are to get help on what are often significant matters to them, they will require that lawyers provide their services free, or at very reduced cost. This Problem first explores whether lawyers have a moral obligation to provide such services. Next, it asks whether there is any basis for putting legal force behind the obligations. Third, it examines the appointment of lawyers as defense counsel in criminal cases and considers whether the legal obligation to serve should be so limited. Finally, it presents some more general efforts to fund delivery of legal services to the poor.

FACTS

The State Bar of Georgia, to which all the state's lawyers are required to belong,[1] has proposed a requirement that each lawyer in the state devote a minimum of 100 hours per year to uncompensated legal assistance in legal aid clinics to be established by the bar. The attorney's time would be scheduled insofar as possible to suit his or her convenience, and no attorney would be required to take an individual case in which there was a conflict of interest. An attorney could begin a case at the legal aid office but credit work done on the case in his or her own office against the 100 hours.

Not pursuant to any formal plan, J.R. Wright was appointed by the court to represent a defendant in a murder case after the

---

1. As described in this problem, the State Bar of Georgia is an "integrated" or "unified" bar, as discussed in the introduction to Chapter II. In Lathrop v. Donohue, 367 U.S. 820, 81 S.Ct. 1826, 6 L.Ed.2d 1191 (1961), the Supreme Court, with no majority opinion, upheld such a bar against an attack based on freedom of association. However, in Keller v. State Bar of California, 496 U.S. 1, 110 S.Ct. 2228, 110 L.Ed.2d 1 (1990), the Court held that the integrated State Bar of California may not constitutionally use compulsory dues to finance political and ideologi-cal causes that the petitioners opposed. The State Bar may use such dues to finance regulation of the legal profession (e.g., to propose ethical codes or discipline Bar members), but not, for example, to endorse gun control or nuclear freeze initiatives. See also, Morrow v. State Bar of California, 188 F.3d 1174 (9th Cir.1999), cert. denied 528 U.S. 1156, 120 S.Ct. 1162, 145 L.Ed.2d 1073 (2000) (constitutional to require membership in bar association that takes positions on public issues if dissenting members can get refund of portion of dues that go to support that function).

defendant refused representation by the public defender. The statutory compensation in such a case is a maximum of $750. Wright believed his client was guilty, but the defendant protested his innocence and the case ultimately required 300 hours of the attorney's time. Wright sued the state for a fee of $30,000 based on his regular hourly fee of $100 per hour. The state's defense was, in part, that the work was part of the inherent duty of an attorney.

QUESTIONS

A. THE MORAL OBLIGATION TO PROVIDE PRO BONO LEGAL SERVICES

1. Do lawyers have any moral obligation to provide free or reduced price legal services?

a. In 1958, the Joint Committee on Professional Responsibility of the ABA and the AALS set out a rationale for pro bono services in clear tones:

"The moral position of the advocate is here at stake. Partisan advocacy finds its justification in the contribution it makes to a sound and informed disposition of controversies. Where this contribution is lacking, the partisan position permitted to the advocate loses its reason for being. The legal profession has, therefore, a clear moral obligation to see to it that those already handicapped do not suffer the cumulative disadvantage of being without proper legal representation, for it is obvious that adjudication can neither be effective nor fair where only one side is represented by counsel.

"In discharging this obligation, the legal profession can help to bring about a better understanding of the role of the advocate in our system of government. Popular misconceptions of the advocate's function disappear when the lawyer pleads without a fee, and the true value of his service to society is immediately perceived. The insight thus obtained by the public promotes a deeper understanding of the work of the legal profession as a whole.

"The obligation to provide legal services for those actually caught up in litigation carries with it the obligation to make preventive legal advice accessible to all. It is among those unaccustomed to business affairs and fearful of the ways of the law that such advice is often most needed. If it is not received in time, the most valiant and skillful representation in court may come too late."[2]

b. Raymond Marks and colleagues at the American Bar Foundation articulated the source of such an obligation this way:

"Given the function that the lawyer has to perform—structuring the conflicts of society so that they are capable of peaceful resolution—

---

2. 44 A.B.A.J. 1159, 1216 (1958).

we feel that even without a monopoly grant of power the legal profession is a public utility. The law is a calling which by definition deals with public interest, not self-interest. The monopoly grant simply makes the need for regulation by self or state more urgent.

"In many ways the legal profession is like that sensitive area of the field of radio and television in which licensees control access to public discussion. In the communications field, the announced public policy—the Communications Act—requires that a commitment be made when a license is granted, that the licensee affirmatively undertake to 'operate its license in the public interest.' * * *

" * * * The absence of controls over the lawyer with respect to what he turns away is socially dangerous. It is more dangerous than the risk involved in drafting or socializing a percentage of a lawyer's time. The latter would be a drastic step but less drastic than socializing all of a lawyer's time. To some this will be a shocking notion. But why?

"A draft of lawyers is not outrageous when one considers that we draft children from the ages of six to sixteen so that they can acquire the skills of good citizens. This is compulsory education. * * * The military draft is supported on the premise that the country's security is involved. Yet when one examines the policies of our country, arrived at without hearing from all, and then sees the lawyers, who possess unique skills for arriving at balanced social policy, exempting themselves from their professional duty or being exempted by others, why *would* a draft for lawyers be outrageous?[3]

2.   Are you persuaded by these arguments that members of the bar have a moral obligation to see that all have access to their services?

a.   Is the obligation, if any, derived from the lawyer's role as advocate? Is it based on the fact that only lawyers are authorized to provide legal services?

b.   Is there a shortage of available legal help such that part of it must be allocated to poor people as one might allocate food after a severe hurricane? Is Marks any longer right that the number of lawyers is as limited as the number of broadcast licenses, for example?

c.   Is there a "market failure" in the provision of legal services? That is, while there are certainly some lawyers who serve poor people, do we see a commercial market to serve them analogous to the marketplace of doctors willing to serve medicaid patients, for example? Does this kind of market failure require a response from lawyers or does it suggest a publicly-funded system such as the one adopted for medical care?

d.   Might lawyers see a moral obligation that flows from the number of persons who had to sacrifice to see that they obtained a legal education?

3. F. Raymond Marks, et al., The Lawyer, the Public and Professional Responsibility 288–92 (1972).

Are any of us truly self-made? Are all members of the bar privileged to have a talent that others badly need and only some can pay for?

B. EFFORTS TO TRANSLATE A MORAL OBLIGATION INTO A LEGAL REQUIREMENT

1. Assuming that lawyers have some moral obligation to use their legally-protected license to practice on behalf of those who cannot afford to pay, do we see that obligation reflected anywhere in the Model Rules?

a. Does Model Rule 6.1 impose such a requirement? Why should a rule be specific—i.e., set a standard of 50 hours per year and prescribe how that standard should be met—if it is not to be made mandatory?

b. Some explanation—if not justification—for the voluntary rule we have comes from an A.B.A. Report on the lawyer's public interest obligation that said in part:

"In August, 1975, in Montreal, the American Bar Association House of Delegates confirmed 'the basic responsibility of each lawyer engaged in the practice of law to provide public interest legal services' without fee, or at a substantially reduced fee, in one or more of the following areas: poverty law, civil rights law, public rights law, charitable organization representation, and administration of justice. * * * We suggest * * * that the ABA encourage each state and local bar association to adopt *specific guidelines* for members of the bar who wish to budget their public interest legal service. * * *

"In this connection, it is important to note that a practicing lawyer may spend from 1,000 to 2,000 hours or more each year on billable client matters (as distinguished from non-client matters such as law firm administration, continuing legal education, bar association activity, and professional writing and speaking). Without focusing on this wide range of legal practice, some commentators have urged every lawyer to budget a flat 5% of client-related time for public interest legal service, yielding 50 to 100 hours per year; others have called for 10% of a lawyer's time, or 100 to 200 hours per year. Still others have suggested that a more realistic and manageable approach would be for the bar to settle on a fixed minimum number of hours, without reference to the time a lawyer spends on fee-producing matters. * * * "[4]

c. To the argument that poverty law is largely its own specialty, unknown to most private practitioners, the Committee responded:

"In our Committee's judgment, the professional responsibility to contribute public interest legal service is inherently an obligation to contribute one's time—one's abilities. Given the breadth of the 1975

---

4. A.B.A. Special Committee on Public Interest Practice, Implementing the Lawyer's Public Interest Obligation 1–7 (June 1977).

definition, few lawyers, if any, can responsibly argue that they are unable to make a useful, personal contribution. * * *

Do you agree?

2.   From what legal authority would a requirement to deliver free legal services be derived?

a.   Is the duty to take cases without compensation "inherent" in being a lawyer? Is the same duty inherent in being a plumber, a funeral director, or some other licensed professional? Do we require landowners to devote their land to public uses without compensation? Do the moral arguments made in the earlier questions translate easily into legal duties?

b.   Schwarz v. Kogan, 132 F.3d 1387 (11th Cir.1998), was an action under 42 U.S.C. § 1983 action challenging the Florida Bar rule that required its members report the number of pro bono hours they worked each year. It encouraged them to do at least 20 hours of such work each year or to pay $350 to a legal aid organization if they did not want to do the work themselves. In upholding the requirement, the Eleventh Circuit said that Florida "undoubtedly has a legitimate interest" in encouraging pro bono service and that "[d]ue to the unique and important role of the legal profession in this country, the free provision of legal services to the poor has long been recognized as an essential component of the practice of law." 132 F.2d at 1391. Indeed, the Court said, "one of the traditions of the legal profession is that a lawyer, as an officer of the Court, is 'obligated to represent indigents for little or no compensation upon court order'." Id. The Florida program was a rational way for the Florida Bar to know how much pro bono service was being done and where in the state more services may be needed. Only reporting, not service, was mandatory, but "even assuming that the reporting requirement may have some implicit coercive effect, and thereby motivates otherwise reluctant lawyers to honor their professional responsibility, this result justifiably furthers the Rule's legitimate purpose." Id. at 1392.

c.   Is *Kogan* precedent for upholding a requirement of providing free legal services to the poor? Does a reporting requirement raise quite different issues? Would you favor adoption of such a reporting requirement in your own state?

3.   If there were a legal obligation to deliver pro bono legal services, on whom should the obligation fall?

a.   Should lawyers not otherwise in practice have the obligation? How about lawyers employed by the government? Law teachers? Judges? Should it matter whether the lawyer is licensed in the jurisdiction of the lawyer's current residence?

b.   Is the likely inability to craft a fair allocation of the burden of pro bono service relevant to the issue of whether there should be such an obligation in the first place?

C. THE TRADITION OF ACCEPTING COURT APPOINTMENT IN A CRIMINAL CASE

1. What is the basis, if any, of the distinction between the "should [do pro bono service]" in Model Rule 6.1 and the "shall [accept court appointments]" in Model Rule 6.2? Do cases holding that defendants have a Constitutional right to counsel necessarily imply that attorneys must bear the uncompensated burden of such representation?

a. Some lawyers have not taken low pay in assigned cases without protest. In re Hunoval, 247 S.E.2d 230 (N.C.1977), for example, concerned an appointed attorney who had seen his client convicted and sentenced to death. The conviction was affirmed by the state Supreme Court, but it then granted a stay of execution for the attorney to seek a writ of certiorari in the U.S. Supreme Court. At that point, the attorney refused to file the petition for certiorari until the state court approved paying him more money, saying "I cannot justify working for * * * a rate less than that received by a garage mechanic." The court turned down the demand for money, and the lawyer failed to file the petition for certiorari on behalf of the condemned man. The court was not sympathetic. It suspended the attorney from practice in the state's appellate courts and barred him from receiving appointments in criminal cases for one year.[5]

b. On the other hand, some attorneys have had greater success protesting low pay in assigned cases. DeLisio v. Alaska Superior Court, 740 P.2d 437 (Alaska 1987), for example, reversed the contempt conviction of lawyer who refused to accept a trial court's order to serve as appointed counsel. Quoting a case from 1854, the court said that a lawyer's "professional services are no more at the mercy of the public, as to remuneration, than are the goods of the merchant, or the crops of the farmer, or the wares of the mechanic." 740 P.2d at 440. The court reasoned that "requiring an attorney to represent an indigent criminal defendant for only nominal compensation unfairly burdens the attorney by disproportionately placing the cost of a program intended to benefit the public upon the attorney rather than upon the citizenry as a whole." Id. at 443. An attorney should receive "just compensation," it said, defined as the rate reflecting compensation received by the average competent attorney operating in the open market.

c. Olive v. Maas, 811 So.2d 644 (Fla.2002), involved an attorney regularly appointed as counsel for death row inmates in postconviction proceedings. In one case, however, he refused to sign the usual engagement contract that contained a cap on the fee he could receive. By a 4–3 vote, the Florida Supreme Court agreed that a mandatory cap on an attorney's fee in postconviction review of a capital case interferes with the prisoner's right

---

5. See also, State v. Richardson, 631 P.2d 221 (Kan.1981) (lawyer indefinitely suspended for failing to take steps to represent defendant for whom he was appointed counsel); Federal Trade Commission v. Superior Court Trial Lawyers Ass'n, 493 U.S. 411, 110 S.Ct. 768, 107 L.Ed.2d 851 (1990) (concerted action by lawyers who regularly volunteered to take assigned cases to withhold their services until rates of compensation raised violates antitrust laws).

to counsel. Such a fee cap discourages an attorney from expending extra time and effort on the defendant's case, the court said, and risks reducing the effectiveness of a defendant's representation. Thus, attorneys may petition the court for additional compensation in appropriate capital cases.[6]

d. Are these results persuasive to you? The timing of the protest in *Hunoval* was clearly inexcusable, but do you agree that courts should listen sympathetically to lawyer's complaints about being forced to work for little or no compensation? Look at Model Rule 6.2(b). Should the lawyer's right to payment be the principal focus of the court, or should the real question be the effect on the client's representation?[7]

e. Should the right to payment of expenses be seen as a separate issue or as simply part of the same question? Compare State v. Lynch, 796 P.2d 1150 (Okla.1990) (lawyers for indigent defendants must be paid expenses, plus same hourly rate that state pays public defenders), with Williamson v. Vardeman, 674 F.2d 1211 (8th Cir.1982) (state may compel lawyer's services without compensation but may not deny reimbursement of litigation expenses).

2. Should appointed counsel in a criminal case be excused from acting where the defendant's conduct puts him in a difficult ethical position?

a. In Chaleff v. Superior Court, 138 Cal.Rptr. 735 (Ct.App.1977), the defendant was trying to represent himself but a deputy public defender had been appointed as "advisory counsel." The lawyer then asked to withdraw because the defendant's conduct allegedly put him in an "untenable ethical position." He said he could not explain further, but it later came out that the client's self-destructive urges caused him to reject the lawyer's suggestions of defenses and to seek imposition of the death penalty. Should the lawyer be relieved in such a case? The court said yes, citing California Rule 2–111 [comparable to Model Rule 1.16]. It noted that "while the attorney's duty is to his client, he cannot be placed in the position where discharging that duty impinges upon his ethical responsibilities as a member of the bar." 138 Cal.Rptr. at 737.

b. Should appointed counsel be excused if he can show he is incompetent? United States v. Wendy, 575 F.2d 1025 (2d Cir.1978), said that he should. The trial court had held a lawyer in contempt for refusing to accept an assignment to defend a felony tax case carrying a potential five year prison term. The lawyer's expertise was in tax and accounting and he had never tried a case "civil or criminal, state or federal." The Second Circuit

---

6. The dissenting justices' concerns went to the issue of declaratory relief and not necessarily to the merits of the court's result. See also, People ex rel. Conn v. Randolph, 219 N.E.2d 337 (Ill.1966) (reimbursement in excess of statutory maximum required where "extraordinary" time and financial burden is required to defend case).

7. See, e.g., Sheppard & White, P.A. v. City of Jacksonville, 827 So.2d 925 (Fla.2002) (rate of pay lawyer entitled to receive must be at rate "that ensures the provision of effective assistance to his client," not the rate lawyers earn for other kinds of work. 827 So.2d at 935.

reversed, saying that a lawyer cannot be required to do what he is incapable of doing.

c.   Zarabia v. Bradshaw, 912 P.2d 5 (Ariz.1996), went so far as to hold the entire Yuma County system for appointing counsel unconstitutional. When there were not enough experienced lawyers who wanted court appointments, the plan required appointments on a "rotational basis" from a pool that included lawyers with no experience in either criminal law or trial work. "Mentors" were available for consultation, but the basic assumption was that any lawyer who worked hard could become competent to conduct a defense once in a while. The court said it did "not share [the county's] optimism that an attorney * * *, who has no trial or criminal experience, can become reasonably competent to represent a defendant * * * charged with a very serious crime." The county had a duty to appoint only competent counsel and then to pay them a reasonable fee.

d.   Do you agree with these results? Look at Model Rule 6.2(a) and Comment [2]. Might courts be too willing to accept an "ethical" excuse for an unwillingness to accept an assigned case? Isn't any lawyer presumed to be able to become competent with sufficient study and preparation? Should it be relevant that if the lawyer does accept an assignment, he or she can later be sued by the client for malpractice? See Ferri v. Ackerman, 444 U.S. 193, 100 S.Ct. 402, 62 L.Ed.2d 355 (1979).

3.   Even though most appointments are made in criminal cases, should courts be able to appoint counsel to serve indigents in civil cases as well?

a.   In Ex parte Dibble, 310 S.E.2d 440 (S.C.App.1983), a prisoner brought civil actions complaining of conditions in the state penitentiary. The trial judge appointed two lawyers to represent the prisoners in those actions. The court of appeals recognized that this was not a criminal case and the defendant had no constitutional right to counsel, but it refused to hold that requiring representation without compensation was a violation of the lawyer's own constitutional rights. The Court noted that lawyers are an "integral and necessary part" of the justice system and concluded that courts have "the inherent power" to appoint lawyers "to serve without compensation where it appears reasonably necessary for the court to do justice." Law is a profession, the court said, and "the chief end of a profession is public service." The case was remanded, however, for a determination by the trial court that (1) the clients in fact required free counsel, (2) no other lawyers were willing to take the case pro bono, and (3) such assignments would be distributed fairly among the bar rather than falling on a limited group of lawyers.

b.   Yarbrough v. Superior Court of Napa County, 702 P.2d 583 (Cal. 1985), involved court appointment of a lawyer to defend a prisoner in a civil suit brought against him for the wrongful death of his murder victim. The facts were very close to the ones for which he had been originally convicted, and the question was whether the defendant could have appointed counsel to defend him in this civil matter as well. The court held that the trial court should consider the inmate's indigency, whether an adverse judgment would affect the prisoner's present or future property rights (i.e., does the indigent have a reasonable likelihood of acquiring property subject to judgment), whether counsel would be helpful in the circumstances of the case before it, and whether the cause of action could be abated until the prisoner is released "and therefore better able to make his own arrangements." The Court did not reach issues of what to do if the attorney were unwilling to be appointed and whether the court can provide compensation to the attorney.

Chief Justice Rose Bird dissented. "As with any other working person, lawyers should be properly compensated for their time and effort," she said. She criticized the majority for avoiding this issue, and quoting the Court of Appeal, went on: "No one would dare suggest courts have the authority to order a doctor, dentist or any other professional to provide free services, while at the same time telling them they must personally pay their own overhead charges for that time. No crystal ball is necessary to foresee the public outrage which would erupt if we ordered grocery store owners to give indigents two months of free groceries or automobile dealers to give them two months of free cars. Lawyers in our society are entitled to no greater privileges than the butcher, the baker and the candlestickmaker; but they certainly are entitled to no less." 702 P.2d at 590.

With which opinion do you agree?

4. Might the rules be different in federal court than in state court?

a.   Some authority for the appointment of counsel is statutory. Federal law provides, for example, that in a civil case the "court may request an attorney to represent any [person claiming *in forma pauperis* status] unable to employ counsel." 28 U.S.C. § 1915(e)(1).

In Mallard v. United States District Court, 490 U.S. 296, 109 S.Ct. 1814, 104 L.Ed.2d 318 (1989), the Court held (5 to 4) that what is now § 1915(e)(1), does *not* authorize federal courts to impose *compulsory* appointment of attorneys in civil cases, in this instance an action brought by inmates against prison guards under 42 U.S.C. § 1983. The statute only authorizes courts to "request", i.e., ask a lawyer to serve voluntarily as appointed counsel in a civil case. In a footnote, the Court said that it did "not reach the question whether the federal courts have inherent authority to order attorneys to represent litigants without pay * * * ." 490 U.S. at 308, n. 4, 109 S.Ct. at 1822, n. 4, 104 L.Ed.2d at 330, n. 4. Justice Kennedy, concurring, stressed lawyers' duty to volunteer their services. Lawyers, he said, "like all those who practice a profession, have obligations to their calling which exceed their obligations to the State. [I]t is precisely because our duties go beyond what the law demands that ours remains a noble profession." 490 U.S. at 310–11, 109 S.Ct. at 1823, 104 L.Ed.2d at 332.

Justices Stevens, Marshall, Blackmun & O'Connor dissented. They believed the word "request" was another way of saying "respectfully command." They said the federal statute made a lawyer's professional obligation compulsory and part of the terms on which any lawyer accepts a law license.

b.   Some lower courts seem impressed with the spirit of the dissent in *Mallard*. In Tabron v. Grace, 6 F.3d 147 (3d Cir.1993), for example, the district court had said that even a request to a lawyer to act as counsel for a prisoner in a 42 U.S.C. § 1983 action against prison officials for failing to protect him against assault by other prisoners required "exceptional circumstances." The Third Circuit found no authority for such a limit on the power to make requests of lawyers. It acknowledged that the number of cases greatly exceeds the number of available lawyers, and it acknowledged the discretion of a district judge to refuse to appoint counsel, but it urged lawyers to serve when asked.

c.   Scott v. Tyson Foods, Inc., 943 F.2d 17 (8th Cir.1991), was an employment discrimination case in which the employee asked that counsel be appointed for him. Citing *Mallard*, the District Court said that it lacked power to do so, but the Eighth Circuit disagreed. Title VII has a special provision for appointment of counsel, the Court said, and the District Court should appoint counsel for Mr. Scott.

d.   In Bothwell v. Republic Tobacco Co., 912 F.Supp. 1221 (D.Neb. 1995), the court released the lawyer it had appointed to represent an indigent prisoner in a civil suit alleging he became ill as a result of using tobacco that lacked an appropriate warning label when he made "roll-your-own" cigarettes. The Court asserted that, in spite of *Mallard*, it had inherent authority to appoint counsel in civil cases. However, it declined to continue to exercise that authority in this case because the reason the plaintiff had not been able to get private counsel was not because of his indigence; it was because trying tobacco cases is expensive and unlikely to be successful.

e.   Where do you come out on the issue of appointing counsel in civil cases? Even if such appointments would be justified in some cases, should judges be cautious about using scarce lawyer resources in cases where there is no constitutional right to counsel at all?

D.   SOURCES OF POSSIBLE OTHER FUNDING FOR LEGAL SERVICES TO THE POOR

1.   Should lawyers expect public funding to be the solution to the lack of adequate legal services for the poor?

a.   Requiring individual lawyers to provide uncompensated legal services is, of course, only one possible way to provide assistance to the poor. The Legal Services Corporation, for example, is a federal agency that provides funding to over 175 local affiliates around the country that hire lawyers to provide a wide variety of legal services. Annual funding for LSC activities was as high as $400 million in 1994–95. It dropped to $278 million in 1996, and rose again to $329 million in 2001.[8]

---

8. This and other information about the LSC can be found at its website www.lsc. gov.

b.   Yet those who live by federal funding may find themselves hand-cuffed by it. Congress imposed statutory restrictions on the LSC's expenditure of funds in the agency's 1996 and 1997 Appropriations Acts. Congress forbade use of LSC funds to aid entities in lobbying, class actions, giving aid to certain aliens, supporting advocacy training, litigating on behalf of prisoners, and suing to reform welfare. The restrictions were imposed on non-federal funds raised by the LSC and its local entities as well.[9]

c.   ABA Formal Ethics Opinion 96–399 (Jan. 18, 1996) analyzed questions presented by reductions in federal LSC funding. Among the conclusions were that lawyers who might lose funding are required to tell their clients and seek alternative funding for existing cases. They also must consider whether to withdraw from "prohibited" cases, i.e., those that would require the office to forfeit LSC funds and thus injure other clients. Offices were told not to take new cases if they cannot effectively handle the cases they have, and to tell clients about requirements that would put some aspects of client confidentiality at risk.

d.   Legal Services Corporation v. Velazquez, 531 U.S. 533, 121 S.Ct. 1043, 149 L.Ed.2d 63 (2001), was a challenge to Congress' prohibiting the use of LSC appropriations to seek to amend or otherwise challenge the existing welfare law. The Second Circuit held that was an unconstitutional content-based restriction on speech and the Supreme Court agreed (5 to 4). In an opinion by Justice Kennedy, the Court acknowledged that Congress has excluded several kinds of cases from LSC jurisdiction, e.g., most criminal cases. However, restricting the kinds of arguments LSC lawyers can make in cases they may take is another story. That "distorts the legal system by altering the traditional role of attorneys * * * [and] threatens severe impairment of the judicial function. * * * The statute is an attempt to draw lines around the LSC program to exclude from litigation those arguments and theories Congress finds unacceptable but which by their nature are within the province of the courts to consider." 531 U.S. at 544–46, 121 S.Ct. at 1050–51, 149 L.Ed.2d at 74–75.

Justice Scalia, joined by Chief Justice Rehnquist and Justices O'Connor and Thomas, argued that the statute did not regulate speech; it defined the scope of a program. Congress routinely says that federal dollars may be used for some things but not others, they observed. Poor people are free to seek welfare reform; they simply may not use LSC dollars to do it.

Which opinion makes more sense to you? If the statute said that welfare cases in general, like most criminal cases, were off limits to LSC lawyers, would the statute have been proper? Is there any limit to the Court's logic? If Congress sets up a system for funding litigation on behalf of the poor, may it impose any limits on use of those funds without intruding on some argument that some lawyer would like to make on behalf of some client?

---

9. Data on the LSC website suggests that those sums amount to another $250 million annually.

2. What is the role of charitable or educational legal clinics in meeting the legal needs of poor citizens?

a. Well before creation of the public Legal Services Corporation, charitable legal services agencies provided free services to the poor. In this country, legal aid is often traced back to 1876 and the formation of a legal aid society for German immigrants living in New York. By 1916, there were legal aid societies in 37 American cities.[10]

b. One common form of those agencies today are law school clinics. They, too, sometimes come under fire from those challenged by their activities on behalf of poor clients.

Southern Christian Leadership Conference v. Supreme Court of Louisiana, 252 F.3d 781 (5th Cir.2001), for example, was an effort of law professors, law students, and community organizations, to challenge an amendment to the student practice rules of the Louisiana Supreme Court adopting a more restrictive definition for the "indigence" of clients whom students could represent. The amendment was seen to have been in response to the Tulane Law School clinic's efforts in environmental cases that angered business interests, but the Fifth Circuit rejected all constitutional challenges to the new rule. The court found that the detailed financial disclosures required before clients could obtain representation did not deny equal protection; wealth classification was rationally related to the purpose of the law to help poor people. Second, although the new rule effectively limited certain kinds of representation by student clinics, it did not implicate the constitutional right of free speech. Even *Velazquez* did not require a different result. A restriction based on client wealth was content neutral, the court reasoned, unlike the restrictions in *Velazquez*.

Do you agree with the court? Should the political purpose behind legislation be relevant to its constitutionality if on its face the legislation is content neutral? Do we want courts trying to discern whether legislators had appropriate motives when they voted for or against a law?

c. Does the existence of the Legal Services Corporation, and of charitable organizations serving the poor, reduce the moral obligation of lawyers generally to provide legal services to the poor? Is the duty to work without fee made more pressing by the relatively modest funding of such agencies?

3. Might the problems of pleasing outside funding sources be avoided by finding "free" money? Might lawyers be required to deposit client trust funds that are small in amount or held only for a short time, in an interest bearing account with the interest going to the Bar and not the client?

a. Voluntary IOLTA (Interest on Lawyer Trust Accounts) programs are in existence in most jurisdictions today, and even though client consent

---

10. The most comprehensive treatments of this early period are Reginald Heber Smith, Justice and the Poor (1919), and Emery A. Brownell, Legal Aid in the United States (1951).

is rarely required or sought, the ABA has said that lawyers may properly participate in such programs. Formal Opinion 348 (July 23, 1982) said:

"* * * [N]othing in the Model Code prohibits a lawyer from placing clients' funds in interest-bearing accounts * * *. [However, in] addition to expenses created by the notification, record keeping and accounting requirements of DR 9–102(B), lawyers may incur other costs in attempting to place clients' funds at interest. Income tax filings may be necessary to enable the client to report the interest earned on the funds, and bank handling fees may further reduce the potential return. It is evident, therefore, that in many—if not most— instances, the accounting and administrative costs, plus any bank charges, will more than offset the potential gains to the client. Thus, while no ethical rule proscribes placing client funds at interest for the benefit of an individual client, administrative costs and practical considerations often will make it self-defeating for the lawyer to attempt to obtain interest on small sums or even on large amounts of clients' funds held for short periods of time. * * *

"* * * The Committee perceives no intention by the drafters of the Model Code to relax in any manner the long-standing restrictions on a lawyer's [own] use of client funds. * * *

"[However, s]uccessful programs using the interest on lawyers' trust accounts for law-related public service projects in Canadian provinces and several British Commonwealth countries have inspired bar groups in the United States to consider the creation of similar programs. Several recent developments have caused the use of this untapped resource to become desirable and feasible. The availability of public funds for law-related public service uses, such as legal services for the indigent, has been reduced. The Internal Revenue Service has ruled that income generated under the circumstances of one program is not taxable to the client. * * *

"The programs being implemented vary in detail but have certain elements in common. All strive to have the pooled funds generate income for remittance to tax-exempt organizations where it will be applied to underwrite law-related public service activities. Under most plans, participation is at the option of the lawyer. Included are funds nominal in amount or to be held for a short period of time; all other funds are outside the scope of the programs. The decision as to what funds will be included is left to the sound discretion of the lawyer to whom the funds are entrusted, and the lawyers' reasonable exercise of discretion often is protected by either judicial or legislative statement. Prior client consent is not required. Notice to clients also is not required but is encouraged where practicable. The funds are placed in interest-bearing accounts in conventionally insured depository institutions and can be withdrawn on request. The banks are directed to remit earnings net of handling charges to a designated receiving entity, usually a bar foundation or similar tax-exempt organization, and to report account activity periodically to both the organization and the participating lawyer. The tax-exempt organizations generally segregate and strictly account for the funds, and apply them as directed by governing boards to law-related uses compatible with section 501(c)(3) of the Internal Revenue Code. * * *

" * * * In the opinion of the Committee, * * * the rationale for the ethical acceptability of these programs is the same as the premise for acceptability in constitutional law and tax law. The client has no right under the circumstances to require the payment of any interest on the funds to himself or herself because the amount of interest which the funds could earn is likely to be less than the appropriate charges for administering the earnings. The practical effect of implementing these programs is to shift a part of the economic benefit from depository institutions to tax-exempt organizations. There is no economic injury to any client. The program creates income where there was none before. For these reasons, the interest is not client funds in the ethical sense any more than the interest is client property in the constitutional sense or client income in the tax law sense. * * *

" * * * The Committee finds no conflict with the principle of careful stewardship when a lawyer participates in the state-authorized programs described. Canon 8 of the Model Code says '[a] lawyer should assist in improving the legal system.' This standard of conduct is advanced when a lawyer participates in a program which puts idle funds to law-related public uses. Moreover, by focusing attention on the earnings potential of lawyer trust accounts, these programs have the added benefit of encouraging lawyers to earn interest for clients on trust funds where the expected interest is more than the cost of administering the account."

b. Do you agree with this analysis? Have lawyers created a special exception for themselves from normal fiduciary standards so as to divert their clients' money to fund services that lawyers would otherwise be morally obliged to provide without compensation? That issue has been before the courts for several years.

c. Lawyers would probably not participate in such programs if their clients explicitly objected. However, because the costs of accounting for each client's share of the interest would exceed the interest earned, clients were said to have no expectation of receiving the interest and thus no "property" that could be deemed unconstitutionally "taken" without just compensation. Cone v. State Bar of Florida, 819 F.2d 1002 (11th Cir.1987), cert. denied 484 U.S. 917, 108 S.Ct. 268, 98 L.Ed.2d 225 (1987) (upholding constitutionality of Florida's Interest on Trust Accounts (IOTA) program).[7]

7. See also, Washington Legal Foundation v. Massachusetts Bar Foundation, 993 F.2d 962 (1st Cir.1993), reaching the same result, and IRS Revenue Ruling 87–2 saying that the sums on deposit in an IOLTA program are not taxable to the client or the lawyer.

4. Do you agree with ABA Formal Opinion 348 and *Cone*, supra, that no "takings" issue is presented by an IOLTA program?

a. In Webb's Fabulous Pharmacies, Inc. v. Beckwith, 449 U.S. 155, 101 S.Ct. 446, 66 L.Ed.2d 358 (1980), Justice Blackmun, for a unanimous Court, invalidated a Florida statute that provided that the county may take for itself the interest accruing on an interpleader fund deposited in the county court. The Court rejected the rationale that the funds deposited were considered to be "public money" from the date of deposit until it left the account: "[A] State, by *ipse dixit*, may not transform private property into public property without compensation, even for the limited duration of the deposit in court. This is the very kind of thing that the Taking Clause of the Fifth Amendment was meant to prevent." 449 U.S. at 164, 101 S.Ct. at 452, 66 L.Ed.2d at 367.

b. Phillips v. Washington Legal Foundation, 524 U.S. 156, 118 S.Ct. 1925, 141 L.Ed.2d 174 (1998), brought the constitutionality of state IOLTA plans to the Supreme Court. The issue before the Court was very specific. The Court assumed that a lawyer was required to put funds into an IOLTA account only if the interest generated on the funds would not be sufficient to offset bank service charges and accounting for the interest. The issue thus was whether the interest was nevertheless "property" of the client so that the Takings Clause could apply.

By a 5 to 4 vote, the Court, per Chief Justice Rehnquist, held that even that little bit of interest on a client's funds in a lawyer's account is property of the client for purposes of the Takings clause. The amount at stake is not the issue, the Court said. "[P]roperty is more than economic value; it also consists of 'the group of rights which the so-called owner exercises in his dominion of the physical thing'." 524 U.S. at 170, 118 S.Ct. at 1933, 141 L.Ed.2d at 187. Rental income would be the property of the owner of a building, for example, even if collecting the rent cost more than the tenant owed. Because other issues had not yet been decided below, the Court left for another day whether, given this view of property, the IOLTA program constituted an unconstitutional taking and what, if any, compensation might be due.

In dissent, Justices Souter, Stevens, Ginsburg and Breyer asserted the Court had reached out unnecessarily to decide an abstract issue, and that it could only properly decide the property issue in light of the issues that were not before the Court. They also believed, however, that it was meaningless to talk of "taking" or calling "property" an asset when it had no practical value to the client.

c. Washington Legal Foundation v. Texas Equal Access to Justice Foundation, 270 F.3d 180 (5th Cir.2001), was the remand of *Phillips*. A Fifth Circuit panel held (2 to 1) that the confiscation of the interest income was a taking of property, because it was not in exchange for any services performed by the state. In addition, the statutory scheme did not allow a client to withdraw any of the interest that his account generated. Thus, the program permanently appropriated the client's income, and that use of the funds constituted a per se taking that was subject to injunction even if not a measurable damage award.

d. The Supreme Court rejected a just compensation challenge to IOLTA programs in Brown v. Legal Foundation of Washington, 123 S.Ct. 1406 (2003). When the Washington supreme court set up this IOLTA program it required: (a) *all* client funds must be deposited in interest-bearing trust accounts, (b) funds that cannot earn net interest for the client must be deposited in an IOLTA account, (c) lawyers must direct banks to pay the net interest on the IOLTA accounts to the Legal Foundation of Washington (Foundation), and (d) the Foundation must use all such funds for tax-exempt law-related charitable and educational purposes. Later, that court made its IOLTA Rules applicable to Limited Practice Officers (LPOs), *i.e.,* nonlawyers who are licensed to act as escrowees in real estate closings. Petitioners, who have funds that are deposited by LPOs in IOLTA accounts, and others sought to enjoin state official from continuing this requirement, alleging, among other things, that the taking of the interest earned on their funds in IOLTA accounts violates the Just Compensation Clause, and requiring that client funds be placed in these accounts is an illegal taking of the beneficial use of those funds.

The Court accepted that the petitioners' funds generated some interest that was paid to the Foundation, but without IOLTA, they would have produced no interest net of bank charges. The Ninth Circuit ruled that there was no taking because petitioners had suffered neither an actual loss nor an interference with any investment-backed expectations, and that if there were such a taking, the just compensation due was zero. The Supreme Court (5 to 4) affirmed.

Justice Stevens, writing for the Court, agreed that a law requiring that the interest on IOLTA accounts be transferred to a different owner for a legitimate public use could be a per se taking requiring the payment of "just compensation" to the client. The use of these funds to benefit "millions of needy Americans" satisfied the "public use" requirement of the Just Compensation Clause.

The court concluded that the requirement that the petitioners' funds be placed in an IOLTA account is merely a transfer of principal and therefore did not effect a confiscation of any interest. The Court assumed that petitioners retained the beneficial ownership of at least a portion of their escrow deposits until the funds were disbursed at closings, that those funds generated interest in the IOLTA accounts, and that the interest was taken for a public use when it was turned over to the Foundation.

However, because just compensation "is measured by the owner's pecuniary loss—which is zero whenever the Washington law is obeyed—there has been no violation of the Just Compensation Clause." The Court concluded that the petitioners were not entitled to any compensation for the nonpecuniary consequences of the taking of the interest on his deposited funds, and that any pecuniary compensation must be measured by the petitioner's net losses rather than the public's gain. Thus, because petitioners' net loss was zero, the compensation due is also zero.

Justice Scalia, joined by Rehnquist, C.J., and Justices Kennedy & Thomas, dissented, objecting that the Court "creates a novel exception to our oft-repeated rule that the just compensation owed to former owners of confiscated property is the fair market value of the property taken." Justice Kennedy, also filed a dissent, raising First Amendment concerns: "One constitutional violation (the taking of property) likely will lead to another (compelled speech). These matters may have to come before the Court in due course." The Washington Supreme Court granted to itself "a monopoly which might then be used for the forced support of certain viewpoints." Under these IOLTA programs, "the true owner cannot even opt out of the State's monopoly."

    e.   With which of these opinions do you agree?

PROBLEM 36

PROBLEMS IN CLASS ACTION REPRESENTATION

Class actions represent a quite different way of delivering legal services to people too poor to pay for them—or people whose individual injuries would not justify hiring lawyers for each. Where several individuals have suffered a similar injury, often whether or not many of them know it, a suit may be filed in the name of some of them but on behalf of all, and in many such cases, the court will require the defendants to pay the plaintiffs' lawyers. This Problem considers some of the ethical issues raised in such class action cases. First, it considers the ethics of recruiting clients to serve as representative plaintiffs, and then, whether the plaintiffs must be warned about the possible dangers of proceeding by class action. Third, it examines the usual rules against a lawyer's paying the expenses of litigation, and finally, it looks at the complex world of setting the fees paid to class action and civil rights lawyers for their services.

FACTS

You know that landlords' failure to pay interest on tenants' damage deposits has cost tenants, in the aggregate, large sums of money each year. You believe that this practice is unconscionable and illegal. You want to stop it by requiring the landlords to pay their tenants interest on the deposits at the average prime rate for the term of the lease. You have put an advertisement in the local newspaper asking any tenant who is interested in filing a suit against his landlord on this basis to come to you for free legal assistance. Three persons come to your office, and you pick the most attractive and articulate one.

You are thinking of filing a class action in the name of this individual and all other tenants similarly situated, but as of now you have not done so and have simply written to your client's landlord threatening suit. The landlord has shown no interest in settlement, and it has become clear that your lawsuit will require a large amount of professional survey work. The requirement of notice to the members of the class may also be expensive. Your named client has no funds with which to pay those expenses, and she has expressed her concern to you about how she can possibly pay your fee.

QUESTIONS

A. **THE USE OF PUBLICITY TO FIND CLIENTS FOR A CLASS ACTION SUIT**

1.   Should lawyers be allowed to advertise to find clients in whose names to bring class action cases?

a.   An early concern for lawyers seeking to file a class action is to advise members of the putative class of their legal rights and to persuade them not to opt out of the class. That sounds a lot like the issues that arose in Problem 31 on lawyer marketing. Indeed, you will find a passing reference to the issue in Model Rule 7.2, Comment [4].

b.   This time, however, the courts have found the authority for contacting potential class members to be implicit in Federal Rule of Civil Procedure 23, rather than the Constitution alone. See, e.g., Coles v. Marsh, 560 F.2d 186, 189 (3d Cir.1977), cert. denied 434 U.S. 985, 98 S.Ct. 611, 54 L.Ed.2d 479 (1977): "We hold * * * that the district court lacked power to impose any restraint on communication for the purpose of preventing the recruitment of additional parties plaintiff or of the solicitation of financial or other support to maintain the action."

c.   The Supreme Court then quoted from *Coles* with approval in Gulf Oil Co. v. Bernard, 452 U.S. 89, 101 S.Ct. 2193, 68 L.Ed.2d 693 (1981). Gulf Oil, pursuant to an agreement with the EEOC, sent notices to alleged victims of racial and gender discrimination offering back-pay in exchange for signed releases of all claims based on discrimination. Respondents then filed a class action on behalf of all present and former employees who had been subject to discrimination. Gulf moved for an order limiting communications between the named class action plaintiffs and their counsel to prospective or actual class members. The district court granted the order but the en banc Fifth Circuit reversed. The Supreme Court agreed with the Fifth Circuit, holding that the order involved an abuse of discretion under Federal Rule 23 and potentially involved serious restraints on expression in violation of the First Amendment:

"The order interfered with their [the class representatives'] efforts to inform potential class members of the existence of this lawsuit, and may have been particularly injurious * * * because the employees at that time were being pressed to decide whether to accept a back-pay offer from Gulf that required them to sign a full release of all liability for discriminatory acts. In addition, the order made it more difficult for respondents, as the class representatives, to obtain information about the merits of the case from the persons they sought to represent.

"Because of these potential problems, an order limiting communications between parties and potential class members should be based on a clear record and specific findings that reflect a weighing of the need for a limitation and the potential interference with the rights of the parties. * * * In addition, such a weighing—identifying the potential abuses being addressed—should result in a carefully drawn order that limits speech as little as possible, consistent with the rights of the parties under the circumstances. * * * [T]he mere possibility of abuses does not justify routine adoption of a communications ban that interferes with the formation of a class or the prosecution of a class action in accordance with the Rules." 452 U.S. at 101–04, 101 S.Ct. at 2200–02, 68 L.Ed.2d at 703–05.

d. Is this holding consistent with the Supreme Court's earlier decisions, In re Primus, 436 U.S. 412, 98 S.Ct. 1893, 56 L.Ed.2d 417 (1978) (upholding solicitation of pro bono cases), and Shapero v. Kentucky Bar Association, 486 U.S. 466, 108 S.Ct. 1916, 100 L.Ed.2d 475 (1988)(upholding direct mail advertising/solicitation), both discussed in Problem 31?[1]

2. Do the same free speech principles justify communication with class members by defense counsel seeking to persuade them to opt out of the class?

a. Resnick v. American Dental Association, 95 F.R.D. 372, 376–78 (N.D.Ill.1982), ordered *defense* counsel, in a class action charging employment discrimination, not to communicate with *plaintiff* class action members because of Model Code of Professional Responsibility DR 7–104(A)(1) [now Model Rule 4.2]. *Gulf Oil* itself, in fact, stated in dictum that DR 7–104 is an example of a "properly impose[d]" restraint on communication. 452 U.S. at 104 n. 21, 101 S.Ct. at 2202 n. 21, 68 L.Ed.2d at 705 n. 21.

b. Kleiner v. First National Bank of Atlanta, 751 F.2d 1193 (11th Cir.1985), was a class action involving alleged violation of an agreement to give small borrowers the "prime rate." To try to limit its liability, the bank

1. The significance of becoming a named class representative may have been somewhat reduced by Devlin v. Scardelletti, 536 U.S. 1, 122 S.Ct. 2005, 153 L.Ed.2d 27 (2002) (non-named class members may appeal settlement where it fixes their legal rights and obligations and where the non-named class members objected to settlement agreement at fairness hearing).

Further, to the extent that recruiting clients has aided a lawyer's chances of being named to represent the class and collect the largest share of the fee award, use of competitive bidding to select class counsel might cut down some early communication. See, e.g., Developments in the Law: The Paths of Civil Litigation, 113 Harvard L. Rev. 1827, 1842 (2000) (bidding rarely used); Third Circuit Task Force on the Selection of Class Counsel (2002) (criticizing the practice).

embarked on a program of calling potential class members to try to persuade them to opt-out of the suit. One loan officer, who was also a lawyer, objected to the pressure tactics being used in the calls and was forced to resign for refusing to participate. The trial judge was incensed and imposed disqualification and a $50,000 fine on the defense lawyer. Although sending the case back for a hearing, the Eleventh Circuit relied on Ohralik v. Ohio State Bar, discussed in Problem 31, to say that sanctions would be appropriate. The defense effort to urge potential plaintiffs to opt out of the class was "inherently conducive to overreaching and duress" and thus not simply the exercise of free speech. 751 F.2d at 1206.

c.   Do you think the courts have been properly even-handed in their treatment of such contacts? Should potential class members be considered represented persons for purposes of Model Rule 4.2 even before they have decided whether to remain part of the class? Why might so considering them be important to carrying out the purposes of Federal Rule 23 and the class action process?

B.   POSSIBLE CONFLICTS OF INTEREST IN CLASS ACTION CASES

1.   Federal Rules of Civil Procedure, Rule 23(a)(4), requires that "the representative parties will fairly and adequately protect the interests of the class." Should that rule be seen as more than merely a procedural rule for the guidance of the court and be found to have a conflict of interest element as well?

a.   In Bachman v. Pertschuk, 437 F.Supp. 973 (D.D.C.1977), a government lawyer tried to act as counsel for a class of employees of which he was also a member. The court found that such representation would violate what is now Model Rule 1.7(a)(2). Any class inevitably consists of people with some interests different from those of others in the class, the court said, concluding:

> "[The attorney] is a present employee seeking relief as a member of a class consisting of persons who are presently employed, were denied employment, or were discharged. Whenever an attorney's personal interest as a class member is limited to the interest of those persons presently employed, the possibility exists that he may favor a settlement which gives preference to the interests of such persons over those denied employment by or discharged from the FTC. Furthermore, he may devote a disproportionate amount of time preparing for trial on the issues relevant to the subgroup to which he belongs. Thus, the varying interests of the class represented coupled with the difficulty of viewing one's own limited interest in the context of the interests of the entire class require that [the attorney] be disqualified as attorney for the class because he may not adequately be able to 'protect the interests of the [entire] class.' Fed.R.Civ.P. 23(a)(4)." 437 F.Supp. at 977.

b.   Amchem Products, Inc. v. Windsor, 521 U.S. 591, 117 S.Ct. 2231, 138 L.Ed.2d 689 (1997), raised another kind of conflict. For many years, asbestos litigation had been a management nightmare for the federal courts. In 1991, the Multi–District Litigation (MDL) panel consolidated all pending asbestos cases in a single federal district. Settlement talks began but the specter of future liability to unknown victims made the defendants unwilling to commit to a figure for current cases. Thus, plaintiffs and defendants together tried to define a class that included everyone who has become ill as a result of asbestos exposure and everyone whose symptoms might only develop in the future. The defendants were prepared to create a huge fund with which to pay all claims. Both sides agreed to a schedule for payments to be made depending on the severity of the illness, and they created an ADR process through which to make payments promptly. The District Court certified the class for settlement purposes only and found the proposed settlement fair. Georgine v. Amchem Products, Inc., 878 F.Supp. 716 (E.D.Pa.1994). However, the Third Circuit reversed. 83 F.3d 610 (3d Cir.1996).

The Supreme Court agreed with the Third Circuit. In an opinion for the six-member majority, Justice Ginsburg acknowledged the problem the District Court faced. However, the Court said, Rule 23 still requires that "common questions" of fact or law "predominate." A shared interest in getting compensation does not, by itself, satisfy the predominance requirement. In the proposed settlement class, issues of both liability and injury were so diverse as to make the class too "sprawling" to certify. The plaintiffs could not represent the class adequately because conflicts of interest within the class abounded. People sick today would want more of the settlement to go to them than to have it saved for future victims, for example. Indeed, the Court found it hard to imagine how future claimants could receive adequate notice and have a basis to decide whether to opt-out of a class of people who did not know they had been injured.[2]

2. Assume that the class action will be governed by Federal Rule 23, subsection (e) of which provides that a class action "shall not be dismissed or compromised without the approval of the court. * * *" Must you warn your client that if you file as a class action, it will no longer be in his discretion when to settle out of court and on what terms?

a. What would you be required to do if you were to represent a number of similarly situated people in other than a class action, and if the defendant proposed an aggregate settlement—a single sum to cover the losses of all of them—an independently-tailored award for this client might not be possible either. See Model Rule 1.8(g).

2. Justices Breyer and Stevens dissented, arguing that the interest in achieving some settlement of this intractable controversy was greater than the court acknowledged. Justice O'Connor did not participate in the decision.

The Amchem case has not completely ended the use of settlement classes, at least if they do not present the case management problems that Amchem involved. See, e.g., Hanlon v. Chrysler Corp., 150 F.3d 1011 (9th Cir. 1998) (class of owners of minivans with defective latches; all death and personal injury victims' cases excluded from class to be sure issues common to all cases).

b.   Assume that the client you have picked—when told of the difficulties of a class action for damages—decides that he wants you to file suit only in his individual capacity. May you "fire" that client and pick another? Is a class action filed for the benefit of the named client, you the lawyer, or the class? Does the rhetoric fit the reality in all cases?

c.   Suppose the landlord whom you have chosen to sue is a major property owner in the community. He offers to settle the case for five times the actual damages of your client or a total of $125, if your client refrains from filing the class action. May you permit your client to settle on that basis? May you ethically refuse to do so? Note that since you have not yet filed the class action, Rule 23(e), quoted above, has not yet formally come into play.

3.   Now assume that you have filed a class action on behalf of construction workers seeking to require the city to institute an affirmative action program for its construction work. City officials are anxious to settle but they do not like the named plaintiff. The city proposes to settle the class action and offers a reasonable affirmative action program for all construction workers, but informs you orally that it will never employ the named plaintiff. As counsel to the entire class, may you—must you—urge acceptance of the plan? What, if anything, should or must you tell the named plaintiff?

a.   Parker v. Anderson, 667 F.2d 1204 (5th Cir.1982), alleged employment discrimination at Bell Helicopter. Class counsel negotiated a settlement worth about $2.5 million, a sum the district court found fair. The named plaintiffs, however, demanded personal payments of up to $100,000 each, and objected when told the proposed settlement would give each much less. The Fifth Circuit affirmed approval of the settlement over the named plaintiffs' objections. "The courts have recognized that the duty owed by class counsel is to the entire class and is not dependent on the special desires of the named plaintiffs," the court said. " * * * [T]he named plaintiffs should not be permitted to hold the absentee class hostage by refusing to assent to an otherwise fair and adequate settlement in order to secure their individual demands." 667 F.2d at 1211

b.   In Blanchard v. EdgeMark Financial Corp., 175 F.R.D. 293 (N.D.Ill.1997), the named plaintiff retained a second lawyer to conduct settlement negotiations of his individual claims. Class counsel sat silent and then proposed to look for a new named plaintiff. The court found that in settling separately, the named plaintiff had violated his fiduciary obligation to the class, and defense counsel had violated Model Rule 4.2 by even talking to the named plaintiff while he was still represented by class counsel. The court forced the named plaintiff to pay attorneys fees and costs of the class created by the litigation over what he had done.

c.   In Lazy Oil Co. v. Witco Corp., 166 F.3d 581 (3d Cir.1999), as well, the named plaintiff objected to the settlement. This time, it tried to disqualify class counsel who wanted to defend the settlement, arguing that the objection rendered class counsel adverse to its former client. The Third

Circuit wrote: "If, by applying the usual rules on attorney-client relations, class counsel could easily be disqualified in these cases, not only would the objectors enjoy great 'leverage,' but many fair and reasonable settlements would be undermined by the need to find substitute counsel after months or even years of fruitful settlement negotiations." 166 F.3d at 589. Absent a finding of "actual prejudice," class counsel may and should remain in the case to conclude the settlement.

C.   LIMITATIONS ON ADVANCING FUNDS NEEDED TO MEET EXPENSES OF LITIGATION

1.   This Problem says your law suit will require a large amount of professional survey work and your named client has no funds with which to pay for it. Should you be able to advance the funds necessary to do that work?

a.   Look at ABA Model Rule 1.8(e). What could possibly be the rationale for forbidding your providing help to a client in need? Restatement Third, The Law Governing Lawyers § 36(2), Comment *c*, says that advancing funds to a client "gives the lawyer the conflicting role of a creditor and could induce the lawyer to conduct the litigation so as to protect the lawyer's interests rather than the client's." See also, Comment [10] to Model Rule 1.8. Are you convinced?

b.   Model Rule 1.8(e)(1) creates an exception for litigation expenses and court costs. Why don't those expenses equally make the lawyer a creditor of the client? In both cases, might the fact that repayment will be "contingent on the outcome of the matter" tend to encourage a lawyer to try to settle a case for a sum certain rather than taking the matter to trial where the client might recover more but the expenses advanced by the lawyer would be at risk?

c.   If the suit is a class action, should a different rule apply? Rand v. Monsanto Co., 926 F.2d 596 (7th Cir.1991), was a securities class action. The District Court denied class certification when the named plaintiff refused to be personally liable for all costs of litigation. The District Court said letting the lawyer advance the expenses violated the local rule counterpart to Model Rule 1.8(e), but the Seventh Circuit reversed. Almost by definition, a class members has a small personal claim, Judge Easterbrook wrote. "A conscientious plaintiff is likely to be willing to make some financial commitment to the case. But no person need be willing to stake his entire fortune for the benefit of strangers." 926 F.2d at 599. DR 5-103(B), the predecessor to Model Rule 1.8(e), is "long in the tooth", he said, a "relic of the rules against champerty and barratry," and inconsistent with Federal Rule 23. Do you agree?

2.   Should you be permitted to you pay your client an allowance for living expenses during the pendency of a case?

a.   The traditional answer has been no. In State of Oklahoma v. Smolen, 17 P.3d 456 (Okla.2000), a lawyer loaned his worker's compensation client $1200 for living expenses after the client's house burned down.

The client agreed to pay the loan back at a rate of $100 per month out of the benefits received in the case. Because the court knew the lawyer had made similar loans to other clients, it was concerned that new clients might choose counsel based on "improper inducements" and suspended him from practice for six months.

b. In Cleveland Bar Ass'n v. Nusbaum, 753 N.E.2d 183 (Ohio 2001), the lawyer was publicly censured for advancing $26,000 in living expenses to a client who was also a friend. The client was out of work and undergoing twenty operations to deal with his injuries. Do you agree that such loans represent a decline in professional standards of the bar? Is it naive to suggest that these cases show that some lawyers retain human compassion?

c. The reporters for the Restatement Third, The Law Governing Lawyers originally suggested in § 36(2), Comment c, that the law should be understood to permit such support, at least where the loan would permit the client "to withstand delay in litigation that otherwise might unjustly induce the client to settle or dismiss a case because of financial hardship rather than on the merits." The ALI membership voted down that proposal, however, after an impassioned appeal that support would be offered by lawyers who were less than scrupulous, thus putting honorable lawyers at a competitive disadvantage. Would you have been moved by that appeal?

d. The law may be becoming more flexible on this issue. Shade v. Great Lakes Dredge & Dock Co., 72 F.Supp.2d 518 (E.D.Pa.1999), was a Jones Act case where the defendant tried to disqualify plaintiff's counsel because counsel paid the plaintiff's apartment rent after the plaintiff lost his house, his job, and his wife was injured as well. After discussing what, if any, continuing justification Rule 1.8(e) might have, the court concluded that the payments would not have an improper effect on the litigation. Discipline, not disqualification, was the way to deal with any violation.

e. Osprey v. Cabana Limited Partnership, 532 S.E.2d 269 (S.C.2000), involved an even more radical approach. When the plaintiff in a lender liability action was short on funds to pay legal bills, the Osprey company loaned it $50,000 and bought "an interest in said lawsuit." Osprey was to get the first $150,000 of any judgment. The case settled for $650,000 and Osprey sought to enforce its claim. The borrower's defense was that the contract constituted common law champerty and thus was void. The court traced the history of champerty back to medieval times[3] and concluded by holding that it would abolish champerty as a defense in the state. Contracts such as the one in this case could be examined as to unconscionability, duress, and fair dealing, the court said, but there was no longer any reason to forbid such contracts per se.

---

3. "[P]ut simply, maintenance is helping another prosecute a suit; champerty is maintaining a suit in return for a financial interest in the outcome; and barratry is a continuing practice of maintenance or champerty." In re Primus, 436 U.S. 412, 424 n. 15, 98 S.Ct. 1893, 1900 n. 15, 56 L.Ed.2d 417, 429 n. 15.

f.   How would you recommend that the issue of loans to clients be resolved? Would you require that all such loans must be repaid? If a lawyer may waive payment of fees even if the case is successfully resolved, why should he or she not be permitted to waive repayment of expenses?

3.   Are the same issues raised if the case also needs the aid of an expert witness and the clients are too poor to hire one? Should you be able to hire the expert witness and make his or her fee contingent on the outcome of the case?

a.   Look at Model Rule 3.4(b). The prohibition of the payment of contingent fees to expert witnesses was attacked in Person v. Association of the Bar of the City of New York, 554 F.2d 534 (2d Cir.1977), cert. denied 434 U.S. 924, 98 S.Ct. 403, 54 L.Ed.2d 282 (1977). The district court struck down the prohibition, but the Court of Appeals reversed, reasoning:

> "States have a compelling interest in regulating the conduct of professionals who practice within their borders. * * * Expert testimony, by its very nature, concerns areas of knowledge with which the ordinary juror and the court are unfamiliar, and perjured expert testimony is particularly difficult for a juror to detect. New York has adopted DR 7–109(C) to lesser the likelihood of false expert testimony. * * *

> "We hold that [the prohibition] has a sufficient rational basis to withstand a constitutional challenge under the equal protection and due process clauses of the fourteenth amendment." 554 F.2d at 538–39.

b.   Is the policy behind the prohibition persuasive to you? Look at Comment [3] to Model Rule 3.4.[4]

D.   CALCULATING FEES FOR PREVAILING IN A CLASS ACTION OR CIVIL RIGHTS CASE

1.   Who should bear attorneys' fees in a class action and civil rights case?

a.   Most non class action, non civil rights cases in this country follow what is called the American Rule; all parties in litigation bear their own costs and attorneys' fees. However, courts have the power to award attorney fees in certain classes of cases.

(1) The "common fund doctrine" says that when the plaintiff's class action creates a fund of money to be distributed to members of the class, the court may allow court costs, other expenses, and counsel

---

4.   First National Bank of Springfield v. Malpractice Research, Inc., 688 N.E.2d 1179 (Ill.1997), makes a simple but important point. Just as a lawyer may not hire an expert on a contingent fee basis, the lawyer may not pay a firm on a contingent basis to procure an expert either. The contingent payment would create an incentive to find an expert who could be "coached," which is why the courts have denied contingent fees to experts themselves.

fees to be paid out of the fund on the theory that those who have benefitted from the fund should pay for the legal services rendered.

(2) Other times, Congress by statute may require the losing party to pay the winner's legal fees, for example, where the plaintiff is treated as a private attorney general vindicating public rights. The lawyer is said to have conferred a benefit upon the public, even if that benefit is not monetary.

(3) Congress has also authorized attorneys' fees in civil rights cases. 42 U.S.C. § 1988 provides that "the court, in its discretion, may allow the prevailing party, other than the United States, a reasonable attorney's fee as part of the costs" in "any action or proceeding" to enforce civil rights laws such as 42 U.S.C. §§ 1981–86, 20 U.S.C. § 1681 et seq., and 42 U.S.C. § 20004 et seq.

b.   The fact that plaintiff is represented free of charge by a nonprofit group, does not preclude the plaintiff from collecting attorneys' fees based on the rates charged by private counsel for the same kind of work. Blum v. Stenson, 465 U.S. 886, 104 S.Ct. 1541, 79 L.Ed.2d 891 (1984). However, a lawyer may not recover attorneys' fees under § 1988 when the lawyer appears pro se. Kay v. Ehrler, 499 U.S. 432, 111 S.Ct. 1435, 113 L.Ed.2d 486 (1991),

c.   In Doe v. Board of Education, 165 F.3d 260 (4th Cir.1998), cert. denied 526 U.S. 1159, 119 S.Ct. 2049, 144 L.Ed.2d 216 (1999), a suit under the Individuals with Disabilities Education Act, the lawyer was the child's father. The court held that *Kay* controlled the result. Granting fees was not necessary to encourage a parent to fight for his child, the court said, and rather than encouraging inexperienced parents to bring cases in the hope of a fee award, the Court denied these fees. See also Kooritzky v. Herman, 178 F.3d 1315 (D.C.Cir.1999) (lawyer appearing pro se not entitled to claim "costs" for his own work as an "expert" in the case).[5]

2.   What kind of relief should be required before a person should be considered a "prevailing party" for purposes of an attorney's fee award?

a.   Hensley v. Eckerhart, 461 U.S. 424, 433, 103 S.Ct. 1933, 1939, 76 L.Ed.2d 40, 50 (1983), quoted a "typical" statement of the prevailing party principle to be: "plaintiffs may be considered 'prevailing parties' for attorney's fees purposes if they succeed on any significant issue in litigation which achieves some of the benefit the parties sought in bringing suit." The Court described this as a "generous formulation." Id.

---

5.   However, Gilbert v. Master Washer & Stamping Co., Inc., 104 Cal.Rptr.2d 461 (Cal.Ct.App.2001), holds that under California law an attorney who is represented by his own law firm may collect reasonable attorney's fees. If the lawyer had represented himself, he would not have been entitled to attorneys' fees at all, but because he was represented by others in his law firm, he got them. The court further said that the fees need not be limited to amounts actually paid by the lawyer; the trial court may assess the fees the firm would have charged an outside client.

b.   However, Buckhannon Board & Care Home v. West Virginia Dept. of Health, 532 U.S. 598, 121 S.Ct. 1835, 149 L.Ed.2d 855 (2001), considered whether the term "prevailing party" applies to someone who did not secure a judgment on the merits but achieved a desired result by another means. Buckhannon sued the state health department claiming that its requirement that residents all be capable of "self-preservation" violated the Fair Housing Amendments Act of 1988. After discovery had begun, the state legislature eliminated the requirement and the case was dismissed as moot. Buckhannon then sought an attorney's fee as the "prevailing party" under the FHAA, arguing based on the "catalyst theory" that a plaintiff is a prevailing party if it achieves a desired result through a voluntary change in the defendant's conduct. Several courts of appeals had adopted that theory, but the Supreme Court rejected it, saying that the catalyst theory "allows an award where there is no judicially sanctioned change in the legal relationship of the parties." 532 U.S. at 605, 121 S.Ct. at 1840, 149 L.Ed.2d at 863. Therefore, it is not a basis for the award of attorney's fees.[6]

c.   The *Buckhannon* decision has now rippled through the federal courts under a number of important federal statutes. Oil, Chemical and Atomic Workers International Union, AFL–CIO v. Department of Energy, 288 F.3d 452 (D.C.Cir.2002), for example, applied it to deny fees under the Freedom of Information Act where the government ultimately turned over the requested documents before a court ordered it to do so.

d.   Brickwood Contractors, Inc. v. United States, 288 F.3d 1371 (Fed. Cir.2002), applied *Buckhannon* to the Equal Access to Justice Act and denied fees where the government withdrew a bid solicitation with the result that the plaintiff's bid protest was dismissed by the Court of Federal Claims without reaching the merits.[7]

e.   What do you think of the *Buckhannon* approach to deciding who has prevailed in a matter? Will lawyers be as willing to bring cases if they know government officials can avoid paying them simply by changing the challenged policy shortly before entry of a decree? Is deterrence of such cases a good thing? Does the ability to have the other side pay the fees tend to create an excessive incentive to bring litigation?

3.   How should the amount of appropriate attorneys fees be calculated?

a.   In determining attorneys fees under 42 U.S.C. § 1988, the Supreme Court said in Hensley v. Eckerhart, 461 U.S. 424, 433, 103 S.Ct.

6.   Justices Scalia and Thomas wrote a concurring opinion. Justice Ginsburg, in an opinion for herself and Justices Stevens, Souter and Breyer, dissented, saying that requiring a "document filed in court" before a plaintiff can be said to "prevail" is not required by the statutory language and will impair the enforcement of civil rights.

7.   See also, Smyth v. Rivero, 282 F.3d 268 (4th Cir.2002) (getting preliminary in-junction against policy doesn't make one a prevailing party under AFDC statute where the government changed policy before a final judgment entered). But see Loggerhead Turtle v. County Council of Volusia County, 307 F.3d 1318 (11th Cir.2002) (*Buckhannon* does not limit grant of attorneys' fees under Endangered Species Act allowing award of fees "where appropriate").

1933, 1939, 76 L.Ed.2d 40, 50 (1983), that the "most useful starting point" is to take the "number of hours reasonably expended on the litigation multiplied by a reasonable hourly rate. This calculation provides an objective basis on which to make an initial estimate of the value of a lawyer's services." This figure is often called the lodestar.

b. Citing Blum v. Stenson, 465 U.S. 886, 104 S.Ct. 1541, 79 L.Ed.2d 891 (1984), the court in Central States Pension Fund v. Central Cartage Co., 76 F.3d 114 (7th Cir.1996), held that the appropriate value to be placed on legal services rendered by in-house counsel is the going rate in the market, regardless of where the client actually turned for legal help. Raney v. Federal Bureau of Prisons, 222 F.3d 927 (Fed.Cir.2000), similarly held that market rates were to be the basis for calculating fees when the litigant was represented by a union lawyer.[8]

c. But the "going rate" for legal services can vary. Davis County Solid Waste Management District v. Environmental Protection Agency, 169 F.3d 755 (D.C.Cir.1999), was tried in the District of Columbia, but most of the work was done by Salt Lake City firms in Utah where legal fees are lower. The Court said the Utah rates should be used because "it produces a result that better reflects the purpose of fee shifting statutes," i.e., to enable parties to get legal help. Davis County could hire lawyers at local rates, the Court reasoned, so those lawyers should not be able to charge D.C. rates. Parties from markets with lawyer rates even higher than those in D.C. should similarly be able to collect at the higher rates.

d. Mahoney v. Pataki, 772 N.E.2d 1118 (N.Y.2002), in turn, asked what fees could properly be included among reimbursable attorneys' fees in capital cases. It held that the time of reasonably necessary paralegals should be included. Prior to this opinion, the state had only been willing to reimburse the time of lead and associate counsel, but the court found it had inherent power to interpret the reimbursement statute more broadly.

4. Would it ever be appropriate to calculate the fee as if it were a contingent fee, i.e., as a percentage of the sum recovered?

a. Swedish Hospital Corp. v. Shalala, 1 F.3d 1261 (D.C.Cir.1993) examined when fees should be set as a percentage of the "common fund" recovery instead of the lodestar method. The class action had recovered $27.8 million for a group of hospitals. The court found a percentage fee appropriate; such a fee reduces the lawyer's incentive for inefficiency and "more accurately reflects the economics of litigation practice." The court approved setting the percentage at 20% but applied it only to the portion of the recovery that reflected the lawyers efforts. Because that portion was found to have been $10 million (the government had conceded the rest), the fee was set at $2 million.

---

8. In State of Wisconsin v. Hotline Industries, 236 F.3d 363 (7th Cir.2000), however, a statute only allowed payment of "actual" attorney's fees and the lawyers used were salaried government attorneys. Because the statute limits fee awards to "actual outlays," not "reasonable" fees, the court said, the State was entitled only to a proportional share of the salaries of its attorneys plus related overhead costs.

b. Welch & Forbes, Inc. v. Cendant Corp. (In re Cendant Corp. Prides Litigation), 243 F.3d 722 (3d Cir.2001), also found that a percentage-fee arrangement would be more appropriate than the lodestar method. The court set out seven factors to consider in deciding what is a reasonable percentage fee award in common fund cases: (1) the complexity and duration of litigation; (2) the range of percentage awards in other cases, (3) the absolute size of other fee awards, (4) how much a percentage award would exceed a lodestar approach, (5) the presence or absence of substantial objections by members of the class to the settlement terms or fees requested by counsel, (6) the skill and efficiency of the attorneys involved, and (7) the amount of time that counsel devoted to the case. In this case, the 3d Circuit found that the trial court abused its discretion when it award a fee (5.7% of the $341 million recovery) that was out of proportion to (i.e. 7 times) what the lodestar approach would have yielded. The case was neither legally nor factually complex, and the entire duration of the case was only four months.

c. Matter of Synthroid Marketing Litigation, 264 F.3d 712 (7th Cir. 2001), involved a district court limiting attorney's fees to 10% of the settlement amount, citing cases that said 10% represented the upper limit in cases with a "megafund" settlement greater than $75 million. In an opinion by Judge Easterbrook, however, the Seventh Circuit overturned the court's award, observing that the Seventh Circuit has tried to make court awards simulate the market price for legal services. The court suggested several ways in which private parties might determine fees in advance, while preserving incentives for the attorney's to act in the best interest of their clients. They might set a declining marginal fee rate as the level of recovery increased. They might take account of the risk of non-payment. Some rates might be set in a competitive bidding process. The court argued that the flat 10% rate applied in this case for cases over $75 million would create illogical distinctions in the amount attorneys earned for settlements that were relatively close in value (e.g., a settlement of $74 million versus one of $76 million). Indeed, the rule would discourage counsel from obtaining settlements above the "megafund" threshold amount.[9]

d. Vizcaino v. Microsoft Corp., 290 F.3d 1043 (9th Cir.2002), on the other hand, expressly rejected the Seventh Circuit's effort to simulate a market-based determination of fees. In upholding an attorney's fee of 28% of the settlement, or over $27 million, the court noted that the case was "extremely risky" and the lawyers had achieved "exceptional results" for the class. The court also used a lodestar calculation as a cross-check of the reasonableness of the fee and found that at normal hourly rates, the fee would have come to less than $7.4 million. In this case, however, the court found a multiplier of 3.65 to be justified.

9. On remand, the district court, 201 F.Supp.2d 861 (N.D.Ill.2002), awarded counsel for the consumer class about 15% of the amount recovered, calculated as 30% of the first $10 million, 25% of the second $10 million, etc., down to 10% of the remainder. This award was based on the range of bids in similar cases, the risk assumed (high) and the relative productivity of the lawyers (low).

e. How would you go about assessing an appropriate fee in such cases? Is there any wholly objective method for doing so? Might some methods tend to create greater incentives for lawyers to place their own interest in collecting a fee above the interest of the class in getting appropriate relief?

5. Might fee provisions in some statutes ever be so low as to be unconstitutional?

a. Boivin v. Black, 225 F.3d 36 (1st Cir.2000), illustrates how arbitrary fee calculation methods can seem to be. The lawyer represented a pretrial detainee who sued a correctional officer for locking him in a restraint chair and impairing his breathing. The jury agreed this conduct violated the plaintiff's constitutional rights but awarded only $1 in nominal damages. The Prison Litigation Reform Act limited the fee award to 150% of the sum recovered or $1.50, while a time-based award would have yielded close to $3,900. The district judge awarded the higher fee, but the First Circuit upheld the fee cap. Lawyers usually do not recover attorneys' fees in litigation at all, the court said; they are paid by the client out of the amount recovered or other funds, so any fee award is better than none. Further, Congress wanted to discourage frivolous suits by prisoners, the court reasoned; it had a legitimate interest in not encouraging litigation where damages were nominal, so the fee limitation did not offend the Fifth Amendment. Hadix v. Johnson, 230 F.3d 840 (6th Cir.2000), and Madrid v. Gomez, 190 F.3d 990 (9th Cir.1999), reached the same conclusion.

b. But in Johnson v. Daley, 117 F.Supp.2d 889 (W.D.Wis.2000), a lone district judge conceded that three courts of appeal had upheld the statute but disagreed and held that the cap violates equal protection because, in her view, there is no non-invidious basis for distinguishing prisoner litigation from other civil rights cases in which fees are not capped.

c. How would you decide this issue? Do you think it is appropriate for Congress to set fee caps so low that most lawyers would be discouraged from taking particular kinds of cases?

6. How should a lawyer respond when presented with a settlement under which the defense has made a good offer to the class but an offer of low or no attorneys' fees? Does that create a conflict of interest between the class and its counsel? What should a court do about that conflict?

a. In Evans v. Jeff D., 475 U.S. 717, 106 S.Ct. 1531, 89 L.Ed.2d 747 (1986), the Court held that a judge in a class action may approve a class settlement even if it is conditioned on the waiver of attorney's fees authorized by statute. In *Jeff D.*, plaintiffs filed a class action to improve conditions of institutionalized handicapped children in Idaho. As part of the settlement agreement, the plaintiffs' lawyers (a public interest law firm) stipulated they would waive attorneys' fees, but only if the court approved. The Ninth Circuit recognized the strong principle in favor of settlements but said that the defendants could not force the plaintiffs to waive statutory attorneys' fees. The district court, said the Ninth Circuit, should have determined what reasonable fees should be in a case like this.

The Supreme Court, however, reversed. In a 6 to 3 opinion written by Justice Stevens, the Court held that the question "derives ultimately from the Fees Act rather than from the strictures of professional ethics." The lawyer had said the tension between a good settlement for the class and a good fee for the public interest law firm put him in an "ethical dilemma." The Court reasoned, however, that the attorney "had no *ethical* obligation to seek a statutory fee award. His ethical duty was to serve his clients loyally and competently. Since the proposal to settle on the merits was more favorable than the probable outcome of the trial, [the attorneys'] decision to recommend acceptance was consistent with the highest standards of our profession. The district court, therefore, correctly concluded that approval of the settlement involved no breach of ethics in this case." 475 U.S. at 728, 106 S.Ct. at 1537–38, 89 L.Ed.2d at 758 (emphasis in original).

Justices Brennan, Marshall and Blackmun, dissented, concerned that the Court's result would likely lead to fewer civil rights actions being brought because lawyers would be uncertain about getting their fees. Do you agree?

b.   In Bernhardt v. County of Los Angeles, 279 F.3d 862 (9th Cir. 2002), the plaintiff complained that the defendant's policy of settling civil rights claims with a lump sum payment that included all attorney's fees meant that she had not been able to find a lawyer. The Ninth Circuit acknowledged that *Evans v. Jeff D.* had upheld a settlement that required waiver of statutory attorney's fees, but it noted that *Evans* specifically recognized that a settlement agreement might be challenged if 1) a government implemented a "statute, policy, or practice" of requiring waiver of attorney's fees in settlement agreements, 2) the settling party required fee waivers as part of a "vindictive effort to deter attorneys from representing plaintiffs in civil rights suits," or 3) such settlement agreements had the overall effect of reducing the number of attorneys willing to accept civil rights claims. The 9th Circuit held that Bernhardt had standing to press her claim. The court dismissed Bernhardt's claim for prospective relief, because her underlying civil rights claim had already been dismissed, but the court observed that Bernhardt might be able to obtain nominal damages based on her inability to obtain counsel in the dismissed case.

c.   Similarly, Johnson v. District of Columbia, 190 F.Supp.2d 34 (D.D.C.2002), refused to dismiss the complaint of a handicapped child and his mother suing the District of Columbia Public Schools (DCPS) under the Individuals with Disabilities Education Act (IDEA). The court found that the defendant's policy of only settling cases on the condition that the plaintiff waive attorneys' fees stated a cause of action for denial of the right to counsel and was not justified by the *Buckhannon* decision, supra.

d.   Bar opinions have consistently said that it is unethical for defense counsel to submit a settlement offer to the plaintiff conditioned on an agreement to waive or limit attorneys fees. E.g., D.C. Bar Ethics Opinion

147 (Jan. 22, 1985); Committee on Professional and Judicial Ethics of the New York City Bar Association, Opinion No. 80–94 ("Defense Counsel * * * are in a uniquely favorable position when they condition settlement on the waiver of the statutory fee: they make a demand for a benefit which the plaintiff's lawyer cannot resist as a matter of ethics and which the plaintiff will not resist due to lack of interest."); Grievance Commission of Board of Overseers of the Bar of Maine, Advisory Opinion No. 17 (1983).

What role should such opinions have in cases like those cited? Do *Jeff D.* and the other cases address the ethical obligations of defense counsel at all?

7.   Can counsel in class action and civil rights cases protect themselves against defense efforts like the ones just described?

a.   *Jeff D.* acknowledged that the client's eligibility for fees from the losing party is a different question than the fee agreement between the lawyer and his or her client. In Blanchard v. Bergeron, 489 U.S. 87, 109 S.Ct. 939, 103 L.Ed.2d 67 (1989), the lawyer and client had negotiated a contingent fee of 40% of any recovery. The amount recovered was $10,000 so the contract fee was $4,000. The Supreme Court unanimously held, however, that under 42 U.S.C.A. § 1988, the contingent fee agreement does not define or impose a limit upon the amount that the defendant can be required to pay; that amount should instead be set by the lodestar method.

b.   Later, in Venegas v. Mitchell, 495 U.S. 82, 110 S.Ct. 1679, 109 L.Ed.2d 74 (1990), plaintiff and attorney again had entered into a contingent fee contract that provided that the attorney would receive 40% of the gross amount of recovery. Any court awarded fee would be applied, dollar for dollar, to offset the contingent fee. A unanimous Court held that § 1988 does not prevent a lawyer from collecting a reasonable contingent fee even if it *exceeds* the statutory fee award. "[N]either *Blanchard* nor any other of our cases has indicated that § 1988, by it own force, protects plaintiffs from having to pay what they have contracted to pay, even though their contractual liability is greater than the statutory award that they may collect from losing opponents." Section 1988 "controls what the losing defendant must pay, not what the prevailing plaintiff must pay his lawyer." 495 U.S. at 89–90, 110 S.Ct. at 1684, 109 L.Ed.2d at 84.

c.   In light of *Blanchard* and *Venegas,* should class action and civil rights lawyers arrange fees by contract and not rely exclusively on a later court award? If lawyers protected themselves in advance by such arrangements, would a settlement for a lump sum that includes attorneys' fees—or a sum that purports to deny such fees—be unfair or improper after all? Might lawyers feel awkward about negotiating such contracts with their clients in cases where fee shifting was supposed to be the rule?

d.   In Uy v. Bronx Municipal Hospital Center, 182 F.3d 152 (2d Cir.1999), an attorney had been retained to represent a plaintiff in an employment discrimination action. During the case, the judge removed him as counsel and appointed a larger firm. The parties then settled for $35,000. At the end of the trial, the lawyer sought a large award of fees pursuant to 42 U.S.C. § 1988 for the work he had done. Rather than award him fees, the district court ruled that sums already paid to the attorney by the plaintiff were unreasonable. The lawyer had received over $43,000 under his contract with the plaintiff, while the trial judge's lodestar calculation justified only $14,200. The Second Circuit held that the district judge could not order a refund of the privately contracted fee. The judge's calculation of a reasonable fee award is not controlling.

Do you agree with this result? If the judge makes the defendant pay the $14,200 that she thinks is fair, should that sum go to the plaintiff or the lawyer?

8. Fee shifting statutes also raise questions of proportionality. If a successful plaintiff can shift the fee to defendant, might there be reason for concern that cases will be brought in which the plaintiff's lawyer has a greater interest in the outcome of the case than the plaintiff does?

a. In Riverside v. Rivera, 477 U.S. 561, 106 S.Ct. 2686, 91 L.Ed.2d 466 (1986), the Supreme Court considered whether attorneys' fees in a civil rights action must be "proportional" to the amount recovered. Two lawyers had recovered $33,350 in damages for a Mexican–American family in a suit against the police department resulting from arrests made at a party. Based on the almost 2,000 hours the lawyers claimed to have worked on the case, the fee award came to $245,456.

In a 5 to 4 decision with no majority opinion, the Supreme Court upheld the fee. The plurality of Justices Brennan, Marshall, Blackmun and Stevens, reasoned that civil rights litigation often produces nonpecuniary benefits. "A rule of proportionality would make it difficult, if not impossible, for individuals with meritorious civil rights claims but relatively small potential damages to obtain redress from the courts." 477 U.S. at 578, 106 S.Ct. at 2696, 91 L.Ed.2d at 482. It was sufficient for these justices that the District Court had found that the case served the public interest and that the hours invested were not inflated.

The dissenting justices cast doubt on the hourly rate claimed by two attorneys only briefly out of law school and questioned whether lawyers should be encouraged to expend time so far beyond a case's economic value. Justice Powell concurred in the judgment but said: "It will probably be the rare case in which an award of private damages can be said to benefit the public interest to an extent that would justify the disproportionality between damages and fees reflected in this case. 477 U.S. at 586 n. 3, 106 S.Ct. at 2700 n. 4, 91 L.Ed.2d at 487 n. 4.

Who had the better of the argument? Why? Is the underlying reality that *many* actions in which fees will be shifted seem to be brought more for the benefit of the lawyers than the clients?

b. In Brandau v. State of Kansas, 168 F.3d 1179 (10th Cir.1999), the plaintiff in a sexual harassment case based on an allegedly hostile environment won a verdict but was only awarded damages of $1. Her attorneys, however, received fees of over $41,500. The Court held that proportionality is not the issue. The plaintiff won her case and changed the practices of her employer. That result justified the lawyers' compensation.

c.   In Kaplan v. Rand, 192 F.3d 60 (2d Cir.1999), on the other hand, after another firm had settled a class action against Texaco and obtained relief for African American workers, this suit was filed against Texaco directors for letting things get bad enough to justify the earlier suit. The case was settled with an agreement that Texaco put a statement of its tolerance objectives in every contract and that, on request, stockholders could get reports of the company's affirmative action efforts. For achieving that victory, the district court awarded the lawyers $1 million in fees and expenses. On appeal, the Second Circuit found the shareholders got no realistic benefit from the settlement and that counsel was entitled to no fee at all.

d.   Can the proportionality issue create its own conflicts problem? Suppose the defendant offers to pay the class only a nominal amount but agrees to pay a generous fee to the lawyer?

Cal Pak Delivery, Inc. v. United Parcel Service, 60 Cal.Rptr.2d 207 (Cal.Ct.App.1997), was a class action alleging that UPS had overcharged its customers. The lawyer for the class had already lost a similar case before the state Public Utilities Commission. The lawyer told UPS he would take $8 to $10 million for himself to settle the class action and give the class nothing. UPS responded with a motion to disqualify the lawyer from representing the class. The court found this to be "a direct, acknowledged, undisputed and indefensible betrayal by counsel of the interests of his client and the putative class." 60 Cal.Rptr.2d at 214. It affirmed the lawyer's disqualification.

e.   How do you believe issues of fee proportionality issues should be handled by the courts? Do you believe courts are well equipped to tell the time spent achieving nonpecuniary benefits for the client class from time spent primarily to justify a high fee award?

PROBLEM 37

THE FUTURE OF THE PRACTICE OF LAW

Will law forever be practiced only by lawyers licensed in individual states and working in traditional law firms? We cannot be sure what the future holds, but a formidable challenge to the present system began in Europe where lawyers may practice across national borders and world-wide accounting firms hold themselves out as providing clients with lawyers in addition to business advise and auditing services. Most of the issues raised by the new service providers, however, transcend competition from large accounting firms. They go to issues of delivering services to ordinary Americans, many of whom are underserved today. That is the context in which this Problem introduces the issues. First, it looks at the concept of unauthorized practice, the principle that reserves legal work to lawyers. Next, it considers jurisdictional limits on a lawyer's practice. Next, it considers the prohibition of a corporation's delivering legal services, and finally, it examines how law firm themselves are offering non-traditional services that are said to be "ancillary" to their regular practice.

FACTS

Victor Dowd is an attorney who believes that persons of even relatively modest means should plan their estates better than they do. He also believes that many people are afraid of the expense of estate planning by present methods of private law practice.

Dowd knows that, even now, financial planners and insurance agents are counseling their clients about basic estate planning issues. He proposes to help them do so more effectively. As another step toward making estate planning available to persons with small estates, Dowd proposes to publish do-it-yourself kits both for planning and administration. He plans to sell these kits only in states for which they have been fully verified as to legal accuracy. The forms and instructions are to be carefully prepared and there is no reason to question the ability of an ordinarily intelligent person, perhaps assisted by a financial planner, to follow them step by step and handle a completely routine case.

A nationwide insurance company thinks Dowd is on to something and has offered to refer its customers to him for preparation of a basic will. The clients might come from any state in the country. Dowd agrees to draft a basic will and any other necessary simple documents for a fee of $225. The fee will be paid to him directly by the insurance agency as part of the $399 fee it charges for its own "complete financial planning services."

Now, Dowd proposes to create an estate planning subsidiary that will work out of his law offices, and employ financial planners and insurance agents. The subsidiary plans to offer a complete package service in ten states consisting of planning before death and estate administration after. Dowd is admitted to practice in only one of those states. All participants will bill at a single hourly rate, no matter which type of specialty is involved. They propose to advertise the service with television commercials that say, "We've all got to go sometime. We might as well do it right."

QUESTIONS

A.   THE UNAUTHORIZED PRACTICE OF LAW

1.   What is the practice of law?

a.   Look at Model Rule 5.5, Comment [2]: "The definition of the practice of law is established by law and varies from one jurisdiction to another." Not much help there!

b. Restatement Third, The Law Governing Lawyers § 4, Comment *c*, is not much better: "The definitions and tests employed by courts to delineate unauthorized practice by nonlawyers have been vague or conclusory, while jurisdictions have differed significantly in describing what constitutes unauthorized practice in particular areas."

c. Perhaps the closest thing to an authoritative definition was provided in ABA Model Code of Professional Responsibility, EC 3–5: "[T]he practice of law relates to the rendition of services for others that call for the professional judgment of the lawyer * * * [consisting of the lawyer's] educated ability to relate the general body and philosophy of law to a specific legal problem of the client."

d. A draft report of an ABA Task Force charged to refine the definition further has suggested that:

"A person is presumed to be practicing law when engaging in any of the following conduct on behalf of another:

"(1) Giving advice or counsel to persons as to their legal rights or responsibilities or to those of others;

"(2) Selecting, drafting, or completing legal documents or agreements that affect the legal rights of a person;

"(3) Representing a person before an adjudicative body, including but not limited to, preparing or filing documents or conducting discovery; or

"(4) Negotiating legal rights or responsibilities on behalf of a person."[1]

e. After reading these definitions, do you know much more than you did before about whether the financial planners and insurance agents in this Problem will be engaged in the practice of law? Estate administration involves following prescribed procedures and filling out legal forms, for example, but are only lawyers capable of knowing how to do that?

2. Why does it matter what constitutes the practice of law?

a. In many states, engaging in the unauthorized practice of law is a crime, typically a misdemeanor. In other states, unauthorized practice is a contempt of court, i.e., engaging in an activity that only a court may license. Under either approach, the usual sanctions are fines and injunctions against further violations.

b. Defining the practice of law may also affect what conduct will expose you to liability for malpractice. When you umpire a children's baseball game, for example, if you make an error in interpreting the rules, it will make the other parents upset but not expose you to a suit for malpractice. When you make a mistake in work denominated the practice of law, however, your exposure to liability will be real.

---

1. ABA Task Force on the Model Definition of the Practice of Law, Draft Definition (Sept. 18, 2002).

c.   Whether the practice of law is involved may also affect whether the attorney-client privilege applies to what you hear. If you are a corporate director, for example, not everything you hear at a board meeting will be protected by the privilege. The privilege will cover only communications made to you in confidence for the purpose of getting legal advice.[2]

d.   Further, a person engaged in the unauthorized practice of law may not collect a fee as if the person were a lawyer. See, e.g., Patton v. Scholl, 1999 WL 431095 (E.D.Pa.1999), that enjoined the work of a "non-attorney bankruptcy preparer" and ordered the return of fees charged in what it held to be the unauthorized practice of law.

e.   Of particular importance to a lawyer's disciplinary exposure is Model Rule 5.5(b), which prohibits a lawyer from assisting a non-lawyer in the unauthorized practice of law. See also, Model Rule 5.4, which prohibits (a) sharing legal fees with a non-lawyer, and (b) forming a partnership with a non-lawyer where any of the firm's activities involve the practice of law.

3.   Does the insurance company program with which Dowd works involve him in assisting the unauthorized practice of law?

a.   Lawline v. American Bar Association, 956 F.2d 1378 (7th Cir.1992), was a suit by a group of lawyers, paralegals, and lay people who had organized a service to answer legal questions from the public over the phone. They had answered over 500,000 calls already. The group also made referrals to legal aid and to lawyers who would charge reduced fees. Their suit alleged that what are now ABA Model Rules 5.4(b) and 5.5(a) were both the product of an illegal conspiracy among lawyers to maintain traditional forms of practice and unconstitutional on their face. The Seventh Circuit affirmed dismissal of the action. The rules only had effect as adopted state supreme courts and thus were immune from antitrust challenge. Further, the rules rationally related to the goal of "safeguard[ing] the public, maintain[ing] the integrity of the profession, and protect[ing] the administration of justice from reproach." 956 F.2d at 1385. Do you agree?

b.   In Florida Bar v. Beach, 675 So.2d 106 (Fla.1996), attorney Beach had a contract with King and King Paralegals, a company that prepared and sold legal documents for consumers. For a flat fee of $75, Beach would review the documents King and King prepared and meet briefly with a King and King client, but clients agreed they had no lawyer-client relationship with Beach. In some cases, Beach met with King to discuss the client's matter but did not meet with the client at all. For assisting King and King to do legal work while unlicensed, the court suspended Beach for ninety days from the practice of law.

c.   The lawyer in Cincinnati Bar Association v. Kathman, 748 N.E.2d 1091 (Ohio 2001), worked as a "review attorney" for the Estate Preserva-

---

2.   On the other hand, if a person talks to someone that he or she reasonably believes is a lawyer, conversations with that person will be privileged even though the non-lawyer is engaged in the unauthorized practice of law. See Restatement Third, The Law Governing Lawyers § 72, Comment e.

tion Group (EPG), a company that sold insurance and living trusts. EPG clients, with the assistance of a non-lawyer, filled out a financial workbook describing their assets and disposition directives. The lawyer would then call the client, explain who he was, and direct EPG to prepare the client's documents. The client sent the fee of $1995 to the lawyer, who kept $200 and remitted the rest to EPG. The court found that the lawyer's actions were aiding the unauthorized practice of law by EPG. No client received the "carefully considered, independent advice" of a lawyer. The payment process constituted illegal fee-sharing with a non-lawyer. The court even held that the lawyer violated state rules against practicing under a trade name by including his name on the company's letterhead. The court suspended him from practice for six months.[3]

d.   Matter of Scott, 739 N.E.2d 658 (Ind.2000), warns about a different way of violating Model Rule 5.5(a). The respondent had hired a disbarred lawyer to assist him in developing his family law practice. Indiana law allows one to delegate functions to a disbarred lawyer as long as the lawyer is supervised and the licensed lawyer retains responsibility for all the work done. In this case, however, the court found that, although respondent claimed to be supervising the disbarred lawyer's work, what he really did was allow the disbarred lawyer to use his office to meet with and counsel people who came in for legal assistance. This action constituted assisting the unauthorized practice of law, so the court suspended the respondent from practice for 18 months.

4.   Should filling in the blanks on prepared forms constitute the practice of law?

a.   In perhaps the most prominent case on this issue, the Arizona Supreme Court held in State Bar of Arizona v. Arizona Land Title and Trust Company, 366 P.2d 1 (Ariz.1961), supplemented 371 P.2d 1020 (Ariz.1962), that real estate agents were engaged in the unauthorized practice of law when they helped buyers and sellers fill in the blanks on preprinted forms for use in real estate transactions. Arizona citizens responded with a ballot initiative that amended the state constitution and reversed the decision. See Arizona Constitution, art. 26, § 1.

b.   In Fifteenth Judicial District Unified Bar Association v. Glasgow, 1999 WL 1128847 (Tenn.App.1999), Ms. Glasgow was filling in the blanks on divorce forms for low income clients who would then represent themselves in court. She charged them a fee of from $99 to $148 and suggested where and "approximately" when the papers should be filed. She even prepared some quit claim deeds if they were necessary to divide real property. Ever vigilant, the Tennessee Bar sued to enjoin Ms. Glasgow's services, and the court complied. The applicable statute defines drafting "any paper, document or instrument affecting or relating to secular rights" as the practice of law, the court said; only lawyers may do that. The statute

---

3.   See also, Matter of Flack, 33 P.3d 1281 (Kan.2001), where a 6 month suspen-   sion was imposed on very similar facts.

is constitutional because "the practice of law by untrained persons endangers the public's personal and property rights, as well as the orderly administration of the judicial system."

Do you agree? Is the public entitled to have only high quality legal services? Should we be at all concerned whether Ms. Glasgow's clients could afford superior services?

c. Bray v. Brooks, 41 S.W.3d 7 (Mo.Ct.App.2001), involved a real estate broker who had helped a family sell a business. As part of the package of services for which he charged an 8% commission, he drafted a sales contract, a corporate resolution authorizing the sale of the corporate assets, a promissory note representing the deferred portion of the sales price, a security agreement for the promissory note, a real estate lease, and a covenant not to compete. Each document bore a legend, "If you do not understand [this document], consult an attorney." The court said that drafting documents constitutes the practice of law, and the evidence supported a finding that the agent was paid for it as part of his commission. However, the court did not award the plaintiffs the treble damages available under state statute because they could not show what portion of the commission was for the illegal activity.

5. Should Dowd's proposed sale of do-it-yourself kits constitute the unauthorized practice of law?

a. Are people likely to be misled by the kits into believing they have had all the legal advice that they need? Can a lay person tell whether he or she has a "completely routine case" for which the kit would be adequate?

b. Books alone have traditionally not been deemed unauthorized practice. The leading case is New York County Lawyers' Association v. Dacey, 283 N.Y.S.2d 984 (App.Div.), reversed 234 N.E.2d 459 (N.Y.1967). Author Norman Dacey had been found guilty of criminal contempt for writing and selling "How to Avoid Probate," a book in which he advised people to put all their property into "living trusts." The book contained 310 pages of forms "perforated for easy removal from the book," and the book told readers the forms "will be suitable for use" to achieve the desired results. "The giving of legal advice * * * including instructions and advice as to the preparation and use of legal instruments, constitutes the practice of law which is forbidden * * * to all but duly licensed New York attorneys," the appellate division said. 283 N.Y.S.2d at 989. "It is immaterial that Dacey has not face-to-face dealings nor a confidential relationship with particular clients." Id. at 991.

The Court of Appeals reversed, adopting the opinion of dissenting appellate Justice Stevens who had said: "It cannot be claimed that the publication of a legal text which purports to say what the law is amounts to legal practice. And the mere fact that the principles or rules stated in the text may be accepted by a particular reader * * * does not affect this. * * * This is the essential of a legal practice—the representation and the advising of a particular person in a particular situation." 283 N.Y.S.2d at 997–98.

With which opinion do you agree?

c. Traditionally, however, it has been unauthorized practice for a lay advisor to go beyond writing books and start giving personalized legal advice. In Matter of Estate of Margow, 390 A.2d 591 (N.J.1978), a long-time legal secretary developed a friendship with an elderly person. Using an old will as a form, the secretary typed a new will that reflected changes allegedly requested by the testator, including naming the secretary as executor of the estate. The court held the secretary's work constituted the unauthorized practice of law and, as a sanction, barred her from service as executor.

d. In Unauthorized Practice of Law Committee v. Parsons Technology, Inc., 1999 WL 47235 (N.D.Tex.1999), a federal district court found the creators of Quicken Family Lawyer guilty of unauthorized practice. The "Family Lawyer" software package contains over 100 legal forms that are represented to be "valid in 49 states." The program asks questions about the user and, based on the responses, generates forms to deal with the user's problem in the user's jurisdiction, while all the while expressly disclaiming providing "specific information for your exact situation." The court held that both the preparation of legal forms and the selection of which form to use constitute the practice of law in Texas. The court found as well that the state had a justifiable interest in not letting people who are not lawyers give legal advice harmful to Texas citizens. Thus, the court said, the prohibition in this case did not burden commercial speech more than was necessary, and it enjoined the sale of the software.

Do you agree with the *Quicken* decision? Was the court defending client protection, lawyer protection, or both?

e. Shortly after the *Quicken* decision, the Texas legislature enacted a law specifically providing that "the 'practice of law' does not include the design, creation, publication, distribution, display, or sale ... [of] computer software, or similar products if the products clearly and conspicuously state that the products are not a substitute for the advice of an attorney." The law was effective immediately. The Fifth Circuit then vacated the lower court injunction and judgment, 179 F.3d 956 (5th Cir.1999) (per curiam), and remanded in light of the statute.

Does the outcome tell you whom lay people tend to think unauthorized practice rules are protecting? Do you agree with their view? Why or why not?

6. May a person represent herself in court? May she act as her own lawyer in negotiating a contract? Why do we let people act pro se if unauthorized practice rules are so important?

a. Restatement Third, The Law Governing Lawyers § 4, Comment *d*, says that "every jurisdiction recognizes the right of an individual to proceed 'pro se' * * * [b]ecause the appearance is personal only." Unauthorized practice, in short, involves assisting another with a legal matter, not handling a matter for one's self.

b. Should it constitute the unauthorized practice of law for a family member who is an officer of a family corporation to represent the corporation in court? Should the answer turn on whether the corporation is large or small? Whether the amount in controversy is large or small? What policies are served by allowing a sole proprietor of an unincorporated business to appear *pro se* but denying the 100% owner of a corporation the same right to appear?

c.   Regardless of the policies served, corporations are usually forced to hire lawyers. See, e.g., Restatement Third, The Law Governing Lawyers § 4, Comment *e* (rule only applies in litigation; corporate officers may negotiate business deals); Merco Construction Engineers, Inc. v. Municipal Court, 581 P.2d 636 (Cal.1978)(statute designed to reverse rule in municipal courts held unconstitutional as invading the judicial power).

7.   Is it time to get rid of the rules against unauthorized practice?

a.   Are unauthorized practice rules anticompetitive? If so, is the reduced competition justified by other considerations? Barlow F. Christensen wrote:

> "Ultimately, the legal profession's traditional unauthorized practice position rests upon either of two serious doubts—or perhaps on both. Lawyers either lack confidence in themselves to meet free and open competition, or they lack faith in the intelligence of the public and in the ability of citizens to determine their lives for themselves. Neither doubt is justified. If we lawyers are the splendid [people] that we claim to be—and, though the claim is immodest, it may even be at least partly true—then we have nothing to fear from open competition. And if the citizen is competent to do important things like govern himself, then surely he is capable of deciding from whom he will purchase legal services. The time has come to let the public choose."[4]

Is Mr. Christensen right? Can you see any solid justifications for unauthorized practice rules?

b.   If a reasonable argument can be made that non-lawyer groups will provide services to middle-class and poor clients who are rarely getting legal services at all today, might we think it is a good idea to have their level of their services improved by lawyer assistance?

c.   Is an important concern the possibility that some non-lawyer groups will seek to exploit a vulnerable client base and that the nominal presence of a lawyer will only facilitate their fraud? Is Model Rule 5.5(a) sufficiently nuanced to prohibit only the assistance of such exploitation? Could you draft a rule to deal better only with issues of legitimate concern?

d.   Richard F. Mallen & Associates, Ltd. v. Myinjuryclaim.com Corp., 769 N.E.2d 74 (Ill.App.Ct.2002), suggests that unauthorized practice laws may be here to stay in spite of relatively low official interest in enforcing them. The case holds that an individual personal injury lawyer has standing to complain about a web site that purports to evaluate the likely

4. Barlow F. Christensen, The Unauthorized Practice of Law: Do Good Fences Really Make Good Neighbors—or Even Good Sense?, 1980 A.B.F.Res.J. 159, 216.

recovery for particular personal injuries. With unusual candor, the court says that "a law license confers a right to practice in the nature of a franchise" that individual lawyers have an interest in protecting against an "unlicensed corporation dispensing legal advice without possessing the requisite expertise or competence" who may cause "irreparable harm to many citizens, as well as to the judicial system itself." 769 N.E.2d at 76.

Do you agree with that assessment of the rights entailed in a law license? Do you agree that a law license should carry with it that enforcement authority?

B. THE MULTIJURISDICTIONAL PRACTICE OF LAW

1. In what jurisdictions may a licensed lawyer regularly practice?

a. To many people, the answer is obvious; admission to the bar of one state should guarantee admission to the bar of another. Under traditional standards, however, that answer is incorrect.

b. The Supreme Court has made clear that states' ability to condition admitting lawyers licensed in other states to practice in their own is not unlimited. Supreme Court of Virginia v. Friedman, 487 U.S. 59, 108 S.Ct. 2260, 101 L.Ed.2d 56 (1988), for example, involved a Maryland resident who challenged a Virginia requirement that, in order to be admitted to the Virginia bar without taking the bar exam, a lawyer had to be a resident of Virginia. The State argued that because a nonresident could be admitted by passing the bar examination, there was no denial of her right to become a member of the Virginia bar. However, the Supreme Court held that making nonresidents take an additional test went to a matter of "fundamental concern" and violated the Privileges and Immunities Clause.[5]

c. As a practical matter, many states automatically admit experienced lawyers who are licensed in other states if the state of licensing will do the same for other states' lawyers. That tit-for-tat system is called "reciprocity." However, states typically require an examination of lawyers from states that do not grant reciprocity or grant it only on certain conditions. So far, most challenges to the constitutionality of such reciprocity requirements have been upheld.[6]

---

5. See also, Barnard v. Thorstenn, 489 U.S. 546, 109 S.Ct. 1294, 103 L.Ed.2d 559 (1989) (same result with respect to a one-year residency with an intent-to-remain rule imposed by the Virgin Islands bar). But see Scariano v. Justices of Indiana Supreme Court, 38 F.3d 920 (7th Cir.1994), cert. denied, 515 U.S. 1144, 115 S.Ct. 2582, 132 L.Ed.2d 831 (1995), upholding rule granting admission only to lawyers who have "practiced predominantly" in Indiana for five years under a conditional license; this rule

establishes to familiarity with Indiana law and is not a residency requirement per se.

6. In other contexts the Supreme Court, using the dormant commerce clause, has invalidated reciprocal barriers to the transfer of goods and services across state lines. Great Atlantic & Pacific Tea Co., Inc. v. Cottrell, 424 U.S. 366, 96 S.Ct. 923, 47 L.Ed.2d 55 (1976), unanimously invalidated a Mississippi law providing that milk from another state may not be sold in Mississippi unless that other state accepts milk processed in Mississippi. If a state concludes that an-

Schumacher v. Nix, 965 F.2d 1262 (3d Cir.1992), for example, upheld the Pennsylvania rule preventing California graduates of non-ABA accredited law schools from sitting for the Pennsylvania bar exam. California does not admit Pennsylvania lawyers without taking the California exam and thus is not a "reciprocal state" under Pennsylvania law. The court agreed that it was hard to see any rational basis for the Pennsylvania rule, but it found one by saying that Pennsylvania may have hoped to "entice states to enter into reciprocal agreements with it and thereby promote its interest in securing similar treatment for its attorneys who are graduates of accredited law schools." 965 F.2d at 1272.

In Matter of Saretsky, 506 N.W.2d 151 (Wis.1993), Michigan required that lawyers maintain a local office; thus, Wisconsin could impose the same requirement. Because the applicant planned to keep his office in Michigan and only wanted to practice in Wisconsin from time to time, he could not be admitted without taking the Wisconsin bar exam.

Do these cases make sense to you? Can they be justified as anything more than an effort by lawyers who already have licenses in a state to make it harder for out-of-state lawyers to become admitted to the bar?

2. Litigators' clients often get sued in states in which the lawyers are not licensed. Should there be a way for them to continue to represent their clients in those cases?

a. In general, if a litigator is not a member of the bar where the litigation is filed, she will file an appearance in court and ask to be admitted *pro hac vice*, i.e., for that particular case.[7] The lawyer so admitted sometimes must associate in that litigation with a lawyer in the state who is admitted in that state for all purposes.

b. Some states try to limit the number of *pro hac vice* appearances so as to prevent lawyers from ignoring the obligation to become admitted to the bar. However, such limits were shown to have a significant adverse effects on the availability of counsel in civil rights cases, and in Sanders v. Russell, 401 F.2d 241 (5th Cir.1968), the court struck down a district court rule limiting *pro hac vice* appearance by out of state lawyers to one case per year.

c. Paciulan v. George, 229 F.3d 1226 (9th Cir.2000), challenged California's rule that permits non-resident lawyers to appear *pro hac vice*, but does not permit lawyers without California licenses who resided in California to so appear. The Ninth Circuit upheld the rule. A state has a

---

other state's rules on milk imports are unfair, the Court said, it should file a lawsuit not impose a trade barrier. Mississippi could require that all milk (including milk imported from other states) meet its standards, but it could not exclude milk that met those standards simply because that other state did not sign a reciprocal trade agreement with Mississippi.

7. As to whether concerns about the lawyer's possible "courtroom demeanor" permit denial of a *pro hac vice* appearance, compare In re Evans, 524 F.2d 1004 (5th Cir. 1975) (insufficiently specific charges and no opportunity for lawyer to defend himself), with In re Admission of Lumumba, 526 F.Supp. 163 (S.D.N.Y.1981) (alleged terrorist denied *pro hac vice* admission and denied access to client at local jail).

significant interest in not letting its residents secure a license elsewhere, the court said, and then regularly practice in California. Granting non-residents occasional *pro hac vice* status is not inconsistent with that interest. Do you agree?

d. However, lawyers admitted *pro hac vice* should not assume they may do everything a lawyer licensed in the jurisdiction may do. In Wellmore Coal Corp. v. Harman Mining Corp., 568 S.E.2d 671 (Va.2002), for example, a notice of appeal had to be signed by a Virginia lawyer. Instead, it was signed by a Kentucky lawyer who was admitted *pro hac vice* in the case. That was not good enough under the appeal statute, the court held, so the appeal was dismissed. Presumably, the Kentucky lawyer's malpractice carrier was not pleased by this mistake.

3. Should transactional lawyers, i.e., those doing deals or other kinds of commercial activity, have a similar way to follow their clients to other jurisdictions?

a. For transactional lawyers giving advice to clients with interests around the country or around the world, the practical problems of state-by-state admission are different. There is no "proceeding" in which one can ask a court to be admitted for purposes of a particular negotiation or closing. In addition, there are often pre-litigation activities (such as interviewing witnesses and other investigation) that may occur before any litigation is filed. Indeed, matters may be resolved in ADR proceedings before a judge ever enters the picture.

b. Birbrower, Montalbano, Condon & Frank, P.C. v. Superior Court, 949 P.2d 1 (Cal.1998), struck terror in the management committees of lots of "national" law firms. Birbrower, a New York law firm, represented ESQ, a California corporation, in claims it had against Tandem Computers, Inc., relating to a software and marketing contract. California law governed the contract and New York firm partners traveled to California on several occasions. The case was to be arbitrated, but the parties ultimately settled the dispute, and the firm asked for its fee which was to be over a million dollars. At that point, the client refused to pay.

To the surprise of many, the court agreed with ESQ that it had no obligation to pay. One remedy for the unauthorized practice of law by non-lawyers is the denial of fees. While the Birbrower lawyers may be competent in New York, "[c]ompetence in one jurisdiction does not necessarily guarantee competence in another." 949 P.2d at 8. Nor was there an exception to the unauthorized practice prohibition for arbitration proceedings, even though there was no way to be admitted *pro hac vice* in such proceedings.

Ultimately, the California Supreme Court made two findings. First, the New York lawyers "practiced" in California. While much of the work was done in the New York office, the lawyers were physically present in California when they advised the California company about the arbitration held in California and governed by California law. Second, even non-physical presence in California can constitute unauthorized practice of law.

One may one may be said to practice in California "although not physically present here [such as] by advising a California client on California law in connection with a California legal dispute by telephone, fax, computer, or other modern technological means." Id. at 5–6. However, the court did "reject the notion that a person automatically practices law 'in California' whenever that person practices California law anywhere, or 'virtually' enters the state by telephone, fax, e-mail, or satellite." Id. at 6. The Court allowed the firm to collect payment for services rendered to the client in New York but only if those could be severed from the rest of the services performed in California.[8]

c. *Birbrower* is a landmark case on this subject, but it does not stand alone. Koscove v. Bolte, 30 P.3d 784 (Colo.Ct.App.2001), for example, involved a lawyer licensed in Wisconsin but not Colorado. The lawyer agreed to pursue royalty payments due to Koscove from an oil company. After obtaining a significant recovery, aided in part by the work of a Colorado lawyer, Koscove moved to get back all fees she had paid to Bolte. The court agreed that, in spite of his efforts and success, Bolte could not collect a fee because he was not licensed to practice in the state. Analyzing the lease in question and giving opinions as to theories for recovery of damages in Colorado, the court found, was the unauthorized practice of law and Bolte could not collect fees based on illegal work.

d. In re Ferrey, 774 A.2d 62 (R.I.2001), involved a lawyer who had appeared several times before a state energy agency in Rhode Island even though he was only licensed to practice law in Massachusetts. The state agency had granted the respondent permission to appear before it, but the Rhode Island supreme court said the permission exceeded agency authority and was invalid. Thereafter, the court granted the respondent *pro hac vice* status to practice before the state agency, holding that he was justified in relying on the permission of the agency. However, on the key issue, the court declined to allow the respondent to obtain fees for any prior appearances because they constituted the unauthorized practice of law.

e. Not all cases have construed unauthorized practice rules this restrictively. Fought & Co. v. Steel Engineering and Erection, Inc., 951 P.2d 487 (Hawaii 1998), for example, involved an Oregon firm acting as general counsel to an international client that built an airport on Maui. The client won a judgment against the state of Hawaii in a case handled by lawyers licensed there, but the Oregon firm sought a portion of the statutory attorneys fees for work it did helping prepare for the litigation. Many clients do work that is interstate and international, the court said. These clients, whether or not based in Hawaii, get important help from law firms who are familiar with their operations, wherever the firms are based. Making it impossible for firms to collect fees for work relating to Hawaii

---

8. The California legislature has reversed *Birbrower* as applied to arbitration cases for work before January 1, 2006. Code of Civil Procedure § 1282.4 and Rule 983.4 of the Rules of Court provide that, until then, with the approval of the arbitrator, an out-of-state lawyer may appear in an arbitration in California without violating the prohibition against unauthorized practice.

would make it hard for all clients to get high quality, efficiently-delivered legal services. Even applying the standards set forth in *Birbrower,* the Court said, the Oregon firm had retained local counsel for work done in Hawaii. It could be seen as simply assisting the Hawaiian counsel and thus it was not barred from collecting a fee.

f.   In the Matter of Opinion 33 of the Committee on Unauthorized Practice of Law, 733 A.2d 478 (N.J.1999), addressed whether out-of-state bond lawyers may advise public entities issuing state and municipal bonds. The unauthorized practice committee had said no; the bond issues raised only issues of New Jersey law. The state supreme court noted that a number of New Jersey firms now have the expertise to advise on bond issues, but ten to twenty out-of-state firms have greater national reputations in the field than any New Jersey firm. Unauthorized practice prohibitions are "not designed to give rise to a professional monopoly, but rather to serve the public right to protection against unlearned and unskilled advice." 733 A.2d at 484. Previously, the court had upheld the right of accountants to prepare inheritance tax returns and real estate brokers to close residential real estate transactions. The court held that here, too, the public interest required that New Jersey law firms be able to involve out-of-state lawyers in bond issues and, in complex cases, issuers could even hire out-of-state lawyers directly.

g.   Condon v. McHenry, 76 Cal.Rptr.2d 922 (Ct.App.1998), somewhat eased concerns about what California courts would do about fees payable to out-of-state lawyers. A Colorado firm had prepared will of a woman who at the time of death lived in California. A Colorado lawyer in that firm was hired by a Colorado co-executor to help administer the estate, most of whose assets were in California. Much of the work of the executor was selling a California business, and the Colorado lawyer helped with that as well. When the time came to award fees to executors' counsel, the California probate court refused to award any to the Colorado lawyer but the Court of Appeals reversed. The lawyer had not set up an office in California to give legal advice, the court said. He represented a Colorado citizen and did most of his work in Colorado; the fact most of the estate was in California did not make his work there improper.

4.   If a transactional lawyer works exclusively on questions of federal law, should state definitions of the practice of law nevertheless be controlling?

a.   Sometimes federal rules govern not only when a federal court will allow *pro hac vice* admission, but also when the court will treat something as not the unauthorized practice of law.

The leading case is Sperry v. Florida Bar, 373 U.S. 379, 83 S.Ct. 1322, 10 L.Ed.2d 428 (1963), where the Supreme Court held that Florida could not enjoin a nonlawyer registered to practice before the United States Patent Office from preparing and prosecuting patent applications in Florida, notwithstanding that such activity, under state law, constituted the "practice of law." The court noted that both a federal statute and Patent Office regulations specifically authorized practice before the Patent Office by nonlawyers. Thus, the Supremacy Clause overrode the state restriction because no state law "can hinder or obstruct the free use of a license granted under an act of Congress." 373 U.S. at 385, 83 S.Ct. at 1326, 10 L.Ed.2d at 433.[9]

b.   In re Desilets, 291 F.3d 925 (6th Cir.2002), is a modern application of the *Sperry* doctrine. A lawyer, Rittenhouse, was licensed in Texas, moved to Wisconsin and opened an office in Michigan to handle only bankruptcy cases. He was not admitted to practice in either Wisconsin or Michigan, but he was admitted in the federal court for the Western District of Michigan. The State Bar of Michigan accused him of the unauthorized practice of law, and the federal bankruptcy court refused to award him fees because he was not an "attorney" where he practiced law. Rittenhouse relied on the fact he only practiced federal law and was admitted in the federal district court. Judge Boggs, speaking for the Sixth Circuit, agreed. Citing *Sperry*, the court held that states may not decide who may practice federal law in federal court. Dissenting, Judge Merritt said that federal court admission does not preclude separate state regulation of a lawyer who opens an office to practice in that state.

c.   State Unauthorized Practice of Law Comm. v. Paul Mason & Assoc., 46 F.3d 469 (5th Cir.1995), dismissed a charge of unauthorized practice brought against a "creditors bankruptcy service" that did clerical work necessary to get creditors' claims filed in bankruptcy cases around Texas. A lawyer's fee for such work would have exceeded the amount of most of the claims, and the "service" handled no disputed claims. The court held that this case, too, was controlled by *Sperry*. Because bankruptcy proceedings were subject to federal rules authorizing non-lawyers do certain administrative chores in bankruptcy, the court affirmed a grant of summary judgment for the respondent.

d.   Schindler v. Finnerty, 74 F.Supp.2d 253 (E.D.N.Y.1999), on the other hand, held that lawyers who did federal patent work were not exempt from jurisdiction of the New York lawyer discipline system when their clients complained of neglect and similar misconduct. The district court acknowledged *Sperry v. Florida*, but it said that state law governs all lawyers to the extent state law does not hinder operation of the patent system. Keeping practitioners honest was consistent with federal objectives, the court said, so the lawyers had to respond in discipline proceedings to their clients' complaints.

5.   Can you derive any practical guidelines from these cases about when a lawyer may represent a client from a jurisdiction— or with respect to work in a jurisdiction—in which the lawyer is not admitted?

a.   Restatement Third, The Law Governing Lawyers § 3, suggested that a lawyer may only act "to the extent the lawyer's activities in the

---

9. Note however, that federal courts often make a part of their own rules for admission to practice before them, a requirement that the lawyers also be admitted in the state where the federal court sits. See "Sample Federal Court Rules" in the Supplement.

matter arise out of or are otherwise reasonably related to the lawyer's practice" in the state in which the lawyer is licensed? Comment *e* explained that several factors are relevant to determining whether a matter is "reasonably related" to the lawyer's home state practice, including:

> "whether the lawyer's client is a regular client of the lawyer or, if a new client, is from the lawyer's home state, has extensive contacts with that state, or contacted the lawyer there; whether a multistate transaction has other significant connections with the lawyer's home state; whether significant aspects of the lawyer's activities are conducted in the lawyer's home state; whether a significant aspect of the matter involves the law of the lawyer's home state; and whether either the activities of the client involve multiple jurisdictions or the legal issues involved are primarily either multistate or federal in nature."

Is that helpful guidance? Does it seem to be consistent with the cases?

b.   The report of American Bar Association Commission on Multijurisdictional Practice (Aug. 2002), in turn, proposed liberalizing the rules on who can practice in a state on a "temporary" basis. Its proposals were adopted by the ABA House of Delegates and the proposed circumstances under which a lawyer may practice in a jurisdiction other than one of the lawyer's admission are now described in Model Rule 5.5(c) and (d). Can you identify any cases that would not fit within at least one of those provisions?

c.   Remember that as a result of a parallel change in ABA Model Rule 8.5, a lawyer who travels to another jurisdiction in handling a matter will be subject to the disciplinary jurisdiction of the state to which she travels. See, e.g., In re Harper, 785 A.2d 311 (D.C.2001) (reciprocal discipline after D.C. lawyer who had never been licensed in Maryland was formally "disbarred" from practicing there in the future because of misconduct during his unauthorized practice).

d.   There may be other consequences to a lawyer's unauthorized practice as well. In re Jackman, 761 A.2d 1103 (N.J.2000), involved a Massachusetts lawyer who had practiced as a senior associate in a New Jersey for seven years without a license to practice there. The court found that he had engaged in the unauthorized practice of law for those seven years and thus withheld his admission to the New Jersey bar for an unlimited period.

e.   The European Union has sought to remove obstacles to the free movement of capital, persons, and services among the member states. Under the Treaty, a qualified EC lawyer may provide legal services in another member state either by visiting on an occasional basis or by setting up a permanent office. He or she may provide this legal service using the qualifications of his or her original home ("home title"), or by obtaining additional qualifications, as an "integrated lawyer" from the place where he or she is setting up the permanent office. * * * A lawyer from one country in the European Community relying on his or her home title while practicing in another country in the EC may give legal advice, "including advice in local law." John Toulmin, Legal Practice in Europe, International Financial Law Review, August, 1989.

Look at ABA Model Rule 5.5(a). Do we have something to learn from the "United States of Europe"?[10]

C.   PROHIBITION OF THE CORPORATE PRACTICE OF LAW

1.   Why might courts be concerned about seeing Dowd, a licensed lawyer, doing general estate planning work for the customers of an insurance company?

a.   Traditionally, lawyer-client relationships have been imagined as personal relationships between one lawyer and one client. Consistent with that model, corporations have been forbidden prohibited from selling legal services. They clearly may have in-house legal departments to handle the company's own legal matters, but they may not let those lawyers represent customers or other third parties. This is the reason, for example, that a bank trust department ordinarily may not draft a will, even if the trust officer is a lawyer.

b.   Is the real concern the conflicts of interest that may be created by or inherent in such a situation? Can a lawyer be expected to give impartial advice on estate planning when his fee is coming from an insurance company? Take a look at Model Rule 5.4(d), for example, and the concern expressed in Model Rule 5.4, Comment [2]. Do you agree that the concern is justified?

c.   In spite of that concern and the traditional prohibition, some cases have upheld the corporate delivery of legal services. Perkins v. CTX Mortgage Company, 969 P.2d 93 (Wash.1999), held that a mortgage company that prepared documents for loan closings was not engaged in the unauthorized practice of law. Only licensed lawyers selected the legal documents and they exercised all legal judgment. Non-lawyers filled in some blanks, and the court held the company to the same standard of practice of a lawyer. In effect, then, at least as to this area of law, a corporation has been allowed to engage in tasks, some of which have traditionally been seen as the practice of law.

d.   The lawyer in State ex rel. Oklahoma Bar Ass'n v. Israel, 25 P.3d 909 (Okla.2001), specialized in obtaining child support orders. He also created a corporation that helped clients collect court-ordered payments. He received 25% of each child support payment for his legal fees and his corporation received another 25% of each payment for its own work. The court held that the lawyer's involvement in the private company was not an impermissible conflict of interest. The corporation's interest was aligned

---

10.   The United States is slowly moving closer to the European model. In response to foreign pressure, and the pressure of American lawyers who want to open access to legal markets abroad, the New York Court of Appeals permits licensing foreign legal consul-tants. The rules allow foreign lawyers to form partnerships with New York lawyers. See Rules of the Court of Appeals for the Licensing of Legal Consultants, 22 N.Y.C.R.R. Part 521.

with the client's interest in collecting the money, and the respondent adequately disclosed his interest in the company through his oral statements to his client and in the fee stipulation in the client's contract.

e. Do you agree that increasing liberality toward corporate legal services is justified? Do such cases simply recognize that there is more to solving a client's problem than can justify an expenditure for expensive legal services? Might the courts be overlooking some protections the law has previously thought were worth providing?

2. How should unauthorized practice of law principles apply to insurance companies who hire full-time employees who are licensed lawyers to work full-time representing the company's policyholders as counsel of record in actions brought by third parties for incidents covered by the terms of the policy? Is that simply a more efficient way to pay the lawyers?

a. Gardner v. North Carolina State Bar, 341 S.E.2d 517 (N.C.1986), was a relatively early case holding that insurance companies cannot employ its lawyer-employees to represent the insured. Nor may the attorney appear as counsel of record for the insured in the prosecution of a subrogation claim for property damage. "Since a corporation cannot practice law directly," the court said, "it cannot do so indirectly by employing lawyers to practice for it." 341 S.E.2d at 521.[11]

b. In re Allstate Insurance Co., 722 S.W.2d 947 (Mo.1987) (en banc), on the other hand, specifically refused to follow *Gardner* and concluded that the insurance company may either hire independent lawyers or use its own employees instead. "An insurer has a very substantial interest in litigation involving its insured, and is entitled to retain counsel of its own choosing to protect its interest." 722 S.W.2d at 950. If an insurer can hire an independent contractor, it may act through its employee. Any danger of conflict of interest is minimized because the company uses its employee-lawyers "only when there is no question of coverage, and when the claim is within policy limits." Id. at 951.

c. In Cincinnati Insurance Co. v. Wills, 717 N.E.2d 151 (Ind.1999), the insurance company provided the lawyers through a "captive" firm called "Berlon & Timmel" whose only practice was on behalf of policyholders of the insurer. The court agreed that Indiana corporations could not practice law; they could, however, hire lawyers to represent themselves, and the only question was whether they could hire lawyers to represent others. Conflicts could arise and be addressed, the court said, but a blanket prohibition was not required. However, the court found it misleading to use a traditional law firm name for a group of lawyers who do all their work for a single company. Change that and the practice may continue.

d. Gafcon, Inc. v. Ponsor & Associates, 120 Cal.Rptr.2d 392 (Ct.App. 2002), also upheld an insurance company's use of captive law firms to

---

11. See also, American Insurance Ass'n v. Kentucky Bar Ass'n, 917 S.W.2d 568, 571 (Ky.1996) (citing the ancient maxim "if it ain't broke don't fix it" to justify retaining the prohibition).

defend its insureds. A lawyer retained to defend an insured owes a fiduciary duty to both insurer and insured, the court said. A corporation may not practice law, but corporations frequently employ house counsel who may appear on their behalf. Where the insured's interest is congruent with the insurer's, and where the lawyers retain independence of professional judgment, counsel employed by an insurance company may also represent policyholders without violating the rule against the corporate practice of law.

e.   Insurance companies are trying to expand the use of in-house lawyers. With which of these cases do you agree? Is what the insurance companies are doing significantly different from the system of prepaid legal insurance discussed in Problem 34?

3.   How do these principles apply to the practice of accounting firms hiring lawyers full-time to give corporate and transactional advice to the firms' business clients?

a.   By far the most important issues of practice by non-lawyer organizations—as well as the most important multidisciplinary practice issues—are raised by the fact that the largest "law firms" in Europe at the turn of the millennium were American accounting organizations. What Model Rules seem to impose the greatest barriers to these firms expanding their practice to the representation of clients in the United States?

b.   Does Model Rule 5.4 stand as a barrier to the delivery of "one-stop business services" by accounting firms? What interests of clients—as distinct from interests of lawyers in traditional law firms—can you see against the phenomenon?

c.   The ABA Commission on Multidisciplinary Practice issued a report in 1999 largely acknowledging the fact of this development and concluding that it inevitably represented a useful new way to deliver legal services to some clients. The Commission went on to propose a new Model Rule 5.8 to regulate such firms.

4.   What would you want to see as the content of such a rule?

a.   Would you want it made clear that lawyers working for accounting firms remain subject to their state's lawyer Rules of Professional Conduct? Would you want to say that the lawyers could not accept direction by non-lawyers over the exercise of the lawyers' professional judgment? Why or why not?

b.   Should accounting firms be subject to the same conflict of interest rules that govern law firms? Should that include the requirement of imputation of all conflicts throughout the accounting firm? Given the small number of large accounting firms, that requirement would probably prohibit the provision of legal services by such firms.

c.   Should client communications with lawyers employed by accounting firms be protected by the attorney-client privilege even though communication with accountants in those firms would not be so protected? Should accountants performing audits of clients to whom legal services are being delivered be deemed to know all confidential information disclosed by the clients to the lawyers in their firm?

d. In February 2000, the ABA summarily rejected the report of the Multidisciplinary Practice Commission, but directed the ABA Ethics Committee to determine whether additional restrictions should be placed on "side-by-side" relationships between law firms and other service providers. In such relationships, the law firm would regularly send its clients to a single economic consulting firm, for example, while the economic consulting firm would regularly recommend the law firm to its clients.

e. The Committee concluded that such arrangements are not per se unethical, although as we saw in Problem 32, it proposed amendments, since adopted, to Rule 7.2 saying that the arrangement must be non-exclusive and that before making a referral to the other service provider, the lawyer "should examine carefully whether his or her representation of clients may be materially limited by obligations to the other professional service provider." If so, the lawyer must get the client's informed consent to the referral.

f. In 2002, the status of multidisciplinary practices was undercut even in Europe where the phenomenon began. Wouters v. Algemene Raad van de Nederlandse Orde van Advocaten, 2002 WL 29971, [2002] All E.R. (EC) 193, [2002] 4 C.M.L.R. 27, held that under European Union law, whether multidisciplinary partnerships may include lawyers is a matter for national law. Arthur Andersen and other large accounting firms were providing legal services all over Europe, and the Netherlands Bar, a national entity, adopted rules prohibiting such partnerships from operating there. The position was challenged as the product of a cartel prohibited by Articles 81 and 82 of the EU Treaty, but the European Court of Justice found that those articles do not limit proper exercise of power by national authorities. The Court believed that whether multidisciplinary partnerships would increase competition among legal service providers or lead to domination of the market by a few firms was far from clear, but it held that it was a matter proper for resolution at a national level. The decision itself thus does not itself outlaw European MDPs, but it does reduce their universal presence. And the implosion of Arthur Andersen, the accounting firm most responsible for the MDP phenomenon, has put the future of such organizations in at least some doubt.

5. Might there remain some appropriate place for multi-disciplinary organizations to deliver legal services to low and middle income clients?

a. Think of an office serving clients like Mrs. Andrews, whom we met in Problem 17, for example. She was the woman in an abusive relationship who had lost custody of her children. Can you see circumstances in which she would be much better served by a social services agency that had a lawyer on its staff than by a traditional private law firm?

b. What about giving banks authority to help their clients prepare their wills and trusts? Is Dowd's non-traditional organization as crazy as it might have sounded when you first read about it? In short, until lawyers figure out a way to deliver legal services at a price most people can afford, do lawyers have much moral authority to stand in the way of people who might deliver such services?

D. LAW FIRM DELIVERY OF ANCILLARY, NOT-TRADITIONALLY-LEGAL SERVICES

1. Could Dowd eliminate all problems with his multidisciplinary organization if he simply ran it out of his law firm?

a. Subsidiaries or law firm "affiliates" are becoming more common today as law firms have gone into the publishing business, financial consulting, and even forms of investment banking. Are these positive developments or do they constitute a threat to the independence and professionalism of lawyers?[12] The debate as to whether law firms should be able to operate non-law entities has become more heated over the years.

b. Washington, D.C. firms initially founded many of the first wave of law firm affiliates. A partner in Arnold & Porter explained a typical reason for creating the subsidiary: the firm wished to hire a departing government official who was not a lawyer; this official would be hired to engage in lobbying activities for clients but "[w]e would have to call him or her a paralegal."

c. An early draft of the Model Rules recommended that non-lawyers be permitted to form partnerships with lawyers if there would be no interference with the lawyers' independent professional judgment or with the lawyer-client relationship, client confidentiality would be maintained, and advising and fee arrangements did not violate the Rules governing lawyers. During the ABA floor debates an ABA delegate asked: "Does this rule mean Sears & Roebuck will be able to open a law office?" Professor Geoffrey C. Hazard, Jr., the Reporter for the Model Rules, answered "Yes." The proposal failed.[13]

2. What advantages and problems can you see with such arrangements?

a. The arguments in favor of such affiliates seem to be four-fold. First, they make the law firm more convenient for the client. When the client has a problem that requires the services of several professionals, as is often the case, it is beneficial and useful for the client be able to engage in one-stop shopping. Second, the law firm wishes to give the non-lawyer professionals the status and titles that they deserve. Third, these entities are perhaps not as constrained in the manner of calculating fees as lawyers

12. There is clearly no ethical restriction on a lawyer's owning a business that is not ancillary to the practice of law. Two lawyers in a law partnership may buy a restaurant, for example, and they presumably may take clients there to dine without the restaurant's becoming law-related?

13. See Rita Henley Jensen, Ethics Row Looms on [Law Firm] Affiliates, Nat'l L. J., Feb. 20, 1989, at 1, 28.

may be. Fourth, having the affiliates may retain existing clients, bring in new clients, and thus offer new sources of revenue.

b.   The arguments against creating such affiliates are both ethical and pragmatic. Ethically, a lawyer who advises a client in dealings with the lawyer's affiliate may not have the independent judgment needed to give sound advice, such as the advice to fire the affiliate. Also, such arrangements inevitably involve the lawyer in business transactions with the client, raising separate problems under Rule 1.8(a).

c.   Pragmatically, law firms must be concerned, first, about the partners' being jointly and severally liable for the acts of the affiliates, ranging from simple negligence to dishonesty of the nonlawyers. When the affiliate is making large sums of money by brokering substantial transactions, the potential exposure to malpractice may look small by comparison, but liability can be enormous.

d.   Next, the affiliate may expand the number of situations disqualifying the law firm, e.g., the affiliate may work on behalf of a client who has an interest that conflicts with a different client of the law firm.

e.   Further, to the extent that law firms become one-stop shopping centers instead of dispensers of a unique service, there is a danger that lawyers will lose their power of self-regulation and that the state supreme courts, which usually claim an inherent power to regulate the practice of law, will lose that claim of authority.

f.   Finally, if a law firm is allowed to set up a non-lawyer affiliate, a non-lawyer entity might be allowed to set up a law firm subsidiary. The fear of becoming a WalMart employee seems to haunt many lawyers.

3.   Take a look at Model Rule 5.7 and its Comments. The ABA adopted a similar rule in 1992, repealed it in 1993, and adopted the present version in 1994. What should constitute "law-related services" within the meaning of the rule?

a.   Is "financial planning" a law-related service, for example? Is the test whether a service is one that some lawyers might offer to some clients? By that definition, is every service performed by any lawyer potentially law-related?

b.   What is the significance of calling something "law-related"? Is a lawyer's title insurance business subject to different in-person solicitation rules than would govern sale of the usual insurance policy, for example? What is the rationale for holding lawyers to a more restrictive standard?

c.   Is there any reason not to call every service a lawyer provides a legal service? Should a lawyer's ancillary business be permitted to do environmental consulting for a customer that may disadvantage one of the lawyer's clients, for example, without the consent of that client?

d.   In Matter of Hear, 755 N.E.2d 579 (Ind.2001), a lawyer entered into a debt collection business with a non-lawyer. He allowed the non-lawyer to solicit clients and to administer and manage the cases that he solicited. He further authorized the non-lawyer to use letterhead captioned

"Charles F. Hear, Attorney at Law" and to collect debtors' payments made out to the lawyer. At some point, the non-lawyer stole funds being held for a client by writing checks to himself from the respondent's account. The court suspended the respondent from the practice of law for 100 days for failure to supervise the non-lawyer properly, failure to make reasonable efforts to ensure that the non-lawyer's conduct complied with the respondent's professional obligations, and for allowing the non-lawyer to solicit work on his behalf.

Do you agree with this result? Does it tend to confirm that if problems arise in the law-related activity, the lawyer will likely be held to traditional lawyer conduct standards?

4. If the law allows law firms to provide non-law services, should law firms be able to admit non-lawyers as partners to perform those services?

a. One jurisdiction permits nonlawyers to be partners of law firms. District of Columbia Court of Appeals Rule 5.4 provides:

(b) A lawyer may practice law in a partnership or other form of organization in which a financial interest is held or managerial authority is exercised by an individual nonlawyer who performs professional services which assist the organization in providing legal services to clients, but only if:

(1) The partnership or organization has as its sole purpose providing legal services to clients;

(2) All persons having such managerial authority or holding a financial interest undertake to abide by these rules of professional conduct;

(3) The lawyers who have a financial interest or managerial authority in the partnership or organization undertake to be responsible for the nonlawyer participants to the same extent as if nonlawyer participants were lawyers under Rule 5.1;

(4) The foregoing conditions are set forth in writing.

b. Comment 5 to this Rule explains that nonlawyer participants "ought not to be confused with nonlawyer assistants under Rule 5.3. Nonlawyer participants are persons having managerial authority or financial interests in organizations which provide legal services."

c. What do you think of this rule? Comment 8 adds that the D.C. Rule "does not permit an individual or entity to acquire all or any part of the ownership of a law practice organization for investment or other purposes" because "such an investor would not be an individual performing professional services within the law firm or other organization." Why not? If a firm can pay a lawyer with a well-known name to meet with potential clients but do little else, why shouldn't the firm be able to pay a passive investor to provide the firm with operating capital?[14]

d. In an important corollary applicable beyond the District of Columbia, ABA Formal Opinion 01–423 (Sep. 22, 2001), advised that U.S. lawyers may form partnerships with lawyers not licensed in the United States, so long as the foreign lawyers are members of a recognized legal profession in a foreign jurisdiction and the arrangement is in compliance with the law of all jurisdictions where the firm practices. If the foreign nation's lawyers are not recognized as a legal profession, they would be deemed "nonlawyers" and making them partners would violate Rule 5.4. The purpose of Rule 5.4 is to protect a lawyer's independence in exercising professional judgment on the client's behalf, the Committee said. As long as a foreign lawyer is a member of a recognized legal profession this objective would be realized.[15]

The opinion says that in order to be deemed a member of a recognized legal profession a person must be specially trained to give advice on the laws of the foreign jurisdiction and licensed to represent clients in its legal system. U.S. lawyers must take reasonable steps to ensure that foreign lawyers meet these requirements, that the arrangement is in compliance with the law of jurisdictions where the firm practices, and that matters in foreign jurisdiction are managed pursuant to all applicable Model Rules that apply to the firm's practice.

e. Why should lawyers be permitted to establish multidisciplinary law firms that hire accountants while accounting firms may not establish multidisciplinary organizations that hire lawyers? Do lawyers have ethical standards that are higher than all accountants? Remember that Enron had lawyers too.

f. What kinds of legal delivery organizations do you see in your future? Is the prospect of using your legal skills to work for many different kinds of organizations a cause for celebration or a cause for apprehension?

---

14. An economic result of this prohibition is that it "can forestall attempts to form the capital structures necessary to make law practice a true consumer product for a mass market. It also prevents competition from banks, insurance companies, title insurance companies and other potential competitors. The prohibition presented a momentary embarrassment when, for tax reasons, it made economic sense for a lawyers to practice in the corporate form. That was gotten around by obtaining state legislation permitting lawyers to form 'professional corporations.'" Charles W. Wolfram, Modern Legal Ethics 840 (1986).

15. New York law has been to this effect for several years. See Rules of the Court of Appeals for the Licensing of Legal Consultants, 22 N.Y.C.R.R. Part 521.

CHAPTER VIII

ETHICAL CONDUCT OF JUDGES

Not all lawyers will be judges. But almost all lawyers will appear before them and public and professional confidence in the integrity of the judiciary is close to the heart of the respect for law. Judicial ethics thus is of central importance to any lawyer, whether or not he or she aspires to be on the bench.

Judges are usually lawyers and continue to be governed by their state version of the ABA Model Rules of Professional Conduct, particularly Rule 8.4. The conduct of lawyers who deal with judges—or who want to become judges—is also the concern of the Model Rules.

More importantly for the issues in this Chapter, however, judicial conduct is regulated by state or federal versions of the ABA Model Code of Judicial Conduct to which this Chapter will introduce you. By this time, it should be clear to you that ethical standards do not draw simple lines between honest persons and crooks. The Model Code of Judicial Conduct is no exception.

As you work through these materials, ask yourself questions such as:

a. Which of the principles of judicial ethics are designed to help assure "correct" or at least disinterested decisions?

b. Which principles are primarily designed to prevent judges from abusing the unusual influence they have over lawyers and in the community?

c. How do issues of judicial misconduct reach official attention and what is the role of lawyers in that process?

d. To what extent would some of the current Code of Judicial Conduct be unnecessary if judges were appointed and not elected?

e. Are any aspects of the Code unnecessarily restrictive on judges? Might any tend to discourage able people from seeking judicial office?

PROBLEM 38

JUDGES' DISQUALIFYING CONFLICTS OF INTEREST

Judges, like everyone else, have financial obligations. They take out a mortgage to buy a house, borrow money to purchase a car, and seek to take advantage of investment opportunities. Their family members lead their own lives and have their own financial relationships and careers, but the judge is likely not to be indifferent to their welfare. Judges also often have strongly-held views on public questions, some of which may come before their court. This Problem first asks what financial relationships create a conflict of interest that requires the judge's disqualification. Next, it asks when interests of the judge's family may create similar problems for the judge. It then examines whether views about policy issues constitute a similarly disqualifying bias, and it closes by exploring when and how a judge's conflict of interest may be waived.

FACTS

Harold Baxter and Martha Anderson met in law school and have been good friends ever since. Baxter has now become a state trial judge and Anderson practices in the same city. Recently, Baxter sought to buy a new house, but the required down payment was higher than he had expected. Anderson, who was attorney for the bank from which Baxter planned to borrow, personally lent Baxter $5,000 evidenced by a demand note that Anderson assured Baxter would not be "called under any conditions I can foresee." Judge Baxter then got his mortgage from the bank.

Anderson is now representing the same bank, which is the plaintiff in a hotly-contested case that has been assigned to Judge Baxter. The case involves a close question of lien priorities and both sides expect the case to go to the state supreme court. Judge Baxter orally informed defense counsel about the loans in an early pre-trial conference and asked, "Do you have any problems with my presiding in this case?" Both Anderson and the defense counsel, who frequently appears before Judge Baxter, replied, "No, sir."

Judge Baxter's niece is 19 and lives with the Baxters while going to college. She has some money of her own that she has invested. She owns 10 shares, a 1/100,000 interest, in the insurance company that is defendant in the lien priorities case before Judge Baxter. The Judge does not know of her interest. "I don't ask my relatives about their business dealings nor tell them about mine," he says.

Before going on the bench, Judge Baxter had been local chair of the "Committee for Responsible Assessment Policy," a committee of citizens who favored correction of what they saw as an inequitable method of making local tax assessments. He is no longer a member of that Committee. Cases are randomly assigned to judges in this district, and Judge Baxter has been assigned to hear a case in which a local taxpayer is challenging the validity of her own assessment. Judge Baxter has taken no steps either to recuse himself from the matter or to determine whether either party believes he should do so.

QUESTIONS

A.   FINANCIAL INTERESTS THAT MAY CREATE DISQUALIFYING BIAS

1.   Was it improper to Anderson to lend money to Judge Baxter to help him buy a house, or for Judge Baxter to accept the loan?

a.   Look at Model Rules 3.5(a) and 8.4(f). Do they tell you that Martha Anderson has to take a good look at the Model Code of Judicial Conduct to know the status of her own conduct under the Model Rules of Professional Conduct?

b.   What will Anderson find when she turns to the Code of Judicial Conduct? Does Canon 4D(1)(b) provide an unambiguous answer to the propriety of the loan? Will Canon 4D(5)(e) give Anderson and Judge Baxter a better sense of the answer to their question? Does the loan create a situation requiring disqualification under Canon 3E?

c.   In re Corboy, 528 N.E.2d 694 (Ill.1988) (per curiam), involved lawyers who gave checks for $1000 each to a state judge. Each of the lawyers testified that they considered the checks to be a gift or loan to the judge's mother to pay the mother's hospital bills so that she could come home for Christmas. The checks were deposited in the judge's own checking account. The funds were not used to pay the hospital bills, which were covered by insurance. The court rejected the argument that gifts to judges are only proscribed if they are motivated by a subjective intent to bribe the judge; such gifts are too subject to abuse to make their propriety turn on later testimony about intent. Similarly, the money given to the judge was not "ordinary social hospitality" under what is now Canon 4D(5)(c) of the ABA Model Code of Judicial Conduct (1990). The transactions were "a far cry from the social dinners, gratuitous rides, birthday recognitions and gifts of books or flowers, which might be genuine instances of social hospitality * * *." 528 N.E.2d at 700. The Court refused to censure any of the attorneys (including prominent lawyers such as Philip Corboy and William James Harte) because "They acted without the guidance of precedent or settled opinion, and there was, apparently, considerable belief among members of the bar that they acted properly." Id. at 701. Do you agree that reasonable lawyers should have been confused about the propriety of such gifts?

d.   In re Alexander, 585 N.E.2d 70 (Ill.1991), involved a Chicago lawyer who had grown up in the same neighborhood with Judge Holzer but did not practice before him. The judge had called the lawyer to his chambers to ask to borrow $11,000 because, the judge said, he "desperately" needed money because he was in arrears on his condominium fees. The lawyer loaned him the loan at a 15% interest rate. When the loan came due, the judge asked for and received an extension to repay. Five years later, Alexander wrote off the loan as uncollectible. While the loan was pending, the judge appointed Alexander a guardian ad litem in a case and later recused himself. Another judge awarded Alexander a $13,684 fee in the matter. Alexander argued that, because all these events occurred before the decision in *Corboy*, he too did not know making the loan was wrong. Further, he had no matter pending before Judge Holzer when he made the loan. The court held that accepting a guardian ad litem appointment before the judge had paid off the loan reflected a lack of "common sense and sound judgment" that required suspending Alexander from practice for six months. Do you think the court might have been closing the door that *Corboy* had appeared to open?

e.   In Lisi v. Several Attorneys, 596 A.2d 313 (R.I.1991), a judge had called twenty–one lawyers at various times, pleading that he desperately needed money to cover some urgent needs. Some of the lawyers had appeared before the judge in family court but several had known him in other settings. Each lent him the money he requested, not knowing others were doing so as well. No reported quid pro quo treatment was shown but some lawyers did have matters pending before the judge while the loans were outstanding. The judge resigned; the court suspended four of the lawyers for a year and imposed public reprimands on seventeen others.

2.   Was it similarly improper for Judge Baxter to get his home mortgage from a bank that might regularly have cases before him?

a.   Look generally at Canon 4D of the ABA Model Code of Judicial Conduct, and particularly at Canon 4D(5)(f). Do you agree that borrowing from a bank—even a litigious bank—should be treated differently from borrowing from the bank's attorney? Why?

b.   In Ausherman v. Bank of America, 216 F.Supp.2d 530 (D.Md. 2002), the plaintiffs claimed that a bank had improperly accessed their credit reports. They sought to disqualify the federal magistrate judge because the defendant bank held his home mortgage, but the judge refused to step down. Citing 28 U.S.C. § 455,[1] the federal law counterpart to Canon 3E of the Model Code of Judicial Conduct, the judge observed, "A loss for the bank, even if ruinous, would not extinguish or reduce the obligation of the mortgagor to repay * * *. Similarly, a victory for the bank, regardless of how substantial, affords no possible benefit to the mortgagor." 216 F.Supp.2d at 533–34. Do you agree?

c.   In re United States, 158 F.3d 26 (1st Cir.1998), involved a government motion to recuse a judge in a criminal trial of officials of a bank at which the judge and her husband had an overdrawn account and a delinquent commercial loan during the period in which the defendants were bank officers. The Court of Appeals heard the request for a writ of mandamus because there had been extensive publicity about the judge's possible partiality. It concluded, however, that there was no showing that the officials on trial had anything to do with granting the loan or that the bank had treated the judge differently from other borrowers. The court thus found the judge's decision not to recuse herself was not an abuse of discretion.

1.   The text of 28 U.S.C. § 455 can be found among the federal statutory materials in the Standards Supplement to this book.

3. How large should the interest have to be before a judge has a disqualifying financial interest in the subject matter of litigation over which the judge is presiding?

a. Look at Canon 3E(1)(c) and the definition of "economic interest" in the Terminology section of the ABA Model Code of Judicial Conduct (1990). What makes an interest "more than de minimis"? The 1972 version of the ABA Model Code of Judicial Conduct, defined "financial interest" as any interest "however small." Do you think the 1990 version is an improvement over the earlier standard? Why or why not?

b. Should a judge be disqualified from hearing a case involving I.B.M. if he or she owns ten shares of I.B.M. stock? Might the process of determining when an interest is "de minimis" intrude on the privacy of the judge? Might what may seem like a large amount to one judge be de minimis to a very rich judge, and thus might litigants need to inquire into the judge's overall financial position? The Reporter's Notes to the 1972 Judicial Code indicate that, to avoid such inquiries, the 1972 Code adopted an absolute prohibition that it thought could then be mitigated by the waiver provisions of Canon 3F, discussed below.

Was that approach was preferable to the current provision? Might that approach give parties too much opportunity to disqualify a judge they did not like for a reason entirely unrelated to the issue of financial interest?

c. Virginia Electric & Power Co. v. Sun Shipbuilding & Dry Dock Co., 539 F.2d 357 (4th Cir.1976), extensively analyzed both 28 U.S.C. § 455 and what is now Canon 3E. The claim was for damages to an electric utility caused by the defendant's fabrication of pump supports. At least in principle, if the utility won the case, the state regulatory commission could require it to lower the electric bills of everyone in Virginia, including the trial judge's bills. The total reduction could have been $100 possibly payable in small amounts over 40 years. The Fourth Circuit held that the trial judge should not be disqualified because he had no "financial" interest in the outcome of the case, because any rate relief was speculative and wholly within the discretion of the Virginia Corporation Commission that sets utility rates. That possibility did constitute an "other interest" that might be a basis for disqualification within the meaning of that section, but that interest was so speculative and remote as not to require the judge's recusal.

d. On the other hand, in Matter of Fuchsberg, 426 N.Y.S.2d 639 (Ct.Jud.1978) (per curiam), a judge of the New York Court of Appeals had engaged in transactions in New York City bonds while cases affecting the value of those bonds were before the New York courts, including his own. On the day the judge took office, he owned $3.4 million in par value in city notes. He redeemed some notes and bought others thereafter. One issue before his court, for example, was the constitutionality of a state law that imposed a three-year freeze on some of these notes. In one of the cases the judge voted against his apparent financial interest and in two others he did not participate. The Court on the Judiciary held that judge's ownership, purchase and sale of municipal and state securities and his participation in cases affecting the value of those holdings violated the "spirit" of the judicial canons that correspond to ABA Canon 2A, 3E(1)(c), and 4D(4), but seeking his removal from office was not warranted. "The record establishes his inattentiveness to and, at times, a cavalier disregard for the necessity of avoiding the appearance of impropriety," the court said, "yet the same record does not show deliberately fraudulent conduct, willful violations of Rules and Canons, or corrupt actions inspired by financial interest." 426 N.Y.S.2d at 649. Do you agree?

4. Should a judge be able to rule on a court challenge to the judge's own pay? Should it matter that the reason for disqualifying this judge extends to all judges, so that no one could decide the case in a wholly impartial manner?

a. In 1976, 140 federal judges filed a lawsuit arguing that since their last pay increase, inflation had reduced the purchasing power of their salaries by over 34%. The failure to grant them cost-of-living pay increases, they said, constituted an unconstitutional reduction of their salaries. Then, as now, 28 U.S.C. § 455(e) said that federal judges could not accept a waiver of recusal in a case involving the judge's personal financial interest. However, the Court of Claims held that under the "rule of necessity," its judges could hear the case. Otherwise, some important legal questions could never be decided. The court then denied the judges' substantive claim. Atkins v. United States, 556 F.2d 1028 (Ct.Cl.1977) (per curiam), cert. denied 434 U.S. 1009, 98 S.Ct. 718, 54 L.Ed.2d 751 (1978).

b. Despite failing to win their first lawsuit, 13 judges filed new suits in a federal district court. The Supreme Court heard their appeal and decided that the "rule of necessity" allowed both the lower courts and the Supreme Court to hear the case, notwithstanding 28 U.S.C.A. § 455. United States v. Will, 449 U.S. 200, 101 S.Ct. 471, 66 L.Ed.2d 392 (1980). The *Will* Court explained: "The Rule of Necessity had its genesis at least five and a half centuries ago. Its earliest recorded invocation was in 1430, when it was held that the Chancellor of Oxford could act as judge of a case in which he was a party when there was no provision for appointment of another judge." 101 S.Ct. at 480. The Rule of Necessity is a "well-settled principle at common law that, as Pollack put it, 'although a judge had better not, if it can be avoided, take part in the decision of a case in which he has any personal interest, yet he not only may but must do so if the case cannot be heard otherwise.' F. Pollack, A First Book of Jurisprudence 270 (6th ed. 1929)." Id. *Will* concluded that Congress did not intend § 455 to change the rule of necessity, "a doctrine that had not been questioned under prior judicial disqualification statutes." Id. at 481. *Will* then decided that for two of the four years in dispute, Congress had unconstitutionally diminished salaries of Article III judges and justices.

c. Does this exception to required recusal make sense to you? Model Code of Judicial Conduct Canon 3E(1) now references the Rule of Necessity in its Comment [3].

5. What other "personal interests" might bias a judge?

a.   Might a judge be found to be biased in one case because he took a bribe in a completely different case? Bracy v. Gramley, 520 U.S. 899, 117 S.Ct. 1793, 138 L.Ed.2d 97 (1997), allowed discovery to show judicial bias during habeas corpus review following a judge's sentencing the defendant to death. The defendant wanted to show that the judge at his state court trial, Judge Thomas J. Maloney, had accepted bribes in other murder cases and thus had a personal bias to convict the defendant so as to deflect attention from those misdeeds. In an opinion for a unanimous Court, Chief Justice Rehnquist concluded that the defendant in this case should be permitted to try to prove his point. This was not a charge of a judge's bias in general; it was an allegation that the defendant did not get a fair trial. Indeed, the Court said, the defense lawyer had been a former associate of Judge Maloney in a law practice that was "familiar and comfortable with corruption." Thus, the lawyer might have furthered the judge's alleged plan by taking this case to trial too quickly. The court remanded the case for further discovery.

b.   Should a judge be considered biased against a defendant because the defendant had threatened to kill the judge? Should we be worried that a defendant might engage in judge-shopping by threatening to kill each judge to whom his case had been assigned? In United States v. Greenspan, 26 F.3d 1001 (10th Cir.1994), the FBI reported that the defendant had taken steps to hire a hit man to kill the trial judge and his family. The trial judge knew of the threats and expedited the sentencing hearing to get the defendant off the streets "immediately." The Court of Appeals held that a defendant may not require a judge's recusal simply by uttering a threat, but in this case—where the facts suggested this was more than a ruse to disqualify the judge—a reasonable person might think the judge's impartiality would be affected. The court held that § 455(a) required that another judge impose the defendant's sentence.

B.   FINANCIAL INTERESTS OF THE JUDGE'S FAMILY

1. What obligation does Judge Baxter have to know his niece's financial holdings?

a.   Should a judge be able to take an "I don't ask" attitude about his or her relatives' financial affairs? Look carefully at Canons 3E(1)(c) & (d) and 3E(2). Is Judge Baxter's 19 year old niece a "member of the judge's family residing in the judge's household"? Is she a minor child? Is she "within the third degree of relationship" to Judge Baxter?

b.   If Judge Baxter had known of the niece's holdings, would he have been obliged to recuse himself in this case? Would his "don't ask, don't tell" approach to others' financial interests subject him to discipline no matter what appropriate inquiry would have revealed?[2]

---

2. You can find out the financial holdings of a federal judge and his or her close relatives. See P.L. 95–521, Title III, Judicial Personnel Financial Disclosure Requirements § 305, in the Standards Supplement. The Fifth Circuit summarily rejected a challenge to these disclosure requirements. Duplantier v. United States, 606 F.2d 654 (5th Cir.1979),

2. Must judges place their assets in a blind trust?

a. Should placing the judge's assets (or his family's assets) in a blind trust satisfy the Code of Judicial Conduct? Why or why not? Does it do so today? Look at Canon 3E(2). Can a judge who puts property into a blind trust be said to be keeping informed about his or her financial holdings?

b. Should a judge be able to "cure" a financial conflict brought on by investments of a relative by having the relative sell the stock? During the discovery period in Union Carbide Corporation v. United States Cutting Service, Inc., 782 F.2d 710 (7th Cir.1986), an antitrust class action, Judge Susan Getzendanner got married. Her husband had a self-managed retirement account that contained stock in IBM and Kodak. At the time, there was no list of class members. When the judge disclosed her husband's holdings in her annual financial disclosure statements, the defendant moved to disqualify her because it knew that IBM and Kodak had bought products from the defendant. Instead, the judge immediately ceased ruling on motions in the case while her husband sold his interest in the two companies. The Court of Appeals upheld that procedure. After the sale, the husband no longer had an interest in the stock, the court reasoned. The majority said "we do not mean to endorse sale as a cure for disqualification in all cases," but in this case there was no basis for saying the judge's impartiality could reasonably be questioned.

The dissent by Judge Flaum argues that nothing in 28 U.S.C. § 455(b)(4)—which corresponds to Canon 3E(1)(c)—permits a judge to "cure" a disqualifying situation in this way. "Congress desired to rid the statute of flexibility where financial interests are concerned." After the case, Congress added 28 U.S.C.A. § 455(f), which largely codified the Seventh Circuit ruling.

3. If Judge Baxter had a daughter who practices federal tax law in a local firm, must he recuse himself whenever his daughter's firm enters an appearance in a case?

a. Does Canon 3E(1)(d) provide an unambiguous answer? Look at the Commentary after Canon 3E(1)(e). Should the answer to the question be the same in a large city with many available judges as in a small town with no other judges within 50 miles?

b. In Bernard v. Coyne, 31 F.3d 842 (9th Cir.1994), Judge Kozinski had to decide when he must disqualify himself in bankruptcy cases arising out of the district in which his wife is the United States Bankruptcy

---

cert. denied 449 U.S. 1076, 101 S.Ct. 854, 66 L.Ed.2d 798 (1981).

Federal judges do not always disqualify themselves when their ethics rules require them to do so. "A number of federal appellate judges have ruled on cases involving companies in which they own stock, despite a federal law designed to prevent judges from taking part in any case in which they have a financial interest." When interviewed, the judges,

"who include some of the nation's best-known jurists, attributed their participation in the cases to innocent mistakes or memory lapses about their financial portfolios." As one judge remarked, "It's embarrassing." See, Joe Stephens, Taking Stock On the Bench: Federal Appeals Court Judges With Conflicts of Interest, Washington Post, Sept. 13, 1999, at p. A1.

Trustee. Most of the Trustee's actual duties are administrative, but she has the right to become involved in any case and some of the cases establish precedents that are important to her office. Judge Kozinski had referred the issue to the Judicial Conference's Committee on the Code of Conduct, which had concluded that, unless a case involved the Trustee as a party or was of such high profile that her career would be affected, no recusal was required. He took that advice and decided that he could hear this case.

c. If there is any question about the issue, how should Judge Baxter determine whether his daughter has "more than a de minimis interest" that will be "substantially affected" by the outcome of a case? May he call his daughter on the telephone and ask her how her firm divides income from such cases? Must the parties be permitted to contact the relative to make a similar inquiry? Must the judge hold a public hearing?[3]

d. Should it matter whether the firm has taken the case on a contingent fee and this its fee may be directly affected by the outcome of the proceedings? Suppose the daughter were "of counsel" to the firm, i.e., she did not automatically share all fees?

e. Does Canon 3E(1)(d)(ii) encourage litigants to use its limitations as a tool of forum shopping? In McCuin v. Texas Power & Light Co., 714 F.2d 1255, 1263–66 (5th Cir.1983), the defendants in an employment discrimination case retained the brother-in-law of Judge Justice who was scheduled to hear the case. Judge Justice recused himself and sent the case to Judge Parker, but Judge Parker found that the lawyer had been retained as a "sham" and a "ploy" to produce the disqualification. Thus, Judge Parker ordered the lawyer disqualified and sent the case back to Judge Justice.

On appeal, the Fifth Circuit found that 28 U.S.C. § 455 was intended to create a bright line rule; thus, Judge Justice had to recuse himself when his brother-in-law entered a notice of appearance in the case. Further, he could not designate his own successor, so the matter was remanded to the district court for reassignment. The Fifth Circuit observed that a certain amount of judge shopping is inherent in the ability of lawyers to decide whether to file in state or federal court and in which judicial district. Further, the right to counsel of one's choice is not easy to override. However, there have to be limits on what a litigant may do that delays a proceeding by obtaining a new judge "by the simple expedient of finding one of the judge's relatives who is willing to act as counsel." 714 F.2d at 1264. "The general rule of law is clear: a lawyer may not enter a case for the primary purpose of forcing the presiding judge's recusal." Id. at 1265.

f. Several Justices of the U.S. Supreme Court have spouses, children or other relatives who practice law and whose law firms may work on matters that will come before the Court. On November 1, 1993, seven Justices[4] announced that, absent "some special factor", they would not

---

3. One federal case that read 28 U.S.C.A. § 455(a) and (b)(5) very broadly to disqualify the judge whenever anyone in his brother's firm appeared before him in virtually any matter was SCA Services, Inc. v. Morgan, 557 F.2d 110 (7th Cir.1977).

4. Justice Blackmun who was about to retire, and Justice Souter, a bachelor, did not sign the statement. 112 S.Ct. at CIX (1993).

recuse themselves solely because a relative of theirs had personally worked on a matter at an earlier stage before it reached the Supreme Court. One "special factor" might be that the relative had been "lead counsel below" because then the outcome of the case "might reasonably be thought capable of enhancing or damaging his or her professional reputation." 112 S.Ct. at *CX* (Dec. 1, 1993) (unbound). See also, 80 A.B.A.J. 18 (Feb. 1994). If the relative is a law firm partner, the rule mandates recusal unless the relative's firm gives "written assurance that income from Supreme Court litigation is, on a permanent basis, excluded from our relative's partnership shares." 112 S.Ct. at *CXI*.

Have the Justices have appropriately balanced the competing interests in establishing these standards? Were they properly concerned that recusing themselves in any more cases might create opportunities for " 'strategizing' recusals, that is, selecting law firms with an eye to producing the recusal of particular Justices." Id. at *CX*.[5]

4. Should a judge be disqualified when someone from the judge's former firm (or the judge's former law clerk) appears before the judge?

a.   Look at Canon 3E(1)(b). In National Auto Brokers Corp. v. General Motors Corp., 572 F.2d 953 (2d Cir.1978), four years into an antitrust case, the plaintiffs moved to recuse the judge because the judge's former law firm represented the defendant. The 2nd Circuit held that while defendant was a client of the firm while the judge was there, he had never represented the defendant and the specific case did not come to the firm until after the judge had left.

b.   Is the judge-clerk relationship likely to have been more close or less than the judge's relationship with his or her law partners?

Monument Builders of Pennsylvania, Inc. v. Catholic Cemeteries Association, Inc., 190 F.R.D. 164 (E.D.Pa.1999), involved a lawyer who had been the judge's clerk in 1984 when the federal district court considered a class action against various cemetery associations. Indeed, she had been the judge's clerk until his retirement in 1998. The parties brought a new case in 1999 to enforce a settlement agreement that the parties had entered into with the judge's approval in 1989. The former clerk was with the firm representing the plaintiff and had been involved in working on the enforcement action. The court held that the enforcement action was the same matter as that begun in 1984 so the lawyer was disqualified under both Rule 1.12 of the ABA Model Rule of Professional Conduct and Canon 2 of the Code of Conduct for federal law clerks. Her law firm, however, was not disqualified because she telecommuted and the firm could easily screen her from further involvement in the matter.

In Bradley v. State of Alaska, 16 P.3d 187 (Alaska Ct.App.2001), the State moved to allow a former appellate court law clerk to represent the

5. See Ronald D. Rotunda, Rubbish About Recusal, Wall Street Journal, December 13, 2000, at A26.

State in the appeal. The proposed lawyer had been a clerk while the appeal was pending, but by the time the appeal had been assigned to a judge within the court, the clerk had finished his clerkship and begun working for the State. The court agreed that the clerk could handle the appeal, even though the state appellate rule seemed to impose a blanket ban on participation in a case that had been pending in the court during the period in which he served. The court looked to the state's later adoption of Model Rule of Professional Conduct 1.12(a), allowing a law clerk to participate in a case that was previously pending in the court in which the clerk served unless he "participated personally and substantially" in the matter during his time as a clerk. The former clerk submitted an affidavit declaring that he had no contact with any of the pleadings in this appeal and that he did not discuss any aspect of this case with any judge, secretary, law clerk, or other court system employee. Thus, the State's motion to let him handle the appeal was granted.

C.   BIAS ARISING FROM PERSONAL VIEWS RATHER THAN FINANCIAL INTEREST

1.   Does Judge Baxter's prior involvement in the Committee for Responsible Assessment Policy require his recusal from the case challenging the plaintiff's assessment?

a.   Do Canons 2B and 3E provide an answer or only suggest more questions? Chief Justice Rehnquist weighed in on the issue shortly after he joined the Supreme Court:

> "Though the Canons of Ethics are extraordinarily detailed and specific about what shall constitute a 'financial interest,' they have virtually nothing to say about what constitutes 'bias.' The Canons state that: 'A judge should disqualify himself in a proceeding in which his impartiality might reasonably be questioned * * *.' [Webster's Dictionary defines 'impartiality' as] 'freedom from bias or favoritism'; one of the definitions of 'bias' in that same volume is 'an inclination of temperament or outlook.' In that broad definition of 'bias,' one can scarcely escape the conclusion that all judges, to a greater or lesser extent, are biased. * * * The late Justice Black was, in this sense of the word, 'biased' in favor of a literal construction of the First Amendment to the United States Constitution, and made no bones about saying so. But it cannot be this sort of 'bias' which would disqualify a judge, else it would be the rare case in which a quorum of a court could be mustered for decision.

> "[The] true distinction is between the concept of attitude or outlook, which is not disqualifying, and the concept of 'favoritism,' which is disqualifying. Favoritism to me means a tendency or inclination to treat a particular litigant more or less generously than a different litigant raising the identical legal issue.

> " * * * It is apparently thought by some that if a judge has spoken publicly on an issue which later comes before him as a judge, he ought to disqualify himself from sitting in the case. * * * If what is sought to

be avoided is any publicly expressed notion of how the judge might vote on a particular issue, the best evidence of his propensities would presumably be previous opinions on the same question or a related question which he has either authored or concurred in as a judge; and yet no one has ever advanced this as a ground for disqualification. Even if the concept be limited to statements made prior to assuming the bench, enforcement of such a rule would scarcely guarantee that the judge's mind would be a *tabula rasa*, even if such were thought desirable; it would merely separate those who might have advanced professional opinions publicly from those who advanced them privately.
* * *

"Even more far afield from any established norm of judicial disqualification is the notion that a sitting judge may not properly engage in private conversations at a social event about matters of general interest, even those with legal overtones, without fear of some sort of professional damnation or the prospect of having to disqualify himself if a case involving some aspect of this general issue should ever come before him. I was sitting with a group of people whom I didn't know very well at a dinner party in Washington this summer, during the time the Watergate hearings were being televised daily. Not long after we sat down, the subject turned, as it doubtless did at most other dinner parties in Washington that evening, to the subject of Watergate and what the various diners thought of the various witnesses. In the midst of the discussion, one of the speakers turned to me and said: 'Wait a minute. We probably shouldn't be talking about this in front of you, because it will probably come to the Supreme Court eventually.'

"I thanked him for his consideration, but added that if listening to this conversation were to render me damaged goods for the purpose of adjudication, it was at most harmless error in view of the damage I had already sustained by being exposed to the daily newspapers and television news programs.

"[Some people] treat judicial disqualification for interest or bias as a matter of personal honor, such that the more ready a judge is to disqualify himself, the higher shall be his standing on the list compiled by that descendant of Abou Ben Adhem who specializes in judges. Once we depart from the area of corruption, or reasonable grounds to suspect corruption, * * * the decision as to disqualification in a particular instance ought, like so many other questions, to be decided by weighing the relevant factors on the appropriate legal scale. The factors favoring disqualification are familiar to us all; the factors which weigh against disqualification are less well advertised.

"Judicial disqualification at the trial court level, and often at the appellate court level where the appellate court does not sit *en banc* can result in docketing and scheduling problems which, while no one would say they outweigh a moral imperative on the other side, ought not to be lightly disregarded. Judicial disqualification at the appellate level has the added disadvantage of causing the decision of the case to be made by less than a full complement of the court charged with responsibility for the decision. [The] standards, both of the statute and of the Canons, pertaining to disqualification for interest and for bias are themselves based on the desire to avoid the appearance of impropriety on the part of a judge, there is no need to throw into the scales, as an additional standard over and above those addressed to disqualification, a desire to 'avoid the appearance of impropriety.'

"During my sixteen years of the private practice of law, the judge who was the most 'sensitive' to the 'appearance of impropriety' of any I knew sat in a court of general jurisdiction in the state where I practiced. He was so 'sensitive' to the appearance of impropriety that if he had so much as shaken hands at a large political gathering with one of the litigants who appeared before him, he would summarily disqualify himself. The principal result of this 'sensitivity' on his part, so far as I could see, was that at least one working day a week he was able to reach the first tee of the golf course before eleven o'clock in the morning, or else get home and do some of those odd jobs which escape the attention of all of us on the weekends. * * * "[6]

b. Do you agree with Chief Justice Rehnquist's approach to policy bias? Will his attempt to distinguish 'bias' from 'favoritism' help Judge Baxter know what he should do? Is he right that any thoughtful person old enough to become a judge is likely to have well formed views on many questions of public policy?

2. Should it be harder to disqualify a judge for a bias based on policy preferences than for bias based on financial or other personal grounds?

a. Sometimes the line between financial grounds for disqualification and the judge's policy preferences grounds is less clear than one might think.

In Aetna Life Insurance Co. v. Lavoie, 475 U.S. 813, 106 S.Ct. 1580, 89 L.Ed.2d 823 (1986), for example, appellees had submitted a health insurance claim to Aetna, which had paid about half of the amount requested. It had failed to pay the rest, about $1,375, on the ground that the length of the hospitalization was unnecessary. Appellant sought punitive damages for the alleged bad faith refusal to pay the claim and the jury awarded $3.5 million in punitive damages. The Alabama Supreme Court affirmed (5 to 4) in an opinion written by Justice Embry.

While the case was pending before the Alabama Supreme Court, Justice Embry had himself filed two actions against other insurance companies making similar allegations and seeking punitive damages. The U.S. Supreme Court held that "only in the most extreme of cases would disqualification [for bias or prejudice] be constitutionally required, and appellant's arguments [based on the judge's general hostility toward insurance companies] here fall well below that level." However, the Court held,

---

6. Hon. William H. Rehnquist, Sense and Nonsense About Judicial Ethics, 28 Record of Assoc. of the Bar of the City of New York 694, 708–713 (1973).

much more than Justice Embry's general hostility was at stake. This was the first case in which the Alabama Supreme Court clearly established the right of action upon which Justice Embry was seeking to rely in his own simultaneous litigation. The Supreme Court held that a decision rendered under these circumstances violated due process. "Justice Embry's opinion for the Alabama Supreme Court had the clear and immediate effect of enhancing both the legal status and the settlement value of his own case," it said. "We hold simply that when Justice Embry made that judgment, he acted as 'a judge in his own case.'" 475 U.S. at 824, 106 S.Ct. at 1586, 89 L.Ed.2d at 834. Three justices concurred but made the point that they would have found Justice Embry's participation improper even if his had not been the deciding vote in the case and even if he had not written the majority opinion.

b. Even interests the judge may have forgotten about might appear to others to constitute an impermissible "bias" in a judge.

Thus, in Liljeberg v. Health Services Acquisition Corp., 486 U.S. 847, 108 S.Ct. 2194, 100 L.Ed.2d 855 (1988), after a bench trial about who owned a hospital corporation, the loser learned that the trial judge was a trustee of Loyola University. During the time the case was pending, the ultimate winner, Liljeberg, was negotiating with Loyola to buy some land for a hospital and prevailing in the litigation was central to Liljeberg's ability to buy Loyola's land. The judge had ruled for Liljeberg, which thereby benefitted Loyola. Health Services thus moved to vacate the judgment, alleging that the trial judge should have disqualified himself under § 455(a). At a hearing to determine what the trial judge knew, he testified that he knew about the land dealings before the case was filed, but that he had forgotten all about them during the pendency of the matter. He learned again of Loyola's interest after his decision, but before the expiration of the 10 days in which the loser could move for a new trial. Even then, the judge did not recuse himself or tell the parties what he knew.

The Court of Appeals reversed the judgement in favor of Liljeberg in the underlying case and the Supreme Court affirmed by a 5–4 vote. The Court held that "[s]cienter is not an element of a violation of § 455(a)." While the trial judge could not have disqualified himself over something about which he was unaware, he was "called upon to rectify an oversight and to take the steps necessary to maintain public confidence in the impartiality of the judiciary." Moreover, while § 455 does not, on its own, authorize the reopening of closed litigation, "Congress has wisely delegated to the judiciary the task of fashioning the remedies that will best serve the purpose of the litigation." The Court recognized that while harmless error could justify failing to reverse a judgment in some cases, in this instance the appearance of impropriety required reversal of the judgment because there was "ample basis in the record for concluding that an objective observer would have questioned" the trial judge's impartiality. Moreover, the trial judge's failure to stay informed of his fiduciary interest in Loyola University "may well constitute a separate violation of § 455. See § 455(c)."

Chief Justice Rehnquist, joined by Justices White & Scalia, dissenting, said that § 455(a) required an "actual knowledge" standard. Justice O'Connor agreed and would have remanded as well to determine whether "extraordinary circumstances" justified a reversal of the underlying case. With which of these opinions do you agree?

c.   Might a judge's religious beliefs arguably "bias" the judge in violation of 28 U.S.C. § 455 and Model Code of Judicial Conduct, Canon 3E?

Idaho v. Freeman, 507 F.Supp. 706 (D.Idaho 1981), involved a judge hearing a case concerning the constitutionality of Congress' extension of the deadline for ratification of the Equal Rights Amendment. The principal leaders of the Church of Jesus Christ of Latter-day Saints (popularly called the "Mormons") had publicly opposed both the ERA and extension of the deadline. The judge was a Mormon; indeed he was a lay regional representative of that church. However, the church was not a party to the case, the judge was neither required nor requested to promote the church's position as a judge, and his duties as a church officer did not relate to the ERA. The judge thus concluded that his religious affiliation did not require him to disqualify himself.

Do you agree that the judge's conclusion was correct? Does the "appearance of bias" standard have to be subject to reasonable limits? Would a conclusion that religious beliefs did constitute impermissible bias lead to consequences worse than having the judge hear the case? For example, if recusal were required in this case, could a judge who believed in God hear a case brought by an atheist objecting to a city display of a Christmas tree? If the judge who believed in God were disqualified, would an atheist be similarly disqualified? The general rule is, then, that religious beliefs (or lack of them) do not mandate disqualification.

3.   Should it matter whether the judge's views on a question were formed outside the courtroom or from information learned in the role of judge?

a.   The "extrajudicial source doctrine," that views formed in the course of trying a case should not normally be disqualifying, is usually traced to United States v. Grinnell Corp., 384 U.S. 563, 583, 86 S.Ct. 1698, 1710, 16 L.Ed.2d 778, 793 (1966): "The alleged bias and prejudice to be disqualifying must stem from an extrajudicial source." The challenge for later courts has been defining when that doctrine should apply and when it should not.

b.   In Liteky v. United States, 510 U.S. 540, 114 S.Ct. 1147, 127 L.Ed.2d 474 (1994), for example, three defendants were charged with spilling human blood on walls and objects at Fort Benning, GA. The judge assigned to preside at their trial had tried and convicted one of the defendants, Father Bourgeois, for similar conduct eight years earlier. During that first trial, the judge had repeatedly admonished the defense to limit its evidence and argument to the issues in the case, not the motivations for the protest. On the basis of those admonitions, it was alleged that the judge's "impartiality might reasonably be questioned" and that 28 U.S.C.A. § 455(a) thus required his recusal. The judge refused to recuse himself, and the defendants were convicted.

Justice Scalia, writing for the Court, observed that a "judge who presides at a trial may, upon completion of the evidence, be exceedingly ill disposed towards the defendant, who has been shown to be a thoroughly reprehensible person. But the judge is not thereby recusable for bias or prejudice, since his knowledge and the opinion it produced were properly and necessarily acquired in the course of the proceedings, and are indeed sometimes (as in a bench trial) necessary to completion of the judge's task." 510 U.S. at 550–51, 114 S.Ct. at 1155, 127 L.Ed.2d at 488.

However, extrajudicial sources are "not the *exclusive* reason a predisposition can be wrongful or inappropriate." A point of view can also constitute "bias or prejudice" even if it comes from a judicial source, if "it is so extreme as to display clear inability to render fair judgment." Id. The Court concluded that judicial rulings alone almost never constitute valid basis for a disqualification motion; "they are proper grounds for appeal, not recusal." And, "opinions formed by the judge on the basis of facts introduced or events occurring in the course of the current proceedings, or of prior proceedings, do not constitute a basis for a bias or partiality motion unless they display a deep–seated favoritism or antagonism that would make a fair judgment impossible." Clearly, "expressions of impatience, dissatisfaction, annoyance, and even anger" such as shown by this judge at the first trial, do not constitute bias. 510 U.S. at 555–56, 114 S.Ct. at 1157, 127 L.Ed.2d at 490–91.

Justice Kennedy, concurring in the judgment on behalf of himself and Justices Blackmun, Stevens and Souter, and found the Court's "impossibility of fair judgment" standard objectively different from the "impartiality might reasonably be questioned" standard of 28 U.S.C. § 455(a). They believed the first might be a fair reading of § 455(b)(1), but that Congress intended § 455(a) to reach any case in which "an objective observer [would] conclude that a fair and impartial hearing is unlikely." In this case, however, the Judge's prior conduct did not require recusal under either standard. 510 U.S. at 564, 114 S.Ct. at 1162, 127 L.Ed.2d at 497.

c. Just two years before *Liteky*, the court in Haines v. Liggett Group, 975 F.2d 81 (3d Cir.1992), ordered a change in trial judges. Judge Lee Sarokin had conducted the trial of, and was assigned to retry, the nation's major cigarette companies who stood accused of producing a product that caused cancer. In a opinion from the bench applying the crime-fraud exception to allegedly privileged documents, he said: "Who are these persons who knowingly and secretly decide to put the buying public at risk solely for the purpose of making profits and who believe that illness and death of consumers is an appropriate cost of their own prosperity! * * * [T]he tobacco industry may be the king of concealment and disinformation." 975 F.2d at 97. The Court of Appeals acknowledged that they believed Judge Sarokin could try the case "free from bias or prejudice," but "that is not the test." Instead, the "polestar is 'impartiality and the appearance of impartiality.' " Id. at 98. Thus, the court ordered a change of judge.

Should a Court reach the same result on these facts after *Liteky*? Was this what Justice Scalia had in mind in leaving open the possibility that even some statements made in the course of judicial proceedings would show that a judge's "fair judgment [is] impossible"?

d. In United States v. Antar, 53 F.3d 568 (3d Cir.1995), a jury had convicted "Crazy Eddie," a well-known consumer electronics retailer, of fraud. At the sentencing hearing, as he considered how much restitution to award, the judge said that "from day one" in the case, his object had been to return to the public what the defendants had "taken" from them. The defendant cited this as evidence of bias and the Third Circuit agreed. The court acknowledged that "[p]ost-*Liteky* cases involving allegations of bias derived from judicial proceedings have construed the exception to the extrajudicial source requirement narrowly." 53 F.2d at 574. Even though the comments came after conviction they reflected a bias that had existed "from day one." If the judge had made the remarks on "day one," they clearly would have been a basis for recusal, so the fact the judge only made them after trial was not controlling. The court reversed the conviction and sent the case sent back for trial before another judge.[7]

e. If you were Judge Baxter, would you now know whether you should sit when issues concerning real estate assessments were before the court? Would you be more confused than ever? What would you do?

D. WAIVING JUDICIAL DISQUALIFICATION

1. Are all circumstances requiring a judge's disqualification subject to waiver by the parties? How about all of the issues raised by this Problem?

a. Is the conflict created by Martha Anderson's loan to Judge Baxter subject to waiver by the parties? Look at Model Code of Judicial Conduct, Canon 3F. Compare 28 U.S.C. § 455(e). Why might the federal statute allow fewer conflicts to be waived than does the Judicial Code?

b. Would any conflicts created by financial interests of the judge's relatives be subject to waiver by the parties? Again, is there any justification for treating state and federal judges differently as to this issue?

c. Would Judge Baxter's possible bias against current assessment practices similarly be subject to waiver? Could his views be said to consti-

---

7. Compare United States v. Microsoft Corporation, 253 F.3d 34, 116 (D.C.Cir.2001) (district judge disqualified only retroactive to order breaking up Microsoft). See also, In re International Business Machines Corp., 45 F.3d 641 (2d Cir.1995) (mandamus issued to recuse judge who was critical of government decision to dismiss case); United States v. Microsoft Corp., 56 F.3d 1448 (D.C.Cir.1995) (new judge required to hear remand of case in which judge had set aside consent decree agreed to by the Antitrust Division); Hathcock v. Navistar International, 53 F.3d 36 (4th Cir.1995) (judge showed bias against tort defendants in speech before Trial Lawyers' Association).

tute "personal bias or prejudice concerning a party"? If not, would his recusal be subject to waiver in both the state and federal systems?

2. How should the judge secure a valid waiver?

a. Compare Model Code of Judicial Conduct, Canon 3F, with 28 U.S.C. § 455(e). What must the judge "disclose" about the grounds for required recusal? Must consent to waive a judge's recusal be as "informed" as consent to waive a lawyer's conflict of interest, for example? See Model Rule of Professional Conduct 1.0(e).

b. May counsel make the waiver orally on the record in the manner defense counsel did in this Problem? Look at Canon 3F. Is there any comparable requirement in § 455(e)? Should lawyers be permitted to waive a disqualifying circumstance on behalf of their clients?

c. Are you satisfied that the procedure specified in the Code of Judicial Conduct will guarantee anonymity to an objector? Is such anonymity important in a setting in which the parties and their counsel may have to appear before the judge again in the future?

PROBLEM 39

THE JUDGE AS A POLITICAL CANDIDATE AND PUBLIC FIGURE

Many states choose their judges by popular election. Judges who run for office have to raise campaign funds, engage in political speeches and participate in other forms of political campaigns. Some people think that it is unseemly for judges to campaign for office; others support election of judges but believe that ethical rules should limit what a judge can say or do in a political campaign. Further, if judges are limited in what they can say about themselves, then arguably others should also be limited in what they may say about the judges. This problem first looks at what judges may say and do in a political campaign. Next, it examines how a judge may raise the funds necessary to participate in electoral politics. Third, it asks what limits lawyers face in making critical comments about a judge. Fourth, it considers what limits are imposed on what a judge may say about others.

FACTS

J. R. Kraft, a local lawyer, was a declared candidate for a vacancy on the trial court at a recent election. Shortly before the primary, the following advertisement appeared in the newspaper in his judicial district:

J. R. KRAFT

(A Working Man's Son)

— The Next Best Thing to Being a Judge Yourself —

I, J. R. Kraft, am a local boy. My Dad died when I was eight, and I worked in a foundry for ten years to earn enough money to go to law school. I have never lost a jury trial in all my time in practice and I have never been a member of a political party. If elected, I will do my best to stop inflation, give the benefit of the doubt to any working man who comes before me, and throw the book at every weirdo and pervert I can find.

Permissiveness is the issue in this campaign. My opponent stupidly gave bail to a 45-year-old low-life who everybody knew had raped a 12-year-old child, but then he slapped a $500 fine on a working man who had been laid off. You can count on me never to do those things!

VOTE FOR J. R. KRAFT

[C2592]

To most people's surprise, Kraft won the primary. To everyone's surprise, the "non-politician" became a party stalwart. He made the rounds of political meetings and gave a five-minute speech at each about how good it was for a working man's son to be on the ticket with the likes of Governor Ford, Senator Barker, and Mayor Black. He called upon "all working people" to support the entire ticket "from the top down to little me at the bottom."

At several meetings, listeners called him aside and pressed $1, $5, $10 or even $20 into his hand to help him meet his campaign expenses. He turned most of the money over to his campaign committee, but he used $389.95 of it to buy a second suit.

Kraft's style appealed to the voters. He won the general election as well and became a judge. He still had some campaign expenses left unpaid, so two weeks after the election he asked his campaign committee to solicit members of the bar to make up the deficit.

After Kraft was on the bench for less than a year, he presided over a major murder trial, which the defense won after Kraft approved unusual jury instructions. Ellen Embers, the State's Attorney, was quite upset. She had no right of appeal, of course, so she called a press conference and said: "Judge Kraft is the most biased, incompetent judge that I have ever seen. He ruled against the people throughout the recent murder trial, and he alone is responsible for letting a maniacal killer out to prey on the citizens of this county."

Two weeks later, State's Attorney Embers issued a statement from her office. "The rumors around the court house have been intense the past several weeks that Judge Kraft tilts his decisions toward Anthony Roberts, the city's leading slum landlord and a regular litigant before Judge Kraft, because Roberts was a major contributor to Kraft's election campaign. I have filed a grievance with the Judicial Inquiry Board to have Judge Kraft investigated and, if the rumors are true, to have him removed from the bench."

In the meantime, one of Kraft's close friends, who was also a major contributor to Kraft's campaign, is now on trial for perjury and bribery in connection with allegedly corrupt labor practices. His defense is that he engaged in an innocent, if careless, oversight. He has asked Judge Kraft to be a character witness. Kraft, who would disqualify himself anyway if the case came before him, said: "Of course, but it would be better if you would subpoena me."

QUESTIONS

A.   THE CONTENT OF JUDICIAL CAMPAIGN SPEECH AND ACTIVITIES

1.   What does the Model Code of Judicial Conduct say about Kraft's advertisement in his campaign to become a state judge?

a.   Should it matter that Kraft was not yet a judge at the time the advertisement was run? Look at Model Rules of Professional Responsibility, Rule 8.2(b). Is such a rule required to assure that no candidate can impair the dignity of a judicial campaign? Does it necessarily favor incumbent judges by making it harder for newcomers to unseat them?

b.   Under the Model Code of Judicial Conduct, will the content of Kraft's advertisement subject him to discipline? Look at Canons 5A(3)(a) & 5A(3)(d). If the advertisement had been extolling the lawyer's credentials for sheriff, would it have violated ethical standards to make these charges and promises? Should the standard be different when the lawyer is instead running for judge?

c.   In re Judicial Campaign Complaint Against Burick, 705 N.E.2d 422 (Ohio Commission of Judges 1999), found that a judicial candidate had (1) said that the incumbent judge had been appointed the previous year by "political bosses," (2) said that she (the candidate) "supports the death penalty and isn't afraid to use it," and (3) accused the incumbent judge of giving a lenient sentence to a convicted rapist when in fact the defendant had receive the maximum sentence for a lesser offense to which the judge had accepted a plea of guilty. The special commission appointed to hear the case held that a judicial candidate could only say things about the appointments process that would "further, not obscure, the public's understanding of the law and legal system." It then found that the incumbent judge had been appointed, not by political bosses, but by the Governor. Further, while a non-judicial candidate could express views about the death penalty, a judicial candidate must refrain from making statements "that adversely reflect on their impartiality." It concluded that the comment about the alleged rape sentence was improper because the case was still pending on appeal. Thus, it publicly reprimanded the candidate, fined her $7,500, and ordered her to pay the complainant $5,000 for attorneys' fees and expenses. Do you agree with this result?

2. Is J.R. Kraft's campaign speech constitutionally protected even if it violated the Model Code of Judicial Conduct?

a. Courts are looking more carefully at the restrictions imposed on judicial campaign speech. In Buckley v. Illinois Judicial Inquiry Board, 997 F.2d 224 (7th Cir.1993), for example, the Seventh Circuit declared unconstitutional a state judicial rule providing that "a candidate, including an incumbent judge, for a judicial office filled by election or retention ... should not make pledges or promises of conduct in office other than the faithful and impartial performance of the duties of the office; announce his views on disputed legal or political issues * * * ." One of the plaintiffs was an appellate judge whose campaign literature accurately stated that he had "never written an opinion reversing a rape conviction." Another was a member of the state legislature who wanted to speak out on "capital punishment, abortion, the state budget and public school education."

The Seventh Circuit, per Judge Posner, said the case required the reconciliation of two principles: candidates for public office should be free to express their views and judges should decide cases on the merits, unaffected by campaign promises they may have made. "[O]nly a fanatic would suppose that one of the principles should give way completely to the other * * * ."

The court noted that the Illinois rule was broader than ABA Model Code of Judicial Conduct, Canon 5A(3)(d)(ii). The Illinois rule, the court said, was overinclusive. The "pledges or promises" clause is not "limited to pledges or promises to rule a particular way * * *; all pledges or promises are forbidden * * * . The 'announce' clause is not limited to declarations as to how the candidate intends to rule in particular cases or classes of case; he cannot 'announce his views on disputed legal or political issues,' period." Curtailing speech this broadly violated the First Amendment. 997 F.2d at 228. The court admitted that its opinion created "undoubted tension" with another circuit, Stretton v. Disciplinary Board, 944 F.2d 137 (3d Cir.1991), which had upheld a similar rule, but *Stretton*, the court said, "is distinguishable, although precariously."

b. In Pittman v. Cole, 267 F.3d 1269 (11th Cir.2001), candidates for seats on Alabama courts sued the state Judicial Inquiry Commission. The Christian Coalition of Alabama wanted to publish voter guides regarding judicial candidates, but the Commission's enforcement policy precluded judges and judicial candidates from responding to the survey from which the organization would create their guides. The plaintiffs claimed that enforcement of the policy would violate their First Amendment rights, while the Commission maintained that the guide was a way for potential judges to announce their prejudgment of certain important issues. The Eleventh Circuit approved certification of the state law issues to the state supreme court before the district court ruled on the First Amendment claims.

c.   Then, in Republican Party of Minnesota v. White, 536 U.S. 765, 122 S.Ct. 2528, 153 L.Ed.2d 694 (2002), the U.S. Supreme Court agreed that state ethics rules that unduly restrict political campaign speech of judicial candidates violate the First Amendment. The parties did not challenge the Minnesota rule that prohibits a judicial candidate or judge from making "pledges or promises" as to how he or she will rule in a particular case. However, the Court declared unconstitutional the rule prohibiting a candidate for judicial office from "announcing" a view on a "disputed legal or political" issue, even as interpreted to apply only to matters likely to come before the candidate's court.

Speaking through Justice Scalia, the 5–person majority said that the announce clause must not "unnecessarily circumscrib[e] protected expression," and that the Minnesota rule did not meet this test. One common view of "impartiality" is an absence of bias toward any party to the proceeding, the Court said, but the announce clause is not tailored to serve that interest because "it does not restrict speech for or against particular parties, but rather speech for or against particular issues." A lack of preconception for or against a particular legal view is not a compelling state interest, the Court said, "since it is virtually impossible, and hardly desirable, to find a judge who does not have preconceptions about the law."[1] 122 S.Ct. at 2536.

Nor does the prohibition promote impartiality in the sense of "open-mindedness" because the announce clause is "woefully underinclusive." For example, a judge may confront a legal issue on which he has expressed an opinion, whether on or off the bench. "Judges often state their views on disputed legal issues outside the context of adjudication, in classes that they conduct, and in books and speeches." Id. at 2537. The Minnesota rule allows a judicial candidate to say, "I think it is constitutional for the legislature to prohibit same-sex marriage" up until "the very day before he declares himself a candidate, and [he] may say it repeatedly (until litigation is pending) after he is elected. As a means of pursuing the objective of open-mindedness that respondents now articulate, the announce clause is so woefully underinclusive as to render belief in that purpose a challenge to the credulous." Id.

1. The Court acknowledged the views of then-Justice Rehnquist described in Prob-   lem 38, supra.

Justice Kennedy, concurring, added: "Minnesota may not * * * censor what the people hear as they undertake to decide for themselves which candidate is most likely to be an exemplary judicial officer. Deciding the relevance of candidate speech is the right of the voters, not the State." Id. at 2545.

Dissenting opinions joined by Justices Stevens, Souter, Ginsburg and Breyer argued that the office of judge is significantly different from a legislative or executive office. Judges are supposed to be elected because they have integrity, not because their views are popular. Thus, they argued, the speech of judges, and those seeking to be judges, can be restricted in ways that the speech of others cannot be.

d. With which of these positions do you agree? Given the logic of these cases, do you believe that other provisions of Canon 5 of the ABA Model Code of Judicial Conduct are likely to be similarly at risk of being successfully challenged?

3. How misleading or inaccurate should judicial advertising have to be before it subjects the judge to discipline? Should the judge be subject to discipline because he makes a statement that his opponents think is incomplete? Should we leave it to the judge's opponents to point that out in the campaign?

a. In an Illinois judicial election, the Chicago Council of Lawyers—a group representing an important segment of the Bar—wrote:

"Judge Elward * * * is *a person of substantial intellectual ability who works hard,* but reports from many lawyers also indicate clearly that he has a terrible judicial temperament characterized by extreme rigidity, unreasonable demands and positions, and closed-mindedness. His efforts *to achieve worthy objectives—such as avoiding delays in the court process* attributable to dilatory lawyers—have in several cases been vitiated by the rigidity and excessive zeal with which he has attempted to pursue them. Because of his clear lack of judicial temperament, the Council concludes that he should not be retained as a judge." (emphasis added).

With the judge's approval, a "Citizens Committee" published an advertisement before the election in certain suburban newspapers and the Chicago Sun Times. The advertisements quoted from an editorial that had appeared in the Chicago Tribune, a statement by a former president of the Chicago Bar Association, and continued:

"* * * a person of substantial intellectual ability who works hard * * * to achieve worthy objectives—such as avoiding delays in the court process."

"CHICAGO COUNCIL OF LAWYERS"

Judge Elward was retained in office and he then faced a complaint for publishing an advertisement that was "materially misleading." The Courts

Commission, a panel of judges established to consider judicial discipline, disagreed:

> "We find analogous the test which has been applied in determining whether in the light of the circumstances under which they were made, omissions to state a material fact in a registration statement, filed with the Securities and Exchange Commission, were misleading. The rule applied is that 'the adequacy of disclosure of material information must be evaluated by a consideration of the "total mix" of all information conveyed or available to the investors [voters].' "

The Commission found that several unrelated news stories and editorials had appeared that were critical of Judge Elward and that several had accurately reported the Chicago Council of Lawyers evaluation. The Commission concluded:

> "Measured against this 'total mix,' we conclude that the respondent, in the use of excerpts from the Council's statements, did not create the false impression that the Council had recommended him for retention or that he had significant Bar Association support.

> " * * * Canon 7 of the Code of Judicial Conduct adopted by the American Bar Association, recognize[s] that a judge seeking retention may find himself confronted with the necessity of mounting a campaign. On this record, we hold that the use of the advertisements in the manner alleged in the Complaint did not constitute conduct that was prejudicial to the administration of justice or that brought the judicial office into disrepute. The Complaint is, accordingly, dismissed."

In re Circuit Judge Paul F. Elward, Case No. 77, Illinois Courts Commission 1 (1977).

b. Do you agree with this result? Is the right issue whether Judge Elward's advertisement was misleading? Whether or not it was misleading, did its use show Judge Elward to be dishonest or otherwise unfit?

c. Is the SEC analogy apt? Would a person charged with misstatements in a registration statement be heard to defend that the investor could have put together the true picture from stories in the *Wall Street Journal*?[2]

4. What other limits are there on other political activities in which a judge may engage?

a. May he or she make speeches on behalf of candidates for nonjudicial public office? Look at ABA Model Code of Judicial Conduct, Canon 5A(1)(b). Do you agree that the public should be concerned about judges making such speeches? Why or why not?

---

2. For a good debate about this case, compare Rubin G. Cohn, Judicial Discipline in Illinois—a Commentary on the Judge Elward Decision, 59 Chi. Bar Rec. 200 (1978), with Donald H. Reuben and Leonard M. Ring, Judges Have Rights Too, Id. at 220.

b. How about contributing money to a political party or to other candidates? Compare Canons 5A(1)(e) and 5C(1)(a). What is the distinction being drawn by those provisions?

c. May a judicial candidate run as part of a party team? See Canon 5C(5).

d. If Judge Kraft wanted to run for Congress, would he be required to resign from the bench first? Look at Canon 5A(2). If a state senator wanted to run for Congress, would he or she similarly be required to resign the state office first? Why do we treat judges differently?

B. JUDGES SOLICITING AND RECEIVING CAMPAIGN CONTRIBUTIONS

1. Are you troubled by the fact that judges receive endorsements and campaign contributions from the lawyers who appear before them?

a. Think back to Problem 38 and the cases condemning lawyers' payments to judges. Why should campaign contributions be distinguished from any other gifts made to a judge?

b. The multi-billion dollar Pennzoil v. Texaco litigation was conducted primarily in the Texas state courts. The trial judge is reported to have received a $10,000 campaign contribution from Pennzoil's chief trial lawyer "[w]ithin days of being assigned the Pennzoil case," a sum the trial judge described as "princely." Wall Street Journal, Nov. 4, 1987, at 1, 20, col. 2. In the three and one-half years prior to their decision in *Pennzoil*, all nine members of the Texas Supreme Court are said to have, consistent with Texas law, "openly accepted campaign contributions from lawyers with cases pending before them." Forbes, Sept. 7, 1987, at 8.

c. If lawyers may make contributions to judges deciding their clients' cases, do the lawyers have any choice but to do so? Do you agree with the last sentence of Commentary [1] following Canon 3C(2) that large campaign contributions from a litigant or lawyer could be a basis for questioning the judge's impartiality?

2. In this Problem, J.R. Kraft accepted campaign contributions pressed into his hand. Was it proper for him to do so?

a. The Model Code of Judicial Conduct prescribes the proper method of handling campaign contributions in Canons 5C(2) to 5C(4). Do you think establishment of a campaign committee will prevent the judge from learning which lawyers support his or her candidacy and the generosity of that support? Are there other reasons to require creating such a committee?

b. Does the requirement of a campaign committee impair free speech? Weaver v. Bonner, 309 F.3d 1312 (11th Cir.2002), held Georgia's version of it unconstitutional, saying:

> "[E]ven if there is a risk that judges will be tempted to rule a particular way because of contributions or endorsements, this risk is not significantly reduced by allowing the candidate's agent to seek these contributions and endorsements on the candidate's behalf rather

than the candidate seeking them himself. Successful candidates will feel beholden to the people who helped them get elected regardless of who did the soliciting of support. Canon [5C(2)] thus fails strict scrutiny because it completely chills a candidate's speech on these topics while hardly advancing the state's interest in judicial impartiality at all." 309 F.3d at 1322–23.

Do you agree with the court's analysis? Whose free speech is limited by requiring that an intermediary be placed between the judge and those who want to give the judge money?

3. May a judge's campaign committee solicit funds from lawyers *after* the election when the winner is known?

a. Look at the penultimate sentence of ABA Model Code of Judicial Conduct, Canon 5C(2). Can you believe the position the provision takes on this question?

b. What arguments could be made in support of the position? Do we want judges starting out a new term of judicial service in substantial debt, for example? Might that put them under financial pressures that could be exploited by others later?

c. Does Commentary [2] following Canon 3C(2) have any teeth? Is its suggestion of good budgeting and self restraint any more than a way to assuage our collective embarrassment at permitting the practice of post-election fund raising at all?

4. Would a "merit system" of judicial selection—i.e., appointing judges, as in the federal system—remove all ethical issues from the selection process?

a. If all judges were appointed, might the "political activity" take other forms? Could a governor's aide properly question a prospective judge about his or her attitudes on bail for "low-lifes," for example? Look at Canon 5B(2).

b. Should it be proper for an attorney to work in a senator's election campaign in the hope of being rewarded with a federal judicial appointment? Is Canon 5B(2)(b) relevant to your answer?

C. LAWYER CRITICISM OF JUDGES

1. Should Ellen Embers, the State's Attorney in this Problem, be subject to discipline for making critical remarks about Judge Kraft at her press conference?

a. Justices of Appellate Division v. Erdmann, 301 N.E.2d 426 (N.Y. 1973) (per curiam), was a case whose facts appear only in the dissenting opinion.

> "The charge was based on [Erdmann's] statements and language used in an article entitled 'I Have Nothing To Do With Justice', which appeared in the March 12, 1971 issue of Life magazine. Lawyer Erdmann said of and concerning the

courts within the First Judicial Department: 'There are so few trial judges who just judge, who rule on questions of law, and leave guilt or innocence to the jury. And Appellate Division judges aren't any better. They're the whores who became madams. I would like to [be a judge] just to see if I could be the kind of judge I think a judge should be. But the only way you can get it is to be in politics or buy it—and I don't even know the going price.' * * * To play the game well, a lawyer must be ruthless. He is working within, but against a system that has been battered to its knees. He must not hesitate to kick it when it's down, and to take advantage of its weakness. * * * The exultation of winning dampens any moral feelings you have." 301 N.E.2d at 427.

The Appellate Division had censured the appellant for these remarks, but the Court of Appeals, in a brief opinion reversed, concluding:

"Without more, isolated instances of disrespect for the law, Judges and courts expressed by vulgar and insulting words or other incivility, uttered, written, or committed outside the precincts of a court are not subject to professional discipline. * * * Perhaps persistent or general courses of conduct, even if parading as criticism, which are degrading to the law, the Bar, and the courts, and are irrelevant or grossly excessive, would present a different issue. No such issue is presented now."

Two judges, however, dissented from that reversal. Judge Burke argued:

"The article, as well as the remarks, violate restrictions placed on attorneys which they impliedly assume when they accept admission to the Bar. * * * To require civility of a lawyer is not arbitrary or a violation of his constitutional rights. Children are repeatedly reprimanded for incivility. Does this amount to an abrogation of Federally protected rights?"

Judge Gabrielli, added:

"[I]t matters not whether the instances of disrespect for the administration of justice by the use of vulgar and insulting words or other acts of incivility, are uttered or committed outside the courtroom. The standard of conduct must remain unchanged even when the lawyer departs from the courtroom."

Would you have imposed discipline on lawyer Erdmann? Why or why not?

b.   In re Holtzman, 577 N.E.2d 30 (N.Y.1991) (per curiam), upheld a letter of reprimand issued to a district attorney who had publicly released a letter charging a trial judge with misconduct. The district attorney had been told by someone, and then repeated in her letter, that the judge in a sexual assault trial had made the complainant get down on the floor and in effect reenact the crime before the judge and counsel. The letter said that doing so made the complainant feel degraded and humiliated. A later investigation determined the charge was not supported by the evidence. N.Y. Times v. Sullivan, 376 U.S. 254, 84 S.Ct. 710, 11 L.Ed.2d 686 (1964), held that a public official cannot recover damages for a defamatory false-hood relating to his official conduct unless he proves that the defendant made the statement with "actual malice," which the Court defined as *scienter*; that is, that the statement was made "with knowledge that it was false or with reckless disregard of whether it was false or not."

The N.Y Court of Appeals, however, refused to apply the *Sullivan* standard to lawyer discipline cases. To do so, it said, "would immunize all accusations, however reckless or irresponsible, from censure as long as the attorney uttering them did not actually entertain serious doubts as to their truth. * * * It is the reasonableness of the belief, not the state of mind of the attorney, that is determinative" 577 N.E.2d at 31.

c. Should a court applying Model Rule 8.2(a) reach the same result? United States District Court v. Sandlin, 12 F.3d 861 (9th Cir.1993), affirmed a lawyer's 6 month suspension from practice before the District Court for falsely charging that the District Judge had ordered important passages deleted from the transcript of a recusal hearing. The lawyer made the statements in a hearing on the lawyer's charges and also in a statement to an Assistant U.S. Attorney. That, in turn, led to FBI scientific tests and a Grand Jury investigation that cleared the judge. The Court agreed that Rule 8.2(a) does not prohibit all criticism of judges, but it refused to read an "actual malice" standard into the "reckless disregard as to its truth or falsity" language of the rule. The test should be "what the reasonable attorney, considered in light of all his professional functions, would do in the same or similar circumstances." 12 F.3d at 867.

Do you agree with this reading of Model Rule 8.2(a)? See Restatement Third, The Law Governing Lawyers § 114, Comment *b* (*N.Y. Times* rule should apply to charges by lawyers about conduct of judges).

d. Standing Committee on Discipline of the United States District Court v. Yagman, 55 F.3d 1430 (9th Cir.1995), provides an interesting contrast to the result in *Sandlin*. Yagman, the lawyer, had tried to disqualify Judge Real from hearing a case. Judge Keller heard and rejected the disqualification motion and also imposed sanctions. Then, Yagman went after Judge Keller as well. He told the L.A. Daily Journal, a legal newspaper, that Judge Keller was "anti-Semitic", has "a penchant for sanctioning Jewish lawyers", and was "drunk on the bench." The district court concluded, after hearing testimony, that Yagman told another lawyer that by conducting this campaign against Judge Keller, he hoped to be able to disqualify Judge Keller from hearing any future cases he filed.

Relying on *Sandlin*, the Disciplinary Committee suspended Yagman from practicing in the Central District of California for 2 years, but the Ninth Circuit reversed. The disciplinary standard—conduct that "impugns the integrity of the Court"—is over broad, Judge Kozinski wrote for the panel. The lawyer's statements were mere opinion and "rhetorical hyperbole," the court said, and it placed the burden on the court to prove them false. "[R]espect for the judiciary [cannot] be won by shielding judges from published criticism." However, the court then went on to impose perhaps the ultimate sanction. It expressly said that Judge Keller was not required to recuse himself from hearing future cases in which Mr. Yagman appeared as counsel.

Do you agree with this result? Why do you suppose courts have such disparate reactions to these cases?

e.   Matter of Reed, 716 N.E.2d 426 (Ind.1999) (per curiam), involved a new judge who announced that she would herself hear cases involving welfare-related child support instead of referring the cases to a commissioner. The prosecuting attorney, who represented the state in such cases, objected to that practice. He gave an interview to the local paper and said about the judge: "Her arrogance is exceeded only by her ignorance." He also suggested the judge had made up a story about liquor being present in court offices. The state supreme court found the charges were inaccurate and made without any reasonable effort to verify them, so it imposed a public reprimand. Two justices dissented and would have suspended the prosecutor who was an experienced public lawyer, not acting under time pressure, who chose to make his remarks so as to get the widest possible circulation.

f.   Should your answers to questions regarding criticism of judges be affected by whether or not judges are elected in your state? Consider Comment [1] to Model Rule 8.2. Does the public have an interest in knowing about the integrity of the judges who stand for election? Would it matter how long it was until these judges next had to face the voters?

On the other hand, are elected judges particularly exposed to unjust vilification and unusually limited in the propriety of their responding to criticism? Should it be the judges with life tenure whom lawyers are most free to criticize?

2.   If another judge believed that Embers' charges against Judge Kraft were true, would that judge have an obligation to report Judge Kraft?

a.   Look at Model Code of Judicial Conduct, Canon 3D(1). Does Model Rule 8.3(b) also give State's Attorney Embers an obligation to move for disciplinary action against Judge Kraft? Should a lawyer be more limited in publicly announcing the filing of charges against a judge than if the charges had been filed against another public official? Is there a public interest in preserving confidence in the judiciary that may distinguish these from ordinary cases? Does the argument cut the other way, i.e., that public confidence in judges is instilled by making it knows that the system aggressively roots out corruption?

b.   If a judge were reckless in her comments accusing a fellow judge of misconduct, could the judge be sanctioned as a lawyer would be for making similar comments? Look at Model Code of Judicial Conduct, Canons 3D(1) and 3D(3). Should the judge's privilege against civil liability extend to immunity from disciplinary prosecution?

3. Should judicial discipline cases be confidential or open to the public?

a. Some states require that judicial discipline proceedings take place behind closed doors. In Illinois, for example, the state constitution provides that "All proceedings of the [Judicial Inquiry] Board shall be confidential except the filing of a complaint with the Courts Commission." Art. 6, sec. 15(c). Should any proceedings against Judge Kraft be closed to the public? Why or why not?

b. The American Bar Foundation published a study of judicial discipline by William T. Braithwaite that argued in favor of confidentiality:

"* * * [W]e may say that the general problem of judicial misconduct includes a range of particular problems, from occasional corruption and major felonies at one extreme to tardiness and discourtesy at the other. To be effective, a removal-discipline procedure should be able to deal with all these problems; that is, it should be capable of a range of dispositions, from informal admonition to formal public censure to termination of service. The procedure should, as well, be capable of operating reasonably expeditiously and with minimum cost and public spectacle.

"Although it is sometimes necessary (and sometimes unavoidable) that a trial of misconduct charges be public—for example, when the charges have been publicly made and are apparently well founded—there is in most cases nothing to be gained, and respect for the judiciary to be lost, by having a public proceeding. It is reasonable to assume that once the charges and evidence are privately made known to them, most judges who are accused of misconduct serious enough to warrant initiating a proceeding to remove them will prefer to resign or retire. After the charges become public, the judge has less to lose by contesting them to the finish. [Our research found that] in most cases where the sanction imposed is discipline rather than removal, it is done confidentially (and often informally) rather than publicly.

"The argument for confidentiality is even stronger in the case of disability. We learned * * * that the legal community finds it unacceptable to deal with the problem of disability by means of formal, public, adversary proceedings. * * *

"Maintaining confidentiality, at least in preliminary proceedings, serves several purposes. First, in those cases where termination of service is warranted, it allows the judge to avoid the time, expense, and spectacle of a public trial by resigning or retiring, a convenient and desirable disposition from the agency's point of view also. * * * Publicizing incidents of minor misconduct serves no purpose in most cases, and contrition and cooperation from the judge are more likely if he is not made needlessly to suffer a public recitation of his professional or personal failings.

"Confidentiality also protects judges from groundless accusations. * * * Many complaints come from losing litigants and jailhouse lawyers. A removal-retirement agency may arguably be serving a therapeutic function by providing these people a means to express their dissatisfaction with the court system. It need not also provide a means for them to defame honest judges.

"Finally, confidentiality may also help protect lawyer-complainants. This research found that some lawyers who appear in court frequently, while they are in a good position to know firsthand about disability and some kinds of misconduct, are reluctant to report it because they believe (whether justifiably is not the point) that if they do, their clients' interests will suffer. A practice of keeping complainants' identity confidential can help allay this anxiety, although there will of course be cases where confidentiality is impossible to maintain, such as a case eventuating in a formal hearing at which the complainant must be called as witness. * * * No complaint should ever be simply ignored; even those that are prima facie trivial or foolish from the staff's point of view should be acknowledged with a letter explaining why the agency cannot act. California's Commission on Judicial Qualifications follows this practice of acknowledging all complaints but goes a step further in public relations by publishing a brief annual report summarizing the Commission's activities. The report does not identify the judges who were the subject of complaints, but states the number of complaints received and investigations conducted and the number of judges who resigned or retired during Commission investigation. Provided it is discreet in substance and language, such a report can help to create public confidence that the agency is carrying out its responsibilities and will conscientiously consider every complaint submitted."[3]

What do you think? People may file frivolous complaints against judges, but people also file frivolous lawsuits against lawyers and others. Those lawsuits are never kept secret. Is making the hearing public a part of the sanction for judges who deserve discipline?

c.   *Kamasinski v. Judicial Review Council*, 44 F.3d 106 (2d Cir.1994), was a challenge to a Connecticut rule against disclosing the filing of a complaint against a judge. The court found the rule to be a content-based regulation of speech and applied strict scrutiny review. The court concluded

---

3.   William T. Braithwaite, Who Judges the Judges? 161–165 (1971).

that until the Judicial Review Council makes a finding of probable cause the state has a compelling interest in not having judges harassed that justifies keeping confidential both the filing and the fact of testifying before the Council. However, after a finding of probable cause, no state interest is compelling enough to prohibit public discussion of the case. See also, Doe v. Florida Judicial Qualifications Commission, 748 F.Supp. 1520 (S.D.Fla. 1990) (unconstitutional to forbid disclosure of fact complaint filed even if finding of probable cause never issued).

4. Would State's Attorney Embers be subject to any different form of discipline if she made her remarks about Judge Kraft to the judge's face or in a letter to the judge?

a. In re Snyder, 472 U.S. 634, 105 S.Ct. 2874, 86 L.Ed.2d 504 (1985), involved a lawyer appointed to handle a case under the Criminal Justice Act. He submitted a claim for fees that was returned with a request for additional information. Because the lawyer had technical problems with his computer software, he did not provide the information in the form requested by the Chief Judge. The lawyer did provide a supplemental application, which the secretary to the Chief Judge again returned. The lawyer then wrote the Judge's secretary complaining of the "extreme gymnastics" required of him to get paid "puny amounts," which allegedly did not even cover overhead. He wrote that he was "extremely disgusted" by the Eighth Circuit's treatment and he asked to be taken off the list of counsel willing to accept appointment. For these "disrespectful remarks," and because he refused to apologize "for what I consider to be telling the truth, albeit in harsh terms," the lawyer was suspended from practice before the federal courts for six months, 734 F.2d 334 (8th Cir.1984).

A unanimous Supreme Court reversed. One intemperate letter does not justify such a sanction, the Court said. The Court did not reach the first amendment issue but rather relied on its interpretation of Federal Rule of Appellate Procedure 46, which authorizes a court to suspend or disbar an attorney "guilty of conduct unbecoming a member of the bar of the court * * * ." The Supreme Court noted that the lawyer's criticisms of the administration of the Criminal Justice Act had merit (a point the Eighth Circuit had conceded) and that such criticism cannot be a cause for discipline or suspension. The Court of Appeals' testy opinion on remand is at 770 F.2d 743 (8th Cir.1985).

b. Williams v. Williams, 721 A.2d 1072 (Pa.1998), is another case involving a lawyer frustrated with a judge's conduct. After an unfavorable ruling on an objection to a question, the lawyer said under his breath, "He's such a [f—a—]." The other lawyer, always concerned about protecting the court's dignity, repeated the remark in a much louder voice to get it on the record. The Pennsylvania Supreme Court said the remark was ill-mannered but caused no significant disruption in the proceeding and therefore did not rise to the level of criminal contempt.

c. Contrast, Morrissey v. Commonwealth, 428 S.E.2d 503 (Va.App. 1993). A prosecutor sought to protect his assistants against what he considered to be a judge's high-handed conduct. After the judge had refused to approve a plea agreement and had publicly called the prosecutor's office "lazy," the Commonwealth Attorney wrote to the judge, saying: "In the future, should you have any criticism of this Office or [one of my assistants], you are directed to set up an appointment with [my deputy] so that you can voice your complaints in a more professional manner. * * * [I]f that behavior ever, ever happens again, I will not be so kind as to merely draft you a letter of indignation." 428 S.E.2d at 504–05.

The Virginia Court of Appeals affirmed the prosecutor's conviction for contempt of court. Even if the letter were not threatening violence but were only threatening to report the judge to the disciplinary commission, the letter was intimidating and thus "calculated to embarrass, hinder or obstruct the court in the administration of justice." Do you agree?

d.   In the *Yagman* case, supra, the Court of Appeals expressly allowed the trial judge to hear cases brought by a lawyer who had publicly criticized the judge. However, other courts have sometimes require recusal of the judge in later cases involving lawyers whose criticism has seemed more justified. In United States v. Anderson, 160 F.3d 231 (5th Cir.1998), for example, the Court vacated the sentence handed down by a judge against whom defense counsel had testified before the Fifth Circuit Judicial Council. See also, United States v. Avilez–Reyes, 160 F.3d 258 (5th Cir.1998) (same result and same judge). Cf. United States v. Vadner, 160 F.3d 263 (5th Cir.1998) (no recusal required where lawyer had not testified but others in his Federal Defender office had).

e.   In MacDraw, Inc. v. CIT Group Equipment Financing, Inc., 138 F.3d 33 (2d Cir.1998), counsel wrote a letter to the judge asking whether the judge had any dealings with John Huang, an Asian businessman accused in the media of illegal campaign contributions to President Clinton. The lawyers who wrote the letter were challenging Clinton Administration policy in another matter. The judge, a Clinton appointee, was Asian–American, and took the inquiry as a challenge to his integrity based on his race. He revoked the lawyers' pro hac vice status and ordered them to show his order to any other judge in the district to whom they might apply for such status. The Second Circuit upheld the order. It said that no one should "charge that a judge is not impartial solely because an attorney is embroiled in a controversy with the administration that appointed the judge" or "because of membership in a particular racial or ethnic group." The attorneys' letter was "insulting and smacked of intimidation" and "Judge Chin was in no way required to tolerate it." Do you agree? Would the answer be the same if there were any indication that John Huang had something to do with the case before the court?

D.   THE JUDGE REWARDING HIS FRIENDS

1.   May Judge Kraft testify as a character witness on behalf of his friend?

a.   Judges are people and often have friends. Some of those friends are in politics. The politicians may wish to have the judge vouch for them. What is the point of Model Code of Judicial Conduct, Canon 2B? When

Kraft said "it would be better if you would subpoena me," did he satisfy his obligation not to testify "voluntarily"?

b. One state bar committee proposed that Canon 2B should read:

"He should not appear as a character witness unless he appears pursuant to compulsory process of law * * * and unless the judge or other official presiding in the proceeding determines that his testimony is needed to protect the constitutional rights of a party or to provide a fair hearing."[4]

Do you see the reason for the different language? Would such an approach make the subpoena more than a formality? Do you agree with the proposed change? How would you have a court make the determination of which witnesses a "fair hearing" requires?

2. Should there be any restrictions on a judge appointing friends to a position that is within the power of the judge to fill, perhaps as a special master, for example?

a. Look at ABA Model Rules of Professional Conduct, Rule 7.6. What is that Rule trying to regulate? Does it apply to seeking a senator's recommendation for a judgeship? Does Rule 7.6 relate to being appointed to a position that a judge may fill?

b. Suppose lawyer Mary has contributed substantial amounts to Kraft's campaign because she and Kraft went to high school together and she wanted her old friend to win the election. May Judge Kraft appoint Mary as a special master in a case in which the fee would be substantial? Mary if asked, could truthfully say that she did not contribute any money "for the purpose of obtaining or being considered" for that appointment by Judge Kraft. May Mary accept the appointment from Judge Kraft under Model Rule 7.6? May Judge Kraft appoint Mary if Mary has contributed more than the amount the state inserts into its version of Canon 3C(5)?

c. Lawyer Harry has given no money to Judge Kraft's campaign, but he has contributed substantial amounts of time. He distributed leaflets, visited various newspapers and urged the editorial departments to endorse Kraft for election as judge. Now, Judge Kraft would like to appoint Harry to become an Associate Judge of the court. Does Model Rule 7.6 limit Harry's ability to accept this appointment? Look particularly at Comment 2. Why should the rule distinguish between cash and in-kind contributions to the judge?

PROBLEM 40

THE ACTIVE FEDERAL JUDGE

Judges are people too. Some have a background in litigation and are tempted to involve themselves in a trial, particularly when it appears that

4. Report and Recommendations of the Joint Illinois State Bar Association–Chicago Bar Association Committee on Rules of Judicial Conduct, April, 1974, at p. 5.

one lawyer is not as effective as the other. Even when judges act more like umpires, they may affect what the jury thinks of the case by the way they treat the litigants and their counsel. Judges often have achieved distinction in fields other than law and may want to write books or participate in civic and educational programs. Unfortunately, still others become most visible when others discover their indiscretions. This problem looks first at the issues surrounding how a judge manages the courtroom and judicial proceedings. It then asks what extrajudicial activities are proper for a judge. Third, it tries to give content to the idea that a judge should act honorably. Finally, it looks at special problems enforcing these rules in the case of federal judges, who have lifetime appointments.

FACTS

L.M. Richardson, Chief Judge of the Federal District Court for the District of Massachusetts, is known behind his back as "Loud Mouth" because of the way he interjects himself into trials. His long experience on the bench has given him what he believes to be an unfailing sense of who is telling the truth. If a witness appears to be lying, Richardson will interrupt to question the witness himself. If a skilled attorney is making an apparently honest witness look bad, Richardson will call a recess.

Judge Richardson can be particularly insensitive in dealing with female lawyers. He typically uses the title "Mr." when addressing male lawyers, while he usually calls female lawyers by their first name. He told one female lawyer who appeared before him: "With a pretty young lady like you in the courtroom, I wonder if the jury will pay any attention to me."

On the other hand, Judge Richardson has had a long-time concern about the homeless. He is an officer of a local organization that runs a homeless shelter, and he has testified before the state legislature that more funds should be appropriated to fund services for the homeless. The organization also tries to raise such funds from local businesses.

Because of his experience and judicial prominence, a Boston-area law school has invited him to teach classes in federal jurisdiction. In class, he tries out new theories he hopes to introduce in upcoming opinions. In substantive fields with which he is less familiar, he plans to ask some of his friends on the faculty to write drafts of opinions in cases he has before him.

Judge Richardson is 65 years of age. Recently he was stopped by local police for traveling 70 miles per hour in a residential zone. He was incoherent and chemical tests showed him to be intoxicated. His companion, a 28–year-old dancer in a local "nude review," attempted to flee when the car was stopped. The story has received front-page newspaper coverage in the Boston area and the dancer has appeared on several television programs to detail her experiences with Judge Richardson. She explained that she met Judge

Richardson through a mutual friend at a dinner at the Owl Club, an athletic club to which the Judge belongs. Owl Club membership is open only to white males. The Judge and his wife of 42 years have been unavailable for comment.

QUESTIONS

A. A JUDGE'S PERFORMANCE OF OFFICIAL DUTIES

1. How much should Judge Richardson insert himself into a trial?

a. Judge Charles Wyzanski once contended that the judge's role should depend on the nature of the case, with the judge generally passive in tort cases, more active in commercial cases (because he is more likely to have a specialized knowledge) and passive in criminal cases until the point of sentencing.[1] Later, Judge Wyzanski had changed his view. As reported by Judge Marvin Frankel, Wyzanski became "confessedly more activist today than [he] was a quarter of a century ago."[2] Frankel himself has admitted:

> "Introspecting, I think I have usually put my penetrating questions to witnesses I thought were lying, exaggerating, or obscuring the facts. Less frequently, I have intruded to rescue a witness from questions that seemed unfairly to put the testimony in a bad light or to confuse its import. * * * [But within] the confines of the adversary framework, the trial judge probably serves best as relatively passive moderator."[3]

b. What limits does the ABA Model Code of Judicial Conduct place on the judge's conduct of a trial? Look at the various parts of Canon 3B. Does Judge Richardson seem to comply with its requirements? Is the proper level of judicial involvement in a trial something that is very hard to capture in a regulatory standard?

c. What protection should a litigant and lawyer have from judicial abuse? Consider the stories of the "active" judges described by Professor Alschuler:

> "During the late nineteenth and early twentieth centuries, appellate courts generally attempted to promote a truly antiseptic atmosphere in America's trial courts. In 1899, for example, a New York court reversed a criminal conviction because the trial judge had instructed an evasive defendant to 'answer the question and stop quibbling.' * * * In 1967, by contrast, a Michigan court found no error when a trial judge, without significant provocation, told a defendant under cross-examination to 'shut up.' * * *

1. Charles Wyzanski, A Trial Judge's Freedom and Responsibility, 65 Harvard L.Rev. 1281, 1283–93 (1952).

2. Marvin Frankel, The Search for Truth: An Umpireal View, 123 U. Pennsylvania L.Rev. 1031, 1045 (1975).

3. Id. at 1043.

"A local magazine for the District of Columbia, The Washingtonian, recently investigated the performance of trial judges in and around that city. Its report provided frequent and striking illustrations of judicial misconduct. * * *

"In suburban Maryland, the reporter investigated the courtroom behavior of Judge William B. Bowie, whose approach to life and to judging was illustrated by a remark that he made in court about certain black defendants: 'If they want to live like animals, let them stay in a pen somewhere.'

"In the District of Columbia, The Washingtonian focused largely on the Court of General Sessions. In the courtroom of Judge Edward A. Beard, two defendants were awaiting trial on a narcotics charge when one of them fell asleep. Judge Beard promptly sentenced both defendants to thirty days' imprisonment for contempt of court.

'But I'm all right,' the non-offending defendant said. 'Why me?'

'You are guilty by association,' the judge replied. 'Get them out of here.' * * *

"These examples are extreme. Nevertheless, similar incidents have occurred throughout the nation. Judges have, for example, asked defense attorneys whether they were not taught better in their first year of law school, referred to their behavior as 'shyster stuff,' called their cross-examination of prosecution witnesses 'just ridiculous,' and characterized them as 'troublesome, like a school boy.' Judges have similarly referred to defendants as drifters, as bamboozlers, * * * and as Sing Sing graduates. * * *

"Courtroom misconduct by prosecutors may merit special condemnation because of the influence that prosecutors commonly have with juries, but juries are undoubtedly even more attentive to the views and prejudices of trial judges. As the Iowa Supreme Court recently remarked, a trial judge's behavior 'may influence the jury more than the evidence.' "[4]

d. Matter of Ross, 428 A.2d 858 (Me.1981) (per curiam), showed that the use of abusive language against persons appearing before the court can indeed subject a judge to professional discipline. In one such case, the judge told a defendant who, while outside the courtroom, had criticized the fine he had received, that "the fine was no longer $50 but rather $200, and he had a choice to pay his fine or serve it at $5 per day." That fine exceeded the court's authority, and to make his displeasure even clearer, the judge used an arguably obscene term and added, "Young man, you will remember that the likes of you I chew up and spit out before breakfast, and I never have breakfast until 8:00 o'clock at night." The Maine Supreme Court acknowledged that "[d]ifferences in style and personality do not of them-

4. Albert W. Alschuler, Courtroom Misconduct by Prosecutors and Trial Judges, 50   Texas L.Rev. 629 (1972).

selves suggest misconduct." However, while "[i]ntemperate language is on occasion understandable, * * * vile and abusive language is inexcusable." There was no showing that the judge had been motivated by personal gain, but the court suspended him for 90 days.

2. Are Judge Richardson's sexist remarks a particular cause for concern?

a. The ABA Journal reports that several years ago, a 27 year old female lawyer from a large, prestigious Chicago law firm, appeared before an Illinois Circuit Court Judge for a pre-trial conference. The judge said: "I am going to hear the young lady's case first. They say I'm a male chauvinist. I don't think that ladies should be lawyers. I believe that you belong at home raising a family. Ladies do not belong down here. Are you married?" "Yes," she replied. "What does your husband think about you working here?" The lawyer was concerned because she feared judicial reprisal against her client's interests. The judge later said, in defense of his actions: "I don't think I did anything wrong." He said: "I have a way of kidding around but some women take on the status of prima donnas and misconstrue what is being done. She said I should call her counsel, not young lady. It's nonsense. If she were 10 or 12 years older, she'd like to be called young lady."[5]

Should the judge be disciplined for his comments to the lawyer? How should Judge Richardson address attorneys who appear before him? Look especially at Canon 3B(5).

b. In Disciplinary Counsel v. Campbell, 623 N.E.2d 24 (Ohio 1993), a judge was found to have told one female prosecutor that her success in cases before him would depend on whether she became his lover. When another female prosecutor said at the start of the day's docket that she was "ready to go," the judge made an overtly sexual response. The Ohio Supreme Court observed that conduct that would be reprehensible in any context is even more so when engaged in by someone with the authority of a judge. The respondent resigned as a judge, and in this case, he was also suspended from the practice of law for a year.[6]

c. In re Rome, 542 P.2d 676 (Kan.1975), involved a magistrate judge who granted a convicted prostitute two years probation. The judge wrote his decision in what he thought was humorous poetic verse. The local newspaper reprinted the decision, and a local group alleged that the judge had held the defendant up to public ridicule. The Kansas Supreme Court upheld a censure of the judge. Pointing to the state version of Canon 3B(4), the court said a judge must be "dignified and courteous" to litigants. It agreed that judges may write opinions in verse, but in this case, the defendant was portrayed in a "ludicrous or comical situation" and her "integrity as an individual, convicted of a crime though she was, was disregarded." 542 P.2d at 685. A judge, of course, has First Amendment

---

5. See Nancy Blodgett, "I Don't Think That Ladies Should be Lawyers," 72 ABA Journal (Dec. 1986), at 48.

6. The court approved his reinstatement as a lawyer in Disciplinary Counsel v. Campbell, 644 N.E.2d 1024 (Ohio 1995).

rights, but the court believed a judge's right to free speech is properly limited by the requirements of the Code of Judicial Conduct. Do you agree?

d.   If a lawyer in Judge Richardson's court refers to a female lawyer as "the little lady," should the judge do anything? Take a look at Canons 3B(6) and 3C(2). Do you agree that judges should have an affirmative duty to see that neither their staff nor lawyers appearing before them manifest bias or prejudice based on race, sex, religion, national origin, disability, age, sexual orientation or socioeconomic status?

e.   The ABA House of Delegates has also recommended that judicial education programs for state and federal judges include "a separate course on the role of the judge in keeping a courtroom free from sex and race bias, and that relevant courses include a discussion of sexual and racial stereotypes that may affect judicial decisions."[7] Do you agree that some judges could use education about such issues?

3.   Should judges be subject to private civil remedies brought by lawyers or litigants injured by their conduct? Should the law instead cloak judges with immunity?

a.   Pulliam v. Allen, 466 U.S. 522, 104 S.Ct. 1970, 80 L.Ed.2d 565 (1984), was a suit for an injunction alleging that a state magistrate's practice of imposing bail on persons arrested for non-jailable offenses was unconstitutional. The federal court agreed, issued an injunction against the magistrate, and charged her with the plaintiff's attorney's fees which amounted to $7,038, plus $653.09 costs. The magistrate asserted that judicial immunity barred the payment of the fees, but the Supreme Court disagreed. Judicial immunity does not prevent obtaining injunctive relief, the Court said, and a judge may be liable for fees incident to the injunction.[8]

b.   Forrester v. White, 484 U.S. 219, 108 S.Ct. 538, 98 L.Ed.2d 555 (1988), considered a state judge's potential liability under Title VII when he fired his female probation officer. The lower courts had held that the decision to fire a close associate of the judge in whom the judge must have confidence is protected by an absolute immunity. The Supreme Court reversed. Judicial immunity is a steadily eroding concept, the Court said, and there is no reason to continue it for administrative decisions that do not relate directly to deciding cases. The Court did not, however, decide whether the judge should be granted a qualified immunity for his action.

c.   In Mireles v. Waco, 502 U.S. 9, 112 S.Ct. 286, 116 L.Ed.2d 9 (1991) (per curiam), a public defender sued a state judge (and two police officers)

---

7.   ABA Journal, Dec. 1986, at 49.

8.   Judges may legitimately be concerned that they will have to buy malpractice insurance against the costs of defending such actions and against the potential awards that may be made against them in spite of their immunity from damage actions. After *Pulliam,* the number of judges buying malpractice insurance has increased, though in only a small number of cases have there been judgments or settlements in favor of plaintiffs suing judges for damages. See generally, Judicial Immunity Insurance Available, 23 Judges Journal 2 (Summer, 1984); Stephen R. Plotkin & Carol D. Mazoral, Judicial Malpractice: Pulliam Is Not the Answer, 20 Trial 24 (Dec. 1984).

for damages in federal court, alleging that the judge requested and authorized the police to use excessive force to bring the attorney into the judge's courtroom. The Court held that the plaintiff cannot overcome judicial immunity for a clearly judicial act by alleging bad faith, malice, or corruption. Unless the state judge acts in the absence of jurisdiction or not in a judicial capacity, there is no federal liability. Justice Stevens dissented, arguing that "[o]rdering a battery has no relation to a function normally performed by a judge."

d. To the extent judges have absolute immunity from civil suits, who should be seen as a "judge"? Wagshal v. Foster, 28 F.3d 1249 (D.C.Cir. 1994), cert. denied, 514 U.S. 1004, 115 S.Ct. 1314, 131 L.Ed.2d 196 (1995), was a claim against a "case evaluator," i.e., a neutral party appointed by the court in a compulsory process designed to try to mediate and settle cases before trial. One of the parties accused the mediator of not being neutral and the mediator withdrew, saying that the case "can and should be settled if the parties are willing to act reasonably." A new mediator was appointed, but after settlement, the plaintiff sued the first one for defamation and infliction of emotional distress that allegedly caused the plaintiff to settle the case for less than if he had gone to trial. The D.C. Circuit held that mediators acting pursuant to a court program clearly perform a "judicial function" and their actions are subject to the same immunity accorded those of a judge.

4. May Judge Richardson speak to the press about a newsworthy case?

a. In United States v. Microsoft Corp., 253 F.3d 34 (D.C.Cir.2001), the trial judge had given interviews to the press while the highly-publicized case was pending in his court. He was apparently making an historical record, because the interviews were not to be publicly released until after he issued his decision in the case. Would such interviews violate the ABA Model Code of Judicial Conduct. Look at Canon 3B(9) and the Commentary thereto.

The D.C. Circuit said that the conduct required the judge's disqualification on remand. The court relied on 28 U.S.C. § 455(a) and acknowledged that ordinarily what a judge learns in his judicial capacity cannot be used to force his later recusal. However, it said that in this case the trial judge's—

> "crude characterizations of Microsoft, his frequent denigrations of Bill Gates, his mule trainer analogy as a reason for his remedy—all of these remarks and others might not have given rise to a violation of the Canons or of § 455(a) had he uttered them from the bench. But then Microsoft would have had an opportunity to object, perhaps even to persuade, and the Judge would have made a record for review on appeal. It is an altogether different matter when the statements are made outside the courtroom, in private meetings unknown to the parties, in anticipation that ultimately the Judge's remarks would be reported. Rather than manifesting neutrality and impartiality, the reports of the interviews with the District Judge convey the impression

of a judge posturing for posterity, trying to please the reporters with colorful analogies and observations bound to wind up in the stories they write. Members of the public may reasonably question whether the District Judge's desire for press coverage influenced his judgments, indeed whether a publicity-seeking judge might consciously or subconsciously seek the publicity-maximizing outcome. We believe, therefore, that the District Judge's interviews with reporters created an appearance that he was not acting impartially as the Code of Conduct and § 455(a) require." 253 F.3d at 115.

b.   Do you agree with the Court of Appeal's analysis? Consider one observer's comments about a hypothetical Judge Loquacious:

"[If Judge Loqacious] discussed his deliberative processes, or his thought-process, or his evaluation of the evidence with a reporter, those statements are part of the published newspaper interview, but are not part of the record. Should a party be able, on appeal, to argue that the judge's factual assumption was wrong, or the party should have a right to * * * counter the judge's evaluation of the evidence, as reported in the newspaper interview? If so, should the other party be able to show (by cross-examining the judge or the reporter) that the judge never really relied on that thought-process or evaluation to the extent or in the way that the reporter believed? * * * Judge Loquacious's ex parte communications during the trial are more troubling than Juror Loquacious's ex parte communications [to other jurors before the trial concludes] * * *. Juror Loquacious will be talking to other jurors. But Judge Loquacious will be communicating with reporters, and these reporters, unlike the jurors, will have been exposed to information that is outside the record. The problem is not simply that the judge is talking to reporters; it is that reporters are talking to the judge. If Judge Loquacious engages in conversations with reporters about the pending case, the very nature of a 'conversation' is that there is give and take. The judge will not only be communicating information to the reporters, they will be communicating information to him. A conversation is a dialogue, a spoken exchange."[9]

c.   May a judge comment publicly about a case over which he or she has not presided? In re Inquiry of Broadbelt, 683 A.2d 543 (N.J.1996), cert. denied 520 U.S. 1118, 117 S.Ct. 1251, 137 L.Ed.2d 332 (1997), reviewed the acts of a municipal court judge in appearing as an uncompensated guest commentator on Court TV and CNBC to discuss the murder prosecution of former football star O.J. Simpson. The New Jersey Supreme Court found that the judge's conduct violated Canon 3B(9) of the ABA Model Code of Judicial Conduct even though the case could not possibly ever come before him. "We find the Canon to be clear and unambiguous: a judge should not comment on pending cases in any court." In particular, his appearance on " 'Geraldo Live' was inappropriate and had the potential to compromise the

9.   Ronald D. Rotunda, Judicial Comments on Pending Cases: The Ethical Restrictions and the Sanctions—A Case Study of the Microsoft Litigation, 2001 U.Ill L. Rev. 611, 612 (2001).

integrity of the judiciary in New Jersey." 643 A.2d at 548. In addition, the Court said, the conduct violated Canon 2B in that the regular appearances caused the judge to become identified with the programs and used the prestige of his judicial office to further the interests of the television producers. The fact that his appearances were educational and consistent with Canon 4 did not, in the court's view, excuse the violations. Do you agree with the Court's analysis?

B. A JUDGE'S PARTICIPATION IN NON-JUDICIAL ACTIVITIES

1. Is it proper for Judge Richardson to be an officer of a civic organization that serves the homeless in his community?

a. In what kinds of non-judicial groups may a judge participate? Is the organization dedicated to the "improvement of the law" within the meaning of Canon 4C(3)? Is it a "civic organization" not conducted for profit? If it is not an organization described in Canon 4C(3), may the judge still remain a member?

b. Should it be important whether the organization is frequently involved in litigation that may come before the federal district court? Look at Canon 4C(3)(a)? If it does file such litigation, must Judge Richardson withdraw from membership in the organization? If so, does that mean that no judge may be a member of the ACLU or the NAACP, because such groups are frequently involved in litigation? May the judge hear a case filed by an organization of which the judge is a member? Remember Canon 3E(1)(a).

c. Could Judge Richardson be appointed to a new commission that the state Governor has created to examine problems of the homeless? Look at Canons 4C(2) and the related Commentary. Does it make sense to you that such commissions should not have judicial participation?

2. May Judge Richardson seek to raise money to help the homeless?

a. May he testify before a public body about the need for more public funds to provide homeless shelters around the state? Look at Canon 4C(1). Why are we worried about having judges provide such testimony? Might Judge Richardson be put in an awkward position if someone were to ask him whether homeless persons have a legal right to shelter?

b. May a judge go alone or with others to local businesses to try to raise private money to help the homeless? Look at Canon 4C(3)(b) and the associated Commentary. Do you agree that it would be excessively awkward for someone whose rights might come before the judge to turn down a fund raising request?

c. Should a judge be able to attend an event if the subject matter is controversial? In Matter of Bonin, 378 N.E.2d 669 (Mass.1978), for example, the chief justice of the state trial court attended a public lecture by writer Gore Vidal on "Sex and Politics in Massachusetts." The lecture was given to raise money for defendants charged with sexual acts between men and boys. Those cases were pending before the superior court over which the judge presided, although none were assigned to this judge for trial. The Massachusetts Supreme Court concluded that the judge, by attending the lecture, had exposed himself to *ex parte* statements and arguments on matters pending before his court in violation of Canon 3B(7). It publicly censured the judge and suspended him while the legislative and executive branches decided whether he should be impeached.

Do you agree that the conduct was that serious? Look at Commentary [1] to Canon 4A and think back to Problem 38. Must judges divorce themselves from public discussions, newspaper commentary, and the like?

It may be worth knowing that the judge also talked with Vidal after the lecture, knowing that he would be photographed in a setting that made it appear that he approved the defendants' cause. Might that be reason enough to criticize the judge's conduct? Remember Canon 3B(9). Might his attendance "at least equally likely * * * be interpreted as being motivated by curiosity or interest in the remarks of the well-known featured speaker."[10]

3. May Judge Richardson work as a part-time law professor?

a. Does Canon 4B eliminate all questions about the propriety of such teaching? Canon 4G, on the other hand, says (subject to a few exceptions) that a "judge shall not practice law." Why should there be a distinction between the two activities?

b. Should a judge be obliged not to take positions in class on unsettled questions of law? Consider Canon 4A. Could those opinions be a basis for disqualifying the judge in later cases? Would you as an advocate before the judge believe you should know the opinions he or she has expressed?

c. May the judge write articles on issues that may come before him? Is it better or worse to encourage students to write the articles? Is the degree of intellectual independence of the law review editors relevant to your answer? Could an ethical rule be made to turn on something that variable?[11]

---

10. Steven Lubet, Beyond Reproach: Ethical Restrictions on the Extrajudicial Activities of State and Federal Judges 44 (1984).

11. Cf. B. Murphy, The Brandeis/Frankfurter Connection: The Secret Political Activities of Two Supreme Court Justices (1982), documenting how Frankfurter and Brandeis "found it impossible to curb their political zeal after their appointment to the bench." While Frankfurter was a law professor, Justice Brandeis enlisted him "as his paid political lobbyist and lieutenant." They "placed a network of disciples in positions of influence and labored diligently for the enactment of their desired programs."

The "adroit use of the politically skillful Frankfurter as an intermediary enabled Brandeis to keep his considerable political endeavors hidden from the public." Frankfurter became the clearing house through which the justice's ideas were passed on to a variety of liberal publications, particularly the *New Republic*. "Frankfurter was instructed by Brandeis to propose those ideas that he liked under his own name at future meetings of *The New Republic*'s board of editors." Thus "Brandeis began to prepare the climate of public opinion for his reform programs [by educating] the editorial board on his views so that the whole slant of the journal would favor his philosophy." Brandeis' letters to Frankfurter were redrafted

4. What do you think of Judge Richardson's plan to ask outside experts to write drafts of his opinions?

a. Look at Canon 3B(7)(b). Are you surprised that a judge may ask an expert on the legal area to suggest how cases should be decided? Does permitting such a practice make sense to you? Is such a practice different from having law clerks write the opinions? See Canon 3B(7)(c). Does the fact that the judge is required to disclose which expert was consulted and what he or she said enough to make the advice little more than an amicus curiae brief?

b. In Matter of Fuchsberg, 426 N.Y.S.2d 639 (Ct.Jud.1978), the evidence showed that a judge of the New York Court of Appeals had consulted with law professors in at least 12 cases. In some, telephone conversations were held about developments in particular areas of the law. In others, the judge sent the briefs to a professor and asked for a draft opinion, substantial portions of which he used in his own opinion. In at least one case the judge sent a draft opinion from another judge to a professor for comments. Do any of these acts violate Canon 3B(7)? Do they violate Canons 2A and 2B as well? Is it revealing that neither the judge nor any of the professors said that they knew the content of these Canons? The Court's opinion concludes that his behavior "properly subjects [Judge Fuchsberg] to censure and disapproval" but not to removal from office.

c. Are there limits on the type of experts the judge may consult? In Collins v. SEC, 532 F.2d 584 (8th Cir.1976), a case considering the economic effects of merging a closed-end investment company into the company whose stock it owned, the Court explained:

> "The Administrative Office of the United States Courts authorized the appointment of Professor Roger B. Upson, Associate Dean of the University of Minnesota College of Business Administration, to serve as a contract consultant in the office of the Circuit Executive. His duties as a contract consultant were to assist the Court in understanding the record in this case and to prepare reports and memoranda for this Court in connection with that function. Dean Upson's report was filed with the Clerk of this Court and copies thereof were submitted to the parties. The parties have been given an opportunity to respond. Dean Upson's consulting fees were paid by the Administrative Office."

532 F.2d at 605, n. 40.

In an opinion finding that the Eighth Circuit had given too little deference to the Commission's own expertise, the Supreme Court specifically commented on the practice.

> "We note that after receiving briefs and hearing oral argument, the Court of Appeals—over the objection of the Commission,

and published in *The New Republic* as unsigned articles and covered such issues as the 1924 Immigration Act, the McNary–Haugen bill on agriculture surplus, and Coolidge's silence on Teapot Dome. Id. at 9–10, 89–91.

Cristiana and du Pont—undertook the unique appellate procedure of employing a university professor to assist the court in understanding the record in this case and to prepare reports and memoranda for the court. Thus, the reports relied upon by that court included a variety of data and economic observations which had not been examined and tested by the traditional methods of the adversary process. We are not cited to any statute, rule, or decision authorizing the procedure employed by the Court of Appeals. Cf. Fed. Rule App.Proc. 16.''

E. I. du Pont de Nemours & Co. v. Collins, 432 U.S. 46, 57, 97 S.Ct. 2229, 2235, 53 L.Ed.2d 100, 109–110 (1977).

Does the Supreme Court's comment surprise you? Might it reflect a concern that a reviewing court not substitute its own judge for that of the relevant agency? Should it be relevant that Dean Upson was not a law professor?

In 1992, the Judicial Conference of the United States adopted a Code of Conduct for United States Judges patterned loosely on the 1990 version of the ABA Model Code of Judicial Conduct. Canon 3A(4) of the U.S. Judges' Code is similar to Canon 3B(7) of the ABA Code. See Code of Conduct for United States Judges, 150 F.R.D. 307 (Sept. 22, 1992). An updated version is reprinted in 175 F.R.D. 364 (1998).

d. Edgar v. K.L., 93 F.3d 256 (7th Cir.), cert. denied sub nom. Duff v. Governor of Illinois, 519 U.S. 1111, 117 S.Ct. 949, 136 L.Ed.2d 837 (1997), was a challenge to the constitutionality of the Illinois mental health system. The trial judge, Brian Duff, had appointed a panel of three experts to investigate the system. The judge and parties had authorized the experts to conduct interviews out of the presence of counsel to get more reliable answers, but then the judge unilaterally decided to meet ex parte with the experts. These meetings became lengthy and substantive, and the judge claimed that "judicial privilege" prevented the parties from learning their substance. The Seventh Circuit put an end to the trial judge's approach. ABA Canon 3B(7) prohibits a judge from initiating or considering ex parte information, the Court said, and 28 U.S.C. § 455(b) requires disqualification if the judge has "personal knowledge of disputed evidentiary facts." Judge Duff violated both provisions, so the court issued a writ of mandamus removing him from the case.

C. A JUDGE'S OBLIGATION TO MODEL PROPER BEHAVIOR

1. Is it proper for Judge Richardson to belong to a private club that only admits white males to membership?

a. Look at Canon 2C and the accompanying Commentary. Do you agree that parties are likely to be concerned about the clubs to which a judge belongs? There is presently nothing in the Model Rules or Model Code that restricts *lawyers* from joining clubs which exclude persons from membership because of race, religion, or sex. Should judges be subject to different standards?

b. In August 1990, the U.S. Senate Judiciary Committee passed a nonbinding resolution declaring that it is "inappropriate" for nominees to the federal bench or to posts in the Justice Department to belong to clubs that discriminate on the basis of race, color, religion, sex, disability, or national origin. The resolution provided that Senators should consider such continued membership "an important factor" in evaluating nominees, but nominees are excused from this requirement if they "are actively engaged in bona fide efforts to eliminate the discriminatory practices" in the clubs to which they belong. The resolution also states: "So as to promote a consistent policy on this issue, any Senator belonging to such a club should resign." Do you think this resolution appropriately deals with the relevant issues? Does it create a standard that is more than window dressing?

2. Should Judge Richardson's arrest for drunk driving and the fact a young dancer was in the car at the time be considered bases for judicial discipline?

a. What operational content should be given to Model Code of Judicial Conduct, Canons 1 and 2A? Are they more than sanctimonious hyperbole?

b. Is there any basis for believing Judge Richardson's effectiveness as a judge may be impaired by one incident of drunk driving? Would your answer be different if you thought Judge Richardson were an alcoholic? Would the case be entirely different if the judge had sought to avoid the ticket by showing the officer his judicial identification card?

c. If Judge Richardson were shown to have had an affair with the young woman who was in his car, should that be a personal matter or a professional offense? Might a judge's open and notorious adulterous relationship be a basis for disciplinary action? In Matter of Dalessandro, 397 A.2d 743 (Pa.1979), the Pennsylvania Supreme Court said no disciplinary action could be taken. Canons 1 & 2A, the court said, "are concerned with the conduct of a judge in his official capacity and not with his conduct in his private life. * * * Conduct of a judge * * * which may be offensive to the personal sensibilities of a segment of the society is properly judged in the privacy of the ballot box." 397 A.2d at 757. One dissenter maintained, however, that "to read these rules of conduct as restricted to activities while a judge is clothed in a robe * * * is pure sophistry."

With which of these positions do you agree? Should it matter that Judge Richardson does not have to face the voters and thus cannot experience the discipline of the ballot box to which the majority referred? Does the Commentary following Canons 1 & 2A support the view of the majority or the dissent?[12]

d. Should someone like Judge Richardson try to avoid the public eye? A clothing store in the small town where a trial judge lived had a wall on which hung pictures of famous local citizens who wore neckties sold at the

---

12. The Pennsylvania Supreme Court has modified its earlier position somewhat. In Matter of Larsen, 616 A.2d 529, 582 (Pa. 1992), the court said: "We reject the implica-tion in [Dalessandro] that matters in one's personal life which legitimately reflect upon the jurists' professional integrity are immune from censure."

store. The judge agreed to have his picture hung on the wall of the store as well, and for doing so, the store gave him a free necktie. Citing Canon 2B, Ohio Supreme Court Opinion 87–42 (1987) held that it is unseemly for a judge to further a private business in this way. Do you agree? Presumably, now the judge either will pay for his neckties or wear open-neck shirts under his robe.

D.   SPECIAL ISSUES INVOLVING FEDERAL JUDGES

1.   What methods exist by which to sanction or discipline a federal judge?

a.   As the cases cited in this chapter reveal, states have various processes to remove their judges. In addition to impeachment and removal by the state legislature, in many states a judicial conduct commission can hear complaints against judges and provide for suitable discipline, ranging from private censure to suspension to removal from office.

b.   It is much harder to discipline a federal judge who has a constitutional guarantee of life tenure and salary protection? Could Congress constitutionally create a panel of federal judges to impose discipline on other federal judges? Should a constitutional amendment be adopted to provide for a fixed term of office for federal judges? Periodic reconfirmation by the Senate?

c.   An ABA committee to study professional discipline of federal judges concluded:

> "The federal judicial system should have an appropriate structure for the discipline of federal judges. This can be accomplished through: (1) limited inherent power of the United States Supreme Court; (2) a constitutional amendment; or (3) a congressional act.

> "With regard to the first alternative, the United States Supreme Court does not have any constitutional authority to remove a judge from office but it may by administrative order provide procedures for the investigation and the discipline by reprimand and declination to assign cases. This authority is derived from the court's inherent power. The United States Supreme Court also after investigation and due process may recommend impeachment of a judge to the Congress of the United States. It is, however, doubtful the court would ever take this action. The view that the United States Supreme Court has the inherent power to discipline the federal judiciary is not widely accepted * * * . Justices Douglas and Black, in a dissent, reflected what may well be a majority opinion of the United States Supreme Court when they stated:

> > 'An independent judiciary is one of this nation's outstanding characteristics. Once a federal judge is confirmed by the Senate and takes his oath, he is independent of every other judge. He commonly works with other federal judges who are likewise sovereign. But neither one alone nor any number banded together can act as censor and

place sanctions on him. Under the Constitution the only leverage that can be asserted against him is impeachment * * * .

'It is time that an end be put to these efforts of federal judges to ride herd on other federal judges. This is a form of "hazing" having no place under the Constitution. Federal judges are entitled, like other people, to the full freedom of the First Amendment. If they break a law, they can be prosecuted. If they become corrupt or sit in cases in which they have a personal or family stake, they can be impeached by Congress. But I search the Constitution in vain for any power of surveillance that other federal judges have over those aberrations * * * . Chandler v. Judicial Council of Tenth Circuit of the United States (Douglas dissenting), 398 U.S. 74, 136–37, 140, 90 S.Ct. 1648, 1680, 26 L.Ed.2d 100, 137, 138 (1970), rehearing denied 399 U.S. 937, 90 S.Ct. 2248, 26 L.Ed.2d 809.'[13]

"The court, however, has stated in a matter involving the discipline of an attorney:

'[T]he courts ought not to hesitate * * * to protect themselves from scandal and contempt and the public from prejudice, by removing grossly improper persons from participation in the administration of the law. Ex Parte Wall, 107 U.S. (17 Otto) 265, 288, 2 S.Ct. 569, 589, 27 L.Ed. 552, 561 (1883).'

"Some writers have gone further and stated that the United States Supreme Court, as part of its implied and inherent powers, has the right to discipline as well as remove federal judges. See Burke Shartel, Federal Judges—Appointment, Supervision, and Removal—Some Possibilities Under the Constitution, 28 Mich. L.Rev. 723 (1930).

"We suggest that the United States Supreme Court consider an appropriate disciplinary structure within its inherent powers to discipline the federal judiciary. Such a structure should provide an accessible means to receive and process complaints from the public and the legal profession in accordance with these standards.

"The second alternative for a federal judicial discipline is the adoption of a constitutional amendment similar to that in effect in nineteen states. The necessary action to obtain a constitutional disciplinary provision for the federal judiciary would be a cumbersome process which would take years to accomplish.

---

13. Ed. Note: In *Chandler* the 10th Circuit Judicial Council refused to assign any cases to a federal judge because of its belief that Judge Chandler was "unable, or unwilling, to discharge his duties efficiently" and the Supreme Court, for procedural reasons, did not reverse the 10th Circuit order.

"The third alternative is the establishment of a disciplinary structure for the federal judiciary by congressional act. There have been and there are now before Congress, congressional acts which would establish such a disciplinary structure. Such a congressional act is subject to possible constitutional attack on the authority of Congress to define 'good behavior' for the judicial branch. See Powell v. McCormack, 395 U.S. 486, 89 S.Ct. 1944, 23 L.Ed.2d 491 (1969), which spells out the powers of Congress to expel one of its own members. We know, however, that the Federal Judicial Conference has approved in principle this approach."

ABA Standards Relating to Judicial Discipline and Disability Retirement, Part 10 (1977).

d.   Congress has enacted a law creating the Judicial Council of each circuit as the body to hear complaints against federal judges. See 28 U.S.C.A. § 372, reprinted in the Standards Supplement. The United States Judicial Conference has also promulgated a Code of Conduct for federal judges, using the format and much of the text of the 1990 ABA Model Code of Judicial Conduct, even though the ABA Code does not directly apply to federal judges. The text of the latest version of the federal judicial Code is published at 175 F.R.D. 364 (1998).

2.   What kinds of circumstances might make discipline of a federal judge appropriate?

a.   Gardiner v. A.H. Robins Co., Inc., 747 F.2d 1180 (8th Cir.1984), involved an effort to control the allegedly intemperate statements of a federal judge. Judge Miles Lord of Minnesota, in approving a settlement of some tort actions arising out of the use of the Dalkon Shield, had read a "speech" to officers of the defendant condemning them for violating "every ethical precept to which every doctor under your supervision must pledge." Later, he read to the defendants from a speech he had written about sin and accused them of conduct for which they should "confess" and "beg forgiveness." The Eighth Circuit struck the prejudicial statements from the record, but imposed no formal discipline. Shortly thereafter, Judge Lord retired. Do you think this conduct merited discipline? Was the Eighth Circuit's approach probably a discrete and humane way to end the matter?

b.   In October of 1986, Federal District Judge Harry Claiborne of Nevada became the first judge in approximately a half century to be impeached by the House and removed by the Senate after he was convicted in Federal court of income tax evasion. Since then, Congress has impeached several other judges, including Judge Walter Nixon who was convicted of perjury but refused to resign and sought review of the manner of his impeachment in the Supreme Court. Nixon v. United States, 506 U.S. 224, 113 S.Ct. 732, 122 L.Ed.2d 1 (1993) (conducting impeachment trial before a committee of senators is a matter for the Senate and not subject to judicial review).

c.   Hastings v. Judicial Conference of the United States, 829 F.2d 91 (D.C.Cir.1987), upheld the constitutionality of the federal judicial discipline system in the context of the Judicial Council of the Eleventh Circuit's investigation of Judge Alcee Hastings of Florida.[14] The Council was investigating allegations of several violations of the Code of Judicial Conduct, including a charge that Judge Hastings conspired to obtain a bribe. The court also upheld the propriety of referring the Hastings matter to the House of Representatives for possible impeachment even though Hastings had been acquitted in a criminal trial of accepting the alleged bribe. Judge Hastings claimed that the charges levied against him were false and racially motivated, but the House voted to impeach and the Senate voted to remove him from office. In October, 1989, Hastings became the first judge impeached and removed from office on the basis of charges for which he had earlier been acquitted, and in November, 1992, he was elected a member of the House of Representatives that had impeached him.

d. McBryde v. Committee to Review Circuit Council Conduct, 264 F.3d 52 (D.C.Cir.2001), involved conduct having some of the elements of this Problem. Judge McBryde had been reprimanded by the Fifth Circuit Judicial Council and barred from hearing cases involving lawyers who had complained of what the council found to be his "pattern of abusive behavior" toward lawyers who appeared before him. In one case, for example, a lawyer had failed to bring one of the parties to a court-ordered mediation in violation of the court's rules. Judge McBryde required the lawyer to attend a reading comprehension course. When she did so, he then required her to list each day that she attended and the name of every person who could verify her attendance. In this case, Judge McBryde challenged the authority of anyone to criticize the exercise what he considered to be his right to run his court as he pleased. The D.C. Circuit rejected that challenge. Quoting the *Chandler* case cited above, the court said: "There can, of course, be no disagreement among us as to the imperative need for total and absolute independence of judges in deciding cases or in any phase of the decisional function. But it is quite another matter to say that each judge in a complex system shall be the absolute ruler of his manner of conducting judicial business."

e. If you were Judge Richardson in this Problem, would you conclude that—even as a federal judge—you had better change some of your ways?

14. Matter of Certain Complaints Under Investigation, 783 F.2d 1488 (11th Cir. 1986).

*

INDEX

ACCOUNTS AND ACCOUNTING
Handling client property and withdrawing from representation, 112 et seq.

ACCREDITED SCHOOLS
Admission to bar, educational and knowledge standards for, 41 et seq.
Development of American legal profession, 2

ACCURACY OR INACCURACY
Advising clients, lawyer liability for inaccurate opinion, 346–350

ACT UTILITARIANISM
Contributions from moral philosophy, consequential versus deontological standards, 21

ADMISSION TO BAR
Regulation of legal profession, 31 et seq.

ADVERTISING
Billing for legal services, fundamentals of lawyer-client relationship, 106, 107
Class action suit, use of publicity to find clients for, 579–581
Delivery of legal services, 502–512, 579–581

ADVISING CLIENTS
Generally, 275 et seq.

ADVOCACY
Advising clients, difference between advice and advocacy, 277–280

AGENCY LAW
Loyalty to client requirement, using confidential client information to make private investments, 208

AGGRAVATION OR MITIGATION
Reporting duty, another lawyer's misconduct, 61

ALCOHOL AND ALCOHOLISM
Admission to bar, other attempts at state and federal limits on, 46, 51 et seq.
Bar application process, candor in, 38, 39
Driving while intoxicated, 56

ALTERNATIVE DISPUTE RESOLUTION
Ethical problems in litigation, consideration of ADR alternatives, 379–382

AMENDMENTS
Standards of professional conduct, 12

AMERICAN BAR ASSOCIATION
Admission to bar, 31 et seq.
Advising clients, specific ABA responses to series of corporate failures, 364–366

AMERICAN BAR ASSOCIATION—Cont'd
Attorneys' liens and other security interests, 127
Billing for legal services, fundamentals of lawyer-client relationship, 98, 101, 109
Commission on Professionalism, 23
Compulsory legal education, 8, 9
Criminal litigation, loyalty to client requirement, 196, 197
Delivery of legal services, generally, 495 et seq.
Development of American legal profession, 10
Educational and knowledge standards for admission to bar, 40–45
Former private lawyer who enters government service, loyalty to client requirement, 268, 269
Handling client property and withdrawing from representation, 114, 116
Hourly-rate fees, fundamentals of lawyer-client relationship, 109–112
Interstate discipline, jurisdiction, 55
Intimate relationships between lawyers and clients, 214
Lawyer-client relationship, fundamentals of, 83 et seq.
Limitations on lawyer's efforts to collect fee, 120, 123
Loyalty to client requirement, 160 et seq.
Malpractice actions, regulation of legal profession, 75
Model Code of Professional Responsibility, generally, 1
Organization as client, privilege and confidentiality, 149
Reporting duty, another lawyer's misconduct, 56 et seq.
Screening to avoid imputation, loyalty to client requirement, 256–260
Special problems of government lawyers, loyalty to client requirement, 261–263
Standards of professional conduct, generally, 12
State and federal limits on admission to bar, 45–82

AMERICANS WITH DISABILITIES ACT (ADA)
Admission to bar, other attempts at state and federal limits on, 51, 53
Bar application process, candor in, 38, 40
Educational and knowledge standards for admission to bar, 44
Mental illness, candor in bar application process, 38

669

ANTITRUST ACTIONS
Admission to bar, educational and knowledge standards for, 41
Billing for legal services, fundamentals of lawyer-client relationship, 101
Loyalty to client, requirement of, 173, 179, 181, 189, 265
Special problems of government lawyers, loyalty to client requirement, 265

APPOINTMENT BY COURT
Delivery of legal services, tradition of accepting court appointment in criminal case, 567–571
Lawyer-client relationship, fundamentals of, 88, 89

APPRENTICESHIP
Development of American legal profession, 7–9

ARBITRATION
Limitations on lawyer's efforts to collect fee, 122

ASBESTOS CASES
Billing for legal services, fundamentals of lawyer-client relationship, 98, 99
Loyalty requirement, former clients, 241

ASCERTAINING CURRENT CLIENT
Loyalty to client requirement, generally, 178

ATTORNEY-CLIENT PRIVILEGE
Corporations, 141 et seq.
Handling client property and withdrawing from representation, 116
Loyalty to client, requirement of, 161
Organization as client, privilege and confidentiality, 142–152
Public health and safety, confidentiality and risks to, 153
Reporting duty, another lawyer's misconduct, 57

ATTORNEYS' LIENS
Generally, 124–127

AUDITS AND AUDITORS
Advising clients, special problems responding to auditor's request for information, 341–346
Criminal prosecution, loyalty to client requirement, 199, 200
Handling client property and withdrawing from representation, 116, 117
Insured and insurer represented, loyalty to client requirement, 227
Loyalty to client requirement, 199, 200, 227

AUTOMOBILE ACCIDENTS
Billing for legal services, fundamentals of lawyer-client relationship, 105
Confidentiality, information protected by attorney-client privilege, 130

AUTOMOBILE ACCIDENTS—Cont'd
Insured and insurer represented, loyalty to client requirement, 223
Loyalty to client requirement, 214, 223

BANKRUPTCY
Criminal prosecution, loyalty to client requirement, 199
Former clients, loyalty requirement, 236, 237
Loyalty to client requirement, 171, 199, 236, 237
Malpractice actions, regulation of legal profession, 76
Organization as client, privilege and confidentiality, 148
Regulation of legal profession, admission to bar, 35

BARRATRY
Malpractice actions, regulation of legal profession, 76

BILLABLE HOURS
Hourly-rate fees, fundamentals of lawyer-client relationship, 111

BILLING FOR LEGAL SERVICES
Lawyer-client relationship, fundamentals of, 95–112

BOARD OF DIRECTORS
Loyalty to client, requirement of, 188

BONDS
Loyalty to client requirement, screening to avoid imputation, 258

BREAKING AND ENTERING
Admission to bar, other attempts at state and federal limits on, 49

BRIBERY
Admission to bar, other attempts at state and federal limits on, 51
Organization as client, privilege and confidentiality, 147

BURGLARY
Loyalty to client requirement, criminal litigation, 195

BURN-OUT SYNDROME
Admission to bar, other attempts at state and federal limits on, 53

BUYING LAW PRACTICE
Delivery of legal services, buying lawyer's or law firm's practice, 555–557

CAMPAIGN CONTRIBUTIONS
Admission to bar, other attempts at state and federal limits on, 49
Judges' ethical conduct, judges soliciting and receiving campaign contributions, 642, 643
Public health and safety, confidentiality and risks to, 153

CAMPAIGNS
Judges' ethical conduct, content of judicial campaign speech and activities, 637–642

CANDIDATES
Judges' ethical conduct, judge as political candidate and public figure, 635–651

CANDOR
Bar application process, regulation of legal profession, 37
Ethical problems in litigation, 402–416

CAR PHONES
Disclosure, how legal protection against disclosure can be lost, 136

CARE
Contributions from moral philosophy, ethic of care, 21
Introductory problem, achieving justice for innocent client, 27

CAUSATION
Malpractice actions, regulation of legal profession, 72

CERTIFIED PUBLIC ACCOUNTANTS
Loyalty to client requirement, criminal prosecution, 201

CHAMPERTY AND MAINTENANCE
Attorneys' liens and other security interests, 126

CHANGE OF NAME
Bar application process, candor in, 39

CHARACTER AND FITNESS
Regulation of legal profession, admission to bar, 32 et seq.

CHARITABLE CONTRIBUTIONS
Loyalty to client requirement, acceptance of unsolicited gifts from happy clients, 211

CHEATING IN LAW SCHOOL
Regulation of legal profession, admission to bar, 34

CHILD CUSTODY
Loyalty to client, requirement of, 162

CHILD MOLESTATION
Loyalty to client, requirement of, 162

CHILD PORNOGRAPHY
Admission to bar, other attempts at state and federal limits on, 49

CHILDREN
Adoption of Child, this index
Loyalty to client requirement, generally, 167

CITIZENSHIP
Admission to bar, other attempts at state and federal limits on, 45

CIVIL RIGHTS AND DISCRIMINATION
Delivery of legal services, calculating fees for prevailing in class action or civil rights case, 586–595
Development of American legal profession, 9
Lawyer-client relationship, fundamentals of, 89
Loyalty requirement, former clients, 234–236

CIVIL WAR
Development of American legal profession, 7

CIVILITY
Ethical problems in litigation, judicial efforts to enforce civility, 398–401

CLASS ACTIONS
Delivery of legal services, problems in class action representation, 578–595
Interstate discipline, jurisdiction, 55
Loyalty requirement, former clients, 240

CLERKSHIPS
Development of American legal profession, 6

CLIENT
Defined, 129

CLOSELY HELD CORPORATIONS
Organization as client, privilege and confidentiality, 149

CO-DEFENDANTS
Loyalty to client, requirement of, 163

COLLECTIONS
Limitations on lawyer's efforts to collect fee, 120 et seq.

COLONIAL AMERICA
Development of American legal profession, 5

COMMERCIAL LOANS
Loyalty to client, requirement of, 172

COMMON ETHICAL STANDARDS
Contributions from moral philosophy, 18

COMMON INTEREST
Multiple organizations, common interest privilege among, 150–152

COMMUNICATIONS
Lawyer-client relationship, fundamentals of, 83 et seq.

COMPENSATION
Delivery of legal services, duty to work for no compensation, 562–578
Ethical problems in litigation, compensation of witnesses, 456–458

COMPETITION
Development of American legal profession, 9, 11

COMPUTERS
Email, this index
Internet, this index
Lawyer-client relationship, fundamentals of, 87

CONFIDENTIAL INFORMATION
Generally, 127–157
Agents, generally, 127
Attorney-client privilege, generally, 127
Client fraud, generally, 155–157
Criminal litigation, loyalty to client require-
ment, 198, 201
Ethical problems in litigation, confidentiality
of client's identity, 417–420
Ethical problems in litigation, using oppo-
nent's inadvertently disclosed confi-
dential information, 395–397
Former clients, loyalty requirement, 234,
236, 243
Imputation within lawyers' families, loyalty
to client requirement, 255
Insured and insurer represented, loyalty to
client requirement, 219–223
Investments, using confidential client infor-
mation to make private, 208, 209
Lawyer-client relationship, fundamentals of,
87, 92
Limitations on lawyer's efforts to collect fee,
120, 121
Loyalty to client requirement, 167, 181 et
seq.
Trustees, generally, 127
Work product immunity, generally, 127

CONFLICTS OF INTEREST
Billing for legal services, fundamentals of
lawyer-client relationship, 100
Contributions from moral philosophy, ethic of
care, 22
Delivery of legal services, possible conflicts of
interest in class action cases, 581–584
Former clients, loyalty requirement, 230–260
Judges' ethical conduct, disqualifying con-
flicts of interest, 618–635
Lawyer-client relationship, fundamentals of,
87, 92
Loyalty to client requirement, 158 et seq.,
230–260

CONGRESS
Former private lawyer who enters govern-
ment service, 270
Loyalty to client requirement, 268, 270
Special problems of government lawyers, 268

CONSENT
Insured and insurer represented, loyalty to
client requirement, 217, 218
Lawyer-client relationship, fundamentals of,
90, 91
Loyalty to client requirement, 160 et seq.

CONSEQUENTIAL STANDARDS
Contributions from moral philosophy, 20

CONSPIRACY
Loyalty to client requirement, criminal litigation, 196

CONSPIRACY—Cont'd
Other significant consequences of negligence
or misconduct by lawyers, regulation
of legal profession, 79

CONSTITUTIONAL LAW
Delivery of legal services, generally, 498–502

CONSUMER FRAUD
Loyalty to client requirement, special problems of government lawyers, 261

CONTEMPT
Loyalty to client requirement, criminal prosecution, 201

CONTINGENT FEES
Billing for legal services, fundamentals of
lawyer-client relationship, 95 et seq.
Hourly-rate fees, fundamentals of lawyer-
client relationship, 111
Limitations on lawyer's efforts to collect fee,
123
Withdrawal from representation, 119

CONVERSION OF FUNDS
Reporting duty, another lawyer's misconduct,
56

COPIES AND COPYING
Billing for legal services, fundamentals of
lawyer-client relationship, 97
Disclosure, how legal protection against disclosure can be lost, 137

CORDLESS TELEPHONES
Disclosure, how legal protection against disclosure can be lost, 136

CORPORATE COUNSEL
Hourly-rate fees, fundamentals of lawyer-
client relationship, 112

CORPORATIONS
Advising clients, 289–293, 364–366
American Bar Association, specific ABA re-
sponses to series of corporate failures,
364–366
Attorney-client relationship, 141 et seq.
Delivery of legal services, prohibition of cor-
porate practice of law, 610–614
Insured and insurer represented, loyalty to
client requirement, 228
Loyalty to client requirement, 179, 228
Securities and Exchange Commission, specific
SEC responses to series of corporate
failures, 364–366
Self-incrimination privilege, 141

CORRECTION OF MISTAKE
Advising clients, duty to volunteer information or correct a misapprehension,
326–332

CRIMINAL CASES
Delivery of legal services, tradition of accepting court appointment in criminal case, 567–571
Loyalty to client requirement, conflict of interest, 189–201

CRIMINAL RECORD
Bar application process, candor in, 39

CRITICISM
Judges' ethical conduct, lawyer criticism of judges, 643–650

DEBT COLLECTION
Handling client property and withdrawing from representation, 114
Limitations on lawyer's efforts to collect a fee, 120
Other significant consequences of negligence or misconduct by lawyers, regulation of legal profession, 80, 81

DECISION-MAKING
Lawyer-client relationship, fundamentals of, 92–95

DEFAMATION ACTION
Billing for legal services, fundamentals of lawyer-client relationship, 108

DEFENSE COUNSEL
Ethical problems in litigation, generally, 477–481
Loyalty to client requirement, conflicts of interest, generally, 201

DELAY
Litigation tactic, ethical status of delay as, 377–379

DELIVERY OF LEGAL SERVICES
Generally, 495 et seq.

DEMOGRAPHICS
Development of American legal profession, 10

DEONTOLOGICAL STANDARDS
Contributions from moral philosophy, 20, 21
Introductory problem, achieving justice for innocent client, 27

DEPOSITIONS
Billing for legal services, fundamentals of lawyer-client relationship, 97

DESTRUCTION OF EVIDENCE
Ethical problems in litigation, 429–432

DIMINISHED CAPACITY
Advising clients, client suffering from diminished capacity, 283–285

DISBARMENT
Admission to bar, other attempts at state and federal limits on, 51
Handling client property and withdrawing from representation, 117
Interstate discipline, jurisdiction, 55

DISCIPLINARY MATTERS
Additional sanctions, 63 et seq.
Admission to bar, other attempts at state and federal limits on, 46 et seq.
Bar application process, candor in, 37
Development of American legal profession, 10
Disbarment, this index
Ethical problems in litigation, sanctions for litigation misconduct, 382–386
Handling client property and withdrawing from representation, 116
Intimate relationships between lawyers and clients, 214
Jurisdiction, interstate discipline, 54–56
Loyalty to client requirement, 162 et seq., 214
Moral philosophy, study of legal ethics, 15
Other significant consequences of negligence or misconduct by lawyers, regulation of legal profession, 77–82
Regulation of legal profession, admission to bar, 34
Reporting duty, another lawyer's misconduct, 56–63
Standards of professional conduct, generally, 12
Suspension, this index

DISCLOSURE
Advising clients, 295–300, 351–356, 366, 367
Attorney-client privilege, confidential relationship forfeiture, 134
Confidentiality and client fraud, 155
Ethical problems in litigation, 395–397, 401–416, 426–429
Loyalty to client, requirement of, 177, 182

DISCOUNTS
Billing for legal services, fundamentals of lawyer-client relationship, 96

DISCOVERY
Ethical problems in litigation, candor about incomplete or inaccurate discovery responses, 410–414

DISCRETION
Criminal prosecution, 201
Loyalty to client requirement, 167, 201
Withdrawal from representation, 117

DISCRIMINATION
Civil Rights and Discrimination, this index

DISGORGEMENT SUIT
Loyalty to client requirement, using confidential client information to make private investments, 209

DISQUALIFICATION
Conflicts of interest, 198, 635
Criminal litigation, 197, 199

DISQUALIFICATION—Cont'd
Former clients, loyalty requirement, 230, 231, 238–245
Imputed disqualification, 244–260
Judges' ethical conduct, 618–635
Lawyer-client relationship, fundamentals of, 87
Loyalty to client requirement, 169 et seq., 184, 197–199, 230, 231, 238–260, 263
Order of disqualification, requirement of loyalty to client, 174
Other significant consequences of negligence or misconduct by lawyers, regulation of legal profession, 81
Special problems of government lawyers, 263
Waiver of judicial disqualification, 634, 635

DIVORCE
Intimate relationships between lawyers and clients, 213
Limitations on lawyer's efforts to collect fee, 121
Loyalty to client requirement, 159, 165, 166, 168, 213
Malpractice actions, regulation of legal profession, 66

DOCUMENTARY EVIDENCE
Ethical problems in litigation, destruction or failing to retain physical or documentary evidence, 429–432

DOCUMENTATION
Lawyer-client relationship, fundamentals of, 90

DOMESTIC RELATIONS
Billing for legal services, fundamentals of lawyer-client relationship, 108

DOONESBURY
Generally, 1

DRIVING WHILE INTOXICATED
Interstate discipline, jurisdiction, 56

DRUGS AND NARCOTICS
Admission to bar, other attempts at state and federal limits on, 51 et seq.
Bar application process, candor in, 38, 39
Handling client property and withdrawing from representation, 114
Loyalty to client requirement, criminal litigation, 193–198
Marijuana, this index
Other significant consequences of negligence or misconduct by lawyers, regulation of legal profession, 79
Regulation of legal profession, admission to bar, 33, 35

DUE PROCESS
Limitations on lawyer's efforts to collect fee, 122

DUTY
Moral philosophy, study of legal ethics, 14

DYSLEXIA
Admission to bar, educational and knowledge standards for, 45

EDUCATION
Admission to bar, educational and knowledge standards for, 40–45
Cheating in law school, admission to bar, 34
Development of American legal profession, 7, 8
Harvard Law School, this index
School Boards, this index

EFFECTIVE OR INEFFECTIVE ASSISTANCE OF COUNSEL
Loyalty to client requirement, criminal litigation, 191, 193, 195, 197
Loyalty to client requirement, criminal prosecution, 202
Other significant consequences of negligence or misconduct by lawyers, regulation of legal profession, 78

EMAIL
Disclosure, how legal protection against disclosure can be lost, 136
Lawyer-client relationship, fundamentals of, 87
Loyalty to client requirement, criminal prosecution, 201

EMBEZZLEMENT
Admission to bar, other attempts at state and federal limits on, 53
Regulation of legal profession, admission to bar, 34

EMPIRICAL EVIDENCE OR STUDIES
Disclosure, how legal protection against disclosure can be lost, 140
Matter of professionalism, 25

EMPLOYMENT DISCRIMINATION
Loyalty requirement, former clients, 234, 236

ENDANGERMENT
Advising clients, client likely to endanger others, 286–289

ENGAGEMENT LETTER
Attorneys' liens and other security interests, 126
Lawyer-client relationship, fundamentals of, 91
Limitations on lawyer's efforts to collect fee, 122

ENVIRONMENTAL MATTERS
EPA. Environmental Protection Agency, this index
Loyalty to client, requirement of, 250, 251

ENVIRONMENTAL PROTECTION AGENCY
Corporations, attorney-client privilege, 141
Multiple organizations, common interest privilege among, 150
Public health and safety, confidentiality and risks to, 153, 154

EPILEPSY
Bar application process, candor in, 40

ESTATE PLANNING
Lawyer-client relationship, fundamentals of, 92
Loyalty to client, requirement of, 166, 167, 171

EVALUATION
Advising clients, lawyer as evaluator, 336–350

EVIDENCE
Ethical problems in litigation, destruction or failing to retain physical or documentary evidence, 429–432
Ethical problems in litigation, handling physical evidence, 416–432

EXECUTORS AND ADMINISTRATORS
Loyalty to client requirement, acceptance of unsolicited gifts from happy clients, 211

EXPERT WITNESSES
Criminal prosecution, loyalty to client requirement, 201
Loyalty to client requirement, 176, 201
Malpractice actions, regulation of legal profession, 70, 71

EXPLOSIVES ILLEGALLY SOLD
Admission to bar, other attempts at state and federal limits on, 48

FACSIMILES
Billing for legal services, fundamentals of lawyer-client relationship, 100
Disclosure, how legal protection against disclosure can be lost, 137

FAIR DEBT COLLECTION PRACTICES ACT
Other significant consequences of negligence or misconduct by lawyers, regulation of legal profession, 80, 81

FAMILIES AND RELATIVES
Children, this index
Husband and Wife, this index
Judges' ethical conduct, financial interests of judge's family, 624–628
Loyalty to client requirement, imputation within lawyers' families, 253–256

FEDERAL COURT
Judges' ethical conduct, active federal judge, 651–667

FEDERAL ELECTION LAWS
Work product immunity, information protected by, 132

FEE FOR SERVICES BASIS
Loyalty to client, requirement of, 178

FEES
Alternatives to referral fees, 527–530
Attorneys' liens, 124–127
Billing for legal services, fundamentals of lawyer-client relationship, 95–112
Calculating fees for prevailing in class action or civil rights case, 586–595
Contingent Fees, this index
Criminal litigation, loyalty to client requirement, 195, 200
Delivery of legal services, 524–530, 586–595
Development of American legal profession, 4, 10
Ethical problems in litigation, fees of criminal defense counsel, 481–486
Former clients, loyalty requirement, 248
Handling client property and withdrawing from representation, 115
Hourly rates, billing for legal services, 95, 99, 104, 109–112
Lawyer-client relationship, fundamentals of, 91
Loyalty to client requirement, 171, 178, 195, 200, 204–208, 248
Malpractice actions, regulation of legal profession, 67, 74, 75
Referral fees, delivery of legal services, 524–530
Stock, accepting payment in form of, 204–208

FELONIES
Admission to bar, other attempts at state and federal limits on, 49
Regulation of legal profession, admission to bar, 34

FIFTH AMENDMENT
Admission to bar, other attempts at state and federal limits on, 51

FILES AND FILING
Billing for legal services, fundamentals of lawyer-client relationship, 97
Civil action, ethical standards governing filing of, 370–376

FILING FEES
Billing for legal services, fundamentals of lawyer-client relationship, 97

FINANCIAL INFORMATION
Confidentiality, lawyer's professional obligation of, 133

FINANCIAL INTERESTS
Judges' ethical conduct, 620–634

FINGERPRINTS
Bar application process, candor in, 39

FIRST AMENDMENT
Admission to bar, educational and knowledge standards for, 41
Regulation of legal profession, admission to bar, 36

FIXED FEES
Hourly-rate fees, fundamentals of lawyer-client relationship, 112

FORECLOSURE PROCEEDINGS
Loyalty to client, requirement of, 172, 173

FOREIGN COUNTRIES
Admission to bar, educational and knowledge standards for, 42

FORGERY
Introductory problem, achieving justice for innocent client, 26

FORMATION OF LAW FIRM
Delivery of legal services, leaving one law firm and forming another, 545–562

FORMER CLIENTS
Loyalty to client requirement, 230–244

FRAUD
Admission to bar, other attempts at state and federal limits on, 48, 50, 51
Advising clients, obligations when client may be engaged in fraud, 350–367
Confidentiality and client fraud, 155–157
Criminal prosecution, 200
Ethical problems in litigation, ambiguous line between creative lawyering and deception, 387–390
Loyalty to client requirement, 171, 200, 261
Other significant consequences of negligence or misconduct by lawyers, regulation of legal profession, 80
Public health and safety, confidentiality and risks to, 152
Regulation of legal profession, admission to bar, 34
Reporting duty, another lawyer's misconduct, 58, 59
Special problems of government lawyers, 261

FRIENDS
Judges' ethical conduct, judge rewarding his friends, 650, 651

FUGITIVES
Regulation of legal profession, admission to bar, 35

FUNDAMENTAL DISAGREEMENT
Withdrawal from representation, 118

GIFTS
Loyalty to client requirement, acceptance of unsolicited gifts from happy clients, 210–212

GOVERNMENT LAWYERS
Advising clients, special issues of disclosure by government lawyer, 366, 367

GOVERNMENT LAWYERS—Cont'd
Loyalty to client requirement, special problems of government lawyers, 260–274

GOVERNMENTAL AGENCIES OR ENTITIES
Disclosure, how legal protection against disclosure can be lost, 135
Loyalty to client, requirement of, 176

GRAND JURY
Disclosure, how legal protection against disclosure can be lost, 137
Loyalty to client requirement, criminal litigation, 196
Organization as client, privilege and confidentiality, 147

GROUP LEGAL SERVICES PLAN
Delivery of legal services, establishing group legal services plan as part of law firm, 557–562

GUARDIANS AND GUARDIANSHIP
Confidentiality, lawyer's professional obligation of, 134
Handling client property and withdrawing from representation, 113
Malpractice actions, regulation of legal profession, 70

HABEAS CORPUS
Loyalty to client requirement, criminal litigation, 195

HARASSMENT
Organization as client, privilege and confidentiality, 145

HARVARD LAW SCHOOL
Admission to bar, educational and knowledge standards for, 40
Development of American legal profession, 8

HEALTH MAINTENANCE ORGANIZATIONS (HMOS)
Delivery of legal services, 559
Loyalty to client requirement, representing insured and insurer, 226

HEROIN SALES
Loyalty to client requirement, criminal litigation, 195

HIT-AND-RUN ACCIDENT
Confidentiality, information protected by attorney-client privilege, 130

HOMICIDE
Murder, this index

HONESTY OR TRUTH
Advising clients, ethics of negotiation, 322–326
Ethical problems in litigation, using deception in search for truth, 390–395

HOT POTATO RULE
Loyalty to client, requirement of, 182–186

HOURLY RATES
Billing for legal services, fundamentals of lawyer-client relationship, 95, 99, 104, 109–112

HUSBAND AND WIFE
Criminal litigation, loyalty to client requirement, 193
Divorce, this index
Former clients, 232, 233
Imputation within lawyers' families, 253–255
Insured and insurer represented, loyalty to client requirement, 219
Intimate relationships between lawyers and clients, 213, 214
Loyalty to client requirement, 162, 165–167, 193, 213, 214, 219, 232, 233, 253–255

IDENTITY OR IDENTIFICATION
Ethical problems in litigation, confidentiality of client's identity, 417–420

IMMIGRANTS
Discrimination in development of American legal profession, 9

IMMUNITY
Privilege or Immunity, this index

IMPUTED DISQUALIFICATION
Loyalty requirement, former clients, 244–260

INCREASES
Billing for legal services, fundamentals of lawyer-client relationship, 99

INDIGENT PERSONS
Delivery of legal services, sources of possible other funding for legal services to the poor, 571–578
Lawyer-client relationship, fundamentals of, 88
Pro Bono, this index

INEFFECTIVE ASSISTANCE OF COUNSEL
Effective or Ineffective Assistance of Counsel, this index

INFORMED CONSENT
Loyalty to client, requirement of, 160, 168, 186

INNOCENCE
Introductory problem, achieving justice for innocent client, 26

INSTITUTIONALIZATION
Development of American legal profession, 7

INSURANCE
Former clients, 238
Loyalty to client requirement, 215–229, 238
Malpractice actions, regulation of legal profession, 69, 70
Regulation of legal profession, admission to bar, 34

INTEGRITY
Fundamentals of lawyer-client relationship, generally, 83

INTEREST ON MONEY
Limitations on lawyer's efforts to collect fee, 123

INTERNET
Disclosure, how legal protection against disclosure can be lost, 136
Email, this index
Lawyer-client relationship, fundamentals of, 87

INTERSTATE DISCIPLINE
Jurisdictions, sanctions, 54–56

INVESTIGATION
Ethical problems in litigation, limits on prosecutors investigating defense attorneys, 477–481

INVESTMENTS
Confidential client information used to make private investments, 208, 209
Criminal prosecution, 199
Handling client property and withdrawing from representation, 115
Lawyer-client relationship, fundamentals of, 84
Loyalty to client requirement, 199, 208, 209

IOLTA PROGRAMS
Constitutionality, 573–578

JOINT REPRESENTATION
Criminal litigation, 190, 191
Loyalty to client requirement, 165–167, 190, 191

JOINT VENTURES
Loyalty requirement, former clients, 236, 237

JUDGES
Conflicts of former judge or third party neutral, 272–274
Contributions from moral philosophy, ethic of care, 22
Criminal litigation, 192, 195
Ethical conduct of judges, generally, 618 et seq.
Loyalty to client requirement, 169, 170, 192, 195, 256, 272–274
Reporting duty, another lawyer's misconduct, 59
Screening to avoid imputation, 256

JURISDICTION
Interstate discipline, 54–56

JURY AND JURORS
Ethical problems in litigation, contacting jurors before or after trial, 454–458
Grand Jury, this index

JUSTICE DEPARTMENT
Disclosure, how legal protection against disclosure can be lost, 135

KNOWLEDGE
Notice or Knowledge, this index

KUTAK COMMISSION
ABA Commission on Evaluation of Professional Standards, 2

LANDLORD AND TENANT
Loyalty to client requirement, representing insured and insurer, 217, 218

LATE PAYMENT PENALTY
Limitations on lawyer's efforts to collect fee, 123

LAW CLERKS
Billing for legal services, fundamentals of lawyer-client relationship, 97
Former clients, 242
Loyalty to client requirement, 242, 256
Screening to avoid imputation, 256

LAW FIRMS
Delivery of legal services, 530–545, 614–617
Former clients, 245–249
Loyalty to client requirement, 172, 187, 245–249
Organization as client, privilege and confidentiality, 148
Reporting duty, another lawyer's misconduct, 62
Roles and responsibilities in modern law firm, 530–545

LAWYER-CLIENT RELATIONSHIP
Generally, 83 et seq.
Fundamentals, 83 et seq.
Loyalty to client, requirement of, 181

LEARNING DISABILITY
Admission to bar, educational and knowledge standards for, 44

LEGAL AID SOCIETY
Malpractice actions, regulation of legal profession, 76

LEGISLATIVE BRANCH OFFICIALS
Loyalty to client requirement, former private lawyer who enters government service, 270

LICENSES
Regulation of legal profession, admission to bar, 32, 34

LIENS
Attorneys' liens, 124–127

LIFE INSURANCE
Malpractice actions, regulation of legal profession, 70

LIMITATION OF ACTIONS
Statute of Limitations, this index

LIMITATIONS
Actions. Statute of Limitations, this index
Admission to bar, other attempts at state and federal limits on, 45–82
Advising clients, 280–283, 332–335
Delivery of legal services, limitations on advancing funds needed to meet expenses of litigation, 584–586
Ethical problems in litigation, limits on prosecutors investigating defense attorneys, 477–481
Fees, limitations on lawyer's efforts to collect, 120
Lawyer-client relationship, fundamentals of, 89
Loyalty to client requirement, criminal litigation, 190
Negotiations, possible limits on results reached in, 332–335

LIMITED LIABILITY COMPANIES
Malpractice actions, regulation of legal profession, 76, 77

LIMITED LIABILITY PARTNERSHIP
Malpractice actions, regulation of legal profession, 76, 77

LIQUIDATION
Handling client property and withdrawing from representation, 115

LITERARY RIGHTS CONTRACT
Loyalty to client requirement, criminal prosecution, 201

LITIGATION
Ethical problems, generally, 368 et seq.

LOANS
Commercial loans, requirement of loyalty to client, 172
Loyalty to client requirement, screening to avoid imputation, 259

LOYALTY
Advising clients, primary loyalty owed by corporate lawyer, 290–293
Client, requirement of loyalty to, 158 et seq.

MALFEASANCE
Malpractice actions, regulation of legal profession, 75

MALPRACTICE
Former clients, 238
Insured and insurer represented, 229
Lawyer-client relationship, fundamentals of, 85

MALPRACTICE—Cont'd

Limitations on lawyer's efforts to collect fee, 122

Loyalty to client requirement, 175, 229, 238

Medical Malpractice, this index

Regulation of legal profession, 65 et seq.

MARIJUANA

Admission to bar, 33, 35, 52

Regulation of legal profession, admission to bar, 33, 35

State and federal limits on admission to bar, other attempts at, 52

MARKETS AND MARKETING

Delivery of legal services, 496–517

MASTERCARD PAYMENTS

Limitations on lawyer's efforts to collect fee, 123

MATERIAL RISKS

Loyalty to client, requirement of, 161

MEDIA

Ethical problems in litigation, media relations, 465–473

MEDICAID FRAUD

Other significant consequences of negligence or misconduct by lawyers, regulation of legal profession, 80

MEDICAL INSURANCE

Malpractice actions, regulation of legal profession, 69

MEDICAL MALPRACTICE

Billing for legal services, fundamentals of lawyer-client relationship, 100, 107

Handling client property and withdrawing from representation, 116

Lawyer-client relationship, fundamentals of, 90

Loyalty requirement, former clients, 234

Organization as client, privilege and confidentiality, 145

Other significant consequences of negligence or misconduct by lawyers, regulation of legal profession, 82

Withdrawal from representation, 118

MENTAL HEALTH

Admission to bar, other attempts at state and federal limits on, 53

Advising clients, client suffering from diminished capacity, 283–285

Bar application process, candor in, 38, 39

Reporting duty, another lawyer's misconduct, 61

MENTALLY RETARDED PERSONS

Loyalty to client, requirement of, 164

MERGERS

Law firm mergers, requirement of loyalty to client, 182

Loyalty to client, requirement of, 182, 184

MILITARY LEGAL OFFICES

Loyalty to client requirement, former private lawyer who enters government service, 270

MINORITIES

Contributions from moral philosophy, consequential versus deontological standards, 20, 21

Development of American legal profession, 10

MISAPPLICATION OF FUNDS

Interstate discipline, jurisdiction, 55

MISAPPROPRIATION OF FUNDS

Disclosure, how legal protection against disclosure can be lost, 138

MISDEMEANORS

Regulation of legal profession, admission to bar, 33

MITIGATION

Reporting duty, another lawyer's misconduct, 61

MORALITY

Introductory problem, achieving justice for innocent client, 28

Lawyer-client relationship, fundamentals of, 88

Organization of book, 30

Philosophy, study of legal ethics, 15

Regulation of legal profession, admission to bar, 35, 36

Six stages of moral development, contributions from moral philosophy, 17

Standards of professional conduct, generally, 11

MORTGAGES

Loyalty to client, requirement of, 172

MULTIJURISDICTIONAL PRACTICE OF LAW

Delivery of legal services, future of practice of law, 603–610

MULTINATIONAL LAW FIRMS

Loyalty to client, requirement of, 172

MULTI-PARTY BUSINESS DEALS

Loyalty to client, requirement of, 177

MULTIPLE CLIENTS

Loyalty to client requirement, former private lawyer who enters government service, 269, 270

MULTIPLE PARTIES

Loyalty to client, requirement of, 159

MULTISTATE LAW FIRMS

Loyalty to client, requirement of, 172

MULTISTATE PROFESSIONAL RE-SPONSIBILITY EXAM
Admission to bar, educational and knowledge standards for, 43

MURDER
Admission to bar, other attempts at state and federal limits on, 49
Attorneys' liens and other security interests, 124
Billing for legal services, fundamentals of lawyer-client relationship, 108
Confidentiality, information protected by attorney-client privilege, 130
Disclosure, how legal protection against disclosure can be lost, 139
Lawyer-client relationship, fundamentals of, 93
Loyalty to client requirement, criminal litigation, 192 et seq.
Other significant consequences of negligence or misconduct by lawyers, regulation of legal profession, 79

NARCOTICS
Drugs and Narcotics, this index

NEGOTIATIONS
Advising clients, ethics of negotiation, 318–335
Bar application process, candor in, 37
Billing for legal services, fundamentals of lawyer-client relationship, 107

NOERR-PENNINGTON DOCTRINE
Admission to bar, educational and knowledge standards for, 41

NON-CLIENTS
Malpractice actions, regulation of legal profession, 70

NONJUDICIAL ACTIVITIES
Judges' ethical conduct, judge's participation in nonjudicial activities, 659–662

NON-LAWYERS
Loyalty to client requirement, screening to avoid imputation, 257

NONREFUNDABLE FEES
Billing for legal services, fundamentals of lawyer-client relationship, 98, 99

NORTH AMERICAN FREE TRADE AGREEMENT (NAFTA)
Foreign lawyers, educational and knowledge standards for admission to bar, 43

NOTES
Work product immunity, information protected by, 133

NOTICE OR KNOWLEDGE
Admission to bar, educational and knowledge standards for, 40–45

NOTICE OR KNOWLEDGE—Cont'd
Ethical problems in litigation, client who intends to commit perjury, 433–436
Handling client property and withdrawing from representation, 113

OBSTRUCTION OF JUSTICE
Other significant consequences of negligence or misconduct by lawyers, regulation of legal profession, 79

OFFERS
Loyalty to client requirement, representing insured and insurer, 223–226

OFFICE OF INDEPENDENT COUNSEL
Disclosure, how legal protection against disclosure can be lost, 140
Organization as client, privilege and confidentiality, 146

OFFICE SPACE
Loyalty requirement, former clients, 248

ORGANIZATION OF BOOK
Generally, 28

ORGANIZED CRIME
Loyalty to client requirement, conflicts of interest, 199

PARALEGALS
Billing for legal services, fundamentals of lawyer-client relationship, 97
Loyalty requirement, former clients, 240

PAROL MATTERS
Billing for legal services, fundamentals of lawyer-client relationship, 97
Disclosure, how legal protection against disclosure can be lost, 136

PARTITION
Billing for legal services, fundamentals of lawyer-client relationship, 108

PARTNERSHIPS
Criminal litigation, 192
Delivery of legal services, leaving one law firm and forming another, 546–548
Loyalty to client requirement, 160, 171, 173, 180, 181, 192, 250, 257, 265
Screening to avoid imputation, 257
Special problems of government lawyers, 265

PASSAGE OF BAR EXAMINATION
Admission to bar, educational and knowledge standards for, 43

PENDING ACTIONS
Withdrawal from representation, 119

PERJURY
Ethical problems in litigation, client who intends to commit perjury, 432–453

PERSONAL ETHICS
Contributions from moral philosophy, generally, 22

PERSONAL INJURY ACTIONS
Former clients, 236
Insured and insurer represented, 216
Loyalty to client requirement, 205, 216, 236, 267
Special problems of government lawyers, 267
Stock, accepting payment in form of, 205

PERSONAL INTEREST OF LAWYER
Loyalty to client requirement, generally, 203

PERSONAL VIEWS
Judges' ethical conduct, bias arising from personal views rather than financial interest, 628–634

PHARMACEUTICALS
Organization as client, privilege and confidentiality, 142–144

PHILOSOPHY
Moral philosophy, study of legal ethics, 14

PHYSICAL EVIDENCE
Ethical problems in litigation, 420–432

PLAGIARISM
Admission to bar, other attempts at state and federal limits on, 51
Bar application process, candor in, 37, 38

PLEA BARGAINING
Advising clients, ethics of negotiation, 320, 321
Bar application process, candor in, 39
Conflicts of interest, 199
Criminal litigation, 193
Loyalty to client requirement, 193, 199, 211

PLEAS
Lawyer-client relationship, fundamentals of, 93
Organization as client, privilege and confidentiality, 149

POLICE OFFICERS
Loyalty to client requirement, criminal litigation, 194

POLITICS
Additional sanctions, 64
Admission to bar, 37, 49
Judges' ethical conduct, judge as political candidate and public figure, 635–651
Regulation of legal profession, admission to bar, 37
State and federal limits on admission to bar, other attempts at, 49

POOR PERSONS
Indigent Persons, this index

PORNOGRAPHY
Admission to bar, other attempts at state and federal limits on, 49

POSITIONAL CONFLICT PROBLEMS
Loyalty to client, requirement of, 186–189

POSSESSION OF DRUGS OR NARCOTICS
Regulation of legal profession, admission to bar, 33

PREPAYMENT PENALTY
Commercial loans, requirement of loyalty to client, 172

PRESIDENT CLINTON
Organization as client, privilege and confidentiality, 146

PRESIDENTIAL PARDONS
Confidentiality, information protected by attorney-client privilege, 131
Reporting duty, another lawyer's misconduct, 63

PRIVATE CONTRIBUTIONS
Loyalty to client requirement, criminal prosecution, 201

PRIVATIZED PROSECUTION FUNCTION
Loyalty to client requirement, conflict of interest, 199

PRIVILEGE OR IMMUNITY
Admission to bar, 41, 51
Attorney-client privilege, handling client property and withdrawing from representation, 116
Bar application process, candor in, 40
Educational and knowledge standards for admission to bar, 41
Reporting duty, another lawyer's misconduct, 63
State and federal limits on admission to bar, other attempts at, 51

PRO BONO
Delivery of legal services, moral obligation to provide pro bono legal services, 563–565
Lawyer-client relationship, fundamentals of, 87

PROBATE PRACTICE
Handling client property and withdrawing from representation, 116

PROMPT NOTICE CLAUSE
Loyalty to client requirement, representing insured and insurer, 221

PROPERTY
Lawyer-client relationship, fundamentals of, 112–127
Real Property, this index

PROSECUTING ATTORNEYS
Advising clients, possibility of special rules applying to federal prosecutors, 313–318
Conflicts of interest, 198–201
Ethical problems in litigation, crusading prosecutor, 464–486
Former clients, 248
Loyalty to client requirement, 175, 198–201, 248

PROSECUTORIAL MISCONDUCT
Loyalty to client, requirement of, 175

PROSPECTIVE CLIENTS
Lawyer-client relationship, fundamentals of, 84 et seq.

PROTECTIVE ORDERS
Reporting duty, another lawyer's misconduct, 59

PSYCHOLOGISTS
Contradictory expectations, matter of professionalism, 24

PUBLIC FIGURES
Judges' ethical conduct, judge as political candidate and public figure, 635–651

PUBLIC HEALTH AND SAFETY
Confidentiality and risks to, 152–155

PUBLIC INTEREST
Loyalty to client requirement, criminal litigation, 196

QUANTUM MERUIT
Limitations on lawyer's efforts to collect fee, 123

REAL PROPERTY
Former private lawyer who enters government service, 270
Loyalty to client requirement, 164, 171, 270
Malpractice actions, regulation of legal profession, 69, 74

REASONABLENESS
Billing for legal services, generally, 100
Withdrawal from representation, 118

RECIPROCITY
Interstate discipline, jurisdiction, 55

RECORDS OR REPORTS
Advising clients, reporting corporate misconduct within and outside client organization, 293–295
Billing for legal services, fundamentals of lawyer-client relationship, 102
Corporations, attorney-client privilege, 141
Discipline, duty to report another lawyer's misconduct, 56–63
Ethical problems in litigation, secret tape recording, 458–461
Lawyer-client relationship, fundamentals of, 83 et seq.

RECORDS OR REPORTS—Cont'd
Loyalty to client, requirement of, 162
Public health and safety, confidentiality and risks to, 154

RECUSAL
Admission to bar, other attempts at state and federal limits on, 50
Loyalty to client requirement, former private lawyer who enters government service, 268

REDUCTION
Billing for legal services, fundamentals of lawyer-client relationship, 103

REFERRALS
Delivery of legal services, ethics of referral to specialist, 517–530

REFUNDS
Billing for legal services, fundamentals of lawyer-client relationship, 98

REGULATION OF LEGAL PROFESSION
Generally, 31

REIMBURSEMENT
Handling client property and withdrawing from representation, 117

REPORTS
Records or Reports, this index

RESERVATION OF RIGHTS
Loyalty to client requirement, representing insured and insurer, 222, 224

RESIDENCY
Admission to bar, other attempts at state and federal limits on, 45
Interstate discipline, jurisdiction, 54

RESIGNATION
Reporting duty, another lawyer's misconduct, 61

RESISTING ARREST
Regulation of legal profession, admission to bar, 37

RESTATEMENT
Admission to bar, other attempts at state and federal limits on, 47
Attorneys' liens and other security interests, 125, 126
Billing for legal services, fundamentals of lawyer-client relationship, 100, 103
Confidentiality, information protected by attorney-client privilege, 128
Disclosure, how legal protection against disclosure can be lost, 136, 137, 139
Gifts from happy clients, acceptance of unsolicited, 210, 212
Insured and insurer represented, 227
Investments, using confidential client information to make private, 208, 209

RESTATEMENT—Cont'd

Lawyer-client relationship, fundamentals of, 94

Limitations on lawyer's efforts to collect fee, 121

Loyalty to client requirement, 159 et seq.

Malpractice actions, regulation of legal profession, 67, 70

Organization as client, privilege and confidentiality, 149

Other significant consequences of negligence or misconduct by lawyers, regulation of legal profession, 81

Public health and safety, confidentiality and risks to, 152, 154

Regulation of legal profession, admission to bar, 33

Standards of professional conduct, 12, 14

Withdrawal from representation, 119

Work product immunity, information protected by, 132, 133

RESUMES

Admission to bar, other attempts at state and federal limits on, 50

RETAINER AGREEMENTS

Loyalty to client, requirement of, 185

Malpractice actions, regulation of legal profession, 75

RETAINING LIEN

Attorneys' liens and other security interests, 124

RETALIATORY DISCHARGE FROM EMPLOYMENT

Loyalty requirement, former clients, 235

Refusal to Violate Law, 534–538

RETENTION OF EVIDENCE

Ethical problems in litigation, destruction or failing to retain physical or documentary evidence, 429–432

RETIREMENT

Loyalty to client requirement, negotiating for post-government employment while still in government, 271, 272

REVOLUTIONARY ERA

Development of American legal profession, 4

REWARDS

Judges' ethical conduct, judge rewarding his friends, 650, 651

ROLE ETHICS

Contributions from moral philosophy, 18

ROYALTIES

Loyalty to client, requirement of, 179

RULE AGAINST PERPETUITIES

Malpractice actions, regulation of legal profession, 65

RULE UTILITARIANISM

Contributions from moral philosophy, consequential versus deontological standards, 21

SAFEKEEPING

Ethical problems in litigation, taking possession of physical evidence for safekeeping, 420–426

SAME OR SUBSTANTIALLY RELATED

Loyalty requirement, former clients, 232–238

SARBANES–OXLEY ACT

SEC Regulation of Lawyers, 364–366

SCHEDULE OF FEES

Billing for legal services, fundamentals of lawyer-client relationship, 101, 107

SCREENING

Loyalty to client requirement, screening to avoid imputation, 256–260

SECRECY

Ethical problems in litigation, secret tape recording, 458–461

SECRETARIES

Billing for legal services, fundamentals of lawyer-client relationship, 97

Disclosure, how legal protection against disclosure can be lost, 137

Former clients, 240, 241

Handling client property and withdrawing from representation, 116

Loyalty requirement, former clients, 240, 241

SECURED CREDITORS

Loyalty to client, requirement of, 171

SECURITIES

Advising clients, special obligations of securities lawyer, 356–364

Confidentiality and client fraud, 157

Loyalty requirement, former clients, 237

SECURITIES AND EXCHANGE COMMISSION

Advising clients, specific SEC responses to series of corporate failures, 364–366

Disclosure, how legal protection against disclosure can be lost, 135

SECURITY INTERESTS

Attorneys' liens and other security interests, 124–127

SELF-INCRIMINATION

Admission to bar, other attempts at state and federal limits on, 51

SENTENCE AND PUNISHMENT

Loyalty to client requirement, criminal litigation, 192

Other significant consequences of negligence or misconduct by lawyers, sentencing guidelines, 79

SETTLEMENT

Advising clients, ethics of negotiation, 321, 322

Attorneys' liens and other security interests, 126

Billing for legal services, fundamentals of lawyer-client relationship, 103, 104, 107

Former clients, 238

Insured and insurer represented, 223–226

Lawyer-client relationship, fundamentals of, 93

Loyalty to client requirement, 166, 223–226, 238

SEX AND SEXUAL MATTERS

Admission to bar, other attempts at state and federal limits on, 50

Bar application process candor, sexual harassment, 40

Disclosure, how legal protection against disclosure can be lost, 140

Loyalty to client requirement, intimate relationships between lawyers and clients, 212–215

Organization as client, sexual harassment, 145

Other significant consequences of negligence or misconduct by lawyers, regulation of legal profession, 81

SHERMAN ACT

Billing for legal services, fundamentals of lawyer-client relationship, 101

SHOPLIFTING

Bar application process, candor in, 38

Regulation of legal profession, admission to bar, 37

SIMULTANEOUS REPRESENTATION

Loyalty to client, requirement of, 159

SIXTH AMENDMENT

Loyalty to client requirement, criminal litigation, 191

SLEEPING THROUGH TRIAL

Other significant consequences of negligence or misconduct by lawyers, regulation of legal profession, 79

SMUGGLING

Handling client property and withdrawing from representation, 114

Regulation of legal profession, admission to bar, 35

SOCIAL ETHICS

Contributions from moral philosophy, personal versus social ethics, 22

SOCIAL LIFE

Loyalty to client requirement, criminal prosecution, 202

SOCIAL RESPONSIBILITY

Generally, 24

Introductory problem, achieving justice for innocent client, 28

SOLICITATION

Delivery of legal services, 502–508, 512–517

Judges' ethical conduct, judges soliciting and receiving campaign contributions, 642, 643

SPECIAL PROBLEMS OF GOVERNMENT LAWYERS

Loyalty to client requirement, 260–274

SPECIALISTS

Delivery of legal services, ethics of referral to specialist, 517–530

STANDARDS OF PROFESSIONAL CONDUCT

Generally, 11

STATE SUPREME COURTS

Admission to bar, 35, 37, 46

Attempts at state and federal limits on admission to bar, other, 46

Bar application process, candor in, 38

Billing for legal services, fundamentals of lawyer-client relationship, 102

Loyalty to client, requirement of, 165

Organization of book, 30

Regulation of legal profession, 31, 35, 37

STATUTE OF LIMITATIONS

Malpractice actions, regulation of legal profession, 69

Regulation of legal profession, admission to bar, 35

STOCK AND STOCKHOLDERS

Accepting payment in form of stock, 204–208

Disclosure, how legal protection against disclosure can be lost, 135

Former clients, 237

Handling client property and withdrawing from representation, 114

Lawyer-client relationship, fundamentals of, 84

Loyalty to client requirement, 204–208, 237

SUBPOENAS

Public health and safety, confidentiality and risks to, 153

SUBSIDIARIES

Loyalty to client, requirement of, 179, 183

SUBSTANCE ABUSE

Admission to bar, other attempts at state and federal limits on, 51 et seq.

Bar application process, candor in, 38

SUBSTANTIAL FACTOR TEST

Malpractice actions, regulation of legal profession, 73

SUBSTANTIAL RELATIONSHIP TEST
Loyalty to client, requirement of, 174

SUICIDE
Lawyer-client relationship, fundamentals of, 94

SUIT-WITHIN-A-SUIT
Malpractice actions, regulation of legal profession, 72, 73

SUPERVISION
Delivery of legal services, obligations of supervisory lawyer and those they supervise, 531–534

SURETY BONDS
Loyalty to client, requirement of, 180

SUSPENSION
Admission to bar, other attempts at state and federal limits on, 50, 51
Handling client property and withdrawing from representation, 117
Interstate discipline, jurisdiction, 55
Lawyer-client relationship, fundamentals of, 93
Reporting duty, another lawyer's misconduct, 57, 62

TAINTED VERDICT
Ethical problems in litigation, 453–464

TAPE RECORDING
Ethical problems in litigation, secret tape recording, 458–461

TARDINESS
Other significant consequences of negligence or misconduct by lawyers, regulation of legal profession, 78

TAXATION
Loyalty to client, requirement of, 186
Malpractice actions, regulation of legal profession, 66
Work product immunity, information protected by, 133

TELEPHONES
Disclosure, how legal protection against disclosure can be lost, 136

TELEVISION
Delivery of legal services, continuing issues in field of lawyer advertising, 511, 512

TEMPORARY EMPLOYMENT
Loyalty requirement, former clients, 243

TERMINATION
Limitations on lawyer's efforts to collect fee, 123
Loyalty to client, requirement of, 182–186

TESTATORS
Malpractice actions, regulation of legal profession, 69

TESTS OR TESTING
Ethical problems in litigation, taking possession of physical evidence for testing, 420–426

THEFT
Bar application process, candor in, 38
Regulation of legal profession, admission to bar, 34
Shoplifting, this index

THIRD PARTIES
Advising clients, duties in preparation of legal opinion for delivery to third party, 339–341
Conflicts of former judge or third party neutral, 272–274
Insured and insurer represented, 223–226
Loyalty to client requirement, 223–226, 272–274

THIRTEENTH AMENDMENT
Limitations on lawyer's efforts to collect fee, 122

THREATS
Reporting duty, another lawyer's misconduct, 58

TRADE ASSOCIATIONS
Loyalty to client, requirement of, 180

TRADE SECRETS
Criminal prosecution, 200
Loyalty to client requirement, 183, 200

TRADEMARKS
Criminal prosecution, 200, 201
Former clients, 242
Lawyer-client relationship, fundamentals of, 86
Loyalty to client requirement, 200, 201, 242

TRAFFIC CITATIONS
Bar application process, candor in, 37

TRAFFICKING IN DRUGS
Loyalty to client requirement, criminal litigation, 193

TRIAL
Lawyer-client relationship, fundamentals of, 94
Loyalty to client requirement, mini-trial, 258
Regulation of legal profession, sleeping through trial, 79

TRUST
Fundamentals of lawyer-client relationship, generally, 83

TRUSTS AND TRUSTEES
Billing for legal services, fundamentals of lawyer-client relationship, 103
Handling client property and withdrawing from representation, 113, 115, 116
Lawyer-client relationship, fundamentals of, 95

TRUSTS AND TRUSTEES—Cont'd

Malpractice actions, regulation of legal profession, 69, 70

Organization as client, privilege and confidentiality, 148, 149

TRUTH

Honesty or Truth, this index

UNITED STATES DISTRICT COURTS

Admission to bar, other attempts at state and federal limits on, 45

UNITED STATES SUPREME COURT

Billing for legal services, fundamentals of lawyer-client relationship, 95

Regulation of legal profession, admission to bar, 37

UTILITARIANISM

Contributions from moral philosophy, consequential versus deontological standards, 20

Introductory problem, achieving justice for innocent client, 27

VALUE BILLING

Fundamentals of lawyer-client relationship, billing for legal services, 109

VERDICTS

Ethical problems in litigation, tainted verdict, 453–464

VERIFICATION

Ethical problems in litigation, candor about factual matters not easily verifiable, 414–416

VOLUNTARINESS

Advising clients, duty to volunteer information or correct a misapprehension, 326–332

WAIVER

Accreditation standards, educational and knowledge standards for admission to bar, 41

Criminal prosecution, 202

Disclosure, how legal protection against disclosure can be lost, 135, 137

Foreign lawyers, educational and knowledge standards for admission to bar, 43

Judges' ethical conduct, waiving judicial disqualification, 634, 635

Loyalty to client requirement, 161 et seq., 202

Malpractice actions, regulation of legal profession, 73, 76

WAIVER—Cont'd

Organization as client, privilege and confidentiality, 148

WARNING DUTY

Confidentiality and client fraud, 157

WEB SITES

Lawyer-client relationship, fundamentals of, 87

WILLS

Disclosure, how legal protection against disclosure can be lost, 139

Loyalty to client requirement, acceptance of unsolicited gifts from happy clients, 211

WIRETAPS

Disclosure, how legal protection against disclosure can be lost, 137

WITHDRAWAL

Lawyer-client relationship, fundamentals of, 112–127

WITNESSES

Compensation of witnesses, 456–458

Ethical problems in litigation, 436–453, 456–458, 461–464

Expert Witnesses, this index

Lawyer as witness at trial, 461–464

Perjury, client who intends to commit, 436–453

WOMEN

Development of American legal profession, 10

Prison inmates, requirement of loyalty to client, 164

WORK PRODUCT

Loyalty requirement, former clients, 243–245

Organization as client, privilege and confidentiality, 142–152

Public health and safety, confidentiality and risks to, 153

WRITINGS OR WRITTEN INSTRUMENTS

Billing for legal services, fundamentals of lawyer-client relationship, 96

Disclosure, how legal protection against disclosure can be lost, 136

Limitations on lawyer's efforts to collect fee, 123

Loyalty to client, requirement of, 162

YALE

Admission to bar, educational and knowledge standards for, 40

†

1–58778–524–2

90000

9 781587 785245